The World Book Atlas of the United States and Canada

The American eagle on the Great Seal of the United States carries a shield on its breast, an olive branch and some arrows in its talons, and a scroll in its beak. The eagle represents freedom. The olive branch stands for the nation's desire for peace, while the arrows symbolize determination in war. The blue in the shield represents all the branches of the U.S. government. The scroll carries the inscription E Pluribus Unum *(One [nation] Out of Many [states]). The national flag, which was adopted in 1777, carries 13 stripes, one for each of the original 13 colonies. The 50 stars on the flag represent the states of the Union* (facing page).

Canada's coat of arms displays a shield bearing 3 red maple leaves and the royal arms of England, Scotland, Ireland, and France (from left to right, top to bottom). A British lion holds the Union Jack and a unicorn holds the fleur-de-lis of France. Below the shield is a scroll with the national motto, A Mari Usque ad Mare *(From Sea to Sea). The national flag, the design for which was officially proclaimed in 1965, carries a red, 11-pointed maple leaf, Canada's national emblem. The leaf appears on a white field. At each end is a broad, vertical red stripe. Red and white are Canada's national colors* (facing page).

The World Book Atlas of the United States and Canada

World Book–Childcraft International, Inc.
A subsidiary of The Scott & Fetzer Company
Chicago London Paris Sydney Tokyo Toronto

Staff

Editorial director
William H. Nault

Editorial

Executive editor
Robert O. Zeleny

Managing editor
Dominic J. Miccolis

Senior editor
Seva Johnson

Assistant editor
Gail Rosicky

Index editor
Jean Babrick

Editorial assistant
Janet T. Peterson

Art

Executive art director
William Dobias

Senior art director
William Hammond

Art director
Joe Gound

Design director
Ronald A. Stachowiak

Designer
Janice Wheeler

Photography director
John S. Marshall

Senior photographs editor
Carol Parden

Cartographic services

H. George Stoll, head
Jill Eilertsen
Amelia R. Gintautas
Eugene Melchert
Toby Roberts
Paul M. Yatabe

Statistics

Robert S. Gauron, chief
Ruth L. Bainbridge
Karen Molohon
Katherine Norgel

Product production

Executive director
Philip B. Hall

Research and development
Henry Koval

Manufacturing
Joseph C. LaCount

Pre-press services
J. J. Stack

Product control
Barbara Podczerwinski

Composition
John Babrick

Film separations
Al Mozdzen

Editorial services

Director
Susan C. Kilburg

Editorial research
Lenore Glanz, head
Edna Capehart
Yogamani Leo Hamm
Max R. Kinsey

Rights and permissions
Mary Norton

Printed in the United States of America

ISBN 0-7166-3114-8
Library of Congress Catalog Card No. 80-54104

Introduction

The World Book Atlas of the United States and Canada is a storehouse of information about two great North American nations. Carefully prepared by the editors of *The World Book Encyclopedia,* this highly illustrated volume not only provides maps of all the United States and Canada but also highlights many of the geographic, historical, political, cultural, and economic features of both countries. The format is easy to use and provides both an enjoyable travel guide and a quick, up-to-date reference.

The opening section is a simple explanation of how to use the maps that appear in the atlas. Detailed illustrations point out various symbols and devices used on these maps. These illustrations help to clarify the use of such aids.

Next follows a highly illustrated overview of both the United States and Canada. The land features, weather, energy resources, agriculture, and peoples of the two nations are described with attention to both each country's individual characteristics and the traits that they hold in common. Travel maps that feature U.S. and Canadian highways provide an aid to vacationers who wish to develop a personal acquaintance with the many interesting areas of both nations.

Then the atlas presents each state of the United States according to four general geographic areas: Northeast, Midwest, South, and West. The Canadian provinces and territories follow.

Each entry in this section contains an illustrated article giving interesting details about the state, province, or territory. Outstanding landmarks are noted, plus important and often unique facts regarding the area's history and economy. A map follows, accompanied by more information such as state, province, and territorial capitals, total land areas, high/low elevations, and official mottoes and songs. Official seals, flags, and other symbols also appear.

This atlas next highlights 50 cities of the United States and Canada, chosen as major cities because of their size and visitor appeal. Details such as each city's date of founding, origin of name, nickname, population, time zone, average winter/summer temperatures, and favorite places to visit make this section a concise travel and study reference.

The volume also features a chronology, or listing of the dates, of the important events in the history of the United States and Canada. Entries include the dates of many significant political, religious, social, philosophical, literary, artistic, scientific, and technological events. Special features include maps showing each country's expansion from colonial times and illustrations with capsule biographies of all the U.S. Presidents and Canadian Prime Ministers.

The index at the back of the atlas, when used with the state, provincial, and territorial maps, pinpoints political and terrain features of the United States and Canada. A metric conversion table ends the volume and provides a final aid to the most effective use of the atlas.

The Editors

Contents

Introduction *5*

Using the atlas *9*
Latitude/longitude/time zones/map reading

United States and Canada: Overview *12*

United States terrain map *14*
Canadian terrain map *16*
Facts about the United States and Canada *18*
United States geography *22*
United States weather *24*
United States energy *26*
United States agriculture *30*
United States people *32*
Canadian geography/weather *35*
Canadian energy *38*
Canadian agriculture *40*
Canadian people *42*
U.S.—Canada highways *44*
Northeast/Southeast/Southwest/Northwest/New England, Alaska, Hawaii

Northeast *56*

Connecticut *58*
Maine *62*
Massachusetts *66*
New Hampshire *70*
New Jersey *74*
New York *78*
Pennsylvania *82*
Rhode Island *86*
Vermont *88*

Midwest *92*

Illinois *94*
Indiana *98*
Iowa *102*
Kansas *106*
Michigan *110*
Minnesota *114*
Missouri *118*
Nebraska *122*
North Dakota *126*
Ohio *130*
South Dakota *134*
Wisconsin *138*

South *142*

Alabama *144*
Arkansas *148*
Delaware *152*

Florida *154*
Georgia *158*
Kentucky *162*
Louisiana *166*
Maryland *170*
Mississippi *174*
North Carolina *178*
South Carolina *182*
Tennessee *186*
Texas *190*
Virginia *194*
West Virginia *198*

West *202*

Arizona *204*
California *208*
Colorado *212*
Idaho *216*
Montana *220*
Nevada *224*
New Mexico *228*
Oklahoma *232*
Oregon *236*
Utah *240*
Washington *244*
Wyoming *248*
Alaska *252*
Hawaii *256*

Canada *260*

Alberta *262*
British Columbia *266*
Manitoba *270*
New Brunswick *274*
Newfoundland *276*
Nova Scotia *280*
Ontario *282*
Prince Edward Island *286*
Quebec *288*
Saskatchewan *292*
Northwest Territories *296*
Yukon Territory *297*

Major cities *298*

U.S. history *314*

Canadian history *341*

Index *352*

Metric conversion table *444*

Acknowledgments *445*

Alphabetical key to states, provinces, and territories

United States

Alabama 144–147
Alaska 252–255
Arizona 204–207
Arkansas 148–151
California 208–211
Colorado 212–215
Connecticut 58–61
Delaware 152–153
Florida 154–157
Georgia 158–161
Hawaii 256–259
Idaho 216–219
Illinois 94–97
Indiana 98–101
Iowa 102–105
Kansas 106–109
Kentucky 162–165
Louisiana 166–169
Maine 62–65
Maryland 170–173
Massachusetts 66–69
Michigan 110–113
Minnesota 114–117
Mississippi 174–177
Missouri 118–121
Montana 220–223
Nebraska 122–125
Nevada 224–227
New Hampshire 70–73
New Jersey 74–77
New Mexico 228–231
New York 78–81
North Carolina 178–181
North Dakota 126–129
Ohio 130–133
Oklahoma 232–235
Oregon 236–239
Pennsylvania 82–85
Rhode Island 86–87
South Carolina 182–185
South Dakota 134–137
Tennessee 186–189
Texas 190–193
Utah 240–243
Vermont 88–91
Virginia 194–197
Washington 244–247
West Virginia 198–201
Wisconsin 138–141
Wyoming 248–251

Canada

Alberta 262–265
British Columbia 266–269
Manitoba 270–273
New Brunswick 274–275
Newfoundland 276–279
Northwest Territories 296
Nova Scotia 280–281
Ontario 282–285
Prince Edward Island 286–287
Quebec 288–291
Saskatchewan 292–295
Yukon Territory 297

Using the atlas

All the state and province maps in this atlas have certain basic features. They are drawn to *scale.* This means that certain distances on the maps represent certain distances on the face of the earth. For example, 1 inch may equal 40 miles (64.4 kilometers). All the maps use *symbols* that represent certain types of information. For example, a dot represents a city and a wavy blue line represents a river. *Color* is another common feature of the state and province maps. Color, for example, helps you tell which part of the map is land and which part is water.

Finally, all the state and province maps use a *geographic grid.* East-west lines measure distances north or south of the equator. These are lines of latitude. Because the lines are parallel, they are also called *parallels of latitude.* Latitude is measured in units called degrees. Points of latitude are always given as so many degrees north or south of the equator. For example, Chicago has a latitude of about 42 degrees (42°) north of the equator.

North-south lines measure degrees east and west. These lines are called *meridians of longitude.* A *meridian* is an imaginary circle passing through the earth's surface and through the North and South poles. Meridians of longitude are counted from the line that passes through Greenwich, England. This is called the prime meridian and has a longitude of zero degrees (0°). Longitude is measured east and west of the prime meridian from 0° to 180°. Chicago is at about 88° west longitude.

Longitude and time are related. The prime meridian is also the place where time zones start. There are 12 time zones east of Greenwich and 12 time zones west of Greenwich. Each time zone represents about 15° of longitude, or 1 hour. The United States has 7 standard time zones and Canada has 6—each about 15° of longitude apart. For convenience, there is some variation in the width of each time zone. Chicago is in the Central Standard Time Zone.

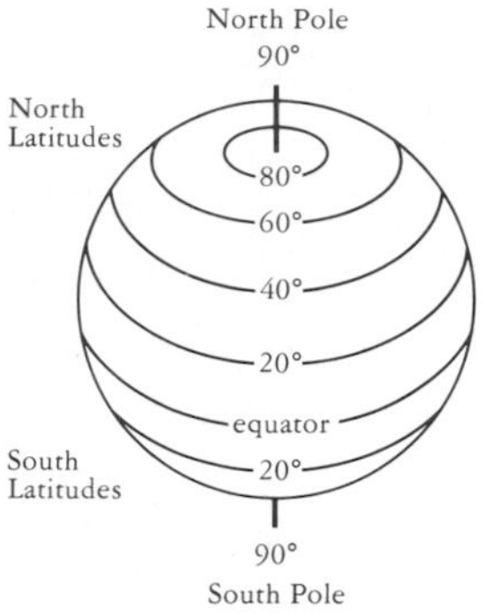

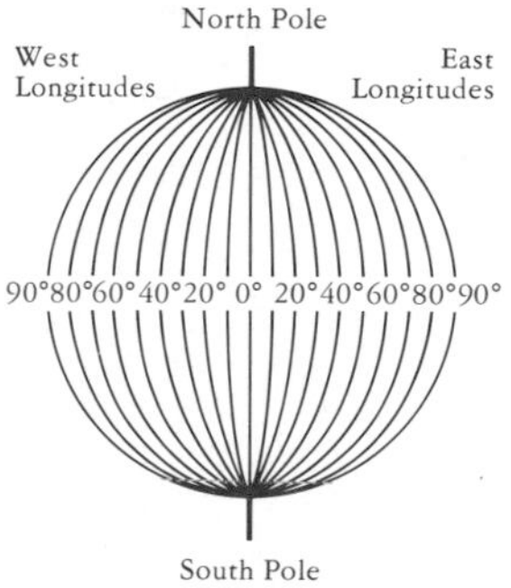

Lines of latitude and longitude are imaginary lines circling the globe. The latitudes run east-west, parallel to the equator (0°). The longitudes run north-south on a globe, beginning with the prime meridian (0°) and intersecting at the poles (above).

WORLD BOOK map

The United States and Canada share some of their standard time zones. Western Alaska uses the Bering time zone, not shown on this map. Zone boundaries are irregular to match the borders of political units that would otherwise be split into separate time zones (left).

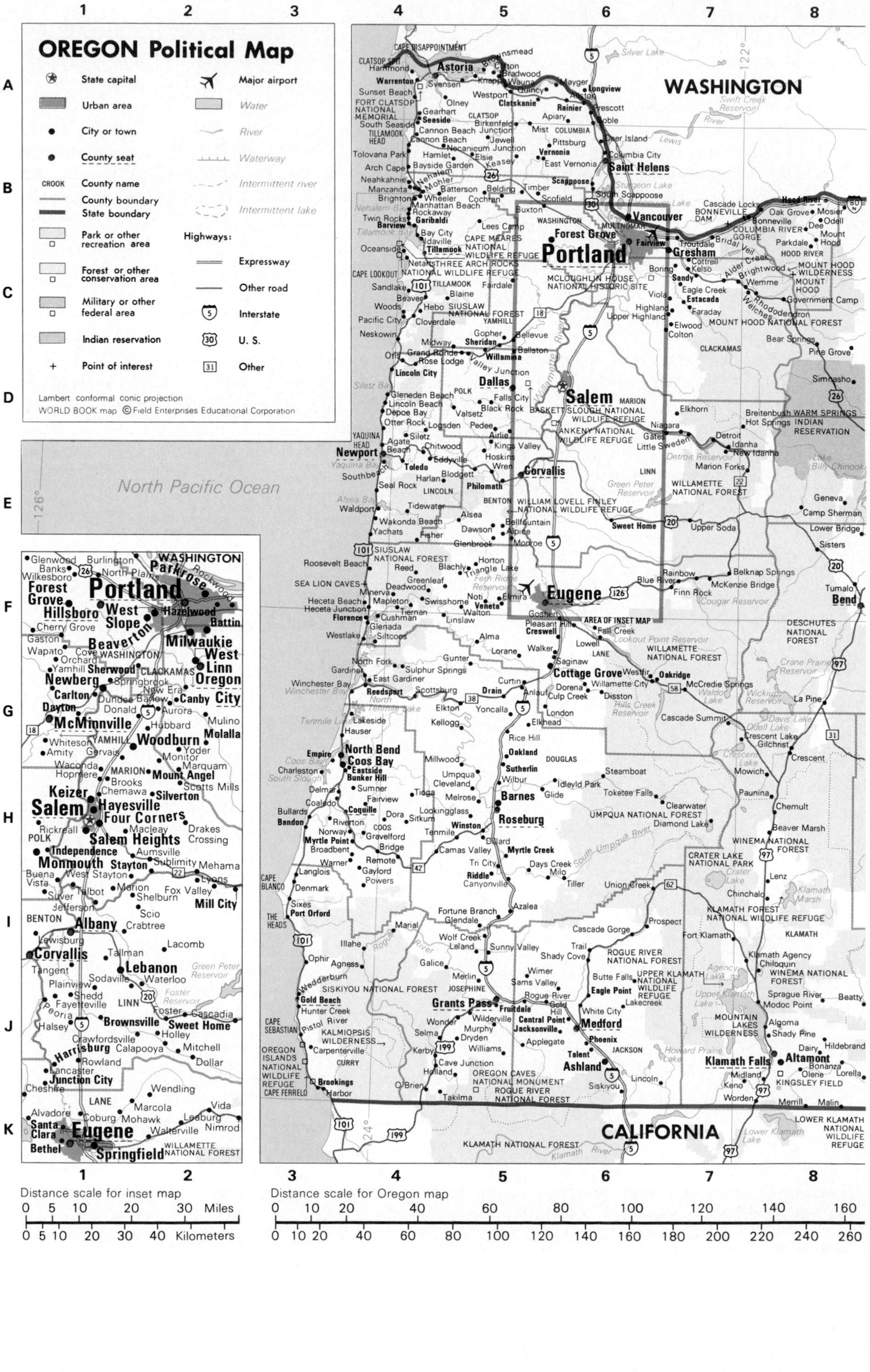

OREGON Political Map
State capital
Urban area
City or town
County seat
CROOK County name
County boundary
State boundary
Park or other recreation area
Forest or other conservation area
Military or other federal area
Indian reservation
Point of interest
Major airport
Water
River
Waterway
Intermittent river
Intermittent lake
Highways:
Expressway
Other road
Interstate
U. S.
Other
Lambert conformal conic projection
WORLD BOOK map © Field Enterprises Educational Corporation
North Pacific Ocean
WASHINGTON
CALIFORNIA
Portland
Salem
Eugene
Astoria
Vancouver
Gresham
Forest Grove
Saint Helens
Tillamook
Lincoln City
Dallas
Newport
Corvallis
Florence
Coos Bay
North Bend
Roseburg
Grants Pass
Medford
Ashland
Klamath Falls
Bend
Cottage Grove
Oakridge
Gold Beach
Brookings
Port Orford
Bandon
Coquille
Myrtle Point
Reedsport
Sweet Home
Albany
Lebanon
Springfield
Hillsboro
Beaverton
Milwaukie
West Linn
Oregon City
Newberg
McMinnville
Woodburn
Keizer
Independence
Monmouth
Silverton
Stayton
Mill City
Brownsville
Harrisburg
Junction City
MOUNT HOOD NATIONAL FOREST
WILLAMETTE NATIONAL FOREST
UMPQUA NATIONAL FOREST
SIUSLAW NATIONAL FOREST
SISKIYOU NATIONAL FOREST
ROGUE RIVER NATIONAL FOREST
WINEMA NATIONAL FOREST
DESCHUTES NATIONAL FOREST
KLAMATH NATIONAL FOREST
CRATER LAKE NATIONAL PARK
OREGON CAVES NATIONAL MONUMENT
WARM SPRINGS INDIAN RESERVATION
AREA OF INSET MAP
Distance scale for inset map
0 5 10 20 30 Miles
0 5 10 20 30 40 Kilometers
Distance scale for Oregon map
0 10 20 40 60 80 100 120 140 160
0 10 20 40 60 80 100 120 140 160 180 200 220 240 260

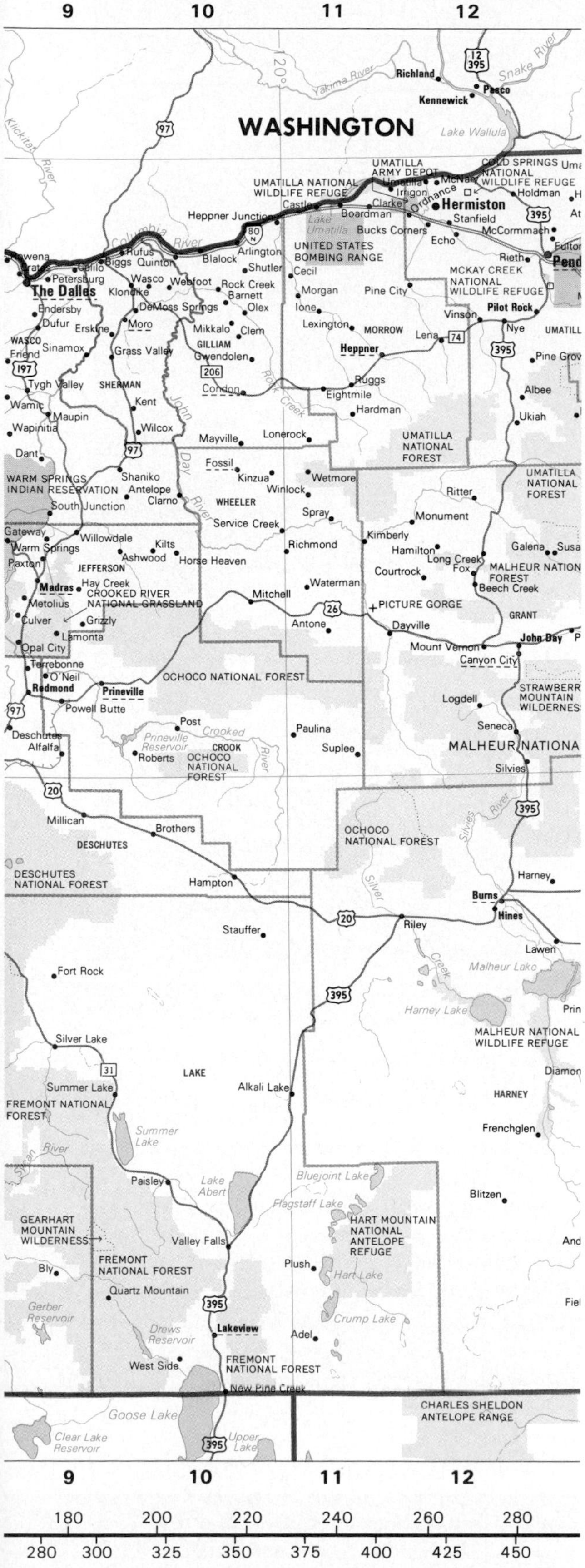

The state and province maps in this atlas were specially designed to make them easy to use. The section of the map of the state of Oregon shows some of the most important features of the main maps in this atlas.

Each map has a legend box in one corner. This box shows you the symbols used on the map and tells you what they stand for. Urban areas, for example, are shown in orange and the locations of major airports are indicated by an airplane symbol.

The distance scale for each map is located in a yellow band across the bottom. The Oregon map has two distance scales, one for the main map and the other for the inset map. Many of the maps in the atlas have insets, such as the one that shows the area between Portland and Eugene. These are used to give you a closer view of areas that have large numbers of place names, such as urban areas around major cities. The areas covered by the inset maps are outlined by a gray border on the main map.

The letters of the alphabet that run vertically along the edge of the map and the numbers that run horizontally are used with the map index to help you locate places on the map. For example, the map index in the back of the atlas tells you that Eugene, Ore., is located at or near F5 on pages 238-9. To find Eugene, simply place one finger at letter *F* and the other at number 5 and move them across and down the map. They will come together near Eugene.

The type used on the atlas maps has been carefully selected for ease of use. City names are in different sizes and weights of type to indicate the relative sizes of each city. For example, the type indicates that Portland is larger than Eugene, which is larger than Medford. The size and weight of the type does not stand for specific population size, as on some maps, but only indicates relative population size. Other kinds of type are used for terrain features, points of interest, and so on.

These maps have many other useful features. Major highways, including parts of the Interstate Highway System, are clearly indicated. So are recreation areas and points of interest. Counties are named and outlined in red.

The study of maps is not only an important school subject, but a vital skill for students and adults alike. In order to get the most out of this atlas, spend some time studying the maps. You will find them not only interesting but useful.

Hope lured settlers from many lands west across North America, perhaps to farmland like this in Oregon (above left).

The clear waters of Moraine Lake in Alberta reflect the snow-capped Rockies, a range that the United States and Canada share (above right).

United States and Canada

The United States and Canada occupy four-fifths of North America. They are separated from the other countries of North America not only by geography, but also by language, culture, and a shared heritage. The two nations are also different from each other, like two neighboring cousins. This section will highlight both nations.

The United States' and Canada's present societies are a product of their European heritage. Indians and Eskimos inhabited both countries long before any white people arrived. Hawaiians also inhabited the United States before the appearance of whites. European immigrants and their descendants overwhelmed the native populations in both Canada and the United States. In the eastern areas, for example, as Europeans moved into both countries, the Indians were pushed out. As the settlers began moving farther west, the Indians became less and less numerous.

Most of the people of Canada and the United States have European ancestry. The earliest settlers in the United States were from England. German, Dutch, French, and Spanish settlers followed. There also were black slaves, brought from Africa to work on southern plantations. Today, the largest groups born in other countries include, in order of size, Italians, Germans, Poles, Russians, Mexicans, and English and Welsh.

Canada's population reflects a lesser mixture of peoples than does the United States'. Half of all Canadians are descendants of British and Irish immigrants. About a third of the population have French ancestry. Southern and middle Europeans immigrated to Canada, but not in the record numbers that came to the United States. Canada also has a black population but, since the nation never practiced slavery, there are fewer blacks than in the United States.

The people of the United States and Canada enjoy a high standard of living. Both countries have large, industrialized, modern cities. Both have well-developed transportation systems. Superhighways cross the countries from coast to coast. Jet airplanes speed travelers across the vast distances within each country's borders. A highly developed communications system links cities, suburbs, and rural areas with one another and with other countries in the world. Television, movies, newspapers, and radios are commonly available.

Geographically, Canada and the United States share many characteristics. The Appalachian Mountains run between the southern United States and the Canadian Atlantic Provinces. The Great Plains occupy the central part of both countries. The mountain ranges in the west—the Rockies and the coastal mountain ranges—extend across both Canada and the United States.

Each country also has unique land formations. Much of northern Canada is a wilderness of forests and frozen wasteland. The part of the United States between the Rocky Mountains and the Sierra Nevada is a vast desert.

Both countries have beautiful lakes and rivers. The Mississippi-Missouri river system in the United States is the longest in North America, but the Mackenzie River in Canada is the longest single North American river. Both countries share four of the five Great Lakes.

Agriculture is important business to both Canada and the United States. Farmers in both countries use the latest equipment and modern scientific techniques to make them leaders in world agriculture. Together, they produce 15 per cent of the world's crops. Both export large amounts of their harvests each year.

Fertile farmland covers from the southern portion of Canada to the southern portion of the United States. The Great Plains of Canada and the United States support valuable crops of wheat, corn, and other grains. Both countries grow fruits and vegetables.

Canada and the United States also have large deposits of fuels. Coal, natural gas, and oil are found in both countries. Canada has expansive timberland, making forestry one of Canada's important industries.

In this section, both the common heritage of the United States and Canada and each country's unique characteristics will be emphasized. The material that follows provides a close look at these two North American neighbors.

Modern, industrialized cities like Vancouver, B.C., are found today in the United States and Canada (top). *Portland Head Light has guided seafarers to Maine's rugged Atlantic coast since 1791* (middle). *A unique U.S. land formation is Monument Valley in Arizona* (bottom).

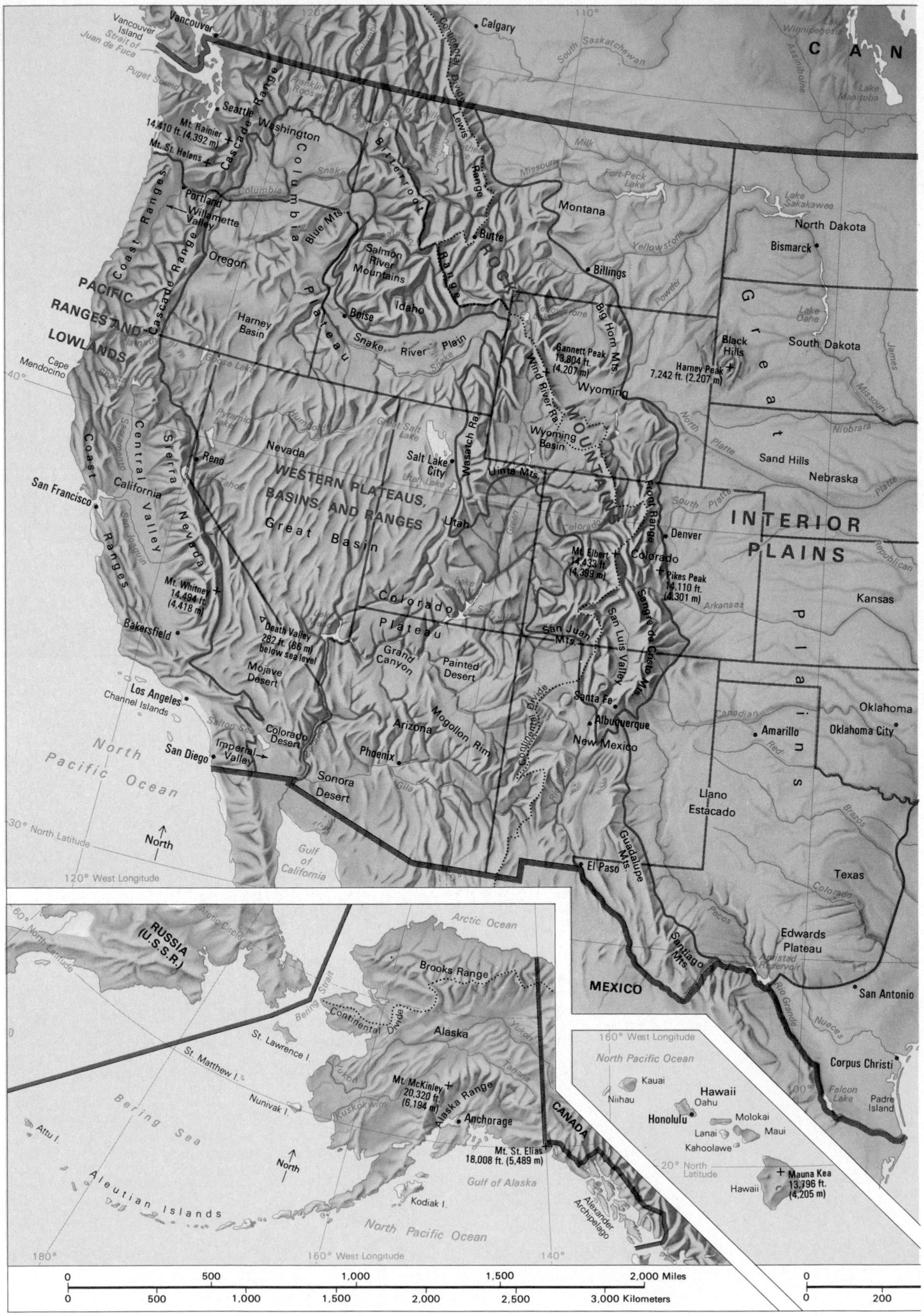
Vancouver Island
Strait of Juan de Fuca
Vancouver
Calgary
Puget Sound
Seattle
Mt. Rainier 14,410 ft. (4,392 m)
Mt. St. Helens
Cascade Range
Washington
Columbia Plateau
Bitterroot Range
Lewis Range
Continental Divide
C A N
Lake Winnipegosis
Lake Manitoba
South Saskatchewan
Missouri
Milk
Fort Peck Lake
Lake Sakakawea
North Dakota
Bismarck
Montana
Yellowstone
Butte
Billings
Portland
Willamette Valley
Coast Ranges
Blue Mts.
Salmon River Mountains
Oregon
Idaho
Boise
Snake River Plain
ROCKY MOUNTAINS
PACIFIC RANGES AND LOWLANDS
Harney Basin
Cape Mendocino
Big Horn Mts.
Gannett Peak 13,804 ft. (4,207 m)
Wind River Ra.
Wyoming
Wyoming Basin
Black Hills
Harney Peak 7,242 ft. (2,207 m)
South Dakota
Lake Oahe
Great Plains
Niobrara
North Platte
Sand Hills
Nebraska
Great Salt Lake
Salt Lake City
Wasatch Ra.
Uinta Mts.
Nevada
Reno
Coast Ranges
Central California Valley
Sierra Nevada
San Francisco
WESTERN PLATEAUS, BASINS, AND RANGES
Great Basin
Utah
Front Range
Denver
INTERIOR PLAINS
Mt. Elbert 14,433 ft. (4,399 m)
Colorado
Pikes Peak 14,110 ft. (4,301 m)
Kansas
Arkansas
Mt. Whitney 14,494 ft. (4,418 m)
Colorado Plateau
Death Valley 282 ft. (86 m) below sea level
Bakersfield
San Juan Mts.
San Luis Valley
Sangre de Cristo Mts.
Grand Canyon
Painted Desert
Mojave Desert
Los Angeles
Channel Islands
Santa Fe
Albuquerque
New Mexico
Amarillo
Oklahoma
Oklahoma City
Arizona
Mogollon Rim
Salton Sea
Colorado Desert
Imperial Valley
San Diego
Phoenix
North Pacific Ocean
Sonora Desert
Llano Estacado
Texas
30° North Latitude
North
Gulf of California
El Paso
Guadalupe Mts.
120° West Longitude
Edwards Plateau
Santiago Mts.
MEXICO
San Antonio
Corpus Christi
Rio Grande
Nueces
Falcon Lake
Padre Island
RUSSIA (U.S.S.R.)
Arctic Circle
Arctic Ocean
Brooks Range
Bering Strait
Continental Divide
Alaska
Yukon
St. Lawrence I.
St. Matthew I.
Nunivak I.
Mt. McKinley 20,320 ft. (6,194 m)
Alaska Range
Anchorage
Bering Sea
CANADA
Mt. St. Elias 18,008 ft. (5,489 m)
Attu I.
North
Gulf of Alaska
Kodiak I.
Aleutian Islands
Alexander Archipelago
North Pacific Ocean
180°
160° West Longitude
140°
160° West Longitude
North Pacific Ocean
Kauai
Niihau
Hawaii
Oahu
Honolulu
Molokai
Lanai
Maui
Kahoolawe
20° North Latitude
Mauna Kea 13,796 ft. (4,205 m)
Hawaii
0 500 1,000 1,500 2,000 Miles
0 500 1,000 1,500 2,000 2,500 3,000 Kilometers
0 200

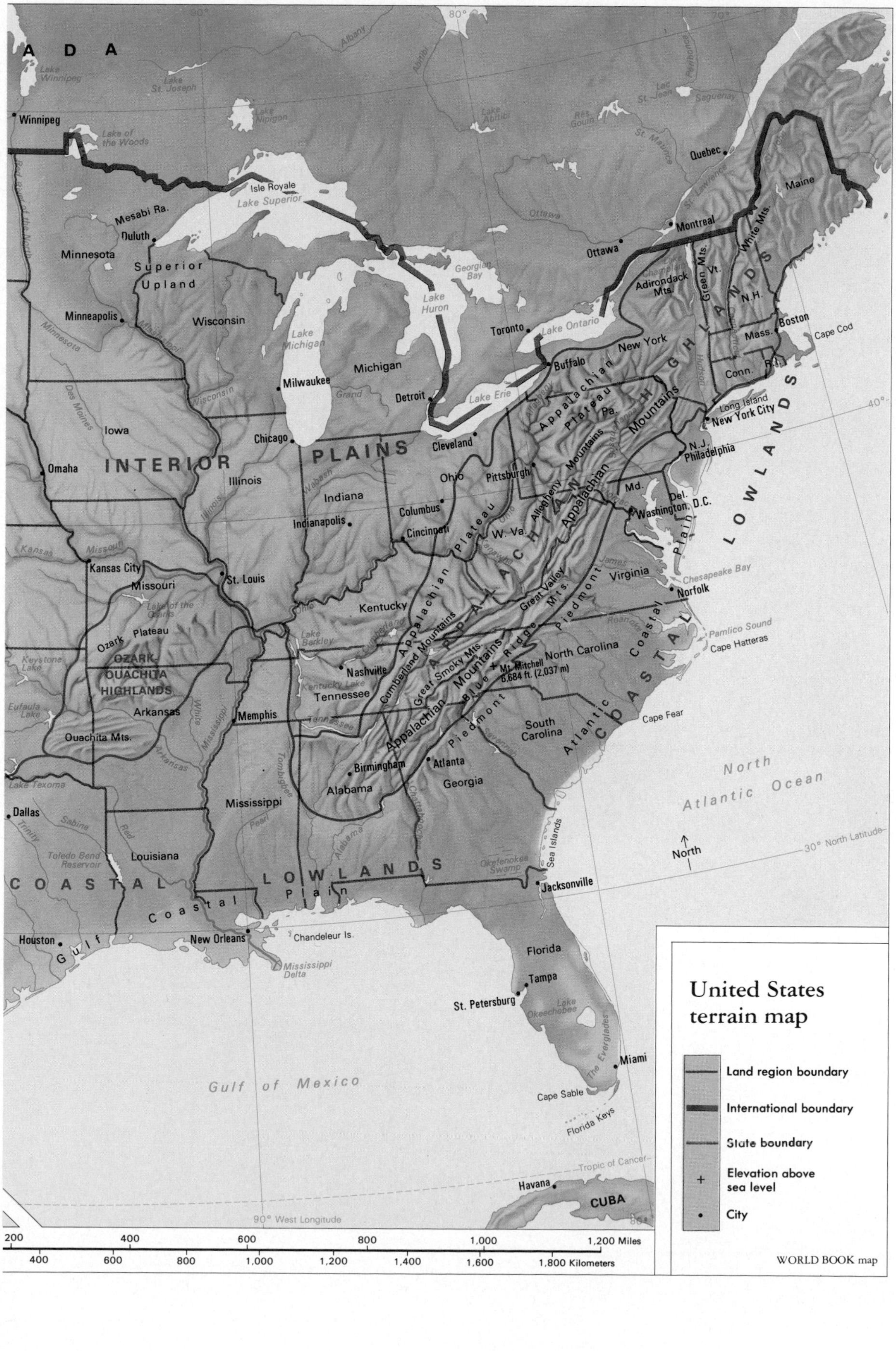
United States terrain map
Land region boundary
International boundary
State boundary
Elevation above sea level
City
WORLD BOOK map
200 400 600 800 1,000 1,200 Miles
400 600 800 1,000 1,200 1,400 1,600 1,800 Kilometers
INTERIOR PLAINS
Superior Upland
APPALACHIAN HIGHLANDS
Appalachian Plateau
Appalachian Mountains
Cumberland Mountains
Allegheny Mountains
Great Smoky Mts.
Blue Ridge Mts.
Great Valley
Piedmont
Adirondack Mts.
Green Mts.
White Mts.
OZARK-QUACHITA HIGHLANDS
Ozark Plateau
Ouachita Mts.
COASTAL LOWLANDS
Atlantic Coastal Plain
Gulf Coastal Plain
Mt. Mitchell 6,684 ft. (2,037 m)
Mesabi Ra.
Isle Royale
Lake Superior
Lake Michigan
Lake Huron
Lake Erie
Lake Ontario
Winnipeg
Duluth
Minneapolis
Milwaukee
Chicago
Detroit
Toronto
Buffalo
Ottawa
Montreal
Quebec
Boston
Cape Cod
New York City
Long Island
Philadelphia
Washington, D.C.
Norfolk
Chesapeake Bay
Pamlico Sound
Cape Hatteras
Cape Fear
Cleveland
Pittsburgh
Columbus
Cincinnati
Indianapolis
St. Louis
Kansas City
Omaha
Nashville
Memphis
Birmingham
Atlanta
Jacksonville
Sea Islands
Dallas
Houston
New Orleans
Chandeleur Is.
Mississippi Delta
Tampa
St. Petersburg
Miami
Cape Sable
Florida Keys
Havana
CUBA
Minnesota
Wisconsin
Michigan
Iowa
Illinois
Indiana
Ohio
Missouri
Kentucky
Tennessee
Arkansas
Mississippi
Alabama
Georgia
Louisiana
Florida
South Carolina
North Carolina
Virginia
W. Va.
Md.
Del.
N.J.
Pa.
New York
Conn.
R.I.
Mass.
Vt.
N.H.
Maine
North Atlantic Ocean
Gulf of Mexico
North
30° North Latitude
Tropic of Cancer
90° West Longitude

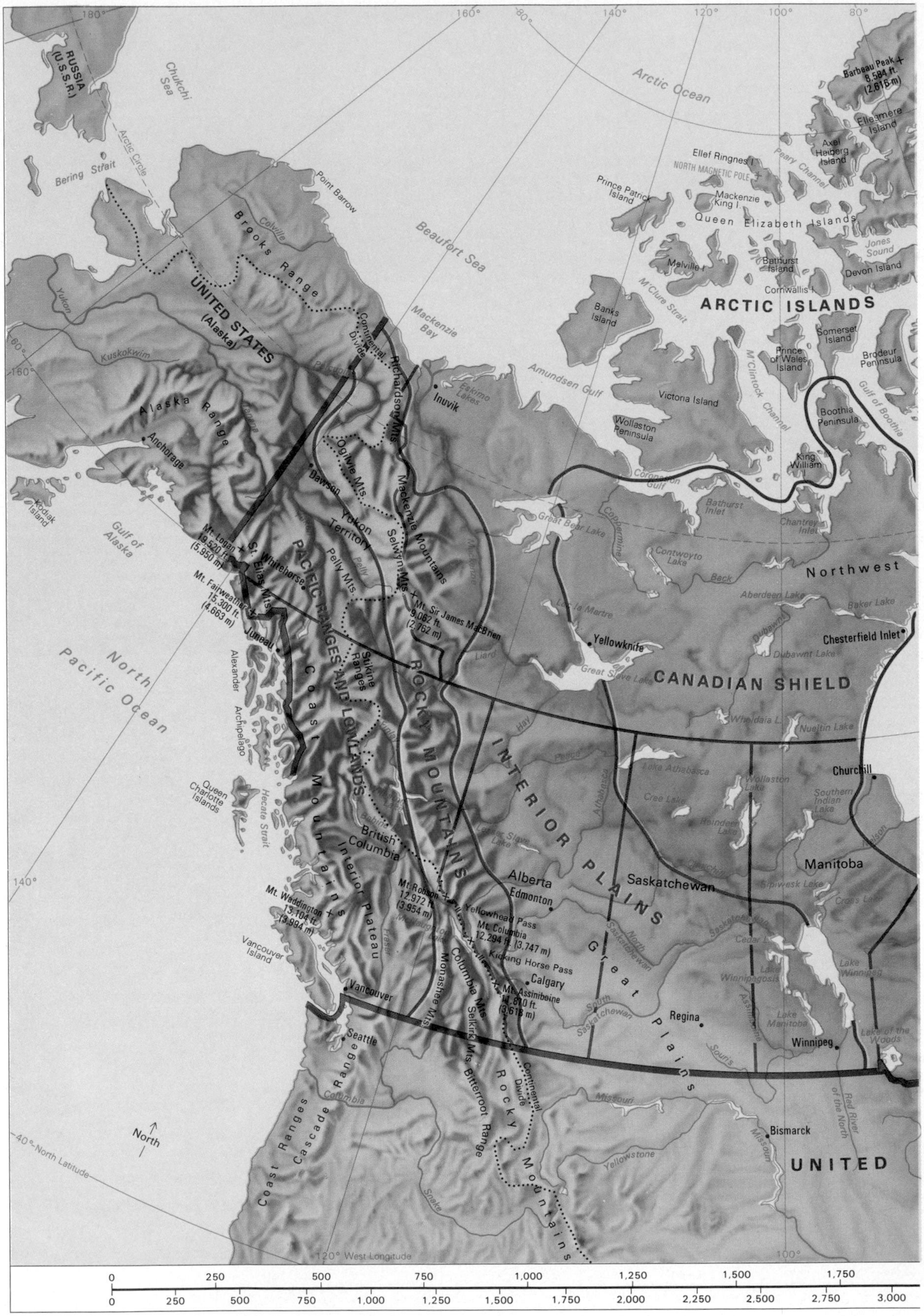
RUSSIA (U.S.S.R.)
Chukchi Sea
Bering Strait
Arctic Circle
Arctic Ocean
Point Barrow
Brooks Range
Beaufort Sea
UNITED STATES (Alaska)
Yukon
Kuskokwim
Alaska Range
Anchorage
Kodiak Island
Gulf of Alaska
Continental Divide
Mackenzie Bay
Richardson Mts
Inuvik
Eskimo Lakes
Amundsen Gulf
Ogilvie Mts
Dawson
Yukon Territory
Mackenzie Mountains
Selwyn Mts
Mt. Logan 19,520 ft. (5,950 m)
St. Elias Mts
Whitehorse
Pelly Mts
Mt. Fairweather 15,300 ft. (4,663 m)
Mt. Sir James MacBrien 9,062 ft. (2,762 m)
Juneau
North Pacific Ocean
Alexander Archipelago
PACIFIC RANGES AND LOWLANDS
Coast Mountains
Stikine Ranges
ROCKY MOUNTAINS
Queen Charlotte Islands
Hecate Strait
British Columbia
Interior Plateau
Mt. Waddington 13,104 ft. (3,994 m)
Vancouver Island
Vancouver
Seattle
Mt. Robson 12,972 ft. (3,954 m)
Yellowhead Pass
Mt. Columbia 12,294 ft. (3,747 m)
Kicking Horse Pass
Mt. Assiniboine 11,870 ft. (3,618 m)
Monashee Mts
Columbia Mts
Selkirk Mts
Bitterroot Range
Rocky Mountains
Coast Ranges
Cascade Range
Columbia
Snake
North
40° North Latitude
120° West Longitude
Prince Patrick Island
Ellef Ringnes I.
NORTH MAGNETIC POLE
Mackenzie King I.
Queen Elizabeth Islands
Barbeau Peak 8,584 ft. (2,616 m)
Ellesmere Island
Axel Heiberg Island
Peary Channel
Jones Sound
Devon Island
Melville I.
Bathurst Island
Cornwallis I.
Banks Island
M'Clure Strait
ARCTIC ISLANDS
Somerset Island
Prince of Wales Island
Brodeur Peninsula
Gulf of Boothia
Boothia Peninsula
M'Clintock Channel
Victoria Island
Wollaston Peninsula
King William I.
Coronation Gulf
Bathurst Inlet
Chantrey Inlet
Great Bear Lake
Coppermine
Contwoyto Lake
Back
Northwest
Aberdeen Lake
Baker Lake
Chesterfield Inlet
Dubawnt Lake
Lac la Martre
Yellowknife
Great Slave Lake
CANADIAN SHIELD
Liard
Hay
Wholdaia L.
Nueltin Lake
INTERIOR PLAINS
Lake Athabasca
Athabasca
Cree Lake
Wollaston Lake
Reindeer Lake
Churchill
Southern Indian Lake
Lesser Slave Lake
Alberta
Edmonton
Saskatchewan
Manitoba
Cedar L.
Lake Winnipegosis
Lake Winnipeg
Lake Manitoba
North Saskatchewan
South Saskatchewan
Great Plains
Calgary
Regina
Winnipeg
Souris
Lake of the Woods
Red River of the North
Missouri
Yellowstone
Bismarck
UNITED
0 250 500 750 1,000 1,250 1,500 1,750
0 250 500 750 1,000 1,250 1,500 1,750 2,000 2,250 2,500 2,750 3,000

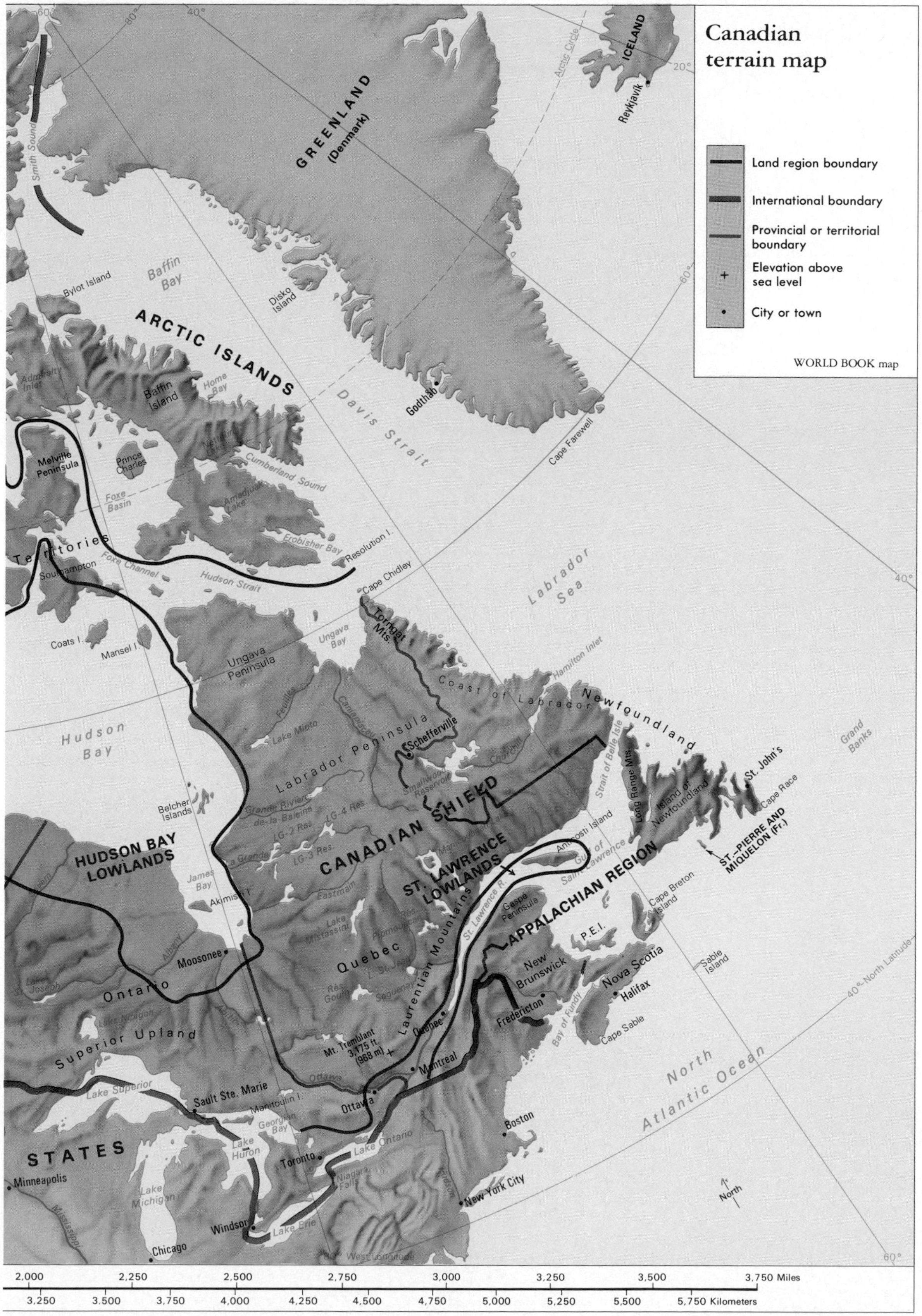
Canadian terrain map
Land region boundary
International boundary
Provincial or territorial boundary
Elevation above sea level
City or town
WORLD BOOK map
GREENLAND (Denmark)
ICELAND
Reykjavik
Arctic Circle
Smith Sound
Baffin Bay
Bylot Island
Disko Island
ARCTIC ISLANDS
Admiralty Inlet
Baffin Island
Home Bay
Davis Strait
Godthåb
Cape Farewell
Melville Peninsula
Prince Charles
Foxe Basin
Cumberland Sound
Amadjuak Lake
Frobisher Bay
Resolution I.
Territories
Southampton
Foxe Channel
Hudson Strait
Cape Chidley
Labrador Sea
Coats I.
Mansel I.
Ungava Peninsula
Ungava Bay
Torngat Mts.
Hamilton Inlet
Coast of Labrador
Newfoundland
Hudson Bay
Lake Minto
Labrador Peninsula
Schefferville
Smallwood Reservoir
Churchill
Strait of Belle Isle
Long Range Mts.
Island of Newfoundland
St. John's
Cape Race
Grand Banks
Belcher Islands
Grande Rivière de-la-Baleine
LG-4 Res.
LG-2 Res.
LG-3 Res.
La Grande
CANADIAN SHIELD
Anticosti Island
ST.-PIERRE AND MIQUELON (Fr.)
HUDSON BAY LOWLANDS
James Bay
Akimiski I.
Eastmain
ST. LAWRENCE LOWLANDS
Gulf of Saint Lawrence
APPALACHIAN REGION
Cape Breton Island
Lake Mistassini
Gaspé Peninsula
St. Lawrence R.
Laurentian Mountains
Quebec
P.E.I.
Albany
Moosonee
New Brunswick
Nova Scotia
Sable Island
Lake St. Joseph
Ontario
Halifax
Fredericton
Bay of Fundy
Cape Sable
Lake Nipigon
Superior Upland
Mt. Tremblant 3,175 ft. (968 m)
Montreal
North Atlantic Ocean
40° North Latitude
Lake Superior
Sault Ste. Marie
Manitoulin I.
Ottawa
Georgian Bay
Lake Huron
Boston
STATES
Toronto
Lake Ontario
Minneapolis
Lake Michigan
Niagara Falls
Hudson
New York City
Mississippi
Windsor
Lake Erie
Chicago
North
60° West Longitude
2,000 2,250 2,500 2,750 3,000 3,250 3,500 3,750 Miles
3,250 3,500 3,750 4,000 4,250 4,500 4,750 5,000 5,250 5,500 5,750 Kilometers

Facts about the United States and Canada

United States

State	Capital	Popular name	Area (sq. mi.)	Area (km²)	Rank in area	Population*	Rank in pop.*	Population density* (sq. mi.)	Population density* (km²)
Alabama	Montgomery	Yellowhammer State	51,609	133,667	29	3,890,061	22	75	29
Alaska	Juneau	Last Frontier	589,757	1,527,464	1	400,481	50	0.7	0.3
Arizona	Phoenix	Grand Canyon State	113,909	295,023	6	2,717,866	29	24	9
Arkansas	Little Rock	Land of Opportunity	53,104	137,539	27	2,285,513	33	43	17
California	Sacramento	Golden State	158,693	411,013	3	23,668,562	1	149	58
Colorado	Denver	Centennial State	104,247	269,998	8	2,888,834	28	28	11
Connecticut	Hartford	Constitution State	5,009	12,973	48	3,107,576	25	620	239
Delaware	Dover	First State	2,057	5,328	49	595,225	47	289	112
Florida	Tallahassee	Sunshine State	58,560	151,670	22	9,739,992	7	166	64
Georgia	Atlanta	Empire State of the South	58,876	152,488	21	5,464,265	13	93	36
Hawaii	Honolulu	Aloha State	6,450	16,705	47	965,000	39	150	58
Idaho	Boise	Gem State	83,557	216,412	13	943,935	41	11	4
Illinois	Springfield	Land of Lincoln	56,400	146,075	24	11,418,461	5	202	78
Indiana	Indianapolis	Hoosier State	36,291	93,993	38	5,490,179	12	151	58
Iowa	Des Moines	Hawkeye State	56,290	145,790	25	2,913,387	27	52	20
Kansas	Topeka	Sunflower State	82,264	213,063	14	2,363,208	32	29	11
Kentucky	Frankfort	Bluegrass State	40,395	104,623	37	3,661,433	23	91	35
Louisiana	Baton Rouge	Pelican State	48,523	125,674	31	4,203,972	19	87	34
Maine	Augusta	Pine Tree State	33,215	86,026	39	1,124,660	38	34	13
Maryland	Annapolis	Old Line State	10,577	27,394	42	4,216,446	18	399	154
Massachusetts	Boston	Bay State	8,257	21,385	45	5,737,037	11	695	268
Michigan	Lansing	Wolverine State	58,216	150,779	23	9,258,344	8	159	61
Minnesota	St. Paul	Gopher State	84,068	217,735	12	4,077,148	21	49	19
Mississippi	Jackson	Magnolia State	47,716	123,584	32	2,520,638	31	53	20
Missouri	Jefferson City	Show Me State	69,686	180,486	19	4,917,444	15	71	27
Montana	Helena	Treasure State	147,138	381,086	4	786,690	44	5	2
Nebraska	Lincoln	Cornhusker State	77,227	200,017	15	1,570,006	35	20	8
Nevada	Carson City	Silver State	110,540	286,297	7	799,184	43	7	3
New Hampshire	Concord	Granite State	9,304	24,097	44	920,610	42	99	38
New Jersey	Trenton	Garden State	7,836	20,295	46	7,364,158	9	940	363
New Mexico	Santa Fe	Land of Enchantment	121,666	315,113	5	1,299,968	37	11	4
New York	Albany	Empire State	49,576	128,401	30	17,557,288	2	354	137
North Carolina	Raleigh	Tar Heel State	52,586	136,197	28	5,874,429	10	112	43

* 1980 census.

State abbr.**	State bird	State flower	State tree	State song
Ala.	Yellowhammer	Camellia	Southern pine	"Alabama"
†	Willow ptarmigan	Forget-me-not	Sitka spruce	"Alaska's Flag"
Ariz.	Cactus wren	Saguaro (Giant cactus)	Paloverde	"Arizona"
Ark.	Mockingbird	Apple blossom	Pine	"Arkansas"
Calif.	California valley quail	Golden poppy	California redwood	"I Love You, California"
Colo.	Lark bunting	Rocky Mountain columbine	Blue spruce	"Where the Columbines Grow"
Conn.	Robin	Mountain laurel	White oak	"Yankee Doodle"
Del.	Blue hen chicken	Peach blossom	American holly	"Our Delaware"
Fla.	Mockingbird	Orange blossom	Cabbage (Sabal) palm	"Swanee River"
Ga.	Brown thrasher	Cherokee rose	Live oak	"Georgia on My Mind"
†	Nene (Hawaiian goose)	Hibiscus	Kukui	"Hawaii Ponoi" (Hawaii's Own)
Ida.	Mountain bluebird	Syringa (Mock orange)	Western white pine	"Here We Have Idaho"
Ill.	Cardinal	Native violet	White oak	"Illinois"
Ind.	Cardinal	Peony	Tulip tree	"On the Banks of the Wabash"
Ia.	Eastern goldfinch	Wild rose	Oak	"The Song of Iowa"
Kans. or Kan.	Western meadow lark	Sunflower	Cottonwood	"Home on the Range"
Ky. or Ken.	Kentucky cardinal	Goldenrod	Kentucky coffeetree	"My Old Kentucky Home"
La.	Brown pelican	Magnolia	Bald cypress	"Give Me Louisiana"
Me.	Chickadee	White pine cone and tassel	White pine	"State of Maine Song"
Md.	Baltimore oriole	Black-eyed Susan	White (Wye) oak	"Maryland, My Maryland"
Mass.	Chickadee	Mayflower	American elm	"Hail Massachusetts"‡
Mich.	Robin	Apple blossom	White pine	"Michigan, My Michigan"‡
Minn.	Common loon	Pink and white lady's-slipper	Norway (Red) pine	"Hail! Minnesota"
Miss.	Mockingbird	Magnolia	Magnolia	"Go Mis-sis-sip-pi"
Mo.	Bluebird	Hawthorn	Flowering dogwood	"Missouri Waltz"
Mont.	Western meadow lark	Bitterroot	Ponderosa pine	"Montana"
Nebr. or Neb.	Western meadow lark	Goldenrod	Cottonwood	"Beautiful Nebraska"
Nev.	Mountain bluebird‡	Sagebrush‡	Single-leaf piñon	"Home Means Nevada"
N.H.	Purple finch	Purple lilac	White birch	"Old New Hampshire"‡‡
N.J.	Eastern goldfinch	Purple violet	Red oak	None
N. Mex. or N.M.	Road runner	Yucca flower	Piñon (Nut pine)	"O, Fair New Mexico"
N.Y.	Bluebird	Rose	Sugar maple	None
N.C.	Cardinal	Flowering dogwood	Pine	"The Old North State"

** For U.S. Postal Service abbreviations, see individual state articles.
† No traditional abbreviation.
‡Unofficial.
‡‡This state has more than one official song. See state article for others.

State	Capital	Popular name	Area (sq. mi.)	Area (km²)	Rank in area	Population*	Rank in pop.*	Population density* (sq. mi.)	Population density* (km²)
North Dakota	Bismarck	Flickertail State	70,665	183,022	17	652,695	46	9	3
Ohio	Columbus	Buckeye State	41,222	106,764	35	10,797,419	6	262	101
Oklahoma	Oklahoma City	Sooner State	69,919	181,089	18	3,025,266	26	43	17
Oregon	Salem	Beaver State	96,981	251,180	10	2,632,663	30	27	10
Pennsylvania	Harrisburg	Keystone State	45,333	117,412	33	11,866,728	4	262	101
Rhode Island	Providence	Ocean State	1,214	3,144	50	947,154	40	780	301
South Carolina	Columbia	Palmetto State	31,055	80,432	40	3,119,208	24	100	39
South Dakota	Pierre	Sunshine State	77,047	199,551	16	690,178	45	9	3
Tennessee	Nashville	Volunteer State	42,244	109,411	34	4,590,750	17	109	42
Texas	Austin	Lone Star State	267,338	692,402	2	14,228,383	3	53	20
Utah	Salt Lake City	Beehive State	84,916	219,931	11	1,461,037	36	17	7
Vermont	Montpelier	Green Mountain State	9,609	24,887	43	511,456	48	53	20
Virginia	Richmond	Old Dominion	40,817	105,716	36	5,346,279	14	131	51
Washington	Olympia	Evergreen State	68,192	176,616	20	4,130,163	20	61	24
West Virginia	Charleston	Mountain State	24,181	62,628	41	1,949,644	34	81	31
Wisconsin	Madison	Badger State	56,154	145,438	26	4,705,335	16	84	32
Wyoming	Cheyenne	Equality State	97,914	253,596	9	470,816	49	5	2

Main outlying areas of the United States

Name	Acquired	Status
American Samoa	1900	Unorganized, unincorporated territory
Canton and Enderbury Islands	1939	Joint administration with Great Britain
Guam	1898	Organized, unincorporated territory
Howland, Baker, and Jarvis islands	1857	Unincorporated territory
Johnston Island and Sand Island	1858	Unincorporated territory
Kingman Reef	1922	Unincorporated territory
Midway Islands	1867	Unincorporated territory
Palmyra Island	1898	Unincorporated territory
Puerto Rico	1898	Commonwealth
Trust Territory of the Pacific Islands	1947	UN trust territory (U.S. administration)
Virgin Islands of the United States	1917	Organized, unincorporated territory
Wake Island	1898	Unincorporated territory

State abbr.**	State bird	State flower	State tree	State song
N. Dak. or N.D.	Western meadow lark	Wild prairie rose	American elm	"North Dakota Hymn"
O.	Cardinal	Scarlet carnation	Buckeye	"Beautiful Ohio"
Okla.	Scissor-tailed flycatcher	Mistletoe	Redbud	"Oklahoma!"
Ore. or Oreg.	Western meadow lark	Oregon grape	Douglas fir	"Oregon, My Oregon"
Pa. or Penn.	Ruffed grouse	Mountain laurel	Hemlock	None
R.I.	Rhode Island Red	Violet	Red maple	"Rhode Island"
S.C.	Carolina wren	Carolina jessamine	Palmetto	"Carolina"
S. Dak. or S.D.	Ring-necked pheasant	American pasqueflower	Black Hills spruce	"Hail, South Dakota"
Tenn.	Mockingbird	Iris	Tulip poplar	"The Tennessee Waltz"‡‡
Tex.	Mockingbird	Bluebonnet	Pecan	"Texas, Our Texas"
Ut.	Sea gull	Sego lily	Blue spruce	"Utah, We Love Thee"
Vt.	Hermit thrush	Red clover	Sugar maple	"Hail, Vermont!"
Va.	Cardinal	Flowering dogwood	Dogwood	"Carry Me Back to Old Virginia"
Wash.	Willow goldfinch	Coast rhododendron	Western hemlock	"Washington, My Home"
W.Va.	Cardinal	Rhododendron	Sugar maple	"The West Virginia Hills"‡‡
Wis.	Robin	Wood violet	Sugar maple	"On, Wisconsin!"
Wyo.	Meadow lark	Indian paintbrush	Cottonwood	"Wyoming"

Canadian provinces

Province	Capital	Area (sq. mi.)	Area (km²)	Rank in area	Population*	Rank in pop.*	Province abbr.	Provincial flower
Alberta	Edmonton	255,285	661,185	4	1,838,037	4	Alta.	Wild rose
British Columbia	Victoria	366,255	948,596	3	2,466,608	3	B.C.	Flowering dogwood
Manitoba	Winnipeg	251,000	650,087	6	1,021,506	5	Man.	Pasqueflower
New Brunswick	Fredericton	28,354	73,437	8	677,250	8	N.B.	Violet
Newfoundland	St. John's	156,185	404,517	7	557,725	9	Nfld.	Pitcher plant
Nova Scotia	Halifax	21,425	55,490	9	828,571	7	N.S.	Trailing arbutus
Ontario	Toronto	412,582	1,068,582	2	8,264,465	1	Ont.	White trillium
Prince Edward Island	Charlottetown	2,184	5,657	10	118,229	10	P.E.I.	Lady's-slipper
Quebec	Quebec	594,860	1,540,680	1	6,234,445	2	Que.	White garden lily
Saskatchewan	Regina	251,700	651,900	5	921,323	6	Sask.	Prairie lily

* 1976 census.

Canadian territories

Territory	Capital	Area (sq. mi.)	Area (km²)	Population*	Territorial flower	Territory abbr.
Northwest Territories	Yellowknife	1,304,903	3,379,683	42,609	Mountain avens	N.W. Terr. or N.W.T.
Yukon Territory	Whitehorse	207,076	536,324	21,836	Fireweed	Y.T.

* 1976 census.

A farm in North Carolina nestles in the smooth, green Appalachians of the eastern United States (above left). *In Death Valley, Calif., shifting sand dunes reach toward the foothills of the Panamint Mountains* (near right). *Harsh terrain gives way to quiet beauty at Lower Falls in Yellowstone National Park, Wyo.* (far right).

United States geography

Imagine a friend planning her first trip to the United States. "Everything," she writes, "I want to see everything. The mountains, the lakes, the ocean, and the desert." Your response, understandably, must be "which ones?"

To the inexperienced traveler, the landscape of the United States is full of surprises, contrasts, and abundance. There are many mountains, some ages old and some just young outcroppings—only a few million years old. The land can stretch for hundreds of miles with little change in elevation. It can also drop from a height of 11,000 feet (3,352 meters) to almost 300 feet (91 meters) below sea level.

Once our traveler leaves one of the many great cities along the East Coast, she may want to head west. Unless she leaves from a point south of Savannah, Georgia, she will eventually run into the Appalachian Mountains. It is impossible to leave from any eastern seaboard city north of Savannah without crossing these wooded, rolling mountains.

The Appalachians are the oldest mountains in the country. They cover a good portion of the eastern quarter of the United States. They almost fill the New England states and seem barely to stop short of the Atlantic Ocean. The names of the Appalachian ranges may change from state to state.

Countless centuries of wind and rain have worn these mountains smooth. Their peaks range over 6,000 feet (1,828 meters). The highest is Mount Mitchell in North Carolina at 6,684 feet (2,037 meters).

Just when our tourist has accustomed herself to seeing green mountain peaks, she has a change of scene. West of the Appalachian ranges the land alters dramatically. Where there were mountains, there may be hills; where there were forests, there is grass. Where peaks may have blocked out the sun, now there seems to be nothing between her and the horizon.

The interior of the United States is covered by plains. Glacier activity millions of years ago formed much of this area. As a result, many midwestern states are flat. Travelers who head west from Ohio can drive for days with little change in scenery. But if our tourist travels through Indiana and Illinois, she will discover something as awesome as the mountains she left behind: the Mississippi River. In a country filled with rivers, it is beyond compare.

In Missouri, the Mississippi River is a wide ribbon of water cutting through the flat interior of the United States.

The Mississippi is the longest river in the United States. It begins as a small, clear stream in northern Minnesota. As it travels southward, rivers in Minnesota, Wisconsin, Iowa, Illinois, and Missouri empty into it. When it reaches near St. Louis, the cloudy, mud-choked waters of the Missouri River join it. From this point on, the river deserves its name the "muddy Mississippi."

Several miles downstream at Cairo, Illinois, the Ohio River empties into the Mississippi. At this point the river is about 4,500 feet (1,370 meters) wide—its widest point. The river continues to pick up additional water until it empties into the Gulf of Mexico.

Beyond the Mississippi, our traveler continues her journey across the Great Plains. The plains stretch from west of the Mississippi for more than 2,000 miles (3,218 kilometers). Just as our wanderer thinks she will never see a rise in the earth's surface again, a group of purple clouds on the horizon catch her eye. Hours later, the clouds have turned into a ragged line of sharp points. They are not cumulus clouds. They are the Rocky Mountains.

The Rockies are as different from the Appalachians as day is from night. Where the Appalachians are old, the Rockies are relatively young. Nowhere are the gentle, rolling formations of the eastern range to be found. The Rockies are rugged. There are 50 to 60 peaks over 14,000 feet (4,267 meters) in the Colorado Rockies alone.

The area around the Rockies offers more breathtaking scenery. The rivers in the vicinity have carved out deep canyons, most notably the Grand Canyon. Directly west of the mountains in Utah lies the Great Salt Lake Desert. At the eastern edge of the desert is one of the natural wonders of the world: Great Salt Lake, an inland sea that, even though fed by freshwater streams, is saltier than the ocean.

The area west of the Rockies is harsher than the land west of the Appalachians. Much of it is desert. By the time our tourist has crossed the Sierras and the Coast Ranges to reach the Pacific Ocean, she feels she has seen the splendor of the United States. But this is not so. She has barely scratched the surface. Nothing's more beautiful than Hawaii in the Pacific Ocean. Nothing's more rugged than Alaska to the north. And still there for her return trip are the Great Lakes, Death Valley, and the swamplands of the South.

United States weather

Because of its size and varied geography, the United States has a variety of weather conditions. Generally, though, most of the contiguous United States can be roughly divided into three sections for winter and summer. In January, the northernmost part is very cold, the middle section is cold, and the southern section is moderate. In July, the northern portion is moderate, the middle hot, and the southern portion extremely hot. The West Coast and Hawaii are moderate in both winter and summer.

Generalizations can also be made about the amount of precipitation in the country. Moderate to heavy amounts of rain and snow fall in the eastern half, but large areas on either side of the Rockies receive little moisture compared to the rest of the country. The driest—and hottest—spot in the United States is Death Valley, California, which receives less than 2 inches (5 centimeters) of rain per year and recorded the country's highest temperature, 134° F. (57° C). Mount Waialeale on Kauai Island in Hawaii, on the other hand, receives about 460 inches (1,170 centimeters) of rain per year.

During the spring and summer months the mid- and southwestern states are threatened with sometimes devastating tornadoes. The coastal areas of the Atlantic Ocean and the Gulf of Mexico are plagued with another kind of destructive storm. Hurricanes can occur from June to November, though most hit the coasts in September. Hurricane winds can blow at speeds of 74 or more miles (119 kilometers) per hour. The winds blow in from the sea, carrying heavy rain and causing huge waves to batter coastlines. Hurricanes affect the weather inland for great distances.

Probably the state with the most extreme weather conditions is Alaska. Its winter temperature averages as low as −30° F. (−34° C) and as high as 48° F. (9° C). The amount of snow is up to 200 inches (508 centimeters) in the southernmost portion of the state.

Hawaii has the most moderate weather of any state. Heavy rain falls on the mountaintops, but less than 10 inches (25 centimeters) fall on the lowlands. There is little temperature change between night and day, winter and summer in this area of tropical beauty.

Regular snowfalls are a winter feature in the northeastern half of the United States (below). *Night and day, winter and summer, Hawaii has little change in its moderate, tropical climate* (below right).

Average January temperatures

Degrees Fahrenheit	Degrees Celsius
Over 60	Over 16
45 to 60	7 to 16
30 to 45	−1 to 7
15 to 30	−9 to −1
0 to 15	−18 to −9
−15 to 0	−26 to −18
Below −15	Below −26

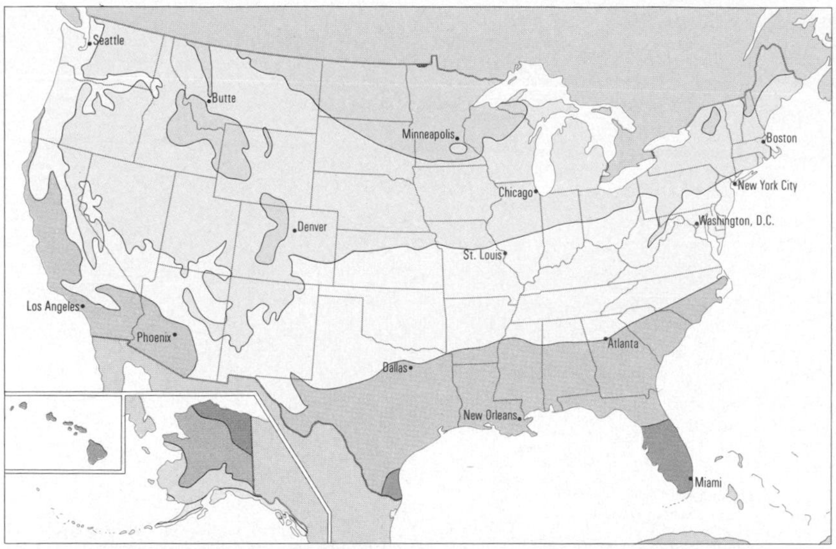

Average July temperatures

Degrees Fahrenheit	Degrees Celsius
Over 90	Over 32
75 to 90	24 to 32
60 to 75	16 to 24
45 to 60	7 to 16
Below 45	Below 7

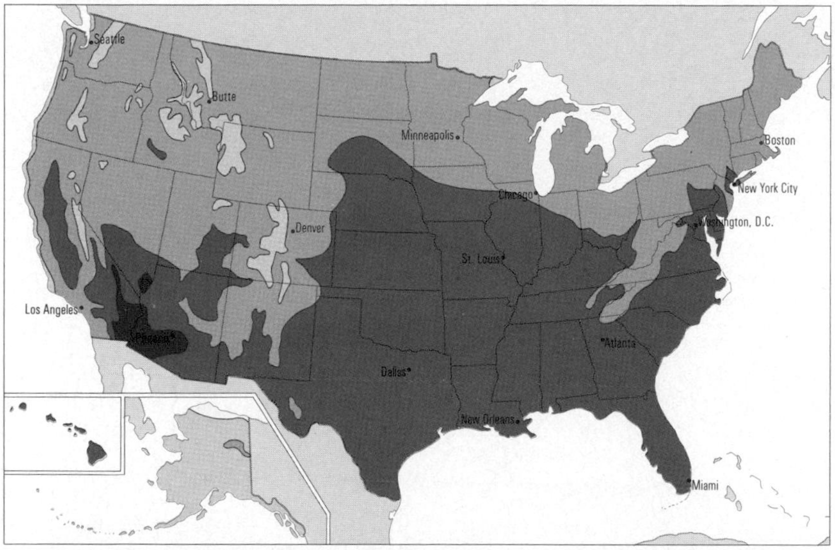

Average yearly precipitation

Inches	Centimeters
More than 80	More than 200
60 to 80	150 to 200
40 to 60	100 to 150
20 to 40	50 to 100
10 to 20	25 to 50
Less than 10	Less than 25

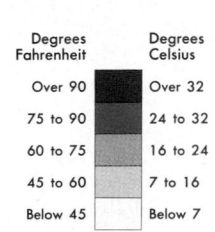

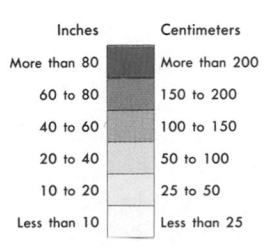

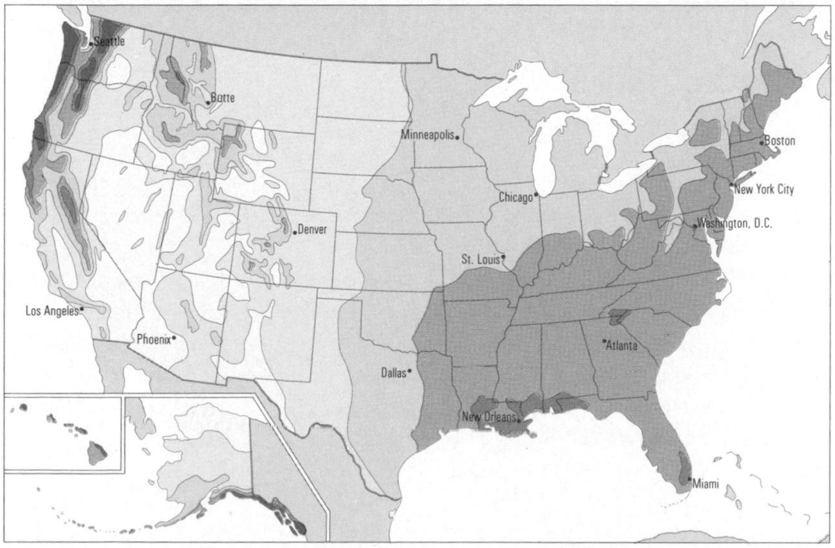

WORLD BOOK maps

Varied U.S. weather conditions *The United States exhibits a variety of weather conditions. January temperatures generally decrease from south to north. The South and West also have milder winters than the rest of the nation.*

In July, the average temperatures in most of the nation are between 75 and 90° F. (24 and 32° C) or 60 and 75° F. (16 and 24° C). Lower temperatures occur in some mountains and most of Alaska. Temperatures are higher in the southwestern desert.

Annual precipitation generally increases from west to east in the United States. Hawaii and the west coast of Alaska, however, receive the most precipitation.

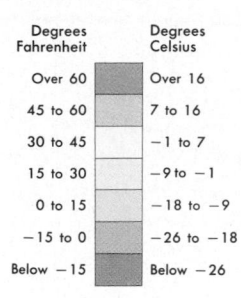

The Trans-Alaska Pipeline was built to help increase U.S. fuel supplies by tapping Alaska's vast oil reserves. The pipeline carries oil about 800 miles (1,300 kilometers) across the state from Prudhoe Bay on the Arctic coast to Valdez on the state's south-central coast.

United States energy

The United States is more than a large country with many interesting geographical features. It is an industrialized and complex nation whose people enjoy a high standard of living. Most U.S. people, whether rich or poor, have driven cars and live in heated residences. People take for granted vacuum cleaners, televisions, washing machines, heated office buildings, and air-conditioned movie theaters. Abundant energy sources are required to fuel these conveniences.

About 90 per cent of U.S. energy comes from fossil fuels. These fuels were formed from the remains of plants and animals that lived millions of years before human beings existed.

Fossil fuels are buried deep in the earth. Extracting them is costly and time consuming. Fossil fuels include petroleum, natural gas, and coal.

About 45 per cent of U.S. energy is supplied by petroleum. This dark liquid contains hundreds of different materials, including gasoline. Thousands of products are in turn made from these materials.

Automobiles, buses, trucks, and tractors use most of the gasoline. Petroleum also provides heating oil for homes and businesses, plus fuel oil for factories, power plants, ships, railroads, and trucks. Jet fuel powers commercial air carriers and military planes. Kerosene is another fuel refined from petroleum.

Thirty-one states produce petroleum commercially. Most of the domestic oil is located in Texas,

Louisiana, California, Oklahoma, Wyoming, New Mexico, Kansas, and Alaska. These states produce about nine-tenths of the nation's domestic oil. The source of much of the United States' petroleum, however, is not the United States itself. The nation consumes much more than it produces, so importing foreign oil to meet its needs is necessary. During the 1970's and 1980's, this increasing dependence on foreign oil became a serious problem for the United States. The high price of foreign oil spurred U.S. efforts to conserve petroleum.

The second important source of U.S. energy is natural gas, which supplies about 25 per cent of the nation's energy needs. This source is not to be confused with gasoline, which is liquid. Natural gas, like other gases, cannot be seen or felt. The same process that formed petroleum created natural gas, and it is usually found along with petroleum deposits.

Industry uses 40 per cent of the natural gas in the United States. This energy source is used in the production of many products including bricks, tile, cement, glass, foods, iron and steel, and textiles. It is also used for diverse purposes such as hardening of nose cones of spacecraft.

The average U.S. consumer has many uses for gas in the home. Gas is the cleanest of all the fossil fuels. It is the easiest to transport to its users and causes very little pollution. Gas is a popular cooking and heating fuel. Many hot water heaters, clothes dryers, and outdoor lamps are fueled by gas. Gas has even been used experimentally to fuel automobiles.

The United States produces more natural gas than any other nation. Texas and Louisiana combined produce more gas than any state and more gas than the next leading foreign producer: the Soviet Union.

In the late 1960's and early 1970's, gas consumption in the United States was greater than the amount of newly discovered gas reserves. Although the United States has supplies of gas for many years, some people became concerned about the declining reserves. The gas industry has been exploring for additional sources of gas in the United States and throughout the world. The industry has also been seeking ways of producing gas from coal.

The third important source of U.S. energy is coal, which supplies about 20 per cent of the country's needs. Coal is a dark-colored rock, some of it buried deep below the earth's surface. Most U.S. coal is found either in the eastern half of the nation or in the Rocky Mountain area. Additional deposits are located in Alaska.

Not all coal is alike. Generally there are four different kinds. The distinction is based on how much carbon the coal contains. The coal with the highest carbon content, called anthracite, has about 98 per cent carbon. In order of decreasing carbon content come bituminous coal, subbituminous coal, and lignite.

Coal is sometimes used as a fuel, as when it is burned to produce heat. There are problems, though, with burning coal. It is more difficult to process than petroleum, and it is dirtier than natural gas.

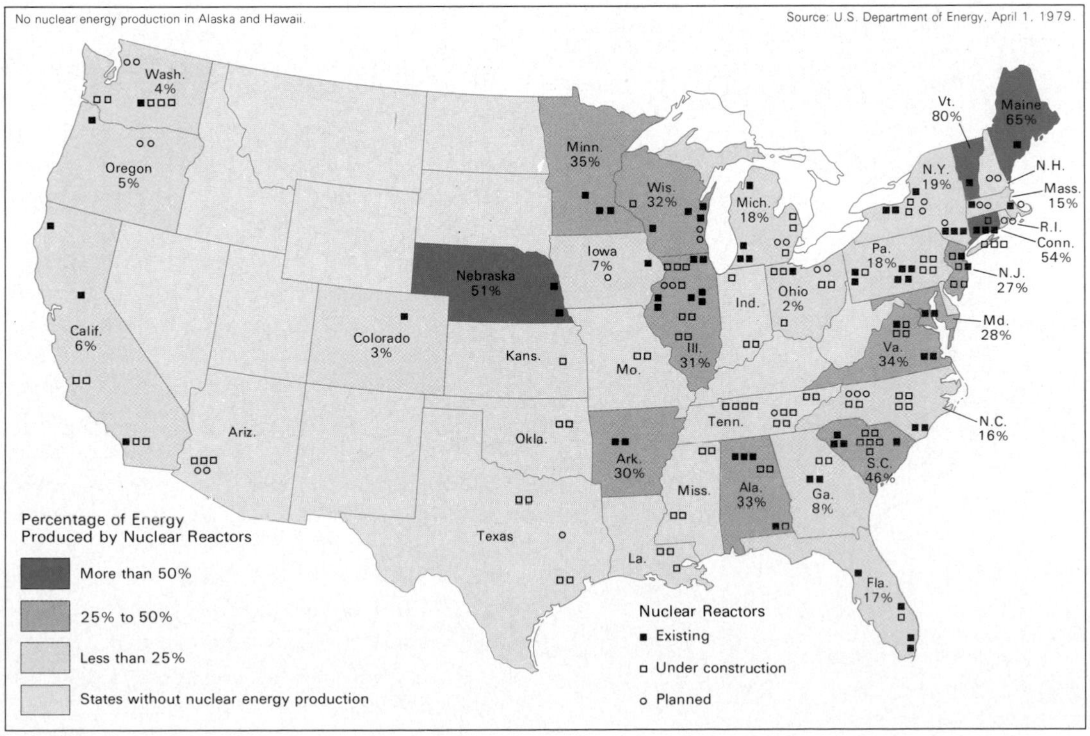

U.S. nuclear facilities and output *An alternative source to petroleum, coal, and natural gas for U.S. energy is nuclear fuel. U.S. nuclear facilities and their output are shown on the map to the left. The United States has more nuclear-powered electric plants than any other nation. They produce an average of 9 per cent of U.S. electric power.*

U.S. coal deposits *After oil and natural gas, coal is the third most important source of U.S. energy, supplying 20 per cent of the nation's needs. Major deposits of the four types of coal found in the United States, plus Canada, are shown on the map to the right.*

Coal deposits in the United States

■ Anthracite

■ Bituminous

▨ Subbituminous

▨ Lignite and brown

WORLD BOOK map

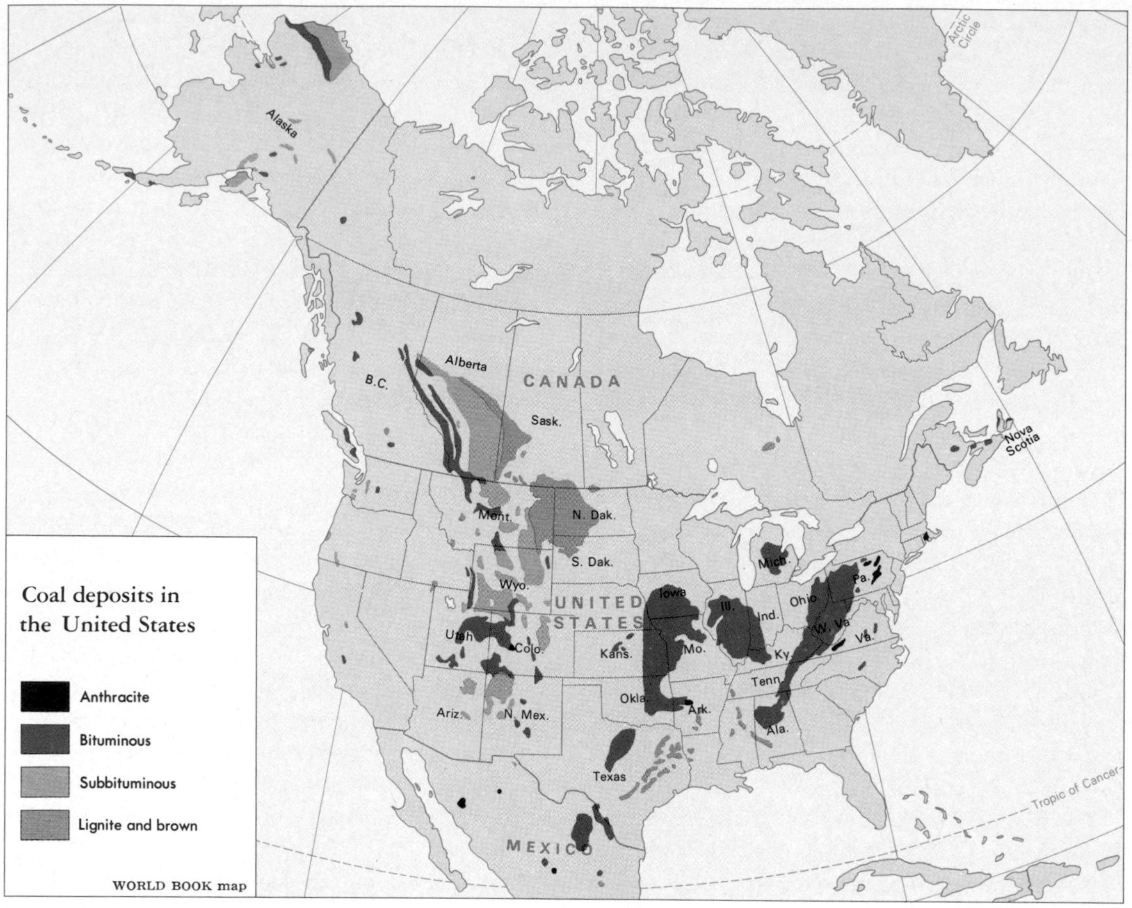

U.S. coal uses *All types of U.S. coal consumed or exported in 1976 totaled 663,228,000 short tons (601,670,300 metric tons). Use of this coal splits into the five general categories shown on the chart to the right.*

Electric power 68%

Coking coal 13%

General industries 9%

Exports 9%

Heating 1%

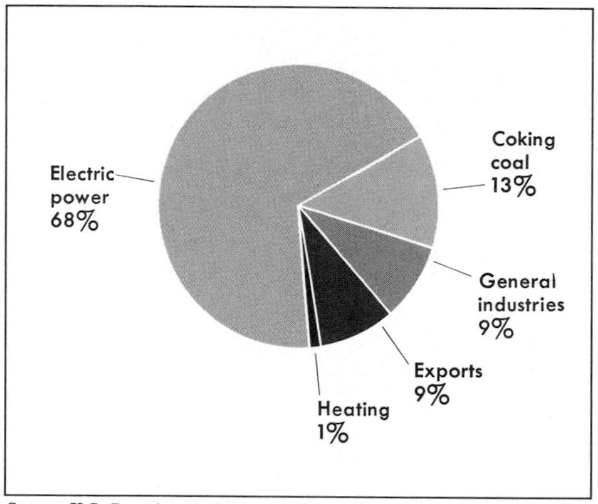

Source: U.S. Department of Energy.

Coal's main use in the United States is as fuel for the production of electricity. Often when you turn on a light switch or start the air conditioner, you have used energy that originated from this hard, dark rock.

Most electric power plants use steam-turbine engines. Water is boiled to produce steam. This steam moves the wheels of turbines. They in turn drive the generators that produce electricity. In most of these steam-turbine plants, coal is the fuel burned to produce the steam.

Coal is in plentiful supply in the United States. But with a current reduction in the use of petroleum and natural gas, the need for coal has increased. If the use of coal continues to grow, mining of hard-to-reach sources to meet demand will force the cost of coal up.

An alternative to coal as a fuel for steam-turbine power plants is nuclear fuel. The United States has more nuclear-powered electric plants than any other nation. They provide about 9 per cent of U.S. electric power. The advantage of nuclear-powered plants is that they use less fuel than coal plants and they do not pollute the air. The disadvantages are that they are costly to build and they pose potential dangers of radioactive leakage.

Another source of power is water. Hydroelectric plants use water from a waterfall or dam to generate electricity. Water power supplies about 4 per cent of U.S. energy.

Some U.S. farmers harness the power of the wind to provide energy. Windmills are generally used to pump water and to drive electric generators for lighting and for charging storage batteries. Research is under way to discover new uses for wind power on farms and elsewhere.

The United States is fortunate that its natural resources offer so many sources of energy. The consumption of energy, however, has so increased that scientists must always look to new technologies to provide different ways to heat U.S. homes or run its automobiles. One of the more promising ways of creating energy is solar power.

There are places in the United States such as the South and West where sunshine seems more abundant than in other areas. Southern and western states could use solar power as an alternative, or a companion, to conventional power.

It is not unusual when traveling in California to see glass plates on the tops of residential buildings. These devices are special collectors that trap the sun's rays. The sunlight caught by the collectors is turned into heat. Houses, water, and swimming pools are heated by this method.

Solar power is being used today on a small scale. Research is under way, however, to discover how to power large electric plants with the sun. This source of energy is accessible, cheap, unthreatened by changing political circumstances, and sure to be around when U.S. fossil fuels have been depleted.

The United States has other potential sources of energy that may become important in future years. The western part of the country has large deposits of oil shale, a type of rock that can be processed to yield petroleum. But oil shale is expensive to mine. Oil-shale mining requires tearing up the land and creates huge piles of waste rock.

The farms of the United States can also serve as a source of energy. Grains such as corn, barley, and oats can be converted to ethyl alcohol, which is used to make a fuel mixture called gasohol. Gasohol is nine-tenths gasoline and one-tenth alcohol. The use of gasohol helps conserve petroleum.

Other long-range possibilities to help replace U.S. dependence on petroleum include geothermal power from underground heat, burning of solid wastes, and hydrogen from ocean water.

Most experts agree, however, that the United States will remain dependent on dwindling and increasingly expensive petroleum for many years. This makes conservation a vital necessity until new sources of energy are found.

Quadrillions of British thermal units*

Total energy†

Nuclear

Natural gas

Petroleum

Coal

Hydroelectric and geothermal

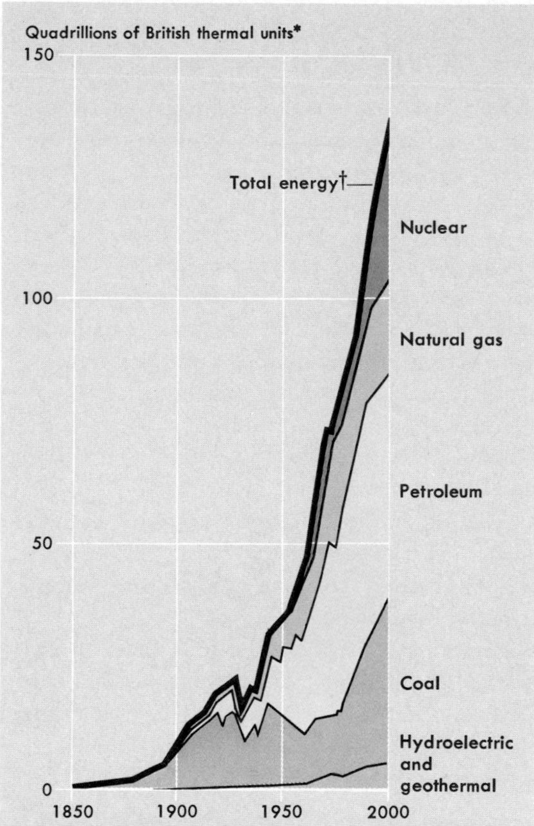

*One British thermal unit (BTU) equals 1,055 joules.
†Total for year 2000 includes 6.9 quadrillion BTU's from oil shale, solar energy, and biomass (burning or gasification of wood and wastes).

Sources: *Annual Report to Congress, 1977*, Energy Information Administration, U.S. Department of Energy, April 1978; *Historical Statistics of the United States, Colonial Times to 1970*, U.S. Bureau of the Census, September 1975; *Monthly Energy Review*, September 1978, U.S. Department of Energy.

Changing U.S. energy sources *Petroleum surpassed coal as the most important U.S. fuel in the 1950's. The graph to the left shows that by the year 2000, nuclear power may fill as much as 25 per cent of all U.S. energy needs.*

Short tons of coal equivalent*

1976: 12.7

United States

1950: 8.5

1976: 2.3

1950: 1.2   World

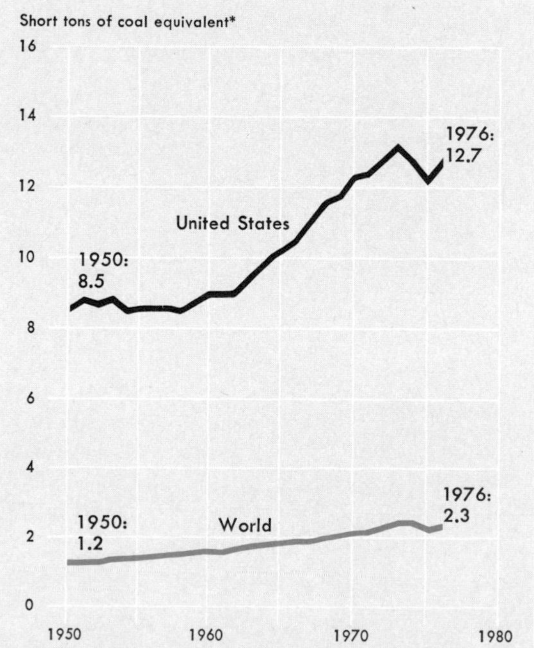

*One short ton of coal equals 0.9071847 metric ton.

Source: *Statistical Yearbooks*, 1960-1977, United Nations.

U.S. energy use per person *In the highly industrialized and technological United States, energy consumption is nearly six times as high per person as in the rest of the world. The graph to the left shows that U.S. energy consumption rose 4.2 per cent between 1950 and 1976, compared to only 1.1 per cent for the rest of the world.*

United States agriculture

If the United States has difficulty keeping its fuel consumption consistent with its production, it enjoys the reverse situation in agriculture. The United States is one of the most important agricultural nations in the world. Approximately 25 per cent of the world's beef, 15 per cent of its milk, 50 per cent of its corn, and 20 per cent of its oats are produced by the United States. The nation makes sizable contributions to the world's supply of other grains, chickens, eggs, cotton, hogs, and tobacco.

There are three basic factors contributing to this situation: U.S. geography and climate, technology, and management.

The land in the United States is fertile and there is much of it. The weather is largely moderate. These two factors combine to produce excellent growing conditions.

Almost one-half of the United States is covered with farmland. Even though so much of the land is devoted to agriculture, only about 4 to 5 per cent of the population is employed on farms.

Traditionally, certain areas of the country have been dominated by one particular crop. The Southeast is the foremost tobacco-growing region of the country. The warm climate and light soil make this area perfect for tobacco growing. North Carolina, Kentucky, Virginia, South Carolina, and Tennessee produce the second largest amount of tobacco in the world.

The United States also ranks among the world's leading rice exporters. The leading rice-growing states are in the South and Southwest: Arkansas, Texas, California, and Louisiana.

Dairy farming prevails in the Northeast. The states from New York and Pennsylvania to Wisconsin and Minnesota produce most of the milk in the country. California also has many dairy farms.

The Midwest enjoys some of the best growing conditions in the world. Much of the land is fertile, flat, and free of rocky surfaces. Most of the land in these states is used for growing crops or grazing cattle. Corn is the area's—and the nation's—most val-

The Midwest's fertile, flat, and rock-free land make for some of the world's best growing conditions. Much of the land is used for grazing cattle and growing crops—especially corn, the area's and the nation's most valuable crop.

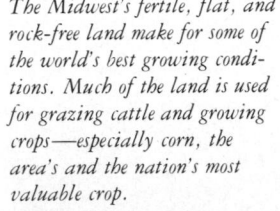

uable crop. Cattle and hogs are the second most important commodity, followed by dairy products.

The West—California, in particular—produces valuable fruits, vegetables, and nuts. Beef and dairy cattle, sheep, and poultry are also raised.

This breakdown of the major agricultural regions in the United States is quite simplified. Every state raises crops. One reason that countrywide agricultural production is possible and profitable is U.S. technology.

Scientific methods and modern machines have helped U.S. farmers profit the most from their efforts and have made U.S. agriculture big business. Farms are decreasing in numbers and increasing in size. Large farms need the latest in mechanized equipment. Power equipment is used to plow and fertilize the land and to plant the crops. This equipment cuts, bales, and chops hay. It unloads grain and milks cows.

Technology turned many areas in California and the rest of the Southwest from semiarid regions to fertile farmland. Almost all of California's crops are grown on land that must be irrigated.

Advances in science have produced fruits and vegetables that can be grown almost anywhere, picked by less-than-delicate machines, and shipped long distances without bruising. Truck farms, which raise vegetables for market, produce the second largest food group in the United States in terms of volume and consumption. The leading truck farming states include California, Florida, New York, and Texas.

Special kinds of grass have been developed that allow the southern states to support grazing cattle. New kinds of winter wheat can be grown. Advances in animal breeding have produced cows with more milk, cattle with more meat, and chickens with bigger drumsticks. Anything that is grown is protected from gnawing bugs with the latest chemical pesticides, often sprayed by airplanes.

Besides the natural advantages and technical skills that have accounted for U.S. agricultural excellence, modern management techniques have also made a significant contribution.

About 95 per cent of U.S. farms specialize in one product. Many farmers already have a buyer for their product before the crop is planted. This arrangement, called contract farming, is common.

Farmers belong to a variety of interest groups from marketing associations to commodity organizations. These groups try to protect the farmers and find markets for their products.

The government has made significant contributions to the well-being of U.S. agriculture. Laws have been passed to protect farm prices. Government publications also make the latest techniques available to all farmers.

Modern technology has helped make U.S. agriculture big business. Power equipment such as this cotton harvester maximize farmers' efforts (left). *Irrigation helped farmers in California turn many semiarid regions into fertile farmland. The state now produces valuable fruits, vegetables, and nuts* (below).

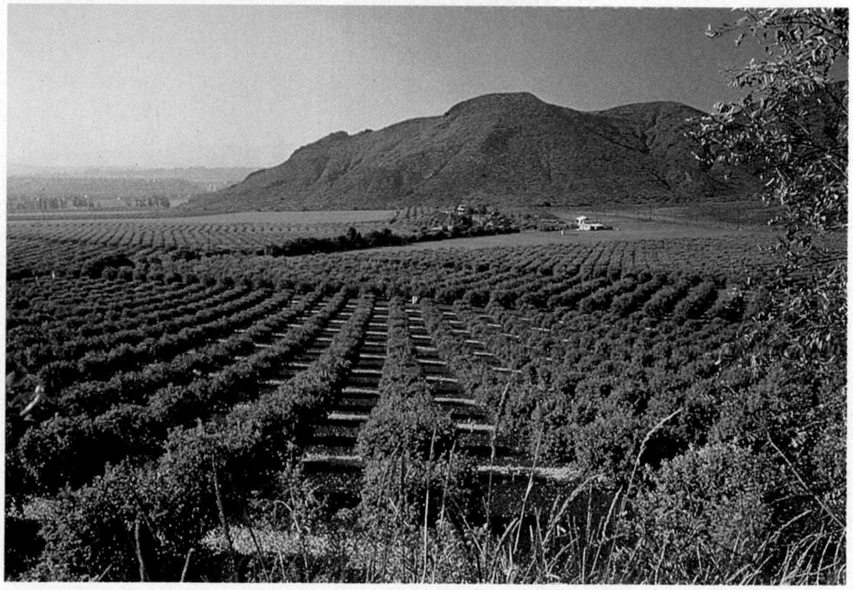

United States people

No country has a people so diverse as the United States'. It has the world's fourth largest population. The nation's inhabitants have increased over the years through great influxes of immigrants, a process that continues today.

Every U.S. inhabitant has roots in another country. Even the Indians', Eskimos', and Hawaiians' ancestors came from other lands thousands of years ago. The U.S. culture reflects the tremendous variety of its people.

In the early 18th century, most settlers in what is now the United States were from Great Britain. They all spoke the same language and shared the same culture. As English settlers continued to arrive on the eastern seaboard, the Indian population began to shrink—either through disease, war, or migration west. This trend continued for the next 100 years as the English settlers and their political beliefs became firmly rooted in New England and elsewhere along the east coast.

Blacks, who now make up the nation's largest minority group, were first brought to the colonies in 1619. Between 1700 and 1750, thousands more were brought each year.

By 1841, other groups were moving to the United States. Germans, Dutch and French were arriving in record numbers. In the mid-1840's, when black immigration was illegal, forced black immigration continued.

Two decades later, after the Civil War, the character of the migration changed again. Italians, Poles, Russians, and central Europeans flooded the U.S. urban areas, bringing with them different languages and customs. A century before the immigrants had arrived and remained largely on the east coast. In the late 19th century some went past New York to Cleveland, Chicago, or to the frontier cities farther west. San Francisco had been admitting hundreds of Chinese for some years.

Large numbers of European immigrants continued to come to the United States before and after World War I. Changes in immigration laws, however, reduced the flow of new citizens during the 1920's. The period after World War II brought

Technology has provided U.S. families with labor-saving devices that increase leisure time. Free hours may be spent in a number of enjoyable activities.

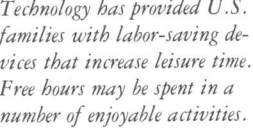

another flood of immigration from war-torn Europe. After the mid-1960's, the character of U.S. immigration changed again, with Mexico, the Carribean, and Asia becoming increasingly important as sources. Many of these recent immigrants were refugees from Communist countries.

About three-quarters of the people of the United States live in urban areas. People cluster in cities for the same reasons they originally came to the United States: cities offer the hope of employment, advancement, and success. Large metropolitan populations were, however, not always the trend. In 1850, 85 out of 100 U.S. inhabitants lived in rural areas. When automation lessened the need for human labor in agriculture, people left the farms to work in industry. They found employment in the factories close to cities, and the trend toward urban living increased.

Most of the large urban areas are centered in the eastern half of the United States. There are large metropolitan areas along the west coast, but most of the western states have small populations. Because of rising fuel, labor, housing, and other costs, many industries began leaving the Northeast and Midwest cities in the mid-1970's. Business—and populations—began shifting to the southern and southwestern states. This trend continues today.

The ability to pack up and move quickly to a new city or state is shared by many U.S. people. The population is largely mobile. Many people in the United States view moving to new communities as a normal, if inconvenient, part of life. Families separated by distance communicate through the advances of technology. The long-distance phone call and the airplane trip "home" at Christmas help keep family members in touch with one another.

Technology has given the average U.S. inhabitant a life free from many menial tasks. No matter the economic level, all U.S. people have probably eaten a frozen TV dinner, used a vacuum cleaner, had access to a washing machine, used a disposable diaper, and baked a cake from a box. These labor-savers have also provided U.S. people with leisure time that they fill with enjoyable activities.

The U.S. people are great sports lovers. The interest of the people has turned sports into a multimillion dollar business in the United States. Cities and towns often provide public tennis courts, football fields, bike paths, running tracks, basketball courts, and swimming pools.

Religion is also an important part of U.S. life. Nearly two-thirds of the people in the United States belong to an organized religion. About 95 per cent of the members of these religious groups are Christians, almost 5 per cent are Jewish, and a small number belong to the Islamic or other Eastern faiths.

Large metropolitan areas in the United States offer a variety of entertainments such as Sea World in San Diego, Calif. (top left). *U.S. cities and towns often provide public facilities for sports-minded people such as these midwestern children* (middle left). *About three-quarters of the U.S. population live in urban areas, making for bustling rush-hour crowds in big cities like Chicago* (bottom left).

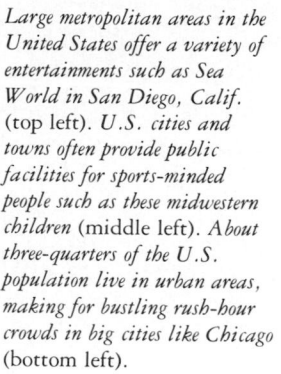

U.S. population growth

The population of the U.S. has risen to about 226.5 million persons since the first U.S. census in 1790. The chart to the right plots this growth and lists population figures for each census year.

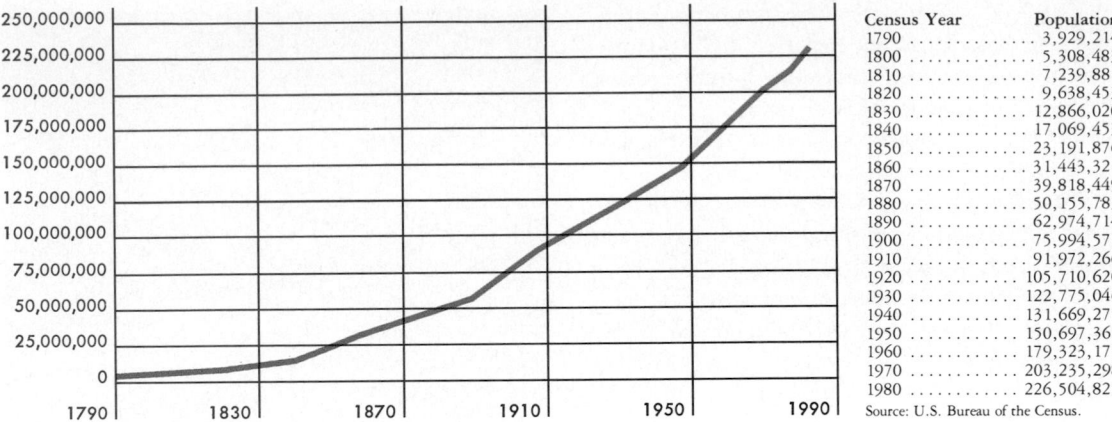

Census Year	Population
1790	3,929,214
1800	5,308,483
1810	7,239,881
1820	9,638,453
1830	12,866,020
1840	17,069,453
1850	23,191,876
1860	31,443,321
1870	39,818,449
1880	50,155,783
1890	62,974,714
1900	75,994,575
1910	91,972,266
1920	105,710,620
1930	122,775,046
1940	131,669,275
1950	150,697,361
1960	179,323,175
1970	203,235,298
1980	226,504,825

Source: U.S. Bureau of the Census.

U.S. population groups

The geographic, racial, and age composition of the U.S. people appear in the charts to the right.

Urban-rural population

Rural 23%
Urban 77%

Racial groups

Whites 86%
Blacks 12%
Others 2%

Age groups by years

0-19 32%   20-39 32%
60 and over 16%   40-59 20%

WORLD BOOK map

U.S. population distribution

Today's U.S. population clusters in the major urban centers shown on the map to the right. The center of population, also shown, has moved steadily westward from 1790.

Persons per sq. mi.	Persons per km²
More than 500	More than 200
250 to 500	100 to 200
50 to 250	20 to 100
10 to 50	4 to 20
Less than 10	Less than 4

Major Urban Centers
● More than 7 million inhabitants
• 1 million to 7 million inhabitants
○ Less than 1 million inhabitants

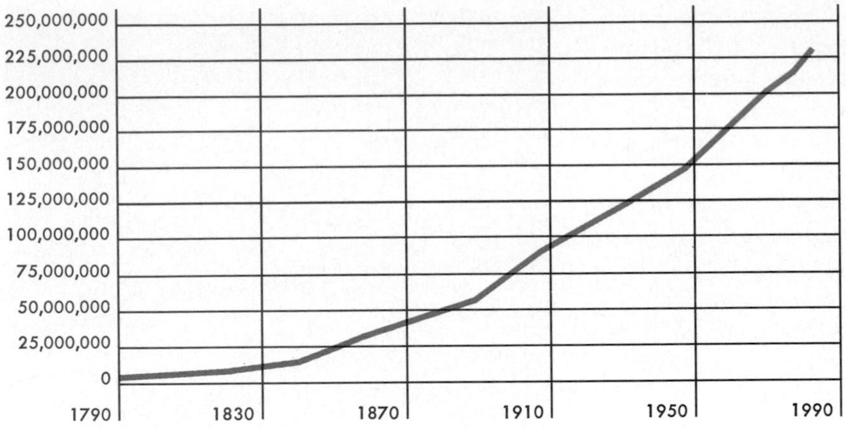

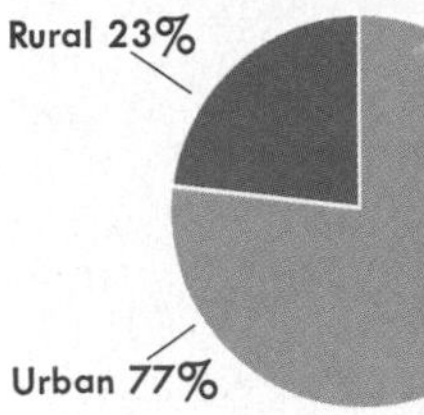

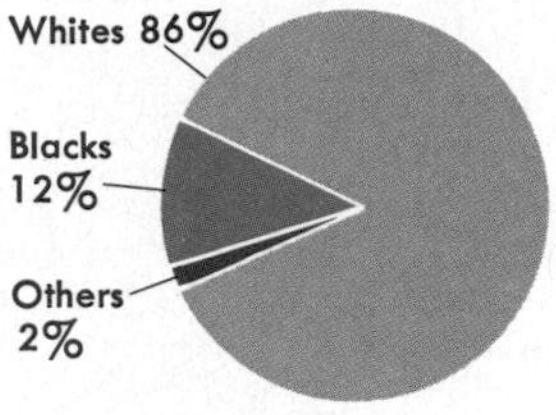

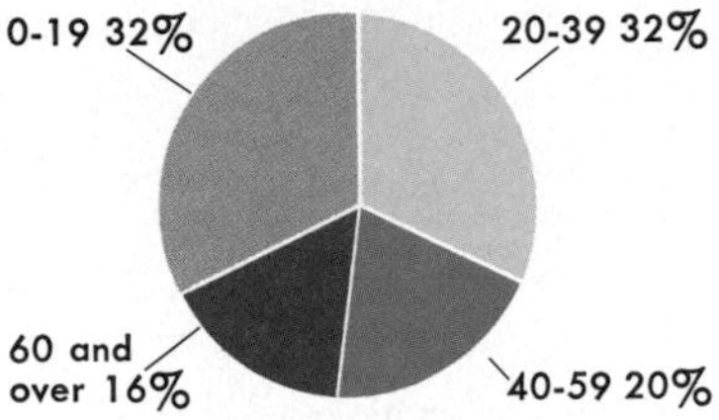

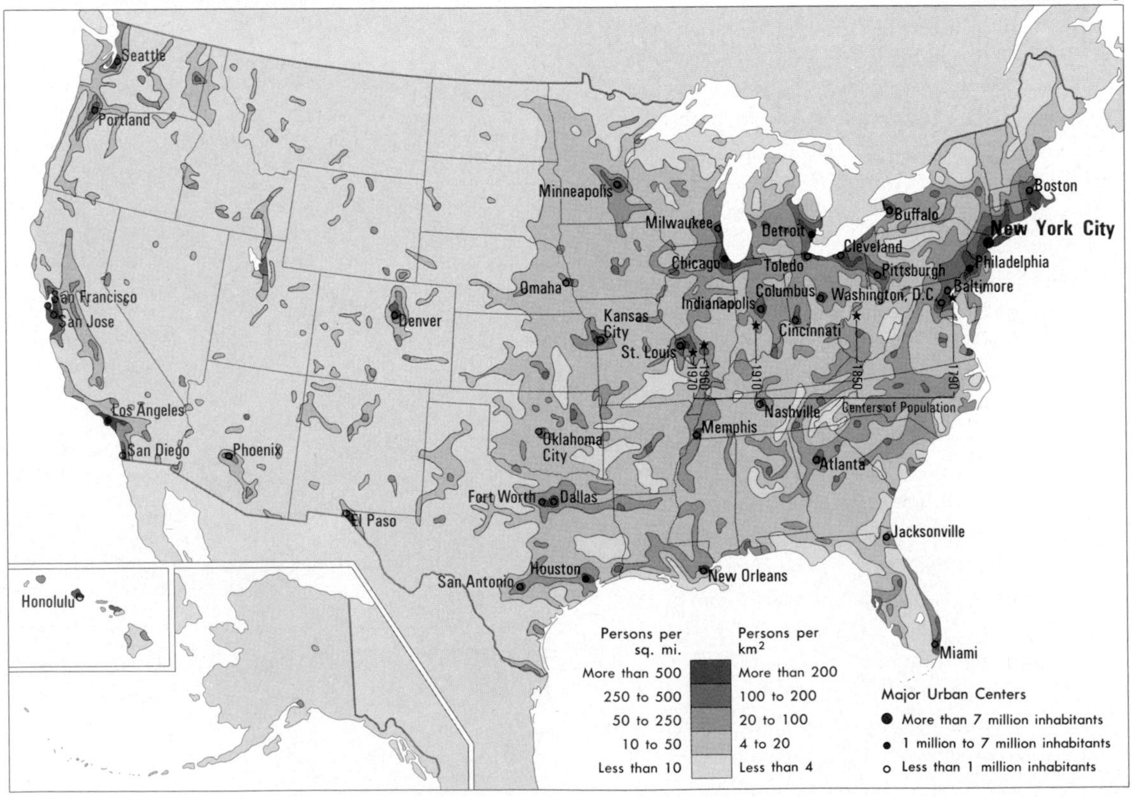

Canadian geography

Canada is big. The second largest country in area in the world, it is about 176,000 square miles (455,800 square kilometers) larger than the United States. Most of the geographical features found in the United States are present in Canada.

In the west, Canada is bounded by the Pacific Ocean. The area near the coast is mountainous. The coast mountains rise up from the deep inlets and bays that mark the coastline. These waters are beautiful, rocky, and difficult to navigate. Even the islands offshore—Queen Charlotte Islands and Vancouver Island—are the tops of an underground mountain range. The highest mountain in Canada, Mount Logan, is in this range. On the southwest corner of the Yukon, Mount Logan is 19,520 feet (6,050 meters) above sea level.

Once past the Coast Range and the deep valleys and basins west of the range, the Canadian half of

The rugged Gaspé Peninsula in Quebec juts into the Gulf of St. Lawrence, providing a wonderland of beauty for nature seekers.

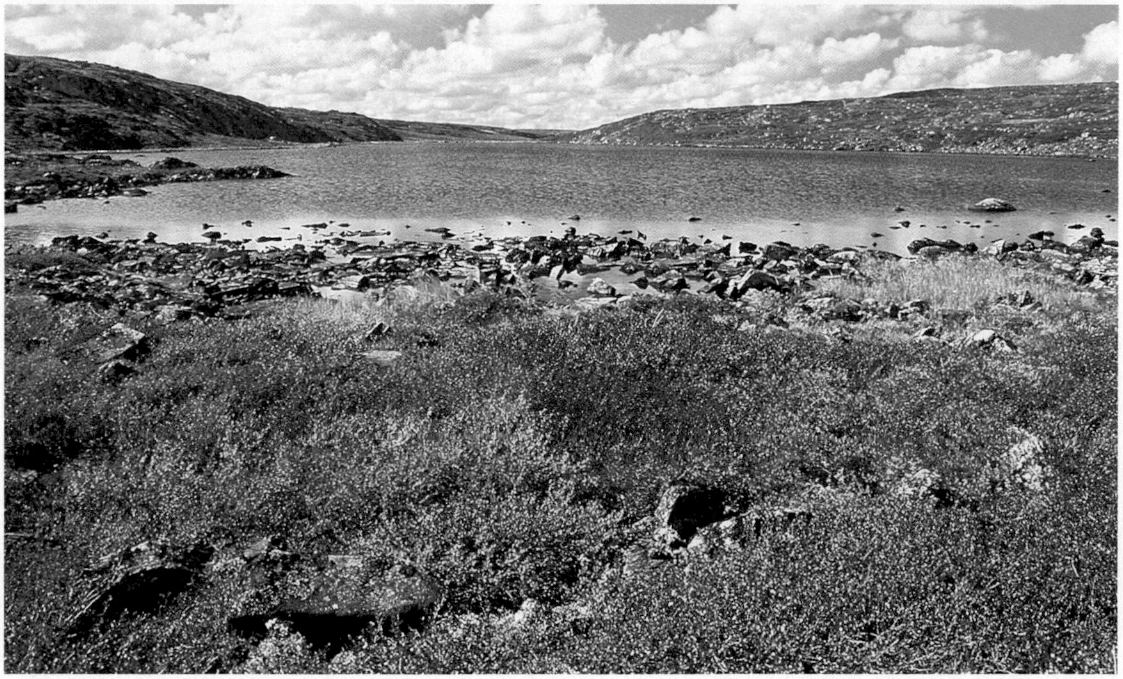

Trees cannot grow in Canada's tundra, where brief summers give way to winter temperatures as low as −20° F. (−29° C).

Fishing boats nest in the foggy waters of this small cove in Nova Scotia, a province known for excellent fishing.

the Rocky Mountains appears. The Rockies cover the western quarter of Canada. They fill the Yukon Territory, British Columbia, part of the Northwest Territories, and part of western Alberta.

Directly east of the Rockies lies the northern extension of the Great Plains. Alberta, Saskatchewan, part of the Northwest Territories, and the lower part of Manitoba are flat, broad grasslands. The unbroken landscape does not hint at the mountainous region directly to the west. The southern part of this plain is called the Prairies. Because of this region's rich earth and large area, it produces most of Canada's crops.

The northern plains do not provide fertile farmlands. The cold climate of the north makes growing any crop impossible. Even in the summer, the temperature reaches only from about 55° to 65° F. (13° to 18° C). The temperature in the winter dips from about −20° to 0° F. (−29° to −18° C). This area is however not a wasteland. It contains valuable deposits of coal, petroleum, potash, and natural gas.

Beyond the plains region, the land changes again. There are no huge mountain ranges, but hills appear from time to time. Hard, rocky soil has replaced fertile grassland. The land cannot support wheat, but forest grows with ease. The rivers of the Prairies have their sources in the many lakes that dot this area. Waterfalls and rapids add to the beauty of the region. This land is called the Canadian Shield. It covers almost half of Canada in a horseshoe-shape, curving around Hudson Bay.

Few people live in this region because the soil cannot be used for farming. Mining and logging are the only industries in the area. The northern parts of the Shield are hazardous in the winter months. In January, the temperature ranges from about −40° to −20° F. (−40° to −29° C). Even in the summer, the temperature rises only from about 45° to 55° F. (7° to 13°C).

East of the Canadian Shield lie lowlands bordering the St. Lawrence River and Lakes Huron, Erie, and Ontario. This small area contains one-half of the Canadian population. The land can be farmed successfully. Valuable fruits and vegetables are grown in these lowlands, and most of Canada's industry is located in the lowland cities of Hamilton, Montreal, and Toronto. So is the historic city of Quebec. One of the most interesting sights of the world—Niagara Falls—attracts tourists to this area all year round.

The eastern edge of Canada is made up of the Atlantic Provinces. Sometimes called the Maritime Provinces, they include Newfoundland, Nova Scotia, Prince Edward Island, and New Brunswick. The Appalachian Mountains extend from these provinces to near Savannah, Georgia, in the United States. The Appalachians in Canada are no more than low hills or lowland plains.

The coastlines in this area have excellent harbors and are known for their fishing. They also offer beautiful beaches and ocean resorts to vacationers and tourists. Inland, this area supports dairy and crop farming. The moderate climates and good soil make growing many products easy. Areas that are not supporting farmland or cities are covered with forests. The wildlife, flowers, and seascape make the Atlantic Provinces beautiful and inviting.

The Atlantic Provinces seem to beckon the interested tourist. The Arctic Islands have the opposite effect. These large islands north of the mainland and Hudson Bay lie within the Arctic Circle. They are frozen nine months of the year. The summers are short and cool. The weather is so cold even farther north that snow is on the ground all year round. Trees never grow in this area, called the Arctic tundra, because the earth is frozen even in the summer.

The Northwest Territories and the Yukon Territory make up more than a third of Canada's land area. Less than 1 per cent of the nation's people live there. Most of these are Eskimos, military personnel, representatives of mining companies, and traders.

The land in the territories is generally low, but some islands have mountains and snowcaps that are from 6,000 to 10,000 feet (1,800 to 3,000 meters) above sea level. The mountains, valleys, wind, and humidity all determine the quality of the winter cold in this area.

Average January temperatures

Degrees Fahrenheit	Degrees Celsius
Over 20	Over −7
10 to 20	−12 to −7
0 to 10	−18 to −12
−10 to 0	−23 to −18
−20 to −10	−29 to −23
Below −20	Below −29

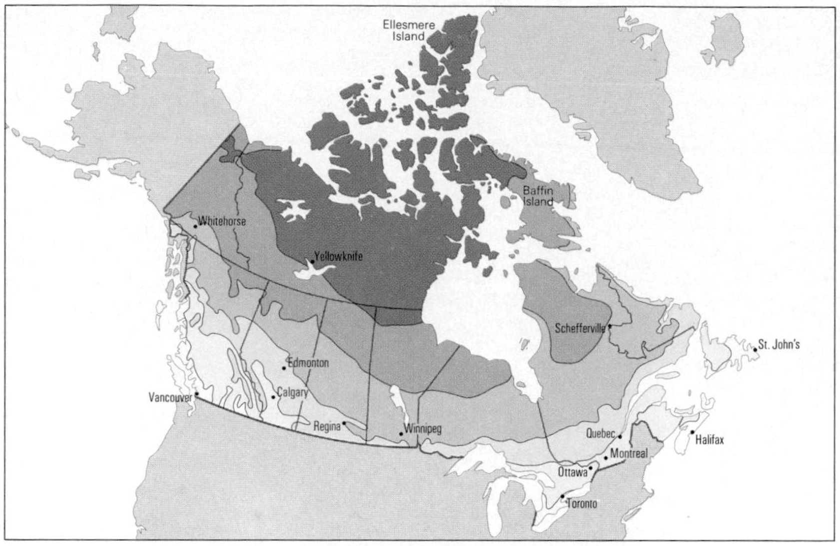

Average July temperatures

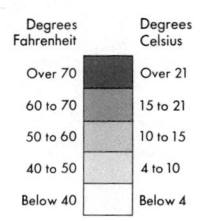

Degrees Fahrenheit	Degrees Celsius
Over 70	Over 21
60 to 70	15 to 21
50 to 60	10 to 15
40 to 50	4 to 10
Below 40	Below 4

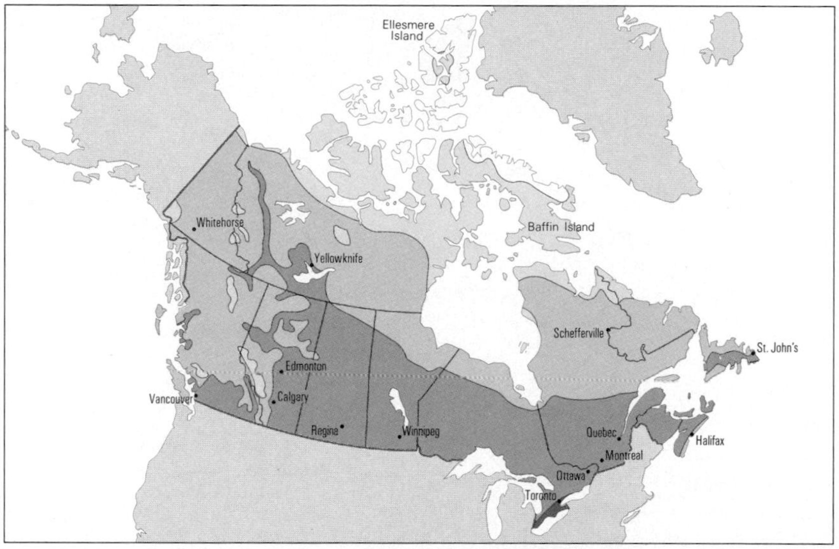

Average yearly precipitation

Inches	Centimeters
More than 80	More than 200
60 to 80	150 to 200
40 to 60	100 to 150
20 to 40	50 to 100
8 to 20	20 to 50
Less than 8	Less than 20

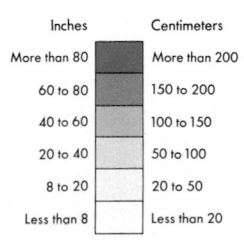

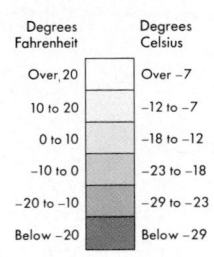

WORLD BOOK maps

Canadian weather conditions *More than two-thirds of Canada has January temperatures averaging below 0° F. (−18° C). The winters in most of Canada are long and cold. British Columbia provides some variation, with its coastal areas having average January temperatures above 32° F. (0° C).*

Sufficiently warm summer temperatures permit farming in Canada's southern areas. But summers are cool in the north. The average July temperatures range from about 70° F. (21° C) in southern Ontario to 40° F. (4° C) in the northern Arctic Islands.

Yearly precipitation is heaviest along the Pacific coast, where it averages more than 80 inches (200 centimeters). The Prairie Provinces receive only 8 to 20 inches (20 to 50 centimeters), mostly during the summer.

The Niagara River plunges across Horseshoe Falls, providing a continuously renewable source of energy. The last 7-mile surge of the river before Niagara Falls is lined with hydroelectric plants.

Canadian energy

Canada is an energy-rich land. Among the nations of the world, it ranks third in the production of electrical power. It ranks fourth in the production of natural gas and in the development of hydroelectric power. It ranks fifth in total output of electricity.

Canada possesses vast coal deposits, most of which remain untapped. New sources of fossil fuels have recently been discovered, and some long-standing resources have only recently been developed.

Much of Canada's energy derives from its abundance of lakes and fast-moving rivers. Remarkably, hydroelectric plants supply about three-fourths of Canada's electricity. In contrast, only about one-seventh of the electricity generated in the United States is so produced. Water-generated power, unlike that supplied by combustion of fossil fuels, is continuously renewable.

Scores of hydroelectric facilities are in operation throughout Canada. The last 7-mile surge of the Niagara River, right before the world-famous Niagara Falls, is lined with generating plants. There, the Sir Adam Beck complex produces about 1,811,000 kilowatts of electricity. (A 100,000 kilowatt generator can supply enough electricity to light a million 100-watt light bulbs.)

A great joint U.S.-Canadian engineering project was undertaken in 1954 to open the St. Lawrence Seaway. The project included the construction of power-generating facilities that have fostered an industrial boom in the Great Lakes regions. The dams in the Seaway produce over 12 trillion kilowatt hours annually.

One of the most spectacular hydroelectric projects was undertaken near Kitimat in British Columbia in the 1950's. The project's goal is to supply power for the energy-intensive production of aluminum. Part of the headwaters of the Fraser River are siphoned through a 10-mile (16-kilometer) channel bored through mountain rock. The waters then plunge 1,600 feet (304.8 meters) to the turbines below.

The Churchill Falls project, which began operations in Labrador in 1971, is the largest single power project in the Western Hemisphere. It has a generating capacity of over 5 million kilowatts. Another grand project is currently under way at the Bay of Fundy, an 180-mile (289.6-kilometer) arm of the Atlantic between New Brunswick and southern Nova Scotia. The highest tides in the world occur in this bay. Its energy-producing potential is enormous.

Those areas of Canada without hydroelectric power generate electricity in steam plants fueled by coal oil or natural gas. Canada's largest thermal operation is the Lakeview plant in Toronto. Canada has had little need for nuclear power, but a full-scale atomic electric plant is in operation at Douglas Point in Ontario. Because of Canada's high latitudes and long winters, its potential for solar energy development is—at best—limited.

Petroleum production came late in Canada. The first major strike was made at Leduc, south of Edmonton, in 1947. Annual production has jumped from about 8 million barrels in 1947 to about 650 million barrels in the mid-1970's. Most of Canada's reserves lie in Prairie Provinces, particularly Alberta, which produces about four-fifths of Canada's oil. Alberta now rivals the state of Texas in output.

As a result of the worldwide increase in petroleum prices, previously uneconomic sources of oil have now become profitable. The region around the Athabasca River in Alberta holds the world's largest known deposits of oil-rich bituminous sands. These deposits extend underground for 19,000 square miles (49,200 square kilometers) and are estimated to contain 300 billion barrels of petroleum: more than the proven oil reserves of all OPEC nations combined. In the late 1970's engineering refinements coupled with runaway prices to provide a new oil bonanza from the tar sands.

In the late 1970's, offshore drilling efforts along the coast of Nova Scotia led to the discovery of large oil reserves in that area. These reserves promise dramatic production potentials for the 1980's. It is also already known that the Arctic regions possess large stores of natural gas. The Arctic regions, too, therefore, may yield significant energy production.

Oil fields in Alberta provide four-fifths of Canada's oil (left). *Alberta's tar-sand plants are now tapping the largest known deposits of bituminous sands, estimated to hold more oil than the proven oil reserves in all OPEC nations combined* (below).

Wheat is by far the most important cereal crop of Canada's Prairie Provinces. Single families can usually operate large farms because of highly developed agricultural machinery.

Canadian agriculture

Canada is a great farming land. Mechanization, specialization, and scientific advances have made the Canadian farmer one of the most productive in the world despite Canada's bitter winters and short growing seasons.

Of all Canada's vast territory, only a small part (about 7 per cent) is suited for agriculture. But that small part, located along the southern belt of the country, produces crops and supports livestock in great abundance and variety.

Two distinct southern regions produce most of Canada's agricultural output. The first centers in the Prairie Provinces of Manitoba, Saskatchewan, and eastern Alberta. The other is located in southeastern Canada, stretching along the lowlands of the St. Lawrence River and reaching into the areas between Lakes Huron, Ontario, and Erie.

The lands of the Prairie Provinces resemble the Great Plains of the United States, from which they are separated politically by the 49th parallel. The prairies are sometimes called the "land of magnificent distances." There, one can see far in every direction. The landscape is almost filled with nothing but endless fields of waving wheat. Farm houses are few in number because farms are large: typically 800 acres (1,976 hectares) or more. These farms, by virtue of sophisticated agricultural machinery, are usually operated by a single family. Brightly painted grain elevators rise every 10 miles (16 kilometers) or so out of the flat prairie land. These elevators, located along railroad spurs, are usually operated by farmers' cooperatives, which manage most of Canada's wheat production.

The fertile black and brown soils of the prairies largely support the growth of cereal crops. Wheat is by far the most important one. Since the turn of this century, hardy strains of protein-rich red wheat have steadily developed to withstand the dry summers and ferocious six-month winters of the prairies. Harvested from late August to mid-September, the wheat is transported by rail to mills, feed lots, or ports, where it is shipped abroad as Canada's major export crop.

In addition to wheat, there are abundant harvests of other grains—barley, oats, rye, and rapeseed—all used mainly for livestock feed. Sunflower fields also brighten the landscape.

Livestock, particularly beef cattle, is the second great product of the prairies. In regions suitable for crops, cattle are grazed on wheat stubble or supported by locally grown grains. In the drier areas to the west, where the plains shoulder against the Canadian Rockies (the Cordillera), cattle graze on enormous ranches.

In addition to beef cattle and cereal cultivation, the prairies support other agriculture on a limited scale. Many farmers raise some vegetables and poultry for sale to nearby towns or cities. A substantial sugar beet crop is grown in specially irrigated fields in southern Alberta. The raising of hogs and sheep, as well as some dairy farming, round out the region's agricultural output. In total, the prairie region accounts for about three-fourths of Canada's agricultural land and well over 60 per cent of its crop production.

The second great agricultural region of Canada is the southeast. The gray sedimentary soils laid down by ancient lakes in this area support a rich variety of crops. Here, however, farming is conducted on a scale smaller than that of the prairies. The southeast's output is used to feed the urban centers of Quebec and Ontario.

The farms in this region are relatively small, ranging from 150 to 300 acres (370.5 to 741 hectares). They resemble the U.S. farms of the Great Lakes and mid-Atlantic states. Farm houses, however, are typically built of brick or stone rather than of wood as is common to the United States.

The output of these farms is far more diversified than their U.S. counterparts, though individual farms can be highly specialized. Dairy farms may abut grainfields, tobacco fields may alternate with potato farms, and orchards may be under cultivation next to corn fields.

Dairy farming and the raising of livestock or poultry are the chief agricultural activities of the region. Barley, oats, rye, soybeans, corn, and hay grow in abundance. The area supplies most of the nation's milk, butter, cheese, eggs, chickens, turkeys, and hogs. Nearly all farmers raise some vegetables. Potatoes are the most important crop. Other important vegetables include cabbage, beans, lettuce, carrots, onions, sweet corn, and tomatoes. Tobacco growing flourishes in Ontario around Lake Erie.

The farms in the valleys of British Columbia supply dairy products, meat, and vegetables to western Canada.

Orchards flourish throughout the area. Apples are the most important fruit crop. The vineyards and orchards of the Niagara fruit belt are celebrated for their cherries, grapes, peaches, plums, pears, and other small fruit. The ever-present maples of the region are tapped in spring for sugar and syrup.

Outside the prairies and southeast lowlands, areas that can be cultivated in Canada are limited. Yet there are other agricultural pockets. The rugged Atlantic, or Maritime, Provinces produce potatoes and apples. Dairy farming exists on a small scale, together with farming of hay and feed grains. Nearly half of Prince Edward Island is under cultivation. Its rich red soil yields potatoes and other crops in abundance. In British Columbia, farms in the lower Fraser Valley supply dairy products, meat, and vegetables to Vancouver.

Okanagen Valley is famous for its orchard fruits: apples, cherries, and pears. The Peace River region produces grain and livestock, and the Kamloops and Cariboo regions have many cattle ranches.

Canadian people

The customs of Canada's people are more mixed than those of the U.S. population. Canadian national and cultural groups have remained well defined over the years. Canadians have not given up the languages and customs of their forebears easily.

Canada's first inhabitants, as those of the United States, were Indians and Eskimos. The Indians lived in nomadic fashion on the grasslands and in the forests of central and southern Canada. Today most of them live on *reserves,* the Canadian term for *reservations.* The Eskimos lived on the northern edge of what is now called the Northwest Territories and in the Arctic Islands. Some still hunt and fish as their ancestors did, but many work in mining or fishing, one of Canada's oldest industries.

The first Europeans to settle in Canada were the French in the early 1600's. France ruled eastern Canada as a colony for almost 160 years. When French rule ended, the French Canadians continued their French way of life. To this day, the descendants of this group speak French and retain many French customs and traditions.

About 30 per cent of Canada's population is French Canadian. Most live in the province of Quebec. Their strong influence is evident in that French is Canada's official language along with English. Many government workers are required to know both languages.

The largest group of Canadians are descendants of British settlers. In the early 17th century, these settlers began arriving in Newfoundland and Nova Scotia. The city of Halifax in Nova Scotia was founded by the English about 14 years before France lost Canada to Great Britain.

Most Canadians live in cities or metropolitan areas. Huge complexes such as the Toronto Eaton Centre provide facilities and goods that appeal to the diverse Canadian population.

Major Urban Centers

● More than 2 million inhabitants

● 500,000 to 2 million inhabitants

○ Less than 500,000 inhabitants

Persons per sq. mi.	Persons per km²
More than 50	More than 20
10 to 50	4 to 20
5 to 10	2 to 4
2 to 5	1 to 2
Less than 2	Less than 1

WORLD BOOK map

Canadian population distribution *Most Canadians live in major urban centers, as the map on the right shows. Ninety per cent occupy the rim of land along the Canada-U.S. border, the Atlantic Provinces, and the eastern bank of the Gulf of St. Lawrence.*

Another large influx of British immigrants arrived after the American Revolutionary War. Thousands of British Americans moved to what is now New Brunswick and Ontario after England lost the war.

In the late 18th century, Scottish settlers arrived in Pictou on the northern shore of Nova Scotia. Scots continued to immigrate in large numbers up to the early 19th century. Many Scot Canadians living on Cape Breton Island still speak Gaelic and continue the customs of their Scottish Highland ancestors.

Other European immigrants arrived in the late 19th century. They by-passed the Atlantic Provinces and settled on the new farmland of the prairies and in the growing industrial cities. On Canada's west coast the cities became homes for large numbers of Chinese who worked on the new Canadian Pacific Railway.

Most Canadians today live in cities or metropolitan areas. Whether urban or rural dwellers, almost all Canadians live in the southern part of their country. Ninety per cent of the population occupy the rim of land along the Canada-U.S. border, the Atlantic Provinces, and the eastern bank of the Gulf of St. Lawrence.

Life in Canada is similar to life in the United States. Canadians enjoy a high standard of living. Family life, religion, and sports are about the same in the two countries. Only when one reaches the Arctic Islands does the style of living alter dramatically.

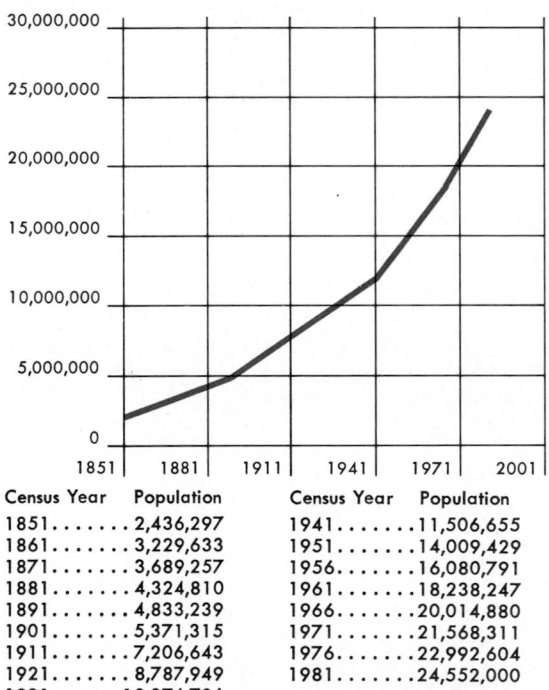

Census Year	Population	Census Year	Population
1851	2,436,297	1941	11,506,655
1861	3,229,633	1951	14,009,429
1871	3,689,257	1956	16,080,791
1881	4,324,810	1961	18,238,247
1891	4,833,239	1966	20,014,880
1901	5,371,315	1971	21,568,311
1911	7,206,643	1976	22,992,604
1921	8,787,949	1981	24,552,000
1931	10,376,786		

Source: Statistics Canada. Figure for 1981 is an estimate.

Canada's growing population *Since Canada's first census in 1851, the nation's population has grown steadily to 24,552,000 in 1981. Especially rapid growth periods were 1851–1861, 1901–1911, and 1951–1961.*

There are no large cities in the Arctic Islands, only trading posts or mining camps. The land is inhabited mostly by Eskimos. Many still hunt and fish the way their ancestors did with kayaks, or skin-covered boats, and *komatiks,* or dog sleds. Farther south, a few meteorologists and military radar technicians work at posts in this isolated region.

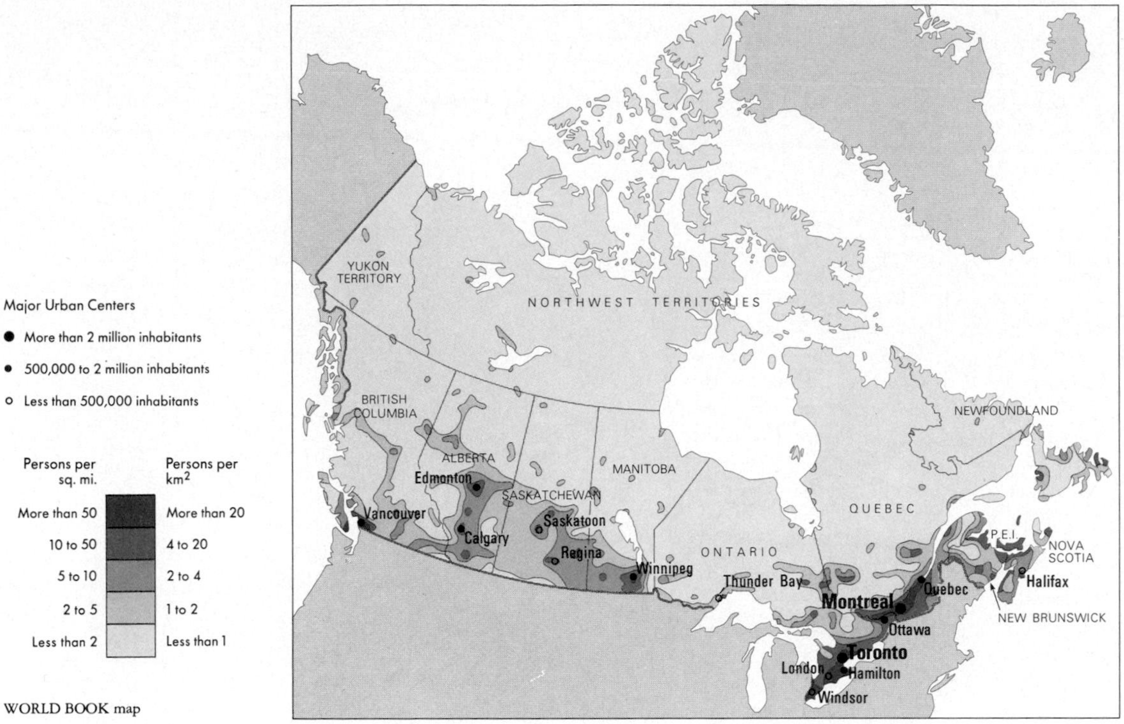

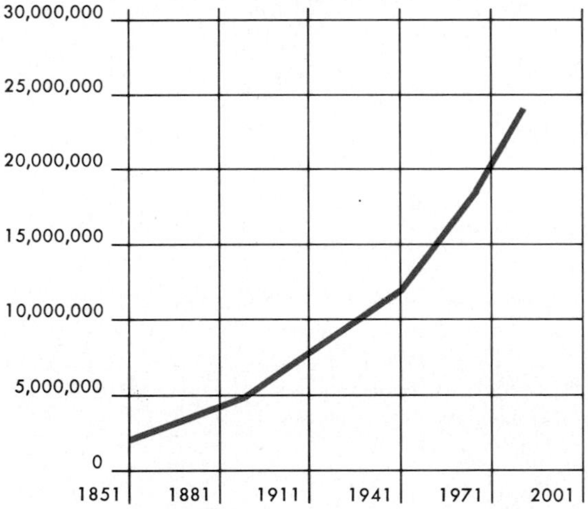

	Atlanta, Georgia	Calgary, Alberta	Chicago, Illinois	Denver, Colorado	Houston, Texas	Kansas City, Missouri	Los Angeles, California	Mexico City, Mexico	Miami, Florida	Montreal, Quebec	New York, New York	San Francisco, California	Seattle, Washington	Washington, D.C.	Winnipeg, Manitoba
Acapulco, Mexico	2152	3298	2346	2097	1300	1941	2178	255	2556	3149	3014	2589	3324	2776	2727
Albuquerque, N. Mexico	1433	1432	1322	437	838	785	851	1405	1984	2183	2096	1146	1539	1887	1532
Anchorage, Alaska	4321	2198	3702	3334	4241	3607	3764	5060	4829	4244	4548	3353	2484	4403	2854
Atlanta, Georgia		2123	671	1436	852	842	2245	1897	663	1249	868	2579	2740	624	1541
Bangor, Maine	1329	2236	1190	2209	2104	1664	3245	3218	1856	386	459	3458	3081	697	1882
Billings, Montana	1839	559	1267	587	1638	909	1176	2411	2419	1869	2146	1179	809	1968	755
Birmingham, Alabama	155	2290	618	1301	701	707	2063	1746	803	1292	1023	2449	2605	779	1488
Bismarck, North Dakota	1422	811	866	688	1405	771	1656	2224	2218	1468	1651	1698	1210	1567	407
Boise, Idaho	2342	794	1832	906	1872	1500	932	2406	2963	3763	2704	635	505	2498	1409
Boston, Massachusetts	1090	2178	992	2016	1865	1400	3004	2979	1615	328	220	3265	3072	460	1758
Calgary, Alberta	2123		1654	1136	2153	1596	1641	3043	2804	2325	2478	1429	733	2355	829
Charleston, S. Carolina	299	2422	970	1735	1155	1141	2544	2196	612	1140	759	2878	2985	521	1840
Charleston, W. Virginia	496	2180	524	1391	1140	797	2375	2266	1059	832	543	2711	2600	382	1401
Charlotte, N. Carolina	237	2360	850	1673	1093	973	2482	2134	743	1006	625	2816	2781	387	1727
Cheyenne, Wyoming	1537	1035	1027	101	1162	695	1069	1925	2225	1818	1899	1226	1350	1715	994
Chicago, Illinois	671	1654		1062	1139	537	2115	2091	1352	804	824	2240	2076	701	877
Cleveland, Ohio	767	1985	331	1393	1372	744	2393	2471	1327	589	493	2571	2378	370	1201
Dallas, Texas	814	1912	923	820	241	518	1476	1168	1367	1776	1580	1790	2136	1446	1304
Denver, Colorado	1436	1136	1062		1061	594	1148	1804	2104	1866	1794	1324	1411	1696	1095
Des Moines, Iowa	962	1484	374	688	1042	254	1823	1940	1684	1178	1259	1866	1731	1075	700
Detroit, Michigan	774	1916	271	1333	1306	780	2415	2351	1437	533	670	2511	2347	547	1136
Edmonton, Alberta	2309	186	1690	1322	2229	1595	1827	3048	2817	2232	2536	1615	919	2391	842
Halifax, Nova Scotia	1849	3185	1710	2729	2624	2184	3765	3738	2376	860	979	3933	3555	1217	2356
Hanover, New Hampshire	1127	2526	960	2040	2019	1391	3040	3103	1654	201	259	3218	2896	497	1697
Houston, Texas	852	2153	1139	1061		788	1585	1045	1256	1839	1714	1950	2377	1476	1618
Indianapolis, Indiana	508	1848	194	1087	1042	493	2071	2149	1171	820	713	2407	2268	613	1062
Kansas City, Missouri	842	1596	537	594	788		1578	1686	1510	1313	1277	1914	1808	1102	859
Las Vegas, Nevada	2021	1336	1905	843	1426	1437	305	1852	2572	2709	2637	624	1198	2475	1688
Los Angeles, California	2245	1641	2115	1148	1585	1578		1923	2841	2948	2784	411	1280	2680	1993
Louisville, Kentucky	394	1962	308	1106	936	512	2190	1981	1057	934	738	2426	2320	604	1176
Memphis, Tennessee	382	2056	579	1054	560	460	1816	1605	1050	1310	1114	2214	2358	980	1319
Mexico City, Mexico	1897	3043	2091	1804	1045	1686	1923		2301	2884	2759	2334	3069	2521	2472
Miami, Florida	663	2804	1352	2104	1256	1510	2841	2301		1749	1395	3192	3421	1130	2222
Milwaukee, Wisconsin	761	1585	90	1152	1229	627	2205	2181	1442	894	914	2330	1984	791	780
Minneapolis, Minnesota	1090	1235	426	921	1291	503	2056	2189	1794	1188	1250	2099	1634	1127	451
Monterrey, Mexico	1345	2453	1501	1458	455	1096	1584	590	1711	2304	2169	1949	2685	1931	1882
Montreal, Quebec	1249	2325	804	1866	1839	1313	2948	2884	1749		381	3044	2695	619	1496
New Orleans, Louisiana	492	2458	981	1326	360	849	1945	1405	896	1650	1360	2296	2669	1116	1721
New York, New York	868	2478	824	1794	1714	1277	2784	2759	1395	381		3045	2852	238	1694
Norfolk, Virginia	593	2591	935	1802	1381	1208	2786	2472	1029	827	446	3122	3011	208	1812
Oklahoma City, Okla.	882	1770	856	674	446	356	1402	1373	1433	1632	1630	1697	2029	1421	1099
Omaha, Nebraska	1043	1395	498	564	911	201	1699	1838	1711	1302	1383	1742	1607	1199	658
Orlando, Florida	442	2565	1113	1865	1017	1271	2602	2062	239	1537	1156	2953	3182	915	1983
Ottawa, Ontario	1236	2207	733	1795	1768	1242	2877	2813	1823	118	489	2973	2577	693	1378
Philadelphia, Penn.	778	2493	766	1770	1624	1176	2726	2669	1278	471	90	3021	2828	148	1636
Phoenix, Arizona	1885	1631	1761	835	1180	1224	415	1563	2454	2622	2535	770	1487	2326	1928
Pittsburgh, Penn.	771	2124	470	1462	1439	868	2446	2524	1358	662	366	2713	2520	243	1343
Portland, Oregon	2765	782	2255	1329	2295	1923	1098	2829	3433	2818	2992	687	182	2921	1508
Quebec, Quebec	1415	2016	970	2032	2005	1479	3114	3050	2470	166	547	3210	2861	785	1662
Rapid City, S. Dakota	1592	890	929	420	1370	706	1423	2224	2216	1763	1815	1525	1075	1628	759
Regina, Saskatchewan	1758	475	1202	878	1741	1107	1639	2560	2329	1744	2048	1642	1014	1903	354
St. Louis, Missouri	562	1850	283	848	856	254	1832	1910	1346	1059	1057	2168	2062	848	1019
Salt Lake City, Utah	1970	890	1485	534	1480	1128	611	2081	2638	2276	2293	768	897	2173	1312
San Francisco, Calif.	2579	1429	2240	1324	1950	1914	411	2334	3192	3044	3045		869	2968	2018
Seattle, Washington	2740	733	2076	1411	2377	1808	1280	3069	3421	2695	2852	869		2777	1368
Syracuse, New York	1088	2268	658	1738	1717	1089	2737	2801	1594	244	260	2916	2763	464	1447
Thunder Bay, Ontario	1343	1273	672	1269	1639	851	2404	2537	2031	1052	1384	2447	1812	1343	444
Toronto, Ontario	972	2123	469	1531	1504	978	2613	2549	1631	335	513	2709	2514	561	1258
Vancouver, B. Columbia	2780	657	2220	1555	2521	1862	1424	3055	3565	2982	2996	1013	144	2921	1486
Washington, D.C.	624	2355	701	1696	1476	1102	2680	2521	1130	619	238	2968	2777		1578
Winnipeg, Manitoba	1541	829	877	1095	1618	859	1993	2472	2222	1496	1694	2018	1368	1578	

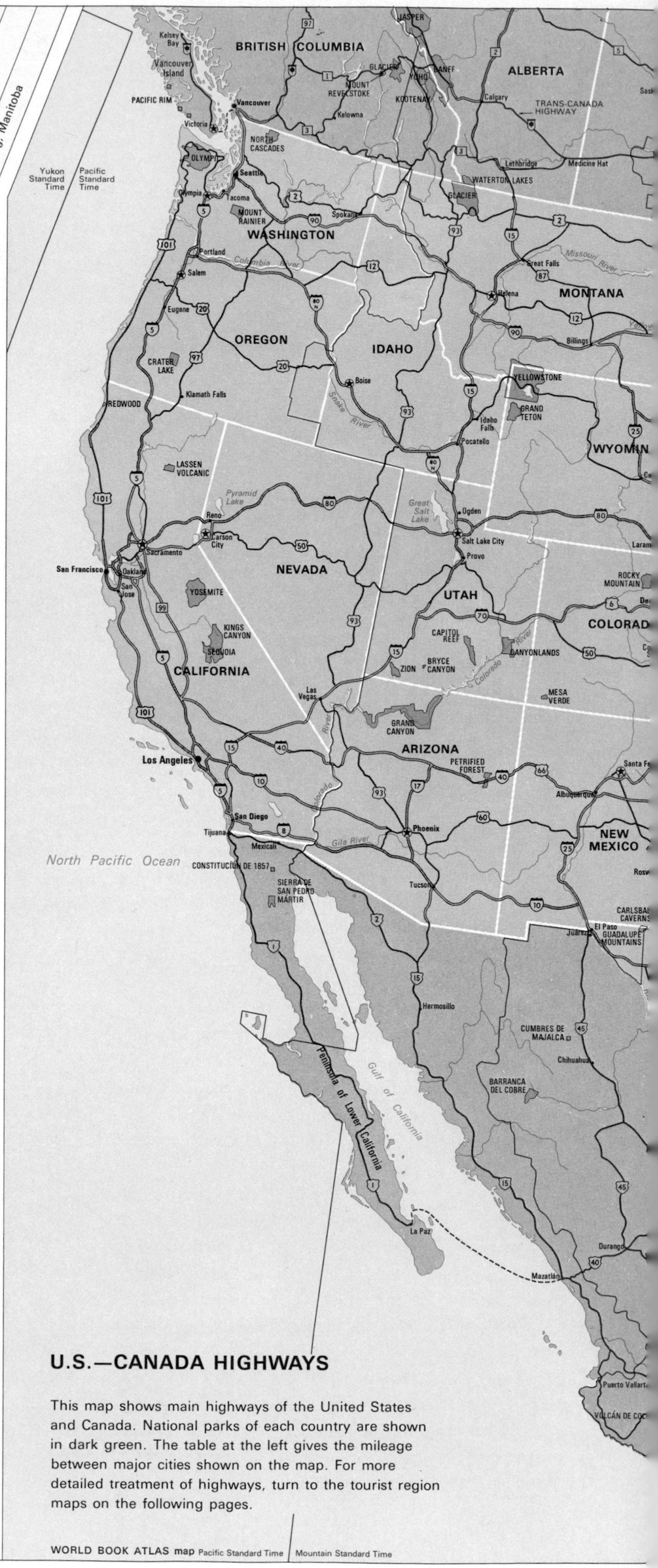

U.S.—CANADA HIGHWAYS

This map shows main highways of the United States and Canada. National parks of each country are shown in dark green. The table at the left gives the mileage between major cities shown on the map. For more detailed treatment of highways, turn to the tourist region maps on the following pages.

CANADA
UNITED STATES
MEXICO
SASKATCHEWAN
MANITOBA
ONTARIO
QUEBEC
NEWFOUNDLAND
Newfoundland Standard Time
PRINCE EDWARD ISLAND
NEW BRUNSWICK
NOVA SCOTIA
CAPE BRETON HIGHLANDS
Anticosti Island
FORILLON
KOUCHIBOUGUAC
PRINCE EDWARD ISLAND
FUNDY
KEJIMKUJIK
YELLOWHEAD HIGHWAY
RIDING MOUNTAIN
TRANS-CANADA HIGHWAY
VOYAGEURS
PUKASKWA
ISLE ROYALE
LA MAURICIE
GEORGIAN BAY ISLANDS
ST. LAWRENCE ISLANDS
ACADIA
James Bay
Lake Winnipeg
Lake Nipigon
Lake of the Woods
Lake Superior
Lake Michigan
Lake Huron
Lake Erie
Lake Ontario
Albany River
Saint Lawrence River
Saskatchewan River
Regina
Brandon
Winnipeg
Portage la Prairie
Thunder Bay
Timmins
Sault Ste Marie
Sudbury
North Bay
Ottawa
Montreal
Quebec
Sherbrooke
Laval
Toronto
Hamilton
London
Windsor
Sept-Îles
Fredericton
Saint John
Halifax
Amherst
Charlottetown
Sydney
NORTH DAKOTA
SOUTH DAKOTA
NEBRASKA
KANSAS
OKLAHOMA
TEXAS
MINNESOTA
IOWA
MISSOURI
ARKANSAS
LOUISIANA
WISCONSIN
ILLINOIS
MICHIGAN
INDIANA
OHIO
KENTUCKY
TENNESSEE
MISSISSIPPI
ALABAMA
GEORGIA
FLORIDA
SOUTH CAROLINA
NORTH CAROLINA
VIRGINIA
WEST VIRGINIA
PENNSYLVANIA
NEW YORK
VERMONT
NEW HAMPSHIRE
MAINE
MASSACHUSETTS
RHODE ISLAND
CONNECTICUT
NEW JERSEY
DELAWARE
MARYLAND
MAINE TURNPIKE
MASSACHUSETTS TURNPIKE
CONNECTICUT TURNPIKE
GARDEN STATE PARKWAY
NEW JERSEY TURNPIKE
NEW YORK STATE THRUWAY
PENNSYLVANIA TURNPIKE
OHIO TURNPIKE
INDIANA TOLL ROAD
GREAT RIVER ROAD
KANSAS TURNPIKE
WILL ROGERS TURNPIKE
TURNER'S TURNPIKE
H. E. BAILEY TURNPIKE
KENTUCKY TURNPIKE
MOUNTAIN PARKWAY
FLORIDA'S TURNPIKE
EVERGLADES PARKWAY (ALLIGATOR ALLEY)
WIND CAVE
POINT PELEE
MAMMOTH CAVE
GREAT SMOKY MOUNTAINS
SHENANDOAH
HOT SPRINGS
EVERGLADES
Minot
Bismarck
Fargo
Grand Forks
Duluth
Aberdeen
Pierre
Rapid City
Sioux Falls
Minneapolis
St. Paul
Green Bay
Madison
Milwaukee
Rockford
Chicago
Gary
Grand Rapids
Lansing
Flint
Detroit
Toledo
Cleveland
Erie
Buffalo
Rochester
Syracuse
Albany
Burlington
Montpelier
Hanover
Concord
Manchester
Worcester
Boston
Providence
Hartford
Bridgeport
New York City
Trenton
Allentown
Harrisburg
Philadelphia
Wilmington
Dover
Baltimore
Annapolis
Washington, D.C.
Arlington
Richmond
Norfolk
Pittsburgh
Columbus
Cincinnati
Covington
Indianapolis
Fort Wayne
Peoria
Springfield
Cedar Rapids
Davenport
Des Moines
Omaha
Lincoln
Grand Island
Kansas City
Topeka
Jefferson City
St. Louis
Louisville
Frankfort
Lexington
Huntington
Charleston
Wichita
Springfield
Tulsa
Oklahoma City
Fort Smith
Little Rock
Pine Bluff
Memphis
Nashville
Knoxville
Huntsville
Winston-Salem
Greensboro
Raleigh
Charlotte
Greenville
Columbia
Charleston
Atlanta
Macon
Savannah
Columbus
Birmingham
Montgomery
Jackson
Shreveport
Baton Rouge
New Orleans
Biloxi
Mobile
Tallahassee
Jacksonville
Orlando
Tampa
Miami
Key West
Amarillo
Lubbock
Lawton
Wichita Falls
Fort Worth
Dallas
Austin
Houston
Galveston
San Antonio
Corpus Christi
Bangor
Augusta
Lewiston
Portland
Lake Okeechobee
North Atlantic Ocean
Gulf of Mexico
Caribbean Sea
BAHAMAS (GREAT BRITAIN)
Nassau
CUBA
Havana
Atlantic Standard Time
DOMINICAN REPUBLIC
HAITI
Port-au-Prince
JAMAICA
Kingston
Eastern Standard Time
Atlantic Standard Time
SIERRA DEL CARMEN
CUMBRES DE MONTERREY
Monterrey
Matamoros
PAN-AMERICAN HIGHWAY
EL SALTO FALLS
EL GOGORRON
San Luis Potosí
Aguascalientes
León
Tampico
Mexico City
PICO DE TANCITARO
NEVADO DE TOLUCA
IXTACHUATL POPOCATEPETL
LA MALINCHE
Puebla
Veracruz
CAÑON DEL RÍO BLANCO
Acapulco
NATIONAL CATHEDRAL
NATIONAL PALACE
PALACE OF FINE ARTS
PLAZA MEXICO (BULLFIGHTING RING)
PLAZA OF THE THREE CULTURES
UNIVERSITY OF MEXICO
ZOCALO (CONSTITUTION PLAZA)
SAN JUAN DE ULÚA FORTRESS
FERRIES
Mérida
Puerto Juárez
MAYAPÁN (MAYAN RUINS)
CHICHÉN ITZÁ (MAYAN RUINS)
Yucatan Peninsula
GUATEMALA
BRITISH HONDURAS
Distance Scale
0 100 200 300 400 500 Miles
0 200 400 600 800 Kilometers
Mountain Standard Time
Central Standard Time
Central Standard Time
Eastern Standard Time

Central Standard Time
Eastern Standard Time
Lake of the Woods
Ignace
SANDBAR LAKE
Lake Nipigon
Geraldton
LONG LAKE
BLACKSAND
NORTHLAND RAILWAY TERMINAL
Fraserdale
Rainy Lake
INWOOD
NAGAGAMISIS
SPRUCE FALLS PAPER COMPANY
Kapuskasing
Matagami
Fort Frances
International Falls
Atikokan
IRON ORE MINE
Nipigon
KIWASSA
TRANS-CANADA HIGHWAY (NORTHERN ROUTE)
GREENWATER
Cochrane
QUETICO PROVINCIAL PARK
FORT WILLIAM HISTORICAL SOCIETY MUSEUM
MOUNT BALDY
KAKABEKA FALLS
Thunder Bay
MOUNT McKAY
MOUNT SIBLEY
LOCH LOMOND
Marathon
PIC POST
WHITE LAKE
TRANS-CANADA HIGHWAY (LAKE SUPERIOR ROUTE)
Tip Top Hill 2,120 ft.
Ansonville
Lake Abitibi
CANADA
UNITED STATES
FORT CHARLOTTE
Mesabi Range
PUKASKWA NATIONAL PARK
OBATANGA
FLYING POST
Timmins
NOTRE-DAME DU NORD SHRINE
AIGUEBELLE
SENNETERRE
Hibbing
Isle Royale (Michigan)
ISLE ROYALE NATIONAL PARK
MISSINAIBI LAKE
PORCUPINE GOLD MINING MUSEUM
ESKER LAKES
Rouyn
COPPER MINE
Lake Superior
FT. FRIENDSHIP
Wawa
MOUNT WAWA
Kirkland Lake
MUSEUM OF NORTHERN HISTORY
Val-d'Or
GOLD MINE
MINNESOTA
THE SHOALS
Chapleau
ROLLET ZOO
FT. WILKINS
Keweenaw Peninsula
APOSTLE ISLANDS N.L.
Hancock
ARCADIAN COPPER MINE
MOUNTBATTEN
Duluth
RED CLIFF
APOSTLE ISLANDS
LAKE SUPERIOR PROVINCIAL PARK
New Liskeard
NORTHERN ONTARIO MINING MUSEUM
Cobalt
Superior
ONTARIO
VILLE MARIE GROTTO CHAPEL
PATTISON
PORCUPINE MOUNTAINS
L'ANSE
THE UPPER CANADA ROUTE
LA VÉRENDRYE PROVINCIAL PARK
Mille Lacs Lake
Ashland
BAD RIVER
BIG POWDERHORN
Mt. Curwood 1,980 ft.
COPPER FALLS
INDIANHEAD
Marquette
PICTURED ROCKS NATL. LAKESHORE
SEARCHMONT VALLEY
MOUNT TELEMARK
AMERICAN SKI HALL OF FAME
TAHQUAMENON FALLS
INTERNATIONAL BRIDGE
Sault Ste. Marie
MISSISSAGI
Temiscaming
SPOONER MUSEUM OF WOODCARVING
LAC COURTE OREILLES
LAC DU FLAMBEAU
THE LAKE MICHIGAN ROUTE
BIG SPRING
INDIAN LAKE
BAY MILLS
FT. BRENTON
SOO CANALS
Elliot Lake
THE BIG NICKEL
COPPER CLIFF
BIG EDDY
Sudbury
NORTHERN ONTARIO FLIGHT PARK
North Bay
LA VASE PORTAGES
Mattawa
ST. CROIX NATL. SCENIC RIVERWAY
Rice Lake
PINE MOUNTAIN
IRON MOUNTAIN
Manistique
Blind River
Espanola
INTERSTATE
RHINELANDER LOGGING MUSEUM
Escanaba
HANNAHVILLE
STRAITS
MACKINAC ISLAND
BIRCH ISLAND INDIAN VILLAGE
KILLARNEY
Lake Nipissing
Minneapolis
St. Paul
Timms Hill 1,952 ft.
MACKINAC BRIDGE
FT. MICHILIMAKINAC
Cheboygan
MANITOULIN HISTORICAL MUSEUM
ALGONQUIN PROVINCIAL PARK
Pembroke
CHAMPLAIN TRAIL MUSEUM
BRUNET ISLAND
POTAWATOMI
GREAT LAKES INDIAN MUSEUM
Washington Island
Manitoulin Island
CASWELL RESORT
Chippewa Falls
Eau Claire
RIB MOUNTAIN
Wausau
WOLF NATL. SCENIC RIVERWAY
PENINSULA
Door Peninsula
Petoskey
OLD PRESQUE ISLE LIGHTHOUSE
Georgian Bay
HIDDEN VALLEY
MADAWASKA VALLEY
WISCONSIN
STOCKBRIDGE
OCONTO MOUND
POTAWATOMI
Sturgeon Bay
SLEEPING BEAR DUNES N.L.
BOYNE MOUNTAIN
Parry Sound
SCHUSS MOUNTAIN
TOBERMORY HARBOR
GEORGIAN BAY ISLANDS NATIONAL PARK
Stevens Point
SLEEPING BEAR DUNES
D.H. DAY
Traverse City
OTSEGO LAKE
Alpena
Muskoka Lakes
Rochester
Winona
Wisconsin Rapids
HARTMAN CREEK
ONEIDA
Green Bay
NATL. RAILROAD MUSEUM
NATL. MUSIC CAMP
INTERLOCHEN
HARTWICK PINES
Lake Huron
BETHEL CHURCH
NECEDAH NATL. WILDLIFE REFUGE
APPLETON PAPER MUSEUM
HIGH CLIFF
POINT BEACH
Manitowoc
SOUTH HIGGINS LAKE
LUMBERMEN'S MEMORIAL
MARTYRS' SHRINE
SAINTE-MARIE RESTORATION
La Crosse
THE LAKE MICHIGAN ROUTE
Oshkosh
Lake Winnebago
CABERFAE
Cadillac
Owen Sound
WASAGA BEACH
COLLINGWOOD
BLUE MOUNTAIN
ORILLIA RESORT
HORSESHOE VALLEY
Kawartha Lakes
REPUBLICAN PARTY BIRTHPLACE
Fond du Lac
Lake Michigan
LUDINGTON
POINT DOUGLAS NUCLEAR POWER PLANT
Lake Simcoe
ACADEMY THEATRE
PETERBOROUGH LOCKS
SERPENT MOUNDS
WISCONSIN DELLS
KETTLE MORAINE
KOHLER
ANDRAE
Sheboygan
THE LAKE MICHIGAN ROUTE
EARL ROWE
CIRCUS WORLD MUSEUM
BEER BREWERIES
MARQUETTE UNIVERSITY
MITCHELL PARK CONSERVATORY
WAR MEMORIAL AND ART CENTER
ZOO
SILVER LAKE
Saginaw Bay
THE UPPER CANADA ROUTE
PRESQU'ILE
OUTLET BEACH
VILLA LOUIS
DEVIL'S LAKE
UNIVERSITY OF WISCONSIN
LITTLE SWITZERLAND
ISABELLA INDIAN RESERVATION
Bad Axe
Goderich
BLACK CREEK PIONEER VILLAGE
Toronto
DOMINION CENTRE
OLD FT. YORK
ONTARIO PLACE
PARLIAMENT BUILDINGS
UNIVERSITY OF TORONTO
MUSEUM OF MEDICAL PROGRESS
KICKAPOO CAVERNS
TALIESIN
Madison
Bay City
AUTOMOBILE PLANTS
COBO HALL
FORD AUDITORIUM
FORT WAYNE
WAYNE STATE UNIVERSITY AND CULTURAL CENTER
MACDONALD INSTITUTE
HOUSE ON THE ROCK
LITTLE NORWAY
CAVE OF THE MOUNDS
AZTALAN
Milwaukee
MUSKEGON
Muskegon
MICHIGAN
Saginaw
WOODSIDE N.H.P.
Lake Ontario
STONEFIELD VILLAGE
NEW GLARUS
KETTLE MORAINE
GRAND HAVEN
NORTON INDIAN MOUNDS
Grand Rapids
Flint
STRATFORD SHAKESPEARE THEATRE
Hamilton
NIAGARA-ON-THE-LAKE
HAMLIN BEACH
EASTMAN KODAK
GEORGE EASTMAN HOUSE
Waterloo
PINERY
ROYAL BOTANICAL GARDENS
BELL MEMORIAL
FT. NIAGARA
ERIE CANAL LOCKS
Rochester
Dubuque
IOWA
Galena
BELOIT COLLEGE
YERKES OBSERVATORY
Racine
ALPINE VALLEY
LAKE GENEVA
Kenosha
WILMOT
ADLER PLANETARIUM
ART INSTITUTE
FIELD MUSEUM
MUSEUM OF SCIENCE AND INDUSTRY
SHEDD AQUARIUM
THE LOOP
UNIVERSITY OF CHICAGO
HOLLAND
WINDMILL ISLAND
Holland
BAKER MUSEUM
YANKEE SPRINGS
Lansing
MICHIGAN STATE UNIVERSITY
Port Huron
FANSHAWE PIONEER VILLAGE
London
MUSEUM OF ARCHEOLOGY
Sarnia
OIL REFINERIES
OIL MUSEUM
NIAGARA FALLS
WELLAND CANAL
Buffalo
STATE UNIVERSITY OF NEW YORK
HOLLAND LAND OFFICE
Cedar Rapids
OLD MARKET HOUSE
U.S. GRANT HOME
MISSISSIPPI PALISADES
ROCK CUT
Rockford
CHAIN O'LAKES
ILLINOIS BEACH
BAHAI TEMPLE
KELLOGG BIRD SANCTUARY
Kalamazoo
Battle Creek
Pontiac
CRANBROOK INSTITUTE
ST. THOMAS CHURCH
TURKEY POINT
LONG POINT
ANSLEY WILCOX HOUSE N.H.S.
BRISTOL MOUNTAIN
BLACKHAWK STATUE
LINCOLN MONUMENT
PROPHETSTOWN
NORTHWESTERN UNIVERSITY
MORTON ARBORETUM
Chicago
HOUSE OF DAVID
ARBORETUM
Jackson
WATERLOO
Ann Arbor
UNIVERSITY OF MICHIGAN
NICHOLS ARBORETUM
Detroit
Windsor
Lake St. Clair
KENT MUSEUM
Lake Erie
CATTARAUGUS
LETCHWORTH
HAMMONDSPORT WINERIES
Davenport
Rock Island
BLACK HAWK VILLAGE
BROOKFIELD ZOO
CHICAGO PORTAGE N.H.S.
FT. MIAMI
WARREN DUNES
INDIANA DUNES N.L.
Gary
NOTRE DAME UNIVERSITY
South Bend
INDIANA TOLL ROAD
GREENFIELD VILLAGE
JACK MINER'S WATERFOWL SANCTUARY
FT. MALDEN N.H.P.
RONDEAU
POINT PELEE N.P.
CASE WESTERN RESERVE UNIVERSITY
SEVERANCE HALL
TERMINAL TOWER
PRESQUE ISLE
Erie
CHAUTAUQUA INSTITUTION
ALLEGANY
Jamestown
HOLIDAY VALLEY
ALLEGANY
OLD KASKASKIA VILLAGE
BISHOP HILL
HENNEPIN
STARVED ROCK
KANKAKEE RIVER
Kankakee
U.S. STEEL CORPORATION
POKAGON
MUSEUM OF ART
Toledo
PERRY'S VICTORY N.M.
KELLEYS ISLAND
EAST HARBOR
CEDAR POINT
GARFIELD HOME
FT. LE BOEUF
PYMATUNING
DRAKE WELL
Oil City
BENTON HILL
THE MID-AMERICA ROUTE
Galesburg
KNOX COLLEGE
GENE STRATTON PORTER MEMORIAL
THE MID-AMERICA ROUTE
BLUE HOLE
Cleveland
THE MIDDLE ATLANTIC ROUTE
Burlington
JUBILEE COLLEGE MEMORIAL
METAMORA COURT HOUSE
BASS LAKE
TIPPECANOE RIVER
HAYES MEMORIAL
EDISON BIRTHPLACE
OBERLIN COLLEGE
OHIO TURNPIKE
MOSQUITO
COOK FOREST
NAUVOO HISTORIC DISTRICT
Peoria
FT. CREVE COEUR
Fort Wayne
LINCOLN LIBRARY AND MUSEUM
CUYAHOGA FALLS
Akron
Youngstown
Williamsport
FT. EDWARDS MONUMENT
ARGYLE LAKE
SPRING LAKE
Bloomington
JEFFERSON STREET BRIDGE
Lima
PORTAGE LAKES
MORAINE
PENNSYLVANIA
PENNSYLVANIA STATE UNIVERSITY
DICKSON MOUNDS
ILLINOIS
PURDUE UNIVERSITY
TIPPECANOE BATTLEFIELD
Lafayette
Marion
LIMBERLOST MEMORIAL
GRAND LAKE ST. MARYS
KINGWOOD CENTER
Mansfield
Canton
McKINLEY MONUMENT
CATHEDRAL OF LEARNING
GOLDEN TRIANGLE
STEEL MILLS
THREE RIVERS STADIUM
MILITARY MUSEUM
Quincy
POSTVILLE COURT HOUSE
FT. QUIATENON
Kokomo
INDIAN LAKE
Marion
HARDING TOMB
MALABAR FARM
FOOTBALL HALL OF FAME
ZOAR VILLAGE
OLD ECONOMY VILLAGE
PRINCE GALLITZIN
SILOAM SPRINGS
MT. PULASKI COURT HOUSE
Champaign
Urbana
UNIVERSITY OF ILLINOIS
KICKAPOO
BENJAMIN HARRISON HOME
SOLDIERS AND SAILORS MONUMENT
FT. RECOVERY
DELAWARE
SCHOENBRUNN VILLAGE
Pittsburgh
ALLEGHENY PORTAGE RAILROAD N.H.S.
Altoona
Hannibal
LINCOLN'S NEW SALEM STATE PARK
Springfield
Decatur
Anderson
Muncie
MOUNDS
OHIO CAVERNS
MOUNT VERNON
CY YOUNG MEMORIAL
Johnstown
JOHNSTOWN FLOOD N. MEM.
LINCOLN HOME N.H.S.
LINCOLN TOMB
OLD STATE CAPITOL
LINCOLN TRAIL HOMESTEAD
COVERED BRIDGE
SHADES
TURKEY RUN
WILBUR WRIGHT MEMORIAL
BATTELLE MEMORIAL INSTITUTE
OHIO STATE UNIVERSITY
OHIO
Columbus
NEWARK EARTHWORKS
BLUE KNOB
PENNSYLVANIA TURNPIKE
MOTOR SPEEDWAY
Indianapolis
JAMES WHITCOMB RILEY HOME
Dayton
AIR FORCE MUSEUM
WRIGHT BROTHERS MEMORIAL
Wheeling
SEVEN SPRINGS
LAUREL HILL
GETTYSBURG N.M.P.
MOORE HOME
Terre Haute
LIEBER
INDIANA
DUNBAR HOUSE
ZANESVILLE ART INSTITUTE
JAMES BUCHANAN BIRTHPLACE
LINCOLN LOG CABIN
LINCOLN TRAIL
McCORMICK'S CREEK
WHITEWATER CANAL
HUESTON WOODS
MIAMISBURG MOUND
FT. NECESSITY N.B.
EISENHOWER N.H.S.
Fulton
PERE MARQUETTE
LOVEJOY MEMORIAL
SHAKAMAK
Bloomington
INDIANA UNIVERSITY
T.C. STEELE MEMORIAL
BROWN COUNTY ART GALLERIES
BROWN COUNTY
FT. ANCIENT
ADENA MEMORIAL
MOUND CITY GROUP N.M.
Chillicothe
CAMPUS MARTIUS MUSEUM
Marietta
Morgantown
WEST VIRGINIA UNIVERSITY
Fairmont
Cumberland
FT. FREDERICK
BERKELEY SPRINGS
Hagerstown
ANTIETAM N.B.S.
Missouri River
St. Louis
East St. Louis
CAHOKIA MOUNDS
VANDALIA STATE HOUSE
STEPHEN A. FORBES
Centralia
RED HILLS
Vincennes
WILLIAM HENRY HARRISON HOME
TERRITORIAL CAPITOL
GEORGE ROGERS CLARK N.H.P.
VERSAILLES
BENJAMIN HARRISON BIRTHPLACE
WILLIAM HOWARD TAFT N.H.S.
Cincinnati
U.S. GRANT BIRTHPLACE
FT. HILL
SERPENT MOUND
ROCK FORK
BUCKEYE FURNACE
Parkersburg
BLENNERHASSETT ISLAND
Clarksburg
JACKSON'S MILL
WESTON GLASS CENTER
TYGART LAKE
ICE MOUNTAIN
CHARLES TOWN
HARPERS FERRY
CHESAPEAKE AND OHIO CANAL N.H.P.
Washington, D.C.
Mt. Vernon
OLD GRIST MILL
PIGEON ROOST MEMORIAL
FRENCH LICK SPA
CLIFTY FALLS
J.F.D. LANIER MEMORIAL
ART MUSEUM
FT. WASHINGTON
RIVERFRONT STADIUM
Portsmouth
POINT PLEASANT MONUMENT
WEST VIRGINIA
BLACKWATER FALLS
SPRUCE KNOB
Spruce Knob 4,862 ft.
SENECA ROCKS
SENECA CAVERNS
Rolla
MISSOURI
FT. CHARTRES
FT. KASKASKIA
PIERRE MENARD HOME
KASKASKIA MEMORIAL
THE MID-AMERICA ROUTE
NEW HARMONY MEMORIAL
WYANDOTTE CAVE
New Albany
Louisville
Frankfort
Ashland
Huntington
ART GALLERY
STATE MUSEUM
Charleston
GREEN BANK RADIO OBSERVATORY
CASS SCENIC RAILROAD
FORD'S THEATRE N. MEM.
FREDERICK DOUGLASS HOME N. MEM.
GEORGETOWN HISTORIC DISTRICT
HOUSE WHERE LINCOLN DIED N. MEM.
JEFFERSON MEMORIAL N. MEM.
KENNEDY CENTER FOR PERFORMING ARTS
LIBRARY OF CONGRESS
LINCOLN MEMORIAL N. MEM.
SMITHSONIAN INSTITUTION
U.S. CAPITOL
U.S. SUPREME COURT
WASHINGTON MONUMENT N. MEM.
WHITE HOUSE
SOUTHERN ILLINOIS UNIVERSITY
Carbondale
GIANT CITY
SHAWNEETOWN MEMORIAL
Evansville
LINCOLN BOYHOOD N.M.
SANTA CLAUS
CORYDON CAPITOL
ANGEL MOUNDS
LINCOLN PIONEER VILLAGE
Owensboro
Lexington
HAWKS NEST
WEST VIRGINIA TURNPIKE
Cape Girardeau
FERNE CLYFFE
CAVE IN ROCK
Bardstown
KENTUCKY
HONEY IN THE ROCK THEATRE
BECKLEY EXHIBITION MINE
PONDEROSA WILDLIFE PRESERVE
WHITE SULPHUR SPRINGS
THE GREENBRIER
Charlottesville
Poplar Bluff
Sikeston
Cairo
FT. DEFIANCE
FORT MASSAC
Paducah
BLUEGRASS PARKWAY
PIPESTEM
BLUESTONE
Lynchburg
Richmond
Hazard
Bowling Green
Somerset
Bluefield
Roanoke
VIRGINIA
Petersburg
ARKANSAS
Clarksville
POCAHONTAS EXHIBITION MINE
Paris
TENNESSEE
Blytheville
Dyersburg
Nashville
Central Standard Time
Eastern Standard Time
Kingsport
Danville
NORTH CAROLINA

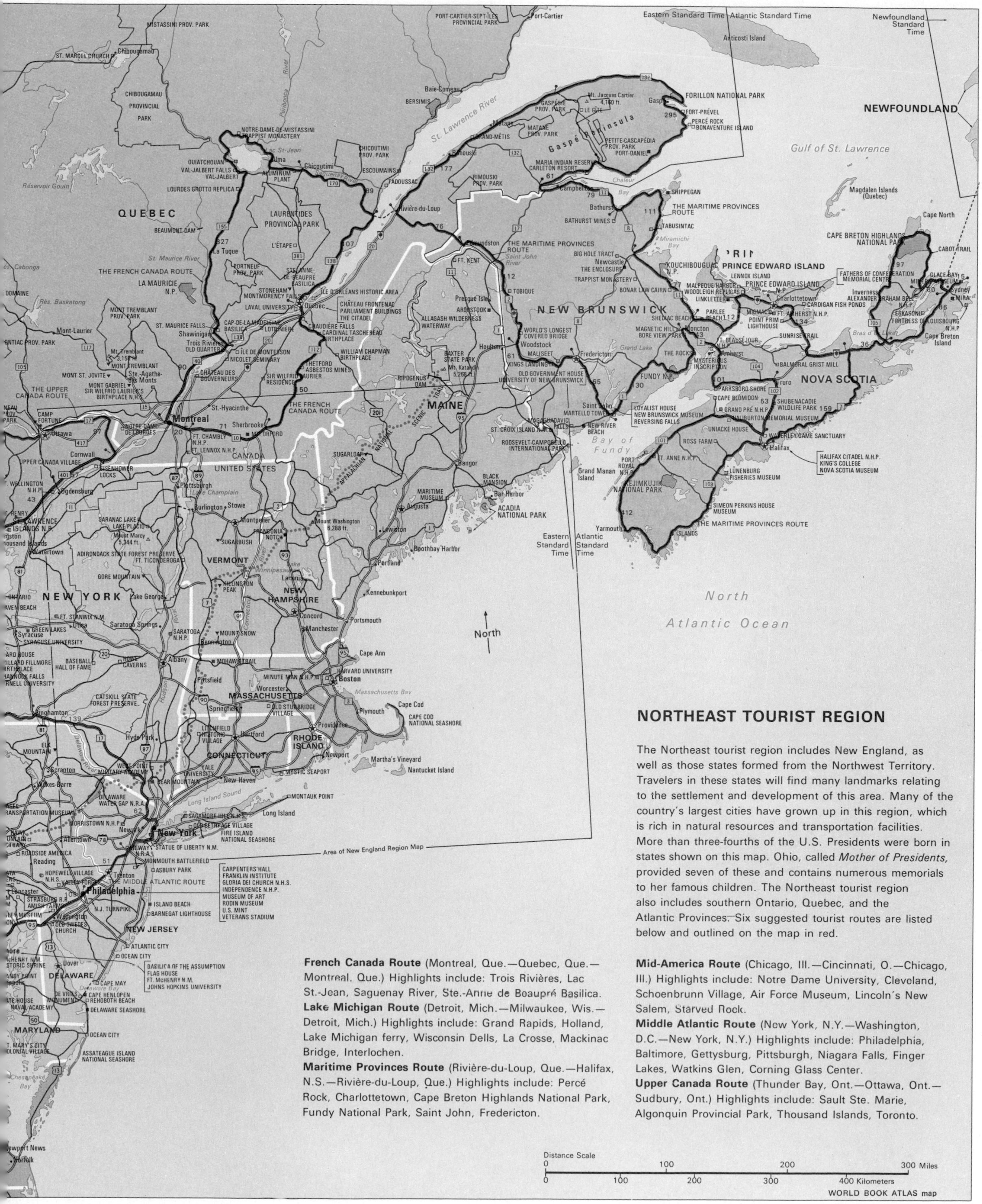

NORTHEAST TOURIST REGION

The Northeast tourist region includes New England, as well as those states formed from the Northwest Territory. Travelers in these states will find many landmarks relating to the settlement and development of this area. Many of the country's largest cities have grown up in this region, which is rich in natural resources and transportation facilities. More than three-fourths of the U.S. Presidents were born in states shown on this map. Ohio, called *Mother of Presidents,* provided seven of these and contains numerous memorials to her famous children. The Northeast tourist region also includes southern Ontario, Quebec, and the Atlantic Provinces. Six suggested tourist routes are listed below and outlined on the map in red.

French Canada Route (Montreal, Que.—Quebec, Que.—Montreal, Que.) Highlights include: Trois Rivières, Lac St.-Jean, Saguenay River, Ste.-Anne de Beaupré Basilica.

Lake Michigan Route (Detroit, Mich.—Milwaukee, Wis.—Detroit, Mich.) Highlights include: Grand Rapids, Holland, Lake Michigan ferry, Wisconsin Dells, La Crosse, Mackinac Bridge, Interlochen.

Maritime Provinces Route (Rivière-du-Loup, Que.—Halifax, N.S.—Rivière-du-Loup, Que.) Highlights include: Percé Rock, Charlottetown, Cape Breton Highlands National Park, Fundy National Park, Saint John, Fredericton.

Mid-America Route (Chicago, Ill.—Cincinnati, O.—Chicago, Ill.) Highlights include: Notre Dame University, Cleveland, Schoenbrunn Village, Air Force Museum, Lincoln's New Salem, Starved Rock.

Middle Atlantic Route (New York, N.Y.—Washington, D.C.—New York, N.Y.) Highlights include: Philadelphia, Baltimore, Gettysburg, Pittsburgh, Niagara Falls, Finger Lakes, Watkins Glen, Corning Glass Center.

Upper Canada Route (Thunder Bay, Ont.—Ottawa, Ont.—Sudbury, Ont.) Highlights include: Sault Ste. Marie, Algonquin Provincial Park, Thousand Islands, Toronto.

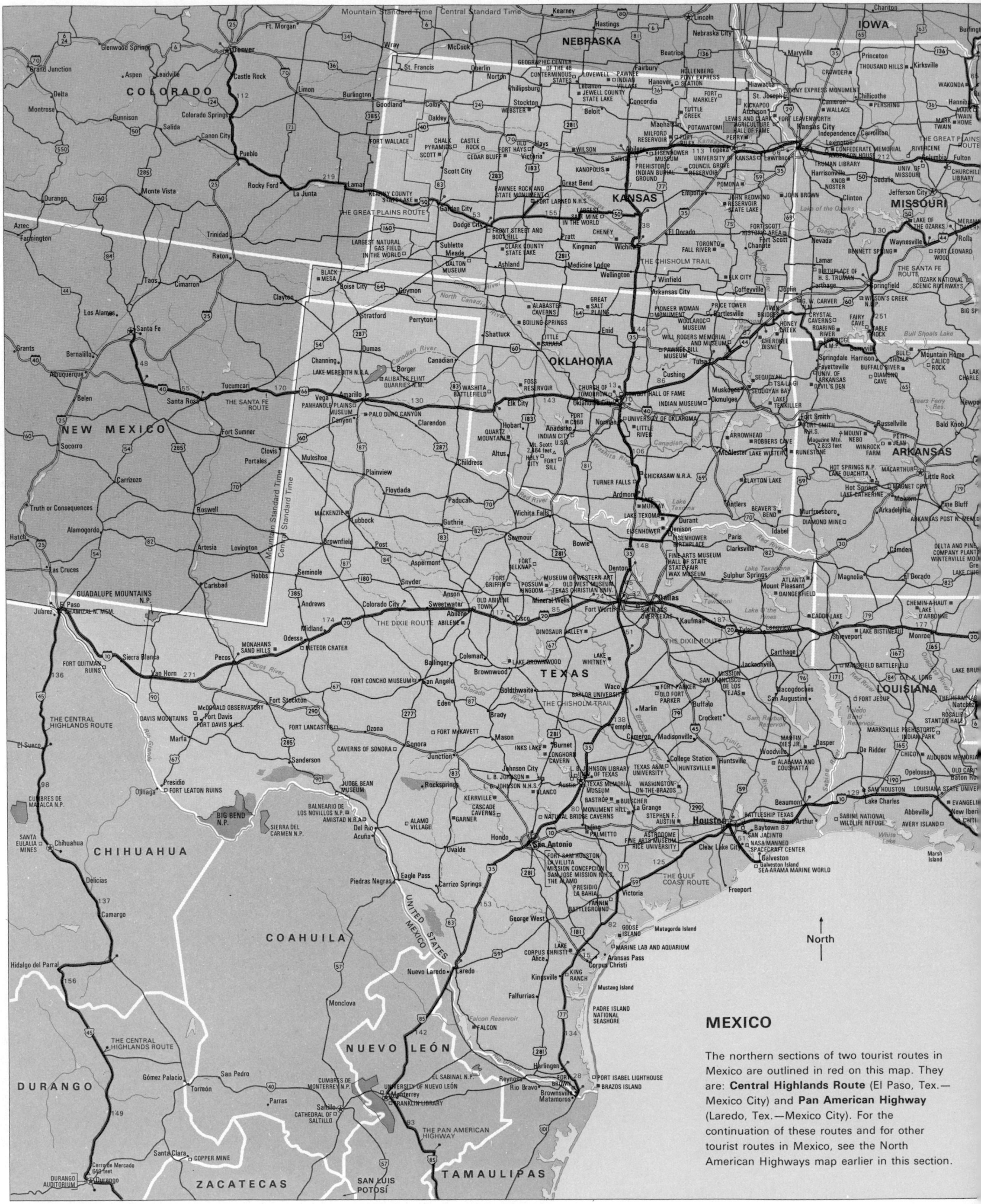

MEXICO

The northern sections of two tourist routes in Mexico are outlined in red on this map. They are: **Central Highlands Route** (El Paso, Tex.—Mexico City) and **Pan American Highway** (Laredo, Tex.—Mexico City). For the continuation of these routes and for other tourist routes in Mexico, see the North American Highways map earlier in this section.

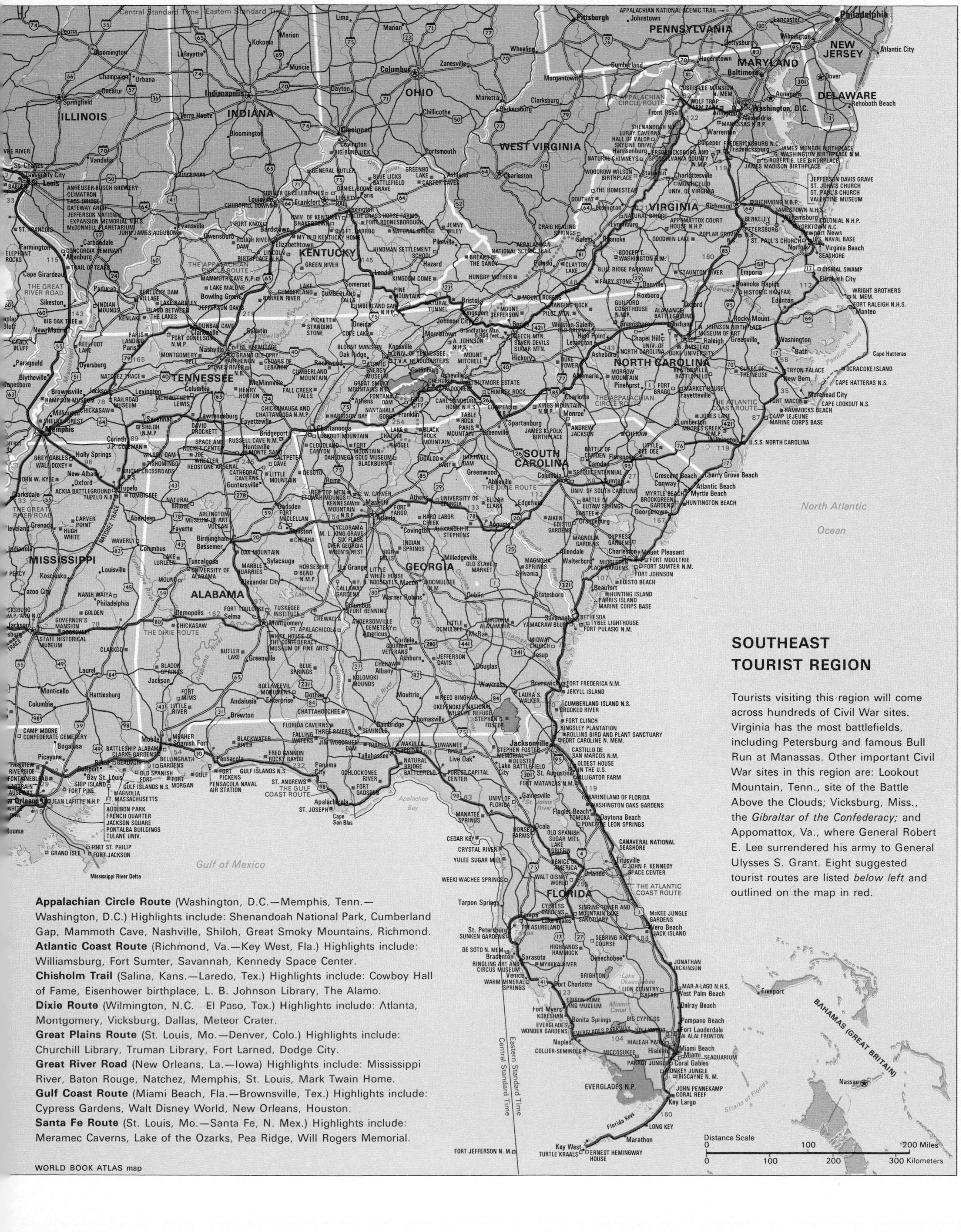

SOUTHEAST TOURIST REGION

Tourists visiting this region will come across hundreds of Civil War sites. Virginia has the most battlefields, including Petersburg and famous Bull Run at Manassas. Other important Civil War sites in this region are: Lookout Mountain, Tenn., site of the Battle Above the Clouds; Vicksburg, Miss., the *Gibraltar of the Confederacy;* and Appomattox, Va., where General Robert E. Lee surrendered his army to General Ulysses S. Grant. Eight suggested tourist routes are listed *below left* and outlined on the map in red.

Appalachian Circle Route (Washington, D.C.—Memphis, Tenn.—Washington, D.C.) Highlights include: Shenandoah National Park, Cumberland Gap, Mammoth Cave, Nashville, Shiloh, Great Smoky Mountains, Richmond.
Atlantic Coast Route (Richmond, Va.—Key West, Fla.) Highlights include: Williamsburg, Fort Sumter, Savannah, Kennedy Space Center.
Chisholm Trail (Salina, Kans.—Laredo, Tex.) Highlights include: Cowboy Hall of Fame, Eisenhower birthplace, L. B. Johnson Library, The Alamo.
Dixie Route (Wilmington, N.C.—El Paso, Tex.) Highlights include: Atlanta, Montgomery, Vicksburg, Dallas, Meteor Crater.
Great Plains Route (St. Louis, Mo.—Denver, Colo.) Highlights include: Churchill Library, Truman Library, Fort Larned, Dodge City.
Great River Road (New Orleans, La.—Iowa) Highlights include: Mississippi River, Baton Rouge, Natchez, Memphis, St. Louis, Mark Twain Home.
Gulf Coast Route (Miami Beach, Fla.—Brownsville, Tex.) Highlights include: Cypress Gardens, Walt Disney World, New Orleans, Houston.
Santa Fe Route (St. Louis, Mo.—Santa Fe, N. Mex.) Highlights include: Meramec Caverns, Lake of the Ozarks, Pea Ridge, Will Rogers Memorial.

WORLD BOOK ATLAS map

SOUTHWEST TOURIST REGION

This region is famous for its many natural landmarks—the giant redwoods of California, the Grand Canyon of the Colorado River, Great Salt Lake, Death Valley, and, of course, the Rocky Mountains. The Southwest is also rich in historical landmarks. In Arizona and New Mexico, tourists can see prehistoric Indian pueblos. In California, 21 beautifully preserved missions recall the days of Spanish exploration and early settlement. Ghost towns—relics of gold rush days—are scattered throughout the area. Nine suggested tourist routes are listed below and outlined on the map in red.

Border Route (Carlsbad, N. Mex.—San Diego, Calif.) Highlights include: Carlsbad Caverns, frontier town of Tombstone, Old Tucson, Casa Grande Ruins, Phoenix, Organ Pipe Cactus National Monument, Mexicali.

Desert Route (Salt Lake City, Ut.—Los Angeles, Calif.) Highlights include: Zion National Park, Las Vegas, Hoover Dam, Death Valley National Monument, Mojave Desert.

Eastern Slope Route (Wyoming—Carlsbad, N. Mex.) Highlights include: Rocky Mountain National Park, Denver, Air Force Academy, Pikes Peak, Taos, Santa Fe.

Great Divide Route (Denver, Colo.—Salt Lake City, Ut.) Highlights include: crossing the Continental Divide, Shadow Mountain, Dinosaur National Monument, Mormon Temple.

High Road (Los Angeles, Calif.—Tucumcari, N. Mex.) Highlights include: Calico ghost town, Grand Canyon National Park, Walnut Canyon, Petrified Forest, Albuquerque.

Pacific Coast Route (Oregon—Baja California) Highlights include: Redwood National Park, Muir Woods, San Francisco, San Simeon, Los Angeles, San Diego, Spanish missions.

Rugged Route (Pueblo, Colo.—southwestern Utah) Highlights include: Black Canyon of the Gunnison, Mesa Verde, Hopi and Navajo Indian reservations, Glen Canyon.

Sierra Route (Oregon—Los Angeles, Calif.) Highlights include: Mount Shasta, Sacramento, Yosemite and Sequoia national parks, Fort Tejon.

Union Pacific Route (San Francisco, Calif.—Salt Lake City, Ut.) Highlights include: Donner Pass, Reno, Carson City, Lake Tahoe, Bonneville Speedway, Great Salt Lake.

WORLD BOOK ATLAS map

IDAHO
WYOMING
NEBRASKA
UTAH
COLORADO
KANSAS
OKLAHOMA
ARIZONA
NEW MEXICO
TEXAS
CHIHUAHUA
SONORA
COAHUILA
Rocky Mountains
Continental Divide
Mountain Standard Time
Central Standard Time
Pacific Standard Time
UNITED STATES
MEXICO
THE GREAT DIVIDE ROUTE
THE RUGGED ROUTE
THE DESERT ROUTE
THE EASTERN SLOPE ROUTE
THE HIGH ROAD
THE BORDER ROUTE
Painted Desert
Gulf of California
Great Salt Lake
Flaming Gorge Reservoir
Salt Lake City
Denver
Colorado Springs
Pueblo
Santa Fe
Albuquerque
Phoenix
Tucson
Flagstaff
El Paso
Juárez
Las Cruces
Gallup
Grand Junction
Cheyenne
Laramie
Rock Springs
Provo
Ogden
Amarillo
Lubbock
Roswell
Carlsbad
Yuma
Nogales
Kingman
Needles
Las Vegas
Durango
Taos
Trinidad
Raton
Pikes Peak 14,110 Ft.
Mt. Elbert 14,431 Ft.
Kings Peak 13,498 Ft.
Humphreys Peak 12,670 Ft.
NAVAJO INDIAN RESERVATION
HOPI INDIAN RESERVATION
FORT APACHE INDIAN RESERVATION
SAN CARLOS INDIAN RESERVATION
PAPAGO INDIAN RESERVATION
UINTAH AND OURAY INDIAN RESERVATION
GRAND CANYON NATIONAL PARK
MESA VERDE N.P.
CARLSBAD CAVERNS N.P.
ZION NATIONAL PARK
BRYCE CANYON NATIONAL PARK
CANYONLANDS NATIONAL PARK
CAPITOL REEF NATIONAL PARK
GLEN CANYON NATIONAL RECREATION AREA
LAKE MEAD NATIONAL RECREATION AREA
WHITE SANDS N.M.
PETRIFIED FOREST N.P.
ROCKY MOUNTAIN N.P.
GREAT SAND DUNES N.M.
SIERRA DEL CARMEN NATIONAL PARK
CUMBRES DE MAJALCA NATIONAL PARK

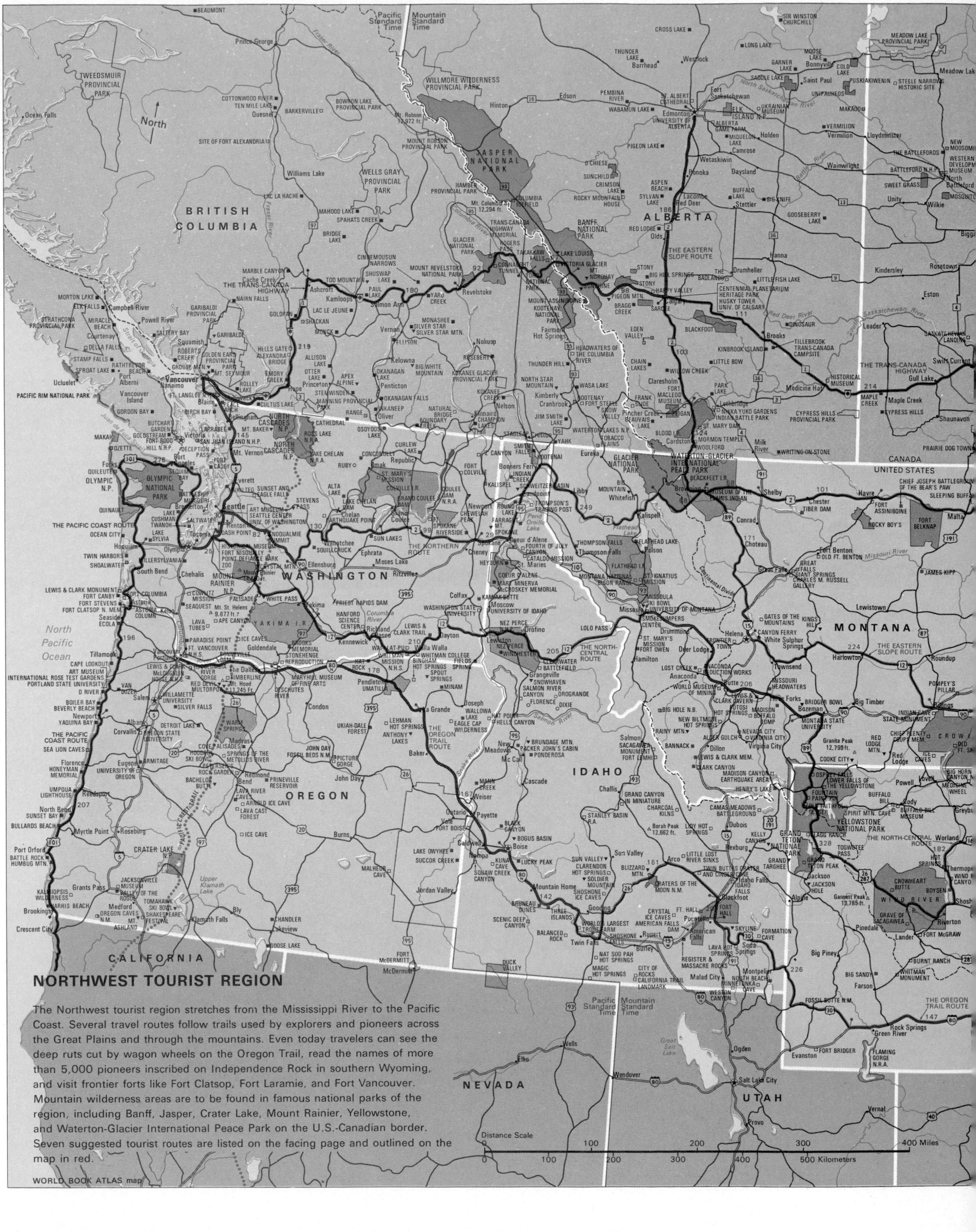

NORTHWEST TOURIST REGION

The Northwest tourist region stretches from the Mississippi River to the Pacific Coast. Several travel routes follow trails used by explorers and pioneers across the Great Plains and through the mountains. Even today travelers can see the deep ruts cut by wagon wheels on the Oregon Trail, read the names of more than 5,000 pioneers inscribed on Independence Rock in southern Wyoming, and visit frontier forts like Fort Clatsop, Fort Laramie, and Fort Vancouver. Mountain wilderness areas are to be found in famous national parks of the region, including Banff, Jasper, Crater Lake, Mount Rainier, Yellowstone, and Waterton-Glacier International Peace Park on the U.S.-Canadian border. Seven suggested tourist routes are listed on the facing page and outlined on the map in red.

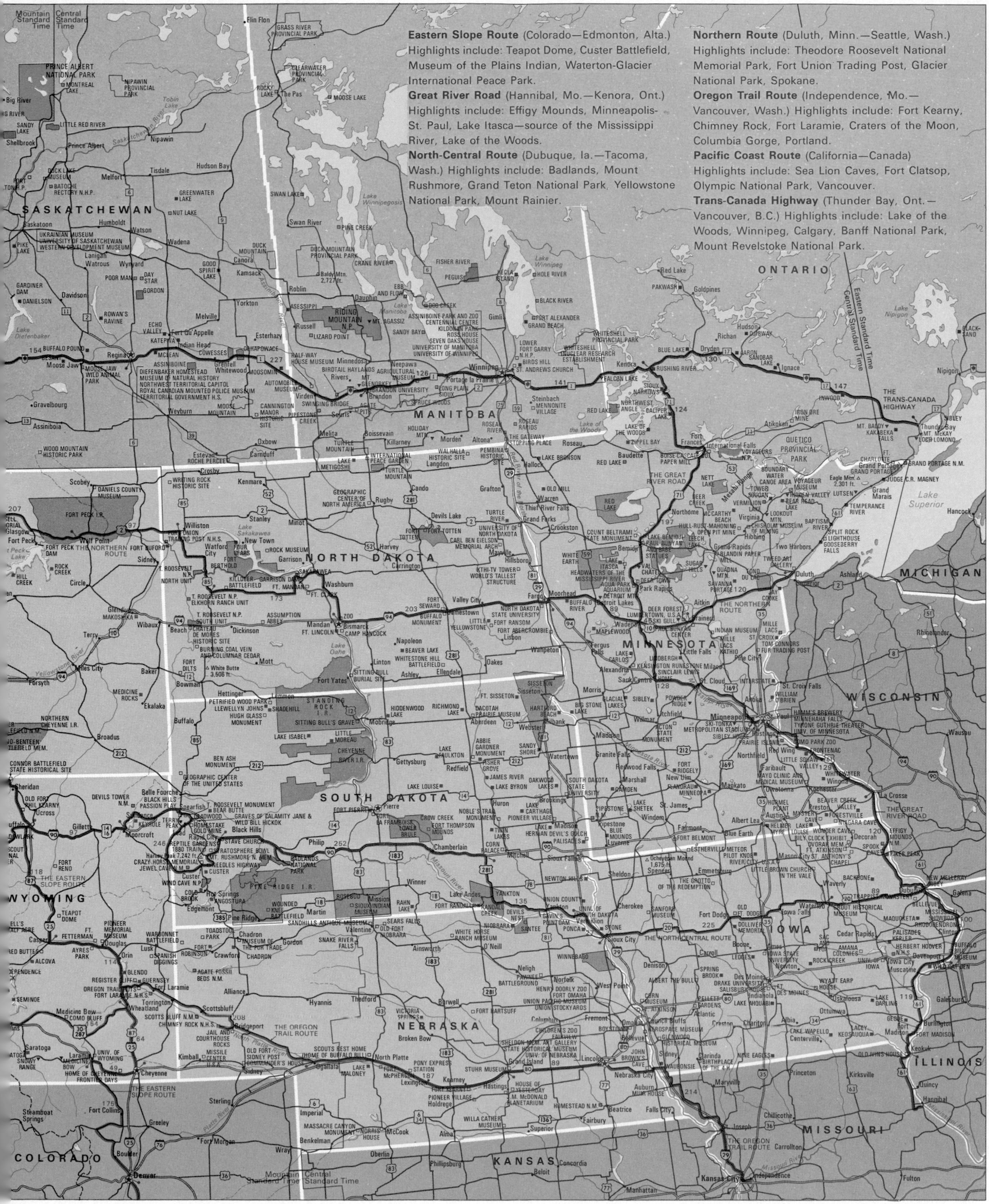
Eastern Slope Route (Colorado—Edmonton, Alta.) Highlights include: Teapot Dome, Custer Battlefield, Museum of the Plains Indian, Waterton-Glacier International Peace Park.
Great River Road (Hannibal, Mo.—Kenora, Ont.) Highlights include: Effigy Mounds, Minneapolis-St. Paul, Lake Itasca—source of the Mississippi River, Lake of the Woods.
North-Central Route (Dubuque, Ia.—Tacoma, Wash.) Highlights include: Badlands, Mount Rushmore, Grand Teton National Park, Yellowstone National Park, Mount Rainier.
Northern Route (Duluth, Minn.—Seattle, Wash.) Highlights include: Theodore Roosevelt National Memorial Park, Fort Union Trading Post, Glacier National Park, Spokane.
Oregon Trail Route (Independence, Mo.—Vancouver, Wash.) Highlights include: Fort Kearny, Chimney Rock, Fort Laramie, Craters of the Moon, Columbia Gorge, Portland.
Pacific Coast Route (California—Canada) Highlights include: Sea Lion Caves, Fort Clatsop, Olympic National Park, Vancouver.
Trans-Canada Highway (Thunder Bay, Ont.—Vancouver, B.C.) Highlights include: Lake of the Woods, Winnipeg, Calgary, Banff National Park, Mount Revelstoke National Park.
SASKATCHEWAN
MANITOBA
ONTARIO
NORTH DAKOTA
MINNESOTA
SOUTH DAKOTA
WISCONSIN
MICHIGAN
WYOMING
NEBRASKA
IOWA
ILLINOIS
MISSOURI
KANSAS
COLORADO
Lake Superior
Mountain Standard Time
Central Standard Time
Eastern Standard Time

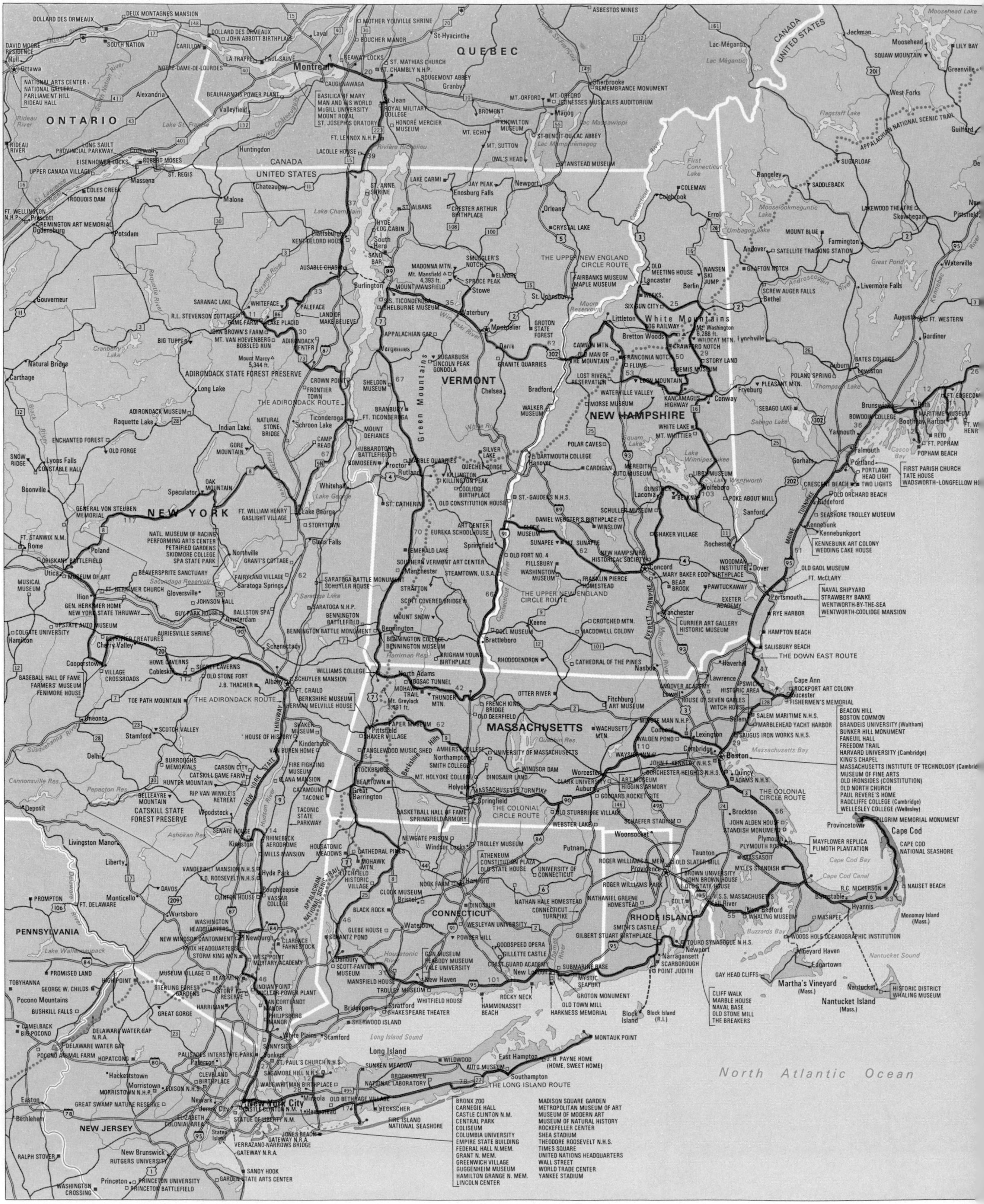
QUEBEC
ONTARIO
CANADA
UNITED STATES
NEW YORK
VERMONT
NEW HAMPSHIRE
MASSACHUSETTS
CONNECTICUT
RHODE ISLAND
PENNSYLVANIA
NEW JERSEY
North Atlantic Ocean
Long Island Sound
Long Island
Massachusetts Bay
Cape Cod Bay
Buzzards Bay
Nantucket Sound
Ottawa
Montreal
Sherbrooke
Granby
St-Hyacinthe
Lac-Mégantic
Jackman
Moosehead
Greenville
West Forks
Guilford
Rangeley
Skowhegan
Pittsfield
Farmington
Waterville
Augusta
Gardiner
Lewiston
Auburn
Brunswick
Bath
Portland
Gorham
Sanford
Biddeford
Kennebunk
Kennebunkport
Portsmouth
Dover
Rochester
Concord
Manchester
Nashua
Keene
Brattleboro
Bennington
Rutland
Burlington
Montpelier
Barre
Stowe
St. Johnsbury
Newport
Lancaster
Berlin
Littleton
Conway
Laconia
Wolfeboro
Hanover
Springfield
Pittsfield
North Adams
Northampton
Holyoke
Worcester
Fitchburg
Lowell
Lawrence
Haverhill
Gloucester
Salem
Lexington
Concord
Cambridge
Boston
Quincy
Brockton
Plymouth
Taunton
Fall River
New Bedford
Providence
Newport
Narragansett
Hyannis
Barnstable
Provincetown
Cape Cod
Martha's Vineyard (Mass.)
Nantucket Island (Mass.)
Block Island (R.I.)
Hartford
Bristol
Waterbury
New Haven
New London
Danbury
Bridgeport
Stratford
Stamford
White Plains
Yonkers
New York City
Newark
Paterson
Jersey City
Elizabeth
Staten Island
New Brunswick
Princeton
Easton
Bethlehem
Hackettstown
Morristown
Mineola
Hempstead
East Hampton
Southampton
MONTAUK POINT
Albany
Schenectady
Amsterdam
Saratoga Springs
Glens Falls
Lake George
Ticonderoga
Plattsburgh
Lake Placid
Saranac Lake
Malone
Massena
Potsdam
Ogdensburg
Watertown
Gouverneur
Carthage
Boonville
Utica
Rome
Ilion
Gloversville
Hamilton
Cooperstown
Cobleskill
Oneonta
Stamford
Delhi
Kingston
Hyde Park
Poughkeepsie
Newburgh
Monticello
Liberty
Wurtsboro
Woodstock
Hudson River
Lake Champlain
Green Mountains
White Mountains
Berkshire Hills
ADIRONDACK STATE FOREST PRESERVE
CATSKILL STATE FOREST PRESERVE
THE ADIRONDACK ROUTE
THE UPPER NEW ENGLAND CIRCLE ROUTE
THE COLONIAL CIRCLE ROUTE
THE DOWN EAST ROUTE
THE LONG ISLAND ROUTE
APPALACHIAN NATIONAL SCENIC TRAIL
NEW YORK STATE THRUWAY
MASSACHUSETTS TURNPIKE
CONNECTICUT TURNPIKE
MAINE TURNPIKE
EVERETT TURNPIKE
PALISADES INTERSTATE PARK
FIRE ISLAND NATIONAL SEASHORE
CAPE COD NATIONAL SEASHORE
Mt. Washington 6,288 ft.
Mt. Mansfield 4,393 ft.
Mount Marcy 5,344 ft.
Mt. Greylock 3,491 ft.
NATIONAL ARTS CENTER
NATIONAL GALLERY
PARLIAMENT HILL
RIDEAU HALL
BASILICA OF MARY QUEEN OF THE WORLD
McGILL UNIVERSITY
MOUNT ROYAL
ST. JOSEPH'S ORATORY
BASEBALL HALL OF FAME
FARMERS' MUSEUM
FENIMORE HOUSE
NATL. MUSEUM OF RACING
PERFORMING ARTS CENTER
PETRIFIED GARDENS
SKIDMORE COLLEGE
SPA STATE PARK
BEACON HILL
BOSTON COMMON
BRANDEIS UNIVERSITY (Waltham)
BUNKER HILL MONUMENT
FANEUIL HALL
FREEDOM TRAIL
HARVARD UNIVERSITY (Cambridge)
KING'S CHAPEL
MASSACHUSETTS INSTITUTE OF TECHNOLOGY (Cambridge)
MUSEUM OF FINE ARTS
OLD IRONSIDES (CONSTITUTION)
OLD NORTH CHURCH
PAUL REVERE'S HOME
RADCLIFFE COLLEGE (Cambridge)
WELLESLEY COLLEGE (Wellesley)
NAVAL SHIPYARD
STRAWBERY BANKE
WENTWORTH-BY-THE-SEA
WENTWORTH-COOLIDGE MANSION
FIRST PARISH CHURCH
TATE HOUSE
WADSWORTH-LONGFELLOW HOUSE
PORTLAND HEAD LIGHT
TWO LIGHTS
MAYFLOWER REPLICA
PLIMOTH PLANTATION
PILGRIM MEMORIAL MONUMENT
HISTORIC DISTRICT
WHALING MUSEUM
CLIFF WALK
MARBLE HOUSE
NAVAL BASE
OLD STONE MILL
THE BREAKERS
BRONX ZOO
CARNEGIE HALL
CASTLE CLINTON N.M.
CENTRAL PARK
COLISEUM
COLUMBIA UNIVERSITY
EMPIRE STATE BUILDING
FEDERAL HALL N.MEM.
GRANT N. MEM.
GREENWICH VILLAGE
GUGGENHEIM MUSEUM
HAMILTON GRANGE N. MEM.
LINCOLN CENTER
MADISON SQUARE GARDEN
METROPOLITAN MUSEUM OF ART
MUSEUM OF MODERN ART
MUSEUM OF NATURAL HISTORY
ROCKEFELLER CENTER
SHEA STADIUM
THEODORE ROOSEVELT N.H.S.
TIMES SQUARE
UNITED NATIONS HEADQUARTERS
WALL STREET
WORLD TRADE CENTER
YANKEE STADIUM
STATUE OF LIBERTY N.M.
WEST POINT MILITARY ACADEMY
YALE UNIVERSITY
WESLEYAN UNIVERSITY
UNIVERSITY OF MASSACHUSETTS
UNIVERSITY OF CONNECTICUT
DARTMOUTH COLLEGE
WILLIAMS COLLEGE
SMITH COLLEGE
MT. HOLYOKE COLLEGE
AMHERST COLLEGE
BOWDOIN COLLEGE
BATES COLLEGE
VASSAR COLLEGE
COLGATE UNIVERSITY
PRINCETON UNIVERSITY
RUTGERS UNIVERSITY
TANGLEWOOD MUSIC SHED
BASKETBALL HALL OF FAME
MYSTIC SEAPORT
SUBMARINE BASE
COAST GUARD ACADEMY
ELEANOR ROOSEVELT
F.D. ROOSEVELT N.H.S.
VANDERBILT MANSION N.H.S.

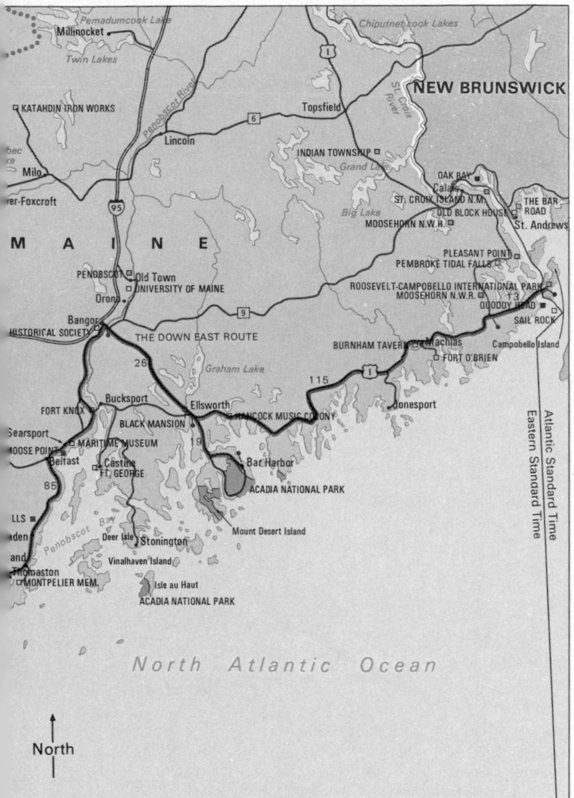

NEW ENGLAND

A tourist visiting this region will find it rich in landmarks of early U.S. history. At Plymouth, where the first Pilgrims landed, you can see a replica of the *Mayflower*. The opening battles of the Revolutionary War were fought at Lexington and Concord near Boston. In Quincy, you can visit the birthplace of two U.S. Presidents: John Adams and John Quincy Adams. New York City and Boston are important tourist centers, offering a variety of entertainment and sightseeing. The eastern part of New York State and Long Island are also shown as part of the New England tourist region. Five suggested tourist routes are listed below and outlined on the map in red.

Adirondack Route (New York City—Montreal, Que.) Highlights include: West Point Military Academy, Hyde Park, Albany, Howe Caverns, Cooperstown, Lake George, Fort Ticonderoga, Lake Placid, Saranac Lake, Lake Champlain.

Colonial Circle Route (Boston, Mass.—New Haven, Conn.—Boston, Mass.) Highlights include: Plymouth, Cape Cod, Newport, Mystic Seaport, New London, New Haven, Litchfield, Pittsfield, Old Sturbridge Village, Wayside Inn, Minute Man National Historic Park.

Down East Route (Boston, Mass.—Campobello Island, N.B.) Highlights include: Cape Ann, Portsmouth, Kennebunk, Portland, Fort Popham, Boothbay Harbor, Camden, Fort Knox, Bar Harbor, Acadia National Park.

Long Island Route (New York City—Montauk Point) Highlights include: Sagamore Hill, Old Bethpage Village, Fire Island, Southampton, Auto Museum.

Upper New England Circle Route (Bennington, Vt.—Concord, N.H.—Bennington, Vt.) Highlights include: Proctor Marble Quarries, Shelburne Museum, Stowe, Franconia Notch, Mt. Washington, Lake Winnipesaukee, Connecticut River Valley, Mohawk Trail.

Distance Scale: 20, 40, 60, 80, 100 Miles; 20, 40, 60, 80, 100, 120, 140 Kilometers

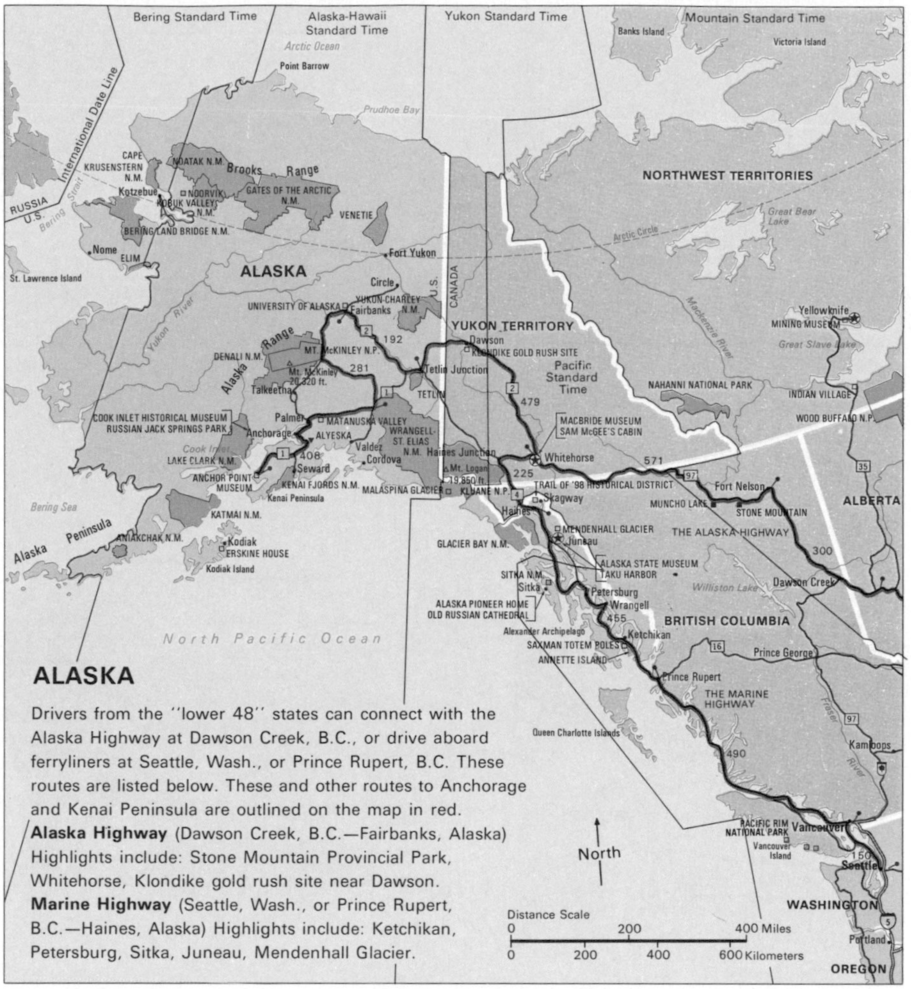

ALASKA

Drivers from the "lower 48" states can connect with the Alaska Highway at Dawson Creek, B.C., or drive aboard ferryliners at Seattle, Wash., or Prince Rupert, B.C. These routes are listed below. These and other routes to Anchorage and Kenai Peninsula are outlined on the map in red.

Alaska Highway (Dawson Creek, B.C.—Fairbanks, Alaska) Highlights include: Stone Mountain Provincial Park, Whitehorse, Klondike gold rush site near Dawson.

Marine Highway (Seattle, Wash., or Prince Rupert, B.C.—Haines, Alaska) Highlights include: Ketchikan, Petersburg, Sitka, Juneau, Mendenhall Glacier.

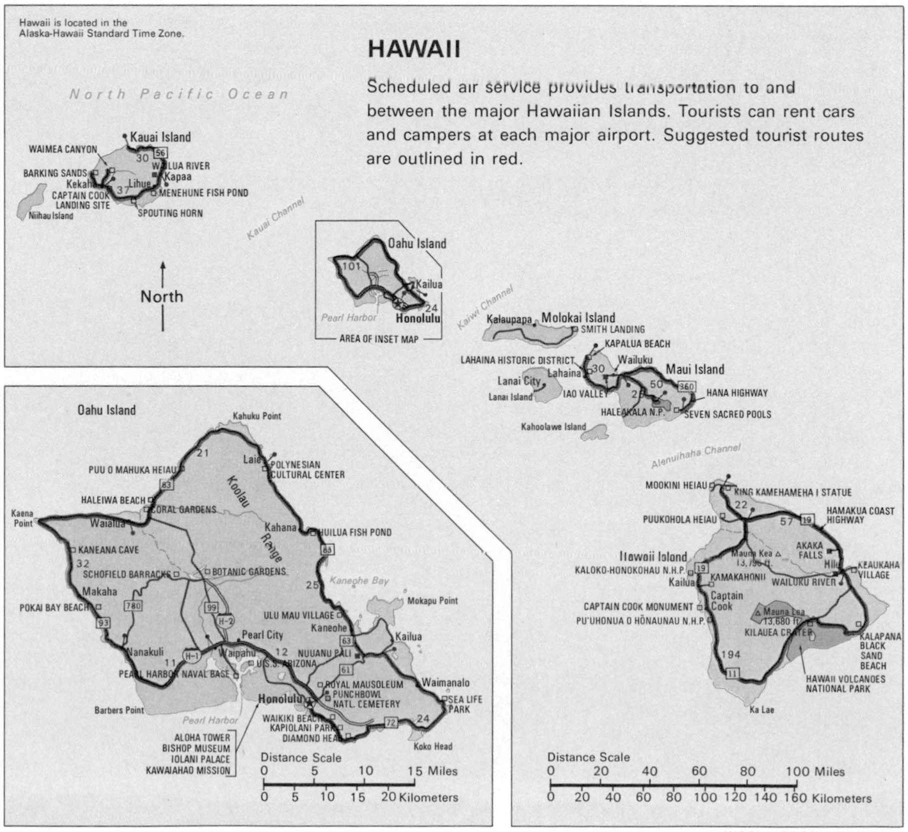

HAWAII

Scheduled air service provides transportation to and between the major Hawaiian Islands. Tourists can rent cars and campers at each major airport. Suggested tourist routes are outlined in red.

WORLD BOOK ATLAS maps

Northeast

Connecticut *58*
Maine *62*
Massachusetts *66*
New Hampshire *70*
New Jersey *74*
New York *78*
Pennsylvania *82*
Rhode Island *86*
Vermont *88*

The Northeast's rugged seacoasts, wooded mountains, and velvety grass provided a haven for early colonists. Birthplace of the Revolutionary War, this region has contributed greatly to the heritage of the United States.

Autumn adds rusty hues to the hills of Vermont, the Green Mountain State (facing page).

Old North Church still stands in Boston, Mass. In 1775, lanterns hung in the steeple warned Paul Revere of a British attack (above left).

Vendors with traveling hot dog stands claim their space in New York City's busy streets. The largest U.S. city, New York is also the fifth largest city in the world (below left).

In 1916, Maine residents donated the land that became Acadia National Park. A lake-strewn haven for wildlife, the area was the first national park east of the Mississippi River (below right).

The sea has always played a major role in Connecticut's heritage. Mystic Seaport is a reconstructed seafaring village of the 1800's—complete with authentic sailing ships of the past.

Connecticut

Connecticut is the third smallest state in area. But it ranks as one of the nation's industrial leaders and has a higher per capita income than any other state.

Connecticut is a leader in the manufacture of many goods. The state's manufacturing tradition goes back to colonial days, when Yankee peddlers traveled in horse-drawn carts across the countryside, selling Connecticut goods such as buttons, clocks, firearms, hats, and pins. These "door-to-door" salespersons were so skillful in promoting the products of Connecticut craftworkers that some people claimed the peddlers could even sell a wooden nutmeg. Such claims earned Connecticut one of its nicknames, the *Nutmeg State.*

Inventors and factory workers in Connecticut have contributed to a variety of pioneering industrial efforts. Eli Whitney introduced mass production to Connecticut—and the world—when he began using a system of interchangeable parts in the production of guns. Another Connecticut inventor, Eli Terry, became the first person to make clocks using mass-production techniques. The first successful repeating pistol was devised by Samuel Colt of Connecticut. And the state was also the home of Charles Goodyear, who found a way to strengthen rubber using a method called vulcanization. The first silk mill in the United States was operated in Mansfield. Connecticut workers were the first in the nation to make bicycles, cigars, copper coins, nuts and bolts, pins and needles, and rubber shoes.

Over the years, Connecticut has kept pace with changing industrial needs. The world's first nuclear-powered submarine was built and launched at Groton. And when U.S. astronauts became the first persons to walk on the moon, they carried supplies in backpacks made in Connecticut.

Connecticut has achieved many firsts in fields other than manufacturing. In 1639, the Connecticut Colony adopted a document called the Fundamental Orders, which gave voters the right to elect government officials. This document is sometimes called the first written constitution. Litchfield was the home of the first law school in the United States. The nation's first free school for the deaf was founded in Hartford by Thomas H. Gallaudet. Citizens in Salisbury can claim what is probably the first free, tax-supported public library in the country. The first insurance policies covering accidents, automobiles, and aircraft were issued in Hartford, a city that became known as *Insurance City*. Today, Hartford hosts the headquarters of about 50 insurance companies.

In addition to all these firsts, Connecticut played a crucial role in the writing of the U.S. Constitution. When a deadlock over representation in the Congress threatened to break up the Constitutional Convention, Roger Sherman proposed the Connecticut Compromise. The compromise established the nation's two-house legislature, with equal representation for all states in the Senate and representation according to population in the House of Representatives. The compromise was adopted, and Sherman's contribution earned Connecticut one of its other nicknames—the *Constitution State.*

The democratic tradition in its purest form is carried out today in small towns throughout Connecticut. Most of the state's small towns have a "town meeting" form of government. At the annual town meeting, citizens gather to elect officials, discuss town business, and vote on local matters.

Long before Europeans settled in what is now Connecticut, various Indian tribes lived in the area. One of Connecticut's best-known historical figures was Uncas, chief of the Mohegan (or Mohican) tribe. James Fenimore Cooper's novel *The Last of the Mohicans* characterizes Uncas as an ideal Indian.

Another famous novelist, Mark Twain, built a sprawling Victorian mansion in Hartford and lived there with his family during the late 1800's. The mansion is one of many historic buildings and other attractions that draw crowds of tourists to Connecticut. The state has many colonial buildings from the 1600's, including Whitfield House in Guilford, which may be the oldest stone house in all New England.

The historic charm of rural Connecticut is a feature of small towns throughout the state. Many small towns center around a village green, frequently surrounded by a white-steepled church, stately colonial homes, and a town meeting hall. Old shipbuilding centers and whaling ports such as Mystic and Groton recall the state's seafaring past, when clipper ships and whaling fleets dotted the horizon along Connecticut's Atlantic coast.

On the old campus of Yale students stroll among stately buildings and memorials, some dating to colonial times.

Connecticut's pride in its rich military history is reflected at Fort Griswold State Park near Groton. The park was the site of a Revolutionary War battle and is also the resting place of the U.S.S. Croaker, *a World War II submarine built in Groton that visitors may tour.*

Connecticut
Constitution State

Capital: Hartford
Area: 5,009 sq. mi. (12,973 km²), including 147 sq. mi. (381 km²) of inland water and excluding 573 sq. mi. (1,484 km²) of Long Island Sound; 48th in size among the states
Elevation: *Highest*—2,380 ft. (725 m) above sea level, on the south slope of Mount Frissell; *lowest*—sea level along the Long Island Sound shore
Statehood: January 9, 1788, the 5th state
Abbreviations: Conn. (traditional); CT (postal)
Motto: *Qui Transtulit Sustinet* (He Who Transplanted Still Sustains)
Song: "Yankee Doodle"
Tree: White Oak

Connecticut's state seal shows three grapevines symbolizing the transplanting of European culture and traditions to the colony of Connecticut. The seal was adopted in 1931. The grapevines also appear on the state flag, adopted in 1897.

CONNECTICUT Political Map

State capital
Urban area in Connecticut
Urban area outside Connecticut
City or town
County courthouse
TOLLAND County name
County boundary
State boundary
Military or other federal area
Point of interest

Major airport
Water
River
Intermittent lake

Highways:
Expressway
Other road
84 Interstate
7 U.S.
25 Other

Polyconic projection
WORLD BOOK map
© Field Enterprises Educational Corporation

Distance Scale

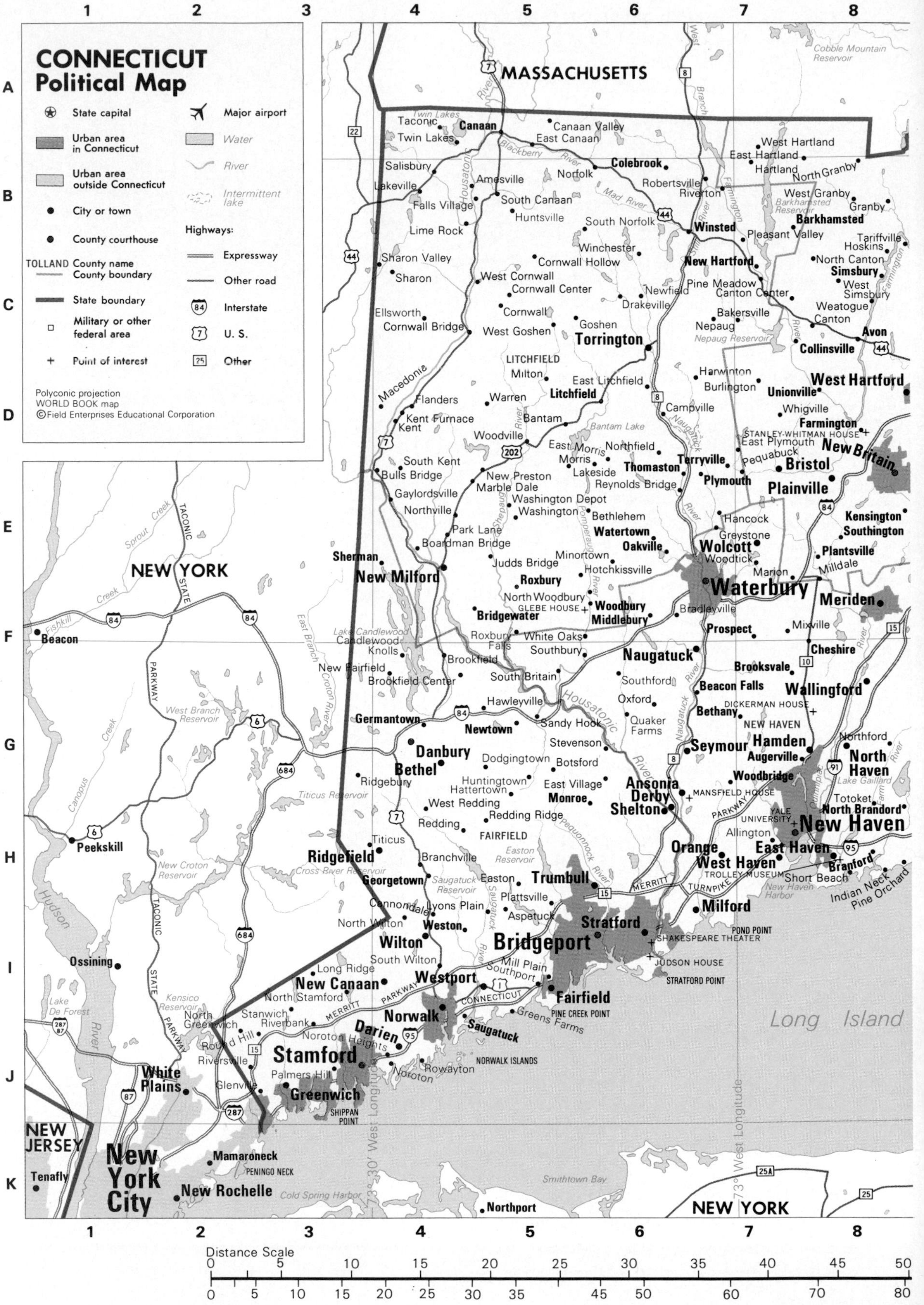

Seal

Flag

Bird: Robin

Flower: Mountain Laurel

9 10 11 12 13 14 15 16

Westfield

Springfield **MASSACHUSETTS**

East Longmeadow

Southbridge

Webster

A

Thompsonville

North Somers   Mashapaug   Quinebaug   Wilsonville
                                        Fabyan

West   Suffield   Somers   North Woodstock   North Grosvenor Dale
Suffield   Hydeville   Staffordville   Union
Enfield   Hazardville   Somers   Grosvenor Dale   Pascoag
          Somersville 190   Orcutts   Stafford   West Woodstock   Thompson
          West Stafford   Grosvenor Dale   Mechanicsville
B
          Stafford Springs   Woodstock Valley   Harrisville   Quaddick
Windsor Locks   Melrose   Crystal Lake   Westford   South Woodstock   Woodstock
TROLLEY MUSEUM   East Granby   Ellington   West Willington   Pomfret   East Putnam
Poquonock   Scantic   Willington Hill   Pomfret Center   Putnam Heights
          Hayden   Windsorville   Phoenixville   Ashford   Ballouville   Greenville
North Bloomfield   Windermere   Tolland   West Willington   Warrenville   Abington   Rogers   Attawaugan
HARTFORD   Rockville   South Willington   West Ashford   Dayville   East Killingly
Bloomfield   East Windsor Hill   Vernon Center   Mansfield   Mount Hope   Killingly Center
Windsor   Wapping   Vernon   Merrow   Storrs   WINDHAM   Danielson   South Killingly
Blue Hills   Talcottville   Mansfield Depot   Spring Hill   Chaplin   East Brooklyn
South Windsor   Coventry   Eagleville   Gurleyville   Hampton   Brooklyn
East   Wilson   Burnside   Mansfield Center   Atwoodville   South Chaplin   Wauregan
Hartford   Manchester   Bolton   South Coventry   Clarks Corner   Central Village   Almyville
C
Hartford   Andover   North Windham   Scotland   Canterbury   Sterling
          Glastonbury   Columbia   Willimantic   Windham   Plainfield   Moosup   Oneco
BUTTOLPH   East Glastonbury   Gilead   Chestnut Hill   South Windham   Packerville   Sterling Hill
WILLIAMS   Wethersfield   Hebron   Liberty Hill   Hanover   Ekonk
HOUSE   Newington   South Glastonbury   Lebanon   North Franklin   Versailles   Hopeville
          Rocky Hill   Marlborough   Goshen Hill   Franklin   Baltic   Occum   Jewett City   Doaneville
Berlin   North Westchester   Amston   Gilman   Taftville   Pachaug   Voluntown
East   Cromwell   Cobalt   East Hampton   Fitchville   Lisbon   Pachaug Pond   Glasgo
Berlin   Westfield   Middle Haddam   Westchester   Bozrah   Long Society
Newfield   Portland   Gardner Lake   Street   Preston City
Rockfall   Middletown   Wopowog   Bashan   Leffingwell   Norwich   Hallville   Laurel Glen
          Middlefield   Leesville   Moodus   Salem   Oakdale   Poquetanuck   Clarks Falls
Durham   Higganum   Millington   Mohegan   NEW LONDON
Durham Center   Haddam   Montville   Allyns Point   North Stonington
Ponset   Shailerville   East Haddam   North Plain   Uncasville   Ledyard
MIDDLESEX   Tylerville   Chesterfield   Gales Ferry   Old Mystic
Rockland   Hadlyme   Chester   Center Groton   Burnetts Corner   Pawcatuck
Killingworth   Deep River   UNITED STATES NAVAL SUBMARINE BASE   Groton   Mystic   Westerly
North Madison   Winthrop   Hamburg   UNITED STATES COAST GUARD ACADEMY   MYSTIC SEAPORT   Wequetequock
          Ivoryton   Essex 156   East Lyme   New London   West   Noank
Guilford   Centerbrook   Morningside Park   Groton   Mystic   Stonington
Stony Creek   Laysville   Waterford   OLD TOWN MILL   Mason Island   Lords Point
East River   9   Old Lyme   Niantic   Poquonock   NAVAL UNDERWATER SYSTEMS CENTER
Leetes Island   Pond Meadow   Bridge   FORT GRISWOLD AND GROTON MONUMENT
HAMMONASSET POINT   WHITFIELD HOUSE CONNECTICUT   Old Saybrook   South Lyme   Millstone   Pleasure
Sachem Head   SALT MEADOW   Fenwick   Sound   Black Point   Beach
          NATIONAL WILDLIFE REFUGE   Westbrook   View   Black Point Beach
          Grove Beach   Saybrook Manor   Saybrook Point
          Westbrook

RHODE ISLAND

44
6
6
95
165
102
TURNPIKE
Scituate Reservoir
Moosup River
Beach Pond
Worden Pond
Watchaug Pond
Ninigret Pond

Greenville

41° 30' North Latitude

42° North Latitude
Wallum Lake
Quaddick Reservoir

D

E

F

G

H

SANDY POINT

Block Island Sound

PLUM ISLAND

BLOCK ISLAND
(RHODE ISLAND)

I

North

Sound

Greenport

Orient Harbor

Gardiners Island

Gardiners Bay

MONTAUK POINT

114

25

SHELTER ISLAND

Little Peconic Bay

27

Napeague Bay

J

41° North Latitude

Sag Harbor

114

LONG ISLAND

North Atlantic Ocean

25

27

K

Riverhead

24

9 10 11 12 13 14 15 16

60 70 80 90 100 Miles
90 100 110 120 130 140 150 160 Kilometers

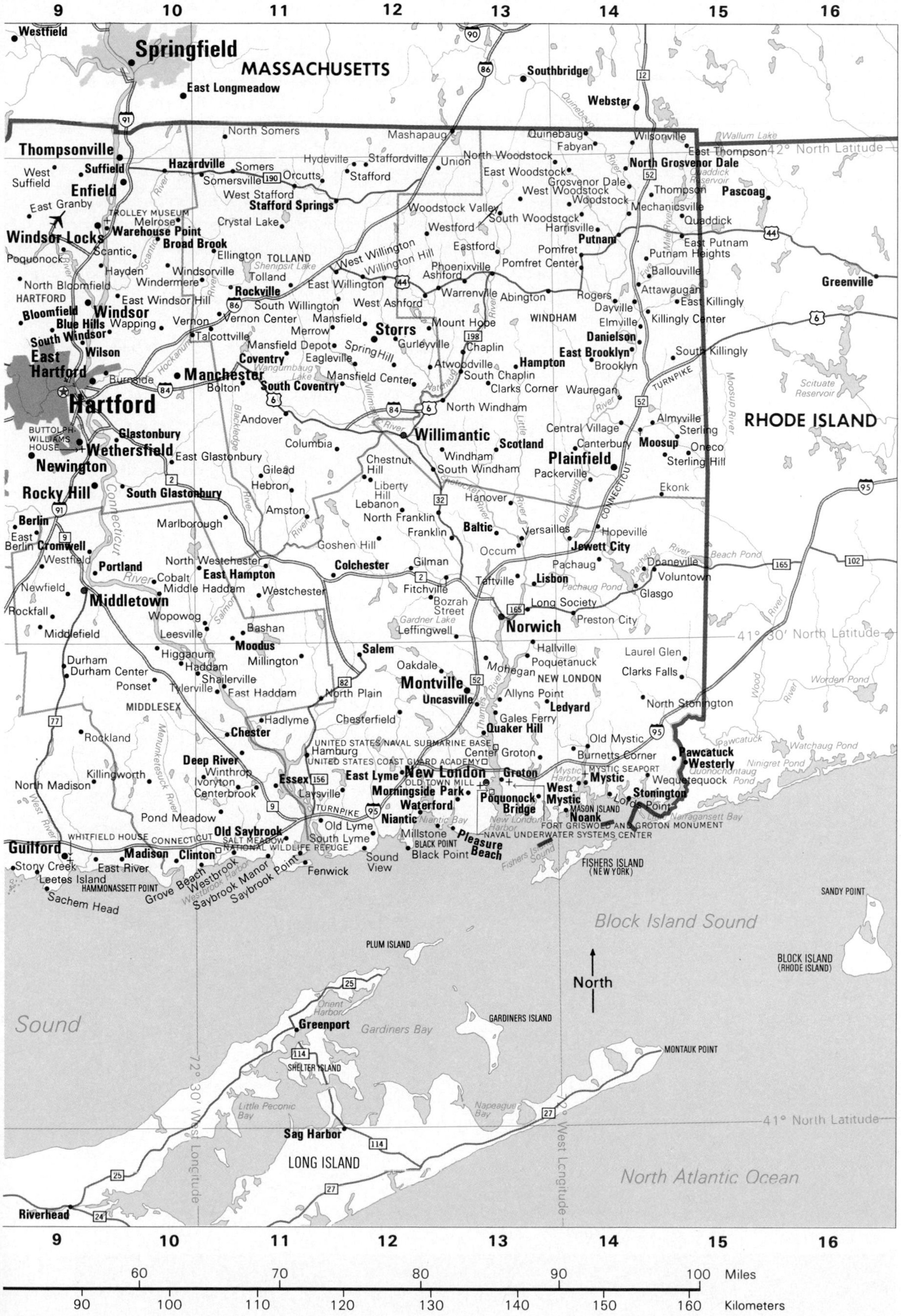

Maine

Maine lies farther east than any other state. The easternmost point in the United States is a small Maine peninsula called West Quoddy Head. Portland, Maine, is 116 miles (186 kilometers) nearer to Europe than any other large U.S. port.

Maine and its people are sometimes referred to in terms that might be confusing to non–New Englanders. In early New England usage, the word *down* meant "north." This probably explains why New Englanders often refer to Maine as Down East, and the people of Maine as Down Easters or Down Easterners.

Some of the earliest English settlements in North America were founded in Maine. Colonists established the Popham Colony near the mouth of the Kennebec River in 1607, but they later abandoned the site because of cold weather and other hardships. Various other settlements were made during the 1620's. In 1641, Gorgeana (now York) became the first chartered English city in what is now the United States. Various disputes over the ownership of Maine were finally resolved in 1677, when Massachusetts bought Maine for about $6,000. Maine remained part of Massachusetts until becoming a state in 1820.

For many years, Maine's political preferences were the subject of national interest. Until 1960, Maine held its election for Congress and governor in September. Its voters often elected persons of the political party that also won most of the November elections in other states. As a result, the slogan developed *As Maine goes, so goes the nation.*

One of Maine's most famous citizens was not a politician, but a poet. The great American poet Henry Wadsworth Longfellow was born in Portland. The Wadsworth-Longfellow House, his boyhood home, still stands in Portland and is a popular tourist attraction.

Over the years, much of Maine's development has depended upon two of its most valuable natural resources: its forests and its waters. Forests cover 90 per cent of Maine, and the state's nickname, the

Maine lobsters, which please the palates of millions, are shipped from fishing villages like this one—replete with traps and buoys.

Pine Tree State, refers to the tall pines that once made up most of the forest land.

The wood-products industry has long been the backbone of Maine's economy. The state's first railroad was built in 1836 to carry lumber between Bangor and Old Town. Today, paper products rank as the most valuable manufactured goods in Maine, and the state has some of the nation's largest newsprint factories. Maine's forests also provide lumber, as well as diverse wood products such as skis, splints, clothespins, matches, and ice cream sticks. Maine produces 125 million toothpicks a day—more than any other state. And many Maine trees become Christmas trees each year.

In early colonial days, Maine's forests provided the raw materials for the state's first industry: shipbuilding. The first boat ever built in America by English colonists was built in Maine in 1607 and launched on the Kennebec River. The tall, straight white pines of Maine made fine masts for sailing ships, and the state soon developed a great shipbuilding tradition. One of the most famous ships ever built was the clipper ship *Red Jacket,* built in Rockland. It set a transatlantic speed record in 1854, sailing from New York City to Liverpool, England, in just over 13 days. The record time of the *Red Jacket* has never been broken by a sailing ship.

Ships and boats are still built in many towns and cities in Maine. And almost every town along the coast has its own fishing fleet. Maine is known for its lobsters, and the state ranks first in the nation in its lobster catch.

Maine's seafaring traditions also contribute to its popularity as a vacation spot. Thousands of visitors come to enjoy seafood festivals, marine museums, historic lighthouses, and other nautical attractions. One of the oldest lighthouses in the country is the Portland Head Light, built in 1791 near Portland. Many vacationers come simply to enjoy the dramatic beauty of Maine's rugged coastline. Maine is famous for its rocky shores, but it also has one of the longest and smoothest sandy beaches on the Atlantic Coast. Old Orchard Beach stretches for 11 miles (17 kilometers) and is one of several sandy beaches on Maine's coast.

In addition to coastal resorts, Maine has more than 2,500 lakes and ponds and 5,000 rivers and streams. Much of the inland forest area of Maine is wilderness where deer, bear, and other wild animals make their homes. Moose live in certain remote areas and are protected by law from hunters. Maine is home for more than 320 kinds of land and sea birds. And every spring and fall, flocks of migratory geese and ducks darken the Maine sky and gather at a place called Merrymeeting Bay before continuing their migratory journey.

Although known for its rugged coastline, Maine also has sandy beaches where bathers frolic in the surf or search the sand for treasures (above).

Quaint shops at the Old Port Exchange in historic Portland are reminders of the city's colonial past. Now the largest city in Maine, Portland was founded in 1632 (left).

Maine
Pine Tree State

Capital: Augusta
Area: 33,215 sq. mi. (86,026 km²), including 2,295 sq. mi. (5,944 km²) of inland water but excluding 1,102 sq. mi. (2,854 km²) of Atlantic coastal water; 39th in size among the states
Elevation: *Highest*—Mount Katahdin, 5,268 ft. (1,606 m) above sea level; *lowest*—sea level along the coast
Statehood: March 15, 1820, the 23rd state
Abbreviations: Me. (traditional); ME (postal)
Motto: *Dirigo* (I Direct or I Guide)
Song: "State of Maine Song"
Tree: White Pine

Maine's state seal shows a farmer and seaman representing two of Maine's chief occupations. The pine tree on the shield symbolizes Maine's many forests, and the moose represents its wildlife. The North Star above the shield stands for the state's northern location. The seal was adopted in 1820. The state flag, adopted in 1909, bears a reproduction of the seal.

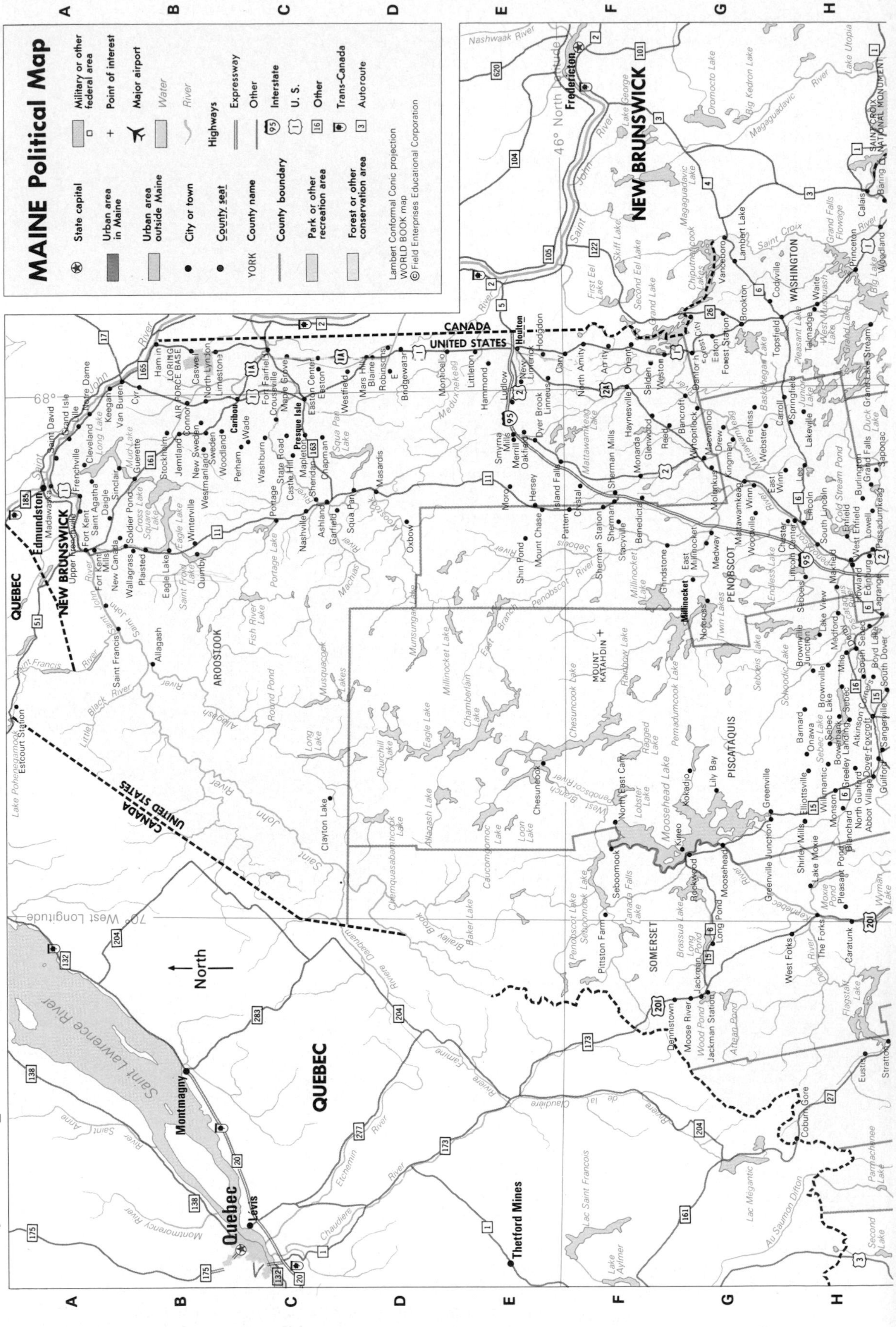

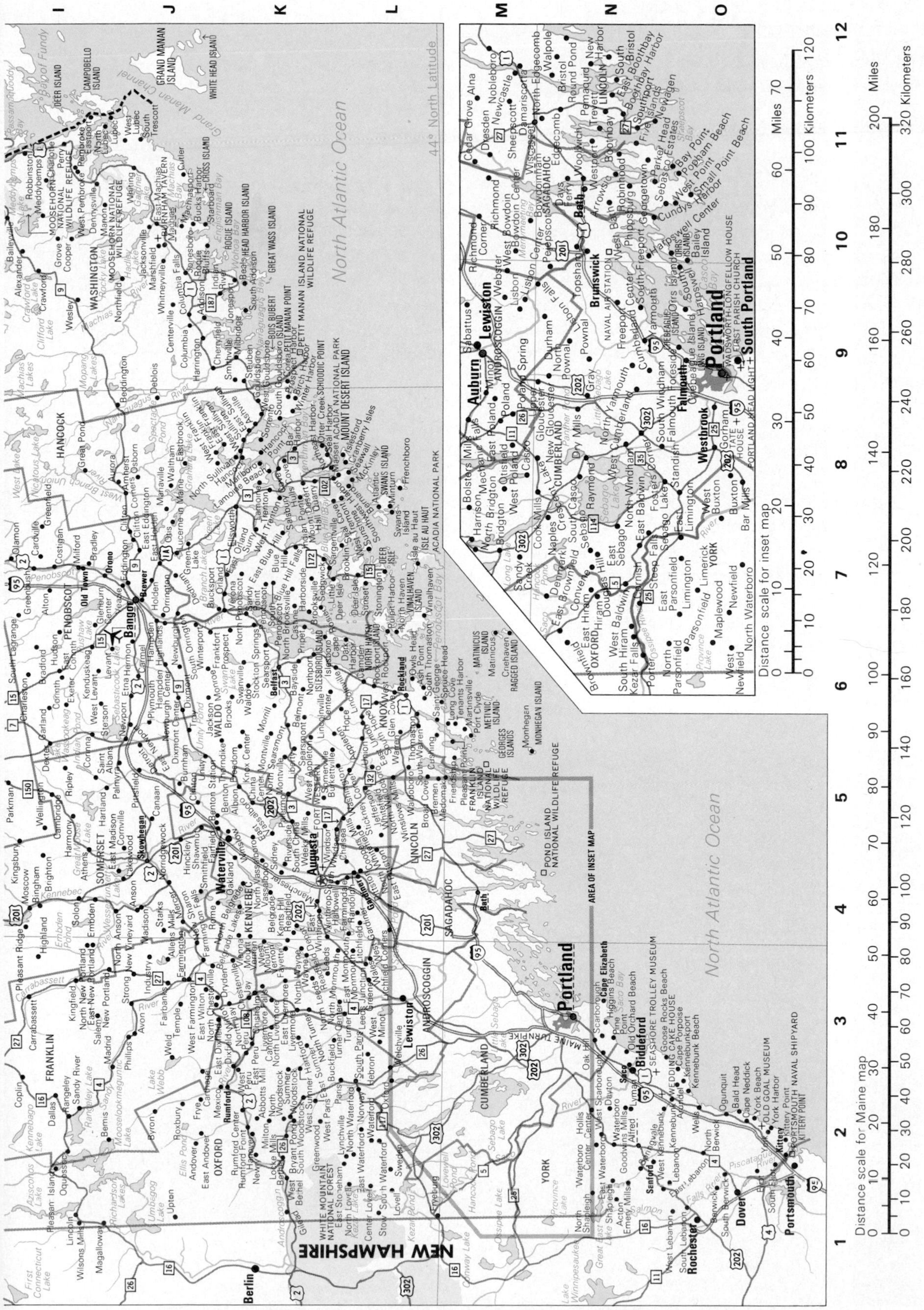

Seal

Flag

Bird: Chickadee

Flower: White Pine Cone and Tassel

Massachusetts

Massachusetts is the sixth smallest state, but it has been the site of some of the most important events in U.S. history. Its citizens have contributed much to the development of the nation.

Massachusetts was named for the Massachusett Indian tribe, which was one of several tribes that lived in the region before the first white settlers arrived. In 1620, the Pilgrims landed at what is now Plymouth, ending a three-month voyage from England aboard the ship *Mayflower.* Their celebration the following autumn to give thanks for a bountiful harvest established the American custom of the Thanksgiving holiday. Ten years after the Pilgrims' arrival, another group of English settlers, the Puritans, established what is now Boston. Boston became the capital of the Massachusetts Bay Colony in 1632 and has been the capital of Massachusetts ever since.

During the 1600's, Massachusetts led the colonies in a series of landmark achievements in education. Citizens of Massachusetts were the first in the world to provide free public education at government expense. A secondary school called the Boston Latin School was the first public school in what is now the United States. The first university in the English colonies in America was Harvard College, established at Newtowne (now Cambridge).

Cambridge was the site of the first printing press in the English colonies. Stephen Daye set up the press in 1639. The following year, he printed *The Bay Psalm Book,* the first English-language book published in America. The first two newspapers in the colonies were published in Boston. The first, established in 1690, was called *Publick Occurrences Both Forreign and Domestick.* About 14 years later, *The Boston News-Letter* appeared.

Massachusetts also played an early role in the economic development of the colonies. The first successful ironworks in North America was established at Hammersmith (now Saugus) around 1646.

Massachusetts is well known for its role in events leading up to the Revolutionary War. Fighting between British soldiers and colonists in Boston led to the killing of several colonists, and the event became known as the Boston Massacre. In 1773, angry colonists protested British tax policies by dumping 340 chests of British tea into Boston Harbor, in an event that became known as the Boston Tea Party. Paul Revere's famous ride across the Massachusetts countryside warned colonists that the British were arriving to seize supplies of gunpowder hidden by the colonists at Concord. The morning after Revere's ride, the first battle of the Revolutionary War was fought at Lexington.

Historic Massachusetts' attractions include Concord Bridge, where Minutemen fought the British in one of the first skirmishes of the Revolutionary War (near left).

Boston abounds with places of interest, including Faneuil Hall Market, where tourists may visit a number of shops and restaurants or simply stop to watch the passersby (far left).

Charming Cape Cod communities such as Provincetown—where the Mayflower *first anchored in the New World—have long lured artists, writers, and theatrical companies.*

Massachusetts can count a number of famous Americans among its citizens over the years. Three U.S. Presidents—John Adams, John Quincy Adams, and John F. Kennedy—were born there. A fourth, Calvin Coolidge, lived there much of his life. Elias Howe invented the sewing machine in Cambridge in 1845, and Alexander Graham Bell invented the telephone in Boston in 1876.

Historic attractions are among the many tourist sites that bring thousands of visitors to Massachusetts each year. Some of the leading attractions include Plimouth Plantation, a reconstruction of the Plymouth Colony, with a replica of the *Mayflower;* the John and Priscilla Alden House, built around 1653; and Bunker Hill Monument, which commemorates one of the early battles of the Revolution.

Massachusetts also has many natural attractions that appeal to vacationers, including the Berkshire Hills and the ocean resorts on Cape Cod. There are more than 1,300 lakes and ponds in Massachusetts. One of the ponds, Walden Pond, is famous as the place where the writer Henry David Thoreau lived alone in a one-room cabin for two years. He wrote of his experiences and his thoughts on nature in the book *Walden.*

Many of Massachusetts' lakes have Indian names. One of the most interesting is Lake Chaubunagungamaug, also called Lake Webster. The long form of the name in the language of the Nipmuc Indians is Chargoggagoggmanchauggagoggchaubunagungamaug. It means, "You fish your side of the lake. I fish my side. Nobody fishes the middle."

The coastal waters of Massachusetts have long played an important role in the state's economy. Fishing and whaling once brought Massachusetts much of its wealth. Today, manufacturing is the most important economic activity. But Massachusetts still ranks among the leading states in its annual commercial fish catch. Cape Cod was named for the codfish. Its importance in the economic development of Massachusetts is symbolized by a five-foot-long wooden cod, called the Sacred Cod, that hangs above the rear of the chamber of the Massachusetts House of Representatives in Boston.

Massachusetts
Bay State

Capital: Boston
Area: 8,257 sq. mi. (21,385 km²), including 431 sq. mi. (1,116 km²) of inland water but excluding 959 sq. mi. (2,484 km²) of Atlantic coastal water; 45th in size among the states
Elevation: *Highest*—Mount Greylock in Berkshire County, 3,491 ft. (1,064 m) above sea level; *lowest*—sea level along the Atlantic Ocean
Statehood: Feb. 6, 1788, the 6th state
Abbreviations: Mass. (traditional); MA (postal)
Motto: *Ense Petit Placidam sub Liberate Quietem* (By the Sword We Seek Peace, but Peace Only Under Liberty)
Song: "Hail Massachusetts"
Tree: American Elm

Massachusetts' state seal, adopted in 1898, shows the coat of arms of the Commonwealth of Massachusetts. An Indian points an arrow downward, symbolizing peace. A star over his right shoulder represents Massachusetts as a state. An arm and sword above the shield stand for the state motto. The state flag, adopted in 1908, has a reproduction of the coat of arms.

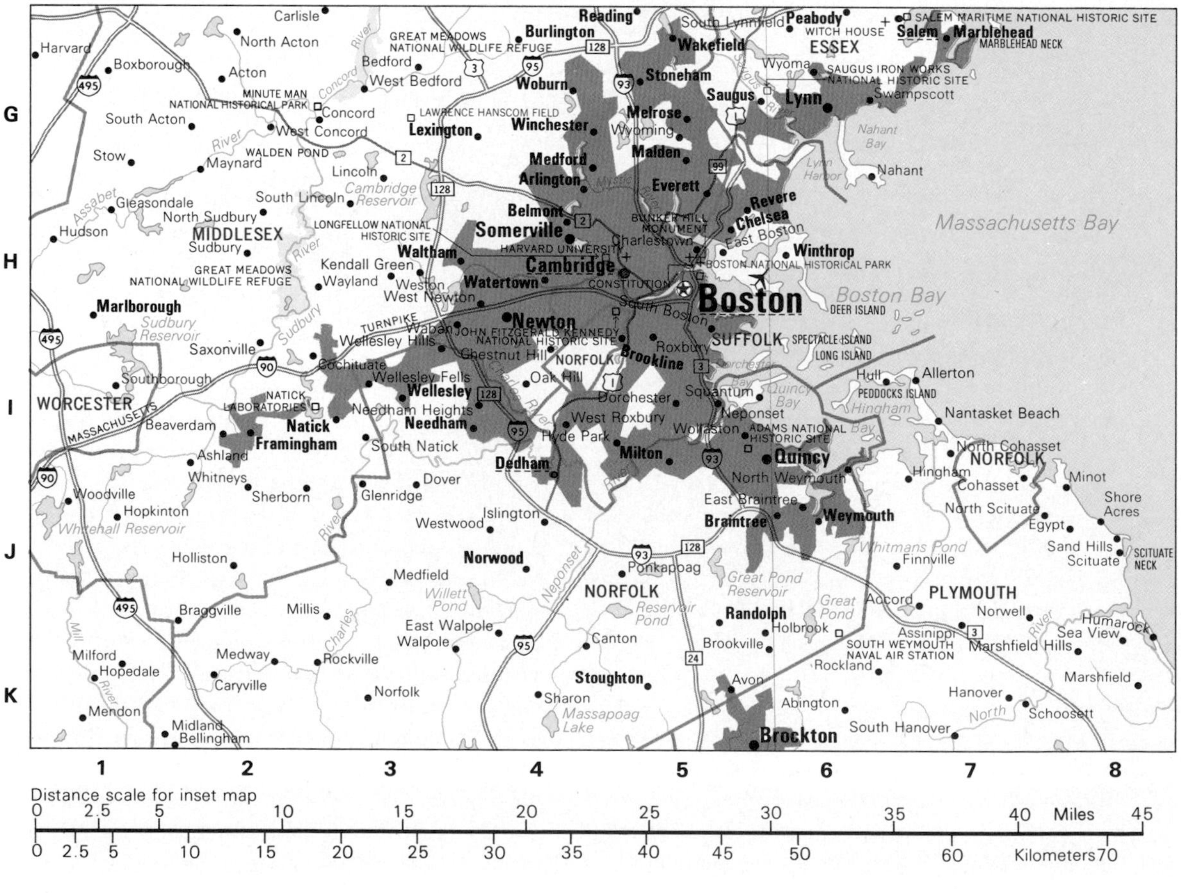

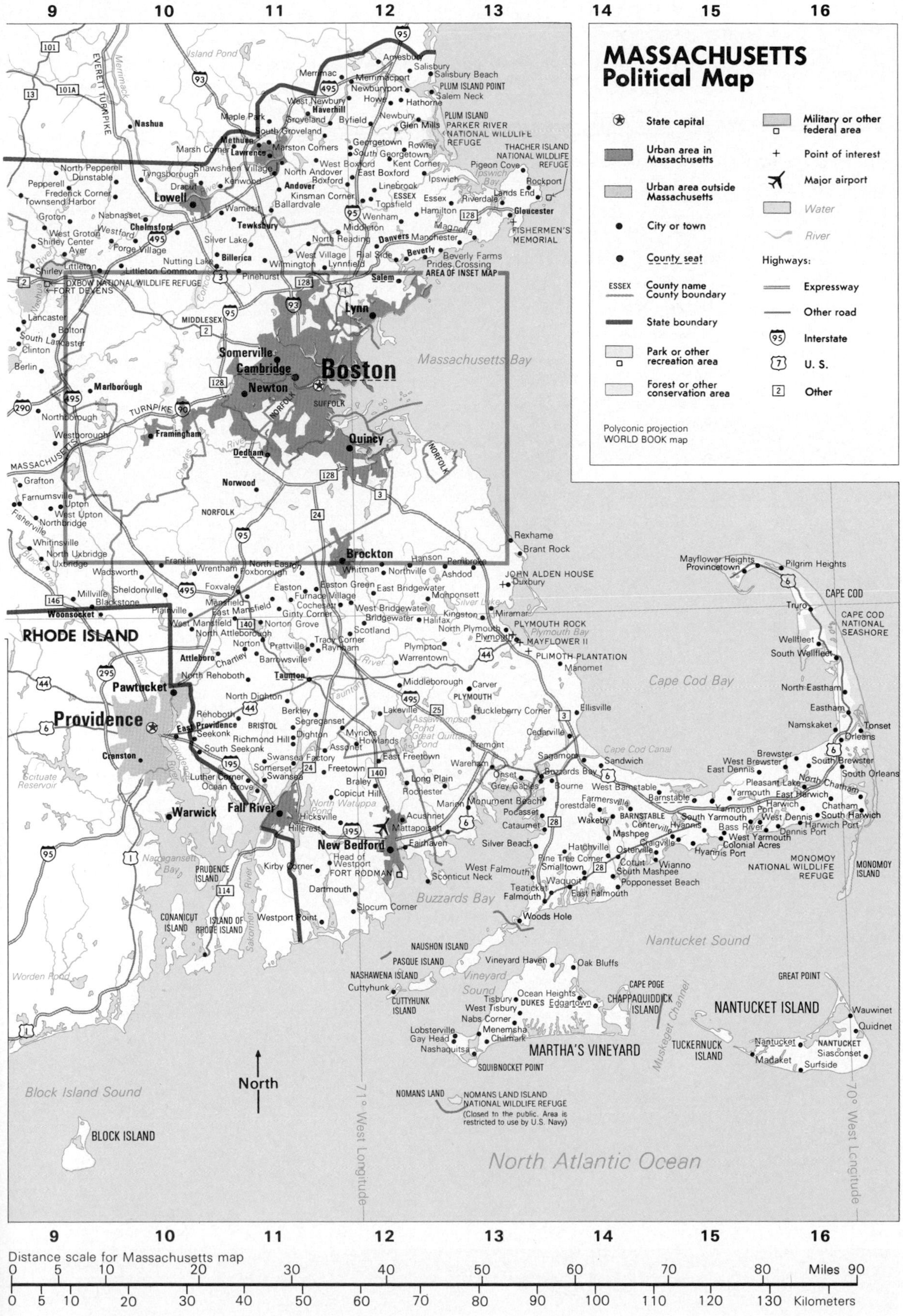
MASSACHUSETTS
Political Map
State capital
Urban area in Massachusetts
Urban area outside Massachusetts
City or town
County seat
ESSEX County name
County boundary
State boundary
Park or other recreation area
Forest or other conservation area
Military or other federal area
Point of interest
Major airport
Water
River
Highways:
Expressway
Other road
Interstate
U. S.
Other
Polyconic projection
WORLD BOOK map
Boston
Cambridge
Somerville
Newton
Quincy
Lynn
Brockton
Lowell
Providence
Pawtucket
Cranston
Warwick
Fall River
New Bedford
RHODE ISLAND
Massachusetts Bay
Cape Cod Bay
Buzzards Bay
Nantucket Sound
Vineyard Sound
Block Island Sound
North Atlantic Ocean
MARTHA'S VINEYARD
NANTUCKET ISLAND
BLOCK ISLAND
CAPE COD
North
71° West Longitude
70° West Longitude
Distance scale for Massachusetts map
Miles
Kilometers

SIGILLUM REIPUBLICÆ MASSACHUSETTENSIS

Seal

Flag

Bird: Chickadee

Flower: Mayflower

New Hampshire

New Hampshire has the highest mountains in New England. Several peaks in the White Mountains of New Hampshire rise up more than a mile. The state's beautiful mountains, forests, and lakes create a picturesque background for year-round recreation activities, and tourism is an important income producer.

The highest mountain in New Hampshire, Mount Washington, is famous for a record-breaking weather occurrence. The strongest winds ever measured on the surface of the earth—188 miles (302 kilometers) per hour—were measured on Mount Washington in 1934. During the measurement, one gust of wind reached 231 miles (371 kilometers) per hour.

New Hampshire's Atlantic coastline extends for only 13 miles (20 kilometers). This is a shorter coastline than that of any other state bordering an ocean. But the U.S. Navy chose Portsmouth, New Hampshire, as the site of its first shipbuilding yard, which was established in 1800.

New Hampshire is nicknamed the *Granite State*

A cog railway carries passengers through the White Mountains to view spectacular scenery—especially vibrant when the trees wear their fall colors.

Gigantic snow sculptures enliven Dartmouth's campus during the annual Winter Carnival held in mid-February (above top).

Scattered throughout New Hampshire are villages and towns with picturesque buildings like this general store built in 1824 at Bath (above bottom).

because of its large beds of red, gray, and other kinds of granite. Mining actually contributes little to New Hampshire's economy. New Hampshire, however, supplied granite used to build the Library of Congress in Washington, D.C., and other famous buildings. A block of New Hampshire granite forms the cornerstone of the main UN building in New York City.

New Hampshire was named by John Mason, who held title to the land in the early 1600's. He named it after his native Hampshire County in England. New Hampshire became the first colony to establish a government wholly independent of Great Britain when the colony adopted a temporary constitution in 1776. It joined the other American colonies in approving the Declaration of Independence about six months later and ratified the Articles of Confederation in 1778.

In 1788, New Hampshire became the ninth state to ratify the U.S. Constitution. It was New Hampshire's action that enabled the Constitution to take effect.

The state constitution of New Hampshire provides for a unique executive branch. New Hampshire has a governor but no lieutenant governor. Instead, voters elect a five-member executive council, which advises the governor. The council must also approve the governor's appointments for the positions of attorney general, comptroller, and other state offices.

Like most other states, New Hampshire has a two-house legislature. But it is unusual in that the state house of representatives has 400 members. The U.S. House of Representatives is the only legislative body in the nation that has more members than New Hampshire's house.

The 222 towns of New Hampshire are sometimes called "little republics" because they have almost complete self-government. They are governed according to one of the purest forms of democracy in existence. Voters gather at an annual town meeting to discuss local business, pass the local budget, and elect local officials.

New Hampshire was the birthplace of Franklin Pierce, the 14th President of the United States. One of the great orators of the 1800's, Daniel Webster, was also born in New Hampshire. The Franklin Pierce Homestead in Hillsboro and Daniel Webster's birthplace near the town of Franklin are among New Hampshire's many historic attractions. Other notable citizens of New Hampshire include Mary Baker Eddy, who founded the Christian Science religion, and Alan B. Shepard, who was the first American to travel in space.

The oldest university in New Hampshire, and one of the oldest in the nation, is Dartmouth College. It was founded in Hanover in 1769 under a charter from King George III. It developed from Moor's Indian Charity School, and its original purpose was to provide education and instruction for the youth of Indian tribes. One of New Hampshire's best-known annual events is the Winter Carnival at Dartmouth. Students build huge snow sculptures as part of the carnival festivities.

The small town of Peterborough, New Hampshire, is famous in the history of libraries in the United States. One of the first free, tax-supported public libraries in America was founded there in 1833.

New Hampshire became the site of a major international gathering in 1944, when representatives of 44 nations met at Bretton Woods to discuss postwar world trade and other economic issues. The gathering, officially called the International Monetary Conference, also led to the establishment of two UN agencies: the International Monetary Fund and the World Bank.

New Hampshire
Granite State

Capital: Concord
Area: 9,304 sq. mi. (24,097 km²), including 277 sq. mi. (717 km²) of inland water; 44th in size among the states
Elevation: *Highest*—Mount Washington, 6,288 ft. (1,917 m) above sea level; *lowest*—sea level, along the Atlantic Ocean
Statehood: June 21, 1788, the 9th state
Abbreviations: N.H. (traditional); NH (postal)
Motto: *Live Free or Die*
Songs: "Old New Hampshire," "New Hampshire, My New Hampshire," "New Hampshire Hills"
Tree: White Birch

New Hampshire's state seal has a reproduction of the Revolutionary War frigate Raleigh *surrounded by a laurel wreath to symbolize victory. The date 1776 is the year the state adopted its first constitution. On the state flag, adopted in 1909, nine stars and a laurel wreath surround an adaptation of the state seal. This symbol shows that New Hampshire was the ninth state to ratify the U.S. Constitution.*

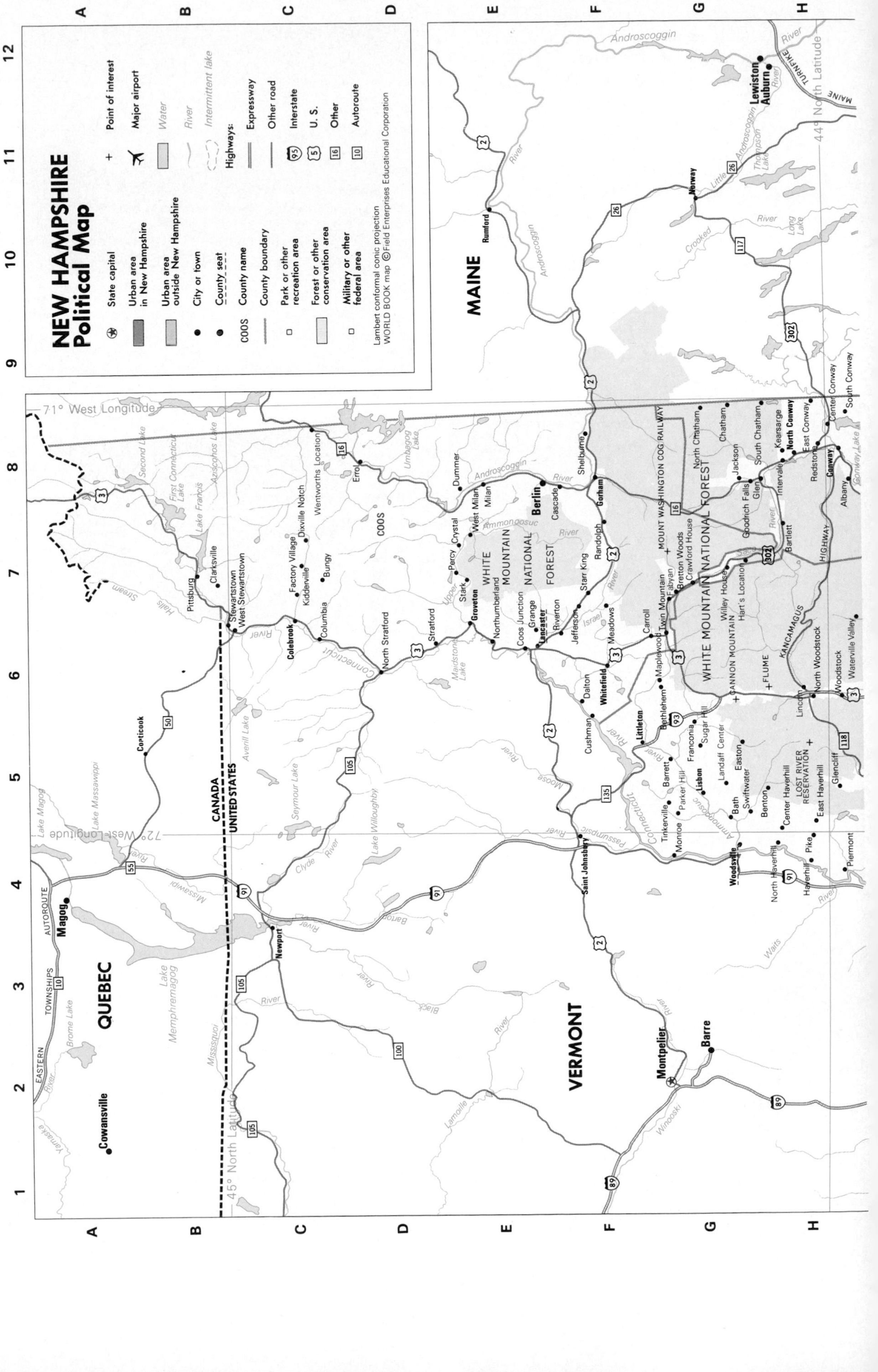

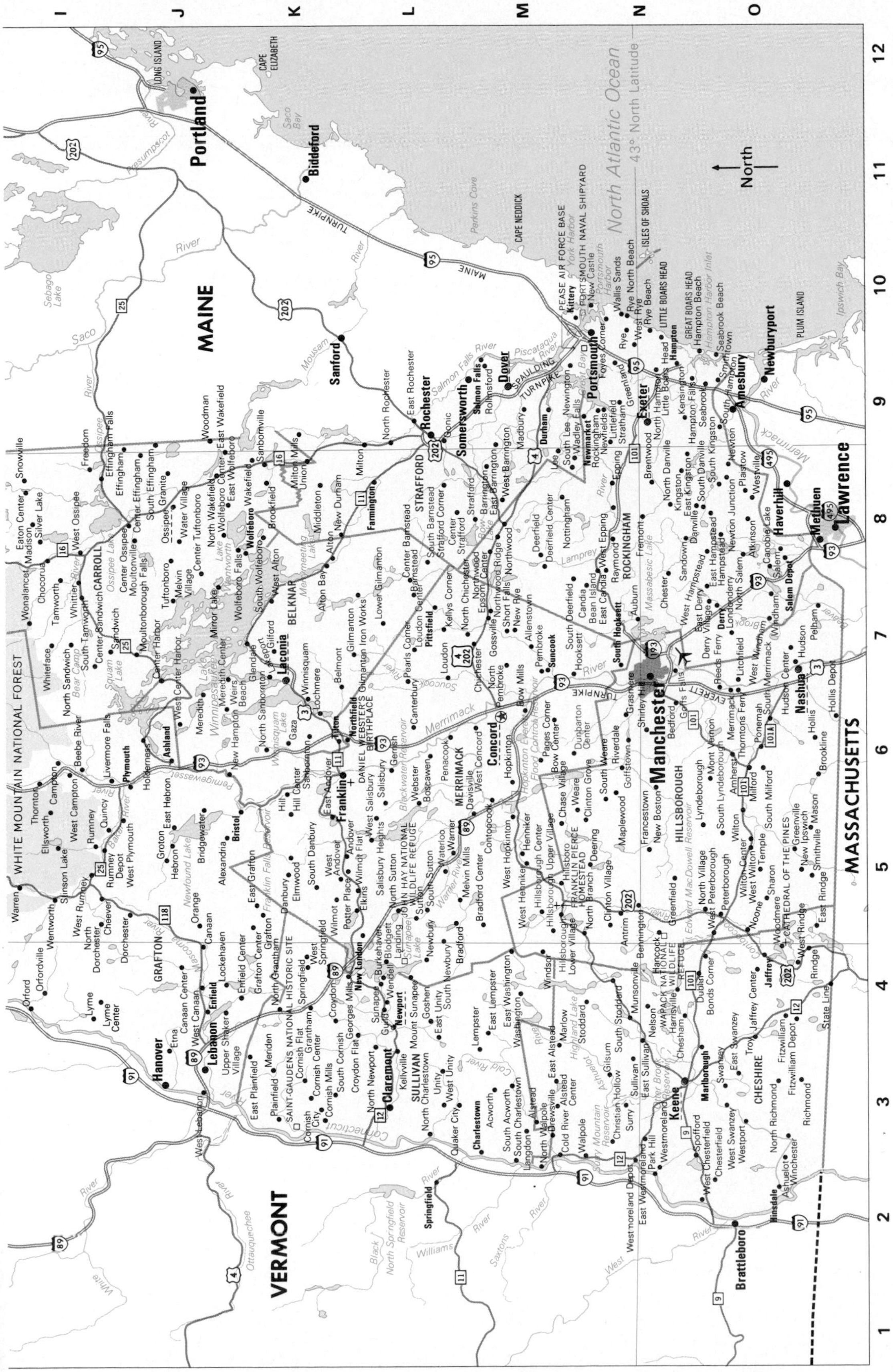

Seal

Flag

Bird: Purple Finch

Flower: Purple Lilac

MAINE
VERMONT
MASSACHUSETTS
WHITE MOUNTAIN NATIONAL FOREST
North Atlantic Ocean
43° North Latitude
North
Portland
Biddeford
Sanford
Rochester
Somersworth
Dover
Portsmouth
Exeter
Hampton
Newburyport
Amesbury
Haverhill
Methuen
Lawrence
Manchester
Concord
Nashua
Laconia
Franklin
Keene
Claremont
Lebanon
Hanover
Brattleboro
CARROLL
GRAFTON
BELKNAP
STRAFFORD
MERRIMACK
SULLIVAN
HILLSBOROUGH
ROCKINGHAM
CHESHIRE
Distance scale
Miles
Kilometers

The boardwalk at Atlantic City, lined with theaters, shops, and restaurants, has contributed for many years to the city's popularity as a seashore resort.

New Jersey

New Jersey is a state of interesting contrasts. It is one of the smallest states in area but ranks high in population. It has some of the nation's most popular vacation resorts and some of its most sprawling industrial complexes.

New Jersey's nickname, the *Garden State,* refers to the many truck farms, orchards, and nurseries that supply food and plants to markets in the eastern United States. But New Jersey has also been called the *Workshop of the Nation* because of the tremendous variety of manufactured goods produced there. Households throughout the United States use products manufactured in New Jersey. The state's factories produce vitamins, paints, soaps, food products, radios, washing machines, and automobiles, among other goods.

New Jersey is also one of the nation's major centers of industrial research. New Jersey researchers developed the first transistor and the "brain" that operates guided missiles. The state has been the home of some of the world's most famous scientists and inventors. Samuel F. B. Morse developed the first successful U.S. telegraph near Morristown. Thomas Edison invented the electric light and the phonograph at his laboratory in Menlo Park. And Albert Einstein worked for many years at the Institute for Advanced Study in Princeton.

New Jersey has played an impressive role in the history of communications in the United States. The first radio impulse was transmitted at Princeton, and the first long-distance telephone call was made from New Brunswick, New Jersey, to New York City. *Telstar I,* the first communications satellite to transmit live television across the Atlantic Ocean, was developed by the Bell Laboratories in New Jersey.

For a brief period in the early 1900's, Fort Lee was the motion picture capital of the world. Stars such as Mary Pickford and "Fatty" Arbuckle made movies there. Thomas Edison had helped develop the motion picture while working in New Jersey.

This state can also claim a number of historic firsts in the field of transportation. The first U.S. submarine was built by John Stevens in Hoboken. The state was the first in the nation to contribute funds to local governments for the construction of roads. And the nation's first regular airline passenger service was inaugurated in 1919 between Atlantic City, New Jersey, and New York City.

The world of sports also owes a great deal to New Jersey. In 1846 at Hoboken, the first professional baseball game was played between the New York Nine and the New York Knickerbockers. In 1869, Rutgers and Princeton played the world's first intercollegiate football game.

The earliest European settlers in what is now New Jersey were the Dutch and the Swedes. The English eventually gained control of the area, and several years afterward a group of English settlers led by Edward Byllynge founded the first Quaker settlement in America, the colony of West Jersey.

New Jersey earned the title *Cockpit of the Revolution* for its role in the Revolutionary War. Nearly 100 battles between American and British forces took place on New Jersey soil. George Washington made his famous crossing of the Delaware River on Christmas Night in 1776, then surprised and defeated a Hessian army the following day. Another major New Jersey battle was the Battle of Monmouth, during which Molly Pitcher took the place of her fallen husband on a cannon crew. Two New Jersey cities served as the U.S. capital during the postwar period. Princeton was the capital for a time during 1783, and Princeton University's Nassau Hall was the meetingplace of the Congress. In 1784, Trenton served as the temporary U.S. capital.

In 1804, Weehawken became the site of one of the most famous duels in history. Aaron Burr, the vice-president of the United States at the time, shot and killed his political rival, Alexander Hamilton.

Two Presidents made their home in New Jersey. Caldwell was the birthplace of Grover Cleveland, who was elected to two non-consecutive terms in 1884 and 1892. Woodrow Wilson was born in Virginia but served as president of Princeton University and governor of New Jersey before being elected to the presidency in 1912. Two of America's most famous literary figures also lived in New Jersey. The novelist James Fenimore Cooper was born in Burlington, and the poet Walt Whitman lived in Camden for several years.

New Jersey's various historic sites are popular with tourists. But millions of people visit the state just to take advantage of its many seaside resorts including Ocean City, Cape May, and Atlantic City, which border New Jersey's sandy Atlantic shore.

Glenmont was the home of America's most revered inventor, Thomas A. Edison. The mansion, located in West Orange, is a national historic site (below top).

In many sections of New Jersey, horseback riders follow trails that take them across scenic mountain streams and through an unspoiled wilderness (below bottom).

New Jersey
Garden State

Capital: Trenton
Area: 7,836 sq. mi. (20,295 km^2), including 315 sq. mi. (816 km^2) of inland water but excluding 384 sq. mi. (995 km^2) of Delaware Bay and New York Harbor; 46th in size among the states
Elevation: *Highest*—High Point, 1,803 ft. (550 m) above sea level; *lowest*—sea level along the Atlantic Ocean
Statehood: Dec. 18, 1787, the 3rd state
Abbreviations: N.J. (traditional); NJ (postal)
Motto: *Liberty and Prosperity*
Tree: Red Oak

New Jersey's state seal, adopted in 1928, shows three plows and the goddess Ceres holding a horn of plenty. These symbols represent the agricultural importance of New Jersey. Liberty stands on the left. A horse's head, which also represents the state's agriculture, appears above a sovereign's helmet. The date 1776 is the year New Jersey signed the Declaration of Independence. Adopted in 1896, the state flag bears an adaptation of the seal.

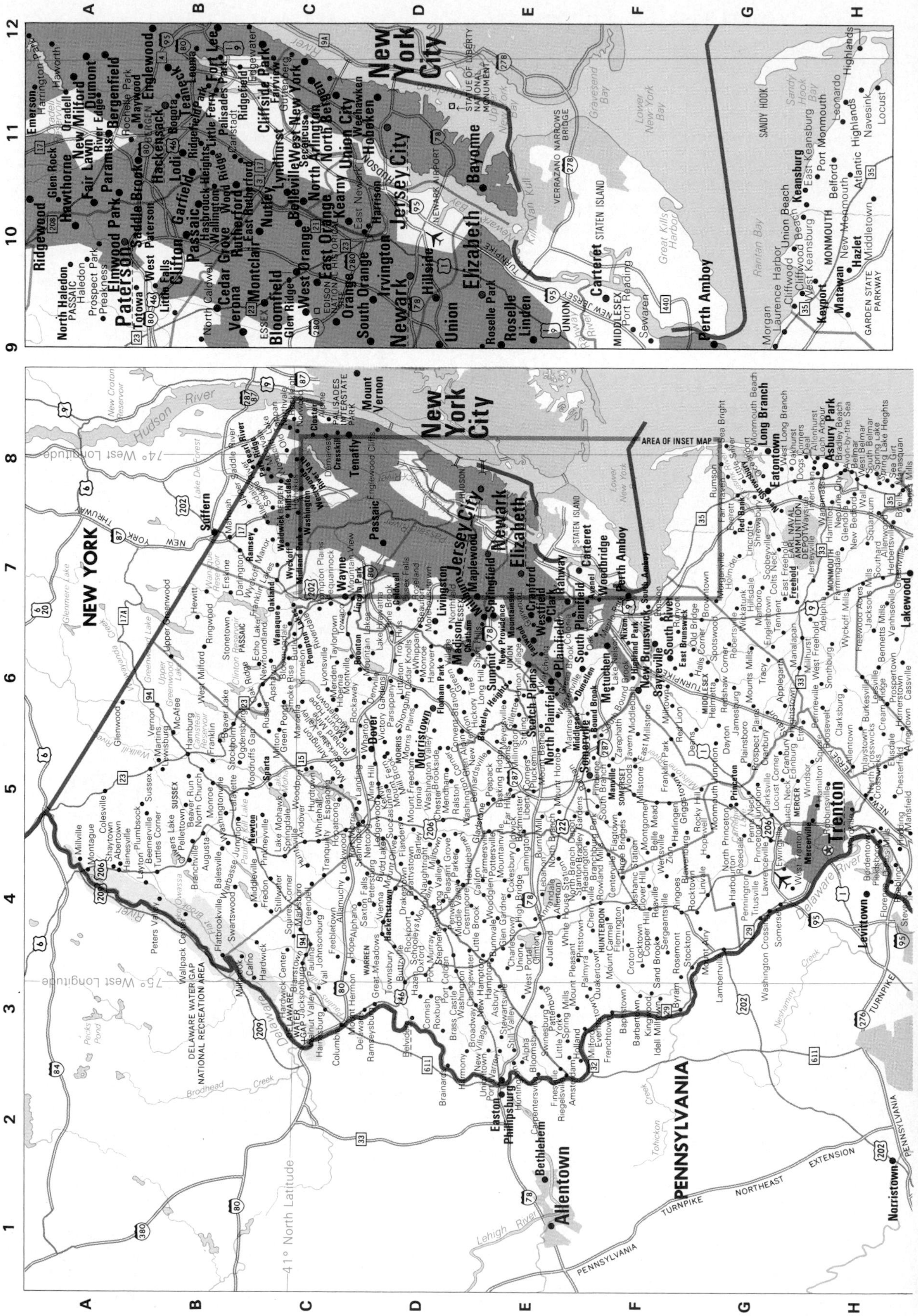

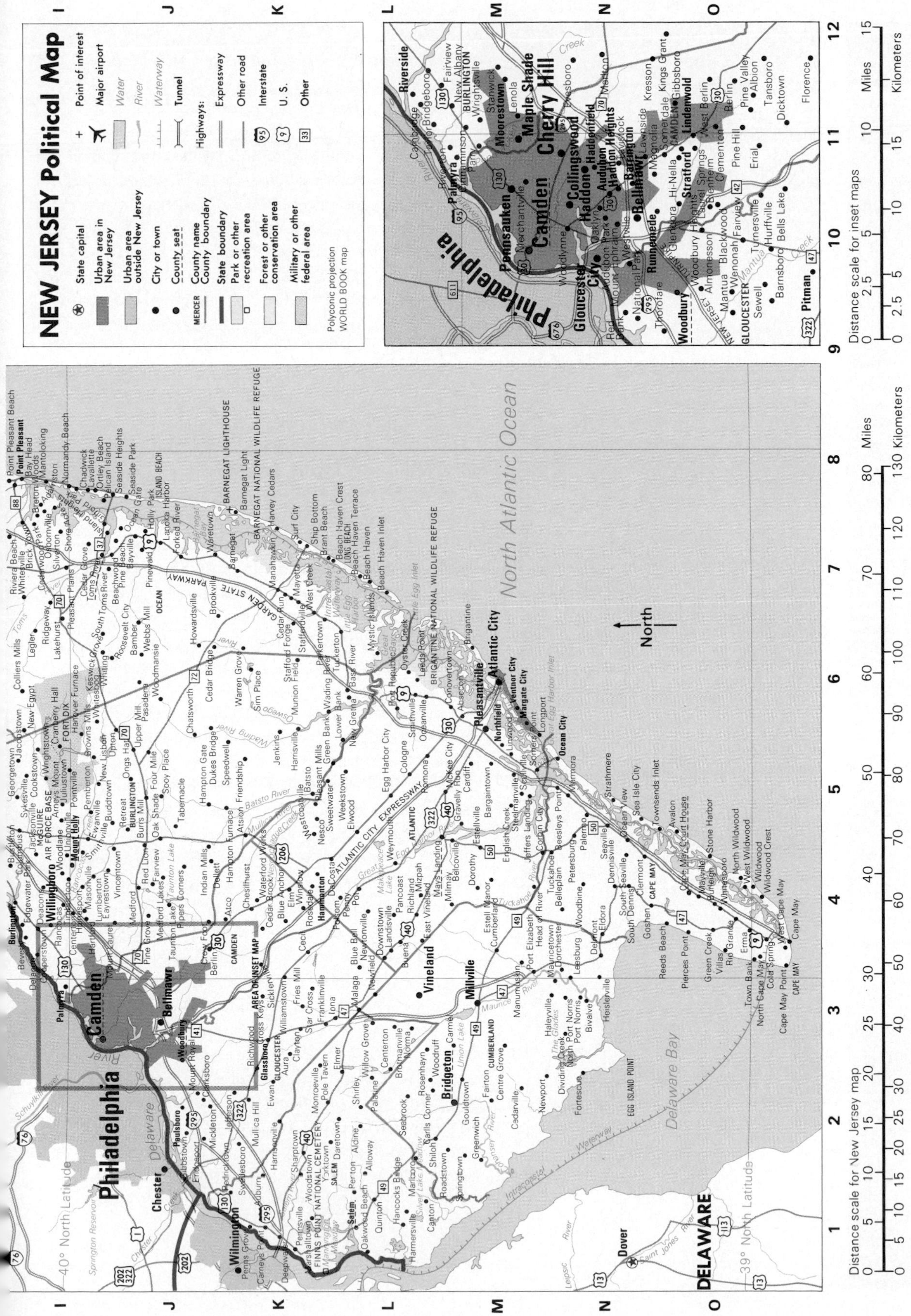

NEW JERSEY Political Map

I   J   K

Point of interest
✈ Major airport
Water / Waterway
River
Waterway
Tunnel

Highways:
Expressway
Other road
95 Interstate
9 U.S.
33 Other

State capital
⊛
Urban area in New Jersey
Urban area outside New Jersey
• City or town
• County seat
MERCER County name
— County boundary
State boundary
□ Park or other recreation area
Forest or other conservation area
Military or other federal area

Polyconic projection
WORLD BOOK map

Distance scale for inset maps
Miles   Kilometers

North Atlantic Ocean

Delaware Bay

DELAWARE

North

Distance scale for New Jersey map
Miles   Kilometers

Seal

Seal

Flag

Flag

Bird: Eastern Goldfinch

Flower: Purple Violet

Immigrants from around the world have quickened with the anticipation of freedom and prosperity when first sighting New York's Statue of Liberty (right).

Cadets stand in formation against a backdrop of the traditionally styled buildings of the U.S. Military Academy at West Point (below).

New York

In 1783, George Washington visited New York and predicted that some day it might become the seat of a new empire. Over the years, the so-called *Empire State* has developed into a leading world center of culture, finance, trade, communications, and manufacturing. The UN headquarters in New York City has put New York into the center of international affairs. The state of New York, and New York City in particular, have attracted immigrants from all over the world. The Statue of Liberty, which stands in the New York City harbor, has long been a symbol of hope and freedom. People of many cultures have come to New York and become part of a "melting pot" that typifies the diversity of the American population as a whole. Thus, in some ways, George Washington's prediction came true.

For many people, New York City is the cultural capital of the world. It is the largest city in the United States and one of the world's five largest. Its Metropolitan Museum of Art is the largest art museum in the nation. The Lincoln Center for the Performing Arts is the home of outstanding cultural organizations such as the Juilliard School of Music, the Metropolitan Opera, and the New York Philharmonic Orchestra. Broadway reigns as the foremost theater center of the United States, and publishing firms in the New York City area produce more than a third of the nation's books each year.

The state of New York has more than 300 museums, including several of the most famous in the nation. The New York State Museum in Albany is the country's oldest state museum. There are more than 1,000 public libraries in the state.

New York holds a prominent position in the field of journalism. The first victory for freedom of the press in the American colonies occurred in 1735 when John Peter Zenger, the editor of the *New York Weekly Journal,* was acquitted of libel charges. Today, *The New York Times* is one of the most influential newspapers in the world, and the *New York Daily News* has the largest circulation of any U.S. newspaper.

The state of New York produces an incredible amount and variety of manufactured goods. Its 40,000 industrial plants employ a million and a half workers. Printing and publishing are the most important industrial activities in the state. New York City has more printing plants than any other U.S.

city. New York also ranks first among the states in the manufacture of clothing.

Away from its glittering cultural centers and bulging industrial complexes, there is a side of New York that many people are unaware of: its farms. New York is one of the leading dairy states in the country and produces huge quantities of milk, butter, and cheese. Its vegetable farms supply the vast markets of eastern cities, and its orchards yield an abundance of apples, cherries, peaches, pears, and other fruits.

New York is also a state of breathtaking waterfalls, forested mountains, and scenic rivers and lakes. Niagara Falls is probably the most famous waterfall in the United States. The worn, rounded peaks of New York's Adirondack Mountains may be among the oldest mountains in the country. The state has more than 8,000 lakes, most of them the result of glacial activity thousands of years ago.

The Dutch were the first European settlers to arrive in what is now New York, and they established the first permanent settlement in the region at Fort Orange (now Albany). Soon afterward, the Dutch began a settlement on Manhattan Island. The Dutch governor, Peter Minuit, bought Manhattan from the Manhattan Indians for trinkets worth about $24.

When Britain threatened to seize the Manhattan settlement, Minuit surrendered without a fight. Britain eventually took over all the Dutch holdings in the region and named the area New York in honor of the Duke of York, who later became King James II.

About a third of all the battles of the Revolutionary War took place in New York. After the war, New York City became the first capital of the new nation under the Constitution. George Washington took his oath of office as the first President of the United States at Federal Hall in New York City.

Four Presidents have been born in New York. Martin Van Buren was born in Kinderhook, Millard Fillmore in Locke, Theodore Roosevelt in New York City, and Franklin D. Roosevelt in Hyde Park.

New York has had several notable citizens in the fields of literature and politics. The poet Walt Whitman was born near Huntington. Mark Twain lived in New York for a time and is buried in Elmira. Robert Louis Stevenson and Edgar Allen Poe both wrote many of their works while living in New York.

Bountiful vineyards straddle Seneca Lake in the Finger Lakes region of upstate New York.

New York
Empire State

Capital: Albany
Area: 49,576 sq. mi. (128,401 km²), including 1,745 sq. mi. (4,520 km²) of inland water but excluding 4,376 sq. mi. (11,334 km²) of Lakes Erie and Ontario, New York Harbor, and Long Island Sound; 30th in size among the states
Elevation: *Highest*—Mount Marcy in the Adirondack Mountains, 5,344 ft. (1,629 m) above sea level; *lowest*—sea level along the Atlantic Ocean
Statehood: July 26, 1788, the 11th state
Abbreviations: N.Y. (traditional); NY (postal)
Motto: *Excelsior* (Ever Upward)
Tree: Sugar Maple

On the left of New York's state seal stands a figure representing Liberty. The crown at her feet signifies that Liberty has rejected monarchies. The figure on the right symbolizes Justice. A typical New York river scene is in the center of the seal, and an American eagle perches on the globe at the top. The seal was adopted in 1778. The state flag, adopted in 1909, has a reproduction of the seal.

NEW YORK Political Map

⊛ State or provincial capital	+ Point of interest
▪ Urban area in New York	✈ Major airport
▪ Urban area outside New York	Water
● City or town	River
◉ County seat	Aqueduct
ALBANY County name	Waterway
County boundary	
▬ State boundary	**Highways:**
▭ Park or other recreation area	Expressway
▫ Military or other federal area	Other road
▫ Indian reservation	81 Interstate
	15 U.S.
	7 Other
	Trans-Canada

Lambert conformal conic projection
WORLD BOOK map

Distance scale for New York map
0 10 20 40 60 80 100 120 140 160 180 200 220
0 10 20 40 60 80 100 120 140 160 180 200 220 240 260 280 300 350

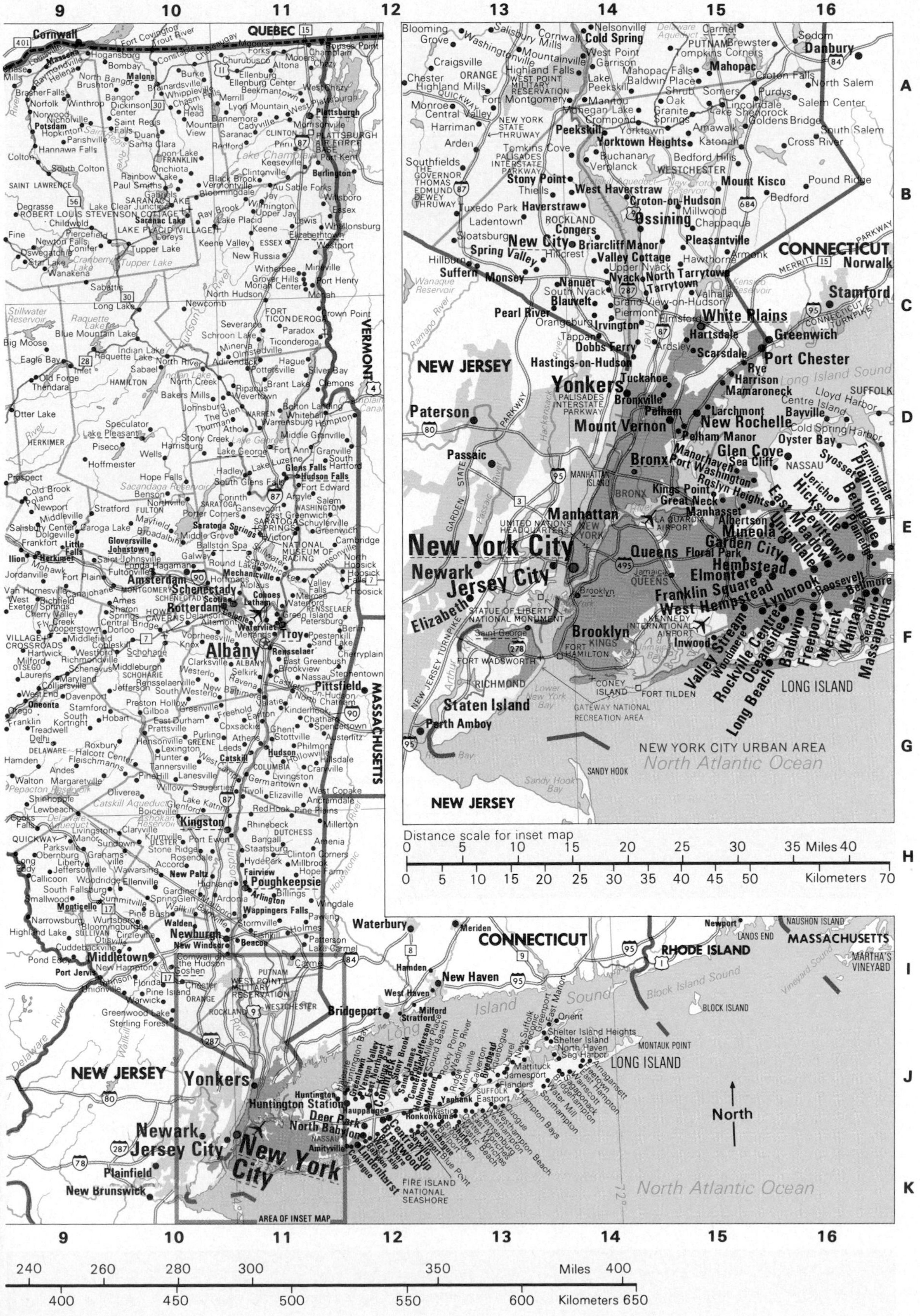

Seal

Flag

Bird: Bluebird

Flower: Rose

QUEBEC
VERMONT
MASSACHUSETTS
CONNECTICUT
RHODE ISLAND
NEW JERSEY
LONG ISLAND
North Atlantic Ocean
NEW YORK CITY URBAN AREA
Distance scale for inset map
Miles
Kilometers
AREA OF INSET MAP
North
Albany
Schenectady
Troy
Amsterdam
Kingston
Poughkeepsie
Newburgh
Middletown
Plattsburgh
Yonkers
New York City
Newark
Jersey City
Paterson
Elizabeth
Manhattan
Bronx
Queens
Brooklyn
Staten Island
White Plains
New Rochelle
Mount Vernon
Stamford
Greenwich
Port Chester
Danbury
Norwalk
Bridgeport
New Haven
Waterbury
Ossining
Peekskill
Long Island Sound
Block Island Sound

The Liberty Bell in Philadelphia tolled for freedom on July 8, 1776. The bell is one of the most treasured symbols of the founding of the United States.

Pennsylvania

Pennsylvania is perhaps best known as the birthplace of the nation. Both the Declaration of Independence and the U.S. Constitution were drafted and signed there. In addition, Pennsylvania is a leading manufacturing and mining state, and contains some of the richest farmland in the United States.

Swedes were the first settlers in Pennsylvania. They established the capital of their colony of New Sweden at Tinicum Island, near what is now Philadelphia. The Dutch later captured New Sweden, and then the British took control of the region.

William Penn was given title to the area in 1681. Penn named it Sylvania, which means "woods," and King Charles II added *Penn* to the name in honor of Penn's father, who was an English admiral. Penn arranged a friendship treaty with the Indians who lived in the region and paid them for most of the land the king had given him.

Penn was a Quaker, and he wanted Pennsylvania to be a place where Quakers and other religious groups could have freedom of worship. As a result, Pennsylvania became known as the *Quaker State.* Today, Pennsylvania has people of all religious backgrounds, including several groups known as the Pennsylvania Dutch. These groups, including the Amish and the Mennonites, are known for their plain dress, traditional lifestyles, and productive farms in southeastern Pennsylvania.

A principal nickname for Pennsylvania is the *Keystone State* because of its location at the center of the arch formed by the original 13 colonies. There is little doubt that Pennsylvania played a key role in the early history of the United States. The First Continental Congress met in Philadelphia in 1774. Two years later, delegates to the Second Continental Congress approved the final draft of the Declaration of Independence in the Pennsylvania State House (now Independence Hall) in Philadelphia. The British captured Philadelphia during the Revolutionary War, and George Washington spent a long, cold winter with his troops at nearby Valley Forge. In 1787, delegates came to Philadelphia again and drafted the U.S. Constitution. Pennsylvania became the second state to ratify the Constitution, and Philadelphia served as the U.S. capital from 1790 to 1800.

Gettysburg Battlefield in southern Pennsylvania is now a peaceful memorial honoring the soldiers who perished there in one of the major battles of the Civil War (above).

Set among rolling hills and the banks of three rivers, Pittsburgh has many parks and recreational areas, plus excellent sports facilities such as Three Rivers Stadium near Point Park (left).

Pennsylvania's many historic sites are among its most popular tourist attractions. Independence National Historical Park in Philadelphia features Independence Hall, the Liberty Bell, and other attractions relating to the nation's founding. Gettysburg National Park commemorates the scene of one of the most famous battles of the Civil War. Abraham Lincoln delivered his famous Gettysburg Address at the battlefield and dedicated part of the battlefield as a cemetery for the soldiers who died there.

Pennsylvania has long been a center of learning and culture. The first newspaper in the American colonies outside of Boston was the *American Weekly Mercury,* founded in Philadelphia in 1719. One of colonial America's most famous citizens, Benjamin Franklin, lived in Philadelphia for many years and published his *Pennsylvania Gazette* and *Poor Richard's Almanac* there. Philadelphia was the home of America's first magazine, called *The American Magazine, or A Monthly View of the Political State of the British Colonies.*

Benjamin Franklin founded the Library Company of Philadelphia in 1731. Members contributed money to buy books but could use the books without charge. During the early 1800's, the Pennsylvania Academy of the Fine Arts was founded in Philadelphia as the nation's first art school.

Pennsylvania's contributions to the economic development of the nation have a long history as well. The first paved road in what is now the United States was a turnpike between Lancaster and Philadelphia. The famous Conestoga wagons that carried settlers westward were first made at the town of Conestoga in what in now Lancaster County. As early as 1750, Pennsylvania was an important center of the iron industry.

Today, Pennsylvania ranks first among the states in the production of steel and pig iron, producing a fourth of the nation's total output. Pittsburgh produces more steel than any other city in the world. All the anthracite, or hard coal, mined in the United States comes from eastern Pennsylvania, and the state mines about a fourth of the nation's bituminous, or soft, coal. The first successful oil well in the United States was drilled at Titusville in 1859. Today, thousands of oil and natural gas wells add to Pennsylvania's tremendous mineral production.

The world's largest chocolate and cocoa factory has made Hershey a well-known Pennsylvania town. A large share of the nation's sausage, pretzels, potato chips, and ice cream also comes from Pennsylvania.

Pennsylvania
Keystone State

Capital: Harrisburg
Area: 45,333 sq. mi. (117,412 km^2), including 367 sq. mi. (951 km^2) of inland water but excluding 735 sq. mi. (1,904 km^2) of Lake Erie; 33rd in size among the states
Elevation: *Highest*—Mount Davis in Somerset County, 3,213 ft. (979 m) above sea level; *lowest*—sea level along the Delaware River
Statehood: Dec. 12, 1787, the 2nd state
Abbreviations: Pa. or Penn. (traditional); PA (postal)
Motto: *Virtue, Liberty, and Independence*
Tree: Hemlock

Pennsylvania's state seal, adopted in 1893, features symbols on both sides. One shows an eagle representing speed, strength, bravery, and wisdom. A ship, plow, and bundles of wheat stand for commerce and agriculture. A cornstalk and olive branch symbolize prosperity and peace. The other side of the seal shows Liberty defeating a lion, the symbol of tyranny, and the words Both Can't Survive. *The state flag, adopted in 1907, shows two horses supporting the state's coat of arms.*

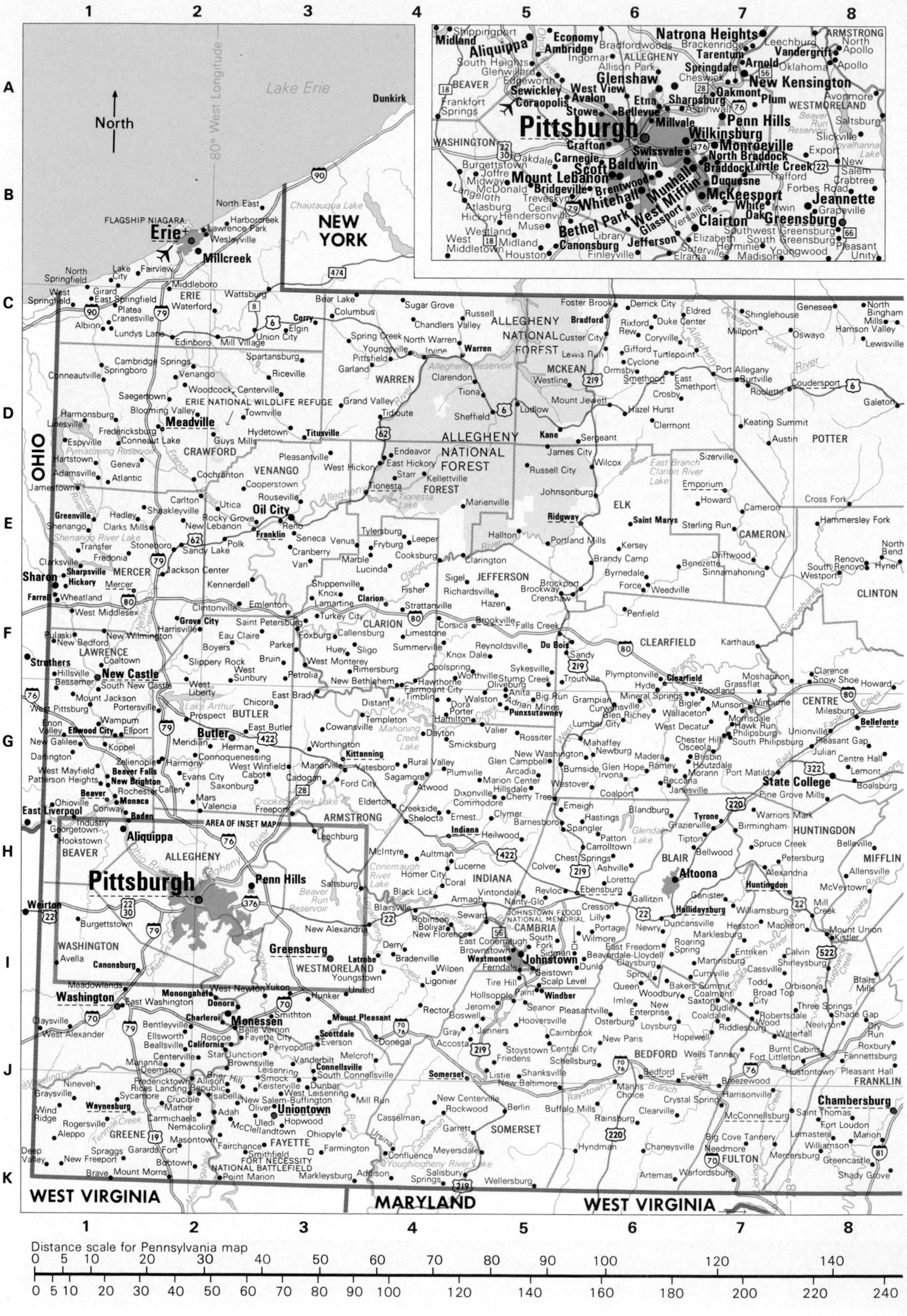

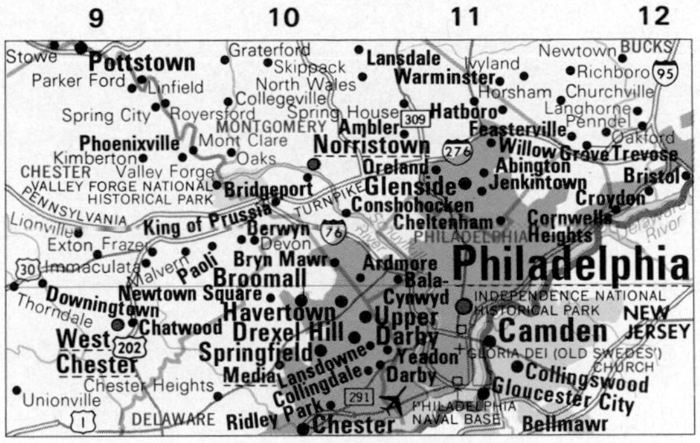

PENNSYLVANIA Political Map

- ✪ State capital
- ▨ Urban area in Pennsylvania
- ▢ Urban area outside Pennsylvania
- ● City or town
- ⬤ County seat
- YORK County name
- County boundary
- State boundary

Lambert conformal conic projection
WORLD BOOK map

- ▨ Park or other recreation area
- ▨ Forest or other conservation area
- ▢ Military or other federal area
- + Point of interest
- ✈ Major airport

- Water
- River

Highways:
- Expressway
- Other road
- 78 Interstate
- 6 U.S.
- 18 Other

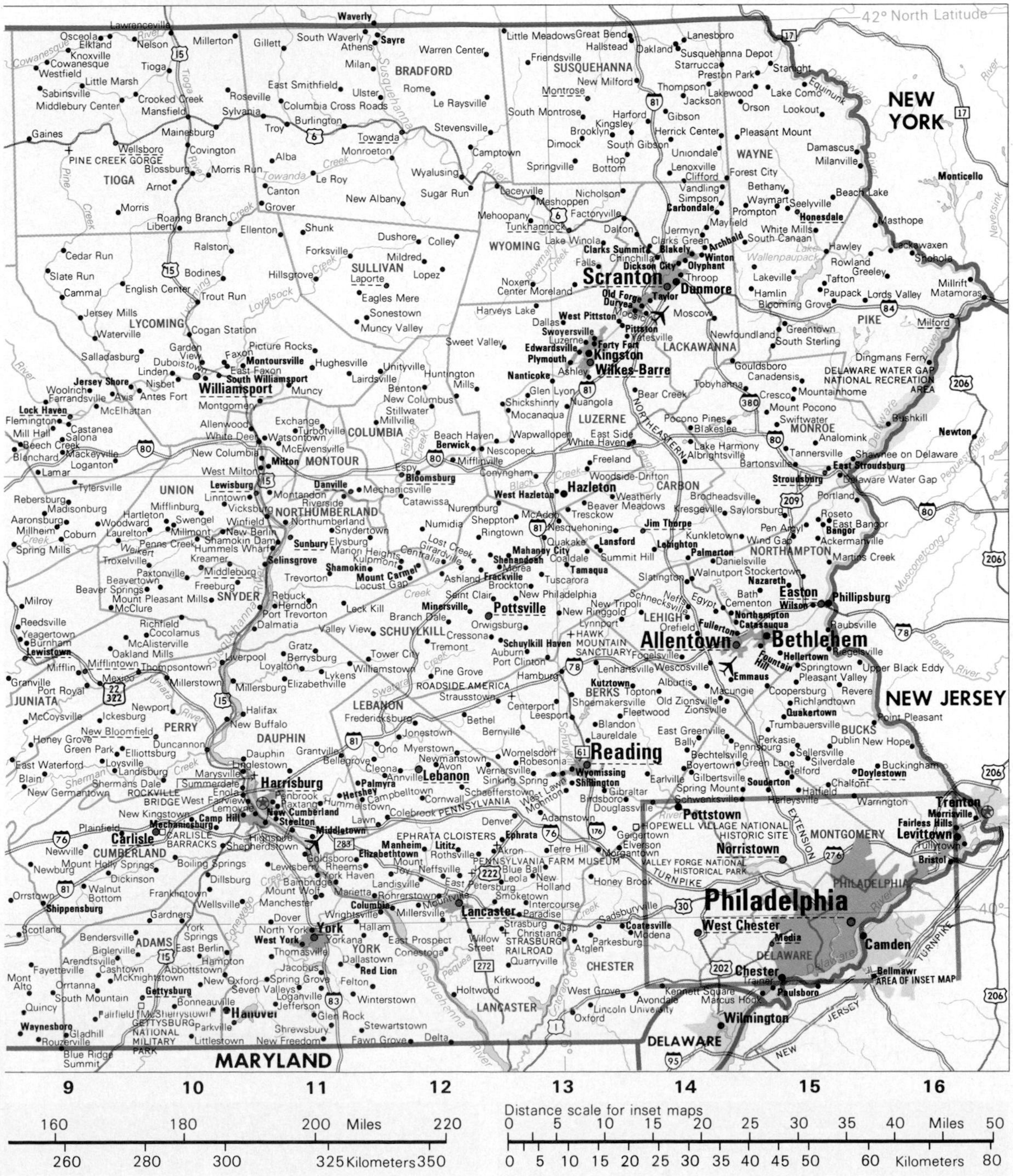

Seal

Flag

Bird: Ruffed Grouse

Flower: Mountain Laurel

Distance scale for inset maps
0 5 10 15 20 25 30 35 40 Miles 50
0 5 10 15 20 25 30 35 40 45 50 60 Kilometers 80

160 180 200 Miles 220
260 280 300 325 Kilometers 350

Ocean State

Capital: Providence
Area: 1,214 sq. mi. (3,144 km^2), including 165 sq. mi. (427 km^2) of inland water but excluding 14 sq. mi. (36 km^2) of coastal water; 50th and smallest in size among the states
Elevation: *Highest*—Jerimoth Hill, 812 ft. (247 m) above sea level; *lowest*—sea level along the Atlantic coast
Statehood: May 29, 1790, the 13th state
Abbreviations: R.I. (traditional); RI (postal)
Motto: *Hope*
Song: "Rhode Island"
Tree: Red Maple

Rhode Island's state seal shows the state motto, Hope, *printed above an anchor, a symbol of hope. The date 1636 is the year Roger Williams founded Providence, the state's first permanent white settlement. The seal was adopted in 1875. The state flag, adopted in 1877, has 13 gold stars that represent the 13 original colonies. The white field symbolizes the Rhode Island soldiers' white uniforms during the Revolutionary War.*

Rhode Island

Rhode Island is the smallest of the 50 states and is often called *Little Rhody*. But it has the longest official name of any state. In 1644, an island in Narragansett Bay was named Rhode Island. Mainland settlements nearby were called the Providence Plantations. As a result, Rhode Island, which includes both areas, took the official name, State of Rhode Island and Providence Plantations.

Narragansett Bay, with its many islands and inlets, once made Rhode Island a major shipping and whaling center. Today, tourists come to enjoy sailing, fishing, and other water sports.

During the late 1800's, a number of wealthy American bankers and industrialists chose Rhode Island's rocky coast as the site of fabulous summer mansions. Two of the most famous are The Breakers, a 70-room house built for Cornelius Vanderbilt, and Marble House, one of the most ornate buildings in the United States.

North Kingston is the site of the Old Narragansett Church, the oldest Episcopal Church in the northern United States. Newport's Touro Synagogue is the nation's oldest existing synagogue. One of the state's most unusual structures is a roofless stone tower called the Old Stone Mill. It isn't really a mill, and archaeologists have been unable to determine its origin. Local historians believe it was built by Vikings around A.D. 1000.

Rhode Island was the first colony to declare its independence from Britain. But it was the last to ratify the U.S. Constitution. Rhode Islanders waited until 1790, when the Bill of Rights was ready to be added to the Constitution, before approving the federal charter.

Over the years, the character of Rhode Island's economy has changed greatly. During the early 1700's, many Rhode Islanders developed large plantations worked by slaves. But in 1774, Rhode Island became the first colony to prohibit the importation of slaves. Around the same time, industrialization began. Samuel Slater, who had worked in England's textile industry, fled to America with the secret of how to build water-powered cotton-spinning machines. From memory, he built the first water-powered cotton-spinning machines in the United States in Pawtucket. In Providence, Nehemiah and Seril Dodge established the first jewelry industry in the United States. The textile industry eventually declined in importance, but the state is still the nation's leading manufacturer of jewelry.

The shift to industry helped make Rhode Island one of the nation's most urban states. There are only eight cities in all of Rhode Island. But about 85 per cent of the state's citizens live in urban areas, and Providence ranks second in size only to Boston among New England cities.

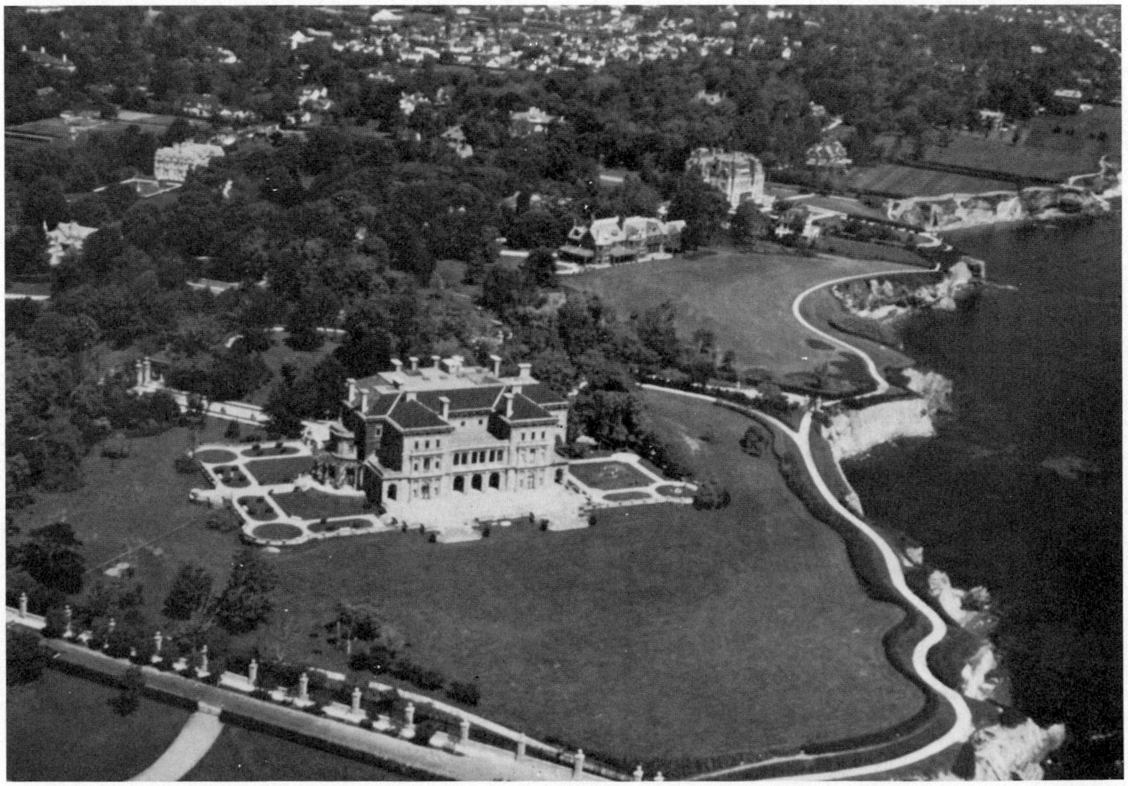

The tiny state of Rhode Island has provided summer homes for many American financial giants such as Cornelius Vanderbilt. His estate—The Breakers—lies along the coast at Newport.

RHODE ISLAND Political Map

Symbol	Meaning
⊛	State capital
	Urban area in Rhode Island
	Urban area outside Rhode Island
●	City or town
●	Seat of county courthouse
KENT	County name
	County boundary
□	Military or other federal area
+	Point of interest
✈	Major airport
	Water
	River
	Roads or highways:
	Expressway
	Other road
95	Interstate
6	U.S.
3	Other

Polyconic projection
WORLD BOOK map
ⓒ Field Enterprises Educational Corporation

Distance scale

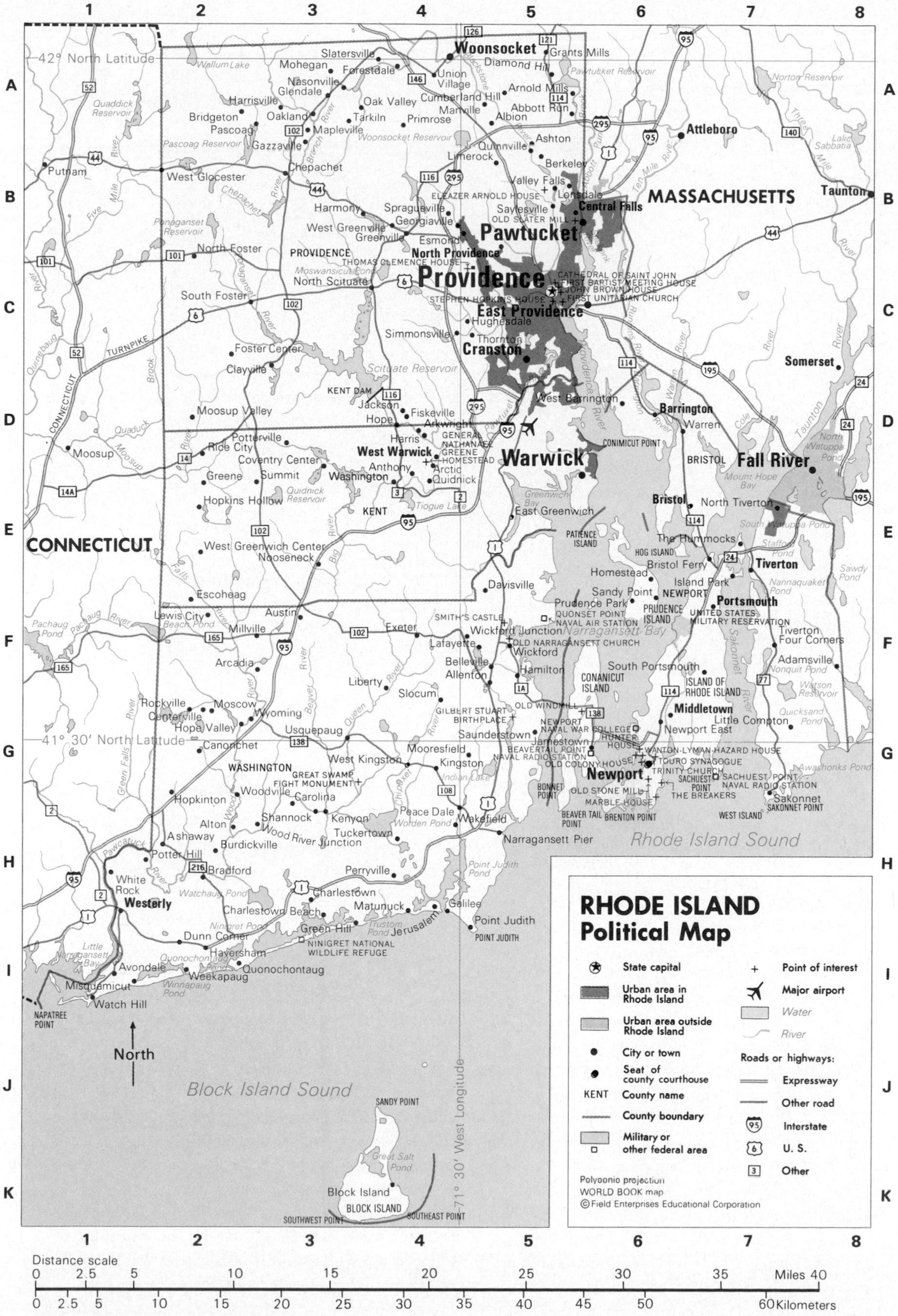

Seal

Flag

Bird: Rhode Island Red

Flower: Violet

The forests and peaks of Vermont's Green Mountains make the area an ideal setting for summer hiking.

Vermont

Vermont is one of the smallest states in population and has the lowest percentage of urban dwellers of any state in the nation. Less than a third of Vermont's residents live in urban areas. The state has a total of eight cities, but only two—Burlington and Rutland—have more than 15,000 persons. Towns in Vermont are geographic divisions rather than political units and may include several communities. There are 237 towns with local government and 5 towns that have too few inhabitants to have governments. Three of the five—Glastenbury, Lewis, and Somerset—have no people at all.

The rural character of Vermont is reflected to a certain degree in its economy. Manufacturing is the single most important income producer in Vermont, but the state derives a greater percentage of its income from agriculture than is the case in any other New England state. Milk is the most important farm product in Vermont, and the state has almost as many cattle as people. Vermont is famous for two other agricultural products: maple syrup and maple sugar.

In the autumn, Vermont's forests of maples and other trees provide brilliant displays of foliage that attract thousands of visitors. Forests cover about three-fourths of the state.

The name *Vermont* comes from the French words *vert mont,* which mean "green mountain." The forested Green Mountains of Vermont rank among the state's most popular recreation areas. They gave Vermont its nickname, the *Green Mountain State.*

Vermont is the only New England state that does not border the Atlantic Ocean. But the Connecticut River forms the entire eastern boundary of the state, and Lake Champlain, in the northwestern corner, is the largest lake in New England.

Vermont ranks among the leading states in the production of asbestos, granite, marble, and slate. The largest granite quarries in the United States are at Barre. Barre also has the largest stone-finishing plant in the world, where visitors can watch blocks of granite being quarried, sawed, polished, and carved. Some of the largest marble quarries in the

Towns like Woodstock, with its graceful buildings and village green, delight not only residents but thousands of out-of-staters each year.

world are located in Proctor, and Lowell has the nation's largest asbestos mine.

The first permanent settlement by whites in Vermont was established by colonists from Massachusetts. They built Fort Dummer in 1724 to warn settlers in western Massachusetts of Indian attacks.

The ownership of Vermont was the subject of a long series of disputes between New York and New Hampshire during the 1700's. The conflicting claims over land led to the establishment of the famous military force, the Green Mountain Boys, who were settlers holding New Hampshire grants. They fought New Yorkers who tried to settle in Vermont. During the Revolutionary War, the Green Mountain Boys, led by Ethan Allen, captured Fort Ticonderoga from the British. Benedict Arnold was among the Green Mountain Boys who took part in the battle.

In 1777, Vermont declared itself an independent republic called New Connecticut. In July of that year, it adopted its present name and its first constitution. The constitution was the most liberal of its time. It forbade slavery and granted voting rights to all males regardless of race, religion, or property ownership.

In spite of Vermont's declaration of independence, New York and New Hampshire still claimed parts of the territory. Vermont ignored the claims, and George Washington wrote that he thought it might be necessary to send in troops to overthrow the Vermont government. But troops were never sent, and Vermont remained an independent republic for 14 years. Eventually, Vermont settled its disputes with New York and New Hampshire and finally joined the Union in 1791 as the 14th state. It was the first state admitted after the original 13 colonies.

In 1864, Vermont became the site of the northernmost land action of the Civil War. A band of 22 Confederate soldiers robbed some banks in St. Albans and fled to Canada with more than $20,000.

During the 1850's, Vermont established the most consistent voting record of any state in the nation. From the early 1800's until 1974, the state elected only Republicans to the U.S. Senate. All of Vermont's U.S. representatives between 1853 and 1959 were Republicans, as were all of its governors between 1854 and 1963. Vermont has voted for Republican presidential nominees in every election since 1856, with the exception of the 1964 election, when its votes went to Lyndon Johnson.

Two Vermont Republicans became Presidents. Chester A. Arthur was born in Fairfield, and Calvin Coolidge was born in Plymouth Notch.

Early spring in 20th-century Vermont recalls lifestyles of times past, especially when the maple sap is boiling in the barn.

Vermont
Green Mountain State

Capital: Montpelier
Area: 9,609 sq. mi. (24,887 km^2), including 342 sq. mi. (886 km^2) of inland water; 43rd in size among the states
Elevation: *Highest*—Mount Mansfield, 4,393 ft. (1,339 m) above sea level; *lowest*—Lake Champlain in Franklin County, 95 ft. (29 m) above sea level
Statehood: March 4, 1791, the 14th state
Abbreviations: Vt. (traditional); VT (postal)
Motto: *Vermont, Freedom and Unity*
Song: "Hail, Vermont!"
Tree: Sugar Maple

Vermont's state seal shows 14 branches on a pine tree. This symbol represents the 13 original states and Vermont. The wavy lines at the top symbolize the sky and those at the bottom stand for Lake Champlain, which forms part of Vermont's western boundary. The cow and sheaves of wheat represent dairying and agriculture. The seal was designed and adopted in 1779, then modified in 1937. The state flag, adopted in 1923, carries the Vermont coat of arms and a view of the Green Mountains.

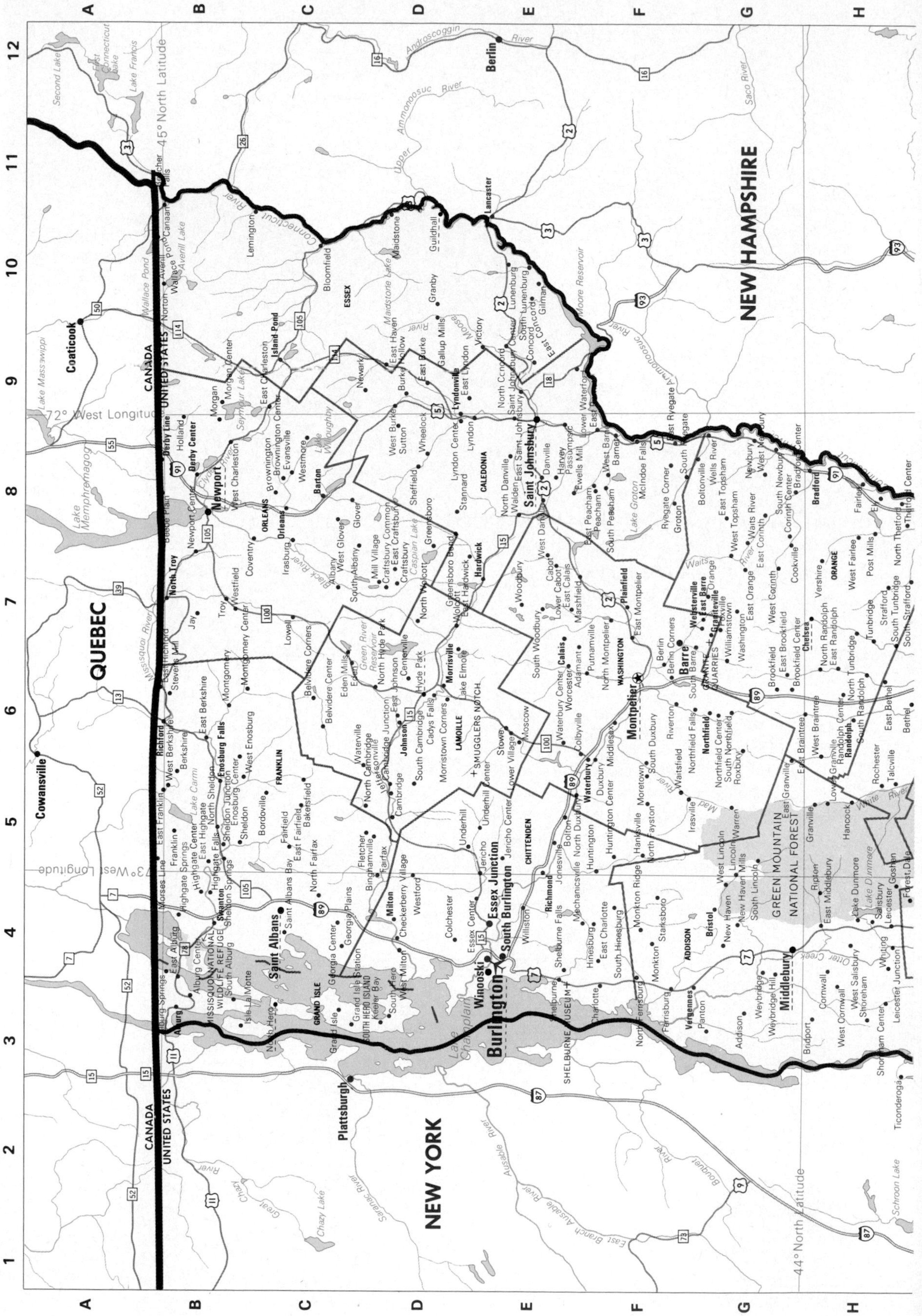

Lambert conformal conic projection
WORLD BOOK map © Field Enterprises Educational Corporation

VERMONT Political Map

Highways:
Expressway
Other road

⊛	State capital
▢	Urban area
•	City or town
●	County seat
ADDISON	County name
	County boundary
	State boundary
	Forest or other conservation area
+	Point of interest
✈	Major airport

97 Interstate
4 U.S.
9 Other
15 Autoroute

Waterway
Intermittent lake
Water
River

North

Distance scale

Miles
Kilometers

NEW HAMPSHIRE

NEW YORK

MASSACHUSETTS

GREEN MOUNTAIN NATIONAL FOREST

Seal

Flag

Bird: Hermit Thrush

Flower: Red Clover

VERMONT FREEDOM & UNITY

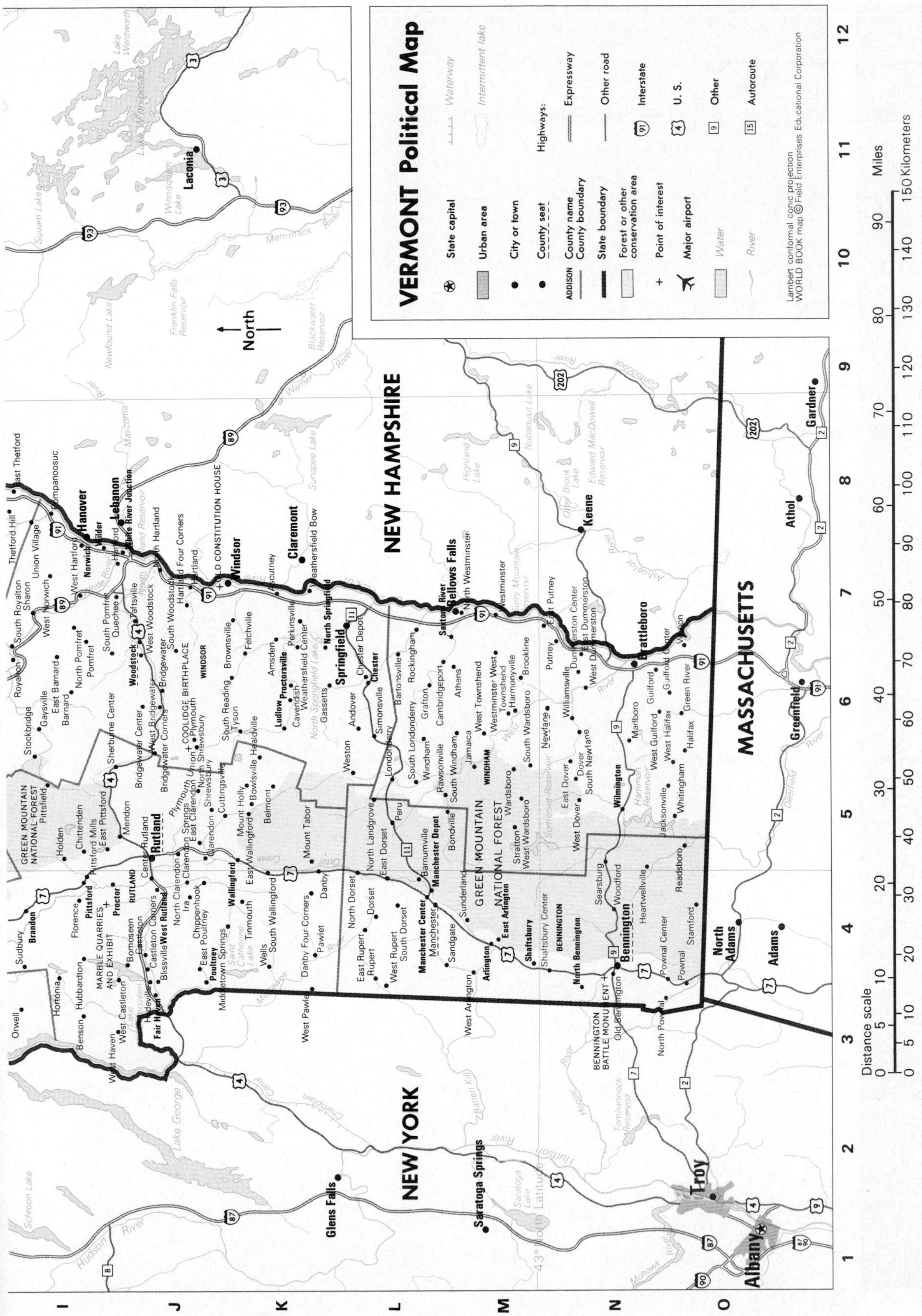

Midwest

Illinois *94*
Indiana *98*
Iowa *102*
Kansas *106*
Michigan *110*
Minnesota *114*
Missouri *118*
Nebraska *122*
North Dakota *126*
Ohio *130*
South Dakota *134*
Wisconsin *138*

The Midwest, at the interior of the United States, is a rich and important region of the world. Hard-working midwestern settlers found rich farmlands, plentiful minerals, and friendly rivers in this promising new home.

The Midwest's rivers and lakes are an angler's delight. Here, vacationers prepare for a try at Birch Lake in Minnesota (facing page).

St. Louis, the busiest inland port on the Mississippi River, houses the state capitol of Missouri and the Gateway Arch, the nation's tallest monument (above left).

Mount Rushmore, a memorial to four Presidents, stands in one of South Dakota's national parks. The stone figures are the largest of any sculpture in the world (below left).

Midwestern manufacturing has prospered in part because of the region's excellent waterways. Riverside mills, such as this one in Indiana, produce more steel than those of any other U.S. region (below right).

Illinois

One of Illinois' nicknames is the *Prairie State* because of the gently rolling plains that cover most of its area. Farms cover more than three-fourths of Illinois, producing huge amounts of soybeans, corn, and other crops. But the state is also an industrial giant known for its production of farm machinery, diesel engines, television sets, and a great variety of other products. Coal lies beneath about two-thirds of Illinois, giving the state the largest deposits of bituminous, or soft, coal in the nation.

In 1858, a series of debates between two contenders running in Illinois for the U.S. Senate drew national attention. One of them, Stephen Douglas, eventually won the senatorial election. The loser was Abraham Lincoln, who was elected the 16th President of the United States two years later. Illinoisans are proud that Abraham Lincoln lived most of his life in Illinois, and they call their state the *Land of Lincoln.* Lincoln's home in Springfield and New Salem State Park are two of Illinois' leading historical attractions.

The world of the past is recaptured at the Field Museum of Natural History in Chicago (above).

New Salem State Park houses a reproduction of a village where Abraham Lincoln once lived. Tourists may use modern phone-tapes to learn about life in the 18th century (right).

Nearly two-thirds of all Illinoisans live in the northern part of the state, a region that was almost not included in the state's original boundaries. In 1818, when Illinois was admitted to the Union as the 21st state, only the southern third of the state was settled. The future state's northern boundary had been set at a line drawn westward from the southern tip of Lake Michigan. At the urging of Nathaniel Pope, the territorial delegate to Congress, the northern boundary was extended to its present location. The change gave Illinois what is now Chicago, plus a rich northern dairy region and valuable lead deposits around Galena.

Today, the sprawling Chicago metropolitan area alone has about 60 per cent of Illinois' population. The Chicago area ranks as the nation's largest manufacturing center. The famous Illinois poet Carl Sandburg gave Chicago the nickname, *City of the Big Shoulders.* The city employs millions of workers in thousands of factories. It is a major center of textbook and paperback book publishing. Chicago is also the leading Great Lakes port and a major railroad center. Chicago-O'Hare International Airport is the busiest airport in the world. The city's museums and libraries rank among the finest in the nation, and its sandy Lake Michigan beaches provide a striking contrast to its towering skyscrapers.

In 1942, Chicago became the site of one of the most important scientific achievements in history. A group of scientists led by Enrico Fermi produced the world's first controlled nuclear chain reaction, ushering in the nuclear age. Their experiment took place in laboratories under the football stadium stands at the University of Chicago. Today, the Fermi National Accelerator Laboratory in suburban Batavia attracts scientists and engineers from around the world as one of the foremost centers for study of the atom.

To a certain extent, Illinois' manufacturing development was encouraged by the work of several noted inventors who lived there. John Deere built the first workable steel plow in 1837 at Grand Detour. He later moved his factory to Moline, a city that became known as the *Farm Implement Capital of the World.* Cyrus McCormick lived in Chicago, where he developed the mechanical reaper. His skill and ingenuity led to the establishment of the International Harvester Company. In Bloomington, George M. Pullman built the first successful railroad sleeping car. Two Illinoisans—Louis Sullivan and Frank Lloyd Wright—became world-renowned for their innovative architectural designs.

Thousands of years before Illinois became a productive agricultural and industrial state, Indians known as Mound Builders lived in the region. More than 10,000 burial and temple mounds still stand in Illinois as reminders of the ancient Indian civilization.

Father Jacques Marquette and Louis Joliet were probably the first white persons in what is now Illinois. Their explorations during the 1670's opened up the area to French Roman Catholic missionaries, who remained as the dominant influence in the region for more than a hundred years.

Illinois changed hands several times during its early history. It was part of the French colony of Louisiana for a time, then was taken over by the British. During the Revolutionary War, George Rogers Clark led a band of frontier dwellers in successful raids on the settlements of Kaskaskia and Cahokia, seizing them from the British. The Illinois region then became a county of Virginia. It later was transferred to the Northwest Territory, the Indiana Territory, and finally the Illinois Territory before becoming a state in 1818.

Separated from the metropolitan sprawl of its cities, most of Illinois is covered with highly productive farms.

Illinois
Land of Lincoln

Capital: Springfield
Area: 56,400 sq. mi. (146,075 km²), including 652 sq. mi. (1,689 km²) of inland water but excluding 1,526 sq. mi. (3,952 km²) of Lake Michigan; 24th in size among the states
Elevation: *Highest*—Charles Mound, 1,235 ft. (376 m) above sea level; *lowest*— along the Mississippi River in Alexander County, 279 ft. (85 m) above sea level
Statehood: Dec. 3, 1818, the 21st state
Abbreviations: Ill. (traditional); IL (postal)
Motto: *State Sovereignty, National Union*
Song: "Illinois"
Tree: White Oak

Illinois' state seal shows an American eagle holding a shield with stars and stripes that represent the 13 original states. The olive branch stands for peace, and the prairie and rising sun represent the plains of Illinois. The dates on the rock tell when Illinois was admitted to the Union (1818) and when the seal was adopted (1868). The state flag, adopted in 1915, has an adaptation of the seal.

ILLINOIS Political Map

* State capital
* Urban area in Illinois
* Urban area outside Illinois
* City or town
* County seat
* KANE County name
  County boundary
* State boundary
* Forest or other conservation area
* Military or other federal area
* Point of interest
* Major airport
* Water
* River
* Waterway
* Highways:
  * Expressway
  * Other road
  * 55 Interstate
  * 61 U.S.
  * 3 Other

Lambert conformal conic projection
WORLD BOOK map

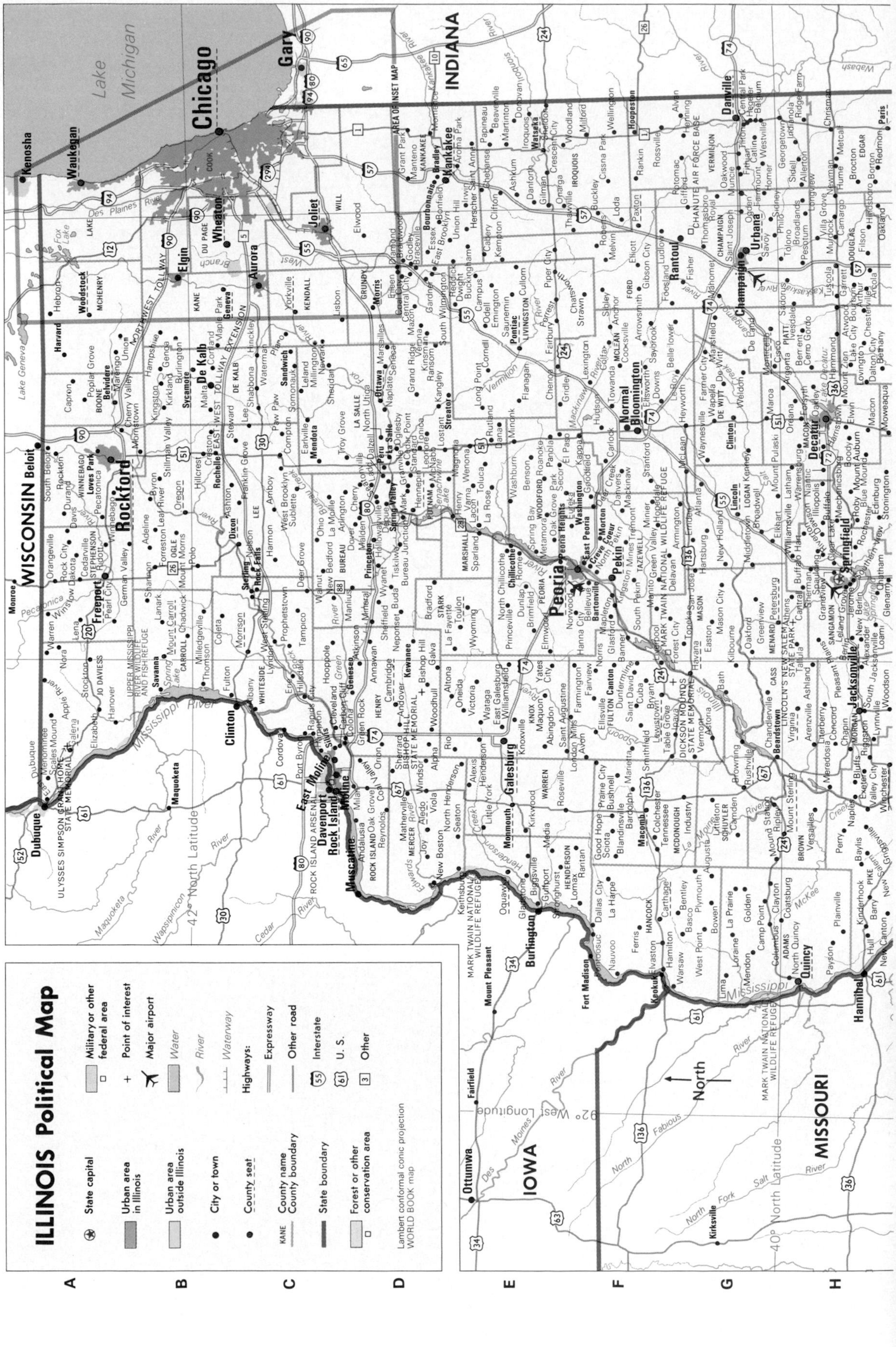

Seal

Flag

Bird: Cardinal

Flower: Native Violet

Distance scale for Illinois map

Distance scale for inset map

88° West Longitude

90° West Longitude

INDIANA

KENTUCKY

WISCONSIN

INDIANA

Terre Haute

Evansville

Paducah

Cape Girardeau

Saint Louis

Chicago

Kenosha

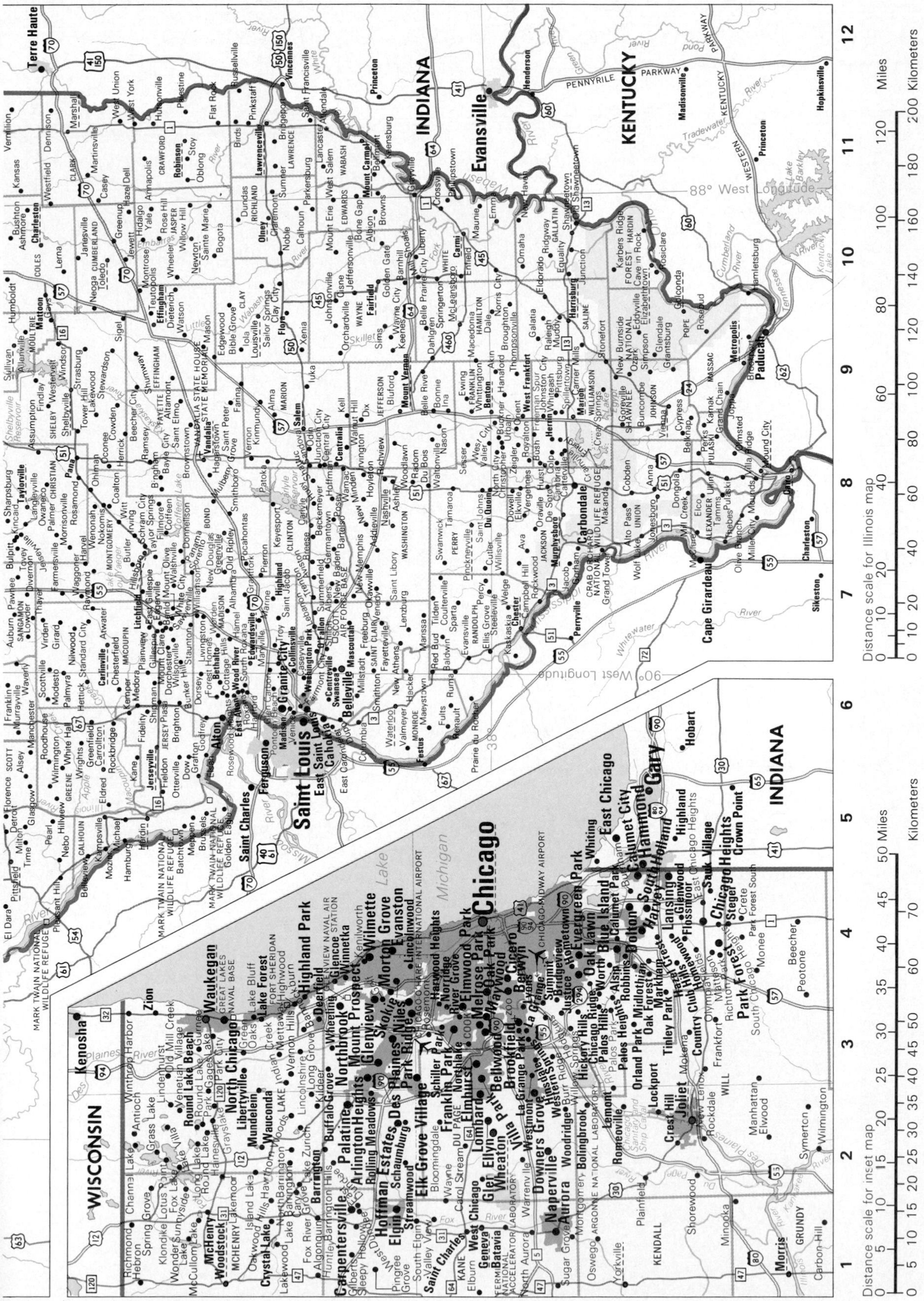

Indiana

Indiana is a state of great diversity. Its fertile farmland produces abundant yields of corn, wheat, soybeans, tomatoes, and other crops. Picturesque Brown County, in the south-central part of the state, is a mecca for artists, who come to paint the seasonal landscapes of the rolling countryside. More than 30 covered bridges add touches of quaint charm to Parke County. But Indiana is also an industrial leader. The state has large beds of coal, active oil wells, and huge limestone quarries. More than half the building limestone produced in the United States comes from Indiana. The sprawling steelmaking complex in the Calumet region, which includes East Chicago, Gary, Hammond, and Whiting, is one of the nation's largest. Indiana factories also turn out aircraft engines, recreational vehicles, electronic equipment, and many other goods.

Indiana's industrial development goes back many years. Clement and Henry Studebaker opened a blacksmith and wagon shop in South Bend in 1852. Their wagon industry eventually became the largest in the country, and the Studebaker Company later manufactured electric and gasoline-powered automobiles. In 1889, the Standard Oil Company built the world's largest oil refinery at Whiting. Several years later, the United States Steel Corporation planned and built the city of Gary and began constructing the world's largest steelworks there.

It wasn't long after the dawn of the automobile age that Indiana began one of its best-known traditions—the world-famous Indianapolis 500 automobile race. The first 500-mile race at the Indianapolis Motor Speedway took place in 1911, with the winning car clocking a speed of just under 75 miles per hour. Today, the annual Memorial Day weekend event draws more than 300,000 spectators.

The popularity of the "Indy 500" led to the establishment of the Indianapolis Motor Speedway Museum, which displays famous racing cars. Indiana has many other museums and places of interest, including the Lincoln Library and Museum in Fort Wayne. Abraham Lincoln lived in Indiana from age 7 to 21, and the state has several sites dedicated to his memory.

The first territorial governor of Indiana, William Henry Harrison, also became the ninth President of the United States. But he served the shortest term of any President. Harrison caught cold on his inauguration day in 1841 and served only 30 full days before he died.

Harrison's grandson, Benjamin Harrison, lived in Indiana for many years before being elected the 23rd President in 1888. He campaigned to the accompaniment of a Republican song called "Grandfather's Hat Fits Ben."

In addition to its political figures, Indiana has been the home of a number of famous writers. James Whitcomb Riley, Theodore Dreiser, Booth Tarkington, and Lew Wallace were all born in Indiana. Riley became known as the Hoosier Poet, writing in the dialect of Indiana country folk.

Indiana ranks among the top 12 states in population. But in area, it is the smallest state west of the Appalachian Mountains except for Hawaii.

The people of Indiana have long been known as Hoosiers, and the state's nickname is the *Hoosier State.* The word *Hoosier* may have come from the traditional Indiana pioneer greeting to visitors: "Who's here?" Or it may have come from the slang word *husher,* meaning a fighting man who could silence, or "hush," others with his fists.

Thousands of years before the first Hoosiers arrived, various Indian tribes lived in what is now In-

Indianapolis, Indiana's capital, is also the state's cultural and educational center. The Indianapolis Museum of Art is but one of the city's many attractions (below top).

Sturdy and simple describes not only the architecture of the tiny farming community of Metamora but also the spirit of the people who settled and prospered in Indiana (below bottom).

Canyons shrouded by an eerie fog are part of the primitive landscape preserved at Turkey Run State Park—one of the more than 20 state parks found in Indiana.

diana. As Europeans began to settle the eastern United States, other Indian tribes that were forced out of the east and north also came to the Indiana region. A Frenchman, Robert Cavelier, Sieur de la Salle, was probably the first white person to arrive in the Indiana area. In 1731, the French established Vincennes, the first permanent settlement in Indiana. Before long, French and British settlers had established a thriving fur trade with the Indians. Competition between the French and British for land and trade rights led to the French and Indian wars. Britain eventually conquered the region. After the Revolutionary War, the area became part of the United States.

Indiana became the 19th state in 1816. Its constitution was the first state constitution to provide for free public schools throughout the state. Several innovative ideas in education were developed in Indiana. An experimental cooperative community at New Harmony operated one of the first nursery schools and conducted the first classes in the United States in which boys and girls were taught together.

Indiana
Hoosier State

Capital: Indianapolis
Area: 36,291 sq. mi. (93,993 km^2), including 194 sq. mi. (502 km^2) of inland water but excluding 228 sq. mi. (591 km^2) of Lake Michigan; 38th in size among the states
Elevation: *Highest*—1,257 ft. (383 m) above sea level, in Wayne County; *lowest*—320 ft. (98 m) above sea level, in Posey County
Statehood: Dec. 11, 1816, the 19th state
Abbreviations: Ind. (traditional); IN (postal)
Motto: *The Crossroads of America*
Song: "On the Banks of the Wabash"
Tree: Tulip Tree

Indiana's state seal features a pioneer scene representing westward expansion. Officials of the Indiana Territory used a version of the seal as early as 1801. The date 1816 was added when Indiana became a state, but the seal was not adopted until 1963. The state flag, adopted in 1917, bears a torch symbolizing freedom and knowledge. The stars surrounding the torch represent Indiana's entry into the Union as the 19th state.

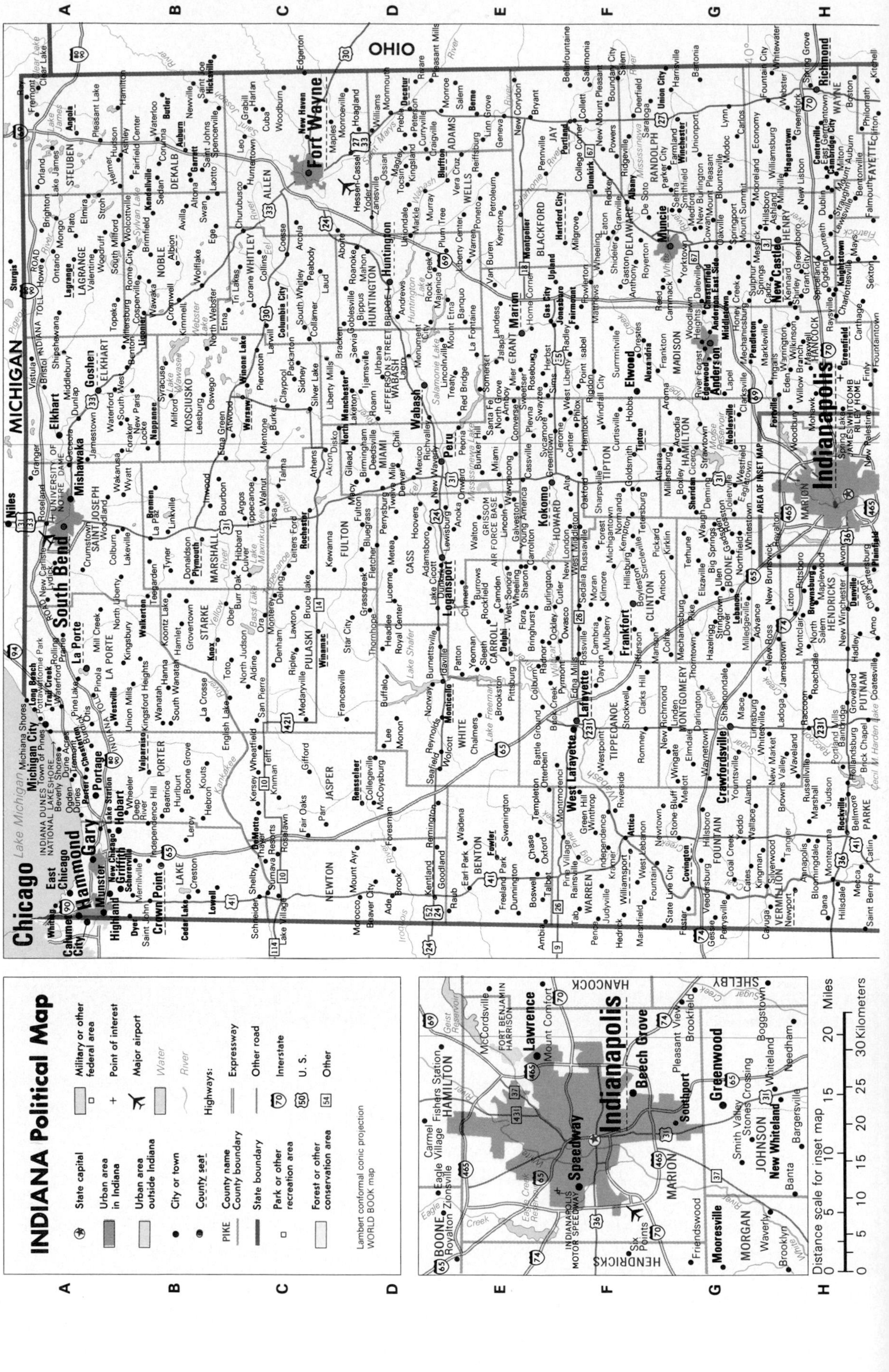

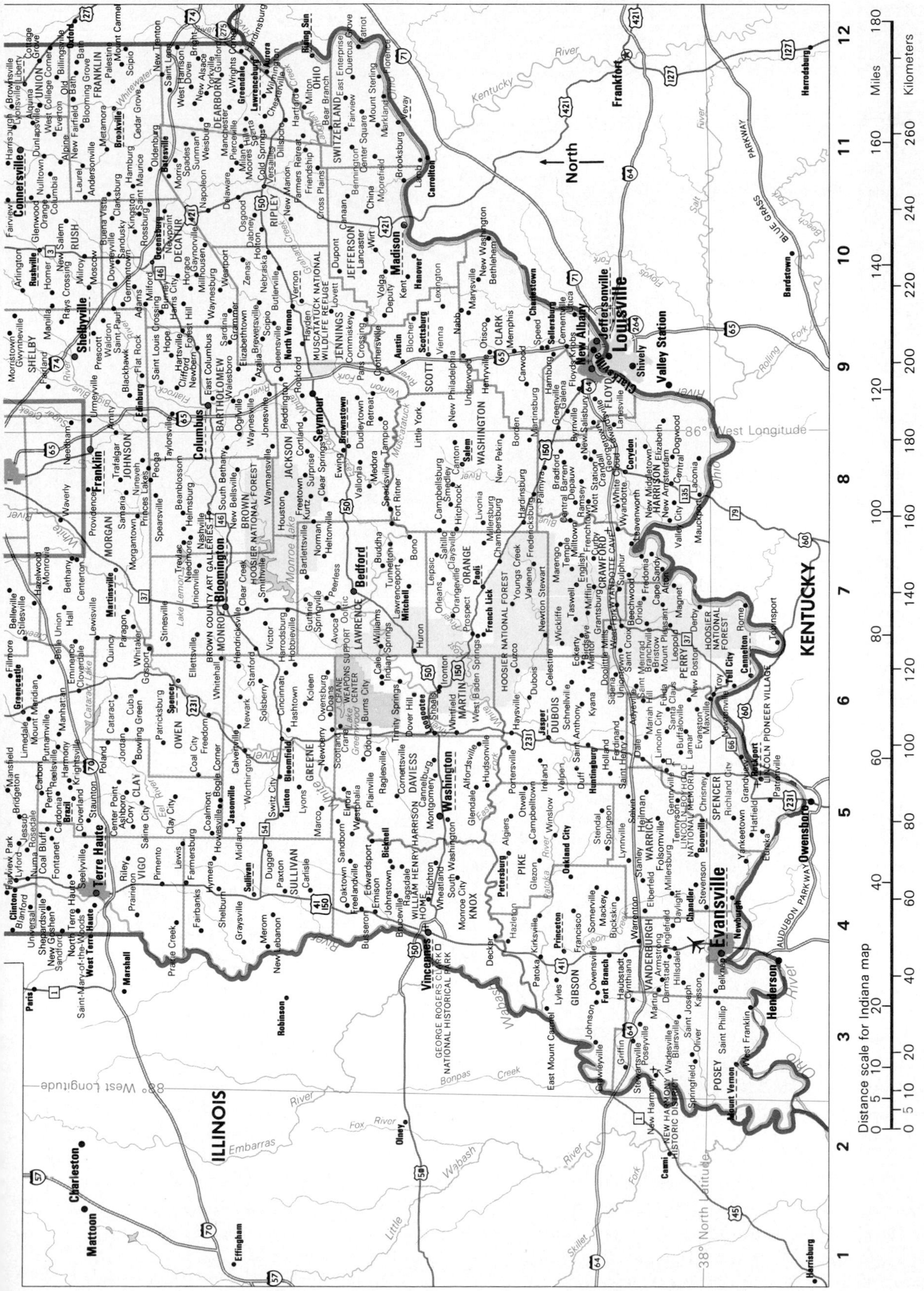

Seal

Flag

Bird: Cardinal

Flower: Peony

ILLINOIS
KENTUCKY
Evansville
Louisville
Terre Haute
Bloomington
Columbus
Vincennes
North
Distance scale for Indiana map
Miles
Kilometers
86° West Longitude
88° West Longitude
38° North Latitude
J
K
M
1
2
3
4
5
6
7
8
9
10
11
12

The Mississippi River marks the eastern boundary of Iowa with dramatic stretches of natural beauty. Recalling times past, a paddlewheeler enters the locks at Keokuk—named for a Sac Indian chief.

Iowa

Iowa is a state of many rivers. They provide Iowans and tourists with enjoyable hours of boating, canoeing, and fishing. Two of the state's borders are formed by the Mississippi River on the east and the Missouri River on the west. Between these two large rivers are many smaller ones, all flowing into the Mississippi-Missouri river system.

In the eastern part of Iowa, rivers are long and winding, rising in the prairies of central Iowa and flowing through shallow valleys bordered by wooded hills and bluffs. The longest of these rivers is the Des Moines River. Other large eastern rivers include the Cedar, Iowa, Maquoketa, and Wapsipinicon. The rivers in western Iowa are much shorter than those in the eastern portion of the state.

The rivers of Iowa provide water for some of the most productive farms of the United States. Corn is the chief crop. So much corn is grown in Iowa that it is often called "the land where the tall corn grows" or the *Corn State.* Iowa farmers raise both food corn, for human consumption, and corn for livestock feed. Much of the livestock feed goes to Iowa hogs, the state's leading source of farm income.

Most of Iowa's industry serves the state's agriculture. Farm machinery is manufactured in the cities of Davenport, Des Moines, and Waterloo. The largest cereal mill in the country is located in Cedar Rapids, and the nation's largest popcorn-processing plant is in Sioux City. Many beef and dairy cattle are also raised by Iowa farmers; thus, Iowa has many meat-packing plants and plants that process dairy products.

Iowa is a state of four distinct seasons, and every season offers travelers interesting sights and activities. Winter finds the International Snow Festival being held in Cresco in late January. It is followed by the Estherville Winter Sports Festival in early February.

In the spring, wild flowers such as blue pasque-flowers, bloodroots, marsh marigolds, and violets color the countryside, and apple trees bloom profusely. Tulip festivals are held in Orange City and Pella in May.

The Iowa State Fair is one of the state's most celebrated summer events. It is held in Des Moines during the last week in August. Visitors to the state fair will see agricultural and industrial exhibits, enjoy amusement park rides and side shows on the midway, and sample many of the food products that are grown and processed in Iowa. In early July, Riverboat Days are held in Clinton. Late July is the time for the Bix Biederbecke Memorial Jazz Festival in Davenport and the Nordic Fest in Decorah.

The Iowa corn fields seem to turn into a sea of green as the plants grow during the summer months. Fall is harvest time. Corn fields have turned an amber color and the leaves of the many hardwood trees have turned to beautiful shades of red, yellow, orange, and rust. Farmers throughout Iowa are busy gathering their bountiful harvests. The Amana Colonies, seven villages located southwest of Cedar Rapids, hold their traditional German *Oktoberfest* in Middle Amana in early October. These colonies are a popular tourist attraction throughout the year. Here visitors can browse through interesting museums, sample popular restaurants, and watch craftworkers build furniture, make yarn, and weave fabrics.

Several famous people are associated with Iowa. President Herbert Hoover, the 31st President of the United States, was born in West Branch in 1874. A park in West Branch surrounds his birthplace. A restored blacksmith shop that his father ran and a library containing Hoover's public papers are also on the park grounds.

Grant Wood, one of the Midwest's most famous artists, was born near Anamosa in 1892. His paintings of rural Iowa, the most famous of which is *American Gothic,* have won him worldwide acclaim.

In 1893, Czech composer Antonín Dvořák visited Spillville. While there, he worked on his *Symphony in E minor: From the New World.* The house in which Dvořák lived has been turned into a memorial to him and now houses a collection of clocks carved by the Bily brothers, Czech craftworkers.

Other interesting places to visit in Iowa include Effigy Mounds National Monument near McGregor. This monument has earthen mounds, some shaped like animals, built by prehistoric Indians who inhabited the area long before any white explorers arrived. Floyd Monument in Sioux City marks the grave of Sargeant Charles Floyd, who died while serving as a member of the Lewis and Clark Expedition. Floyd is the first known white man to be buried in Iowa. The Grotto of the Redemption in West Bend is a religious structure built by Father Paul M. Dobberstein in 1912. Rocks used to build the grotto come from countries throughout the world.

With more than 90 per cent of Iowa's land devoted to agriculture, nothing identifies the state more than farming. Visitors may sample farm life of the 1800's by touring living history farms like this one near Des Moines (above top).

Before 1857, when the capital of Iowa was moved to Des Moines, Old Capitol in Iowa City housed the government offices of both the state and the territory of Iowa. Today, Old Capitol provides administrative offices for the University of Iowa (above bottom).

Iowa
Hawkeye State

Capital: Des Moines
Area: 56,290 sq. mi. (145,790 km²), including 349 sq. mi. (904 km²) of inland water; 25th in size among the states
Elevation: *Highest*—1,670 ft. (509 m) above sea level, along the north boundary of Osceola County; *lowest*—480 ft. (146 m) above sea level, at the junction of the Mississippi and Des Moines rivers in Lee County
Statehood: Dec. 28, 1846, the 29th state
Abbreviations: Ia. (traditional); IA (postal)
Motto: *Our Liberties We Prize and Our Rights We Will Maintain*
Song: "The Song of Iowa"
Tree: Oak

Iowa's state seal shows a prairie scene representing Iowa's pioneer days. An eagle flies over the scene carrying a streamer bearing the state motto. The seal was adopted in 1847. The state flag was adopted in 1921. It bears a reproduction of the flying eagle.

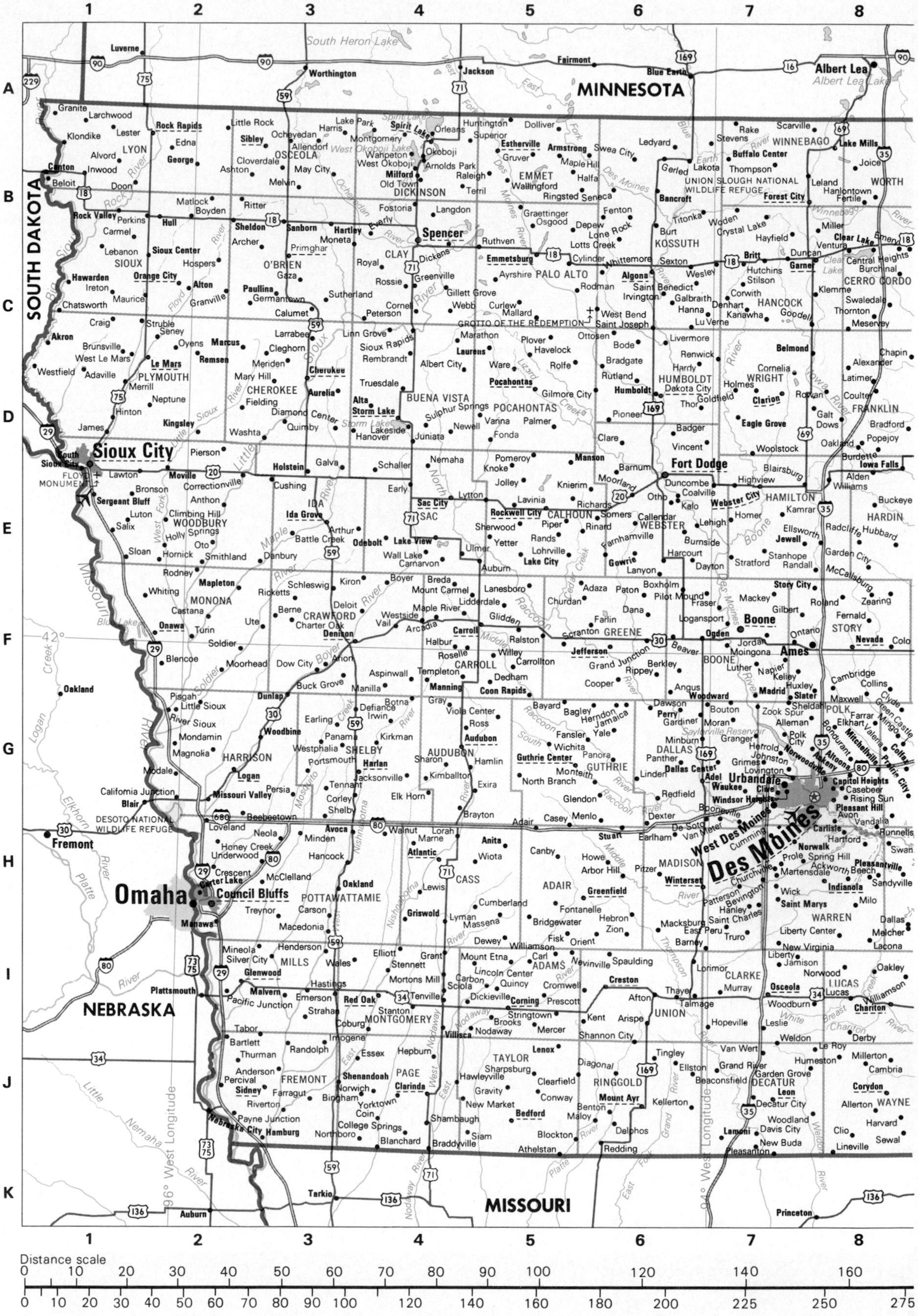

IOWA Political Map

★ State capital
■ Indian reservation
Urban area in Iowa
+ Point of interest
Urban area outside Iowa
✈ Major airport
● City or town
Water
● County seat
River
SAC County name
Intermittent river
County boundary
Flood control reservoir
State boundary
Highways:
Expressway
Other road
□ Park or other recreation area
㉙ Interstate
㉖⑦ U. S.
㉔ Other
□ Forest or other conservation area

Lambert conformal conic projection
WORLD BOOK map
© Field Enterprises Educational Corporation

Seal

Flag

Bird: Eastern Goldfinch

Flower: Wild Rose

North

Kansas

Kansas is known by many names. The word *Kansas* itself is an Indian word meaning "people of the south wind." These people were the Kansa, or Kaw, Indians, who once lived in the region. Kansas is also known as the *Midway U.S.A.* because it lies midway between the Atlantic and Pacific oceans.

Because it leads all the United States in wheat production, Kansas is known as the *Wheat State* and the *Breadbasket of America.* In early summer, vast wheat fields on the state's prairies become golden seas of grain.

Loneliness, Indian attacks, and uncertain food supplies are among the many hardships endured by the determined Kansas pioneer women honored by this statue on Topeka's capitol grounds.

DEDICATED TO THE
PIONEER WOMEN OF
KANSAS

Kansas is probably best known as the *Sunflower State.* These tall, yellow flowers thrive in almost all areas of the state and have become a symbol of the hot, sunny summer days on the Great Plains.

Dodge City, a famous Kansas town, has as its nickname, *Cowboy Capital of the World,* suggesting Kansas' background as cattle country. When pinned with this name, Dodge City was a brawling cattle center, the largest in the world. Today, the state remains a leader in the production of beef cattle.

This state is also a leader in manufacturing, its most important economic activity. The oil industry is also strong, with about 50,000 oil and gas wells dotting Kansas' fertile prairies.

Kansas is rich in natural resources. The most important of these are fertile soil, rich mineral deposits, and water. Large herds of buffalo once roamed the plains of the state, but by the 1870's most were killed by hunters.

Kansas' weather in winter can be cold and unpredictable. Blizzards, hail, and tornadoes are not uncommon on the flat plains of Kansas during the winter and spring months. But summertime in this Great Plains state is usually warm and most pleasant.

Kansas is sometimes called the *Jayhawker State.* It is uncertain as to what this nickname means, but it appears to stem from the state's turbulent history during a time of political conflict. Persons who fought to make Kansas a free, rather than a slave, state were called Jayhawkers. This violence over the slavery issue in Kansas attracted nationwide attention and the area become known as *Bleeding Kansas.*

Most of present-day Kansas was part of the territory known as the Louisana Purchase, which France sold to the United States in 1803. Its first permanent white settlement was Fort Leavenworth. The fort, near Leavenworth, Kansas, now houses the U.S. Army Command and Leavenworth Prison. In 1861, Kansas became the 34th state admitted to the Union.

During the 1860's and 1870's, railroads were influential in Kansas' development. They provided transportation for settlers coming into the state and for products going out. Cattle drives began from Texas to Kansas railroad towns. The towns, cattle trails, and people of Kansas' past have provided the state with a colorful history. Books, TV, and motion pictures have made famous now-familiar names such as: Wyatt Earp, Wild Bill Hickok, and Bat Masterson—lawmen known for taming the wild Kansas "cow towns"; Chisholm, Western, and Santa Fe trails—famous cattle trails; and Abilene, Dodge City, and Wichita—prominent Kansas cow towns.

As the railroad reached Texas, the cattle drives ended, since ranchers no longer needed to drive their cattle to Kansas towns. But visitors can still see wagon ruts on the Santa Fe Trail, and Front Street, the colorful main street of Dodge City, is still a popular tourist attraction.

Wichita is now Kansas' largest city; Topeka is its capital. Abilene is the boyhood home of President Dwight D. Eisenhower. His mementos and papers are housed in the Eisenhower Library and Museum there.

The annual fairs and rodeos held throughout the state are reminiscent of the western farm background of Kansas. Hutchinson is the site of the Kansas State Fair and the Mid-America Fair is staged in Topeka, both in mid-September. In Hanover, travelers enjoy visiting Hollenberg Station, the only station on the pony express route that looks as it did in the early 1860's.

Other Kansas sites of interest to travelers might be the Chalk Beds in Gove and Trego counties, containing the fossilized remains of many prehistoric animals; Fort Riley, near Junction City, a famous cavalry center and site of General George A. Custer's home; John Brown Memorial State Park in Osawatomie, which marks the site of an early slavery battle and houses Brown's cabin; and Fort Larned, which is a fort built to protect travelers on the Santa Fe Trail.

Wichita originally flourished as a cow town along the shores of the Arkansas River. Today, it is a modern, industrialized area and Kansas' largest city (above top).

Wheat storage elevators in Haven break the stark horizon of the Kansas plains (above bottom).

Kansas
Sunflower State

Capital: Topeka
Area: 82,264 sq. mi. (213,063 km²), including 477 sq. mi. (1,235 km²) of inland water; 14th in size among the states
Elevation: *Highest*—Mount Sunflower, 4,039 ft. (1,231 m) above sea level; *lowest*—680 ft. (207 m) above sea level, along the Verdigris River in Montgomery County
Statehood: Jan. 29, 1861, the 34th state
Abbreviations: Kans. or Kan. (traditional); KS (postal)
Motto: *Ad Astra per Aspera* (To the Stars Through Difficulties)
Song: "Home on the Range"
Tree: Cottonwood

Kansas' state seal shows the rising sun representing the East, from which most Kansas settlers came. The buffalo, log cabin, riverboat, wagons, and the farmer plowing suggest the region's early history. The seal was adopted in 1861. To represent the Louisiana Purchase, the state flag, adopted in 1927, has a wreath above an adaptation of the seal. The yellow sunflower stands for the state's prairies and for the golden future.

KANSAS Political Map

Legend:
- State capital
- Urban area in Kansas
- Urban area outside Kansas
- City or town
- County seat
- FORD County name / County boundary
- State boundary
- Park or other recreation area
- Forest or other conservation area
- Military or other federal area
- Indian reservation
- Point of interest
- Major airport
- Water
- River
- Intermittent river
- Intermittent lake
- Highways: Expressway; Other road; 35 Interstate; 77 U.S.; 7 Other

Lambert conformal conic projection
WORLD BOOK map © Field Enterprises Educational Corporation

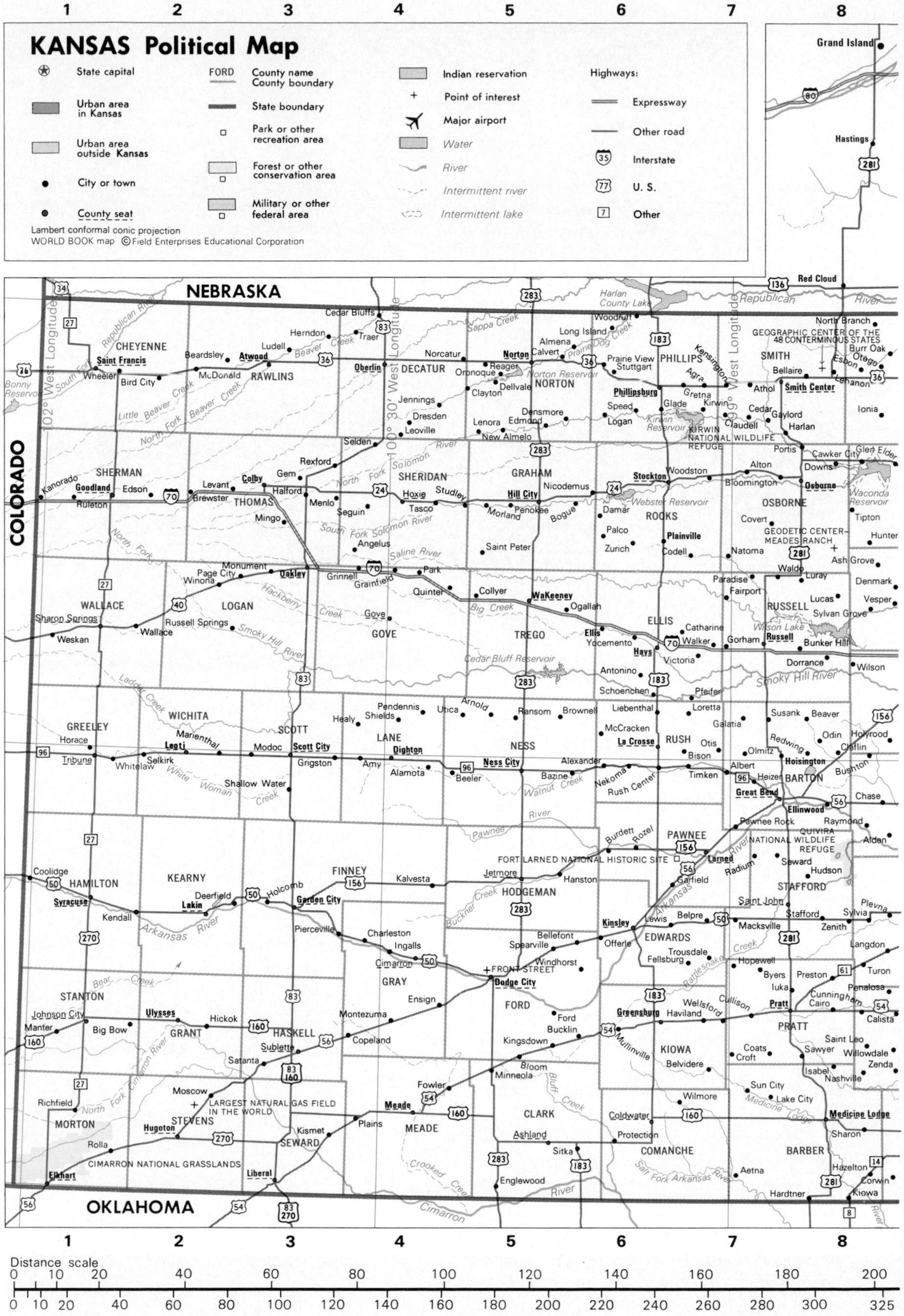

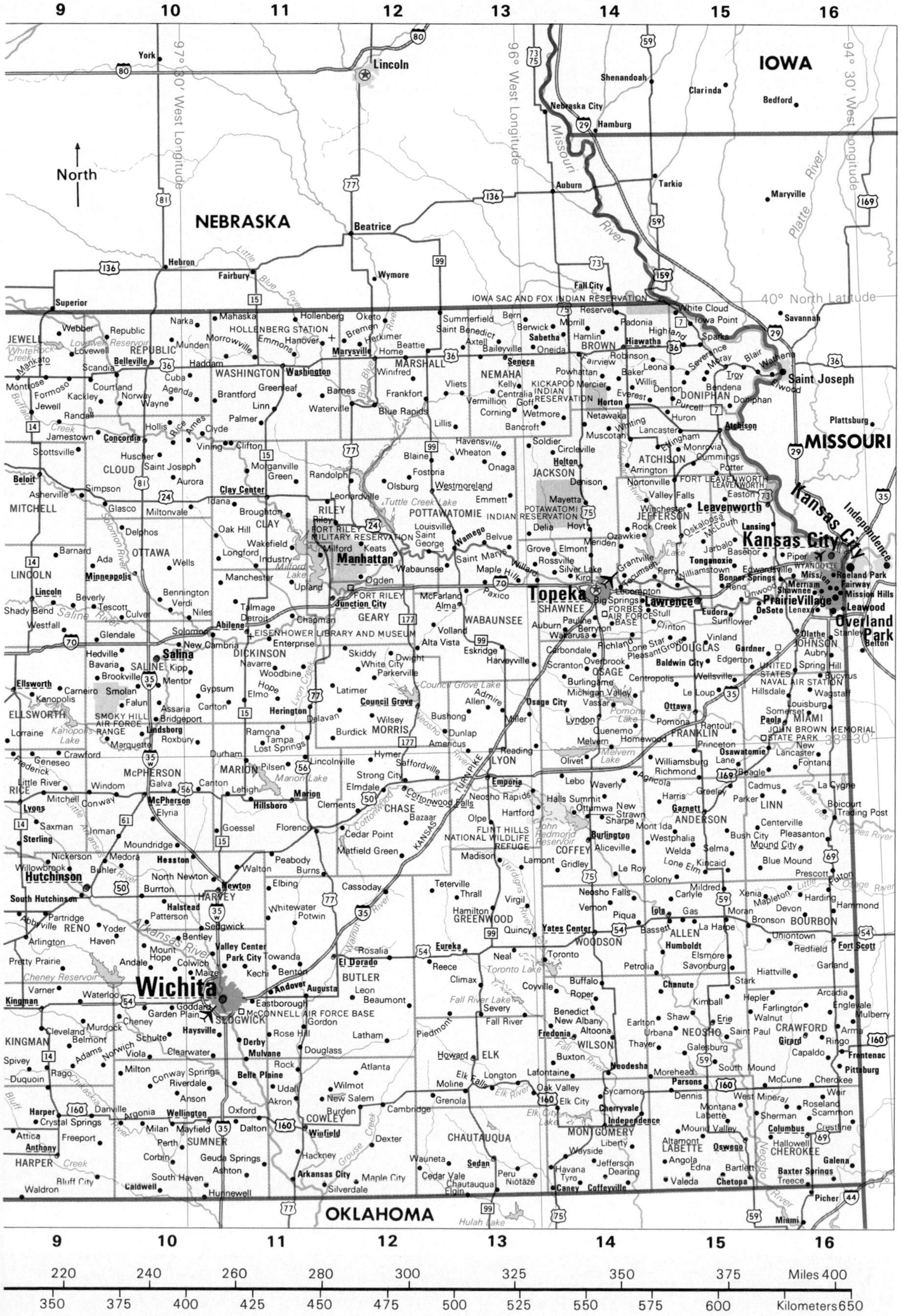

Seal

Flag

Bird: Western Meadow Lark

Flower: Sunflower

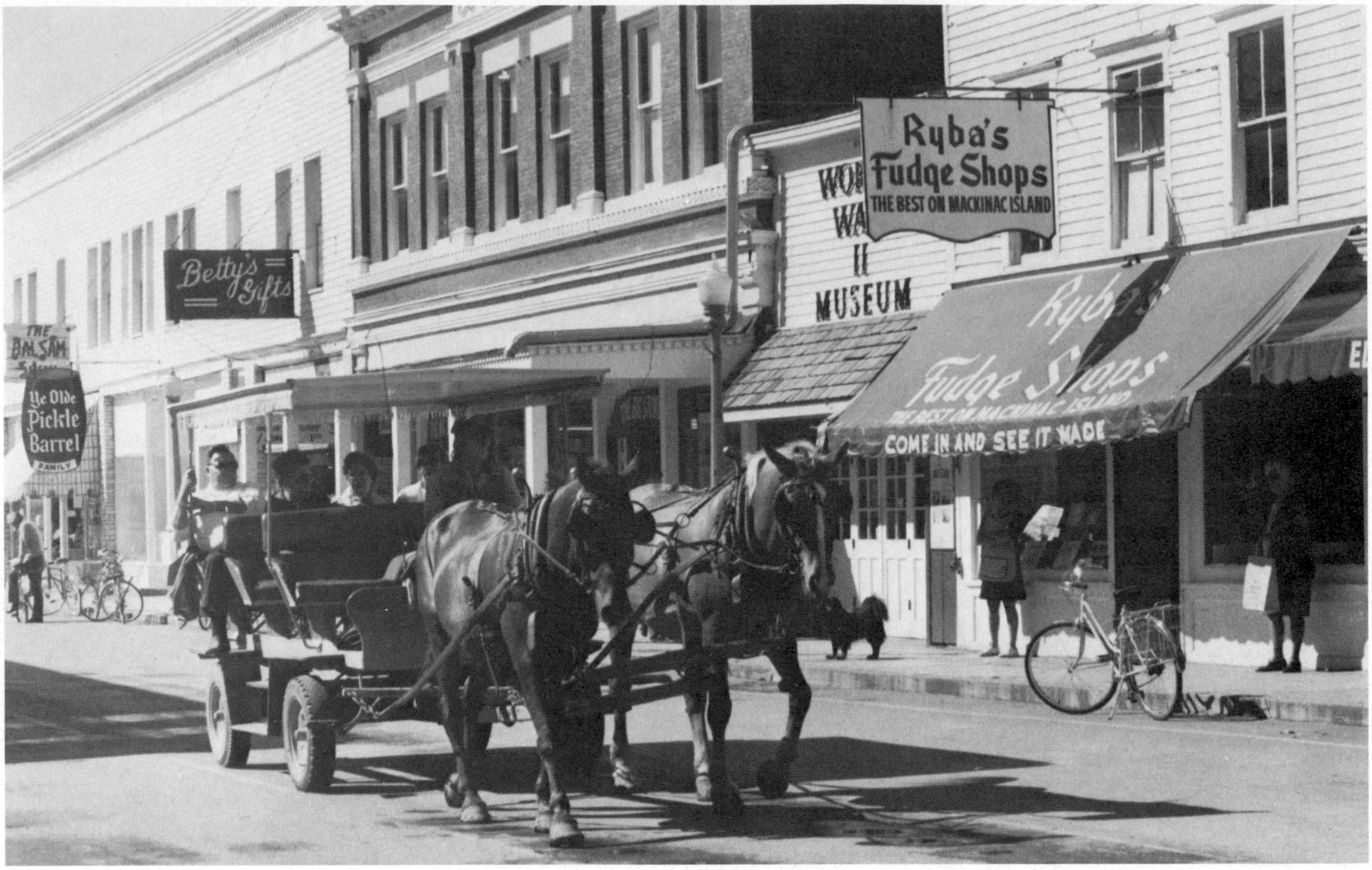

The serenity of a long-gone era persists on Mackinac Island, a resort where automobiles are forbidden.

Michigan

Michigan is well known as the center of automobile manufacturing in the United States. The manufacture of transportation equipment accounts for about a third of the state's manufacturing income and employs about a fourth of all industrial workers in Michigan. Detroit, the state's largest city, is called the *Automobile Capital of the World* and *Motor City.* A number of other Michigan cities also produce automobiles, but Detroit has been an automotive center since the 1890's. Henry Ford built his first workable automobile in Detroit in 1896. In 1899, Ranson E. Olds established the state's first automobile factory there.

In addition to automobile production, Michigan has other claims to manufacturing fame. Battle Creek is called the *Cereal Center of the World* because of its huge output of cereal products. Fremont has the nation's largest baby food factory, and Muskegon has the largest U.S. plant for the manufacture of bowling alley equipment.

Michigan also ranks among the leading states in its agricultural and mineral output. Its orchards produce more cherries than those of any other state. It also ranks high in apples, pears, strawberries, dry beans, and celery. One of the world's greatest iron ore regions lies in Michigan and neighboring Wisconsin. Michigan's rich copper deposits have been supplying ore for thousands of years. Indians were the first copper miners in Michigan, fashioning tools from the valuable metal.

The city of Detroit stands atop one of the world's huge salt deposits. Michigan probably has enough salt to satisfy the entire world demand for a million years. The world's biggest limestone quarry is in Michigan. The state ranks first in U.S. production of gypsum, peat, and magnesium.

Water is probably Michigan's single most valuable resource. The state was named for Lake Michigan. Chippewa Indians originally named the lake Michigama, meaning "great lake" or "large lake." Michigan accurately calls itself a *Water Wonderland,* one of its popular names. It has more water within its boundaries than any other state in the nation. Michigan touches four of the five Great Lakes and has the longest shoreline of any inland state.

In addition to the Great Lakes, there are more than 11,000 smaller lakes in Michigan. Michigan territory actually consists of two separate masses of land divided by water. The Mackinac Bridge over the Straits of Mackinac links the Upper Peninsula and Lower Peninsula of Michigan.

For millions of Americans, Michigan means vacationland. The state has over 13,000 campgrounds—more than any other state. Many of its Lake Michigan beaches are swept by vast dunes, with sand covering the tops of trees in some areas. One of the largest dunes, Sleeping Bear Dune, has sand so fine people can ski down it in the summer. Mackinac Island, a famous resort in the Straits of Mackinac, forbids automobiles. People travel in horse-and-buggies, on foot, or by bicycle on this tranquil island. Iron Mountain has one of the highest artificial ski jumps in the world.

Michigan's Upper Peninsula has about 150 waterfalls. Tahquamenon Falls are among the most picturesque. The American poet Henry Wadsworth Longfellow wrote about them in his poem *The Song of Hiawatha.* Longfellow's poem gave the Upper Peninsula its nickname—the *Land of Hiawatha.*

In the Lake Superior waters north of the Upper Peninsula lies Isle Royale, a national park that includes about 200 islands. One of the country's largest remaining herds of great-antlered moose lives in the park.

Michigan's waterways provided easy means of transportation for the various Indian tribes who lived in the region before white settlers arrived. The first whites were French explorers and missionaries, who traveled about in canoes. Father Jacques Marquette founded the first permanent settlement in the area at Sault Ste. Marie in 1668. After the city's founding, the French kept control of the Michigan region for nearly 100 years before the British defeated them in the French and Indian War. The British made the Michigan area part of Quebec. After the Revolutionary War, the region was turned over to U.S. control. The British were reluctant, however, completely to give up their valuable fur-trading centers at Detroit and Fort Mackinac. They didn't surrender those settlements to the Americans until 1796. Michigan entered the Union as the 26th state in 1837.

The fur trade that first made Michigan such a valuable prize eventually gave the state its official nickname, the *Wolverine State.* Wolverine pelts were among the many precious furs that trappers offered for sale. Even today, Michigan has many kinds of wild fur-bearing animals, including bears, minks, muskrats, raccoons, and red foxes.

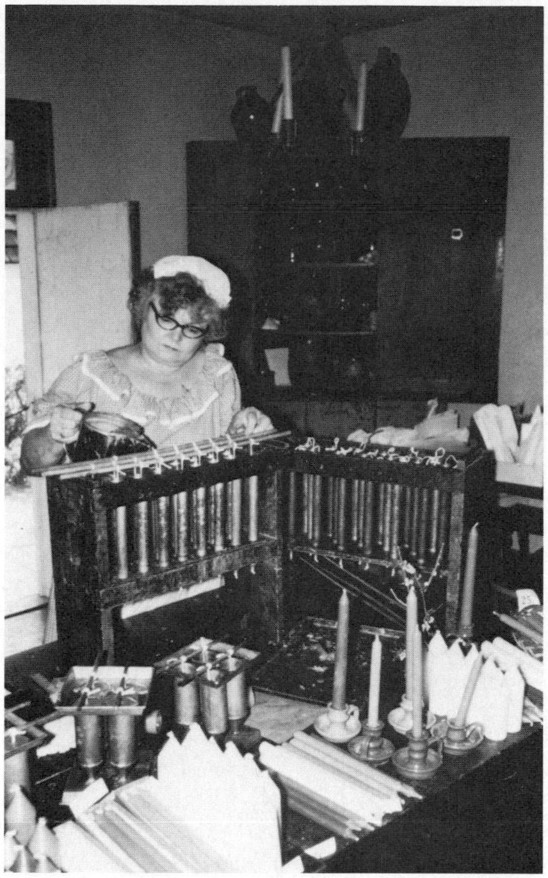

Greenfield Village in Dearborn recreates a colonial community, complete with a candle-making shop.

Holland, Mich., is known as the tulip capital of the United States. During the annual mid-May Tulip Festival, people from around the world visit this colorful city.

Michigan
Wolverine State

Capital: Lansing
Area: 58,216 sq. mi. (150,779 km²), including 1,399 sq. mi. (3,623 km²) of inland water but excluding 38,575 sq. mi. (99,909 km²) of Lakes Erie, Huron, Michigan, St. Clair, and Superior; 23rd in size among the states
Elevation: *Highest*—Mt. Curwood, 1,980 ft. (604 m) above sea level; *lowest*—572 ft. (174 m) above sea level along Lake Erie
Statehood: Jan. 26, 1837, the 26th state
Abbreviations: Mich. (traditional); MI (postal)
Motto: *Si Quaeris Peninsulam Amoenam, Circumspice* (If You Seek a Pleasant Peninsula, Look About You)
Song: "Michigan, My Michigan" (unofficial)
Tree: White Pine

The shield on Michigan's state seal shows the sun rising over water and a man in a field. An elk and a moose support the shield. These symbols represent Michigan's wealth, resources, and people. An eagle above the shield symbolizes the superior authority and jurisdiction of the U.S. Government over state governments. The Latin word Tuebor means "I will defend." The seal was adopted in 1835. The state flag, adopted in 1911, has a reproduction of the state seal.

MICHIGAN Political Map

State capital
Urban area in Michigan
Urban area outside Michigan
City or town
County seat
IRON County name
County boundary
State boundary
Park or other recreation area
Forest or other conservation area
Military or other federal area

Indian reservation
Point of interest
Major airport
Water
River

Highways:
Expressway
Other road
75 Interstate
10 U.S.
21 Other
Trans-Canada

Lambert conformal conic projection
WORLD BOOK map © Field Enterprises Educational Corporation

Distance scale for inset map
0 5 10   20   30   40   50   60   70   80   90   100 Miles 110
0 5 10 20 30 40 50 60 70 80 90 100 110 120 130 140 150 160 Kilometers 180

Distance scale for Michigan map
0 20 60 100 150 200 250 300 Miles
0 20 60 100 150 200 250 300 350 400 450 Kilometers

Seal

Flag

Bird: Robin

Flower: Apple Blossom

Minnesota

From the Crystal Court—a shopping arcade at the base of the IDS Center in downtown Minneapolis—pedestrians may walk in glass-enclosed skyways to other city blocks.

The word *Minnesota* comes from two Sioux Indian words that mean "sky-tinted waters." This name is most appropriate for the state because Minnesota has thousands of clear, blue inland lakes. The largest lake in Minnesota is Red Lake. It covers 430 square miles (1,110 square kilometers). Lake Itasca, located in the north-central part of the state, is the source of the Mississippi River. The Mississippi is just a small stream when it flows out of the lake. By the time the Mississippi River reaches St. Paul, it is a wide, deep river that can accommodate the numerous barges that carry products to and from Minnesota.

Minnesota's many clear, blue lakes make it one of America's favorite vacationlands, to which boaters, water skiers, and swimmers are attracted yearly. A large variety of game fish can be found in abundance in the cool northern waters. Hunters can find many kinds of game animals in the dense forests that surround the lakes. The state has many parks and forests to accommodate campers and hikers as well. Among these are Voyageurs National Park in northern Minnesota and Superior National Forest in the northeast. Other popular parklands include, on the northwestern shore of Lake Superior, Grand Portage National Monument, which marks the site of a historic canoe route and trading post; and, in southwestern Minnesota, Pipestone National Monument, where Indians once made peace pipes from the red pipestone found there.

Minnesota is also the home of beautiful waterfalls. The highest that is entirely within the state is Cascade Falls on the Cascade River. Minnehaha Falls on the Minnehaha Creek is located in Minneapolis. This waterfall was made famous in the poem *The Song of Hiawatha* by Henry Wadsworth Longfellow. High Falls, another famous Minnesota waterfall, is located along the Minnesota-Ontario border on the Pigeon River.

Minnesota is one of America's largest producers of food. Its chief crops include corn, potatoes, soybeans, and sugar beets. One of Minnesota's most important industries is the processing of its farm products.

Minnesota is often called the *Bread and Butter State.* It received this nickname because of its wheat crops, flour mills, and dairy products. More butter is made in Minnesota than in any other state. Milk and cheese are also important products.

Minnesota farmers raise many beef cattle and hogs, and Minnesota is one of the nation's leading meat-packing states. Southern Minnesota is also the site of many large poultry processing plants.

Mining is an important source of Minnesota's income as well. The world's largest open-pit iron mine, Hull-Rush-Mahoning Mine, is located near Hibbing. The four iron-ore ranges in Minnesota produce about 70 per cent of the total iron ore mined in the United States.

Forests cover a large percentage of the land in Minnesota, and lumber production has always been an important industry to Minnesotans. Lumbertown, U.S.A., located in Brainerd, is a reconstruction of a typical early logging town. In Bemidji, huge statues of Paul Bunyan and Babe, his giant blue ox, can be viewed. Paul Bunyan, a giant lumberjack, is a great legendary character in American folklore. Legend has it that Paul Bunyan invented logging and that he scooped out the Great Lakes to provide drinking water for Babe.

Minnesota winters are long and cold, making the weather ideal for winter sports and various other winter activities. Ice fishing on many of the frozen lakes is a popular sport during the winter months in Minnesota. The Victorian Christmas Fair is held in Minneapolis during November and December. The St. Paul Winter Carnival begins during the last week in January. Featured activities include ice-skating races, ski-jumping contests, and snowmobile races. Every January, sled-dog races are held in Ely, and there is a winter carnival in Bemidji. The Red River Valley Winter Show is an annual February event in Crookston.

Aside from all of its natural beauty, Minnesota also has some interesting cities. St. Paul is the capital of Minnesota, and Minneapolis is its largest city. This booming twin-city metropolis provides visitors and residents with a multitude of varied activities. For those with cultural interests, the Guthrie Theater is a popular spot. This strikingly designed playhouse has a permanent company of actors that perform a series of plays in repertory every year. The Walker Art Center is another popular tourist attraction and contains one of the country's finest collections of modern art. A famous historical site near Minneapolis is Fort Snelling, a restored military post built in the 1820's. Here, visitors can view demonstrations dealing with military life of that period.

Rochester is the home of the Mayo Clinic, founded in 1889 by William Worall Mayo and his sons, William James and Charles Horace Mayo. The clinic's original purpose was to care for surgical patients. It is now one of the greatest medical research centers in the world. The medical center has cared for about 3 million patients since its founding. Tours of the medical center are available, and the Mayo Medical Museum in Rochester is also an interesting tourist attraction.

Vacationers hop from rock to rock in Itasca State Park, where the mighty Mississippi begins its course south as a peaceful stream (above).

At Duluth, the St. Louis River meets Lake Superior. This aerial lift bridge rises much like an elevator to allow the passage of tall vessels through a ship canal (left).

Minnesota
Gopher State

Capital: St. Paul
Area: 84,068 sq. mi. (217,735 km²), including 4,799 sq. mi. (12,378 km²) of inland water but excluding 2,212 sq. mi. (5,729 km²) of Lake Superior; 12th in size among the states
Elevation: *Highest*—Eagle Mountain, 2,301 ft. (701 m) above sea level in Cook County; *lowest*—602 ft. (183 m) above sea level along Lake Superior
Statehood: May 11, 1858, the 32nd state
Abbreviations: Minn. (traditional); MN (postal)
Motto: *L'Etoile du Nord* (Star of the North)
Song: "Hail! Minnesota"
Tree: Norway (Red) Pine

Minnesota's state seal shows an Indian riding into the sunset and a farmer who symbolize the white settlers' rise and the Indians' decline in the state's pioneer days. The waterfall and the forest represent Minnesota's natural features. The seal was adopted in 1858. The present state flag, adopted in 1957, has an adaptation of the seal and 19 stars. The stars symbolize Minnesota's entry into the Union as the 19th state after the original 13 states. The date 1819 is that of the establishment of Fort Snelling. The year 1893 is when the state flag was adopted that showed the basic symbol retained in the 1957 flag.

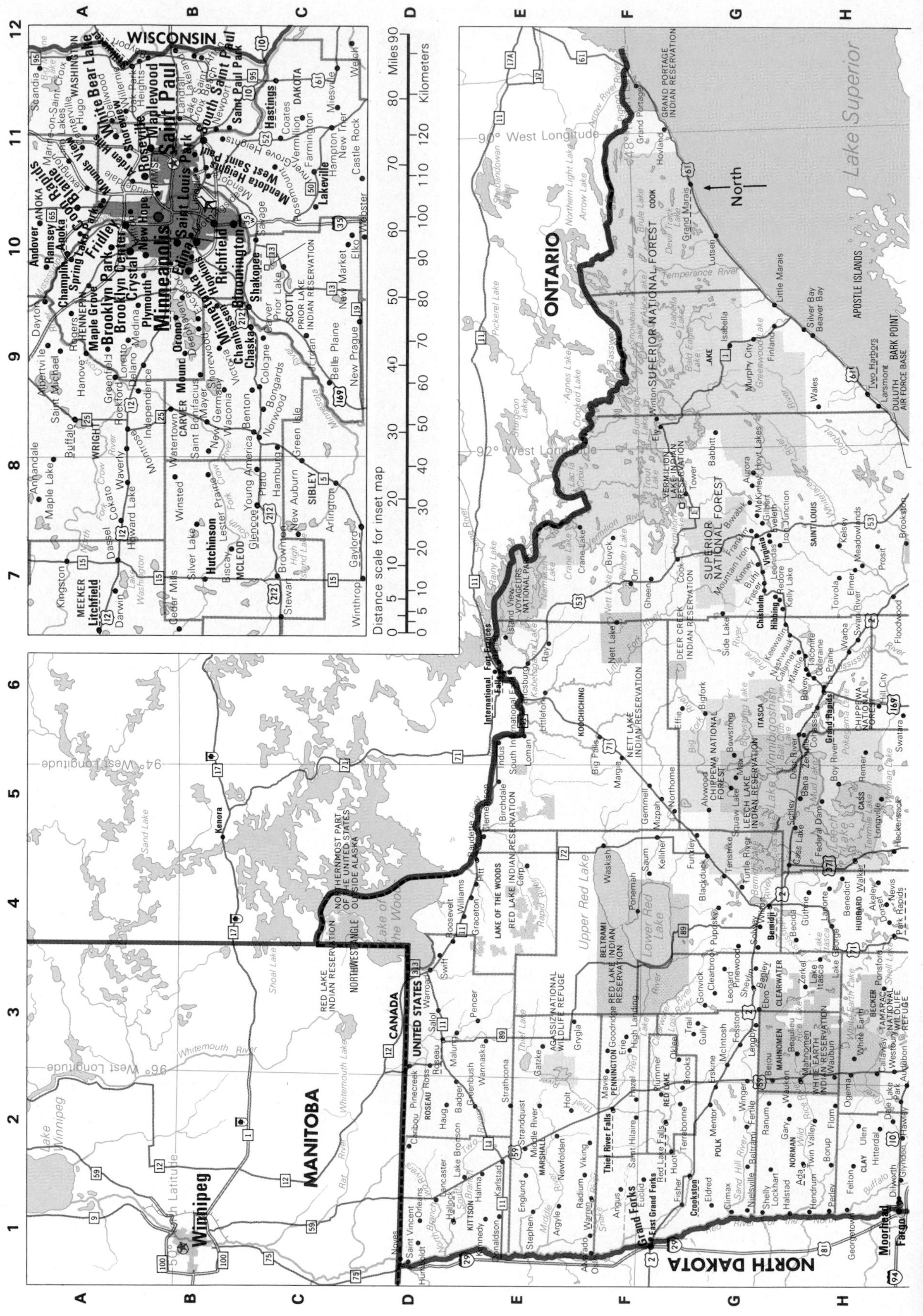

MINNESOTA
Political Map

⊛ State capital
+ Point of interest
✈ Major airport

Urban area in Minnesota
Urban area outside Minnesota
● City or town
● County seat

Water
River
Waterway
Intermittent river

PINE County name
County boundary
State boundary

Highways:
Expressway
Other road

🛡54 Interstate
⬡26 U.S.
▢17 Other
⬡ Trans Canada

Park or other recreation area
Forest or other conservation area
Military or other federal area
Indian reservation

Lambert conformal conic projection
WORLD BOOK map
© Field Enterprises Educational Corporation

Distance scale for Minnesota map

Miles   Kilometers

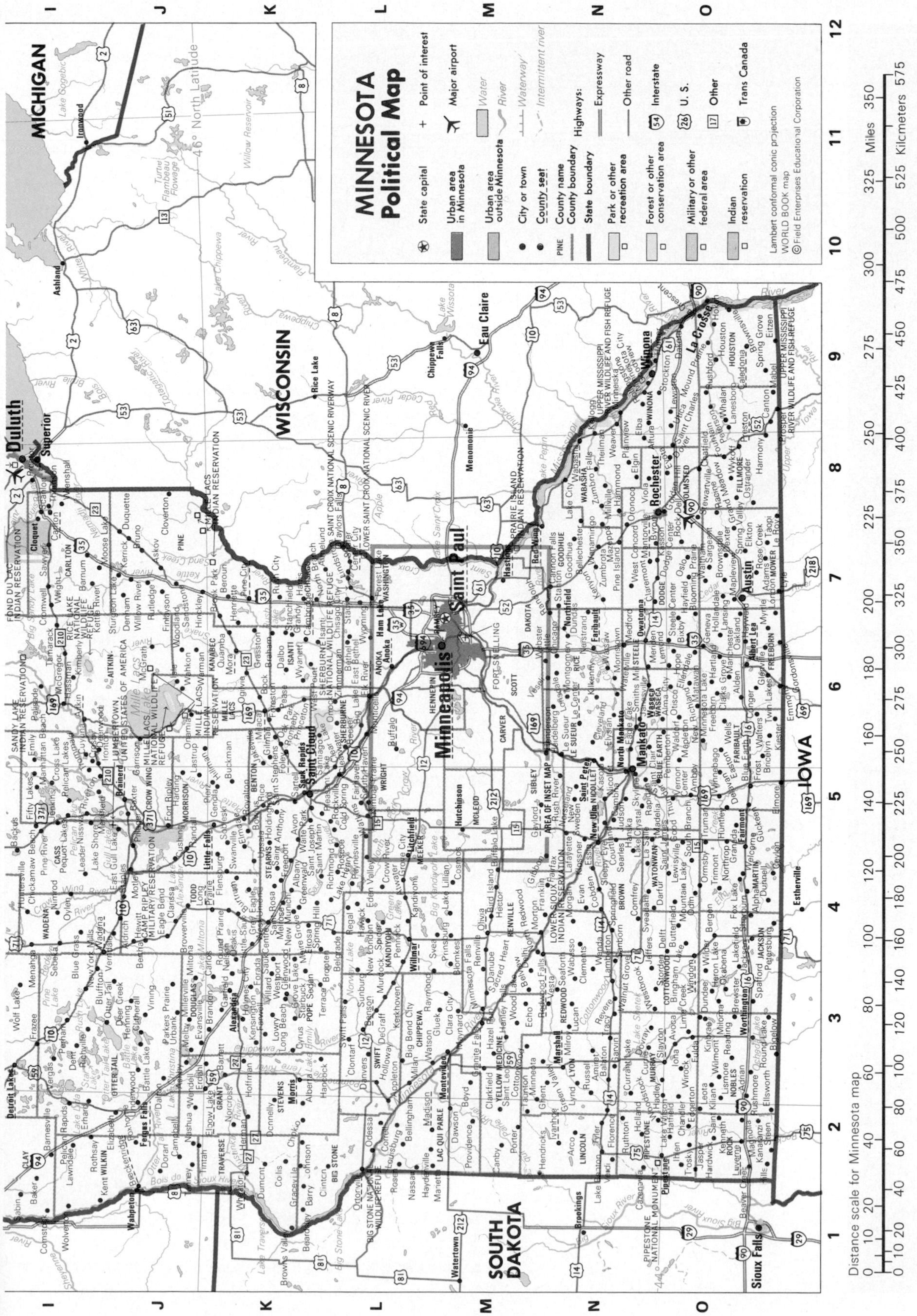

Seal

Flag

Bird: Common Loon

Flower: Pink and White Lady's-Slipper

MICHIGAN

WISCONSIN

IOWA

SOUTH DAKOTA

Duluth
Superior
Saint Paul
Minneapolis
Saint Cloud
Rochester
Mankato
Austin
Winona
La Crosse
Eau Claire
Chippewa Falls

Rocks that the forces of nature have carved into bizarre formations lie strewn in Elephant Rocks State Park in southeastern Missouri (above top).

At the foot of Cardiff Hill in Hannibal stands a life-sized memorial to Tom Sawyer and Huckleberry Finn, beloved characters immortalized by Mark Twain (above bottom).

Missouri

In part, Missouri owes its successful development as an important commercial and industrial state to its two great rivers, the Mississippi and the Missouri—the largest rivers in the United States. These rivers and their branches provide water highways for transportation, water supplies for cities and industries, and hydroelectric power for homes and factories.

The Missouri River flows across the state from west to east. The Mississippi River forms Missouri's eastern border and is a favorite waterway for sightseeing trips on old-time stern-wheel boats. The presence of these two great rivers, coupled with Missouri's geographic location, has made the state a center of water, land, and air transportation. Two of Missouri's large cities, St. Louis and Kansas City, are famous as important air, rail, and trucking centers.

Important products manufactured in Missouri include transportation equipment, food products, shoes, chemicals, and machinery. Missouri is also a leader among agricultural states. Soybeans are its leading crop with corn ranking second. Livestock, including dairy cows, beef cattle, hogs, and chickens, provides a profitable income for the state. As a mining state, Missouri produces more lead than any other state.

Missouri is also a state of scenic beauty. The wooded plateau of southern Missouri, called the Ozarks, is a major vacation and recreation area of the Midwest. In its heart is the Lake of the Ozarks, Missouri's largest lake. Entirely artificial, it has a shoreline of more than 1,300 miles (2,092 kilometers) and covers about 60,000 acres (24,281 hectares). The Current River, also in the Ozarks, is one of Missouri's most beautiful rivers.

Besides beautiful, rushing waterways, the Ozarks is also famous for over 1,450 caves formed by underground streams. Marvel Cave, near Branson, is one of the largest and contains an underground railroad winding through its 10 miles (16 kilometers). Bridal Cave, near Camdenton, is the site of about 20 marriages a year. And Meramec Caverns, near Sullivan, is the legendary hideout of the outlaw Jesse James.

Because it once lay at the gateway to the western frontier, Missouri is sometimes called the *Mother of the West.* The historic Santa Fe and Oregon trails both began at Independence, Missouri. The Gateway Arch in St. Louis, the tallest monument constructed in the United States, commemorates westward expansion and St. Louis' role in the settlement of the West. Silver Dollar City, near Branson, is a reconstruction of an early mining town. Craft-

At the Missouri Botanical Garden in St. Louis, a reflecting pool frames the geodesic dome Climatron, a greenhouse where tropical plants thrive.

workers demonstrate the skills and culture depicting life in those historic times.

Many varied Indian tribes inhabited the Missouri region long before white people arrived. Prehistoric Indians known as Mound Builders built large earthwork mounds still visible in several areas of the state. Other tribes included the Missouri, the Osage, the Fox, and the Sauk. The state is named for the Missouri River, but the word *Missouri* most likely came from an Indian word meaning the "town of the large canoes."

Present-day Missouri was part of the Louisiana Territory sold to the United States by France in the transaction known as the Louisiana Purchase. Because of the region's great waterways, it was an important fur-trading area during its early settlement.

Many famous Americans have lived in Missouri. Harry S. Truman, the 33rd President of the United States, was born in Lamar and spent his childhood years in Independence. His birthplace and the Harry S. Truman Library can be viewed in those two towns, respectively. Mark Twain, famous author and humorist, and creator of Tom Sawyer and Huckleberry Finn, grew up in Hannibal, Missouri. His home and museum, the legendary cave in which Tom Sawyer and Becky Thatcher became lost, and other spots made famous in his writings can be toured in Hannibal.

Other famous Missourians include Eugene Field, children's poet; General John J. Pershing, commander of U.S. forces in Europe during World War I; Joseph Pulitzer, famous journalist; George Washington Carver, celebrated black scientist; and Thomas Hart Benton and George Caleb Bingham, noted painters.

Missouri's capital is Jefferson City and its largest city is St. Louis. It has as its nickname the *Show Me State.* This tag has been traced to a Missouri politician who said in a speech in 1899, ". . . frothy eloquence neither convinces nor satisfies me. I am from Missouri. You have got to show me."

Missouri
Show Me State

Capital: Jefferson City
Area: 69,686 sq. mi. (180,486 km²), including 691 sq. mi. (1,790 km²) of inland water; 19th in size among the states
Elevation: *Highest*—Taum Sauk Mountain, 1,772 ft. (540 m) above sea level; *lowest*—230 ft. (70 m) above sea level, along the St. Francis River near Cardwell
Statehood: Aug. 10, 1821, the 24th state
Abbreviations: Mo. (traditional); MO (postal)
Motto: *Salus Populi Suprema Lex Esto* (The Welfare of the People Shall Be the Supreme Law)
Song: "Missouri Waltz"
Tree: Flowering Dogwood

Missouri's state seal, adopted in 1822, shows two grizzly bears representing the state. They hold shields of the United States and Missouri to show that the state supports itself and the Union. A helmet symbolizes enterprise and hardiness. Stars show that Missouri was the 24th state in the Union. The Roman numerals give the date (1820) that Missouri's first constitution was adopted. The state flag, adopted in 1913, has an adaptation of the seal.

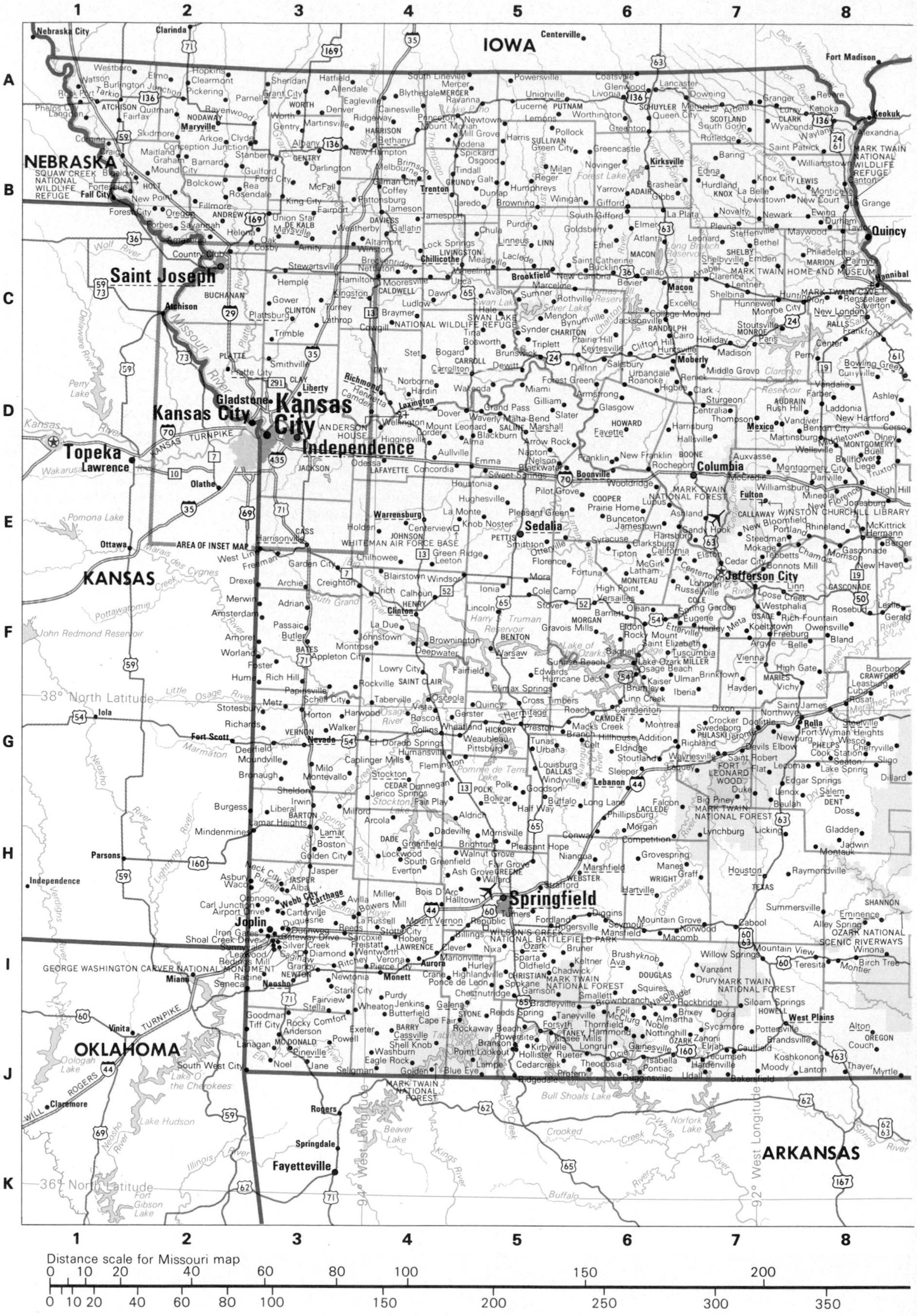

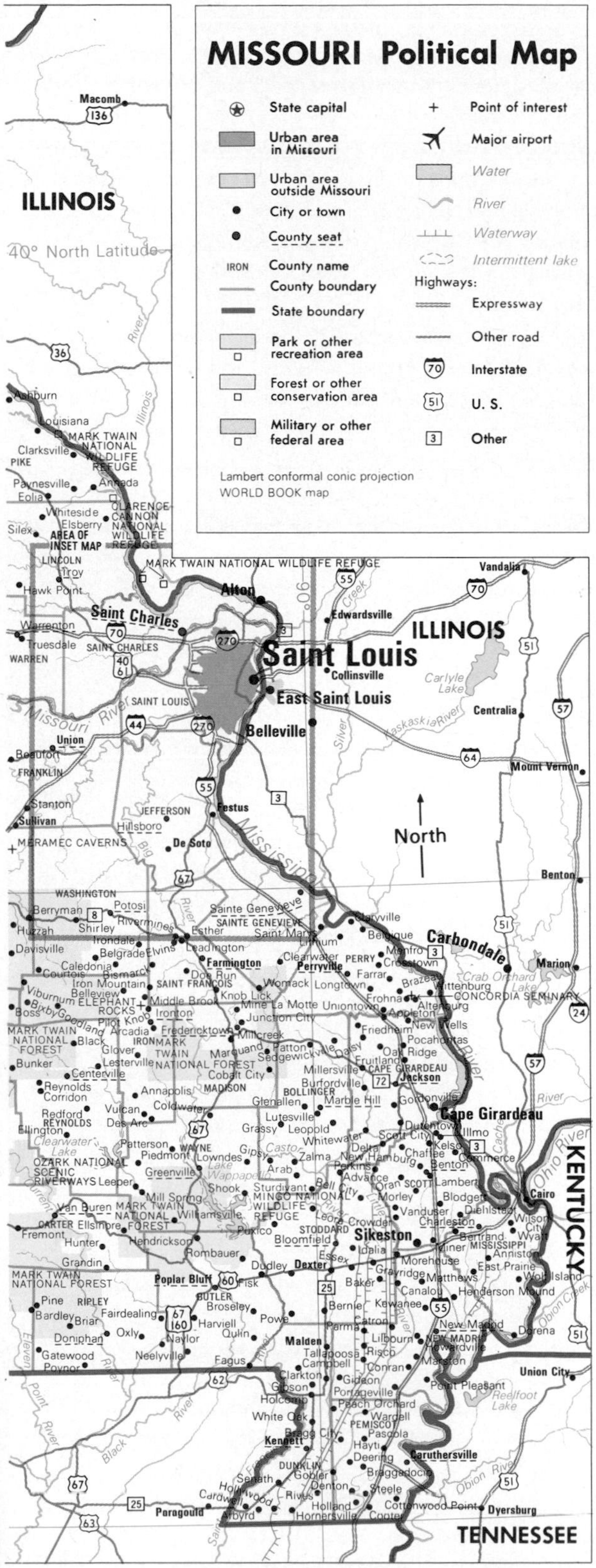

13 14 15 16

Distance scale for inset maps

0 5 10 20 30 40 50 Miles

0 5 10 20 30 40 50 60 70 Kilometers

250 300 Miles 350

400 450 500 Kilometers 550

Seal

Flag

Bird: Bluebird

Flower: Hawthorn

A landmark of the Oregon Trail, Chimney Rock stood like a beacon as pioneers trudged past in their covered wagons.

Nebraska

The Oregon Trail winds through Nebraska, entering at the state's southeastern border and traveling in a northwesterly course to Fort Kearny and up the Platte River. As pioneers began following the Oregon Trail westward in the early 1840's, some of them settled in Nebraska. In the 1860's, the area's population increased more when government land grants lured many homesteaders to the area to claim free land.

Nebraska once was considered part of the "Great American Desert." Much of the land was flat and dry and not much could be grown there. Life, therefore, was not easy for the early settlers. Summers were hot and dry and winters were cold and brutal.

Most of the early settlers built their homes out of Nebraska sod because there were few trees growing on the flat, grassy land. In the spring, blossoming sod plants decorated the houses with flowers. Many of the farmers' early crops failed, but the determined settlers planted more. Their hard work did much to help make Nebraska what it is today.

Many settlers came from heavily wooded eastern states. They missed the trees and so they started programs to plant trees in Nebraska. J. Sterling Morton originated the idea of Arbor Day, a day set aside each year for planting trees. Nebraska was the first state to celebrate Arbor Day. Morton's home, Arbor Lodge, in Nebraska City is a popular point of interest. It is a 52-room mansion built in 1855 as a 4-room house and then enlarged several times.

Today Nebraska is one of the leading farming states in America. Farmers grow wheat, corn, and soybeans in the eastern and south-central sections. The large amount of corn grown in the state and the annual fall cornhusking contests once held in many rural communities have given Nebraska its official nickname, the *Cornhusker State.* Huge herds of beef cattle also graze on large ranches in the Sand Hills region north of the Platte River in the Great Plains.

Nebraska was much a part of the historic Old West. Pony Express riders rode through Nebraska on the Oregon Trail as they carried mail from Missouri to California. Buffalo Bill fought Indians on the Platte River and later formed a traveling wild west circus with headquarters near North Platte. Buffalo Bill's home, where his wild west circus rehearsed, still stands near North Platte.

Throughout the years many dams have been built in Nebraska to provide water for livestock and irrigation. The building of dams created many artificial lakes. Nebraska's largest, Lake McConaughy, was formed on the North Platte River when Kingsley Dam was built. Other large artificial lakes in Nebraska include Johnson, Swanson, Harlan County, and Harry Strunk lakes. There are also hundreds of small natural lakes and swift-moving streams in the Sand Hills region.

Nebraska offers its visitors a great variety of sights and activities. Each year thousands of tourists visit this state. They travel the historic Oregon Trail, where ruts left by the Conestoga wagons of the early pioneers can still be seen along the roadside.

Campers and hikers enjoy the forests and rugged rocks of the Pine Ridge in western Nebraska. People who enjoy fishing can catch bass, pike, and other game fish in the lakes and streams of the Sand Hills region. Hunters can find pheasants and quail in the prairie grasses of the Great Plains.

June through September is a busy and happy time for Nebraskans and visitors alike. In June, a week-long celebration, Nebraskaland Days, takes place in North Platte. Activities during the week include old-time wild west shows and a rodeo. The Days of '56 Rodeo and Celebration is held in Ponca, and the Swedish Festival takes place in Stromsburg. From late June through early July, the Arrows to Aerospace Celebration is held in Bellevue. The Johnson Lake Regatta in Lexington, Old Mill Days in Neligh, and Oregon Trail Days in Gering all take place in July. In August, Nebraska's Biggest Rodeo is held in Burwell, and the Omaha Pow Wow takes place in the town of Macy. The Nebraska State Fair is an annual September event in Lincoln. The fair features crop and livestock exhibits as well as exhibits of farm machinery and household equipment. Also in September are the Ak-Sar-Ben Livestock Show and Rodeo in Omaha, the Applejack Festival in Nebraska City, and Hay Days in Cozad.

Boys Town, near Omaha, is a famous home for neglected and homeless boys of all races and creeds. It was established in 1917 by Edward J. Flanagan, a Roman Catholic priest, who believed that boys would grow up to be useful adults if they were given the best possible home, education, and training. More than 14,000 boys have received care at Boys Town, Nebraska.

Other interesting sights throughout the state include Stuhr Museum of the Prairie Pioneer near Grand Island; Toadstool Park in the Badlands near Crawford; Bellevue, the oldest town in Nebraska; Chimney Rock National Historic Site near Bayard; and Lincoln, the state capital.

At the foot of Scotts Bluff National Monument is a noble memorial to the thousands who crossed Nebraska in their "prairie schooners" (below top).

John Brown's hatred of slavery carried the radical abolitionist to many parts of the United States in his struggle to rally support for his cause. John Brown's Cave in Nebraska commemorates this early proponent of civil rights, who died in 1859 (below bottom).

Nebraska
Cornhusker State

Capital: Lincoln
Area: 77,227 sq. mi. (200,017 km²), including 744 sq. mi. (1,927 km²) of inland water; 15th in size among the states
Elevation: *Highest*—5,426 ft. (1,654 m) above sea level in southwestern Kimball County; *lowest*—840 ft. (256 m) above sea level in Richardson County
Statehood: March 1, 1867, the 37th state
Abbreviations: Nebr. or Neb. (traditional); NE (postal)
Motto: *Equality Before the Law*
Song: "Beautiful Nebraska"
Tree: Cottonwood

Nebraska's state seal, adopted in 1867, shows a smith representing the mechanical arts. The settler's cabin, the growing corn, and the shocks of grain stand for agriculture. The steamboat and train symbolize transportation. The state flag, adopted in 1925, bears a silver and gold reproduction of the seal.

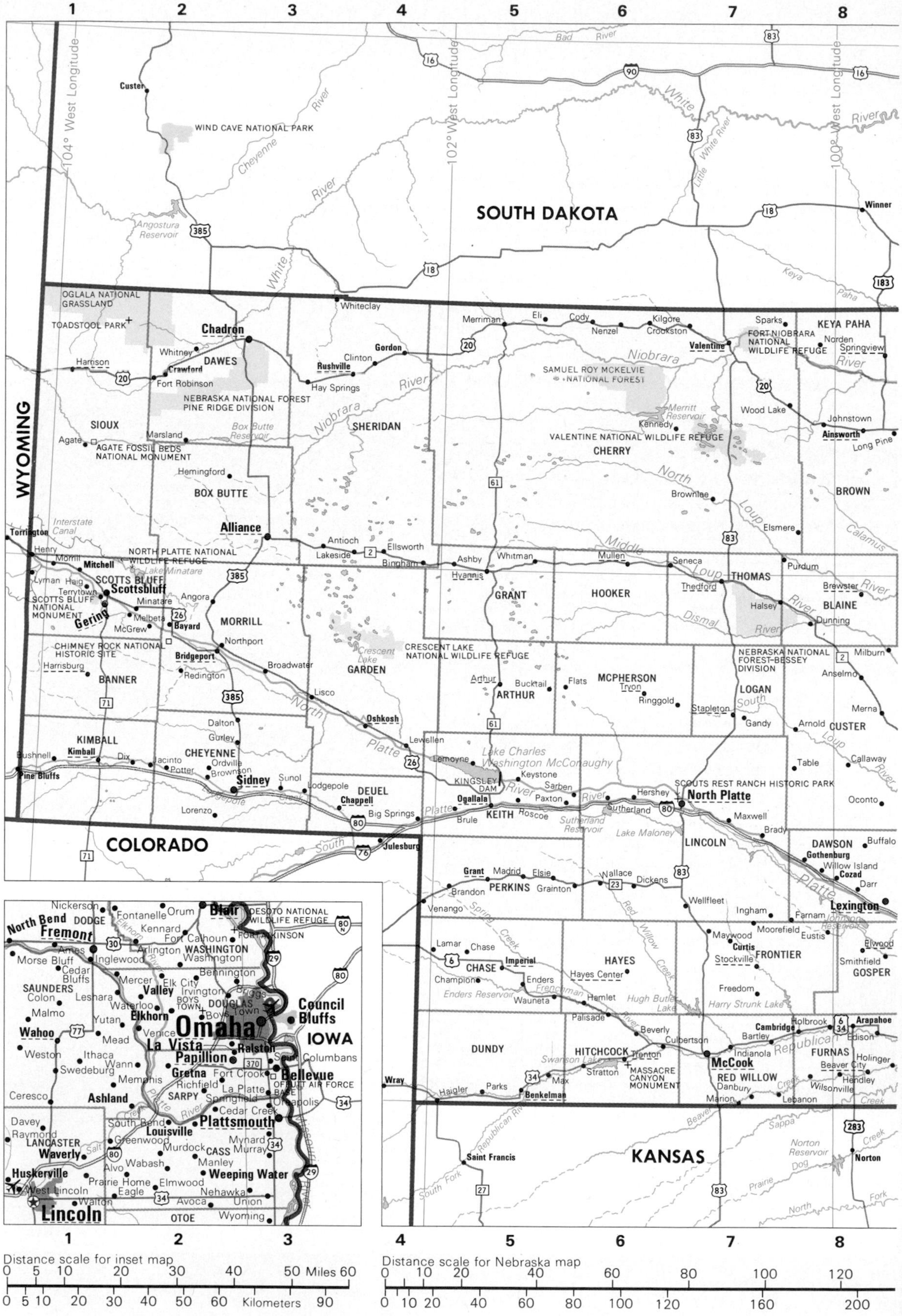

NEBRASKA Political Map
State capital
Urban area in Nebraska
Urban area outside Nebraska
City or town
County seat
POLK County name
County boundary
State boundary
Park or other recreation area
Forest or other conservation area
Military or other federal area
Indian reservation
Point of interest
Major airport
Water
River
Intermittent river
Intermittent lake
Highways:
Expressway
Other road
Interstate
U. S.
Other
Lambert conformal conic projection
WORLD BOOK map © Field Enterprises Educational Corporation
SOUTH DAKOTA
IOWA
KANSAS
MISSOURI
North
Omaha
Lincoln
Council Bluffs
Sioux City
Grand Island
Kearney
Hastings
Norfolk
Columbus
Fremont
Bellevue
Beatrice
Nebraska City
Fall City
Papillion
Plattsmouth
York
Seward
McCook
Holdrege
Wayne
Blair
SANTEE INDIAN RESERVATION
WINNEBAGO INDIAN RESERVATION
OMAHA INDIAN RESERVATION
IOWA, SAC AND FOX INDIAN RESERVATION
DESOTO NATIONAL WILDLIFE REFUGE
HOMESTEAD NATIONAL MONUMENT OF AMERICA
AREA OF INSET MAP
44° North Latitude
42° North Latitude
40° North Latitude
98°
96° West Longitude
Missouri River
Niobrara
Elkhorn River
Loup River
Platte River
Republican River
Big Blue River
160 200 240 280 320 Miles 360
240 280 320 360 400 440 480 520 Kilometers 560

GREAT SEAL OF THE STATE OF NEBRASKA
MARCH 1ST 1867
Seal

Flag

Bird: Western Meadow Lark

Flower: Goldenrod

North Dakota

North Dakota is a state with fertile farmland and an abundance of mineral resources. Farms and ranches stretch from the Red River Valley in the east to the Badlands in the west. North Dakota ranks among the nation's top producers of wheat, flaxseed, barley, and rye. Its economy depends more heavily on farming than that of any other state in the nation. Sheep are raised in North Dakota's southeastern counties and hogs in south and south-central areas, where corn is plentiful.

Petroleum was discovered in western North Dakota in 1951. Since then it has become the state's most valuable mineral. Southwestern North Dakota has great amounts of clay. Fine pottery, as well as common bricks, are made of North Dakota clay.

Western North Dakota has large lignite coal deposits. The most famous are the Burning Lignite Beds near Amidon, which have been burning for years. It is thought that they were probably set afire by lightning, prairie fires, or campfires.

In the early days of North Dakota's history, transportation to the area was poor. Few settlers—who were also afraid of Indians—went there. People began moving into North Dakota in the 1870's, when the Northern Pacific Railroad was being built across the Dakota Territory. Large wheat farms were established in the Red River Valley by some families and eastern corporations. They were so profitable, they became known as bonanza farms.

As people heard about the farms, settlers rushed to North Dakota to establish more. In less than 20 years, farming had become North Dakota's major industry. Ranching began in North Dakota at about the same time, and much of North Dakota's western range lands were used to fatten Texas cattle.

The Red and Missouri rivers are North Dakota's major rivers. The Red River flows northward through eastern North Dakota. The Missouri runs through the western part of the state. The Garrison Dam, one of the largest dams in the world, spans

Buttes shatter the monotony of the North Dakota plains in this view across the "wide Missouri."

the Missouri near Riverdale. The dam helps control floods and provides water for irrigation and hydroelectric power.

There are many small lakes in the north-central and eastern parts of North Dakota. The largest natural one is Devils Lake. Having no outlet, its water is salty.

The geographic center of North America is near the center of Pierce County, just southwest of Rugby. A stone pile called a cairn marks the spot.

North Dakota was inhabited by Indians long before settlers moved into the territory. The state was named for the Sioux Indians, who called themselves the *Dakota* or *Lakota*, meaning "allies" or "friends." One of North Dakota's nicknames is the *Sioux State*. Today there are several Indian reservations in the state. One of the largest that is completely within the state is the Fort Berthold Indian Reservation. It is located in the west on Lake Sakakawea. Turtle Mountain Indian Reservation is in the north near Rolla. Fort Totten Indian Reservation, which has the country's only restored cavalry square, is south of Devils Lake.

Every summer, visitors to North Dakota are entertained by the colorful Indian ceremonies that are conducted on the reservations. In July and August, Indian powwows are held in Bismarck, Fort Totten, Fort Yates, Mandaree, and New Town.

North Dakota was a part of America's historic wild west and, during the summer, North Dakota cowboys participate in many rodeos to keep this heritage alive. The White Earth Rodeo takes place in June. In July there are rodeos in Dickinson, Fort Totten, Fort Ransom, Fort Yates, Mandan, New Town, and Raleigh.

Visitors to North Dakota can visit 12 state parks and campgrounds. There are also many historic and military sites. One of the most important of these is Fort Abraham Lincoln State Park near Mandan. In 1876, General George A. Custer left this fort on the expedition that ended in the Battle of Little Bighorn. Fort Abercrombie, established in 1857 at Abercrombie, was the first military post in present-day North Dakota.

In the autumn, thousands of hunters travel to North Dakota's lakes and streams to hunt migrating ducks and geese that stop there to rest on their way south. Game birds are plentiful on the Great Plains, while rivers and streams have abundant fish. North Dakota's official nickname, the *Flickertail State*, was coined because of the many flickertail ground squirrels that live in the central portion of the state.

Several summer-resort areas attract many tourists each year. Among the favorites are the Badlands, Devils Lake, and the Kildeer, Pembina, and Turtle mountains.

This blockhouse at Fort Abercrombie near Fargo is a relic of the first U.S. military post built in present-day North Dakota. The fort was established in 1857 (above top).

A bronze memorial to the courageous pioneer families who struggled to settle the west beautifies the grounds of Bismarck's capitol building (above bottom).

North Dakota
Flickertail State

Capital: Bismarck
Area: 70,665 sq. mi. (183,022 km^2), including 1,392 sq. mi. (3,605 km^2) of inland water; 17th in size among the states
Elevation: *Highest*—White Butte, 3,506 ft. (1,069 m) above sea level in Slope County; *lowest*—750 ft. (229 m) above sea level in Pembina County
Statehood: Nov. 2, 1889, the 39th state
Abbreviations: N. Dak. or N.D. (traditional); ND (postal)
Motto: *Liberty and Union, Now and Forever, One and Inseparable*
Song: "North Dakota Hymn"
Tree: American Elm

North Dakota's state seal shows an elm tree and a setting sun that represent the state's landscape. The plow, sheaves of wheat, and anvil symbolize agriculture. The bow and arrows and the Indian hunting a buffalo represent North Dakota's history. The seal was adopted in 1889. North Dakota adopted the regimental flag of the First North Dakota Infantry as its state flag in 1911. The design is a modified version of the U.S. coat of arms.

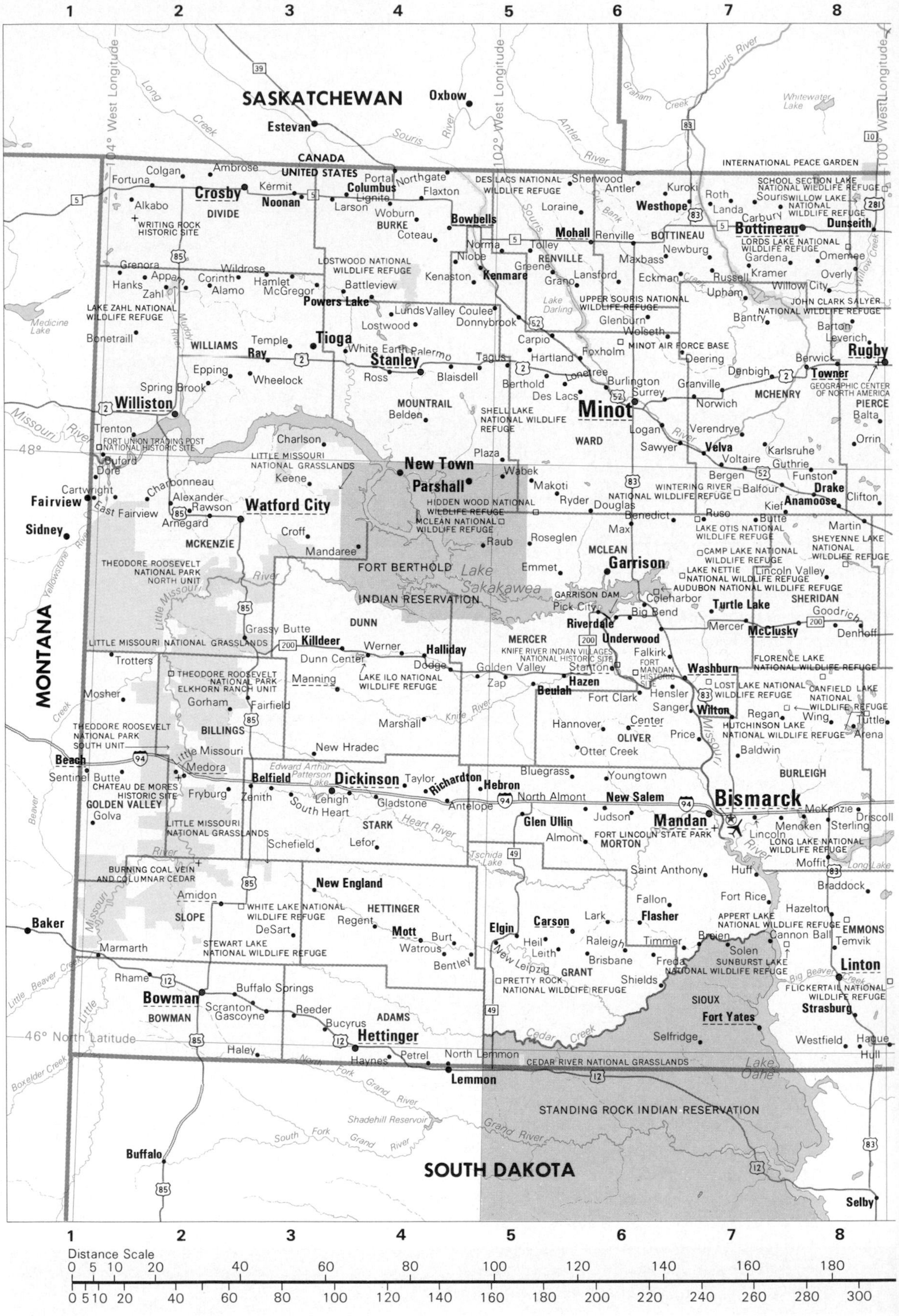

NORTH DAKOTA
Political Map

★	State capital		Indian reservation
	Urban area in North Dakota	+	Point of interest
	Urban area outside North Dakota	✈	Major airport
•	City or town		River
●	County seat		Water
			Intermittent river
DUNN	County name		Intermittent lake
	County boundary	Highways:	
	State boundary		Expressway
	Park or other recreation area		Other road
	Forest or other conservation area	29	Interstate
	Military or other federal area	2	U.S.
		11	Other

Lambert conformal conic projection
WORLD BOOK map

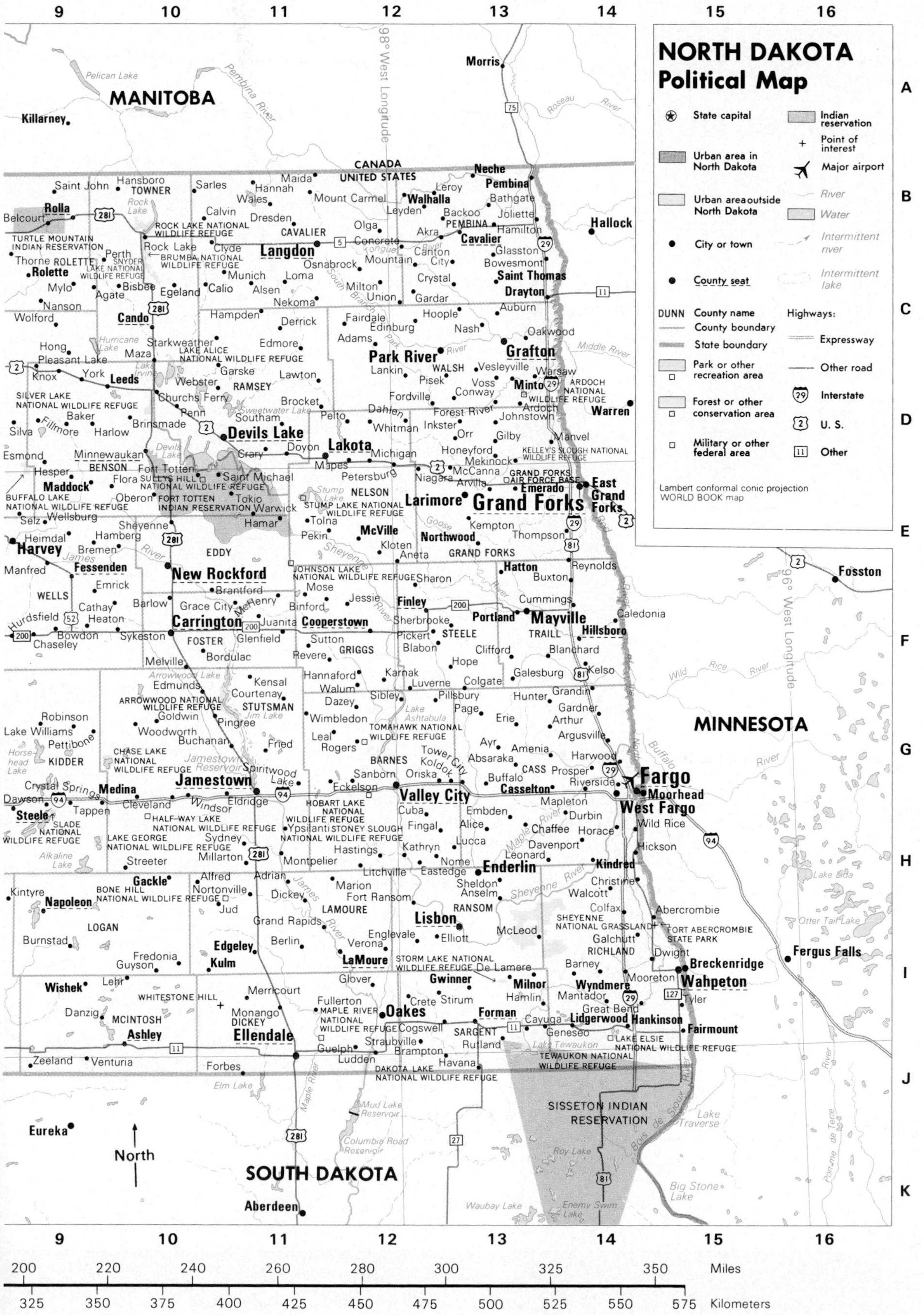

Seal

Flag

Bird: Western Meadow Lark

Flower: Wild Prairie Rose

9   10   11   12   13   14   15   16

North

200   220   240   260   280   300   325   350   Miles
325   350   375   400   425   450   475   500   525   550   575   Kilometers

MANITOBA

CANADA
UNITED STATES

MINNESOTA

SOUTH DAKOTA

SISSETON INDIAN RESERVATION

Ohio

Ohio was the first state west of the Allegheny Mountains. It was carved out of the Northwest Territory and admitted to the Union in 1803 as the 17th state. The first settlement by whites in Ohio had been made at Marietta in 1788.

Some of Ohio's most interesting history goes back to long before the first white settlers arrived. Beginning several thousand years ago, various Indian tribes called Mound Builders lived in Ohio. Many of them had advanced forms of civilization. They left more than 6,000 burial mounds, forts, and other earthworks in the region that is now Ohio. A well-known prehistoric structure is the Great Serpent Mound, which lies near Hillsboro. It curves in the shape of a snake. Another Indian landmark, Fort Ancient, stands near Lebanon. It is the largest hill-top earth structure in the country.

One of the nation's finest collections of American, Asian, and European sculptures and paintings, as well as the Severance collection of arms and armor, are at the Cleveland Museum of Art (above).

Commodore Oliver Perry secured control of Lake Erie for the United States during the War of 1812 and later coined his famous statement, "We have met the enemy and they are ours." Perry's Victory Memorial stands at Put-in-Bay on South Bass Island, near the spot where the battle for the lake was fought against the British in 1813 (right).

Ohio took its name from the Iroquois word *ohio,* meaning "something great." The Indians had used the word to refer to the Ohio River.

The many buckeye, or horse chestnut, trees that the settlers found in the region gave the state its nickname, the *Buckeye State.* The settlers cut down many of the buckeyes to build log cabins. It wasn't long before Ohio also became known as the *Gateway State* because of its strategic location as a pathway from the eastern United States to the western frontier. Zane's Trace, a road built by Ebenezer Zane for the federal government, opened in 1797. It cut across southern Ohio, providing a link with the road that led to New Orleans. The National Road, or Cumberland Road, led many settlers westward across central Ohio beginning in the early 1800's. Later, canals and railroads further enhanced Ohio's position as a key state in the movement of goods and people between the East and the West.

Ohio claims another title for itself: *Mother of Presidents.* More U.S. Presidents have come from Ohio than from any other state except Virginia. Ulysses S. Grant was born at Point Pleasant, Rutherford B. Hayes at Delaware, James A. Garfield at Orange, Benjamin Harrison near North Bend, William McKinley at Niles, William H. Taft at Cincinnati, and Warren G. Harding near Blooming Grove. An eighth President, William Henry Harrison, was living at North Bend when he was elected. In the 1920 Presidential election, both candidates were Ohioans. Warren G. Harding defeated Governor James M. Cox of Dayton.

In addition to its Presidents, Ohio has been the home of many other famous Americans. The great inventor Thomas Alva Edison was born at Milan. Orville and Wilbur Wright made test flights of their first power-driven plane at a field near Dayton. Benjamin F. Goodrich established his first successful rubber industry in Akron. John Glenn, the first American astronaut to orbit the earth, was born in Cambridge. The town of Wapakoneta was the birthplace of Neil A. Armstrong, the first person to set foot on the moon.

Many noteworthy developments in education and related fields took place in Ohio. For many years, school children throughout the country learned to

Set at the mouth of the Maumee River where it empties into Lake Erie, Toledo forms a water gateway between the eastern seaboard and the West.

read by using the *McGuffey Readers,* written by Ohioan William H. McGuffey. In 1833, Oberlin College became the first coeducational college in the nation. The country's first presidential library is the Rutherford B. Hayes Library in Fremont. Ohio State University established WOSU, the first educational radio station in North America, in 1922. The first newspaper published in the region north and west of the Ohio River was the *Centinel of the North-Western Territory,* founded in Cincinnati.

Ohio has also left its mark on the history of sports. In 1869, the Cincinnati Red Stockings (now the Cincinnati Reds) became the first all-professional basebell team in the nation.

Ohio ranks high among the states as an industrial center. No other state produces as many machine tools and glass products as Ohio. Ohio has the nation's largest factories for the production of soap, golf balls, and weighing scales. The state also produces about a fourth of the nation's rubber tires. Dayton is the home of the cash register. James Ritty invented the machine there in 1879. Today Dayton manufactures more cash registers than any other city in the United States.

Agriculture has been important to Ohio's economy since the earliest days of settlement. The legendary Johnny Appleseed traveled through northern and central Ohio distributing apple seeds and seedlings that grew into some of the state's first orchards. About 1,000 acres (404.7 hectares) of Ohio land are cultivated under glass, and the state is the nation's leader in the production of hothouse vegetables. It also produces more wool than any other state east of the Mississippi River.

Ohio
Buckeye State

Capital: Columbus
Area: 41,222 sq. mi. (106,764 km²), including 247 sq. mi. (640 km²) of inland water but excluding 3,457 sq. mi. (8,954 km²) of Lake Erie; 35th in size among the states
Elevation: *Highest*—Campbell Hill in Logan County, 1,550 ft. (472 m) above sea level; *lowest*—433 ft. (132 m) above sea level along the Ohio River in Hamilton County
Statehood: March 1, 1803, the 17th state
Abbreviations: O. (traditional); OH (postal)
Motto: *With God, All Things Are Possible*
Song: "Beautiful Ohio"
Tree: Buckeye

Ohio's state seal shows a sheaf of wheat representing the richness of the state's land. A bundle of arrows symbolizes Ohio's admission to the Union as the 17th state. The sun rising behind the mountains shows that Ohio was the first state west of the Allegheny Mountains. The seal was adopted in 1868 and revised in 1967. The state flag, adopted in 1902, displays a white circle for O, the state's initial. The red circle represents the buckeye nut. Ohio is the only state with a pennant-shaped flag.

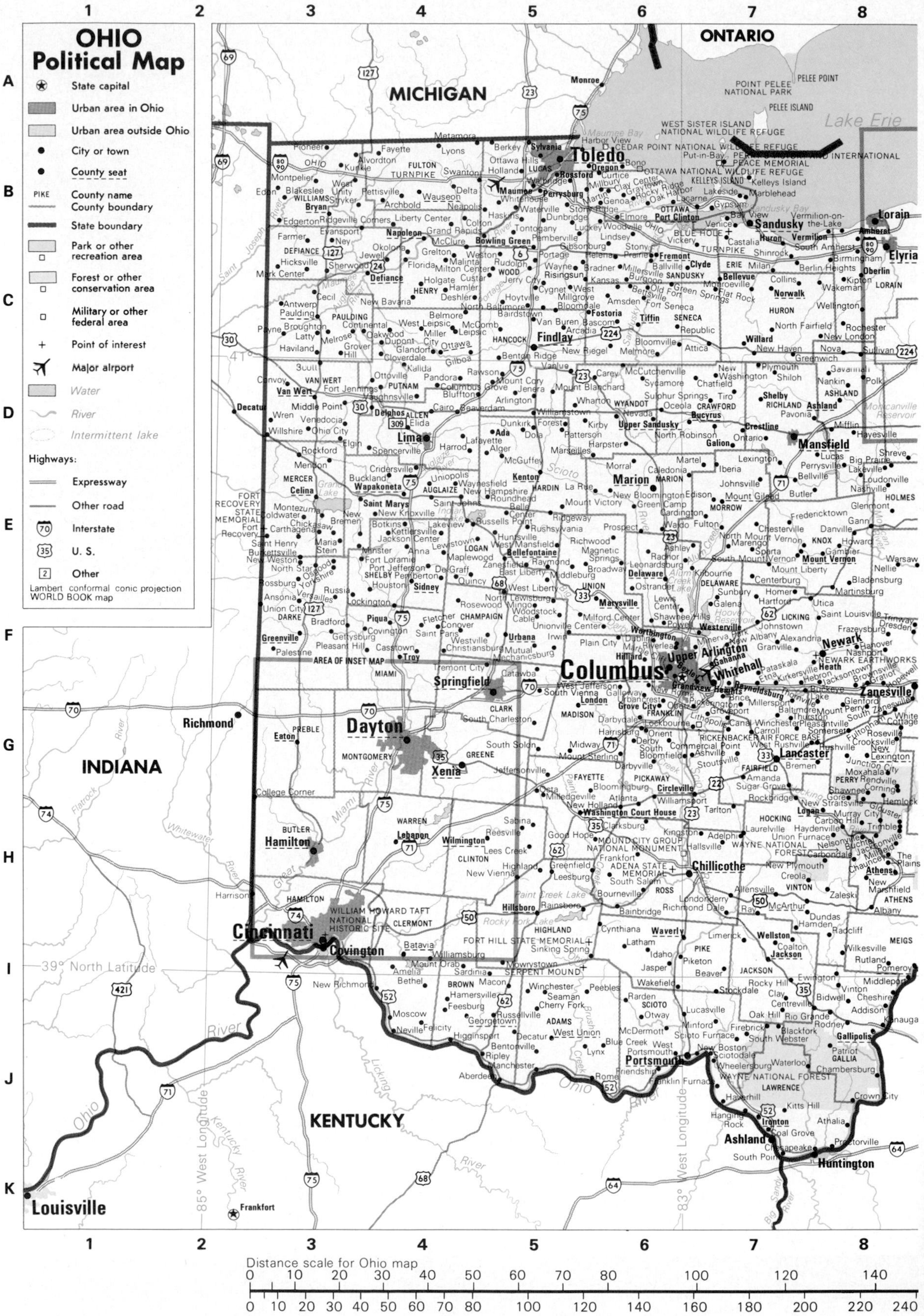

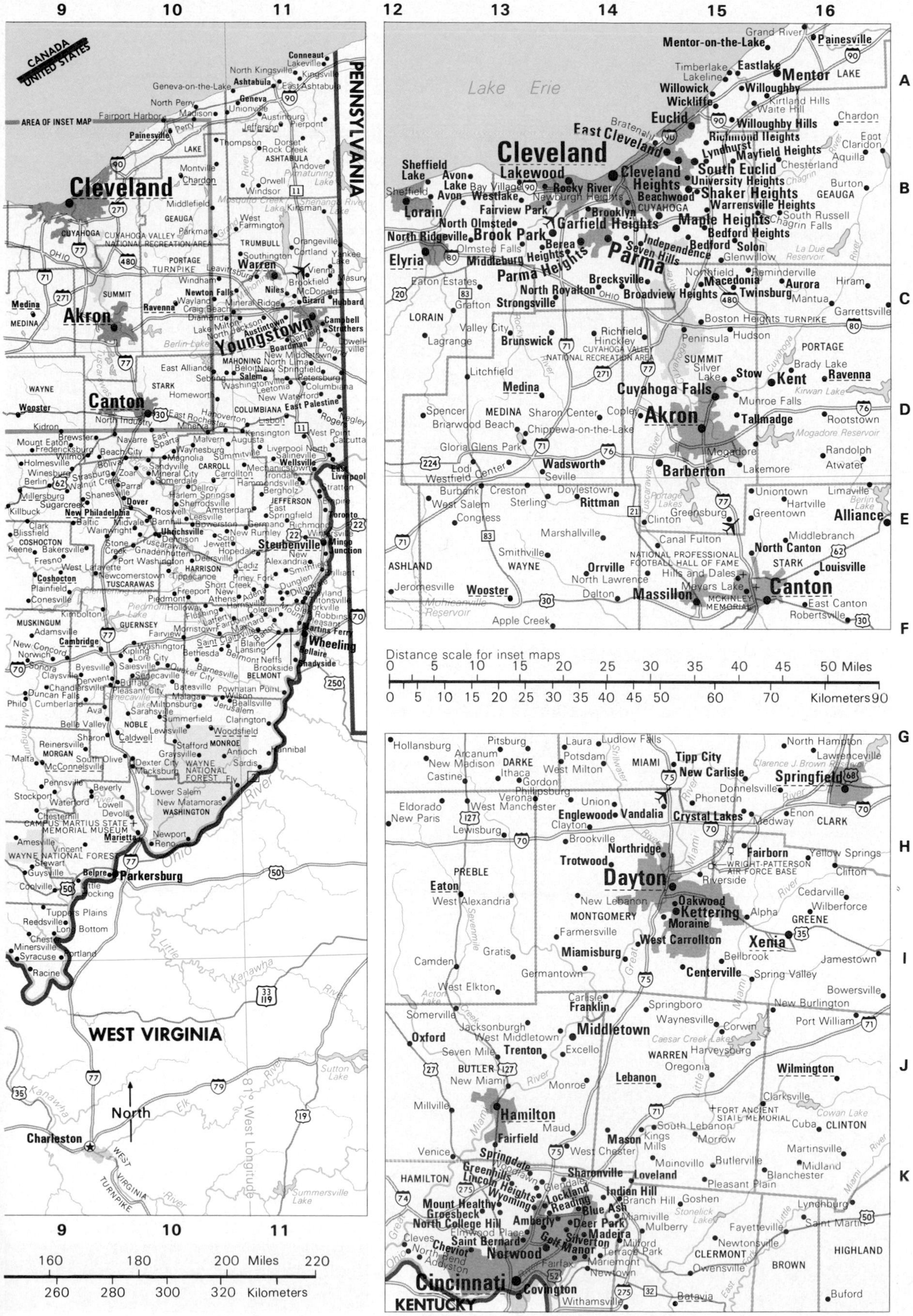

Seal

Flag

Bird: Cardinal

Flower: Scarlet Carnation

South Dakota

South Dakota is called the *Sunshine State,* an appropriate nickname for a state with a bright, sunny climate. The state's most important metallic mineral is also bright and shining: gold. This mineral was first discovered in the Black Hills in 1874. Two years later the rich Homestake lode was discovered at Lead. The Homestake Mine is still one of the largest gold-producing mines in the Western Hemisphere.

The Black Hills are a range of low mountains in southwestern South Dakota and eastern Wyoming. The Sioux Indians gave the mountains the name Black Hills because the pine forests that grew on the slopes appeared black when seen from the plains. Once part of a reservation for the Sioux, the land was bought by the federal government in 1876 after the discovery of gold. Thousands of settlers then rushed in to search for this desirable mineral. Mining towns sprang up all over the area. Later the forests were logged, and farmers planted crops.

The infamous town of Deadwood became the center of mining operations in the Black Hills in the mid-1870's. Deadwood was a wild, brawling town that had the reputation of being the most lawless settlement on the frontier.

South Dakota's history is filled with names associated with the Old West. Colorful characters such as Wild Bill Hickok, Calamity Jane, and Preacher Smith became legends partly because of their association with Deadwood. They are buried in Deadwood's Boot Hill Cemetery.

Today the Black Hills are one of America's most popular vacationlands, a beautiful region with deep canyons and towering rock formations. Here visitors are attracted to Mount Rushmore National Memorial near Rapid City, which is also called the *Shrine of Democracy.* Huge heads of George Washington, Thomas Jefferson, Theodore Roosevelt, and Abraham Lincoln have been carved out of a granite mountain. Near Custer, Korczak Ziolkowski is now blasting out of another granite mountain a gigantic sculpture of the great Sioux chief, Crazy Horse.

Wind Cave National Park and Jewel Cave are two other popular Black Hills tourist attractions. The famous Black Hills Passion Play, staged annually at Spearfish, is a popular event attended by many tourists. Days of '76 is an annual celebration held in Deadwood every August.

While many tourists go to South Dakota just to see the Black Hills, many others find numerous interesting and exciting things to do and see in other parts of the state as well. Millions of visitors travel to the state each year. South Dakota offers visitors breath-taking scenery, fascinating historical sights,

A stone shaft marks the geographic center of the United States, about 17 miles (27 kilometers) west of Castle Rock. The mound was moved twice in 1959—once when Alaska became a state and again after Hawaii's statehood (right).

Decorated with murals made of corn and other grains, the Corn Palace in Mitchell emphasizes the importance of agriculture in South Dakota's economy (below).

and recreational facilities for swimming, fishing, boating, and hunting.

With its wide variety of landscapes, South Dakota is often called the *Land of Infinite Variety.* Visitors, for example, can view a desolate but weirdly beautiful land area at the Badlands National Monument in southwestern South Dakota. Wind and water have worn away the land and left deep ravines, steep ridges, and colorful cliffs. Little plant or animal life is evident in this region. Immediately north of the Black Hills, near Castle Rock, a stone shaft shows tourists the geographic center of the United States.

South Dakota has rich, fertile soil and excellent grazing land. It is one of America's leading states in raising beef cattle, hogs, sheep, and lambs. Grazing pastures cover almost half the state. Cattle can be seen grazing on huge ranches in the western Great Plains section. The many sheep and lambs raised in the northwest portion of the state make South Dakota one of the country's largest producers of wool.

The determined, courageous farmers of South Dakota have been important characters throughout the state's history. They steadfastly held their land through droughts, depressions, and blizzards. They have made South Dakota one of the nation's great agricultural states.

Indians play an important role in South Dakota's history as well. The Sioux Indians called themselves *Dakota* or *Lakota,* meaning "allies" or "friends," thus giving the state its name. Indian uprisings led by the famous chiefs Crazy Horse and Sitting Bull were caused by the white settlers' invasion of the Black Hills.

After 1876 most of the Sioux surrendered and settled west of the Missouri River. Indian fairs, rodeos, and roundups are popular events throughout the state, keeping the state's frontier heritage alive.

A popular point of interest in South Dakota is the Corn Palace in Mitchell. This magnificent structure is where concerts, dances, and other events are held. The Corn Palace is redecorated every fall with murals made of different colors of corn and other grains. The "Great Lakes of South Dakota" is another favorite attraction, formed by huge dams on the Missouri River. Pierre, the state capital, also draws many tourists every year.

The Cathedral Spires are but a small sampling of the startling natural formations in the famous Black Hills of South Dakota.

South Dakota
Sunshine State

Capital: Pierre
Area: 77,047 sq. mi.
(199,551 km²), including
1,092 sq. mi. (2,828 km²)
of inland water; 16th in size
among the states
Elevation: *Highest*—Harney
Peak, 7,242 ft. (2,207 m)
above sea level; *lowest*—Big
Stone Lake, 962 ft. (293 m)
above sea level
Statehood: Nov. 2, 1889,
the 40th state
Abbreviations: S. Dak. or
S.D. (traditional); SD
(postal)
Motto: *Under God the People
Rule*
Song: "Hail, South Dakota"
Tree: Black Hills Spruce

*South Dakota's state seal was
adopted in 1889. The smelter
chimney represents mining, the
plowman farming, and the
riverboat transportation. The
state flag, adopted in 1963,
has an adaptation of the seal.
The gold circle around the seal
represents the blazing rays of the
sun. The blue field symbolizes
South Dakota's clear skies.*

SOUTH DAKOTA Political Map

- ⭐ State capital
- ▦ Urban area in South Dakota
- ▢ Urban area outside South Dakota
- ● City or town
- ● County seat
- CLAY County name
- County boundary
- State boundary
- Park or other recreation area
- ▢ Forest or other conservation area
- ▢ Military or other federal area
- ▦ Indian reservation
- ✈ Major airport
- Water
- River
- Intermittent river
- + Point of interest

Highways:
- Expressway
- Other road
- 90 Interstate
- 20 U.S.
- 73 Other

Lambert conformal conic projection
WORLD BOOK map

Distance scale

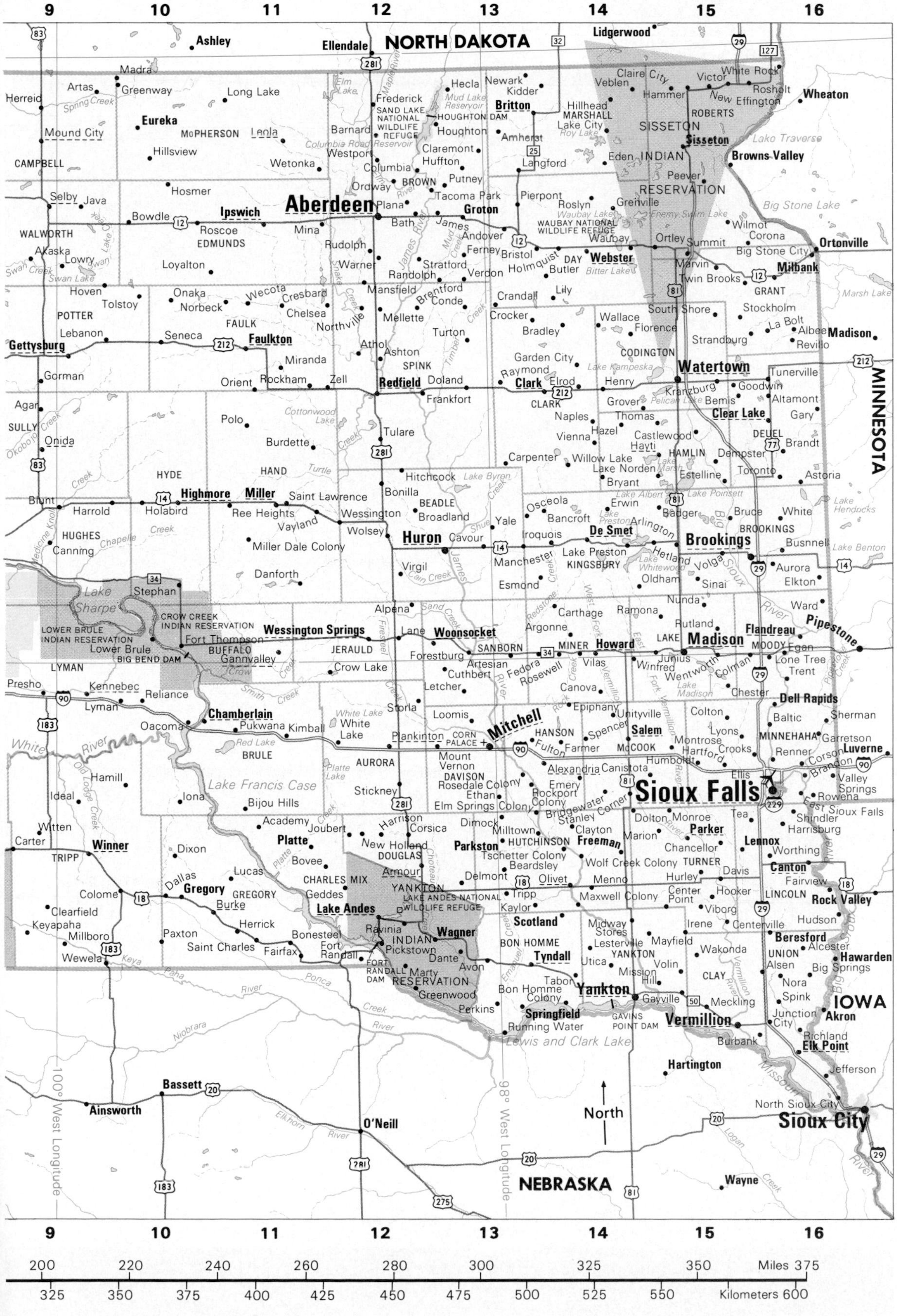

Seal

Flag

Bird: Ring-necked Pheasant

Flower: American Pasqueflower

Wisconsin

Wisconsin is commonly known as *America's Dairyland*—and with good reason. It ranks first among the states in dairy production, providing more milk than any other state. About a fifth of the nation's butter and about two-fifths of its cheese come from the prosperous dairy farms of Wisconsin. The state's cheese-making industry was begun in the 1800's by settlers from New York. Swiss immigrants who settled in New Glarus also contributed to the development of Wisconsin's thriving dairy industry. The Wisconsin Dairymen's Association was founded in 1872 to improve and promote the dairy industry. Today, Wisconsin has the headquarters of more than 500 farm cooperatives.

In addition to dairy products, farmers in Wisconsin grow more sweet corn, peas, green beans, and beets than farmers in any other state. The state ranks first in cranberry production and is also a leader in honey. Wisconsin is also a great "ranch" state. Its mink ranches have made it the nation's top mink-raising state.

In spite of its agricultural prominence, Wisconsin earns far more income from manufacturing than from agriculture. Nonelectric machinery such as engines, farm machinery, and construction equipment is the number-one manufactured product in Wisconsin. But the state's breweries are probably among its best-known factories. Wisconsin brews more beer

Carved by ancient glaciers, much of Wisconsin's land surface is a contrast of gentle valleys and rocky outcroppings such as Gibralter Rock in Columbia County.

than any other state, and Milwaukee is known as the *Beer Capital* of the nation. German immigrants in Milwaukee helped start the beer industry. The city has one of the nation's largest German-American populations.

Wisconsin has had a reputation as a progressive state for many years. It can point to a long list of pioneer achievements in education, social legislation, and other fields. The first kindergarten in the United States was founded for German-speaking children in Watertown. The University of Wisconsin established one of the nation's first correspondence schools, and the first vocational schools were also set up in this state. Wisconsin approved the first primary election law, the first pensions for mothers and teachers, the first minimum wage laws, and the first worker's unemployment compensation program. It also pioneered in the regulation of railroads and public utilities. It was the first state to adopt numbers for its highways and the first to require seatbelts in automobiles sold in the state. The first state-wide press service was the Wisconsin Press Association, established in 1853. At Appleton, Wisconsin built the first hydroelectric plant in the nation.

Three Milwaukee inventors—Carlos Glidden, Christopher Latham Sholes, and Samuel W. Soule—made a lasting contribution to the business world with their invention of the first practical typewriter in 1867. And the town of Baraboo was the scene of an important first in the world of entertainment. The Ringling brothers staged their first circus there in 1884. Today, Baraboo displays interesting circus items at Circus World Museum.

Some of the most popular attractions in Wisconsin are its beautiful lakes and woodlands. The state has more than 8,000 lakes, many of which were created by glaciers thousands of years ago. One of the state's most picturesque regions is the Wisconsin Dells. The Wisconsin River has carved a deep gorge through the Dells region, creating unusual rock formations with names such as Grand Piano, Devil's Elbow, and Fat Man's Misery. Winnebago Indians perform ceremonial dances at the Dells during the summer vacation season.

The Winnebago were one of many Indian tribes that lived in Wisconsin long before the first whites arrived. A French explorer, Jean Nicolet, was the first white person to come to the region. He arrived while looking for a water route to China. Believing he had reached his goal, he put on a Chinese robe and fired pistols into the air as he landed on shore. To his surprise and disappointment, Winnebago Indians, not Chinese, greeted him.

Other French explorers and missionaries followed the path of Jean Nicolet. After Britain defeated France in the French and Indian War, Britain took

Milwaukee's breweries are a legacy of Wisconsin's German immigrants and a testimony to the state's pure lake waters (above).

Boating of all kinds is a popular pastime along the dramatic shorelines of Wisconsin's Door County, a fingerlike peninsula that juts out between Green Bay and Lake Michigan (left).

control of the Wisconsin area. It eventually became part of the province of Quebec. The Wisconsin area became U.S. territory after the Revolutionary War ended. It wasn't until 1848, however, that Wisconsin was admitted to the Union as the 30th state. Six years later, antislavery meetings held in Ripon contributed to the development of the Republican Party.

Wisconsin's nickname, the *Badger State*, dates back to the 1820's, when valuable lead deposits in the southwestern part of the state lured many miners. Some lived in shelters dug out of the hillsides. The miners reminded people of badgers burrowing holes in the ground. And so, all Wisconsinites eventually came to be known as *Badgers*.

Wisconsin
Badger State

Capital: Madison
Area: 56,154 sq. mi. (145,438 km²), including 1,690 sq. mi. (4,377 km²) of inland water but excluding 10,062 sq. mi. (26,060 km²) of Lakes Michigan and Superior; 26th in size among the states
Elevation: *Highest*—Timms Hill, 1,952 ft. (595 m) above sea level, in Price County; *lowest*—581 ft. (177 m) above sea level, along the western shore of Lake Michigan
Statehood: May 29, 1848, the 30th state
Abbreviations: Wis. (traditional); WI (postal)
Motto: *Forward*
Song: "On, Wisconsin!"
Tree: Sugar Maple

Wisconsin's state seal, adopted in 1851, shows a sailor and a miner holding a shield. Symbols on the shield represent Wisconsin's agriculture (a plow), mining (a pick and shovel), manufacturing (an arm and hammer), and navigation (an anchor). A horn of plenty stands for prosperity, and a pyramid of pig lead symbolizes the state's mineral wealth. A badger represents Wisconsin's popular name, the Badger State. *The state flag, adopted in 1913, has an adaptation of the state seal.*

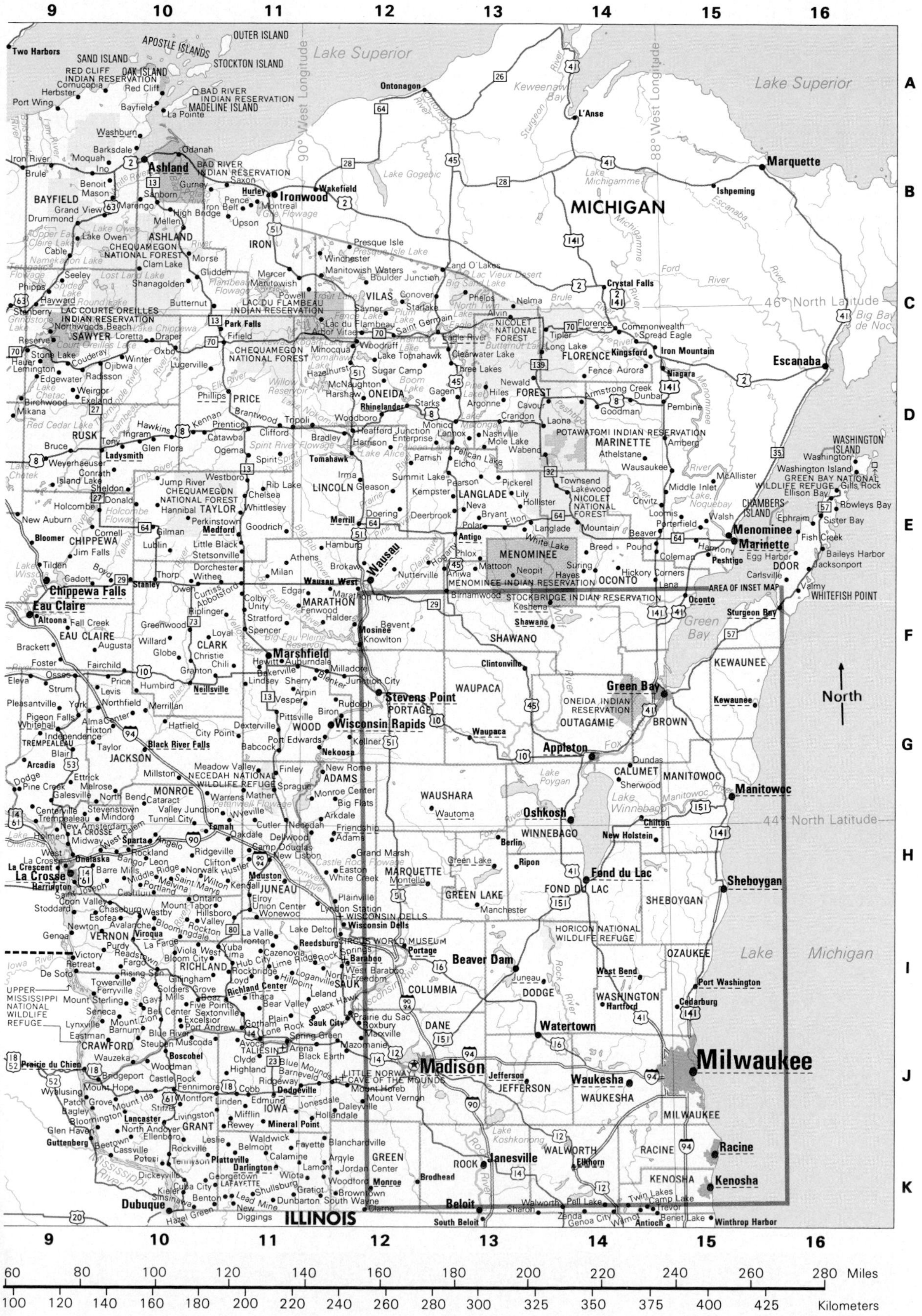

Seal

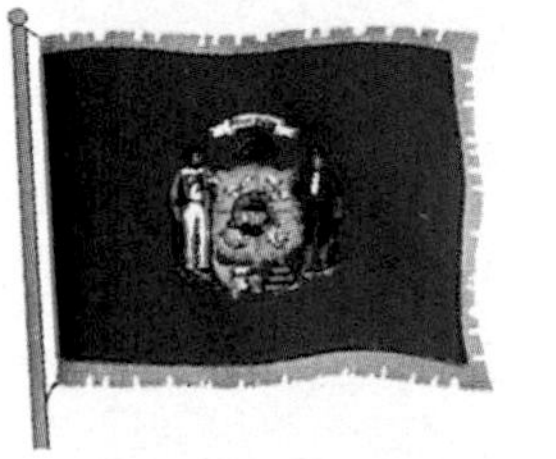
Flag

Bird: Robin

Flower: Wood Violet

9
10
11
12
13
14
15
16
C
H
J
K
Lake Superior
MICHIGAN
ILLINOIS
Lake Michigan
Green Bay
North
46° North Latitude
44° North Latitude
90° West Longitude
88° West Longitude
APOSTLE ISLANDS
OUTER ISLAND
STOCKTON ISLAND
MADELINE ISLAND
Ashland
Ironwood
Marquette
Escanaba
Menominee
Marinette
Eau Claire
Chippewa Falls
Wausau
Marshfield
Stevens Point
Wisconsin Rapids
Green Bay
Appleton
Oshkosh
Manitowoc
Sheboygan
Fond du Lac
La Crosse
Beaver Dam
Madison
Watertown
Waukesha
Milwaukee
Racine
Kenosha
Janesville
Beloit
Dubuque
MENOMINEE
WASHINGTON ISLAND
CHAMBERS ISLAND
WHITEFISH POINT
AREA OF INSET MAP
60 80 100 120 140 160 180 200 220 240 260 280 Miles
100 120 140 160 180 200 220 240 260 280 300 325 350 375 400 425 Kilometers

South

Alabama *144*
Arkansas *148*
Delaware *152*
Florida *154*
Georgia *158*
Kentucky *162*
Louisiana *166*
Maryland *170*
Mississippi *174*
North Carolina *178*
South Carolina *182*
Tennessee *186*
Texas *190*
Virginia *194*
West Virginia *198*

A moderate area of rolling hills, mossy trees, and sandy coastlines, the South began as a farming region. Since the Civil War, Southerners have added major U.S. manufacturing to their contributions to the nation's economy.

Cumberland Gap lies at the meeting point of Virginia, Kentucky, and Tennessee. A natural pass through the Appalachians, the gap served as a gateway west for pioneers (facing page).

Atlanta, Ga., is the distribution, manufacturing, and transportation center of the Southeast and the center of one of the nation's fastest growing urban areas (above left).

Florida's swaying palm trees and warm ocean breezes each year attract thousands of tourists to beaches like this one on Sanibel Island (below left).

Vacationers escape the southern sun in the cool twilight of South Carolina's many artificial lakes (below right).

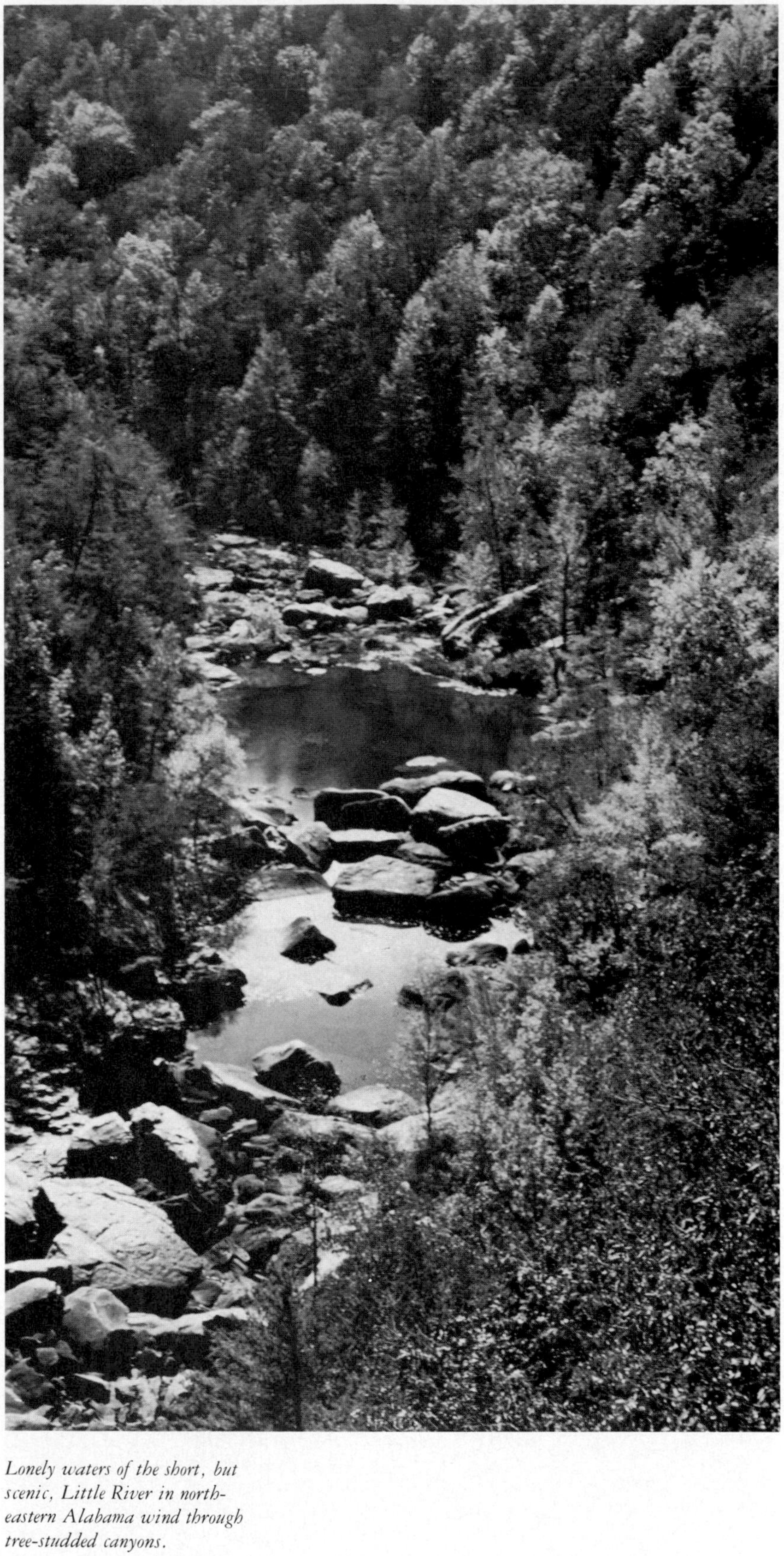

Lonely waters of the short, but scenic, Little River in northeastern Alabama wind through tree-studded canyons.

Alabama

Alabama is famous as the birthplace of the Confederate States of America in 1861. For this reason, the state is sometimes called the *Heart of Dixie.* Its capital, Montgomery, is called the *Cradle of the Confederacy.* Disagreements with the federal government over slavery and other issues led Alabama to secede from the United States early in 1861 and declare itself an independent republic. It then invited other southern states to attend a convention. The convention adopted the constitution of the Confederate States of America and chose Montgomery as its first capital. Jefferson Davis took office as the president of the Confederacy on the steps of the Alabama state capitol. The end of the Civil War brought an end to the Confederacy. Alabama was readmitted to the Union in 1868.

Today, Alabama is an important steel-producing state. One of the nation's largest steel complexes is located in Birmingham. The steel industry helped make Alabama one of the first southern states to develop an industrial economy. Alabama has large deposits of coal, iron ore, and limestone—the three key ingredients for steel. As early as the 1800's, blast furnaces were operating in Birmingham, and Alabama was on its way to becoming an industrial state. Today, many Alabama cities in addition to Birmingham produce iron, steel, and other metal products. Paper products, food products, and chemical products are also important to Alabama's economy.

Much of the nation's space research and engineering takes place in Alabama at the Redstone Arsenal and the George C. Marshall Space Flight Center in Huntsville, which is called *Rocket City, U.S.A.* because of its prominent role in the development of the U.S. space program. Among their many achievements, Huntsville scientists developed the *Saturn V* rocket that carried the first astronauts to the moon.

One of Alabama's largest cities is Mobile, which ranks as a leading U.S. port on the Gulf of Mexico. The Alabama State Docks at Mobile can handle as many as 35 ocean-going ships at one time. The Tennessee Valley Authority operates one of the largest nuclear power plants in the world at Browns Ferry.

Alabama is probably one of the few places in the world that has a monument to a destructive insect. Farmers in Alabama erected the Boll Weevil Monument in the town of Enterprise in appreciation of the role this insect played in the development of the state's agriculture. At one time, Alabama farmers relied almost exclusively on cotton for their income. But with the arrival of the destructive boll weevil around 1915, farmers were forced to diversify and plant other crops as well. Today, Alabama farmers harvest a variety of crops. The state is a leader in the production of pecans and peanuts. Soybeans rank as the number-one income producer for Alabama farmers. The state also produces broiler chickens, beef cattle, hogs, corn, wheat, hay, potatoes, peaches, sweet corn, and other agricultural products.

One of the nation's most famous institutes of higher education, the Tuskegee Institute, was founded by Alabama in 1881. Booker T. Washington, a former slave, directed the school for over 30 years. The famous black scientist George Washington Carver was on the institute's staff from 1896 until his death in 1943. Today, Tuskegee is a national historic site that includes Booker T. Washington's home and the George Washington Carver Museum.

Another historic attraction in Alabama shows visitors what life in Alabama may have been like thousands of years ago. At the Russell Cave National Monument, archaeologists have found tools and other items used by prehistoric peoples. Cliff-dwelling Indians lived in the cave itself as early as 6000 B.C.

Cherokee, Creek, Choctaw, and Chickasaw Indians lived in Alabama around the time the first whites arrived. Various Spanish explorers sailed along the Gulf coast during the early 1500's, and the Spaniard Hernando de Soto was the first to explore the interior. Temporary settlements were set up by Spaniards seeking gold. But it was the French who were the first to establish permanent settlements in the Alabama region. They founded Fort Louis on the Mobile River in 1702. Nine years later they moved their settlement to the present-day site of Mobile.

For the next hundred years or so, various parts of Alabama were controlled by the French, the British, the Spanish, the Americans, and the Indians. Some parts changed hands several times. It wasn't until 1813 that all of present-day Alabama came under control of the United States. The Creek Indians continued to fight for their land until 1814, when U.S. forces under General Andrew Jackson finally defeated them. In 1819, Alabama became the 22nd state in the Union.

The Alabama Space and Rocket Center houses the world's largest collection of missiles, space equipment, and related exhibits (above).

The stillness of a summer's day at Tuscumbia is broken by actors performing The Miracle Worker *at Helen Keller's birthplace, Ivy Green* (left).

Alabama Yellowhammer State

Capital: Montgomery
Area: 51,609 sq. mi. (133,667 km²), including 901 sq. mi. (2,334 km²) of inland water but excluding 560 sq. mi. (1,450 km²) of Gulf of Mexico coastal water; 29th in size among the states
Elevation: *Highest*—Cheaha Mountain, 2,407 ft. (734 m) above sea level; *lowest*—sea level, along the Gulf of Mexico
Statehood: Dec. 14, 1819, the 22nd state
Abbreviations: Ala. (traditional); AL (postal)
Motto: *Audemus Jura Nostra Defendere* (We Dare Defend Our Rights)
Song: "Alabama"
Tree: Southern Pine

Alabama's state seal features a circled map showing the state's boundaries and rivers. The seal was used from 1819 to 1868, then readopted in 1939. The Alabama state flag, adopted in 1895, displays the cross that was the principal feature of the Confederate battle flag.

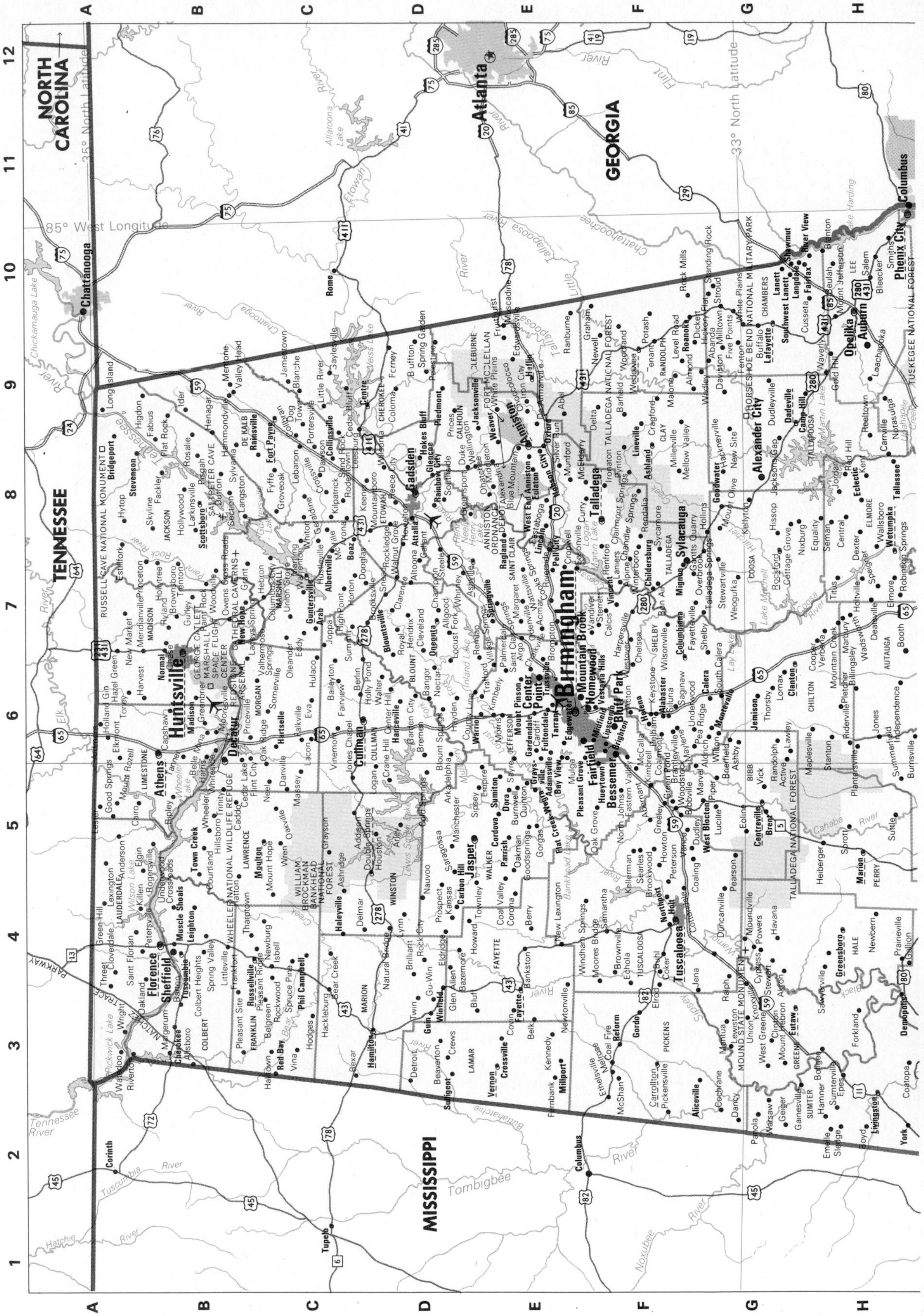

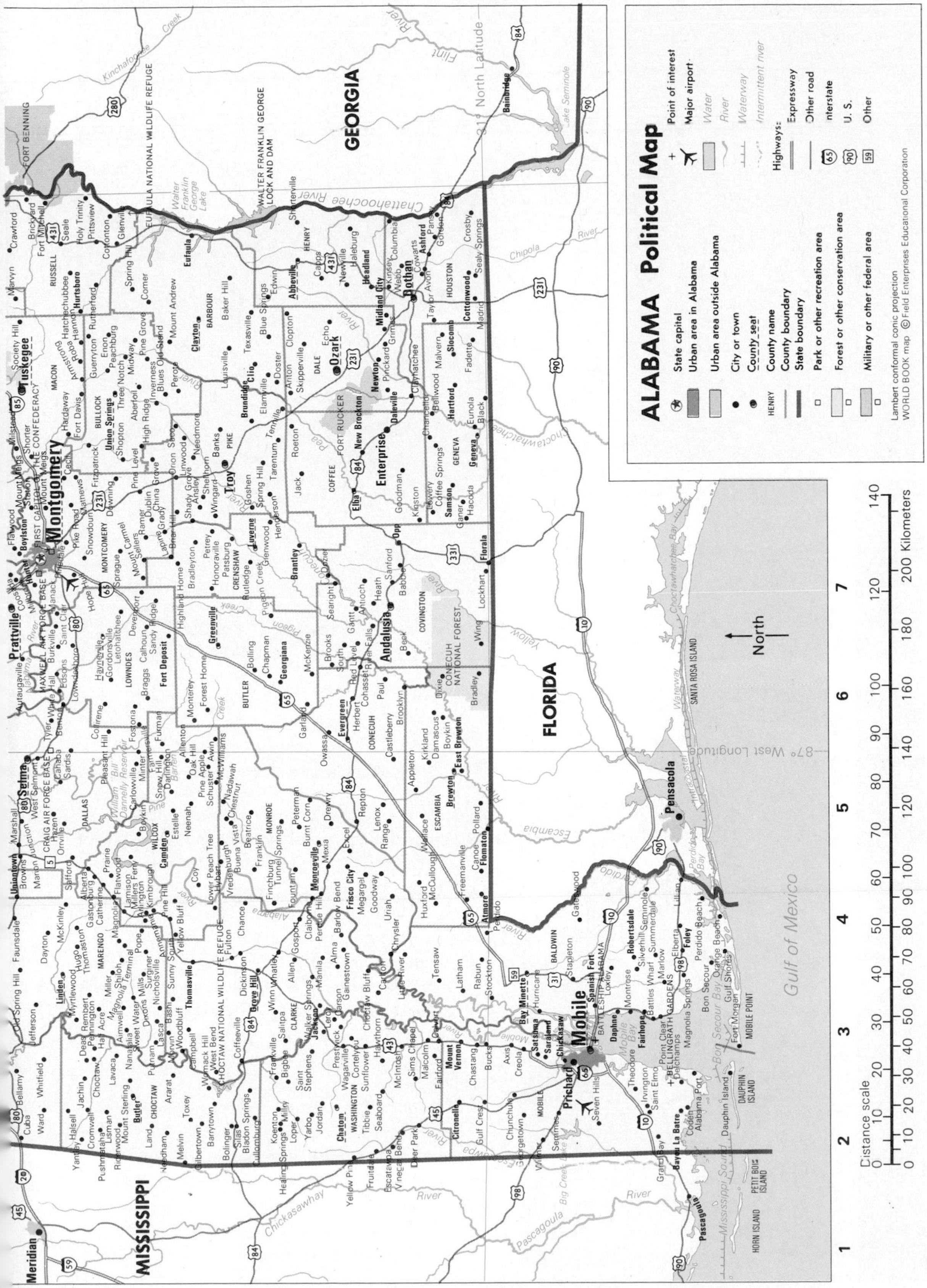
ALABAMA Political Map
State capital
Urban area in Alabama
Urban area outside Alabama
City or town
County seat
County name
County boundary
State boundary
Park or other recreation area
Forest or other conservation area
Military or other federal area
Point of interest
Major airport
Water
River
Waterway
Intermittent river
Highways:
Expressway
Other road
Interstate
U. S.
Other
Lambert conformal conic projection
WORLD BOOK map © Field Enterprises Educational Corporation
GEORGIA
FLORIDA
MISSISSIPPI
Gulf of Mexico
Montgomery
Mobile
North
Distance scale
Kilometers

ALABAMA
GREAT SEAL

Seal

Flag

Bird: Yellowhammer

Flower: Camellia

Although peaceful now, Pea Ridge National Military Park is the site of Arkansas' most savage Civil War battle, when, in March 1862, victorious Union troops forced the Confederates into southern Arkansas (above).

Said to have curative powers, the soothing waters of Hot Springs have made the city famous (right).

Arkansas

Arkansas is a popular tourist state, known for its mountains, lakes, caverns, forests, and especially for its mineral springs. At the famous Hot Springs resort, 47 different springs bubble up from the earth, producing about a million gallons of water a day with a temperature of about 143° F. (62° C). Mammoth Springs in the Ozark Mountains is one of the world's largest springs. It yields about 865 million gallons of water a day.

Many of the natural lakes in Arkansas are oxbow lakes, which are created when a river gradually changes course over a period of many years. Forests cover about half of Arkansas. The state's beautiful mountains and woods abound in wild plant and animal life. On Magazine Mountain, the highest mountain in the state, a kind of fern called *Woodsia scopulina* grows. This particular kind of fern is found nowhere else between the Allegheny and Rocky mountains. The state's native animals include bobcats, foxes, deer, minks, wild turkeys, wild geese, wild ducks, pheasants, and quail.

Farmers in Arkansas produce about a third of the nation's rice crop—more than any other state. They also produce huge crops of soybeans and cotton. Arkansas has more irrigated land than it needs to grow crops, so some farmers flood unused fields and raise fish in them. Arkansas also ranks as the country's leading producer of broiler chickens.

Arkansas' mineral deposits include the only U.S. diamond mine, located near Murfreesboro. John Huddleston found the first diamond on his farm in 1906. The mine is not commercially mined, but visitors may hunt for diamonds. Some tourists have actually found valuable gems.

Oil, bromine, and natural gas are the most important Arkansas minerals. The state produces about 90 per cent of the U.S. supply of bauxite, the ore used in making aluminum. Bauxite was first discovered near Little Rock in 1887.

The first white person in Arkansas was the Spanish explorer Hernando de Soto, who reached the area in 1541. More than a hundred years later, French explorers and missionaries came to the region. In 1682, France claimed the area called Louisiana, which included Arkansas. Henri de Tonti founded the first permanent settlement in the Arkansas region at Arkansas Post in 1686.

The Louisiana Territory, including Arkansas, came under Spanish control, then was returned to the French before the United States purchased it in 1803. Under U.S. control, the Arkansas region was part of the Louisiana Territory, the Missouri Territory, and the Arkansaw Territory before finally becoming the nation's 25th state in 1836. The state's name comes from an Indian word meaning "downstream people."

During the years before the Civil War, pro- and antislavery sentiments divided the people of Arkansas. The state first voted to remain within the Union and then, two months later, voted to secede. But the divisions within Arkansas' population remained throughout the war. In 1864, the Confederates moved the state capital from Little Rock to the town of Washington. Another group then formed a Union government in Little Rock, which was occupied by Union troops. Arkansas had two governments—one Confederate and one Union—until the war ended in 1865.

In 1872, a hotly contested governor's race threatened to tear Arkansas apart. Two Republicans, Elisha Baxter and Joseph Brooks, ran against each other. Baxter won but Brooks charged fraud. Brooks forced Baxter out of the statehouse at gunpoint, and citizens quickly took sides, clashing in street fights. President Ulysses S. Grant finally had to resolve the issue by proclaiming Baxter governor.

Meandering through the Ozark Plateau, this stretch of the Buffalo River has waters calm enough even for inexperienced canoeists.

After the Reconstruction period, Arkansas established a sustained record of support for the Democratic Party. Since 1874, only two Republicans have been elected governor of Arkansas. The overwhelming majority of the state's senators and representatives have also been Democrats.

An Arkansas woman was the first woman ever elected to the U.S. Senate. Hattie Caraway won a special election in 1932 and filled the Senate seat that her husband had occupied before his death.

One of Arkansas' most famous citizens was General Douglas MacArthur, who was born in Little Rock. His birthplace, now the Museum of Science and History, is part of a park dedicated to his memory.

Arkansas

Land of Opportunity

Capital: Little Rock
Area: 53,104 sq. mi. (137,539 km²), including 1,159 sq. mi. (3,002 km²) of inland water; 27th in size among the states
Elevation: *Highest*—Magazine Mountain in Logan County, 2,753 ft. (839 m) above sea level; *lowest*—Ouachita River in Ashley and Union counties, 55 ft. (17 m) above sea level
Statehood: June 15, 1836, the 25th state
Abbreviations: Ark. (traditional); AR (postal)
Motto: *Regnat Populus* (The People Rule)
Song: "Arkansas"
Tree: Pine

The shield of Arkansas' state seal shows a steamboat, plow, beehive, and sheaf of wheat. These symbolize the state's industrial and agricultural wealth. The Angel of Mercy and the Sword of Justice guard an American eagle. The goddess Liberty stands above in a circle of stars. The seal in its present form was adopted in 1907. The state flag, adopted in 1913, bears a diamond-shaped design representing Arkansas as the only diamond-producing state. The large star above "Arkansas" commemorates the Confederacy. The smaller stars below have two meanings. First, they signify the three nations to which the state successively belonged: Spain, France, and the United States. Second, they show Arkansas as the third state formed from the Louisiana Purchase.

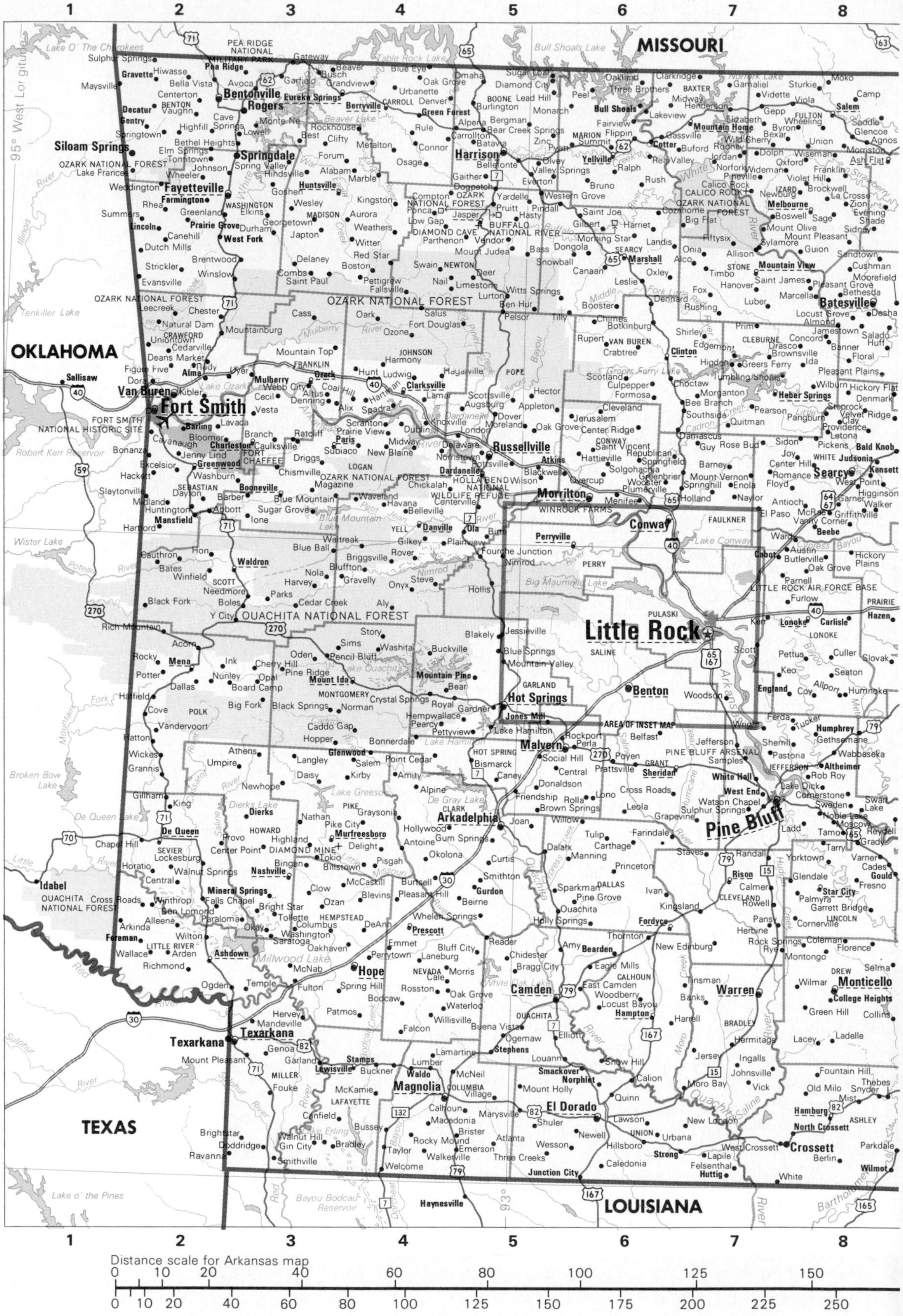

ARKANSAS Political Map

Symbol	Description	Symbol	Description
✪	State capital	+	Point of interest
(urban)	Urban area in Arkansas	✈	Major airport
(urban)	Urban area outside Arkansas	Water	Water
●	City or town	River	River
●	County seat	Waterway	Waterway
POLK	County name County boundary	Intermittent river	Intermittent river
	State boundary	Flood control reservoir	Flood control reservoir
(park)	Park or other recreation area	Highways:	
(forest)	Forest or other conservation area	Expressway	Expressway
(military)	Military or other federal area	Other road	Other road
		40	Interstate
		65	U.S.
		7	Other

Lambert conformal conic projection
WORLD BOOK map © Field Enterprises Educational Corporation

North

Distance scale for inset map
0   5   10   15   20   25   30   35   40   45 Miles 50
0 5 10 15 20 25 30 35 40 45 50   60   70 Kilometers

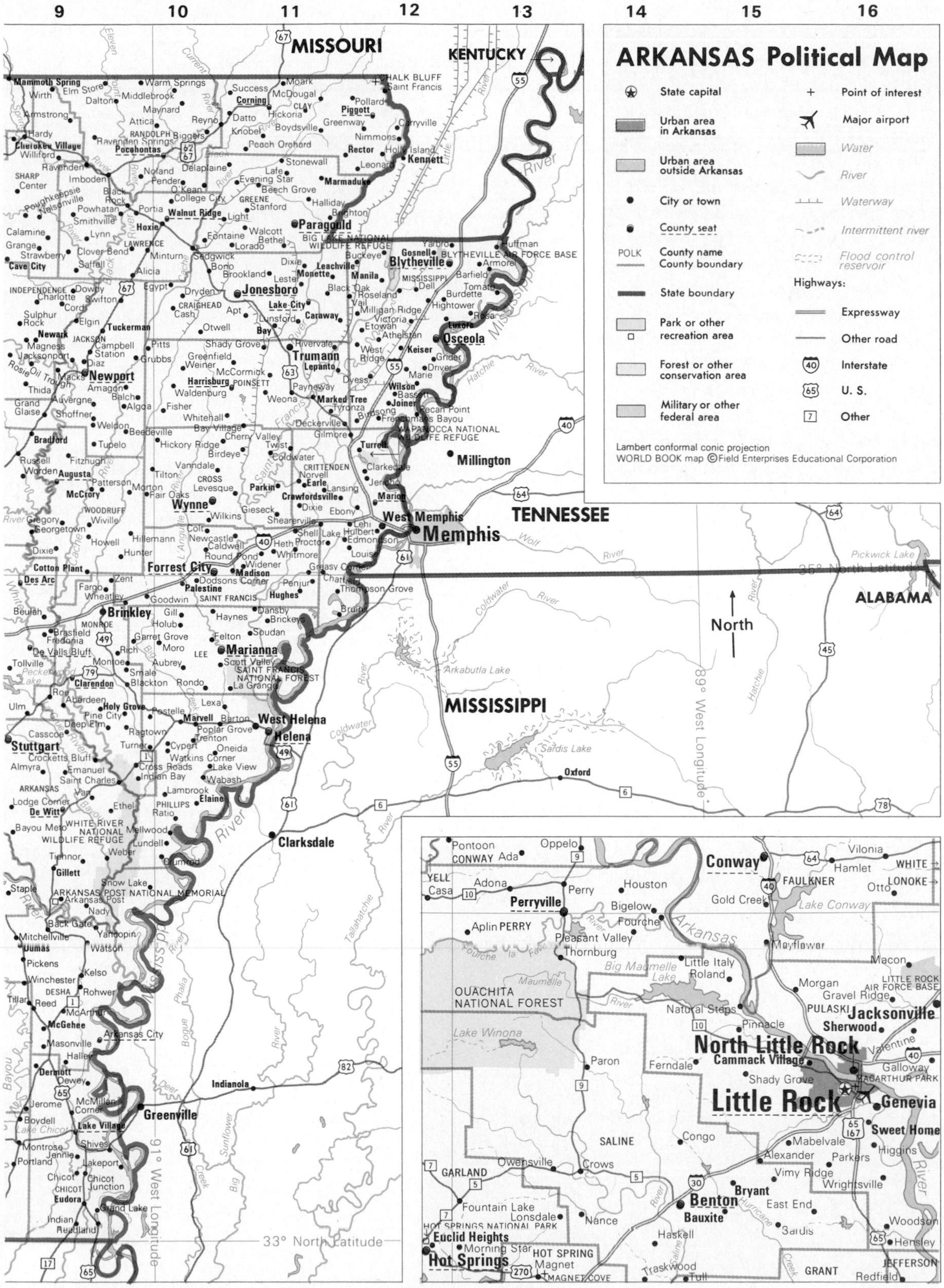

175   200   225   Miles
275   300   325   350   375 Kilometers

Seal

Flag

Bird: Mockingbird

Flower: Apple Blossom

Delaware

First State

Capital: Dover
Area: 2,057 sq. mi. (5,328 km^2), including 75 sq. mi. (194 km^2) of inland water but excluding 350 sq. mi. (906 km^2) of Delaware Bay; 49th in size among the states
Elevation: *Highest*—442 ft. (135 m) above sea level on Ebright Road in New Castle County; *lowest*—sea level along the coast
Statehood: Dec. 7, 1787, the 1st state
Abbreviations: Del. (traditional); DE (postal)
Motto: *Liberty and Independence*
Song: "Our Delaware"
Tree: American Holly

Delaware's state seal shows a sheaf of wheat, an ear of corn, and an ox. These symbolize Delaware's early farms. A farmer and rifleman represent the duties of the people of Delaware both as productive workers and as defenders of their rights. The seal was originally adopted in 1777 and modified in 1793, 1847, and 1907. The flag, adopted in 1912, has an adaptation of the seal. The date "December 7, 1787" shows that Delaware was the first state to ratify the U.S. Constitution.

Delaware is called the *First State* because it was the first of the original 13 states to ratify the U.S. Constitution. Delaware approved the charter on December 7, 1787.

During the days of early colonial settlement, Delaware was the site of the first log cabins built in America. They were constructed in 1638 by a group of Swedes who had founded New Sweden, the first permanent settlement in the Delaware region. The Swedish settlers were led by Netherlander Peter Minuit. New Sweden was eventually taken over by the Dutch, then the British. Delaware was ruled as part of the colony of New York, then as part of Pennsylvania before becoming a state in 1776.

Delaware joined other American colonies in approving the Declaration of Independence, and Delaware soldiers fought in battles throughout the Revolutionary War. But only one minor skirmish actually occurred on Delaware soil.

The early 1800's brought the birth of Delaware's chemical industry, which eventually became the most important industry in the state. In 1802, French immigrant Éleuthère Irénée du Pont established a powder mill near Wilmington. Du Pont's mill was the start of the present-day Du Pont Company, the largest chemical company in the world. Over the years, other chemical companies established headquarters and research laboratories in or near Wilmington, and the city gained the nickname *Chemical Capital of the World.*

Delaware is the second smallest state in the nation after Rhode Island. It is divided into only three counties that, in turn, are divided into units called hundreds. Delaware is the only state that uses hundreds. These divisions have no governing function but serve as units for zoning and property location. Delaware is also the only state in which legislators may amend the state constitution without the voters' approval.

Methodism was founded in Delaware as a result of a meeting in 1784 between Francis Asbury and Thomas Coke in Barratt's Chapel near Frederica. The chapel today is one of Delaware's historic attractions. Another is the Henry Francis du Pont Winterthur Museum near Wilmington. It has an extensive collection of early American furniture displayed in more than a hundred rooms.

Every year, millions of Americans follow a Christmas tradition that began in Delaware in 1907. That year, Emily Bissell, a nurse, introduced the first Christmas seals during a local tuberculosis fund-raising drive.

The golden glow of a shimmering sunset starkly outlines the Delaware Memorial Bridge, which spans the Delaware River and links the state with New Jersey.

DELAWARE Political Map

✪	State capital		
▮	Urban area in Delaware	▢	Military or other federal area
▢	Urban area outside Delaware	+	Point of interest
●	City or town	✈	Major airport
◉	County seat		Water
KENT	County name		River
	County boundary		Waterway
▢	Forest or other conservation area		**Highways:**
		══	Expressway
		—	Other road
		68	Interstate
		10	U.S.
		34	Other

Transverse Mercator projection

WORLD BOOK map ©Field Enterprises Educational Corporation

Seal

Flag

Bird: Blue Hen Chicken

Flower: Peach Blossom

Distance scale

0 5 10 15 20 25 30 35 40 Miles

0 5 10 15 20 25 30 35 40 50 60 Kilometers

Peering into the tangled growth and murky waters of the Everglades, sightseers hope to spot some of the unique wildlife of the swamps.

Florida

Florida is officially nicknamed the *Sunshine State.* Its warm, sunny weather and beautiful coastal resorts make it one of the most popular tourist states. The beaches at resort areas such as Miami Beach, Palm Beach, Daytona Beach, St. Petersburg, and Fort Lauderdale are among the finest in the world. About 30 million persons visit Florida annually, making tourism the number-one industry in the state.

Florida is also called the *Peninsula State* because it is largely a peninsula that juts 400 miles (643.7 kilometers) into the sea. It has a longer coastline than any other state except Alaska and is the southernmost state in the contiguous United States. Lake Okeechobee in south-central Florida is the second-largest lake that lies entirely within the United States. Only Lake Michigan is larger.

In addition to its beaches, Florida has many other natural features that attract tourists. One of them, Everglades National Park, gives the state a third nickname—the *Everglade State.* The Everglades form the largest subtropical wilderness in the United States. Other natural wonders of Florida include Big Cypress Swamp, numerous tropical gardens, and the John Pennekamp Coral Reef State Park, where visitors can see living reef formations by diving underwater or looking through glass-bottom boats.

The area's lush plant life inspired Spanish explorer Ponce de León to give Florida its name, using a Spanish word that means "full of flowers." Among the many flowers that grow wild in Florida are orchids, lilies, irises, morning glories, sunflowers, and lupines.

Florida is the home of black bears, deer, Florida panthers, wildcats, alligators, and other animals. The state has flocks of many large water birds such as egrets, herons, ibises, pelicans, and water turkeys.

More kinds of freshwater and ocean fish swim in Florida waters than anywhere else in the world. Commercial fishing is important to the state's economy. Shrimp, lobsters, and red snappers are among the valuable catches.

Florida is well known for its contributions to the nation's citrus crop. About three-fourths of all the oranges and grapefruit grown in the United States come from Florida, and the state produces virtually all the frozen orange juice concentrate in the country. Franciscan friars were the first to plant citrus groves in Florida. During the 1600's, they grew oranges, lemons, figs, and other fruits that hadn't grown in the region before. Today, citrus groves thrive throughout central and southern Florida. The state also produces large amounts of peanuts, pecans, soybeans, corn, cotton, tomatoes, and other vegetables, as well as tropical fruits such as bananas, guavas, mangoes, papayas, and pineapples. Florida ranks first in U.S. sugar cane production.

About three-fourths of the phosphate mined in the United States comes from Florida's huge deposits. Most of it is used for agricultural fertilizers.

Florida has played a vital role in the U.S. space program. Cape Canaveral, on Florida's Atlantic coast, has been the launching site of many satellites and rockets, including *Explorer I,* the first U.S. earth satellite. In 1969, the U.S. astronauts who landed on the moon began their trip on the launching pad at Cape Canaveral.

Various Indian tribes may have lived in the Florida region as long as 10,000 years ago. Burial mounds in the state give evidence of their ancient settlements.

Ponce de León was the first white person to set foot on Florida soil. He arrived in 1513 in search of a legendary fountain of youth. Although he never found the fountain, he claimed the area for Spain. In 1565, the Spanish founded their first permanent Florida settlement at St. Augustine. It became the oldest city in the entire United States.

Spain held onto its Florida possessions for about 200 years. The region came under British control in 1763 but was returned to Spain 20 years later. During the early 1800's, the Florida area was the only part of the Southeast not within the United States. Spain refused to yield the territory until 1819. Florida officially became part of the United States in 1821. Congress established the Florida Territory a year later.

Statehood for Florida had to wait until Iowa was also ready to become a state. In 1839, Florida drafted a constitution to prepare for statehood. But Congress wanted to maintain a balance between slave states and free states. In 1845, Florida was finally admitted to the Union as the 27th state. Iowa was admitted as a free state the next year.

During the Civil War, Florida joined the Confederacy. Tallahassee was the only Confederate state capital east of the Mississippi that was not captured by Union troops. Florida was readmitted to the Union in 1868.

A fantasyland for young and old alike, Walt Disney World near Orlando welcomes thousands of visitors each year—many from outside the United States.

History comes to life in a restored Spanish section of St. Augustine.

Florida
Sunshine State

Capital: Tallahassee
Area: 58,560 sq. mi. (151,670 km²), including 4,470 sq. mi. (11,577 km²) of inland water but excluding 1,735 sq. mi. (4,494 km²) of Atlantic and Gulf of Mexico coastal water; 22nd in size among the states
Elevation: *Highest*—345 ft. 105 m) above sea level in Walton County; *lowest*—sea level along the Atlantic Ocean
Statehood: March 3, 1845, the 27th state
Abbreviations: Fla. (traditional); FL (postal)
Motto: *In God We Trust* (unofficial)
Song: "Swanee River"
Tree: Cabbage (Sabal) Palm

The sun on Florida's state seal represents glory and splendor, and the authority of the state government. The steamboat is a sign of commerce and growth, and the palm tree symbolizes victory, justice, and honor. The flowers stand for hope and joy, and the Indian girl strewing flowers shows the influence of various tribes on Florida's history. Adopted in 1868, the seal also appears on the state flag, adopted in 1899. On the flag, the seal lies in a white field crossed by diagonal red bars. These stand for the bars of the Confederate flag.

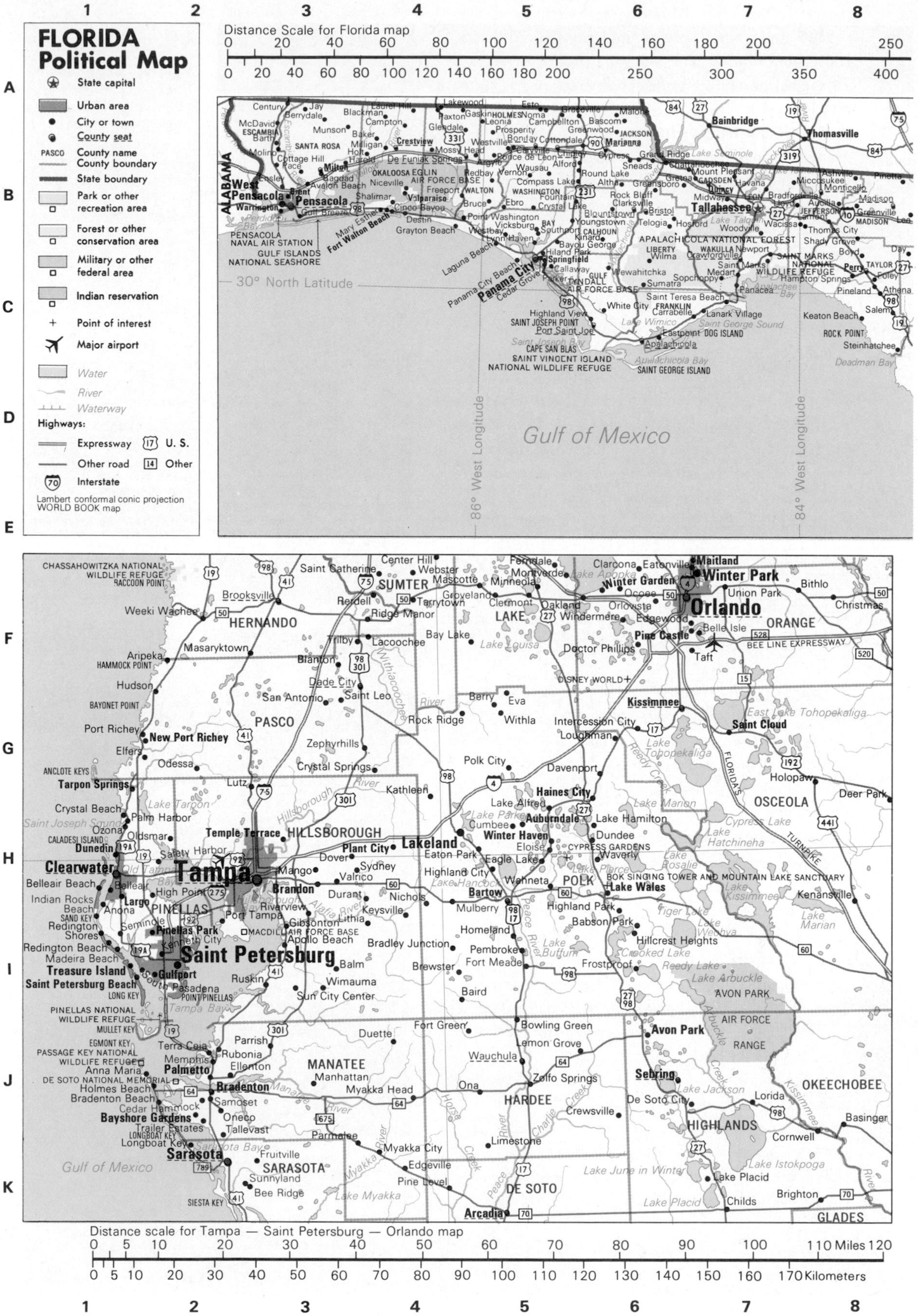

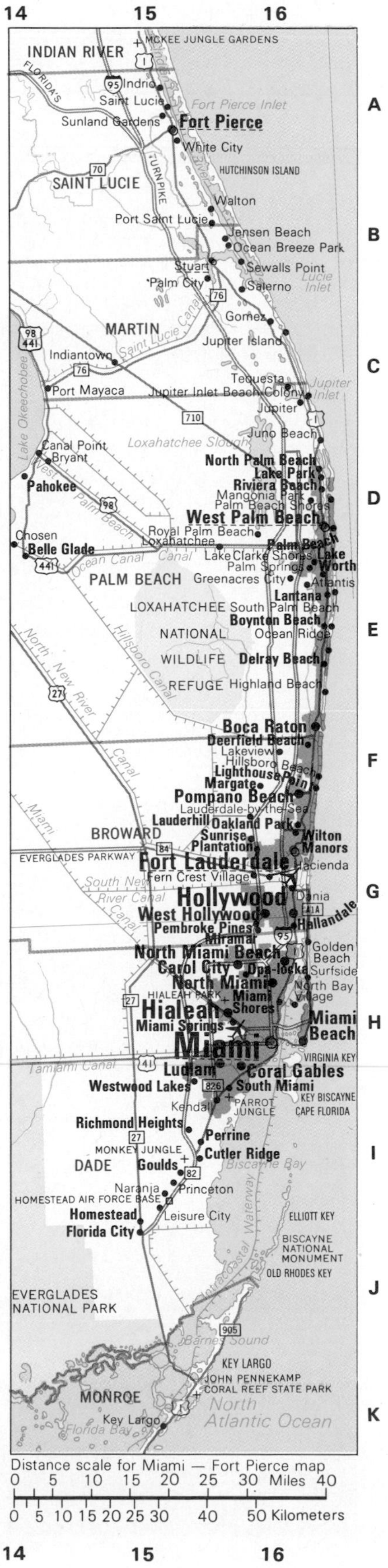

Seal

Flag

Bird: Mockingbird

Flower: Orange Blossom

Carved into the side of the granite dome known as Stone Mountain, this memorial sculpture to Confederate leaders Jefferson Davis, Robert E. Lee, and Stonewall Jackson is an eternal tribute to the South's Civil War heroes (below top).

Cascaded stones form a temporary obstacle for these hikers in the deep woods of Cloudland Canyon State Park (below bottom).

Georgia

At one time Georgia was primarily a cotton-raising state. Almost all of its people grew cotton for a living. Then other crops such as corn, fruit, and tobacco became important. As manufacturing expanded, weaving cotton became more profitable than growing it. Since 1940, Georgia has changed from mainly an agricultural state to an industrial one, and cotton and other textile mills are now Georgia's major source of income.

Other industries important to the state include processing foods and manufacturing transportation equipment and clothing. Called the *Empire State of the South* because of its large size and thriving industries, Georgia has become one of the leading manufacturing states of the South.

Farming, however, remains important to Georgia's economy. The state is a leading producer of pecans and tobacco. It is sometimes called the *Peach State* because it is a leading peach producer. Georgia is also known as the *Goober State* since it produces more peanuts, or goobers, than any other state.

Georgia is one of the nation's leading producers of forest products. It is famous for its pine and hardwood trees, which account for the often-used

expression "tall as a Georgia pine." Forests cover about 70 per cent of the land area of Georgia.

Natural resources are also important to Georgia. It ranks first among all the states in granite output. Stone Mountain in the Piedmont region near Atlanta is a major tourist attraction. It is one of the largest domes of exposed granite in North America. On its sides are carved huge figures of Confederate leaders.

Marble is another important natural resource to come from this state. Georgia marble was used in building the Lincoln Memorial in Washington, D.C., and several state capitols. Two of the largest blocks of marble in the world, each weighing 90 tons, have been taken from this state.

Georgia is well known for its mild, sunny year-round climate, its magnolias, and its moss-draped trees. These, teamed with its natural beauty and famous resorts, make Georgia an attractive vacation spot. The "Golden Isles" along Georgia's coast are popular with tourists. Warm Springs is a favorite spot. People suffering from various illnesses often find relief in its soothing waters. President Franklin D. Roosevelt, a polio victim, built his Little White House in Warm Springs. The house, where he died, and the nearby Franklin D. Roosevelt Museum contain mementos of the President and are open to visitors.

Other interesting Georgia sites include Callaway Gardens, acres of green meadows, rolling hills, lakes, and woodlands—all near Pine Mountain; the famous Okefenokee Swamp, where visitors may explore water trails on guided boat tours; the Old Slave Market in Louisville, one of the few slave-market buildings still standing; and Westville, a reconstructed farming village in Lumpkin that shows the handicrafts and culture of Georgia in the 1850's.

Georgia is rich in history. It was the last of the original 13 American colonies and was named for King George II of England. Eli Whitney invented the cotton gin near Savannah. The machine saved much work among cotton farmers and led to great expansion in the farming of cotton. Dahlonega was the site of the first gold rush in the United States when prospectors discovered gold deposits in 1828. Visitors may pan for gold in any of the three private mines that are about 3 to 5 miles (4.8 to 8 kilometers) from the museum.

During the Civil War in America, General William T. Sherman of the Union Army began his famous march across Georgia to the sea. The result was the burning of the entire city of Atlanta and the destruction of $100 million worth of property.

Georgia is the birthplace of the Girl Scouts of America, founded by Juliette Gordon Low of Savannah; the departure point of the first steamship to cross the Atlantic, the S.S. *Savannah,* which traveled from Savannah, Georgia, to Liverpool, England, in 1819; and the home of Jimmy Carter, the 39th President of the United States, born in Plains.

Georgia has been the inspiration for numerous songs and tales. Stephen Foster made the Suwannee River near Waycross famous in his song, "Old Folks at Home." Georgia influenced Joel Chandler Harris while writing his famous Uncle Remus stories.

Other Georgia writers include poet Sidney Lanier and novelists Margaret Mitchell and Erskine Caldwell. Mitchell wrote the celebrated Civil War saga, *Gone with the Wind.*

Shifting sands piled into dunes line the shores of Cumberland Island, one of the many "Golden Isles" that fringe Georgia's coastline.

Georgia
Empire State of the South

Capital: Atlanta
Area: 58,876 sq. mi. (152,488 km²), including 803 sq. mi. (2,080 km²) of inland water but excluding 48 sq. mi. (124 km²) of Atlantic coastal water; 21st in size among the states
Elevation: *Highest*—Brasstown Bald Mountain, 4,784 ft. (1,458 m) above sea level; *lowest*—sea level on the Atlantic coast
Statehood: Jan. 2, 1788, the 4th state
Abbreviations: Ga. (traditional); GA (postal)
Motto: *Wisdom, Justice, and Moderation*
Song: "Georgia on My Mind"
Tree: Live Oak

Georgia's state seal features symbols on both sides. One shows an arch representing the state constitution. Three columns bear Georgia's motto. The date 1776 is the year Georgia signed the Declaration of Independence. On the other side of the seal, a ship represents Georgia's exports. A boat represents internal commerce. A man plowing and sheep grazing represent Georgia's agriculture. The state adopted its seal in 1914. The state flag, adopted in 1956, displays the seal and the Confederate battle flag.

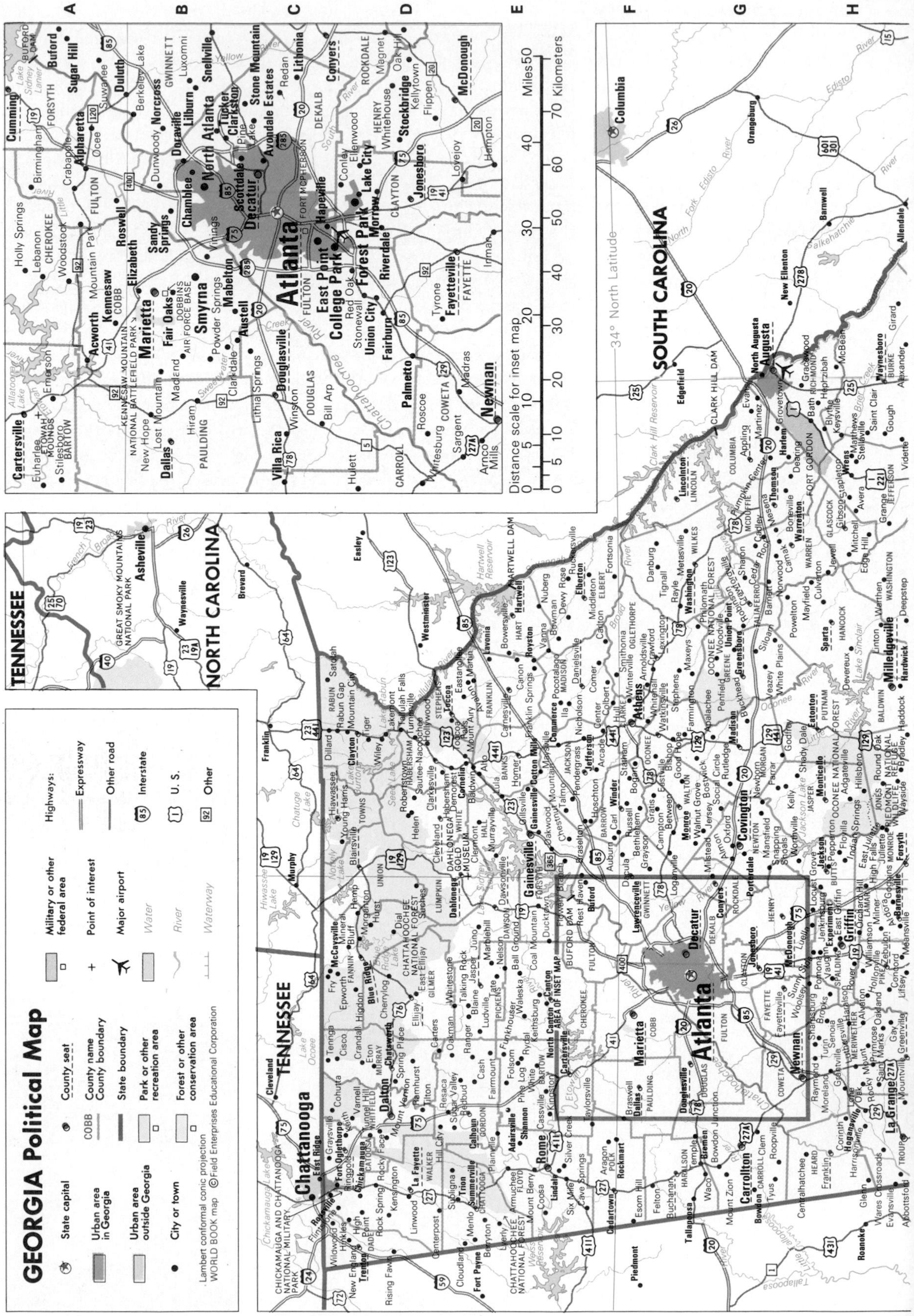

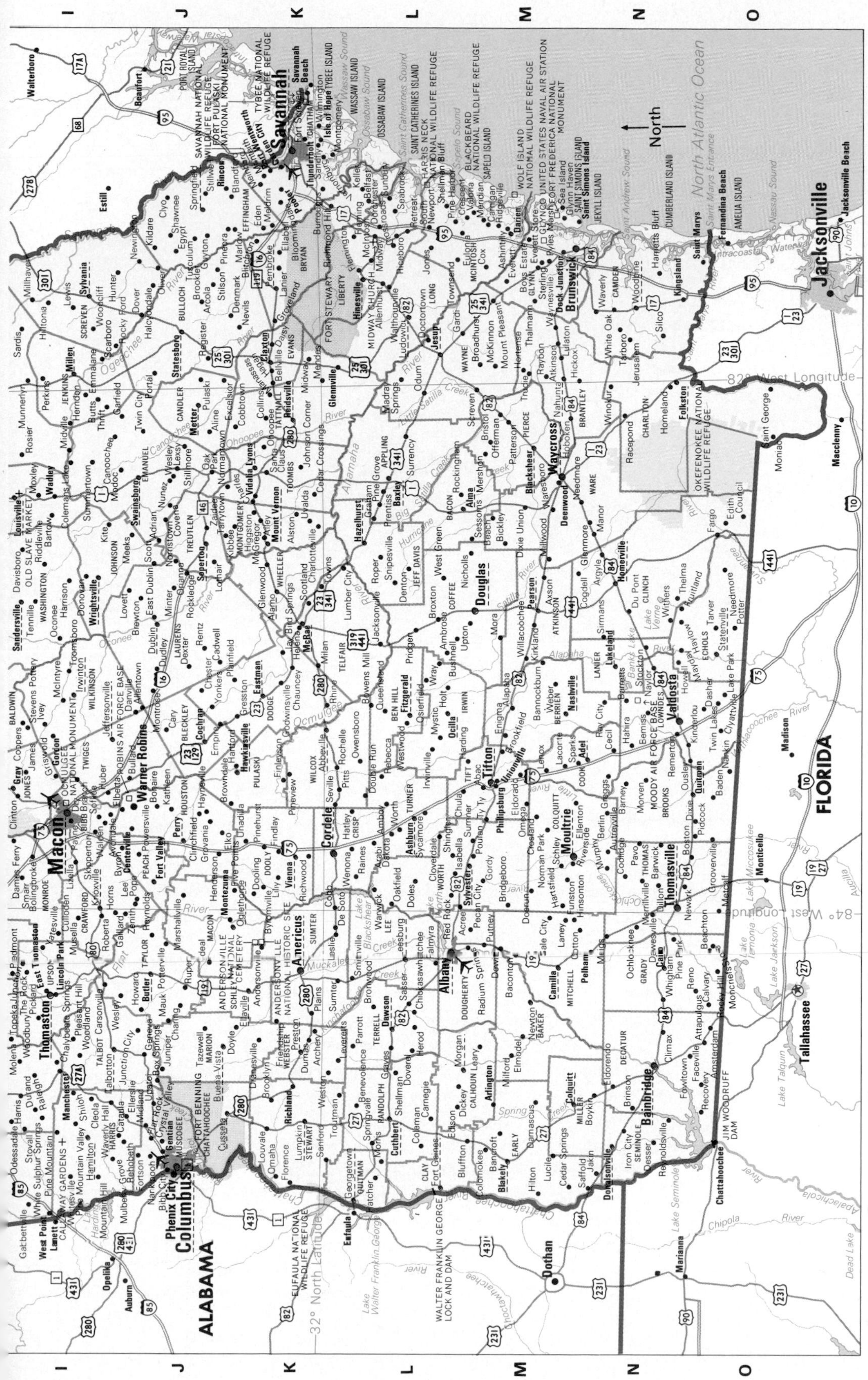

Seal

Flag

Bird: Brown Thrasher

Flower: Cherokee Rose

For generations, the bluegrass pastures of Kentucky have been heralded as outstanding breeding grounds for race horses.

Kentucky

Nicknamed the *Bluegrass State,* Kentucky is covered to a large extent by areas of rolling pastures of rich grass called bluegrass, so named because of its dusty blue blossoms. These pastures are the grazing ground for many champion Thoroughbred race horses, for which Kentucky is famous. More than 4,000 Thoroughbreds are born every year on farms in the Lexington area. These farms—including Darby Dan, Dixiana Farm, Domino Stud, and King Ranch—are open to the public and are among Kentucky's most interesting sites.

Churchill Downs in Louisville is another popular tourist attraction. It is the home of the Kentucky Derby, the most famous of all U.S. horse races.

Kentucky is known, however, for more than champion race horses. The state is the nation's leader in the production of coal and ranks second among all the states in total tobacco produced. Coal is mined mainly in Kentucky's eastern and northwestern counties, while tobacco is raised in almost every county of the state. Kentucky is also the leading producer of whiskey in the United States.

Kentucky is a state of great natural beauty. Scenic attractions and natural wonders abound. The most famous and probably most popular of these is Mammoth Cave in central Kentucky. The cave is now part of Mammoth Cave National Park.

Other attractions include, near Corbin, Cumberland Falls, the state's highest waterfall and often called the *Niagara of the South;* Natural Bridge, located in a scenic state park in the beautiful Red River Valley; and Cumberland Gap, where parts of three different states—Kentucky, Virginia, and Tennessee—can be viewed from a scenic overlook in what is now an historical park.

Kentucky's name has a Cherokee Indian background, but its meaning is somewhat of a mystery. Possible translations include "land of tomorrow," "meadowland," and the "dark and bloody ground." The third is occasionally used as a nickname for the state since Kentucky has a history of much bloody fighting.

Many battles were fought between the Indians and the early settlers of the state. During the Civil War, the state of Kentucky remained in the Union, but many Kentucky residents joined the Confederate armies and, occasionally, members of the same family fought one another in battle.

A number of Civil War battles were fought on Kentucky soil. Several of the Indian and Civil War battlefields are favorite visitor attractions. In 1900, Kentucky came close to fighting a civil war of its own when Governor William Goebel was assassinated after a turbulent political election.

Both Abraham Lincoln, President of the United States, and Jefferson Davis, President of the Confederate States, were born in Kentucky, not 100 miles (161 kilometers) apart. Abe Lincoln's birthplace is now a national historic site near Hodgenville.

Rivers are an important part of Kentucky's geography. The Ohio River forms the state's entire northern border. Its western border is formed by the Mississippi River, while the Big Sandy and Tug Fork rivers form Kentucky's northeastern border. The state's southeastern border touches another great land feature, the Appalachian Mountains.

Other principal rivers in Kentucky are all westward flowing tributaries of the Ohio River including the Cumberland, Green, Kentucky, Licking, Salt, and Tennessee rivers. The Breaks of the Sandy is an interesting site where the Russell Fork River joins the Big Sandy River in a plunging drop of about 350 feet (106.7 meters). Frankfort, Kentucky's capital, lies on the Kentucky River. Its capitol building overlooks this scenic waterway.

Many lakes can also be seen dotting the Kentucky landscape. Many of these are favorite spots for fishing and boating. Kentucky Lake, in western Kentucky, was created by the Tennessee Valley Authority and is the state's largest artificial lake.

There are other interesting historic places to visit in Kentucky. Among these are My Old Kentucky Home in Bardstown, the home of Stephen Foster's cousin and the inspiration for Foster's famous song, "My Old Kentucky Home," now the state song of Kentucky; Fort Knox, south of Louisville, where the nation's gold reserves are stored; Shakertown, or Pleasant Hill, an old Shaker settlement near Lexington; and Washington, a town with many restored structures built in the late 1700's and open to the public.

Picnickers relax under a shady canopy in the recreational area between Kentucky and Barkley lakes (above).

Surprises such as Natural Bridge await those who follow the trails through Kentucky's numerous forests and parks (left).

Kentucky
Bluegrass State

Capital: Frankfort
Area: 40,395 sq. mi. (104,623 km²), including 745 sq. mi. (1,930 km²) of inland water; 37th in size among the states
Elevation: *Highest*—Black Mountain, 4,145 ft. (1,263 m) above sea level; *lowest*—257 ft. (78 m) above sea level along the Mississippi River in Fulton County
Statehood: June 1, 1792, the 15th state
Abbreviations: Ky. or Ken. (traditional); KY (postal)
Motto: *United We Stand, Divided We Fall*
Song: "My Old Kentucky Home"
Tree: Kentucky Coffeetree

Kentucky's state seal shows the state motto and two men greeting each other. These symbolize brotherhood. The seal was adopted in 1792. The state flag was first adopted in 1918 and again in 1962. It bears the state flower and an adaptation of the state seal.

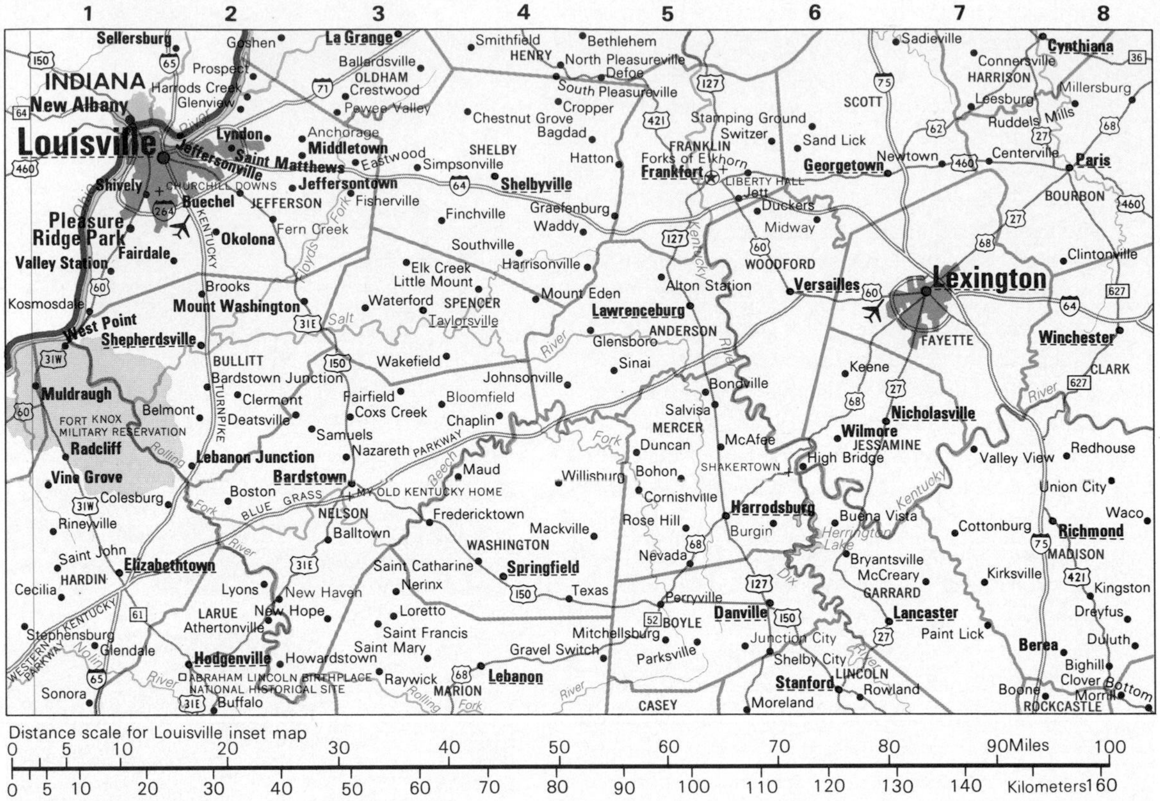

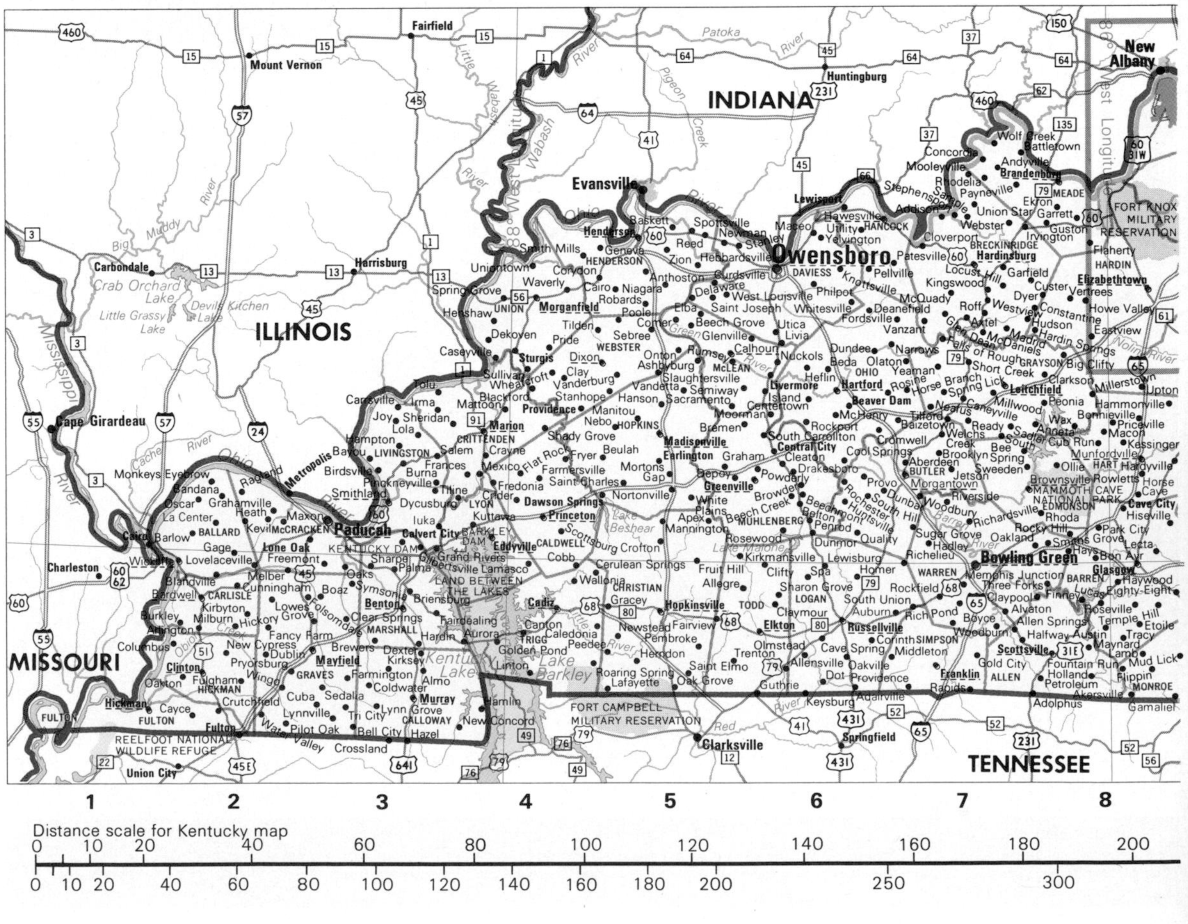

KENTUCKY Political Map

Symbol	Description
★	State capital
	Urban area in Kentucky
	Urban area outside Kentucky
•	City or town
•	County seat
BARREN	County name
	County boundary
	State boundary
	Park or other recreation area
	Forest or other conservation area

Symbol	Description
	Military or other federal area
+	Point of interest
✈	Major airport
	Water
	River

Highways:
Symbol	Description
	Expressway
	Other road
75	Interstate
421	U.S.
80	Other

Lambert conformal conic projection
WORLD BOOK map © Field Enterprises Educational Corporation

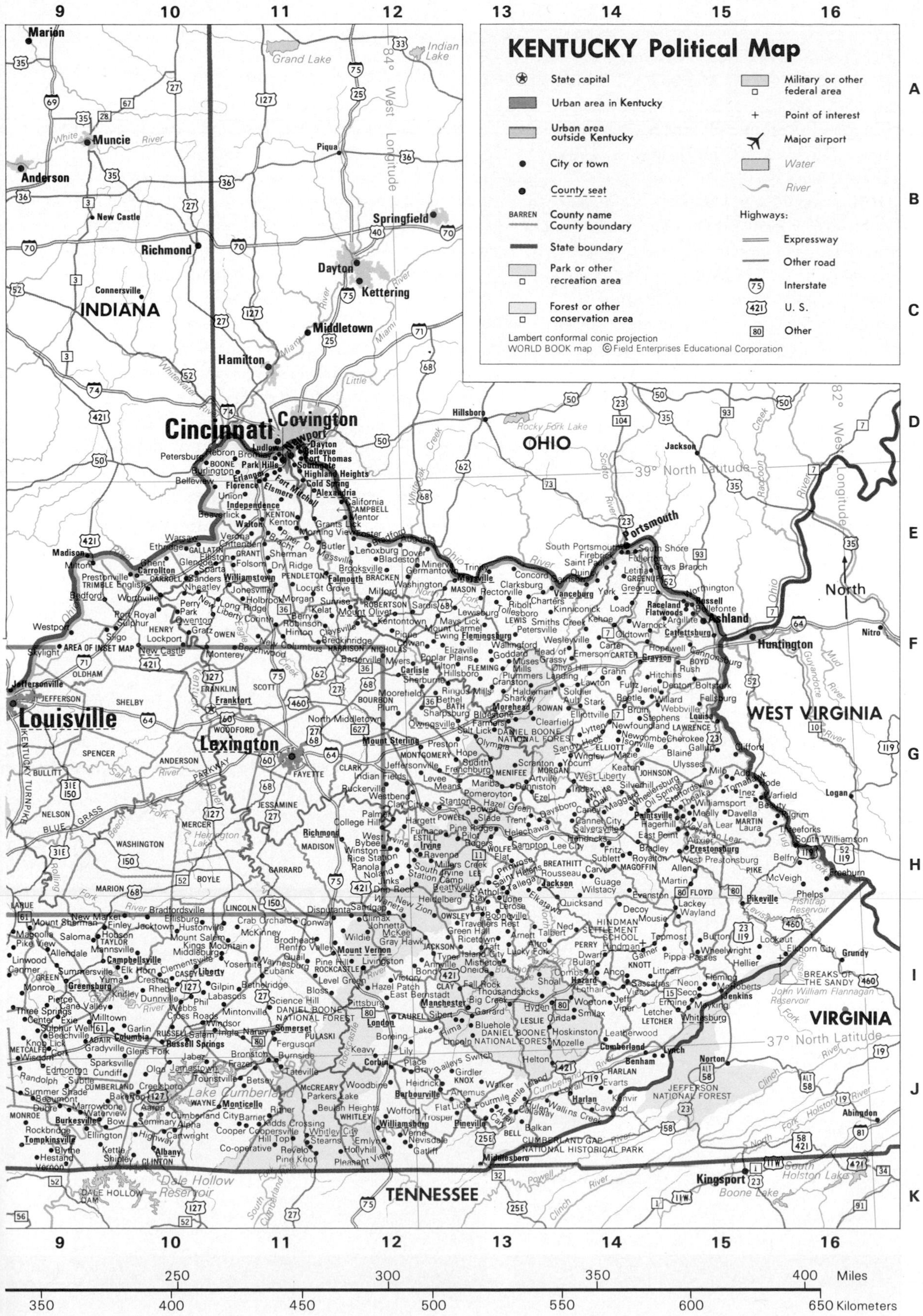

Seal

Flag

Bird: Kentucky Cardinal

Flower: Goldenrod

250   300   350   400 Miles
350   400   450   500   550   600   650 Kilometers

Louisiana

Most of present-day Louisiana was once part of an ancient bay of the Gulf of Mexico. Over thousands of years, however, rivers such as the Mississippi flowing from the north deposited huge amounts of soil or silt. These account for the present size and formation of the state.

The Mississippi River has been a major factor in making Louisiana one of the nation's busiest commercial areas. This supreme waterway, which empties into the Gulf of Mexico at Louisiana's southern tip, links the state with the heart of America as well as lands across the sea. Louisiana's largest city, New Orleans, is one of the world's busiest seaports. Even Baton Rouge, the state capital, situated about 235 miles (378.2 kilometers) upriver, can accommodate ocean-going ships.

The rich soil deposited by the Mississippi and other rivers has given Louisiana one of the world's largest regions of fertile farmland. Louisiana ranks as one of the leaders in the production of sugar cane. It has occasionally been called the *Sugar State.* Other important agricultural products include soybeans, cotton, rice, and sweet potatoes.

Louisiana's greatest source of income, however, is mineral production—chiefly oil and natural gas. Wells can be seen mainly in the southern marshlands of the state. Louisiana is also the nation's leader in the production of salt.

Wildlife is abundant in this state, making Louisiana the nation's leader in the production of fur from wild animals, primarily muskrats and nutrias, which are beaverlike animals. But minks, opossums, and raccoons also live in the wooded lowlands. Louisiana maintains well over a million acres of land supervised for hunting. The coastal marshes are the winter home of half of North America's wild ducks and geese. The brown pelican—Louisiana's state bird and the source of the state's official nickname, the *Pelican State*—also makes its home there.

Louisiana contains an interesting mixture of people, culture, and customs. It was first settled by the French in 1682 and was named in honor of

Tending to his gear, this sportsman of the Mississippi Delta is preparing for the duck-hunting season (near right).

The sweet harvest from extensive sugar cane fields in central Louisiana will soon be processed into refined sugar products (far right).

Louis XIV, the king of France. In 1803, it was sold to the United States along with the Mississippi Valley region in the transaction known as the Louisiana Purchase. Most of southern Louisiana is now inhabited by descendants of the original French and Spanish settlers, called Creoles, or by descendants of French settlers from Canada called Cajuns. The culture of these people still has an important influence on the area. In fact, Louisiana is often called the *Creole State.* Most of the population of northern Louisiana, on the other hand, has ancestors who were pioneers from neighboring states and are of Anglo-Saxon descent.

New Orleans, often called *America's Most Interesting City,* is famous for its Old World charm. The French Quarter, fine restaurants featuring creole and cajun cooking, and Old World architecture depict the influence on New Orleans of Louisiana's colonial past. As a tourist center, the city has much to offer. New Orleans is the home of superb museums and of the famous Mardi Gras celebration held just before Lent. It is also the *Cradle of Jazz,* where New Orleans-style jazz can be heard almost incessantly at famous night spots and concert halls.

White-columned mansions can be seen throughout Louisiana's countryside and are symbols of the state's past glory as a leader of the Old South before the Civil War. Much of Louisiana's history involves the Mississippi River itself. It was an important route for traders and fur trappers in colonial days. It also provided a highway for colorful paddle-wheel steamboats carrying passengers or shipments of cotton. In the early 1800's, the pirates of Jean Laffite terrorized the entire Louisiana coast. Today, a few of their descendants live in the village of Grand Isle south of New Orleans at the entrance to Barataria Bay. Grand Isle is one of Louisiana's top tourist attractions.

Louisiana has a number of other spots of interest to visitors. One is Chalmette National Historic Park in Chalmette, the site where General Andrew Jackson directed the American forces in the Battle of New Orleans during the War of 1812. The Evangeline Country, around St. Martinsville, is the home of the Cajuns and was made famous by Henry Wadsworth Longfellow in his poem *Evangeline.* The Evangeline Monument marks the spot where the Acadians from Canada landed.

Also of interest is the Feliciana Country, where John J. Audubon sketched. It has many old plantation homes that are open to the public. Natchitoches Country in west-central Louisiana includes the oldest town in Louisiana. The Lake Pontchartrain Causeway, the world's longest bridge, extends approximately 29 miles (46.7 kilometers) between New Orleans and Mandeville, Louisiana.

Lacy iron grillwork encloses Jackson Square, which fronts the St. Louis Cathedral in New Orleans' French Quarter.

Louisiana
Pelican State

Capital: Baton Rouge
Area: 48,523 sq. mi. (125,674 km²), including 3,593 sq. mi. (9,306 km²) of inland water but excluding 1,016 sq. mi. (2,631 km²) of Gulf of Mexico coastal water; 31st in size among the states
Elevation: *Highest*—Driskill Mountain, 535 ft. (163 m) above sea level; *lowest*—5 ft. (1.5 m) below sea level at New Orleans
Statehood: April 30, 1812, the 18th state
Abbreviations: La. (traditional); LA (postal)
Motto: *Union, Justice, and Confidence*
Song: "Give Me Louisiana"
Tree: Bald Cypress

Louisiana's state seal, adopted in 1902, shows a mother pelican feeding and protecting her brood. This design represents the state's role as the protector of its people and resources. The seal also carries the state motto. The state flag, adopted in 1912, has an adaptation of the state seal.

Seal

Flag

Bird: Brown Pelican

Flower: Magnolia

LOUISIANA Political Map

⭐ State capital

■ Urban area in Louisiana

□ Urban area outside Louisiana

● City or town

◉ Parish seat

ORLEANS Parish name

Parish boundary

State boundary

□ Park or other recreation area

□ Forest or other conservation area

□ Military or other federal area

□ Indian reservation

✛ Point of interest

✈ Major airport

Water

River

Waterway

Highways:

Expressway

Other road

🛣10 Interstate

🛣165 U.S.

🛣14 Other

Lambert conformal conic projection
WORLD BOOK map © Field Enterprises Educational Corporation

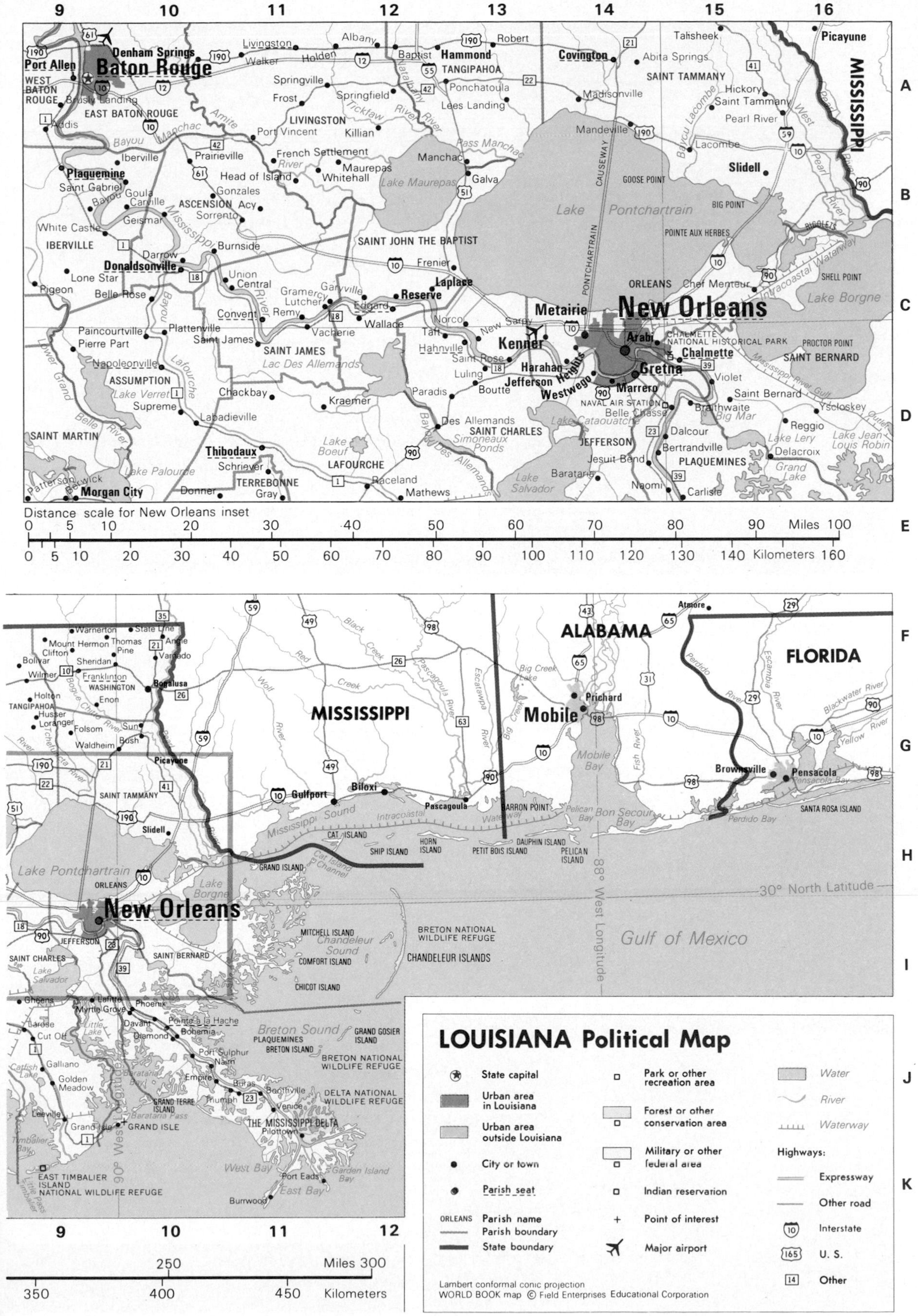

Trotting to the starting gate, jockey and horse are ready for the Preakness Stakes at Pimlico Race Track in Baltimore.

Maryland

Maryland is cut almost in two by the Chesapeake Bay, a huge arm of the Atlantic Ocean. The area west of the bay is called the Western Shore, and the area to the east is called the Eastern Shore. The William P. Lane, Jr., Memorial Bridge links the two shores.

Maryland has an Atlantic coastline of only 31 miles (49.9 kilometers). But the many deep inlets of the Chesapeake Bay give the state a total coastline of 3,190 miles (5,133.8 kilometers). The bay provides Maryland with many harbors including Baltimore, one of the nation's leading seaports, and Annapolis, the state capital and home of the U.S. Naval Academy. The bay also provides valuable catches of oysters, crabs, bluefish, striped bass, and other fish. Maryland leads the nation in its oyster catch and ranks second only to Maine in soft-shell clams.

The United States owes its national anthem to Maryland and to the city of Baltimore in particular. During the War of 1812, British forces bombarded Fort McHenry in Baltimore harbor. Seeing the American flag still flying over the fort after the successful defense of the city, Francis Scott Key was inspired to write "The Star-spangled Banner."

Baltimore has a number of other places of interest. The Peale Museum, one of the oldest museums in the country, was founded by Rembrandt Peale, son of the painter Charles Willson Peale. The Baltimore Museum of Art has the world's largest public collection of works by the French painter Henri Matisse. Baltimore is also the site of the first major Roman Catholic cathedral in the United States. The Basilica of the Assumption of the Blessed Virgin Mary was designed by Benjamin Latrobe and completed in 1821.

Spanish explorers of the 1500's were the first Europeans to reach the Chesapeake Bay. But the English were the first to settle in what is now Maryland. The state was named for Queen Henrietta Maria, wife of King Charles I of England. Charles granted a charter for the Maryland region to Cecil Calvert, the second Lord Baltimore. Lord Baltimore sent colonists to Maryland in 1634, and they founded St. Marys City.

Maryland quickly became known as a religious haven for groups persecuted elsewhere. Lord Baltimore was a Roman Catholic, and he wanted freedom of worship for Catholics and other groups as well. In 1649, he issued a religious toleration law that granted freedom of religion to all Christians in Maryland.

Reminders of the Lords Baltimore are found on various symbols of Maryland, including the state flag and the state seal. Even the state bird, the Bal-

During the War of 1812, Fort McHenry in Baltimore Harbor was the target of fierce British bombardment through the night of September 13, 1814. Francis Scott Key was so moved when he saw the American flag still flying at the fort the next morning, he wrote the lyrics to the "Star-spangled Banner."

timore oriole, was chosen because of the colonial leaders. Baltimore orioles are not particularly common in Maryland, but their colors—orange and black—were the family colors of the Baltimores.

Shortly before the Revolutionary War began, Marylanders staged their own version of the Boston Tea Party. They burned the British ship *Peggy Stewart* and its cargo of tea in Annapolis harbor in 1774. The Continental Congress met in Baltimore during the war, and Annapolis served as the U.S. capital for a time in 1783 and 1784. George Washington resigned his commission as commander in chief of the Continental Army in the Maryland State House. The state house still stands in Annapolis and is the oldest state capitol still in use in the United States.

Maryland became the seventh state when it ratified the U.S. Constitution in 1788. Three years later, it gave up part of its territory to the federal government for the new national capital at the District of Columbia.

Maryland's boundary with Pennsylvania is the famous Mason-Dixon Line, which has commonly come to be known as the dividing line between southern and northern states. Maryland's southern traditions caused deep divisions among its people during the Civil War. Maryland was a slave-holding state, but it voted to stay within the Union. Many Marylanders nevertheless joined the Confederate forces. One of the costliest battles of the Civil War occurred in Maryland. On a single day, during the Battle of Antietam, more than 12,000 Union soldiers and 10,000 Confederate soldiers were killed or wounded. The battle stopped a Confederate invasion of the North.

Over the years, Maryland has made a number of important contributions to the fields of transportation and communication. The Baltimore and Ohio Railroad was the first railroad in the Western Hemisphere to carry both freight and passengers. In 1830, the B & O tested the *Tom Thumb,* the first U.S. coal-powered steam locomotive, on a track near Baltimore. The first ocean-going iron steamship in the nation was the *De Rosset,* launched from Baltimore in 1839. The first telegraph line in the United States was established in 1844 between Baltimore and Washington, D.C.

Bushels of oysters wait to be shucked and eaten at this outdoor restaurant on Maryland's eastern shores.

Maryland
Old Line State

Capital: Annapolis
Area: 10,577 sq. mi. (27,394 km²), including 686 sq. mi. (1,777 km²) of inland water but excluding 1,726 sq. mi. (4,470 km²) of Chesapeake Bay; 42nd in size among the states
Elevation: *Highest*—Backbone Mountain, 3,360 ft. (1,024 m) above sea level, in the southwestern corner of the state; *lowest*—sea level, along the ocean
Statehood: April 28, 1788, the 7th state
Abbreviations: Md. (traditional); MD (postal)
Motto: *Fatti Maschii Parole Femine* (Manly Deeds, Womanly Words), Italian motto of the Calvert family
Song: "Maryland, My Maryland"
Tree: White (Wye) Oak

Maryland's state seal, adopted in 1876, features symbols on both sides. One shows Lord Baltimore, founder of Maryland, as a knight. A shield on the other side bears the coats of arms of the Calvert and Crossland families. Lord Baltimore was related to both families and used the combined arms. A farmer beside the shield symbolizes Maryland. A fisherman represents Lord Baltimore's Avalon colony in Newfoundland. The state flag, with an adaptation of Baltimore's arms, was adopted in 1904.

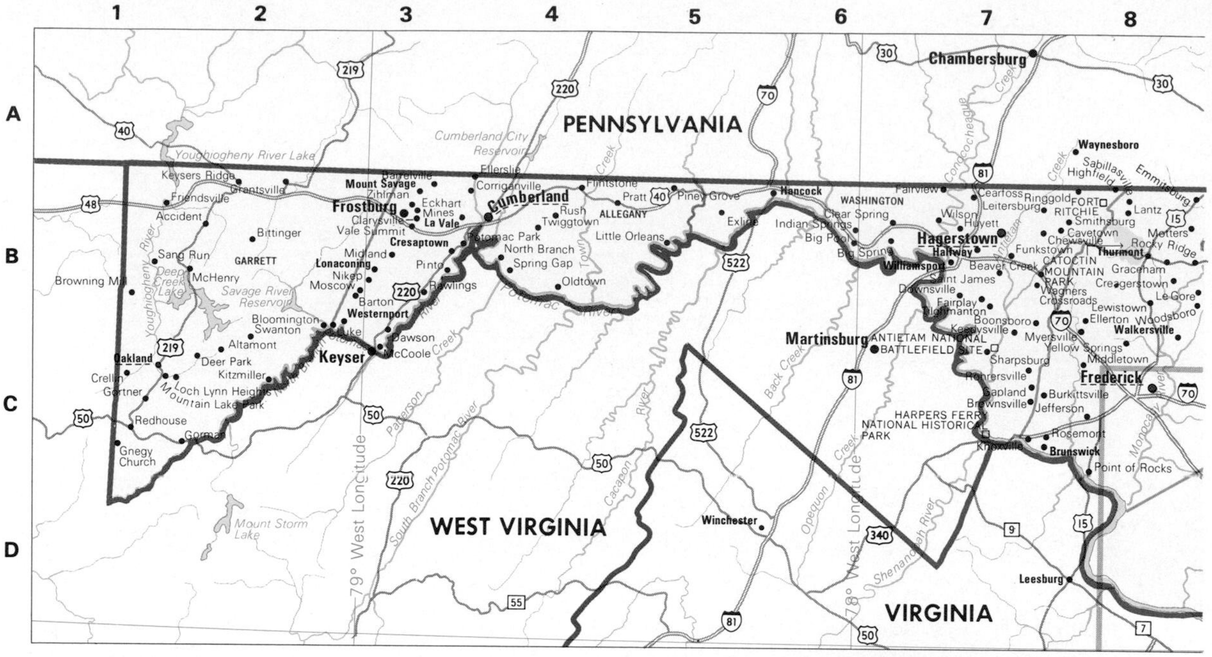

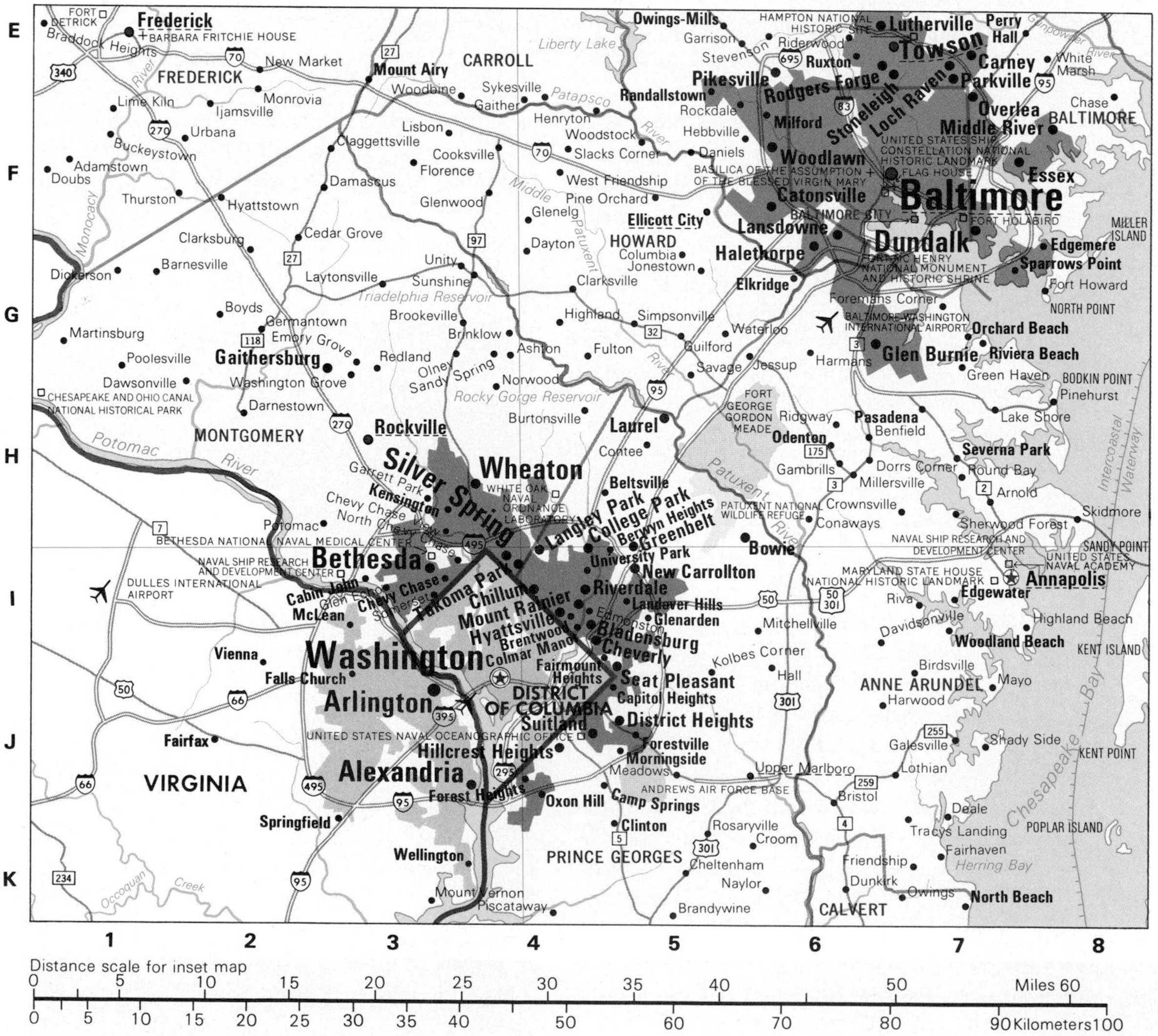

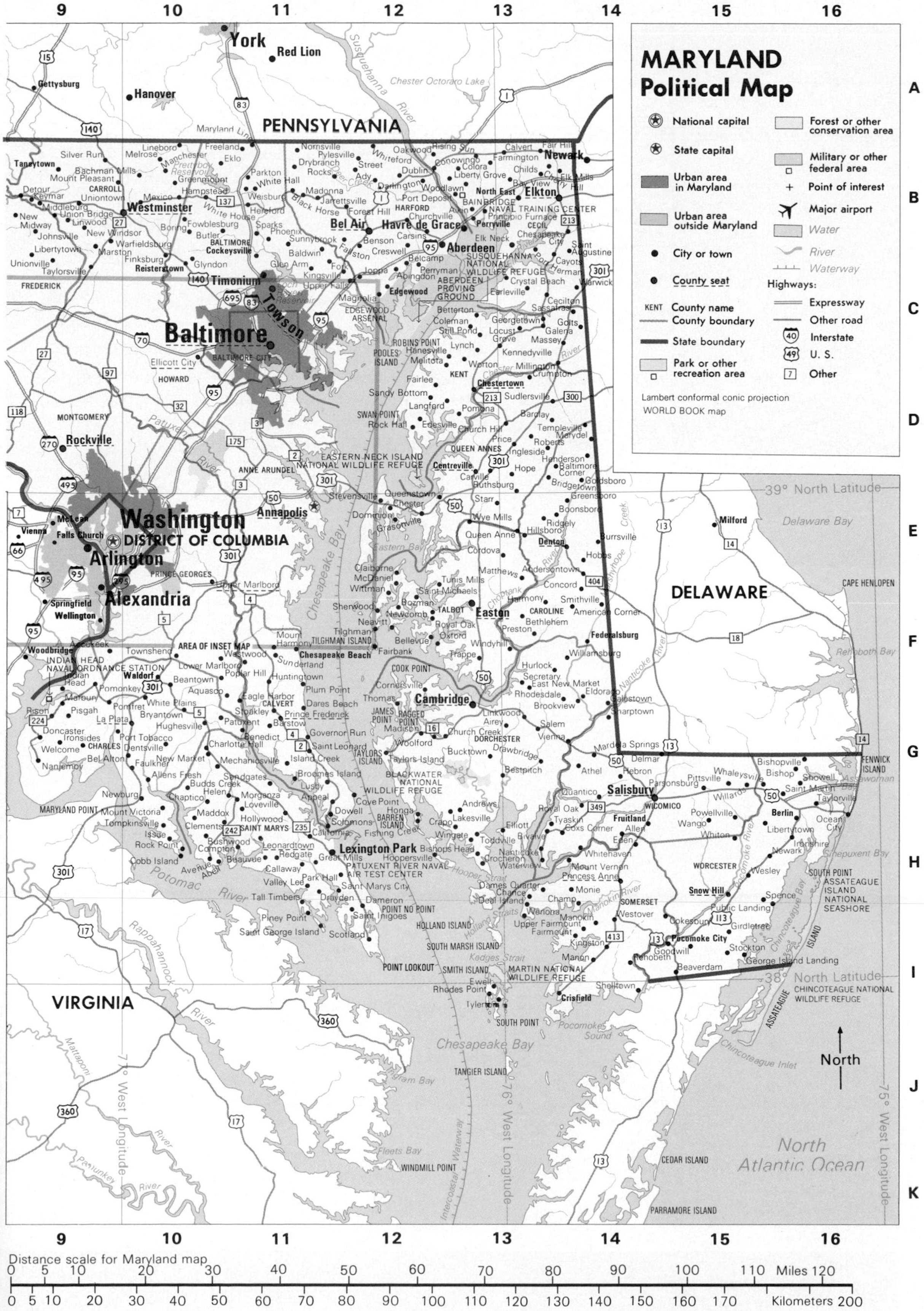
MARYLAND
Political Map
National capital
State capital
Urban area in Maryland
Urban area outside Maryland
City or town
County seat
KENT County name
County boundary
State boundary
Park or other recreation area
Forest or other conservation area
Military or other federal area
Point of interest
Major airport
Water
River
Waterway
Highways:
Expressway
Other road
Interstate
U. S.
Other
Lambert conformal conic projection
WORLD BOOK map
PENNSYLVANIA
DELAWARE
VIRGINIA
York
Red Lion
Gettysburg
Hanover
Westminster
Bel Air
Havre de Grace
Aberdeen
Elkton
Newark
Timonium
Towson
Baltimore
Rockville
Washington
DISTRICT OF COLUMBIA
Arlington
Alexandria
Annapolis
Chestertown
Centreville
Easton
Cambridge
Denton
Salisbury
Snow Hill
Pocomoke City
Berlin
Lexington Park
Crisfield
Milford
Chesapeake Bay
North Atlantic Ocean
Delaware Bay
39° North Latitude
38° North Latitude
77° West Longitude
76° West Longitude
75° West Longitude
North
Distance scale for Maryland map
0 5 10 20 30 40 50 60 70 80 90 100 110 Miles 120
0 5 10 20 30 40 50 60 70 80 90 100 110 120 130 140 150 160 170 Kilometers 200

SCUTIS · BONAE · VOLUNTATIS · CORONASTI · NOS
TERRAE · MARIAE · ET · AVALONIAE · BARO · DE · BALTIMORE

Seal

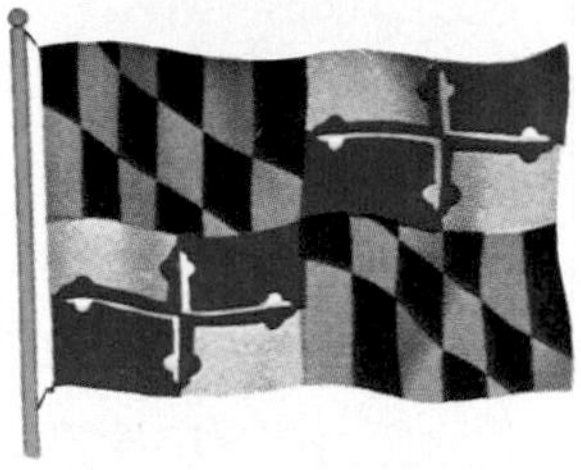

Flag

Bird: Baltimore Oriole

Flower: Black-eyed Susan

Vicksburg National Military Park honors the siege of Vicksburg with monuments to each state represented in the battle. The Union victory here was a major turning point of the Civil War (right).

A curved, flower-laced road leads to stately Stanton Hall, one of the many antebellum mansions in the Natchez area (below).

Mississippi

History is highly important to the state of Mississippi and its residents. They have a great deal of pride in the traditions of their state and in the many reminders of the Old South. Old Mississippi plantations and stately mansions dating back to pre–Civil War days provide memories of those historic times.

Many monuments have been erected throughout the state to commemorate the heroic Confederate soldiers who fought numerous battles on Mississippi soil during the Civil War. Probably the most important of the confrontations was the Battle of Vicksburg, where the Union Army besieged and finally took the city. Along with the Union victory at Gettysburg, this battle marked the turning point of the Civil War. Vicksburg is often called the *Gibraltar of the Confederacy*. Today, Vicksburg National Military Park honors the siege, which lasted from May 18 to July 4, 1863.

Jefferson Davis, the President of the Confederate States, was from Mississippi. His boyhood home, Rosemont, can be seen near Woodville, and in Biloxi is Davis' last home, Beauvoir, which is now a shrine and museum. Visitors can tour other lovely mansions and plantations, where they can see what life might have been like in pre–Civil War Mississippi.

Some of the mansions and plantations in the Natchez area include Richmond, built in 1786; Auburn, built in 1812; D'Evereux, built in 1840; and Stanton Hall, built in 1857. There are many others throughout the state including Cedar Grove in Vicksburg, Waverly near Columbus, Grey Gables in Holly Springs, and Hampton Hall near Woodville.

Mississippi has numerous other historical points of interest. Ackia Battleground in northeastern Mississippi, for instance, marks the site of the Chickasaw Indian fort that the French attacked in 1736. The Old Spanish Fort in Pascagoula dates from 1718, and Fort Massachusetts, on Ship Island, was a Union stronghold during the Civil War. Jackson, Mississippi's capital and largest city, is the site of the Old Capitol, now the State Historical Museum, and the New Capitol. Built in 1903, New Capitol houses the present state legislature and the governor's offices.

Mississippi's name comes from the Mississippi River, which forms the major portion of the state's western border. *Mississippi* is an Indian word meaning "great water" or the "father of waters." Over the years, the river's flood waters have deposited soil or silt on the land, making the Mississippi Alluvial Plain one of the richest, most fertile areas in the

United States. Soybeans are probably Mississippi's most valuable crop, but the state is also one of the nation's leading cotton-growing regions.

Since 1930, however, Mississippians have been working hard to build an industrial economy. The state is now becoming one of busy factories and cities. Its rich natural resources have been important in the rapid industrial growth of the state.

Other than abundant water supplies and rich soil, petroleum is the most valuable mineral resource of Mississippi. Petroleum supplies much of the fuel used by rapidly growing manufacturing industries. Among the goods manufactured in Mississippi are transportation equipment, food products, chemicals, and clothing.

The sunny beaches and fine hotels of Mississippi's Gulf coast have made this part of the state famous as a popular winter resort region. Mississippi's mild climate with short winters and long summers has helped attract many tourists.

Biloxi is a particularly attractive resort town on the Gulf of Mexico. It is also the site of the annual Shrimp Festival held during the first week of June. The festival marks the opening of the shrimp-fishing season and includes parades, balls, and varied celebrations topped by the blessing of the shrimp fleet.

Mississippi's warm, moist climate also accounts for its beautiful gardens, where azaleas, camellias, and especially magnolias thrive. Mississippi gets its official nickname, the *Magnolia State,* from these beautiful trees, which grow in most parts of the state.

Other tourist attractions in Mississippi include, near Scott, the Delta and Pine Land Company Plantation, one of the largest cotton plantations in the world; and, near Flora, the Petrified Forest, which contains giant petrified trees dating back 30 million years.

Sports enthusiasts are often attracted by the excellent hunting and fishing available in the 25 wildlife management areas of the state. Found in abundance are wild doves, ducks, geese, quails, turkeys, deer, rabbits, raccoons, and squirrels.

Just off the white sands of Biloxi Beach, sailboats skitter across the Gulf of Mexico.

Mississippi
Magnolia State

Capital: Jackson
Area: 47,716 sq. mi. (123,584 km²), including 420 sq. mi. (1,088 km²) of inland water but excluding 556 sq. mi. (1,440 km²) of Gulf of Mexico coastal water; 32nd in size among the states
Elevation: *Highest*—Woodall Mountain, 806 ft. (246 m) above sea level in Tishomingo County; *lowest*—sea level along the coast
Statehood: Dec. 10, 1817, the 20th state
Abbreviations: Miss. (traditional); MS (postal)
Motto: *Virtute et Armis* (By Valor and Arms)
Song: "Go Mis-sis-sip-pi"
Tree: Magnolia

Mississippi's state seal features an American eagle holding an olive branch that represents peace. Three arrows symbolize war. The seal was adopted in 1817. The state flag, adopted in 1894, reflects Mississippi's ties to the United States and to the Confederacy. The red, white, and blue bars stand for the colors of the national flag. A replica of the Confederate Army's battle flag occupies the upper left portion.

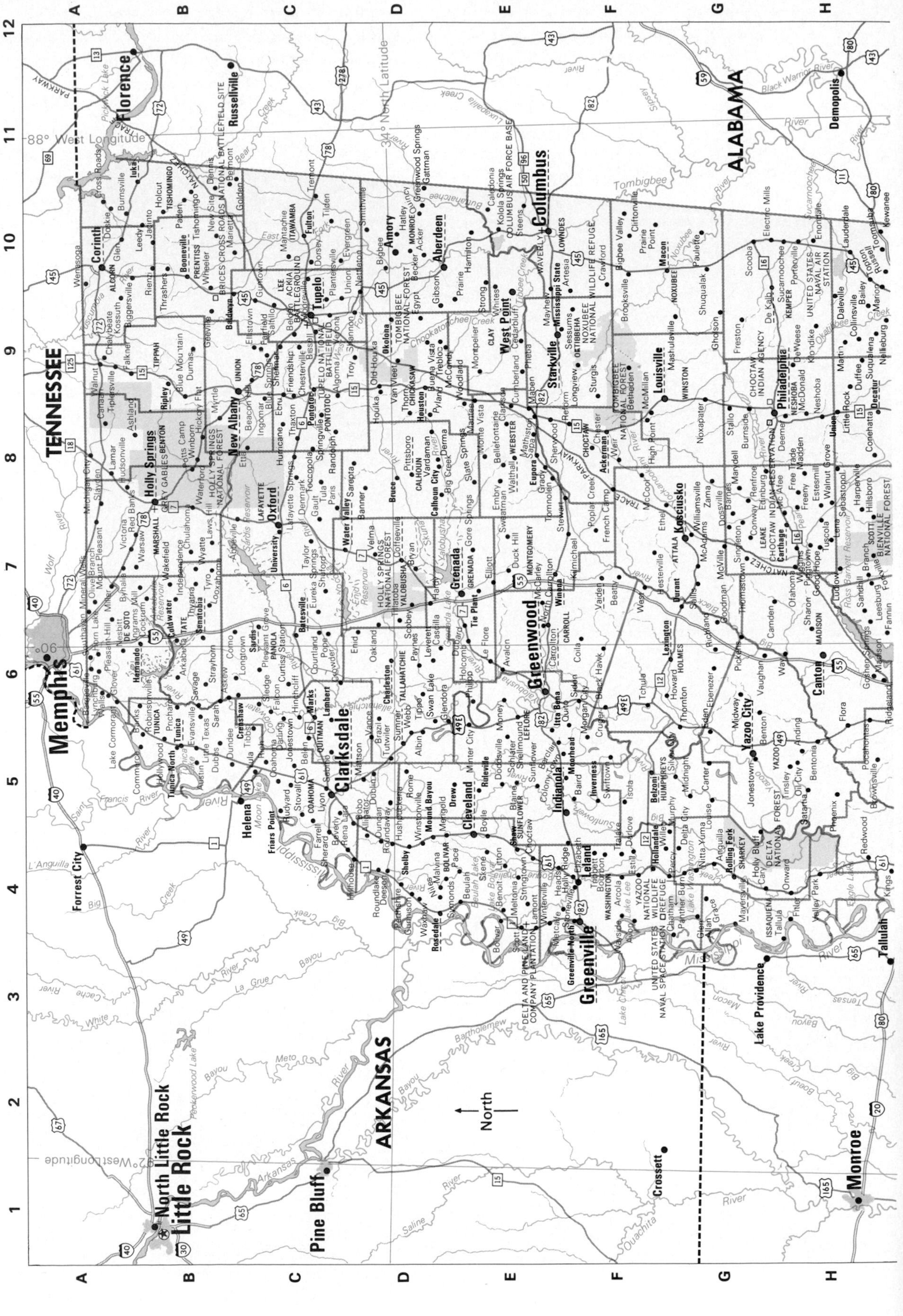

Seal

Flag

Bird: Mockingbird

Flower: Magnolia

MISSISSIPPI Political Map

✱	State capital	
	Urban area in Mississippi	
	Urban area outside Mississippi	
•	City or town	
	County seat	
	County name	
	County boundary	
	Forest or other conservation area	
	Military or other federal area	
	Indian reservation	
+	Point of interest	

✈	Major airport	
	Water	
	River	
	Waterway	
	Intermittent lake	

Highways:
	Expressway
	Other road
55	Interstate
84	U.S.
26	Other

BENTON

Lambert conformal conic projection
WORLD BOOK map © Field Enterprises Educational Corporation

Distance scale
Miles 200
300 Kilometers

LOUISIANA

New Orleans

Gulf of Mexico

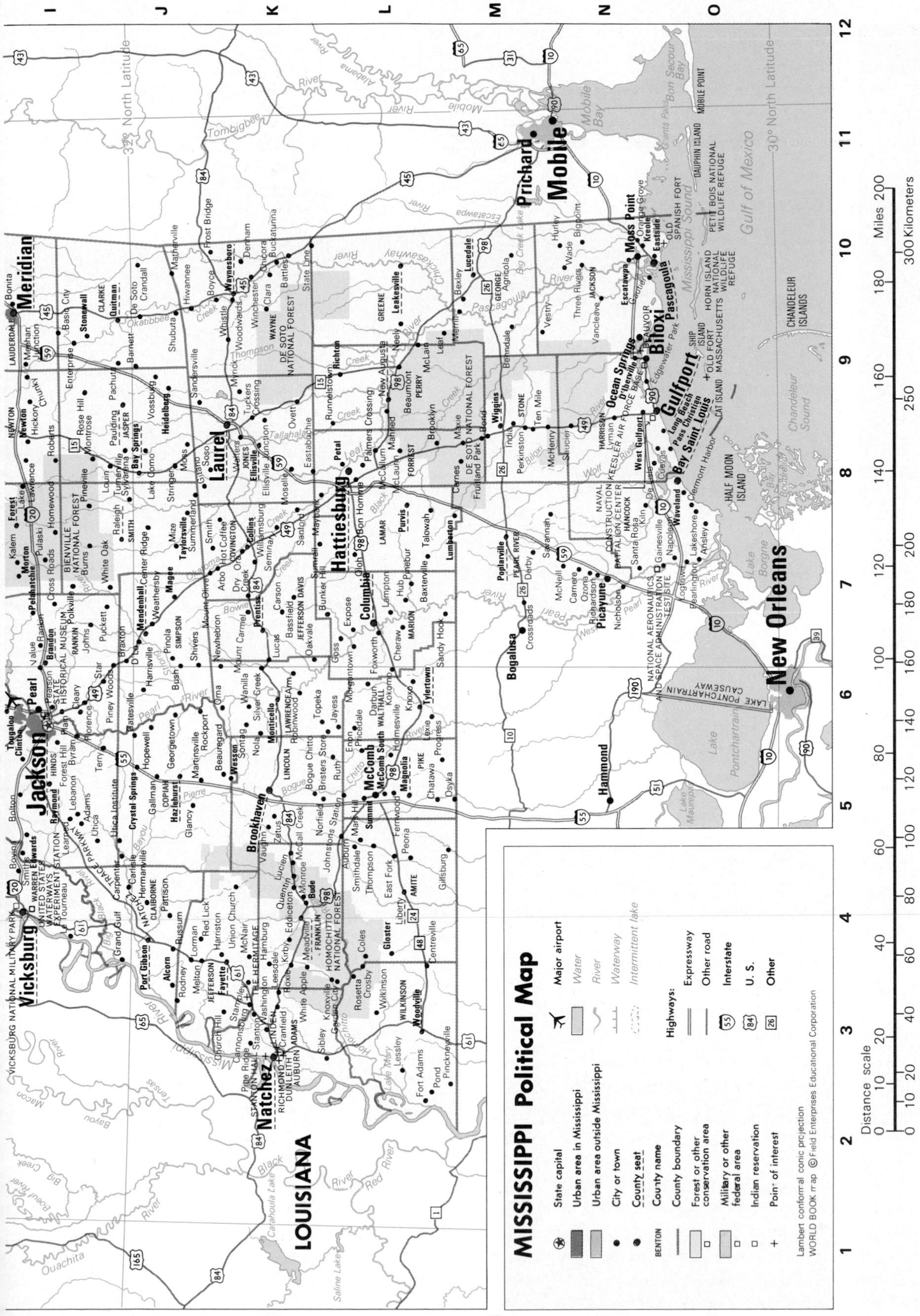

Old Salem, a restored village in Winston-Salem, tells the story of departed days of early America. The Moravians, who settled the area in 1766, cooked and ate in kitchens like this one, which dates from 1784.

North Carolina

North Carolina was the first area in America to be settled by the English. A group of settlers established a colony on Roanoke Island off the North Carolina coast in 1585. They were however forced to return to England in 1586. A second expedition was sent to the same spot in 1587. John White, governor of the colony, sailed back to England for supplies. Three years later, when he returned to Roanoke Island, the colony had disappeared. What happened to the 100 men, women, and children remains a mystery to this day. They have come to be called the Lost Colony. Virginia Dare, the first child born to English parents in America, was a member of the Lost Colony. An historical drama, the story of the Lost Colony, is staged nightly during July and August at Fort Raleigh in Manteo. It has become one of North Carolina's most popular annual events.

North Carolina has a long, interesting history that spans from early colonial times to the present. Many battles, including some from the colonial wars, the Revolutionary War, and the Civil War, were fought on North Carolina soil. Alamance Battlefield near Burlington was the scene of a battle shortly before the Revolutionary War. Bentonville Battlefield near Smithfield was the scene of one of the last important Civil War battles. Both sites are notable points of interest in North Carolina.

North Carolina's official nickname, the *Tar Heel State,* comes from the Civil War era. The North Carolinians supposedly threatened to put tar on the heels of other Confederate troops after they had retreated during a fierce battle, leaving North Carolina forces to fight alone. The North Carolinians hoped the tar would help the retreated Confederate troops "stick better in the next fight."

Prior to these wars, during the late 1600's and early 1700's, early settlers had to deal with pirates who terrorized North Carolina's coastline. The famous pirate Blackbeard met his death in a battle near Ocracoke Island in 1718, putting an end to most piracy along the Atlantic coast. Ocracoke Island, which was Blackbeard's hideout and the site of many shipwrecks, is an interesting tourist spot. It lies about 20 miles (32.2 kilometers) offshore, southeast of Pamlico Sound.

The islands, reefs, and sandbars along North Carolina's Atlantic coast are called outer banks. They make the state's shores some of the most treacherous in the world. The rough seas and difficult currents around Cape Hatteras have been the cause of numerous shipwrecks and have given Cape Hatteras the nickname *Graveyard of the Atlantic*. Other outer banks are equally treacherous, as their names imply: Cape Fear, Cape Lookout, Nags Head.

The state of North Carolina has some varied land regions. One is the coastal plain in the east, which includes swamps, prairies, and rich farmland. The Dismal Swamp in the northeast is one of the country's largest swamps. The Piedmont region in the central portion of the state contains most of the state's manufacturing industries. The Blue Ridge or Mountain region in the west is named for the Blue Ridge Mountains, North Carolina's chief range. Here is the site of Mount Mitchell, the highest peak east of the Mississippi River. Chimney Rock, in Rutherford County, offers an excellent view of the Blue Ridge Mountains.

Tobacco is North Carolina's most famous product. The state is the nation's leader in tobacco farming as well as in the manufacture of tobacco products. The heart of the coastal plain is known as *Tobaccoland* because of its fertile soil, but tobacco is raised in most parts of the state. North Carolina also leads the nation as the number-one manufacturer of cloth and wooden furniture.

As important as manufacturing is to the state, however, it is dependent on other industries and particularly on the state's natural resources. Cotton and tobacco farms with rich soils and North Carolina's thick forests provide manufacturing plants with the necessary raw materials.

North Carolina's mild climate, its beautiful, blossoming gardens, and its historic sites attract many visitors yearly. The mountains provide excellent hunting and beautiful autumn colors. Pinehurst and Southern Pines are popular winter resort areas located in the sandhills region. Other interesting sites include the Cherokee Indian Reservation at Cherokee; Grandfather Mountain near Linville; Nantahala Gorge in Swain County; Old Salem, a restored colonial village in Winston-Salem; Market House in Fayetteville, once a slave market; Tryon Palace in New Bern, a restored governor's mansion built in the 1700's; and the Wright Brothers National Memorial near Kitty Hawk, which honors the first powered airplane flight.

The magic of flight captivates these youngsters as they sail their kite at the Wright Brothers National Memorial near Kitty Hawk (below top).

The Lumbee Indians of Robeson County present Strike at the Wind *yearly near Pembroke. This outdoor musical drama by Randolph Umberger tells the story of Henry Berry Lowrie, a Lumbee Indian folk hero of the Civil War and Reconstruction eras* (below bottom).

North Carolina
Tar Heel State

Capital: Raleigh
Area: 52,586 sq. mi. (136,197 km²), including 3,788 sq. mi. (9,811 km²) of inland water; 28th in size among the states
Elevation: *Highest*—Mount Mitchell in Yancey County, 6,684 ft. (2,037 m) above sea level; *lowest*—sea level, along the Atlantic coast
Statehood: Nov. 21, 1789, the 12th state
Abbreviations: N.C. (traditional); NC (postal)
Motto: *Esse Quam Videri* (To Be, Rather Than to Seem)
Song: "The Old North State"
Tree: Pine

North Carolina's state seal, adopted in 1971, shows two figures. The one standing represents Liberty and holds a scroll inscribed "Constitution." The seated figure symbolizes Plenty. The date "May 20, 1775" honors the supposed Mecklenburg Declaration of Independence. Citizens of Mecklenburg are said to have held a meeting in Charlotte on this date, the result of which was their declaration of independence from Great Britain. The state flag, adopted in 1885, bears the dates of the two North Carolina declarations of independence that were made before the national Declaration.

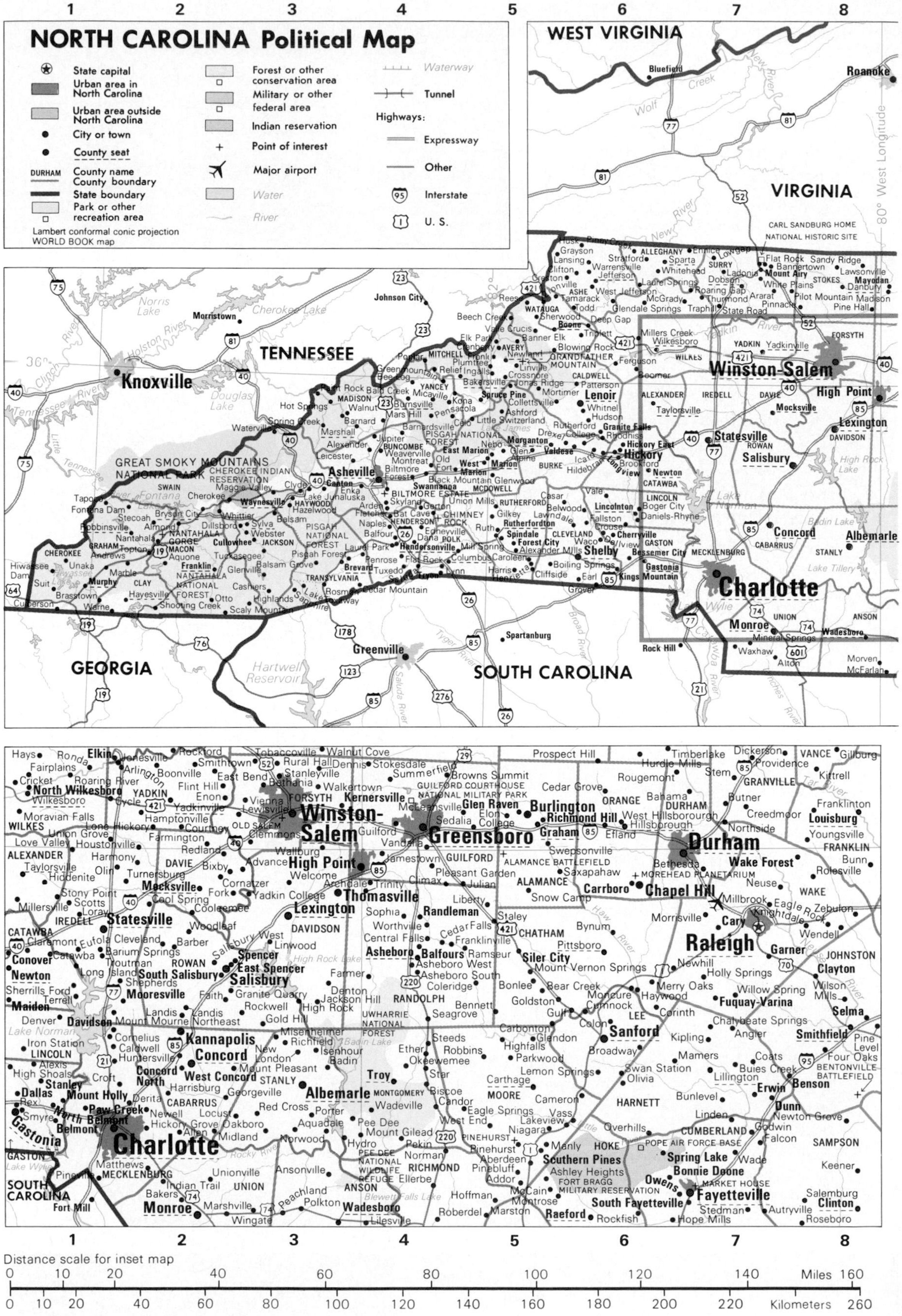

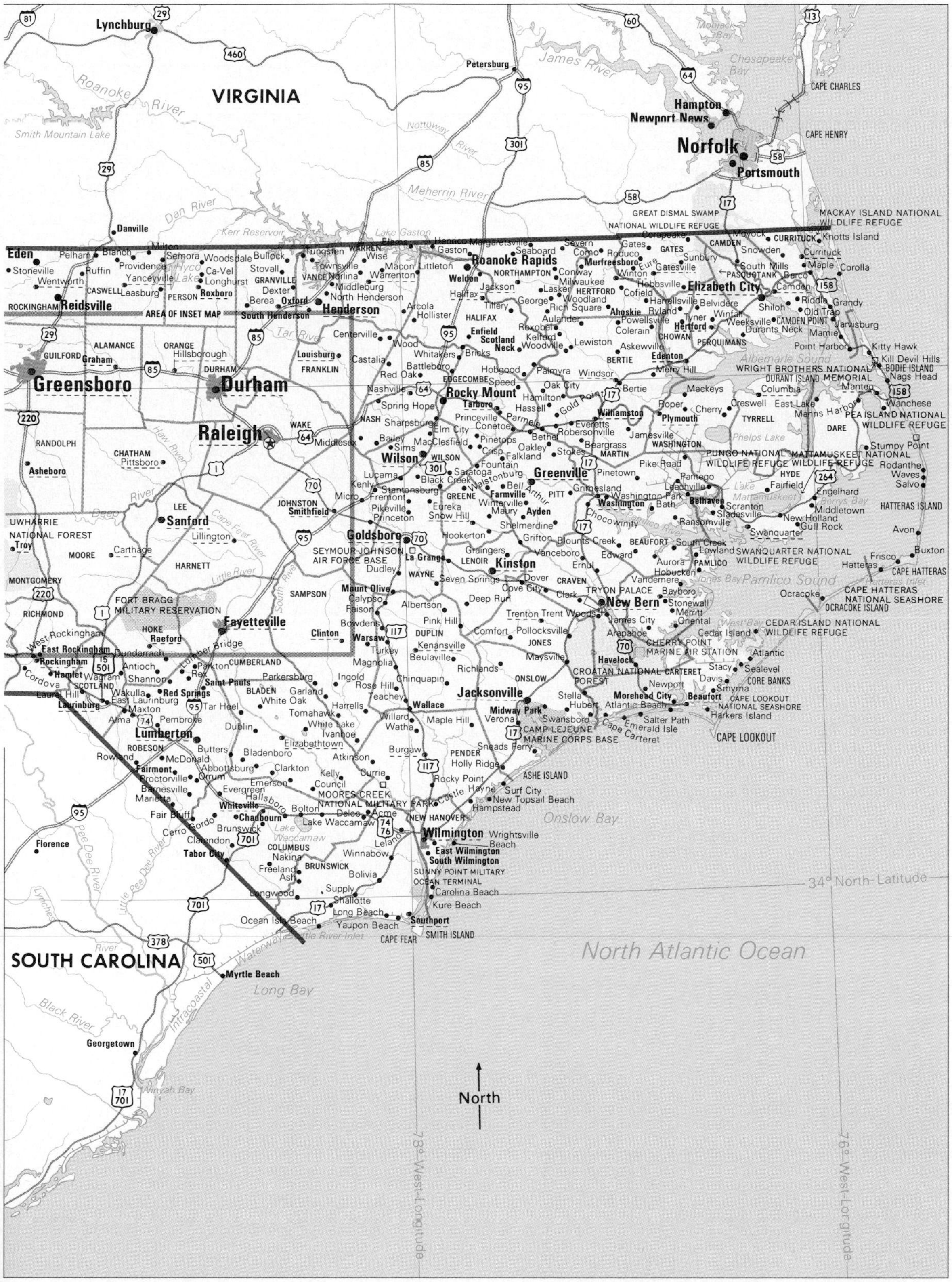

Distance scale for North Carolina map

0 10 20 40 60 80 100 120 140 160 180 200 220 240 Miles

0 10 20 40 60 80 100 120 140 160 180 200 220 240 260 280 300 325 Kilometers

Seal

Flag

Bird: Cardinal

Flower: Flowering Dogwood

South Carolina

Defending their newborn country, colonists bravely fought off the British here at Fort Moultrie in Charleston Harbor (below top).

This modern waterfront park in historic Beaufort stands in sharp contrast to city sections with buildings dating from the early 1700's (below bottom).

South Carolina's name is derived from *Carolina,* a Latin form of *Charles.* In 1629, the area was named Province of Carolana (land of Charles) in honor of King Charles I of England. The spelling was changed to *Carolina* in 1663 and the word *South* was added in 1730, when North and South Carolina became separate colonies. South Carolina's first permanent white settlement was established at Albemarle Point, near present-day Charleston, in 1670. The colonists moved to Oyster Point in 1680 and named the settlement Charles Town, changed to *Charleston* in 1783.

Over the years, many battles have been fought on South Carolina soil. There are numerous battlefields and monuments now marking these historic sites. Two of these that recall South Carolina's part in the Revolutionary War are Kings Mountain National Military Park and Cowpens National Battlefield, both near Gaffney. These two points of interest mark the sites of major battles that were turning points of the Revolutionary War in the South.

Fort Moultrie in Charleston Harbor is the site of a brave defense by the colonists against the British during the Revolutionary War. It was probably here that South Carolina earned its official nickname, the *Palmetto State.* After the colonists had defeated the British fleet, it is said that William Moultrie, the colonial commander, saw a column of smoke rising from a British ship burning in the harbor. The shape of the smoke reminded Moultrie of the palmetto tree, which grows abundantly in the state and whose logs were used to build the fort. Thus, the nickname was born.

Probably the most well-known and most popular of South Carolina's historic sites is in Charleston Harbor: Fort Sumter, where the Civil War began. The Confederate troops attacked Fort Sumter on April 12, 1861, and the first shots of the Civil War were fired. The fort is now a national monument. Other interesting historic points include Fort Johnson, also in Charleston, and Windmill Point, near Charleston.

South Carolina is a major manufacturing state. Outside of North Carolina, South Carolina produces more textiles than any other state. Agriculture ranks second as the state's chief economic activity, followed by the tourist industry. Tobacco is South Carolina's most valuable crop. Soybeans is the second leading crop, and South Carolina ranks second only to California in peach production.

Contour farming, an important method of farming used to prevent soil erosion, can be seen widely in the hilly Piedmont region of South Carolina. By planting alternate strips of crops that are harvested at different times, the Piedmont farmer always has a soil-holding crop on the land.

The Atlantic Coastal Plain, however, which covers most of the eastern portion of the state, has some of South Carolina's best farmland. Deposits of silt from rivers in the region have left a rich black soil along the river valleys. The northwestern corner of the state is covered by the Blue Ridge Mountains, part of the Appalachian system. Not as rugged as the Blue Ridge Mountains in North Carolina, they remain beautifully topped with forests and are the location of some large, lovely waterfalls.

Oaks draped in Spanish moss line the path that leads to Boone Hall Plantation near Charleston.

South Carolina's mountains, seashore, and historic sites all make the state a popular vacation spot. The state's warm, sunny weather is a boon to the tourist industry. Myrtle Beach, South Carolina's largest seaside resort, and Myrtle Beach State Park attract year-round sunbathers and visitors. Other popular beaches include Cherry Grove, Ocean Drive, Crescent, Atlantic, Windy Hill, Isle of Palms, and Hilton Head Island.

South Carolina is also famous for its beautiful flower gardens, reminders of the leisurely southern life in pre–Civil War days. Of these, Middleton Place Gardens near Charleston are probably the most notable. They are the oldest landscaped gardens in the United States and feature azaleas, camellias, and ancient oak trees. Other famous and attractive gardens include Cypress Gardens and Magnolia Gardens, both also near Charleston; Brookgreen Gardens, north of Georgetown; and Edisto Gardens, in Orangeburg.

A trip to South Carolina would not be complete without viewing some of the graceful buildings and stately mansions erected before the Civil War. Beaufort and Charleston are two cities renowned for these beautiful structures. Large plantations, once the basis for the economy of the South, also remain in several parts of the state. The state capitol is in Columbia, and there visitors will also find Woodrow Wilson's boyhood home, now a museum.

South Carolina
Palmetto State

Capital: Columbia
Area: 31,055 sq. mi. (80,432 km²), including 830 sq. mi. (2,150 km²) of inland water but excluding 138 sq. mi. (357 km²) of Atlantic coastal water; 40th in size among the states
Elevation: *Highest*— Sassafras Mountain, 3,560 ft. (1,085 m) above sea level; *lowest*—sea level along the Atlantic coast
Statehood: May 23, 1788, the 8th state
Abbreviations: S.C. (traditional); SC (postal)
Mottoes: *Animis Opibusque Parati* (Prepared in Mind and Resources); *Dum Spiro Spero* (While I Breathe, I Hope)
Song: "Carolina"
Tree: Palmetto

South Carolina's state seal, authorized in 1776, shows a palmetto tree towering over an uprooted oak. The palmetto is the state tree. On the seal, it symbolizes the successful defense in 1776 of the palmetto-log fort on Sullivan's Island against the oaken ships of the British. The figure of Hope carrying a laurel branch across a sword-covered beach represents the wish to remain forever independent. The state flag, adopted in 1777, also bears a palmetto as well as a crescent moon. The crescent moon represents the silver crescent that decorated the caps of the South Carolina troops, for whom Colonel Moultrie originally designed the flag.

SOUTH CAROLINA Political Map

- ⊛ State capital
- Urban area in South Carolina
- Urban area outside South Carolina
- • City or town
- ● County seat
- LEE County name
- ── County boundary
- ━━ State boundary
- ◻ Park or other recreation area
- Forest or other conservation area

- Military or other federal area
- + Point of interest
- ✈ Major airport
- Water
- River
- Waterway

Highways:
- ── Expressway
- ── Other road
- 🛡26 Interstate
- 🛡25 U.S.
- 🛡11 Other

Lambert conformal conic projection
WORLD BOOK map © Field Enterprises Educational Corporation

Distance scale for inset map

0 5 10   20   30   40   50   60   70 Miles 80

0 5 10 20 30 40 50 60 70 80 90 100 110 Kilometers 130

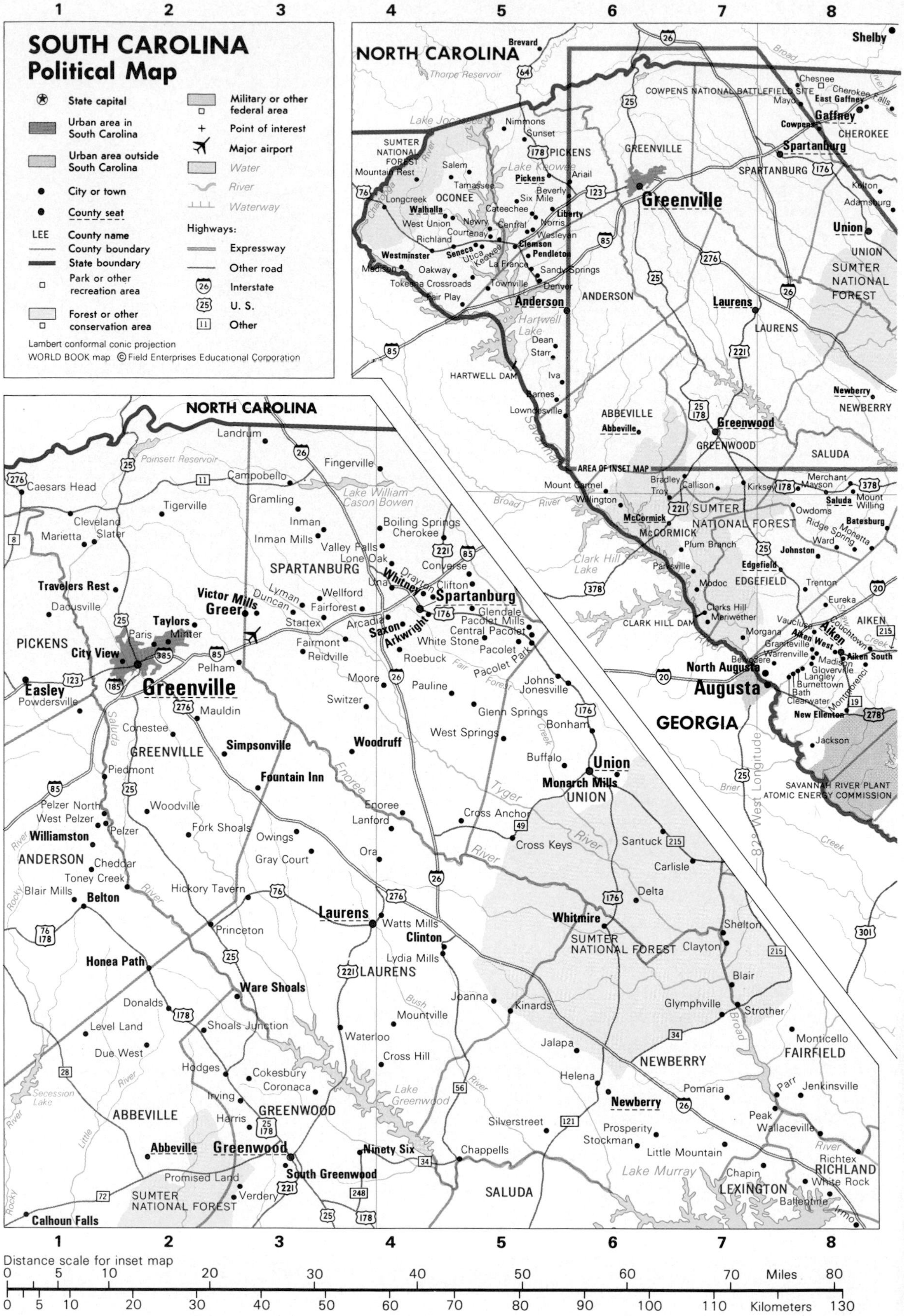

Seal

Flag

Bird: Carolina Wren

Flower: Carolina Jessamine

North

Distance scale for South Carolina map

| 0 | 10 | 20 | 30 | 40 | 60 | 80 | 100 | 120 | 140 | Miles | 160 |

| 0 | 10 | 20 | 40 | 60 | 80 | 100 | 120 | 140 | 160 | 180 | 200 | 220 | Kilometers | 260 |

Dazzling with their infinite variety of natural splendor, the Great Smoky Mountains also offer excursionists a cool respite from summer heat.

Tennessee

Tennessee's name comes from Tanasie, the name of a Cherokee Indian village in the region. The Cherokee were one of several tribes that once roamed Tennessee's mountains and forests. They had claimed middle Tennessee as their hunting ground. The Chickamauga Indians lived near present-day Chattanooga, and the Chickasaw inhabited west Tennessee. The earliest known people to occupy the region, more than one thousand years ago, were Indians now known as the Mound Builders. They are so called because they used mounds to support their temples and chiefs' houses. Today, Tennessee is sometimes called the *Big Bend State* because of the sudden bend in the Tennessee River that causes it to flow through the state twice. Tennessee's official nickname, however, is the *Volunteer State* because of its outstanding military traditions.

The military tradition of honor and bravery was established in Tennessee by great leaders such as John Sevier in the Revolutionary War, Andrew Jackson in the War of 1812, and Alvin C. York in World War I. Two great heroes of the Texas Revolution grew up in Tennessee and served its people faithfully: Davy Crockett and Sam Houston.

More Civil War battles were fought in Tennessee than in any other state except Virginia. During the Civil War, Tennessee loyalties were divided between the North and the South. Tennessee was the last Confederate state to leave the Union but the first to return.

Several military parks in the state commemorate historic battles from the past. One is Shiloh National Military Park in Pittsburg Landing. Others include Chickamauga and Chattanooga parks, which Tennessee shares with Georgia, and Fort Donelson near Dover. Lookout Mountain at the Moccasin Bend of the Tennessee River near Chattanooga marks the site where Union forces won an important victory during the Civil War in the "Battle Above the Clouds." Three national cemeteries in the state—Fort Donelson, Shiloh, and Stone River—are popular attractions.

Tennessee began as a wild frontier region. In 1772, a group of Tennessee's first settlers formed the Watauga Association to provide law and order in the wilderness. They drew up one of the first written constitutions in North America. Three Presidents of the United States, Andrew Jackson, James K. Polk, and Andrew Johnson, all lived in the state and played key roles in its development.

Today, over 200 years later, a series of more than 20 dams have been built by the Tennessee Valley Authority to furnish electric power and control floods. In Oak Ridge there is the atomic energy plant as well as the American Museum of Atomic Energy, which features exhibits on the peaceful uses of nuclear energy. Other atomic plants operate elsewhere in the state.

Tennessee's economy depends primarily on manufactured goods such as chemicals, food products, machinery, and clothing. The chief industrial centers are large cities such as Memphis, Nashville, Chattanooga, and Knoxville. Tennessee is also a rich agricultural and mining state. The most prosperous farms are in the western half of the state, and mining occurs mainly in the eastern and central portions. Coal and stone are the chief minerals mined.

Major cities of Tennessee provide many interesting sites for visitors. Nashville, the capital of Tennessee and a recording center for country music, has: the Grand Ole Opry House and Opryland; the Hermitage, President Andrew Jackson's home; and the Parthenon, the world's only reproduction of the ancient temple in Athens, Greece.

Memphis, situated on the Mississippi River, is Tennessee's largest city. It has the Fontaine House, a stately mansion built in 1871 by Amos Woodruff, a prominent businessman. Memphis is also the home of the Cotton Carnival held each May and often called the "Nation's Party in the Land of Cotton." The celebration includes a river pageant, grand parade, concerts, and horse shows.

Many visitors are attracted to Tennessee each year by the rugged mountains, thick forests, and beautiful lakes and rivers that provide excellent hunting, camping, fishing, boating, or swimming for sports enthusiasts and vacationers. The Great Smoky Mountains National Park, which Tennessee shares with North Carolina, itself attracts over 6 million visitors yearly. Clingmans Dome, near Gatlinburg in the Smokies, is the state's tallest peak and a popular tourist attraction.

Celebrated in song, the Chattanooga Choo-choo no longer rides the rails. But would-be passengers may climb aboard to relive railroading of yesteryear (above).

In the heartland of country music, performers at Opryland near Nashville entertain outdoors. The Nashville area has spawned many star performers (left).

Tennessee
Volunteer State

Capital: Nashville
Area: 42,244 sq. mi.
(109,411 km²), including
916 sq. mi. (2,372 km²) of
inland water; 34th in size
among the states
Elevation: *Highest*—
Clingmans Dome, 6,643 ft.
(2,025 m) above sea level;
lowest— 182 ft. (55 m) above
sea level along the Mississippi River in Shelby County
Statehood: June 1, 1796,
the 16th state
Abbreviations: Tenn.
(traditional); TN (postal)
Motto: *Agriculture and Commerce*
Songs: "The Tennessee
Waltz," "When It's Iris
Time in Tennessee," "My
Tennessee"
Tree: Tulip Poplar

*Tennessee's state seal shows a
plow, a sheaf of wheat, and a
cotton plant that represent agriculture. The river boat symbolizes commerce. The Roman
numerals show that Tennessee
was the 16th state of the
Union. The date 1796 is the
year the state approved its first
constitution. The seal was
adopted in 1801. The state
flag, adopted in 1905, shows
three stars standing for East,
Middle, and West Tennessee.
The circle represents unity.*

TENNESSEE Political Map

Symbol	Description
✪	State capital
	Urban area in Tennessee
	Urban area outside Tennessee
•	City or town
•	County seat
KNOX	County name / County boundary
	State boundary
	Park or other recreation area
	Forest or other conservation area

Symbol	Description
□	Military or other federal area
+	Point of interest
✈	Major airport
	Water
	River
	Waterway

Highways:
Expressway
Other road
40 Interstate
64 U.S.
20 Other

Lambert conformal conic projection
WORLD BOOK map

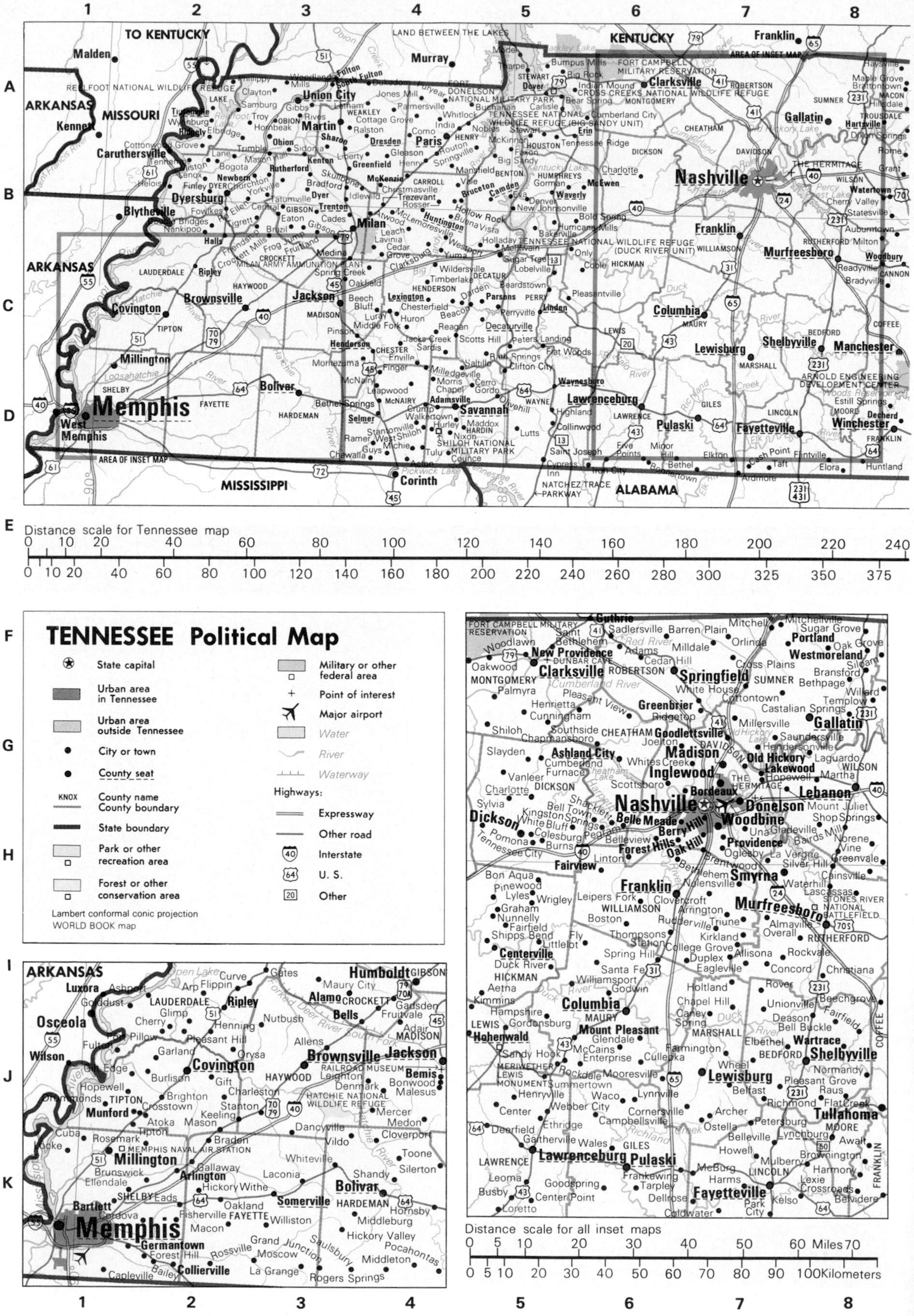

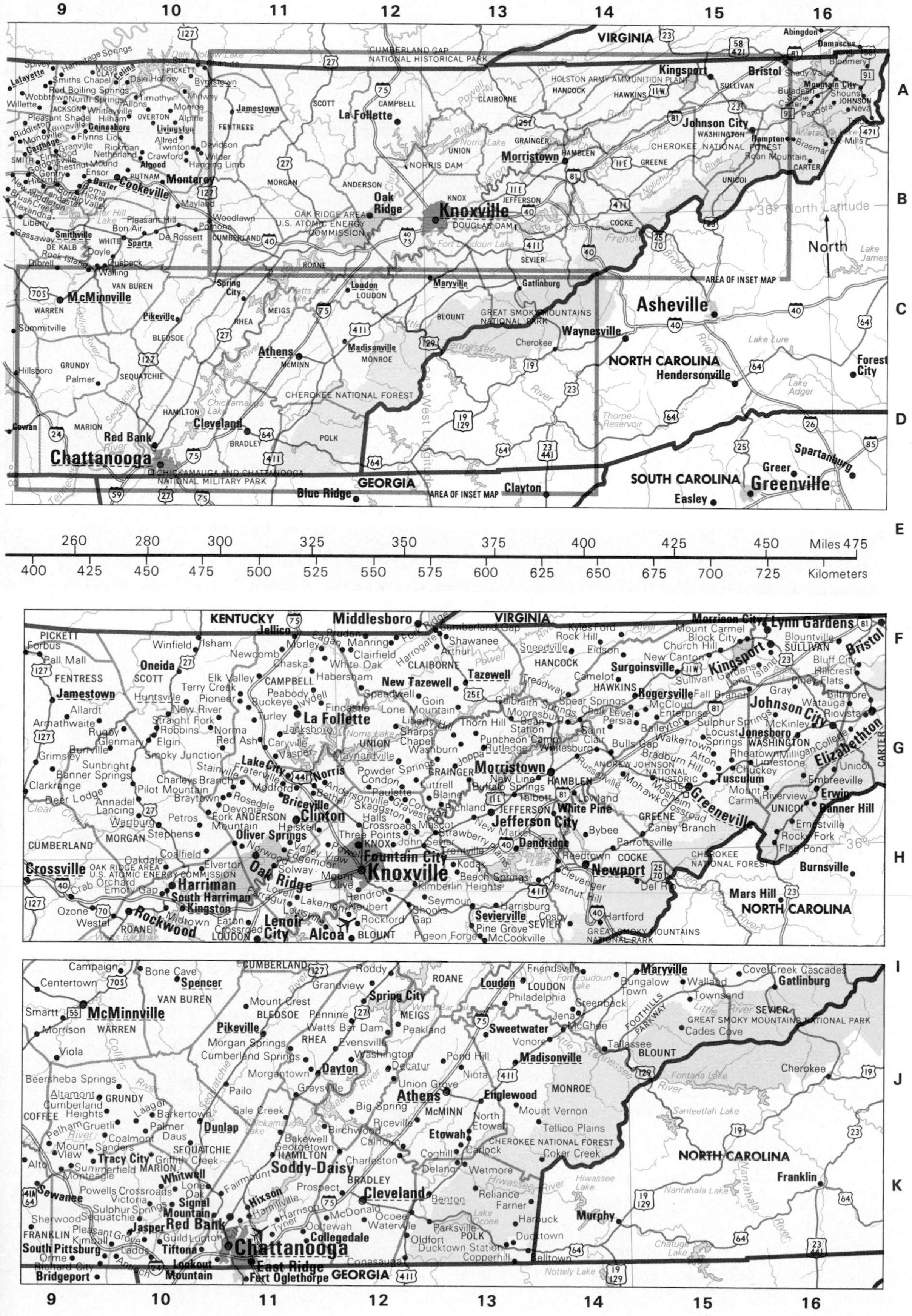

Seal

Flag

Bird: Mockingbird

Flower: Iris

VIRGINIA
KENTUCKY
NORTH CAROLINA
SOUTH CAROLINA
GEORGIA
Knoxville
Chattanooga
Kingsport
Bristol
Johnson City
Morristown
Oak Ridge
Cookeville
McMinnville
Cleveland
Athens
Asheville
Greenville
Spartanburg
GREAT SMOKY MOUNTAINS NATIONAL PARK
CHEROKEE NATIONAL FOREST
CUMBERLAND GAP NATIONAL HISTORICAL PARK
CHICKAMAUGA AND CHATTANOOGA NATIONAL MILITARY PARK
OAK RIDGE AREA U.S. ATOMIC ENERGY COMMISSION
AREA OF INSET MAP
North
36° North Latitude
Miles
Kilometers
THE GREAT SEAL OF THE STATE OF TENNESSEE
XVI
AGRICULTURE
COMMERCE
1796

Texas

Texas is famous for its bigness, and rightly so. It is the largest state in the United States except for Alaska, and it ranks fourth in population. Texas is the nation's leader in the production of cattle, cotton, sheep, and wool, and it has more farms and farmed area than any other state in the country. Texas is also the leader among all the states in the production of oil and natural gas.

Texas has a colorful history. Known as the *Lone Star State* because of the single star on its flag, Texas has flown the flags of six different nations through the years. These are Spain, France, Mexico, the Republic of Texas, the Confederate States of America, and the United States. Texas holds the distinction, along with Hawaii and Vermont, of once being an independent republic. Its history goes back more than 450 years to when the Spanish first explored the region. The name *Texas* comes from the Spanish pronunciation of the Indian word *tejas,* meaning "friends" or "allies."

Probably the most famous of all Texas' historical sites is the Alamo. In 1836 this old Spanish mission chapel in San Antonio was the site of a famous battle of the Texas revolution, when Texans were fighting for freedom from Mexico. Famous American heroes such as Davy Crockett and Jim Bowie died at the Alamo.

Another point of interest commemorating the Texas revolution is the San Jacinto Monument near Houston. It honors those who, led by Sam Houston, fought in the Battle of San Jacinto, in which Texas won its independence from Mexico. Their battle cry was, "Remember the Alamo!"

Texas has a history of cattle and cowboys. Texas longhorn cattle were driven on the Chisholm Trail northward to Kansas in the 1870's. Today, cowhands still ride the plains driving herds of cattle, although not as abundantly. The Cowboy is a life-size bronze statue by Constance Whitney Warren honoring the Texas cowboy. It stands on the capitol grounds in Austin.

Cowboy boots and hats are still the general garb of many Texans. Rodeos, too, are a favorite pastime and may be found in progress somewhere in the state throughout the year.

Cattle are still important in Texas. They feed on the mesquite and grasses of the Great Plains in the western part of the state. Beef cattle are the state's

Like a gigantic mirror, this section of the Rio Grande River in Big Bend National Park reflects sheer canyon walls, whose layers mark geological time.

largest source of farm income. Because the winters are so mild, cattle can graze outdoors all year. Other agricultural income comes from sorghum grain, cotton, poultry, sheep, and wool.

Texas' land has helped make it wealthy. Besides providing fertile soil and rich grasslands, the land also contains some of the greatest deposits of petroleum, natural gas, and other minerals. The Panhandle natural-gas field is one of the largest known natural-gas reservoirs in the world. But the chief source of income for the state is manufacturing, particularly of chemicals and petroleum products. Plants are located mainly in cities along the Gulf coast.

Texas, with its frontier history, is today involved in a new frontier: space. Houston is the home of the Lyndon B. Johnson Space Center, the headquarters for all manned spacecraft projects of the National Aeronautics and Space Administration (NASA). An interesting visitors' center displays spacecraft equipment and shows films about space flights and moon landings.

Texas is also a popular vacation spot in terms of its natural beauty and scenic recreational areas. Some highly popular resort centers are on Texas' Gulf coast. Padre Island National Seashore extends 80 to 100 miles (128.7 to 160.9 kilometers) along the Gulf coast on Padre Island and includes dunes and beaches. The seashore helps protect the coast from damage by waves. The coastal cities of Aransas Pass, Corpus Christi, and Galveston are favorite starting points for deep-sea fishers, who try their best at hooking marlin, sailfish, and tarpon. Texas also has some beautiful national parks and forests. Big Bend National Park lies within the great bend of the Rio Grande River, which forms the dividing line between the United States and Mexico. Guadalupe Mountains National Park lies in Culberson and Hudspeth counties and contains Guadalupe Peak, the highest point in the state.

Other interesting sites throughout the state of Texas include Astroworld in Houston; Fair Park in Dallas, the home of Texas' State Fair and location of gardens, museums, an aquarium, and other sites; Lion Country Safari near Grand Prairie, where jungle animals roam free; Mission San Jose in San Antonio, established in 1720 and said to be the most beautiful Texas mission; Texas Memorial Museum in Austin; and the Lyndon B. Johnson Library, also in Austin.

Areas like the Paseo del Rio (River Walk) in San Antonio show the influence of Spain and Mexico on the city's development (above top).

The visitors' center at the Lyndon B. Johnson Space Center offers films and exhibits about the U.S. space program (above bottom).

Texas
Lone Star State

Capital: Austin
Area: 267,338 sq. mi. (692,402 km²), including 5,204 sq. mi. (13,478 km²) of inland water but excluding 7 sq. mi. (18 km²) of Gulf of Mexico coastal water; 2nd in size among the states
Elevation: *Highest*—Guadalupe Peak, 8,751 ft. (2,667 m) above sea level; *lowest*—sea level, along the Gulf of Mexico
Statehood: Dec. 29, 1845, the 28th state
Abbreviations: Tex. (traditional); TX (postal)
Motto: *Friendship*
Song: "Texas, Our Texas"
Tree: Pecan

Texas' state seal features symbols on both sides. One side, adopted in 1846, carries the single star that gives Texas its popular name, the Lone Star State. *The oak branch on the left symbolizes strength, and the olive branch on the right represents peace. The other side of the seal was adopted in 1961. It shows a shield with symbols of the Texan war for independence from Mexico. The six flags that have flown over Texas surround the symbols. The state flag, adopted in 1839, also displays a single star. The blue stands for loyalty, the white for strength, and the red for bravery.*

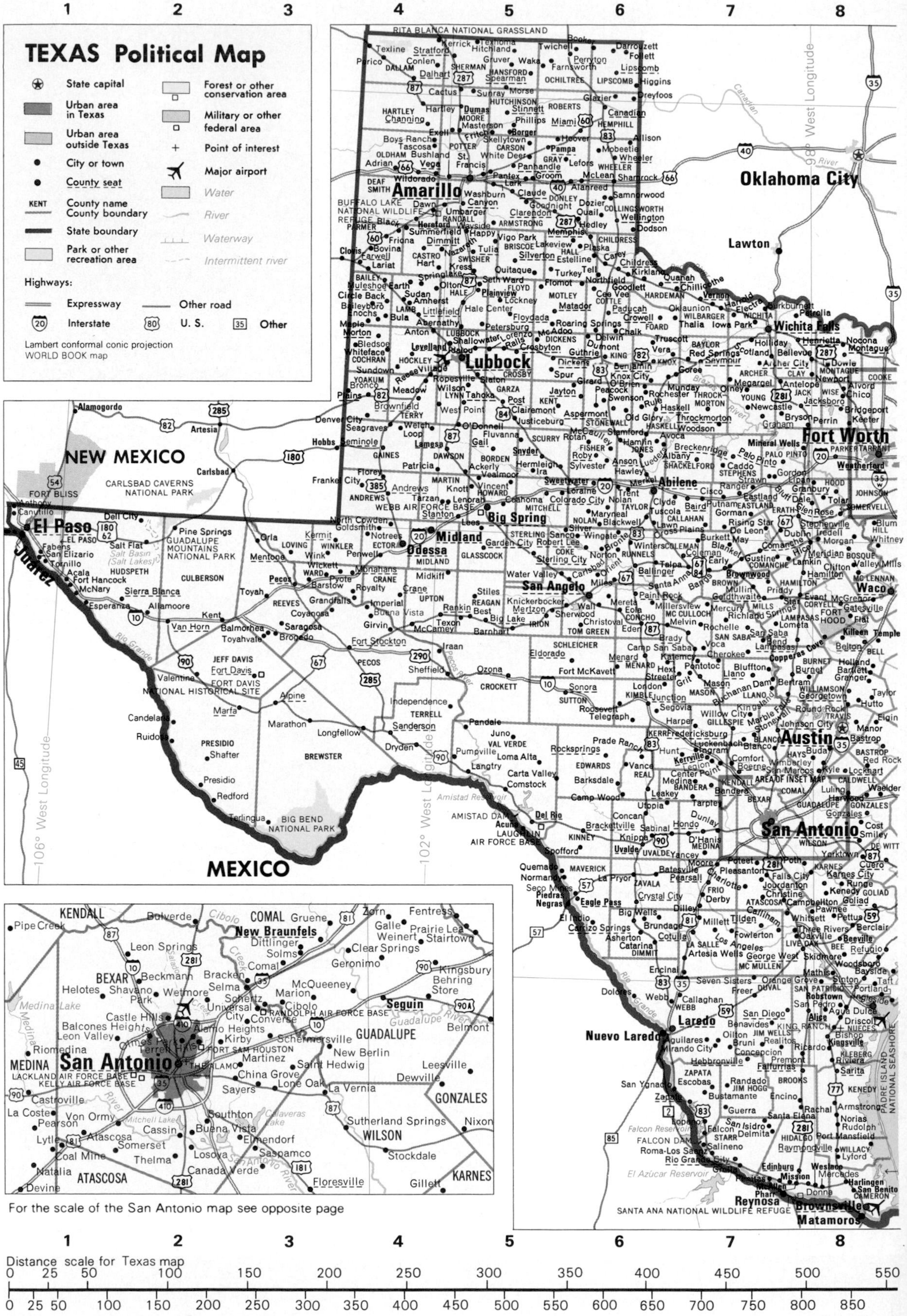

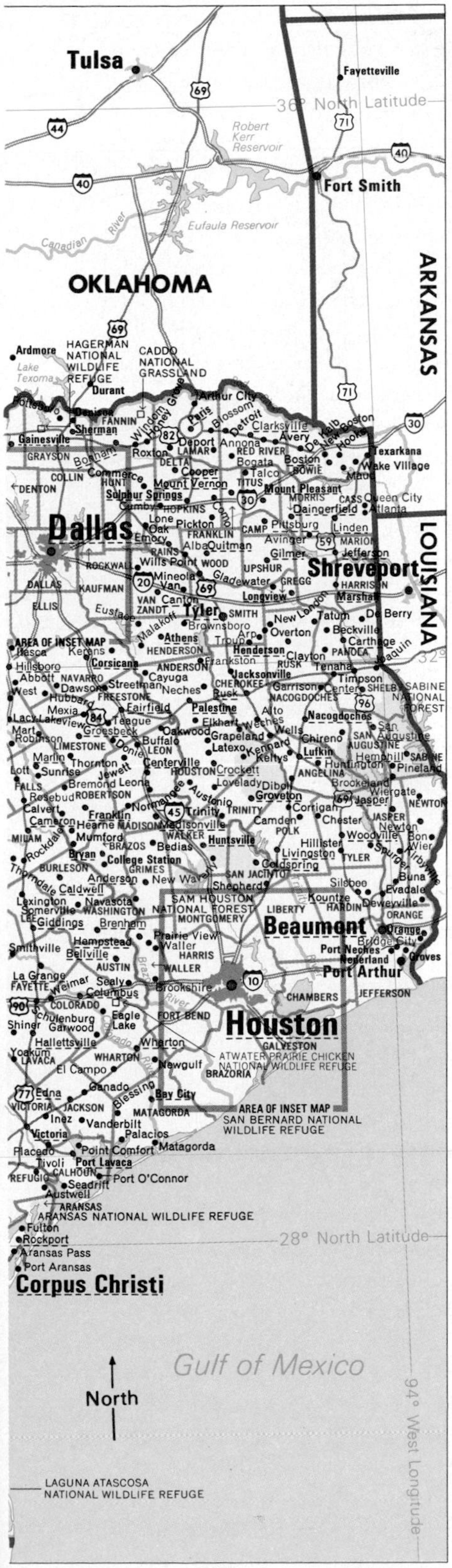

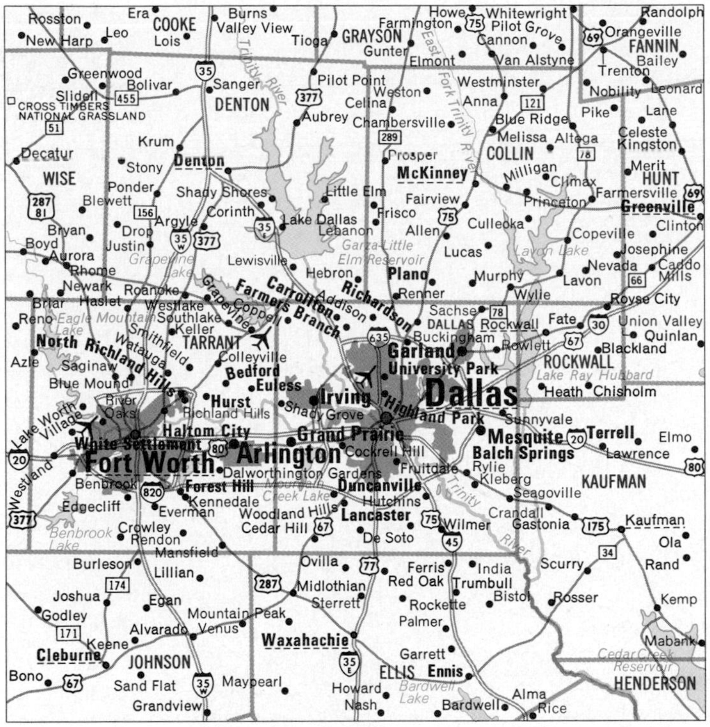

600 650 700 Miles 750

900 950 1000 1050 1100 Kilometers 1200

Distance scale for inset maps

0 5 10 20 30 40 50 60 70 Miles 80

0 5 10 20 30 40 50 60 70 80 90 100 110 Kilometers

Seal

Flag

Bird: Mockingbird

Flower: Bluebonnet

Virginia

Virginia is most famous for its historic past and the important events in American history that took place there. The first permanent English settlement in America was made at Jamestown in 1607, and the first representative legislature in America was established there in 1619. Jamestown Festival Park on the James River is a popular tourist attraction. It has reproductions of old James Fort and of the three ships that brought the first settlers from England.

Virginia was named for Queen Elizabeth I of England, the *Virgin Queen.* The state's name is believed to have been the suggestion of Sir Walter Raleigh after Elizabeth gave him permission to colonize the Virginia region in 1584. One of the state's nicknames is *Old Dominion,* a term coined by King Charles II because Virginia remained loyal to the crown during the English Civil War of the mid-1600's.

Recalling the past, reproductions of the ships that brought the first settlers from England in 1607 rest along the dock at Jamestown Festival Park.

Another of Virginia's nicknames is *Mother of Presidents.* This name evolved because eight U.S. Presidents were born there. This list includes four of the first five Presidents—George Washington, Thomas Jefferson, James Madison, and James Monroe—plus William Henry Harrison, John Tyler, Zachary Taylor, and Woodrow Wilson.

The homes of several of these great statespeople are among some of Virginia's most interesting sites. George Washington's Mount Vernon is near Alexandria; Thomas Jefferson's Monticello is near Charlottesville; and Berkeley, near Richmond, was the birthplace of President William Henry Harrison. Other famous Virginia homes of interest to tourists include Carter's Grove, one of the most beautiful old plantations along the James River; Gunston Hall near Lorton, the home of George Mason, author of the Virginia Bill of Rights; the John Marshall House in Richmond, the home of the great chief justice of the United States; and Stratford Hall near Montross, the birthplace of Robert E. Lee.

A large part of Virginia's history stems from its role in the Revolutionary and Civil wars. Some of the greatest battles of these wars were fought on Virginia soil and an end to both wars came in Virginia. The Revolutionary War ended when Lord Cornwallis was forced to surrender at Yorktown in 1781. Again in 1865, peace prevailed when Confederate troops surrendered at Appomattox. Appomattox Court House is now a national historical park and includes the McLean House, the site of the signing of the Civil War surrender agreement. Yorktown is part of Colonial Historical Park, which also includes most of Jamestown Island.

Historic churches in Virginia are notable points of interest. St. John's Church in Richmond was the site of the Second Virginia Convention in 1775 and the spot where Patrick Henry gave his famous call for liberty or death. George Washington and Robert E. Lee worshiped at Christ Church in Alexandria. St. Luke's Church near Smithfield is said to be the oldest remaining church in the original 13 states. Williamsburg's Burton Parish Church is one of the oldest Episcopal churches in the nation.

Other interesting places to visit in Virginia include the Tomb of the Unknown Soldier and the grave of President John F. Kennedy in Arlington National Cemetery. Colonial Williamsburg has also been a popular visiting ground for tourists. The city was Virginia's second colonial capital and has been restored to look as it did in the 1700's, displaying home furnishings, modes of transportation, and the dress of the period.

Richmond, the state capital of Virginia, draws

The rolling hills that bore the brunt of the Revolutionary and Civil wars are now a part of Virginia's extensive farmlands.

Under a dusting of snow, the Governor's Palace is one of the most imposing structures of Williamsburg, which is restored to look much as it did in the 1700's.

many tourists. Historic battlefields are also favorite sites. Most are now national parks and include those at Manassas, Richmond, Petersburg, and Fredericksburg.

About 50 million tourists visit Virginia every year, accounting for a good portion of the state's income. Its economy, however, is based chiefly on manufacturing and federal government activities. Virginia is also a major tobacco-producing state, and coal is its most important mineral resource. Newport News is the home of the largest ship-building and ship-repairing yard in the world.

Virginia abounds with scenic beauty and natural wonders. Two scenic drives, Skyline Drive in the north and the Blue Ridge Parkway in the south, afford lovely views in springtime and fall. Natural Bridge near Lexington, Natural Chimneys near Mount Solon, and Natural Tunnel near Gate City are wonders of nature.

For water sports, the Atlantic Ocean, Chesapeake Bay, and the tidal rivers are all popular. Vacationers particularly enjoy Virginia Beach, a famous ocean resort southeast of Norfolk.

Virginia
Old Dominion

Capital: Richmond
Area: 40,817 sq. mi. (105,716 km^2), including 1,037 sq. mi. (2,686 km^2) of inland water but excluding 1,511 sq. mi. (3,913 km^2) of Chesapeake Bay; 36th in size among the states
Elevation: *Highest*—Mount Rogers in Grayson and Smyth counties, 5,729 ft. (1,746 m) above sea level; *lowest*—sea level
Statehood: June 25, 1788, the 10th state
Abbreviations: Va. (traditional); VA (postal)
Motto: *Sic Semper Tyrannis* (Thus Always to Tyrants)
Song: "Carry Me Back to Old Virginia"
Tree: Dogwood

Virginia's state seal features symbols on both sides. One shows a standing figure representing Virtue dressed as a woman warrior. She is triumphant over Tyranny. On the other side of the seal, three figures represent Eternity, Liberty, and Agriculture. Perseverando, *the Latin motto above the figures, means "By persevering." George Wythe, a signer of the Declaration of Independence, designed the seal. It was first adopted in 1776. The present version was authorized in 1930. The state flag probably was first used in the mid-1800's, but it was not adopted until 1930. The flag has an adaptation of the state seal.*

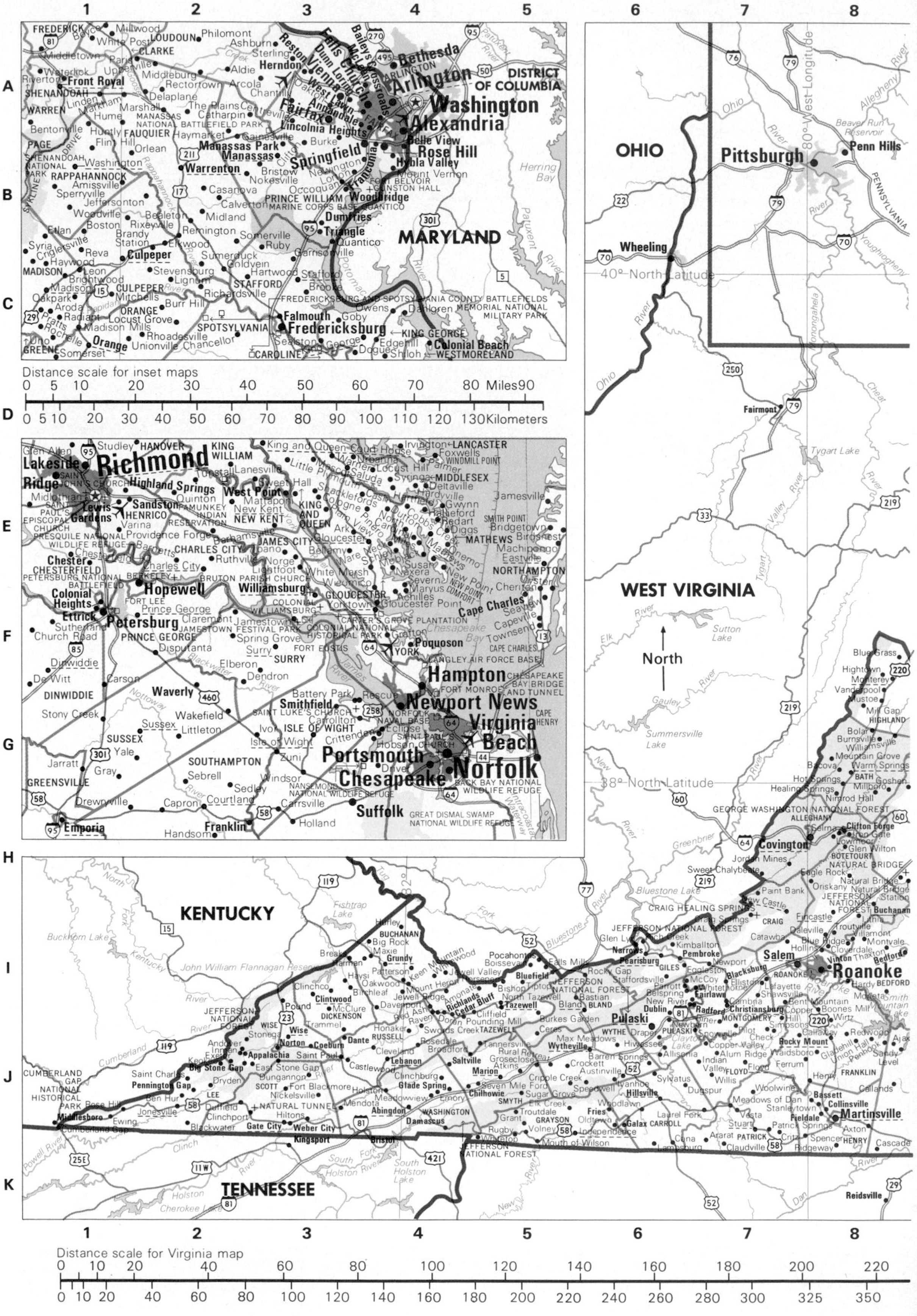

VIRGINIA Political Map

Symbol	Description
★	National capital
★	State capital
	Urban area in Virginia
	Urban area outside Virginia
•	City or town
•	County seat

SCOTT County name
County boundary
State boundary
Park or other recreation area
Forest or other conservation area
Military or other federal area

Indian reservation
Point of interest
Major airport
Water
River
Waterway
Intermittent lake
Tunnel

Highways:
Expressway
Other road
81 Interstate
17 U.S.
15 Other

Lambert conformal conic projection
WORLD BOOK map ©Field Enterprises Educational Corporation

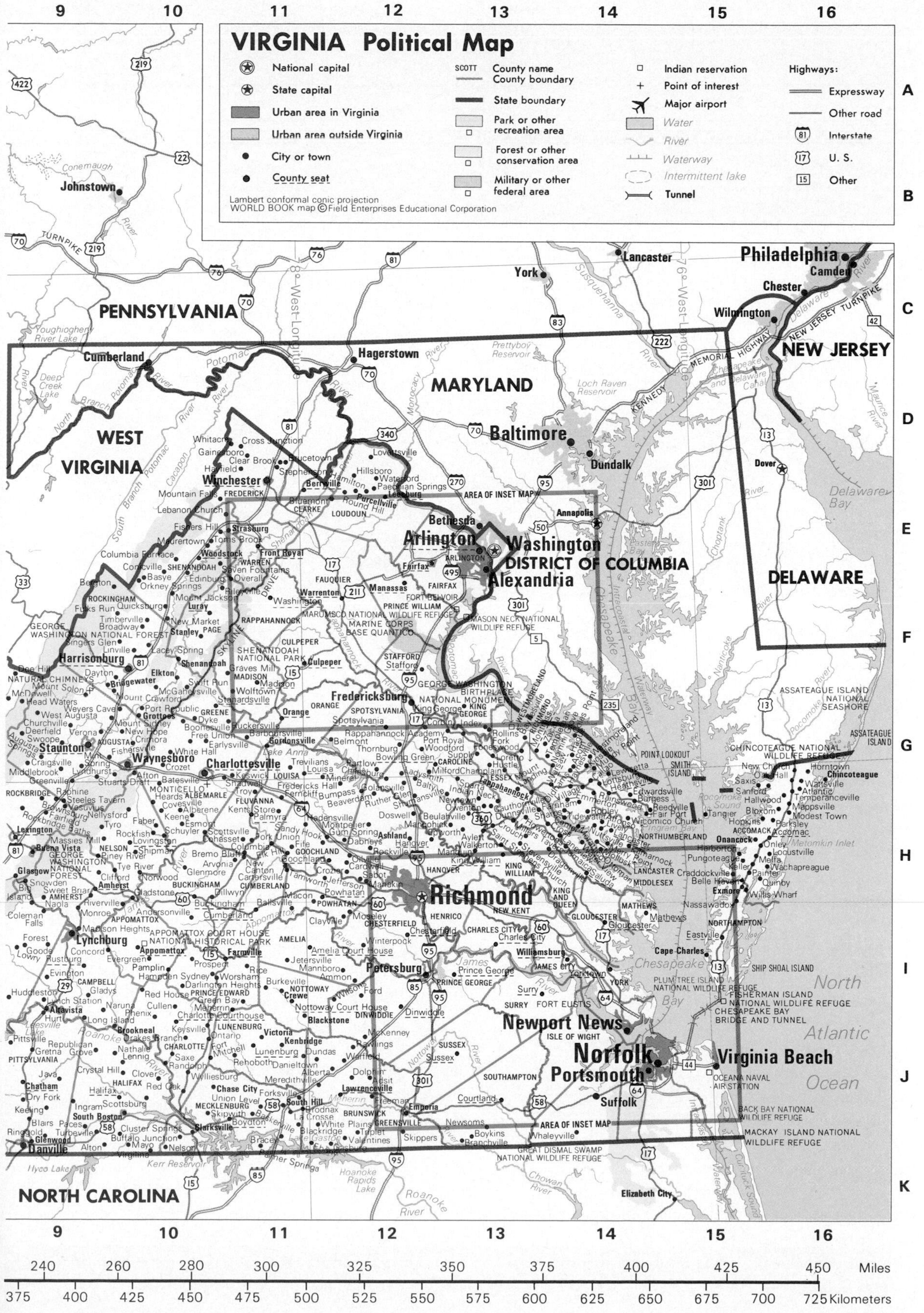

Seal

Flag

Bird: Cardinal

Flower: Flowering Dogwood

PENNSYLVANIA

MARYLAND

WEST VIRGINIA

NEW JERSEY

DELAWARE

DISTRICT OF COLUMBIA

Richmond

Norfolk

NORTH CAROLINA

North Atlantic Ocean

240	260	280	300	325	350	375	400	425	450	Miles
375	400	425	450	475	500	525	550	575	600	625	650	675	700	725	Kilometers

Rugged terrain and an abundance of rivers have joined to create churning torrents of white water throughout West Virginia. Although some are safe enough for a family adventure, others can be too treacherous.

West Virginia

West Virginia became a state in the midst of the Civil War. For more than 250 years, West Virginia had been part of the colony, then the state, of Virginia. But in 1861, at the start of the Civil War, settlers in the west refused to accept Virginia's decision to secede from the Union. They formed their own government instead and adopted a state constitution in 1862. A year later, West Virginia was admitted to the Union as the 35th state.

Over the years, West Virginia's development has been strongly influenced by its terrain. Rugged hills and mountains cover most of the state, giving it what became its official nickname, the *Mountain State.* West Virginia's rugged beauty attracts many tourists. And the mountains and hills are storehouses of valuable minerals.

Coal lies under about half of West Virginia's territory, and the state ranks second only to Kentucky in its coal production. West Virginia also has oil, natural gas, limestone, sand, salt, and other minerals. Altogether, mineral products make up more than half the value of the state's economic production. The minerals have also provided the raw materials for various manufacturing industries in the state.

West Virginia's rough landscape has caused problems for the state. The development of manufacturing industries and large cities has been largely limited to areas along river valleys, where the land is relatively level. Transportation through the rugged terrain has long been a problem. Many isolated areas had no paved roads until the early 1900's. In the 1800's, the Baltimore and Ohio Railroad overcame serious obstacles to lay track through the state. Between the cities of Cumberland and Wheeling, a distance of about 200 miles (321.9 kilometers), railroad workers had to build 11 tunnels and 113 bridges.

Today, partly as a result of the gradual development of a transportation network, West Virginia has a number of important manufacturing industries. Chemical products and steel are among its leading manufactured goods. Factories turn out famous table glassware, bottles, crystalware, stained glass, glass bricks, and other glass products.

Clarksburg and Parkersburg make millions of glass marbles each year.

West Virginia has limited farmland, but the far eastern part of the state lies within one of the best apple-growing regions in the country. West Virginia farmers were the first in the United States to grow Golden Delicious and Grimes Golden apples.

The state's colonial history dates back to 1606, when King James I of England included the region as part of the Virginia Colony. But a German explorer, John Lederer, was the first European to actually reach the area. Around 1670, when Lederer and other explorers roamed over the region, various Indian tribes were using it as a summer hunting ground.

The West Virginia area remained unsettled until about 1726, when Morgan Morgan arrived from Delaware. He built a log cabin at Bunker Hill. Within the next few years, Germans from Pennsylvania and Scotch-Irish from Northern Ireland founded settlements.

As a young surveyor, George Washington surveyed part of the West Virginia area for Lord Fairfax in 1748. Washington noticed the healthful qualities of mineral springs at the town of Bath (now Berkeley Springs). People came to the springs for the supposed health benefits, and Lord Fairfax himself bathed in a separate rock-lined hollow that is now called the "Fairfax Bathtub."

Charles Town was founded by Charles Washington, a brother of George Washington. It has several historic homes once owned by members of the Washington family. Charles' home, Mordington, was built around 1774. George Washington designed Harewood house for his brother Samuel. Dolley and James Madison were married at Harewood in 1794.

The West Virginia town of Harpers Ferry is famous in Civil War history. John Brown led his unsuccessful raid on a federal arsenal there in an attempt to begin a slave rebellion. Harpers Ferry is now part of a national historical park.

Many early Civil War battles occurred in West Virginia, and Confederate forces often raided the state for salt, food, and other supplies. The little town of Romney in the northeastern part of the state changed hands 56 times during the course of the war.

After the war had ended, Virginia wanted to reunite with West Virginia, but the new state refused. Virginia then demanded that West Virginia pay its share of the state debt at the time it had separated. Court battles over this issue continued until 1915, when the U.S. Supreme Court decided that West Virginia owed Virginia more than $12 million. West Virginia made its final payment to Virginia in 1939.

At this luxurious private resort in White Sulphur Springs, guests sample the elegance that surrounded the fashionable people of the Old South (left).

Although the rough landscape of West Virginia limits farming, it does provide a perfect setting for ski resorts (below).

West Virginia
Mountain State

Capital: Charleston
Area: 24,181 sq. mi.
(62,628 km²), including
111 sq. mi. (287 km²) of
inland water; 41st in size
among the states
Elevation: *Highest*—Spruce
Knob in Pendleton County,
4,862 ft. (1,482 m) above
sea level; *lowest*—240 ft. (73
m) above sea level along the
Potomac River in Jefferson
County
Statehood: June 20, 1863,
the 35th state
Abbreviations: W. Va.
(traditional); WV (postal)
Motto: *Montani Semper Liberi*
(Mountaineers Are Always
Free)
Songs: "The West Virginia
Hills," "This is My West
Virginia," "West Virginia,
My Home Sweet Home"
Tree: Sugar Maple

*West Virginia's state seal,
adopted in 1863, features symbols on both sides. One displays
a rock and ivy representing stability and continuity. The rock
bears the date West Virginia
became a state. The farmer and
miner symbolize the state's industries. On the seal's other side,
a landscape showing a farm-
house, derrick and factory, some
livestock, and a wooded mountain represents the state's industries. An adaptation of the front
of the seal appears on the state
flag, adopted in 1929.*

WEST VIRGINIA Political Map

★ State capital
Urban area in West Virginia
Urban area outside West Virginia
● City or town
● County seat
MINGO County name
County boundary
State boundary
Park or other recreation area
Forest or other conservation area

□ Military or other federal area
+ Point of interest
✈ Major airport
Water
River
Highways:
Expressway
Other road
79 Interstate
60 U.S.
4 Other

Lambert conformal conic projection
WORLD BOOK map ©Field Enterprises Educational Corporation

Distance scale for West Virginia map

Miles: 0 10 20 40 60 80 100 120 140 160 180
Kilometers: 0 10 20 40 60 80 100 120 140 160 180 200 220 240 260 300

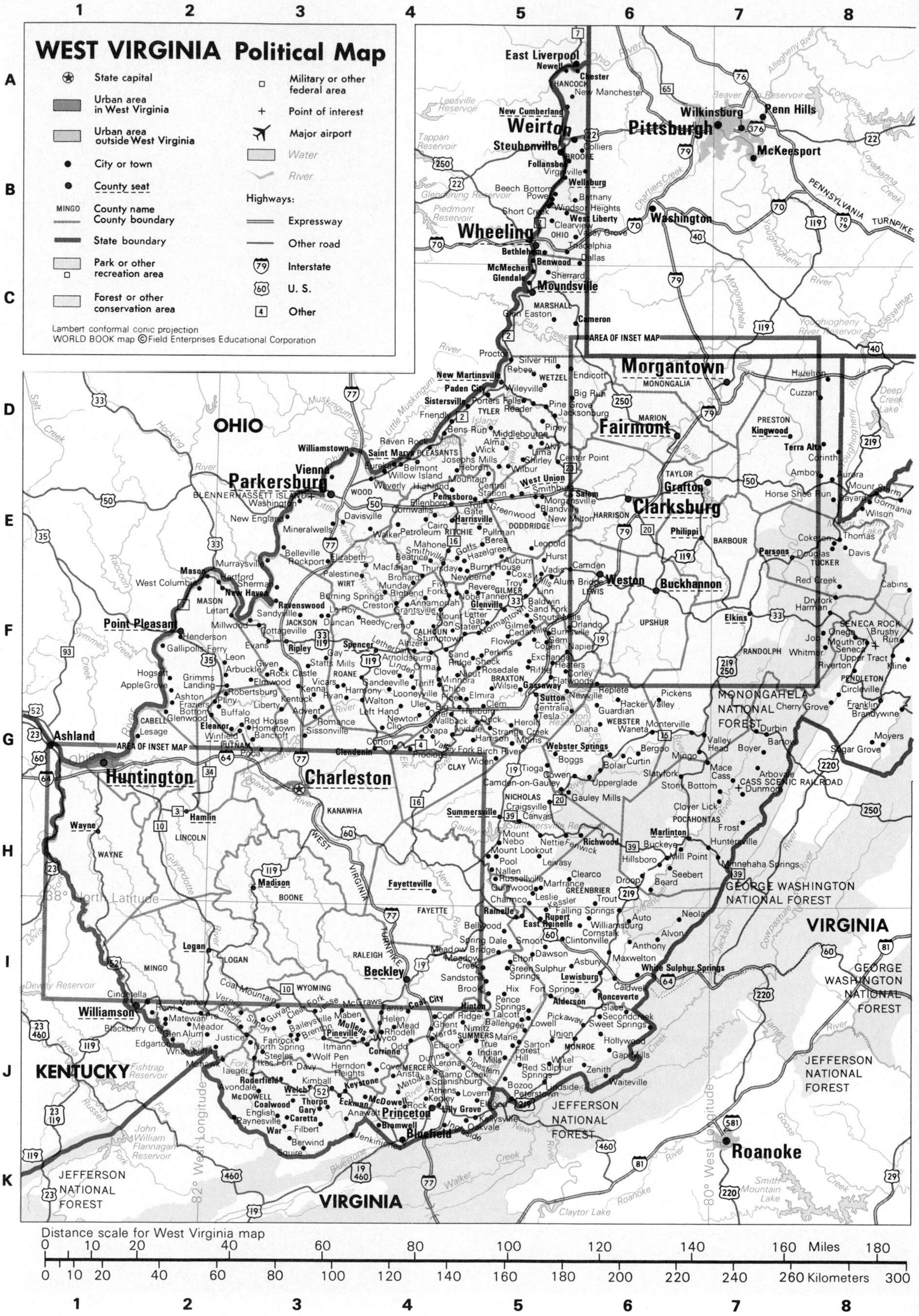

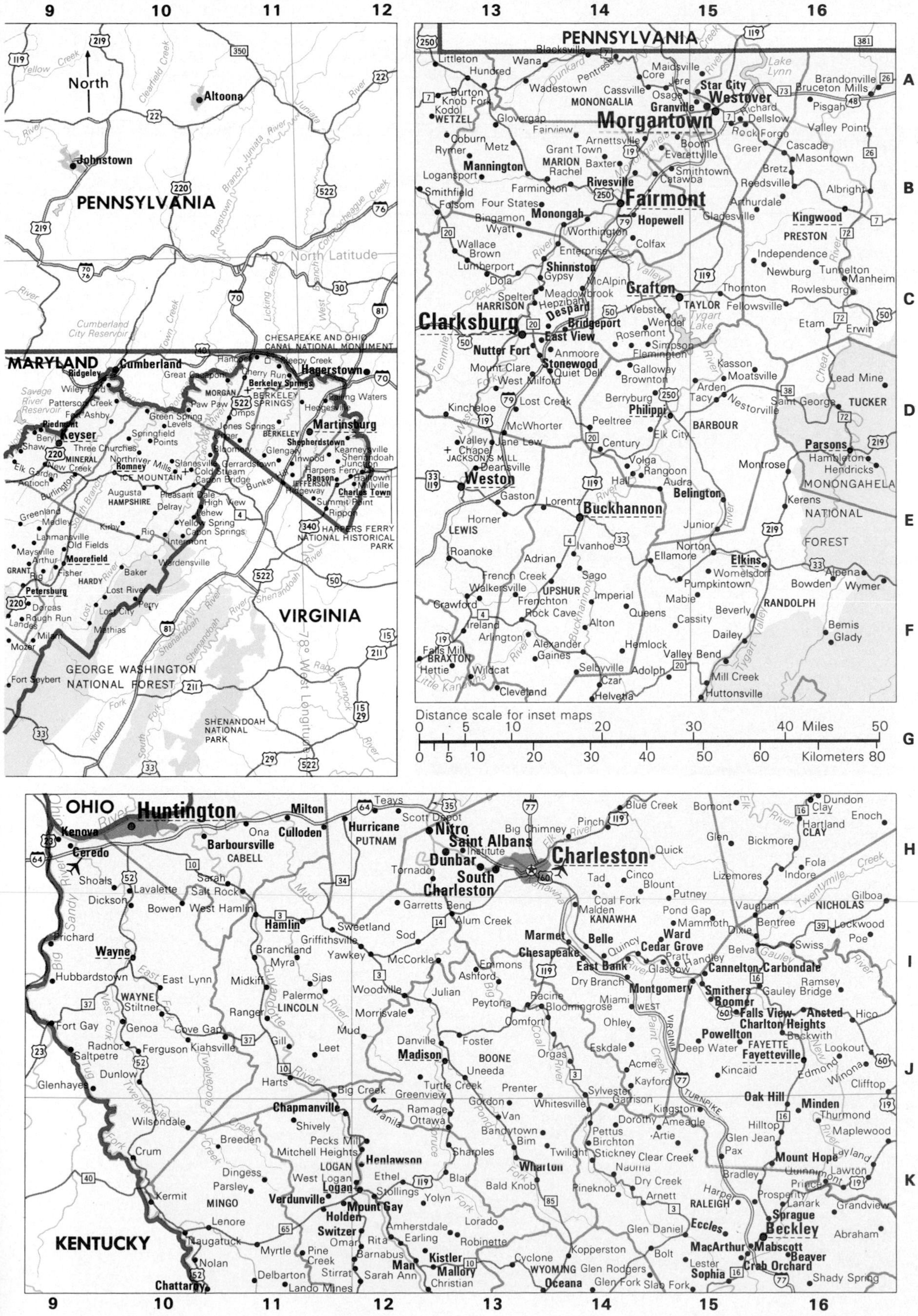

Seal

Flag

Bird: Cardinal

Flower: Rhododendron

9 10 11 12 13 14 15 16

North

Altoona

Johnstown

PENNSYLVANIA

40° North Latitude

Cumberland City Reservoir

MARYLAND

Ridgeley Cumberland Hagerstown

Wiley Ford Great Cacapon Hancock Cherry Run Sleepy Creek

Fort Ashby Green Spring Berkeley Springs Falling Waters

Piedmont MORGAN Paw Paw Omps

Beryl Keyser Patterson Creek Levels Hedgesville

Shaw Three Churches Springfield BERKELEY Martinsburg

New Creek Northriver Jones Springs Glengary Inwood Kearneysville Shenandoah Junction

MINERAL Stanleyville Cold Stream Shepherdstown

Antioch Romney Gerrardstown Harpers Ferry

Elk Garden HAMPSHIRE Pleasant Dale Capon Bridge Bunker JEFFERSON Millville

Greenland Augusta High View Summit Point Rippon

Medley Kirby Delray Ridgeway Charles Town

Lahmansville Old Fields Intermont Yellow Spring

Maysville Rio Capon Springs

Arthur Moorefield

GRANT Fisher Baker 522

Petersburg HARDY Lost River 50

Dorcas Lost City Perry

Rough Run Landes

Mozer Milam Mathias

Fort Seybert

GEORGE WASHINGTON NATIONAL FOREST

VIRGINIA

78° West Longitude

SHENANDOAH NATIONAL PARK

PENNSYLVANIA

Littleton Wana Blacksville Maidsville

Hundred Pentress Core Star City

Wadestown Cassville Osage Westover

Kodol MONONGALIA Richard Dellslow

WETZEL Glovergap Fairview Rock Forge

Coburn Metz Grant Town Greer Cascade

Ryner Arnettsville Booth Everettville Masontown

Mannington MARION Baxter Bretz

Logansport Rachel Reedsville

Smithfield Farmington **Rivesville** Arthurdale

Folsom Four States **Fairmont** Gladesville **Kingwood**

Bingamon Monongah Hopewell PRESTON

Wyatt Worthington Independence

Wallace Enterprise Newburg Tunnelton Manheim

Brown **Shinnston** McAlpin Thornton Rowlesburg

Lumberport Dola Spelter Meadowbrook **Grafton** Etam Erwin

HARRISON Hepzibah Webster TAYLOR

Clarksburg Despard **Bridgeport** Rosemont

Nutter Fort **East View** Anmoore Flemington

Mount Clare **Stonewood** Quiet Dell Simpson

West Milford Galloway Kasson Moatsville

Kincheloe Lost Creek Brownton Arden Tacy Lead Mine

McWhorter Berryburg TUCKER

Philippi Peeltree BARBOUR Saint George

Weston Jane Lew Century Elk City Montrose **Parsons**

Gaston Volga Hamilton Hendricks

Horner Lorentz Rangoon Audra MONONGAHELA

LEWIS Hall **Belington** Junior Kerens

Roanoke Ivanhoe NATIONAL

Adrian Sago Norton FOREST

French Creek **Elkins**

Walkersville Imperial Ellamore Womelsdorf Alpena

Crawford Frenchton Mabie Beverly RANDOLPH Bowden Wymer

Ireland Rock Cave Queens Cassity Bemis

Arlington Alton Dailey Glady

Falls Mill Alexander Gaines Hemlock Valley Bend

Hettie Wildcat Selbyville Adolph Mill Creek

Cleveland Czar Huttonsville

Helvetia

Distance scale for inset maps

0 5 10 20 30 40 Miles 50

0 5 10 20 30 40 50 60 Kilometers 80

OHIO **Huntington** **Milton** Teays Blue Creek Bomont Dundon CLAY

Kenova Ona Hurricane Scott Depot Pinch Hartland Enoch

Ceredo Culloden PUTNAM Big Chimney Glen Bickmore Fola

Barboursville **Nitro** **Saint Albans** Quick Indore

Shoals CABELL Tornado **Dunbar** Institute Tad Lizemores Gilboa

Lavalette Sarah **South** **Charleston** Cinco Putney NICHOLAS

Dickson Salt Rock **Charleston** Blount Pond Gap Vaughan Lockwood

Bowen West Hamlin Garretts Bend Coal Fork Mammoth Dixie Poe

Hamlin Sweetland Alum Creek Malden KANAWHA Bentree Swiss

Branchland Sod Belle Ward Belva

Wayne Myra Griffithsville **Marmet** **Cedar Grove** Smithers Gauley Bridge

Yawkey **Chesapeake** Quincy **Cannelton** **Carbondale**

Hubbardstown East Lynn McCorkle **East Bank** Pratt Glasgow Handley Ramsey

Fort Gay Midkiff Woodville Dry Branch **Montgomery** **Roomer** Hico

Genoa Ranger LINCOLN Emmons Racine Miami FAYETTE **Falls View** **Ansted**

Radnor Cove Gap Julian Bloomingrose Ohley **Charlton Heights** Lookout

Saltpetre Gill Morrisvale **Powellton** Backwith

Dunlow Mud Comfort Eskdale Deep Water **Fayetteville** Edmond

Glenhayes Harts Leet Foster Orgas Kincaid Winona Clifftop

Madison BOONE Acme Kayford Oak Hill

Big Creek Uneeda Prenter Sylvester Garrison **Minden**

Greenview Whitesville Kingston Hilltop Thurmond

Chapmanville Ramage Van Dorothy Maplewood

Shively Ottawa Bandytown Bim Artie Glen Jean

Wilsondale Manila Birchton Pax Layland

Breeden Pecks Mill Sharples Stickney Clear Creek **Mount Hope** Bradley

Crum Mitchell Heights Naoma Dry Creek Quinnimont

Dingess LOGAN **Henlawson** Blair Bald Knob **Wharton** Arnett Prince

Parsley West Logan Ethel 119 Yolyn Pineknob RALEIGH Lanark

Verdunville **Logan** **Mount Gay** Prosperity Grandview

Kermit MINGO **Holden** Lorado Eccles Sprague

Lenore **Switzer** Amherstdale Earling Glen Daniel **Beckley**

Naugatuck Myrtle Omar Rita Robinette Abraham

Pine Creek Barnabus **Man** Cyclone **MacArthur** **Mabscott**

Nolan Delbarton Stirrat **Kistler** **Mallory** WYOMING Glen Rodgers Lester **Sophia** Beaver **Crab Orchard**

Chattaroy Lando Mines Sarah Ann Christian **Oceana** Glen Fork Slab Fork Shady Spring

KENTUCKY

9 10 11 12 13 14 15 16

A B C D E F G H I J K

West

Arizona *204*
California *208*
Colorado *212*
Idaho *216*
Montana *220*
Nevada *224*
New Mexico *228*
Oklahoma *232*
Oregon *236*
Utah *240*
Washington *244*
Wyoming *248*
Alaska *252*
Hawaii *256*

The West's open land, rugged peaks, and big, blue skies lured hardy pioneers until the United States stretched from coast to coast and beyond. The statehood of Alaska and Hawaii completed the formation of today's United States.

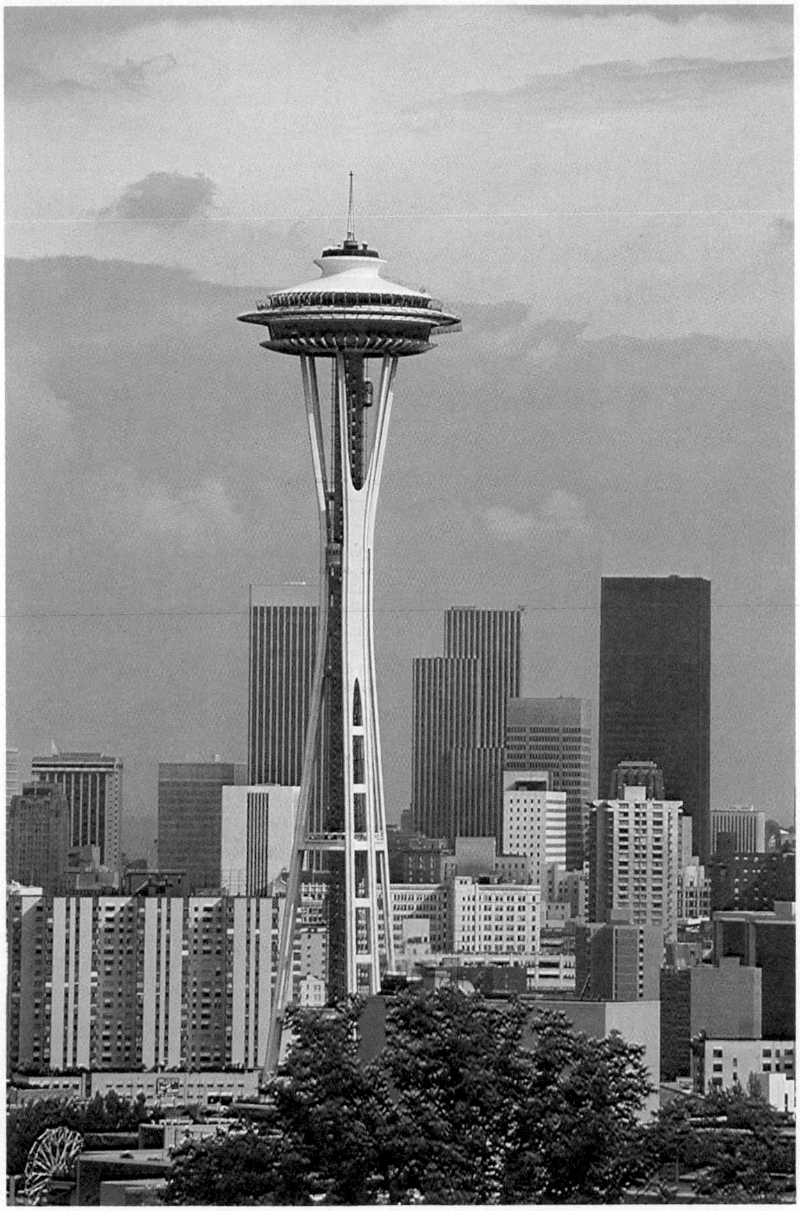

The narrow gauge railroad between Durango and Silverton, Colo., carries visitors through the rugged Colorado Rockies (facing page).

Saguaro cacti stand vigil over Arizona's southern desert as dude ranchers pass near Tucson (above left).

Cypress Point on California's Monterey Peninsula is one of the most photographed pieces of real estate in the United States. The picturesque Monterey cypress, named for the peninsula, is a favorite subject of artists (above right).

Seattle, Wash., is the state's largest city, a gateway to Alaska, and the home of the Space Needle. Its observation deck offers a splendid view of Mt. Rainier, Puget Sound, and Lake Washington (below left).

Arizona

Mention of Arizona may conjure up thoughts of the magnificent Grand Canyon of the Colorado River in northwestern Arizona. One of the Seven Natural Wonders of the World, this giant gorge is 217 miles (349.2 kilometers) long and 1 mile (1.6 kilometers) or more deep. Now a national park, it attracts millions of visitors every year. It is also the source of Arizona's official nickname, the *Grand Canyon State*. Tributaries of the Colorado River have cut other beautiful canyons through Arizona rock. Two of the most popular are Oak Creek Canyon and Canyon de Chelly, where red rock formations can be viewed.

Arizona also brings to mind vast areas of colorful, sunny desert. In northeastern Arizona lies the famous Painted Desert, which also attracts millions of tourists yearly. The Arizona-Sonora Desert Museum west of Tucson features interesting exhibits on desert plants and animals.

The majority of Arizona's population is found in the desertlike areas around Tucson and Phoenix, the state's capital and largest city. The climate here is very hot in the summer. The desert winters, however, are extremely pleasant. The warm temperatures and sunny skies attract many visitors when other parts of the nation are battling cold winter winds. In fact, so many people have been attracted by the climate that, in the 20 years between 1950 and 1970, Arizona's population more than doubled.

Arizona's large area of desert once made people believe the state to be worthless. Huge irrigation systems have, however, turned dry desert soil into rich farmland. Water is one of Arizona's leading natural resources, and dams have been built on many streams and rivers to conserve this water supply and to provide the all-important irrigation systems. The dams have also created many large, artificial lakes such as Theodore Roosevelt and San Carlos lakes.

Beef cattle, cotton, milk, and hay are Arizona's major farm products. Cattle and sheep can frequently be seen grazing along the countryside. They use about 80 per cent of the state's land for grazing.

With the advent of air conditioning, manufacturing has become an important part of Arizona's economy. The production of nonelectric machinery is the leading manufacturing activity, the primary metals industry comes next, and the production of electric and electronic equipment is third. Copper is the leading mineral product of Arizona. Many open-pit copper mines can be seen in various counties.

More than half of this state consists of mountains and plateaus. These higher, cooler areas are the home of some of the largest ponderosa pine forests in the United States. One interesting sight in northeastern Arizona is the Petrified Forest, now a national park. It is made up of ancient logs that were buried in mud, sand, or volcanic ash and have since been calcified.

Rising in lonely majesty, the red-rock formations of Oak Creek Canyon rival the beauty of the famed Grand Canyon.

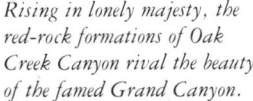

Southwest of Tucson is the Kitt Peak National Observatory. Here astronomers use a number of sophisticated devices, including the world's largest solar telescope.

Besides being an area of scenic natural beauty, Arizona is also a land rich in the history of the American Indians and Spanish influence. Indian reservations cover about a fourth of the state's land. Oraibi in Navajo County is probably the oldest continuously inhabited settlement in the nation. It was built by the Hopi Indians during the 1100's. The Apache Trail is a scenic mountain highway that passes interesting Tonto Indian ruins in the rugged Tonto National Forest. And the Navajo Indian Reservation in northeastern Arizona houses the Monument Valley Navajo Tribal Park.

Cochise and Geronimo are two prominent figures from Arizona's past. They were the last of the hostile Indian chiefs to continue fighting for their land. The name *Arizona* probably comes from an Indian word, *arizonac,* believed to mean "small spring."

Tombstone is a popular tourist attraction located in Cochise County. This western boom town, complete with cemetery, was made famous by the gunfighter Wyatt Earp.

Spanish and Mexican influence throughout Arizona is evidenced by customs, food, and place names. The Walled City of Tucson was originally a Spanish fort established in 1776 for defense against hostile Indians. It now provides historic points of interest. Near Tucson is the San Xavier del Bac Mission, probably the best preserved of the state's early missions. In it are beautiful and unusual carvings and paintings.

The Arizona desert, which was once considered by many to be worthless, now nurtures bountiful vineyards, due primarily to the construction of massive irrigation projects.

Other notable points of interest throughout Arizona include Kitt Peak National Observatory on the Papago Indian Reservation southwest of Tucson; Meteor Crater, a large hole in Coconino County formed when a huge object from space struck the earth; and any of the 15 national monuments throughout the state such as Montezuma Castle, Casa Grande, Organ Pipe Cactus, and Saguaro.

Arizona
Grand Canyon State

Capital: Phoenix
Area: 113,909 sq. mi. (295,023 km^2), including 492 sq. mi. (1,274 km^2) of inland water; 6th in size among the states
Elevation: *Highest*—Humphreys Peak, 12,633 ft. (3,851 m) above sea level; *lowest*—70 ft. (21 m) above sea level, along the Colorado River in Yuma County
Statehood: Feb. 14, 1912, the 48th state
Abbreviations: Ariz. (traditional); AZ (postal)
Motto: *Ditat Deus* (God Enriches)
Song: "Arizona"
Tree: Paloverde

Arizona's state seal, adopted in 1910, shows a miner standing in the mountains. He symbolizes the state's minerals industry. Irrigated fields and a cow represent agriculture. The state flag, adopted in 1917, has a copper-colored star representing Arizona's chief mineral product. Rays of a setting sun stand for the state's western location. The flag's red and gold colors suggest the Spanish flag early explorers carried.

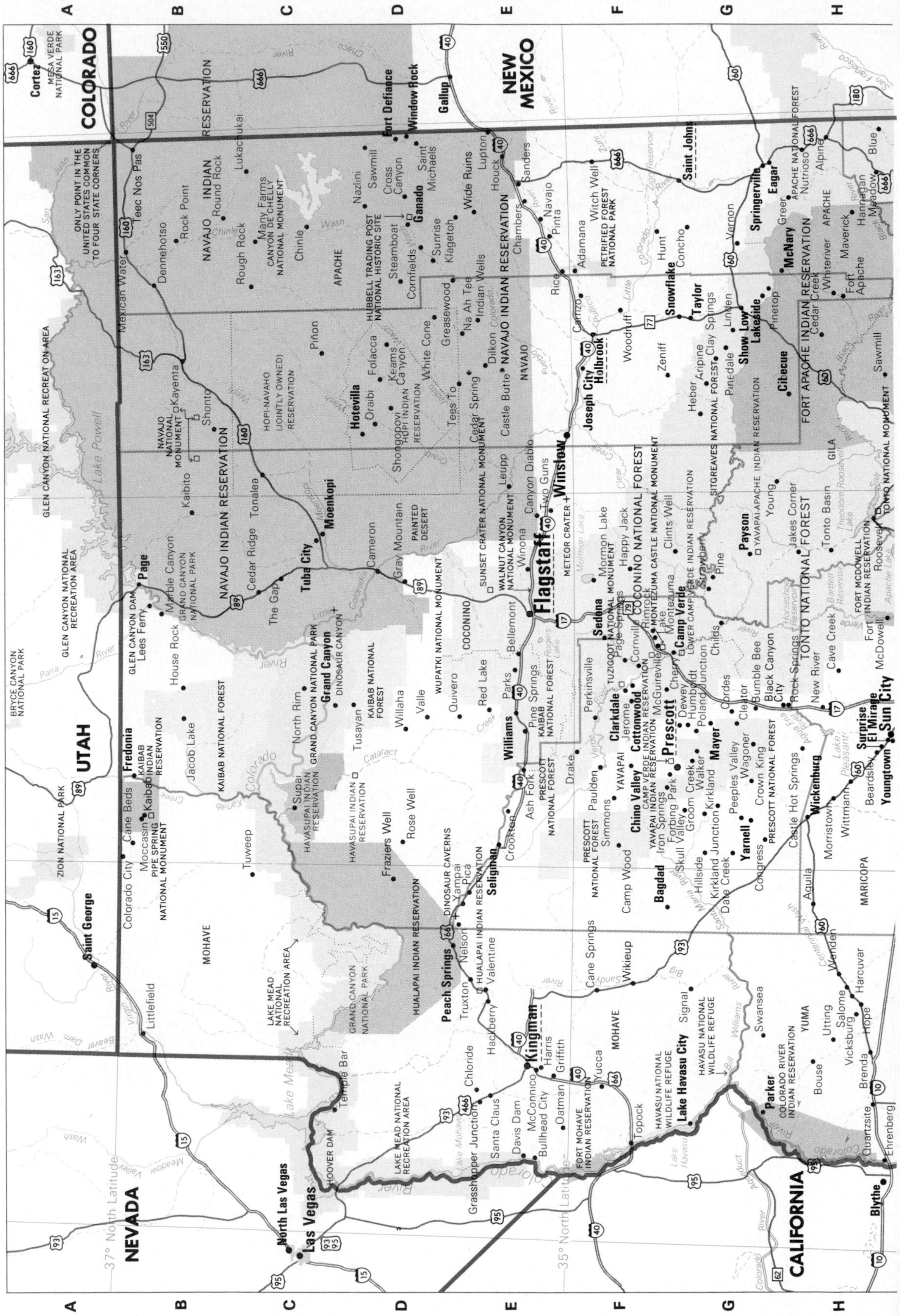

ARIZONA Political Map

⊛	State capital
	Urban area in Arizona
	Urban area outside Arizona
•	City or town
○	County seat
GILA	County name
	County boundary
	State boundary

	Park or other recreation area
	Forest or other conservation area
	Military or other federal area
	Indian reservation
+	Point of interest
✈	Major airport

	River
	Waterway
	Aqueduct
	Intermittent river
	Intermittent lake

Highways:
	Expressway
	Other road
40	Interstate
95	U.S.
15	Other
	Water

Distance scale

Lambert conformal conic projection
WORLD BOOK map ©Field Enterprises Educational Corporation

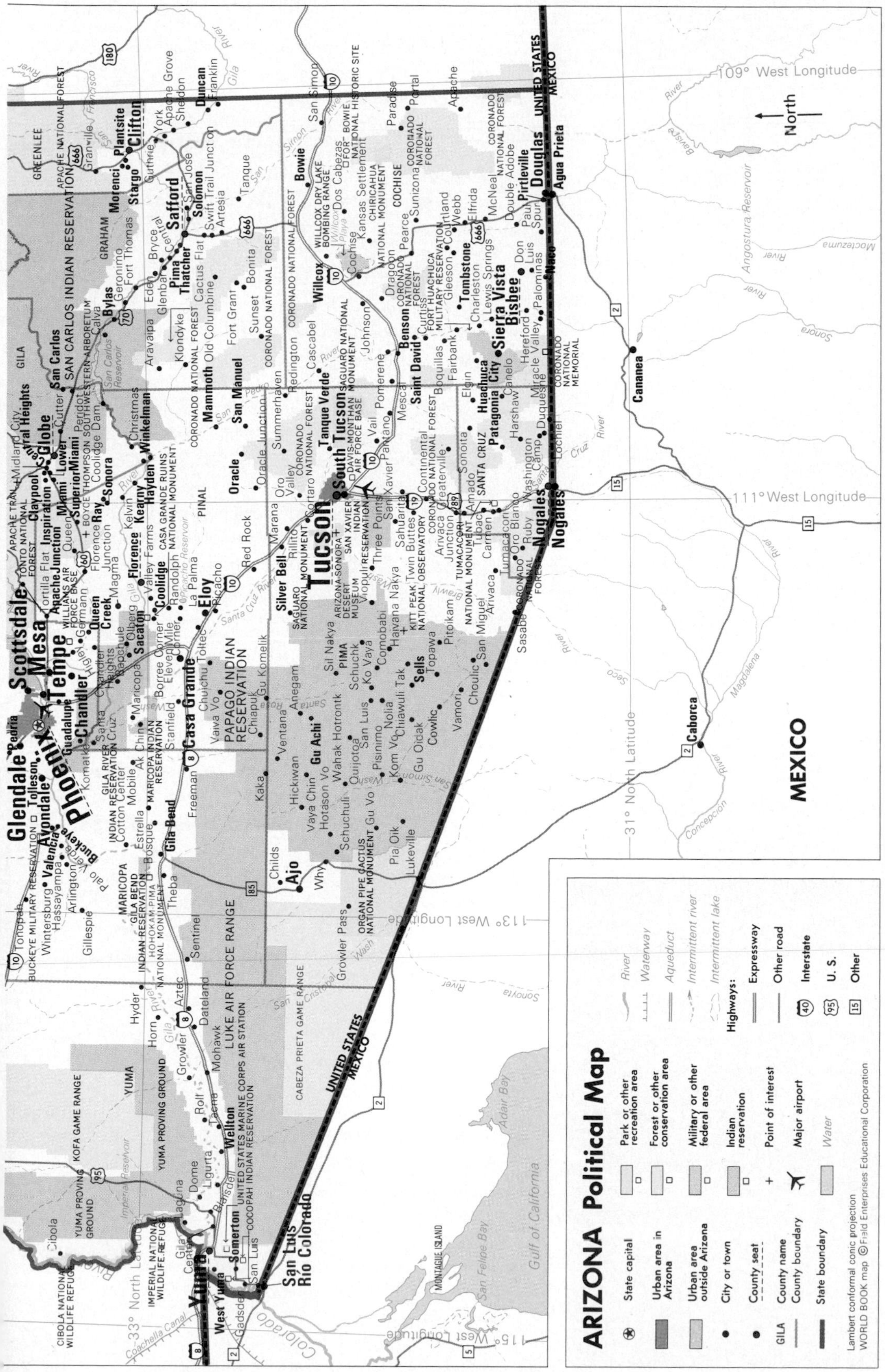

Seal

Flag

Bird: Cactus Wren

Flower: Saguaro (Giant Cactus)

California

Made famous in films and fiction, Chinatown is a bustling center frequented by tourists and native San Franciscans alike (left).

Enticing travelers away from the congested freeways, boating facilities such as this one at San Pedro are strung along the California coast (below).

California is a state of greatly varied landscapes, climates, wildlife, economic sources, ways of life, and points of interest. Large cities such as Los Angeles and San Francisco, among the greatest in the nation, provide visitors with the hustle and bustle of exciting city life. More remote areas of the state such as the redwood forests of the northwest or the barren deserts of the southeast, provide vacationers with tranquility and natural beauty.

Spanish explorers first sailed along California's coast in the 1500's. They are responsible for the state's name, probably taken from the name of a treasure island in a popular Spanish tale. California's official nickname, the *Golden State,* comes from the gold fields that attracted thousands of miners during the gold rush of 1849. The nickname also suggests California's famous golden sunshine and its golden pastures in autumn.

The many old Spanish missions built by Franciscan friars beginning in 1769 are evidence of California's Spanish history. Probably the most famous of these is Mission San Juan Capistrano. Others include San Diego de Alcalá, San Antonio de Padua, Santa Barbara, and San José de Guadalupe. Other Spanish influence can be seen on the Monterey Peninsula in Monterey, which has buildings dating from Spanish colonial days. Olvera Street in Los Angeles has been restored as a typical old Mexican market where shoppers can browse in colorful stalls.

Los Angeles, California's largest city, and the surrounding area provide visitors with more attractions such as Disneyland, Knott's Berry Farm, and Marineland.

San Francisco, situated on steep hillsides overlooking San Francisco Bay, is the site of interesting places such as the Golden Gate Bridge, Chinatown, and Fisherman's Wharf.

California's economy is based on a variety of sources. It leads the nation in manufactured goods. California also ranks first among the states in farm income. The huge variety of climates, soil, and water conditions account for the 200 or more different crops grown by California farmers. The state leads all others in the output of peaches and pears. Grapes are California's most valuable fruit.

The Central Valley is the primary farming region of the state. Cattle and sheep can also be seen grazing on the fertile pastures of this area. California is a major mining state as well, particularly of petroleum and natural gas, and it ranks second only to Alaska in commercial fishing.

Scenic beauty abounds throughout California, from the glittering beauty of the big cities at night to the natural beauty of the state's mountains, valleys, and deserts. Along California's eastern border lie the rugged Sierra Nevada Mountains containing Mount Whitney, the nation's highest point south of Alaska. Also within this area lies spectacular Yosemite National Park, containing several breathtaking waterfalls. One of these, Ribbon Falls, is the highest on the continent. Others include Bridalveil, Illilouette, Nevada, Silver Strand, Vernal, and Upper and Lower Yosemite.

California's coastline also varies from steep cliffs and terraces in the north and central areas of the state to wide sandy beaches in the south. Two great natural harbors are a part of California's coastline at San Francisco and San Diego. Redwood National Park is located on the far northern coast of the state. In this area grow California's famous giant redwood trees. Redwood Highway, or U.S. 101, runs from San Francisco to Oregon through groves of these magnificent trees, the tallest in the world.

The barren desert areas of the state provide visitors with other spectacular scenic attractions. One of these is Death Valley National Monument near the California-Nevada border, part of which is the lowest point in North America. Scotty's Castle, located there, was built by Walter E. Scott, who lived in Death Valley for over 30 years. In the middle of this desert wasteland of southern California lies the lush resort city of Palm Springs, which attracts many vacationers every year.

Climates vary widely in California as well. They range from mild along the southern coast, to hot and dry in the southeast, to mild but cooler in the north and central areas of the state.

Other interesting sights within California's borders include San Simeon, the estate near San Luis Obispo of newspaper owner William Randolph Hearst; the San Diego Zoo, containing the largest collection of birds, mammals, and reptiles in the world; Kings Canyon, Lassen Volcanic, and Sequoia national parks; and more national monuments including Lava Beds, Muir Woods, and Pinnacles.

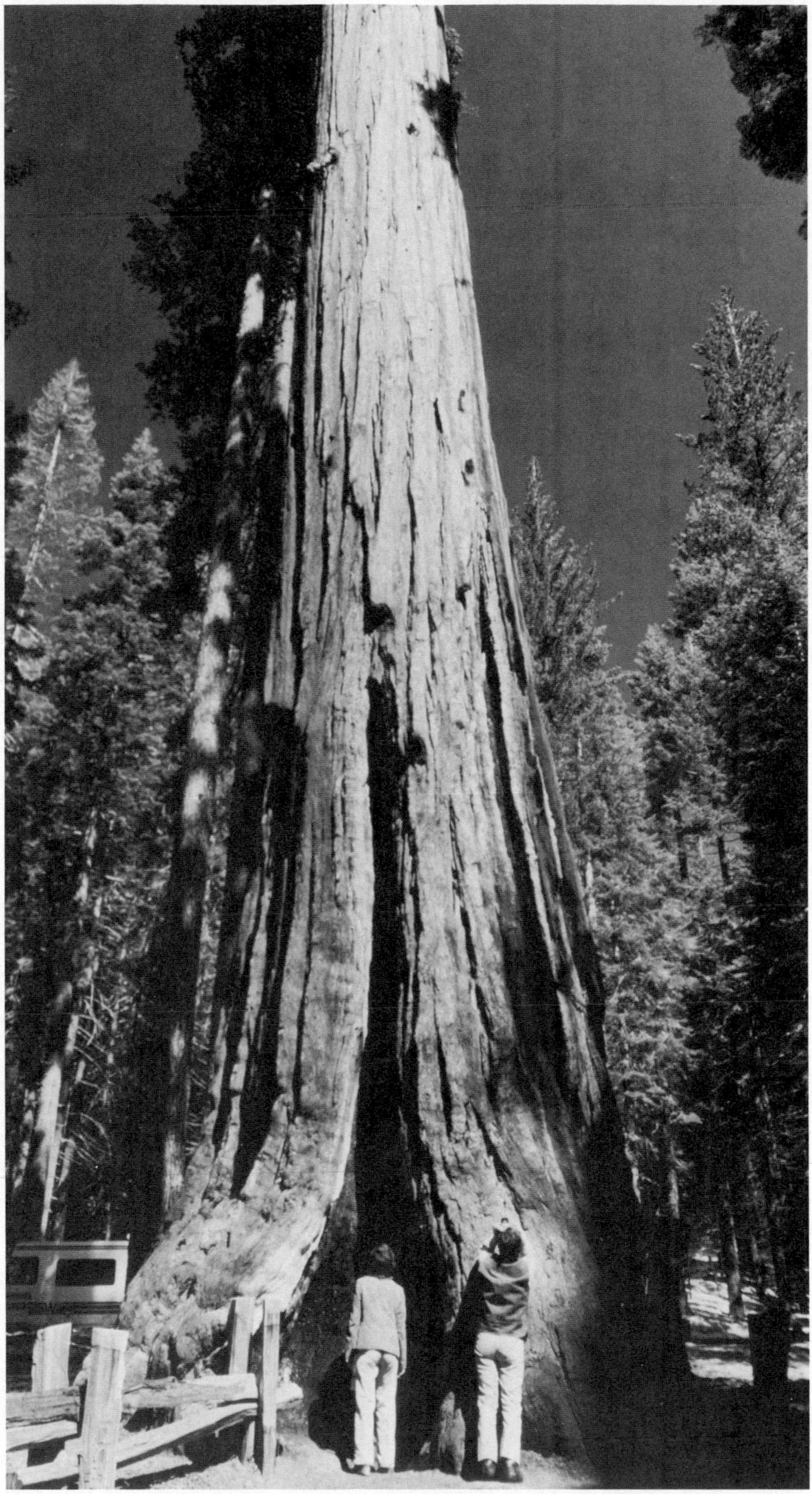

Stretching toward the heavens, this giant sequoia in Yosemite National Park is one of the mammoth sequoias found only on the western slopes of the Sierra Nevada mountain range.

California
Golden State

Capital: Sacramento
Area: 158,693 sq. mi. (411,013 km²), including 2,332 sq. mi. (6,040 km²) of inland water but excluding 69 sq. mi. (179 km²) of Pacific coastal water; 3rd in size among the states
Elevation: *Highest*—Mount Whitney, 14,494 ft. (4,418 m) above sea level; *lowest*—282 ft. (86 m) below sea level in Death Valley
Statehood: Sept. 9, 1850, the 31st state
Abbreviations: Calif. (traditional); CA (postal)
Motto: *Eureka* (I Have Found It)
Song: "I Love You, California"
Tree: California Redwood

California's state seal, adopted in 1849, features the grizzly bear. A symbol of determination, the bear stands near the seated figure of Minerva, the Roman goddess of wisdom. A miner represents the state's mining industry, and ships symbolize commercial greatness. The peaks in the background represent the Sierra Nevada. The state flag was adopted in 1911. Americans revolting against Mexican rule first raised this banner in 1846. The grizzly bear appears on the flag, as well as a single star, after the lone star of Texas.

CALIFORNIA Political Map

Lambert Conformal Conic projection
WORLD BOOK map © Field Enterprises Educational Corporation

State capital
Urban area in California
Urban area outside California
City or town
County seat

FRESNO County name
County boundary
State boundary

Park or other recreation area
Forest or other conservation area
Military or other federal area
Indian reservation
Point of interest
Major airport
Water

Highways:
Expressway
Other road
Interstate
U.S.
Other

River
Waterway
Aqueduct
Intermittent river
Intermittent lake

Distance scale for inset maps

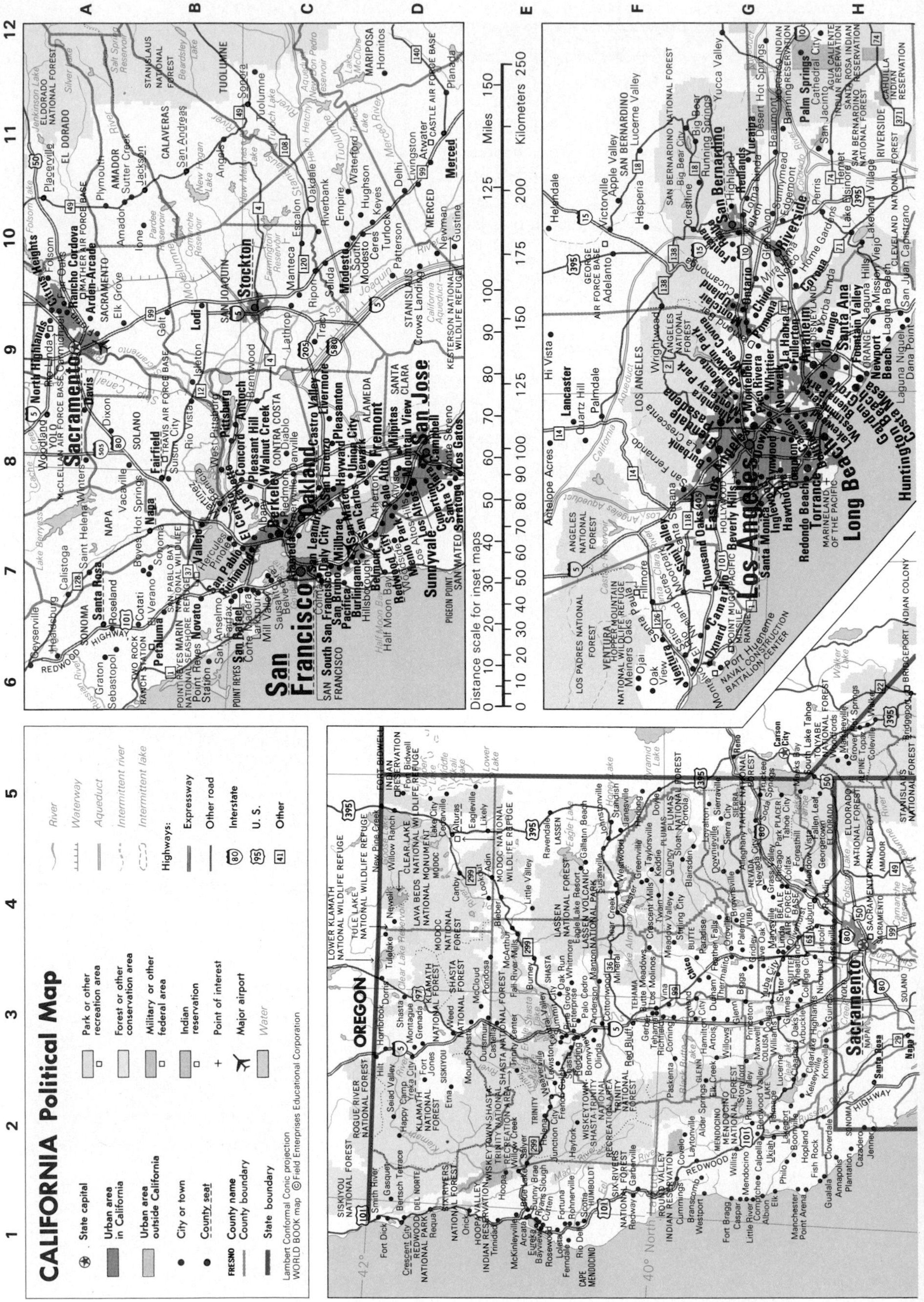

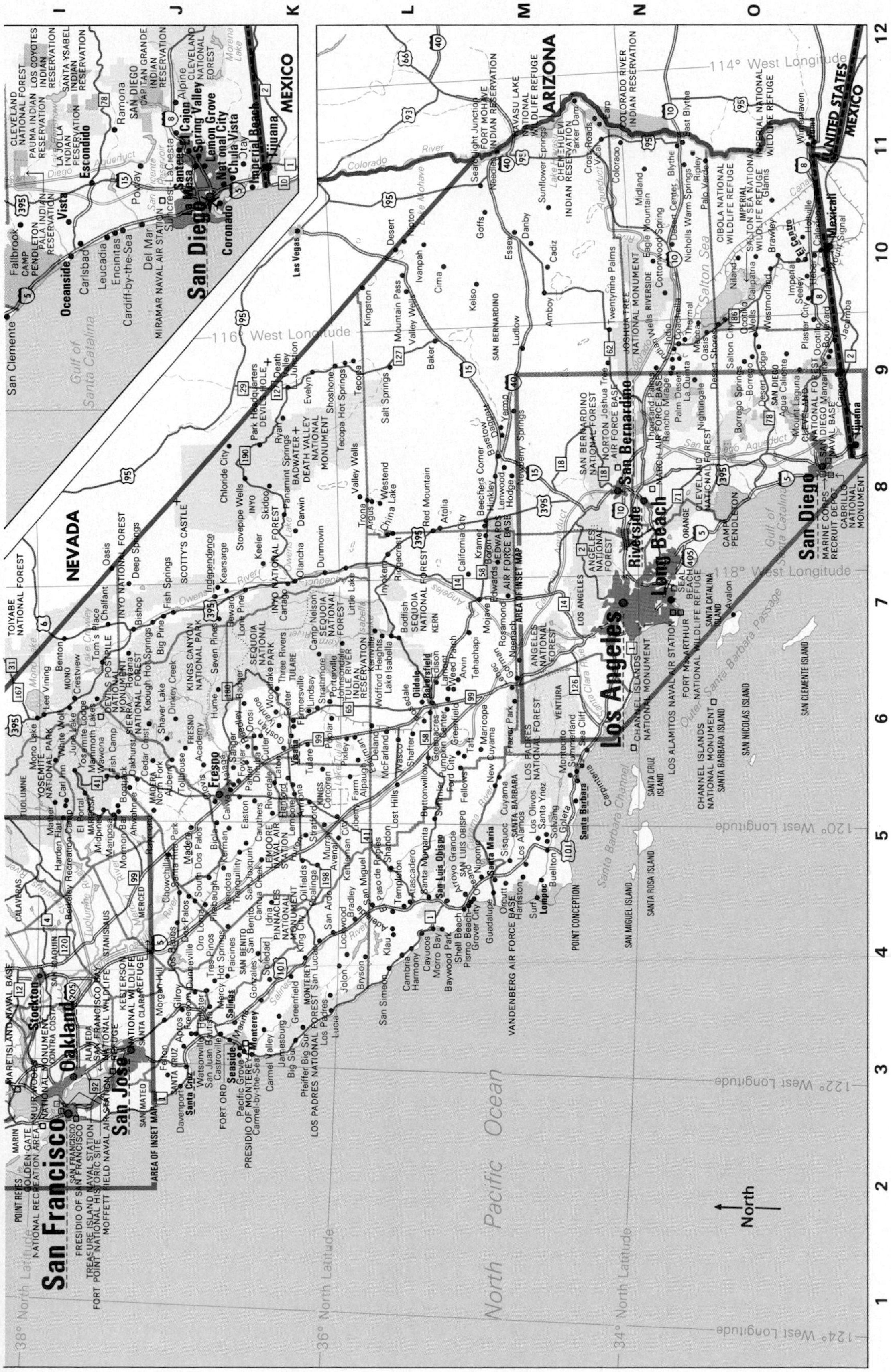

Seal

Flag

Bird: California Valley Quail

Flower: Golden Poppy

Perched high upon canyon walls, the Cliff Palace in Mesa Verde National Park was inhabited by Cliff Dweller Indians almost 1,000 years ago. A great drought forced the Indians to leave the area in the late 1200's.

Colorado

Indians roamed present-day Colorado long before white explorers arrived. Mesa Verde National Park near Cortez preserves some ancient Indian cliff dwellings that are almost 1,000 years old. Spanish explorers arrived in the 1500's but left without settling the area when they failed to find gold.

The word *colorado* is a Spanish word meaning "colored red." The name was first given to the Colorado River, which flows through canyons of red rock. The state was then named for the river. Colorado is officially nicknamed the *Centennial State* because it joined the Union in 1876, the centennial, or 100th anniversary, of the Declaration of Independence.

After the United States had acquired the land that is now known as Colorado, Zebulon M. Pike, an army officer, was one of the first to explore the region. In the records of his trip, he described a mighty mountain, and so Pikes Peak was given his name. This peak is probably the most famous of all Colorado's mountains.

Pikes Peak is part of the beautifully rugged range known as the Rocky Mountains. Colorado's Rocky Mountain National Park encompasses just a small portion of this huge range. The unusual natural beauty of the mountains, teamed with the sports activities that they accommodate, are probably Colorado's greatest attractions. The Rocky Mountains are one of the nation's most popular areas for camping, mountain climbing, hunting, fishing, and especially skiing. The deep, powdery snow of the long winter attracts skiers to many world-famous Colorado resort towns such as Aspen, Vail, and Winter Park. The brilliant yellow aspen trees in the fall, the cool, pleasant climate of the summer, and the scenic wonders of the area make Colorado a tourist haven all year round.

Rushing rivers and gorges, rugged mountains and valleys, and beautiful red rock formations and mesas are plentiful throughout the state. The Garden of the Gods near Colorado Springs is a breathtaking cluster of huge red sandstone rocks. An Easter Sunday sunrise service in the garden is popular among worshipers. Royal Gorge, near Canon City, is a massive canyon cut by the Arkansas River. The gorge is more than 1,000 feet (304.8 meters) deep and is crossed by the world's highest suspension bridge. Other attractions throughout the state have been designated as national monuments. These include the Black Canyon of the Gunnison, the Great Sand Dunes, Hovenweep, and Florissant Fossil Beds.

The Continental Divide runs through the Colorado Rockies. Streams and rivers east of this imaginary dividing line flow into the Atlantic Ocean. Those west of it flow into the Pacific Ocean. More important rivers begin in Colorado than in any other state. A few of these include the Colorado, the Arkansas, and the South Platte.

Not all of Colorado is mountainous. Roughly two-fifths of the state is a part of the Great Plains. This region comprises the state's major crop-growing area, although it was once thought to be too dry for farming. Irrigation projects have made agriculture possible. Colorado's chief crops are wheat, corn, and sugar beets. Potatoes and lettuce are grown in the San Luis Valley of southern Colorado. The land of the plains area is also important grazing land for cattle and sheep. Herds are also a familiar sight on the plateaus and mesas of western Colorado.

Manufacturing is the leading source of income in Colorado, which is the leading manufacturing state in the entire Rocky Mountain region of the United States. The major manufacturing centers are located in the eastern portion of the state, particularly around Denver. Mining is important to the state's economy as well. Petroleum is the major mineral product, but gold and silver ores are also mined. Mining of one sort or another takes place in all but one of Colorado's 63 counties.

Mining played an important part in Colorado's history and accounted for its rapid growth during the 1850's. When gold was discovered in 1858 along Cherry Creek near present-day Denver, prospectors rushed to the area. *Pikes Peak or Bust* became their slogan. Central City, once a rich gold camp, is now a rustic western resort town. A theater and music festival are held each summer in the old-time opera house.

Other notable points of interest in Colorado include: east of La Junta, Bent's Old Fort, a reconstructed trading post and national historic site; on top of Lookout Mountain near Golden, Buffalo Bill's Grave, honoring the famous scout and showman William F. Cody; north of Colorado Springs, the Air Force Academy; and in Denver, the U.S. Mint.

Crackling clear winter air, plentiful snow, and steep slopes like these at Copper Mountain have made Colorado synonymous with skiing (above).

As a tribute to the rough-and-tumble frontiersmen who helped tame Colorado, the Bucking Bronco statue adorns Denver's Civic Center (left).

Colorado
Centennial State

Capital: Denver
Area: 104,247 sq. mi. (269,998 km^2), including 481 sq. mi. (1,246 km^2) of inland water; 8th in size among the states
Elevation: *Highest*—Mount Elbert, 14,433 ft. (4,399 m) above sea level; *lowest*—3,350 ft. (1,021 m) above sea level along the Arkansas River in Prowers County
Statehood: Aug. 1, 1876, the 38th state
Abbreviations: Colo. (traditional); CO (postal)
Motto: *Nil sine Numine* (Nothing Without Providence)
Song: "Where the Columbines Grow"
Tree: Blue Spruce

Colorado's state seal shows a triangular figure representing the "all-seeing" eye of God. The fasces, *or "bound rods," are a symbol of power. The three mountains stand for the state's rugged land, and the pick and hammer for the importance of mining. The seal was adopted in 1877. On the state flag, adopted in 1911, the red C stands for* Colorado, *the Spanish word for "colored red." The golden ball is said to represent the state's gold production.*

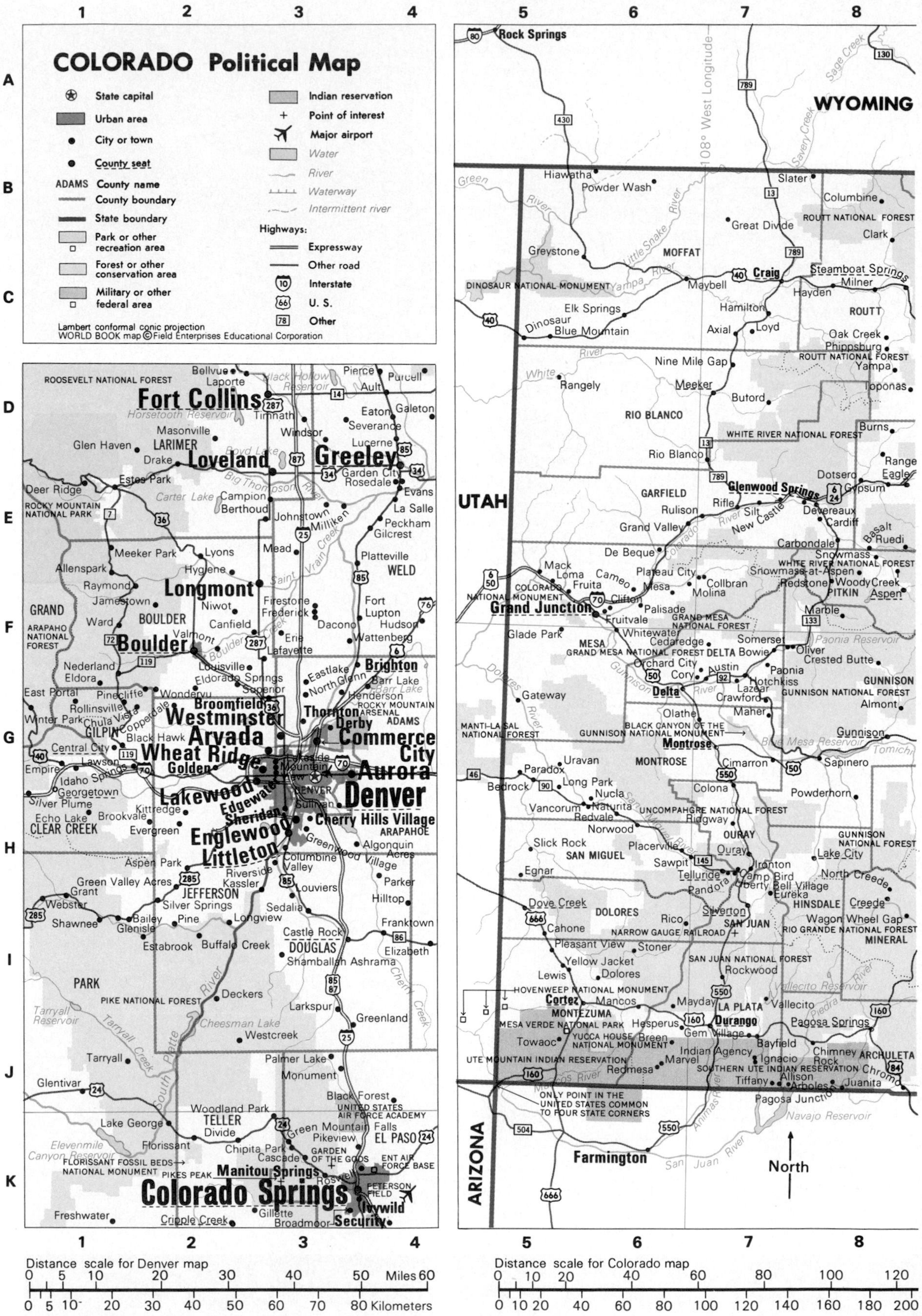

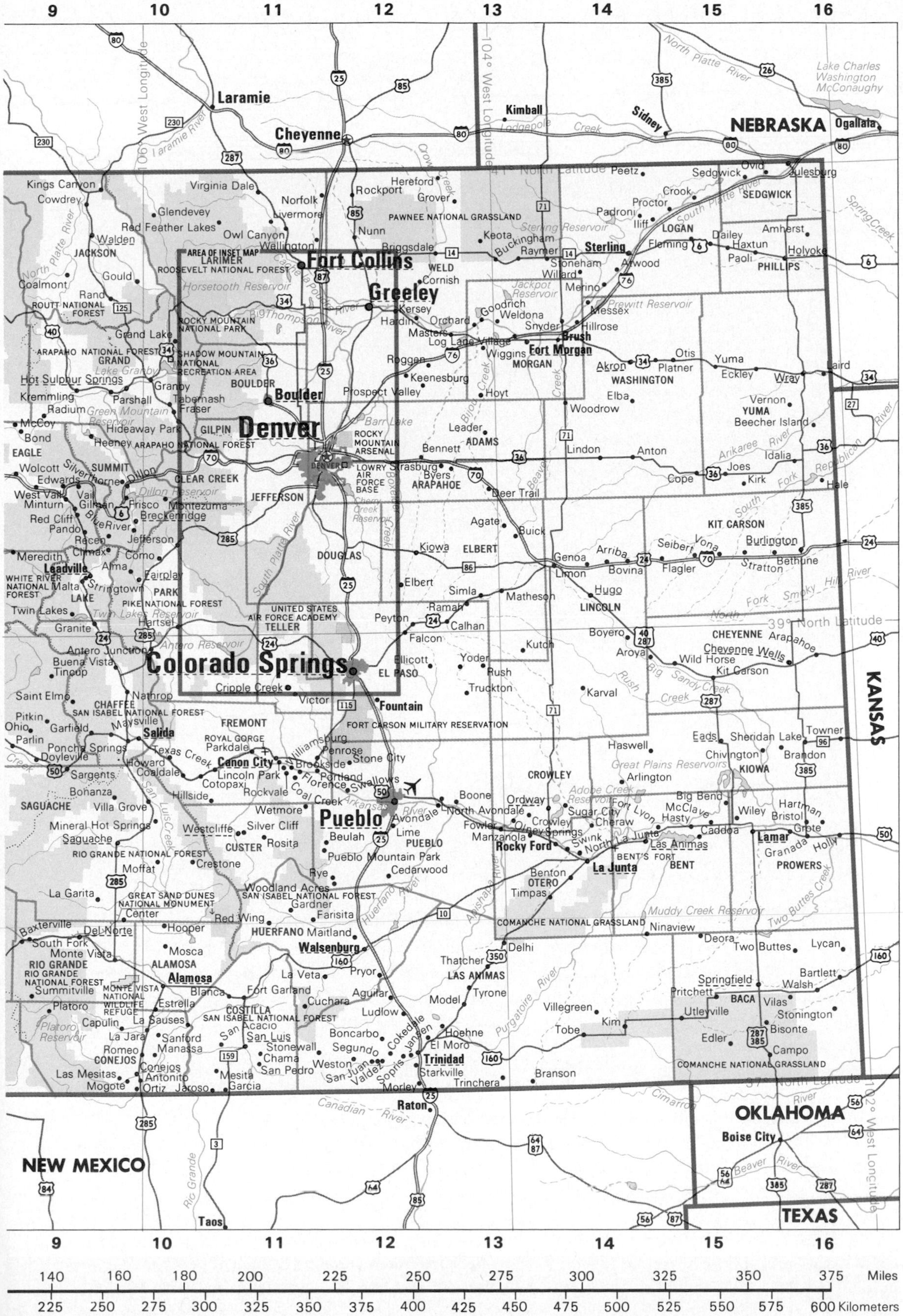

Seal

Flag

Bird: Lark Bunting

Flower: Rocky Mountain Columbine

Idaho's fertile soil and abundant water supplies enable farmfields like this to produce golden wheat and the famous Idaho potato.

Idaho

Idaho, the *Gem State,* is rich in natural resources. Its fertile soil is probably the most important of these and is the basis for Idaho's agricultural economy. Other major natural resources include valuable minerals, thick forests, and excellent water supplies.

About half the people of Idaho live in cities and towns, but Idaho has only 35 cities of more than 2,500 persons. The state has no great manufacturing industries to encourage the growth of big cities. But manufacturing is expanding, and large companies have set up operations.

Agriculture is the state's leading industry. Most farming is done on the fertile soil of the Columbia Plateau region, which follows the sweeping path of the Snake River across southern Idaho. Little rain falls in this area, but irrigation has played a key role in developing productive fields. Golden fields of wheat can be seen covering many parts of this region. Potatoes, however, are Idaho's most important—and probably most famous—agricultural product. Idaho ranks first among all the states in potato production. Other major crops include sugar beets, barley, beans, and hay. Grazing cattle and sheep also dot the landscape of this region.

Idaho's rich deposits of minerals provide a good portion of the state's income. It leads the nation in the production of silver and is also a leader in the production of lead and zinc. The Sunshine Mine in Shoshone County is the nation's largest silver mine, and the Bunker Hill Mine at Kellogg is one of the largest lead mines in the nation. Rich deposits of various minerals have been found in 42 of Idaho's 44 counties.

Thick forests cover about 40 per cent of Idaho's land area and have made it a major timber-producing state. Idaho has some of the world's largest white-pine forests, and its mills and factories turn out vast quantities of fiberboard, pulp, paper, and other forest products.

Idaho is one of the few states that have abundant water supplies. Vast underground water resources are among them. Idaho's Salmon River is the longest river that lies entirely in one state. This waterway has been called the *River of No Return* because at one time travelers could not navigate up-

In the Sawtooth Mountains of south-central Idaho lies Sun Valley, a winter sports center known for its brilliant sunshine and frequent snowfalls.

stream against its raging current and rapids. Now it is a popular spot for guided raft and boat trips.

Other waterways and lakes are among Idaho's popular scenic attractions. Peaceful Coeur d'Alene Lake in the northern mountains may be one of the world's most beautiful lakes. Most of Idaho's rivers are lovely, rushing mountain streams dotted with many areas of whitewater rapids. Hundreds of large waterfalls can also be viewed along these rivers. Shoshone Falls, on the Snake River near Twin Falls, is one of the most popular, taking a breathtaking plunge from a height greater than that of Niagara Falls. Other spectacular waterfalls include Twin Falls, also on the Snake River, and Mesa Falls, on the North Fork of the Snake. These quiet lakes and streams provide excellent fishing.

Several areas, called primitive areas, in the Rocky Mountain region of the state have been preserved without roads, logging developments, or modern improvements. These areas can be explored only on foot, on horseback, in boats, or from planes.

Snow-capped mountains and plunging canyons and gorges are also among Idaho's natural wonders. Hells Canyon on the Snake River south of Lewiston is the deepest canyon in the nation. Idaho also has hundreds of underground caverns with frozen rivers and waterfalls, other formations of ice and stone, and huge chambers that look like gothic halls. These caves lie under lava fields and include Crystal Ice Cave near American Falls, Minnetonka Cave near Paris, and Shoshone Ice Caves near Shoshone.

Still other natural wonders of Idaho are: near Castleford, Balanced Rock, a balloon-shaped rock 40 feet (12.1 meters) high that rests on a small stone block; in southern Idaho, Craters of the Moon National Monument, which resembles the surface of the moon; and, near Gooding, Little City of Rocks, a collection of weird rock formations carved by nature to resemble towers, cathedrals, and castles.

Idaho's colorful history as an old western mining area also provides the state with many interesting sites. Mining towns such as Silver City in Owyhee County and Idaho City in Boise County once bustled with activity. They are now ghost towns. Other historical points of interest include, west of Kellogg, Cataldo Mission, Idaho's oldest building, dating from the 1800's; near Lewiston, Nez Perce National Historical Park, which honors the history and life of the Nez Perce Indian region and the Lewis and Clark Expedition; and, in Pocatello, Old Fort Hall, a reconstructed trading post that was once an important stop on the Oregon Trail.

Idaho
Gem State

Capital: Boise
Area: 83,557 sq. mi. (216,412 km²), including 880 sq. mi. (2,279 km²) of inland water; 13th in size among the states
Elevation: *Highest*—Borah Peak, 12,662 ft. (3,859 m) above sea level; *lowest*— Snake River at Lewiston in Nez Perce County, 710 ft. (216 m) above sea level
Statehood: July 3, 1890, the 43rd state
Abbreviations: Ida. (traditional); ID (postal)
Motto: *Esto Perpetua* (It Is Forever)
Song: "Here We Have Idaho"
Tree: Western White Pine

Idaho's state seal, adopted in 1891, shows two figures. The woman holding the scales and spear symbolizes freedom and equality. The miner represents Idaho's mineral resources. The trees and river in the shield stand for Idaho's natural beauty. The elk's head represents wildlife. The horns of plenty and sheaves of grain symbolize agricultural wealth. The state flag, adopted in 1907, has a reproduction of the seal.

IDAHO Political Map

Highways:
- Expressway
- Other road
- Interstate
- U.S.
- Other

- Water
- River
- Intermittent river

- Park or other recreation area
- Forest or other conservation area
- Military or other federal area
- Indian reservation
- Point of interest
- Major airport

- State capital
- Urban area in Idaho
- Urban area outside Idaho
- City or town
- Ghost town
- County seat
- County name
- County boundary
- State boundary

Lambert conformal conic projection
WORLD BOOK map © Field Enterprises Educational Corporation

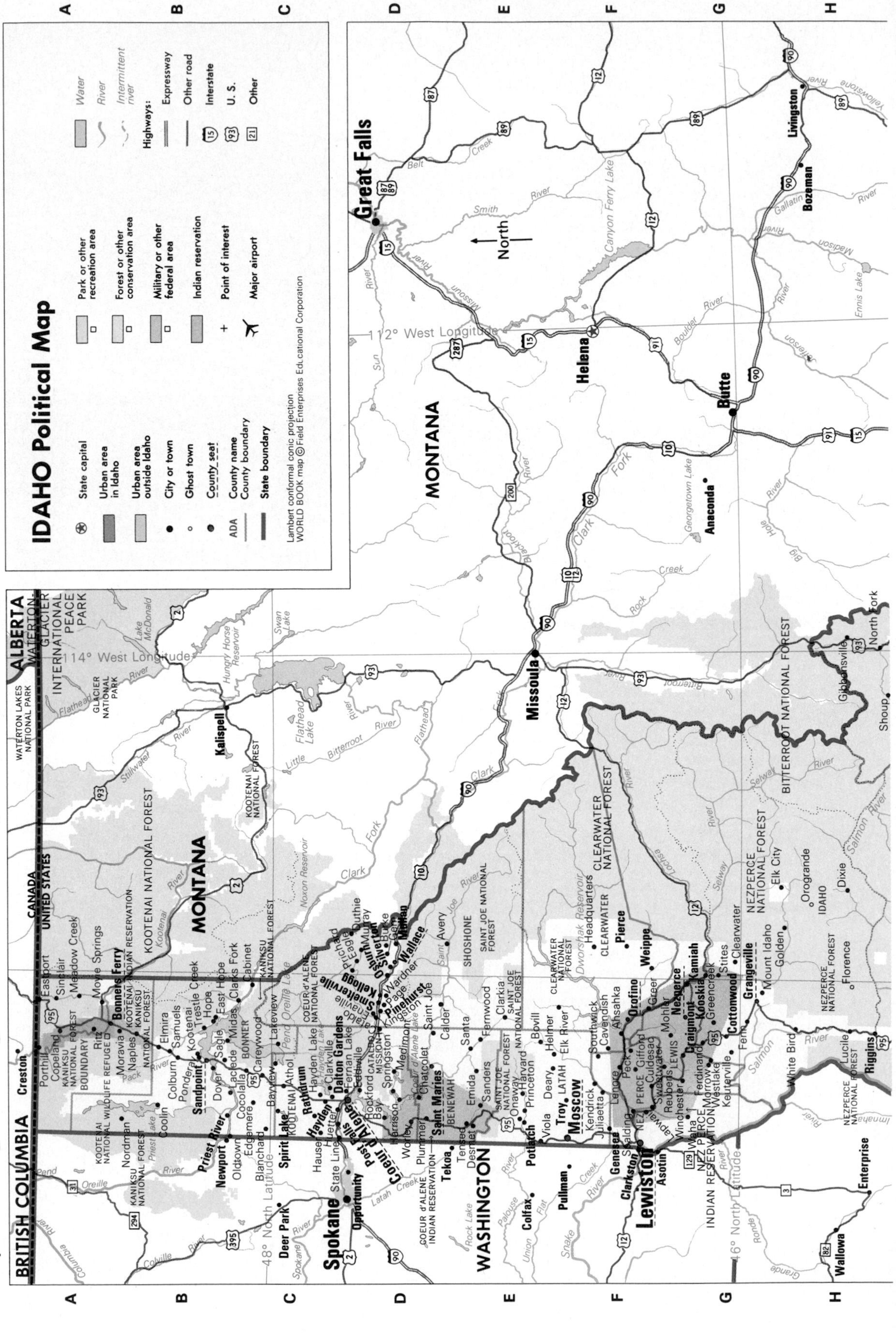

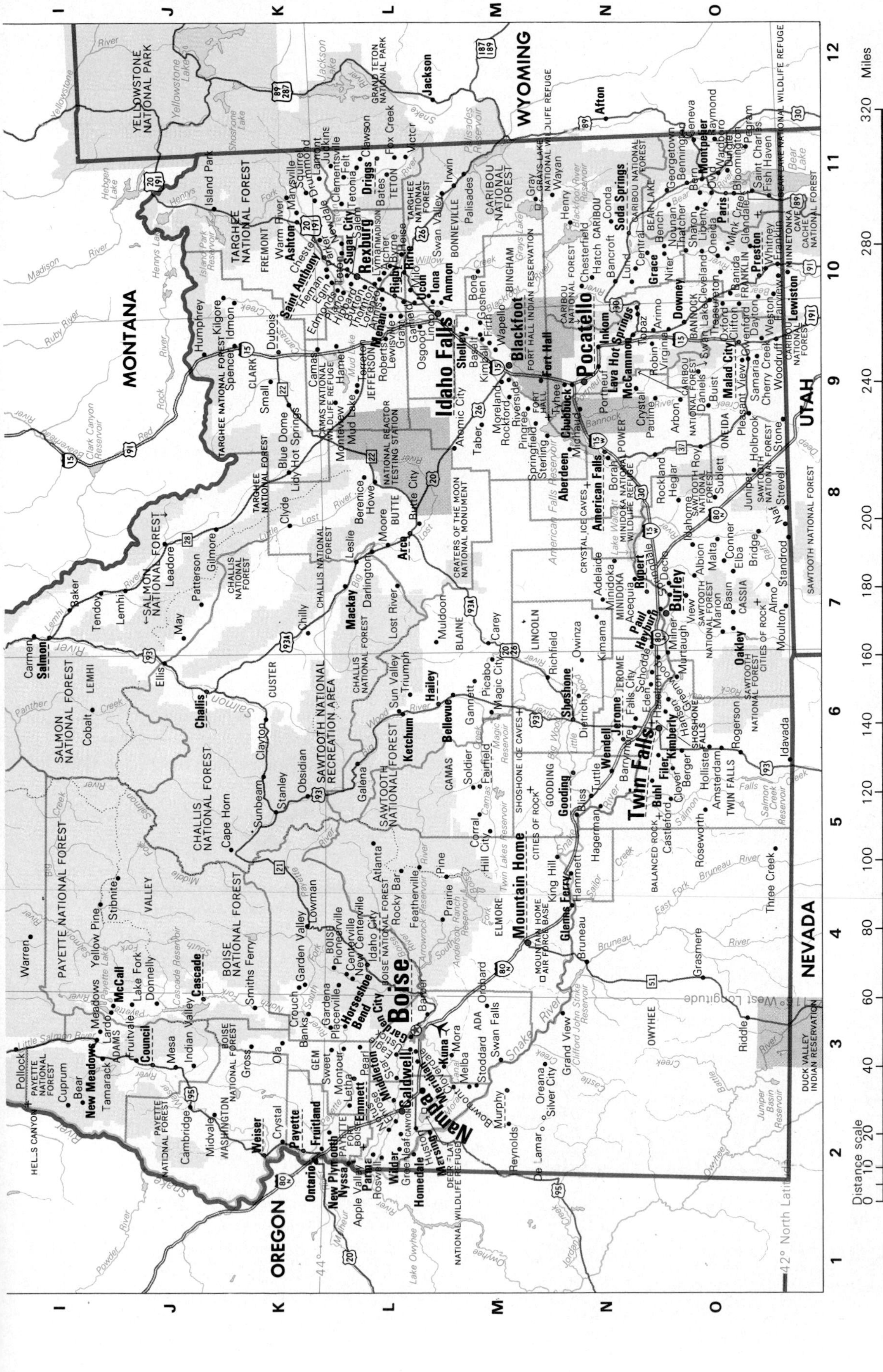

Seal

Flag

Bird: Mountain Bluebird

Flower: Syringa (Mock Orange)

Montana

Montana was called the *Land of the Shining Mountains* by early travelers who saw the sun glistening on the area's snow-capped mountain peaks. The name *Montana* comes from a Spanish word meaning "mountainous." Montana's official nickname, the *Treasure State,* comes from the abundance of gold and silver found in the mountains.

The discovery of gold in Montana did much to give the state a place in U.S. history. It also helped to make Montana truly a part of the Wild West. After gold was discovered in southwestern Montana, wild mining camps grew up around the mines, attracting outlaws. Since the mining camps had virtually no effective law enforcement, the citizens took the law into their own hands. They formed a vigilance committee, called vigilantes, and hanged many outlaws and drove others out of Montana.

Virginia City near Dillon was one of America's richest gold camps in 1865. It has been restored and is now a popular tourist attraction. The main street in Helena, Montana's capital, is called Last Chance Gulch. It is named for the gold camp that once stood on that site.

Mining still plays an important part in Montana's economy. Vast deposits of copper, gold, and silver are found in western Montana, while petroleum and coal are abundant in the eastern portion of the state. Anaconda is the location of Anaconda Reduction Works, one of the world's largest copper smelters. During the summer, tours through the facility are conducted twice a day.

During frontier days, one of the most famous Indian wars in American history was fought near the Little Bighorn River in Montana. On June 25, 1876, the Battle of Little Bighorn was fought between the Sioux and Cheyenne Indians and Captain George A. Custer's Seventh Cavalry. Custer and about 225 of the soldiers under his command were killed in the battle. The battle is known as "Custer's Last Stand." Custer Battlefield National Monument, south of Hardin, is now a popular point of interest.

The rugged Rocky Mountains run through western Montana, providing visitors to the state with many magnificent views of Montana's natural beauty. Glacier National Park in northwestern Montana is the site of some of the most majestic scenery in the United States. The more than 50 glaciers on the mountain slopes give the park its name. Located in the park are several peaks so steep and rugged that they have never been climbed.

Giant Springs near Great Falls is one of Montana's most popular natural wonders. The springs, which discharges over a quarter of a million gallons of water a minute, was sighted by Lewis and Clark

Breathtaking, glacier-covered mountain slopes and valleys strewn with wild flowers attract thousands to Glacier National Park each summer.

A shepherd on horseback guides his sheep across the nourishing grasslands that Indian hunters once roamed.

in 1805. Another of Montana's natural wonders is the Great Falls of the Missouri, the highest waterfall on the Missouri River. It is located near the city bearing its name.

In contrast to the rugged, mountainous landscape in the west, eastern Montana is part of America's Great Plains. The landscape consists of broad prairies and golden wheat fields occasionally dotted with oil wells. Large herds of beef cattle and flocks of sheep can be seen grazing on sprawling ranches. Farmers in Montana raise wheat as their major crop. Sweet black cherries are the state's major fruit crop. Farmers also produce eggs, milk, and wool.

Huge forests and swift-flowing streams make western Montana an excellent haven for hunters and fishers. Visitors who enjoy the outdoors may take advantage of Montana's national parks and forests, dude ranches, summer resorts, and ski lodges. Those who are interested in history enjoy trips to the sites of famous Indian battles, old ghost towns, and museums. The Montana Historical Society in Helena has a large collection of paintings and sculptures by the famous cowboy artist, Charles M. Russell.

Montana has many annual events that reflect its cowboy and Indian background. There are rodeos in almost all towns in Montana. Some of the rodeos are large and draw riders from all over the country, while others are so small that just a few local riders participate. Indians on Montana's reservations also perform colorful dances and hold ceremonies throughout the state.

Most of the annual "cowboy and Indian" events take place from May through September, which is a busy time for Montana citizens and an interesting and enjoyable time for visitors. In May, rodeo owners buy wild horses in a Bucking Horse Sale in Miles City. The Vigilante Parade in Helena and Whoop-up Days in Conrad are also held in May.

The Flathead Lake Showboat in Polson, North American Indian Days in Browning, and Yellowstone River Float from Livingston to Billings are all held in July. In August, visitors to Montana may attend the Festival of Nations in Red Lodge, the Midland Empire Fair and Rodeo in Billings, and the State Fair and Rodeo in Great Falls.

Western Montana has its roots deep in mining. Many of the old mines, like this one in Jardine, were abandoned long ago. Others flourish and play a major role in the state's economy.

Montana
Treasure State

Capital: Helena
Area: 147,138 sq. mi. (381,086 km²), including 1,551 sq. mi. (4,017 km²) of inland water; 4th in size among the states
Elevation: *Highest*—Granite Peak in Park County, 12,799 ft. (3,901 m) above sea level; *lowest*—1,800 ft. (549 m) above sea level, along the Kootenai River in Lincoln County
Statehood: Nov. 8, 1889, the 41st state
Abbreviations: Mont. (traditional); MT (postal)
Motto: *Oro y Plata* (Gold and Silver)
Song: "Montana"
Tree: Ponderosa Pine

Montana's state seal, adopted in 1893, shows a plow, a pick, and a shovel resting on the soil. These symbols represent the state's agricultural opportunities and its mineral industries. The Great Falls of the Missouri River and the mountain scenery stand for Montana's natural beauty and resources. The state motto appears on a ribbon. The state flag, adopted in 1905, bears an adaptation of the seal.

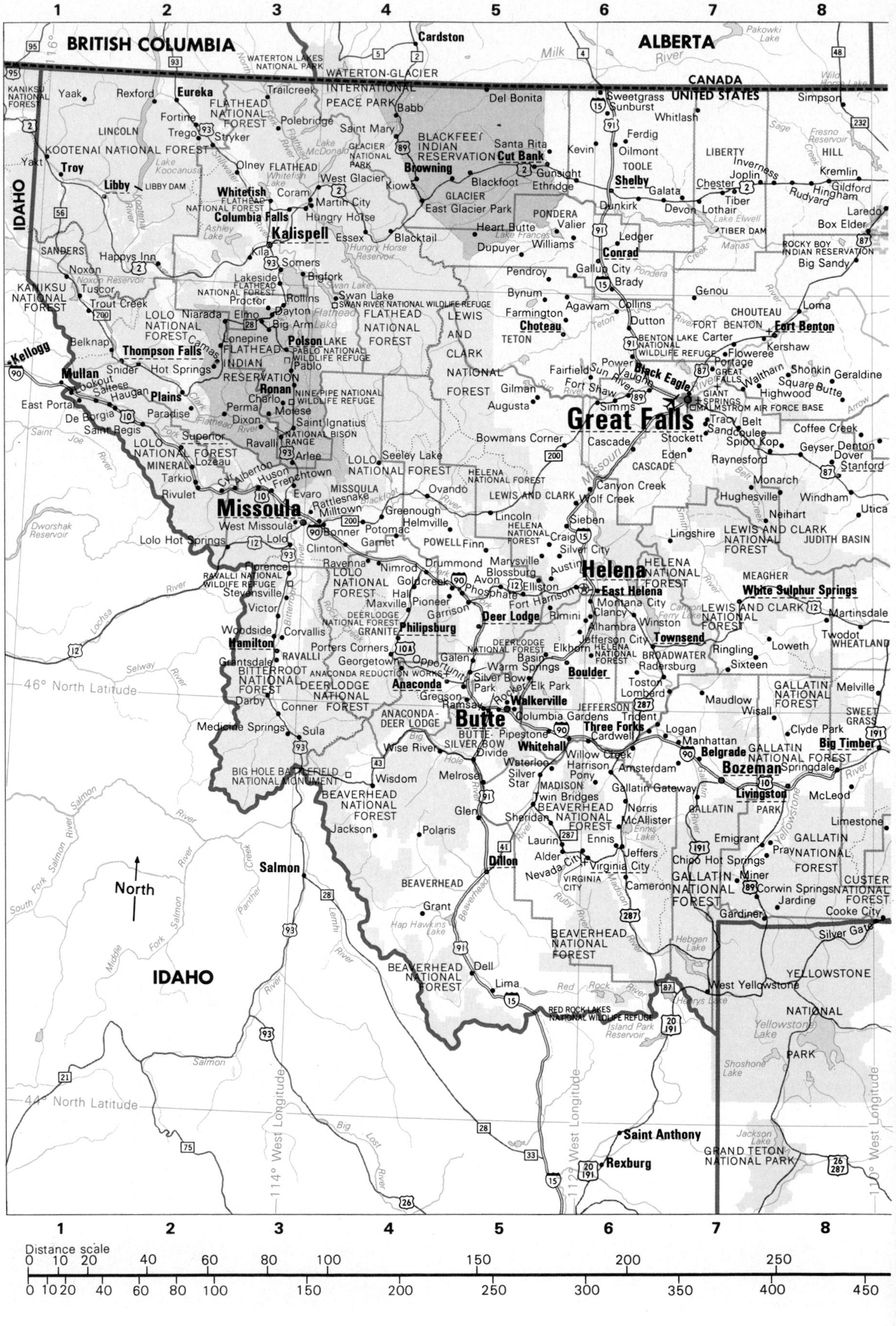

Seal

Flag

Bird: Western Meadow Lark

Flower: Bitterroot

9   10   11   12   13   14   15   16

SASKATCHEWAN

CANADA
UNITED STATES

CREEDMAN COULEE
NATIONAL WILDLIFE REFUGE
Hogeland   Turner   Loring   Thoeny   Opheim   Glentana   Four   DANIELS   Whitetail   Daleview   Westby
HILL   North   Havre   Whitewater   Richland   Buttes   Madoc   Redstone   Outlook   Raymond   Plentywood
233   Lake Thibadeau   National Wildlife Refuge   Scobey   Flaxville   Navajo   SHERIDAN   Coalridge   Antelope   Reserve   Dagmar

Big Muddy Lake

Morgan

Peerless

BLACK COULEE
NATIONAL WILDLIFE REFUGE

Chinook   Harlem   HEWITT LAKE
NATIONAL WILDLIFE REFUGE   Saco   Hinsdale   Larslan   FORT PECK INDIAN RESERVATION   Medicine Lake   MEDICINE LAKE
NATIONAL WILDLIFE REFUGE
Havre   Zurich   Nelson Reservoir   Homestead   Froid
ROCKY BOYS
INDIAN RESERVATION   BLAINE   Wagner   Malta   Bowdoin
NATIONAL WILDLIFE REFUGE   Vandalia   Tampico   ROOSEVELT   Culbertson   Bainville   McCabe   Williston
Rocky Boy   Lloyd   Cleveland   PHILLIPS   Glasgow   Brockton   Lake Sakakawea
FORT BELKNAP   Nashua   Frazer   Wolf Point   Poplar
INDIAN RESERVATION   Fort Peck   Oswego   Wiota   Nohly
Lodge Pole   FORT PECK DAM   Sioux Pass   Fairview

Hays   Regina   Vida   RICHLAND
Landusky   Zortman   Enid   Lambert   Sidney
UL BEND   Crane
Winifred   NATIONAL WILDLIFE   MCCONE   Richey   Savage
Suffolk   REFUGE   Circle   Bloomfield   Burns
CHARLES MARION RUSSELL   CHARLES MARION RUSSELL   Intake
Christina   NATIONAL WILDLIFE   NATIONAL WILDLIFE REFUGE   DAWSON
FERGUS   REFUGE   Brusett   Brockway   Lindsay
Danvers   Hilger   GARFIELD   Jordan   200   2003
Kolin   Roy   Benzien   Glendive
Grass Range   PETROLEUM   22   Cohagen   Wibaux
Lewistown   Cat Creek   WAR HORSE   Hodges   Beach
Ross Fork   Teigen   NATIONAL WILDLIFE   Sand Springs   WIBAUX
Moore   Forestgrove   REFUGE   200   Saint Phillip
Hobson   Winnett   Mosby   Rock Springs   PRAIRIE   Fallon   LAMESTEER NATIONAL
Casin   WAR HORSE   Flatwillow   Angela   Blatchford   Terry   WILDLIFE REFUGE   Carlyle
Buffalo   LEWIS AND CLARK   NATIONAL WILDLIFE REFUGE   Bonfield   Benz   Mildred
Garneill   NATIONAL FOREST   Flatwillow   Kinsey   Ismay
Judith Gap   LAKE MASON   Shirley   Plevna
Oxford   NATIONAL WILDLIFE REFUGE   Sumatra   Ingomar   Locate   FALLON
WHEATLAND   Melstone   22   Knowlton   Baker
Harlowton   Rothiemay   MUSSELSHELL   Vananda   Sheffield   Miles City   Willard
Winnecook   Delphia   Musselshell   Thurlow   CUSTER
Shawmut   Roundup   Cartersville   Forsyth   Hathaway   Mizpah
Ryegate   Sanders   Myers   Rosebud   O'Neill   MEDICINE ROCKS
Slayton   Cushman   Lavina   Bighorn   Garland
GOLDEN VALLEY   Hysham   94   Ekalaka   Mill Iron
HAILSTONE   YELLOWSTONE   Custer   TREASURE   ROSEBUD   Volburg   CUSTER
NATIONAL WILDLIFE REFUGE   Broadview   Powderville   NATIONAL
SWEET   Acton   Pompeys Pillar   Colstrip   FOREST
GRASS   Rapelje   Worden   Ballantine   CARTER
HALFBREED LAKE   Shepherd   Huntley   Lame   Capitol
NATIONAL WILDLIFE REFUGE   Molt   CUSTER
STILLWATER   Laurel   Billings   Hardin   NATIONAL FOREST
Greycliffe   Reedpoint   Youngs   Crow Agency   Deer   Ashland   Olive   Broadus
Columbus   Point   Park City   Busby   Epsie
Abasarokee   Montagua   Silesia   Garryowen   NORTHERN CHEYENNE   Sonnette   Boyes
Nye   Joliet   Rockvale   CUSTER BATTLEFIELD   INDIAN RESERVATION   POWDER RIVER   Hammond
Dean   Fishtail   Boyd   NATIONAL MONUMENT   Birney   Sayle   Alzada
Beehive   Edger   Saint Xavier   BIG HORN   Kirby
Roberts   Fromberg   Lodge Grass   Otter   Biddle
Luther   Roscoe   Pryor   CROW INDIAN   Ridge
Red Lodge   CARBON   Bridger   RESERVATION   Wyola   Boxelder   Moorhead
Washoe   Bearcreek   310   BIGHORN CANYON   212
CUSTER NATIONAL FOREST   Belfry   Warren   NATIONAL RECREATION AREA   Decker
Powell   14   90   59   WYOMING

BEARTOOTH
HIGHWAY

Cody   Bighorn Lake

WYOMING   Buffalo Bill Reservoir

NORTH DAKOTA

SOUTH DAKOTA

A
B
C
D
E
F
G
H
I
J
K

44° North Latitude

MONTANA Political Map

✴ State capital

■ Urban area

● City or town

● County seat

TETON   County name

County boundary

State boundary

Lambert conformal conic projection
WORLD BOOK map

Park or other
recreation area

Forest or other
conservation area

Military or other
federal area

Indian reservation

+ Point of interest

✈ Major airport

Water

River

Intermittent lake

Intermittent river

Highways:

Expressway

Other road

15 Interstate

91 U. S.

28 Other

300   350   400   450   500   Miles 550
500   550   600   650   700   750   800   850 Kilometers 900

With a little imagination, visitors to the Valley of Fire State Park can see an elephant trunk shaped in red rock.

Nevada

Nevada's landscape is a collection of canyons, mountains, prairies, and deserts. The state's scenic beauty is one of its major natural resources and attracts millions of visitors to Nevada yearly. The rugged, snow-capped mountains, grassy valleys, and sandy deserts provide special tourist attractions for hunters, campers, and other sports enthusiasts and sightseers.

Nevada's name comes from a Spanish word meaning "snow-clad." Boundary Peak in Esmeralda County is the highest point in the state at 13,143 feet (4,006 meters). Skiing is popular on the snowy slopes of Mount Rose near Reno, Mount Charleston near Las Vegas, and Ward Mountain near Ely.

Lehman Caves National Monument in the mountains near Baker is one of Nevada's beautiful natural wonders, where visitors may see limestone caverns with tunnels and corridors. A popular scenic attraction near Overton is Valley of Fire State Park, where the weather has worn the rocks into unusual shapes.

Between the mountains lie buttes, or lone hills, and mesas, or flat, tablelike mountains. Lake Tahoe and other mountain lakes in west-central Nevada are popular vacation spots. Lake Tahoe, Pyramid Lake, and, in the southeast, Lake Mead are all favorite spots for swimming and water-skiing. Lake Mead is particularly interesting. It is one of the world's largest artificially created lakes and Nevada's only lake with an outlet to the sea. It was formed when Hoover Dam, one of the world's highest concrete dams, was built across a canyon.

Hot springs and geysers are seen in many areas of Nevada and are evidence of dying volcanoes. Geyser Basin near Beowawe has active geysers, hot springs, and bubbling mud.

The northeast corner of Death Valley National Monument is also in Nevada. Some of the state's desert areas, although largely barren, are frequently splashed with color from the blossoms of the cactus, yucca, and sagebrush plants. Nevada is sometimes called the *Sagebrush State* because of these gray-green desert plants.

In contrast to all this natural splendor is the glittering beauty of resorts like Lake Tahoe, Reno, and Las Vegas, Nevada's largest city and chief tourist attraction. Las Vegas is the home of sparkling hotels, gambling casinos, and nightclubs that feature outstanding Broadway and Hollywood performers. Some of these restaurants and casinos never close.

The tourist industry is Nevada's greatest source of income, but Las Vegas and Reno are also important manufacturing centers. Farming is another source of income for Nevada. Due to the state's lack of rainfall, this industry depends primarily on irrigation for necessary water. Less rain falls in Nevada than in any other state in the country. The Newlands Irrigation Project near Reno was the first system of its kind built by the federal government. These irrigation systems have turned large areas of Nevada wasteland into fertile fields. Important crops include alfalfa seed, hay, potatoes, and wheat. Livestock provides the state's major source of agricultural income. Cattle and sheep can be seen grazing on huge ranches in the central and eastern areas of Nevada.

Mining, too, plays an important part in Nevada's economy. Copper is its most valuable mineral. Ruth Copper Pit near Ely is one of the largest open-pit copper mines in the world and a notable point of interest. Other important minerals include gold, sand and gravel, gypsum, and mercury.

At one time, Nevada ranked as an important silver-mining state. Its official nickname, the *Silver State,* comes from the large amounts of silver taken from its mines. These discoveries of gold and silver ore in the mid-1800's brought hundreds of prospectors westward to "strike it rich." Some managed to achieve their goal but most found little or no wealth. Colorful ghost towns and historic mining towns are all that remain of this once profitable industry. Virginia City, once a mining boom town, was the home of the famous Comstock Lode, a rich deposit of gold and silver. It is now a ghost town that attracts many visitors every year. Hamilton, another ghost town, lies between Eureka and Ely. Now abandoned, it once housed nearly 15,000 persons. A third ghost town, Rhyolite, is near Beatty.

Other interesting sights within the state of Nevada include, at the University of Nevada in Reno, the Atmospherium-Planetarium, which shows realistic motion pictures of hurricanes, tornadoes, and other weather conditions; near Carson City, Bowers Mansion, a large Italian-style home built by "Sandy" Bowers, a silver miner who became a millionaire via the Comstock Lode; and Carson City, the capital of Nevada.

Rafting and swimming are but two of the activities sports enthusiasts enjoy at Lake Tahoe.

Holding back the Colorado River, Hoover Dam is one of the highest concrete dams in the world.

Nevada
Silver State

Capital: Carson City
Area: 110,540 sq. mi. (286,297 km²), including 651 sq. mi. (1,686 km²) of inland water; 7th in size among the states
Elevation: *Highest*—Boundary Peak, in Esmeralda County, 13,143 ft. (4,006 m) above sea level; *lowest*—470 ft. (143 m) above sea level along the Colorado River in Clark County
Statehood: Oct. 31, 1864, the 36th state
Abbreviations: Nev. (traditional); NV (postal)
Motto: *All for Our Country*
Song: "Home Means Nevada"
Tree: Single-Leaf Piñon

Nevada's state seal shows a plow and a sheaf of wheat representing Nevada's agricultural resources. The quartz mill, mine tunnel, and carload of ore symbolize the mineral wealth of the state. The 36 stars around the outside show that Nevada was the 36th state to enter the Union. The seal was adopted in 1866. The state flag, adopted in 1929, carries the words Battle Born. *They recall that Nevada gained statehood during the Civil War.*

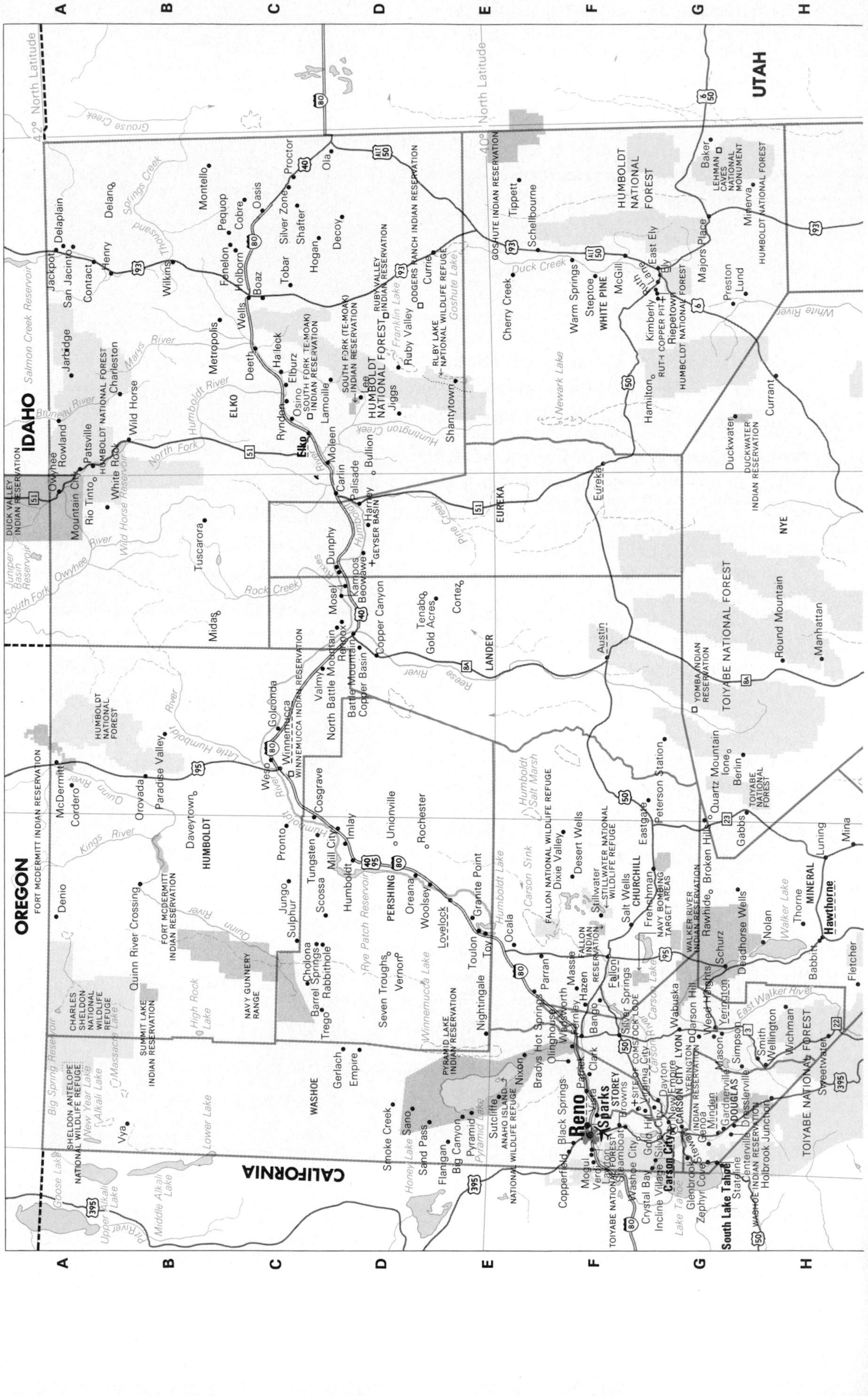

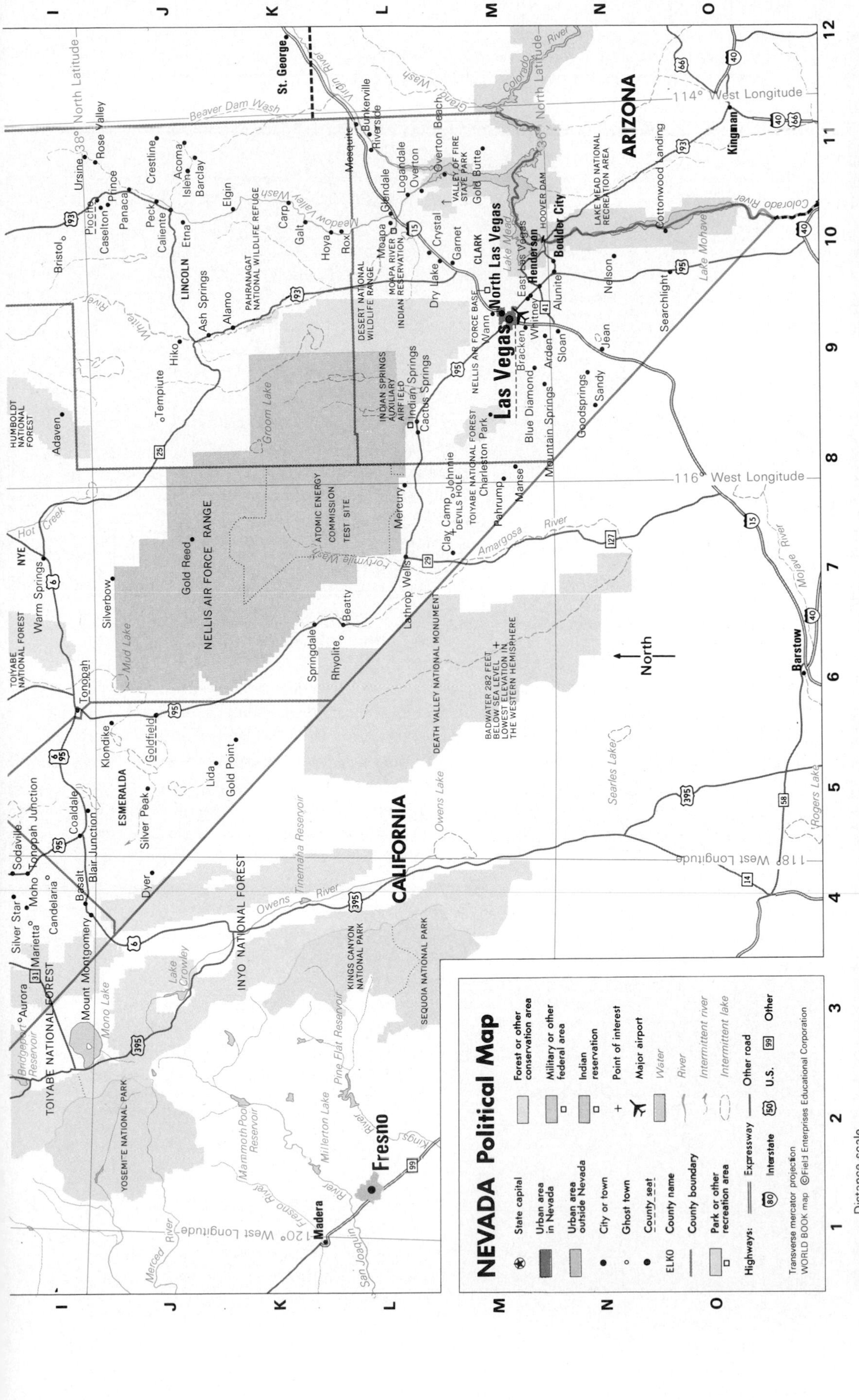

Seal

Flag

Bird: Mountain Bluebird

Flower: Sagebrush

NEVADA Political Map

⊛ State capital	☐ Forest or other conservation area
▮ Urban area in Nevada	☐ Military or other federal area
▮ Urban area outside Nevada	☐ Indian reservation
• City or town	+ Point of interest
○ Ghost town	✈ Major airport
● County seat	▮ Water
ELKO County name	River
— County boundary	Intermittent river
▮ Park or other recreation area	Intermittent lake

Highways:
⎓⎓ Expressway   ⎓⎓ Other road
⟨80⟩ Interstate   ⟨50⟩ U.S.   ⟨99⟩ Other

Transverse mercator projection
WORLD BOOK map ©Field Enterprises Educational Corporation

Distance scale

New Mexico

New Mexico has a number of exhibits and museums devoted to the atomic age. Shown here is the National Atomic Museum near Albuquerque (below top).

Inhabited for centuries before the arrival of white people, pueblos survive throughout New Mexico. Taos Indians still cook in this pueblo's rounded ovens (below bottom).

New Mexico is a land rich in history. Ancient Indians are the oldest known residents of the state. Spearheads found in the northeastern area of the state indicate that Indians hunted there more than 10,000 years ago. Some of the remains of the ancient Indian civilizations are now national monuments and attract many visitors every year. These monuments include Aztec Ruins, an ancient pueblo; Bandelier, the ruins of four pueblos; Chaco Canyon, the site of 18 pueblo ruins; and the Gila Cliff Dwellings, once an Indian settlement. The Puyé Cliff Dwellings west of Española are ancient Indian "apartment houses." One building is estimated to have had 800 rooms.

Spanish influence is abundant throughout New Mexico. The Spanish explored the area as early as the 1500's and eventually ruled the land for more than 250 years. Today, New Mexican place names, customs, holidays, churches, and foods are all indicative of this early Spanish history.

San Miguel Mission in Santa Fe was built by the Spaniards in 1636. Restored in 1710, it is an interesting tourist spot. Santa Fe, New Mexico's capital, was also the capital of a Spanish province in 1610. Albuquerque, the state's largest city, was founded by the Spaniards in 1706. New Mexico is also the home of the oldest road in the United States, El Camino Real, the Royal Road, which served travelers in 1581. Now Highway 85, it runs from Santa Fe to Chihuahua, Mexico.

The frontier days of America's past were also an important part of New Mexico's history. A part of this history included colorful characters such as Kit Carson, a frontier scout who played a key role in dealing with the Indians of the area; Billy the Kid, an infamous outlaw of the West; and Geronimo, one of the last hostile Apache chiefs. Interesting tourist attractions that give visitors a taste of the Old West include Glorieta Battle Site west of Pecos, where Union and Confederate troops fought for control of New Mexico during the Civil War, and Fort Union National Monument, an old military post.

Interesting events such as Spanish fiestas, Indian ceremonies, and rodeos are popular with visitors to this state. These attractions can be found going on throughout the year in most areas of New Mexico. Visitors have also always been attracted to New Mexico because of its scenic beauty and natural wonders. These, along with its colorful history, have given the state its official nickname, the *Land of Enchantment.*

Much of New Mexico is covered by beautiful mountain ranges, rugged canyons, and rocky deserts. One of the most famous of New Mexico's natural wonders—and probably one of the greatest in the world—is Carlsbad Caverns National Park in southeastern New Mexico. Here, a series of huge caves with lighted trails provide visitors with a view of fantastic rock formations. Tens of thousands of bats fly out of the cavern at dusk and return at dawn.

The Gila Wilderness near Silver City is also an interesting sight. It was the first area in the country set aside as a national wilderness to be kept in its natural condition. Another magnificent scenic wonder is White Sands National Monument near Alamogordo. This is a vast area of huge shifting dunes of white gypsum sand.

Much of New Mexico's landscape consists of deep canyons, sharp cliffs, and lonely, flat-topped hills called mesas. The most famous mesa in the state is Acoma on the Acoma Indian Reservation. The Indians built a fascinating city on top of this mesa. Ship Rock in San Juan County is another famous landmark. This is a steep hill resembling a ship in full sail.

Besides providing a natural wonderland, New Mexico's land is also the basis for its economy. Its main sources of income are mining and agriculture. The most important minerals produced are petroleum and natural gas. New Mexico is also a leader in the production of uranium and potash, two important minerals for the future.

Little farming is done in New Mexico because of the lack of rainfall. Most farming that is done depends to a great extent on irrigation. But much of the land unsuitable for crop farming provides excellent grazing land for ranchers. Ranching is the most important agricultural activity in the state. New Mexico has almost twice as many cattle and sheep as it has people.

New Mexico has been an important area for nuclear science. The world's first atomic bomb was built at Los Alamos and was exploded in 1945 near Alamogordo. The Los Alamos Bradbury Science Hall and Museum is an interesting tourist attraction and shows the development of atomic energy. New Mexico is still an important center of research into rockets and nuclear energy.

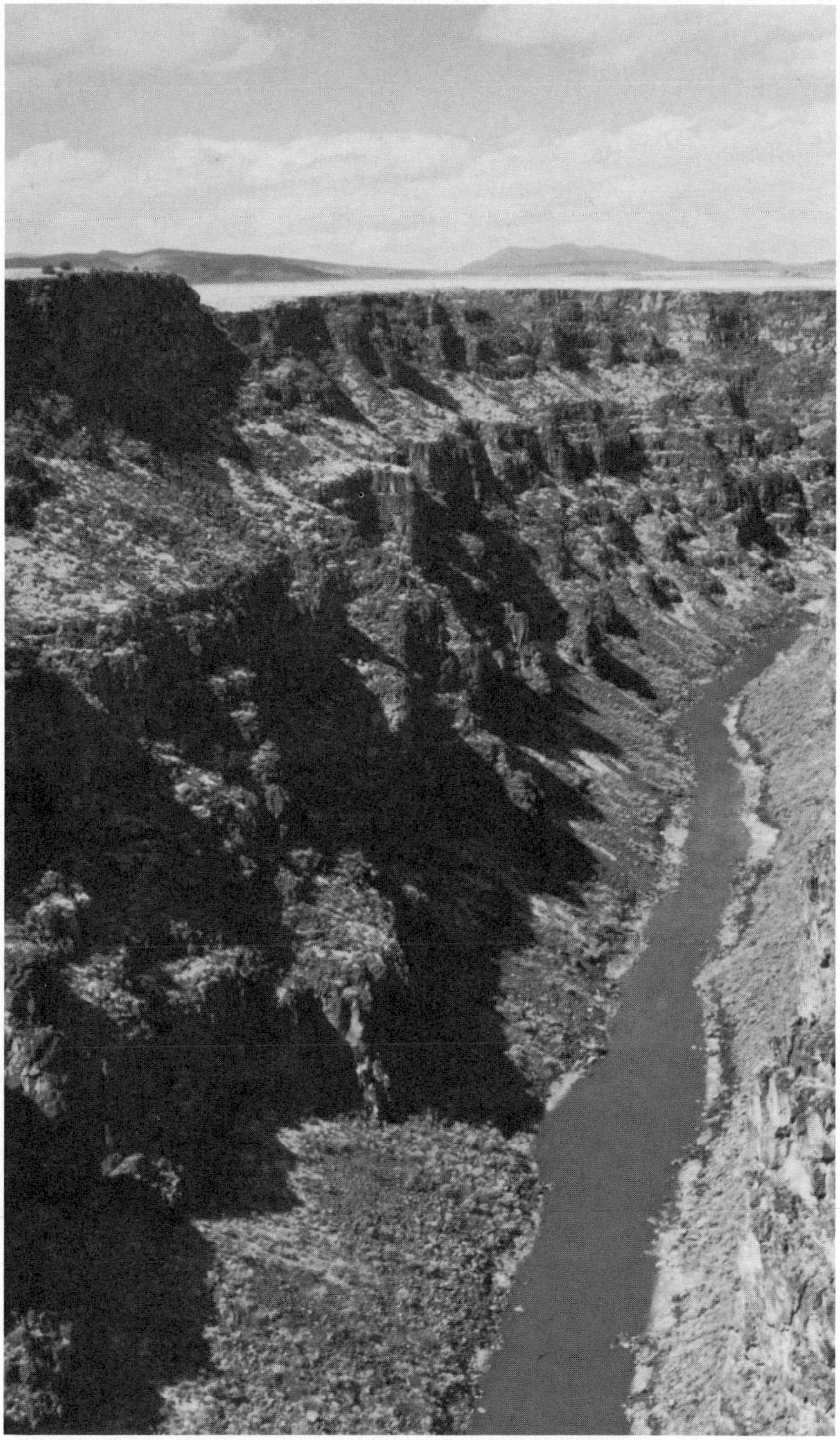

Chiseled by ever-flowing waters, harsh canyons line the Rio Grande's pathway.

New Mexico
Land of Enchantment

Capital: Santa Fe
Area: 121,666 sq. mi. (315,113 km²), including 254 sq. mi. (658 km²) of inland water; 5th in size among the states
Elevation: *Highest*—Wheeler Peak in Taos County, 13,161 ft. (4,011 m) above sea level; *lowest*—2,817 ft. (859 m) above sea level at Red Bluff Reservoir in Eddy County
Statehood: Jan. 6, 1912, the 47th state
Abbreviations: N. Mex. or N.M. (traditional); NM (postal)
Motto: *Crescit Eundo* (It Grows As It Goes)
Song: "O, Fair New Mexico"
Tree: Piñon (Nut Pine)

New Mexico's state seal, adopted in 1913, shows two eagles representing the U.S. annexation of New Mexico. The scroll beneath the birds bears the state's motto. On the state flag, adopted in 1925, the ancient sun symbol of the Zia pueblo of Indians appears in red on a yellow field. The colors represent the Spanish flag, a reminder that New Mexico was once Spanish territory.

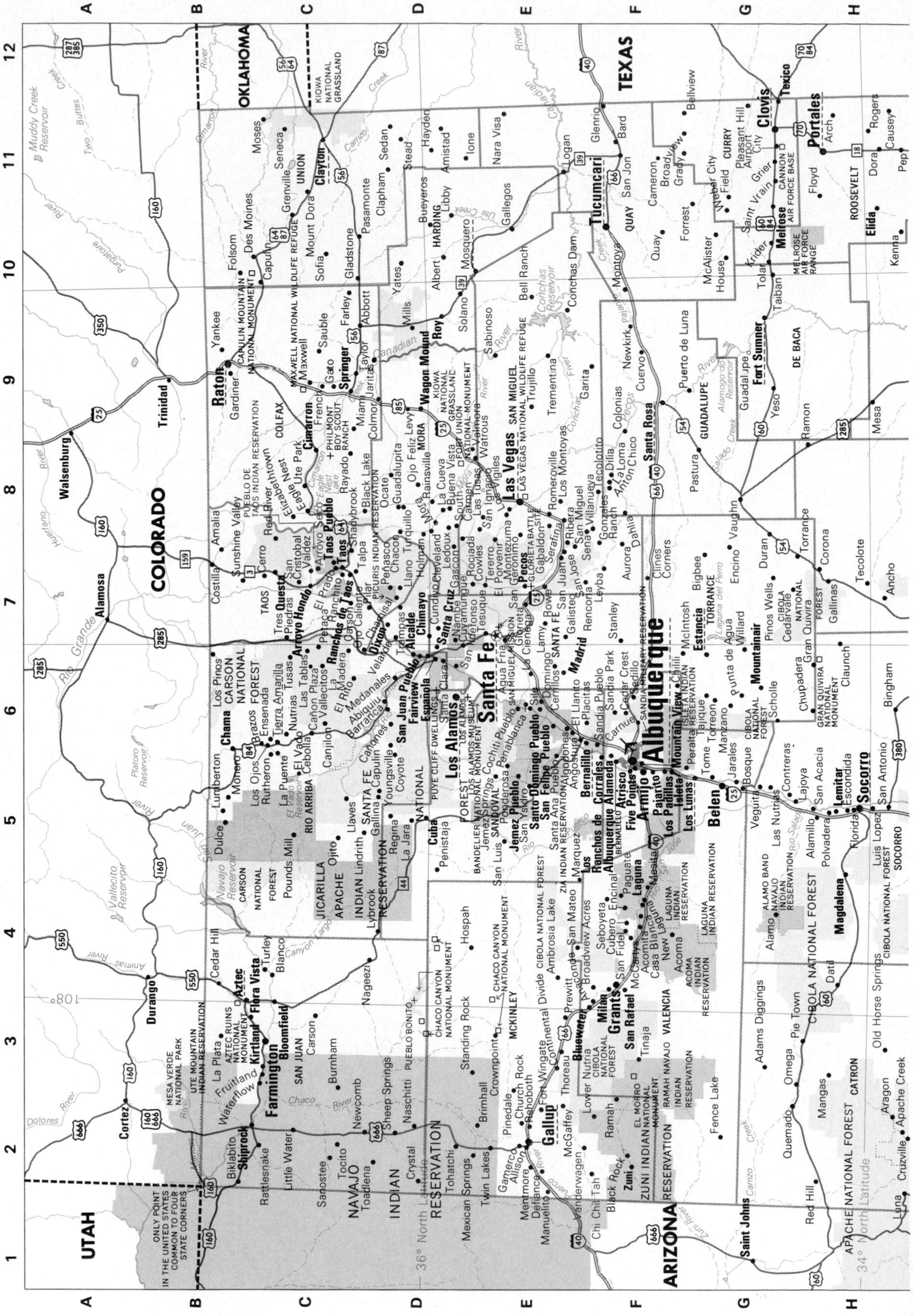

NEW MEXICO Political Map

State capital ⊛
Urban area in New Mexico
Urban area outside New Mexico
City or town ●
Ghost town ○
County seat ◉
County name EDDY
County boundary
Park or other recreation area
Forest or other conservation area
Military or other federal area

Indian reservation
Point of interest +
Major airport ✈
Water
River
Intermittent river
Intermittent lake

Highways:
Expressway
Other road
Interstate 40
U. S. 66
Other 24

Lambert conformal conic projection
WORLD BOOK map ©Field Enterprises Educational Corporation

Miles

Kilometers

Distance scale

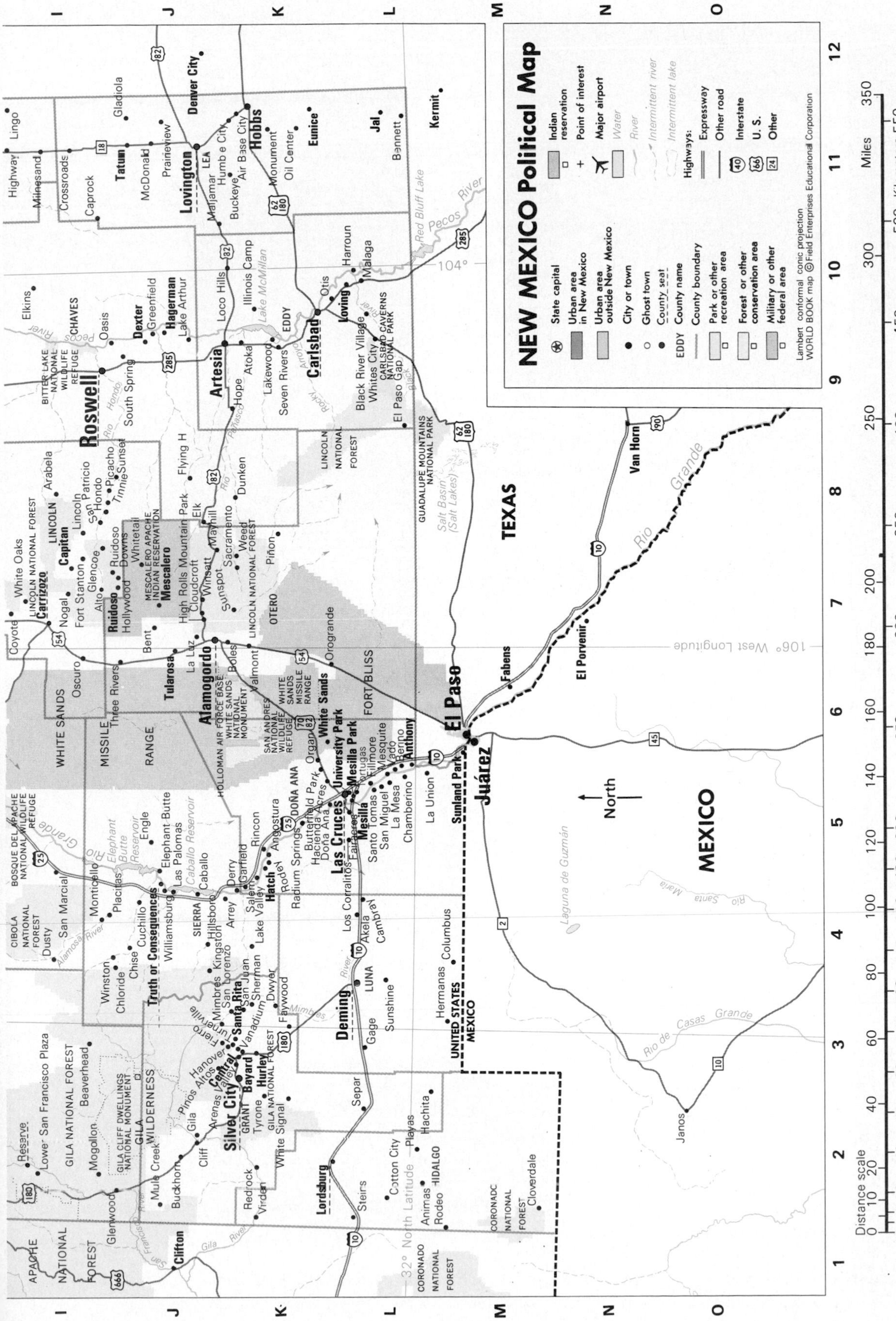

Seal

Flag

Bird: Road Runner

Flower: Yucca Flower

Remnants of the Old West with its cattle drives and cowboys still survive in Oklahoma, where rodeos are commonplace even today.

Oklahoma

Oklahoma is a state of many contrasts. Golden wheat fields cover much of its plains region, while thousands of wells pump oil and natural gas on its prairies. Oklahoma's land varies widely across the state, with mountains occasionally wedged between hills and plains. The land regions include some beautiful natural settings that attract many visitors. The Wichita Mountains in southwestern Oklahoma rise from a fertile plain and contain many rough granite boulders. The high sand stone ridges in the Ouachita Mountains of the southeast form the roughest land areas in the state. The highest point in Oklahoma is Black Mesa in the High Plains.

Oklahoma's oil reserves are among the largest in the nation. The first producing oil well in Oklahoma was drilled in 1889 near Chelsea. Since then, over 100,000 wells have been sunk throughout the state. Pipelines carry the crude oil to refineries for processing.

Petroleum and natural gas deposits have been found in 70 of the state's 77 counties. Even the state capitol in Oklahoma City is located in an area that is now a major oil field, and wells operate on the capitol's front lawn. Oil derricks can also be seen on some of Oklahoma's lakes, where wells pump oil from beneath the water. Nor is it unusual to stand near a derrick on an Oklahoma prairie and see the skyscrapers of a large nearby city in the background.

Huge, golden fields of winter wheat can be seen as they are harvested early each summer in Oklahoma, one of the nation's leading wheat-producing states. Beef cattle, however, is the state's main source of farm income. A frequent sight on Oklahoma's flat plains and low hills is that of a herd of white-faced beef cattle grazing on the rich grass. Present-day ranching is now a modern business, but cowhands still occasionally ride the range as they once did.

The early days in Oklahoma began with the Indians. In the 1800's, the federal government persuaded a number of Indian tribes to move west, giving up their eastern lands. Most of Oklahoma was made into a huge Indian reservation for the tribes. Each established a nation with its own government, and treaties protected the Indian nations from white settlement.

The name Oklahoma is a combination of two Choctaw Indian words: *okla,* meaning "people," and *homma,* meaning "red." Today the Tsa-La-Gi Indian Village southeast of Tahlequah is an interesting tourist attraction. It re-creates an ancient Cherokee village. The Indians themselves give tours. Creek Capitol in Okmulgee is the building from which Creek Indians ruled their republic. Many of Oklahoma's museums own excellent collections on Indian history. The Woolaroc Museum near Bartlesville owns one of the world's finest collections of Indian blankets.

The Civil War destroyed the protection the Indians of Oklahoma once enjoyed. They were forced to give up some of their lands because they had supported the South. Great land rushes began in the late 1800's when the government first opened Oklahoma to white settlement. Thousands of settlers waited at the border for the opening, which was signaled by a pistol shot at noon on April 22, 1889. The race began, and in a single day Guthrie and Oklahoma City became cities of 10,000 persons. Oklahoma's official nickname, the *Sooner State,* came from a number of settlers who were there "sooner" than the land was opened.

Oklahoma has a reputation as a state of cattle drives and cowboys. The Chisholm Trail ran north from Texas through Oklahoma to Abilene, Kansas, and was used for driving millions of cattle in the 1870's. The Cowboy is a famous statue by Constance Whitney Warren and stands in front of the state capitol in Oklahoma City. Also in Oklahoma City is the National Cowboy Hall of Fame and Western Heritage Center, which houses famous paintings and sculptures.

Will Rogers was a famous cowboy humorist from Oklahoma. He was once quoted as saying, "There ought to be a law against anybody going to Europe until they have seen the things we have in this country." The Will Rogers Memorial is in Claremont and contains paintings, manuscripts, and other memorabilia of this native Oklahoman. Rogers is also buried there.

One of the state's most popular annual events is the National Finals Rodeo (World Series of Rodeo) held each December in Oklahoma City. Interesting sites in Oklahoma include, in Oklahoma City, the Church of Tomorrow, which has a 1,500-seat sanctuary, an educational building, and a theater-in-the-round; near Lawton, Fort Sill, a military center established in 1869; and, near Cheyenne, Washita Battlefield, which marks the site of an 1868 Indian fight.

A sight unique to Oklahoma City is an oil well operating on the front lawn of the Oklahoma state capitol building (above).

Mindful of their rich and colorful heritage, Indians at Anadarko present an American Indian Exposition each August (left).

Oklahoma
Sooner State

Capital: Oklahoma City
Area: 69,919 sq. mi.
(181,089 km²), including
1,137 sq. mi. (2,945 km²)
of inland water; 18th in size
among the states
Elevation: *Highest*—Black
Mesa in Cimarron County,
4,973 ft. (1,516 m) above
sea level; *lowest*—along the
Little River in McCurtain
County, 287 ft. (87 m)
above sea level
Statehood: Nov. 16, 1907,
the 46th state
Abbreviations: Okla.
(traditional); OK (postal)
Motto: *Labor Omnia Vincit*
(Labor Conquers All Things)
Song: "Oklahoma!"
Tree: Redbud

*Oklahoma's state seal features
an Indian and a white man
shaking hands before Justice to
show the cooperation of all
Oklahomans. The large star has
symbols of the Five Civilized
Tribes, which first settled the
region. The seal was adopted in
1907. The state flag, adopted
in 1925, has two symbols of
peace: a peace pipe and an olive
branch. The shield behind these
symbols stands for defensive
warfare.*

OKLAHOMA Political Map

✪ State capital
▮ Urban area in Oklahoma
▮ Urban area outside Oklahoma
• City or town
● County seat
LOVE County name
County boundary
□ Park or other recreation area
▮ Forest or other conservation area
▮ Military or other federal area

□ Indian reservation
+ Point of interest
✈ Major airport
▮ *Water*
River
Intermittent river
Highways:
Expressway
Other road
35 Interstate
66 U.S.
9 Other

Lambert conformal conic projection
WORLD BOOK map
ⒸField Enterprises Educational Corporation

Distance scale for inset map
0 5 10   20   30   40   50 Miles 60
0 5 10   20   30   40   50   60   70   80 Kilometers

Distance scale for Oklahoma map
0 10 20   40   60   80   100
0 10 20   40   60   80   100   125   150   175

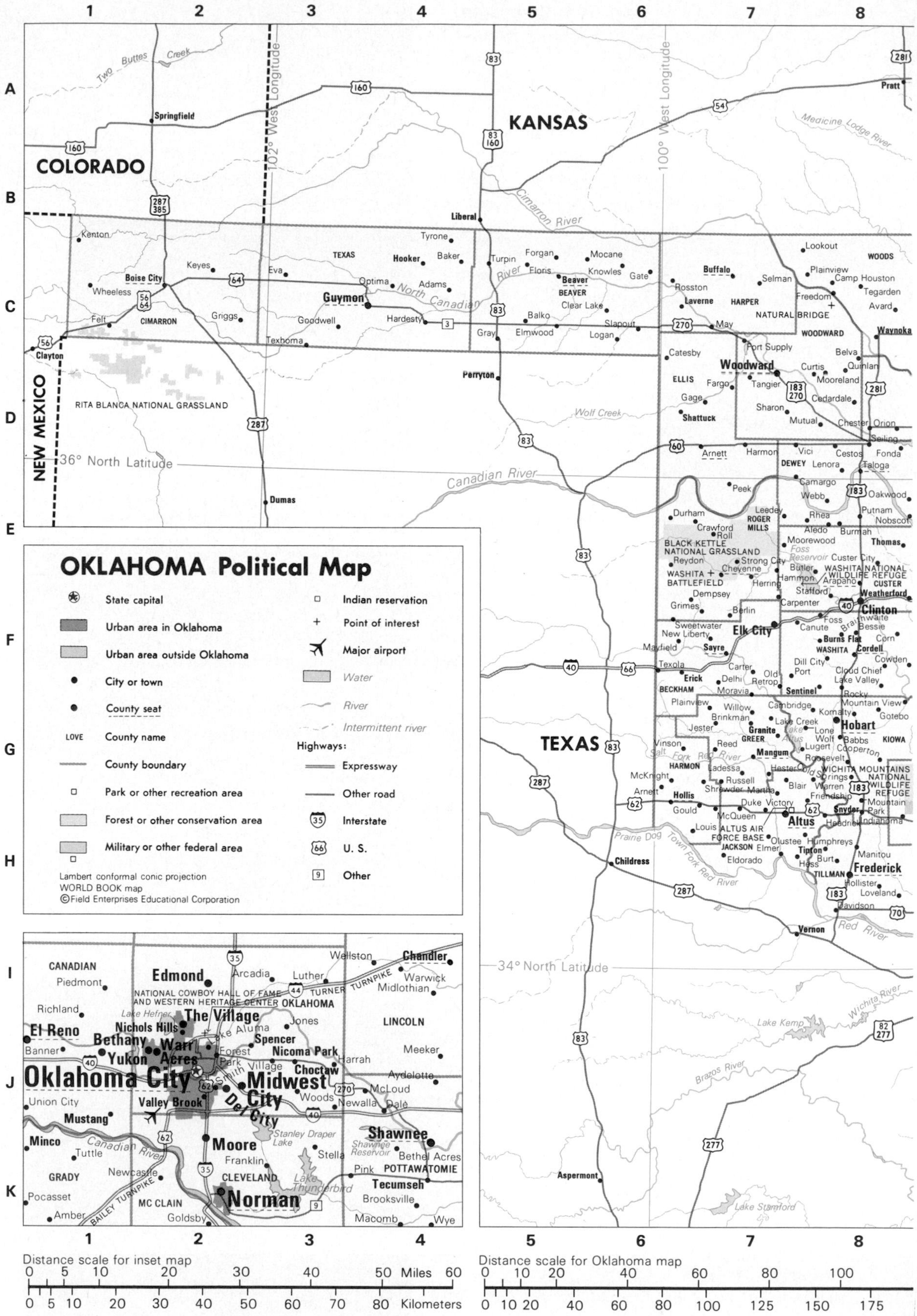

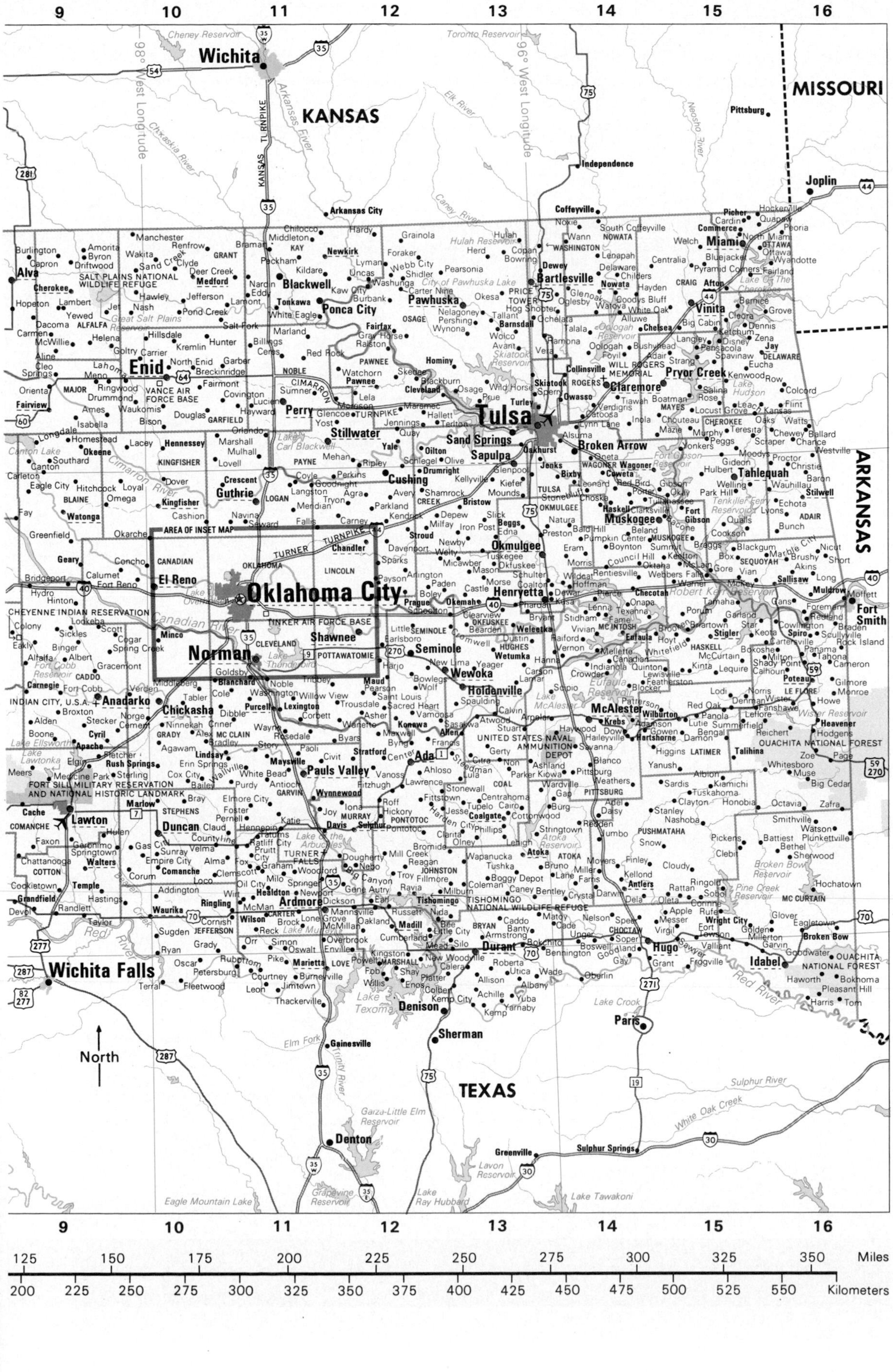

MISSOURI

KANSAS

Wichita

Joplin

Independence

Coffeyville

ARKANSAS

Bartlesville

Enid

Tulsa

Stillwater

Oklahoma City

Norman

Shawnee

El Reno

McAlester

Lawton

Ardmore

Wichita Falls

Paris

Sherman

Denison

TEXAS

Gainesville

Denton

Greenville

Sulphur Springs

North

Seal

Flag

OKLAHOMA

Bird: Scissor-tailed Flycatcher

Flower: Mistletoe

9   10   11   12   13   14   15   16

125	150	175	200	225	250	275	300	325	350	Miles
200	225	250	275	300	325	350	375	400	425	450	475	500	525	550	Kilometers

Oregon

For thousands of early pioneers, the end of the Oregon Trail was Oregon's Willamette Valley. Starting in Independence, Missouri, the settlers traveled to this precious farmland by covered wagon on a northwesterly course through prairies and deserts, across rivers and mountains, and into the fertile valley of Oregon's Willamette River.

The Willamette Valley was, and still is, a land of fertile soil and plentiful water. Today, it is Oregon's greatest center for trade and industry. Flower bulbs, fruits, and vegetables grow there. Most of Oregon's large cities are located in the Willamette Valley, including Portland, Oregon's largest, and Salem, its capital.

To tourists, Oregon is a place of rare beauty. This state is famous for its beautiful mountains, rugged coastal scenery, and vast evergreen forests. Steep cliffs rise along much of the Pacific coast, while other parts of the coast offer sandy beaches and protected harbors.

Oregon's huge timber reserves are one of its most important natural resources. Almost half the state is covered by forests, and every large city has factories that produce wood products. This makes Oregon the leading lumber producer in the nation.

Besides thick forests, Oregon's landscape is also dotted with areas of golden wheat fields. Wheat is the state's most valuable farm product and is grown chiefly in the north-central portion of the state. Cowhands branding cattle on large livestock ranches in eastern Oregon are a familiar sight.

Often called the *Pacific Wonderland,* Oregon has many outstanding natural wonders. A number of these are nestled within the magnificent Cascade Mountain Range. One of the most popular sights is that of majestic Mount Hood, an inactive volcano located east of Portland. U.S. Highway 26 skirts Mount Hood and offers spectacular views of its glacier-covered slopes. Crater Lake National Park in south-central Oregon is another famous tourist attraction. Crater Lake, the deepest lake in the United States, is located in the crater of Mount Mazama,

The sea gently laps Oregon's rock-studded shores, where evergreen forests meet the Pacific Ocean.

another inactive volcano. The Columbia River cuts through the Cascade Mountains to form the breathtaking Columbia River Gorge. Colorful basalt cliffs line the deep gorge, and several lovely waterfalls tumble into it. Other scenic attractions of Oregon include, near Dayville, Picture Gorge, a canyon named for the Indian pictures on the walls; in the Siskiyou Mountains in southwestern Oregon, Oregon Caves National Monument, containing beautiful stone formations; and, on the Snake River in eastern Oregon, Hells Canyon.

More than 10 million tourists visit Oregon each year. People who like to hunt find elk, deer, and other game animals in Oregon's thick forests. Those who favor fishing can do so in Oregon's sparkling lakes and rivers and in the Pacific Ocean. Sea Lion Caves, a favorite tourist site, is located on the Pacific coast near Florence. Hundreds of sea lions live in this area.

The skiing season in Oregon begins in December and lasts through April. Ski enthusiasts find excellent skiing on the slopes in the Cascades, Wallowas, and other mountains. Timberline on Mount Hood is probably the most famous ski area in the state.

The mighty Columbia River forms most of the border between Oregon and Washington. The Snake River forms much of the Oregon-Idaho border and joins the Columbia in Washington. Bonneville Dam, east of Portland on the Columbia River, is a popular Oregon point of interest. The dam raised the water level, enabling large ships to travel up the Columbia River for 188 miles (203 kilometers). The dam has a series of fish ladders that salmon use on their way upstream to spawn.

Throughout the year, Oregon offers many activities for participants and spectators alike. In January, there are ski tournaments at Mount Ashland near Ashland, at Mount Bachelor near Bend, and at Government Camp near Mount Hood. Sled Dog Races are held in Bend and Union Creek in January and February. In mid-May, the All-Indian Rodeo is held in Tygh Valley.

The Shakespearean Festival in Ashland is held from mid-June through mid-September. It is one of Oregon's most famous events. Shakespearean plays are presented in an Elizabethan theater and in the Angus Bowmer indoor theater. The Portland Rose Festival in early June features a spectacular Grand Floral Parade. The Pendleton Round-Up and Happy Canyon Pageant in mid-September is a four-day rodeo featuring an Indian historical pageant. The World Championship Timber Carnival is held in Albany each July.

For pioneers traveling west, coming upon a log cabin in central Oregon signaled the nearness of the Willamette Valley and, for many, the end of the Oregon Trail (above).

The product of a once-active volcano, Crater Lake beckons to those who seek solitude and sweeping vistas (left).

Oregon
Beaver State

Capital: Salem
Area: 96,981 sq. mi.
(251,180 km²), including
797 sq. mi. (2,064 km²) of
inland water but excluding
48 sq. mi. (124 km²) of
Pacific coastal water; 10th in
size among the states
Elevation: *Highest*—Mount
Hood in Clackamas and
Hood River counties,
11,235 ft. (3,424 m) above
sea level; *lowest*—sea level,
along the Pacific Ocean
Statehood: Feb. 14, 1859,
the 33rd state
Abbreviations: Ore. or
Oreg. (traditional); OR
(postal)
Motto: *The Union*
Song: "Oregon, My Oregon"
Tree: Douglas Fir

*Oregon's state seal carries 33
stars representing the state's
entry into the Union as the
33rd state. The departing
British man-of-war and arriving American merchant ship
symbolize the end of British
influence and the rise of
American power. The sheaf of
grain, the pickax, and the plow
represent Oregon's mining and
agricultural resources. The seal
was adopted in 1859. The state
flag, adopted in 1925, has a
reproduction of the seal. The
reverse side of the flag shows a
beaver, which represents the
state's popular name.*

OREGON Political Map

✴ State capital	✈ Major airport
▨ Urban area	▨ Water
● City or town	∿ River
● County seat	⊢⊢⊢ Waterway
CROOK County name	⌐ ⌐ Intermittent river
County boundary	Intermittent lake
State boundary	
▨ Park or other recreation area	Highways:
▨ Forest or other conservation area	═══ Expressway
▨ Military or other federal area	─── Other road
▨ Indian reservation	⑤ Interstate
	㉚ U.S.
+ Point of interest	㉛ Other

Lambert conformal conic projection

WORLD BOOK map © Field Enterprises Educational Corporation

Distance scale for inset map
0 5 10   20   30   Miles
0 5 10 20   30   40 Kilometers

Distance scale for Oregon map
0 10 20   40   60   80   100   120   140   160 Miles
0 10 20 40 60 80 100 120 140 160 180 200 220 240 260 Kilometers

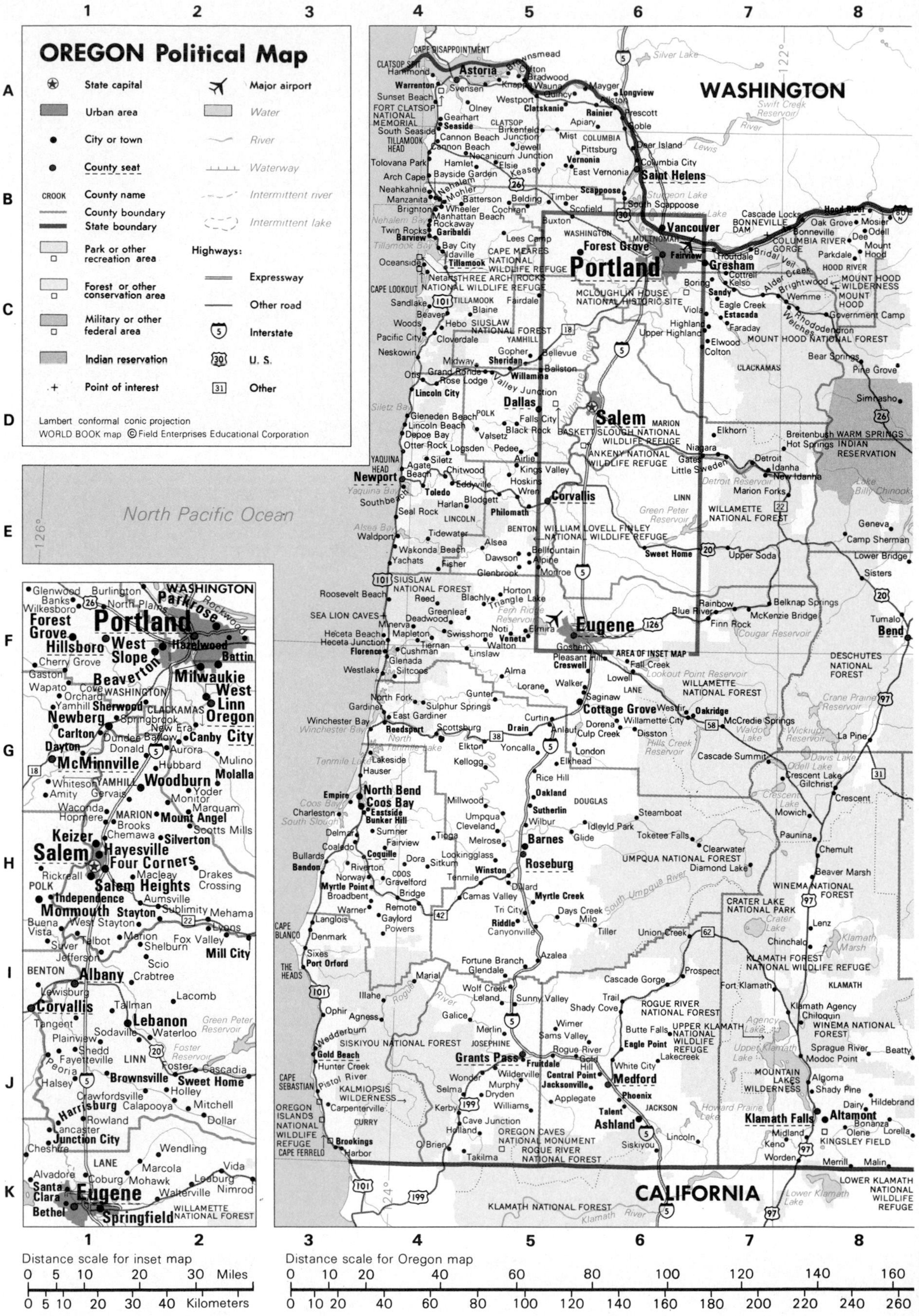

9   10   11   12   13   14   15   16

A
B
C
D
E
F
G
H
I
J
K

WASHINGTON

IDAHO

NEVADA

North

9   10   11   12   13   14   15   16

| | 180 | 200 | 220 | 240 | 260 | 280 | 300 | | 325 | 350 | 375 | Miles |

| 280 | 300 | 325 | 350 | 375 | 400 | 425 | 450 | 475 | 500 | 525 | 550 | 575 | 600 | Kilometers |

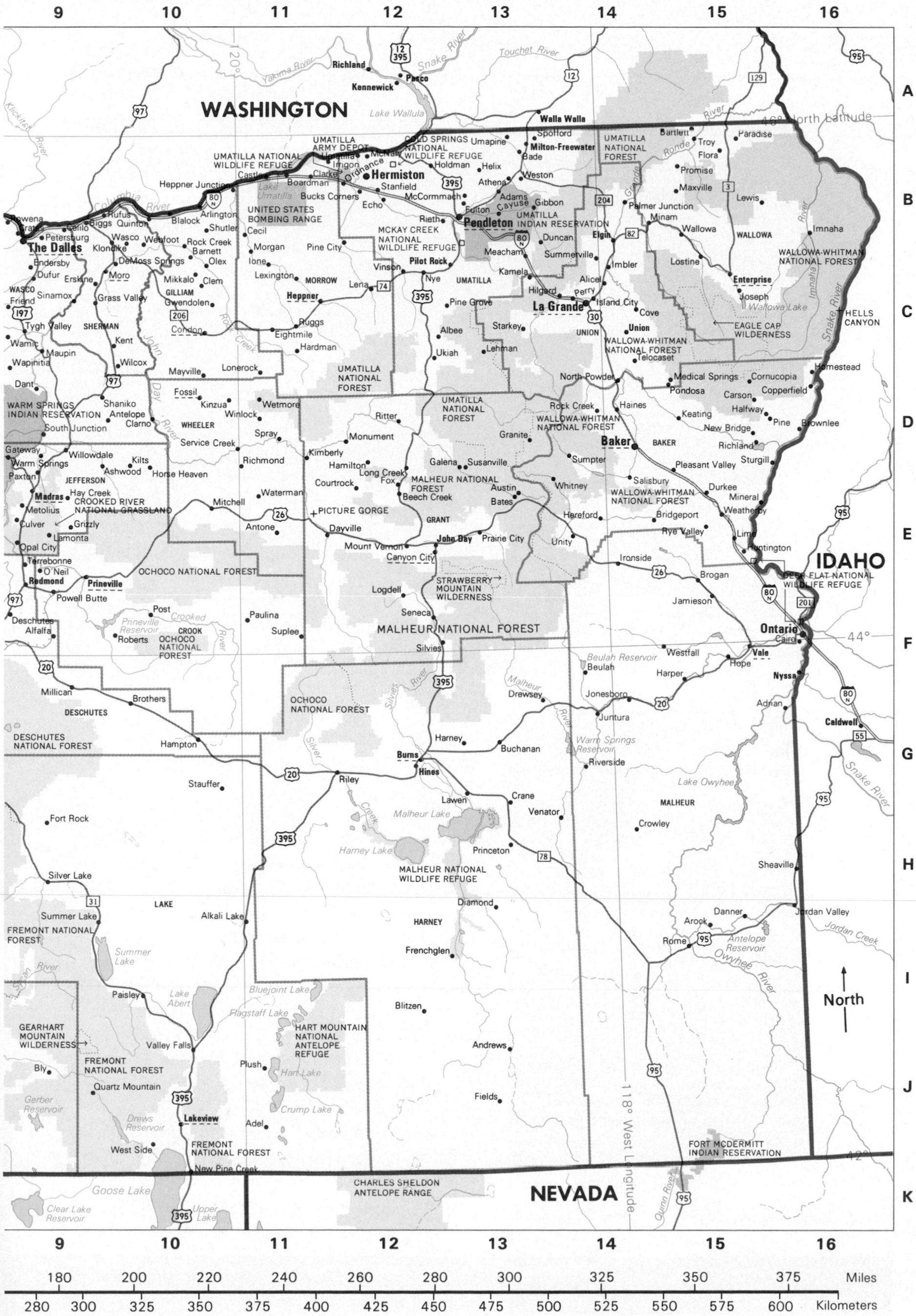

Seal

Flag

Bird: Western Meadow Lark

Flower: Oregon Grape

Utah's natural wonders include gorgeous canyons, this one carved by the Colorado River (above).

The majestic Mormon Temple is one of Utah's most popular sights. The temple, which took 40 years to build, stands in Salt Lake City's Temple Square (right).

Utah

Utah's name comes from the Ute Indians, a tribe that lived in the area hundreds of years ago. Today, ruins of Indian cliff dwellings can be seen lining mountain ledges near Blanding, Bluff, Kanab, Moab, Parowan, Price, and Vernal.

Utah's first permanent white settlers were the Mormons, a religious group belonging to the Church of Jesus Christ of Latter-day Saints. This group, led by Brigham Young, came west from New York looking for religious freedom. They had been persecuted nearly everywhere they had gone. Finally, upon seeing Utah's Great Salt Lake, Brigham Young chose the area for the new Mormon community. The group settled there in 1847. The Mormons called the area *Deseret,* a Mormon word meaning "honeybee" and representing hard work and industry. Thus, Utah's official nickname became the *Beehive State.*

The Mormons played an important part in the development of Utah, especially in what is now the Salt Lake City area. They began the irrigation that is a necessary process in much of the state's farming industry, an important part of the state's economy. A good portion of Utah's land can also be farmed without irrigation by using dry-farming methods.

Most of the irrigated farmland in Utah lies in a north-south line across the center of the state. This land is irrigated by water stored in large reservoirs. Wheat, hay, and sugar beets are the chief crops that can be seen growing in the north and central areas of the state.

Salt Lake City, Utah's capital and largest city, is probably the state's greatest attraction. The headquarters of the Mormon Church, it provides tourists with many interesting sights. Temple Square, the center of Mormonism, is one of the most popular. Standing in the square are three important Mormon church buildings: the majestic Mormon Temple, which took 40 years to build; the Salt Lake Tabernacle, famous for its huge organ and choir; and the Visitor Center. Also in Salt Lake City are the Beehive House, the restored home of Brigham Young; Trolley Square, a colorful center of shops and restaurants in a remodeled trolley service area; and Pioneer Trails State Park.

Near the capital is the largest natural lake west of the Mississippi River: the Great Salt Lake. Its water is four to seven times saltier than any ocean because the lake is not drained by outflowing streams. Instead, some of the water evaporates, leaving salt deposits behind.

The Great Salt Lake is not the only natural wonder in Utah to attract visitors. Much of Utah's landscape consists of snow-covered mountains, beautifully colored canyons, and barren deserts. The Great Salt Lake Desert is one of the most desolate regions in the world.

Stretching over the hard salt beds of the Great Salt Lake Desert is the Bonneville Speedway. Here in 1947, John Cobb, a British driver, was the first to travel more than 400 miles (643.7 kilometers) per hour on land. The speedway is now famous for its racing trials in August.

Some of the gorgeous canyons throughout Utah were formed by glaciers that once covered the area, while others were cut by rivers. Two of the most breathtaking are Bryce and Zion canyons, both national parks in southwestern Utah. Monument Valley, a Navajo Indian tribal park in the southeastern corner of the state, is another color-splashed scenic wonder. Here tourists can view red sandstone formations that rise 1,000 feet (304.8 meters). In the evening, a formation called totem pole casts a shadow 35 miles (56.3 kilometers) long. Other glimpses of Utah's spectacular natural beauty can be had at spots such as Arches National Park, Canyonlands National Park, Natural Bridges National Monument, Cedar Breaks National Monument, and Timpanogos Cave National Monument.

The Rocky Mountains area near Salt Lake City provides sports enthusiasts with excellent skiing and hunting. The beautiful lakes and rivers of this area also furnish some fine boating and swimming facilities as well as excellent fishing.

Utah has many rich mineral deposits and ranks as a leader in mining among the states of the Rocky Mountain region. Utah is second only to Arizona in the production of copper. Bingham Canyon Copper Pit near Salt Lake City is the largest open-pit copper mine in North America and produces a seventh of all the nation's copper. The pit, a popular tourist stop, is nearly ½-mile (.8 kilometer) deep and over 2 miles (3.2 kilometers) across at its widest point. Utah also ranks among the leading states in gold, lead, and uranium ore production.

Antelope Island, the largest island in the Great Salt Lake, provides breeding grounds for flocks of birds, farmlands for alfalfa and cattle raising, and plenty of camping facilities for visitors.

Utah
Beehive State

Capital: Salt Lake City
Area: 84,916 sq. mi. (219,931 km²), including 2,820 sq. mi. (7,304 km²) of inland water; 11th in size among the states
Elevation: *Highest*—Kings Peak, 13,528 ft. (4,123 m) above sea level; *lowest*—Beaverdam Creek, in Washington County, 2,000 ft. (610 m) above sea level
Statehood: Jan. 4, 1896, the 45th state
Abbreviations: Ut. (traditional); UT (postal)
Motto: *Industry*
Song: "Utah, We Love Thee"
Tree: Blue Spruce

Utah's state seal bears a shield with a beehive representing industry. The sego lilies surrounding the beehive symbolize the time when Mormon pioneers ate lily bulbs to avoid starvation. The date 1847 is the year the Mormons came to Utah. The seal was adopted in 1896. The state flag, adopted in 1913, has an adaptation of the state seal.

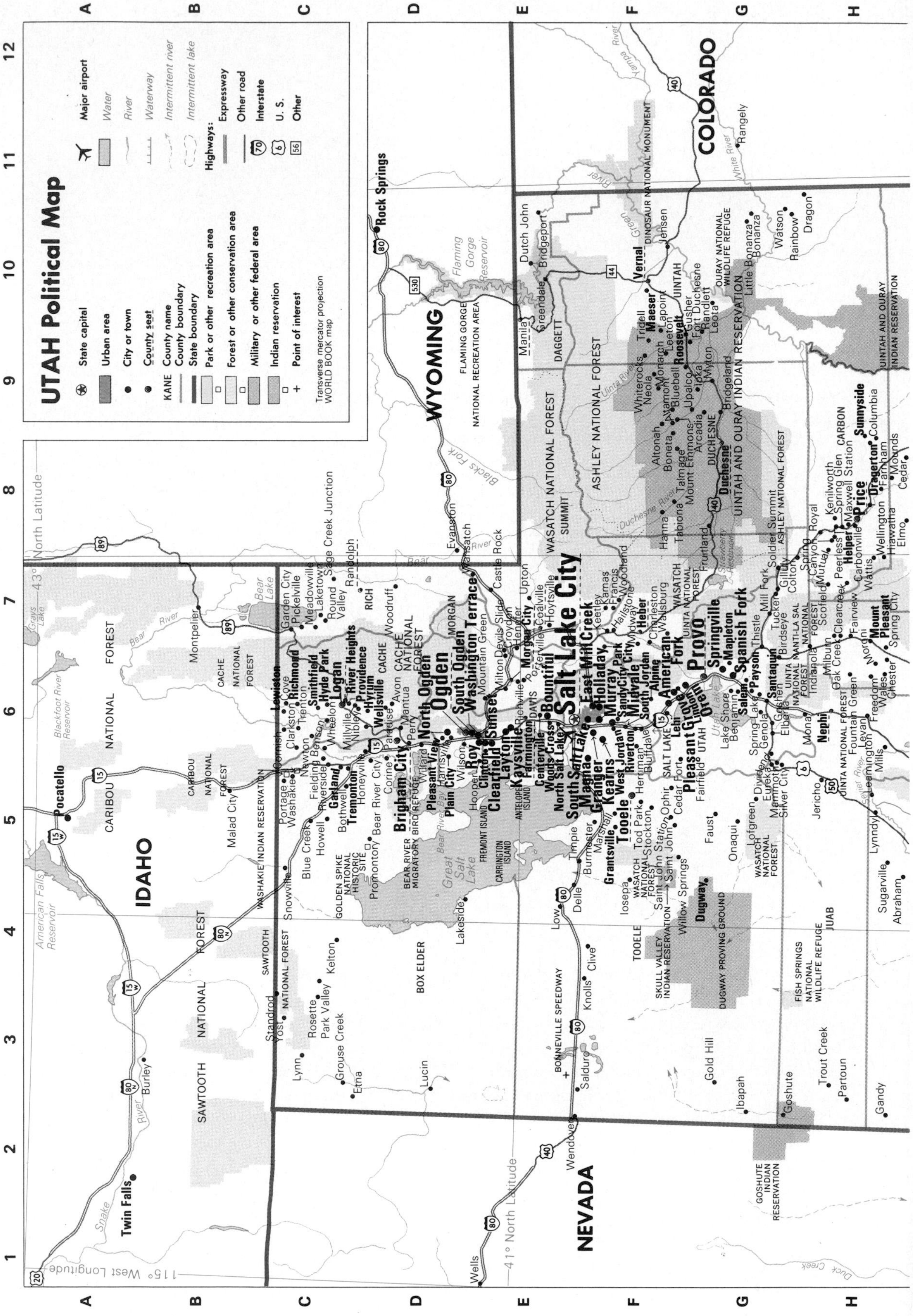

COLORADO

NEW MEXICO

NEVADA

ARIZONA

Seal

Flag

Bird: Sea Gull

Flower: Sego Lily

North

Distance scale
Miles
Kilometers

39° North Latitude

37° North Latitude

109° West Longitude

111° West Longitude

113° West Longitude

Grand Junction
Harley Dome
Westwater
Crescent Junction
Sego
Thompson
GRAND JUNCTION
Elgin
Green River
Woodside
Cleveland
Castle Dale
Lawrence
Orangeville
Clawson
Ferron
Moore
Emery
Huntington
Castle
Molen
Hanksville
Caineville
Fremont
Lyman
Bicknell
Teasdale
Loa
Grover
Boulder
Escalante
Henrieville
Cannonville
Tropic
Bryce Canyon
Hatch
Ruby's Inn
Long Valley Junction
Glendale
Orderville
Mount Carmel
Mount Carmel Junction
Kanab
Page

Moab
MANTI-LA SAL NATIONAL FOREST
La Sal
La Sal Junction
CANYONLANDS NATIONAL PARK
ARCHES NATIONAL PARK
SAN JUAN
Monticello
Verdure
Ucolo
Lockerby
Blanding
INDIAN CLIFF RUINS
NATURAL BRIDGES NATIONAL MONUMENT
HOVENWEEP NATIONAL MONUMENT
Bluff
Aneth
MESA VERDE NATIONAL PARK
Cortez
ONLY POINT IN THE UNITED STATES COMMON TO FOUR STATE CORNERS
Mexican Hat
MONUMENT VALLEY
RAINBOW BRIDGE NATIONAL MONUMENT
GLEN CANYON NATIONAL RECREATION AREA
WHITE CANYON
WAYNE
EMERY
GARFIELD
KANE
GRAND CANYON NATIONAL PARK
HOPI-NAVAHO (JOINTLY-OWNED) RESERVATIONS
CANYON DE CHELLY NATIONAL MONUMENT

Ely
Garrison
Hinckley
Delta
Oasis
Deseret
Clear Lake
Black Rock
Oak City
Scipio
Fillmore
Meadow
Kanosh
Holden
FISHLAKE NATIONAL FOREST
KANOSH INDIAN RESERVATION
Flowell
Hatton
Fayette
Gunnison
Centerfield
Redmond
Aurora
Salina
Manti
Ephraim
SANPETE
MANTI-LA SAL NATIONAL FOREST
Sterling
Mayfield
Axtell
Scipio
Milford
Minersville
Adamsville
Beaver
BEAVER
Greenville
Manderfield
Cove Fort
Richfield
Monroe
Elsinore
Central
Joseph
Sevier
Sigurd
Venice
Glenwood
Annabella
Austin
FISHLAKE NATIONAL FOREST
Koosharem
Greenwich
Burrville
Marysvale
Junction
Circleville
Kingston
Angle
Antimony
PIUTE
SEVIER
Thompsonville
Alunite
Latimer
Lund
Zane
Beryl
Modena
Uvada
Newcastle
Enterprise
Pinto
New Harmony
Central
Pine Valley
Gunlock
Shiwits
Santa Clara
Saint George
Ivins
Washington
WASHINGTON
Leeds
La Verkin
Hurricane
Virgin
Springdale
Grafton
Toquerville
ZION NATIONAL PARK
Rockville
Pintura
Kanarraville
DIXIE NATIONAL FOREST
Cedar City
Enoch
Summit
Parowan
IRON
Iron Springs
Hamilton Fort
CEDAR BREAKS NATIONAL MONUMENT
Paragonah
Panguitch
Spry
Orton
INDIAN CLIFF RUINS
MILLARD

Gunnison River
Colorado River
Green River
Price River
San Rafael River
Dirty Devil River
Fremont River
Escalante River
Sevier River
Clear Creek
Beaver River
Sevier Lake
Paria River
Kanab Creek
Lake Powell
Lake Mead
Dolores River
San Miguel River
San Juan River
Virgin River
Santa Clara River
Meadow Valley Wash
Hamlin Valley Wash

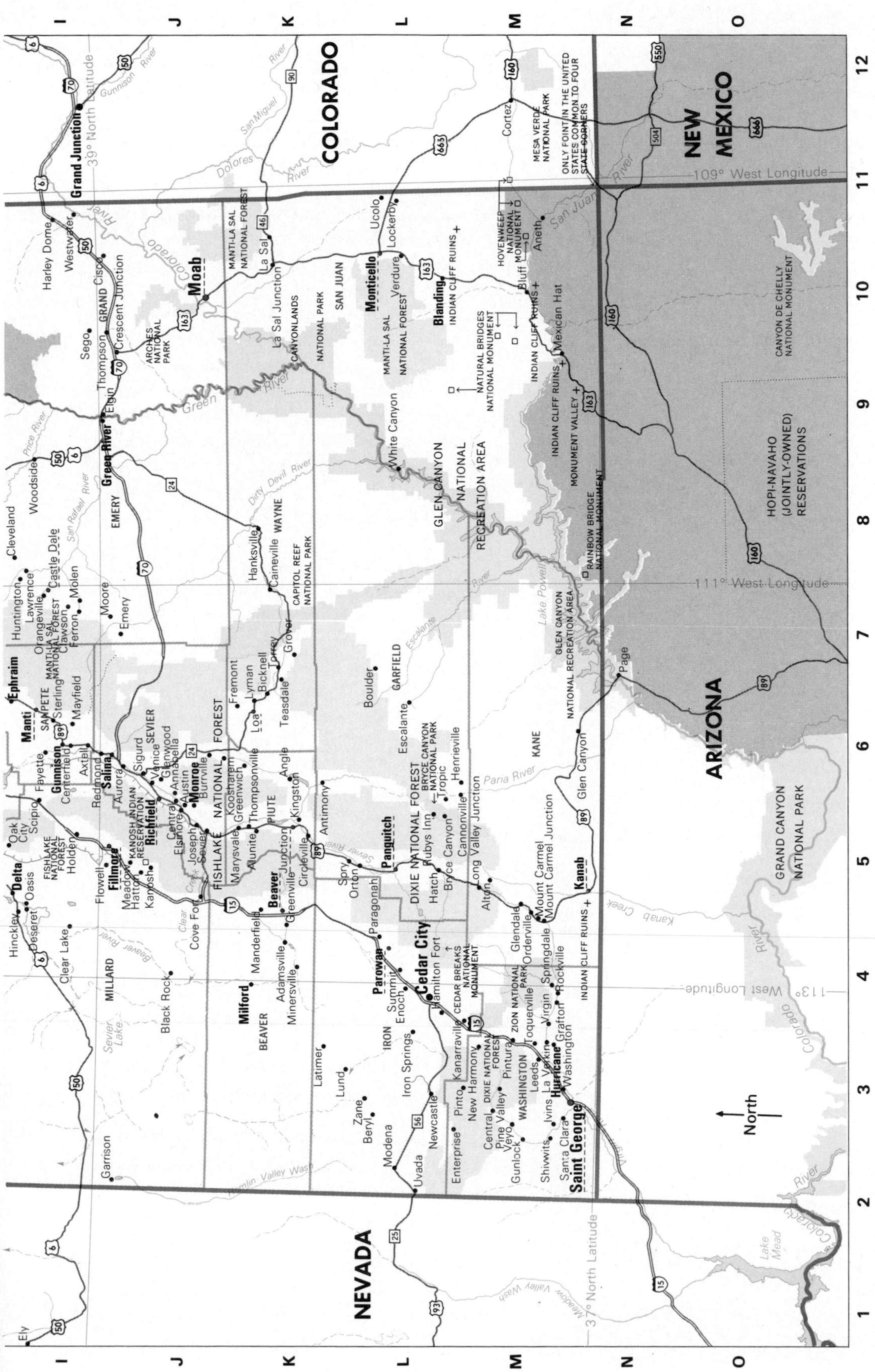

Washington

Plying Puget Sound, a ferry briefly blends with Seattle's skyline. The Space Needle, a noted landmark, stands to the right (below top).

These rolling, fertile hills in southeastern Washington were created by lava that poured from the earth's crust thousands of years ago (below bottom).

Washington is a state of great diversity. It has beautiful mountains, dense evergreen forests, sparkling waters, fertile farmland, flat, semidesert land, abundant recreational areas, and the Pacific Coast. The state's location on the Pacific Coast in the northwestern part of the United States makes it a gateway for travel to Alaska and countries across the Pacific Ocean.

Washington is divided into two major regions by the Cascade Mountains, which extend southward through the western part of the state. Located in the western region of Washington is Puget Sound, a large inlet in the northwest corner of the state. It is famous for the fisheries and lumber mills along its shores. Many ships from all parts of the world dock at cities along Puget Sound, making it one of America's leading shipping centers. Seattle, Tacoma, Bremerton, Olympia, and Everett are centers for trade, fishing, and shipbuilding. Seattle, Washington's largest city, also has a large aircraft construction industry. Olympia is the state capital.

Fish packing and canning, and lumbering are among the most important industries in the western region of Washington. The state's nickname, the *Evergreen State,* comes from the many firs, hemlocks, pines, and other evergreen trees that cover the western slopes of the Cascade Mountains. The nickname also suggests the lush green lowlands of western Washington. Dairy farms are a familiar sight in this region as well. Farmers in the area also produce great numbers of flower bulbs.

Important agricultural areas lie east of the Cascades. Farmers here raise large crops of wheat, fruits, and vegetables. Many beef cattle can be seen grazing on large ranches in this region. Washington is also famous for the apple orchards east of the Cascades. More apples are grown in Washington than in any other state. Spokane, the largest city in eastern Washington, is an important financial and marketing center.

Visitors to the state of Washington are treated to some of the most breathtaking scenery in the country. The ruggedly beautiful Cascade Mountains are a major vacation area. Many of the peaks are dormant volcanoes. Mount Rainier is the highest point in Washington and one of the highest peaks in the United States. It rises southeast of the cities of Seattle and Tacoma. On clear days, residents and visitors in Seattle can view Mount Baker to the north, the Olympic Mountains to the west, and the Cascades to the east. On the Olympic Peninsula, Olympic National Park features junglelike forests. The San Juan Islands near Canada's Vancouver Island are a famous resort area noted for their scenic beauty.

Every year skiers flock to the excellent slopes in the Cascade Mountains. Popular ski areas include Crystal Mountain, Mission Ridge, Mount Baker, Snoqualmie Pass, Stevens Pass, and White Pass. Washington's skiing season lasts from early December until late spring.

Several engineering wonders are among Washington's special attractions. The most famous of these is probably Grand Coulee Dam. The largest concrete dam in the United States, it ranks as the mightiest piece of masonry built. It is located on the Columbia River 92 miles (148 kilometers) west of Spokane. Other engineering wonders include, near Wenatchee in central Washington, Rocky Reach Dam, which has a museum and an underground room where visitors can watch salmon swim upstream to spawning areas each year; and running under the Cascade Range in Chelan and King counties, the Cascade Tunnel, the longest tunnel in the Western Hemisphere. This tunnel cuts through 7.79 miles (12.54 kilometers) of granite and was built by the Great Northern Railway in 1929.

Several of Washington's annual events center around flowers. In April, the Daffodil Festival is held in Puyallup. The Apple Blossom Festival takes place in Wenatchee during the first week in May. The Lilac Festival in Spokane, the Blossom Time Festival in Bellingham, and the Rhododendron Festival in Port Townsend are also held in May.

The Seafair, held in Seattle in late July and early August, is probably the most celebrated annual event in Washington. The show features parades, water carnivals, and boat races on Lake Washington.

Other popular tourist attractions throughout the state include, in Maryhill, Maryhill Castle, an art museum housed in an elaborate mansion overlooking the Columbia River Gorge; and, in Seattle, Seattle Center. This includes the Pacific Science Center from the Century 21 Exposition, a world's fair held in 1962; the towering Space Needle with its observation deck; and a monorail linking the center to downtown Seattle.

Its peak covered by glaciers that sporadically melt into sparkling pools, Mount Rainier is one of Washington's most imposing spectacles.

Washington
Evergreen State

Capital: Olympia
Area: 68,192 sq. mi. (176,616 km²), including 1,622 sq. mi. (4,201 km²) of inland water but excluding 2,397 sq. mi. (6,208 km²) of Pacific coastal water, Puget Sound, and Straits of Georgia and Juan de Fuca; 20th in size among the states
Elevation: *Highest*—Mount Rainier, 14,410 ft. (4,392 m) above sea level; *lowest*—sea level, along the Pacific Ocean
Statehood: Nov. 11, 1889, the 42nd state
Abbreviations: Wash. (traditional); WA (postal)
Motto: *Alki* (Bye and Bye)
Song: "Washington, My Home"
Tree: Western Hemlock

Washington's state seal bears a portrait of George Washington, for whom the state was named. The date 1889 beneath the portrait is the year the state entered the Union. The seal was adopted in 1889. The state flag, adopted in 1925, has a reproduction of the seal. The flag's green field represents the green of Washington's forests.

WASHINGTON Political Map

Lambert conformal conic projection
WORLD BOOK map © Field Enterprises Educational Corporation

Distance scale for inset map
0 5 10   20   30   40   Miles 40
0 5 10   20   30   40   50 Kilometers 70

Distance scale for Washington map
0 10 20   40   60   80   100   120
0 10 20   40   60   80   100   120   140   160   180   200

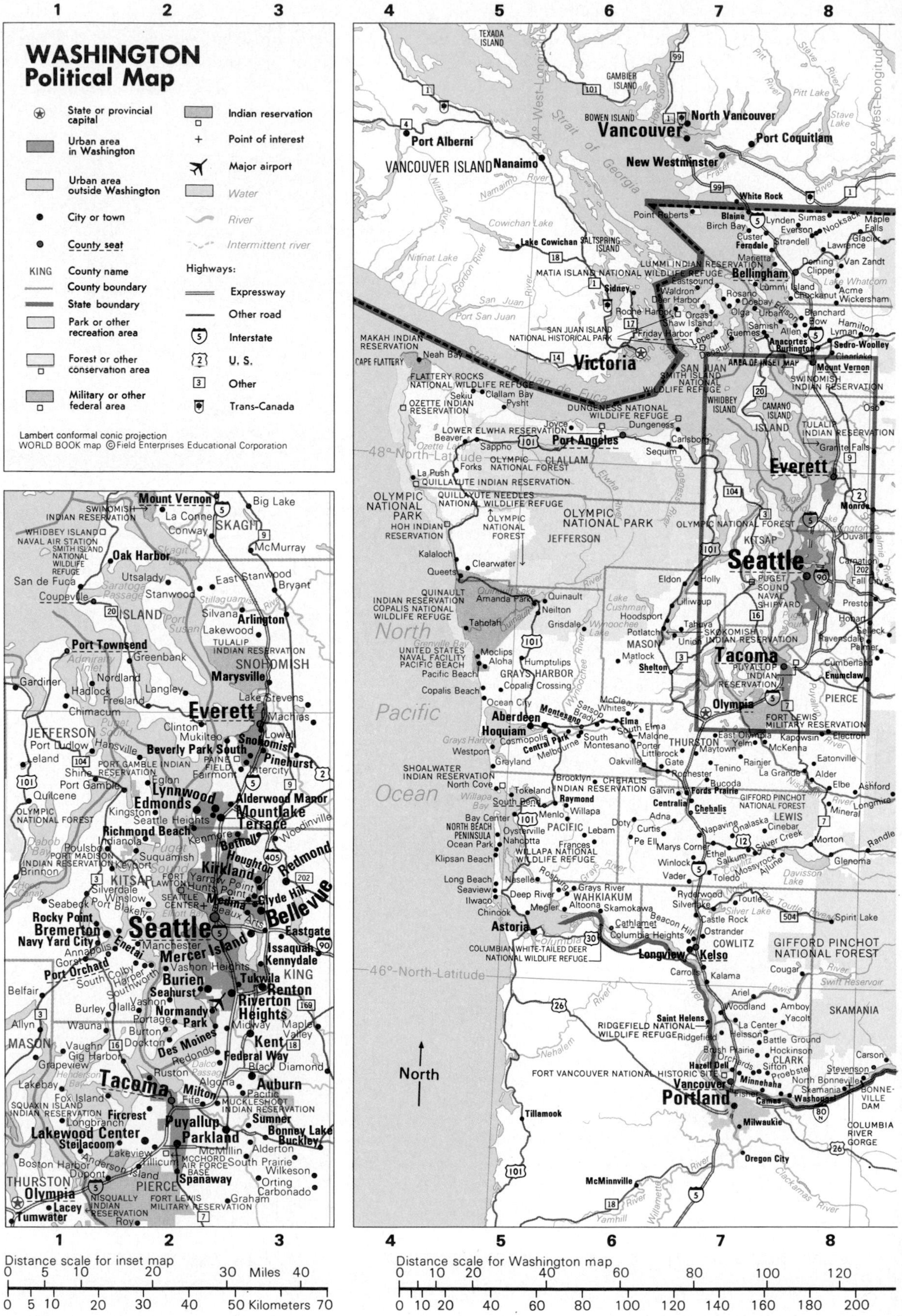

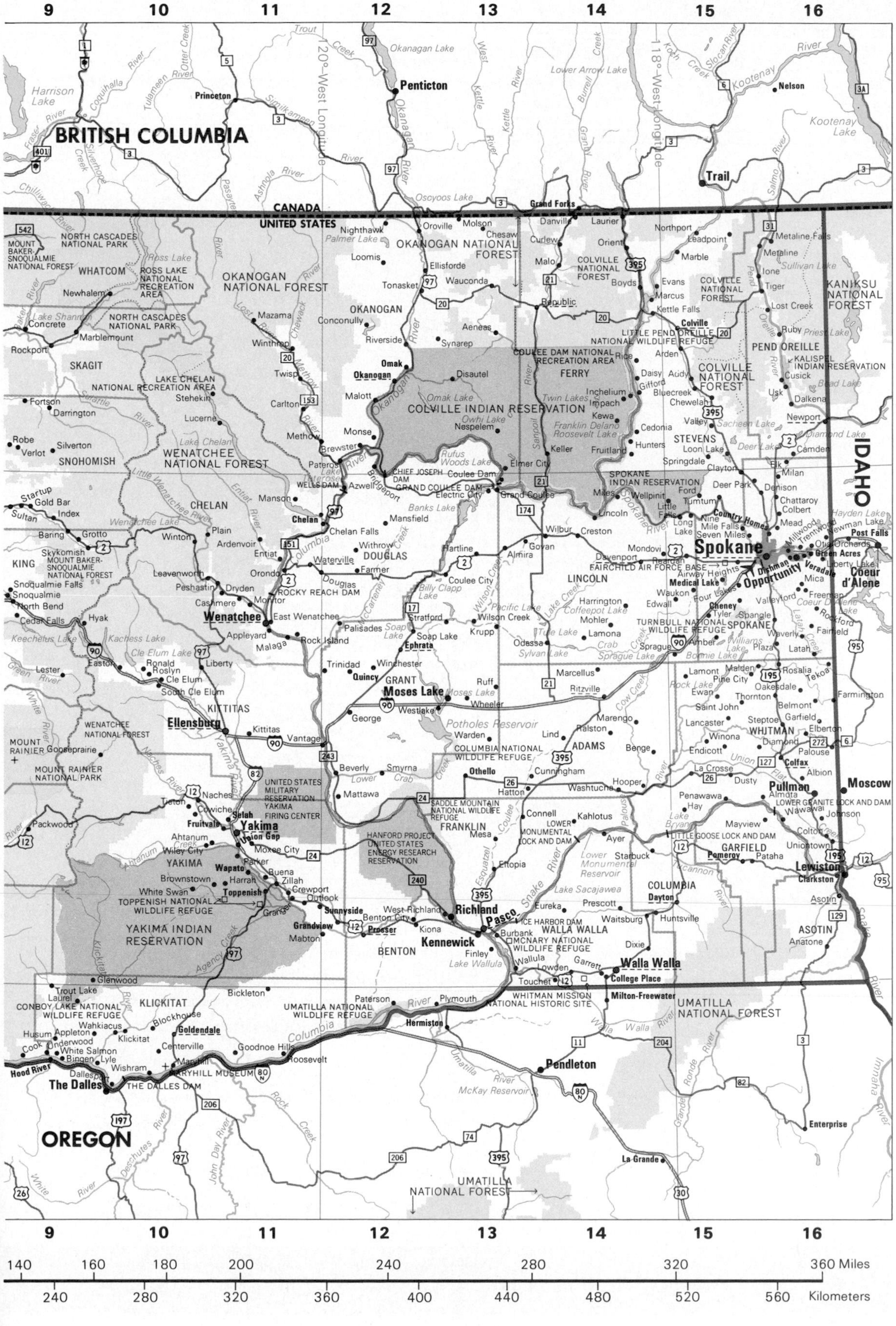

Seal

Flag

Bird: Willow Goldfinch

Flower: Coast Rhododendron

Spewing a stream of boiling water formed by the earth's inner fires, Yellowstone National Park's Old Faithful is North America's most famous geyser.

Wyoming

Wyoming is the home of many "firsts" for the United States. Devils Tower, a volcanic tower that rises from the hills that border the Belle Fourche River in northeastern Wyoming, was established as the country's first national monument in 1906. America's first national forest, Shoshone National Forest, is located in the northwestern part of Wyoming. It is the largest national forest completely within the state. In 1904, Sheridan, Wyoming, became the home of Eaton Ranch, the first dude ranch in the west.

Women have played a large part in making Wyoming a state of many firsts. Wyoming is nicknamed the *Equality State* because its women were the first in the United States to vote, hold public office, and serve on juries. Wyoming's Esther H. Morris became the nation's first woman justice of the peace in 1870, and Mrs. Nellie Tayloe Ross was elected by Wyoming voters as the first woman governor in 1924.

In 1872, this state became the location of the country's first national park, Yellowstone National Park in northwestern Wyoming. This national park is also the country's largest and contains more geysers and hot springs than any other location in the world.

Old Faithful is the most famous geyser in Yellowstone National Park, erupting on the average of every 65 minutes. Other natural features of the park include towering waterfalls, sparkling clear lakes, deep canyons, and vast areas of evergreen forests. Lower Falls of the Yellowstone River is one of the park's particularly beautiful sights.

In spite of threats of attack by Indians and other hardships of early travel, settlers began visiting the park soon after it was established. Today, Yellowstone is one of America's favorite national parks. More than two million tourists visit there each year. Summer vacationers in Yellowstone Park may go hiking on the many trails, take free guided bus tours, ride horseback or take stagecoach rides, and enjoy cookouts and campfire programs.

Wyoming is famous for the scenic beauty of its majestic mountains. Grand Teton National Park in northwestern Wyoming is another of the state's special attractions. Here the Teton Mountains rise in splendor from a beautiful valley called Jackson Hole.

Wyoming, however, contains a variety of landscapes. Besides the rugged ranges of the Rocky Mountains, there are treeless basins dotted with lonely towers of rock called buttes, and broad, flat plains and vast prairies spotted with oil wells and grazing cattle.

Devils Tower, the first national monument of the United States, rises in splendid majesty behind the bank of the Belle Fourche River in northeast Wyoming.

Oil and cattle are the basis of Wyoming's economy. About 95 per cent of the state's land is used for grazing. Much of the land is owned by the federal government. Logging, grazing, and mining in these areas are therefore controlled by federal agencies.

Other scenic attractions throughout the state include, west of Kemmerer, Fossil Butte National Monument, which contains the remains of fishes that lived in the water that covered the area about 50 million years ago; near Casper, Hell's Half Acre, a rugged depression where wind and water have created unusual rock gullies, ridges, and towers; and, south of Thermopolis, Wind River Canyon, where cliffs rise 2,000 feet (609.6 meters) above the river.

Wyoming played a large part in the early cowboy and Indian days in the old west. Thousands of pioneers traveled through Wyoming on three famous trails, the California, the Mormon, and the Oregon trails. All of these took pioneers through South Pass, famous as the easiest route across the Rocky Mountains.

Plains Indians living in Wyoming during this time were upset by the settlers. The Indians saw them as intruders who killed or frightened the animals that the Indians depended upon for food. The Indians watched the prairies being destroyed by fires that were caused by careless settlers, and many Indians were killed or crippled by diseases they had not known before. The Indians often attacked and raided wagon trains. They fought soldiers that had been sent to protect the pioneers.

Today Wyoming has many museums that contain relics of early pioneer and Indian days. Wyoming State Museum in Cheyenne, Fort Casper Museum in Casper, and Fort Bridger State Museum in Fort Bridger all have large collections of mementos of Wyoming's early days.

Regional museums have exhibits that pertain to specific areas. These museums provide a close look at some of America's early history. Relics from the days of pioneer wagon trains are displayed at the Fort Laramie National Historic Site near Fort Laramie. The National Park Service runs the Fur Trade Museum at Moose and the Coulter Bay Museum in the Grand Teton National Park, which contains a fine collection of Indian art.

A lone cowhand follows his herd as it drifts over the flatlands of eastern Wyoming. Much of this area is suitable only for grazing cattle and sheep.

Wyoming
Equality State

Capital: Cheyenne
Area: 97,914 sq. mi. (253,596 km²), including 711 sq. mi. (1,814 km²) of inland water; 9th in size among the states
Elevation: *Highest*—Gannett Peak in Fremont County, 13,804 ft. (4,207 m) above sea level; *lowest*—Belle Fourche River in Crook County, 3,100 ft. (945 m) above sea level
Statehood: July 10th, 1890, the 44th state
Abbreviations: Wyo. (traditional); WY (postal)
Motto: *Equal Rights*
Song: "Wyoming"
Tree: Cottonwood

Wyoming's state seal shows a woman and the state motto declaring the equal rights women have held in the state. The two men represent Wyoming's livestock and mining industries. The dates are those on which Wyoming became a territory (1869) and a state (1890). The seal was adopted in 1893. The state flag, adopted in 1917, has a adaptation of the seal on a buffalo representing the branding of livestock. The red border symbolizes Indians and the blood of the pioneers.

WYOMING Political Map

State capital
City or town
County seat
UINTA **County name**
County boundary
State boundary
Park or other recreation area
Forest or other conservation area
Military or other federal area
Indian reservation

Point of interest
Water
River
Waterway
Intermittent river
Intermittent lake

Highways:
Expressway
Other road
41 **Interstate**
66 **U. S.**
84 **Other**

Lambert conformal conic projection
WORLD BOOK map © Field Enterprises Educational Corporation

Distance scale for inset map
0 5 10 20 30 40 50 Miles 60
0 5 10 20 30 40 50 60 70 Kilometers 100

Distance scale for Wyoming map
0 10 20 40 60 80 100 120
0 10 20 40 60 80 100 120 140 160 180 200

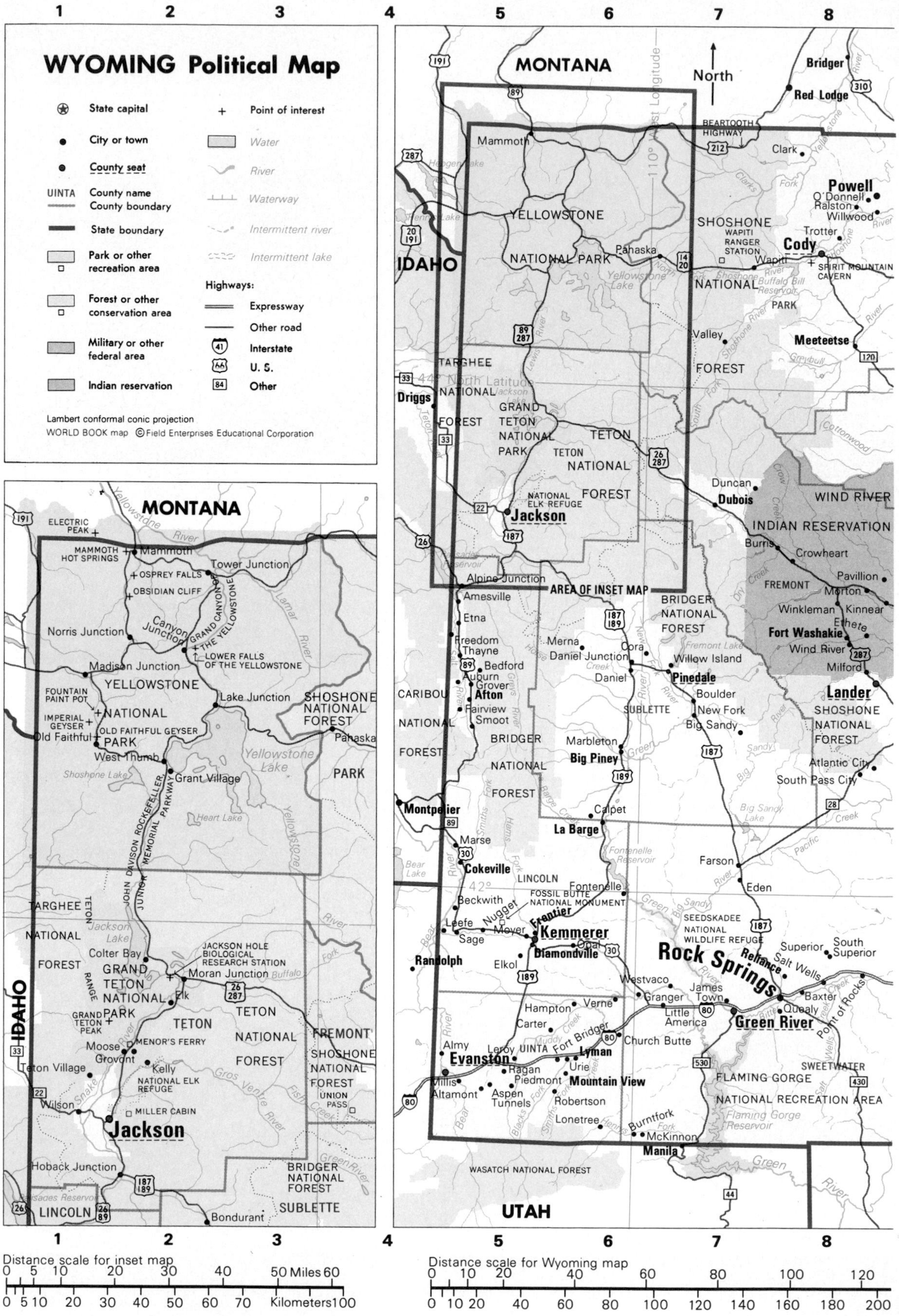

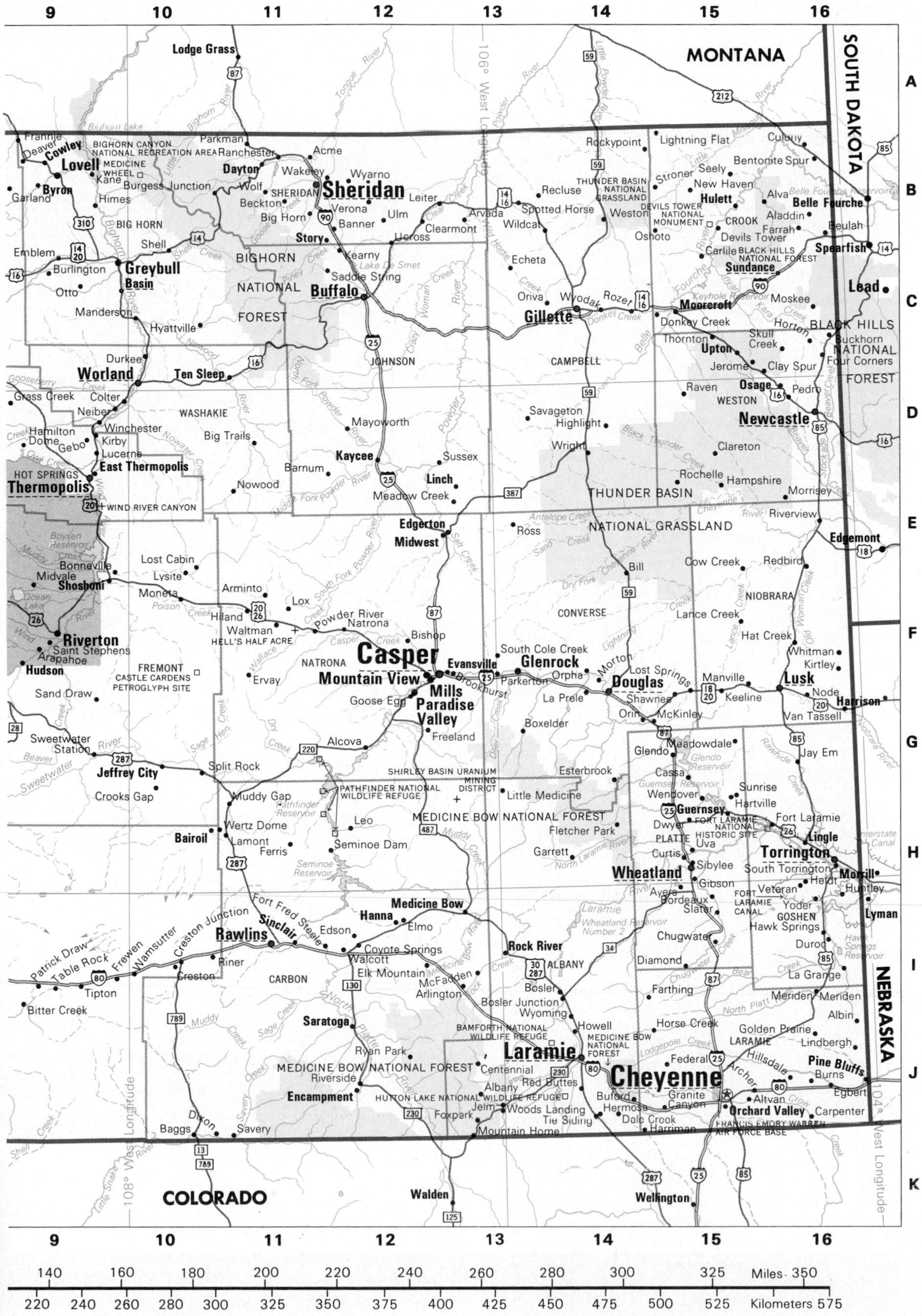

Seal

Flag

Bird: Meadow Lark

Flower: Indian Paintbrush

9 10 11 12 13 14 15 16

MONTANA

SOUTH DAKOTA

Lodge Grass

Frannie
Deaver Cowley
Lovell
MEDICINE
WHEEL
Byron Kane BIGHORN CANYON
Garland NATIONAL RECREATION AREA
Burgess Junction
Himes

Emblem
Burlington
Greybull
Basin
Otto
Manderson
Hyattville

Worland
Grass Creek Colter
Neiber
Hamilton Winchester
Dome Kirby
Gebo Lucerne
East Thermopolis
HOT SPRINGS
Thermopolis
WIND RIVER CANYON

Bonneville
Midvale
Shoshoni
OCEAN
LAKE

Riverton
Saint Stephens
Arapahoe
Hudson
Sand Draw

Sweetwater
Station

Jeffrey City
Crooks Gap

Bairoil

A

B

C

D

E

F

G

H

I

J

K

Parkman
Ranchester
Dayton
Wolf
SHERIDAN
Beckton
Big Horn
Story
Kearny
Lake De Smet
Saddle String

BIGHORN

NATIONAL

FOREST
Buffalo

Shell
BIG HORN

Durkee
Ten Sleep

WASHAKIE
Big Trails

Mayoworth

Kaycee
Barnum
Nowood
Sussex
Linch
Meadow Creek

Edgerton
Midwest

Lost Cabin
Lysite
Moneta
Armino
Lox
Hiland
Waltman
HELL'S HALF ACRE
Powder River
Natrona
Bishop

Casper
NATRONA
Mountain View
Evansville
Mills
Paradise
Valley
Goose Egg
Freeland

Alcova

Split Rock

Muddy Gap
Wertz Dome
Lamont
Ferris
Leo
Seminoe Dam

Wakeley
Acme
Wyarno
Leiter
Banner
Ulm
Clearmont
Ucross

Echeta

Recluse
Spotted Horse
Arvada
Wildcat

Oriva
Wyodak
Rozet
Gillette

JOHNSON

CAMPBELL

Savageton
Highlight
Wright

THUNDER BASIN

Ross
Sand Creek

Bill

Dry Fork

CONVERSE
South Cole Creek
Glenrock
Orpha
Parkerton
Douglas
Shawnee
La Prele
Orin
Boxelder McKinley

Esterbrook

MEDICINE BOW NATIONAL FOREST
Fletcher Park
Little Medicine
Garrett

Rockypoint Lightning Flat Culony
Stroner Seely
Bentonite Spur
New Haven
Hulett Alva
Aladdin
Devils Tower
THUNDER BASIN DEVILS TOWER
NATIONAL NATIONAL
GRASSLAND MONUMENT
Weston Oshoto
Carlile BLACK HILLS
NATIONAL
Sundance FOREST
Moorcroft
Donkey Creek
Thornton
Upton
Jerome
Clay Spur
Raven
Osage
WESTON
Clareton

Rochelle Hampshire
Morrisey

NATIONAL GRASSLAND

Riverview

Cow Creek Redbird
NIOBRARA
Lance Creek
Hat Creek

Manville
Lost Springs
Keeline
Lusk
Node
Van Tassell

Meadowdale
Cassa
Wendover
Glendo Hartville
Sunrise
Guernsey
Dwyer FORT LARAMIE
PLATTE NATIONAL
Uva HISTORIC SITE

Belle Fourche
Beulah
Farrah
Spearfish
Lead
Moskee

BLACK HILLS

Buckhorn
Four Corners
FOREST

Newcastle

Edgemont

Whitman
Kirtley
Harrison

Jay Em

Fort Laramie
Lingle
Torrington
South Torrington
Morrill
Huntley
Lyman

Wheatland
Ayers
Bordeaux
Slater
FORT
Curtis LARAMIE
CANAL Gibson
Sibylee
Veteran
Yoder
Hawk Springs
Duroc

Medicine Bow
Hanna
Elmo
Sinclair
Rawlins Edson
Coyote Springs
Walcott
Elk Mountain
McFadden
Arlington
Bosler
Rock River
ALBANY

Saratoga
Ryan Park
BAMFORTH
WILDLIFE REFUGE
Laramie
Riverside
Centennial
Albany Red Buttes
Encampment HUTTON LAKE NATIONAL WILDLIFE REFUGE
Dixon
Baggs Savery
Jelm Woods Landing
Foxpark

COLORADO Walden

Diamond

Farthing
Bosler Junction
Wyoming
Howell
MEDICINE BOW
NATIONAL
FOREST
Buford
Hermosa
Jelm Tie Siding
Mountain Home

Chugwater

Horse Creek

Federal

Cheyenne
Granite
Canyon
Altvan
Dale Crook
Harriman
FRANCIS EMORY WARREN
AIR FORCE BASE

La Grange

Meriden Meriden
Albin

Golden Prairie
LARAMIE
Lindbergh
Hillsdale
Pine Bluffs
Burns
Egbert
Carpenter

Orchard Valley

Wellington

NEBRASKA

---

9 10 11 12 13 14 15 16

140 160 180 200 220 240 260 280 300 325 Miles 350
220 240 260 280 300 325 350 375 400 425 450 475 500 525 Kilometers 575

Alaska

Alaska is officially nicknamed the *Last Frontier*. Much of the state has not yet been settled. Almost a third of Alaska is north of the Arctic Circle. For this reason, people often think of Alaska as a place that is very cold, although much of the state has a wide temperature range. Some points in Alaska have temperatures as low as −80° F. (−62° C). In other places the high temperature can reach 100° F. (38° C).

Farmers can raise livestock and crops in Alaska as far north as the Arctic Circle. The growing season is short, but crops grow and ripen quickly in the central part of the state because the sun shines about 20 hours a day during the summer. Livestock products such as milk, eggs, and beef cattle account for the majority of Alaska's agricultural income. Chief crops include potatoes, barley, and oats.

The cold waters surrounding Alaska's lacelike coastline teem with fishing boats. The state has an annual fish catch valued at about $145 million.

Because approximately 500 miles (800 kilometers) of Canadian territory separate Alaska and the state of Washington, native Alaskans call the continental United States the "lower 48." Until 1942, there were no highways providing access to Alaska from Canada or the United States. During World War II, however, the federal government built the Alaska Highway as a military supply route. The highway was first used to carry military and other supplies to the thousands of people who had been sent to Alaska to build and maintain military installations. Today, the Alaska Highway runs 1,422 miles (2,288 kilometers) between Dawson Creek, British Columbia, and Delta Junction. The Richardson Highway links Delta Junction and Fairbanks.

Alaska is an interesting mixture of the old and the new. Eskimos who live along the Arctic coast in the north and west still hunt and fish in much the same way their ancestors did. These Alaskan natives use animal skins to make clothing such as parkas and mukluks, the soft sealskin boots that Alaskan natives have traditionally worn.

Many of the remote Alaskan villages have airstrips where bush pilots can land planes to deliver messages, passengers, and supplies. Radar and communication stations housing modern scientific equipment can also be seen dotting the Alaskan landscape. These stations protect the United States and Canada against air attacks from across the North Pole region.

Many people travel to Alaska each year to view its beautiful mountain scenery or to visit its historic coastal towns. Mount McKinley National Park, featuring majestic Mount McKinley, the highest peak in North America, is a popular tourist spot. Two interesting coastal towns are Ketchikan, which houses a large totem pole collection, and Sitka, which was the Russian capital of Alaska and has a historic Russian Orthodox Church. These and other coastal towns are accessible to visitors via the Marine Highway, a system of ocean-going ferryliners that carry cars and passengers along a scenic route between forested islands and the steep, fiord-cut mainland coast.

People who love the great outdoors are attracted to Alaska's untamed wilderness areas. Here they can hunt brown bears and caribou, or fish for record-

sized salmon and trout. Awesome Mount McKinley and other high mountain peaks attract expert mountain climbers yearly.

Alaska has thousands of glaciers, which range from 1 to 30 miles (1.6 to 48 kilometers) long, filling the state's mountain valleys and canyons. Most of the glaciers are along the coast in southern and southeastern Alaska. North America's largest glacier, Malaspina, is in the Saint Elias Range. Many glaciers in Alaska are easy to reach, and scientists from all over North America venture there to study them.

Tourists and Alaskans alike enjoy many annual events in this state. From January to May, ski races are held at the major ski areas. The ten-day-long Anchorage Fur Rendezvous is held in February. Athletic contests and sled dog races are among the events featured during the festival. A March event is the Alaskan Arts and Crafts Show in Juneau. The Little Norway Festival is held in Petersburg each May. The Golden Days Celebration is an annual July event in Fairbanks. On October 18, Sitka's Alaska Day Festival is held. It commemorates the transfer of Alaska from Russia to the United States in 1867.

The purchase of Alaska from Russia marks an important event in U.S. history. Secretary of State William H. Seward paid $7,200,000 for the land, or about 2 cents an acre. Many people thought the area was a snow-covered wasteland and called it "Seward's Folly" and "Seward's Icebox." Alaska, however, proved to be rich in fish, minerals, timber, and water supplies. Oil, particularly, is Alaska's chief source of wealth. The value of these natural resources has paid back the purchase price of Alaska hundreds of times.

Rivers of ice flow in symmetrical patterns from the multitude of glaciers that fill Alaska's mountain valleys and canyons (above top).

Oxen of the Arctic, dogs provided early Alaskan transportation. Here at Mount McKinley National Park, tourists are given an explanation and demonstration of sledding maneuvers (above bottom).

Alaska
Last Frontier

Capital: Juneau
Area: 589,757 sq. mi. (1,527,464 km²), including 20,157 sq. mi. (52,206 km²) of inland water; 1st in size among the states
Elevation: *Highest*—Mount McKinley, 20,320 ft. (6,194 m) above sea level; *lowest*—sea level, along the Pacific
Statehood: Jan. 3, 1959, the 49th state
Abbreviation: AK (postal)
Motto: *North to the Future*
Song: "Alaska's Flag"
Tree: Sitka Spruce

Alaska's state seal shows the rising sun shining on forests, a lake, a fishing boat and merchant ship, and mining and agricultural activities. These symbols represent Alaska's principal resources and occupations. The seal was adopted in 1913. The state flag, designed by a 13-year-old schoolboy, was adopted in 1927. Seven gold stars representing Alaska's gold-mining industry form the Big Dipper. An eighth star in the corner is the North Star, symbolizing the state's location in the far north.

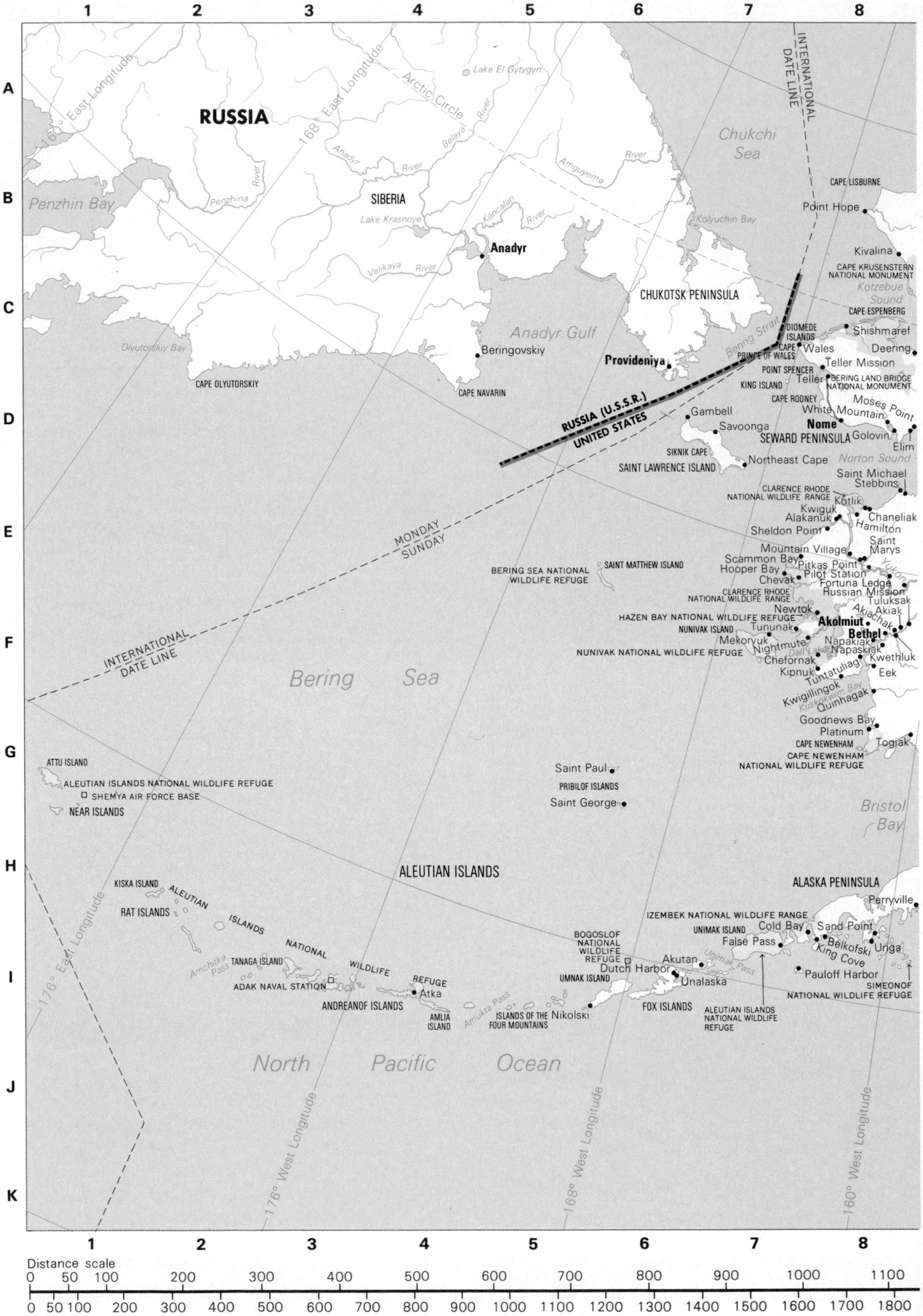

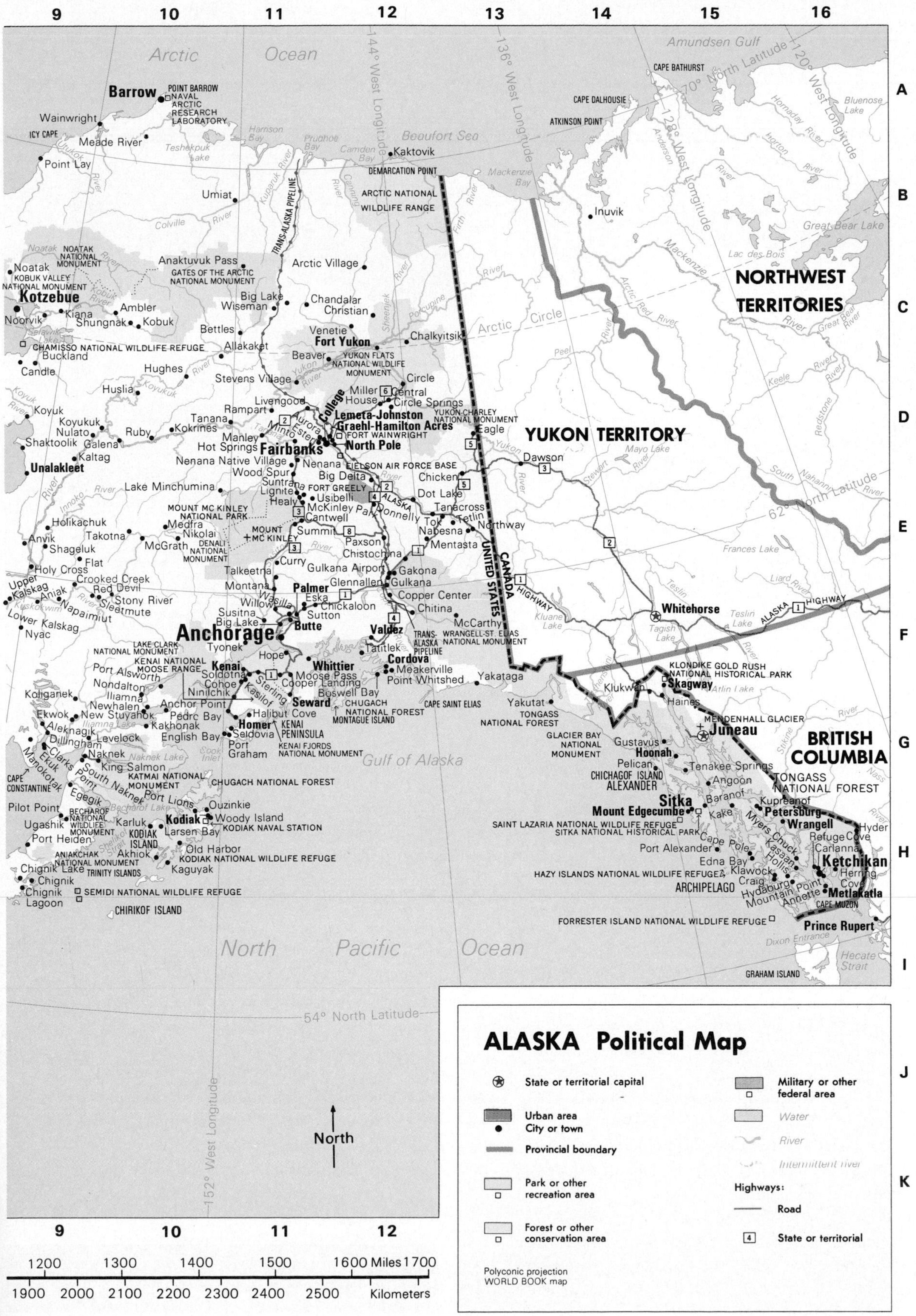

Seal

Flag

Bird: Willow Ptarmigan

Flower: Forget-Me-Not

9 10 11 12 13 14 15 16

Arctic   Ocean

Barrow
POINT BARROW
NAVAL ARCTIC RESEARCH LABORATORY
Wainwright
ICY CAPE
Meade River
Point Lay

Amundsen Gulf
CAPE BATHURST
70° North Latitude
CAPE DALHOUSIE
ATKINSON POINT

A

Harrison Bay
Prudhoe Bay
Beaufort Sea
Kaktovik

144° West Longitude
136° West Longitude
128° West Longitude
120° West Longitude

Bluenose Lake

B

DEMARCATION POINT
ARCTIC NATIONAL WILDLIFE RANGE
Inuvik

Mackenzie Bay
Great Bear Lake

Umiat
Colville River
NOATAK NATIONAL MONUMENT
Noatak
KOBUK VALLEY NATIONAL MONUMENT
Kotzebue
Noorvik Kiana Shungnak Kobuk
Ambler
Anaktuvuk Pass
GATES OF THE ARCTIC NATIONAL MONUMENT
Arctic Village
Big Lake Wiseman
Chandalar Christian

Lac des Bois
NORTHWEST TERRITORIES

C
Arctic Circle

CHAMISSO NATIONAL WILDLIFE REFUGE
Buckland
Candle
Huslia
Hughes
Bettles
Allakaket
Venetie
Fort Yukon
YUKON FLATS NATIONAL WILDLIFE MONUMENT
Beaver
Stevens Village
Chalkyitsik
Circle

Great Bear River
Keele River
Redstone River

D

Koyuk Koyukuk Nulato Ruby Kokrines
Shaktoolik Galena Kaltag
Unalakleet
Tanana
Rampart
Livengood
Manley Hot Springs
Nenana Native Village
Miller House
College
Lemeta-Johnston
Graehl-Hamilton Acres
FORT WAINWRIGHT
North Pole
Central
Circle Springs
YUKON-CHARLEY NATIONAL MONUMENT
Eagle
Aurora
Ester
Fairbanks
YUKON TERRITORY
Dawson

62°
South Nahanni River
Mayo Lake
North Latitude

E

Wood Spur
Lignite
MOUNT MC KINLEY NATIONAL PARK
Lake Minchumina
Nenana
Big Delta
FORT GREELY
McKinley Park
Cantwell
Usibelli
Healy
Suntrana
Summit
Donnelly
ALASKA
Dot Lake
Chicken
Tanacross
Tok
Tetlin
Nabesna
Northway
Mentasta
Chistochina
Gulkana Airport
Paxson
MOUNT MC KINLEY
DENALI NATIONAL MONUMENT
Holikachuk
Takotna
Medfra
Nikolai
McGrath
Flat
Anvik
Shageluk

CANADA
UNITED STATES
Frances Lake
Liard River

Holy Cross
Crooked Creek
Red Devil
Stony River
Sleetmute
Napaimiut
Upper Kalskag
Aniak
Lower Kalskag
Nyac
Talkeetna
Montana
Curry
Willow
Sutton
Susitna
Palmer
Eska
Gakona
Glennallen
Gulkana
Copper Center
Chitina
McCarthy
WRANGELL-ST ELIAS NATIONAL MONUMENT
TRANS-ALASKA PIPELINE
HIGHWAY
Whitehorse
ALASKA HIGHWAY

Teslin Lake
Kluane Lake
Tagish Lake
Atlin Lake

F

Anchorage
Tyonek
Big Lake
Butte
Chickaloon
Hope
Moose Pass
Valdez
Tatitlek
Cordova
Meakerville
Point Whitshed
Yakataga
Klukwan
Skagway
KLONDIKE GOLD RUSH NATIONAL HISTORICAL PARK
Haines

BRITISH COLUMBIA

G
Kolganek
Newhalen
Nondalton
Iliamna
Levelock
Kenai
Kasilof
Soldotna
Cohoe
Sterling
Cooper Landing
Boswell Bay
Whittier
Seward
CHUGACH NATIONAL FOREST
MONTAGUE ISLAND
CAPE SAINT ELIAS
Yakutat
TONGASS NATIONAL FOREST
GLACIER BAY NATIONAL MONUMENT
Gustavus
Hoonah
Pelican
Tenakee Springs
Angoon
CHICHAGOF ISLAND
ALEXANDER
Baranof
Juneau
MENDENHALL GLACIER
TONGASS NATIONAL FOREST

Ekwok New Stuyahok
Dillingham
Naknek
King Salmon
Ekuk
Anchor Point
Halibut Cove
Homer
Seldovia
Port Graham
English Bay
KENAI PENINSULA
KENAI FJORDS NATIONAL MONUMENT

Gulf of Alaska

Sitka
Mount Edgecumbe
SAINT LAZARIA NATIONAL WILDLIFE REFUGE
SITKA NATIONAL HISTORICAL PARK
Port Alexander
Kake
Cape Pole
Kupreanof
Petersburg
Wrangell
Myers Chuck
Hyder
Refuge Cove
Carlanna

H

NATIONAL WILDLIFE REFUGE
Clarks Point
CAPE CONSTANTINE
Nakuotok
Pilot Point
Ugashik
Port Heiden
BECHAROF NATIONAL MONUMENT
KATMAI NATIONAL MONUMENT
Egegik
Pedro Bay
Port Lions
Ouzinkie
Kodiak
Larsen Bay
Karluk
KODIAK ISLAND
KODIAK NAVAL STATION
Woody Island
Old Harbor
ANIAKCHAK NATIONAL MONUMENT
Akhiok
Kaguyak
Chignik Lake
TRINITY ISLANDS
Chignik
SEMIDI NATIONAL WILDLIFE REFUGE
Chignik Lagoon
CHIRIKOF ISLAND
Edna Bay
Craig
Klawock
Hydaburg
Mountain Point
Annette
HAZY ISLANDS NATIONAL WILDLIFE REFUGE
ARCHIPELAGO
Ketchikan
Herring Cove
Metlakatla
CAPE MUZON

North   Pacific   Ocean

152° West Longitude
FORRESTER ISLAND NATIONAL WILDLIFE REFUGE
Prince Rupert
Dixon Entrance
GRAHAM ISLAND
Hecate Strait

I

54° North Latitude

J

North ↑

ALASKA Political Map

⊛ State or territorial capital

▢ Urban area
• City or town
━ Provincial boundary

▢ Park or other recreation area

▢ Forest or other conservation area

▢ Military or other federal area

▢ Water

〜 River

〜 Intermittent river

Highways:
━ Road

4 State or territorial

Polyconic projection
WORLD BOOK map

K

1200 1300 1400 1500 1600 Miles 1700
1900 2000 2100 2200 2300 2400 2500 Kilometers

On December 7, 1941, the Japanese attacked Pearl Harbor in Honolulu. The U.S.S. Arizona *Memorial stands over the partially submerged battleship in tribute to those who died on that day.*

Hawaii

Hawaii is called the *Aloha State.* The word *aloha* means "love" in the Hawaiian language. The word is also used to say "greetings," "welcome," and "farewell." The friendly people of Hawaii live up to their state's nickname. When visitors arrive in Hawaii, they are often greeted warmly and presented with leis, or floral wreaths. The Hawaiians then try their best to make certain that the visitors enjoy themselves.

Hawaii, the only state that does not lie on the mainland of North America, is made up of 132 islands, all formed by volcanoes that were built up from the floor of the Pacific Ocean. Of the 132 islands, eight are considered the main islands. They are Hawaii, Maui, Kahoolawe, Molokai, Lanai, Oahu, Kauai, and Niihau. People live on seven of the eight main islands. Only Kahoolawe has no permanent residents.

Each of the inhabited islands has its own nickname. The island of Hawaii is the largest island in the state. It is called the *Big Island.* Maui is called the *Valley Island* because many canyons cut into the volcanic mountains that form the island. Molokai is called the *Friendly Island* because people who live there are especially friendly to visitors. Lanai is the *Pineapple State.* The island is owned by the Dole Company, and all the cultivated land there is used for growing pineapple. Kauai is known as the *Garden Island.* It has rich greenery and many beautiful gardens. Niihau is known as the *Forbidden Island.* It is a private island, most of which is owned by descendants of Mrs. Elizabeth Sinclair, who bought the land from King Kamehameha V in 1864. No one can visit Niihau without the owners' permission.

Cool trade winds keep the climate of Hawaii mild throughout the year. There is little difference in temperature between night and day or between summer and winter. The mild climate and Hawaii's beautiful scenery make the state one of the world's favorite year-round vacationlands. Visitors to the islands can enjoy feasts called *luaus,* folk dancing, parades, hula dancing, sightseeing, island hopping, or relaxing on Waikiki Beach in Honolulu. There are excellent hotel accommodations on the islands of Hawaii, Kauai, Maui, Molokai, and Oahu.

While on the island of Hawaii, vacationers may visit many beautiful and interesting sites. Akaka

Falls near Hilo is a long, slender waterfall on the Kolekole stream. It plunges over a tall cliff into a densely wooded gorge. The Hamakua Coast lies between Hilo and Honokoa. A scenic highway runs through sugar cane plantations and around the base of Mauna Kea, Hawaii's highest mountain. Glistening black lava sand forms Kaimi Black Sand Beach, which is near one of Hawaii's largest coconut palm groves. Kealakekua Bay is the site where Captain James Cook, the first European to reach Hawaii, was killed in 1779. A monument at the bay honors Captain Cook.

The City of Refuge National Historic Park shows the history of the Polynesian people, the original settlers of Hawaii, and Puukohola Heiau National Historic Site preserves one of Hawaii's most historic temples. One of Hawaii's two national parks, Hawaii Volcanoes National Park, is also located on Hawaii Island. Haleakala National Park is on Maui.

The island of Oahu also has many interesting sites for tourists. Honolulu, the state's capital and largest city, is the home of Aloha Tower. The tower rises above a docking area for passenger ships. Visitors have a beautiful view of Honolulu and its harbor from the top of the tower. Kapiolani Park is between Waikiki and Diamond Head, an extinct volcano. Visitors to the park may attend concerts and pageants that are presented there. A zoo is also located in the park. Nuuanu Pali offers tourists a magnificent view of Oahu's northeastern coast from a high cliff. There is a highway to the top of the cliff. The Polynesian Cultural Center includes six Polynesian villages inhabited by people from Fiji, Tonga, Hawaii, New Zealand, Samoa, and Tahiti.

Hawaii is the only state that was once an independent monarchy. The remains of five Hawaiian kings and the only queen who ruled Hawaii are interred in the Royal Mausoleum in Honolulu.

The island of Kauai offers visitors several interesting sites. Barking Sands is a beach that is sometimes quite dry. At these times, the sand, when walked on, makes a sound like a barking dog. Menehune Fish Pond has walls of cut stone. The pond, near Lihue, was supposedly built by the first Polynesian settlers. Waimea Canyon's beautifully colored gorge can be viewed from several lookouts along a highway.

Each year thousands of tourists are attracted to Hawaii by its many celebrations and festivals. The most important of these is the annual Aloha Festival. It is held from mid-September through mid-October on the islands of Hawaii, Kauai, Maui, Molokai, and Oahu. Feasts, folk and street dancing, and parades are offered on the islands during the festival.

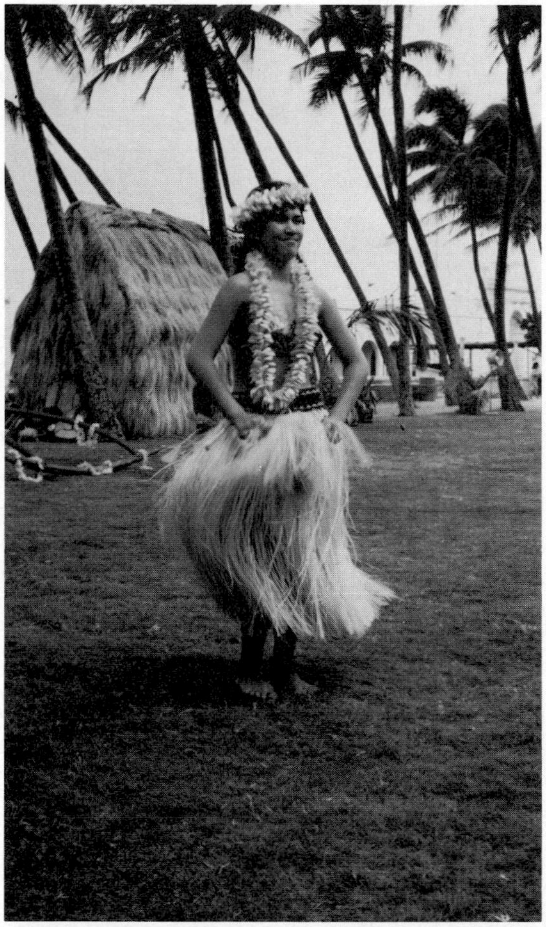

Bedecked in leis and grass skirt, this young Hawaiian performs the traditional hula dance (left).

Stretching for miles, pineapple plantations thrive on the rich, volcanic soil of Hawaii. The succulent fruit is picked by hand and placed on a conveyor belt that carries it to waiting trucks (below).

Hawaii
Aloha State

Capital: Honolulu
Area: 6,450 sq. mi. (16,705 km²), including 25 sq. mi. (65 km²) of inland water; 47th in size among the states
Elevation: *Highest*—Mauna Kea, 13,796 ft. (4,205 m) above sea level; *lowest*—sea level
Statehood: Aug. 21, 1959, the 50th state
Abbreviation: HI (postal)
Motto: *Ua Mau Ke Ea O Ka Aina I Ka Pono* (The Life of the Land Is Perpetuated in Righteousness)
Song: "Hawaii Ponoi" (Hawaii's Own)
Tree: Kukui

Hawaii's state coat of arms was adopted in 1959. It shows the figure of King Kamehameha I on the left and the goddess Liberty on the right. In Hawaiian, the state motto appears. The state flag was also adopted in 1959. The Kingdom, Republic, and Territory of Hawaii all used this flag. The eight stripes represent the state's main islands.

HAWAII Political Map

Symbol	Description
☆	State capital
▨	Urban area
•	City or town
●	County seat
KAUAI	County name
	County boundary

☐	Park or other recreation area
☐	Military or other federal area
+	Point of interest
✈	Major airport
☐	Water

River
Intermittent river
Highways:
Expressway
Other road
H1 Interstate
55 Other

Lambert conformal conic projection
WORLD BOOK map

Distance scale for
0 50 100 200
0 50100 200

KURE ISLAND   MIDWAY ISLANDS (UNITED STATES)
PEARL AND HERMES REEF
INTERNATIONAL DATE LINE — 180° West Longitude
175° West Longitude

North Pacific Ocean

LEHUA ISLAND
NIIHAU ISLAND
Islands west of Kaula Island are part of Honolulu county
KAUAI
PUEO POINT
KAWAIHOA POINT
KAULA ISLAND

Hanalei Bay HANALEI NATIONAL WILDLIFE REFUGE
HAENA POINT Haena Hanalei Kilauea
Wainiha Kolihiwai
BARKING SANDS Moloaa
NOHILI POINT KAUAI Anahola
Manaa WAIMEA CANYON Kumukumu
550 Kealia
Kekaha Kapaa KAUAI ISLAND
Waimea Wailua
Kaumakani Lihue Ahukini
Hanapepe Niumalu Nawiliwili
Port Allen Kukuiula MENEHUNE FISH POND
Koloa HULEIA NATIONAL WILDLIFE
Poipu REFUGE
Koloa Landing
SPOUTING HORN

Kauai Channel

KAHUKU POINT Kahuku
Waialua KAENA POINT OAHU ISLAND
Wahiawa HONOLULU Kaneohe
Honolulu ☆ Kailua
AREA OF INSET MAP KOKO HEAD

OAHU ISLAND
KAHUKU POINT
Kawela
Waialee
Paumalu Kahuku
Sunset Beach MOKUAUIA ISLAND
Pupukea Laie Bay
Waimea Maunawai Laie
Kawailoa Beach POLYNESIAN CULTURAL CENTER
83 Waimea Camp
Kawailoa Hauula
Kaiaka Bay Haleiwa Haleaha
Mokuleia Punaluu
KAENA POINT 930 Kamooloa Kahana Kahana Bay
Waialua 82 Puuiki Kaaawa
99
930 Poamoho Camp 83
930 Waikane
Makaha Whitmore Village
Wahiawa KAPAPA ISLAND
SCHOFIELD BARRACKS KANEOHE BAY MOKUMANU ISLANDS
Schofield Barracks MILITARY RESERVATION MARINE CORPS MOKAPU POINT
780 Waipio Acres AIR STATION
NAVAL Kunia WHEELER AIR FORCE BASE Kahaluu Mokapu
Waianae RESERVATION Mililani HONOLULU
Maili Town Kaneohe Kailua
750 99 Pacific 630 Lanikai
Nanakuli Palisades MOKULUA ISLANDS
MAILI POINT Pearl City Aiea 61
Waipahu Halawa Heights CAMP H. M. SMITH 83 Pohakupu Keolu Hills
Makakilo City Honolulu Waimalu 63 72
Lower Village Foster Village NUUANU PALI Maunawili
Ewa PEARL HARBOR TRIPLER FORT SHAFTER
Barbers Point Housing 760 PEARL HARBOR ARMY MILITARY RESERVATION Waimanalo Waimanalo Beach
CAMPBELL INDUSTRIAL PARK H1 93 NAVAL BASE HOSPITAL 90 61
Iroquois Point HICKAM Hickam Housing MANANA ISLAND
Ewa Beach AIR FORCE BASE ROYAL MAUSOLEUM MAKAPUU POINT
BARBERS POINT KAMEHAMEHA ALOHA PUNCHBOWL NATIONAL MEMORIAL
NAVAL AIR STATION FORT TOWER CEMETERY OF THE PACIFIC
BARBERS POINT MILITARY RESERVATION 92 Honolulu ☆ Kuliouou 72 Maunalua
Keehi Lagoon H1 Hawaii Kai 740
Mamala Bay WAIKIKI BEACH Maunalua Bay KOKO HEAD
DIAMOND HEAD KAPIOLANI PARK Kaiwi Channel

Kaneohe Bay
Kailua Bay
Maunawili
Waimanalo Bay

Distance scale for Oahu Island map
0 2.5 5 10 15 20 25 30 35 40 Miles
0 2.5 5 10 15 20 25 30 35 40 45 50 55 60 Kilometers

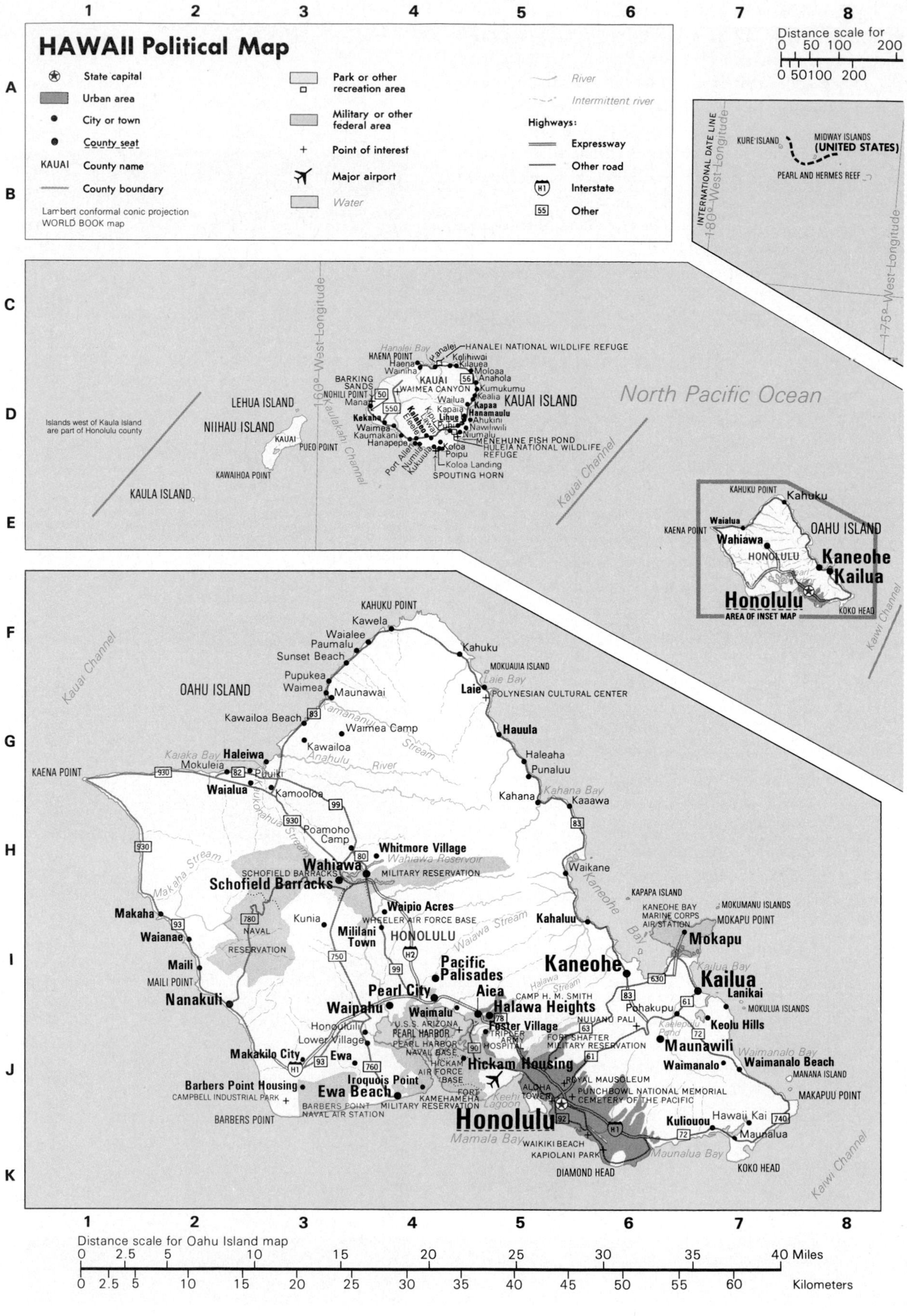

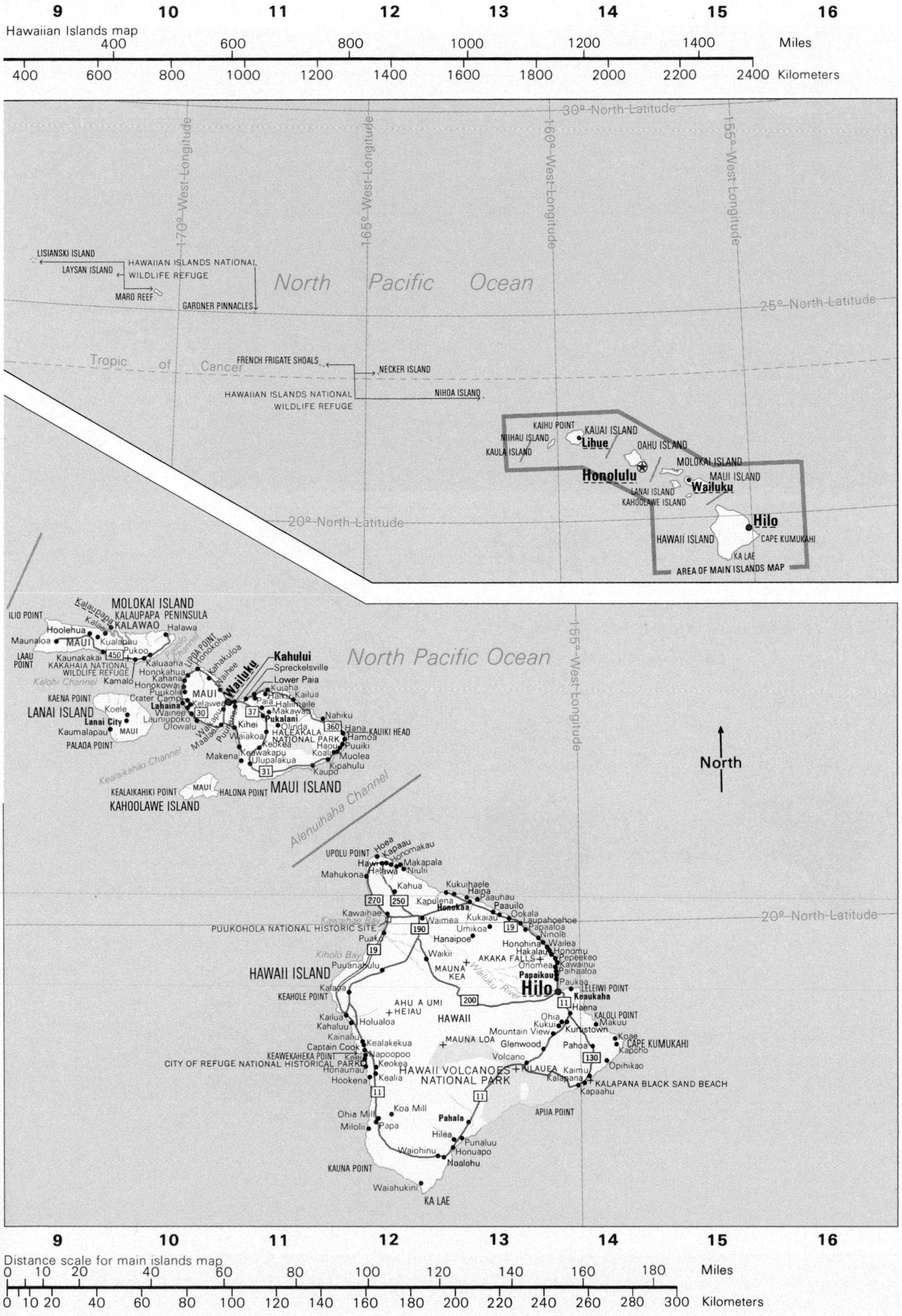

Hawaiian Islands map

9   10   11   12   13   14   15   16

400   600   800   1000   1200   1400   Miles
400   600   800   1000   1200   1400   1600   1800   2000   2200   2400   Kilometers

A

30° North-Latitude

B

STATE OF HAWAII
1959
UA MAU KE EA O KA AINA I KA PONO

Seal

Flag

LISIANSKI ISLAND
LAYSAN ISLAND
HAWAIIAN ISLANDS NATIONAL
WILDLIFE REFUGE
North   Pacific   Ocean

MARO REEF
GARDNER PINNACLES

25° North-Latitude

C

170° West-Longitude
165° West-Longitude
160° West-Longitude
155° West-Longitude

Tropic   of   Cancer
FRENCH FRIGATE SHOALS
NECKER ISLAND
HAWAIIAN ISLANDS NATIONAL
WILDLIFE REFUGE
NIHOA ISLAND

D

KAIHU POINT
NIIHAU ISLAND   KAUAI ISLAND
KAULA ISLAND   Lihue   OAHU ISLAND
MOLOKAI ISLAND
Honolulu   MAUI ISLAND
LANAI ISLAND   Wailuku
KAHOOLAWE ISLAND

20° North-Latitude
Hilo
HAWAII ISLAND   CAPE KUMUKAHI
KA LAE
AREA OF MAIN ISLANDS MAP

E

Bird: Nene (Hawaiian Goose)

F

ILIO POINT
MOLOKAI ISLAND
KALAUPAPA PENINSULA
Kalaupapa   KALAWAO
Kalae   Halawa
Hoolehua
Maunaloa   MAUI   Kualapu   Pukoo
Kaunakakai   Kaluaaha   ILIO POINT
KAKAHAIA NATIONAL   Honokahua   Honakuloa
WILDLIFE REFUGE   Kahana
LAAU   Kalohi Channel   Kamalo   Honokowai
POINT   Puukolii
Kahului
Spreckelsville
Lower Paia
MAUI   Waiehu   Kuiaha
LANAI ISLAND   Lanai City   Wailuku   Haiku Halimaile
Koele   MAUI   Pukalani
Launiupoko   Lahaina   Kelawea   Olinda   Makawao
Kaumalapau   MAUI   Waikapu   Kihei   HALEAKALA   Nahiku
PALAOA POINT   Waiakoa   NATIONAL PARK   Hana   KAUIKI HEAD
Olowalu   Keokea   Haou   Puuiki
North   Keawakapu   Koali
Makena   Ulupalakua   Kaupo   Kipahulu
Muolea
KEALAIKAHIKI POINT   MAUI   HALONA POINT   MAUI ISLAND
KAHOOLAWE ISLAND

North Pacific Ocean

155° West-Longitude

G

Kealaikahiki Channel

H

Alenuihaha Channel

UPOLU POINT   Hoea   Kapaau
Hawi   Honomakau
Mahukona   Halawa   Makapala
Niulii
Kukuihaele
Kahua   Haina
Kapulena   Paauhau
Kawaihae   Waimea   Kukaiau   Paauilo
270   250   Ookala
PUUKOHOLA NATIONAL HISTORIC SITE   Umikoa   Laupahoehoe
Kawaihae Bay   Ninole
Puako   190   Honohina   Wailea
19   Hanaipoe   Honomu
Kiholo Bay   Waikii   AKAKA FALLS   Pepeekeo
HAWAII ISLAND   MAUNA   Onomea   Kawainui
KEA   Papaikou   Pahaaloa
Puuanahulu   200   Wailuku River   Hilo   Paukaa
KEAHOLE POINT   AHU A UMI   LELEIWI POINT
Kalaoa   HEIAU   HAWAII   Keaukaha
Kailua   11   Haena
Kahaluu   Holualoa   KALOLI POINT
Kainaliu   Ohia   Makuu
Captain Cook   Kealakekua   Mountain View   Kukui   Kurtistown
KEAWEKAHEKA POINT   Napoopoo   Glenwood   Pahoa   Koae   CAPE KUMUKAHI
CITY OF REFUGE NATIONAL HISTORICAL PARK   Keokea   MAUNA LOA   Volcano   Kapoho
Honaunau   130   Keaau   Opihikao
Hookena   Kealia   HAWAII VOLCANOES   KILAUEA   Kaimu
NATIONAL PARK   Kalapana   KALAPANA BLACK SAND BEACH
Ohia Mill   Koa Mill   11   Kapaahu
Miloli   Papa   Pahala   APUA POINT
Hilea   Punaluu
Waiohinu   Honuapo
KAUNA POINT   Naalehu

Waiahukini
KA LAE

I

J

K

Flower: Hibiscus

9   10   11   12   13   14   15   16

Distance scale for main islands map
0 10 20   40   60   80   100   120   140   160   180   Miles
0 10 20   40   60   80   100   120   140   160   180   200   220   240   260   280   300   Kilometers

Canada

Alberta *262*
British Columbia *266*
Manitoba *270*
New Brunswick *274*
Newfoundland *276*
Nova Scotia *280*
Ontario *282*
Prince Edward Island *286*
Quebec *288*
Saskatchewan *292*
Northwest Territories *296*
Yukon Territory *297*

Huge, beautiful, and prosperous—Canada is all of these. Wonders of scenic loveliness and plentiful natural resources fill this exciting nation of rich cultural mix.

Striped bass, tuna, salmon, and trout lure sportspeople to the many coves of Nova Scotia, no part of which is more than 35 miles (56 kilometers) from the sea (facing page).

Wheat, Canada's main crop, travels through the Rockies via unit train from the Prairie Province of Alberta to eastern markets (above left).

Traditional parkas and modern snowmobiles help people face the below-zero temperatures at Repulse Bay in the Northwest Territories (above right).

The old European charm of Quebec City's stone houses and crooked streets help make it a major tourist center. Canada's oldest city, Quebec City was founded by Samuel de Champlain in 1608 (below left).

Alberta

Alberta is a wealthy province of Canada. It has huge deposits of oil, natural gas, and coal; fertile farmland; large, dense forests; and abundant wildlife. The home of five national parks, Alberta is also an area of majestic scenery.

This province is the largest oil-producing region in Canada and one of the largest in North America. Oil production and related industries have helped to give Alberta's people a higher standard of living than that of any other Canadians.

Alberta's fertile soil helps make it a wealthy agricultural region. In the plains area, golden wheat fields stretch as far as the eye can see. Wheat is the province's leading crop, although Alberta farmers grow more barley and rye than any other Canadian province or state in the United States. Large herds of cattle may also be seen grazing on huge ranches in this rolling plains region. Alberta is one of Canada's largest producers of beef cattle.

The region's abundant, thick forests contribute to another of the provinces leading industries: forestry. The forest industry operates mainly in the timberlands that cover a large part of the province north of the North Saskatchewan River and in the western foothills of the Canadian Rockies. Poplar, spruce, and pine are the most important trees to the industry. Most of the trees that are cut are used for lumber. Sawmills operate in the Peace River region and west of Red Deer. Edmonton and Grande Prairie have plywood mills.

Alberta is famous for its wealth of sunshine. The province has more hours of sunshine throughout the year than any other Canadian province. The unusually clear skies and the long hours of sunshine have given the province its nickname, *Sunny Alberta.*

The province was named Alberta in 1882 in honor of Princess Louise Caroline Alberta, a daughter of Queen Victoria and the wife of the Canadian governor general. Her first name was also given to what is now Alberta's most famous lake, Lake Louise. Edmonton is the province's capital and Calgary is its largest city.

Millions of tourists every year are attracted to Alberta by its beautiful scenery. Located on the province's southwestern border, the majestic Canadian Rockies contain snow-capped peaks, steep slopes,

With the towering Rockies in the background, sunbathers at a resort in Banff National Park relax amid scenic grandeur.

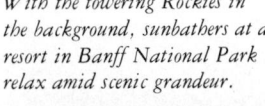

and bare, jagged rocks. The foothills are covered with thick forests of aspen, balsam fir, pine, poplar, and spruce. The rugged Rockies beckon to many mountain climbers, and even the most expert are challenged by the rough terrain. Fishers are attracted to the high lakes and mountain streams, while hunters venture into the mountains for wild goats and sheep. In winter, slopes near Banff and Jasper are open to entice skiing enthusiasts.

More land is devoted to national parks in Alberta than in any other province. Three of Alberta's five national parks are located in the Rockies. They are Banff, Jasper, and Waterton Lakes. These are the most popular of Alberta's tourist attractions. Other national parks include Wood Buffalo in northern Alberta and Elk Island east of Edmonton. In Banff National Park, visitors may view the incredible Victoria Glacier, which towers peacefully above beautiful Lake Louise. Waterton Lakes National Park lies within the Canadian-U.S. International Peace Park.

There are numerous hiking trails throughout Alberta. Each summer, many backpackers trek through the province. Less adventuresome tourists may stay at guest ranches, dude ranches, and farms in various parts of the province.

Alberta offers its tourists other interesting sites. The Badlands in the Red Deer River Valley are a popular attraction, where visitors may view strange but beautiful shapes that wind and water have worn into the rocky soil. The huge Columbia Ice Field is located between Banff and Jasper national parks. The field consists of large glaciers from the Ice Age. Tourists may ride in snowmobiles over Athabasca Glacier, part of the ice field.

Frank Slide is another fascinating point of interest. Located near the southwestern border of Alberta, it is the site of a 1903 landslide. At that time, the top of Turtle Mountain crashed down into Crowsnest Pass and buried part of the town of Frank.

At Fort Macleod, history buffs might enjoy visiting a full-size replica of the Alberta region's first North-West Mounted Police post. The post was established in 1874. Also in Fort Macleod is a museum dealing with the history of the Mounties.

In July of each year, Alberta's most popular annual event, the Calgary Stampede, takes place. This famous, 10-day rodeo features exciting chuck wagon races every evening.

Reliving Alberta's pioneer days, contestants in a chuck wagon competition furiously urge their horses on. These races are a favored event at the annual Calgary Stampede (above top).

In Edmonton, blessed with abundant sunshine, residents engage in a host of pastimes including lawn bowling (above bottom).

Alberta

Capital: Edmonton
Area: 255,285 sq. mi. (661,185 km²), including 6,485 sq. mi. (16,796 km²) of inland water; 4th in size among the provinces
Elevation: *Highest*—Mount Columbia, 12,294 ft. (3,747 m) above sea level: *lowest*—557 ft. (170 m) above sea level along the Slave River in northern Alberta
Entered the Dominion: Sept. 1, 1905, with Saskatchewan as the 8th and 9th provinces
Abbreviation: Alta.

Alberta's provincial coat of arms, adopted in 1907, shows the cross of St. George at the top. The cross symbolizes Alberta's historic association with Great Britain. The mountains and foothills in the center stand for the Canadian Rockies. The field of wheat at the bottom represents Alberta's chief agricultural crop. The provincial flag, adopted in 1968, has a reproduction of the provincial coat of arms.

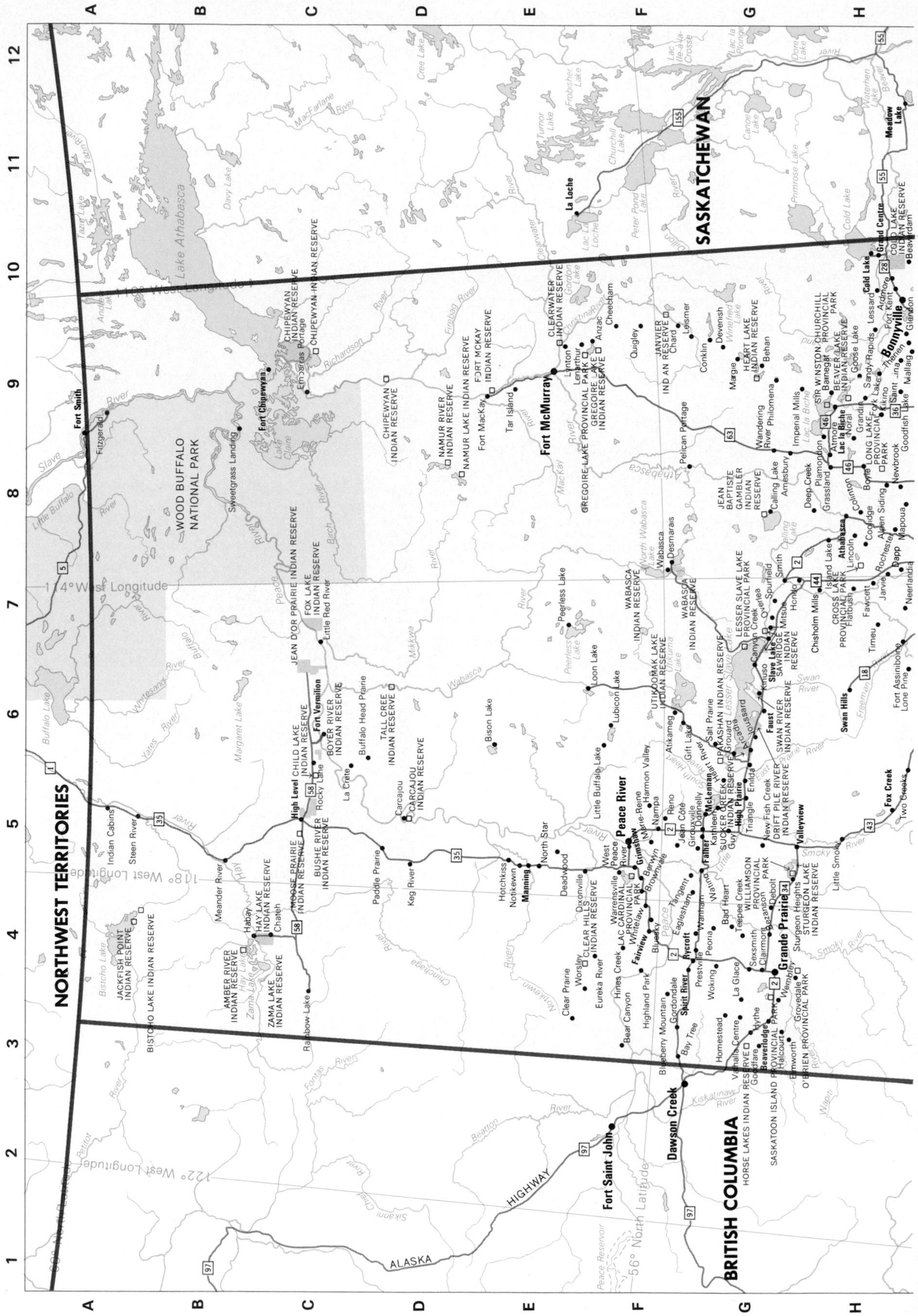

Coat of Arms

Flag

Flower: Wild Rose

ALBERTA Political Map

⊛	Provincial capital	+	Point of interest
•	City or town	✈	Major airport
	Provincial boundary		Water
	Urban area		River
	Park or other recreation area		Intermittent river
	Indian reserve		Reservoir under construction

Highways:
	Expressway		Other road
	Trans-Canada	
● 9	Other
15	Interstate
89	U.S.

Distance scale

Polyconic projection
WORLD BOOK map: © Field Enterprises Educational Corporation

North

BRITISH COLUMBIA

SASKATCHEWAN

MONTANA

CANADA
UNITED STATES

Edmonton

Calgary

Red Deer

Lethbridge

Medicine Hat

BANFF NATIONAL PARK

JASPER NATIONAL PARK

52° North Latitude

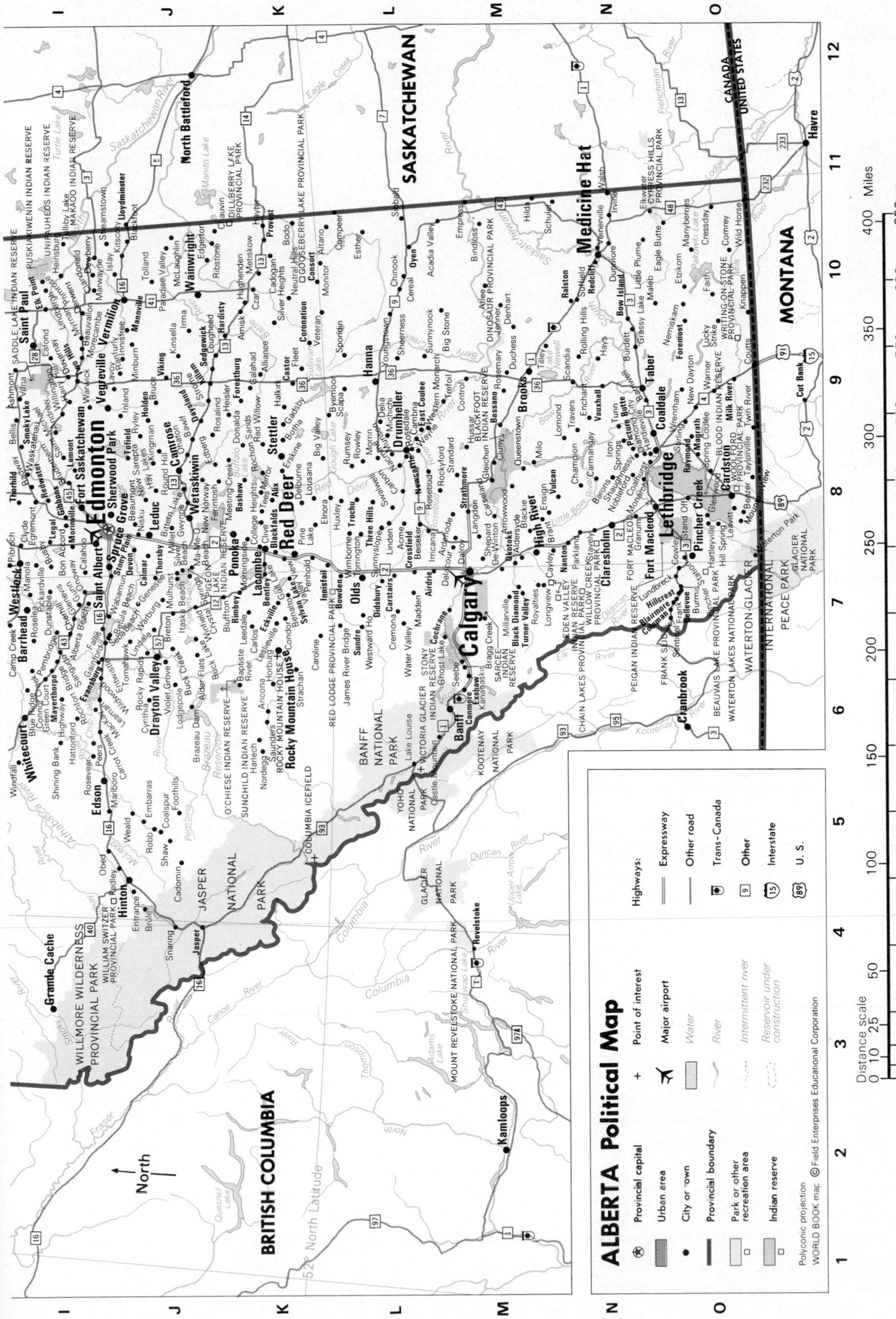

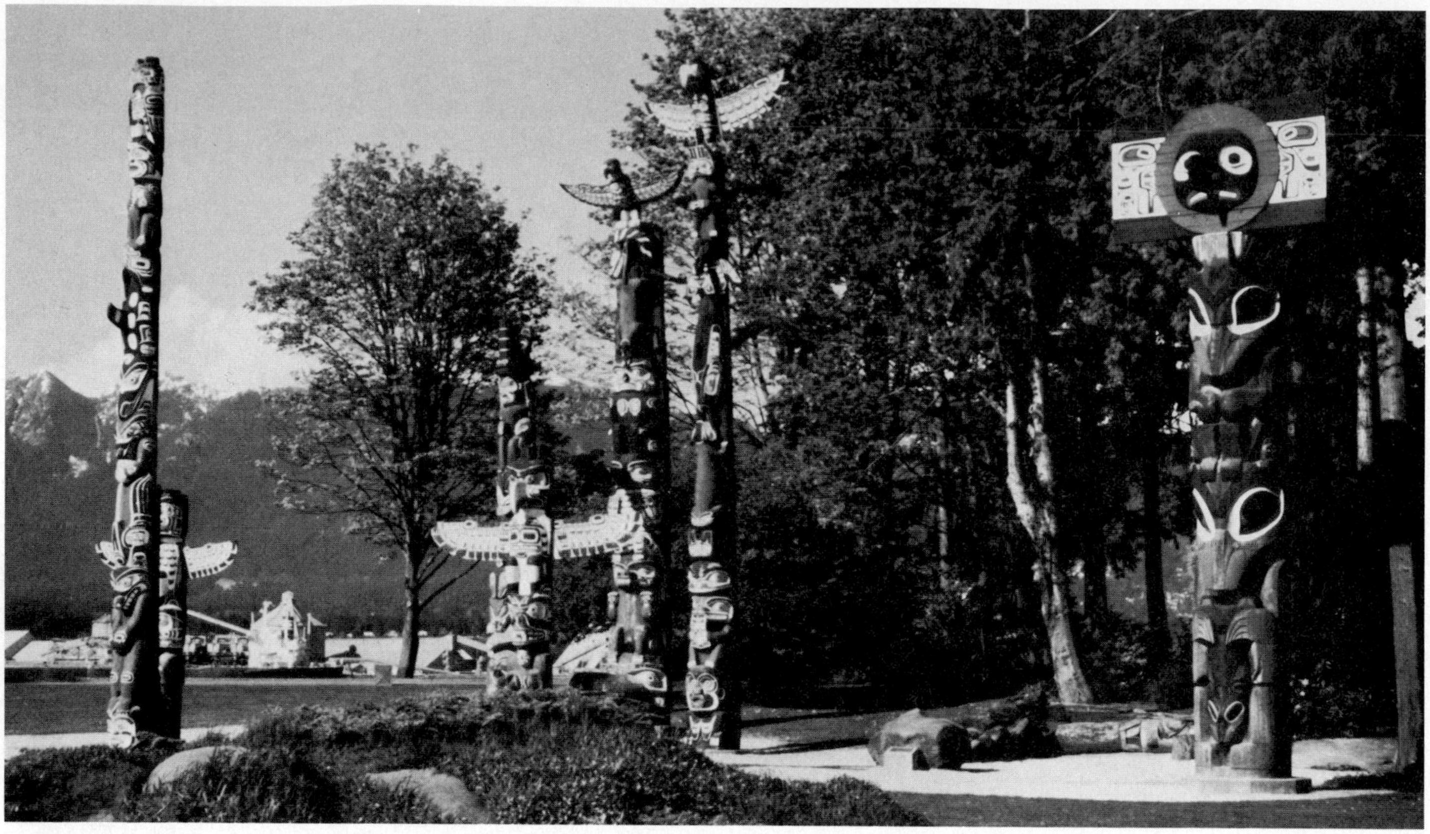

Indians of the Pacific Northwest carved their clan emblems onto wooden totem poles. One of the finest collections of these poles is in Victoria.

British Columbia

British Columbia, the rugged Canadian province that lies along the Pacific Ocean, is almost covered by the mountain mass called the Cordillera. Steep, forested peaks rise up from the shore of the southern coastline, and narrow arms of the sea reach far inland, winding among the mountain ranges. In the north, a narrow strip of Alaska separates the province from the Pacific.

Many of the jewel-like islands that dot the province's western coast are part of a largely submerged mountain range called the Insular Mountains. The Queen Charlotte Islands, 60 miles (97 kilometers) from mid-mainland, are part of this range, as is Vancouver Island, near the southwestern coast.

Mount Fairweather, the highest point in British Columbia, is part of the Coast Mountains. The Canadian Rockies form part of the Eastern Mountains.

The people of British Columbia often call their province by its initials, "B.C." Many have ancestors who came from Great Britain. Some of the towns and streets are named for places in England and for members of Great Britain's royal families.

The southwest corner of British Columbia has a mild climate, where farmers raise dairy cattle and vegetables. Victoria, the province's capital, and Vancouver, its largest city, are located here.

Victoria is a haven for shoppers searching for imported British goods and antiques. Horse-drawn carriages carry sightseers on tours of the city. Called "a bit of old England," Victoria has winding streets, trim gardens, and stone parliament buildings.

Thunderbird Park in Victoria contains many examples of Indian art. Its collection of carvings, together with those in the Provincial Museum, form the finest group of totem poles in existence. The collection contains examples of carvings by the Bella Coola, Haida, Nootka, Salish, and Tsimshian Indians.

Vancouver is the busiest port on the Pacific Coast of North America. Called *Canada's Gateway to the Pacific,* it lies on the southern shore of Burrard Inlet. The city's beautiful setting, near the Coast Mountains and the ocean, attracts visitors year-round. The protective mountains and warm winds blowing in from the Pacific help provide a surprisingly mild climate for a city so far north. Ships can use the port of Vancouver year-round because the harbor's waters never freeze.

Queen Elizabeth Park is located on a hill in Vancouver. On clear days, it offers visitors a beautiful view of the city. The park has an arboretum that includes a lovely sunken garden. Stanley Park, also in this city, is an area of forests, formal gardens, and picnic grounds.

Vancouver's Pacific National Exhibition is held in late August and early September each year. It is famous as the largest fair in western Canada. The fair features agricultural and industrial displays and offers many kinds of entertainment.

British Columbia has a colorful frontier history, and the pioneer spirit is still alive today. Although more than half of all British Columbians live in the Vancouver-Victoria region, present-day pioneers are building towns in several areas that until recently had remained unsettled. Roads and railroads are being built to reach distant parts inland to the north. Huge dams and power projects are also being constructed.

The large inland area, frequently called the interior, has the high mountains and rugged plateaus characteristic of the province. Cold winds from the Yukon Territory make the area severely cold in the winter. The winter weather and the rugged terrain have made transportation and settlement of the interior difficult.

It is precisely this rugged terrain, however, that is also one of the province's major attractions. Campers and hikers enjoy the unspoiled wilderness of the interior. Hunters travel inland in search of deer, moose, and game birds. Fishing enthusiasts venture into the interior to fish in the clear mountain lakes and streams.

British Columbia offers visitors spectacular scenic beauty, making it a favorite vacation spot for people from all parts of Canada and the United States. Several highways offer motorists splendid views of mountains, forests, lakes, and streams. Ships and ferries carry passengers along colorful coastal routes among forested islands, stopping at many of the coastal cities. The Inside Passage to Alaska is one of the most scenic water routes in the world. It extends from Seattle, Washington, and Vancouver to Prince Rupert, then on to Juneau and other Alaskan ports. Tourists may make the trip up the Inside Passage to Alaska on ferryliners.

Motorists may also travel the Historic Cariboo Highway through rugged canyon country to Barkerville in the Cariboo Mountains. Barkerville is a restored gold rush town with a museum that features items from the area's gold rush days. Fort Steele, located near Cranbrook, is a reconstruction of a town in the East Kootenay District in the 1890's. Featured here are a museum and a steam railroad.

Visitors to one of Vancouver Island's ornamental gardens are prepared for a rainstorm. The island's abundant rainfall and moderate temperatures sustain a profusion of flowers.

Neither nature seekers nor industry is discouraged by British Columbia's rugged terrain.

British Columbia

Capital: Victoria
Area: 366,255 sq. mi. (948,596 km^2), including 6,976 sq. mi. (18,068 km^2) of inland water; 3rd in size among the provinces
Elevation: *Highest*—Mount Fairweather, 15,300 ft. (4,663 m) above sea level; *lowest*—sea level along the coast
Entered the Dominion: July 20, 1871, the 6th province
Abbreviation: B.C.
Motto: *Splendor sine Occasu* (Splendor Without Diminishment)

British Columbia's provincial coat of arms was granted by royal warrant in 1906. The crown and the Union Jack show the province's link with Great Britain. The setting sun indicates that British Columbia is the westernmost Canadian province. An American elk, or Wapiti, and a big horned sheep support the shield. Both are familiar animals of British Columbia. The provincial flag, adopted in 1960, has a reproduction of the shield in the coat of arms.

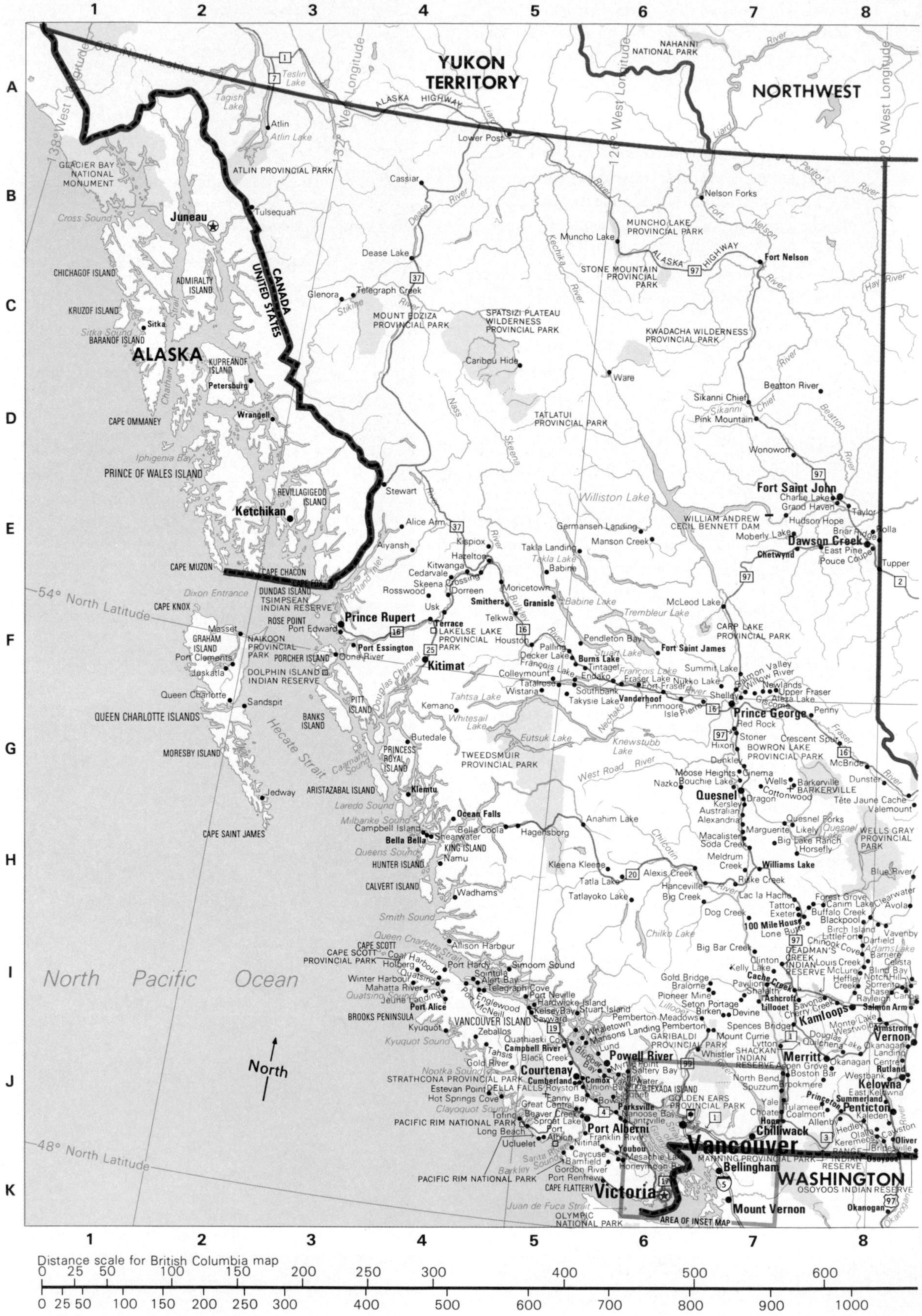

Coat of Arms

Flag

Flower: Flowering Dogwood

BRITISH COLUMBIA
Political Map

★	Provincial or state capital		Water
	Urban area in British Columbia	～	River
	Urban area outside British Columbia		Highways:
●	City or town	═══	Expressway
━━━	Provincial boundary	───	Other road
	Park or other recreation area	🛡	Trans-Canada
	Indian reserve	97	Autoroute
+	Point of interest	5	Interstate
✈	Major airport	2	U.S.

Transverse mercator projection
WORLD BOOK map

Distance scale for inset map

0 5 10 20 30 40 50 60 70 80 90 100 Miles

0 5 10 20 30 40 50 60 70 80 90 100 110 120 130 140 150 Kilometers

700 800 900 Miles

1100 1200 1300 1400 Kilometers

TERRITORIES
ALBERTA
WOOD BUFFALO NATIONAL PARK
GARIBALDI PROVINCIAL PARK
WASHINGTON
Vancouver
Victoria
Nanaimo
Chilliwack
Bellingham
SASKATCHEWAN
Saskatoon
North Battleford
Lloydminster
Wetaskiwin
Red Deer
Calgary
Medicine Hat
Lethbridge
IDAHO
MONTANA
Kalispell

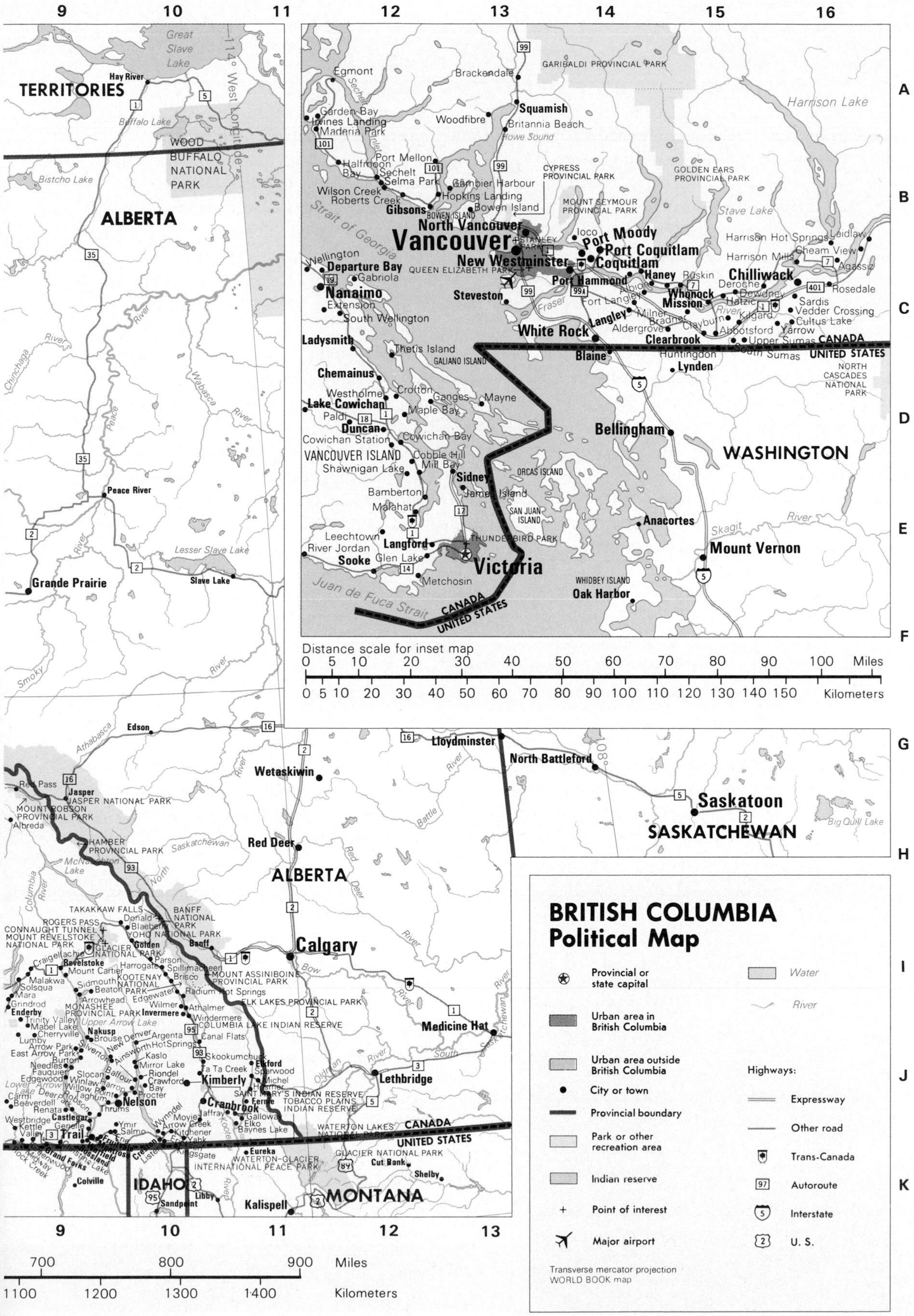

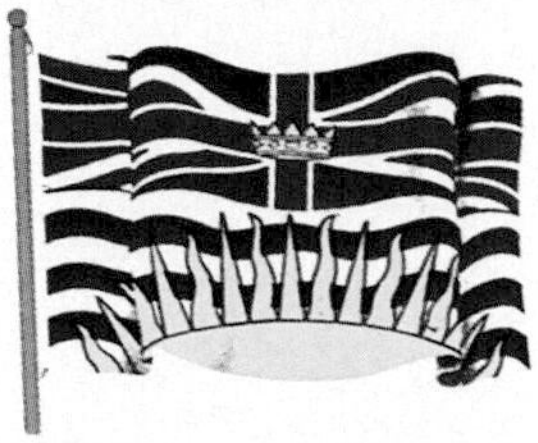

Manitoba

Manitoba, one of Canada's Prairie Provinces, is midway between the Atlantic and Pacific oceans. Winnipeg, its capital and largest city, is the main transportation center linking eastern and western Canada. It is also the province's main industrial center.

The prairie that rolls across Manitoba's southern section has some of the area's richest farmland. Vast fields of wheat have been growing in the province since the early 1800's, when Irish and Scottish farmers began breaking up the plains. They planted wheat in the fertile soil of the Red River Valley and soon began exporting their valuable crop. Before long, Manitoba wheat became famous for its high quality. Today the province has about 35,000 farms, and Manitoba farmers grow barley, rye, flaxseed, mustard seed, rapeseed, and sunflower in addition to wheat.

Large herds of beef cattle graze in pastures on the plains. The raising of beef cattle has become one of Manitoba's most valuable agricultural activities. Manitoba farmers also raise dairy cattle, hogs, and poultry.

Food processing is Manitoba's major industry. Large meat-packing plants are located in cities in the plains area. Winnipeg has the largest stockyard in Canada. Large flour mills are located in Steinbach, Virden, and Winnipeg.

Manitoba is more than a rich farming area. It is also a province of great mineral wealth. Nickel is the most valuable mineral mined. In the mid-1950's, a huge nickel deposit was found in the Mystery Lake-Moak Lake area of north-central Manitoba. Due to the discovery, a mining center called Thompson developed. Other mines in the area produce copper, zinc, cobalt, gold, and silver.

Large, dense forests are located in the southern part of Manitoba. Lumberjacks cut balsam, fir, spruce, and many other kinds of trees from the forests. The trees provide wood for the province's furniture, lumber, and paper industries.

Manitoba has many rivers and lakes. Three of the lakes are so large that they are often called the *Great Lakes of Manitoba.* Lake Winnipeg is the largest body of water entirely within any province or state. It covers 9,398 square miles (24,341 square kilometers). Lake Winnipegosis and Lake Manitoba complete the trio.

The many rivers and lakes of Manitoba have helped to make the province a desirable vacationland. Tourists enjoy boating and swimming at popular summer resorts on the area's beautiful lakes. People who like to fish find a never-ending supply of bass, pike, and trout. Hunters find excellent hunting ground in the dense forests of Manitoba, where there are elk, caribou, moose, and many small game animals. Ducks, geese, and partridges are plentiful in the marshes and prairies.

In the 1600's fur trapping and trading were important in the province. English fur traders traveled into Manitoba from the Hudson Bay. French-Canadian traders went westward from Quebec during the 1700's, paddling their canoes up Manitoba's rivers and traveling through unexplored forests and plains. They traded with the Indians and built forts and trading posts.

Today, much of the fur industry in Manitoba is agricultural in nature. Southern Manitoba has many fur farms, almost all of which raise minks. A great deal of the province's fur production, however, still comes from trapping. Muskrat is the most common fur produced by trappers.

Manitoba offers visitors a multitude of interesting sites and activities. Tourists may visit old forts and trading posts of the fur-trading days. In Winnipeg, the Basilica of St. Boniface, probably the most beautiful cathedral in western Canada, stands on the site of the first Roman Catholic church in western Canada. Many people who helped make Manitoba history are buried in the churchyard.

Mushrooming at the junction of the Assiniboine and Red rivers, modern Winnipeg is a major Canadian cultural and transportation center.

Tourists in Manitoba may visit many other sites reminiscent of the area's colorful history. Fort Prince of Wales near Churchill overlooks Hudson Bay. It contains the remains of the northernmost fortress in North America. The stone fortress was built by the Hudson's Bay Company between 1733 and 1770. Lower Fort Garry, the only stone fur-trading fort in Canada still standing complete, is located 20 miles (32 kilometers) north of Winnipeg. It was built on the Red River during the 1830's by the Hudson's Bay Company. Norway House stands at the northern end of Lake Winnipeg. This old Hudson's Bay Company post, built in 1826, contains many articles from fur-trading days. The Pas is a historic northern crossroads town northwest of Cedar Lake. Its name came from the Cree Indian word *opas,* which means "narrows."

The World Championship Dog Derby, a dog-sled race over snow, is probably Manitoba's most outstanding annual event. It is part of the famous Trappers' Festival that is held in The Pas each February.

In northern Manitoba, tilled fields bring forth large harvests of oil-bearing rapeseed (above).

A bronze tribute at Memorial Park in Winnipeg honors the fur traders and missionaries who battled adversities to settle the region (left).

Manitoba

Capital: Winnipeg
Area: 251,000 sq. mi. (650,087 km²), including 39,225 sq. mi. (101,592 km²) of inland water; 6th in size among the provinces .
Elevation: *Highest*—Baldy Mountain, 2,729 ft. (832 m) above sea level; *lowest*—sea level, along Hudson Bay
Entered the Dominion: July 15, 1870, the 5th province
Abbreviation: Man.

Manitoba's provincial coat of arms was adopted in 1870. The buffalo symbolizes the position of Manitoba as a Prairie Province and the importance of the Red River buffalo in the province's history. The cross of St. George represents Manitoba's bond with Great Britain. The provincial flag, adopted in 1965, has a reproduction of Manitoba's coat of arms and the British Union Jack.

MANITOBA Political Map

Symbol	Description
✪	Provincial capital
■	Urban area
●	City or town
▬	Provincial boundary
	Park or other recreation area
	Indian reserve
+	Point of interest
	Water
┼┼┼	Canal
∿	River

Highways:
Expressway
Other road
Trans-Canada
11 Autoroute
1 Other
29 Interstate
83 U.S.

For an enlarged map of southern Manitoba see the map on the opposite page.
Albers conic projection

Distance scale for Manitoba map
0 25 50 100 150 200 250 300 350 400 450 Miles
0 25 50 100 150 200 250 300 350 400 450 500 550 600 650 700 750 Kilometers

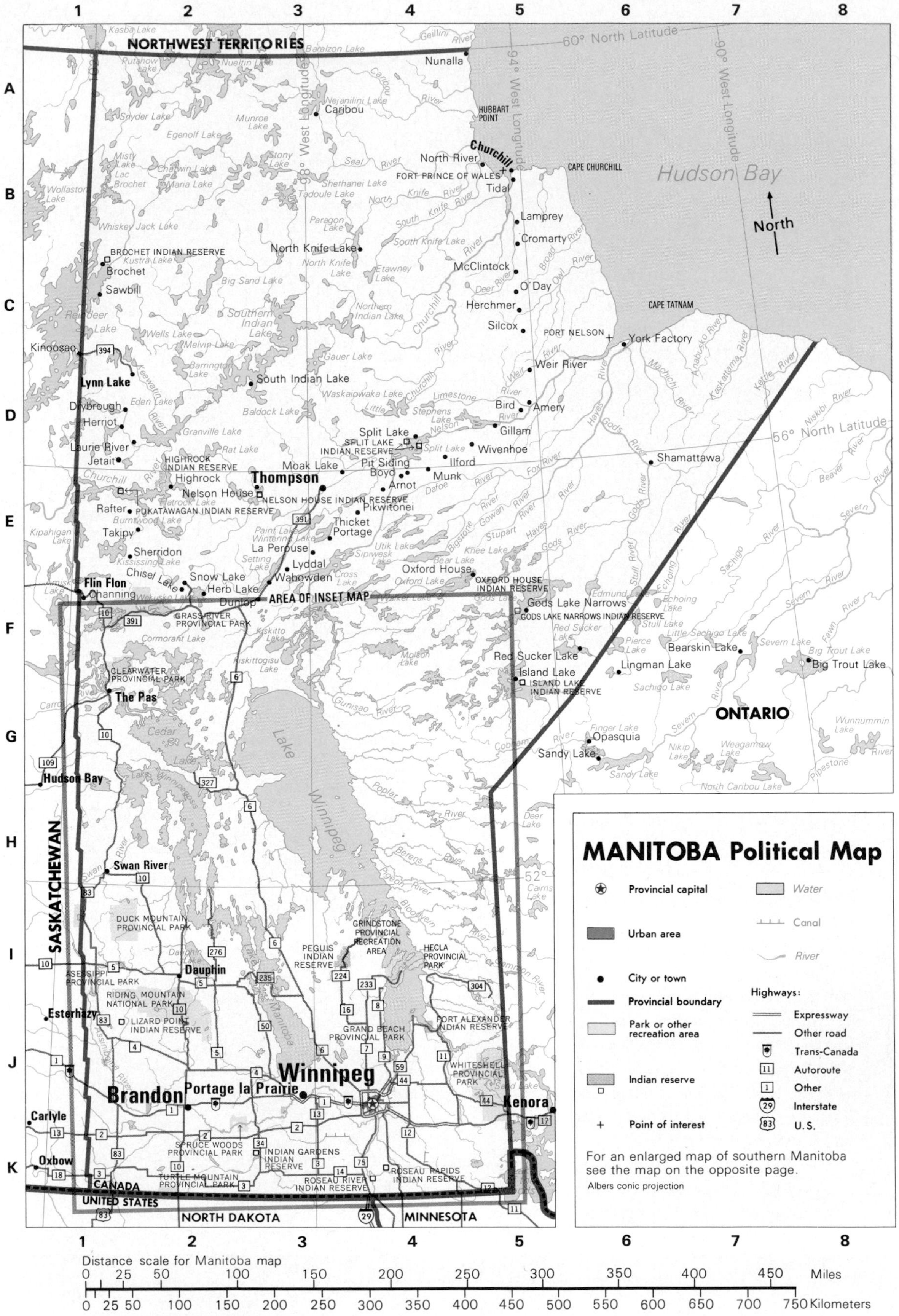

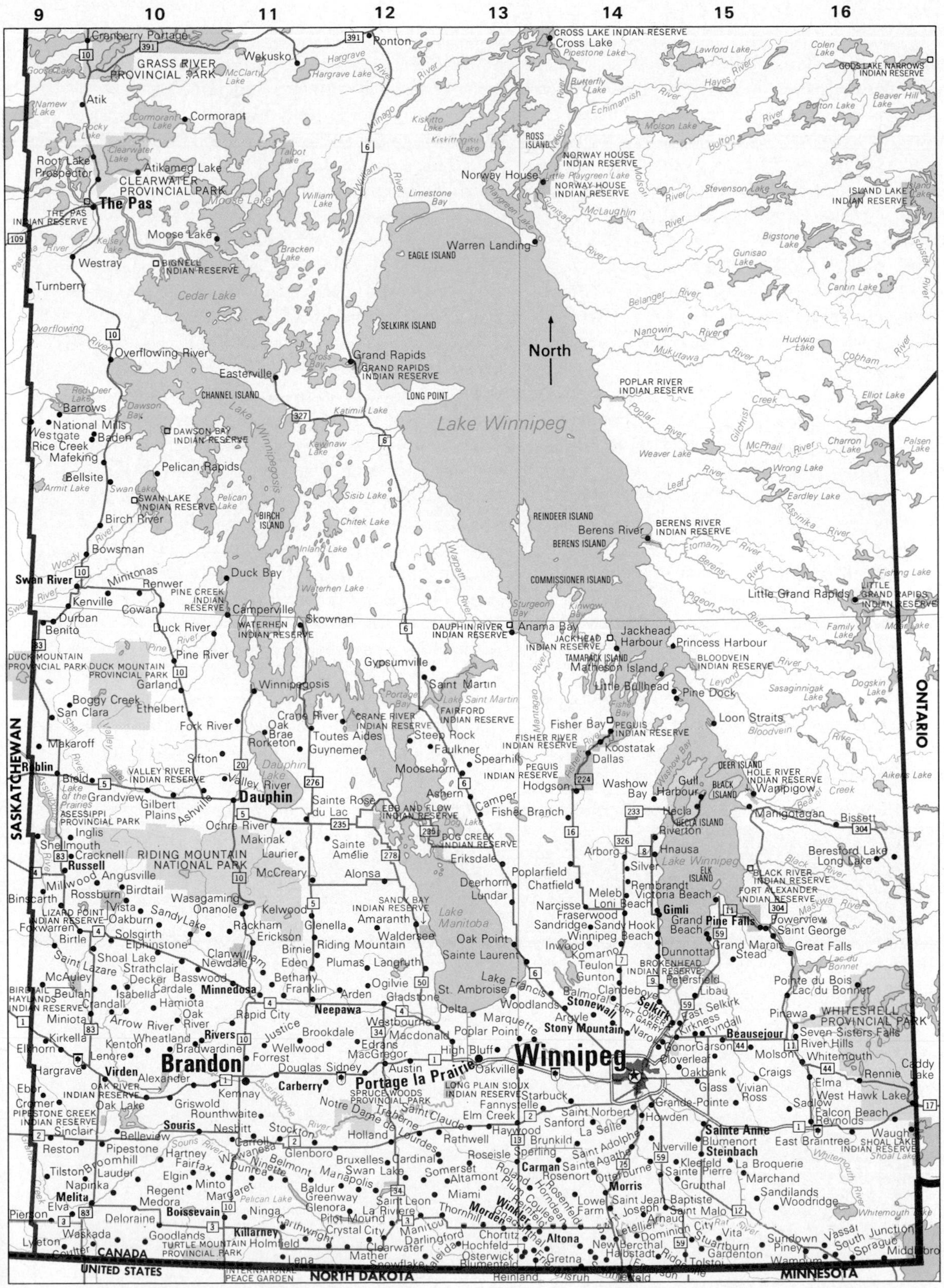

Distance scale for Southern Manitoba map

0	20	40	60	80	100	125	150	175	200	225	250 Miles	275			
0	20	40	60	80	100	125	150	175	200	225	250	275	300	325	350

375, 400 Kilometers 450

Coat of Arms

Flag

Flower: Pasqueflower

Capital: Fredericton
Area: 28,354 sq. mi. (73,437 km²), including 519 sq. mi. (1,344 km²) of inland water; 8th in size among the provinces
Elevation: *Highest*—Mount Carleton, 2,690 ft. (820 m) above sea level; *lowest*—sea level, along the Atlantic coast
Entered the Dominion: July 1, 1867, one of the original four provinces
Abbreviation: N.B.
Motto: *Spem Reduxit* (Hope Was Restored)

New Brunswick's provincial coat of arms, adopted in 1868, shows a crown symbolizing the province's ties with Canada. The British lion represents New Brunswick's link with Great Britain. The galley stands for the province's early shipbuilding industry. The provincial flag, adopted in 1965, has an adaptation of the coat of arms.

New Brunswick

Often called the *Picture Province,* New Brunswick is an area of great natural beauty. Clear rivers rush down steep hills and cut through deep valleys. Waterfalls are abundant throughout the province. The rocks at Hopewell Cape are carved into fantastic forms by the tides from the Bay of Fundy. Dense, green forests also cover much of the land in this province.

Logs cut from these forests provide New Brunswick with two of its major industries: lumber and paper products. The province also has rich farmland. Farmers produce large crops of potatoes and process many dairy products. The Bay of Fundy and the Gulf of St. Lawrence provide commercial fishing fleets with large numbers of crab and herring. Lobsters, also, are an important New Brunswick catch.

New Brunswick was one of the original provinces of Canada. Most of its first settlers were American colonists who had remained loyal to England during the American Revolution. The settlers, called loyalists, began moving into New Brunswick in 1783. The people of New Brunswick celebrate the landing of the loyalists in St. John on May 18 each year. Loyalist House, a popular tourist site, was built in St. John between 1810 and 1817 by David Merritt. It has been restored and is open to the public.

Kings Landing Historical Settlement in Prince William is another popular historical point of interest. This restored village shows how people in the area lived during the 1800's. It was established after the American Revolution by the Kings American Dragoons, a unit of the Royal Provincial Army that aided the British Army during the war.

Each year thousands of tourists visit New Brunswick. They enjoy swimming and boating near the shores or relaxing on the beaches. Campobello, Deer, and Grand Manan islands in the Bay of Fundy are particularly fine spots for these activities. Tourists can also take advantage of the many camping facilities offered in the dense forests. Fishing enthusiasts will find paradise in New Brunswick, one of the finest fishing areas in North America.

Visitors to New Brunswick can tour many interesting sites. One of the most unusual is Magnetic Hill near Moncton. Magnetic Hill offers a remarkable optical illusion. An automobile, left in neutral at what seems to be the bottom of the hill, will appear to roll uphill to the top. Roosevelt Campobello International Park, located on Campobello Island, is the site of President Franklin D. Roosevelt's summer home. Covered Bridge, believed to be the longest in the world, crosses St. John River in Hartland. St. John, New Brunswick's largest city and chief industrial and shipping center, is also an interesting stopping point, along with Fredricton, the province capital.

This sawmill of the 1800's at Kings Landing Historical Settlement depended only on river power to slice logs into lumber.

Coat of Arms

Flag

Flower: Purple Violet

NEW BRUNSWICK
Political Map
Provincial capital
Major airport
Urban area
Water
City or town
River
County seat
Highways:
KENT County name
County boundary
Expressway
Other road
Provincial boundary
Trans - Canada
Park or other recreation area
Autoroute
Indian reserve
Interstate
U. S.
Point of interest
Other
Lambert conformal conic projection
WORLD BOOK map
North
QUEBEC
MAINE
PRINCE EDWARD ISLAND
NOVA SCOTIA
ANTICOSTI ISLAND
Saint Lawrence River
Gaspé Passage
GASPÉ PENINSULA
FORILLON NATIONAL PARK
Gaspé
Cap-Chat
CAP D'ESPOIR
Chandler
Rimouski
Campbellton
Dalhousie
Atholville
Chaleur Bay
MISCOU ISLAND
Miscou Centre
Pigeon Hill
Caraquet
Shippegan
Bathurst
Tracadie
Gulf of Saint Lawrence
Edmundston
Madawaska
Saint-Quentin
MADAWASKA
RESTIGOUCHE
GLOUCESTER
MOUNT CARLETON PROVINCIAL PARK
VICTORIA
Grand Falls
BIG HOLE TRACT INDIAN RESERVE
Newcastle
Chatham
Chatham Head
Nelson-Miramichi
NORTHUMBERLAND
PORTAGE ISLAND NATIONAL WILDLIFE AREA
POINT ESCUMINAC
KOUCHIBOUGUAC NATIONAL PARK
TOBIQUE INDIAN RESERVE
Perth-Andover
Presque Isle
CARLETON
Richibucto
Buctouche
KENT
Summerside
Woodstock
Houlton
YORK
SUNBURY
Chipman
Moncton
Shediac
Dieppe
Riverview
WESTMORLAND
Cap-Pelé
Fredericton
Oromocto
Minto
Sussex
KINGS
QUEENS
Petitcodiac
ALBERT
Sackville
Amherst
FUNDY NATIONAL PARK
Hampton
Saint John East
Saint John
CHARLOTTE
Saint Stephen
Calais
Saint Andrews
McAdam
Millinocket
Old Town
Bangor
DEER ISLAND
ROOSEVELT CAMPOBELLO INTERNATIONAL PARK
GRAND MANAN ISLAND
Bay of Fundy
Minas Channel
CAPE SPLIT
ILE HAUTE
Kentville
48° North Latitude
46°
66° West Longitude
64° West Longitude
68° West Longitude
Distance scale
Miles
Kilometers
SPEM · REDUXIT

With an outlet to the sea and a sheltered harbor, this hamlet in Newfoundland is a haven for fishing crews and their boats.

Newfoundland

The province of Newfoundland includes the island of Newfoundland and the coast of Labrador, which is part of the Canadian mainland. St. John's, one of the oldest communities in North America, is Newfoundland's capital and largest city.

Newfoundland has a long history. Vikings are thought to have established settlements on the island as early as A.D. 1000. Archaeologists have discovered the ruins of a Viking settlement on the northern tip of the island near St. Anthony. The village, L'Anse aux Meadows, dates to about A.D. 1000. Port au Choix, on the Great Northern Peninsula, is the site of an Indian burial ground that is 4,000 years old.

English settlement of Newfoundland began after John Cabot, an Italian who was exploring for England in 1497, took news of the rich fishing ground near Newfoundland back to Europe. Fishermen were attracted to the waters surrounding the island and many of them settled there.

Most of the people who live in Newfoundland today are descendants of these early fishermen. They have kept alive much of the language and many of the customs of their forefathers.

The waters around Newfoundland are still rich fishing grounds, and fishing is one of the province's major industries. Crews catch cod, salmon, bluefin tuna, flounder, herring, sole, and lobster along Newfoundland's shores. Processors prepare salted and frozen fish and pack live lobsters for shipment to other countries. Fishing crews from as far away as Europe and Japan fish on Newfoundland's Grand Banks, an underwater plateau.

The climate in Newfoundland is generally cool because of Arctic winds and ocean currents. There are many storms, and fog often covers the coast. Because of this, the people of Newfoundland have been made hardy by their struggle to earn a living from the sea.

Mining, however, is the province's chief source of income. The area has some of the world's largest iron-ore deposits, making Newfoundland Canada's leading producer of this mineral. Open pit iron ore mines dot Labrador's landscape. One of the largest

Signal Hill near St. John's saw the last battle of the French and Indian War and the first reception of a transatlantic wireless telegraph message.

of these is located in the border town known in Labrador as Knob Lake. At Buchans near Red Indian Lake, mines produce gold, silver, lead, copper, and zinc.

Dense forests cover much of the province of Newfoundland. The forests include trees such as aspen, birch, larch, pine, white spruce, and balsam fir. Balsam fir and spruce are the woods most used in Newfoundland's pulp and paper industry. Corner Brook in western Newfoundland is the site of one of the world's largest pulp and paper mills. Another mill is located at Grand Falls, and a newsprint plant is in Stephenville.

Much of Newfoundland's landscape is rugged, particularly its rocky coast. Almost all of the province's residents live near the sea. Hundreds of remote fishing villages are nestled in small, sheltered bays along the jagged coast. Some of these cozy towns have unusual names such as Dragon Bay, Blow-Me-Down, and Little Heart's Ease. The names alone reveal the towns' quaint beauty.

Tourists are attracted to Newfoundland by a variety of sights and activities. The many bays and inlets along the island's coast provide colorful scenes for photographers and artists. One of the most scenic areas is Port de Grave on Conception Bay. Visitors also enjoy some of the province's well-known fishing communities, where enthusiasts can fish in the coastal waters. Guides are available to lead sportspeople inland to hunt bears, caribou, and moose, or to fish for salmon and trout.

Tourists may take boat trips from Witless Bay, a small fishing village 20 miles (32 kilometers) south of St. John's, to view sea-bird nesting colonies on offshore islands, or they may visit Placentia on the west coast of the Avalon Peninsula. Placentia was established by the French in 1662. In 1941, Prime Minister Winston Churchill and President Franklin D. Roosevelt met on a warship near Placentia and drew up the Atlantic Charter. Another interesting sight in Newfoundland is Gander Airport, once a strategic terminal for air travel between North America and Europe. The airport now contains an exhibit of transatlantic aviation.

On the west coast of Newfoundland lies Gros Morne National Park, while Terra Nova National Park is located on the eastern shore. Three of the province's national historic parks and sites are Castle Hill near Placentia, and, near St. John's, Cape Spear and Signal Hill. Castle Hill contains French and British fortifications of the 1700's. Cape Spear is a lighthouse marking Canada's most easterly point. Signal Hill is the site of the last battle of the French and Indian War (1754–1763) and the point where, in 1901, the first transatlantic wireless telegraph message was received.

Newfoundland

Capital: St. John's
Area: 156,185 sq. mi.
(404,517 km²); the island of
Newfoundland, 43,359 sq.
mi. (112,299 km²); Lab-
rador, 112,826 sq. mi.
(292,218 km²); 7th in size
among the provinces
Elevation: *Highest*—Mont
d'Iberville, 5,400 ft. (1,646
m) above sea level; *lowest*—
sea level
Entered the Dominion:
March 31, 1949, the 10th
province
Abbreviation: Nfld.
Motto: *Quaerite Prime Regnum
Dei* (Seek Ye First the Kingdom of God)
Song: "The Ode to Newfoundland"

*Newfoundland's provincial coat
of arms shows a shield with
two lions and two unicorns representing the province's ties to
Great Britain. Indians symbolize Newfoundland's first inhabitants. King Charles I of
England granted the coat of
arms in 1638. The British
Union Jack was adopted as the
provincial flag in 1952.*

NEWFOUNDLAND Political Map

- ✦ Provincial capital
- • City or town
- Provincial boundary
- Park or other recreation area
- Forest or other conservation area
- ✈ Major airport
- Water
- River
- Highways:
  - Road
  - ⊙ Trans-Canada
  - 73 Autoroute

Lambert conformal conic projection
WORLD BOOK map

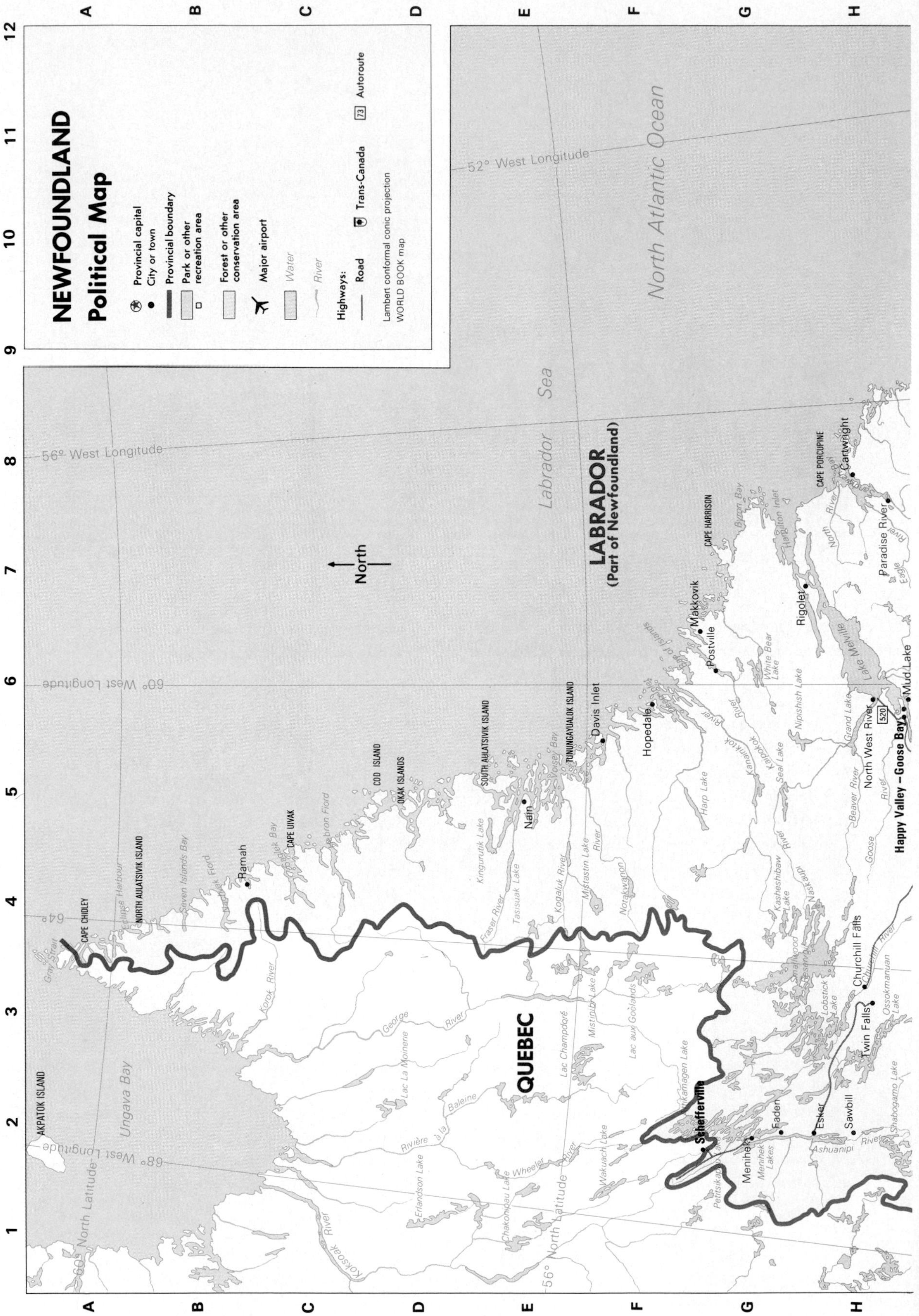

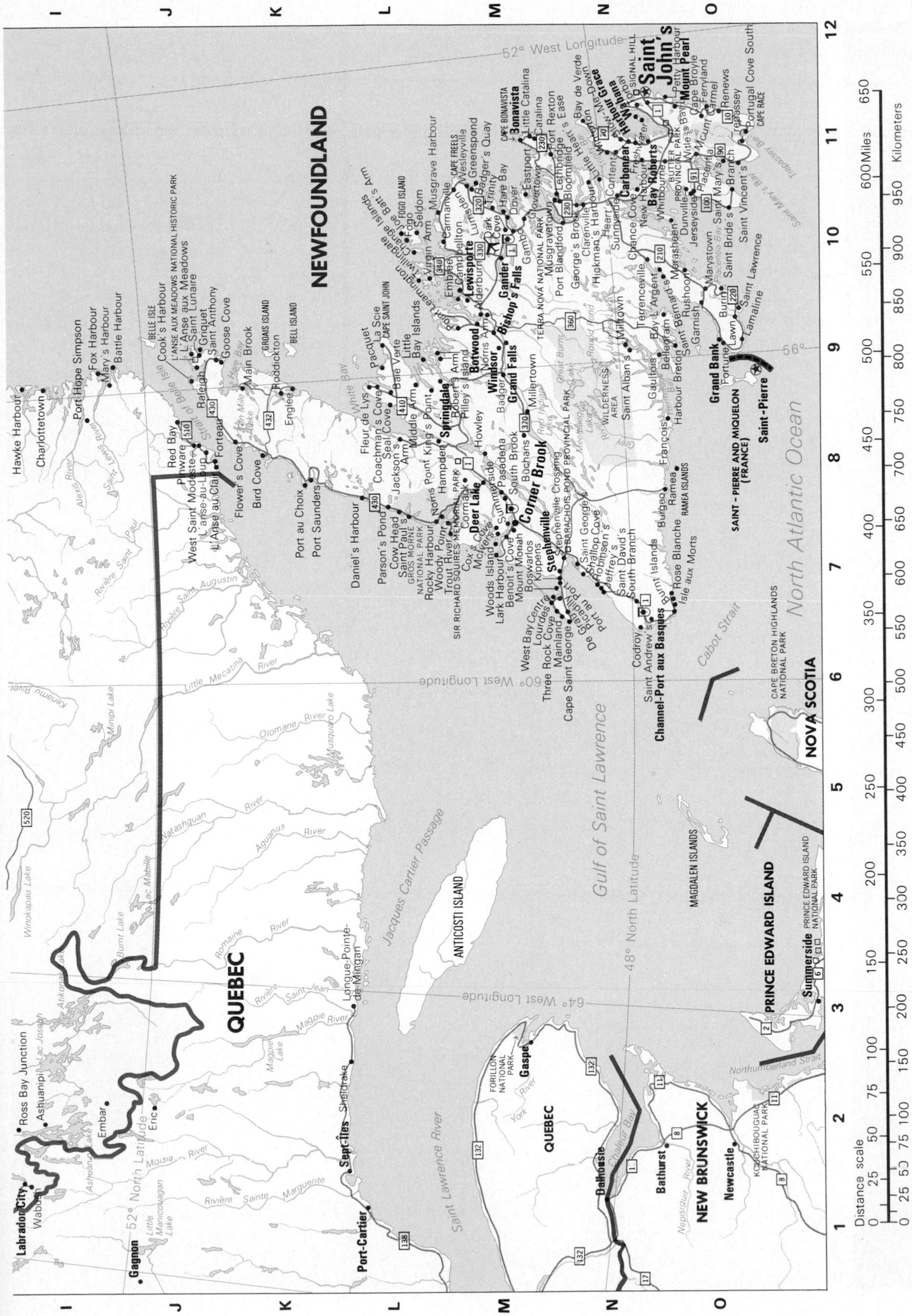

Coat of Arms

Flag

Flower: Pitcher Plant

NEWFOUNDLAND
QUEBEC
NEW BRUNSWICK
NOVA SCOTIA
PRINCE EDWARD ISLAND
ANTICOSTI ISLAND
MAGDALEN ISLANDS
SAINT - PIERRE AND MIQUELON (FRANCE)
Saint-Pierre
Gulf of Saint Lawrence
North Atlantic Ocean
Cabot Strait
Jacques Cartier Passage
Saint Lawrence River
Northumberland Strait
52° West Longitude
60° West Longitude
64° West Longitude
48° North Latitude
52° North Latitude
56°
Saint John's
Corner Brook
Grand Falls
Gander
Stephenville
Channel-Port aux Basques
Bay Roberts
Carbonear
Harbour Grace
Bonavista
Lewisporte
Botwood
Bishop's Falls
Windsor
Springdale
Deer Lake
Grand Bank
Mount Pearl
Labrador City
Wabush
Gagnon
Port-Cartier
Sept-Îles
Longue-Pointe-de-Mingan
Gaspé
Dalhousie
Bathurst
Newcastle
Summerside
Charlottetown
Hawke Harbour
Port Hope Simpson
Fox Harbour
Mary's Harbour
Battle Harbour
Red Bay
Pinware
West Saint Modeste
L'Anse-au-Loup
L'Anse au Clair
Forteau
Flower's Cove
Bird Cove
Port au Choix
Port Saunders
Daniel's Harbour
Parson's Pond
Cow Head
Rocky Harbour
Woody Point
Trout River
Lark Harbour
Pasadena
Howley
Baie Verte
La Scie
Fogo
Twillingate
Musgrave Harbour
Wesleyville
Greenspond
Clarenville
Placentia
Marystown
Burin
Fortune
Saint Lawrence
Lamaline
Trepassey
Ferryland
Renews
Portugal Cove South
CAPE RACE
CAPE BONAVISTA
Harbour Breton
Burgeo
Ramea
Rose Blanche
Codroy
Saint Andrew's
Saint George's
Saint Alban's
Cook's Harbour
Saint Anthony
Goose Cove
Raleigh
Main Brook
Roddickton
Englee
BELLE ISLE
L'ANSE AUX MEADOWS NATIONAL HISTORIC PARK
GROS MORNE NATIONAL PARK
TERRA NOVA NATIONAL PARK
FORILLON NATIONAL PARK
KOUCHIBOUGUAC NATIONAL PARK
PRINCE EDWARD ISLAND NATIONAL PARK
CAPE BRETON HIGHLANDS NATIONAL PARK
Ross Bay Junction
Ashuanipi
Embar
Eric
Sheldrake
Distance scale
Miles 0 25 50 75 100 150 200 250 300 350 400 450 500 550 600
Kilometers 0 25 50 75 100 150 200 250 300 350 400 450 500 550 600 650 700 750 800 850 900 950
1 2 3 4 5 6 7 8 9 10 11 12
I J K L M N O

Capital: Halifax
Area: 21,425 sq. mi. (55,490 km²), including 1,023 sq. mi. (2,650 km²) of inland water; 9th in size among the provinces
Elevation: *Highest*—1,747 ft. (532 m) above sea level in Cape Breton Highlands National Park; *lowest*—sea level
Entered the Dominion: July 1, 1867, one of the original four provinces
Abbreviation: N.S.
Motto: *Munit Haec et Altera Vincit* (One Defends and the Other Conquers)

Nova Scotia's provincial coat of arms shows a shield bearing the blue cross of St. Andrew and a lion representing the province's ties with Scotland. An Indian, symbolizing Newfoundland's first inhabitants, and a unicorn, representing England, flank the shield. Charles I of England granted the coat of arms to Nova Scotia in 1626. The provincial flag, granted by royal charter in 1621, bears the cross of St. Andrew and the lion of the Scottish kings.

Nova Scotia

Nova Scotia means "New Scotland." In 1629, the first British settlers arrived in Nova Scotia from Scotland. Later, after the American Revolution, many people who had been loyal to Britain moved to the area from the United States. These loyalists nicknamed the Nova Scotians "bluenoses." It is thought that the nickname came from the bluenose potatoes that were grown by the Nova Scotians. Today, residents still call themselves bluenoses.

The province of Nova Scotia includes a peninsula of the Canadian mainland, as well as Cape Breton Island. No part of the province is more than 35 miles (56 kilometers) from the sea. Ocean tides may rise higher in Nova Scotia than anywhere else in the world. At the head of the Bay of Fundy, the tide sometimes rises more than 50 feet (15 meters). The sea around Nova Scotia also has a moderating effect on the climate. The weather is never extremely hot or cold.

The many beaches and shoreline resorts throughout the province attract great numbers of visitors, who can sample lobster, scallops, and other seafood caught off Nova Scotia's shores. The province's forests, which attract many hunters, abound with deer, snowshoe rabbits, and grouse.

In 1606, French explorer Samuel de Champlain founded a social organization in Nova Scotia called the Order of the Good Time. The organization still exists, and tourists who spend three or more days in Nova Scotia may become members.

Nova Scotia has three major highways that are popular tourist routes. Cabot Trail winds through the wilderness areas of northern Cape Breton Island. It provides motorists with a magnificent view of the sea. Sunrise Trail runs for 212 miles (341 kilometers) along the shore of the Northumberland Strait between Amherst and the Strait of Canso. The Lighthouse Route runs between Yarmouth and Halifax. It passes through many small, interesting fishing villages.

The Annapolis-Cornwallis Valley in New Brunswick is famous for its apple orchards. Each year in late May or early June, the Annapolis Apple Blossom Festival is held in Wolfville and nearby towns. It is one of the province's best-known annual events. Other yearly events in Nova Scotia center around its Scottish heritage. The Gathering of the Clans is held in Pugwash on July 1 each year, and the Highland Games are an annual July event in Antigonish.

Blending the old with the new, Halifax is both one of Canada's most historic cities and a modern port and military base.

NOVA SCOTIA Political Map

- ⊛ Provincial capital
- Urban area in Nova Scotia
- Urban area outside de Nova Scotia
- • City or town
- DIGBY County name
- County seat
- County boundary
- ✈ Major airport
- Point of interest
- Water
- River
- Park or other recreation area
- Forest or other conservation area
- Indian reserve

Highways:
- Expressway
- Other road
- Trans-Canada
- Autoroute
- U.S.
- Other

Lambert conformal conic projection
WORLD BOOK map © Field Enterprises Educational Corporation

Distance scale

Miles / Kilometers

North

Gulf of Saint Lawrence

North Atlantic Ocean

Bay of Fundy

PRINCE EDWARD ISLAND

NEW BRUNSWICK

MAINE

UNITED STATES / CANADA

Halifax · **Dartmouth** · **Sydney** · **New Waterford** · **Glace Bay** · North Sydney · Sydney Mines · Truro · New Glasgow · Stellarton · Amherst · Yarmouth · Kentville · Bridgewater · Liverpool · Shelburne · Digby · Antigonish · Port Hawkesbury · Inverness · Louisbourg · Springhill · Parrsboro · Charlottetown

CAPE BRETON ISLAND · SABLE ISLAND · CAPE SABLE ISLAND · CAPE NORTH · CAPE GEORGE · CAPE BRETON

ACADIA NATIONAL PARK · CAPE BRETON HIGHLANDS NATIONAL PARK · KEJIMKUJIK NATIONAL PARK · FUNDY NATIONAL PARK

60° West Longitude · 62° West Longitude · 64° · 66° West Longitude · 68° West Longitude
46° · 44° North Latitude

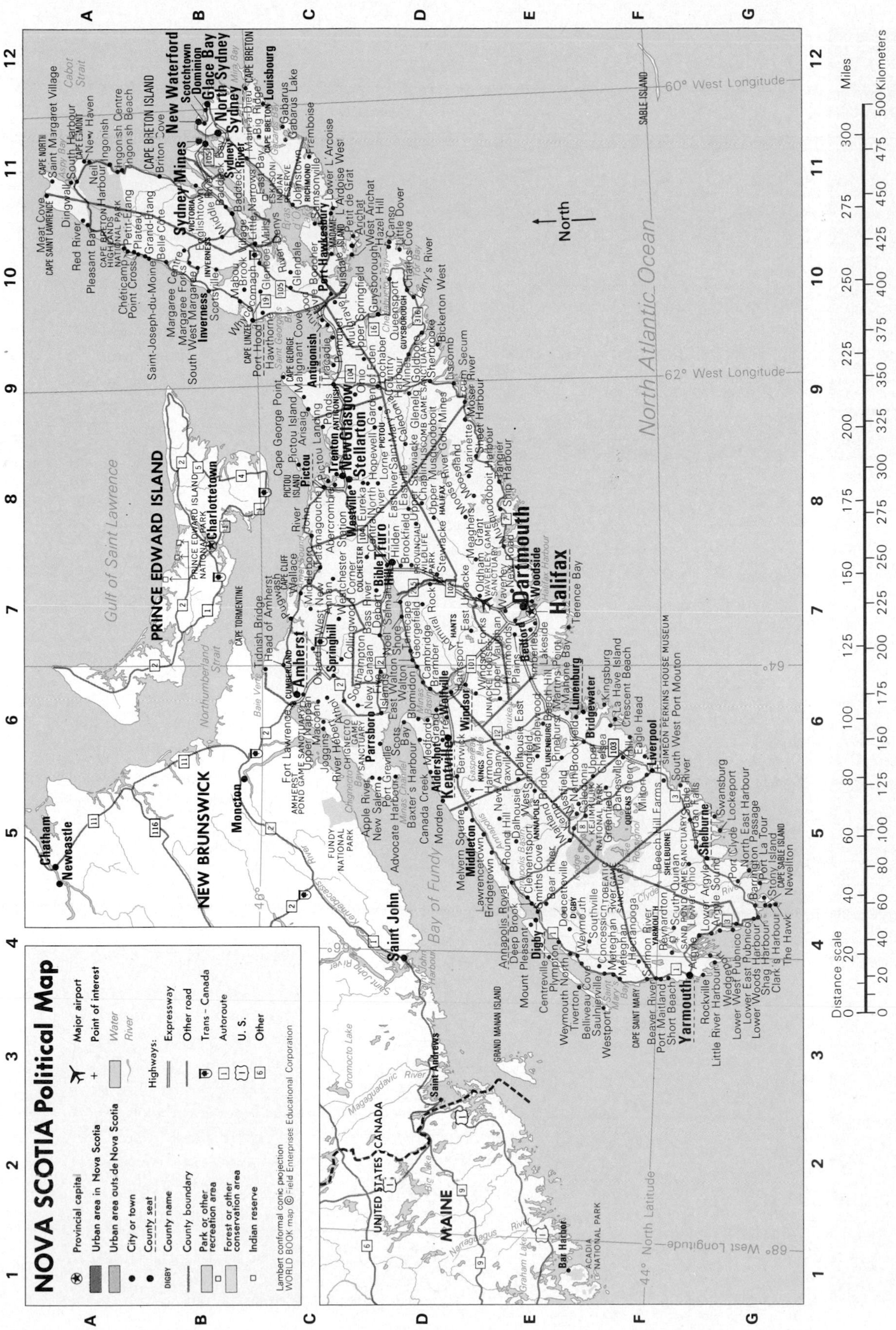

Coat of Arms

Flag

Flower: Trailing Arbutus

Covered by an armor of ice, Ottawa's Rideau Canal is a skaters' highway in winter. In summer the canal provides water access between the Ottawa River and Lake Ontario (above top).

The changing of the guards at Ottawa's Parliament Hill is a popular tourist attraction (above bottom).

Ontario

Ontario is often called the *Workshop of the Nation.* It received this nickname because of the many factories, mills, and plants that provide Ontario with its major industries. Many automobiles are manufactured in Ontario. Most of the automobile plants are located in the Golden Horseshoe, a section of Ontario that curves around the western shores of Lake Ontario. Canada's largest iron and steel center is located in Hamilton, also in the Golden Horseshoe.

Ontario is a province rich with water, forests, and fertile soil. The province has several hundred thousand lakes and many rivers and waterfalls. Its name is believed to be an Iroquois Indian word meaning "beautiful lake." The most important of Ontario's lakes are the Great Lakes. The Ontario border runs through Lakes Superior, Huron, Erie, and Ontario. Of the Great Lakes, only Lake Michigan is not at least partially located in Ontario.

The St. Lawrence River is part of the St. Lawrence Seaway, a major commercial waterway linking the Atlantic Ocean with the Great Lakes. The St. Lawrence River and Seaway help make the ports on the Great Lakes, including those located in Ontario, some of the busiest in the world.

Ontario's most famous waterfall is the mighty Horseshoe Falls—the largest part of Niagara Falls—located on the Niagara River near the Ontario-New York border. The Niagara River and its famous falls make up one of the most beautiful natural regions in the world.

Ontario's bountiful waterways provide a variety of vacation attractions. Millions of people visit Ontario each year to fish in the clear lakes and rushing rivers. The southernmost resort region in Ontario is along Lakes Erie and Ontario. It is known as *Canada's Sun Parlor.* Many tourists visit this area yearly and take boat cruises through the Thousand Islands and other islands in Ontario's waters.

Other popular resort areas include Lake Kawartha and Lake Muskoka near Toronto. The shores of these lakes are lined with low, wooded hills, which are especially beautiful during the fall. Wooded areas around the far northern lakes in the province are good hunting grounds for bear, geese, moose, and other game. Hunters fly into this area by seaplane. Manitoulin Island, probably the world's largest island located in fresh water, is in Lake Huron.

Herds of beef and dairy cattle can be seen grazing on the rich pastures between Lakes Huron and Ontario. Tobacco fields dot the landscape along Lake Erie, and colorful orchards are plentiful in the famous Niagara fruit belt. The thick forests that produce many paper products are located in the north.

Ontario is Canada's second largest province and is

an important area for mining. No other province or state produces more gold. Near Lake Elliot lies one of the largest known uranium deposits in the world.

Some of Ontario's cities are major tourist attractions. Toronto is the capital of the province, and Ottawa, the nation's capital, lies on the Ottawa River in southeastern Ontario. Ontario Place in Toronto is an interesting cultural and recreational complex that features concerts, an ultramodern movie theater, and facilities for boating and picnics. The Royal Botanical Gardens in Hamilton attracts world-wide visitors.

Ontario also has many historic sites for tourists to visit. Bell Homestead in Brantford was Alexander Graham Bell's home, where he worked on his invention, the telephone, in 1874. The home is now a telephone museum. Martyrs' Shrine near Midland is a church built in honor of martyred missionaries who once lived at the Jesuit mission of Asinte-Marie. The mission was destroyed during a war between the Huron and Iroquois Indians in 1649.

Upper Canada Village near Morrisburg demonstrates how people in the Ontario region lived from 1784 to 1867. Some buildings in the village were moved there from the area now covered by Lake St. Lawrence.

Many old forts in Ontario have been restored and are open to the public. Among them are Fort Erie in Fort Erie, Fort George in Niagara-on-the-Lake, Fort Henry in Kingston, Fort Wellington in Prescott, Fort William in Thunder Bay, and Fort York in Toronto.

Throughout the year, Ontario offers tourists interesting and exciting activities. From January through March, winter carnivals are held throughout the province. The Maple Syrup Festival in Elmira and the Spring Festival in Guelph are held in April. The Stratford Festival, probably Ontario's most famous annual event, is held in Stratford from June through October. The dramas of William Shakespeare and other noted playwrights are staged, featuring famous actors.

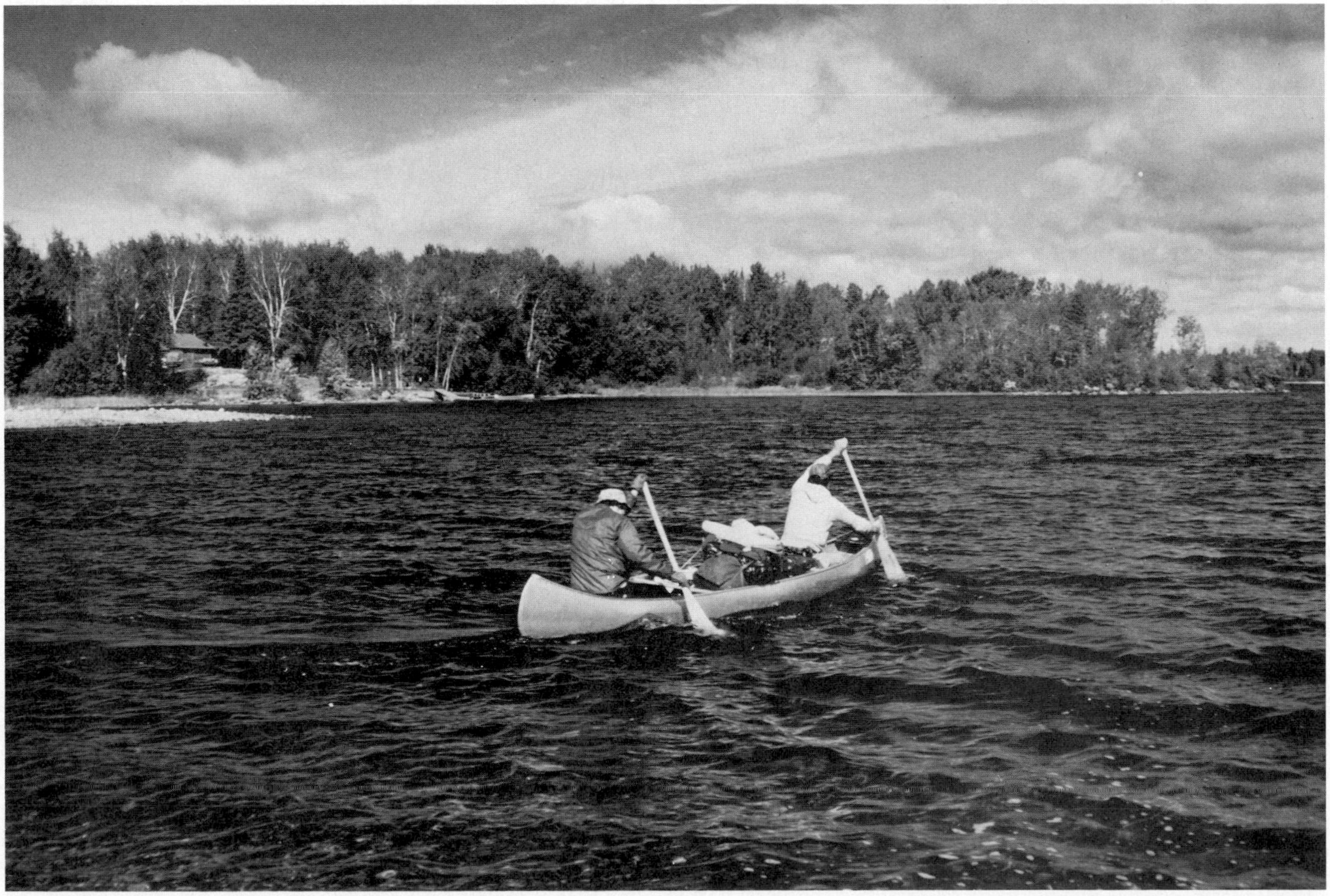

Gifts of prehistoric glaciers, Ontario's multitude of lakes, streams, and rivers are a paradise for canoeists.

Ontario

Capital: Toronto
Area: 412,582 sq. mi. (1,068,582 km²), including 68,490 sq. mi. (177,388 km²) of inland water; 2nd in size among the provinces
Elevation: *Highest*—2,275 ft. (693 m) above sea level in Timiskaming District; *lowest*—sea level
Entered the Dominion: July 1, 1867, one of the original four provinces
Abbreviation: Ont.
Motto: *Ut Incepit Fidelis Sic Permanet* (As Loyal It Began, So Loyal It Remains)

Ontario's provincial coat of arms was adopted in 1868. The shield's red and white cross of St. George represents the province's ties with Great Britain. The three maple leaves symbolize Canada. The bear above the shield stands for strength. A moose and a Canadian deer support the shield. Both are indigenous to Ontario. The provincial flag, adopted in 1965, has the British Union Jack and an adaptation of the provincial shield.

ONTARIO Political Map

- ⊛ National capital
- ⊛ Provincial or state capital
- Urban area in Ontario
- Urban area outside Ontario
- ● City or town
- ● County seat
- ESSEX County, United County, District or Regional Municipality name
- County, United County, District or Regional Municipality boundary
- Provincial boundary
- Park or other recreation area
- Forest or other conservation area
- Indian reserve
- ✛ Point of interest
- ✈ Major airport
- Water
- River
- Waterway
- Highways:
- Expressway
- Other road
- Trans-Canada
- 17 Autoroute
- 75 Interstate
- 71 U. S.
- 21 Other

Lambert conformal conic projection
WORLD BOOK map © Field Enterprises Educational Corporation

Distance scale for Ontario map

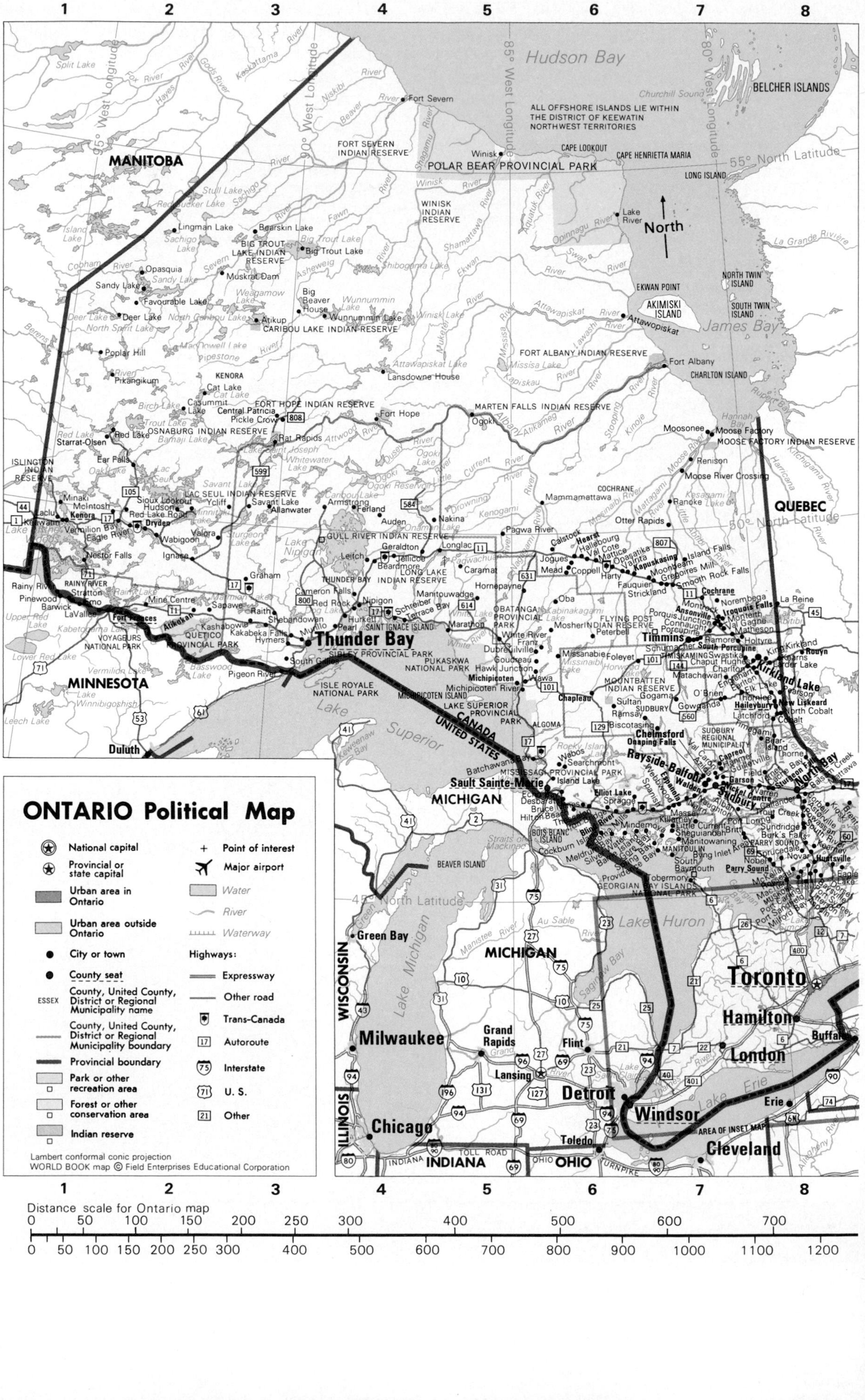

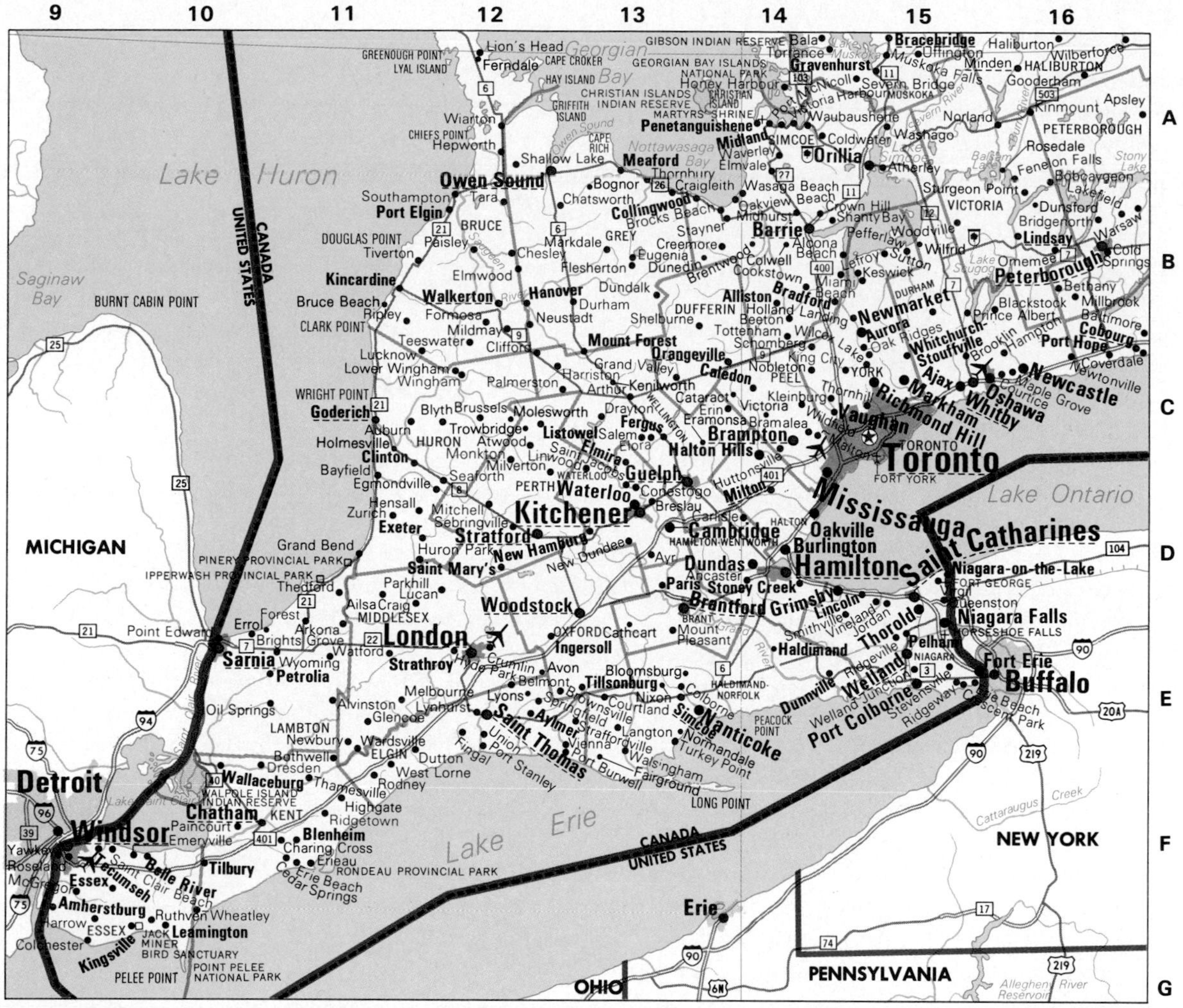

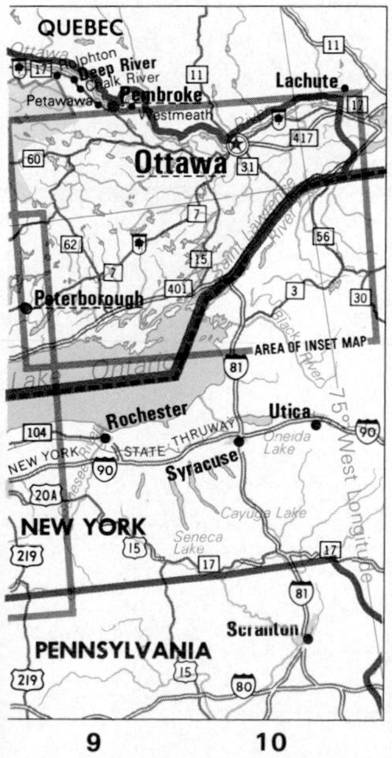

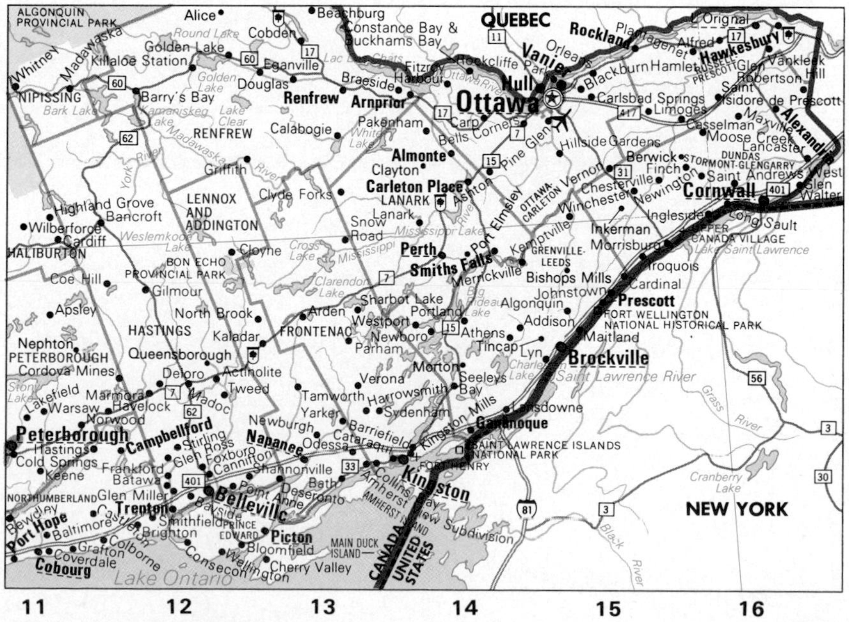

800 900 Miles

1300 1400 Kilometers

Distance scale for inset maps

0 10 20 30 40 50 70 90 110 130 150 170 Miles 190

0 10 20 30 40 50 70 90 110 130 150 170 190 210 230 250 270 Kilometers

Coat of Arms

Flag

Flower: White Trillium

Capital: Charlottetown
Area: 2,184 sq. mi. (5,657 km²); 10th and smallest in size among the provinces
Elevation: *Highest*—465 ft. 142 m) above sea level in Queens County; *lowest*—sea level along the coasts
Entered the Dominion: July 1, 1873, the 7th province
Abbreviation: P.E.I.
Motto: *Parva sub Ingenti* (The Small Under the Protection of the Great)

Prince Edward Island's provincial coat of arms shows three oak saplings standing for the three provincial counties. The oak tree symbolizes Canada and England. The British lion stretches across the top of the shield. The coat of arms was adopted in 1905. The provincial flag, adopted in 1964, has an adaptation of the coat of arms.

Prince Edward Island

Prince Edward Island is the only Canadian province that is completely separated from the mainland. Located in the Gulf of St. Lawrence, it is also the smallest of all the Canadian provinces. Charlottetown is its capital and only city.

Most of the island's landscape is a gently rolling plain with fertile red soil that is ideal for growing potatoes, the province's major crop. Farmers on Prince Edward Island also grow hay and produce hogs, cattle, and milk. Agriculture is the province's chief source of income.

Prince Edward Island has a large fishing industry as well. Lobsters are its most valuable catch, and the province ranks among the leading oyster suppliers in the United States and Canada. The Canadian government controls the oyster beds and operates an oyster research center and hatchery at Ellerslie. The island's chief oyster farm is located in Malpeque Bay. The Gulf of St. Lawrence also yields cod, flounder, sole, mackerel, red fish, tuna, and scallops. North Lake near Elmira is known as the *Tuna Fishing Capital of the World.*

Many features of Prince Edward Island combine to attract visitors to the province each year. The island has a mild climate and is surrounded by warm ocean currents. Long stretches of red or white sandy beaches form much of its coastline. During the summer the water temperature along the coast may reach 70° F. (21° C). Streams in the area have many game fish, while motorboats take people to deep-sea fishing areas where cod, halibut, and mackerel are plentiful. There are fine golf courses on the island and good sailing off the coast.

Tourists can reach the island in several ways. Three ferryboat lines carry passengers and cars across the Northumberland Strait between Prince Edward Island and the Canadian mainland. Airline service is available between Charlottetown and major cities in eastern Canada, as well as to and from the Magdalen Islands in the Gulf of St. Lawrence.

Once on the island, tourists can drive along the scenic roads and highways of the province. They can travel the length of the island on the Canadian National Railway.

Many fascinating points of interest await tourists on Prince Edward Island. Province House in Charlottetown contains Confederation Chamber. This room, called the *Birthplace of Canada,* is where the Fathers of Confederation first met in 1864 to plan the union of Canada. A Micmac Indian reservation is located on Lennox Island in Malpeque Bay. Micmac Village, a reproduction of an Indian settlement of the 1700's, can be visited near Rocky Point. Woodleigh Replicas near Burlington is the site of many miniature reproductions of British castles, churches, and inns.

Completely surrounded by northern waters, residents of Prince Edward Island reach out for the sea's offerings. Lobsters, oysters, flounder, and sole are but a sampling of the catch.

PRINCE EDWARD ISLAND
Political Map

Legend:
- ⊛ Provincial capital
- ● City or town
- County seat
- KINGS County name
- County boundary
- Park or other recreation area
- Indian reserve
- + Point of interest
- ✈ Major airport
- Water
- River
- Highways:
- Roads
- Trans-Canada
- Autoroute

Transverse mercator projection
WORLD BOOK map ©Field Enterprises Educational Corporation

Coat of Arms

PARVA·SUB·INGENTI

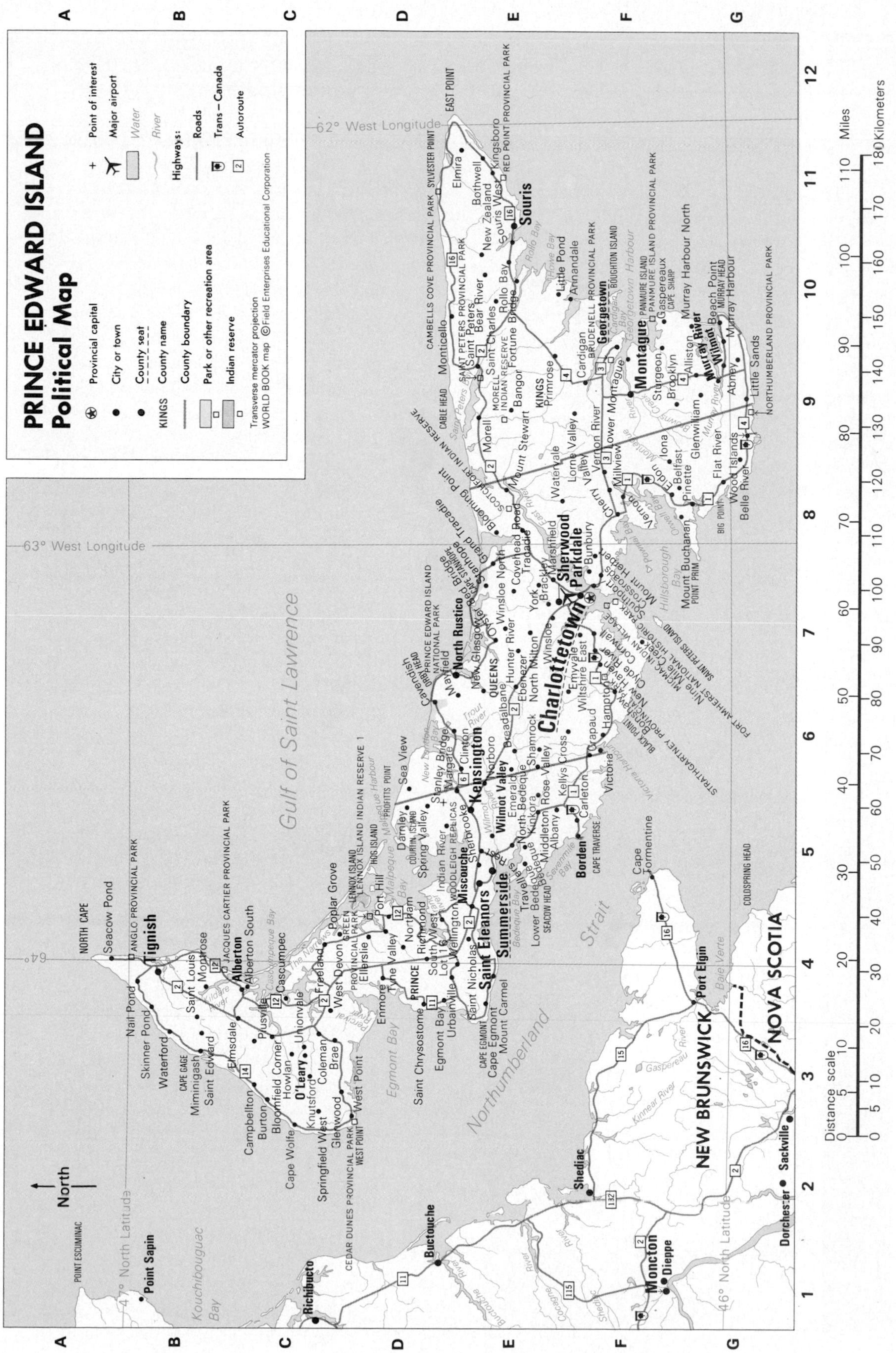

Flag

Flower: Lady's-Slipper

Quebec

Quebec is one of the four original Canadian provinces. The largest province in Canada, it is also the home of Canada's first permanent settlement. The French explorer, Samuel de Champlain, founded Quebec City in 1608. Today, the 300-year-old city, now called Quebec, is the capital of the province. Montreal is the province's largest city.

Most of Quebec's residents are French Canadians, descendants of the French settlers who went to the Quebec region during the 1600's and 1700's. After the French colony in Quebec came under British control in 1763, emigration from France nearly ceased.

The colonists in Quebec had developed a strong sense of their own nationality and considered themselves French Canadians. They did not want to mix with the British settlers. The French Canadians lived apart from the British and continued to follow their own ways of life.

Today, the strong French influence makes the province quite different from the rest of Canada. Many people in Quebec still follow the customs and traditions of France. Most Quebec schools use French as the language of instruction. Old buildings in Quebec are French in architecture, and French-style homes, mills, and outdoor ovens can still be seen throughout the province. Almost every village has a Roman Catholic church, and crosses and shrines are familiar sights along the roadsides.

Sleighing in the snow, nostalgic roamers traverse the outskirts of Montreal's contemporary core.

Quebec is rich in natural resources. Its mines produce asbestos, copper, gold, and zinc. Huge deposits of iron ore are found in the far northern wilderness. Immense forests cover almost half the province. The St. Lawrence River Valley and the Eastern Townships that lie south of the river have rich soil. Quebec is one of North America's greatest producers of apples, dairy cattle, and milk. Quebec is also the leading producer of maple syrup in North America.

Water has always been one of Quebec's most important natural resources. The province has a larger area of fresh water than any other Canadian province. The St. Lawrence, called the *Mother of Canada,* is Quebec's principal river. It enters the province at the point where Quebec, New York, and Ontario meet.

The St. Lawrence River has been one of Canada's major trade routes. It has influenced the life and development of Canada and Quebec since the early 1500's, when the French explorer, Jacques Cartier, sailed up the river into Canada. The word *Quebec* is a derivation of the Algonkian Indian word *kebec,* meaning "place where the river narrows." Samuel de Champlain heard the Indians use this word for a place on the St. Lawrence River and gave the name to the settlement of Quebec City.

Because of its rich historical background, Quebec is often called the *Storied Province.* Almost seven million tourists visit Quebec each year to see the province's many historical points of interest. Winding cobblestone streets make Quebec City seem European. The Citadel, a major landmark, is a walled fortress that overlooks the city. Another major landmark is a square called Palace Royal. The area includes several houses that date from the 1600's and 1700's as well as the Notre-Dame-de-Victoires Church, which was completed in 1688. The church stands on the site where the first log cabin of the French explorer Samuel de Champlain once stood. Ste.-Anne-de-Beaupré is a Roman Catholic shrine in Montmorency County. Shipwrecked French sailors built a chapel there in 1658.

Montreal is a favorite tourist city in Quebec. Vacationers may travel to many of its attractions via the Métro, one of the world's most attractive subways. Brightly colored mosaics and basket-weave designs decorate many of the subway's ceramic

walls. Because of these decorations, the Métro has been called "the largest underground art gallery in the world."

One attraction in Montreal is Man and His World, a cultural exhibition that is a continuation of Expo 67, the 1967 international exposition. Mount Royal Park is a lovely wooded area, where only horse-drawn vehicles are allowed. The top of Mount Royal offers a magnificent view of Montreal and the St. Lawrence River.

Vacationers in the province of Quebec will find many scenic attractions. Artists, hikers, and mountain climbers enjoy the rugged Gaspé Peninsula, while other vacationers take canoe trips down the rushing rivers of the Laurentian Mountains. Bonaventure Island, off the Gaspé Peninsula near Percé, is a popular spot where tourists can view one of the largest water-bird refuges open to the public. More than 60,000 gannets, gulls, and other birds nest on the island in the summer.

Ile d'Orléans is in the middle of the St. Lawrence River near Quebec City. There are many old Norman-style houses, many churches, and numerous religious shrines on the island.

Those weary of urban life may travel to the Gaspé Peninsula, where the St. Lawrence River and the Atlantic Ocean meet (above top).

The Eskimos of northern Quebec ice-fish with the help of modern equipment (above bottom).

Quebec

Capital: Quebec (Quebec City)

Area: 594,860 sq. mi. (1,540,680 km²), including 71,000 sq. mi. (183,889 km²) of inland water; 1st in size among the provinces

Elevation: *Highest*—Mont d'Iberville, 5,400 ft. (1,646 m) above sea level; *lowest*— sea level

Entered the Dominion: July 1, 1867, one of the four original provinces

Abbreviation: Que.

Motto: *Je Me Souviens* (I Remember)

Tree: Sugar Maple

Quebec's provincial coat of arms, adopted in 1939, combines the emblems of France, Great Britain, and Canada. The three fleur-de-lis represent the coat of arms of the French kings. The British lion stands across the center. The three maple leaves at the bottom symbolize Canada. The provincial flag, adopted in 1948, bears a fleur-de-lis in each corner. The white cross stands for the one that Jacques Cartier planted on Quebec's soil after reaching the Gulf of St. Lawrence in 1534.

QUEBEC Political Map

National capital	Indian reserve
Provincial capital	Point of interest
Urban area in Quebec	Major airport
Urban area outside Quebec	River
City or town	Water
County seat	**Roads or Highways:**
HULL County name	Expressway
County boundary	Other road
Provincial boundary	36 Autoroute
Park or other recreation area	2 U.S.
Forest or other conservation area	64 Interstate
	48 Other

Lambert conformal conic projection
WORLD BOOK map

Distance scale for Quebec map
0 50 100 200 300 400 500 600 700 800 900 Miles
0 50 100 200 300 400 500 600 700 800 900 1000 1100 1200 1300 1400 Kilometers 1600

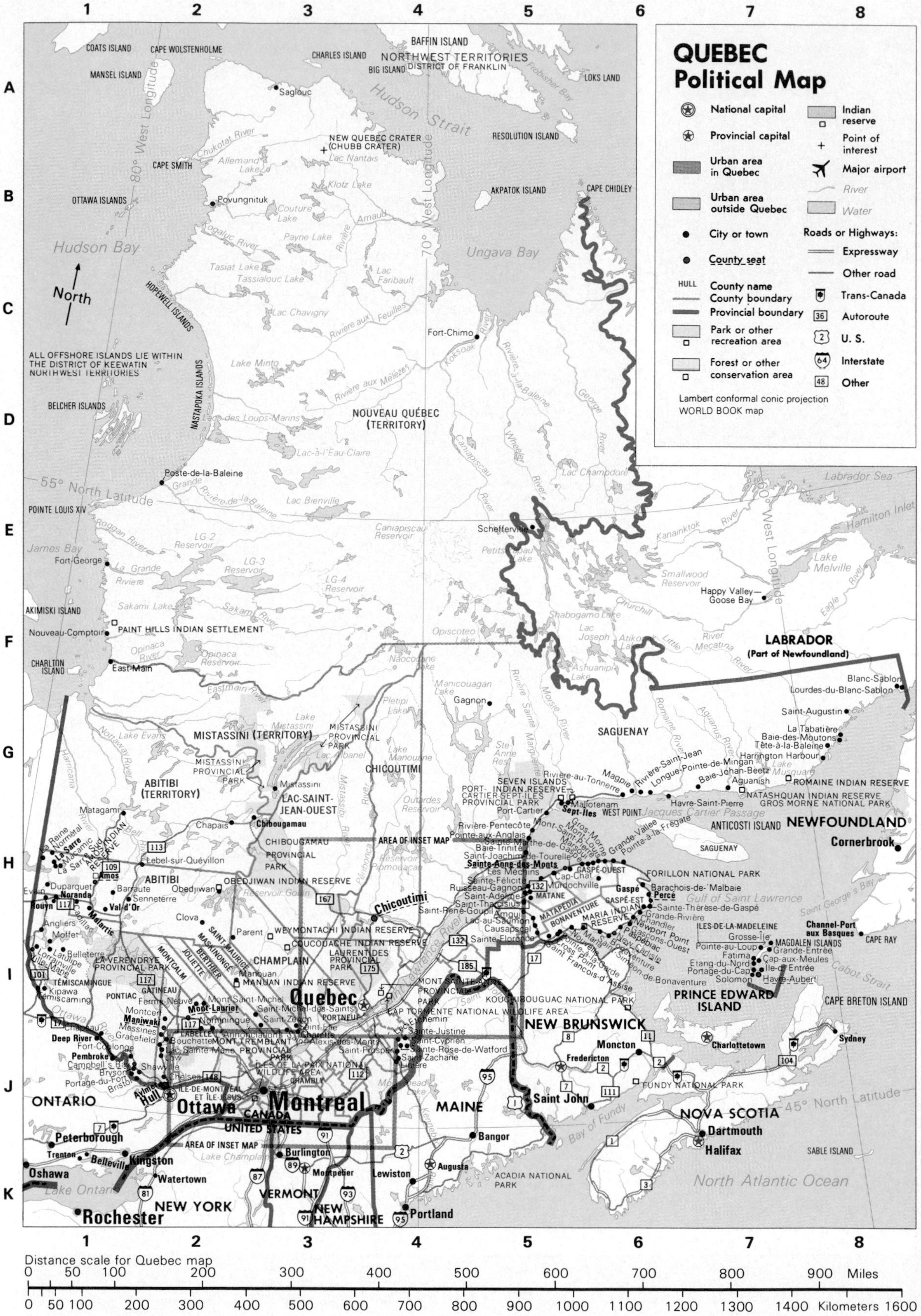

9 10 11 12 13 14 15 16

Coat of Arms

JE ME SOUVIENS

Flag

Flower: White Garden Lily

A B C D E F G H I J K

SAGUENAY
Godbout
Franquelin
Labrieville
Hauterive · Baie-Comeau
Chute-aux-Outardes · Pointe-Lebel
BERSIMIS INDIAN RESERVE · Les Buissons
Pointe-aux-Outardes
Baie aux Outardes
Petite-Matane
Matane
Saint-Luc
Saint-Ulric
Baie-des-Sables · MATANE
Saint-Damase-de-Matane
Saint-Octave · Noël
Mont-Joli · Price · Sayabec
Saint-Angèle-de-Mérici
Saint-Donat-de-Rimouski · Luceville · Val-Brillant
Pointe-au-Père · Rimouski-Est
Sainte-Odile · Rimouski · La Rédemption
Sainte-Blandine · RIMOUSKI · Saint-Léon-le-Grand
Lac-Humqui · MATAPEDIA
Sainte-Françoise
La Trinité-des-Monts
Esprit-Saint
Saint-Médard · Lac-des-Aigles

Labrieville
Forestville
Saint-Thérèse-de-Colombier
Betsiamis River
Rivière-Portneuf
Pointe-au-Boisvert
Sault-au-Mouton
Escoumins
ESCOUMAINS INDIAN RESERVE
Sainte-Rose-du-Nord
Grandes-Bergeronnes
Rivière-Sainte-Marguerite
Tadoussac
Saint-Jean-de-Dieu
Saint-Éloi
L'Isle-Verte
Saint-Arsène
RIVIÈRE-DU-LOUP
Saint-Clément
Saint-Épiphane
Notre-Dame-du-Portage
Rivière-du-Loup
Saint-Antonin · ÎLE AUX LIÈVRES
Saint-Hubert-de-Témiscouata · Lejeune
Saint-Cyprien
Sainte-Rita
Saint-Louis-du-Ha! Ha!
Cabano
Notre-Dame-du-Lac
Dégelis
Edmundston
Saint-Honoré-de-Témiscouata
TÉMISCOUATA
Estcourt
Notre-Dame-de-Kamouraska
Saint-Alexandre-de-Kamouraska
Kamouraska
Saint-Eusèbe
Saint-Pascal
KAMOURASKA
Mont-Carmel
Saint-Philippe-de-Néri
La Pocatière
Sainte-Anne
Saint-Onésime

CHICOUTIMI
LAC-SAINT-JEAN-OUEST
Girardville
Saint-Thomas-Didyme
Saint-Edmond-les-Plaines
Dolbeau
Albanel
Mistassini · Saint-Ludger
Normandin
Saint-Méthode
Notre-Dame-de-la-Doré
Sainte-Jeanne-d'Arc · Bégin
Péribonka
Saint-Félicien · Sainte-Monique
Saint-Prime · Saint-Coeur-de-Marie · L'Ascension
Notre-Dame-du-Rosaire
Saint-David-de-Falardeau
OUIATCHOUAN INDIAN RESERVE
Alma · Saint-Ambroise
Roberval · Desbiens · Saint-Bruno
Saint-Jean-Vianney
Sainte-Hedwidge-de-Roberval
Métabetchouan
Jonquière · Rivière-du-Moulin · Chicoutimi
Saint-André-du-Lac-Saint-Jean · Laterrière
Lac-Bouchette
LAC-SAINT-JEAN-EST · La Baie
Jonquière-Sud-Ouest
Jonquière-Est
Boilleau

CHAMPLAIN
La Tuque
Wayagamac
QUÉBEC
MONTMORENCY I
LAURENTIDES PROVINCIAL PARK
CHARLEVOIX-OUEST
CHARLEVOIX-EST
Saint-Georges-de-Cacouna
Saint-Siméon
Port-au-Persil
Saint-Fidèle
Cap-à-l'Aigle
La Malbaie
Pointe-au-Pic
Clermont
Saint-Irénée
Saint-Urbain-de-Charlevoix
Saint-Hilarion
Les Éboulements
Baie-Saint-Paul
ÎLE AUX COUDRES
Saint-Joseph-de-la-Rive
Saint-Denis-de-la-Boutellerie

PORTNEUF PROVINCIAL PARK
PORTNEUF
Rivière-à-Pierre
Notre-Dame-des-Anges
Saint-Raymond
Montauban
Sainte-Thècle
Saint-Gérard-de-Laurentides
Saint-Joseph-de-Mékinac
Baie-de-Shawinigan
Grand-Mère
Shawinigan
Sainte-Geneviève-de-Batiscan
Saint-Tite
Saint-Casimir
Pont-Rouge
Cap-Santé
Portneuf
Donnacona
Sainte-Croix
Champlain
Batiscan
La Pérade

Charlesbourg
Beauport
Québec
Sainte-Foy
Sillery
Lauzon
Lévis
Saint-Romuald-d'Etchemin
Charny
MONTMORENCY II
BELLECHASSE
Berthier-sur-Mer
Montmagny
Saint-Pierre
Notre-Dame-du-Rosaire
Sainte-Apolline
Saint-Marcel
Saint-Adalbert
Saint-Eugène
Saint-Ignace
Sainte-Perpétue
Saint-Pamphile
ÎLE D'ORLÉANS
Sainte-Famille
Saint-Joachim
Sainte-Anne-de-Beaupré
Saint-Jean-Port-Joli
ÎLE AUX OIES
Saint-Aubert
L'Islet
L'Islet-sur-Mer
Tourville

MAINE
NEW BRUNSWICK
CANADA
UNITED STATES

Saint-Léon-de-Standon
Saint-Malachie
DORCHESTER
Saint-Luc
Saint-Camille
Saint-Gédéon
Saint-Léonard
Saint-Anselme
Saint-Isidore
Saint-Damien-de-Buckland
Sainte-Claire-de-Joliette
Saint-Juste-de-Bretenières
Sainte-Lucie-de-Beauregard
Saint-Fabien
Saint-Raphaël
Lac-Frontière

Distance scale for inset maps

Miles
0 10 20 60 80 100 120 140 160 180 200 220

Kilometers
0 10 20 40 60 80 100 120 140 160 180 200 220 240 260 280 300 350

La Minerve
MONTCALM
Saint-Charles-de-Mandeville
Trois-Rivières
Cap-de-la-Madeleine
Dosquet · LOTBINIÈRE · Sainte-Marie
DORCHESTER
MONT-TREMBLANT PROVINCIAL PARK
Saint-Émélie-de-l'Énergie
Saint-Côme
JOLIETTE
MASKINONGE
Yamachiche
Bécancour
Manseau
Sainte-Agathe
Sainte-Sylvestre
Saint-Odilon
PAPINEAU-LABELLE
Mont-Tremblant
LABELLE
Lac-Carré
Saint-Alphonse
Saint-Gabriel
SAINT-MAURICE
Nicolet
NICOLET
Saint-Sylvère
Laurierville
MÉGANTIC
Inverness
Leeds
173
Notre-Dame-du-Laus
Saint-Faustin
Saint-Félix-de-Valois
BERTHIER
Louiseville
Nicolet-Est
Saint-François-du-Lac
BEAUCE
Beauceville
Sainte-Agathe-des-Monts
Val-David
Notre-Dame-de-la-Merci
Rawdon
Saint-Pierre
Berthierville
Baieville
Plessisville
265 · St-Ferdinand
Victoriaville
St-Georges
PAPINEAU-LABELLE PROVINCIAL PARK
Huberdeau
Arundel
Sainte-Julienne
Saint-Jacques
Lanoraie
Yamaska
ARTHABASKA
Arthabaska
Warwick
Ham-Nord
Chesterville
Fortune
Black-Lake
Thetford Mines
Saint-Ephrem-de-Tring
Bolduc
Chénéville
Namur
Saint-Adolphe-d'Howard
Terrebonne
Saint-Esprit
Saint-Roch
RICHELIEU
Saint-Guillaume
WOLFE
Wottonville
Saint-Adrien
Disraeli
Beaulac
Saint-Gédéon
FRONTENAC
Saint-André-Avellin
Montpellier
Montebello
David
L'ASSOMPTION
Crabtree
Saint-Hugues
DRUMMOND
Danville
Windsor
Melbourne
RICHMOND
Wolfe
112
Nantes
204
Saint-Pierre-de-Wakefield
Montebello
Papineauville
Saint-Jérôme
Mirabel
Saint-Eustache
Repentigny
Terrebonne
Saint-Hyacinthe
Drummondville
Kingsey Falls
Saint-Libore
Asbestos
Richmond
Weedon-Centre
Marbleton
Saint-Ludger
Lac-Mégantic
Gatineau
309
Cantley
Perkins
Buckingham
Hawkesbury
Laval
Lachine
Deux-Montagnes
Pierrefonds
Pincourt
Pointe-Fortune
Rigaud
Longueuil
Saint-Césaire
Saint-Pie
Sainte-Rosalie
Acton Vale
BAGOT
Roxton Falls
Sainte-Pudentienne
Saint-Grégoire
Windsor
Compton
East-Angus
Scotstown
Notre-Dame-des-Bois
Woburn
27
Ottawa
417
ONTARIO
Sainte-Justine-de-Newton
Montréal
Verdun
La Prairie
Marieville
ROUVILLE
Granby-Nord
Sherbrooke
Ascot Corner
Bury
Cookshire
Coteau-Landing
34
Vaudreuil
Dorion
20
IBERVILLE
Valcourt
Granby
SHEFFORD
Waterloo
Eastman
Magog
Deauville
Lennoxville
Sawyerville
COMPTON
Salaberry-de-Valleyfield
SOULANGES
Saint-Polycarpe
Beauharnois
Châteauguay
Maricourt
Saint-Jean
Napierville
Iberville
Farnham
Cowansville
Foster
Brome
Knowlton
North-Hatley
STANSTEAD
Sainte-Edwidge
Saint-Malo
MAINE
Cornwall
401
Huntingdon
Ormstown
CHÂTEAUGUAY
15
Lacolle
Sabrevois
Dunham
Sutton
Bedford
Philipsburg
Ayer's Cliff
Coaticook
Dixville
143
Henryville
MISSISQUOI
Beebe-Plain
Stanstead
Rock-Island
Abercorn
3
Aziscohos Lake
Brockville
INDIAN RESERVE
LAC SAINT-FRANÇOIS NATIONAL WILDLIFE AREA
Franklin Centre
Hemmingford
CANADA · UNITED STATES
105
16
NEW YORK
87
VERMONT
89
114
NEW HAMPSHIRE
Lake Champlain
Lake Memphremagog
Mooselookmeguntic Lake
91

9 10 11 12 13 14 15 16

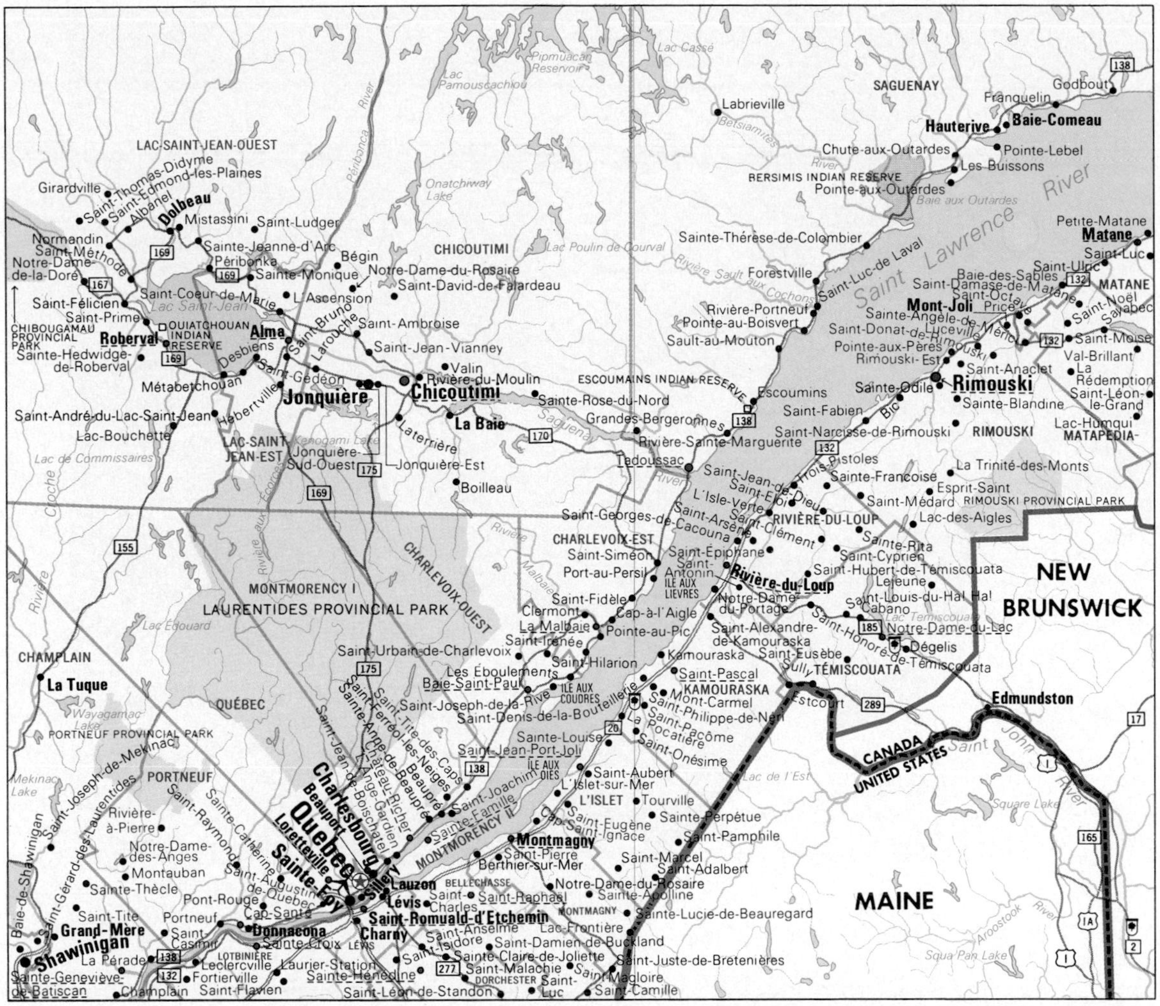

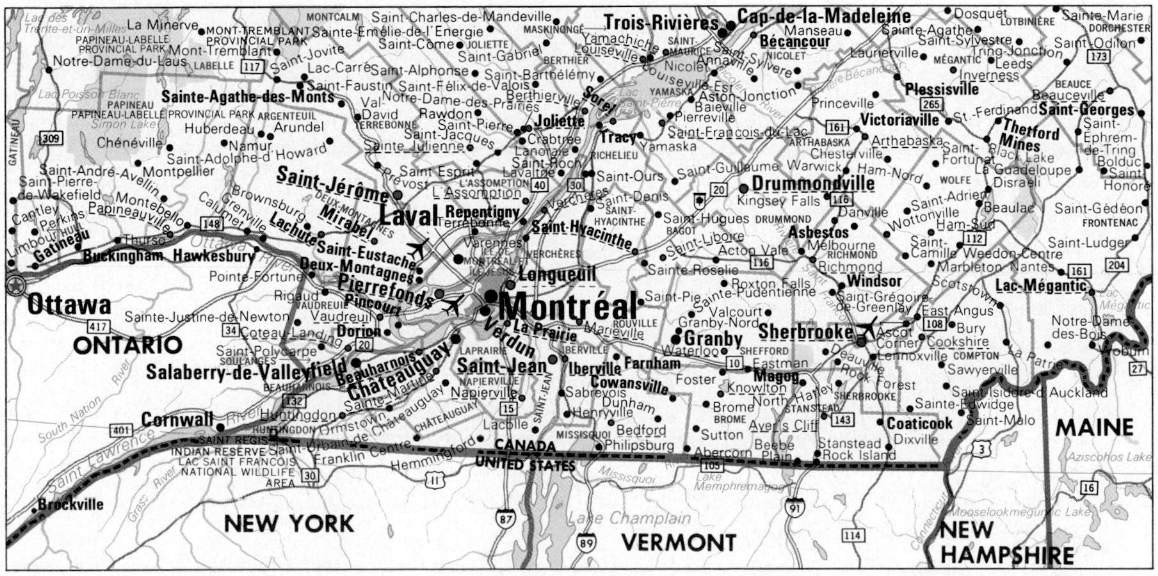

Regina, Saskatchewan's capital and largest city, takes pride in its imposing Legislative Building, which is set among spectacular gardens.

Saskatchewan

Saskatchewan is one of Canada's Prairie Provinces. It is one of the greatest wheat-growing areas in North America. Saskatchewan farmers produce so much wheat that the province has been nicknamed *Canada's Breadbasket.*

Saskatchewan has more farmland than any other province: about two-fifths of Canada's total. Its farms are on the flat southern prairie, where most of Saskatchewan's people live. More of Saskatchewan's land is used to grow wheat than any other crop. In many areas wheat fields stretch in all directions as far as the eye can see. Saskatchewan farmers raise barley, flaxseed, and rye in smaller amounts. They also raise large herds of beef cattle. The raising of beef cattle is the province's second-ranking agricultural activity. Hogs are also an important source of farm income.

Saskatchewan has many natural resources. Fertile soils, valuable minerals, and forests are the most important of these. Major oil fields were discovered in the province in the 1950's. Soon after this discovery, oil wells and drilling rigs became a common sight in the golden wheat fields. Today Saskatchewan is one of the leading producers of oil in North America. This province also has the largest potash fields in the world. Potash is mined near Allen, Belle Plaine, Colonsay, Delisle, Esterhazy, Lanigan, Rocanville, and Saskatoon. Most of the potash is used in fertilizers. Uranium, sodium sulfate, gold, salt, silver, zinc, and coal are also mined in Saskatchewan.

Saskatchewan's large forests are valuable as a source of raw material for the province's logging industry. They are also important as a home for large game animals such as caribou, elk, and moose. Lakes in the northern forests have an abundance of northern pike, pickerel, trout, and whitefish. People from Canada and the United States fly into the rugged northern wilderness to hunt and fish.

Saskatchewan played an important part in Canada's frontier days. The Canadian Pacific Railway crossed the area in 1882 and 1883 and opened the region to agricultural settlement. Many small towns were established along the railway route. Métis, persons of mixed Indian and white descent, and Indians feared that the settlers would destroy the buffalo, their main source of food and clothing. The métis were also afraid that they would lose their homes to the white settlers. In 1885, the métis and some Indians, led by Louis Riel, joined in the Saskatchewan Rebellion against the Canadian government. The métis were defeated, and Riel was hanged for treason. After the Saskatchewan Rebellion, the métis were given legal titles to their lands.

Today, motorists may drive along the highways of Saskatchewan and see more than a hundred historic markers that honor battlefields, forts, missions, and other reminders of Saskatchewan's colorful past. Many markers along the roads identify early trails used by hunters, fur traders, and patrols of the old North-West Mounted Police.

Many vacationers visit Saskatchewan each year. They travel to the sparkling lakes of the Qu'Appelle Valley, where popular summer resorts offer boating, swimming, and golfing. Or they venture to northern Saskatchewan to some of the best hunting and fishing areas in North America.

Saskatchewan has many interesting sites. Fort Walsh, a reconstruction of a North-West Mounted Police fort built in 1875, is located in the Cypress Hills. The fort is surrounded by a high stockade and includes a number of historical exhibits. Moose Jaw Wild Animal Park is the largest animal park in Saskatchewan. It has lions, monkeys, and many animals that live in the province.

The Royal Canadian Mounted Police Training Center is located in Regina, the province's capital and largest city. The center is the Mounties' training headquarters and houses a museum containing historic documents, uniforms, and weapons. The Western Development Museum in Saskatoon has a collection of antique cars, pioneer household equipment, and steam engines.

The opening of the fishing season in Saskatchewan is a popular outdoor event. It takes place in early May in the south and later in the month in the north. During July and August, Saskatchewan holds events that reflect its frontier past. Frontier Days Rodeo is an annual July event in Swift Current. The Territorial Days Celebration in North Battleford is also held in July, and Buffalo Days in Regina takes place in late July and early August.

Grain-storage facilities dot Saskatchewan's wheat fields. One of the greatest wheat-growing regions in North America, the province has been nicknamed Canada's Breadbasket (above).

Canada's emergence as a self-governing, united dominion owes much to John A. Macdonald. This statue erected in Regina honors Macdonald's accomplishments (left).

Saskatchewan

Capital: Regina
Area: 251,700 sq. mi. (651,900 km²), including 31,518 sq. mi. (81,631 km²) of inland water; 5th in size among the provinces
Elevation: *Highest*—4,567 ft. (1,392 m) above sea level, in the Cypress Hills; *lowest*—700 ft. (213 m), at Lake Athabasca
Entered the Dominion: Sept. 1, 1905, with Alberta as the 8th and 9th provinces
Abbreviation: Sask.
Bird: Prairie Sharp-tailed Grouse

Saskatchewan's provincial coat of arms shows the British lion, symbolizing the British Crown, and three sheaves of wheat, a provincial resource. The color red stands for prairie fires, green for grass, and golden yellow for wheat fields. The coat of arms was adopted in 1906. The provincial flag was adopted in 1969. The green stripe represents Saskatchewan's forests. The gold stripe stands for the province's wheat fields. The flag also shows the provincial flower and an adaptation of the provincial coat of arms.

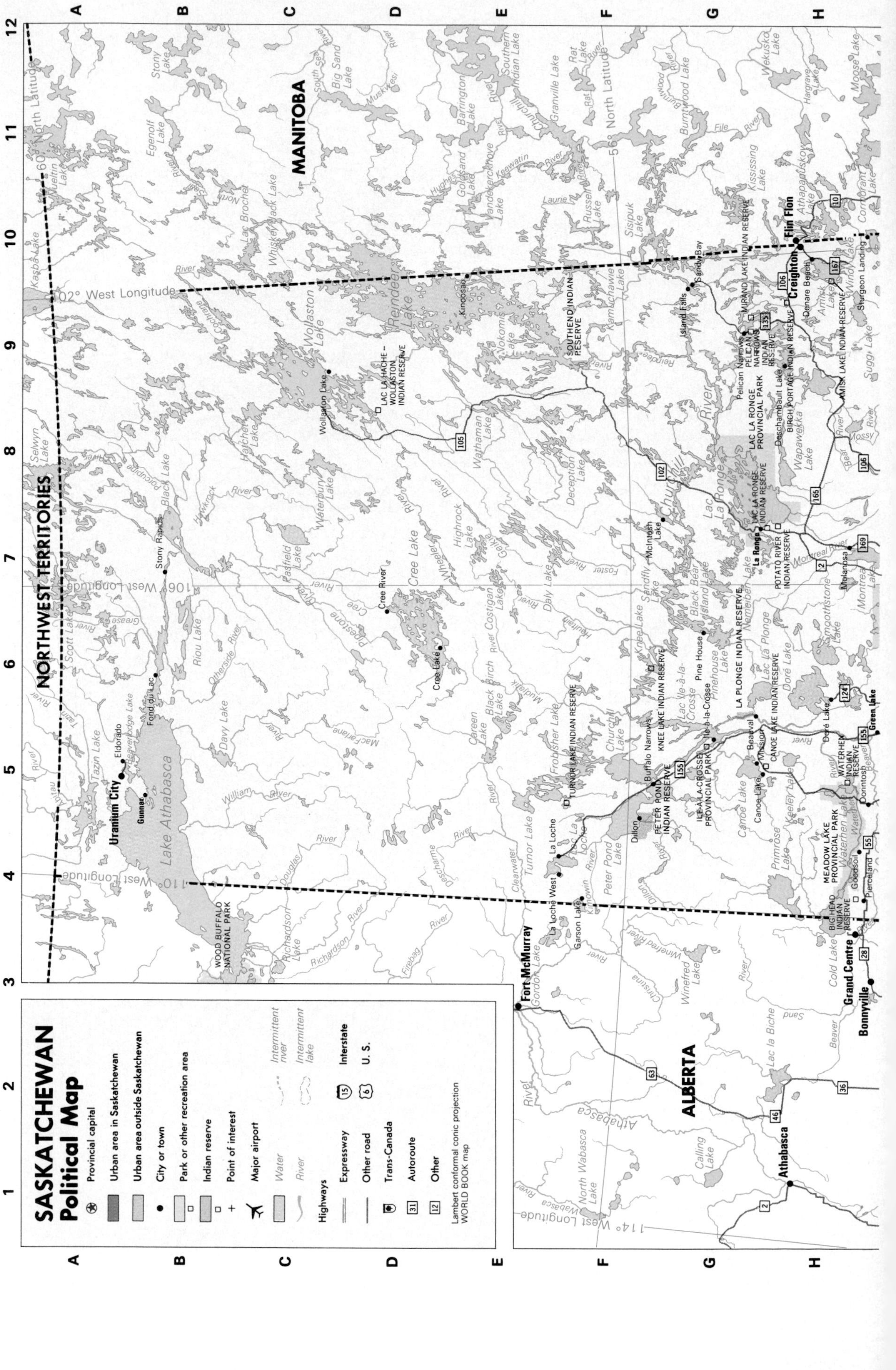

Coat of Arms

Flag

Flower: Prairie Lily

MANITOBA
ALBERTA
MONTANA
NORTH DAKOTA
CANADA
UNITED STATES
Saskatoon
Regina
Moose Jaw
Prince Albert
North Battleford
Swift Current
Yorkton
Medicine Hat
Lethbridge
Edmonton
North
Distance scale
Miles
Kilometers

Capital: Yellowknife
Area: 1,304,903 sq. mi. (3,379,683 km²), including 51,465 sq. mi. (133,294 km²) of inland water
Elevation: *Highest*—Mount Sir James MacBrien in the Mackenzie Mountains, 9,062 ft. (2,762 m) above sea level; *lowest*—sea level along the coast
Abbreviation: N.W. Terr.
Flag: Adopted in 1969, has two blue vertical panels right and left and a white panel in the center. Center of white panel has shield from coat of arms.
Flower: Mountain Avens

Northwest Territories

The Northwest Territories is a region that covers about one-third of Canada, stretching from the northern boundaries of the Canadian provinces to within 500 miles (800 kilometers) of the North Pole. This area was one of the world's last undeveloped frontiers until the 1950's, when modern-day pioneers began tapping its great mineral wealth.

The Territories is divided into three geographic districts. The District of MacKenzie is in the southwestern portion of the region. It includes the

rugged MacKenzie Mountains and the MacKenzie River, Canada's longest waterway. The Franklin Mountains lie along the east bank of the MacKenzie River. Two of Canada's largest lakes, Great Bear Lake and Great Slave Lake, also lie in this district, east of the plain of the MacKenzie River.

The District of Keewatin covers the southeastern part of the Territories. Its name is a Cree Indian word meaning "north wind." The landscape here is primarily a rocky, sparsely vegetated plateau called the Barrens.

The District of Franklin includes all of the Canadian Arctic islands and the northeastern peninsulas of the Territories. This area is extremely desolate with not one tree growing in the entire district. A multitude of colorful flowers, however, can be seen growing in some places during the summer. The northern portion of the district is almost uninhabited.

Scheduled air services operate in each of the three districts of the Territories. Seaplanes take supplies to prospecting communities during the summer, when they can land on lakes. During the winter, airplanes use skis for landing on the frozen lakes.

Yellowknife, the Northwest Territories' capital and largest city, was founded in the mid-1930's, about 20 years before modern pioneers began developing the Territories' mineral wealth. Today, the city is a growing metropolis.

Coat of Arms

Northwest Territories' coat of arms, granted in 1956, shows two golden narwhals guarding the compass rose. Bars of gold stand for mineral resources, and a fox for the fur industry.

★ Territorial Capital
● Other City or Town
----- District Boundaries
— Road
+—+ Rail Line
~ River

All islands in Hudson Bay, James Bay, and Ungava Bay are part of the Northwest Territories.

WORLD BOOK map

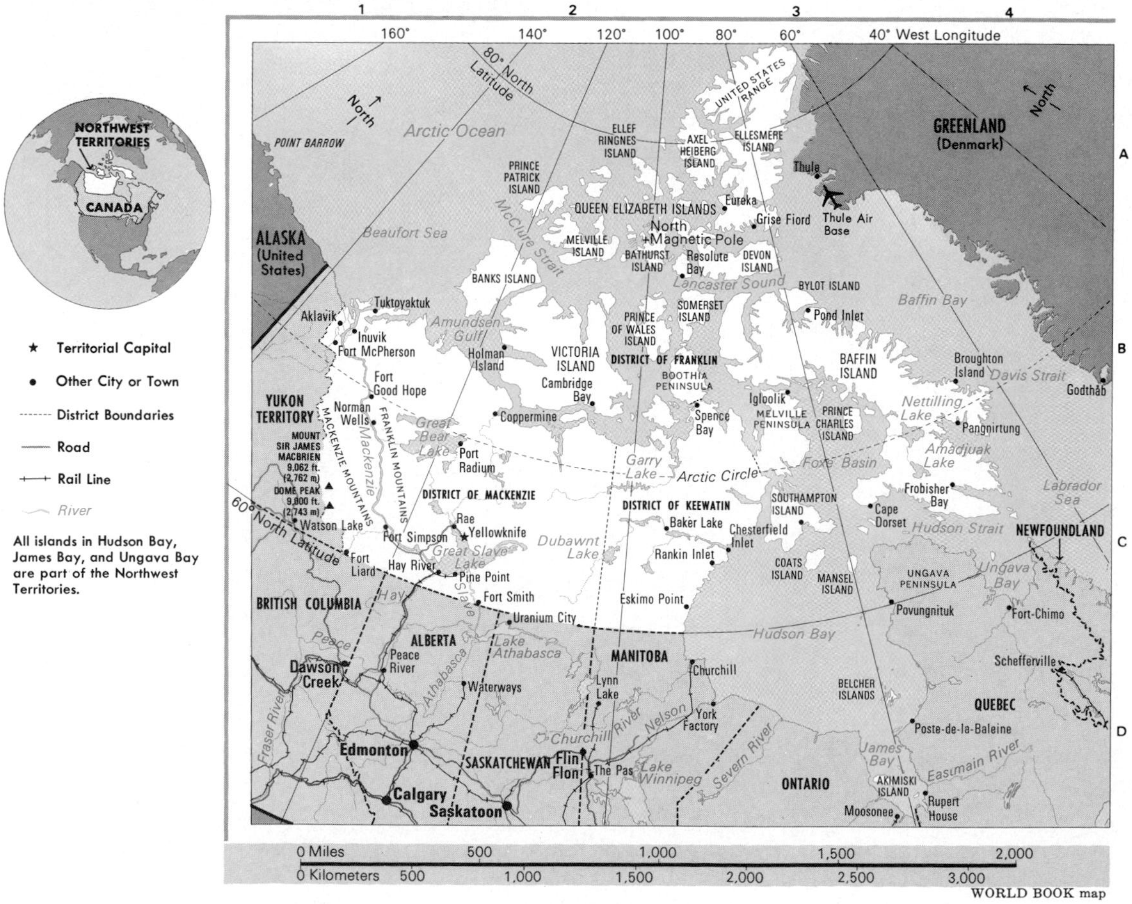

Yukon Territory

The Yukon Territory is located north of British Columbia and east of Alaska. The northernmost part of the territory lies north of the Arctic Circle. Large mountains cover much of the land area. Mount Logan, the highest point in Canada, is located in the St. Elias Mountains in the southwest.

This territory is named for the Yukon River. The word *yukon* itself is believed to have originated from the Indian word *youcon,* meaning "greatest river" or "big river."

The Yukon has short, warm summers and extremely long, cold winters. Because of the Territory's severe climate, Yukoners must wear warm clothing and keep their homes well heated in order to survive.

There had not been much settlement in the Yukon Territory until 1897, when gold was discovered on Bonanza Creek, a tributary of the Klondike River. This discovery led to the Klondike Gold Rush of 1897 and 1898. Prospectors poured into the Yukon Territory by the thousands after news of the discovery reached the rest of the world.

At the height of the Klondike Gold Rush in 1898, an estimated 35,000 persons lived in the Yukon Territory. Soon after much of the surface gold had been exhausted, however, many prospectors sold their claims and moved away.

Each year thousands of tourists visit the Yukon Territory as they travel across the Alaska Highway. The Yukon portion is believed by many to be the most scenic of the entire highway. Visitors enjoy seeing scenes of the Klondike Gold Rush. Many landmarks of the Gold Rush era have been preserved in Dawson. Other popular tourist attractions include the MacBride Museum at Whitehorse, the capital city of the Yukon Territory, and Kluane National Park in the southwest.

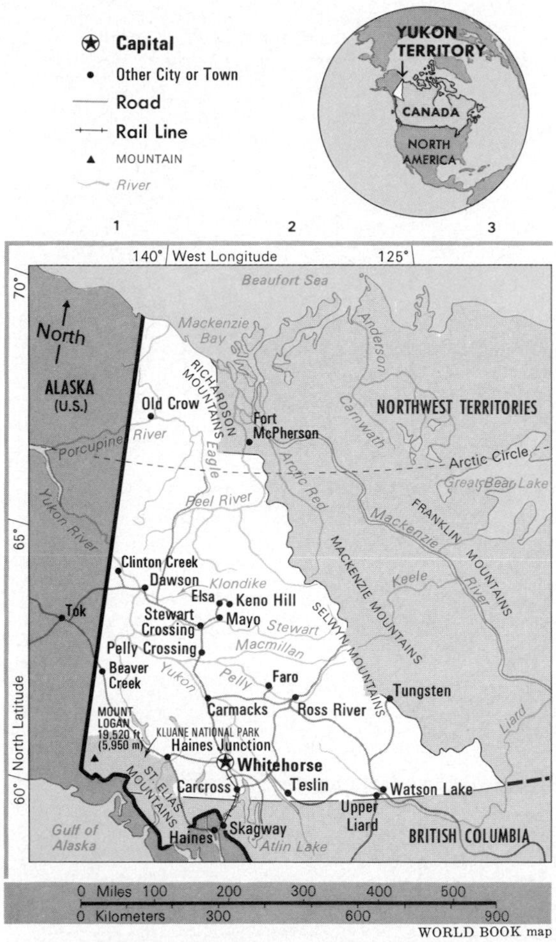

WORLD BOOK map

Capital: Whitehorse
Area: 207,076 sq. mi. 536,324 km²), including 1,730 sq. mi. (4,481 km²) of inland water
Elevation: *Highest*—Mount Logan in the Saint Elias Mountains, 19,520 ft. (5,950 m) above sea level; *lowest*—sea level, along the Beaufort Sea
Abbreviation: Y.T.
Flag: Adopted in 1967, has, from left to right, a green, white, and blue vertical panel. White panel has coat of arms above a wreath of fireweed.
Flower: Fireweed

Yukon Territory's coat of arms, granted in 1956, shows a crest with a black and white malamute above. A shield carries a wavy, blue vertical stripe representing the Yukon River. Red "steeples" stand for the mountains and gold balls for mineral resources. A cross of St. George symbolizes the fur trade of the early English explorers.

Coat of Arms

The glitter and glamour of gold have urged many to hasten to the Yukon Territory. Sternwheelers such as this one still transport hopeful prospectors, as well as sightseers, to Whitehorse—the Yukon's capital city.

Major cities

This section provides thumbnail descriptions of 50 U.S. and Canadian cities. Information given includes popular name, founding date, population, time zone, average low/high temperatures, and important sites.

Magnificent monuments like the Jefferson Memorial help make Washington, D.C., the U.S. capital, one of the nation's most striking, beautiful cities (facing page).

City Hall stands in downtown Toronto, Ont. This modern complex consists of two curved office buildings and an oyster-shaped city council chambers (above left).

Detroit, Mich., is the home of Renaissance Center. One of the largest renewal projects in U.S. history, it includes four 39-story office buildings and a circular 73-story hotel (above right).

A cable car makes its stiff climb en route through San Francisco, Calif. Some of the world's steepest streets lie in this interesting city, sometimes called "America's favorite" (below left).

United States

Atlanta, Georgia
Dogwood City

The capital of Georgia and its largest city. Distribution, manufacturing, and transportation center of the Southeast. The center of one of the nation's fastest growing urban areas. Famous for its large old homes and beautiful flower gardens.
Founded 1837 at the southern end of the Western and Atlantic Railroad. Named Terminus; in 1845 J. Edgar Thompson, a railroad engineer, renamed the city Atlanta after the Western and Atlantic; incorporated 1847.
City proper—436,057 persons; *metropolitan area*—1,595,517 persons
Eastern Standard Time; *Low/high temp.:* Jan.—36/53F. (2/12C), July—70/89F. (21/32C)
What to see—Peachtree Center, Peachtree Street, Underground Atlanta, Five Points, Atlanta Memorial Arts Center, Grant Park, Atlanta Historical Society, Grave of Martin Luther King, Jr., Toy Museum of Atlanta, Wren's Nest

Baltimore, Maryland

The largest city in Maryland and the seventh largest in the nation. Commerce, education, and industry center of Maryland. One of the nation's principal port cities. Has one of the world's largest natural harbors. The only U.S. port with two links to the Atlantic Ocean. Site of the inspiration for the "Star-spangled Banner" during the War of 1812.
Founded 1729 by the Maryland colonial government as a trading center for the tobacco farmers of southern Maryland; named in honor of the Lords Baltimore, heads of the family that founded and controlled the colony of Maryland; incorporated 1796.
City proper—851,698 persons; *metropolitan area*—2,071,016 persons
Eastern Standard Time; *Low/high temp.:* Jan.— 26/43F. (−3/6C), July—66/87F. (19/31C)
What to see—Star-spangled Banner Flag House and 1812 War Museum, Basilica of the Assumption of the Blessed Virgin Mary, Edgar Allan Poe House, Lexington Market, Johns Hopkins University, Babe Ruth Birthplace Shrine and Museum, Fort McHenry National Monument, Baltimore Seaport

Boston, Massachusetts
Hub of the Universe, Athens of America, Cradle of Liberty

The capital of Massachusetts and New England's largest city. Business, financial, government, and transportation center of New England. One of the nation's great educational centers and one of its oldest and most historic cities. A birthplace of the American Revolutionary War.
Founded by the Puritans 1630; named after Boston, England, where many of the Puritans had lived; incorporated 1822.
City proper—636,725 persons; *metropolitan area*—2,899,101 persons; *consolidated metropolitan area*—3,526,349 persons
Eastern Standard Time; *Low/high temp.:* Jan.—20/40F. (−7/4C), July —60/84F. (16/29C)
City sections—Downtown Boston; Back Bay; Beacon Hill; North End; South Boston; East Boston; Charlestown, Brighton-Allston; Roxbury, Dorchester, and Jamaica Plain; Southwestern Boston
What to see—Freedom Trail, Boston Common, Prudential Center, Bunker Hill Monument, USS *Constitution,* Boston Tea Party Ship and Museum, Haymarket Square, Tremont Street, New England Aquarium, Plymouth Rock and the *Mayflower II* in Plymouth

Charleston, South Carolina

An important Atlantic seaport and South Carolina's second largest city. Famous for its preservation of buildings and homes of the 1700's and 1800's and for some of the nation's oldest landscaped gardens. The birthplace of the Confederacy in 1861.
Founded 1670 by settlers from England and the British West Indies; named for King Charles II of England; first called Charles Town, then changed to Charleston in 1783.
City proper—57,818 persons; *metropolitan area*—336,125 persons
Eastern Standard Time; *Low/high temp.:* Jan.—44/59F. (7/15C), July—75/88F. (24/31C)
What to see—Edmondston-Alston House, Provost Dungeon, Heyward-Washington House, Old Slave Mart Museum and Gallery, Gateway Walk, Middleton Place Gardens, Magnolia Plantation, Fort Sumter National Monument, Charleston Museum, Charles Towne Landing, Cypress Gardens, aircraft carrier *Yorktown*

Note: All statistics are taken from the latest available figures.

Chicago, Illinois
Second City, City of the Big Shoulders

The nation's second largest city and its leading industrial and transportation center. Produces more steel, cookies, candy, paint, and radios and TV sets than any other area of the country. More goods transported in and out of Chicago than any other U.S. city. Has one of the world's most beautiful lakefronts and its tallest building, largest grain market, biggest post office building, and busiest airport.

Founded 1803 at the south bank of what is now known as the Chicago River; named after the river, which the Potawatomi Indians called the Checagou; incorporated 1837.

City proper—3,099,391 persons; *metropolitan area*—6,978,947 persons; *consolidated metropolitan area*—7,621,647 persons

Central Standard Time; *Low/high temp.:* Jan.—17/33F. (−8/1C), July—64/75F. (18/29C)

City sections—Downtown Chicago, North Side, West Side, South Side

What to see—Museum of Science and Industry, Shedd Aquarium, Adler Planetarium, Art Institute of Chicago, Lincoln Park Zoo, Buckingham Fountain, Sears Tower, Chicago Board of Trade, Dearborn Street plazas, Magnificent Mile, Water Tower Place, Hancock Building, State Street Mall, Chicago Public Library Cultural Center, Chicago Symphony, Navy Pier, Old Town

Skyscrapers like the Hancock Building in Chicago, Ill., form a magnificent skyline against one of the world's most beautiful lakefronts.

Cincinnati, Ohio
Queen City of the West

Ohio's third largest city and a major industrial and commercial center of the Midwest. World's leading producer of soap and playing cards and the nation's leading producer of machine tools. One of the nation's most beautiful cities.

Founded 1788 by early settlers and called Losantiville; name changed to Cincinnati by General Arthur St. Clair, governor of the Northwest Territory, in 1790 in honor of the Society of the Cincinnati, an organization of army officers of the Revolutionary War; incorporated 1819.

City proper—412,564 persons; *metropolitan area*—1,385,103 persons; *consolidated metropolitan area*—1,611,310 persons

Eastern Standard Time; *Low/high temp.:* Jan.—25/41F. (−4/5C), July—66/87F. (19/31C)

What to see—Riverfront Stadium, Carew Tower, *Delta Queen,* Skywalk System, William Howard Taft National Historic Site, Public Landing, Stowe House State Memorial, Cincinnati Zoo, Eden Park and Krohn Conservatory, Museum of Natural History

Cleveland, Ohio

Ohio's largest city and one of the nation's leading industrial centers. An important producer of steel because of its nearness to Lake Erie and the Cuyahoga River, and to huge supplies of coal and iron ore. A transportation and cultural center of the Midwest. A chief port and one of the busiest on the Great Lakes. Receives more iron ore than any other U.S. port.

Founded 1796 by Moses Cleaveland, a surveyor for the Connecticut Land Company; named after Cleaveland, but a newspaper printer misspelled the name in 1831 and it has remained Cleveland ever since; incorporated 1836.

City proper—638,793 persons; *metropolitan area*—

2,063,729 persons; *consolidated metropolitan area*—2,999,811 persons
Eastern Standard Time; *Low/high temp.:* Jan.—21/36F. (−6/2C), July—63/85F. (17/29C)
What to see—"The Mall," Public Square, Terminal Tower, Dunham Tavern Museum, Cleveland Health Museum and Education Center, Lakeview Cemetery, Cleveland Museum of Art, Rockefeller Park and Cleveland Cultural Gardens, Cleveland Orchestra, high-level bridges

Columbus, Ohio

The capital of Ohio and its second most populated city. Has a larger land area than any other city in the state. A leading industrial center of the state. Home of one of the nation's largest universities, the Ohio State University.
Founded 1812 as the capital of Ohio because of the site's proximity to all major cities in the state; named by the state legislators in honor of the explorer Christopher Columbus; incorporated 1834.
City proper—535,610 persons; *metropolitan area*—1,017,847 persons
Eastern Standard Time; *Low/high temp.:* Jan.—25/41F. (−4/6C), July—63/87F. (17/32C)
What to see—Leveque-Lincoln Tower; Avenue of the Flags; Ohio State University; Gallery of Fine Arts; Park of Roses; state capitol; Ohio Village, City Hall, and Plaza; German Village

Dallas, Texas
Big D

The second largest city in Texas and the eighth largest in the United States. One of the nation's major centers of banking, fashion, manufacturing, trade, and transportation. One of the country's leading manufacturers of electronics and electrical equipment, aircraft and missile parts, and women's clothing. The headquarters of more oil firms than any other U.S. city and of more insurance companies than any other southern city. A cultural center and the area's most important transportation center.
Founded 1841 by John Neely Bryan, a lawyer and trader, when he built a trading post on the Trinity River; believed by historians to be named for George M. Dallas, the vice-president of the United States under President James K. Polk; incorporated 1871.
City proper—822,461 persons; *metropolitan area*—2,378,353 persons
Central Standard Time; *Low/high temp.:* Jan.—36/55F. (2/13C), July—76/95F. (24/35C)
What to see—Reunion Tower, Dealey Plaza, Summer Rodeo, State Fair Park, Dallas Theater Center

Denver, Colorado
Mile High City

The capital of Colorado and a central point for snow sports. Distribution, manufacturing, and transportation center for the Rocky Mountain area. The national or regional headquarters of more federal agencies than any other city in the United States except Washington, D.C. One of the nation's major livestock centers is located at the Denver Union Stockyards.
Founded 1858 by prospectors after gold was discovered at Cherry Creek; named for James W. Denver, a governor of the territory; incorporated 1861.
City proper—488,434 persons; *metropolitan area*—1,239,477 persons
Mountain Standard Time; *Low/high temp.:* Jan.—16/42F. (−9/6C), July—58/87F. (14/31C)
What to see—Denver Art Museum, Colorado Heritage Center, Denver Museum of Natural History, U.S. Mint, state capitol, Larimer Square

Detroit, Michigan
Automobile Capital of the World, Motor City, Arsenal of Democracy

The largest city in Michigan and the sixth largest in the nation. One of the world's greatest industrial centers and its leading producer of automobiles. Michigan's largest port and one of the most important in the United States. Became an international seaport with the opening of the St. Lawrence Seaway in 1959. The Detroit River, along which the city lies, ranks as one of the world's busiest inland waterways. A major center of transportation. A leading producer of military equipment during World War II. Under the city lies one of the largest salt mines in the country.
Founded 1701 by Antoine de la Mothe Cadillac, a French colonist who, with a group of settlers, built Fort Pontchartrain on the Detroit River; name derived from *détroit,* the French word for "strait"; incorporated 1806.
City proper—1,335,085 persons; *metropolitan area*—4,435,051 persons; *consolidated metropolitan area*—4,669,154 persons
Eastern Standard Time; *Low/high temp.:* Jan.—19/32F. (−7/0C), July—63/84F. (17/29C)
What to see—Automobile plants, Cultural, Civic, and Renaissance centers, Detroit Institute of Arts, Belle Isle, Detroit Zoological Park, Masonic Temple

Fort Worth, Texas
Cowtown

One of the largest industrial cities in the state and one of the chief aircraft producers in the United

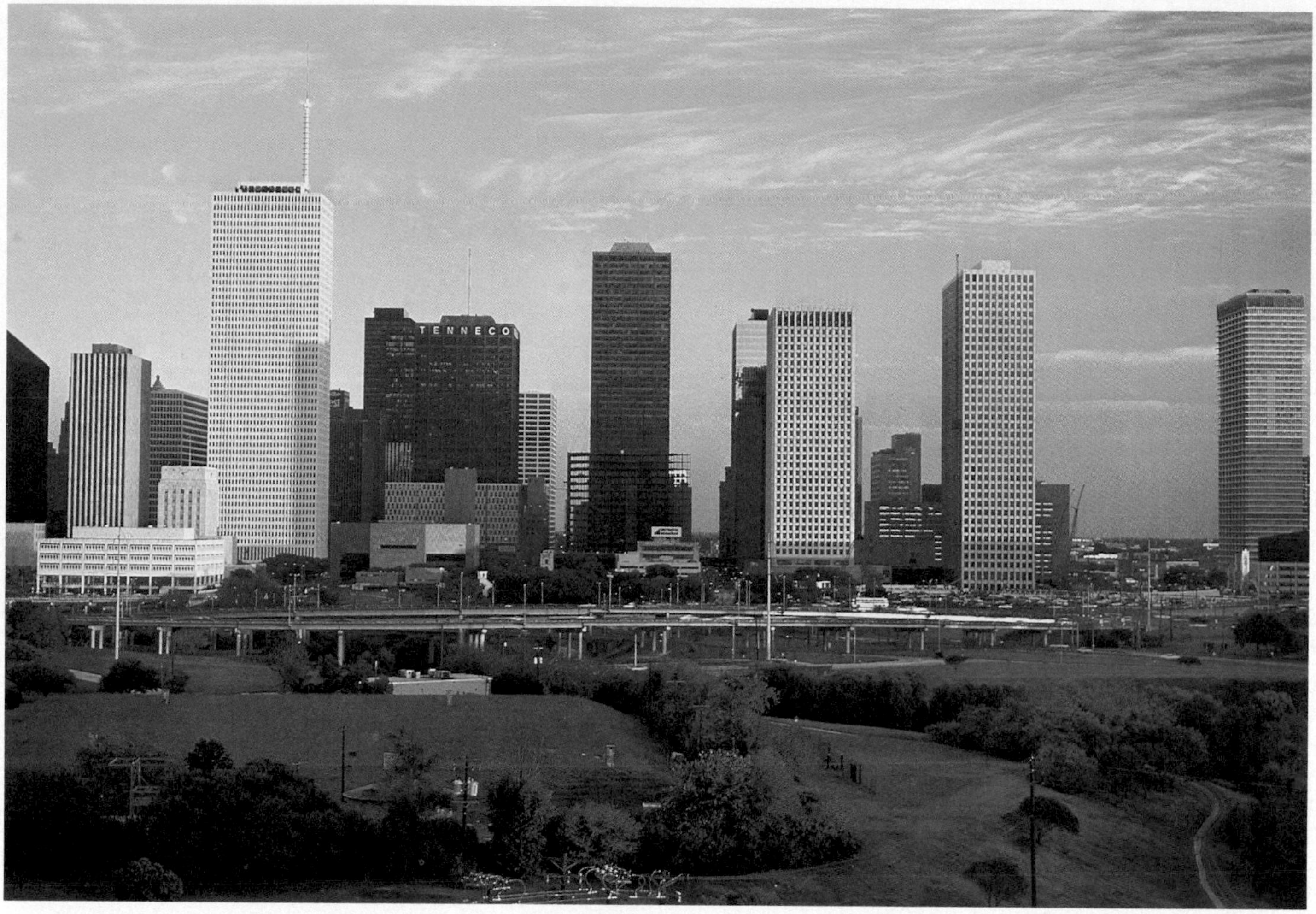

Looping freeways around downtown Houston, Tex., link the city with its suburbs. Houston is Texas' largest city, and its metropolitan area is the home of a sixth of all Texans.

States. Its aircraft plants rank among the largest in the nation. A leading market for grain and oil among cities in the region. Has a history of being a cattle-marketing center and has become one of the fastest growing urban centers in Texas. A major wholesale outlet for the region.

Founded 1849 by Major Ripley A. Arnold as an army post to protect settlers from Indian attacks; named for Major General William J. Worth, a hero of the Mexican War; incorporated 1873.

City proper—358,364 persons; *metropolitan area*—2,378,353 persons

Central Standard Time; *Low/high temp.:* Jan.—36/55F. (2/13C), July—76/95F. (24/35C)

What to see—Fort Worth Museum of Science and History, Will Rogers Memorial Center, Tarrant County Convention Center, Fort Worth Water Gardens, Fort Worth Zoological Park

Honolulu, Hawaii
Crossroads of the Pacific

The capital, largest city, and chief port of Hawaii. Home of four-fifths of Hawaii's entire population. A popular tourist spot and one of the nation's fastest growing cities. The center of U.S. military operations in the Pacific, as well as the Pacific's center of air and sea travel. Site of the bombing of Pearl Harbor, which marked the U.S. entrance into World War II.

Founded 1794 by Captain William Brown of England, who sailed into what is now Honolulu Harbor and found shelter; *honolulu* is a Hawaiian word meaning "sheltered bay"; incorporated 1907

City and county of Honolulu—705,381 persons

Alaska-Hawaii Standard Time; *Low/high temp.:* Jan.—67/77F. (19/25C), July—74/82F. (23/28C)

What to see—Pearl Harbor, Diamond Head Crater, Iolani Palace, Waikiki Beach, Foster Botanical Gardens, Queen Emma's Summer Palace, Kapiolani Park, Punchbowl National Memorial, state capitol, Royal Mausoleum

Houston, Texas

The largest city in Texas and the fifth largest in the nation. One of the world's major seaports in spite of its location 50 miles (80.5 kilometers) inland. The Houston Ship Channel links it to the Gulf of

Las Vegas, Nev., is famous for its gambling casinos and night-clubs. A major U.S. tourist center, the city entertains about 10 million visitors yearly.

Mexico. Ranks third in cargo handled among port cities of the United States. The leading trade center of the region. A major industrial city and, with the Southeast Texas Gulf Coast, the nation's top oil-refining center. Serves as a center of the U.S. space program. Leads the nation in the manufacture of fertilizers, insecticides, and oil field equipment. Founded 1836 by Augustus C. and John K. Allen, brothers and real estate promoters; named by them in honor of General Samuel Houston, commander of the army that won Texas' independence from Mexico; incorporated 1839.
City proper—1,388,929 persons; *metropolitan area*—1,999,316 persons; *consolidated metropolitan area*—2,169,128 persons
Central Standard Time; *Low/high temp.:* Jan.—50/61F. (10/16C), July—76/88F. (24/31C)
What to see—Lyndon B. Johnson Space Center, Port of Houston, San Jacinto Battleground State Park, Battleship *Texas,* Houston Civic Center, Astrodome, Old Market Square, Houston Zoological Gardens

Indianapolis, Indiana
Crossroads of America

The capital and largest city of Indiana. One of the chief centers of manufacturing, transportation, and the distribution of goods in the Midwest. One of the largest cities in the nation not on navigable water. Home of the famous Indianapolis 500 automobile race held during the Memorial Day weekend. World's leading producer of telephones. Founded 1820 by the George Pogue and John McCormick families, the first white settlers in the area; name conceived by Jeremiah Sullivan, an Indiana Supreme Court judge, by combining *Indiana* with *polis,* the Greek word for "city"; incorporated 1847.
City proper—714,878 persons; *metropolitan area*—1,111,352 persons
Eastern Standard Time; *Low/high temp.:* Jan.—21/37F. (−6/3C), July—64/88F. (18/31C)
What to see—Indianapolis Motor Speedway and Museum, World War Memorial Plaza, Soldiers and Sailors Monument, Children's Museum, Scottish

Rite Cathedral, Conner Prairie Pioneer Settlement and Museum, Benjamin Harrison Memorial Home, Garfield Park

Jacksonville, Florida

The largest city in Florida and its financial and insurance capital. An important seaport and a major center for transportation and distribution in the Southeast. Florida's second busiest port. Ranks second among all U.S. cities in land area.
Founded 1822 by Isaiah D. Hart, a Georgia plantation owner; named after Andrew Jackson, the provisional governor of the Territory of Florida and later the seventh President of the United States; incorporated 1859.
City proper—535,030 persons; *metropolitan area*—621,827 persons
Eastern Standard Time; *Low/high temp.:* Jan.—48/70F. (9/21C), July—74/90F. (23/32C)
What to see—St. Johns River Park and Marina, Friendship Fountain, Fort Caroline National Memorial, Cummer Gallery of Art, Jacksonville Children's Museum, Treaty Oak, Kingsley Plantation State Historical Memorial

Kansas City, Missouri
Heart of America

The second largest city in Missouri and a commerce, industry, and transportation center of the Midwest. Its location in the center of the United States helped it become a national distribution, transportation, and warehouse center. The largest winter-wheat market in the nation. The city's Livestock Exchange is also one of the largest in the United States. Beneath the metropolitan area lies a vast system of limestone caves, some of which have been converted into warehouses for frozen food storage.
Founded 1821 by employees of the American Fur Company, who established a trading post on the site; named the Town of Kansas for the Kansa Indians, who once lived in the area; incorporated 1853 as the city of Kansas; name officially changed to Kansas City 1889.
City proper—472,529 persons; *metropolitan area*—1,273,926 persons
Central Standard Time; *Low/high temp.:* Jan.—21/39F. (−6/4C), July—71/91F. (22/33C)
What to see—Kansas City Livestock Exchange and Stockyards, Liberty Memorial, Nelson Gallery-Atkins Museum, Swope Park, City Market, Country Club Plaza, Crown Center

Las Vegas, Nevada

Nevada's largest city and a major tourist center of the United States. Famous for its gambling casinos and nightclubs. A shipping center for the surrounding mining and ranching area.
Founded 1905 as a station in the middle of a fertile grassland on what is now the Union Pacific Railroad route; name derived from the Spanish words meaning "the meadows"; incorporated 1911.
City proper—146,030 persons; *metropolitan area*—273,288 persons
Pacific Standard Time; *Low/high temp.:* Jan.—33/55F. (1/13C), July—76/105F. (24/41C)
What to see—The Strip, Convention Center, Behind-the-Scenes Tour—Del Webb's Mint Hotel, Red Rock Canyon Recreation Area, University of Nevada, Las Vegas, Museum of Natural History

Los Angeles, California

The nation's third largest city and the business, financial, and trade center of the western United States. Home of some of the largest banks and financial institutions in the country. The nation's leader in the production of aircraft and equipment for space exploration. World famous for its television and motion-picture industry. The busiest port on the West Coast and the nation's leading fishing port.
Founded 1781 by a group of pioneers from Guaymas, Mexico; name derived from the original Spanish name for the area, Neustra Señora la Reina de Los Angeles de Porciúncula, meaning "Our Lady the Queen of the Angels of Porciúncula"; incorporated 1850.
City proper—2,727,399 persons; *metropolitan area*—7,032,075 persons; *consolidated metropolitan area*—9,972,037 persons
Pacific Standard Time; *Low/high temp.:* Jan.—45/65F. (7/18C), July—62/83F. (17/28C)

Few U.S. cities have grown as rapidly as Los Angeles, Calif. Its pleasant climate attracts thousands of new residents each year.

City sections—Downtown Los Angeles; South-Central Los Angeles; Central Los Angeles; San Fernando Valley; West Los Angeles; South Bay; Port of Los Angeles; East Los Angeles
What to see—Griffith Park and the Los Angeles Zoo, Spanish missions, Farmers Market, Universal Studios, television broadcasting stations, Disneyland, Chinatown, Busch Gardens, La Brea Pits, Marineland, Music Center for the Performing Arts, Los Angeles County Museum of Art

Louisville, Kentucky
Falls City

Kentucky's largest city and a major industrial center of the Southeast. An important transportation link between the North and the South. Home of the world-famous horse race, the Kentucky Derby, held yearly on the first Saturday in May. The tobacco manufacturing center of the world and one of the largest producers of gin and whiskey in the United States.
Founded 1778 by a group of pioneers led by the explorer George Rogers Clark; named by Clark for King Louis XVI of France in gratitude for France's help to the colonies during the American Revolutionary War; incorporated 1828.
City proper—335,954 persons; *metropolitan area*—867,330 persons
Eastern Standard Time; *Low/high temp.:* Jan.—26/44F. (−3/7C), July—67/89F. (19/32C)
What to see—Churchill Downs, Riverfront Plaza, Founders Square, Cave Hill Cemetery, Locust Grove, boat excursion—*Belle of Louisville,* distillery tours

Memphis, Tennessee
City of Churches

The largest city in Tennessee and the chief commercial and industrial center of western Tennessee and parts of neighboring states. The world's largest market for cotton and hardwood lumber. About a third of the nation's cotton bought or sold in Memphis each year. One of the South's largest livestock, meat-packing, and wholesale marketing centers. Ranks second, behind St. Louis, as the busiest inland port on the Mississippi River. An important center of medical care, motel development, and recorded music.
Founded 1819 by General Andrew Jackson, Judge John Overton, and General James Winchester, who became owners of the land when the U.S. Government bought much of western Tennessee from the Chickasaw Indians; named for the ancient Egyptian capital Memphis on the Nile River; incorporated 1849.
City proper—661,319 persons; *metropolitan area*—834,103 persons
Central Standard Time; *Low/high temp.:* Jan.—33/51F. (0/10C), July—70/91F. (21/31C)
What to see—Overton Park Zoo and Aquarium, Memphis Cotton Exchange, Beale Street, Magevney House, Victorian Village, Mississippi River excursion—*Memphis Queen,* Chucalissa Indian Village and Museum

Miami, Florida

The second largest city in Florida and a world-famous resort city. Ranks second among U.S. cities in the production of clothing. An important center of international banking.
Founded 1896 when Julia D. Tuttle agreed to give Henry Flagler half her land in return for his bringing the Florida East Coast Railroad to the area around Biscayne Bay; named for the Miami River; incorporated 1896.
City proper—365,082 persons; *metropolitan area*—1,267,792 persons
Eastern Standard Time; *Low/high temp.:* Jan.—58/76F. (14/24C), July—75/89F. (24/32C)
What to see—Miami Beach, Bay cruise, Vizcaya, Museum of Science and Space Transit Planetarium, Historical Museum of Southern Florida, Parrot Jungle, Bayfront Park, Seaquarium, Serpentarium

Milwaukee, Wisconsin
Beer Capital, Cream City

The largest city in Wisconsin and one of the nation's major industrial centers. A leading manufacturer of automobile parts and electrical equipment. The nation's largest beer producer and an important Great Lakes port.
Founded 1833 by Solomon Juneau, a French-Canadian fur trader; later combined with other villages to become Milwaukee; name derived from Algonquin Indian name, *Millioke,* translated by some historians as "good land" and by others as "great council place"; incorporated 1846.
City proper—665,796 persons; *metropolitan area*—1,403,884 persons; *consolidated metropolitan area*—1,574,722 persons
Central Standard Time; *Low/high temp.:* Jan.—15/29F. (−9/−2C), July—61/81F. (16/27C)
What to see—Milwaukee Public Museum, Milwaukee War Memorial, Milwaukee Harbor, Mitchell Park Horticultural Conservatory, Milwaukee County Zoo, Court of Honor, brewing company tours, Greek Orthodox Church of the Annunciation, St. Joan of Arc Chapel

Minneapolis, Minnesota
City of Lakes, Vacation Capital

The largest city in Minnesota and home of one of the nation's largest universities, the University of Minnesota. A finance, industry, trade, and transportation center of the Midwest. The nation's leading market center for farm equipment. With its twin city, St. Paul, ranks among the nation's top trucking terminals. Home of Minnehaha Falls, made famous by the U.S. poet Henry Wadsworth Longfellow in his poem *The Song of Hiawatha.*
Founded 1849 by settlers who were lumber workers from Maine; they called the village All Saints; residents changed the name to Minneapolis in 1852; Minneapolis comes from the Indian word *minne,* meaning "water," and the Greek word *polis,* meaning "city"; so named because of the 22 natural lakes that lie within the city limits; incorporated 1866.
City proper—378,112 persons; *metropolitan area*—1,965,391 persons
Central Standard Time; *Low/high temp.:* Jan.—6/23F. (−14/−5C), July—63/85F. (17/29C)
What to see—Nicollet Mall, IDS Tower, University of Minnesota, Minnehaha Park and Falls, St. Anthony Falls, Walker Art Center, Guthrie Theater, Science Museum and Planetarium

Nashville, Tennessee
Athens of the South, Music City

Tennessee's capital and its second largest city. A recording and broadcasting center for country music. Ranks as one of the nation's largest cities in land area. Famous for its buildings in the Greek classical style.
Founded 1779 by settlers from North Carolina looking for fertile farmland; called Fort Nashborough after Brigadier General Francis Nash, an American Revolutionary War hero and friend of one of the settlers; renamed Nashville in 1784; incorporated 1806.
City proper—423,426 persons; *metropolitan area*—699,271 persons
Central Standard Time; *Low/high temp.:* Jan.—31/49F. (−1/9C), July—69/91F. (21/33C)
What to see—Opryland USA, Grand Ole Opry House, Hermitage, Parthenon, Tennessee Game Farm, Country Music Hall of Fame and Museum, Tennessee State Museum, state capitol, Belle Meade Mansion, Tennessee Botanical Gardens and Fine Arts Center

The Miami, Fla., metropolitan area is famous for its sandy beaches and beautiful year-round weather. Tourism produces about $4 billion annually in this major U.S. resort city.

New Orleans, Louisiana
America's Most Interesting City, Crescent City

Louisiana's largest city and the oldest major city in the South. An important shipping center and one of the world's busiest ports. A business, cultural, and industrial center of the South. Famous for its annual Mardi Gras celebration. Helped give birth to jazz in the early 1900's.
Founded 1718 by Jean Baptiste le Moyne, Sieur de Bienville, governor of the French colony of Louisiana; named after Phillipe, Duke of Orléans, who ruled France as regent for King Louis XV; incorporated 1805.
City proper—559,770 persons; *metropolitan area*—1,046,470 persons
Central Standard Time; *Low/high temp.:* Jan.—48/64F. (9/18C), July—76/90F. (24/32C)
What to see—French Quarter, Preservation Hall, St. Louis Cathedral, Pirate's Alley, Cabildo, Madame John's Legacy, levees and docks, city park and Lake Pontchartrain, Garden District, International Trade Mart, Louisiana Superdome, Mardi Gras Museum, New Orleans Jazz Museum, Moss-Pitot House

New York City, New York
Big Apple

The nation's largest city and the fifth largest in the world. One of the world's greatest cultural centers and the home of some of the nation's largest museums and art galleries. Its Broadway area is the center of professional theater in the United States. Nation's most important communications center and one of the chief printing and publishing centers in the United States. One of the world's largest and busiest seaports. Handles more cargo than any other U.S. port. One of the world's most important centers of business and finance. Its financial institutions help provide the money used by most of the nation's large corporations.
Founded 1624 by Dutch settlers; originally named New Amsterdam; renamed New York by the English; incorporated 1653.
City proper—7,481,613 persons; *metropolitan area*—11,571,899 persons; *consolidated metropolitan area*—18,565,136 persons
Eastern Standard Time; *Low/high temp.:* Jan.—26/40F. (−3/4C), July—67/82F. (19/28C)
City sections—Manhattan, Brooklyn, Bronx, Queens, Staten Island
What to see—Statue of Liberty, Empire State Building, Rockefeller Center, St. Patrick's Cathedral, U.N. Headquarters, Greenwich Village, Museum of Modern Art, Broadway, Times Square, Lincoln Center for the Performing Arts, Central Park, Guggenheim Museum

Omaha, Nebraska

Nebraska's largest city and one of the nation's busiest railroad terminals. A leading cattle market and meat-packing center of the world. The trading center for eastern Nebraska and western Iowa.
Founded 1854 through an Indian treaty; site chosen because of its rich farmland and location favorable to trading; named for the Omaha Indians; incorporated 1857.
City proper—371,455 persons; *metropolitan area*—542,646 persons
Central Standard Time; *Low/high temp.:* Jan.—14/32F. (−10/0C), July—68/89F. (20/32C)
What to see—Boys Town, Joslyn Art Museum, Union Pacific Historical Museum, Old Market, Mormon Cemetery, Fontenelle Forest, historic Bellevue

Philadelphia, Pennsylvania
City of Brotherly Love, Quaker City

The fourth largest city in the nation and one of its most historic cities. The birthplace of the United States and the capital of the American colonies during most of the American Revolutionary War. A culture, education, finance, and industry center of the United States. One of the world's busiest ports. The biggest oil-refining district on the East Coast and a major center of shipbuilding in the nation.
Founded 1682 by William Penn, an English Quaker, as a center for religious freedom; *philadelphia* means "brotherly love" in Greek; incorporated 1701.
City proper—1,815,808 persons; *metropolitan area* 4,824,110 persons; *consolidated metropolitan area*—5,672,719 persons
Eastern Standard Time; *Low/high temp.:* Jan.—25/41F. (−4/5C), July—66/87F. (19/31C)
What to see—Independence National Historical Park, City Hall, observation deck—Penn Mutual Tower, Academy of Natural Sciences of Philadelphia, Franklin Institute, Rodin Museum, Fairmount Park, Betsy Ross House, Christ Church, U.S. Mint, Society Hill area, Germantown, Philadelphia Orchestra, Norman Rockwell Museum, Living History Center, Walnut Street Theater

Phoenix, Arizona

The capital and largest city of Arizona. A major resort center of the country and a leading manufacturer of computers and electronic equipment. One of the fastest growing cities of the United States.
Founded 1871 by Darrell Duppa; named for the phoenix, a Greek mythological bird that supposedly burned itself every 500 years and then rose to life again with renewed youth and beauty; incorporated 1881.
City proper—664,721 persons; *metropolitan area*—971,228 persons
Mountain Standard Time; *Low/high temp.:* Jan.—35/65F. (2/18C), July—75/105F. (24/41C)
What to see—State capitol, Hall of Flame, Desert Botanical Garden, Heard Museum of Anthropology and Primitive Arts, Pueblo Grande Museum, Taliesin West, Rawhide Western Town, Phoenix Zoo, Camelback Mountain

Pittsburgh, Pennsylvania
Hearth of the Nation, Iron City, Steel City, Arsenal of the World

Pennsylvania's second largest city and a leading industrial city of the United States. One of the great steelmaking centers of the world and the heart of the nation's chief steel area. The center of Pennsylvania's inland waterway system. Features 720 bridges—more than the number found in any other city in the nation.
Founded 1758 by British settlers who established a community outside Fort Pitt; named for William Pitt, then prime minister of Great Britain; incorporated 1816.
City proper—458,651 persons; *metropolitan area*—2,401,362 persons
Eastern Standard Time; *Low/high temp.:* Jan.—21/37F. (−6/3C), July—62/83F. (17/28C)
What to see—Point State Park, Carnegie Institute, Buhl Planetarium and Institute of Popular Science, Gateway Center, Civic Arena, Monongahela and Duquesne inclined planes, Alcoa Building, Schenley Park, Old Post Office Museum, Stephen Foster Memorial, Cathedral of Learning, Highland Park zoos

Portland, Oregon
City of Roses

The largest city in Oregon and its major center of industry, trade, finance, and medicine. An important West Coast port. Handles more grain and lumber than any other port in the Pacific Northwest. Famous for its public and private rose gardens. Served as a supply point for gold miners in Alaska and the Yukon Territory of Canada during the late 1890's and early 1900's.
Founded 1845 by two land developers, Asa L. Lovejoy of Boston and Francis W. Pettygrove of Portland, Maine; named for Pettygrove's home city after he won the flip of a penny; incorporated 1851.
City proper—356,732 persons; *metropolitan area*—1,007,130 persons
Pacific Standard Time; *Low/high temp.:* Jan.—35/44F. (2/7C), July—58/79F. (14/26C)
What to see—Civic Auditorium Forecourt and Fountain, Oregon Museum of Science and Industry, Oregon Historical Society, Pittock Mansion, Council Crest Park, Sanctuary of Our Sorrowful Mother, St. Johns Bridge, International Rose Test Garden, Hoyt Arboretum

St. Louis, Missouri

The largest city in Missouri and a leading industrial and transportation center of the nation. Ranks second as a rail and trucking center among U.S. cities. The busiest inland port on the Mississippi River. One of the nation's top hog-shipping centers. The finance center of the central Mississippi River Valley. One of the few cities in the United States that is not in a county.
Founded 1764 by fur traders who built a post on its site, chosen because Indians bringing furs to trade could reach it easily by canoe; named for King Louis IX, who had been made a saint; incorporated 1822.
City proper—524,964 persons; *metropolitan area*—2,410,492 persons
Central Standard Time; *Low/high temp.:* Jan.—26/41F. (−3/5C), July—72/90F. (22/32C)
What to see—Gateway Arch, Old Courthouse, Jefferson National Expansion Memorial, Old Cathedral, Missouri Botanical Garden, Forest Park, St. Louis Zoo, St. Louis Cathedral, Aloe Plaza, Laclede's Landing, Grant's Farm, National Museum of Transport, river excursions

Salt Lake City, Utah

The capital and largest city of Utah. World headquarters of the Church of Jesus Christ of Latter-day Saints, commonly known as the Mormon Church. One of the chief centers of culture, finance, industry, and transportation of the Rocky Mountain states. Home of the largest open-pit copper mines in North America. Founded 1847 by Mormon pioneers, led by Brigham Young, who were fleeing from religious persecution; named for Great Salt Lake; incorporated 1851.
City proper—175,885 persons; *metropolitan area*—705,458 persons
Mountain Standard Time; *Low/high temp.:* Jan.—17/36F. (−8/2C), July—61/92F. (16/33C)
What to see—Temple Square, grave of Brigham Young, Salt Palace, state capitol, Pioneer Trails State Park, International Peace Gardens, Utah State Historical Society, Great Salt Lake, Bingham Canyon Mine, ZCMI Shopping Center, Trolley Square

San Antonio, Texas
Alamo City

The tenth largest city in the United States and one of its most historic cities. Site of the famous Battle of the Alamo in 1836. One of the leading cultural and trade centers of the region and one of its leading science centers. Home of some of the nation's largest military bases. One of the region's leading convention cities.

Called the Gateway to the North, *Edmonton, Alta., is a major distributing point to and from Alaska and northwestern Canada. It is the most northern major city in North America.*

Founded 1718 by Father Antonio Olivares when he established a Spanish mission on the site; chosen because of its location midway between the Spanish missions in eastern Texas and the Spanish military posts in northern Mexico; named for St. Anthony of Padua; incorporated 1837.
City proper—773,248 persons; *metropolitan area*—888,179 persons
Central Standard Time; *Low/high temp.:* Jan.—42/66F. (5/20C), July—72/96F. (22/36C)
What to see—Alamo, Menger Hotel, Hemis-Fair Plaza, Tower of the Americas, La Villita, Old San Antonio Museum, Paseo del Rio, Mexican Quarter, San Jose Mission State and Historic Site, Steves Homestead, Brackenridge Park, Fort Sam Houston

San Diego, California
Cradle of Californian Civilization

The Pacific Coast's second largest city and the ninth largest in the nation. One of the country's fastest growing major cities. One of the chief naval and aircraft centers of the United States with one of the world's finest natural deepwater harbors serving ocean-going ships, tuna fleets, and U.S. Navy vessels. A major industrial center of the nation and one of its leading tourist centers. World's leader in avocado production.
Founded 1769 by Spanish soldiers who built California's first presidio, or military fort, on the site; chosen because of its fine harbor; named after San Diego de Alcalá, a Spanish saint; incorporated 1850.
City proper—774,489 persons; *metropolitan area*—1,357,854 persons
Pacific Standard Time; *Low/high temp.:* Jan.—45/65F. (7/18C), July—62/83F. (17/28C)
What to see—San Diego Zoo, Cabrillo National Monument, Rosecroft Begonia Gardens, Mission San Diego de Alcalá, Mission San Luis Rey, Old Town, Balboa Park, Old Globe Theater, Sea World, San Diego Bay and the Embarcadero, San Diego Harbor excursions, whale-watching trips, Maritime Museum Association

San Francisco, California
City by the Golden Gate, City by the Bay

The second largest metropolitan area on the Pacific Coast. One of the world's most interesting cities and a leading U.S. tourist center because of its mild climate and scenic beauty. Downtown area has some of the world's steepest streets. A leading center of culture, finance, and industry in the United States and one of its leading publishing centers. A busy mining supply center during the gold rush of 1849. Destroyed by earthquake and fire in 1906 but quickly rebuilt.
Founded 1776 by Spanish settlers and called Pueblo de San Francisco or "Town of St. Francis" in honor of St. Francis of Assisi; incorporated 1850.
City proper—664,520 persons; *metropolitan area*—3,108,782 persons; *consolidated metropolitan area*—4,425,224 persons
Pacific Standard Time; *Low/high temp.:* Jan.—40/56F. (4/13C), July—52/69F. (11/21C)
What to see—Mission Dolores, Twin Peaks, Civic Center, Transamerica Pyramid, Golden Gate Park, Golden Gate Bridge, San Francisco-Oakland Bay Bridge, Old Mint, Cow Hollow, Chinatown, Fisherman's Wharf, Russian Hill, Nob Hill, Cable Car Barn, Presidio, California Historical Society, Alcatraz Island

San Jose, California

A major industrial city of the nation and one of its chief centers of aerospace manufacturing. California's first capital from 1849 to 1851.
Founded 1777 by a group of Spanish colonists as the first Spanish town in what is now California; named Pueblo de San Jose de Guadalupe in honor of St. Joseph; incorporated 1850.
City proper—555,707 persons; *metropolitan area*—1,065,313 persons
Pacific Standard Time; *Low/high temp.:* Jan.—40/56F. (4/13C), July—52/69F. (11/21C)
What to see—Park Center, Alum Rock Park, Kelley Park, Rosicrucian Park, San Jose Municipal Rose Garden, Winchester Mystery House, San Jose Historical Museum

Seattle, Washington

The largest city in the state of Washington and a gateway to Alaska and the Far East. An important manufacturing, trade, and transportation center of the Pacific Northwest. Home port of a large fishing fleet, famous for its halibut catch. Home of the largest university in the Pacific Northwest, the University of Washington.
Founded 1851 by pioneers from Illinois who chose the site because of its many natural resources; named for Chief Sealth, a Duwamish Indian who had befriended the settlers; incorporated 1869.
City proper—487,091 persons; *metropolitan area*—1,424,605 persons; *consolidated metropolitan area*—1,836,949 persons
Pacific Standard Time; *Low/high temp.:* Jan.—31/43F. (−1/6C), July—53/75F. (12/24C)
What to see—Seattle Center, Pike Place Market, Seattle Art Museum, Woodland Park, Volunteer Park, Waterfront Drive, Pioneer Square Historic District, Museum of History and Industry, Seattle Harbor Tour

Washington, D.C.

Capital of the United States and headquarters of its federal government. One of the world's leading centers of tourism and one of the nation's most beautiful and historic cities. A symbol of the unity, history, and democratic tradition of the United States. Its museums together house the world's largest collection of items from the U.S. and colonial past. The only U.S. city or town that is not part of a state, and one of the few cities in the world that was designed before it was built.
Founded 1791 on site chosen by George Washington, who hired Pierre Charles L'Enfant, a French engineer, to plan the physical layout of the city; named by Congress in honor of George Washington; became capital 1800.
City proper—711,518 persons; *metropolitan area*—2,925,521 persons
Eastern Standard Time; *Low/high temp.:* Jan.—29/44F. (−2/7C), July—68/87F. (20/31C)
What to see—U.S. Capitol, Supreme Court Building, U.S. Botanic Garden, Folger Shakespeare Library, J. Edgar Hoover Building, Smithsonian museums, Washington Monument, Lincoln Memorial, Jefferson Memorial, White House, Ford's Theater, John F. Kennedy Center for the Performing Arts, National Shrine of the Immaculate Conception, Georgetown, Pentagon Building, Arlington National Cemetery, Marine Corps War Memorial, Mount Vernon

Canada

Calgary, Alberta
Foothills City

The largest city in the province of Alberta and the oil center of Canada, housing the headquarters of most Canadian oil firms. A transportation and shipping center and a major distribution point of western Canada. One of Alberta's major cattle centers and famous for its annual Calgary Exhibition and Stampede. A major financial center, housing the western headquarters of most Canadian banks. Has probably more U.S. citizens than any other city outside the United States.
Founded 1875 when the North-West Mounted Police—now the Royal Canadian Mounted Police—established a fort on its site; named by Colonel James F. Macleod after his ancestors' home, Calgary, in Scotland; *calgary* is a Gaelic word meaning "clear, running water"; incorporated 1893.
City proper—469,917 persons
Mountain Standard Time; *Low/high temp.:* Jan.—5/26F. (−15/−3C), July—49/76F. (9/24C)
What to see—Calgary Tower, Calgary Zoo, Heritage Park, Aquarium, Planetarium, Glenmore Park, University of Calgary, Fish Creek Provincial Park

Edmonton, Alberta
Gateway to the North

The capital and second largest city of Alberta. The northernmost major city in North America and a major distribution point between Alaska and northwestern Canada. A center of Canada's oil industry and one of its major meat-packing centers. Lies in the heart of one of Canada's richest farm regions.
Founded 1795 when the Hudson's Bay Company built a fur-trading post on the North Saskatchewan River; city rebuilt on its present site after the Blackfoot Indians destroyed the original fort; named after the English city of Edmonton; incorporated 1904.
City proper—461,361 persons; *metropolitan area*—554,228 persons
Mountain Standard Time; *Low/high temp.:* Jan.—−1/17F. (−18/−8C), July—51/75F. (11/24C)
What to see—Edmonton Civic Center, Alberta Legislative Building, Provincial Museum and Archives, Historical Exhibits Building, Al Rachid Mosque, Queen Elizabeth Planetarium, Storyland Valley Zoo, Alberta Game Farm, Fort Edmonton Historic Park, Elk Island National Park

Halifax, Nova Scotia

Nova Scotia's capital and the largest city in Canada's four Atlantic Provinces. Canada's main naval base and its busiest east coast port. Its harbor remains open in winter, when ice closes most other eastern ports of Canada. One of Canada's most historic cities, it served as a British naval base during the American Revolutionary War and the War of 1812. Home of Canada's first Protestant church and first newspaper.
Founded 1749 by British settlers; named for George Dunk, Earl of Halifax, who headed the government board that supervised the colony; incorporated 1841.
City proper—117,882 persons; *metropolitan area*—267,991 persons
Atlantic Standard Time; *Low/high temp.:* Jan.—17/32F. (−8/0C), July—56/74F. (13/23C)
What to see—Halifax City Hall, Scotia Square, Province House, Citadel, Point Pleasant Park, Prince of Wales Martello Tower, York Redoubt, Public Archives of Nova Scotia, Nova Scotia Museum, Dalhousie University Arts Centre, Halifax Harbor

Hamilton, Ontario

Ontario's second largest city and a leading Canadian industrial center. A center of Canada's steel industry, producing about half the nation's steel. An important link in the St. Lawrence Seaway route. Ranks third in trade handled among Canada's inland ports. One of Canada's major manufacturing and marketing centers because of its position in the center of Ontario's most populated area. Its growth has been limited due to its proximity to Toronto less than 50 miles (80.5 kilometers) away.
Founded 1813 by George Hamilton, a pioneer farmer who bought the land and had it surveyed for a town; named for him; incorporated 1846.
City proper—312,003 persons; *metropolitan area*—529,371 persons
Eastern Standard Time; *Low/high temp.:* Jan.—15/35F. (−10/−2C), July—63/83F. (17/28C)
What to see—Lloyd D. Jackson Square, Hamilton Place, Art Gallery of Hamilton, Royal Botanical Gardens, Dundurn Park, Dundurn Castle, Central Market, Canadian Football Hall of Fame

Montreal, Que., Canada's largest city, has some of the nation's tallest office buildings, largest department stores, and most luxurious hotels. Beneath the downtown area also lies the world's largest underground network of stores and restaurants.

Montreal, Quebec

The largest city in Canada and, next to Paris, the largest French-speaking city in the world. One of the world's largest inland seaports and Canada's chief transportation center. A major business, industry, culture, and education center of Canada. The only city on the continent built around a mountain. Home of the world's largest network of underground stores and restaurants.
Founded 1642 by French Roman Catholic missionaries sent to convert the Indians to Christianity; named Ville-Marie, "Mary's City," in honor of the Virgin Mary; name later changed to Montreal after the mountain Mont Réal, "Mount Royal"; incorporated 1832.
City proper—1,080,546 persons; *metropolitan area*—2,802,485 persons
Eastern Standard Time; *Low/high temp.:* Jan.—8/23F. (−13/−5C), July—62/79F. (17/26C)
What to see—Old Montreal, Notre Dame Parish Church, Notre-Dame-de-Bon-Secours Church, Place Ville Marie, Place des Arts, Underground City, Royal Bank of Canada Building, Montreal Museum of Fine Arts, Mount Royal Park, St. Joseph's Oratory, Man and His World, Olympic Park, Montreal Harbor

Ottawa, Ontario

The capital and eighth largest city of Canada. Home of the buildings of the Canadian parliament. The Canadian government ranks as the city's largest employer. An important center of scientific research.
Founded 1826 by British troops who came to build the Rideau Canal; originally called Bytown; name changed by residents to Ottawa, an English version of the Algonkian Indian word *adawe,* meaning "to trade"; incorporated 1855.
City proper—304,462 persons; *metropolitan area*—693,288 persons
Eastern Standard Time; *Low/high temp.:* Jan.—3/21F. (−16/−6C), July—58/80F. (14/27C)
What to see—Parliament buildings, Royal Canadian

Mint, Canadian Supreme Court Building, National War Memorial, National Arts Centre, Rockcliffe Park, Sparks Street Mall, National Museum of Science and Technology

Regina, Saskatchewan
Queen City of the Plains

The capital and largest city of Saskatchewan. Commercial, financial, and industrial center of the province. Lies in the center of Canada's richest wheat-growing region and houses the headquarters of the Saskatchewan Wheat Pool, the largest grain-handling cooperative in the world. Trade and distribution center for the surrounding region and an important oil center. Home of the training headquarters of the Royal Canadian Mounted Police.
Founded 1882 when the Canadian Pacific Railway reached the site and the Canadian government moved the capital of the North West Territories there; *regina* means "queen" in Latin; named in honor of Queen Victoria of England; incorporated 1903.
City proper—149,593 persons; *metropolitan area*—151,191 persons
Central Standard Time; *Low/high temp.:* Jan.—−7/12F. (−22/−11C), July—52/81F. (11/27C)
What to see—Wascana Centre, Legislative Building, Saskatchewan Museum of Natural History, Saskatchewan Centre of the Arts, Royal Canadian Mounted Police Training Center

Toronto, Ontario

The capital of Ontario and Canada's second largest city. One of the busiest Canadian ports on the Great Lakes. The chief manufacturing, financial, and communications center of Canada and the leader among all Canadian cities in printing, publishing, and television and film production. A major cultural center of the nation with Canada's largest museum and public library system.
Founded 1793 by John Graves Simcoe, who chose the site to replace Newark as the capital of the province of Upper Canada; named York after the Duke of York; in 1834; renamed after *toronto,* a Huron Indian word meaning "meeting place"; incorporated 1834.
City proper—633,318 persons; *metropolitan area*—2,803,101 persons
Eastern Standard Time; *Low/high temp.:* Jan.—18/31F. (−8/−1C), July—61/81F. (16/27C)
What to see—Ontario Place, Exhibition Park, Old Fort York, City Hall, Provincial Parliament Buildings, CN Tower, University of Toronto, Art Gallery of Ontario, Royal Ontario Museum, Marine Museum of Upper Canada, Toronto Islands Park, Casa Loma

Vancouver, British Columbia
Canada's Gateway to the Pacific

British Columbia's largest city and the sixth largest in the nation. Commerce, culture, industry, and transportation center of British Columbia and North America's busiest Pacific Coast port. Handles nearly all of Canada's trade with Japan and other Asian nations. An important center of finance, it houses more financial institutions than any other city in western Canada.
Founded 1865 by lumber workers who built a sawmill on its site; named for Captain George Vancouver, a British explorer who had sailed into Burrard Inlet in 1792; incorporated 1886.
City proper—410,188 persons; *metropolitan area*—1,166,348 persons
Pacific Standard Time; *Low/high temp.:* Jan.—33/42F. (1/6C), July—55/74F. (13/23C)
What to see—Stanley Park Zoo, Vancouver Public Aquarium, Robson Street, Gastown, Queen Elizabeth Theater, Centennial Museum, H. R. MacMillan Planetarium, Maritime Museum, Queen Elizabeth Park, Pacific Centre

Winnipeg, Manitoba
Gateway to the West

The capital of Manitoba and Canada's third largest city. A leading culture, finance, industry, and trade center of the nation and Canada's main grain market. An important transportation center because of its central location midway between the Atlantic and Pacific oceans. About half of Manitoba's entire population live in Winnipeg.
Founded 1870 when Manitoba entered the Dominion of Canada and the settlement around a fur-trading post on the Red River became known as Winnipeg and was made capital of the province; named after Lake Winnipeg; name derived from Cree Indian words meaning "muddy water"; incorporated 1873.
City proper—560,874 persons; *metropolitan area*—578,217 persons
Central Standard Time; *Low/high temp.:* Jan.—−8/9F. (−22/−13C), July—57/80F. (14/27C)
What to see—Civic Centre, Legislative Building, Centennial Arts Centre, Museum of Man and Nature, Winnipeg Art Gallery, Assiniboine Park and Zoo, Lower Fort Garry, St. Boniface Basilica, Royal Winnipeg Ballet

U.S. history

This section chronicles many important dates in U.S. history. The events highlighted include political, religious, social, philosophical, literary, artistic, scientific, and technological milestones for the United States.

1492 **Columbus sees New World**
Christopher Columbus sails from Spain and lands in the Western Hemisphere.

1513 **Florida explored**
Ponce de Léon of Spain searches for the Fountain of Youth in the West Indies; he finds instead a place that he names Florida.

1521 **Cortés defeats the Aztecs**
The Spanish conquistador Hernando Cortés defeats the Aztec Indians in Mexico.

1534 **Cartier reaches Canada**
Jacques Cartier of France reaches the Gulf of St. Lawrence.

1540–1542 **American Southwest explored**
Francisco Coronado of Spain explores the American Southwest.

1565 **Oldest U.S. city founded**
Spaniards in the area Ponce de Léon called Florida found St. Augustine, the oldest city in what is now the United States.

1585–1586 **Raleigh settlement fails**
Sir Walter Raleigh fails in his attempt to establish a permanent English settlement in what is now the United States.

1600s **Folk arts flourish**
Folk arts and household arts flourish in the colonies. Craftworkers produce furniture, pottery, silverware, quilts, embroidery, signs, weather vanes and some glassware—to name just a few crafts.

1600s **Colonial architecture**
Many buildings, like the Paul Revere House in Boston, Massachusetts Colony, are built in the colonies. The various European styles of architecture are blended, and the resulting new style is called "colonial architecture."

1600–1700 **Limners ply trade**
Folk artists called "limners" travel through the colonies, painting simple portraits of local residents.

1600–1700s **Gravestone carvings**
On gravestones, stonecutters make ornamental carvings in various decorative motifs.

1607 **Jamestown founded**
The first permanent English settlement is founded at Jamestown.

1607 **Colonists worship**
The Anglican Church begins holding regular services in Jamestown.

1608 **Smith on the colonies**
John Smith's book *A True Relation of such occurrences and accidents . . . as hath hapned in Virginia* is published in England; it is probably the first personal account of life in the colonies.

1619 **First blacks arrive**
A Dutch vessel brings the first blacks in the English colonies to Jamestown.

1619 **First representative legislature founded**
Virginia establishes the House of Burgesses.

1620 **Mayflower Compact signed**
English Pilgrims sign the Mayflower Compact, the first agreement for self-government in America.

1621 **Blast furnace built**
The first blast furnace in the colonies is placed in operation at Falling Creek, Virginia Colony.

1636 **First college founded**
Harvard College, the first college in the colonies, is founded on October 28.

1638 **Baptist church founded**
The religious leader Roger Williams founds a Baptist church in Providence, Rhode Island Colony.

1640 **First book published**
The Bay Psalm Book, a collection of psalms in verse, is published. It is the first book published in the colonies.

1646 **Ironworks built**
The first successful American ironworks is built north of Boston, Massachusetts Colony.

1647 **Public schools started**
The first public school system supported by taxes is set up in Massachusetts.

1649 **Religious freedom provided**
Maryland passes the first religious tolerance act in North America.

1650 **First poetry book**
Anne Dudley Bradstreet publishes the first volume of original poetry written in the colonies.

1654 **Jews arrive**
A group of 24 Jews land in New Amsterdam (now New York City) in the New World. The governor does not want them to perform military service, but he is overruled by the Dutch West India Company.

1658 **Jews to Rhode Island**
Jews found a second community in the colonies, this one in Newport, Rhode Island Colony.

1672 **Major cities linked**
The completion of the Boston Post Road links Boston and New York City.

1681 **Pennsylvania founded**
Quaker William Penn founds the colony of Pennsylvania as a haven for English Quakers suffering from persecution.

1689 **Mather on witchcraft**
Cotton Mather publishes his *Memorable Providences Relating to Witchcraft and Possessions.* This work is credited with stirring up hatred of "witches" in Salem, Massachusetts Colony.

1690s **Salem witch trials held**
Twenty persons are executed as a result of the Salem witch trials.

1701 **Mather fired**
Increase Mather is removed from his post as president of Harvard College. He and his son Cotton, both conservative Congregationalists, have been outspoken in attacking their liberal colleagues.

1702 **Cotton Mather's famous book**
Cotton Mather, a minister, publishes what may be his greatest work, *Magnalia Christi Americana (Ecclesiastical History of New England).*

1706 **Presbyterians meet**
Presbyterians in the colonies of Maryland, Delaware, and Pennsylvania form an informal presbytery, or church body.

c. 1724 **Irrigation employed**
South Carolina rice growers use irrigation systems to increase the size of their rice crops.

1725–1775 **Revivalism grows**
In New England, the sermons of Jonathan Edwards, a Puritan minister, inspire the spread of the religious revival movement called "The Great Awakening."

1728 **First botanical garden**
John Bartram, a famous botanist, plants the first botanical garden in America.

1731 **Franklin founds library**
Benjamin Franklin founds the first subscription library in the colonies, the Library Company of Philadelphia. Members pay dues, which are pooled to buy books.

1733–1758 **Franklin's almanac**
Benjamin Franklin publishes his *Poor Richard's Almanac.* The almanac contains a great number of brief proverbs, many of them witty. Taken as a whole, Franklin's proverbs have a strong influence on the political and social philosophy of the colonies.

1735 **Freedom of press affirmed**
New York newspaper publisher John Peter Zenger is acquitted of a libel charge that grew out of his criticism of the British government.

1739 **First glass factory**
The first successful American glass factory is started in Salem County, New Jersey Colony.

1743 **Science group formed**
Benjamin Franklin founds the American Philosophical Society, which becomes the chief center of colonial science.

1751 **Hospital started**
One of the first public hospitals in America is chartered in Philadelphia, Pennsylvania Colony.

1752 **Franklin's famous kite**
In a basic experiment Benjamin Franklin flies a kite during a storm. He proves that lightning is a form of electricity.

1754 **Edwards publishes**
Jonathan Edwards, a Puritan minister, publishes his major philosophical work, *Freedom of Will.*

1756 **Stagecoach line opens**
A stagecoach line links New York City and Philadelphia.

c. 1757 **City lights up**
The first street lights in the colonies are installed in Philadelphia.

c. 1760 **Conestoga wagons built**
Conestoga wagons are built in Pennsylvania. The pioneers use these sturdy covered wagons in their move westward.

1763 **Treaty of Paris signed**
France loses most of its possessions in North America after defeat by the British and Americans.

1763 **Synagogue dedicated**
The Jewish synagogue at Newport, Rhode Island Colony, is dedicated. It is the oldest synagogue still standing in the United States.

1765 **Stamp Act unites Americans**
Colonists protest taxation without representation after Parliament passes the Stamp Act.

1765 **First medical school**
The first medical school in the colonies is established in Philadelphia.

1766 **Copley shows in London**
John Singleton Copley, perhaps the greatest portrait painter in the colonies, exhibits his work in London.

1769 **Missions in California**
Junípero Serra, a Franciscan missionary from Spain, establishes the first Catholic mission in California, near what is today San Diego.

1770 **Boston Massacre occurs**
On March 5, British troops fire on and kill American civilians.

1770 **Wheatley's first poem**
Black poet Phillis Wheatley publishes her first poem, "An Elegiac Poem on the Death of that celebrated Divine . . . George Whitefield."

1771–1790 **Franklin on his life**
Benjamin Franklin begins writing his autobiography in 1771 and works on it, without finishing it, for the rest of his life. The book remains a classic.

1773 **Colonists dump tea**
Rebelling against British laws, colonists disguised as Indians dump British tea in the harbor at Boston on December 16.

1774 **Intolerable Acts passed**
Parliament passes the Intolerable Acts as a punishment for colonial rebellion.

1774 **The colonies organize**
Meeting in Philadelphia, delegates from 12 colonies hold the First Continental Congress.

1774 **Jefferson on rights**
Thomas Jefferson's pamphlet, *A Summary View of the Rights of British America,* is printed. In this pamphlet, Jefferson sets forth a political philosophy that will lead to revolution: namely, that Great Britain has no right to govern the colonies from afar.

1775 **Revolutionary War begins**
The Revolutionary War begins on April 19, as British soldiers attack the patriots at Lexington and Concord.

1775 **Battle of Bunker Hill**
On June 17, the British army defeats the patriots.

1775 **Iron production grows**
Colonial ironworks are producing one-seventh of the world's iron.

Thirteen colonies in the mid-1700s

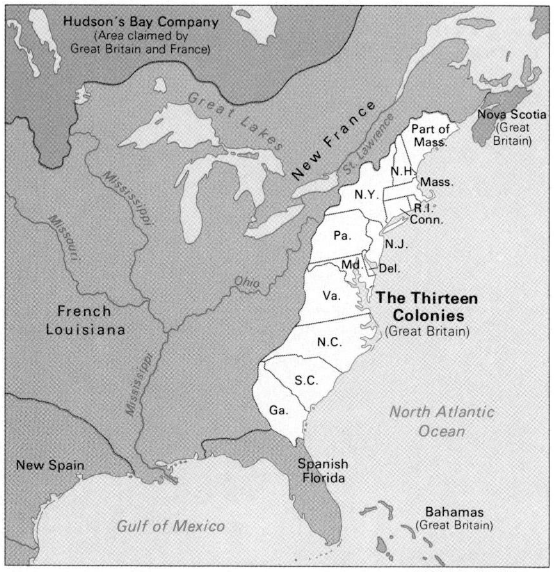

WORLD BOOK map

The 13 colonies stretched from what is now Maine in the north to Georgia in the south. Spanish territory lay to the south of the colonies, and French territory lay to the north and west.

1 George Washington

Born—Feb. 22, 1732. Died—Dec. 14, 1799. Place of birth—Westmoreland County, Va. Political party—none. Terms—1789–1797. Electoral votes—69; 132. Vice-president—John Adams.

1776 **Paine's rallying statement**
Tom Paine's pamphlet, *Common Sense,* is published. The pamphlet contains a stirring demand for independence and lists reasons why independence is absolutely necessary.

1776 **Independence declared**
On July 4, the Declaration of Independence is adopted.

1776 **Smith on economics**
Adam Smith publishes the first systematic classification of classical economics.

1777 **Burgoyne defeated**
Britain's General John Burgoyne surrenders at Saratoga on October 17.

1777 **Winter at Valley Forge**
General George Washington leads his army to its winter quarters at Valley Forge, Pennsylvania, on December 19.

1778 **France allies with patriots**
The United States and France sign an alliance on February 6.

1779 **Patriots win at sea**
Captain John Paul Jones captures a major British ship, the *Serapis,* on September 23.

1781 **British fleet defeated**
The French drive a British naval force from the Chesapeake Bay on September 15.

1781 **British army surrenders**
A British army surrenders at Yorktown, Virginia, on October 19, ending the last major battle of the Revolutionary War.

1781 **Articles signed**
The first U.S. central government is established by the Articles of Confederation.

1782 **Crèvecoeur on America**
Jean de Crèvecoeur publishes his *Letters from an American Farmer.* The book presents a vivid description of life in the young nation.

1783 **Treaty of Paris signed**
The Americans and the British sign the Treaty of Paris on September 3; the Revolutionary War is officially over.

1785 **Madison on liberty**
James Madison writes his *Memorial and Remonstrance on the Religious Rights of Man.* This is a statement advocating religious freedom and defining civil rights as separate from religion.

1787 **Constitution signed**
The Constitution of the United States is signed on September 17 in Philadelphia; it replaces the Articles of Confederation.

1787 **First steamboat**
John Fitch demonstrates the first workable steamboat in the United States.

1787 **Prison reformers meet**
A group of Philadelphia Quakers organizes a prison reform group; it is later called the Pennsylvania Prison Society.

1787–1788 **The Federalist papers**
Alexander Hamilton, James Madison, and John Jay write most of the essays that are later published as *The Federalist.* In the Federalist papers, the authors lay out their political philosophy—especially, the need for a strong central government.

1789 **Washington elected President**
In February, George Washington is elected the first President of the United States.

1789 **Catholic bishop elected**
United States Roman Catholic priests elect John Carroll as the first bishop in the United States.

c. 1790 **Political parties formed**
Disputes over government policies lead to the formation of political parties.

1790 **Cotton-spinning machine**
Samuel Slater builds the country's first successful water-powered machine for spinning cotton.

1791 **Bill of Rights adopted**
By December 15, ten amendments to the Constitution are approved, guaranteeing freedom of speech, religion, press, and peaceful assembly.

1791 **Banneker and the Capital**
Benjamin Banneker, a free black and a mathematician, helps survey the city of Washington, D.C. He later publishes an annual almanac of weather predictions and tide calculations.

1792 **Washington re-elected**
George Washington is re-elected President.

1792 **First local union founded**
Philadelphia, Pennsylvania, shoemakers organize the first local union in the United States.

2 John Adams

Born—Oct. 30, 1735. Died—July 4, 1826. Place of birth—Braintree, Mass. Political party—Federalist. Term—1797–1801. Electoral vote—71. Vice-president—Thomas Jefferson.

1793 **Cotton gin invented**
Eli Whitney builds the first cotton gin. This machine cleans cotton faster than 50 persons working by hand.

1795 **Peale's master work**
Painter Charles Willson Peale completes his picture *The Staircase Group,* a portrait of his family.

1795–1796 **Stuart and Washington**
President George Washington sits for three different portraits by artist Gilbert Stuart.

c. 1798 **Mass production**
Using the first mass-production methods, Eli Whitney makes muskets.

1800 **Capital moved**
The federal government is moved from Philadelphia to Washington, D.C.

1800 **Library of Congress founded**
The Library of Congress is established by Congress; the library is to serve as the national library and to provide research assistance to Congress.

1803 **Judicial review provided**
In deciding the case *Marbury v. Madison,* the Supreme Court establishes the principle of judicial review.

1803 **Louisiana Purchase**
The size of the United States doubles when President Jefferson buys the Louisiana Territory from France.

United States in 1783

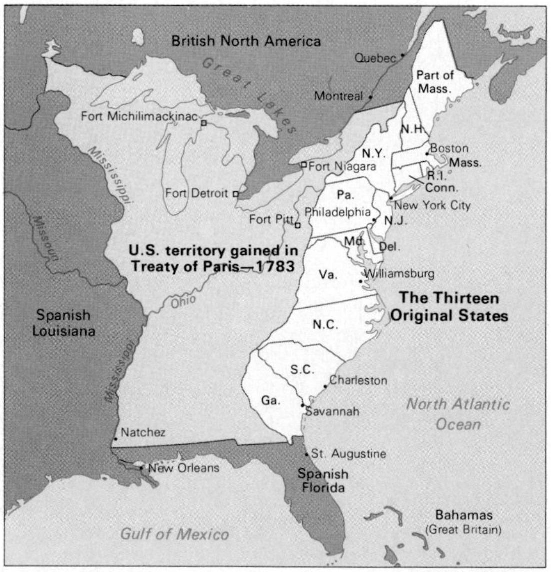

WORLD BOOK map

As a result of the Treaty of Paris in 1783, the United States controlled all of North America from the Atlantic Ocean to the Mississippi River between Canada and Florida. Spanish territory lay to the west and south. British territory lay to the north.

1804–1806 **West explored**
The Lewis and Clark Expedition explores the lands west of the Mississippi River.

1807 **Steamboat perfected**
Robert Fulton demonstrates the first commercially successful steamboat. It revolutionizes the shipping industry of the new nation.

1811 **National Road begun**
Work begins on the National Road, which will eventually link the East and the Midwest.

1812–1814 **War of 1812 waged**
The United States goes to war with Great Britain to protect freedom of the seas and the American shipping trade.

1814 **National anthem composed**
During the War of 1812, Francis Scott Key writes "The Star-spangled Banner."

1817 **"Thanatopsis" published**
William Cullen Bryant writes "Thanatopsis," a brilliant poem about death.

1819 **Plow improved**
Jethro Wood produces an improved cast-iron plow, which features replaceable pieces at points of greatest wear.

1820–1821 **Missouri Compromise**
Congress approves the Missouri Compromise in March 1820; Missouri is admitted as a slave state (1820), Maine is admitted as a free state (1821), and,

3 Thomas Jefferson

Born—April 13, 1743. Died—July 4, 1826. Place of birth—Albemarle County, Va. Political party—Democratic-Republican. Terms—1801–1809. Electoral votes—73; 162. Vice-presidents—Aaron Burr; George Clinton.

4 James Madison

Born—March 16, 1751. Died—June 28, 1836. Place of birth—Port Conway, Va. Political party—Democratic-Republican. Terms—1809–1817. Electoral votes—122; 128. Vice-presidents—George Clinton; Elbridge Gerry.

except in the state of Missouri, slavery is forbidden from the Louisiana Purchase north of the southern boundary of Missouri, the line of the 36° 30′ north latitude.

1820 **Short story created**
Washington Irving completes "Rip Van Winkle." With this piece, he creates a new literary form, the short story.

1820 **Great actor's debut**
One of the first great American actors, Edwin Forrest, makes his initial stage appearance.

1823 **Monroe Doctrine issued**
On December 2, President James Monroe announces the Monroe Doctrine, which warns European nations not to interfere with free nations in the Western Hemisphere.

1823–1841 **Cooper on the frontier**
James Fenimore Cooper writes a series of five novels about the frontier called *The Leatherstocking Tales.* The five include *The Deerslayer* and *The Last of the Mohicans.*

1824 **Sunday School Union**
The American Sunday School Union is formed, as the Sunday school movement grows.

1825 **Erie Canal completed**
The Erie Canal is opened, providing a water passage between New York City and the Great Lakes.

1825 **Unitarian Church founded**
Clergyman William Ellery Channing organizes the American Unitarian Association.

1825 **Recognition for Cole**
Painter Thomas Cole receives first recognition for his landscapes of the Hudson River Valley in New York state.

1830s **Five Civilized Tribes uprooted**
Troops drive thousands of Indians from the Five Civilized Tribes from their homes and west across the Mississippi River on a "Trail of Tears."

1830 **Mormon Church founded**
Joseph Smith and his associates start the Church of Jesus Christ of Latter-day Saints, or Mormon Church, on April 6.

1830 **Alcott publishes**
Bronson Alcott publishes his *Observations on the Principles and Methods of Infant Instruction.*

1830 **Passenger train travel**
Peter Cooper builds the "Tom Thumb," the first American-made steam locomotive to operate on a common carrier. It pulls one of the first passenger trains.

1832 **Catlin on Indians**
George Catlin completes his portrait of The Four Bears, a Mandan chief. Catlin paints many Indian chiefs and tribesmen during his career.

United States in 1803

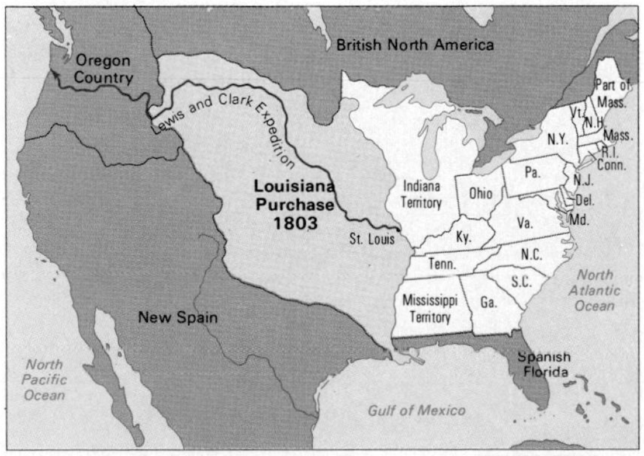

WORLD BOOK map

The Louisiana Purchase of 1803 added the territory between the Mississippi River and the Rocky Mountains to the United States. The size of the country doubled.

5 James Monroe

Born—April 28, 1758. Died—July 4, 1831. Place of birth—Westmoreland County, Va. Political party—Democratic-Republican. Terms—1817–1825. Electoral votes—183; 231. Vice-president—Daniel D. Tompkins.

6 John Quincy Adams

Born—July 11, 1767. Died—Feb. 23, 1848. Place of birth—Braintree, Mass. Political party—Democratic-Republican. Term—1825–1829. Electoral vote—84. Vice-president—John C. Calhoun.

7 Andrew Jackson

Born—March 15, 1767. Died—June 8, 1845. Place of birth—Waxhaw settlement, S.C.? Political party—Democrat. Terms—1829–1837. Electoral votes—178; 219. Vice-presidents—John C. Calhoun; Martin Van Buren.

1834 **Convent burned**
Amid an atmosphere of fear and prejudice, the townspeople in Charlestown, Massachusetts, burn down a Roman Catholic convent of the Ursuline order.

1834 **Reaper helps farming**
Cyrus McCormick patents a reaping machine that makes harvesting larger wheat crops possible.

1834 **Threshing machine**
John and Hiram Pitts patent an early threshing machine on which modern threshing machines are based; the development of large-scale farming advances.

1834–1839 **Alcott runs school**
Philosopher Bronson Alcott operates the experimental Temple School in Boston, Massachusetts.

1835 **Colt perfects revolver**
Samuel Colt develops the first successful repeating pistol.

1836 **First child labor law**
Massachusetts passes the first law limiting child labor in the United States.

1837 **Steel plow developed**
John Deere builds the first steel plow effectively to turn heavy American sod. This plow is especially suitable for the heavy prairie sod.

1837 **First telegraph message**
Samuel F. B. Morse demonstrates the first successful telegraph, which proves to be the fastest communication available to date.

1838 **Mormons to Nauvoo**
Ordered out of Missouri, about 15,000 Mormons migrate to Illinois and found the city of Nauvoo.

1838 **Missionary to Indians**
Jesuit Pierre De Smet begins his long career of converting Indians to Christianity. Other Catholic orders and other denominations also send missionaries to work among the Indians.

1839 **Rubber industry advanced**
Charles Goodyear makes rubber stronger through a process called vulcanization.

1839–1844 **Fuller lectures**
Margaret Fuller, a transcendentalist philosopher, conducts a series of "conversations" for women in Boston, Massachusetts. The lectures—which cover philosophy, literature, and education—are a successful experiment in adult education.

1840s **Immigration increased**
Great waves of immigration to the United States begin; Germany, Ireland, Great Britain, and France are countries from which the migrants come.

1840s **Minstrels entertain**
Minstrel shows become a popular form of musical entertainment. Troupes such as Christy's Minstrels dance and sing, usually in blackface makeup.

8 Martin Van Buren

Born—Dec. 5, 1782. Died—July 24, 1862. Place of birth—Kinderhook, N.Y. Political party—Democrat. Term—1837–1841. Electoral vote—170. Vice-president—Richard M. Johnson.

9 William Henry Harrison

Born—Feb. 9, 1773. Died—April 4, 1841. Place of birth—Charles City County, Va. Political party—Whig. Term—1841. Electoral vote—234. Vice-president—John Tyler.

1840 **Fuller edits magazine**
Margaret Fuller becomes the editor of *The Dial,* a magazine of transcendentalist philosophy.

1840 **Trinity Church**
In New York City, building begins on the Trinity Church, which was designed by architect Richard Upjohn. The architect has adapted traditional Gothic design to the New World.

1840 **A Greenough sculpture**
Horatio Greenough completes his massive sculpture of George Washington.

1840–1900 **Religious composition altered**
The religious composition of the country changes. The Roman Catholic Church increases in size, as many Catholics, including great numbers of Irish Catholics, arrive from central and eastern Europe. The Lutheran Church also grows, as many Lutherans arrive from the Scandinavian countries.

1841 **Mental patients aided**
Dorothea Dix begins her drive to provide better care for the mentally ill.

1841 **Emerson's first essays**
The transcendentalist philosopher Ralph Waldo Emerson publishes his brilliant *Essays, First Series.* The famed essay "Self-Reliance" appears in this series.

1841–1847 **Brook Farm founded**
A group of transcendentalists, led by philosopher George Ripley, operate Brook Farm, an experimental community. Brook Farm is located near West Roxbury, Massachusetts.

1842 **Unions ruled legal**
A Massachusetts court legalizes labor unions.

1842 **Ether kills pain**
Crawford Long uses ether as an anesthetic in surgery.

1844 **Joseph Smith killed**
In Nauvoo, Illinois, the office of a newspaper that has opposed Mormon leader Joseph Smith is burned down. Smith and his brother are jailed at Carthage for the crime; a mob breaks into the jail and kills Smith and his brother.

1844 **Emerson's second essays**
Essays, Second Series, by Ralph Waldo Emerson, is published.

1845 **"Manifest destiny" rises**
Many Americans come to believe that it is their "destiny" to control all of North America.

1845 **Southern Baptists meet**
The Southern Baptist Convention is organized in Augusta, Georgia. Baptists in the South have been arguing with Baptists in the North over the slavery issue.

1845 **"The Raven" by Poe**
Edgar Allan Poe writes "The Raven," a sad poem about a man who feels haunted after the death of his love.

1845–1846 **Emerson lectures**
Ralph Waldo Emerson delivers a lecture series called *Representative Men.*

1846 **Smithsonian founded**
The Smithsonian Institution is founded in Washington, D.C.; the Smithsonian is a national institution devoted to research and learning.

1846 **Poems by Emerson**
Ralph Waldo Emerson publishes *Poems,* a volume of his verse.

1846 **Song hit by Foster**
Composer Stephen Foster writes the song "Oh! Susanna," perhaps the most popular of his 200-plus songs.

1846 **Sewing machine improved**
Elias Howe patents a practical sewing machine.

1846–1848 **Mexican War fought**
In a dispute over territory, the United States goes to war with Mexico. The new land that is gained becomes a portion of what is to be the southwestern United States.

10 John Tyler

Born—March 29, 1790. Died—Jan. 18, 1862. Place of birth—Greenway, Va. Political party—Whig. Term—1841–1845. Electoral vote—none. Vice-president—none.

11 James K. Polk

Born—Nov. 2, 1795. Died—June 15, 1849. Place of birth—near Pineville, N.C. Political party—Democrat. Term—1845–1849. Electoral vote—170. Vice-president—George M. Dallas.

1847 **Mormons settle in Utah**
Brigham Young, the new Mormon leader, starts a Mormon settlement in the Great Salt Lake Valley in what is now the state of Utah.

1847 **Longfellow's poetry**
Henry Wadsworth Longfellow publishes one of his best poems, *Evangeline.*

1848 **Gold Rush begins**
On January 24, the discovery of gold at Sutter's Mill in California triggers a frantic gold rush.

1848 **Feminists organize**
Meeting in Seneca Falls, New York, delegates to the first Women's Rights Convention publicly declare that "all men and women are created equal."

1848 **Oneida group formed**
John Humphrey Noyes founds a cooperative religious settlement called the Oneida Community in Oneida, New York. The community is based on personal communication with God and harmonious living with peers.

1849 **Apply for statehood**
The Mormons, who have set up a civil government in the Great Salt Lake Valley, apply for admission to the Union as the "State of Deseret." Instead of granting statehood, Congress sets up the Territory of Utah the next year.

United States in the mid-1800s

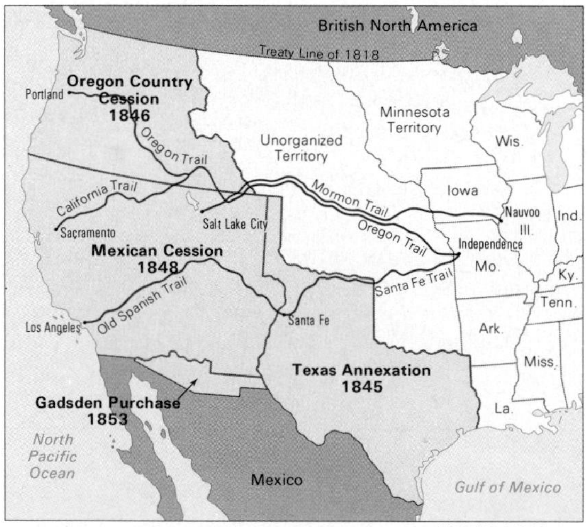

Expansion in the mid-1800s extended the United States to the Pacific Ocean in the west. Britain ceded the Oregon Country to the United States in 1846. The remainder of the new territory came from Mexico in 1845 and 1848.

1849 **Parkman on Indians**
Historian Francis Parkman publishes *The Oregon Trail,* an account of life among the Indians of the Northwest.

1850 **The Compromise of 1850**
A series of laws are passed to deal with the issue of slavery in the new territory acquired from Mexico. The chief terms are the banning of slavery from California and the enactment of the Fugitive Slave Law to tighten the slavery system.

1850 **Hawthorne on sin**
Nathaniel Hawthorne's *The Scarlet Letter* is published. It is a novel about the tragic consequences of sin.

1851 **Melville's masterpiece**
Moby Dick, by Herman Melville, is published. *Moby Dick* is a novel about whaling and about the nature of life.

1851–1852 **Stowe on slavery**
Harriet Beecher Stowe writes *Uncle Tom's Cabin,* a famous antislavery novel.

1852 **Otis improves elevator**
Elisha Otis builds an elevator that uses safety devices to protect against falling.

1854 **Kansas-Nebraska Act**
Congress passes the Kansas-Nebraska Act, which sets up the two territories of Kansas and Nebraska and allows the citizens of those territories to vote on whether they wish to have slavery.

1854 **Major work by Thoreau**
Henry David Thoreau publishes a book of essays called *Walden;* the book discusses nature and the human spirit.

1855 **Poetry by Walt Whitman**
Walt Whitman publishes a volume of poetry called *Leaves of Grass.* It contains the moving poem "Song of Myself."

12 Zachary Taylor

Born—Nov. 24, 1784. Died—July 9, 1850. Place of birth—near Barboursville, Va. Political party—Whig. Term—1849–1850. Electoral vote—163. Vice-president—Millard Fillmore.

1857 **Dred Scott ruling**
In the Dred Scott decision, the Supreme Court rules that blacks are not citizens.

1859 **John Brown raids arsenal**
John Brown, a radical abolitionist, captures the arsenal at Harpers Ferry, Virginia, hoping to start a slave revolt.

1859 **Darwin on evolution**
Charles R. Darwin publishes his theory of evolution in *On the Origin of Species by Means of Natural Selection, or the Preservation of Favoured Races in the Struggle for Life.* Though Darwin is a British naturalist, *The Origin of Species*—as it comes to be known—has a profound impact on U.S. philosophy and psychology.

1859 **Petroleum industry**
The first commercially successful oil well is drilled near Titusville, Pennsylvania.

1860 **Lincoln elected President**
Abraham Lincoln, a Republican from Illinois, is elected 16th President of the United States; he is dedicated to preserving the Union.

1860 **South Carolina secedes**
In December, the state of South Carolina becomes the first state to secede from the Union.

1860 **Lectures published**
Ralph Waldo Emerson's lectures are published under the title *The Conduct of Life.* The lectures were first given in 1851.

1861 **Confederacy formed**
On February 4, South Carolina and five other states that have seceded from the Union meet in Montgomery, Alabama, and declare the formation of a new nation, the Confederate States of America; a total of 11 states eventually joins the Confederacy.

1861 **Civil War begins**
On April 12, Southern troops fire on Fort Sumter in Charleston Harbor. The Civil War begins.

1861 **First Battle of Bull Run**
One of the first major battles of the war occurs at Manassas, Virginia; the army of the North is defeated at Bull Run.

1861 **Dickinson begins writing**
Emily Dickinson begins writing poetry seriously and in volume. Only a few of her poems, however, are published during her lifetime.

1861 **Telegraph across nation**
The transcontinental telegraph line, connecting the eastern United States with California, is completed.

1862 **Monitor and Merrimack**
On March 8 the Confederate ironclad ship *Merrimack* sinks two Northern ships, but on March 9 the Union ironclad *Monitor* appears and fights the *Merrimack* to a draw.

1862 **Union wins at Shiloh**
On April 6 and 7, General Ulysses S. Grant gains a Union victory in the Battle of Shiloh at Pittsburg Landing, Tennessee.

13 Millard Fillmore

Born—Jan. 7, 1800. Died—March 8, 1874. Place of birth—Locke Township, N.Y. Political party—Whig. Term—1850–1853. Electoral vote—none. Vice-president—none.

14 Franklin Pierce

Born—Nov. 23, 1804. Died—Oct. 8, 1869. Place of birth—Hillsboro, N.H. Political party—Democrat. Term—1853–1857. Electoral vote—254. Vice-president—William R. King.

15 James Buchanan

Born—April 23, 1791. Died—June 1, 1868. Place of birth—near Mercersburg, Pa. Political party—Democrat. Term—1857–1861. Electoral vote—174. Vice-president—John C. Breckinridge.

16 Abraham Lincoln

Born—Feb. 12, 1809. Died—April 15, 1865. Place of birth—Hardin County, Ky. Political party—Republican. Terms—1861–1865. Electoral votes—180; 212. Vice-presidents—Hannibal Hamlin; Andrew Johnson.

1862 **Lands in the West open**
The Homestead Act is passed, offering free land to settlers in the West.

1862 **Bull Run revisited**
The Second Battle of Bull Run takes place August 29 and 30; the South wins again.

1862 **Land-Grant colleges founded**
The Morrill, or Land-Grant, Act of 1862 provides land to each state; the land is to be sold to finance a college for agriculture and the mechanical arts in each state.

1862 **Popular Civil War song**
Walter Kittredge writes the rousing Civil War song "Tenting on the Old Camp Ground."

1863 **North wins in the West**
From May 19 to July 4, General Grant leads the Union army to victory in the Siege of Vicksburg, Mississippi.

1863 **Slaves freed**
President Lincoln issues the Emancipation Proclamation on January 1; slaves in the Confederate States designated as being in rebellion are declared free.

1863 **North wins at Gettysburg**
Confederate General Robert E. Lee leads his army in an attack in and primarily around Gettysburg, Pennsylvania, July 1–3; the Northern victory here is a turning point in the war.

1864 **Truth visits White House**
Sojourner Truth, a former slave who has traveled widely to speak out against slavery, visits President Lincoln in the White House

1864 **Grant forges on**
On May 5 and 6, the North under General Grant and the South under General Lee fight the inconclusive Battle of the Wilderness in a heavily wooded area of northern Virginia; Grant and his army continue moving south.

1864 **Sherman marches**
Union General William Tecumseh Sherman begins his "March through Georgia" by leaving Atlanta in flames on November 15 and moving southeast through the state.

1865 **Civil War ends**
On April 9, General Lee surrenders to General Grant at Appomattox Court House, a town in Virginia.

1865 **Lincoln assassinated**
On April 14, John Wilkes Booth shoots President Abraham Lincoln at Ford's Theatre in Washington, D.C.

1865 **Railway sleeping cars**
George Pullman introduces a new sleeping car for overnight train travel.

1865–1877 **Reconstruction proceeds**
The South is gradually returned to the Union in the Reconstruction era; amendments to the U.S. Constitution abolish slavery, make blacks citizens, and grant them voting rights.

1866 **Whittier's "Snow-Bound"**
Poet John Greenleaf Whittier publishes what may be

U.S. Civil War (1861–1865)

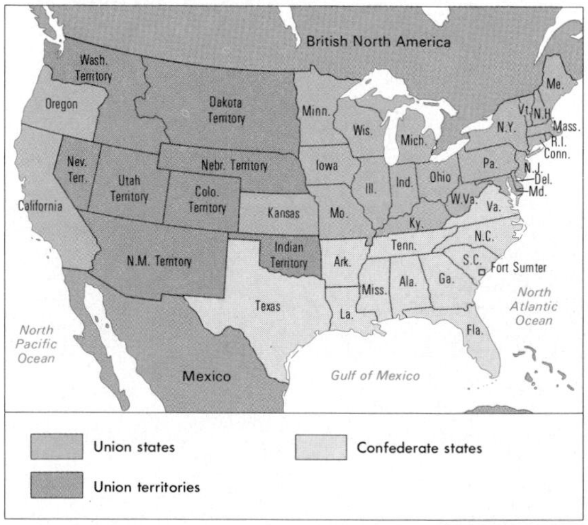

WORLD BOOK map

The Civil War split the United States into two parts, the Confederacy and the Union. In 1860 and 1861, 11 southern states withdrew from the Union to form the Confederacy.

his best work, "Snow-Bound," a long poem about winter in a Quaker community.

1866 **Cable across Atlantic**
After four unsuccessful attempts, Cyrus Field lays a telegraph cable across the Atlantic Ocean.

1869 **Women seek vote**
To help win the vote for women, Susan B. Anthony and Elizabeth Cady Stanton found the National Woman Suffrage Association.

1869 **Transcontinental railway**
In Promontory, Utah, the

17 Andrew Johnson

Born—Dec. 29, 1808. Died—July 31, 1875. Place of birth—Raleigh, N.C. Political party—Democrat (National Union). Term—1865–1869. Electoral vote—none. Vice-president—none.

1866 **Black Baptists meet**
A state convention of black Baptists is formed in North Carolina.

1867 **Alaska purchased**
The United States buys Alaska from Russia for $7.2 million.

1867 **Farmers organize**
The National Grange is founded that later assists farmers in obtaining fairer prices for their products.

1867 **Currier and Ives**
Home for Thanksgiving, a Currier and Ives print, is first published.

1867 **Typewriter developed**
Christopher Sholes plays a major role in developing the typewriter; it is patented in 1868.

1868 **Andrew Johnson on trial**
The House of Representatives votes impeachment charges against President Andrew Johnson, but the Senate votes not to remove him from office.

1868 **Air brakes perfected**
Trains are made faster and safer with the addition of new air brakes, perfected by George Westinghouse.

last spike is driven into the first transcontinental railway line.

1870s **Birth of pragmatism**
The term *pragmatism* is added to the language of philosophy. American philosopher Charles Sanders Peirce coins the term to refer to a particular method of logic.

1870 **Philosophy club formed**
A group of philosophers, including Charles Sanders Peirce, William James, Chauncey Wright, and Oliver Wendell Holmes, Jr., meet in Cambridge to discuss philosophy; they call their group the "Metaphysical Club."

1870–1916 **Population doubles**
More than 25 million immigrants enter the United States; the country's population more than doubles.

1872 **Whistler's famous work**
James Abbott McNeill Whistler paints the portrait *Whistler's Mother.*

1875 **Eddy publishes**
Mary Baker Eddy publishes her major work, *Science and Health with Key to the Scriptures.*

1876 **Custer defeated**
In June, a band of Sioux and Cheyenne defeats Lieutenant Colonel George Armstrong Custer at the Little Bighorn River in Montana.

1876 **ALA founded**
The American Library Association (ALA) is founded to help organize and encourage U.S. libraries; in the same year, Melvil Dewey publishes his Dewey Decimal Classification system.

1876 **Twain on the river**
Mark Twain's novel *The Adventures of Tom Sawyer* is published. The book portrays a boy's adventures on the Mississippi River.

1876 **Winslow Homer**
Painter Winslow Homer completes one of his famous paintings of the sea, *Breezing Up.*

1876 **Telephone invented**
Alexander Graham Bell invents the telephone.

1877 **Federal troops leave South**
The Reconstruction period ends officially as federal troops are withdrawn from the South.

18 Ulysses S. Grant

Born—April 27, 1822. Died—July 23, 1885. Place of birth—Point Pleasant, Ohio. Political party—Republican. Terms—1869–1877. Electoral votes—214; 286. Vice-presidents—Schuyler Colfax; Henry Wilson.

1877 **Wright publishes**
A collection of the writings of Chauncey Wright is published; the book is called *Philosophical Discussions.*

1877 **Phonograph invented**
Thomas Edison, the "Wizard of Menlo Park," creates the phonograph, which he calls his favorite invention.

1879 **Willard seeks temperance**
Frances E. Willard, an educator and social reformer, becomes president of the Woman's Christian Temperance Union; she organizes a drive toward national prohibition.

1879 **Christian Science Church founded**
Mary Baker Eddy and her husband found the Church of Christ, Scientist, also known as the Christian Science Church.

1879 **Electric light invented**
Thomas Edison adds the electric light to his long list of inventions.

1879–1888 **Philosophy school operates**
The Concord Summer School of Philosophy and Literature goes into operation. The school begins in the home of Bronson Alcott, a leading transcendentalist philosopher. Later the school is moved to a center dedicated to transcendentalism.

1880s **Barnum joins Bailey**
Two "greats" in the circus world, P. T. Barnum and James A. Bailey, become partners. Their joint circus is called Barnum & Bailey's Greatest Show on Earth.

1880 **Salvation Army arrives**
The Salvation Army, founded in England in 1878, is introduced in the United States. The Army provides, within a religious framework, food, shelter, and other types of aid to the poor.

1880 **Sousa leads band**
John Philip Sousa, the "March King," is appointed leader of the U.S. Marine Band.

19 Rutherford B. Hayes

Born—Oct. 4, 1822. Died—Jan. 17, 1893. Place of birth—Delaware, Ohio. Political party—Republican. Term—1877–1881. Electoral vote—185. Vice-president—William A. Wheeler.

20 James A. Garfield

Born—Nov. 19, 1831. Died—Sept. 19, 1881. Place of birth—Orange, Ohio. Political party—Republican. Term—1881. Electoral vote—214. Vice-president—Chester A. Arthur.

1881 **Red Cross started**
Clara Barton, a nurse known as "the Angel of the Battlefield" in the Civil War, helps establish the American branch of the Red Cross.

1881 **Tuskegee Institute founded**
In Alabama, Booker T. Washington, an influential black leader and educator, starts the Tuskegee Institute, a vocational school for blacks.

1881 **James in flower**
The Portrait of a Lady, a novel by Henry James, is published.

1881 **Another Twain classic**
The Prince and the Pauper, a novel by Mark Twain, is published.

1883 **Civil service reformed**
Congress passes the Civil Service Reform Act, also called the Pendleton Act; it eventually improves the morale and efficiency of the federal civil service.

1883 **Met founded**
The Metropolitan Opera House opens in New York City, with *Faust* as its first offering.

1884 **Statue of Liberty erected**
The people of France give a 150-foot statue to the United States as a symbol of friendship.

1884 **Twain's masterpiece**
Mark Twain's novel, *The Adventures of Huckleberry Finn,* is published. Like *Tom Sawyer, Huck Finn* is set on the Mississippi River.

1884 **Linotype patented**
Ottmar Mergenthaler patents the linotype, which speeds the printing process. Two years later, the New York City *Tribune* uses the new machine to set type.

1884–1885 **Early skyscraper**
The Home Insurance Building, designed by William Le Baron Jenney, is erected in Chicago. This building is considered one of the first skyscrapers.

21 Chester A. Arthur

Born—Oct. 5, 1829. Died—Nov. 18, 1886. Place of birth—Fairfield, Vt. Political party—Republican. Term—1881–1885. Electoral vote—none. Vice-president—none.

1885 **Howells on success**
William Dean Howells' novel, *The Rise of Silas Lapham,* is published. The work deals with the life of a self-made success.

1885–1887 **Richardson masterwork**
The Marshall Field and Company Wholesale Warehouse in Chicago, designed by architect H. H. Richardson, is completed.

1886 **Labor group formed**
The American Federation of Labor (AFL) is founded by Samuel Gompers in Columbus, Ohio.

1886 **Bible school founded**
Dwight L. Moody founds the Moody Bible Institute in Chicago; the Institute is a school for training workers in various fields of Christian service.

1886–1889 **Adler and Sullivan**
The Auditorium Building, designed by Dankmar Adler and Louis H. Sullivan, is erected in Chicago.

1887 **Catholic University founded**
The Catholic University of America is established in Washington, D.C. It is designated the official Roman Catholic university in the United States.

1887 **Residential architecture**
The firm of McKim, Mead, & White designs the W. G. Low house in Bristol, Rhode Island.

1889 **Hull House founded**
Jane Addams and Ellen Starr found a Chicago settlement house called Hull House; they use Hull House as a base from which to work with slum dwellers.

1889 **Twain on King Arthur**
Mark Twain publishes *A Connecticut Yankee in King Arthur's Court,* Twain's take-off on the Arthurian legends.

1890 **Abandon polygamy**
The Mormons outlaw the practice of polygamy, or having more than one wife at the same time. Congress has blocked statehood for Utah because of strong feelings in the United States against polygamy.

c. 1892 **Work by Cassatt**
Mary Cassatt completes her famed painting *The Bath.*

1892 **Lynching at peak**
Mobs execute some 230 persons, mostly blacks, without trial. This is the peak of lynching, which continues to 1968.

1892 **Labor deaths at Homestead**
Ten persons die when guards attack strikers at the steel mills in Homestead, Pennsylvania.

1892 **Idealism movement begins**
Josiah Royce, leader of the movement called "idealism," publishes *The Spirit of Modern Philosophy,* the first of five famous books.

1893 **Famed Stieglitz photo**
Winter on Fifth Avenue, New York, a photograph by Alfred Stieglitz, first appears.

1893 **Columbian Exposition**
The World's Columbian Exposition opens in Chicago. Featured is the White City, which contains vast buildings designed by famous architects. Also featured are large statues by prominent sculptors like Augustus Saint-Gaudens and Daniel Chester French.

1894 **Pullman clash violent**
Federal troops battle strikers at the Pullman plant in Chicago and elsewhere, with heavy loss of life and considerable property damage.

1895 **Baptists organize**
The National Baptist Convention of America is formed to bring unity to black Baptists in the United States.

1896 **Segregation upheld**
The Supreme Court rules in *Plessy v. Ferguson* that a state may provide "separate but equal" facilities for whites and blacks.

22 Grover Cleveland

Born—March 18, 1837. Died—June 24, 1908. Place of birth—Caldwell, N.J. Political party—Democrat. Terms—1885–1889; 1893–1897. Electoral votes—219; 277. Vice-presidents—Thomas A. Hendricks; Adlai E. Stevenson.

23 Benjamin Harrison

Born—Aug. 20, 1833. Died—March 13, 1901. Place of birth—North Bend, Ohio. Political party—Republican. Term—1889– 1893. Electoral vote—233. Vice-president—Levi P. Morton.

24 Grover Cleveland

Second term: 1893– 1897. For full entry, see page 327.

1896 **"A cross of gold"**
Asking the delegates not to "crucify mankind upon a cross of gold," Populist leader William Jennings Bryan makes an impassioned speech before the Democratic National Convention in Chicago; Bryan supports free coinage of silver to benefit "the producing masses."

1896 **Essay on pragmatism**
Philosopher William James publishes the essay "The Will to Believe," a major work on pragmatism.

1896 **Ford builds first car**
Henry Ford completes his first automobile, paving the way for later mass production.

1897 **First U.S. subway built**
The first U.S. subway is built in Boston.

1898 **Hawaii annexed**
The Hawaiian Islands are annexed by the United States.

1898 **U.S. battleship sinks**
In February, the battleship *Maine* explodes in the harbor at Havana, Cuba; "yellow journalists" in the United States use this event to agitate for war with Spain.

1898 **War with Spain**
On April 25, the United States declares war with Spain.

1898 **War ends**
On December 10, the Paris Peace Treaty is signed, ending the Spanish-American War; the United States gains possession of Guam, Puerto Rico, and the Philippines as part of the settlement.

1898 **Work by Eakins**
Realist painter Thomas Eakins completes *The Clinic of Dr. Agnew*.

1899 **Dewey on education**
In his book *School and Society,* John Dewey sets forth the principles of progressive education.

1901 **McKinley assassinated**
President William McKinley is assassinated in September.

1901 **Pentecostal landmark**
A worshiper at an evangelical meeting of the Holiness movement in Topeka, Kansas, begins "speaking in tongues," or speaking unintelligible words in a spirit of religious ecstasy. This incident is the start of the spread of the Pentecostal movement.

1901 **Realism from Norris**
Frank Norris' novel *The Octopus* is published. The book is a realistic account of the struggles surrounding railroad expansion.

1901–1902 **James lectures**
William James delivers a series of lectures in Scotland compiled in a book called *Varieties of Religious Experience*.

1903 **University founded**
The University of Puerto Rico is founded in San Juan; a branch campus is later opened in Mayagüez.

1903 **Classic by London**
Jack London's novel *The Call of the Wild* is published.

1903 **New James novel**
Henry James's novel *The Ambassadors* is published.

1903 **Remington painting**
Painter Frederic Remington completes his *Fight for the Waterhole.* Remington mostly paints scenes of the American frontier.

25 William McKinley

Born—Jan. 29, 1843. Died—Sept. 14, 1901. Place of birth—Niles, Ohio. Political party—Republican. Terms—1897– 1901. Electoral votes—271; 292. Vice-presidents—Garret A. Hobart; Theodore Roosevelt.

1903 **First airplane**
Wilbur and Orville Wright fly the first airplane at Kitty Hawk, North Carolina.

1903 **Canal land leased**
The United States purchases the rights to the land in Central America on which the Panama Canal is scheduled to be built.

1905–1906 **Santayana publishes**
Philosopher George Santayana completes a five-volume work, *The Life of Reason*.

1909 **NAACP founded**
The National Association for the Advancement of Colored People (NAACP) is founded to work for the rights of blacks.

1909 **Pragmatism debated**
William James publishes *The Meaning of Truth*, a collection of writings debating various aspects of pragmatism.

1909 **Peary reaches North Pole**
On April 6, Commander Robert E. Peary of the U.S. Navy is the first person to reach the North Pole.

1910 **Black orchestra**
James Reese Europe, leader of a black dance band, starts a black symphony orchestra.

1910 **Urban League founded**
The National Urban League is founded to assist blacks in getting jobs and housing.

1911 **Ives's *Symphony No. 3***
Charles Edward Ives completes his *Symphony No. 3*. It is not until 1947, however, that he receives the Pulitzer prize for music for this work.

1911–1913 **Woolworth Building**
The Woolworth Building is erected in New York City. The building is a Gothic skyscraper designed by Cass Gilbert.

1912 **Empiricism explored**
A series of essays by William James is published posthumously under the title *Essays in Radical Empiricism*.

1913 **Major poem by Lindsay**
Vachel Lindsay's poem "General William Booth Enters into Heaven" is published. Lindsay's poetry features strong rhythms and vivid images.

1914 **Canal opened**
On August 15, the United States opens the Panama Canal.

1914 **Family planning aided**
Margaret Sanger founds the American Birth Control League to provide birth control information and devices. The group later changes its name to Planned Parenthood-World Population (PPWP).

1914 **Amy Lowell's poetry**
Amy Lowell publishes *Sword Blades and Poppy Seeds*, a volume of imagist poetry.

1914 **"St. Louis Blues"**
Black composer W. C. Handy writes "The Saint Louis Blues." Handy's work has a major effect on ragtime and jazz music.

1915 **Baptists split**
The National Baptist Convention of America loses a large portion of its membership in a dispute over church property and church publications. The splinter group forms the National Baptist Convention, U.S.A. It proves to be a larger group than the parent organization.

1916 **Child labor law passed**
Congress passes the first federal law regulating child labor.

1916 **Wright hotel**
The Imperial Hotel in Tokyo, Japan, is begun; the quakeproof hotel was designed by the American architect Frank Lloyd Wright.

1916 **Carver receives acclaim**
George Washington Carver is honored by the Royal Society of Arts in London for his agricultural research with peanuts and other products.

1917 **United States enters World War I**
Following a period of unlimited submarine warfare by Germany, the United States enters World War I on the Allied side.

26 Theodore Roosevelt

Born—Oct. 27, 1858. Died—Jan. 6, 1919. Place of birth—New York, N.Y. Political party—Republican. Terms—1901–1909. Electoral vote—336. Vice-president—Charles W. Fairbanks.

27 William Howard Taft

Born—Sept. 15, 1857. Died—March 8, 1930. Place of birth—Cincinnati, Ohio. Political party—Republican. Term—1909–1913. Electoral vote—321. Vice-president—James S. Sherman.

28 Woodrow Wilson

Born—Dec. 29, 1856. Died—Feb. 3, 1924. Place of birth—Staunton, Va. Political party—Democrat. Terms—1913–1921. Electoral votes—435; 277. Vice-president—Thomas R. Marshall.

29 Warren Gamaliel Harding

Born—Nov. 2, 1865. Died—Aug. 2, 1923. Place of birth—near Blooming Grove, Ohio. Political party—Republican. Term—1921–1923. Electoral vote—404. Vice-president—Calvin Coolidge.

1917 **O. Henry collected**
The complete works of O. Henry, mainly short stories, are published.

1917 **Ryder dies**
Romantic painter Albert Pinkham Ryder dies.

1918 **Fourteen Points listed**
President Woodrow Wilson announces his Fourteen Points necessary to conclude a peace settlement to World War I.

1918 **Armistice signed**
The armistice ending World War I is signed in France on November 11.

1918 **Sandburg on war**
Carl Sandburg's poem "Grass" is published. The poem deals with the horrors of war.

1918 **Cather on the prairie**
Willa Cather's novel *My Ántonia* is published; it deals with the struggles of an immigrant girl on the prairie.

1919 **First public strike**
Police in Boston, Massachusetts, go on strike; this is the first strike by public workers in the United States.

1919 **Adams wins Pulitzer**
Philosopher and historian Henry Brooks Adams wins a Pulitzer prize for his best-known work, *The Education of Henry Adams.*

1919 **Anderson's short stories**
Sherwood Anderson publishes his first collection of short stories, entitled *Winesburg, Ohio.*

1919 **Pulitzer for Tarkington**
Booth Tarkington wins the Pulitzer prize for literature for his novel *The Magnificent Ambersons.*

1920s **Jazz in flower**
Jazz composers and artists win a wide audience. Popular jazz personalities include Louis Armstrong, Sidney Bechet, Bix Beiderbecke, Edward (Duke) Ellington, Earl (Fatha) Hines, and Joseph (King) Oliver.

1920 **Prohibition goes into effect**
The 18th Amendment to the U.S. Constitution goes into effect, prohibiting the manufacture and sale of alcoholic beverages.

1920 **Women receive vote**
The 19th Amendment to the U.S. Constitution is adopted, granting women the vote.

1920 **Versailles Treaty spurned**
The Senate votes not to ratify the Treaty of Versailles, drawn up after the German armistice in World War I.

1920 **Romantic poet**
A Few Figs from Thistles, a volume of poetry by Edna St. Vincent Millay, is published.

1920 **Panama Canal opens**
The Panama Canal opens with official proclamation on July 12; work began in 1904. Presidential proclamation took place in 1914.

1920–1940 **Blues flourish**
Singer Bessie Smith reigns as "empress of the blues." Other prominent blues performers include Billie Holiday, Blind Lemon Jefferson, and Huddie (Leadbelly) Ledbetter.

1921 **Famed Steichen photo**
Photographer Edward Steichen takes his photograph *Three Pears and an Apple.*

1921 **Einstein honored**
Albert Einstein wins the Nobel prize in physics for his study of quanta, the smallest amounts of energy capable of existing independently.

1922 **McPherson builds temple**
Evangelist Aimee Semple McPherson builds the Angelus Temple in Los Angeles. She is the founder of the International Church of the Foursquare Gospel and is well known for her revival meetings.

1923 **Cummings innovates**
Tulips and Chimneys, a book of poems by e e cummings, is published. The literary world is startled by cummings' revolutionary approach to titles, punctuation, and line breaks.

1924 **Teapot Dome scandal**
A Senate investigation in February and March uncovers a major offense called the Teapot Dome scandal in the Administration of President Warren G. Harding.

1924 **Indians made citizens**
By Act of Congress, Indians born in the United States are declared citizens.

1924 **Whitehead to Harvard**
English philosopher Alfred North Whitehead joins the faculty of Harvard University in Cambridge, Massachusetts.

1924 **Gershwin's major work**
On a commission from jazz bandleader Paul Whiteman, composer George Gershwin completes his *Rhapsody in Blue*.

1924 **Varèse experiments**
Edgard Varèse composes *Octandre,* an instrumental piece that utilizes disordered sounds.

1925 **The Great Gatsby appears**
F. Scott Fitzgerald publishes the novel *The Great Gatsby*.

1925 **Dreiser's naturalism**
Theodore Dreiser, a leading writer in the naturalism movement, publishes the novel *An American Tragedy*.

1926 **Durant publishes**
Will Durant publishes the major work *The Story of Philosophy*.

1926 **Hemingway emerges**
Publication of *The Sun Also Rises* signals the emergence of Ernest Hemingway as a major novelist.

1926 **Lewis wins, refuses prize**
Sinclair Lewis is awarded the Pulitzer prize for literature for the novel *Arrowsmith*. He turns down the prize, apparently feeling he should have received it sooner for *Main Street* or *Babbitt.*

1926 **Rocket launched**
Space pioneer Robert H. Goddard launches the first successful liquid-fuel rocket.

1927 **Sacco and Vanzetti die**
Nicola Sacco and Bartolomeo Vanzetti are executed in August for killing a paymaster and his guard during a robbery in South Braintree, Massachusetts; many believe they have been condemned for their political ideas.

1927 **Kern's major hit**
Show Boat, perhaps the greatest musical by composer Jerome Kern, is first produced.

1927 **Lindbergh's flight**
Charles A. Lindbergh makes the first nonstop solo flight across the Atlantic Ocean.

1927 **Compton honored**
American scientist Arthur Holly Compton is cowinner of the Nobel prize in physics. He is honored for discovering "the Compton effect," or variations in the wavelengths of X rays.

30 Calvin Coolidge

Born—July 4, 1872. Died—Jan. 5, 1933. Place of birth—Plymouth Notch, Vt. Political party—Republican. Terms—1923– 1929. Electoral vote—382. Vice-president—Charles G. Dawes.

1928 **Summary work**
V. L. Parrington's important work *Main Currents in American Thought* is acclaimed. The work surveys the important trends in American philosophy.

1928 **Mickey Mouse**
Cartoonist Walt Disney produces the film *Steamboat Willie,* in which he introduces the character of Mickey Mouse, who proves to be a beloved figure in U.S. popular culture.

1928 **Earhart's flight**
Amelia Earhart becomes the first woman to fly across the Atlantic Ocean.

1929 **Stock market crashes**
On October 24, the stock market crashes, ruining many investors; the crash heralds the beginning of the Great Depression.

1929 **Whitehead's major work**
While on the faculty of Harvard University, English philosopher Alfred North Whitehead publishes the book *Process and Reality*.

1929 **Hammett begins**
Dashiell Hammett publishes two detective novels, *Red Harvest* and *The Dain Curse*.

1929 **Wolfe on youth**
Thomas Wolfe's first novel, *Look Homeward, Angel,* is published.

1929 **Thurber and White unite**
Is Sex Necessary?, a humorous book by James Thurber and E. B. White, is published.

1929 **A classic by Faulkner**
The novel *The Sound and the Fury,* by William Faulkner, is published. The novel uses the stream-of-consciousness technique in a striking manner.

1929–**Plastics industry grows**
1937 Chemists make cellulose

acetate, acrylics, and polystyrene in commercial quantities.

1930s **Black Muslims founded**
Elijah Muhammad and W. D. Farad found the Nation of Islam, or the Black Muslim movement.

1930–1936 **Trilogy on U.S. culture**
John Dos Passos writes the three novels that make up the trilogy *U.S.A.*

1931 **Cohen publishes**
Morris R. Cohen, a noted defender of reason and scientific thinking, publishes the book *Reason and Nature.*

1931 **Buck novel**
Pearl Buck's novel *The Good Earth* is published. The story is set in China and is the first in a series.

1931 **Still premiere**
The Afro-American Symphony, by black composer William Grant Still, is first performed.

1932 **Injunctions limited**
The Norris-La Guardia Act limits the use of federal court injunctions in strikes and labor disputes.

1933 **New Deal begins**
President Franklin D. Roosevelt begins the "New Deal" in an effort to end the depression.

1933 **Day founds paper**
Dorothy Day founds the *Catholic Worker,* a monthly publication. Day is a leader in the Catholic Worker movement in the United States and works to further social change in New York City.

1934 **Urey honored**
Harold C. Urey wins the Nobel prize in chemistry for the discovery of deuterium, or heavy hydrogen.

1934–1951 **Mumford published**
Lewis Mumford, philosopher and social critic, completes *The Renewal of Life,* a four-volume philosophy of civilization.

1935 **NLRB created**
Congress passes the National Labor Relations Act, or Wagner Act, to protect the rights of labor; the National Labor Relations Board (NLRB) is created to settle disputes.

1935 **Peirce's papers published**
The Collected Papers of Charles Sanders Peirce are published posthumously. The *Papers* are edited by Charles Hartshorne and Paul Weiss.

31 Herbert C. Hoover

Born—Aug. 10, 1874. Died—Oct. 20, 1964. Place of birth—West Branch, Iowa. Political party—Republican. Term—1929– 1933. Electoral vote—444. Vice-president—Charles Curtis.

32 Franklin Delano Roosevelt

Born—Jan. 30, 1882. Died—April 12, 1945. Place of birth—Hyde Park, N.Y. Political party—Democrat. Terms—1933– 1945. Electoral votes—472; 523; 449; 432. Vice-presidents—John Nance Garner; Henry A. Wallace; Harry S. Truman.

1935 **Maxwell Anderson**
Winterset, a play by Maxwell Anderson, is published. The play is based on the Sacco-Vanzetti case, a world-famous trial of the 1920's which resulted in the execution of two political anarchists.

1936 **Balanchine on Broadway**
The ballet *Slaughter on Tenth Avenue,* by choreographer George Balanchine, is produced as part of the musical *On Your Toes.*

1937 **Catholic Unionists meet**
The Association of Catholic Trade Unionists is formed to extend the church's influence and ideology to labor matters.

1937 **Vitamin C**
Albert Szent-Györgyi wins the Nobel prize in physiology or medicine for the isolation of vitamin C, or ascorbic acid.

1938 **Alcott published**
Selected writings of transcendentalist philosopher Bronson Alcott are published posthumously under the title *The Journals of Bronson Alcott.*

1938 **Play by Thornton Wilder**
Our Town, a play by Thornton Wilder, receives the Pulitzer prize for drama.

1938 **Nobel for Fermi**
Enrico Fermi wins the Nobel prize in physics for his discovery of radioactive elements.

1938–1940 **Blood plasma research**
Black physician Charles Drew conducts research on blood plasma. Dr. Drew helps set up blood banks, which save many lives.

1939 **Dewey on culture**
Freedom and Culture, a book by John Dewey, is published.

1939 **Sandburg on Lincoln**
Carl Sandburg's *Abraham*

Lincoln: The War Years is published in four volumes.

1939–1940 Neutrality weighed
The United States remains officially neutral as Germany invades Poland and World War II begins.

1940 Landmark in black fiction
Richard Wright's first novel, *Native Son,* is published.

1940 Pulitzer for Steinbeck
John Steinbeck receives the Pulitzer prize for literature for his novel *The Grapes of Wrath.*

1941 Lend-Lease begins
The United States decides to expand its aid to the Allies. The Lend-Lease Act gives the President the power to transfer arms and food to the Allies.

1941 Pearl Harbor attacked
On December 7, Japan launches a surprise attack on the United States military installations at Pearl Harbor on the island of Oahu in Hawaii.

1941 Europeans declare war
On December 11, Germany and Italy declare war on the United States, which then declares war on Germany and Italy.

1941 Hellman on Nazism
Lillian Hellman's play *Watch on the Rhine* is published. The play centers on a man of integrity pursued by Nazis.

1942 Japan takes Philippines
From January to May, Japan's troops successfully battle U.S. troops for control of the Philippine Islands.

1942 Allies land in Africa
In the largest amphibious invasion to date in World War II, American and British troops land in North Africa in early November.

33 Harry S. Truman

Born—May 8, 1884. Died—Dec. 26, 1972. Place of birth—Lamar, Mo. Political party—Democrat. Terms—1945–1953. Electoral votes—303. Vice-president—Alben W. Barkley.

1942 Solomon Islands won
United States forces claim victory on November 12 after a three-day naval battle for control of the Solomon Islands.

1942 Japanese interned
The U.S. government moves all Japanese on the West Coast, including aliens and native born, to relocation camps in Arkansas, Colorado, Utah, and other states.

1942 Manhattan Project
The Manhattan Project is organized by the U.S. Army Corps of Engineers to supervise the development of an atomic bomb.

1943 Allies land on Sicily
In the second largest amphibious invasion of the war, American, British, and Canadian troops land on Sicily July 10.

1943 Saroyan on life
William Saroyan's novel *The Human Comedy* is published.

1943 Frost wins Pulitzer
Robert Frost is awarded the Pulitzer prize for poetry for the fourth time.

1943 Robeson on stage
Black actor and singer Paul Robeson stars in the title role of *Othello,* a dramatic play that becomes a long-running hit.

1944 Normandy invaded
On June 6, D-day, Allied troops invade the Normandy coast of France.

1944 Philippines recaptured
In the first stage of the battle to recapture the Philippine Islands, U.S. troops led by General Douglas MacArthur land on Leyte October 20.

1944 Allies hold the line
American and British troops hold back the German army at the Battle of the Bulge in December.

1944 Rodgers and Hammerstein
Richard Rodgers and Oscar Hammerstein II win a Pulitzer special citation for their musical play *Oklahoma!*

1944 Mark I developed
The Mark I digital computer is developed after years of research.

1945 Iwo Jima captured
In February and March, U.S. troops battle in the Pacific to capture the island of Iwo Jima from the Japanese.

1945 Okinawa invaded
The United States invades the island of Okinawa near Japan; the battle lasts for almost three months.

1945 Victory in Europe
Following the April 30 death of Germany's dictator Adolf Hitler, German military leaders sign surrender terms on May 7 in Reims, France.

1945 United Nations founded
Fifty nations meeting in San Francisco, California, adopt the United Nations (UN) Charter on June 26.

1945 **Atomic bombs dropped**
Atomic bombs are dropped on Hiroshima, Japan, on August 6, and on Nagasaki, Japan, on August 9.

1945 **Japan surrenders**
Japan offers to surrender on August 14. The official terms of surrender are signed on September 2.

1945 **Gwendolyn Brooks**
A Street in Bronzeville, the first book of poems by Gwendolyn Brooks, is published. *Bronzeville* deals with life in the black ghettos of Chicago.

1945 **Williams to the fore**
The Glass Menagerie, a play by Tennessee Williams, is first performed.

1946 **New suburb started**
Construction begins on the town of Levittown, New York, a new type of suburb; a "planned community," Levittown features a master plan for streets and highways, and mass-produced houses that look much alike.

1947 **Cold War heats up**
President Harry S. Truman announces his "Truman Doctrine"; the United States will give aid to any nation striving to resist Communism; the United States and Russia are engaged in the Cold War.

1947 **Taft-Hartley Act passed**
The Labor-Management Relations Act, or Taft-Hartley Act, is passed by Congress and passed again over the veto of President Harry S. Truman; the act limits union activities in a variety of ways.

1948 **Marshall Plan begins**
The European Recovery Program, or Marshall Plan, begins supplying massive amounts of financial aid to Western European nations.

1948 **Brandeis opens**
Brandeis University is founded; located in Waltham, Massachusetts, Brandeis is sponsored by the American Jewish community but is a nonsectarian institution.

1948–1949 **Berlin blockade broken**
The Russians blockade West Berlin on June 24, 1948, hoping to drive out the Western allies; the allies use an airlift of gigantic proportions to break the blockade.

1949 **NATO organized**
The United States and 11 European nations form the North Atlantic Treaty Organization (NATO).

1949 **Graham begins crusades**
Billy Graham, an evangelist preacher, begins his large-scale campaigns for converts throughout the world.

1949 ***Death of a Salesman* appears**
Arthur Miller's play *Death of a Salesman* is published. The play is a tragedy about the life of salesman Willy Loman.

1949–1951 **Television expands**
The number of television sets in American homes expands from 1 million to 10 million in just two years.

1950s **Bishop Sheen on TV**
Roman Catholic Bishop Fulton J. Sheen is the host for a television series called "Life Is Worth Living"; Bishop Sheen becomes a well-known personality in America.

1950 **"McCarthyism" in flower**
Senator Joseph R. McCarthy, Republican from Wisconsin, accuses the U.S. Department of State of harboring Communists.

1950 **Troops to Korea**
On June 30, President Truman sends troops to South Korea, which was invaded by North Korea on June 25.

1950 **Troops land at Inchon**
In September U.S. troops land at Inchon, Korea, behind enemy lines and move north to the Yalu River.

1950 **Allies retreat**
China enters the war on the side of North Korea on October 25; the Chinese attack the allies, who begin retreating on November 26.

1950 **Unity sought**
The National Council of the Churches of Christ in the U.S.A. is formed. A number of Protestant and Eastern Orthodox denominations form the Council to promote Christian unity.

1950 **Graham goes on radio**
Evangelist Billy Graham starts a radio program called "The Hour of Decision."

1950 **Bradbury and fantasy**
The Martian Chronicles, a book of stories by Ray Bradbury, is published.

1951 **MacArthur fired**
President Truman removes General Douglas MacArthur as commander in chief of U.N. forces in Korea.

1951 **Major article by Quine**
The American philosopher Willard Van Orman Quine publishes his article "Two Dogmas of Empiricism." This article is one of Quine's chief contributions to epistemology, or the study of knowledge.

1951 **Salinger's major work**
J. D. Salinger's novel *The Catcher in the Rye* is published.

1951 **Cage's music**
Composer John Cage completes *Music of Changes.* In his work, Cage breaks away from many of the old conventions regarding sound.

1951 **Two share Nobel prize**
Glenn T. Seaborg and Edwin M. McMillan win the Nobel prize in chemis-

try for the discovery of plutonium and other transuranic elements, or radioactive chemical elements whose atomic numbers are higher than that of uranium.

1951 **UNIVAC computer**
The UNIVAC is first of a variety of electronic computers mass-produced during the 1950's.

1952 **Vonnegut's first novel**
Player Piano, the first novel by Kurt Vonnegut, Jr., appears.

1953 **Korean truce signed**
A truce ending the Korean War is signed on July 27.

1953 **HEW founded**
A new department is added to the U.S. Cabinet: the Department of Health, Education, and Welfare (HEW). It is designed to coordinate federal policies in those three broad areas.

1953 **Book by Quine**
Willard Van Orman Quine, the influential logician and philosopher, publishes the book *From a Logical Point of View.*

1953 **Pollock's painting**
Jackson Pollock, the abstract painter, completes his *Ocean Grayness.*

1953 **Color broadcasts begin**
The first color television broadcasts begin.

1954 **Army-McCarthy hearings**
Senator Joseph R. McCarthy begins nationally televised hearings in April on possible Communist influences in the U.S. Army; he accuses the army of "coddling Communists."

1954 **Court says desegregate**
On May 17, the Supreme Court rules in *Brown v. Board of Education of Topeka* that segregated public schools are a denial of blacks' civil rights.

1954 **Condemn McCarthy**
In December, the Senate votes to condemn Senator Joseph R. McCarthy for "contemptuous" conduct.

1954 **Nagel publishes**
Sovereign Reason, a book by science philosopher Ernest Nagel, is published.

1954 **Bellow emerging**
Saul Bellow wins the National Book Award for fiction for his novel *The Adventures of Augie March.*

1954 **Landmark jazz festival**
The first large American jazz festival is held in Newport, Rhode Island.

1954 **Solar energy explored**
Bell Telephone Laboratories develops the solar battery.

1954 **Nuclear submarine built**
The United States launches the *Nautilus,* the first nuclear-powered submarine.

1955 **King begins crusade**
Dr. Martin Luther King, Jr., begins organizing a movement to protest discrimination against blacks.

34 Dwight David Eisenhower

Born—Oct. 14, 1890. Died—March 28, 1969. Place of birth—Denison, Tex. Political party—Republican. Terms—1953–1961. Electoral votes—442; 457. Vice-president—Richard M. Nixon.

1955 **AFL-CIO created**
The Congress of Industrial Organizations (CIO), a collection of industrial unions, merges with the American Federation of Labor (AFL), a collection of craft unions, to form one "umbrella" organization, the AFL-CIO.

1955 **Polio vaccine safe**
Dr. Jonas Salk's polio vaccine is declared safe.

1957 **Crisis at Little Rock**
Arkansas Governor Orval E. Faubus sends the National Guard to block black students from entering Central High School in Little Rock, Arkansas; the students are admitted after President Dwight D. Eisenhower sends federal troops to the school.

1957 **O'Neill's final work**
Long Day's Journey into Night, a play by Eugene O'Neill, is published four years after the playwright's death.

1957 **Pulitzer for Wilbur**
Richard Wilbur receives the Pulitzer prize for poetry for his volume *Things of This World.*

1957 **Nuclear energy**
The first full-scale U.S. nuclear power plant opens in Shippingport, Pennsylvania.

1958 **Randall on function**
In his book *Nature and Historical Experience,* John Herman Randall presents a traditional concept of the function of philosophy.

1958 **Satellite orbits earth**
The first U.S. satellite orbits the earth.

1958 **Heredity studies**
Americans George W. Beadle, Edward L. Tatum, and Joshua Lederberg win the Nobel prize in physiology or medicine. The three are honored for their studies of heredity.

35 John Fitzgerald Kennedy

Born—May 29, 1917. Died—Nov. 22, 1963. Place of birth—Brookline, Mass. Political party—Democrat. Term—1961–1963. Electoral vote—303. Vice-president—Lyndon B. Johnson.

36 Lyndon Baines Johnson

Born—Aug. 27, 1908. Died—Jan. 22, 1973. Place of birth—near Stonewall, Tex. Political party—Democrat. Terms—1963–1969. Electoral vote—486. Vice-president—Hubert H. Humphrey.

1959 **Two new states added**
Alaska and Hawaii are admitted to the Union; they are the 49th and 50th states.

1959 **Roth to prominence**
Goodbye, Columbus, a book of stories by Philip Roth, is published.

1959 **Updike's first novel**
The Poorhouse Fair, a novel by John Updike, appears.

1959 **Two honored on DNA**
Severo Ochoa and Arthur Kornberg win the Nobel prize in physiology or medicine. The two are honored for their synthesis of ribonucleic acid and deoxyribonucleic acid (DNA).

1960s **Mexican Americans elected**
Four Mexican Americans are elected to Congress and work for civil rights for Latin Americans; they are Senator Joseph Montoya (New Mexico) and Representatives Eligio de la Garza (Texas), Henry B. Gonzales (Texas), and Edward R. Roybal (California).

1960s **Catholic Church changes**
In the wake of the Second Vatican Council, the Roman Catholic Church in the United States undergoes a series of changes. The liturgy of the Mass is changed from Latin to mainly English, special Masses utilize folk music and folk dancing, and dress codes for nuns are relaxed.

1960 **Communications satellite**
The United States launches *Echo I,* the first passive communications satellite.

1960 **Pentecostal revival**
Father Dennis Bennett tells his congregation at St. Mark's Episcopal Church in Van Nuys, California, that he has experienced the Pentecostal spirit. The Pentecostal movement, which emphasizes faith healing and speaking in tongues, grows with momentum in the United States for the second time.

1961 **Peace Corps started**
President John F. Kennedy obtains congressional approval to start the Peace Corps, a government agency that sends American citizens to foreign countries to promote peace, health, and welfare.

1961 **Heller published**
Joseph Heller's comic novel *Catch-22* is published.

1961 **Major work by Kahn**
The Richards Medical Research Building at the University of Pennsylvania is completed. The building was designed by architect and planner Louis I. Kahn.

1962 **Cuban missile crisis**
The United States learns that the Soviet Union has missile bases in Cuba; President John F. Kennedy orders a naval blockade of Cuba and forces removal of the missiles.

1962 **Meredith enrolls**
James Meredith becomes the first black to enroll in the University of Mississippi at Oxford. Attorney General Robert F. Kennedy sends U.S. marshals to maintain order when whites riot.

1962 **Chavez organizes**
Cesar Chavez founds the National Farm Workers Association to organize farm laborers in the grape fields. The group organizes strikes and boycotts against California grape growers.

1962 **School prayer banned**
The Supreme Court rules that required prayers and devotional Bible readings in public schools are unconstitutional.

1962 **Glenn in orbit**
Astronaut John Glenn becomes the first American to orbit the earth.

1962 **Watson honored**
American scientist James D. Watson shares the Nobel prize in physiology or medicine with two British colleagues. The three are cited for their research on the molecular structure of DNA.

1963 **Rights marchers to capital**
On August 28, in Washington, D.C., more than 200,000 persons take part in the civil rights demonstration called the March on Washington.

1963 **President Kennedy slain**
President John F. Kennedy is shot and killed in Dallas, Texas, on November 22; Lee Harvey Oswald is arrested for the crime and is then himself shot and killed.

1963 **Equal pay required**
The Federal Equal Pay Act requires employers to pay the same wages to men and women who perform the same duties.

1963 **Right to counsel**
In *Gideon v. Wainwright,* the Supreme Court rules that states must provide free legal counsel to any person accused of a felony who cannot afford to pay for counsel.

1963 **Moral responsibility probed**
The *Journal of Philosophy,* a publication associated with Columbia University in New York City, publishes the "Symposium on Human Action." The symposium discusses moral freedom and responsibility and the relationship of knowledge to action.

1963 **Baldwin essays**
The Fire Next Time, a nonfiction work on race relations by James Baldwin, is published.

1964 **Civil rights laws passed**
Congress passes the Civil Rights Act of 1964 and other legislation guaranteeing blacks equal protection under the law.

1964 **Gulf of Tonkin incident**
North Vietnamese PT boats attack U.S. destroyers in the Gulf of Tonkin.

1964 **Gulf of Tonkin resolution**
Congress passes the Gulf of Tonkin resolution, which authorizes the President to "take all necessary measures to repel any armed attack against the forces of the United States and to prevent further aggression."

1964 **"Freedom summer" violence**
A number of civil rights groups, including the Student Nonviolent Coordinating Committee (SNCC), send students to Mississippi to register black voters; whites kill three workers.

1964 **"War on Poverty" designed**
President Lyndon B. Johnson initiates the creation of the Office of Economic Opportunity (OEO), a government agency designed to wage the "War on Poverty."

1964 **Townes and lasers**
American scientist Charles H. Townes shares the Nobel prize in physics with two Russian scientists. The three are honored for their research on lasers and on masers, which are devices that amplify or generate electromagnetic waves with great stability and accuracy.

1965 **Bomb North Vietnam**
President Lyndon B. Johnson orders the bombing of military targets in North Vietnam.

1965 **LBJ sends troops**
In March President Johnson sends U.S. Marines to Da Nang, South Vietnam. They are the first U.S. ground troops, as opposed to advisers, to be sent to Vietnam.

1965 **Rights confrontation**
Police use tear gas and whips to turn back voting rights marchers near Selma, Alabama.

1965 **Voting Rights Act**
In August, Congress passes the Voting Rights Act of 1965 to equalize standards for voting in the 50 states.

1965 **Urban riots touched off**
In August, blacks riot in the Watts section of Los Angeles, California, calling national attention to conditions in U.S. inner city areas.

1965 **Vintage O'Connor**
Everything That Rises Must Converge, a book of short stories by Flannery O'Connor, is published a year after her death.

1965 **COMSAT launches satellite**
COMSAT puts the first commercial communications satellite into orbit.

1966 **"Black power" urged**
Stokely Carmichael is elected head of the Student Nonviolent Coordinating Committee (SNCC); he urges that blacks be militant in seeking "black power," politically and economically.

1966 **NOW founded**
The National Organization for Women (NOW) is founded by a group of persons including Betty Friedan, author of *The Feminine Mystique.*

1966 ***Miranda* expands rights**
Ruling in the case *Miranda v. Arizona,* the Supreme Court states that criminal suspects must be fully informed of their rights when they are arrested; otherwise, confessions or statements by the suspect may not be used in court.

1966 **Quine's papers**
Various papers by Willard Van Orman Quine are published in two volumes, *Selected Logic Papers* and *The Ways of Paradox and Other Essays.*

1966 **Mulliken and molecules**
Robert S. Mulliken wins the Nobel prize in chemistry for his research on the structure of molecules.

1967 **More riots hit cities**
In the "long, hot summer," riots occur in about 75 U.S. cities.

1967 **Presbyterians publish**
The United Presbyterian Church, U.S.A., meets and adopts the Book of Confessions. This is a new statement of the essentials of the Presbyterian faith.

1967 **Pulitzer for Albee**
Playwright Edward Albee is voted the Pulitzer prize for drama for his play *A Delicate Balance.*

1967 **Geodesic dome**
An innovative and startling structure, the geodesic dome, is erected as the American exhibit at Expo 67 in Montreal, Canada. The dome is designed by R. Buckminster Fuller.

1967 **Rock culture**
The rock musical *Hair* is first performed.

1968 **Dr. King slain**
On April 4, in Memphis, Tennessee, civil rights leader Dr. Martin Luther King, Jr., is shot and killed.

1968 **Peace talks begin**
Preliminary peace talks begin between the United States and North Vietnam.

1969 **Troops massed**
Some 543,000 U.S. troops, the largest number of the war, are in Vietnam by February.

1969 **Antiwar protests escalate**
Peace demonstrators march in major U.S. cities on Moratorium Day, October 15; about 300,000 persons march on Washington, D.C., on November 15 to protest the continuation of the war and the bombing of Cambodia.

1969 **Desegregation ordered**
The Supreme Court rules that desegregation of all public school systems must take place "at once."

1969 **Mies dies**
Architect Ludwig Mies van der Rohe dies. Mies, who worked by the principle "less is more," is often considered the leading U.S. contemporary architect.

1969 **Wall murals**
The Wall of Truth, a wall mural by black artist William Walker, is completed in Chicago. Wall murals flourish as an artistic expression of community pride.

1969 **Man walks on moon**
Astronaut Neil Armstrong becomes the first person to walk on the moon.

1969 **Nobel for Gell-Mann**
Murray Gell-Mann wins the Nobel prize in physics for his discoveries relating to subatomic particles.

1970 **Senate acts on war**
On June 24, the U.S. Senate repeals the Gulf of Tonkin resolution, which gave the President broad powers to wage war.

1970 **Latin party founded**
La Raza Unida, a political party for Chicanos, or Mexican Americans, is established in Texas.

1971 **Prisoners revolt**
Demanding a series of prison reforms, prisoners take over the New York State Attica Correctional Facility; law enforcement officers storm the prison, and 43 persons are killed.

1971 **Essays published**
The U.S. philosopher Horace M. Kallen publishes a volume of essays, *What I Believe and Why—Maybe.*

1971 **A new look at history**
Dee Brown's *Bury My Heart at Wounded Knee* is printed and becomes a best seller. The book is a nonfiction account of U.S. actions against the American Indians in the 19th century.

1972 **Watergate burglary foiled**
On June 17, a group of persons are arrested for breaking into the Democratic Party headquarters in the Watergate complex in Washington, D.C.; the men arrested prove to be employees of President Richard M. Nixon's reelection committee.

1972 **Indians protest**
To protest the U.S. Bureau of Indian Affairs' policies, the American Indian

37 Richard M. Nixon

Born—Jan. 9, 1913. Place of birth—Yorba Linda, Calif. Political party—Republican. Terms—1969–1974. Electoral votes—301; 520. Vice-presidents—Spiro T. Agnew; Gerald R. Ford.

38 Gerald R. Ford

Born—July 14, 1913. Place of birth—Omaha, Nebr. Political party—Republican. Term—1974–1977. Electoral vote—none. Vice-president—Nelson A. Rockefeller.

Movement (AIM) and other Indian rights groups hold a sit-in at the bureau's headquarters in Washington, D.C.

1972 **Death penalty halted**
The Supreme Court rules that the death penalty as currently written and administered in most states is "cruel and unusual punishment" in violation of the Constitution.

1972 **"Jesus movement" grows**
The International Student Congress on Evangelism is held in Dallas, Texas, and more than 75,000 young persons attend. Evangelist Billy Graham says the event proves the power of the "Jesus revival" among the nation's youth.

1972 **Yearbook established**
Marshall Cohen establishes *Philosophy and Public Affairs,* a yearbook of philosophy, at Princeton University, Princeton, New Jersey.

1972 **Women as philosophers**
The Society for Women in Philosophy holds its first conference in Chicago, Illinois.

1972 **Bardeen wins again**
John Bardeen becomes the first person to win the Nobel prize in physics twice. He is honored this year for his work in superconductivity; in 1956, he was honored for discovering the transistor effect.

1973 **War ends officially**
The United States, North Vietnam, South Vietnam, and the Viet Cong sign a cease-fire agreement in January.

1973 **Vice-president resigns**
Vice-president Spiro T. Agnew resigns from office on October 10, while he is under investigation on bribery charges in Maryland.

1973 **Ford appointed**
Gerald R. Ford is appointed vice-president by President Nixon; Ford is the first person to be appointed under the terms of the 25th Amendment to the Constitution.

1973 **Seize Wounded Knee**
Members of the American Indian Movement (AIM) seize the village of Wounded Knee, South Dakota; they demand the return of certain lands taken from Indians in violation of treaty agreements.

1973 **Abortion rights ruling**
The Supreme Court rules that states may not prohibit a woman's right, under certain conditions, to have an abortion during the first six months of pregnancy.

1973 **Major art sale**
Fifty contemporary American paintings from the collection of Robert C. Scull are sold for more than $2 million. The artists represented in the sale include Andy Warhol, Franz Kline, Jasper Johns, and Robert Rauschenberg.

1973–1974 **Watergate facts disclosed**
Investigators reveal that high officials of the Nixon Administration were involved in covering up the Watergate break-in in 1972.

1974 **Nixon resigns**
On August 8, President Nixon announces to the nation that he is resigning from office effective the following day; he denies any wrongdoing, but most observers link his resignation to threats of impeachment.

1974 **Guru gains followers**
The Guru Maharaj Ji, leader of the Divine Light Mission, claims that he now has 50,000 followers in the United States and 8 million worldwide. Most of these followers are young persons. Maharaj Ji's movement is based very loosely on several spiritual movements found in his native India.

1974 **Women ordained**
On July 29, eleven women are ordained priests of the Episcopal Church by three bishops jointly celebrating a service in Philadelphia, Pennsylvania; the ordinations are considered "irregular" because the denomination has not yet approved ordination for women.

1974 **Graham to Far East**
The U.S. Department of State sponsors a tour of the Far East by modern dancer Martha Graham and her troupe.

1974 **Flory wins Nobel**
Paul J. Flory is awarded the Nobel prize for chemistry for his research on the physical chemistry of macromolecules.

1975 **More women ordained**
On September 7, four more women are ordained priests in the Episcopal Church in a service performed by the Right Reverend George W. Barrett in Washington, D.C.

1975 **Eastern philosophy**
Robert M. Pirsig's book, *Zen and the Art of Motorcycle Maintenance: An Inquiry into Values,* is published. The novel deals in a popularized form with Oriental and classical Greek philosophy. The popularity of Pirsig's book is but one indication of a current interest in Eastern philosophy.

1976 **America celebrates**
The United States celebrates its 200th birthday. Bicentennial observances of all kinds are held in many cities and towns throughout the United States.

39 James Earl Carter, Jr.

Born—Oct. 1, 1924. Place of birth—Plains, Ga. Political party—Democrat. Term—1977–1981. Electoral vote—297. Vice-president—Walter F. Mondale.

1976 **Death penalty approved**
On July 2, the Supreme Court rules that the death penalty may be used again in the United States; the Court says that state laws passed in Florida, Georgia, and Texas since its 1972 decision are fair and just in the laws' application of capital punishment.

1976 **Haley's Roots**
The biographical novel *Roots,* by Alex Haley, is published. *Roots* is a fictional account of Haley's family saga, ranging from Africa to the United States.

1976 **Calder show**
"Calder's Universe," an exhibition of more than 200 works by the American sculptor Alexander Calder, opens in New York City.

1976 **Hammond honored**
The Priestly Medal of the American Chemical Society is awarded to George S. Hammond for his work in photochemistry.

1977 **Robert Lowell dies**
Poet Robert Lowell, generally considered the leading contemporary American poet, dies in September.

1977 **Human-powered flight**
A group of Californians headed by Paul MacCready, Jr., sponsor a successful test flight of the Gossamer Condor. The Condor is a human-powered aircraft.

1978 **Camp David accords**
Egypt and Israel agree to a framework for peace as a result of 12-day talks mediated by President Carter at Camp David, Maryland. The two nations sign a peace treaty the following year, ending more than 30 years of a state of war.

1978 **Bakke decision**
In the case *Regents of the University of California v. Allan Bakke,* the Supreme Court rules that rigid quota systems used to achieve racial balance may constitute unfair discrimination against nonminority persons.

1979 **Canal Zone returned**
The United States returns sovereignty over the Panama Canal Zone to Panama. The United States had governed the zone since 1903.

1979 **U.S.-China ties**
The United States and China establish full diplomatic relations after a break of nearly 30 years.

1979 **Three Mile Island**
A failure in the cooling system of the Three Mile Island nuclear power plant near Harrisburg, Pennsylvania, causes the worst nuclear accident in U.S. history. The incident spurs widespread protests against nuclear power.

1979 **Gasoline crisis**
Shortages of gasoline lead to sharp price increases and long lines of motorists waiting for service at gas stations.

1979 **Iran seizes hostages**
Militant Iranians seize 53 Americans and hold them hostage at the U.S. embassy in Teheran, Iran.

1979 **Inflation rate soars**
The inflation rate tops 13%, the highest rate since 1946.

1979 **Nobel to Cormack**
Allan McLeod Cormack is cowinner of the Nobel prize in physiology or medicine for the development of an X-ray scanning technique used in medical diagnosis.

1979 **Cheever wins Pulitzer**
The Pulitzer prize for fiction goes to John Cheever for *The Stories of John Cheever.* The collection brings together short stories written from 1946 to 1978.

1980 **Rescue attempt fails**
Eight U.S. soldiers die in an unsuccessful attempt to rescue the American hostages in Iran.

1980 **Cuban refugees**
Thousands of refugees flee Cuba aboard boats and land in Florida. The migration occurs with the concurrence of Cuban President Fidel Castro.

40 Ronald Reagan

Born—Feb. 6, 1911. Place of birth—Tampico, Ill. Political party—Republican. Term—1981– Electoral vote—489. Vice-president— George Bush.

Canadian history

This section chronicles many important dates in Canadian history. The events highlighted include political, religious, social, philosophical, literary, artistic, scientific, and technological milestones for Canada.

A.D. 1000s **Viking voyages**
Vikings from Iceland and Greenland sail along the eastern coast of Canada, possibly establishing a temporary settlement at the northern tip of Newfoundland.

1497 **Cabot lands in Canada**
Italian explorer John Cabot, sailing under the English flag, lands on Newfoundland or Cape Breton Island. As a result of this landing, Britain lays claim to all Canada.

1500s 1600s **Fish and furs**
French sailors fish off the eastern coast of Canada and begin trading with the Indians for furs. French merchants seek fur-trading rights from the king in return for their help in establishing colonies in Canada.

1524 **Verrazano explores coast**
The Italian explorer Giovanni da Verrazano sails along the eastern coast of Canada on behalf of King Francis I of France.

1534 **Cartier makes claim**
French explorer Jacques Cartier lands on the Gaspé shore of what is now Quebec. Cartier is the first European to reach the Gulf of St. Lawrence. He claims the surrounding territory for France.

1583 **Gilbert on Newfoundland**
Sir Humphrey Gilbert lands on Newfoundland and claims it for Queen Elizabeth I of England.

1603 **Champlain claims island**
French explorer Samuel de Champlain lands at what is now Prince Edward Island and claims it for France. He names the island Ile St. Jean.

1608 **Quebec founded**
Champlain founds Quebec on the banks of the St. Lawrence River. His volume *Des Sauvages, ou Voyage de Samuel de Champlain* provides early information about the Indians of North America.

1610 **Hudson reaches bay**
English explorer Henry Hudson arrives at the great bay that later bears his name. He and his crew explore the bay area.

1620 **First school**
Madame Samuel de Champlain, wife of the explorer, begins teaching French and Roman Catholicism to a group of Indians in what is probably the first school in Canada.

1621 **Settlers on Newfoundland**
George Calvert, later Lord Baltimore, establishes the first permanent settlement in Newfoundland.

1629 **Scots arrive**
The first British settlers arrive in Nova Scotia from Scotland.

1642 **Montreal established**
A group of Roman Catholic missionaries led by former French army officer Paul de Chomeday, Sieur de Maisonneuve, founds the settlement of Ville-Marie, later renamed Montreal.

1663 **New France proclaimed**
King Louis XIV of France officially declares Canada to be a province of France. The North American colonies are called New France.

1663 Laval founded
Laval University is founded at Ste. Foy, near Quebec City, as the Seminary of Quebec. The French-language institution is the oldest university in Canada.

1670 Bay company obtains charter
King Charles II of England grants a charter to the Hudson's Bay Company, giving the company sole trading rights in all lands drained by streams that flow into Hudson Bay. The company builds trading posts and forts in the area, which becomes known as Rupert's Land, and establishes a fur trade with the Indians.

1672 Frontenac to New France
Comte de Frontenac is named governor of New France. He becomes a leader in the fight against the Iroquois Indians for the territory of New France.

1674 Laval named bishop
Monsignor François Xavier de Laval de Montmorency becomes the first Roman Catholic bishop of Quebec City.

1689–1763 French and Indian Wars
British and French forces clash over territorial claims in a series of four wars known collectively as the French and Indian Wars.

1713 Britain wins territory
The Treaty of Utrecht gives Britain control of the mainland of Nova Scotia, Newfoundland, and the Hudson Bay region.

1734 First highway
The first Canadian highway links Montreal and Quebec City.

1752 First newspaper
The *Halifax Gazette* (now the *Royal Gazette*) is founded in Nova Scotia. It is the first newspaper published in Canada.

1755 Acadians banished
In Nova Scotia, British colonial troops from New England drive out French settlers, called Acadians, who refuse to swear allegiance to Britain. The Acadians go to Prince Edward Island, Quebec, the French colony of Louisiana, and British colonies farther south.

Canada in the 1500s and 1600s

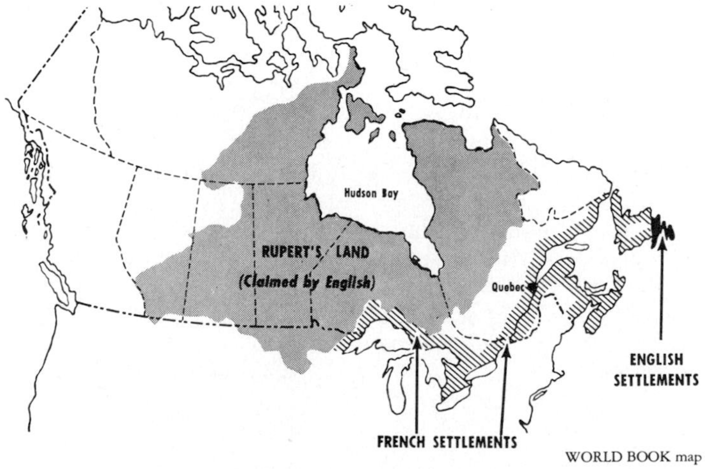

WORLD BOOK map

Early immigrants to Canada included French fur trappers followed by thousands of French settlers. English settlers established only a few villages in the east. The Hudson's Bay Company claimed Rupert's Island, the area around Hudson Bay.

1759 Battle of Quebec
French forces led by the Marquis de Montcalm are defeated by the British under General James Wolfe at the Battle of Quebec. The French defeat marks a turning point in the continuing battle for control of Canada.

1760 France loses empire
British forces close in on Montreal, and the French governor, the Marquis de Vaudreuil-Cavagnal, surrenders New France.

1763 Treaty ends wars
The Treaty of Paris brings a formal end to the French and Indian Wars. Under the terms of the treaty, Britain wins control of Canada. France is allowed to retain control of two tiny islands south of Newfoundland: Saint Pierre and Miquelon.

1769 English novel appears
Frances Brooke publishes *The History of Emily Montague,* the first English-language novel about Canadian life.

1770s North West Company formed
Independent fur traders in Canada set up the North West Company to compete with the Hudson's Bay Company. The new company operates mainly in Canada's far western and Pacific coast regions.

1774 French win rights
The Quebec Act guarantees freedom of religion to Roman Catholic French Canadians. It also makes French civil law valid in British courts in Quebec.

1778 Cook on Vancouver
Captain James Cook, in search of a trade route to the Orient, lands on Vancouver Island.

1779 **First public library**
At Quebec City, British Canadians and French Canadians establish the first public library in Canada.

1789 **Mackenzie reaches Arctic**
Sir Alexander Mackenzie travels from Lake Athabasca to Great Slave Lake, then continues along the Mackenzie River to the Arctic Ocean.

1791 **Quebec divided**
The province of Quebec is divided into Upper Canada (now Ontario) and Lower Canada (now Quebec) through the Constitutional Act of 1791. Each section has its own government. British Canadians live primarily in Upper Canada, and French Canadians live mainly in Lower Canada.

1793 **Toronto settled**
Lieutenant Governor John Simcoe sends British troops to establish a permanent settlement at York (now Toronto).

1793 **Mackenzie reaches Pacific**
Sir Alexander Mackenzie reaches the Pacific Ocean. He becomes the first white person to reach the Pacific by crossing the northern part of North America.

1800s-1914 **European immigration**
Large numbers of European settlers migrate to Canada, settling chiefly on the prairie farmlands and in the growing industrial cities.

1804 **Cathedral opens**
The Anglican Cathedral of the Holy Trinity opens its doors in Quebec. It is the first cathedral of the Church of England built outside Great Britain.

1812 **War with the United States**
U.S. forces based in Detroit, on the Niagara River, and at the foot of Lake Champlain launch a 3-point invasion of Canada at the start of the War of 1812. The invasion attempts fail completely.

Canada in 1791

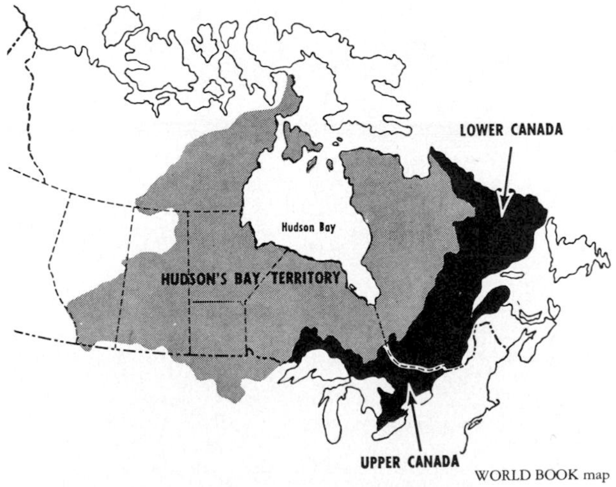

WORLD BOOK map

The Constitutional Act of 1791 split Quebec into two self-governing parts: Upper Canada and Lower Canada. British settlers occupied Upper Canada, which included the area along the Great Lakes and the upper St. Lawrence River. Former French settlements to the northeast became Lower Canada.

1813 **United States seizes Toronto**
U.S. troops capture York (now Toronto) and hold the city for a short time, burning several public buildings.

1814 **Treaty returns status quo**
The Treaty of Ghent ends the War of 1812. Conditions of the treaty return all territorial holdings of the two sides to their prewar status. Neither side gains anything.

1821 **Companies consolidate**
The Hudson's Bay Company takes over control of the rival North West Company.

1827 **King's College founded**
King's College is founded as an English-language institution in Toronto. It later changes its name to the University of Toronto and becomes the largest university in Canada.

1829 **Welland Canal**
The Welland Canal links Lakes Erie and Ontario, enabling commercial ships to travel from one waterway to the other.

1832 **Novel by Richardson**
John Richardson publishes *Wacousta,* a historical novel about an Indian conspiracy organized by the Ottawa chief Pontiac at the end of the French and Indian Wars. *Wacousta* ranks as the first important English-Canadian novel.

1836 **First railroad**
Canada's first railroad begins operations between Laprairie and St. Jean, Quebec.

1837-1838 **Rebellions erupt**
Louis Joseph Papineau leads a brief, unsuccessful rebellion against British rule in Lower Canada. In Upper Canada, William Lyon Mackenzie leads an unsuccessful revolt demanding more self-government.

1839 Lord Durham's report
Lord Durham arrives in Canada in 1838 and studies the problems of discontent in the colonies. In 1839, he submits a report to Queen Victoria urging Britain to grant self-government to the North American colonies. He predicts they will stay within the British Empire if they are granted self-government.

1840 Canada reunited
The British Parliament adopts the Act of Union, which combines Upper and Lower Canada into the new province of Canada. Each section receives equal representation in a provincial legislative assembly.

1842 Museum in New Brunswick
The New Brunswick Museum is founded in St. John. The oldest museum in Canada, it features exhibits of cultural, historical, and scientific interest.

1843 Vancouver settlement
The Hudson's Bay Company establishes the first permanent settlement on Vancouver Island at what is now Victoria.

1845–1860 Kane paints Indians
Artist Paul Kane paints a number of pictures of Plains and Pacific Coast Indians. In 1859, he publishes an account of his travels called *Wanderings of an Artist Among the Indians of North America.*

1846 Telegraph service begins
The first Canadian telegraph service begins operating between Toronto and Hamilton, Ontario.

1848 Bilingual university
The College of Bytown is founded. Now called the University of Ottawa, it is the largest bilingual university in Canada.

1850s Oil strike
Canada's first oil field is developed in Lambton County, Ontario.

c. 1857 Gold in British Columbia
The discovery of gold in the Fraser River region of British Columbia leads to a gold rush.

1857 Ottawa proclaimed capital
Queen Victoria of England designates Ottawa as the capital of the province of Canada.

1858 Crémazie's "Le Drapeau"
Octave Crémazie writes the poem "Le Drapeau de Carillon," which later becomes the lyric for one of the best-loved songs of French Canadians.

1860s Poetry movement
A group of poets establish the School of Quebec, which draws its inspiration from French-Canadian patriotism.

1860 Art museum founded
The Montreal Museum of Fine Arts, Canada's oldest art museum, is founded.

1864 Confederation conferences
Leaders of British North American colonies meet at Charlottetown on Prince Edward Island, then at Quebec City. At the Quebec Conference, they draw up a plan to form a confederation called the Dominion of Canada. Newfoundland and Prince Edward Island later reject the plan.

1866 Constitution framed
The Fathers of Confederation meet in London to draw up the British North America Act, which becomes the written portion of the Canadian constitution.

1867 Dominion proclaimed
The British Parliament passes the British North America Act, formally establishing the Dominion of Canada. The act is formally proclaimed on July 1, which becomes known as Dominion Day. The new

Canada after 1867

WORLD BOOK map

With the British North America Act in 1867, four provinces became the Dominion of Canada. Other provinces were added up to the entrance of Newfoundland in 1949. Canada divided the Hudson's Bay Territories in 1912. Adjoining provinces took part of the land, and the remainder became the Northwest Territories.

1 Sir John A. Macdonald

Born—Jan. 11, 1815. Died—June 6, 1891. Place of birth—Glasgow, Scotland. Political party—Conservative. Terms—1867–1873; 1878–1891.

2 Alexander Mackenzie

Born—Jan. 28, 1822. Died—April 17, 1892. Place of birth—Logierait, Scotland. Political party—Liberal. Term—1873–1878.

3 Sir John A. Macdonald

Second term: 1878–1891. For full entry, see above.

nation consists of four provinces: Quebec (formerly Lower Canada), Ontario (formerly Upper Canada), Nova Scotia, and New Brunswick.

1867 First prime minister
Sir John A. Macdonald, who was leader of the Conservative Party in Upper Canada, becomes the first prime minister of the Dominion of Canada.

1867 "Maple Leaf" composed
Alexander Muir writes the words and music for the song "Maple Leaf Forever!" It becomes one of Canada's favorite national songs, especially in Ontario and other predominantly English-speaking areas.

1869–1870 Red River Rebellion
Louis Riel, a leader of the *métis* (persons of mixed Indian and European descent), leads a rebellion against the Canadian government in what is now Manitoba. The revolt delays the creation of a new province.

1873 Mounties organized
The Canadian parliament establishes the North-West Mounted Police, later called the Royal Canadian Mounted Police.

1880 Roberts begins career
Sir Charles G. D. Roberts publishes *Orion and Other Poems,* launching a literary career that spans 60 years.

1880 National Gallery opens
The National Gallery of Canada is established in Ottawa. It eventually houses the largest collection of Canadian art in the world.

1880 "O Canada" written
Calixa Lavallée composes the tune that eventually becomes known as "O Canada," the country's national anthem.

1883 Ore found in Ontario
The world's largest copper-nickel reserves are discovered near Sudbury, in Ontario.

1885 Railroad links coasts
The Canadian Pacific Railway is completed, linking Canada's Atlantic and Pacific coasts.

1885 Riel Rebellion
Louis Riel leads a second revolt of the métis, this time in Saskatchewan. The revolt is unsuccessful, and Riel is later hanged in spite of widespread protests among French Canadians.

1891 Educators join forces
The Dominion Educational Association (later called the Canadian Education Association) is founded to promote cooperation among the provincial education authorities.

4 Sir John J. C. Abbott

Born—March 12, 1821. Died—Oct. 30, 1893. Place of birth—St. Andrews, Lower Canada (now Quebec). Political party—Conservative. Term—1891–1892.

5 Sir John S. D. Thompson

Born—Nov. 10, 1844. Died—Dec. 12, 1894. Place of birth—Halifax, N.S. Political party—Conservative. Term—1892–1894.

6 Sir Mackenzie Bowell

Born—Dec. 27, 1823. Died—Dec. 10, 1917. Place of birth—Rickinghall, England. Political party—Conservative. Term—1894–1896.

1893 **Bliss Carman emerges**
Bliss Carman begins his career as one of Canada's best-known poets with the volume *Low Tide on Grand Pré.*

c. 1895 **Poets explore psychology**
A group of French-Canadian poets form the School of Montreal, which emphasizes the psychology of the individual.

1896 **Laurier leads Canada**
Sir Wilfrid Laurier, head of the Liberal party, becomes the first French Canadian to serve as prime minister of Canada.

1896 **Gold in the Klondike**
Gold is discovered on Bonanza Creek, a tributary of the Klondike River in what is now the Yukon Territory, near the present site of Dawson. The discovery leads to the Klondike Gold Rush of 1897 and 1898, and thousands of prospectors pour into the region.

1897 **Habitant poetry**
W. H. Drummond publishes a collection of poetry called *The Habitant.* Drummond becomes known as the poet of the habitant, or French-Canadian farmer, as a result of his vivid descriptions of the habitants' legends and ways of life.

1898 **Novels of the West**
Charles W. Gordon, writing under the pseudonym Ralph Connor, publishes his first novel, *Black Rock,* which establishes him as one of Canada's most popular novelists.

1899 **Lampman on nature**
Archibald Lampman, one of Canada's finest nature poets, dies at age 38, after publishing three volumes of poetry: *Among the Millet, Lyrics of Earth,* and *Alcyone.*

1902 **Radio station built**
Italian inventor Guglielmo Marconi builds the first transatlantic radio station at Glace Bay, Nova Scotia.

1909 **Treaty with the United States**
Canada and the United States sign the Boundary Waters Treaty, which establishes the International Joint Commission. The commission settles boundary problems and handles questions about the use of boundary waters for water power, navigation, sanitation, and irrigation.

1912 **Boundaries extended**
The boundaries of Quebec, Ontario, and Manitoba are expanded to include land that had been part of the old Hudson's Bay Company territory.

1913 **Hémon's classic**
Louis Hémon completes *Maria Chapdelaine,* a classic story of pioneers.

1914 **Canada enters war**
Canada joins the British war effort in World War I and sends its troops overseas.

1914 **Oil strike in Alberta**
A major oil discovery in Alberta is made in Turner Valley.

1915 **War poem published**
John McCrae's poem "In Flanders Fields" appears in the English magazine *Punch.*

1917 **Union Government**
The Liberal and Conservative parties join to form the Union Government to promote the war effort.

1917–1919 **Prohibition**
The Canadian government bans the import and manufacture of alcoholic beverages.

7 Sir Charles Tupper

Born—July 2, 1821. Died—Oct. 30, 1915. Place of birth—Amherst, N.S. Political party—Conservative. Term—1896.

8 Sir Wilfrid Laurier

Born—Nov. 20, 1841. Died—Feb. 17, 1919. Place of birth—St. Lin (now Laurentides), Que. Political party—Liberal. Term—1896–1911.

9 Sir Robert L. Borden

Born—June 26, 1854. Died—June 10, 1937. Place of birth—Grand Pré, N.S. Political parties—Conservative; Unionist. Terms—1911–1917; 1917–1920.

10 Sir Robert L. Borden

Second term: 1917–1920. For full entry, see above.

11 Arthur Meighen

Born—June 16, 1874. Died—Aug. 5, 1960. Place of birth—near St. Mary's, Ont. Political party—Unionist. Terms—1920–1921; 1926.

1918 **Women win voting rights**
The Canadian parliament grants women the right to vote in federal elections.

1919 **War comes to an end for Canada**
Canada takes part in the negotiations leading to the Treaty of Versailles, bringing an end to World War I for Canada.

1919 **Radio broadcasts begin**
Station CFCF, the first Canadian radio station, begins regular broadcasts from Montreal.

1920 **Canada joins League**
Canada becomes a charter member of the League of Nations.

1920 **Group of Seven exhibits**
The Group of Seven, a group of Canadian painters known primarily for their large, bold landscapes of the Canadian countryside, stage their first exhibition.

1923 **Banting wins Nobel**
Sir Frederick Grant Banting shares the Nobel prize for physiology or medicine with John J. R. Macleod of Scotland for the discovery of insulin, the hormone used to treat diabetes.

1925 **United Church founded**
The United Church of Canada is established as a result of an act of parliament passed the year before. The church is a union of the Methodist Church in Canada with most Canadian Congregationalist and Presbyterian congregations. It becomes the largest Protestant denomination in Canada.

1926 **Crisis and conference**
A constitutional crisis arises over the question of the power of the governor. William Lyon Mackenzie King attends the Imperial Conference in London, where representatives declare that all British dominions have equal status and are completely self-governing.

1927 **Canadian-U.S. ties**
Canada exchanges diplomatic representatives with the United States. The exchange marks the first time Canada has handled its own diplomatic relations rather than working through the British diplomatic service.

1927 **Carr exhibits paintings**
An exhibition of works by painter Emily Carr shows her careful portrayal of Indian life and culture in British Columbia.

1927 **Whiteoaks' debut**
Author Mazo de la Roche introduces the Whiteoak family in *Jalna,* the first of a series of 16 related novels.

12 W. L. Mackenzie King

Born—Dec. 17, 1874. Died—July 22, 1950. Place of birth—Berlin (now Kitchener), Ont. Political party—Liberal. Terms—1921–1926; 1926–1930; 1935–1948.

13 Arthur Meighen

Second term: 1926. For full entry, see above.

14 W. L. Mackenzie King

Second term: 1926–1930. For full entry, see above.

1928 Grove and realism
Frederick Philip Grove helps establish the trend toward realism in fiction with the publication of *Our Daily Bread*.

1929 Depression strikes
Canada, like countries throughout the world, begins to suffer from the Great Depression.

1930s New parties formed
Three new political parties—the Cooperative Commonwealth Federation, the Social Credit party, and the Union Nationale party—are formed.

1932 Trade accords signed
At the Imperial Conference in Ottawa, Canada signs an agreement with other Commonwealth nations to adjust tariffs and encourage trade.

1933 Group of Seven expands
Several new painters join the Group of Seven, and the group changes its name to the Canadian Group of Painters.

1936 CBC founded
The Canadian Broadcasting Corporation (CBC) is established with headquarters in Ottawa. Funded primarily by the government, the CBC operates radio and television networks that broadcast programs in both French and English.

1937 Airline begins service
Trans-Canada Air Lines (now Air Canada) is established as Canada's first commercial airline.

1939 Canada at war
Canada declares war on Germany on September 10.

1939–1945 Armed forces join Allies
All branches of the Canadian armed forces contribute to the Allied effort in World War II.

15 Richard B. Bennett

Born—July 3, 1870. Died—June 26, 1947. Place of birth—near Hopewell Cape, N.B. Political party—Conservative. Term—1930–1935.

1940 Draft takes effect
Parliament passes a law to draft for home military service. Many Canadians also join the British and U.S. armed forces.

1940 Defense board established
Canada and the United States establish the Permanent Joint Board on Defense, which surveys the defense requirements on the coasts of both countries.

1941 War on Japan declared
Canada declares war on Japan on December 8, one day after the Japanese attack Pearl Harbor in Hawaii.

1942 Raid on Dieppe
Canadian troops suffer heavy casualties during a raid on Dieppe, on the northern coast of France.

1942 Highway to Alaska
The Alaska Highway is completed, linking Dawson Creek, British Columbia, and Delta Junction, Alaska. The highway serves as an important route for military supplies.

1943 Mutual Aid Act
Parliament passes the Mutual Aid Act, which provides about $2 billion worth of supplies to Allied countries in addition to supplies for which they can pay.

1943 Smith's anthology published
A. J. M. Smith publishes the first edition of *The Book of Canadian Poetry: A Critical and Historical Anthology*. The book becomes a standard college text and strongly influences critical attitudes toward Canadian poetry.

1944 D-day
Canadian troops join British and U.S. forces in the invasion of Normandy, launched on June 6.

1945 Canada joins the United Nations
Canada joins 49 other countries to become a charter member of the United Nations.

16 W. L. Mackenzie King

Third term: 1935–1948. For full entry, see page 347.

17 Louis S. Saint Laurent

Born—Feb. 1, 1882. Died—July 25, 1973. Place of birth—Compton, Que. Political party—Liberal. Term—1948–1957.

1945 **MacLennan on conflicts**
Novelist Hugh MacLennan explores a theme of major social importance in *Two Solitudes,* which deals with the conflicts between French and English Canadians.

1945–1955 **Canada aids recovery**
Canada lends nearly $4 billion to help the post–World War II recovery efforts. The country also sends food and other supplies abroad.

1945–1961 **European influx**
About 2 million European immigrants settle in Canada after the end of World War II. The immigrants include Dutch, Germans, Italians, Poles, Russians, and Scandinavians.

1947 **Oil in Alberta**
A major oil strike is made at Leduc, south of Edmonton, Alberta.

1948 **King resigns**
W. L. Mackenzie King resigns as prime minister of Canada after serving more than 20 years—longer than any other prime minister in the Commonwealth.

1949 **New Supreme Court power**
The Supreme Court of Canada becomes the country's final court of appeals. Before this time, the Privy Council in England had heard appeals of Canadian cases.

1949 **Amendment right won**
Canada wins the right to amend its constitution in federal matters.

1949 **NATO membership**
Canada becomes a charter member of the North Atlantic Treaty Organization (NATO).

1950–1953 **Canadians in Korea**
Canadian troops fight with UN forces in Korea.

1951 **Award to Callaghan**
Morley Callaghan wins the Governor General's Award for *The Loved and the Lost,* a novel that explores the relationship between guilt and innocence.

1952 **Massey named**
Vincent Massey is named governor of Canada. He is the first Canadian-born person to hold the position.

1952 **Uranium strike in Ontario**
Geologists discover one of the world's largest single fields of uranium-bearing ore at Elliot Lake in Ontario.

1952 **Pratt's railroad epic**
Poet E. J. Pratt publishes *Towards the Last Spike,* an epic that some consider to be Canada's great national poem. It describes the construction of the Canadian Pacific Railway in the 1800's.

1952 **First TV broadcast**
The first Canadian television stations, CBFT in Montreal and CBLT in Toronto, begin operating.

1953 **National Library founded**
The National Library of Canada is established in Ottawa. It publishes *Canadiana,* a monthly and annual listing of all new books, pamphlets, and music published in Canada or relating to Canada.

1956 **Burns at Suez**
Canadian Major General E. L. M. Burns commands the UN Emergency Force sent to Egypt during the Suez Canal crisis.

1956 **Labor group formed**
The Canadian Labour Congress (CLC) is formed as a result of the merger of the Trades and Labour Congress of Canada and the Canadian Congress of Labour.

1956 **Cable from Newfoundland**
The first transatlantic telephone cable links Clarenville, Newfoundland, with Oban, Scotland.

1957 **Peace prize to Pearson**
Lester Pearson becomes the first Canadian to win the Nobel peace prize. The award cites his work in resolving the Suez Canal crisis of 1956.

1959 **Seaway opened**
Queen Elizabeth II and U.S. President Dwight D. Eisenhower preside at the official opening of the St. Lawrence Seaway.

1959 **Vanier appointed**
Georges Philias Vanier becomes the first French-Canadian governor of Canada.

18 John G. Diefenbaker

Born—Sept. 18, 1895. Died—Aug. 16, 1979. Place of birth—Neustadt, Ont. Political party—Progressive Conservative. Term—1957–1963.

19 Lester B. Pearson

Born—April 23, 1897. Died—Dec. 27, 1972. Place of birth—Toronto, Ont. Political party—Liberal. Term—1963–1968.

1960s **Economic plan launched**
The government launches a program to revitalize Canada's sagging economy. The program includes devaluation of the Canadian dollar, increased tariffs on imports, and greatly expanded trade with Communist nations.

1960s **French-Canadian demands**
French Canadians increase their demands for greater recognition and guaranteed civil rights. Small bands of extremists stage bombings to dramatize their protest.

1960 **Bill of Rights approved**
The government approves a Bill of Rights for Canada. The document includes a provision that no individual may be denied rights because of sex, race, national origin, color, or religion.

1961 **National insurance plan**
A national hospitalization insurance plan takes effect.

1961 **Viking remains unearthed**
Archaeologists discover the remains of an apparent Viking settlement at L'Anse aux Meadows in northern Newfoundland. The ruins are believed to date from about A.D. 1000.

1962 **Highway spans Canada**
Canada's first transcontinental highway—the Trans-Canada Highway—is opened. It extends about 5,000 miles (8,046 kilometers) between St. John's, Newfoundland, and Victoria, British Columbia.

1962 **First atomic power plant**
Canada's first atomic electric power plant is completed in Rolphton, Ontario. It is built for experimental purposes.

1962 **Third award to Reaney**
James Reaney wins the Governor General's Award for poetry for the third time. He won the award previously in 1949 and 1958.

1963 **Commission appointed**
Prime Minister Lester Pearson appoints the Royal Commission on Bilingualism and Biculturalism to study the relations between French-speaking and English-speaking Canadians.

1964 **Flag debate resolved**
After a 33-day parliamentary debate, the government decides to adopt a new flag, which eliminates any symbols of Canada's ties to Britain.

1964 **Ore deposits discovered**
Huge deposits of copper, silver, and zinc are discovered near Timmins, Ontario.

1965 **Commission reports**
The Royal Commission on Bilingualism and Biculturalism reports that a wide gap exists between French-speaking and English-speaking Canadians. The commission states that if the situation continues, most French Canadians might favor the creation of an independent, French-speaking nation.

1965 **New flag adopted**
Canada's new flag is officially adopted on February 15. It features a red maple leaf as its motif.

1966 **Award-winning poems**
Margaret Atwood publishes *The Circle Game,* a collection of poems that wins the Governor General's Award.

1967 **Centennial observed**
In Montreal, Canada observes its centennial with a variety of celebrations, including a world's fair, *Expo 67*.

1967 **Power plant opens**
Canada's first full-scale commercial nuclear power station opens in Douglas Point, near Kincardine, Ontario.

1967 **McLuhan's message**
Marshall McLuhan publishes *The Medium Is the Message,* one of his several books that examine the impact of communications media on individuals and society.

1968 **Parti Québécois formed**
Various French-Canadian separatist groups led by René Lévesque join to form the Parti Québécois.

1968 **Churches merge**
The Canada Conference of the Evangelical United Brethren Church joins the United Church of Canada.

1969 **Languages Act**
Parliament passes the Official Languages Act, requiring all federal facilities to provide service in French in districts where at least 10 per cent of the population speak French and service in English where at least 10 per cent of the population speak English.

1970 **Election Act**
Parliament passes a new Election Act, which lowers the minimum voting age in federal elections from 21 to 18 and allows 18-year-olds to run for seats in the House of Commons.

1970 **Terrorist crisis**
A national crisis erupts when members of the militant French-Canadian separatist group, the Front de Libération du Québec (FLQ), kidnap two government officials and murder one.

1971 **Nobel to Herzberg**
Gerhard Herzberg wins the Nobel prize for chemistry for his research on the structure of molecules, particularly for his work on the fragments of some molecules called free radicals.

1974 **Language laws in Quebec**
The provincial legislature in Quebec enacts laws making French the sole official language for education, commerce, and government.

1975 **Church union rejected**
The Anglican Church in Canada rejects a "plan of union" to join the United Church of Canada.

1975–1978 **Economic controls set**
The government establishes a program of wage and price controls in an attempt to lessen inflation.

1976 **Separatists win in Quebec**
The Parti Québécois, a separatist party, wins control of the provincial government of Quebec. The party's attempts to make Quebec a separate nation lead to tensions between the provincial and federal governments.

1976 **CN Tower caps renewal**
Toronto's Canadian National (CN) Tower, one of the tallest structures in the world, is completed. The 1,815-foot (553-meter) concrete structure is part of Metro Centre, one of the largest downtown redevelopment projects in North America.

1978 **Referendum planned**
The Quebec provincial assembly passes a bill that provides for holding a referendum on the question of independence for Quebec.

1979 **Committee urges action**
A special government committee, the Task Force on Canadian Unity, urges federal and provincial governments to act quickly in restructuring the nation's political institutions to accommodate regional differences.

1980 **Quebec rejects secession**
Voters in a referendum in Quebec vote overwhelmingly against withdrawing from Canada and becoming an independent nation. Canadian Prime Minister Pierre Elliott Trudeau calls for a period of national healing and announces plans to study possible constitutional revision to meet provincial needs.

20 Pierre E. Trudeau

Born—Oct. 18, 1919. Place of birth—Montreal, Que. Political party—Liberal. Terms—1968–1979; 1980–

21 Charles Joseph Clark

Born—June 5, 1939. Place of birth—High River, Alta. Political party—Progressive Conservative. Term—1979–1980.

22 Pierre E. Trudeau

Second term: 1980– . For full entry, see above.

Index

This index provides an easy-to-use list of place names that appear in this atlas, along with the information you need to locate these places on the maps. All cities and towns that appear on the state, province, and territory maps are included. The index also lists all county names, which are identified in the index by the abbreviation "co." In addition, the index includes selected geographic features and points of interest, such as important rivers, lakes, bays, islands, dams, and mountains.

All cities, towns, counties, and geographical features are listed together in one alphabetical order. To help you easily locate names in the index, guide words at the top of each page indicate the first name and the last name that appear on that page.

The index listing for each place name includes—

1. the *name* of the city, town, county, or geographic feature;
2. an abbreviation for the *state, province, or territory* in which it appears;
3. *locator numbers and letters* indicating its approximate location on the map;
4. the *pages* on which the state, province, or territory map may be found.

When you wish to locate a specific place on a map, use the guide words at the top of the index pages to find the index listing for that place. Turn to the page numbers given in the listing to find the appropriate map. Then use the locator number and letter given in the index listing to find the area of the map in which the place appears. Simply put one finger on the appropriate number at the top of the map and another finger on the appropriate letter at the side of the map. Then move your fingers across and down the map; they will come together at or near the place you are seeking.

The index also provides information for some cities and towns that are not labeled on the maps. An asterisk (*) following a town name indicates that the town is not labeled on the map. The index listings for such towns do, however, provide locator letters and numbers to indicate their general location.

In some listings, a town name is followed by a second town name that appears in brackets, indicating that the two towns are in the same general location. In many cases, the town shown in brackets is not labeled on the map; its approximate location can be found, however, since it is located near the town with which it is listed.

To simplify its use, this index employs as few abbreviations as possible. The abbreviations for the names of the states, provinces, and territories—along with the few other common abbreviations used—are listed here for your reference.

State, province, and territory abbreviations

Ala. Alabama
Alta. Alberta
Ariz. Arizona
Ark. Arkansas
B.C. British Columbia
Calif. California
Colo. Colorado
Conn. Connecticut
Del. Delaware
Fla. Florida
Ga. Georgia
Ia. Iowa
Ida. Idaho
Ill. Illinois
Ind. Indiana
Kans. Kansas
Ky. Kentucky
La. Louisiana
Man. Manitoba
Mass. Massachusetts
Md. Maryland
Me. Maine
Mich. Michigan
Minn. Minnesota
Miss. Mississippi
Mo. Missouri
Mont. Montana
N.B. New Brunswick
N.C. North Carolina
N. Dak. North Dakota
Nebr. Nebraska
Nev. Nevada
Nfld. Newfoundland
N.H. New Hampshire
N.J. New Jersey
N. Mex. New Mexico
N.S. Nova Scotia
N.W. Terr. Northwest Territories
N.Y. New York
O. Ohio
Okla. Oklahoma
Ont. Ontario
Ore. Oregon
Pa. Pennsylvania
P.E.I. Prince Edward Island
Que. Quebec
R.I. Rhode Island
Sask. Saskatchewan
S.C. South Carolina
S. Dak. South Dakota
Tenn. Tennessee
Tex. Texas
Ut. Utah
Va. Virginia
Vt. Vermont
Wash. Washington
Wis. Wisconsin
W. Va. West Virginia
Wyo. Wyoming
Y.T. Yukon Territory

Other abbreviations

co. county
Isl. Island or Islands
Mt. Mount or Mountain
Mts. Mountains
R. River
Res. Reservoir
St. Saint
Ste. Sainte

Notes: *Alaska* and *Hawaii* have not been abbreviated in this index.

An asterisk (*) identifies a place that does not appear on the map; locators show its general location.

A

Abanda, Ala. G9 146-7
Abasarokee, Mont. H9 222-3
Abbeville, Ala. K10 146-7
Abbeville, Ga. K6 160-1
Abbeville, La. I5 168-9
Abbeville, Miss. B7 176-7
Abbeville, S.C. K2 184-5
Abbeville, co., S.C. D6 184-5
Abbey, Sask. M4 294-5
Abbot*, Me. H5 64-5
Abbot Village, Me. H5 64-5
Abbotsford, Wis. F11 140-1
Abbotts Mill, Me. K2 64-5
Abbottsburg, N.C. G11 180-1
Abbyville, Kans. I9 108-9
Abel, Ala. E9 146-7
Abell, Md. H11 172-3
Abercorn, Que. J13 290-1
Abercrombie, N. Dak. I15 128-9
Abercrombie, N.S. C8 281
Aberdeen, Ark. F9 150-1
Aberdeen, Ida. N8 218-9
Aberdeen, Md. B13 172-3
Aberdeen, Miss. D10 176-7
Aberdeen, N.C. K5 180-1
Aberdeen, O. J5 132-3
Aberdeen, Sask. K7 294-5
Aberdeen, S. Dak. B12 136-7
Aberdeen, Wash. G5 246-7
Aberdeen Proving Ground, Md. C13 172-3
Aberfoil, Ala. J9 146-7
Abernathy, Tex. C5 192-3
Abernethy, Sask. M9 294-5
Abie, Nebr. G13 124-5
Abilene, Kans. F11 108-9
Abilene, Tex. E6 192-3
Abingdon, Ill. E5 96-7
Abingdon, Md. C12 172-3
Abingdon, Va. J4 196-7
Abington, Conn. C13 60-1
Abington, Mass. K6 68-9
Abington, Pa. A11 84-5
Abiquiu, N. Mex. D6 230-1
Abita Springs, La. A14 168-9
Abitibi, co., Que. H2 290-1
Abney, P.E.I. G9 287
Abraham, Ut. H4 242-3
Abraham, W. Va. K16 200-1
Abrams, Wis. D4 140-1
Abrams [Village]*, P.E.I. E4 287
Absecon, N.J. M6 76-7
Academy, S. Dak. H11 136-7
Acadia, co., La. G4 168-9
Acadia Valley, Alta. L10 264-5
Acadie Siding, N.B. G5 275
Acadieville, N.B. G6 275
Accident, Md. B2 172-3
Accokeek, Md. F10 172-3
Accomac, Va. H16 196-7
Accomack, co., Va. H15 196-7
Accord, Mass. J7 68-9
Acequia, Ida. N7 218-9
Achille, Okla. I13 234-5
Achilles, Va. F4 196-7
Ackerman, Miss. F8 176-7
Ackley, Ia. D9 104-5
Ackworth, Ia. H8 104-5
Acmar, Ala. E7 146-7
Acme, Alta. L8 264-5
Acme, La. E6 168-9
Acme, Mich. F12 112-3
Acme, N.C. G12 180-1
Acme, Wash. C8 246-7
Acme, W. Va. J14 200-1
Acme, Wyo. B11 250-1
Acoma, Nev. J11 226-7
Acoma, N. Mex. F4 230-1
Acomita, N. Mex. F4 230-1
Actinolite, Ont. J12 284-5
Acton, Me. N1 64-5
Acton, Mass. G2 68-9
Acton, Mont. G10 222-3
Acton Vale, Que. I14 290-1
Acushnet, Mass. H12 68-9
Acworth, Ga. A9 160-1
Acworth, N.H. M3 72-3
Acy, La. B11 168-9
Ada, Ark. H13 150-1
Ada, Kans. E9 108-9
Ada, La. B3 168-9
Ada, Minn. H2 116-7
Ada, O. D5 132-3
Ada, Okla. G12 234-5
Ada, co., Ida. M3 218-9
Adair, Ia. H5 104-5
Adair, Okla. C15 234-5
Adair, Tenn. J4 188-9
Adair, co., Ia. H5 104-5
Adair, co., Ky. J9 164-5
Adair, co., Mo. B6 120-1
Adair, co., Okla. E16 234-5
Adairsville, Ga. E3 160-1
Adairville, Ky. K6 164-5
Adak Station*, Alaska I3 254-5
Adamana, Ariz. F10 206-7
Adamant, Vt. E7 90-1
Adams, Ind. J10 100-1
Adams, Kans. J9 108-9
Adams, Mass. B2 68-9
Adams, Minn. O7 116-7
Adams, Nebr. I14 124-5
Adams, N.Y. C7 80-1
Adams, N. Dak. C12 128-9
Adams, Okla. C4 234-5
Adams, Ore. B13 238-9
Adams, Tenn. F6 188-9
Adams, Wis. H12 140-1
Adams, co., Colo. D13 214-5
Adams, co., Ida. J3 218-9
Adams, co., Ill. G4 96-7
Adams, co., Ind. E11 100-1
Adams, co., Ia. I5 104-5
Adams, co., Miss. K3 176-7
Adams, co., Nebr. I11 124-5
Adams, co., N. Dak. J4 128-9
Adams, co., O. I5 132-3
Adams, co., Pa. I10 84-5
Adams, co., Wash. G14 246-7
Adams, co., Wis. G12 140-1
Adams Run, S.C. I12 184-5
Adamsburg, S.C. B9 184-5
Adamson, Okla. G14 234-5
Adamstown, Md. F1 172-3
Adamstown, Pa. I13 84-5
Adamsville, Ala. E6 146-7
Adamsville, N.B. H6 275
Adamsville, R.I. F8 87
Adamsville, Tenn. D4 188-9
Adamsville, Ut. K4 242-3
Adaven, Nev. I8 226-7
Addington, Okla. H10 234-5
Addis, La. A9 168-9
Addison, Ala. C5 146-7
Addison*, Ill. B10 96-7
Addison, Me. J9 64-5
Addison*, Mich. K13 112-3
Addison, N.Y. G5 80-1
Addison, Ont. I14 284-5
Addison, Vt. G3 90-1
Addison, co., Vt. F4 90-1
Addor, N.C. K5 180-1
Addy, Wash. D15 246-7
Addyston, O. K12 132-3
Adel, Ga. N6 160-1
Adel, Ia. G7 104-5
Adel, Ore. J11 238-9
Adelaide, Ida. N7 218-9
Adelanto, Calif. F10 210-1
Adeline, La. I6 168-9
Adell, Wis. H5 140-1
Adelphi, O. H7 132-3
Adelphia, N.J. H7 76-7
Adena, O. F11 132-3
Adirondack Mts. 14-15
Adler, Mont. H6 222-3
Admiral, Sask. O5 294-5
Admire, Kans. G13 108-9
Adna, Wash. H7 246-7
Adner, La. B2 168-9
Adobe, Ariz. H6 206-7
Adolph, W. Va. F15 200-1
Adolphus, Ky. K8 164-5
Adona, Ark. H13 150-1
Adrian, Ga. J8 160-1
Adrian, Mich. K14 112-3
Adrian, Minn. O2 116-7
Adrian, Mo. F3 120-1
Adrian, N. Dak. H11 128-9
Adrian, Ore. G16 238-9
Adrian, W. Va. E14 200-1
Advance, Ind. G7 100-1
Advance, Mo. I11 120-1
Advance, N.C. H3 180-1
Advent, W. Va. G3 200-1
Aeneas, Wash. C13 246-7
Aetna, Kans. K7 108-9
Afton, Ia. I6 104-5
Afton, La. C7 168-9
Afton, Mich. E13 112-3
Afton, Minn. B12 116-7
Afton*, Mo. E10 120-1
Afton, N.Y. G8 80-1
Afton, Okla. C15 234-5
Afton, Va. G10 196-7
Afton, Wis. K2 140-1
Afton, Wyo. G5 250-1
Agar, S. Dak. D9 136-7
Agate, Colo. E13 214-5
Agate Beach, Ore. D4 238-9
Agawam, Mass. E5 68-9
Agawam, Mont. C6 222-3
Agawam, Okla. G10 234-5
Agency, Ia. I11 104-5
Agency, Mo. G14 120-1
Agenda, Kans. D10 108-9
Agness, Ore. I4 238-9
Agnew, Nebr. H14 124-5
Agnos, Ark. A8 150-1
Agra, Kans. D7 108-9
Agra, Okla. E12 234-5
Agricola, Kans. G14 108-9
Agricola, Miss. M10 176-7
Agua Dulce, Tex. I8 192-3
Agua Fria, N. Mex. E7 230-1
Aguanish, Que. G7 290-1
Aguila, Ariz. H4 206-7
Aguilar, Colo. I12 214-5
Ahloso, Okla. G12 234-5
Ahmeek, Mich. B9 112-3
Ahoskie, N.C. C14 180-1
Ahsahka, Ida. F3 218-9
Ahtanum, Wash. H10 246-7
Aiea, Hawaii J5 258-9
Aiken, S.C. F8 184-5
Aiken, co., S.C. F8 184-5
Aiken South, S.C. F8 184-5
Aiken West, S.C. F8 184-5
Aikin, Md. B13 172-3
Ailey, Ga. K8 160-1
Ailsa Craig, Ont. D12 284-5
Aimwell, La. D5 168-9
Ainsworth, Ia. H13 104-5
Ainsworth, Nebr. D8 124-5
Air Base City, N. Mex. K11 230-1
Air Ronge*, Sask. G7 294-5
Airdrie, Alta. L7 264-5
Airey, Md. G13 172-3
Airlie, Ore. D5 238-9
Airport Drive, Mo. H3 120-1
Airway Heights, Wash. E15 246-7
Aitkin, Minn. I6 116-7
Aitkin, co., Minn. J6 116-7
Ajax, La. D2 168-9
Ajax, Ont. C15 284-5
Ajo, Ariz. K5 206-7
Ak Chin, Ariz. J6 206-7
Akaska, S. Dak. C9 136-7
Akeley, Minn. H4 116-7
Akhiok, Alaska H10 254-5
Akiachak, Alaska F8 254-5
Akiak, Alaska F8 254-5
Akolmiut, Alaska F8 254-5
Akron, Ala. G4 146-7
Akron, Colo. D14 214-5
Akron, Ind. C8 100-1
Akron, Ia. C1 104-5
Akron, Kans. J11 108-9
Akron, Mich. H14 112-3
Akron, N.Y. E3 80-1
Akron, O. C9 132-3
Akron, Pa. J12 84-5
Akudlik (Camp 20)*, Man. B10 272-3
Akutan, Alaska I7 254-5
Alabam, Ark. B3 150-1
Alabama Port, Ala. O3 146-7
Alabaster, Ala. F6 146-7
Alachua, Fla. C10 156-7
Alachua, co., Fla. D10 156-7
Aladdin, Wyo. B16 250-1
Alakanuk, Alaska E8 254-5
Alamance, co., N.C. C9 180-1
Alameda, Calif. C7 210-1
Alameda, N. Mex. F6 230-1
Alameda, Sask. O10 294-5
Alameda, co., Calif. I3 210-1
Alamillo, N. Mex. H5 230-1
Alamo, Ga. K7 160-1
Alamo, Ind. G5 100-1
Alamo, Nev. K9 226-7
Alamo, N. Mex. G4 230-1
Alamo, N. Dak. C2 128-9
Alamo, Tenn. I3 188-9
Alamo*, Tex. K8 192-3
Alamo-Danville*, Calif. C8 210-1
Alamo Heights, Tex. J2 192-3
Alamogordo, N. Mex. J7 230-1
Alamosa, Colo. I10 214-5
Alamosa, co., Colo. I10 214-5
Alamosa East*, Colo. I10 214-5
Alamota, Kans. G4 108-9
Alanson, Mich. E13 112-3
Alapaha, Ga. M6 160-1
Alba, Mich. F12 112-3
Alba, Mo. H3 120-1
Albanel, Que. B10 290-1
Albany, Calif. C7 210-1
Albany, Ga. L4 160-1
Albany, Ill. C6 96-7
Albany, Ind. F11 100-1
Albany, Ky. K10 164-5
Albany, La. A12 168-9
Albany, Minn. K4 116-7
Albany, Mo. B3 120-1
Albany, N.H. H8 72-3
Albany, N.Y. F11 80-1
Albany, O. H8 132-3
Albany, Okla. I13 234-5
Albany, Ore. I1 238-9
Albany, P.E.I. E5 287
Albany, Tex. D7 192-3
Albany, Vt. C7 90-1
Albany, Wis. K1 140-1
Albany, Wyo. J13 250-1
Albany, co., N.Y. F11 80-1
Albany, co., Wyo. I14 250-1
Albee, Ore. C12 238-9
Albee, S. Dak. C16 136-7
Albemarle, N.C. E8 180-1
Albemarle, co., Va. G10 196-7
Albemarle Sound, N.C. C15 180-1
Albers, Ill. K7 96-7
Albert, Kans. G7 108-9
Albert, N. Mex. D10 230-1
Albert, Okla. F9 234-5
Albert, co., N.B. I7 275
Albert City, Ia. D4 104-5
Albert Head*, B.C. E4 268-9
Albert Lea, Minn. O6 116-7
Alberta, Ala. I4 146-7
Alberta, Minn. K2 116-7
Alberta, Va. J12 196-7
Alberta Beach, Alta. I7 264-5
Alberton, Mont. E3 222-3
Alberton, P.E.I. C4 287
Alberton South, P.E.I. C4 287
Albertson, N.Y. E16 80-1
Albertson, N.C. F12 180-1
Albertville, Ala. C8 146-7
Albertville, Minn. A9 116-7
Albertville, Sask. J7 294-5
Albia, Ia. I10 104-5
Albin, Wyo. J16 250-1
Albion, Ida. O7 218-9
Albion, Ill. L10 96-7
Albion, Ind. B10 100-1
Albion, Ia. F9 104-5
Albion, Me. K5 64-5
Albion, Mich. J13 112-3
Albion, Mont. H16 222-3
Albion, Nebr. F12 124-5
Albion, N.J. O11 76-7
Albion, N.Y. E3 80-1
Albion, Okla. G15 234-5
Albion, Pa. C1 84-5
Albion, R.I. A5 87
Albion, Wash. G16 246-7
Albion, Wis. J2 140-1
Albright, W. Va. B16 200-1
Albuquerque, N. Mex. F6 230-1
Alburg, Vt. B3 90-1
Alburg Springs, Vt. B4 90-1
Alburnett, Ia. F12 104-5
Alburtis, Pa. H14 84-5
Alcalde, N. Mex. D7 230-1
Alcester, S. Dak. I16 136-7
Alco, Ark. C7 150-1
Alco, La. E3 168-9
Alcoa, Tenn. I12 188-9
Alcolu, S.C. F12 184-5
Alcona, co., Mich. F14 112-3
Alcona Beach*, Ont. I8 284-5
Alcorn, Miss. J3 176-7
Alcorn, co., Miss. A10 176-7
Alcot, S.C. D12 184-5
Alcova, Wyo. G12 250-1
Alda, Nebr. H11 124-5
Aldan*, Pa. J15 84-5
Alden, Ia. D8 104-5
Alden, Kans. H9 108-9
Alden, Mich. F12 112-3
Alden, Minn. O6 116-7
Alden, N.Y. F3 80-1
Alden Bridge, La. A2 168-9
Alder, Wash. G8 246-7
Alder Creek, Ore. C7 238-9
Alder Flats, Alta. J7 264-5
Aldercrest Survey*, Ont. D14 284-5
Aldershot, N.S. D6 281
Alderson*, Okla. G14 234-5
Alderson, W. Va. I5 200-1
Aldersyde, Alta. M7 264-5
Alderwood Manor, Wash. H3 246-7
Aldie, Va. A2 196-7
Aldora, Ga. H4 160-1
Aldrich, Ala. G6 146-7
Aldrich, Minn. J4 116-7
Aldrich, Mo. H4 120-1
Aledo, Ill. D5 96-7
Aleknagik, Alaska G9 254-5
Alençon*, Que. H13 290-1
Alert Bay, B.C. I4 268-9
Aleutian Isl., Alaska H4 254-5
Alex, Okla. G10 234-5
Alexander, Ark. J15 150-1
Alexander, Ia. D8 104-5
Alexander, Kans. G6 108-9
Alexander, Me. I10 64-5
Alexander, Man. J10 272-3
Alexander, N.C. D4 180-1
Alexander, N. Dak. E2 128-9
Alexander, W. Va. F14 200-1
Alexander, co., Ill. O8 96-7
Alexander, co., N.C. D6 180-1
Alexander City, Ala. G8 146-7
Alexander Mills, N.C. E5 180-1
Alexandria, Ala. E8 146-7
Alexandria, B.C. H7 268-9
Alexandria, Ind. F9 100-1
Alexandria, Ky. E11 164-5
Alexandria, La. E4 168-9
Alexandria, Minn. K3 116-7
Alexandria, Mo. A8 120-1
Alexandria, Nebr. J13 124-5
Alexandria, N.H. J5 72-3
Alexandria*, N.J. E3 76-7
Alexandria, O. F7 132-3
Alexandria, Ont. H16 284-5
Alexandria*, P.E.I. F8 287
Alexandria, S. Dak. G14 136-7
Alexandria, Tenn. B9 188-9
Alexandria, Va. E13 196-7
Alexandria Bay, N.Y. B7 80-1
Alexandria Southwest*, La. E4 168-9
Alexis, Ill. E5 96-7
Alexis, N.C. J1 180-1
Alexis Creek, B.C. H6 268-9
Alfalfa, Okla. F9 234-5
Alfalfa, Ore. F9 238-9
Alfalfa, co., Okla. C9 234-5
Alfonso, Va. H14 196-7
Alford, Fla. B6 156-7
Alford, Mass. D1 68-9
Alfordsville, Ind. M6 100-1
Alfred, Me. N2 64-5
Alfred, N.Y. G4 80-1
Alfred, N. Dak. H10 128-9
Alfred, Ont. H16 284-5
Alger, O. D5 132-3
Alger, co., Mich. D10 112-3
Algerie Four Corners, Mass. E3 68-9
Algoa, Ark. D10 150-1
Algodones, N. Mex. E6 230-1
Algoma, Miss. C9 176-7
Algoma, Ore. J8 238-9
Algoma, Wis. D6 140-1
Algoma Mills, Ont. H6 284-5
Algona, Ia. C6 104-5
Algona, Wash. J3 246-7
Algonac, Mich. I8 112-3
Algonquin, Ill. K1 96-7
Algonquin, Ont. I15 284-5
Algood, Tenn. B10 188-9
Algrove, Sask. K9 294-5
Alhambra, Calif. G8 210-1
Alhambra, Ill. K7 96-7
Alhambra, Mont. F6 222-3
Alice, N. Dak. H13 128-9
Alice, Ont. G12 284-5
Alice, Tex. I8 192-3
Alice Southwest*, Tex. I8 192-3
Alicel, Ore. C14 238-9
Aliceville, Ala. G3 146-7
Aliceville, Kans. H14 108-9
Alicia, Ark. C10 150-1

Alida, Sask. O11 294-5
Aline, Okla. C9 234-5
Aliquippa, Pa. H1 84-5
Alix, Alta. K8 264-5
Alix, Ark. D3 150-1
Alkabo, N. Dak. B2 128-9
Alkali Lake, Ore. I11 238-9
Allagash, Me. B6 64-5
Allakaket, Alaska C10 254-5
Allamakee, co., Ia. B13 104-5
Allamuchy, N.J. C4 76-7
Allan, Sask. L7 294-5
Allardt, Tenn. G9 188-9
Allardville, N.B. E6 275
Alleene, Ark. I2 150-1
Allegan, Mich. J12 112-3
Allegan, co., Mich. J11 112-3
Allegany, N.Y. G3 80-1
Allegany, co., Md. B4 172-3
Allegany, co., N.Y. G3 80-1
Alleghany, co., N.C. B6 180-1
Alleghany, co., Va. H8 196-7
Allegheny, co., Pa. H2 84-5
Allegheny Mts. 14-15
Allegheny Res., Pa. C5 84-5
Allegre, Ky. J6 164-5
Alleman, Ia. G8 104-5
Allen, Ala. K4 146-7
Allen, Kans. G13 108-9
Allen, Ky. H15 164-5
Allen, La. D2 168-9
Allen, Md. H14 172-3
Allen, Mich. K13 112-3
Allen, Nebr. D14 124-5
Allen, N.C. J2 180-1
Allen, Okla. G13 234-5
Allen, S.C. E15 184-5
Allen, S. Dak. H5 136-7
Allen, Tex. B15 192-3
Allen, Wash. C8 246-7
Allen, co., Ind. C11 100-1
Allen, co., Kans. I15 108-9
Allen, co., Ky. K7 164-5
Allen, co., La. G3 168-9
Allen, co., O. D4 132-3
Allen Park, Mich. K6 112-3
Allendale, Mo. A3 120-1
Allendale, N.J. C8 76-7
Allendale, S.C. H9 184-5
Allendale, co., S.C. H9 184-5
Allenhurst, Ga. L10 160-1
Allenhurst, N.J. H8 76-7
Allens Fresh, Md. G10 172-3
Allens Grove, Wis. K3 140-1
Allens Mills, Me. J4 64-5
Allenspark, Colo. E1 214-5
Allenstown, N.H. M7 72-3
Allensville, Ky. K6 164-5
Allenton, Ala. J6 146-7
Allenton, Mich. G6 112-3
Allenton, R.I. F5 87
Allenton, Wis. H4 140-1
Allentown, Ga. J6 160-1
Allentown, N.J. H5 76-7
Allentown, Pa. H14 84-5
Allenwood, N.J. H8 76-7
Allerton, Ia. J8 104-5
Allgood, Ala. D7 146-7
Alliance, Alta. K9 264-5
Alliance, Nebr. E3 124-5
Alliance*, N.C. E14 180-1
Alliance, O. E16 132-3
Alligator, Miss. D5 176-7
Allington, Conn. H7 60-1
Allison, Colo. J7 214-5
Allison, Ia. D10 104-5
Allison, N. Mex. E2 230-1
Allison, Pa. J2 84-5
Alliston, Ont. B14 284-5
Alliston, P.E.I. G9 287
Allons, Tenn. A10 188-9
Allouez, Mich. B9 112-3
Allouez*, Wis. G15 140-1
Alloway, N.J. L2 76-7
Allport, Ark. F8 150-1
Allred, Tenn. B10 188-9
Allston, Ore. A6 238-9
Alluwe, Okla. C14 234-5
Allview*, Md. D10 172-3
Allyn, Wash. J1 246-7
Alma, Ark. D2 150-1
Alma, Colo. E10 214-5
Alma, Ga. M8 160-1
Alma, Kans. F13 108-9
Alma, Mich. E1 112-3
Alma, Mo. D4 120-1
Alma, Nebr. J9 124-5
Alma, N.B. I7 275
Alma, N.C. G10 180-1
Alma, Okla. H11 234-5
Alma, Ore. F5 238-9
Alma, Que. C11 290-1
Alma, W. Va. D5 200-1
Alma, Wis. G8 140-1
Alma Center, Wis. G10 140-1
Almaville, Tenn. I7 188-9
Almedia*, Pa. F12 84-5
Almena, Kans. C6 108-9
Almena, Wis. D8 140-1
Almeria, Nebr. F9 124-5
Almira, Wash. E13 246-7
Almo, Ida. O7 218-9
Almo, Ky. K3 164-5
Almon, Ga. C5 160-1
Almond, N.Y. G4 80-1
Almond, N.C. E2 180-1
Almond, Wis. E1 140-1
Almond Gardens*, B.C. J6 268-9
Almonesson, N.J. O10 76-7
Almont, Colo. G8 214-5
Almont, Mich. G6 112-3
Almont, N. Dak. H6 128-9
Almonte, Ont. H14 284-5
Almy, Wyo. J4 250-1
Almyra, Ark. G9 150-1
Almyville, Conn. D14 60-1
Alna, Me. M11 64-5
Aloha, La. D4 168-9
Aloha, Wash. F5 246-7
Alondra Park*, Calif. N7 210-1
Alonsa, Man. H12 272-3
Alorton*, Ill. K6 96-7
Alpena, Ark. A4 150-1
Alpena, Mich. F14 112-3
Alpena, S. Dak. F12 136-7
Alpena, W. Va. E16 200-1
Alpena, co., Mich. F14 112-3
Alpha, Ill. D5 96-7
Alpha, Mich. D9 112-3
Alpha, Minn. O4 116-7
Alpha, N.J. E3 76-7
Alpha, Wis. D7 140-1
Alpharetta, Ga. A11 160-1
Alpine, Ala. F7 146-7
Alpine, Ariz. H11 206-7
Alpine, Ark. G4 150-1
Alpine, Calif. J11 210-1
Alpine, N.J. C8 76-7
Alpine, Ore. E5 238-9
Alpine, Tenn. A10 188-9
Alpine, Tex. G3 192-3
Alpine, Ut. F6 242-3
Alpine, co., Calif. H5 210-1
Alpine Junction, Wyo. F5 250-1
Alquina, Ind. I11 100-1
Alsask, Sask. L3 294-5
Alsatia, La. B7 168-9
Alsea, Ore. E5 238-9
Alsen, N. Dak. C11 128-9
Alsip, Ill. N4 96-7
Alstead, N.H. M3 72-3
Alston, Ga. K8 160-1
Alta, Ia. D4 104-5
Alta*, Ut. F6 242-3
Alta Hill*, Calif. G4 210-1
Alta Loma, Tex. J15 192-3
Alta Vista, Ia. B10 104-5
Alta Vista, Kans. F12 108-9
Altadena*, Calif. G8 210-1
Altamont, Ill. J9 96-7
Altamont, Kans. K15 108-9
Altamont, Man. K12 272-3
Altamont, Mo. B4 120-1
Altamont, N.Y. F10 80-1
Altamont, Ore. J8 238-9
Altamont, S. Dak. D16 136-7
Altamont, Tenn. J9 188-9
Altamont, Ut. F9 242-3
Altamont, Wyo. J5 250-1
Altamonte Springs, Fla. E11 156-7
Altavista, Va. I9 196-7
Altbergthal*, Man. K3 272-3
Altenburg, Mo. G11 120-1
Altha, Fla. B6 156-7
Altheimer, Ark. G8 150-1
Altizer, W. Va. F4 200-1
Alto, Ga. E6 160-1
Alto, La. C6 168-9
Alto, N. Mex. I7 230-1
Alto, Tenn. K9 188-9
Alto, Tex. E10 192-3
Alto, Wis. G3 140-1
Alto Park-Garden Lakes*, Ga. E2 160-1
Alton, Ill. J6 96-7
Alton, Ind. O7 100-1
Alton, Ia. C2 104-5
Alton, Kans. E7 108-9
Alton, Me. I7 64-5
Alton, Mo. J8 120-1
Alton, N.H. K8 72-3
Alton, R.I. H2 87
Alton, Ut. M5 242-3
Alton, Va. K9 196-7
Alton, W. Va. F14 200-1
Alton Bay, N.H. K8 72-3
Alton Station, Ky. B5 164-5
Altona, Ind. B11 100-1
Altona, Man. K14 272-3
Altonah, Ut. F9 242-3
Altoona, Ala. D7 146-7
Altoona, Ia. G8 104-5
Altoona, Kans. J14 108-9
Altoona, Pa. H6 84-5
Altoona, Wash. H6 246-7
Altoona, Wis. F9 140-1
Altro, Ky. I14 164-5
Altura, Minn. O8 116-7
Alturas, Calif. D5 210-1
Altus, Ark. D3 150-1
Altus, Okla. H7 234-5
Altvan, Wyo. J15 250-1
Alum Creek, W. Va. I13 200-1
Alum Ridge, Va. J7 196-7
Alum Rock*, Calif. J3 210-1
Alunite, Nev. N10 226-7
Alva, Okla. C8 234-5
Alva, Wyo. B16 250-1
Alvadore, Ore. K1 238-9
Alvarado, Minn. F1 116-7
Alvarado, Tex. E13 192-3
Alvaton, Ga. H3 160-1
Alvena, Sask. K7 294-5
Alvin, S.C. G13 184-5
Alvin, Tex. I14 192-3
Alvinston, Ont. E11 284-5
Alvo, Nebr. K1 124-5
Alvon, W. Va. I6 200-1
Alvord, Ia. B1 104-5
Alvord, Tex. D8 192-3
Alvordton, O. B3 132-3
Aly, Ark. F4 150-1
Alzada, Mont. H16 222-3
Amado, Ariz. L8 206-7
Amador, Calif. A10 210-1
Amador, co., Calif. H4 210-1
Amagon, Ark. D10 150-1
Amalga*, Ut. C6 242-3
Amalia, N. Mex. B7 230-1
Amana, Ia. G12 104-5
Amanda, O. G7 132-3
Amanda Park, Wash. F5 246-7
Amaranth, Man. H12 272-3
Amarillo, Tex. B5 192-3
Amasa, Mich. D9 112-3
Amazonia, Mo. B2 120-1
Amber, Okla. K1 234-5
Amber, Wash. F15 246-7
Amberg, Wis. D15 140-1
Amberly, O. K14 132-3
Ambia, Ind. E4 100-1
Ambler, Alaska C10 254-5
Ambler, Pa. A11 84-5
Amboy, Ill. C8 96-7
Amboy, Ind. E9 100-1
Amboy, Minn. O5 116-7
Amboy, Wash. I7 246-7
Amboy, W. Va. E8 200-1
Ambridge, Pa. A5 84-5
Ambrose, Ga. L7 160-1
Ambrose, N. Dak. B2 128-9
Ambrosia Lake, N. Mex. E4 230-1
Ameagle, W. Va. K15 200-1
Amelia, La. I7 168-9
Amelia, Nebr. E10 124-5
Amelia, O. I4 132-3
Amelia, co., Va. I11 196-7
Amelia Court House, Va. I11 196-7
Amenia, N.Y. H11 80-1
Amenia, N. Dak. G14 128-9
American Falls, Ida. N8 218-9
American Falls Res., Ida. M8 218-9
American Fork, Ut. F6 242-3
Americus, Ga. K4 160-1
Americus, Kans. G13 108-9
Amery, Wis. E7 140-1
Ames, Ia. F8 104-5
Ames, Kans. D10 108-9
Ames, Nebr. I1 124-5
Ames, Okla. D9 234-5
Ames, Tex. G16 192-3
Amesbury, Mass. A12 68-9
Amesville, Conn. B4 60-1
Amesville, O. H9 132-3
Amesville, Wyo. F5 250-1
Amherst, Me. J8 64-5
Amherst, Mass. D5 68-9
Amherst, Nebr. H9 124-5
Amherst, N.H. O6 72-3
Amherst, N.S. C6 281
Amherst, O. B8 132-3
Amherst, S. Dak. A13 136-7
Amherst, Tex. C4 192-3
Amherst, Va. H9 196-7
Amherst, Wis. E1 140-1
Amherst, co., Va. H9 196-7
Amherst Junction, Wis. E1 140-1
Amherst Point*, Ont. G10 284-5
Amherst View Subdivision, Ont. J13 284-5
Amherstburg, Ont. F9 284-5
Amherstdale [-Robinette], W. Va. K13 200-1
Amidon, N. Dak. H2 128-9
Amisk, Alta. K10 264-5
Amissville, Va. B1 196-7
Amistad, N. Mex. D11 230-1
Amistad Res., Tex. G5 192-3
Amite, Miss. L4 176-7
Amite City, La. G8 168-9
Amity, Ark. G4 150-1
Amity, Ind. J8 100-1
Amity, Me. F9 64-5
Amity, Mo. B3 120-1
Amity, Ore. G1 238-9
Amityville, N.Y. K12 80-1
Ammon, Ida. M10 218-9
Ammon, Va. I12 196-7
Amo, Ind. H7 100-1
Amonate, Va. I5 196-7
Amoret, Mo. F3 120-1
Amorita, Okla. B9 234-5
Amory, Miss. D10 176-7
Amos, Que. H1 290-1
Amos-Est*, Que. H1 290-1
Amqui, Que. H5 290-1
Amsden, Vt. K7 90-1
Amsterdam, Ga. O4 160-1
Amsterdam, Ida. O6 218-9
Amsterdam, Mo. F3 120-1
Amsterdam, Mont. G7 222-3
Amsterdam, N.Y. E10 80-1
Amsterdam, O. E11 132-3
Amsterdam, Sask. L10 294-5
Amston, Conn. E11 60-1
Amy, Ark. I5 150-1
Amy, Kans. G4 108-9
Anacoco, La. E2 168-9
Anaconda, Mont. G4 222-3
Anaconda, N. Mex. F3 230-1
Anaconda-Deer Lodge, co., Mont. G4 222-3
Anacortes, Wash. C7 246-7
Anadarko, Okla. G9 234-5
Anagance, N.B. I6 275
Anaheim, Calif. H9 210-1
Anahola, Hawaii D5 258-9
Anahuac, Tex. H16 192-3
Anaktuvuk Pass, Alaska C11 254-5
Anamoose, N. Dak. E8 128-9
Anamosa, Ia. F13 104-5
Anandale, La. E4 168-9
Anatone, Wash. I16 246-7
Anawalt, W. Va. J3 200-1
Ancaster, Ont. D14 284-5
Ancho, N. Mex. H7 230-1
Anchor Bay Gardens, Mich. I7 112-3
Anchor Point, Alaska G11 254-5
Anchorage, Alaska F11 254-5
Anchorage, Ky. A3 164-5
Anchorage, The*, R.I. G6 87
Anchorville, Mich. H7 112-3
Ancienne-Lorette*, Que. G11 290-1
Anco, Ky. I14 164-5
Andale, Kans. I10 108-9
Andalusia, Ala. L7 146-7
Andalusia, Ill. D5 96-7
Anderson, Ala. A5 146-7
Anderson*, Alaska D11 254-5
Anderson, Calif. F3 210-1
Anderson, Ind. G9 100-1
Anderson, Mo. J3 120-1
Anderson, S.C. C6 184-5
Anderson, Tex. G10 192-3
Anderson, co., Kans. H15 108-9
Anderson, co., Ky. G10 164-5
Anderson, co., S.C. C6 184-5
Anderson, co., Tenn. B12 188-9
Anderson, co., Tex. E10 192-3
Anderson Island, Wash. K1 246-7
Anderson Road, N.B. G3 275
Andersonville, Ga. K4 160-1
Andersonville, Ind. J11 100-1
Andersonville, Tenn. G12 188-9
Andersonville, Va. I10 196-7
Anding, Miss. H5 176-7
Andover, Conn. D11 60-1
Andover, Ia. F16 104-5
Andover, Kans. I11 108-9
Andover, Me. J2 64-5
Andover, Mass. B11 68-9
Andover, Minn. A10 116-7
Andover, N.H. K5 72-3
Andover*, N.J. C5 76-7
Andover, N.J. C5 76-7
Andover, N.Y. G4 80-1
Andover, O. B11 132-3
Andover, S. Dak. B13 136-7
Andover, Vt. L6 90-1
Andover, Va. J2 196-7
Andrew, Alta. I9 264-5
Andrew, Ia. F15 104-5
Andrew, co., Mo. B2 120-1
Andrews, Ind. D10 100-1
Andrews, Md. J5 172-3
Andrews, N.C. E1 180-1
Andrews, Ore. J13 238-9
Andrews, S.C. F14 184-5
Andrews, Tex. E4 192-3
Andrews, co., Tex. E4 192-3
Andrewsville, Del. H3 153
Androscoggin, co., Me. L3 64-5
Anegam, Ariz. K6 206-7
Aneroid, Sask. O6 294-5
Aneta, N. Dak. E12 128-9
Aneth, Ut. M11 242-3
Ange-Gardien*, Que. J13 290-1
Angela, Mont. E13 222-3
Angelica, N.Y. G4 80-1
Angelina, co., Tex. F11 192-3
Angelo, Wis. H10 140-1
Angels, Calif. B11 210-1
Angelus, Kans. E4 108-9
Angelus, S.C. C12 184-5
Angie, La. F10 168-9
Angier, N.C. J7 180-1
Angle, Ut. K6 242-3
Angleton, Tex. J13 192-3
Angleton South*, Tex. H10 192-3
Angliers, Que. I1 290-1
Angola, Del. I6 153
Angola, Ind. A11 100-1
Angola, Kans. K15 108-9
Angola, La. F6 168-9
Angola, N.Y. F2 80-1
Angola on the Lake*, N.Y. F2 80-1
Angoon, Alaska G15 254-5
Angora, Nebr. F2 124-5
Anguilla, Miss. G4 176-7
Angus, Nebr. J12 124-5
Angus*, Ont. B14 284-5
Angusville, Man. H9 272-3
Angwin*, Calif. H2 210-1
Aniak, Alaska F9 254-5
Animas, N. Mex. L2 230-1
Anita, Ia. H5 104-5
Aniwa, Wis. E13 140-1
Anjou*, Que. I12 290-1
Ankeny, Ia. G8 104-5
Anlauf, Ore. G5 238-9
Anmoore, W. Va. C14 200-1
Anmore*, B.C. J6 268-9
Ann Arbor, Mich. J14 112-3
Anna, Ill. N8 96-7
Anna, O. E4 132-3
Anna, Tex. A15 192-3
Anna Maria, Fla. J2 156-7
Annabella, Ut. J6 242-3
Annada, Mo. D9 120-1
Annaheim, Sask. K8 294-5
Annamoriah, W. Va. F4 200-1
Annandale, Minn. A8 116-7
Annandale, N.J. E4 76-7
Annandale, Va. A3 196-7
Annapolis, Md. E11 172-3
Annapolis, Mo. H10 120-1
Annapolis, co., N.S. E5 281
Annapolis Basin, N.S. E4 281

Annapolis Royal, N.S. E5 281
Annaville, Que. H14 290-1
Annawan, Ill. D6 96-7
Anne Arundel, co., Md. E11 172-3
Anneta, Ky. I8 164-5
Annette, Alaska H16 254-5
Annis, Ida. L10 218-9
Anniston, Ala. E8 146-7
Anniston, Mo. I12 120-1
Anniston Northwest*, Ala. E8 146-7
Annville, Ky. I12 164-5
Annville, Pa. I12 84-5
Anoka, Minn. L6 116-7
Anoka, Nebr. C10 124-5
Anoka, co., Minn. L6 116-7
Anola*, Man. J15 272-3
Anona, Fla. H1 156-7
Anse-Bleue, N.B. E6 275
Anselmo, Nebr. F8 124-5
Ansley, La. B4 168-9
Ansley, Miss. O8 176-7
Ansley, Nebr. G9 124-5
Anson, Kans. J10 108-9
Anson, Me. J4 64-5
Anson, Tex. D6 192-3
Anson, co., N.C. F8 180-1
Ansonia, Conn. G6 60-1
Ansonia, O. F3 132-3
Ansonville, N.C. K3 180-1
Ansted, W. Va. I16 200-1
Anston, Wis. D4 140-1
Antelope, Mont. A15 222-3
Antelope, Ore. D9 238-9
Antelope, co., Nebr. E11 124-5
Anthon, Ia. E2 104-5
Anthony, Kans. K9 108-9
Anthony, N. Mex. L6 230-1
Anthony, R.I. E4 87
Anthony, Tex. E1 192-3
Anthony, W. Va. I6 200-1
Anthoston, Ky. H5 164-5
Anticosti Isl., Que. H6 290-1
Antigo, Wis. E13 140-1
Antigonish, N.S. C9 281
Antigonish, co., N.S. C9 281
Antimony, Ut. K6 242-3
Antioch, Calif. B8 210-1
Antioch, Ill. J2 96-7
Antioch, Nebr. E3 124-5
Antioch, N.C. F10 180-1
Antioch, Okla. G11 234-5
Antioch, Tenn. K10 188-9
Antioch, W. Va. E9 200-1
Antler, N. Dak. B6 128-9
Antler, Sask. O11 294-5
Antler Lake*, Alta. I8 264-5
Antlers, Okla. H14 234-5
Antoine, Ark. H4 150-1
Anton, Colo. D14 214-5
Anton, Tex. C4 192-3
Anton Chico, N. Mex. F8 230-1
Antone, Ore. E11 238-9
Antonia, La. D4 168-9
Antonino, Kans. F6 108-9
Antonito, Colo. J10 214-5
Antrim, La. A2 168-9
Antrim, N.H. N5 72-3
Antrim, co., Mich. F12 112-3
Antwerp, N.Y. C8 80-1
Antwerp, O. C3 132-3
Anvik, Alaska E9 254-5
Anvil Location, Mich. D7 112-3
Anzac, Alta. F9 264-5
Apache, Ariz. L11 206-7
Apache, Okla. G9 234-5
Apache, co., Ariz. H10 206-7
Apache Creek, N. Mex. H2 230-1
Apache Grove, Ariz. J11 206-7
Apache Junction, Ariz. I7 206-7
Apalachee, Ga. G6 160-1
Apalachicola, Fla. C6 156-7
Apalachin, N.Y. G7 80-1
Apex*, N.C. D10 180-1
Apiary, Ore. A6 238-9
Aplin, Ark. H12 150-1
Aplington, Ia. D9 104-5
Apohaqui*, N.B. I6 275
Apollo, Pa. A8 84-5
Apollo Beach, Fla. I3 156-7
Apopka, Fla. E11 156-7
Apostle Isl., Wis. A10 140-1
Appalachia, Va. J2 196-7
Appalachian Mts. 14-15
Appanoose, co., Ia. J9 104-5
Apple Creek, O. F14 132-3
Apple Grove, W. Va. G2 200-1
Apple Valley, Calif. E10 210-1
Apple Valley, Ida. L2 218-9
Apple Valley*, Minn. M6 116-7
Applegate, Mich. E7 112-3
Applegate, Ore. J5 238-9
Appleton, Ark. D5 150-1
Appleton, Me. L6 64-5
Appleton, Minn. L2 116-7
Appleton, Mo. H11 120-1
Appleton, S.C. H9 184-5
Appleton, Wash. J9 246-7
Appleton, Wis. G14 140-1
Appleton City, Mo. F4 120-1
Applewood*, Colo. D11 214-5
Appleyard, Wash. F11 246-7
Appling, Ga. G8 160-1
Appling, co., Ga. L8 160-1
Appomattox, Va. I10 196-7
Appomattox, co., Va. I10 196-7
Apsley, Ont. I11 284-5
Aptos*, Calif. J3 210-1
Aquadale, N.C. J3 180-1
Aquasco, Md. G11 172-3
Aquilla, O. B16 132-3
Aquone, N.C. E2 180-1
Arab, Ala. C7 146-7
Arabi, Ga. L5 160-1
Arabi, La. C15 168-9
Aragon, Ga. F2 160-1
Aragon, N. Mex. H2 230-1
Aragon Mills, S.C. B10 184-5
Aransas, co., Tex. I9 192-3
Aransas Pass, Tex. I9 192-3
Arapaho, Okla. E8 234-5
Arapahoe, Colo. F16 214-5
Arapahoe, Nebr. J8 124-5
Arapahoe, N.C. F14 180-1
Arapahoe, Wyo. F9 250-1
Arapahoe, co., Colo. E12 214-5
Ararat, N.C. C7 180-1
Ararat, Va. K7 196-7
Aravaipa, Ariz. J9 206-7
Arbela, Mo. A7 120-1
Arbo, Miss. K7 176-7
Arboles, Colo. J7 214-5
Arbon, Ida. O9 218-9
Arbor Vitae, Wis. C12 140-1
Arborfield, Sask. J9 294-5
Arborg, Man. H14 272-3
Arbovale, W. Va. G7 200-1
Arbuckle, Calif. H3 210-1
Arbuckle, W. Va. F2 200-1
Arbury Hills*, Ill. C10 96-7
Arbutus*, Md. B11 172-3
Arbyrd, Mo. K10 120-1
Arcade, Ga. F6 160-1
Arcade, N.Y. F3 80-1
Arcadia*, Calif. G9 210-1
Arcadia, Fla. G11 156-7
Arcadia, Ind. G8 100-1
Arcadia, Ia. F4 104-5
Arcadia, Kans. I16 108-9
Arcadia, La. B3 168-9
Arcadia, Mich. G11 112-3
Arcadia, Mo. H10 120-1
Arcadia, Nebr. G10 124-5
Arcadia, O. C5 132-3
Arcadia, Okla. I3 234-5
Arcadia, R.I. F3 87
Arcadia, S.C. F4 184-5
Arcadia, Wis. G9 140-1
Arcadia Lakes, S.C. E10 184-5
Arcanum, O. G13 132-3
Arcata, Calif. E1 210-1
Arch Cape, Ore. B4 238-9
Archbald, Pa. E14 84-5
Archbold, O. B4 132-3
Archdale, N.C. H4 180-1
Archer, Fla. D10 156-7
Archer, Ida. L10 218-9
Archer, Ia. B3 104-5
Archer, Mont. A15 222-3
Archer, Nebr. G11 124-5
Archer, Tenn. J7 188-9
Archer, Wyo. J15 250-1
Archer, co., Tex. D7 192-3
Archer City, Tex. D7 192-3
Archerwill, Sask. K9 294-5
Archibald, La. C6 168-9
Archie, La. D5 168-9
Archie, Mo. F3 120-1
Archuleta, co., Colo. J8 214-5
Arco, Ida. L8 218-9
Arco, Minn. N2 116-7
Arcola, Ill. H10 96-7
Arcola, Ind. C10 100-1
Arcola, La. G8 168-9
Arcola, Miss. F4 176-7
Arcola, Mo. H4 120-1
Arcola, N.C. C12 180-1
Arcola, Sask. O10 294-5
Arcola, Va. A3 196-7
Arctic, R.I. E4 87
Arctic Village, Alaska C12 254-5
Arden, Ark. I2 150-1
Arden, Del. A4 153
Arden, Man. I11 272-3
Arden, Nev. N9 226-7
Arden, N.C. E4 180-1
Arden, Ont. I13 284-5
Arden, Wash. C15 246-7
Arden, W. Va. D15 200-1
Arden-Arcade, Calif. A9 210-1
Arden Hills, Minn. A11 116-7
Ardenvoir, Wash. E11 246-7
Ardincaple, S.C. E10 184-5
Ardmore, Ala. A6 146-7
Ardmore, Alta. H10 264-5
Ardmore, Okla. I11 234-5
Ardmore, Pa. B10 84-5
Ardmore, S. Dak. I2 136-7
Ardmore, Tenn. E7 188-9
Ardoch, N. Dak. D13 128-9
Ardrossan*, Alta. I8 264-5
Ardsley, N.Y. C15 80-1
Aredale, Ia. C9 104-5
Arelee*, Sask. K5 294-5
Arena, Wis. J11 140-1
Arenac, co., Mich. G14 112-3
Arenas Valley, N. Mex. K3 230-1
Argenta, B.C. J10 268-9
Argenta, Ill. G9 96-7
Argenta, Mont. H5 222-3
Argenteuil, co., Que. H11 290-1
Argentine, Mich. H3 112-3
Argonia, Kans. J10 108-9
Argonne, Wis. D13 140-1
Argos, Ind. C8 100-1
Argusville, N. Dak. G14 128-9
Argyle, Ga. N8 160-1
Argyle, Man. I14 272-3
Argyle, Mich. H15 112-3
Argyle, Minn. E1 116-7
Argyle, Mo. F7 120-1
Argyle, Wis. K12 140-1
Ariail, S.C. B6 184-5
Arichat, N.S. C10 281
Ariel, Wash. I7 246-7
Arimo, Ida. N10 218-9
Arion, Ia. F3 104-5
Aripine, Ariz. G9 206-7
Arispe, Ia. I6 104-5
Arista, W. Va. J4 200-1
Ariton, Ala. K9 146-7
Arivaca, Ariz. M7 206-7
Arivaca Junction, Ariz. L8 206-7
Arizona, La. A3 168-9
Arjay, Ky. J13 164-5
Ark, Va. E3 196-7
Arkabutla, Miss. B6 176-7
Arkabutla Res., Miss. B6 176-7
Arkadelphia, Ark. H5 150-1
Arkansas, co., Ark. G9 150-1
Arkansas City, Ark. I9 150-1
Arkansas City, Kans. K11 108-9
Arkansas R., Ark. F7 150-1
Arkansas R., Kans. H2 108-9
Arkansaw, Wis. F8 140-1
Arkinda, Ark. I1 150-1
Arkoe, Mo. B2 120-1
Arkoma*, Okla. F16 234-5
Arkona, Ont. E11 284-5
Arkport, N.Y. G4 80-1
Arkwright, R.I. D4 87
Arkwright, S.C. F4 184-5
Arlee, Mont. E3 222-3
Arley, Ala. D5 146-7
Arlington, Ala. J4 146-7
Arlington, Ariz. I5 206-7
Arlington, Ga. M3 160-1
Arlington, Ind. I10 100-1
Arlington, Ia. D12 104-5
Arlington, Kans. I9 108-9
Arlington, Ky. J2 164-5
Arlington, Mass. G4 68-9
Arlington, Minn. C8 116-7
Arlington, Nebr. I2 124-5
Arlington, N.Y. H11 80-1
Arlington, N.C. G1 180-1
Arlington, O. D5 132-3
Arlington, Okla. E12 234-5
Arlington, Ore. B10 238-9
Arlington, S. Dak. E15 136-7
Arlington, Tenn. K2 188-9
Arlington, Tex. D13 192-3
Arlington, Vt. M4 90-1
Arlington, Va. E13 196-7
Arlington, Wash. F3 246-7
Arlington, W. Va. F13 200-1
Arlington, Wis. I1 140-1
Arlington, Wyo. I13 250-1
Arlington, co., Va. E13 196-7
Arlington Heights, Ill. L3 96-7
Arlington Heights*, O. H3 132-3
Arlington Heights-Pocono Park*, Pa. G15 84-5
Arm, Miss. K6 176-7
Arma, Kans. J16 108-9
Armada, Mich. H7 112-3
Armagh*, Que. G12 290-1
Armathwaite, Tenn. G9 188-9
Armijo, N. Mex. F5 230-1
Arminto, Wyo. F11 250-1
Armistead, La. C2 168-9
Armona, Calif. K5 210-1
Armorel, Ark. B13 150-1
Armour, S. Dak. H12 136-7
Armstrong, Ala. I9 146-7
Armstrong, B.C. I8 268-9
Armstrong, Del. C2 153
Armstrong, Ia. B6 104-5
Armstrong, Mo. D6 120-1
Armstrong, Okla. I13 234-5
Armstrong, Ont. E3 284-5
Armstrong, co., Pa. H3 84-5
Armstrong, co., Tex. B5 192-3
Armstrong Creek, Wis. D14 140-1
Armuchee, Ga. E2 160-1
Arnaud, Man. K14 272-3
Arnaudville, La. G5 168-9
Arnco Mills, Ga. E9 160-1
Arnegard, N. Dak. E2 128-9
Arnett, Okla. D7 234-5
Arnett, Okla. G6 234-5
Arnett, W. Va. K14 200-1
Arnold, Kans. G5 108-9
Arnold, Md. H7 172-3
Arnold, Mich. D10 112-3
Arnold, Mo. C15 120-1
Arnold, Nebr. G8 124-5
Arnold, Pa. A7 84-5
Arnold Mills, R.I. A5 87
Arnold's Cove*, Nfld. N10 278-9
Arnolds Park, Ia. B4 104-5
Arnoldsburg, W. Va. F4 200-1
Arnoldsville, Ga. F6 160-1
Arnott, Wis. E1 140-1
Arnprior, Ont. H14 284-5
Arock, Ore. I15 238-9
Aroda, Va. C1 196-7
Aroma Park, Ill. D11 96-7
Aroma Park Northwest*, Ill. D11 96-7
Aroostook, N.B. G3 275
Aroostook, co., Me. B6 64-5
Arp, Tenn. I2 188-9
Arp, Tex. E10 192-3
Arpelar, Okla. G14 234-5
Arpin, Wis. G11 140-1
Arran, Sask. L10 294-5
Arrey, N. Mex. K4 230-1
Arriba, Colo. E14 214-5
Arrington, Kans. D14 108-9
Arrington, Tenn. I7 188-9
Arrow Creek, Mont. D8 222-3
Arrow Rock, Mo. D6 120-1
Arrowsic, Me. N11 64-5
Arrowwood, Alta. M8 264-5
Arroyo Grande, Calif. M5 210-1
Arroyo Hondo, N. Mex. C7 230-1
Arroyo Seco, N. Mex. C7 230-1
Artas, S. Dak. A9 136-7
Artemus, Ky. J13 164-5
Artesia, Ariz. J10 206-7
Artesia*, Calif. H9 210-1
Artesia, Miss. F10 176-7
Artesia, N. Mex. K9 230-1
Artesian, S. Dak. F13 136-7
Arthabaska, Que. H15 290-1
Arthabaska, co., Que. H14 290-1
Arthur, Ill. H9 96-7
Arthur, Ia. E3 104-5
Arthur, Nebr. F5 124-5
Arthur, N. Dak. G14 128-9
Arthur, Ont. C13 284-5
Arthur, Tenn. F13 188-9
Arthur, W. Va. E9 200-1
Arthur, co., Nebr. G5 124-5
Arthurdale, W. Va. B16 200-1
Arthurette, N.B. G3 275
Arundel, Me. O2 64-5
Arvada, Colo. G3 214-5
Arvada, Wyo. B13 250-1
Arvilla, N. Dak. E13 128-9
Arvin, Calif. M6 210-1
Arvonia, Va. H11 196-7
Asbestos, Que. I15 290-1
Asbury, Ia. D14 104-5
Asbury, Mo. H3 120-1
Asbury, N.J. E3 76-7
Asbury, W. Va. I5 200-1
Asbury Park, N.J. H8 76-7
Ascension, co., La. H7 168-9
Ascot Corner, Que. J15 290-1
Ascutney, Vt. K7 90-1
Ash Flat, Ark. B8 150-1
Ash Fork, Ariz. E5 206-7
Ash Grove, Kans. E8 108-9
Ash Grove, Mo. H4 120-1
Ash Point, Me. L6 64-5
Ash Springs, Nev. J9 226-7
Asharoken*, N.Y. J12 80-1
Ashaway, R.I. H2 87
Ashburn, Ga. L5 160-1
Ashburn, Mo. C9 120-1
Ashburn, Va. A3 196-7
Ashburnham, Mass. B8 68-9
Ashby, Ala. G6 146-7
Ashby, Mass. B8 68-9
Ashby, Minn. J2 116-7
Ashby, Nebr. E4 124-5
Ashcroft, B.C. I7 268-9
Ashdod, Mass. E13 68-9
Ashdown, Ark. I2 150-1
Ashe, co., N.C. C6 180-1
Asheboro, N.C. D9 180-1
Asheboro South, N.C. I4 180-1
Asheboro West, N.C. I4 180-1
Ashepoo, S.C. I11 184-5
Asher, Okla. G12 234-5
Ashern, Man. G13 272-3
Asherton, Tex. I6 192-3
Asherville, Kans. E9 108-9
Asheville, N.C. E4 180-1
Ashfield, Mass. C4 68-9
Ashford, Ala. L10 146-7
Ashford, Conn. C13 60-1
Ashford, N.C. D5 180-1
Ashford, Wash. G8 246-7
Ashford, W. Va. I13 200-1
Ashford, Wis. H4 140-1
Ashippun, Wis. I3 140-1
Ashkum, Ill. E11 96-7
Ashland, Ala. F8 146-7
Ashland*, Calif. I3 210-1
Ashland, Ill. H6 96-7
Ashland, Kans. K5 108-9
Ashland, Ky. F15 164-5
Ashland, La. C3 168-9
Ashland, Me. C8 64-5
Ashland, Mass. I2 68-9
Ashland, Miss. B8 176-7
Ashland, Mo. E7 120-1
Ashland, Mont. H13 222-3
Ashland, Nebr. J2 124-5
Ashland, N.H. J6 72-3
Ashland, O. D8 132-3
Ashland, Okla. G13 234-5
Ashland, Ore. J6 238-9
Ashland, Pa. G12 84-5
Ashland, S.C. D12 184-5
Ashland, Va. H12 196-7
Ashland, Wis. B10 140-1
Ashland, co., O. D8 132-3
Ashland, co., Wis. B10 140-1
Ashland City, Tenn. G6 188-9
Ashleigh, S.C. G9 184-5
Ashley, Ill. L8 96-7
Ashley, Ind. A11 100-1
Ashley, Mich. F1 112-3
Ashley, N. Dak. J10 128-9
Ashley, O. E6 132-3
Ashley, Pa. F13 84-5
Ashley, co., Ark. J8 150-1
Ashley Falls, Mass. E1 68-9
Ashley Heights, N.C. K5 180-1
Ashmont, Alta. I9 264-5
Ashmore, Ill. I10 96-7
Ashport, Tenn. I2 188-9
Ashridge, Ala. C4 146-7
Ashtabula, O. A11 132-3
Ashtabula, co., O. B11 132-3
Ashton, Ida. K10 218-9

Ashton, Ill. B8 96-7
Ashton, Ia. B2 104-5
Ashton, Kans. K11 108-9
Ashton, Md. G4 172-3
Ashton, Nebr. G10 124-5
Ashton, Ont. H14 284-5
Ashton, R.I. B5 87
Ashton, S.C. H10 184-5
Ashton, S. Dak. C12 136-7
Ashton, W. Va. G2 200-1
Ashton Creek*, B.C. J5 268-9
Ashuelot, N.H. O2 72-3
Ashville, Ala. D7 146-7
Ashville, Me. K8 64-5
Ashville, Man. G10 272-3
Ashville, O. G6 132-3
Ashwaubenon*, Wis. G15 140-1
Ashwood, Ore. D9 238-9
Askew, Miss. B6 176-7
Askewville, N.C. C14 180-1
Askov, Minn. J7 116-7
Asotin, Wash. H16 246-7
Asotin, co., Wash. I16 246-7
Aspen, Colo. F9 214-5
Aspen Hill*, Md. D9 172-3
Aspen Park, Colo. H2 214-5
Aspen Tunnels, Wyo. J5 250-1
Aspermont, Tex. D6 192-3
Aspetuck, Conn. I5 60-1
Aspinwall, Ia. F4 104-5
Aspinwall, Pa. A6 84-5
Asquith, Sask. K6 294-5
Assaria, Kans. G10 108-9
Assiniboia, Sask. O7 294-5
Assiniboine R., Man. J1 272-3
Assinippi, Mass. K7 68-9
Assonet, Mass. G11 68-9
Assumption, Ill. I8 96-7
Assumption, Nebr. I11 124-5
Assumption, co., La. I7 168-9
Astatula, Fla. E11 156-7
Astle, N.B. G4 275
Astoria, Ill. G6 96-7
Astoria, Ore. A4 238-9
Astoria, S. Dak. E16 136-7
Astorville, Ont. H8 284-5
Atalissa, Ia. G14 104-5
Atascadero, Calif. L4 210-1
Atascosa, co., Tex. H7 192-3
Atchison, Kans. D15 108-9
Atchison, co., Kans. D15 108-9
Atchison, co., Mo. A1 120-1
Atco, N.J. K4 76-7
Athabasca, Alta. H8 264-5
Athalia, O. J8 132-3
Athalmer, B.C. I10 268-9
Athelstan, Ia. K5 104-5
Athelstane, Wis. D14 140-1
Athena, Ore. B13 238-9
Athens, Ala. B6 146-7
Athens, Ark. G3 150-1
Athens, Ga. F6 160-1
Athens, Ill. H7 96-7
Athens, La. B3 168-9
Athens, Me. I5 64-5
Athens, Mich. J12 112-3
Athens, N.Y. G11 80-1
Athens, O. H8 132-3
Athens, Ont. J14 284-5
Athens, Pa. C11 84-5
Athens, Tenn. D11 188-9
Athens, Tex. E10 192-3
Athens, Vt. M6 90-1
Athens, W. Va. J4 200-1
Athens, Wis. E11 140-1
Athens, co., O. H8 132-3
Atherley, Ont. A15 284-5
Atherton, Calif. D8 210-1
Athertonville, Ky. E2 164-5
Athol, Ida. C3 218-9
Athol, Kans. D7 108-9
Athol, Mass. B6 68-9
Athol, S. Dak. C12 136-7
Atholville, N.B. D4 275
Atikameg, Alta. F6 264-5
Atikokan, Ont. F2 284-5
Atironto*, Ont. I14 284-5
Atka, Alaska I4 254-5
Atkins, Ark. D5 150-1
Atkins, Ia. F12 104-5
Atkins, Va. J5 196-7
Atkinson, Ill. D6 96-7
Atkinson*, Me. H6 64-5
Atkinson, Nebr. D10 124-5
Atkinson, N.H. O8 72-3
Atkinson, N.C. G12 180-1
Atkinson, co., Ga. M7 160-1
Atkinson Corners, Me. H6 64-5
Atlanta, Ark. K5 150-1
Atlanta, Del. I3 153
Atlanta, Ga. G4 160-1
Atlanta, Ida. L5 218-9
Atlanta, Ill. G8 96-7
Atlanta, Ind. F8 100-1
Atlanta, Kans. J12 108-9
Atlanta, La. D4 168-9
Atlanta, Mich. F13 112-3
Atlanta, Mo. B6 120-1
Atlanta, Nebr. I9 124-5
Atlanta, Tex. D11 192-3
Atlantic, Ia. H4 104-5
Atlantic, Me. L8 64-5
Atlantic, N.C. F15 180-1
Atlantic, Va. G16 196-7
Atlantic, co., N.J. L5 76-7
Atlantic Beach, Fla. B11 156-7
Atlantic Beach*, N.Y. K11 80-1
Atlantic Beach, N.C. F14 180-1
Atlantic Beach, S.C. E16 184-5
Atlantic City, N.J. M6 76-7
Atlantic City, Wyo. G8 250-1
Atlantic Highlands, N.J. H11 76-7
Atlantis, Fla. E16 156-7
Atlas, Mich. G4 112-3
Atlas*, Pa. G12 84-5
Atlin, B.C. A3 268-9
Atmore, Ala. M4 146-7
Atoka, N. Mex. K9 230-1
Atoka, Okla. H13 234-5
Atoka, Tenn. J2 188-9
Atoka, co., Okla. H14 234-5
Atomic City, Ida. M8 218-9
Atrisco, N. Mex. F5 230-1
Attala, co., Miss. G7 176-7
Attalla, Ala. D8 146-7
Attapulgus, Ga. O3 160-1
Attawaugan, Conn. C14 60-1
Attica, Ind. F5 100-1
Attica, Kans. K9 108-9
Attica, Mich. G6 112-3
Attica, N.Y. F3 80-1
Attica, O. C7 132-3
Attleboro, Mass. F10 68-9
Atwater, Calif. D11 210-1
Atwater, Minn. L4 116-7
Atwater, Sask. M10 294-5
Atwood, Ill. H9 96-7
Atwood, Ind. B8 100-1
Atwood, Kans. D3 108-9
Atwood, Okla. G13 234-5
Atwood, Ont. C12 284-5
Atwood, Tenn. B4 188-9
Atwoodville, Conn. D12 60-1
Au Gres, Mich. G14 112-3
Au Train, Mich. D10 112-3
Aubrey, Ark. F10 150-1
Aubrey, Tex. A14 192-3
Aubry, Kans. F16 108-9
Auburn, Ala. H9 146-7
Auburn, Calif. H4 210-1
Auburn, Ga. F5 160-1
Auburn, Ill. I7 96-7
Auburn, Ind. B11 100-1
Auburn, Ia. E5 104-5
Auburn, Kans. F14 108-9
Auburn, Ky. J7 164-5
Auburn, Me. M9 64-5
Auburn, Mass. E8 68-9
Auburn, Mich. H14 112-3
Auburn, Miss. L5 176-7
Auburn, Nebr. I16 124-5
Auburn, N.H. N7 72-3
Auburn, N.Y. E6 80-1
Auburn, Ont. C12 284-5
Auburn, Wash. J3 246-7
Auburn, W. Va. E5 200-1
Auburn, Wyo. F5 250-1
Auburn Heights, Mich. I5 112-3
Auburndale, Fla. H5 156-7
Auburndale, Wis. F11 140-1
Auburntown, Tenn. B8 188-9
Auden, Ont. E4 284-5
Audra, W. Va. E15 200-1
Audrain, co., Mo. D7 120-1
Audubon, Ia. G4 104-5
Audubon, Minn. I2 116-7
Audubon, N.J. N10 76-7
Audubon, co., Ia. G4 104-5
Audubon Park*, Ky. G9 164-5
Audubon Park, N.J. N10 76-7
Auglaize, co., O. E4 132-3
August School Area*, Calif. I4 210-1
Augusta, Ark. D9 150-1
Augusta, Ga. G9 160-1
Augusta, Ill. G4 96-7
Augusta, Kans. I11 108-9
Augusta, Ky. E12 164-5
Augusta, Me. K4 64-5
Augusta*, Mich. J12 112-3
Augusta, Mo. C14 120-1
Augusta, Mont. D5 222-3
Augusta, W. Va. E10 200-1
Augusta, Wis. F9 140-1
Augusta, co., Va. G9 196-7
Augusta Springs, Va. G9 196-7
Augustine Cove*, P.E.I. F5 287
Aulander, N.C. C13 180-1
Aullville, Mo. D4 120-1
Ault, Colo. D4 214-5
Ault Field*, Wash. D7 246-7
Aumsville, Ore. H1 238-9
Aurelia, Ia. D3 104-5
Aurelius, Mich. I1 112-3
Aurora, Ark. B3 150-1
Aurora, Colo. G3 214-5
Aurora, Ill. C10 96-7
Aurora, Ind. K12 100-1
Aurora, Ia. D12 104-5
Aurora, Kans. E10 108-9
Aurora, Me. J8 64-5
Aurora, Minn. G8 116-7
Aurora, Mo. I4 120-1
Aurora, Nebr. H12 124-5
Aurora, N.Y. F6 80-1
Aurora, N.C. E14 180-1
Aurora, O. C16 132-3
Aurora, Ont. B15 284-5
Aurora, Ore. G2 238-9
Aurora, S. Dak. E16 136-7
Aurora, Ut. J6 242-3
Aurora, W. Va. E8 200-1
Aurora, co., S. Dak. G12 136-7
Auroraville, Wis. F2 140-1
Austell, Ga. B9 160-1
Austin, Ark. E7 150-1
Austin, Colo. F7 214-5
Austin, Ind. L9 100-1
Austin, Ky. J8 164-5
Austin, Man. I12 272-3
Austin, Minn. O7 116-7
Austin, Miss. B5 176-7
Austin, Mont. E6 222-3
Austin, Nev. F6 226-7
Austin, Ore. E13 238-9
Austin, R.I. F3 87
Austin, Tex. G8 192-3
Austin, Ut. J6 242-3
Austin, co., Tex. G9 192-3
Austintown, O. C11 132-3
Austinville, Va. J6 196-7
Australian, B.C. H7 268-9
Autauga, co., Ala. H6 146-7
Autaugaville, Ala. I6 146-7
Auto, W. Va. I6 200-1
Autryville, N.C. K7 180-1
Auvergne, Ark. D9 150-1
Auxier, Ky. H15 164-5
Auxvasse, Mo. D7 120-1
Ava, Ill. M7 96-7
Ava, Mo. I6 120-1
Avalon, Calif. O7 210-1
Avalon, Ga. E6 160-1
Avalon, Miss. E6 176-7
Avalon, N.J. O5 76-7
Avalon, Pa. A6 84-5
Avalon, Wis. K2 140-1
Avant, Okla. C13 234-5
Avard, Okla. C8 234-5
Avella, Pa. I1 84-5
Avenal, Calif. K5 210-1
Avenel, N.J. F7 76-7
Avenel-Hillandale, Md. E10 172-3
Avenue, Md. H10 172-3
Avera, Ga. H8 160-1
Averill, Vt. B10 90-1
Averill Park*, N.Y. F11 80-1
Avery, Ida. D4 218-9
Avery, Ia. I10 104-5
Avery, Okla. E12 234-5
Avery, co., N.C. C5 180-1
Avery Island, La. I5 168-9
Averys Gore*, Vt. B10 90-1
Avilla, Ind. B11 100-1
Avilla, Mo. H3 120-1
Avinger, Tex. D11 192-3
Avis, Pa. F9 84-5
Aviston, Ill. K7 96-7
Avoca, Ark. A3 150-1
Avoca, Ind. L7 100-1
Avoca, Ia. H3 104-5
Avoca, Mich. G7 112-3
Avoca, Minn. O3 116-7
Avoca, Nebr. K2 124-5
Avoca, N.Y. G5 80-1
Avoca*, Pa. E14 84-5
Avoca, Wis. J11 140-1
Avocado Heights*, Calif. N7 210-1
Avola, B.C. H8 268-9
Avon, Ala. L10 146-7
Avon, Conn. C8 60-1
Avon, Ill. F5 96-7
Avon, Ia. H8 104-5
Avon, Me. J3 64-5
Avon, Mass. K5 68-9
Avon, Minn. K5 116-7
Avon, Miss. F4 176-7
Avon, N.Y. F4 80-1
Avon, N.C. E16 180-1
Avon, O. B13 132-3
Avon, Ont. E12 284-5
Avon, Pa. I12 84-5
Avon, S.C. C9 184-5
Avon, S. Dak. I13 136-7
Avon, Ut. D6 242-3
Avon-by-the-Sea, N.J. H8 76-7
Avon Lake, O. B13 132-3
Avon Park, Fla. J6 156-7
Avondale, Ariz. I6 206-7
Avondale, Colo. H13 214-5
Avondale, Mo. I15 120-1
Avondale*, Nfld. O11 278-9
Avondale*, O. G4 132-3
Avondale, Pa. K14 84-5
Avondale, R.I. I1 87
Avondale, W. Va. J3 200-1
Avondale Estates, Ga. C11 160-1
Avondale-Mooreland*, S.C. I13 184-5
Avonlea, Sask. N8 294-5
Avonmore, Pa. A8 84-5
Avoyelles, co., La. F5 168-9
Awendaw, S.C. H14 184-5
Axial, Colo. C7 214-5
Axis, Ala. M3 146-7
Axson, Ga. M8 160-1
Axtell, Kans. C13 108-9
Axtell, Nebr. I10 124-5
Axtell, Ut. I6 242-3
Axton, Va. J8 196-7
Aycock, La. B3 168-9
Aydelotte, Okla. J4 234-5
Ayden, N.C. E13 180-1
Ayer, Mass. C9 68-9
Ayer, Wash. H14 246-7
Ayers, Wyo. H15 250-1
Ayer's Cliff, Que. J14 290-1
Aylesbury, Sask. M7 294-5
Aylett, Va. H13 196-7
Aylmer, Ont. E12 284-5
Aylmer, Que. J2 290-1
Aylsham, Sask. J9 294-5
Aynor, S.C. E15 184-5
Ayr, Nebr. I11 124-5
Ayr, N. Dak. G13 128-9
Ayr, Ont. D13 284-5
Ayrshire, Ia. C5 104-5
Ayton*, Ont. C13 284-5
Azalea, Ore. I5 238-9
Azalea Park*, Fla. E11 156-7
Azle, Tex. C12 192-3
Aztec, Ariz. J4 206-7
Aztec, N. Mex. B3 230-1
Azusa*, Calif. G9 210-1
Azwell, Wash. E12 246-7

B

B-Say-Tah, Sask. M9 294-5
Babb, Mont. A4 222-3
Babbie, Ala. L7 146-7
Babbitt, Minn. G8 116-7
Babbitt, Nev. H3 226-7
Babbs, Okla. G8 234-5
Babcock, Wis. G11 140-1
Babson Park, Fla. I6 156-7
Babylon, N.Y. K12 80-1
Baca, co., Colo. I15 214-5
Bach, Mich. H14 112-3
Back Bay, N.B. J4 275
Backus, Minn. I5 116-7
Bacon, co., Ga. L8 160-1
Bacone, Okla. E15 234-5
Bacons, Del. K3 153
Baconton, Ga. M4 160-1
Bacova, Va. G8 196-7
Bad Axe, Mich. H15 112-3
Baddeck, N.S. B11 281
Bade, Ore. B13 238-9
Baden, Man. D9 272-3
Baden*, Ont. D13 284-5
Baden, Pa. H1 84-5
Badger, Ia. D6 104-5
Badger, Minn. D2 116-7
Badger, Nfld. M9 278-9
Badger, S. Dak. E15 136-7
Badger's Quay, Nfld. M11 278-9
Badger's Quay-Valleyfield-Pool's Island*, Nfld. M11 278-9
Badham, S.C. G11 184-5
Badin, N.C. J3 180-1
Baffin Isl., N.W. Terr. B3 296
Bagdad, Ariz. F4 206-7
Bagdad, Fla. A3 156-7
Bagdad, Ky. A5 164-5
Bagdad, La. E4 168-9
Baggs, Wyo. K10 250-1
Bagley, Ia. G6 104-5
Bagley, Minn. G3 116-7
Bagley, Wis. J9 140-1
Bagnell, Mo. F6 120-1
Bagot*, Man. J13 272-3
Bagot, co., Que. I13 290-1
Bahama, N.C. G7 180-1
Baie-Comeau, Que. A16 290-1
Baie-de-Shawinigan, Que. G9 290-1
Baie-des-Sables, Que. B16 290-1
Baie-d'Urfé*, Que. J12 290-1
Baie-St.-Paul, Que. E12 290-1
Baie-Ste.-Anne*, N.B. F7 275
Baie-Trinité, Que. H5 290-1
Baie Verte, Nfld. L9 278-9
Baieville, Que. H13 290-1
Bailey, Colo. I1 214-5
Bailey, Mich. I12 112-3
Bailey, Miss. H9 176-7
Bailey, N.C. D12 180-1
Bailey, Okla. G10 234-5
Bailey, co., Tex. C4 192-3
Bailey Island, Me. O10 64-5
Bailey Lakes*, O. D8 132-3
Baileys Crossroads, Va. A4 196-7
Baileys Harbor, Wis. E16 140-1
Baileys Switch, Ky. J12 164-5
Baileysville, W. Va. J3 200-1
Baileyton, Ala. C6 146-7
Baileyton, Tenn. G15 188-9
Baileyville, Kans. D13 108-9
Baileyville, Me. I10 64-5
Bainbridge, Ga. N3 160-1
Bainbridge, Ind. H6 100-1
Bainbridge, N.Y. G8 80-1
Bainbridge, O. H6 132-3
Bainbridge Center*, Md. B13 172-3
Bains, La. F7 168-9
Bains Corner, N.B. J6 275
Bainville, Mont. B16 222-3
Baird, Miss. F5 176-7
Baird, Tex. E7 192-3
Bairdsville, N.B. G3 275
Bairoil, Wyo. H10 250-1
Baker, Calif. L9 210-1
Baker, Fla. B4 156-7
Baker, Ida. I7 218-9
Baker, Kans. D14 108-9
Baker, La. G7 168-9
Baker, Mo. I11 120-1
Baker, Mont. F16 222-3
Baker, Nev. G11 226-7
Baker, N. Dak. D9 128-9
Baker, Okla. C4 234-5
Baker, Ore. D14 238-9
Baker, W. Va. E10 200-1
Baker, co., Fla. B10 156-7
Baker, co., Ga. M3 160-1
Baker, co., Ore. D15 238-9
Baker Brook, N.B. F2 275
Baker Hill, Ala. K10 146-7
Baker Lake, N.W. Terr. C2 296
Bakers, N.C. K2 180-1
Bakers Narrows*, Man. F1 272-3
Bakersfield, Calif. L6 210-1
Bakersfield, Mo. J7 120-1
Bakersfield, Vt. C5 90-1
Bakersville, Conn. C7 60-1
Bakersville, N.C. D5 180-1
Bakerville, Wis. F11 140-1
Bakewell, Tenn. K11 188-9

Bal Harbour*, Fla. H16 156-7
Bala, Ont. A14 284-5
Bala-Cynwyd, Pa. B11 84-5
Balaton, Minn. N2 116-7
Balcarres, Sask. M9 294-5
Balch, Ark. D10 150-1
Balch Springs, Tex. D15 192-3
Balcones Heights, Tex. J2 192-3
Bald Creek, N.C. D4 180-1
Bald Head, Me. O2 64-5
Bald Hill, Okla. E14 234-5
Bald Knob, Ark. D8 150-1
Bald Knob, W. Va. K13 200-1
Baldock, S.C. H9 184-5
Baldur, Man. K11 272-3
Baldwin, Fla. B11 156-7
Baldwin, Ga. E6 160-1
Baldwin, Ia. F14 104-5
Baldwin, La. I6 168-9
Baldwin*, Me. N7 64-5
Baldwin, Md. C11 172-3
Baldwin, Mich. H11 112-3
Baldwin, N.Y. F16 80-1
Baldwin, N. Dak. G7 128-9
Baldwin, Pa. B6 84-5
Baldwin, W. Va. F5 200-1
Baldwin, Wis. E7 140-1
Baldwin, co., Ala. N4 146-7
Baldwin, co., Ga. I6 160-1
Baldwin-Aragon Mills, S.C. B9 184-5
Baldwin City, Kans. F15 108-9
Baldwin Park, Calif. G9 210-1
Baldwin Park*, Mo. E3 120-1
Baldwinsville, Mass. B7 68-9
Baldwinsville, N.Y. E7 80-1
Baldwinton, Sask. K4 294-5
Baldwyn, Miss. B10 176-7
Balfour, B.C. J10 268-9
Balfour, N. Dak. E8 128-9
Balfour [-Druid Hills], N.C. E4 180-1
Balfours, N.C. I4 180-1
Balgonie, Sask. N8 294-5
Balkan, Ky. J13 164-5
Balko, Okla. C5 234-5
Ball, La. E4 168-9
Ball Ground, Ga. E4 160-1
Ballantine, Mont. G11 222-3
Ballard, Okla. D16 234-5
Ballard, co., Ky. J2 164-5
Ballardsville, Ky. A3 164-5
Ballardvale, Mass. B11 68-9
Ballengee, W. Va. J5 200-1
Ballentine, S.C. K8 184-5
Ballinger, Tex. E6 192-3
Ballouville, Conn. C14 60-1
Ballston, Ore. D5 238-9
Ballston Spa, N.Y. E11 80-1
Ballsville, Va. H11 196-7
Balltown, Ia. D14 104-5
Ballville, O. C6 132-3
Ballwin, Mo. C15 120-1
Bally, Pa. I14 84-5
Ballydown Beach*, Ont. B14 284-5
Balm Beach*, Ont. A14 284-5
Balmertown*, Ont. D2 284-5
Balmoral, Man. I14 272-3
Balmoral, N.B. D4 275
Balmorhea, Tex. F3 192-3
Balmville, N.Y. I11 80-1
Balsam, N.C. E3 180-1
Balsam Grove, N.C. E3 180-1
Balsam Lake, Wis. D7 140-1
Balta, N. Dak. D8 128-9
Baltic, Conn. E13 60-1
Baltic, O. E9 132-3
Baltic, S. Dak. G16 136-7
Baltimore, Md. C11 172-3
Baltimore, O. G7 132-3
Baltimore, Ont. K11 284-5
Baltimore*, Vt. K6 90-1
Baltimore, co., Md. B11 172-3
Bamberg, S.C. G10 184-5
Bamberg, co., S.C. G10 184-5
Bamfield, B.C. K5 268-9
Bancroft, Ida. N10 218-9
Bancroft, Ia. B6 104-5
Bancroft, Kans. D13 108-9
Bancroft*, Ky. A2 164-5
Bancroft, La. G1 168-9
Bancroft, Me. G9 64-5
Bancroft, Mass. D3 68-9
Bancroft, Mich. H3 112-3
Bancroft, Nebr. E14 124-5
Bancroft, Ont. I12 284-5
Bancroft, S. Dak. E14 136-7
Bancroft, W. Va. G3 200-1
Bancroft, Wis. E1 140-1
Bandana, Ky. I2 164-5
Bandera, Tex. G7 192-3
Bandera, co., Tex. G7 192-3
Bandon, Ore. H3 238-9
Bandytown, W. Va. K13 200-1
Banff, Alta. M6 264-5
Bango, Nev. F3 226-7
Bangor, Ala. D6 146-7
Bangor, Me. J7 64-5
Bangor, Mich. J11 112-3
Bangor, Pa. G15 84-5
Bangor, P.E.I. E9 287
Bangor, Sask. M10 294-5
Bangor, Wis. H10 140-1
Bangs, Tex. E7 192-3
Banida, Ida. O10 218-9
Bankend, Sask. L9 294-5
Banks, Ala. K8 146-7
Banks, Ark. I7 150-1
Banks, Ida. K3 218-9
Banks, Miss. B6 176-7
Banks, Ore. F1 238-9
Banks, co., Ga. E5 160-1
Bankston, Ala. E4 146-7
Bankston, Ia. D14 104-5
Banner, Ark. C8 150-1
Banner, Miss. D8 176-7
Banner, Okla. J1 234-5
Banner, Wyo. B12 250-1
Banner, co., Nebr. F1 124-5
Banner Elk, N.C. C5 180-1
Banner Hill, Tenn. H16 188-9
Banner Springs, Tenn. G9 188-9
Bannertown, N.C. C7 180-1
Banning, Calif. G11 210-1
Bannister, Mich. F1 112-3
Bannock, co., Ida. O10 218-9
Bannockburn, Ill. K3 96-7
Bantam, Conn. D5 60-1
Bantry, N. Dak. C7 128-9
Banty, Okla. I13 234-5
Bapchule, Ariz. I7 206-7
Baptist, La. A12 168-9
Baptist Village, Mass. F5 68-9
Baptistown, N.J. F3 76-7
Bar Harbor, Me. K8 64-5
Bar Mills, Me. O8 64-5
Baraboo, Wis. I12 140-1
Barachois*, N.B. H7 275
Barada, Nebr. J16 124-5
Baraga, Mich. C8 112-3
Baraga, co., Mich. C9 112-3
Baranof, Alaska H15 254-5
Barataria, La. E14 168-9
Barataria Bay, La. J10 168-9
Barber, Ark. E3 150-1
Barber, Ida. L3 218-9
Barber, Mont. F9 222-3
Barber, N.C. I2 180-1
Barber, co., Kans. K8 108-9
Barbers Point Housing, Hawaii J3 258-9
Barberton, O. D15 132-3
Barbour, co., Ala. J9 146-7
Barbour, co., W. Va. E7 200-1
Barbourmeade*, Ky. G9 164-5
Barboursville, Va. G11 196-7
Barboursville, W. Va. H10 200-1
Barbourville, Ky. J13 164-5
Barclay, Md. D14 172-3
Barclay, Nev. J11 226-7
Barco, N.C. C15 180-1
Bard, N. Mex. F11 230-1
Bardstown, Ky. D3 164-5
Bardwell, Ky. J2 164-5
Bardwell, Mass. C4 68-9
Barfield, Ala. F9 146-7
Barfield, Ark. C13 150-1
Bargaintown, N.J. M5 76-7
Bargersville, Ind. H2 100-1
Barhamsville, Va. E3 196-7
Baring, Me. I10 64-5
Baring, Mo. B7 120-1
Baring, Wash. E9 246-7
Barium Springs, N.C. I1 180-1
Bark River, Mich. E10 112-3
Barker, N.Y. E3 80-1
Barker Heights*, N.C. E4 180-1
Barkersville, S.C. I10 184-5
Barkertown, Tenn. J10 188-9
Barkerville, Mass. C2 68-9
Barkhamsted, Conn. B7 60-1
Barkley Dam, Ky. J4 164-5
Barling, Ark. D2 150-1
Barlow*, B.C. G7 268-9
Barlow, Ky. J2 164-5
Barlow, N. Dak. F10 128-9
Barlow, Ore. G2 238-9
Barlow Bend, Ala. L4 146-7
Barnabus, W. Va. K12 200-1
Barnaby River, N.B. G6 275
Barnard, Kans. E9 108-9
Barnard, Me. H6 64-5
Barnard, Mo. B2 120-1
Barnard, N.C. D3 180-1
Barnard, S. Dak. A12 136-7
Barnard, Vt. I6 90-1
Barnardsville, N.C. D4 180-1
Barnegat, N.J. K7 76-7
Barnegat Bay, N.J. J7 76-7
Barnegat Light, N.J. K8 76-7
Barnes, Kans. D11 108-9
Barnes, Ore. H5 238-9
Barnes, co., N. Dak. G12 128-9
Barnes City, Ia. H10 104-5
Barnesboro, Pa. H5 84-5
Barneston, Nebr. I14 124-5
Barnesville, Ga. H4 160-1
Barnesville, Md. G1 172-3
Barnesville, Minn. I2 116-7
Barnesville, Miss. A6 176-7
Barnesville, N.B. I5 275
Barnesville, N.C. G10 180-1
Barnesville, O. F10 132-3
Barnet, Vt. F9 90-1
Barnett, Miss. J9 176-7
Barnett, Mo. F6 120-1
Barnett, Ore. C10 238-9
Barnetts, Va. E2 196-7
Barneveld, Wis. J11 140-1
Barney, Ga. N6 160-1
Barney, N. Dak. I14 128-9
Barnhill, O. E10 132-3
Barnsboro, N.J. O10 76-7
Barnsdall, Okla. C13 234-5
Barnstable, Mass. H15 68-9
Barnstable, co., Mass. H14 68-9
Barnstead, N.H. L7 72-3
Barnum, Ia. D6 104-5
Barnum, Minn. I7 116-7
Barnum, Wyo. E12 250-1
Barnumville, Vt. L4 90-1
Barnwell, Alta. N9 264-5
Barnwell, S.C. G9 184-5
Barnwell, co., S.C. G9 184-5
Baroda, Mich. K11 112-3
Baron, Okla. E16 234-5
Barons, Alta. N8 264-5
Barr Haven*, Ont. H14 284-5
Barr Lake, Colo. F4 214-5
Barrackville*, W. Va. D6 200-1
Barranca, N. Mex. D6 230-1
Barraute, Que. H1 290-1
Barre, Mass. C7 68-9
Barre*, Vt. F7 90-1
Barre, Vt. F7 90-1
Barrel Springs, Nev. C3 226-7
Barrelville, Md. B3 172-3
Barren, co., Ky. J8 164-5
Barren Plain, Tenn. F6 188-9
Barren R., Ky. I7 164-5
Barren Springs, Va. J6 196-7
Barrett, Minn. K2 116-7
Barrett, Tex. H15 192-3
Barrhead, Alta. I7 264-5
Barrie, Ont. B14 284-5
Barriefield, Ont. J14 284-5
Barriere, B.C. I8 268-9
Barrington, Ill. K2 96-7
Barrington, N.H. M8 72-3
Barrington, N.J. N11 76-7
Barrington, R.I. D6 87
Barrington Hills, Ill. K2 96-7
Barrington Passage, N.S. G4 281
Barron, Wis. D8 140-1
Barron, co., Wis. E8 140-1
Barronett, Wis. D8 140-1
Barrow, Alaska A10 254-5
Barrow, co., Ga. F5 160-1
Barrows, Man. D9 272-3
Barrowsville, Mass. F11 68-9
Barry, Ill. H4 96-7
Barry, Minn. K1 116-7
Barry, co., Mich. J12 112-3
Barry, co., Mo. J4 120-1
Barrymore, Ida. N6 218-9
Barry's Bay, Ont. H12 284-5
Barryton, Mich. H12 112-3
Barryville, N.B. F6 275
Barstow, Calif. M8 210-1
Barstow, Md. G11 172-3
Bartholomew, co., Ind. J9 100-1
Bartlesville, Okla. C13 234-5
Bartlett*, Ill. L2 96-7
Bartlett, Kans. K15 108-9
Bartlett, Nebr. F11 124-5
Bartlett, N.H. H7 72-3
Bartlett, N. Dak. D11 128-9
Bartlett, Ore. A15 238-9
Bartlett, Tenn. K1 188-9
Bartlett, Tex. F8 192-3
Bartley, Nebr. J7 124-5
Barton, Ala. B3 146-7
Barton, Ark. F10 150-1
Barton, Md. B3 172-3
Barton, N. Dak. C8 128-9
Barton, S.C. H9 184-5
Barton, Vt. C8 90-1
Barton, co., Kans. G8 108-9
Barton, co., Mo. H3 120-1
Barton City, Mich. F14 112-3
Barton Hills, Mich. J3 112-3
Bartonsville, Vt. L6 90-1
Bartonville, Ill. F7 96-7
Bartow, Fla. F11 156-7
Bartow, Ga. I8 160-1
Bartow, W. Va. G7 200-1
Bartow, co., Ga. E3 160-1
Barview, Ore. B4 238-9
Barwick, Ga. N5 160-1
Barwick, Ont. F1 284-5
Basalt, Colo. E8 214-5
Basalt, Ida. M9 218-9
Basalt, Nev. I4 226-7
Basco, Wis. J1 140-1
Bascom, Fla. A6 156-7
Basehor, Kans. E16 108-9
Bashan, Conn. F11 60-1
Bashaw, Alta. K8 264-5
Bashi, Ala. J3 146-7
Basile, La. G4 168-9
Basin, Ida. O7 218-9
Basin, Mont. F5 222-3
Basin, Wyo. C10 250-1
Basin Corner, Del. B3 153
Baskerville, Va. J11 196-7
Baskett, Ky. H5 164-5
Baskin, La. C6 168-9
Basking Ridge, N.J. E6 76-7
Bass River, Mass. H16 68-9
Bass River, N.B. G6 275
Bass River, N.J. L6 76-7
Bass River, N.S. D7 281
Bassano, Alta. M9 264-5
Bassett, Ark. D12 150-1
Bassett, Ia. C10 104-5
Bassett, Kans. I15 108-9
Bassett, Nebr. D9 124-5
Bassett, Va. J8 196-7
Bassfield, Miss. K7 176-7
Basswood, Man. I11 272-3
Bastian, Va. I5 196-7
Bastrop, La. A5 168-9
Bastrop, Tex. G8 192-3
Bastrop, co., Tex. G8 192-3
Basye, Va. E10 196-7
Bat Cave, N.C. E4 180-1
Batavia, Ark. A5 150-1
Batavia, Ill. M1 96-7
Batavia, Ia. I11 104-5
Batavia, N.Y. E3 80-1
Batavia, O. I4 132-3
Batavia, Wis. H5 140-1
Batawa, Ont. K12 284-5
Batchelor, La. F6 168-9
Bates, Ark. E2 150-1
Bates, Ida. L11 218-9
Bates, Ore. E13 238-9
Bates, co., Mo. F3 120-1
Bates City, Mo. J16 120-1
Batesburg, S.C. E9 184-5
Batesland, S. Dak. I5 136-7
Batesville, Ark. C8 150-1
Batesville, Ind. J11 100-1
Batesville, Miss. C6 176-7
Batesville, Va. G10 196-7
Bath, Me. M4 64-5
Bath, Mich. H1 112-3
Bath, N.B. G3 275
Bath, N.H. G5 72-3
Bath, N.Y. G5 80-1
Bath, N.C. E14 180-1
Bath, Ont. K13 284-5
Bath, Pa. G15 84-5
Bath, S.C. F8 184-5
Bath, S. Dak. B12 136-7
Bath, co., Ky. G13 164-5
Bath, co., Va. G8 196-7
Bath Springs, Tenn. D5 188-9
Bathgate, N. Dak. B13 128-9
Bathurst, N.B. E5 275
Baton Rouge, La. G7 168-9
Batterson, Ore. B4 238-9
Battery Park, Va. G3 196-7
Battiest, Okla. H16 234-5
Battin, Ore. F2 238-9
Battle Creek, Ia. E3 104-5
Battle Creek, Mich. J12 112-3
Battle Creek, Nebr. E12 124-5
Battle Ground, Ind. E6 100-1
Battle Ground, Wash. J7 246-7
Battle Lake, Minn. J3 116-7
Battle Mountain, Nev. D6 226-7
Battleboro, N.C. D12 180-1
Battlefield*, Mo. H5 120-1
Battleford, Sask. K5 294-5
Battles, Miss. K10 176-7
Battles Wharf, Ala. N3 146-7
Battletown, Ky. G8 164-5
Battleview, N. Dak. C4 128-9
Baudette, Minn. E4 116-7
Bauxite, Ark. K15 150-1
Bavaria, Kans. F10 108-9
Bawcomville, La. B5 168-9
Bawlf, Alta. J9 264-5
Baxley, Ga. L8 160-1
Baxter, Ia. G9 104-5
Baxter, Minn. J5 116-7
Baxter, Tenn. B9 188-9
Baxter, W. Va. B14 200-1
Baxter, Wyo. I8 250-1
Baxter, co., Ark. A7 150-1
Baxter Estates*, N.Y. J11 80-1
Baxter Springs, Kans. K16 108-9
Baxterville, Colo. I9 214-5
Baxterville, Miss. L7 176-7
Bay, Ark. C11 150-1
Bay, O. B13 132-3
Bay, co., Fla. B5 156-7
Bay, co., Mich. H14 112-3
Bay Bulls*, Nfld. O11 278-9
Bay Center, Wash. H5 246-7
Bay City, Mich. H14 112-3
Bay City, Ore. B4 238-9
Bay City, Tex. H10 192-3
Bay City, Wis. F7 140-1
Bay de Verde, Nfld. N11 278-9
Bay Harbor Islands*, Fla. H16 156-7
Bay Head, N.J. I8 76-7
Bay Lake*, Fla. E12 156-7
Bay L'Argent, Nfld. N10 278-9
Bay Minette, Ala. M4 146-7
Bay of Fundy, N.S. D4 281
Bay of Islands, Nfld. F6 278-9
Bay Point, Me. O11 64-5
Bay Port, Mich. H14 112-3
Bay Roberts, Nfld. N11 278-9
Bay Shore, Mich. E12 112-3
Bay Shore, N.Y. K12 80-1
Bay Springs, Miss. J8 176-7
Bay St. Louis, Miss. O8 176-7
Bay View, Ala. E6 146-7
Bay View, Md. B13 172-3
Bay View, O. B7 132-3
Bay View Beach, Del. C3 153
Bay Village, Ark. D11 150-1
Bayard, Del. K6 153
Bayard, Ia. G5 104-5
Bayard, Nebr. F2 124-5
Bayard, N. Mex. K3 230-1
Bayard, W. Va. E8 200-1
Bayboro, N.C. E14 180-1
Bayfield, Colo. J7 214-5
Bayfield, Ont. C11 284-5
Bayfield, Wis. A10 140-1
Bayfield, co., Wis. B9 140-1
Baylor, co., Tex. C7 192-3
Bayonne, N.J. E11 76-7
Bayou Cane, La. J8 168-9
Bayou Chicot, La. F4 168-9
Bayou Current, La. F6 168-9
Bayou Goula, La. B9 168-9
Bayou La Batre, Ala. O2 146-7
Bayou Nezpique, La. G3 168-9
Bayou Sorrel, La. H7 168-9
Bayou Vista*, La. I7 168-9
Bayport, Minn. B12 116-7
Bayport, N.Y. K12 80-1
Bayport Park-Lakeside*, Mich. I14 112-3
Bayshore Estates*, Ont. B14 284-5

Bayshore Gardens, Fla.	J2	156-7
Bayside, Me.	K6	64-5
Bayside, Ont.	K12	284-5
Bayside*, Wis.	J15	140-1
Bayside Garden, Ore.	B4	238-9
Baysville, Ont.	I8	284-5
Baytown, Tex.	H15	192-3
Bayview*, Fla.	C5	156-7
Bayview, Ida.	C3	218-9
Bayview [-Pine Hills], Calif.	E1	210-1
Bayville, Del.	K6	153
Bayville, N.J.	J7	76-7
Bayville, N.Y.	D16	80-1
Baywood, La.	G8	168-9
Baywood-Los Osos*, Calif.	L4	210-1
Bazaar, Kans.	H12	108-9
Bazemore, Ala.	D4	146-7
Bazile Mills, Nebr.	D12	124-5
Bazine, Kans.	G6	108-9
Beach, N. Dak.	G1	128-9
Beach City, O.	D9	132-3
Beach Haven, N.J.	L7	76-7
Beach Point, P.E.I.	G10	287
Beachburg, Ont.	G13	284-5
Beachville*, Ont.	D13	284-5
Beachwood, N.J.	J7	76-7
Beachwood, O.	B15	132-3
Beacon, Ia.	H10	104-5
Beacon, N.Y.	I11	80-1
Beacon, Tenn.	C5	188-9
Beacon Falls, Conn.	G7	60-1
Beacon Hill, Miss.	C9	176-7
Beacon Hill, Wash.	I7	246-7
Beacon Squier*, Fla.	F10	156-7
Beaconia*, Man.	K5	272-3
Beaconsfield, Ia.	J6	104-5
Beaconsfield*, Que.	J12	290-1
Beadle, co., S. Dak.	E12	136-7
Beagle, Kans.	G16	108-9
Beale East*, Calif.	G4	210-1
Beale West*, Calif.	G4	210-1
Bealeton, Va.	B2	196-7
Beallsville, O.	G11	132-3
Beals, Me.	K10	64-5
Beaman, Ia.	E9	104-5
Bean Station, Tenn.	G14	188-9
Bear, Del.	B3	153
Bear, Ida.	I2	218-9
Bear Creek, Ala.	C4	146-7
Bear Creek, N.C.	I5	180-1
Bear Creek, Wis.	D3	140-1
Bear Hollow Village*, Ark.	D2	150-1
Bear Island, N.B.	I4	275
Bear-Island, Ont.	G8	284-5
Bear Lake*, B.C.	F5	268-9
Bear Lake, Mich.	G11	112-3
Bear Lake, co., Ida.	N11	218-9
Bear River, N.S.	E4	281
Bear River City, Ut.	D6	242-3
Bear Spring, Tenn.	A5	188-9
Bear Springs, Ore.	C8	238-9
Bearcreek, Mont.	H10	222-3
Beard, W. Va.	H6	200-1
Bearden, Ark.	I6	150-1
Bearden, Okla.	F13	234-5
Beardmore, Ont.	F4	284-5
Beardsley, Ariz.	H6	206-7
Beardsley, Kans.	D3	108-9
Beardsley, Minn.	K1	116-7
Beardstown, Ill.	G5	96-7
Beardstown, Tenn.	C5	188-9
Beargrass, N.C.	D13	180-1
Bearmouth, Mont.	E4	222-3
Béarn*, Que.	I1	290-1
Beatrice, Ala.	K5	146-7
Beatrice, Nebr.	I14	124-5
Beatrice, W. Va.	E4	200-1
Beattie, Kans.	C12	108-9
Beatty, Miss.	F7	176-7
Beatty, Nev.	L7	226-7
Beatty, Ore.	J8	238-9
Beatty, Sask.	J8	294-5
Beattyville, Ky.	H13	164-5
Beaubier, Sask.	O9	294-5
Beauce, co., Que.	H16	290-1
Beauceville, Que.	H16	290-1
Beaufort, N.C.	F14	180-1
Beaufort, S.C.	J11	184-5
Beaufort, co., N.C.	E14	180-1
Beaufort, co., S.C.	J10	184-5
Beaufort Station*, S.C.	J11	184-5
Beauharnois, Que.	J12	290-1
Beauharnois, co., Que.	J11	290-1
Beaulac, Que.	I16	290-1
Beaulieu*, Que.	F11	290-1
Beaumont, Alta.	J8	264-5
Beaumont, Calif.	G11	210-1
Beaumont, Kans.	I12	108-9
Beaumont, Ky.	J9	164-5
Beaumont, Miss.	L9	176-7
Beaumont*, Que.	G12	290-1
Beaumont, Tex.	G11	192-3
Beauport*, Que.	F11	290-1
Beaupré, Que.	F12	290-1
Beauregard, Miss.	K5	176-7
Beauregard, co., La.	G2	168-9
Beausejour, Man.	I15	272-3
Beauty, Ky.	H15	164-5
Beauval, Sask.	G6	294-5
Beauvue, Md.	H11	172-3
Beaux Arts, Wash.	I3	246-7
Beaver, Alaska	C12	254-5
Beaver, Ark.	A3	150-1
Beaver, Ia.	F6	104-5
Beaver, Kans.	G8	108-9
Beaver, La.	F4	168-9
Beaver, O.	I7	132-3
Beaver, Okla.	C5	234-5
Beaver, Ore.	C4	238-9
Beaver, Pa.	H1	84-5
Beaver, Ut.	K3	242-3
Beaver, Wash.	D5	246-7
Beaver, W. Va.	K16	200-1
Beaver, co., Okla.	C5	234-5
Beaver, co., Pa.	H1	84-5
Beaver, co., Ut.	K3	242-3
Beaver Bay, Minn.	H9	116-7
Beaver City, Nebr.	J8	124-5
Beaver Creek, Md.	B7	172-3
Beaver Creek, Minn.	O2	116-7
Beaver Creek, Y.T.	C1	297
Beaver Crossing, Nebr.	H13	124-5
Beaver Dam, Ky.	I6	164-5
Beaver Dam, Wis.	I13	140-1
Beaver Falls*, B.C.	J6	268-9
Beaver Falls, Pa.	G1	84-5
Beaver Isl., Mich.	E11	112-3
Beaver Lake, Ark.	A3	150-1
Beaver Lake*, Sask.	N10	294-5
Beaver Marsh, Ore.	H8	238-9
Beaver Meadows, Pa.	G13	84-5
Beaverbank*, N.S.	E7	281
Beaverbank Villa*, N.S.	E7	281
Beaverdale-Lloydell, Pa.	I6	84-5
Beaverdam, O.	D4	132-3
Beaverdam, Va.	G12	196-7
Beaverdell, B.C.	J9	268-9
Beaverhead, co., Mont.	H4	222-3
Beaverlodge, Alta.	G3	264-5
Beaverton, Ala.	D3	146-7
Beaverton, Mich.	H13	112-3
Beaverton, Mont.	B12	222-3
Beaverton*, Ont.	B15	284-5
Beaverton, Ore.	F2	238-9
Bebee, W. Va.	D5	200-1
Bécancour, Que.	H14	290-1
Beckemeyer, Ill.	K7	96-7
Becker, Minn.	L5	116-7
Becker, Miss.	D10	176-7
Becker, co., Minn.	H3	116-7
Becket, Mass.	D3	68-9
Becket Center, Mass.	D3	68-9
Beckham, co., Okla.	F6	234-5
Beckley, W. Va.	I4	200-1
Beckton, Wyo.	B11	250-1
Beckwith, W. Va.	J16	200-1
Beckwith, Wyo.	H5	250-1
Beda, Ky.	I6	164-5
Beddington, Me.	J9	64-5
Bedeque, P.E.I.	E5	287
Bedford, Ind.	L7	100-1
Bedford, Ia.	J5	104-5
Bedford, Ky.	F9	164-5
Bedford, Mass.	G3	68-9
Bedford, N.H.	N6	72-3
Bedford, O.	B15	132-3
Bedford, Pa.	J6	84-5
Bedford, Que.	J13	290-1
Bedford, Tex.	C13	192-3
Bedford, Va.	I8	196-7
Bedford, Wyo.	F5	250-1
Bedford, co., Pa.	J6	84-5
Bedford, co., Tenn.	C8	188-9
Bedford, co., Va.	I8	196-7
Bedford Heights, O.	B15	132-3
Bedminster, N.J.	E5	76-7
Bee, Nebr.	H13	124-5
Bee, Okla.	I12	234-5
Bee, co., Tex.	I8	192-3
Bee Bayou, La.	B6	168-9
Bee Branch, Ark.	D6	150-1
Bee Log, N.C.	D4	180-1
Bee Ridge, Fla.	K3	156-7
Bee Spring, Ky.	I8	164-5
Beebe, Ark.	E8	150-1
Beebe Plain, Que.	K14	290-1
Beebe Plain, Vt.	B8	90-1
Beebe River, N.H.	I6	72-3
Beech Bluff, Tenn.	C4	188-9
Beech Bottom, W. Va.	B5	200-1
Beech Creek, Ky.	I6	164-5
Beech Creek, Ore.	E12	238-9
Beech Grove, Ark.	B11	150-1
Beech Grove, Ind.	F2	100-1
Beech Grove, Ky.	H5	164-5
Beech Springs, Tenn.	H13	188-9
Beecher, Ill.	O4	96-7
Beecher Falls, Vt.	B11	90-1
Beechgrove, Tenn.	I8	188-9
Beechwood*, Mich.	I11	112-3
Beechwood, Wis.	H4	140-1
Beechwood Village*, Ky.	G9	164-5
Beechy, Sask.	M6	294-5
Beedeville, Ark.	D10	150-1
Beehive, Mont.	H9	222-3
Beekman, La.	A6	168-9
Beeler, Kans.	G5	108-9
Beemer, Nebr.	F14	124-5
Beersheba Springs, Tenn.	J10	188-9
Beesleys Point, N.J.	N5	76-7
Beeton, Ont.	B14	284-5
Beetown, Wis.	K10	140-1
Beeville, Tex.	I8	192-3
Beggs, La.	G5	168-9
Beggs, Okla.	E13	234-5
Beirne, Ark.	H4	150-1
Beiseker, Alta.	L8	264-5
Bejou, Minn.	G2	116-7
Bel, La.	G3	168-9
Bel Air, Md.	B12	172-3
Bel Air North*, Md.	B12	172-3
Bel Air South*, Md.	B12	172-3
Bel Alton, Md.	G10	172-3
Bel-Nor*, Mo.	E10	120-1
Bel-Ridge*, Mo.	E10	120-1
Beland, Okla.	E14	234-5
Belcamp, Md.	C12	172-3
Belcher, La.	A1	168-9
Belcher Isl., N.W. Terr.	D3	296
Belchertown, Mass.	D6	68-9
Belcourt, N. Dak.	B9	128-9
Belden, Miss.	C9	176-7
Belden, Nebr.	D13	124-5
Beldenville, Wis.	F7	140-1
Belding, Mich.	I12	112-3
Belding, Ore.	B5	238-9
Belen, Miss.	C5	176-7
Belen, N. Mex.	G5	230-1
Belfair, Wash.	I1	246-7
Belfast, Ark.	G6	150-1
Belfast, Me.	K6	64-5
Belfast, Tenn.	J7	188-9
Belfield, N. Dak.	G3	128-9
Belford, N.J.	H11	76-7
Belfry, Ky.	H16	164-5
Belfry, Mont.	H10	222-3
Belgium, Ill.	G11	96-7
Belgium, Wis.	H5	140-1
Belgrade, Me.	K4	64-5
Belgrade, Minn.	L4	116-7
Belgrade, Mont.	G7	222-3
Belgrade, Nebr.	G11	124-5
Belgrade Lakes, Me.	K4	64-5
Belgreen, Ala.	C3	146-7
Belhaven, N.C.	E14	180-1
Belington, W. Va.	E15	200-1
Belk, Ala.	E3	146-7
Belknap, Mont.	C1	222-3
Belknap, co., N.H.	K7	72-3
Belknap Springs, Ore.	F7	238-9
Belkofski, Alaska	I8	254-5
Bell*, Calif.	G8	210-1
Bell, Fla.	C9	156-7
Bell, co., Ky.	K13	164-5
Bell, co., Tex.	F8	192-3
Bell Acres*, Pa.	H2	84-5
Bell Buckle, Tenn.	J8	188-9
Bell Center, Wis.	I10	140-1
Bell City, La.	H3	168-9
Bell City, Mo.	I11	120-1
Bell Ewart*, Ont.	B15	284-5
Bell Gardens*, Calif.	G8	210-1
Bell Ranch, N. Mex.	E10	230-1
Bella Coola, B.C.	H5	268-9
Bella Villa*, Mo.	F10	120-1
Bella Vista, Ark.	A2	150-1
Bellaire, Kans.	D8	108-9
Bellaire, Mich.	F12	112-3
Bellaire, O.	F11	132-3
Bellaire, Tex.	H13	192-3
Bellamy, Ala.	I3	146-7
Bellamy, Va.	E3	196-7
Bellbrook, O.	I15	132-3
Belle, Mo.	F8	120-1
Belle, W. Va.	I14	200-1
Belle Center, O.	E5	132-3
Belle Chasse, La.	D15	168-9
Belle Fourche, S. Dak.	D1	136-7
Belle Glade, Fla.	H13	156-7
Belle Haven, Va.	H15	196-7
Belle Isle, Fla.	F7	156-7
Belle Mead, N.J.	F5	76-7
Belle Meade, Tenn.	H7	188-9
Belle Mina, Ala.	B6	146-7
Belle Plaine, Ia.	F11	104-5
Belle Plaine, Kans.	J11	108-9
Belle Plaine, Minn.	C9	116-7
Belle Plaine*, Sask.	N7	294-5
Belle River, Ont.	F10	284-5
Belle River, P.E.I.	G8	287
Belle Rose, La.	C10	168-9
Belle Terre*, N.Y.	J12	80-1
Belle Valley, O.	G9	132-3
Belle Vernon, Pa.	J2	84-5
Belle View, Va.	B4	196-7
Belleair, Fla.	H1	156-7
Belleair Beach, Fla.	H1	156-7
Belleair Bluffs*, Fla.	F9	156-7
Belleair Shores*, Fla.	H1	156-7
Bellechasse, co., Que.	G12	290-1
Bellechester, Minn.	N7	116-7
Belledune*, N.B.	D5	275
Bellefeuille*, Que.	I11	290-1
Bellefond, N.B.	F6	275
Bellefont, Kans.	I6	108-9
Bellefontaine, Miss.	E8	176-7
Bellefontaine, O.	E5	132-3
Bellefontaine Neighbors, Mo.	B16	120-1
Bellefonte, Ark.	B5	150-1
Bellefonte, Del.	A4	153
Bellefonte, Ky.	F15	164-5
Bellefonte, Pa.	G8	84-5
Bellegarde, Sask.	O11	294-5
Bellemeade*, Ky.	G9	164-5
Bellemont, Ariz.	E7	206-7
Belleoram, Nfld.	O9	278-9
Belleplain, N.J.	N4	76-7
Bellerive*, Mo.	E10	120-1
Bellerose*, N.Y.	J11	80-1
Belleterre, Que.	I1	290-1
Belleview, Fla.	D10	156-7
Belleview, Ky.	E10	164-5
Belleview, Tenn.	H6	188-9
Belleville, Ark.	E4	150-1
Belleville, Ill.	L6	96-7
Belleville, Ind.	I7	100-1
Belleville, Kans.	D10	108-9
Belleville, Mich.	K5	112-3
Belleville, N.J.	C10	76-7
Belleville, Ont.	K12	284-5
Belleville, Pa.	H8	84-5
Belleville, R.I.	F5	87
Belleville, Tenn.	K7	188-9
Belleville, W. Va.	E3	200-1
Belleville, Wis.	J1	140-1
Bellevue, Alta.	O7	264-5
Bellevue, Ida.	M6	218-9
Bellevue, Ill.	F7	96-7
Bellevue, Ia.	E15	104-5
Bellevue, Ky.	D11	164-5
Bellevue, La.	B2	168-9
Bellevue, Md.	G12	172-3
Bellevue, Mich.	J13	112-3
Bellevue, Nebr.	G15	124-5
Bellevue, O.	C7	132-3
Bellevue, Ore.	C5	238-9
Bellevue, Pa.	A6	84-5
Bellevue*, Que.	B9	290-1
Bellevue, Sask.	K7	294-5
Bellevue, Wash.	I3	246-7
Bellewood*, Ky.	G9	164-5
Bellflower, Calif.	H8	210-1
Bellflower, Mo.	D8	120-1
Bellfountain, Ore.	E5	238-9
Bellglade Camp*, Fla.	H13	156-7
Bellinger, S.C.	K10	184-5
Bellingham, Mass.	K1	68-9
Bellingham, Minn.	L2	116-7
Bellingham, Wash.	C8	246-7
Belliveau Cove, N.S.	E4	281
Bellmawr, N.J.	J3	76-7
Bellmead*, Tex.	E8	192-3
Bellmore, Ind.	H5	100-1
Bellmore, N.Y.	F16	80-1
Bellows Falls, Vt.	M7	90-1
Bellport, N.Y.	J13	80-1
Bells, Tenn.	J4	188-9
Bells*, Tex.	C9	192-3
Bellsite, Man.	D9	272-3
Bellview, N. Mex.	F11	230-1
Bellville, Ga.	K9	160-1
Bellville, O.	E7	132-3
Bellville, Tex.	G9	192-3
Bellvue, Colo.	D2	214-5
Bellwood, Ala.	L9	146-7
Bellwood, Ill.	M3	96-7
Bellwood, La.	E3	168-9
Bellwood, Nebr.	G13	124-5
Bellwood, Pa.	H7	84-5
Bellwood, W. Va.	I5	200-1
Belmar, N.J.	H8	76-7
Belmond, Ia.	C8	104-5
Belmont, Calif.	D7	210-1
Belmont, Kans.	J9	108-9
Belmont, Ky.	C2	164-5
Belmont, La.	D2	168-9
Belmont, Me.	K6	64-5
Belmont, Man.	J11	272-3
Belmont, Mass.	H4	68-9
Belmont, Miss.	B11	176-7
Belmont, Mont.	F10	222-3
Belmont, N.H.	K7	72-3
Belmont, N.Y.	G4	80-1
Belmont, N.C.	J1	180-1
Belmont, O.	F11	132-3
Belmont, Ont.	E12	284-5
Belmont, Vt.	K5	90-1
Belmont, Va.	G12	196-7
Belmont, Wash.	G16	246-7
Belmont, W. Va.	D4	200-1
Belmont, Wis.	K11	140-1
Belmont, co., O.	F11	132-3
Belmont South*, N.C.	C8	180-1
Belmont-South Rosemary*, N.C.	C12	180-1
Belmore, O.	C4	132-3
Beloeil*, Que.	I12	290-1
Beloit, Kans.	E9	108-9
Beloit, O.	D11	132-3
Beloit, Wis.	K13	140-1
Beloit West*, Wis.	K13	140-1
Belpre, Kans.	I7	108-9
Belpre, O.	H9	132-3
Belspring, Va.	I6	196-7
Belt, Mont.	D7	222-3
Belton, Ky.	I6	164-5
Belton, Mo.	K15	120-1
Belton, S.C.	H1	184-5
Belton, Tex.	F8	192-3
Beltrami, Minn.	G2	116-7
Beltrami, co., Minn.	F4	116-7
Beltsville, Md.	H5	172-3
Belva, Okla.	C8	234-5
Belva, W. Va.	I15	200-1
Belvedere, Calif.	C7	210-1
Belvedere, S.C.	F7	184-5
Belvidere, Ill.	A9	96-7
Belvidere, Kans.	J7	108-9
Belvidere, Nebr.	J12	124-5
Belvidere, N.J.	D3	76-7
Belvidere, N.C.	C14	180-1
Belvidere, S. Dak.	G7	136-7
Belvidere, Tenn.	K8	188-9
Belvidere*, Vt.	C6	90-1
Belview, Minn.	M3	116-7
Belvue, Kans.	E13	108-9
Belwood, N.C.	E6	180-1
Belzoni, Miss.	F5	176-7
Bement, Ill.	H9	96-7
Bemidji, Minn.	G4	116-7
Bemis, S. Dak.	D15	136-7
Bemis, Tenn.	J4	188-9
Bemis, W. Va.	F16	200-1
Bemiss, Ga.	N6	160-1
Ben Avon*, Pa.	H2	84-5
Ben Hill, co., Ga.	L6	160-1
Ben Hur, Ark.	C5	150-1
Ben Hur, Va.	J2	196-7
Ben Lomond, Ark.	H2	150-1
Ben Lomond*, Calif.	J3	210-1
Bena, Minn.	H5	116-7
Benavides, Tex.	J7	192-3
Benbrook, Tex.	D12	192-3
Bench, Ida.	O10	218-9
Benchland, Mont.	E8	222-3
Bend, Ore.	F8	238-9

Bendale, S.C. E10 184-5
Bendena, Kans. D15 108-9
Benedict, Kans. I14 108-9
Benedict, Md. G11 172-3
Benedict, Nebr. H12 124-5
Benedict, N. Dak. E7 128-9
Benedicta, Me. F8 64-5
Benevolence, Ga. L3 160-1
Benewah, co., Ida. D2 218-9
Benfield, Md. H6 172-3
Bengal, Okla. G15 234-5
Benge, Wash. G15 246-7
Bengough, Sask. O8 294-5
Benham, Ky. J14 164-5
Benicia, Calif. B8 210-1
Benito, Man. F9 272-3
Benjamin, Tex. D6 192-3
Benjamin, Ut. G6 242-3
Benkelman, Nebr. J5 124-5
Benld, Ill. J7 96-7
Benndale, Miss. M9 176-7
Bennet, Nebr. H14 124-5
Bennett, Colo. D12 214-5
Bennett, Ia. G14 104-5
Bennett, N. Mex. L11 230-1
Bennett, N.C. I5 180-1
Bennett, co., S. Dak. . . . H5 136-7
Bennetts Pier, Del. G5 153
Bennettsville, S.C. C14 184-5
Bennettsville Southwest, S.C. C13 184-4
Bennington, Ida. O11 218-9
Bennington, Kans. F10 108-9
Bennington, Mich. G2 112-3
Bennington, Nebr. I2 124-5
Bennington, N.H. N5 72-3
Bennington, Okla. I13 234-5
Bennington, Vt. N4 90-1
Bennington, co., Vt. . . . N4 90-1
Benoit, Miss. E4 176-7
Benoit's Cove, Nfld. . . . M7 278-9
Bens Run, W. Va. D4 200-1
Bensenville*, Ill. B10 96-7
Benson, Ariz. L9 206-7
Benson, La. D2 168-9
Benson, Md. C12 172-3
Benson, Minn. L3 116-7
Benson, N.C. J7 180-1
Benson, Sask. O9 294-5
Benson, Ut. C6 242-3
Benson*, Vt. I3 90-1
Benson, co., N. Dak. . . . D9 128-9
Bent, N. Mex. J7 230-1
Bent, co., Colo. H15 214-5
Bent Mountain, Va. I7 196-7
Bentley, Alta. K7 264-5
Bentley, Kans. I10 108-9
Bentley, La. E4 168-9
Bentley, Mich. G13 112-3
Bentley, N. Dak. I5 128-9
Bentley, Okla. H13 234-5
Bentleyville*, O. B10 132-3
Bentleyville, Pa. J2 84-5
Benton, Ala. I6 146-7
Benton, Ark. F6 150-1
Benton, Ill. M9 96-7
Benton, Ind. B9 100-1
Benton, Ia. J6 104-5
Benton, Kans. I11 108-9
Benton, Ky. J3 164-5
Benton, La. B2 168-9
Benton, Me. K5 64-5
Benton, Miss. G6 176-7
Benton, Mo. I12 120-1
Benton, N.B. H3 275
Benton, N.H. H5 72-3
Benton, Pa. F12 84-5
Benton, Tenn. K13 188-9
Benton, Wis. K11 140-1
Benton, co., Ark. A2 150-1
Benton, co., Ind. E4 100-1
Benton, co., Ia. F11 104-5
Benton, co., Minn. K5 116-7
Benton, co., Miss. B8 176-7
Benton, co., Mo. F5 120-1
Benton, co., Ore. E5 238-9
Benton, co., Tenn. B5 188-9
Benton, co., Wash. I12 246-7
Benton Central*, Mich. . J11 112-3
Benton City, Mo. D8 120-1
Benton City, Wash. I12 246-7
Benton Harbor, Mich. . . J11 112-3
Benton Ridge, O. C5 132-3
Benton South*, Mich. . . J11 112-3
Benton Station, Me. K5 64-5
Bentonia, Miss. H5 176-7
Bentonite Spur, Wyo. . . . B16 250-1
Bentonville, Ark. A2 150-1
Bentonville, Va. A1 196-7
Bentree, W. Va. I15 200-1
Benwood, W. Va. C5 200-1
Benz, Mont. E14 222-3
Benzie, co., Mich. F11 112-3
Benzien, Mont. D11 222-3
Benzonia, Mich. F11 112-3
Beowawe, Nev. D7 226-7
Berclair, Miss. E5 176-7
Berdell Hills*, Mo. E10 120-1
Berea, Ky. E8 164-5
Berea, N.C. C11 180-1
Berea, O. B13 132-3
Berea*, S.C. F2 184-5
Berea, W. Va. E5 200-1
Berenice, Ida. L8 218-9
Berens River, Man. E14 272-3
Beresford*, N.B. E5 275
Beresford, S. Dak. I16 136-7
Bergen, N.Y. E4 80-1
Bergen, N. Dak. D7 128-9
Bergen, co., N.J. C8 76-7
Bergenfield, N.J. A12 76-7
Berger, Ida. O6 218-9
Berger, Mo. E8 120-1
Bergholz, O. E11 132-3
Bergland, Mich. C7 112-3
Bergman, Ark. A5 150-1
Bergoo, W. Va. G6 200-1
Bergton, Va. F10 196-7
Berino, N. Mex. L6 230-1
Berkeley, Calif. C7 210-1
Berkeley*, Ill. B11 96-7
Berkeley, Mo. B15 120-1
Berkeley*, N.J. I7 76-7
Berkeley, R.I. B5 87
Berkeley, co., S.C. H13 184-5
Berkeley, co., W. Va. . . . D11 200-1
Berkeley Heights, N.J. . . E6 76-7
Berkeley Lake, Ga. B11 160-1
Berkeley Springs, W. Va. D11 200-1
Berkey, O. A5 132-3
Berkley, Ia. F6 104-5
Berkley, Mass. G11 68-9
Berkley, Mich. I6 112-3
Berks, co., Pa. H13 84-5
Berkshire, Mass. C2 68-9
Berkshire, Vt. B6 90-1
Berkshire, co., Mass. . . . D2 68-9
Berlin, Conn. E9 60-1
Berlin, Ga. N5 160-1
Berlin, Md. H16 172-3
Berlin, Mass. D9 68-9
Berlin, Nev. G5 226-7
Berlin, N.H. E8 72-3
Berlin*, N.J. J4 76-7
Berlin, N.J. J4 76-7
Berlin, N. Dak. I11 128-9
Berlin, Okla. F7 234-5
Berlin, Pa. J5 84-5
Berlin, Vt. F6 90-1
Berlin, Wis. H13 140-1
Berlin Heights, O. C7 132-3
Bern, Ida. O11 218-9
Bern, Kans. C13 108-9
Bernalillo, N. Mex. F6 230-1
Bernalillo, co., N. Mex. . F5 230-1
Bernard, Ia. E14 104-5
Bernard, Me. L8 64-5
Bernards*, N.J. E5 76-7
Bernardston, Mass. B5 68-9
Bernardsville, N.J. E5 76-7
Berne, Ind. E11 100-1
Bernice, La. A4 168-9
Bernice, Okla. C15 234-5
Bernie, Mo. J11 120-1
Bernierville, Que. H15 290-1
Berrien, co., Ga. M6 160-1
Berrien, co., Mich. K11 112-3
Berrien Springs, Mich. . . K11 112-3
Berry, Ala. E4 146-7
Berry, Ky. F11 164-5
Berry Head, Port au Port*, Nfld. N7 278-9
Berry Hill, Tenn. H7 188-9
Berryburg, W. Va. D15 200-1
Berry's Chapel*, Tenn. . . B7 188-9
Berryton, Ga. E2 160-1
Berryton, Kans. F14 108-9
Berrytown, Del. G3 153
Berryville, Ark. A4 150-1
Berryville, Va. E11 196-7
Bertha, Minn. J4 116-7
Berthier, co., Que. I2 290-1
Berthier-sur-Mer, Que. . . F12 290-1
Berthierville, Que. H13 290-1
Berthold, N. Dak. D5 128-9
Berthoud, Colo. E3 214-5
Bertie, co., N.C. C14 180-1
Bertram, Ia. F13 104-5
Bertram, Tex. F8 192-3
Bertrand, Mo. I12 120-1
Bertrand, Nebr. I9 124-5
Bertrand*, N.B. E6 275
Bertrandville, La. D15 168-9
Bertsch Terrace, Calif. . . D1 210-1
Berville, Mich. G6 112-3
Berwick, Kans. C14 108-9
Berwick, La. E9 168-9
Berwick, Me. O2 64-5
Berwick, N. Dak. D8 128-9
Berwick, N.S. D5 281
Berwick, Ont. H16 284-5
Berwick, Pa. F12 84-5
Berwind, W. Va. K3 200-1
Berwyn, Alta. F5 264-5
Berwyn, Ill. M3 96-7
Berwyn, Nebr. G9 124-5
Berwyn Heights, Md. . . . I5 172-3
Beryl, Ut. L3 242-3
Beryl, W. Va. D9 200-1
Bessemer, Ala. F6 146-7
Bessemer, Mich. D7 112-3
Bessemer, Pa. G1 84-5
Bessemer City, N.C. . . . E6 180-1
Bessie, Okla. F8 234-5
Bessmay-Buna*, Tex. . . . G11 192-3
Bethalto, Ill. J6 96-7
Bethania, N.C. G3 180-1
Bethany, Conn. G7 60-1
Bethany, Ill. H9 96-7
Bethany, Ind. I7 100-1
Bethany, La. B1 168-9
Bethany, Man. I11 272-3
Bethany, Mo. B4 120-1
Bethany, Okla. J1 234-5
Bethany, Ont. B16 284-5
Bethany*, Sask. K6 294-5
Bethany, W. Va. B5 200-1
Bethany Beach, Del. . . . J6 153
Betheden, Miss. F9 176-7
Bethel, Alaska F8 254-5
Bethel, Conn. G4 60-1
Bethel, Del. E3 153
Bethel, Del. J3 153
Bethel, Ky. G13 164-5
Bethel, Me. K2 64-5
Bethel, Minn. L6 116-7
Bethel, Mo. B7 120-1
Bethel, N.C. D13 180-1
Bethel, O. I4 132-3
Bethel, Okla. H16 234-5
Bethel, Ore. K1 238-9
Bethel, Tenn. E7 188-9
Bethel, Tenn. H11 188-9
Bethel, Vt. I6 90-1
Bethel Acres, Okla. K4 234-5
Bethel Heights, Ark. . . . A2 150-1
Bethel Island*, Calif. . . . I3 210-1
Bethel Park, Pa. B6 84-5
Bethel Springs, Tenn. . . . D4 188-9
Bethera, S.C. G13 184-5
Bethesda, Ark. C8 150-1
Bethesda, Md. I3 172-3
Bethesda, N.C. H7 180-1
Bethesda, O. F10 132-3
Bethlehem, Conn. E6 60-1
Bethlehem, Ga. F5 160-1
Bethlehem, Md. F13 172-3
Bethlehem, N.H. G6 72-3
Bethlehem*, N.J. E3 76-7
Bethlehem, Pa. H15 84-5
Bethlehem, Tenn. H7 188-9
Bethlehem, W. Va. C5 200-1
Bethpage, N.Y. E16 80-1
Bethpage, Tenn. F8 188-9
Bethune, Colo. E16 214-5
Bethune, Sask. M7 294-5
Bethune, S.C. C12 184-5
Bettendorf, Ia. H15 104-5
Betterton, Md. C13 172-3
Bettles, Alaska C11 254-5
Bettsville, O. C6 132-3
Between, Ga. F5 160-1
Beulah, Ala. H10 146-7
Beulah, Ark. F9 150-1
Beulah, Colo. H11 214-5
Beulah, Ky. I5 164-5
Beulah, Man. I9 272-3
Beulah, Mich. F11 112-3
Beulah, Miss. E4 176-7
Beulah, N. Dak. F5 128-9
Beulah, Ore. F14 238-9
Beulah, Wyo. B16 250-1
Beulah Heights, Ky. J11 164-5
Beulahville, Va. H13 196-7
Beulaville, N.C. F12 180-1
Bevent, Wis. F12 140-1
Beverly, Kans. F9 108-9
Beverly, Mass. C12 68-9
Beverly, Miss. C5 176-7
Beverly, N.J. I4 76-7
Beverly, O. G9 132-3
Beverly, Sask. N5 294-5
Beverly, S.C. B6 184-5
Beverly, Wash. G12 246-7
Beverly, W. Va. F15 200-1
Beverly Beach, Fla. D12 156-7
Beverly Farms, Mass. . . . C13 68-9
Beverly Hills, Calif. G8 210-1
Beverly Hills, Mich. I5 112-3
Beverly Hills*, Mo. E10 120-1
Beverly Hills*, Tex. E8 192-3
Beverly Shores, Ind. A6 100-1
Bevier, Mo. C6 120-1
Bevil Oaks*, Tex. G11 192-3
Bevington, Ia. H7 104-5
Bewdley, Ont. K11 284-5
Bexar, Ala. C3 146-7
Bexar, Ark. A7 150-1
Bexar, co., Tex. H7 192-3
Bexley, Miss. M10 176-7
Bexley, O. F6 132-3
Bibb, co., Ala. G5 146-7
Bibb, co., Ga. I5 160-1
Bibb City, Ga. J2 160-1
Bibbville, Ala. F5 146-7
Bible Hill, N.S. D7 281
Bic, Que. C15 290-1
Bickerton West, N.S. . . . D9 281
Bickleton, Wash. I11 246-7
Bickley, Ga. M8 160-1
Bickmore, W. Va. H16 200-1
Bicknell, Ind. L5 100-1
Bicknell, Ut. K6 242-3
Biddeford, Me. N3 64-5
Biddle, Mont. H15 222-3
Biddles Corner, Del. . . . C3 153
Bideford*, P.E.I. D4 287
Bield, Man. G9 272-3
Bienfait, Sask. O10 294-5
Bienville, La. B3 168-9
Bienville, co., La. B3 168-9
Big Arm, Mont. C3 222-3
Big Bay, Mich. C9 112-3
Big Bear, Calif. F11 210-1
Big Bear City, Calif. . . . F11 210-1
Big Beaver*, Pa. G1 84-5
Big Beaver, Sask. O8 294-5
Big Bend, La. F6 168-9
Big Bend, N. Dak. F6 128-9
Big Bend*, Wis. J14 140-1
Big Black River*, Man. . G4 272-3
Big Bow, Kans. J2 108-9
Big Cabin, Okla. C15 234-5
Big Cane, La. F5 168-9
Big Canyon, Nev. E2 226-7
Big Cedar, Okla. G16 234-5
Big Chimney, W. Va. . . . H14 200-1
Big Clifty, Ky. H8 164-5
Big Creek, Ky. I13 164-5
Big Creek, Miss. D8 176-7
Big Creek, W. Va. J12 200-1
Big Delta, Alaska E12 254-5
Big Eddy*, B.C. K9 268-9
Big Eddy*, Man. B10 272-3
Big Falls, Minn. F6 116-7
Big Falls, Wis. D2 140-1
Big Flat, Ark. B7 150-1
Big Flats, N.Y. G5 80-1
Big Fork, Ark. G3 150-1
Big Horn, Wyo. B11 250-1
Big Horn, co., Mont. . . . H11 222-3
Big Horn, co., Wyo. . . . B10 250-1
Big Island, Va. H9 196-7
Big Lake, Alaska C11 254-5
Big Lake, Alaska F11 254-5
Big Lake, Minn. L6 116-7
Big Lake, Tex. F5 192-3
Big Lake, Wash. E3 246-7
Big Oak Corner, Del. . . . E3 153
Big Otter, W. Va. G4 200-1
Big Pine, Calif. J7 210-1
Big Piney, Wyo. G6 250-1
Big Pool, Md. B6 172-3
Big Prairie*, Alta. G6 264-5
Big Rapids, Mich. H12 112-3
Big River, Sask. I6 294-5
Big Rock, Tenn. A5 188-9
Big Rock, Va. I4 196-7
Big Run, W. Va. D5 200-1
Big Sandy, Mont. C8 222-3
Big Sandy, Tenn. B5 188-9
Big Sandy*, Tex. E10 192-3
Big Sandy, Wyo. G7 250-1
Big Spring, Md. B6 172-3
Big Spring, Tenn. J12 188-9
Big Spring, Tex. E5 192-3
Big Springs, Kans. F14 108-9
Big Springs, Nebr. H4 124-5
Big Stone, co., Minn. . . . L2 116-7
Big Stone Beach, Del. . . G5 153
Big Stone City, S. Dak. . C16 136-7
Big Stone Gap, Va. J2 196-7
Big Sur, Calif. K3 210-1
Big Timber, Mont. G8 222-3
Big Trails, Wyo. D11 250-1
Big Valley, Alta. K8 264-5
Big Wells, Tex. I6 192-3
Bigbee, Miss. D10 176-7
Bigbee Valley, Miss. . . . F10 176-7
Bigbend, W. Va. F4 200-1
Bigelow, Ark. H14 150-1
Bigelow, Minn. O3 116-7
Bigelow, Mo. B1 120-1
Bigfork, Minn. G6 116-7
Bigfork, Mont. C3 222-3
Biggar, Sask. L5 294-5
Biggers, Ark. A10 150-1
Biggersville, Miss. B10 176-7
Biggs, Calif. G3 210-1
Biggs, Ore. B9 238-9
Biggs*, Tex. E1 192-3
Bighorn, Mont. F12 222-3
Bighorn R., Mont. G11 222-3
Biglerville, Pa. J10 84-5
Bigpoint, Miss. N10 176-7
Bill, Wyo. E14 250-1
Billerica, Mass. C11 68-9
Billings, Mo. I4 120-1
Billings, Mont. G10 222-3
Billings, Okla. C11 234-5
Billings, co., N. Dak. . . . G2 128-9
Billingsley, Ala. H6 146-7
Billington Heights*, N.Y. F3 80-1
Billstown, Ark. H4 150-1
Biloxi, Miss. N9 176-7
Biltmore, Tenn. G17 188-9
Biltmore Forest, N.C. . . E4 180-1
Bim, W. Va. K13 200-1
Binford, N. Dak. F11 128-9
Bingamon, W. Va. B13 200-1
Bingen, Wash. J9 246-7
Binger, Okla. F9 234-5
Bingham, Me. I4 64-5
Bingham, Nebr. E4 124-5
Bingham, N. Mex. H6 230-1
Bingham, S.C. C14 184-5
Bingham, co., Ida. M10 218-9
Bingham Canyon*, Ut. . . F6 242-3
Bingham Farms*, Mich. . J14 112-3
Bingham Lake, Minn. . . . O4 116-7
Binghamton, N.Y. G7 80-1
Binscarth, Man. H9 272-3
Bippus, Ind. D10 100-1
Birch Bay, Wash. B7 246-7
Birch Harbor, Me. K9 64-5
Birch Hills, Sask. J7 294-5
Birch Hills Park*, Alta. . J7 264-5
Birch Island, B.C. I8 268-9
Birch River, Man. E9 272-3
Birch River, W. Va. G5 200-1
Birch Run, Mich. F3 112-3
Birch Tree, Mo. I8 120-1
Birchleaf, Va. I3 196-7
Birchton, W. Va. K14 200-1
Birchwood, Alaska F11 254-5
Birchwood*, Minn. L7 116-7
Birchwood, Tenn. K12 188-9
Birchwood, Wis. D9 140-1
Birchwood City*, Md. . . E10 172-3
Bird, Man. D5 272-3
Bird City, Kans. D2 108-9
Bird Island, Minn. M4 116-7
Birdeye, Ark. D11 150-1
Birds Hill*, Man. I14 272-3
Birdsboro, Pa. I14 84-5
Birdseye, Ind. N6 100-1
Birdseye, Ut. G7 242-3
Birdsnest, Va. E5 196-7
Birdsong, Ark. D12 150-1
Birdsville, Ky. I3 164-5

Birdsville, Md. J7 172-3
Birkenfeld, Ore. A5 238-9
Birmingham, Ala. E6 146-7
Birmingham, Ga. A11 160-1
Birmingham, Ia. J12 104-5
Birmingham, Mich. I5 112-3
Birmingham, Mo. I15 120-1
Birnamwood, Wis. F13 140-1
Birney, Mont. H13 222-3
Birnie, Man. I11 272-3
Biron, Wis. G12 140-1
Birsay, Sask. M6 294-5
Birta, Ark. E5 150-1
Birtle, Man. H9 272-3
Bisbee, Ariz. M10 206-7
Bisbee, N. Dak. C10 128-9
Biscay, Minn. B7 116-7
Biscayne Park*, Fla. H16 156-7
Biscoe, N.C. J4 180-1
Biscotasing, Ont. G7 284-5
Bishop, Calif. J7 210-1
Bishop, Ga. F6 160-1
Bishop, Md. G16 172-3
Bishop, Tex. J8 192-3
Bishop, Va. I5 196-7
Bishop, Wyo. F12 250-1
Bishops Corner, Del. E3 153
Bishop's Falls, Nfld. M9 278-9
Bishops Head, Md. H13 172-3
Bishops Mills, Ont. I15 284-5
Bishopville, Md. G16 172-3
Bishopville, S.C. D12 184-5
Bismarck, Ark. G5 150-1
Bismarck, Mo. G10 120-1
Bismarck, N. Dak. H7 128-9
Bison, Kans. G7 108-9
Bison, Okla. D10 234-5
Bison, S. Dak. B4 136-7
Bissell, Miss. C9 176-7
Bissett, Man. G16 272-3
Bitely, Mich. H11 112-3
Bithlo, Fla. F8 156-7
Bitter Creek, Wyo. I9 250-1
Bittern Lake, Alta. J8 264-5
Bittinger, Md. B2 172-3
Bivalve, Md. H13 172-3
Biwabik, Minn. G8 116-7
Bixby, N.C. H2 180-1
Bixby, Okla. E14 234-5
Bjorkdale, Sask. K9 294-5
Blachly, Ore. F5 238-9
Black, Ala. M9 146-7
Black Creek, B.C. J5 268-9
Black Creek, N.C. D12 180-1
Black Creek, Wis. E3 140-1
Black Diamond, Alta. M7 264-5
Black Diamond, Wash. J3 246-7
Black Eagle, Mont. D7 222-3
Black Earth, Wis. J12 140-1
Black Forest, Colo. J4 214-5
Black Hawk, Colo. G1 214-5
Black Hawk, La. F6 168-9
Black Hawk, Miss. F6 176-7
Black Hawk, S. Dak. F2 136-7
Black Hawk, co., Ia. E11 104-5
Black Hills, S. Dak. E2 136-7
Black Horse, Md. B11 172-3
Black Jack*, Mo. B15 120-1
Black Lake, Que. H15 290-1
Black Lick, Pa. H4 84-5
Black Mountain, N.C. D4 180-1
Black Oak, Ark. C11 150-1
Black Oak*, Ind. A5 100-1
Black Point, Conn. H12 60-1
Black River, Mich. F14 112-3
Black River, N.Y. C7 80-1
Black River Falls, Wis. G10 140-1
Black Rock, Ark. B10 150-1
Black Rock, N. Mex. F2 230-1
Black Rock, Ore. D5 238-9
Black Rock, Ut. J4 242-3
Black Springs, Ark. G3 150-1
Black Springs, Nev. F2 226-7
Blackberry City, W. Va. J2 200-1
Blackbird, Del. D3 153
Blackburn, La. A3 168-9
Blackburn, Mo. D5 120-1
Blackburn, Okla. D12 234-5
Blackburn Hamlet*, Ont. H15 284-5
Blackduck, Minn. G4 116-7
Blackfalds, Alta. K8 264-5
Blackfoot, Alta. J10 264-5
Blackfoot, Ida. M9 218-9
Blackfoot, Mont. B5 222-3
Blackford, Ky. I4 164-5
Blackford, co., Ind. E10 100-1
Blackgum, Okla. E15 234-5
Blackhawk, Ind. J9 100-1
Blackhead Road*, Nfld. N11 278-9
Blackie, Alta. M8 264-5
Blackiston, Del. E3 153
Blacklick Estates*, O. F7 132-3
Blackridge, Va. J11 196-7
Blacks Harbour, N.B. J4 275
Blacksburg, S.C. A9 184-5
Blacksburg, Va. I7 196-7
Blackshear, Ga. M9 160-1
Blackstock, S.C. C10 184-5
Blackstone, Mass. F9 68-9
Blackstone, Va. I11 196-7
Blacksville, W. Va. A14 200-1
Blacktail, Mont. B4 222-3
Blackton, Ark. F10 150-1
Blackville, N.B. G5 275
Blackville, S.C. G9 184-5
Blackwater, Mo. D5 120-1
Blackwater, Va. J2 196-7
Blackwell, Ark. D5 150-1
Blackwell, Okla. C11 234-5
Blackwood, N.J. O10 76-7
Bladen, Nebr. I11 124-5
Bladen, co., N.C. F11 180-1
Bladenboro, N.C. G11 180-1
Bladenboro North*, N.C. G11 180-1
Bladensburg, Md. I4 172-3
Blades, Del. J3 153
Bladon Springs, Ala. K2 146-7
Bladworth, Sask. L7 294-5
Blaine, Kans. D12 108-9
Blaine, Ky. G15 164-5
Blaine, Me. D9 64-5
Blaine, Minn. A10 116-7
Blaine, Miss. E5 176-7
Blaine, Ore. C4 238-9
Blaine, Tenn. H12 188-9
Blaine, Wash. B7 246-7
Blaine, co., Ida. M7 218-9
Blaine, co., Mont. B10 222-3
Blaine, co., Nebr. F8 124-5
Blaine, co., Okla. E9 234-5
Blaine Lake*, Sask. K6 294-5
Blainville*, Que. I12 290-1
Blair, Kans. D15 108-9
Blair, Nebr. F15 124-5
Blair, Okla. G7 234-5
Blair, S.C. I7 184-5
Blair, W. Va. K13 200-1
Blair, Wis. G9 140-1
Blair, co., Pa. H6 84-5
Blair Junction, Nev. I5 226-7
Blair Mills, S.C. H1 184-5
Blairmore, Alta. O7 264-5
Blairs, Va. J9 196-7
Blairsburg, Ia. E7 104-5
Blairstown, Ia. F11 104-5
Blairstown, Mo. E4 120-1
Blairstown, N.J. C4 76-7
Blairsville, Ga. D5 160-1
Blairsville, Ind. O3 100-1
Blairsville, Pa. I3 84-5
Blaisdell, Ariz. J2 206-7
Blaisdell, N. Dak. D5 128-9
Blakely, Ark. F5 150-1
Blakely, Ga. M2 160-1
Blakely, Pa. E14 84-5
Blakesburg, Ia. I10 104-5
Blalock, Ore. B10 238-9
Blanca, Colo. I11 214-5
Blanch, N.C. C10 180-1
Blanchard, Ida. C2 218-9
Blanchard, Ia. K4 104-5
Blanchard, La. B1 168-9
Blanchard, Me. H5 64-5
Blanchard, Mich. H12 112-3
Blanchard, N. Dak. F14 128-9
Blanchard, Okla. F10 234-5
Blanchard, Wash. C8 246-7
Blanchardville, Wis. K12 140-1
Blanche, Ala. C9 146-7
Blanchester, O. K16 132-3
Blanco, N. Mex. C4 230-1
Blanco, Okla. G14 234-5
Blanco, Tex. G7 192-3
Blanco, co., Tex. G7 192-3
Bland, Mo. F8 120-1
Bland, Va. I6 196-7
Bland, co., Va. I6 196-7
Blandford, Mass. E3 68-9
Blanding, Ut. L10 242-3
Blandinsville, Ill. F4 96-7
Blandon, Pa. I13 84-5
Blandville, Ky. J2 164-5
Blandville, W. Va. E5 200-1
Blaney Park, Mich. D11 112-3
Blanford, Ind. I4 100-1
Blanks, La. G6 168-9
Blasdell, N.Y. F2 80-1
Blatchford, Mont. E14 222-3
Blauvelt, N.Y. C14 80-1
Blawenburg, N.J. G5 76-7
Blawnox*, Pa. H2 84-5
Bleckley, co., Ga. J6 160-1
Bledsoe, co., Tenn. C10 188-9
Bleecker, Ala. H10 146-7
Blencoe, Ia. F2 104-5
Blenheim, N.J. O10 76-7
Blenheim, Ont. F11 284-5
Blenheim, S.C. C14 184-5
Blenker, Wis. F11 140-1
Blennerhassett Isl., W. Va. E3 200-1
Blevins, Ark. H4 150-1
Blind Bay, B.C. I8 268-9
Blind River, Ont. H6 284-5
Bliss, Ida. N5 218-9
Blissfield, Mich. K14 112-3
Blissfield, N.B. G5 275
Blissville, Vt. J4 90-1
Blitzen, Ore. I12 238-9
Blocher, Ind. L9 100-1
Block City, Tenn. F15 188-9
Block Isl., R.I. K3 87
Block Island, R.I. K4 87
Blocker, Okla. G14 234-5
Blockhouse, Wash. J10 246-7
Blockton, Ia. K5 104-5
Blodgett, Mo. I12 120-1
Blodgett, Ore. E5 238-9
Blomkest, Minn. M4 116-7
Bloom, Kans. J5 108-9
Bloom City, Wis. I10 140-1
Bloomdale, O. C5 132-3
Bloomer, Ark. D2 150-1
Bloomer, Wis. E9 140-1
Bloomery, W. Va. D10 200-1
Bloomfield, Conn. C9 60-1
Bloomfield, Ind. K6 100-1
Bloomfield, Ia. J10 104-5
Bloomfield, Ky. C4 164-5
Bloomfield, Mo. I11 120-1
Bloomfield, Mont. D15 222-3
Bloomfield, Nebr. D12 124-5
Bloomfield, N.J. C10 76-7
Bloomfield, N. Mex. C3 230-1
Bloomfield, Nfld. N10 278-9
Bloomfield, Ont. K12 284-5
Bloomfield, Pa. I10 84-5
Bloomfield, Vt. C10 90-1
Bloomfield Corner, P.E.I. C3 287
Bloomfield Hills, Mich. I5 112-3
Bloomfield Ridge, N.B. I5 275
Blooming Grove*, Tex. E9 192-3
Blooming Prairie, Minn. O7 116-7
Bloomingburg, O. G6 132-3
Bloomingdale, Ga. K11 160-1
Bloomingdale, Ill. L2 96-7
Bloomingdale, Ind. H5 100-1
Bloomingdale, Mich. J11 112-3
Bloomingdale, N.J. C7 76-7
Bloomingdale, N.Y. B10 80-1
Bloomingdale*, O. E11 132-3
Bloomingdale*, Tenn. A15 188-9
Bloomingdale, Wis. I10 140-1
Bloomingrose, W. Va. I13 200-1
Bloomington*, Calif. N8 210-1
Bloomington, Ida. O11 218-9
Bloomington, Ill. F8 96-7
Bloomington, Ind. K7 100-1
Bloomington, Kans. E8 108-9
Bloomington, Md. C2 172-3
Bloomington, Minn. B10 116-7
Bloomington, Nebr. J10 124-5
Bloomington*, Tex. H9 192-3
Bloomington, Wis. J10 140-1
Bloomsburg, Pa. F12 84-5
Bloomsbury, N.J. E3 76-7
Bloomsdale, Mo. E16 120-1
Bloomville, O. C6 132-3
Blossburg, Mont. F5 222-3
Blossburg, Pa. D10 84-5
Blossom, Tex. C10 192-3
Blount, W. Va. H14 200-1
Blount, co., Ala. D6 146-7
Blount, co., Tenn. C13 188-9
Blount Springs, Ala. D6 146-7
Blounts Creek, N.C. E14 180-1
Blountstown, Fla. B6 156-7
Blountsville, Ala. D7 146-7
Blountsville, Ind. G11 100-1
Blountville, Tenn. F16 188-9
Blowing Rock, N.C. C5 180-1
Bloxom, Va. H16 196-7
Blue, Ariz. H11 206-7
Blue Anchor, N.J. K4 76-7
Blue Ash, O. K14 132-3
Blue Ball, Ark. E3 150-1
Blue Brick, S.C. D14 184-5
Blue Creek, Ut. C5 242-3
Blue Creek, W. Va. H14 200-1
Blue Diamond, Nev. M9 226-7
Blue Dome, Ida. K8 218-9
Blue Earth, Minn. O5 116-7
Blue Earth, co., Minn. O5 116-7
Blue Eye, Ark. A4 150-1
Blue Eye, Mo. J5 120-1
Blue Grass, Ia. H15 104-5
Blue Grass, Va. F8 196-7
Blue Hill, Me. K7 64-5
Blue Hill, Nebr. I11 124-5
Blue Hill Falls, Me. K7 64-5
Blue Island, Ill. N4 96-7
Blue Lake, Calif. E1 210-1
Blue Mesa Res., Colo. G7 214-5
Blue Mound, Ill. H8 96-7
Blue Mound, Kans. H15 108-9
Blue Mound, Tex. C13 192-3
Blue Mounds, Wis. J12 140-1
Blue Mountain, Ala. E8 146-7
Blue Mountain, Ark. E3 150-1
Blue Mountain, Colo. C5 214-5
Blue Mountain, Miss. B9 176-7
Blue Rapids, Kans. D12 108-9
Blue Ridge, Alta. I6 264-5
Blue Ridge, Ga. D4 160-1
Blue Ridge, Va. I8 196-7
Blue Ridge Manor*, Ky. F9 164-5
Blue Ridge Mts. 14-15
Blue River, B.C. H8 268-9
Blue River, Colo. E10 214-5
Blue River, Ore. F7 238-9
Blue River, Wis. J10 140-1
Blue Springs, Ala. K9 146-7
Blue Springs, Ark. F5 150-1
Blue Springs, Miss. C9 176-7
Blue Springs, Mo. J16 120-1
Blue Springs, Nebr. J14 124-5
Blue Summit*, Mo. D3 120-1
Bluebell, Ut. F9 242-3
Blueberry Creek*, B.C. J10 268-9
Bluecreek, Wash. D15 246-7
Bluefield, Va. I5 196-7
Bluefield, W. Va. K4 200-1
Bluehole, Ky. J13 164-5
Bluejacket, Okla. C15 234-5
Bluemont, Va. E12 196-7
Bluesky, Alta. F4 264-5
Bluewater, N. Mex. F3 230-1
Bluff, Ut. M10 242-3
Bluff City, Ark. I5 150-1
Bluff City, Kans. K9 108-9
Bluff City, Tenn. F16 188-9
Bluff Park, Ala. F6 146-7
Bluffdale, Ut. F6 242-3
Bluffs, Ill. H5 96-7
Bluffton, Alta. K7 264-5
Bluffton, Ark. E4 150-1
Bluffton, Ga. M3 160-1
Bluffton, Ind. D11 100-1
Bluffton, Minn. I3 116-7
Bluffton, O. D4 132-3
Bluffton, S.C. J10 184-5
Blumenfeld, Man. K13 272-3
Blumenheim*, Sask. K6 294-5
Blumenhof, Sask. N5 294-5
Blumenort, Man. J15 272-3
Blumenort*, Man. K13 272-3
Blumenort, Sask. N5 294-5
Blumenthal, Sask. K6 294-5
Blunt, S. Dak. E9 136-7
Bly, Ore. J9 238-9
Blyth, Ont. C12 284-5
Blythe, Calif. N11 210-1
Blythe, Ga. H9 160-1
Blythedale, Mo. A4 120-1
Blytheville, Ark. B12 150-1
Blythewood, S.C. D10 184-5
Board Camp, Ark. F2 150-1
Boardman, O. C11 132-3
Boardman, Ore. B11 238-9
Boardman, Wis. E7 140-1
Boardman Bridge, Conn. E4 60-1
Boatman, Okla. D15 234-5
Boaz, Ala. C8 146-7
Boaz, Nev. C9 226-7
Boaz, Wis. I10 140-1
Bobcaygeon, Ont. A16 284-5
Bobo, Miss. D5 176-7
Bobtown, Pa. K2 84-5
Boca Chica*, Fla. K11 156-7
Boca Grande, Fla. H10 156-7
Boca Raton, Fla. F16 156-7
Bock, Minn. K6 116-7
Bodcaw, Ark. I4 150-1
Bode, Ia. C6 104-5
Boelus, Nebr. H11 124-5
Boerne, Tex. G7 192-3
Bogalusa, La. G10 168-9
Bogard, Mo. C5 120-1
Bogart, Ga. F6 160-1
Bogata, Tex. D10 192-3
Boger City, N.C. E6 180-1
Boggs, W. Va. G5 200-1
Boggstown, Ind. G3 100-1
Boggy Creek, Man. F9 272-3
Boggy Depot, Okla. H13 234-5
Bognor, Ont. B13 284-5
Bogota, N.J. B11 76-7
Bogota, Tenn. B2 188-9
Bogue, Kans. E6 108-9
Bogue Chitto, Miss. K5 176-7
Bohemia, La. J10 168-9
Bohemia*, N.Y. K12 80-1
Bohners Lake*, Wis. K14 140-1
Bohon, Ky. D5 164-5
Boicourt, Kans. H16 108-9
Boiestown, N.B. G4 275
Boiling Spring Lakes*, N.C. H12 180-1
Boiling Springs, N.C. E5 180-1
Boiling Springs, Pa. J10 84-5
Boiling Springs, S.C. E4 184-5
Bois-des-Filion*, Que. I12 290-1
Boisbriand*, Que. J3 290-1
Boise, Ida. L3 218-9
Boise, co., Ida. K4 218-9
Boise City, Okla. C2 234-5
Boissevain, Man. K10 272-3
Boissevain, Va. I5 196-7
Bokchito, Okla. I13 234-5
Bokhoma, Okla. I16 234-5
Bokoshe, Okla. F16 234-5
Bolair, W. Va. G6 200-1
Bolar, Va. G8 196-7
Bolckow, Mo. B2 120-1
Bold Spring, Tenn. B6 188-9
Bolduc, Que. H16 290-1
Boles, Ark. F2 150-1
Boles, N. Mex. K7 230-1
Boley, Okla. F13 234-5
Boligee, Ala. H3 146-7
Bolingbrook, Ill. N2 96-7
Bolinger, Ala. K2 146-7
Bolinger, La. A2 168-9
Bolivar, La. F9 168-9
Bolivar, Miss. E4 176-7
Bolivar, Mo. G5 120-1
Bolivar, N.Y. G3 80-1
Bolivar, O. D10 132-3
Bolivar, Tenn. D3 188-9
Bolivar*, W. Va. E12 200-1
Bolivar, co., Miss. D4 176-7
Bolivia, N.C. H12 180-1
Bolling, Ala. K6 146-7
Bollinger, co., Mo. H11 120-1
Bolsters Mills, Me. M8 64-5
Bolt, W. Va. K15 200-1
Bolton, Conn. D11 60-1
Bolton, Mass. C9 68-9
Bolton, Miss. I5 176-7
Bolton, N.C. G11 180-1
Bolton, Vt. E5 90-1
Boltonville, Wis. H4 140-1
Boma, Tenn. B9 188-9
Bombay Hook Point, Del. D4 153
Bomont, W. Va. H15 200-1
Bomoseen, Vt. J4 90-1
Bon Accord, Alta. I8 264-5
Bon Air, Ala. F7 146-7
Bon Air, Tenn. B10 188-9
Bon Air*, Va. H12 196-7
Bon Aqua, Tenn. H5 188-9
Bon Homme, Miss. L8 176-7
Bon Homme, co., S. Dak. I13 136-7
Bon Homme Colony, S. Dak. I14 136-7
Bon Secour, Ala. O4 146-7
Bon Secours*, Ont. B14 284-5
Bonaire, Ga. J6 160-1

Bonanza, Ark. D2 150-1
Bonanza, Colo. G10 214-5
Bonanza, Ore. J8 238-9
Bonanza, Ut. G11 242-3
Bonaparte, Ia. J12 104-5
Bonaventure, Que. I6 290-1
Bonaventure, co., Que. I5 290-1
Bonavista, Nfld. M11 278-9
Boncarbo, Colo. J12 214-5
Bond, Ky. I12 164-5
Bond, co., Ill. J8 96-7
Bondhead*, Ont. A14 284-5
Bondsville, Mass. E6 68-9
Bonduel, Wis. D3 140-1
Bondurant, Ia. G8 104-5
Bondurant, Wyo. K2 250-1
Bondville, Ky. C5 164-5
Bondville, Vt. M5 90-1
Bone, Ida. M10 218-9
Bone Cave, Tenn. I10 188-9
Bonesteel, S. Dak. I11 136-7
Boneta, Ut. F9 242-3
Boneville, Ga. G8 160-1
Bonfield, Mont. E14 222-3
Bonfield*, Ont. H8 284-5
Bonham, S.C. G6 184-5
Bonham, Tex. D9 192-3
Bonifay, Fla. B5 156-7
Bonilla, S. Dak. E12 136-7
Bonita, Ariz. K10 206-7
Bonita, La. A6 168-9
Bonita, Miss. I10 176-7
Bonita Springs, Fla. I11 156-7
Bonlee, N.C. I5 180-1
Bonne Terre, Mo. F15 120-1
Bonneau, S.C. G13 184-5
Bonner, Mont. E3 222-3
Bonner, co., Ida. C3 218-9
Bonner Springs, Kans. E16 108-9
Bonners Ferry, Ida. A3 218-9
Bonnertown, Tenn. D6 188-9
Bonneville, Ore. B7 238-9
Bonneville, Wyo. E10 250-1
Bonneville, co., Ida. M10 218-9
Bonneville Dam, Wash. J8 246-7
Bonney Lake, Wash. K3 246-7
Bonnie Doone, N.C. K6 180-1
Bonnie Rigg Corners, Mass. D3 68-9
Bonnieville, Ky. I8 164-5
Bonnyview, Calif. F3 210-1
Bonnyville, Alta. H10 264-5
Bono, Ark. C10 150-1
Bonshaw, P.E.I. F6 287
Bonwood, Tenn. J4 188-9
Book, La. E5 168-9
Booker, Tex. A6 192-3
Boomer, N.C. D6 180-1
Boomer, W. Va. I15 200-1
Boon, Mich. G12 112-3
Boone, Colo. H13 214-5
Boone, Ia. F7 104-5
Boone, Ky. E8 164-5
Boone, Nebr. F12 124-5
Boone, N.C. C5 180-1
Boone, Okla. G9 234-5
Boone, co., Ark. A5 150-1
Boone, co., Ill. A9 96-7
Boone, co., Ind. G7 100-1
Boone, co., Ia. F7 104-5
Boone, co., Ky. D11 164-5
Boone, co., Mo. D7 120-1
Boone, co., Nebr. F11 124-5
Boone, co., W. Va. H3 200-1
Boones Mill, Va. I8 196-7
Boonesville, Va. G10 196-7
Booneville, Ark. E3 150-1
Booneville, Ky. I13 164-5
Booneville, Miss. B10 176-7
Boonsboro, Md. B7 172-3
Boonsboro, Md. E14 172-3
Boonton*, N.J. D6 76-7
Boonton, N.J. D6 76-7
Boonville, Calif. G2 210-1
Boonville, Ind. O5 100-1
Boonville, Mo. D6 120-1
Boonville, N.Y. D8 80-1
Boonville, N.C. G2 180-1
Booth, Ala. H7 146-7
Booth, W. Va. B15 200-1
Boothbay, Me. N11 64-5
Boothbay Harbor, Me. N11 64-5
Boothville, La. J11 168-9
Borah, Ida. N8 218-9
Bordeaux, Tenn. G7 188-9
Bordeaux, Wyo. H15 250-1
Bordelonville, La. F5 168-9
Borden, P.E.I. F5 287
Borden, Sask. K6 294-5
Borden, S.C. E12 184-5
Borden, co., Tex. D5 192-3
Borden [New Providence], Ind. M9 100-1
Bordentown*, N.J. H5 76-7
Bordentown, N.J. H5 76-7
Bordulac, N. Dak. F10 128-9
Boreing, Ky. J12 164-5
Borger, Tex. A5 192-3
Boring, Md. B10 172-3
Boring, Ore. C7 238-9
Boron, Calif. M8 210-1
Borree Corner, Ariz. J7 206-7
Borrego Springs, Calif. O9 210-1
Borup, Minn. H2 116-7
Boscawen, N.H. L6 72-3
Bosco, La. C5 168-9
Boscobel, Wis. J10 140-1
Bosler, Wyo. I14 250-1
Bosler Junction, Wyo. I14 250-1
Bosque, Ariz. J5 206-7
Bosque, N. Mex. G5 230-1
Bosque, co., Tex. E8 192-3
Bossier, co., La. A2 168-9
Bossier City, La. B2 168-9
Bostic*, N.C. E5 180-1
Boston, Ga. O5 160-1
Boston, Ind. H12 100-1
Boston, Ky. D2 164-5
Boston, Mass. D11 68-9
Boston, Tenn. I6 188-9
Boston, Tex. D11 192-3
Boston, Va. B1 196-7
Boston Bar, B.C. J7 268-9
Boston Harbor, Wash. K1 246-7
Boston Heights, O. C15 132-3
Bostwick, Ga. G6 160-1
Bostwick, Nebr. J11 124-5
Boswell, Ind. E4 100-1
Boswell, Okla. I14 234-5
Boswell, Pa. J5 84-5
Boswell Bay, Alaska F12 254-5
Bosworth, Mo. C5 120-1
Botetourt, co., Va. H8 196-7
Botha, Alta. K9 264-5
Bothell, Wash. H3 246-7
Bothwell, Ont. E11 284-5
Bothwell, Ut. C5 242-3
Botkinburg, Ark. C6 150-1
Botkins, O. E4 132-3
Botsford, Conn. G5 60-1
Bottineau, N. Dak. B8 128-9
Bottineau, co., N. Dak. B6 128-9
Botwood, Nfld. M9 278-9
Boucherville*, Que. I12 290-1
Boudreau*, N.B. H7 275
Boulder, Colo. D11 214-5
Boulder, Mont. F6 222-3
Boulder, Ut. L7 242-3
Boulder, Wyo. G7 250-1
Boulder, co., Colo. D11 214-5
Boulder City, Nev. N10 226-7
Boulder Creek*, Calif. J3 210-1
Boulder Junction, Wis. C12 140-1
Boulogne, Fla. B10 156-7
Bound Brook, N.J. F6 76-7
Boundary, co., Ida. A3 218-9
Boundary Dam*, Sask. O9 294-5
Bountiful, Ut. E6 242-3
Bounty, Sask. L6 294-5
Bourbon, Ind. B8 100-1
Bourbon, Miss. F4 176-7
Bourbon, Mo. F9 120-1
Bourbon, co., Kans. I16 108-9
Bourbon, co., Ky. G12 164-5
Bourbonnais, Ill. D11 96-7
Bourg, La. J8 168-9
Bourget*, Ont. H15 284-5
Bourne, Mass. G14 68-9
Bouse, Ariz. H3 206-7
Boutiliers Point*, N.S. E7 281
Bouton, Ia. G7 104-5
Boutte, La. D13 168-9
Bovey, Minn. H6 116-7
Bovill, Ida. E3 218-9
Bovina, Miss. I4 176-7
Bovina, Tex. C4 192-3
Bow*, N.H. M6 72-3
Bow, Wash. C8 246-7
Bow Island, Alta. N10 264-5
Bow Mar*, Colo. H3 214-5
Bow Valley, Nebr. D13 124-5
Bowbells, N. Dak. B4 128-9
Bowden, Alta. L7 264-5
Bowden, W. Va. F16 200-1
Bowdens, N.C. F12 180-1
Bowdle, S. Dak. B10 136-7
Bowdoin*, Me. M10 64-5
Bowdoin Center, Me. M10 64-5
Bowdoinham, Me. M10 64-5
Bowdon, Ga. G2 160-1
Bowdon, N. Dak. F9 128-9
Bowdon Junction, Ga. G2 160-1
Bowen, W. Va. I10 200-1
Bowen Island, B.C. B13 268-9
Bowerbank, Me. H6 64-5
Bowers, Del. G4 153
Bowers Beach, Del. G4 153
Bowerston, O. E10 132-3
Bowersville, Ga. E7 160-1
Bowersville, O. I16 132-3
Bowesmont, N. Dak. C14 128-9
Bowie, Ariz. K11 206-7
Bowie, Colo. F7 214-5
Bowie, Md. I6 172-3
Bowie, Tex. D8 192-3
Bowie, co., Tex. D11 192-3
Bowlegs, Okla. F12 234-5
Bowler, Wis. C2 140-1
Bowling Green, Fla. J5 156-7
Bowling Green, Ind. J5 100-1
Bowling Green, Ky. J7 164-5
Bowling Green, Mo. C8 120-1
Bowling Green, O. B5 132-3
Bowling Green, S.C. A9 184-5
Bowling Green, Va. G12 196-7
Bowlsville, Vt. K5 90-1
Bowlus, Minn. K5 116-7
Bowman, Ga. E7 160-1
Bowman, N. Dak. I2 128-9
Bowman, S.C. G11 184-5
Bowman, co., N. Dak. J2 128-9
Bowman-Auburn North*, Calif. H4 210-1
Bowmans Corner, Mont. D6 222-3
Bowmont, Ida. M3 218-9
Bowring, Okla. C13 234-5
Bowser, B.C. J6 268-9
Bowsman, Man. E9 272-3
Box, Okla. E15 234-5
Box Butte, co., Nebr. E2 124-5
Box Elder, Mont. B8 222-3
Box Elder, S. Dak. F3 136-7
Box Elder, co., Ut. D3 242-3
Boxborough, Mass. G1 68-9
Boxelder, Wyo. G13 250-1
Boxford, Mass. B12 68-9
Boxholm, Ia. F6 104-5
Boy River, Minn. H5 116-7
Boyce, La. E4 168-9
Boyce, Va. A1 196-7
Boyceville, Wis. E8 140-1
Boyd, Ala. H2 146-7
Boyd, Minn. M2 116-7
Boyd, Mont. H10 222-3
Boyd, Tex. B12 192-3
Boyd, Wis. F10 140-1
Boyd, co., Ky. F15 164-5
Boyd, co., Nebr. C10 124-5
Boyd Lake, Me. H7 64-5
Boydell, Ark. J9 150-1
Boyden, Ia. B2 104-5
Boyden Arbor, S.C. E10 184-5
Boyds, Md. G2 172-3
Boyds, Wash. C14 246-7
Boyds Corner, Del. C3 153
Boydsville, Ark. A11 150-1
Boydton, Va. J11 196-7
Boyer, S.C. G12 184-5
Boyer, W. Va. G7 200-1
Boyero, Colo. F14 214-5
Boyertown, Pa. I14 84-5
Boyes, Mont. H15 222-3
Boyes Hot Springs, Calif. B7 210-1
Boykin, Ala. J5 146-7
Boykin, Ala. M6 146-7
Boykin, Ga. N3 160-1
Boykins, Va. K13 196-7
Boyle, Alta. H8 264-5
Boyle, Miss. E5 176-7
Boyle, co., Ky. H10 164-5
Boyleston, Ind. F7 100-1
Boylston, Ala. I7 146-7
Boylston, Mass. D8 68-9
Boyne City, Mich. F12 112-3
Boyne Falls, Mich. F12 112-3
Boynton, Okla. E14 234-5
Boynton Beach, Fla. E16 156-7
Boys Town, Nebr. I2 124-5
Boysen Bay*, N.Y. E7 80-1
Bozeman, Mont. G7 222-3
Bozman, Md. F12 172-3
Bozoo, W. Va. J5 200-1
Bozrah, Conn. F12 60-1
Bozrah Street, Conn. F12 60-1
Bracebridge, Ont. A15 284-5
Braceville, Ill. D10 96-7
Bracey, Va. K11 196-7
Bracken, Nev. M9 226-7
Bracken, Sask. O5 294-5
Bracken, co., Ky. E12 164-5
Brackendale, B.C. A13 268-9
Brackenridge, Pa. A7 84-5
Brackett, Wis. F9 140-1
Brackettville, Tex. H6 192-3
Brackley, P.E.I. E7 287
Bradburn Hill, Tenn. G15 188-9
Bradbury*, Calif. G9 210-1
Braddock, N. Dak. H8 128-9
Braddock, Pa. B7 84-5
Braddock Heights, Md. E1 172-3
Braddock Hills*, Pa. I2 84-5
Braddyville, Ia. K4 104-5
Braden, Okla. F16 234-5
Braden, Tenn. K2 188-9
Bradenton, Fla. J2 156-7
Bradenton Beach, Fla. J2 156-7
Bradford, Ark. D9 150-1
Bradford, Ill. D7 96-7
Bradford, Ind. N8 100-1
Bradford, Ia. D8 104-5
Bradford, Me. I6 64-5
Bradford, N.H. L5 72-3
Bradford, O. F3 132-3
Bradford, Ont. B14 284-5
Bradford, Pa. C6 84-5
Bradford, R.I. H2 87
Bradford, Tenn. B3 188-9
Bradford, Vt. H8 90-1
Bradford, co., Fla. C10 156-7
Bradford, co., Pa. C12 84-5
Bradford Woods, Pa. A6 84-5
Bradfordsville, Ky. I10 164-5
Bradgate, Ia. D6 104-5
Bradley, Ala. M6 146-7
Bradley, Ark. K3 150-1
Bradley, Ga. H6 160-1
Bradley, Ill. D11 96-7
Bradley, Ky. H14 164-5
Bradley, Me. I7 64-5
Bradley, Okla. G10 234-5
Bradley, S.C. E7 184-5
Bradley, S. Dak. C14 136-7
Bradley, W. Va. K16 200-1
Bradley, co., Ark. I7 150-1
Bradley, co., Tenn. D11 188-9
Bradley Beach, N.J. H8 76-7
Bradley Gardens, N.J. F5 76-7
Bradley Junction, Fla. I4 156-7
Bradleyton, Ala. J7 146-7
Bradleyville, Conn. F6 60-1
Bradleyville, Mo. I6 120-1
Bradner, O. C5 132-3
Bradshaw, Nebr. H12 124-5
Bradshaw*, W. Va. J3 200-1
Bradwardine, Man. I10 272-3
Bradwell, Sask. L7 294-5
Bradwood, Ore. A5 238-9
Brady, Mont. C6 222-3
Brady, Nebr. H7 124-5
Brady, Tex. F7 192-3
Brady, Wash. G6 246-7
Brady Lake, O. D16 132-3
Bradys Hot Springs, Nev. F3 226-7
Bradyville, Tenn. C8 188-9
Braemar [-Hampton], Tenn. A16 188-9
Braeside, Ont. H14 284-5
Bragg City, Ark. I5 150-1
Bragg City, Mo. J11 120-1
Bragg Creek, Alta. M7 264-5
Braggs, Ala. J6 146-7
Braggs, Okla. E15 234-5
Braggville, Mass. J1 68-9
Braham, Minn. K6 116-7
Braidwood, Ill. D10 96-7
Brainard, Nebr. G13 124-5
Brainards, N.J. D3 76-7
Brainerd, Minn. J5 116-7
Braintree, Mass. J6 68-9
Braintree*, Vt. H6 90-1
Braithwaite, La. D15 168-9
Bralorne, B.C. I7 268-9
Braman, Okla. B11 234-5
Bramber, N.S. D6 281
Brampton, Mich. D10 112-3
Brampton, N. Dak. J13 128-9
Brampton, Ont. C14 284-5
Bramwell, W. Va. J4 200-1
Branch, Ark. D3 150-1
Branch, La. H5 168-9
Branch*, Minn. K7 116-7
Branch, Miss. H7 176-7
Branch, Nfld. O10 278-9
Branch, Wis. F5 140-1
Branch, co., Mich. K12 112-3
Branchburg*, N.J. F5 76-7
Branchburg Park, N.J. F5 76-7
Branchland, W. Va. I11 200-1
Branchville*, Ala. E7 146-7
Branchville, Conn. H4 60-1
Branchville, N.J. B5 76-7
Branchville, S.C. G11 184-5
Branchville, Va. K13 196-7
Brandenburg, Ky. G8 164-5
Brandon, Colo. G16 214-5
Brandon, Fla. H3 156-7
Brandon, Ia. E11 104-5
Brandon, Man. J2 272-3
Brandon, Minn. K3 116-7
Brandon, Miss. I6 176-7
Brandon, Nebr. H4 124-5
Brandon, S. Dak. G16 136-7
Brandon, Vt. I4 90-1
Brandon, Wis. G3 140-1
Brandonville, W. Va. A16 200-1
Brandsville, Mo. J8 120-1
Brandt, S. Dak. D16 136-7
Brandy Station, Va. B2 196-7
Brandywine, Del. A3 153
Brandywine, Md. K5 172-3
Brandywine, W. Va. G8 200-1
Brandywine Village*, Pa. J15 84-5
Branford, Conn. H8 60-1
Branford, Fla. C9 156-7
Bransford, Tenn. F8 188-9
Branson, Colo. J13 214-5
Branson, Mo. J5 120-1
Brant, Mich. F2 112-3
Brant, co., Ont. E14 284-5
Brant Rock, Mass. E13 68-9
Brantford, Kans. D10 108-9
Brantford, N. Dak. F10 128-9
Brantford, Ont. D13 284-5
Brantley, Ala. K7 146-7
Brantley, co., Ga. N9 160-1
Brantleyville, Ala. F6 146-7
Brantville, N.B. F6 275
Bras d'Or Lake, N.S. C10 281
Braselton, Ga. F5 160-1
Brasfield, Ark. F9 150-1
Brashear, Mo. B7 120-1
Brass Castle, N.J. D3 76-7
Brasstown, N.C. F1 180-1
Braswell, Ga. F2 160-1
Bratenahl, O. A14 132-3
Brattleboro, Vt. N6 90-1
Brattontown, Tenn. A9 188-9
Brawley, Calif. O10 210-1
Braxton, Miss. J6 176-7
Braxton, co., W. Va. F5 200-1
Bray, Okla. H10 234-5
Braymer, Mo. C4 120-1
Brayton, Ia. H4 104-5
Braytown, Tenn. H11 188-9
Brazil, Ind. I5 100-1
Brazil, Miss. D6 176-7
Brazil, Tenn. B3 188-9
Brazoria, Tex. K13 192-3
Brazoria, co., Tex. H10 192-3
Brazos, N. Mex. C6 230-1
Brazos, co., Tex. F9 192-3
Brazos R., Tex. G9 192-3
Brea*, Calif. G9 210-1
Breadalbane, P.E.I. E6 287
Breaks, Va. I3 196-7
Breathitt, co., Ky. H14 164-5
Breaux Bridge, La. H5 168-9
Breckenridge, Colo. E10 214-5
Breckenridge, Mich. E1 112-3
Breckenridge, Minn. J1 116-7
Breckenridge, Mo. C4 120-1
Breckenridge, Tex. D7 192-3
Breckenridge Hills*, Mo. E10 120-1
Breckinridge, Okla. D10 234-5
Breckinridge, co., Ky. H7 164-5
Brecksville, O. C14 132-3
Breda, Ia. E4 104-5
Bredenbury, Sask. M10 294-5
Breeden, W. Va. K11 200-1
Breedsville*, Mich. J11 112-3

Breese, Ill. K7 96-7
Breitenbush Hot Springs, Ore. D7 238-9
Bremen, Ga. G2 160-1
Bremen, Ind. B8 100-1
Bremen, Kans. C12 108-9
Bremen, Ky. I6 164-5
Bremen, Me. L5 64-5
Bremen, N. Dak. E10 128-9
Bremen, O. G8 132-3
Bremer, co., Ia. D10 104-5
Bremerton, Wash. I1 246-7
Bremo Bluff, Va. H11 196-7
Bremond, Tex. F9 192-3
Brenda, Ariz. H3 206-7
Brenford, Del. E3 153
Brenham, Tex. G9 192-3
Brent, Ala. G5 146-7
Brent, Fla. B3 156-7
Brentford, S. Dak. C12 136-7
Brenton, W. Va. J3 200-1
Brentwood, Calif. C9 210-1
Brentwood, Md. I4 172-3
Brentwood, Mo. B16 120-1
Brentwood, N.H. N8 72-3
Brentwood, N.Y. J12 80-1
Brentwood, Ont. B14 284-5
Brentwood, Pa. B6 84-5
Brentwood, Tenn. H7 188-9
Breslau, Ont. D13 284-5
Brethren, Mich. G11 112-3
Breton, Alta. J7 264-5
Breton Woods, N.J. I8 76-7
Bretton Woods, N.H. G7 72-3
Bretz, W. Va. B16 200-1
Brevard, N.C. E3 180-1
Brevard, co., Fla. F12 156-7
Brevort, Mich. D12 112-3
Brewer, Me. J7 64-5
Brewers Mills*, N.B. H4 275
Brewerton, N.Y. E7 80-1
Brewster, Kans. E2 108-9
Brewster, Mass. G16 68-9
Brewster, Minn. O3 116-7
Brewster, Nebr. F8 124-5
Brewster, N.Y. A16 80-1
Brewster, O. D9 132-3
Brewster, Wash. D12 246-7
Brewster, co., Tex. G3 192-3
Brewster Heights*, N.Y. I11 80-1
Brewster Hills*, N.Y. I11 80-1
Brewsters Trailer Court*, Sask. J7 294-5
Brewton, Ala. M5 146-7
Brewton, Ga. J7 160-1
Briar, Tex. C12 192-3
Briar Hill, Ala. J8 146-7
Briarcliff Manor, N.Y. B15 80-1
Briartown, Okla. F15 234-5
Briarwood*, Ky. G9 164-5
Briarwood Beach, O. D13 132-3
Bricelyn, Minn. O6 116-7
Briceville, Tenn. H11 188-9
Brick*, N.J. I8 76-7
Brick Town, N.J. I7 76-7
Brickeys, Ark. F11 150-1
Bricks, N.C. C12 180-1
Brickyard, Ala. I11 146-7
Bridal Veil, Ore. B7 238-9
Bridesville, B.C. K8 268-9
Bridge, Ida. O8 218-9
Bridge, Ore. H4 238-9
Bridge City, Tex. G11 192-3
Bridgeboro, Ga. M5 160-1
Bridgeland, Ut. G9 242-3
Bridgenorth, Ont. B16 284-5
Bridgeport, Ala. A9 146-7
Bridgeport, Calif. I6 210-1
Bridgeport, Conn. I6 60-1
Bridgeport, Ill. K11 96-7
Bridgeport, Kans. G10 108-9
Bridgeport, Mich. F3 112-3
Bridgeport, Nebr. F2 124-5
Bridgeport, N.J. J2 76-7
Bridgeport*, O. F11 132-3
Bridgeport, Okla. F9 234-5
Bridgeport, Ore. E14 238-9
Bridgeport, Pa. A10 84-5
Bridgeport, Tex. D8 192-3
Bridgeport, Ut. E11 242-3
Bridgeport, Wash. E12 246-7
Bridgeport, W. Va. C14 200-1
Bridger, Mont. H10 222-3
Bridgeton, Ind. I5 100-1
Bridgeton, Mo. B15 120-1
Bridgeton, N.J. M2 76-7
Bridgeton*, N.C. E14 180-1
Bridgeton, R.I. A2 87
Bridgeton Terrace*, Mo. E10 120-1
Bridgetown, N.S. E5 281
Bridgetown*, O. I3 132-3
Bridgetown, Va. E5 196-7
Bridgeview, Ill. M3 96-7
Bridgeville, Del. I3 153
Bridgeville, Pa. B6 84-5
Bridgewater, Conn. F5 60-1
Bridgewater, Ia. I5 104-5
Bridgewater, Me. D9 64-5
Bridgewater, Mass. F12 68-9
Bridgewater, Mich. K3 112-3
Bridgewater, N.H. J6 72-3
Bridgewater*, N.J. E5 76-7
Bridgewater*, N.Y. F8 80-1
Bridgewater, N.S. F6 281
Bridgewater*, Pa. G1 84-5
Bridgewater, S. Dak. G14 136-7
Bridgewater, Vt. J6 90-1
Bridgewater, Va. F9 196-7
Bridgman, Mich. K11 112-3
Bridgton, Me. M7 64-5
Bridport, Vt. H3 90-1
Brielle, N.J. H8 76-7
Briensburg, Ky. J3 164-5
Brier, Mass. B3 68-9
Brier*, Wash. E8 246-7
Briercrest, Sask. N7 294-5
Brierfield, Ala. G6 146-7
Brigantine, N.J. M6 76-7
Brigden*, Ont. E10 284-5
Briggsdale, Colo. C13 214-5
Briggsville, Ark. E4 150-1
Briggsville, Mass. B3 68-9
Briggsville, Wis. G1 140-1
Brigham City, Ut. D6 242-3
Bright, Ind. J12 100-1
Bright Star, Ark. H3 150-1
Brighton, Ala. F6 146-7
Brighton, Ark. B11 150-1
Brighton, Colo. F4 214-5
Brighton, Ill. J6 96-7
Brighton, Ind. A10 100-1
Brighton, Ia. I12 104-5
Brighton, Me. I5 64-5
Brighton, Mich. I3 112-3
Brighton, Ont. K12 284-5
Brighton, Ore. B4 238-9
Brighton, S.C. I9 184-5
Brighton, Tenn. J2 188-9
Brighton*, Vt. C9 90-1
Brights Grove, Ont. E10 284-5
Brightstar, Ark. K2 150-1
Brightwaters*, N.Y. K12 80-1
Brightwood, Ore. C7 238-9
Brightwood, Va. C1 196-7
Brigus*, Nfld. N11 278-9
Brill, Wis. D8 140-1
Brilliant, Ala. D4 146-7
Brilliant, O. E11 132-3
Brillion, Wis. F4 140-1
Brimfield, Ill. E7 96-7
Brimfield, Ind. B10 100-1
Brimfield, Mass. E6 68-9
Brimhall, N. Mex. E2 230-1
Brimley, Mich. D13 112-3
Brimson, Mo. B4 120-1
Brinckerhoff*, N.Y. I11 80-1
Bringhurst, Ind. E7 100-1
Brinkley, Ark. E9 150-1
Brinklow, Md. G4 172-3
Brinkman, Okla. G7 234-5
Brinnon, Wash. H1 246-7
Brinsmade, N. Dak. D10 128-9
Brinson, Ga. N3 160-1
Briny Breezes*, Fla. H13 156-7
Brisbane*, Calif. I3 210-1
Brisco, B.C. I10 268-9
Briscoe, co., Tex. C5 192-3
Bristers Store, Miss. L6 176-7
Bristol, Colo. H16 214-5
Bristol, Conn. D7 60-1
Bristol, Fla. B6 156-7
Bristol, Ga. M9 160-1
Bristol, Ind. A9 100-1
Bristol, Me. N12 64-5
Bristol*, N.B. G3 275
Bristol, N.H. K6 72-3
Bristol, Pa. J16 84-5
Bristol, R.I. E7 87
Bristol, S. Dak. B13 136-7
Bristol, Tenn. A16 188-9
Bristol, Vt. G4 90-1
Bristol, Va. K4 196-7
Bristol, Wis. K5 140-1
Bristol, co., Mass. G11 68-9
Bristol, co., R.I. D7 87
Bristol Ferry, R.I. E7 87
Bristow, Ia. D9 104-5
Bristow, Nebr. C10 124-5
Bristow, Okla. E13 234-5
Bristow, Va. B3 196-7
Britannia Beach, B.C. A13 268-9
Britt, Ia. C7 104-5
Britt, Ont. H7 284-5
Britton, Mich. K14 112-3
Britton, S. Dak. A13 136-7
Britton Neck, S.C. E15 184-5
Broad Brook, Conn. B10 60-1
Broad Cove, Me. L5 64-5
Broad Creek, Del. J3 153
Broad Fields*, Ky. G9 164-5
Broad Valley*, Man. I3 272-3
Broadalbin, N.Y. E10 80-1
Broadbent, Ore. H4 238-9
Broadford, Va. J5 196-7
Broadhurst, Ga. M9 160-1
Broadkill Beach, Del. H6 153
Broadland, S. Dak. E12 136-7
Broadmoor, Colo. K3 214-5
Broadus, Mont. H15 222-3
Broadview*, Ill. B11 96-7
Broadview*, Ind. K7 100-1
Broadview, Mont. G10 222-3
Broadview, N. Mex. F11 230-1
Broadview, Sask. N10 294-5
Broadview Acres, N. Mex. F3 230-1
Broadview Heights, O. C14 132-3
Broadview Park-Rock Hill*, Fla. I13 156-7
Broadwater, Nebr. F3 124-5
Broadwater, co., Mont. F7 222-3
Broadway, N.J. E3 76-7
Broadway, N.C. J6 180-1
Broadway, Va. F10 196-7
Brock, Nebr. I15 124-5
Brock, Sask. L5 294-5
Brocket, N. Dak. D11 128-9
Brockport, N.Y. E4 80-1
Brockton, Mass. E12 68-9
Brockton, Mont. C15 222-3
Brockville, Ont. J15 284-5
Brockway, Mont. D14 222-3
Brockway, Pa. F5 84-5
Brockwell, Ark. B8 150-1
Brocton, N.Y. G1 80-1
Broderick, Sask. L6 294-5
Broderick-Bryte*, Calif. H3 210-1
Brodhead, Ky. I11 164-5
Brodhead, Wis. K12 140-1
Brodnax, Va. J11 196-7
Brogan, Ore. E15 238-9
Brohard, W. Va. F4 200-1
Brohman, Mich. H12 112-3
Brokaw, Wis. E12 140-1
Broken Arrow, Okla. D14 234-5
Broken Bow, Nebr. G8 124-5
Broken Bow, Okla. I16 234-5
Broken Hills, Nev. G5 226-7
Brome, co., Que. J14 290-1
Bromhead*, Sask. O10 294-5
Bromide, Okla. H13 234-5
Bromley, Ky. D11 164-5
Bromont*, Que. J13 290-1
Bromptonville*, Que. J15 290-1
Bronaugh, Mo. G3 120-1
Bronson, Fla. D10 156-7
Bronson, Ia. E1 104-5
Bronson, Kans. I15 108-9
Bronson, Mich. K12 112-3
Bronston, Ky. J11 164-5
Bronte, Tex. E6 192-3
Bronwood, Ga. L4 160-1
Bronx, N.Y. E14 80-1
Bronx, co., N.Y. E14 80-1
Bronxville, N.Y. D15 80-1
Brook, Ind. D4 100-1
Brook Park, Minn. K7 116-7
Brook Park, O. B14 132-3
Brookdale, Man. I11 272-3
Brooke, Va. C3 196-7
Brooke, co., W. Va. B5 200-1
Brooken, Okla. F15 234-5
Brooker, Fla. C10 156-7
Brookeville, Md. G4 172-3
Brookfield, Conn. F4 60-1
Brookfield, Ga. M6 160-1
Brookfield, Ill. M3 96-7
Brookfield, Mass. E7 68-9
Brookfield, Mo. C5 120-1
Brookfield, N.H. K8 72-3
Brookfield, N.S. D7 281
Brookfield, Vt. G6 90-1
Brookfield, Wis. J4 140-1
Brookfield Center, Conn. F4 60-1
Brookford, N.C. D6 180-1
Brookgreen, S.C. F15 184-5
Brookhaven, Miss. K5 176-7
Brookhaven, N.Y. J13 80-1
Brookhaven*, Pa. K15 84-5
Brookhurst, Wyo. F13 250-1
Brookings, Ore. K3 238-9
Brookings, S. Dak. E15 136-7
Brookings, co., S. Dak. E15 136-7
Brookland, Ark. C11 150-1
Brooklawn*, N.J. N10 76-7
Brooklet, Ga. J10 160-1
Brooklin, Me. L7 64-5
Brookline, Mass. I5 68-9
Brookline*, Mo. H5 120-1
Brookline, N.H. O6 72-3
Brookline, Vt. M6 90-1
Brooklyn, Ala. L6 146-7
Brooklyn, Conn. C14 60-1
Brooklyn*, Ill. K6 96-7
Brooklyn, Ind. H1 100-1
Brooklyn, Ia. G10 104-5
Brooklyn*, Md. D11 172-3
Brooklyn, Mich. K2 112-3
Brooklyn, Miss. M8 176-7
Brooklyn, N.Y. F14 80-1
Brooklyn*, N.S. F6 281
Brooklyn, O. B14 132-3
Brooklyn, Wis. J1 140-1
Brooklyn Center, Minn. A10 116-7
Brooklyn Heights*, Mo. H3 120-1
Brooklyn Heights*, O. B9 132-3
Brooklyn Park, Minn. A10 116-7
Brookneal, Va. J10 196-7
Brookport, Ill. O9 96-7
Brooks, Ala. L6 146-7
Brooks, Alta. M9 264-5
Brooks, Ga. H4 160-1
Brooks, Ky. B2 164-5
Brooks, Me. K6 64-5
Brooks, Minn. G2 116-7
Brooks, Ore. H1 238-9
Brooks, W. Va. I5 200-1
Brooks, Wis. G1 140-1
Brooks, co., Ga. N5 160-1
Brooks, co., Tex. J8 192-3
Brooksburg, Ind. L11 100-1
Brookshire, Tex. G10 192-3
Brookside*, Ala. E6 146-7
Brookside, Colo. G11 214-5
Brookside, N.J. D5 76-7
Brookside, O. F11 132-3
Brookside*, Tex. G10 192-3
Brookside Park, Del. B2 153
Brookston, Ind. E6 100-1
Brookston, Minn. I7 116-7
Brooksvale, Conn. F7 60-1
Brooksville, Fla. E10 156-7
Brooksville, Ky. E12 164-5
Brooksville, Me. K7 64-5
Brooksville, Miss. F10 176-7
Brooksville, Okla. K4 234-5
Brookton, Me. G9 64-5
Brookvale, Colo. H2 214-5
Brookview, Md. G14 172-3
Brookville, Ind. J11 100-1
Brookville, Kans. F9 108-9
Brookville, Mass. K6 68-9
Brookville*, N.Y. J11 80-1
Brookville, O. H14 132-3
Brookville, Pa. F5 84-5
Brookwood, Ala. F5 146-7
Broome, co., N.Y. G7 80-1
Broomes Island, Md. G11 172-3
Broomfield, Colo. G3 214-5
Brooten, Minn. L4 116-7
Brossard*, Que. I12 290-1
Brothers, Ore. G10 238-9
Brothertown, Wis. F4 140-1
Broughton Isl., N.W. Terr. B4 296
Brouse, B.C. J9 268-9
Broussard, La. H5 168-9
Broward, co., Fla. I13 156-7
Browardale*, Fla. I13 156-7
Browder, Ky. I6 164-5
Browerville, Minn. J4 116-7
Brown, W. Va. C13 200-1
Brown, co., Ill. H5 96-7
Brown, co., Ind. K8 100-1
Brown, co., Kans. C14 108-9
Brown, co., Minn. N4 116-7
Brown, co., Nebr. E8 124-5
Brown, co., O. I4 132-3
Brown, co., S. Dak. B12 136-7
Brown, co., Tex. F7 192-3
Brown, co., Wis. G15 140-1
Brown City, Mich. F6 112-3
Brown Deer, Wis. I5 140-1
Brownell, Kans. G6 108-9
Brownfield, Me. N6 64-5
Brownfield, Tex. D4 192-3
Browning, Mo. B5 120-1
Browning, Mont. B5 222-3
Brownington, Mo. F4 120-1
Brownington, Tenn. K8 188-9
Brownington, Vt. C8 90-1
Brownlee, La. B2 168-9
Brownlee, Nebr. E7 124-5
Brownlee, Ore. D16 238-9
Brownlee, Sask. M7 294-5
Brownlee Park*, Mich. J12 112-3
Browns, Ala. I5 146-7
Browns, Nev. F2 226-7
Browns Flat, N.B. I5 275
Browns Lake*, Wis. K14 140-1
Browns Mills, N.J. I5 76-7
Browns Summit, N.C. G4 180-1
Browns Valley, Minn. K1 116-7
Browns Village*, Fla. J13 156-7
Brownsboro, Ala. B7 146-7
Brownsboro*, Ky. G9 164-5
Brownsboro Farm*, Ky. G9 164-5
Brownsburg, Ind. H7 100-1
Brownsburg, Que. I11 290-1
Brownsburg, Va. H9 196-7
Brownsdale, Minn. O7 116-7
Brownsmead, Ore. A5 238-9
Brownson, Nebr. G2 124-5
Brownstown, Ill. J8 96-7
Brownstown, Ind. L8 100-1
Brownstown, Pa. I5 84-5
Brownstown, Wash. H11 246-7
Brownsville, Ark. C7 150-1
Brownsville, Del. H3 153
Brownsville, Ind. I11 100-1
Brownsville, Ky. I8 164-5
Brownsville, Md. C7 172-3
Brownsville, Minn. O9 116-7
Brownsville, Miss. H5 176-7
Brownsville, Ont. E13 284-5
Brownsville, Ore. J1 238-9
Brownsville, Pa. J2 84-5
Brownsville, S.C. C14 184-5
Brownsville, Tenn. C3 188-9
Brownsville, Tex. K8 192-3
Brownsville, Vt. K7 90-1
Brownsville, Wis. H3 140-1
Brownton, Minn. C7 116-7
Brownton, W. Va. D14 200-1
Browntown, Wis. K12 140-1
Brownvale, Alta. F4 264-5
Brownville*, Ala. F6 146-7
Brownville, La. B5 168-9
Brownville, Me. H6 64-5
Brownville, Nebr. I16 124-5
Brownville, N.Y. C7 80-1
Brownville Junction, Me. H6 64-5
Brownwood, Tex. E7 192-3
Broxton, Ga. L7 160-1
Broxton, Okla. G9 234-5
Bruce, Alta. J9 264-5
Bruce, Miss. D8 176-7
Bruce, S. Dak. E15 136-7
Bruce, Wis. D9 140-1
Bruce, co., Ont. B12 284-5
Bruce Crossing, Mich. C8 112-3
Bruce Mines, Ont. H6 284-5
Bruceton, Tenn. B4 188-9
Bruceton Mills, W. Va. A16 200-1
Brucetown, Va. D11 196-7
Bruceville, Ind. L4 100-1
Brudenell*, P.E.I. F9 287
Bruderheim, Alta. I8 264-5
Brule, Nebr. H4 124-5
Brule, Wis. B9 140-1
Brule, co., S. Dak. G11 136-7
Brumley, Mo. F6 120-1
Brundidge, Ala. K9 146-7
Bruneau, Ida. N4 218-9
Bruning, Nebr. I12 124-5
Brunkild, Man. J14 272-3
Bruno, Ark. B6 150-1
Bruno, Minn. J7 116-7
Bruno, Nebr. G13 124-5
Bruno, Okla. H13 234-5

Bruno, Sask. K7 294-5
Brunson, S.C. H10 184-5
Brunsville, Ia. C1 104-5
Brunswick, Ga. N10 160-1
Brunswick, Me. N10 64-5
Brunswick, Md. C7 172-3
Brunswick, Mich. H11 112-3
Brunswick, Mo. C5 120-1
Brunswick, Nebr. E12 124-5
Brunswick, N.C. G11 180-1
Brunswick, O. C14 132-3
Brunswick, Tenn. K2 188-9
Brunswick*, Vt. C9 90-1
Brunswick, co., N.C. H11 180-1
Brunswick, co., Va. J12 196-7
Brunswick Station*, Me. N10 64-5
Brusett, Mont. D12 222-3
Brush, Colo. C14 214-5
Brush Creek, Tenn. B9 188-9
Brush Hollow, Mass. D3 68-9
Brush Prairie, Wash. J7 246-7
Brushton, N.Y. A10 80-1
Brushy, Okla. E16 234-5
Brushy Run, W. Va. F8 200-1
Brusly Landing, La. A9 168-9
Brussels, Ont. C12 284-5
Brussels, Wis. D6 140-1
Brutus, Mich. E13 112-3
Bruxelles, Man. J12 272-3
Bryan, Miss. D7 176-7
Bryan, O. B3 132-3
Bryan, Tex. F9 192-3
Bryan, co., Ga. K10 160-1
Bryan, co., Okla. I13 234-5
Bryant, Ark. J15 150-1
Bryant, Fla. D14 156-7
Bryant, Ind. E11 100-1
Bryant, Okla. F13 234-5
Bryant, S. Dak. E14 136-7
Bryant, Wash. F3 246-7
Bryant Pond, Me. K2 64-5
Bryantown, Md. G10 172-3
Bryantsville, Ky. D6 164-5
Bryce, Ariz. J10 206-7
Bryce Canyon, Ut. L5 242-3
Bryceland, La. B3 168-9
Bryenton, N.B. G5 275
Bryn Athyn*, Pa. J15 84-5
Bryn Mawr, Pa. B10 84-5
Bryson, Que. J1 290-1
Bryson City, N.C. E2 180-1
Buchanan, Ga. F2 160-1
Buchanan, Mich. K11 112-3
Buchanan, N.Y. B14 80-1
Buchanan, N. Dak. G11 128-9
Buchanan, Ore. G13 238-9
Buchanan, Sask. L10 294-5
Buchanan, Tenn. A5 188-9
Buchanan, Va. H8 196-7
Buchanan, co., Ia. D12 104-5
Buchanan, co., Mo. C2 120-1
Buchanan, co., Va. I4 196-7
Buchans, Nfld. M8 278-9
Buchans*, Nfld. M8 278-9
Buchtel, O. H8 132-3
Buck Creek, Ind. E6 100-1
Buck Grove, Ia. F3 104-5
Buck Lake, Alta. J7 264-5
Buckatunna, Miss. K10 176-7
Buckeye, Ariz. I5 206-7
Buckeye, Ia. E8 104-5
Buckeye, La. E5 168-9
Buckeye, N. Mex. K11 230-1
Buckeye, Tenn. G11 188-9
Buckeye, W. Va. H6 200-1
Buckeye Lake, O. F8 132-3
Buckeystown, Md. F1 172-3
Buckfield, Me. L3 64-5
Buckhannon, W. Va. F6 200-1
Buckhead, Ga. G6 160-1
Buckhorn, N. Mex. J2 230-1
Buckhorn, Wyo. C16 250-1
Buckingham, Colo. C13 214-5
Buckingham, Que. I9 290-1
Buckingham, Va. H10 196-7
Buckingham, co., Va. H10 196-7
Buckland, Alaska C9 254-5
Buckland, Mass. B4 68-9
Buckley, Ill. F10 96-7
Buckley, Mich. G12 112-3
Buckley, Wash. K3 246-7
Bucklin, Kans. J6 108-9
Bucklin, Mo. C6 120-1
Buckman, Minn. K5 116-7
Buckner, Ark. J4 150-1
Buckner, Mo. I16 120-1
Bucks, Ala. M3 146-7
Bucks, co., Pa. I15 84-5
Bucks Corners, Ore. B12 238-9
Bucks Harbor, Me. J10 64-5
Buckskin, Ind. N4 100-1
Bucksport, Me. K7 64-5
Bucksport, S.C. F15 184-5
Bucktail, Nebr. F5 124-5
Bucoda, Wash. G7 246-7
Buctouche, N.B. G7 275
Bucyrus, Kans. F16 108-9
Bucyrus, N. Dak. J3 128-9
Bucyrus, O. D6 132-3
Buda, Ill. D7 96-7
Budd Lake, N.J. D5 76-7
Bude, Miss. K4 176-7
Buechel, Ky. B2 164-5
Buell, Mo. D8 120-1
Buellton, Calif. M5 210-1
Buel's Gore*, Vt. F5 90-1
Buena, N.J. L4 76-7
Buena, Wash. H11 246-7
Buena Park, Calif. H9 210-1
Buena Vista, Ala. K5 146-7
Buena Vista, Ark. J5 150-1
Buena Vista, Colo. F10 214-5
Buena Vista*, Fla. F10 156-7
Buena Vista, Ga. J3 160-1
Buena Vista, Ind. J11 100-1
Buena Vista, Miss. D9 176-7
Buena Vista*, N.J. L4 76-7
Buena Vista, N. Mex. D8 230-1
Buena Vista, Ore. I1 238-9
Buena Vista*, Sask. M8 294-5
Buena Vista, Tenn. B4 188-9
Buena Vista, Va. H9 196-7
Buena Vista, co., Ia. D4 104-5
Bueyeros, N. Mex. D10 230-1
Buffalo, Ind. D6 100-1
Buffalo, Ia. H15 104-5
Buffalo, Kans. I14 108-9
Buffalo, Ky. E2 164-5
Buffalo, Minn. L5 116-7
Buffalo, Mo. G5 120-1
Buffalo, Mont. E9 222-3
Buffalo, N.Y. F2 80-1
Buffalo, N. Dak. G13 128-9
Buffalo, Okla. C7 234-5
Buffalo, S.C. G6 184-5
Buffalo, S. Dak. B2 136-7
Buffalo, Tex. F10 192-3
Buffalo, W. Va. G2 200-1
Buffalo, Wis. G8 140-1
Buffalo, Wyo. C12 250-1
Buffalo, co., Nebr. H9 124-5
Buffalo, co., S. Dak. F10 136-7
Buffalo, co., Wis. G8 140-1
Buffalo Center, Ia. B7 104-5
Buffalo Creek, B.C. H8 268-9
Buffalo Creek, Colo. I2 214-5
Buffalo Gap, S. Dak. H2 136-7
Buffalo Grove, Ill. K3 96-7
Buffalo Junction, Va. K10 196-7
Buffalo Lake, Minn. M4 116-7
Buffalo Narrows, Sask. F5 294-5
Buffalo Springs, Tenn. G13 188-9
Buffalo Valley, Tenn. B9 188-9
Buford, Ark. B6 150-1
Buford, Colo. D7 214-5
Buford, Ga. F5 160-1
Buford, Wyo. J14 250-1
Buhl, Ala. F4 146-7
Buhl, Ida. N5 218-9
Buhl, Minn. G7 116-7
Buhler, Kans. H10 108-9
Buhler, La. H2 168-9
Buick, Colo. E13 214-5
Buies Creek, N.C. J7 180-1
Buist, Ida. O9 218-9
Buladeen, Tenn. A16 188-9
Bulan, Ky. I14 164-5
Bull Shoals, Ark. A6 150-1
Bull Shoals Lake, Ark. A5 150-1
Bullard, Ga. J6 160-1
Bullards, Ore. H3 238-9
Bullhead, S. Dak. A7 136-7
Bullhead City, Ariz. E2 206-7
Bullitt, co., Ky. G9 164-5
Bulloch, co., Ga. J10 160-1
Bullock, N.C. C11 180-1
Bullock, co., Ala. I9 146-7
Bulls Bay, S.C. H14 184-5
Bulls Bridge, Conn. D4 60-1
Bulls Gap, Tenn. G14 188-9
Bulyea, Sask. M8 294-5
Bumble Bee, Ariz. G6 206-7
Bumpass, Va. G12 196-7
Bumpus Mills, Tenn. A5 188-9
Bunavista*, Tex. A5 192-3
Bunbury, P.E.I. F7 287
Bunceton, Mo. E6 120-1
Bunch, Okla. E16 234-5
Bunche Park*, Fla. J13 156-7
Buncombe, co., N.C. D4 180-1
Bungalow Town, Tenn. I14 188-9
Bunker, Mo. H9 120-1
Bunker Hill, Ill. J6 96-7
Bunker Hill, Ind. E8 100-1
Bunker Hill, Kans. F8 108-9
Bunker Hill, Miss. L7 176-7
Bunker Hill, Ore. H3 238-9
Bunker Hill, Tex. H13 192-3
Bunker Hill, W. Va. E11 200-1
Bunkerville, Nev. L11 226-7
Bunkie, La. F5 168-9
Bunlevel, N.C. J7 180-1
Bunn, N.C. H8 180-1
Bunnell, Fla. D12 156-7
Bunnvale, N.J. E4 76-7
Bunny Run, Mich. H6 112-3
Buras [-Triumph], La. J11 168-9
Burbank, Calif. G8 210-1
Burbank*, Ill. B11 96-7
Burbank, O. E13 132-3
Burbank, Okla. C12 234-5
Burbank, S. Dak. J16 136-7
Burbank, Wash. I13 246-7
Burchard, Nebr. J15 124-5
Burden, Kans. J12 108-9
Burdett, Alta. N9 264-5
Burdett, Kans. H6 108-9
Burdette, Ark. C12 150-1
Burdick, Kans. G12 108-9
Burdickville, R.I. H2 87
Bureau, co., Ill. C7 96-7
Burford*, Ont. E13 284-5
Burg, Okla. H14 234-5
Burgaw, N.C. G12 180-1
Burgeo, Nfld. O8 278-9
Burgess, Mo. H3 120-1
Burgess, S.C. F15 184-5
Burgess, Va. H14 196-7
Burgess Junction, Wyo. B10 250-1
Burgettstown, Pa. I1 84-5
Burgin, Ky. D6 164-5
Burien, Wash. I2 246-7
Burin, Nfld. O10 278-9
Burkburnett, Tex. C7 192-3
Burke, Ida. D4 218-9
Burke, S. Dak. I11 136-7
Burke*, Vt. D9 90-1
Burke, Va. A3 196-7
Burke, co., Ga. H9 160-1
Burke, co., N.C. D5 180-1
Burke, co., N. Dak. B4 128-9
Burke Hollow, Vt. D9 90-1
Burkes Garden, Va. I5 196-7
Burkesville, Ky. J9 164-5
Burket, Ind. C9 100-1
Burkettsville, O. E3 132-3
Burkettville, Me. L5 64-5
Burkeville, Va. I11 196-7
Burkittsville, Md. C7 172-3
Burkley, Ky. J2 164-5
Burk's Falls, Ont. H8 284-5
Burkville, Ala. I7 146-7
Burleigh, N.J. O4 76-7
Burleigh, co., N. Dak. G8 128-9
Burleson, Tex. D13 192-3
Burleson, co., Tex. G9 192-3
Burley, Ida. O7 218-9
Burley, Wash. I1 246-7
Burlingame, Calif. C7 210-1
Burlingame, Kans. F14 108-9
Burlington, Colo. E16 214-5
Burlington, Conn. D7 60-1
Burlington, Ind. E7 100-1
Burlington, Ia. J14 104-5
Burlington, Kans. H14 108-9
Burlington, Ky. E11 164-5
Burlington, Me. H8 64-5
Burlington, Mass. F4 68-9
Burlington, Mich. J12 112-3
Burlington*, N.J. I4 76-7
Burlington, N.J. I4 76-7
Burlington, N.C. H5 180-1
Burlington, N. Dak. D6 128-9
Burlington, Okla. C9 234-5
Burlington, Ont. D14 284-5
Burlington, Ore. E1 238-9
Burlington, Vt. E4 90-1
Burlington, Wash. C8 246-7
Burlington, W. Va. E9 200-1
Burlington, Wis. K4 140-1
Burlington, Wyo. C9 250-1
Burlington, co., N.J. J5 76-7
Burlington Junction, Mo. A2 120-1
Burlison, Tenn. J2 188-9
Burmah, Okla. E8 234-5
Burmester, Ut. F5 242-3
Burmis, Alta. O7 264-5
Burna, Ky. I3 164-5
Burnet, Tex. F8 192-3
Burnet, co., Tex. F8 192-3
Burnett, Wis. H3 140-1
Burnett, co., Wis. C8 140-1
Burnettown, S.C. F8 184-5
Burnetts Corner, Conn. G14 60-1
Burnettsville, Ind. D7 100-1
Burney, Calif. E4 210-1
Burney, Ind. J10 100-1
Burneyville, Okla. I11 234-5
Burnham, Ill. N4 96-7
Burnham, Me. J5 64-5
Burnham, N. Mex. C3 230-1
Burnham, Pa. H9 84-5
Burning Springs, W. Va. F4 200-1
Burnips, Mich. I12 112-3
Burns, Colo. D8 214-5
Burns, Kans. H11 108-9
Burns, Miss. I7 176-7
Burns, Mont. D16 222-3
Burns, Ore. G12 238-9
Burns, Tenn. H5 188-9
Burns, Wyo. J16 250-1
Burns City, Ind. L6 100-1
Burns Flat, Okla. F8 234-5
Burns Harbor*, Ind. A5 100-1
Burns Lake, B.C. F5 268-9
Burnside, Conn. D9 60-1
Burnside, Ky. J11 164-5
Burnside, Miss. G8 176-7
Burnstad, N. Dak. I9 128-9
Burnsville, Ala. H6 146-7
Burnsville*, Minn. M6 116-7
Burnsville, Miss. A10 176-7
Burnsville, N.C. D4 180-1
Burnsville, Va. G8 196-7
Burnsville, W. Va. F5 200-1
Burnt Corn, Ala. K5 146-7
Burnt House, W. Va. E5 200-1
Burnt Islands, Nfld. O7 278-9
Burntfork, Wyo. K6 250-1
Burnwell, Ala. E5 146-7
Burr, Nebr. I15 124-5
Burr Ferry, La. F2 168-9
Burr Hill, Va. C2 196-7
Burr Oak, Ind. C7 100-1
Burr Oak, Kans. C9 108-9
Burr Oak, Mich. K12 112-3
Burr Ridge, Ill. M3 96-7
Burrillville*, R.I. A3 87
Burris, Wyo. E8 250-1
Burroughs, Ga. K11 160-1
Burrows, Ind. E7 100-1
Burrsville, Md. E14 172-3
Burrton, Kans. H10 108-9
Burrville, Tenn. G10 188-9
Burrville, Ut. J6 242-3
Burrwood, La. K11 168-9
Burstall, Sask. M3 294-5
Burt, Ia. B6 104-5
Burt, Mich. F3 112-3
Burt, N. Dak. I4 128-9
Burt, Okla. H8 234-5
Burt, co., Nebr. F15 124-5
Burt Lake, Mich. E13 112-3
Burton, B.C. J9 268-9
Burton, Ida. L10 218-9
Burton, Ky. I15 164-5
Burton*, Mich. G3 112-3
Burton, Nebr. C9 124-5
Burton, N.B. I5 275
Burton, O. B16 132-3
Burton, P.E.I. C3 287
Burton, S.C. J11 184-5
Burton, Wash. J2 246-7
Burton, W. Va. A13 200-1
Burtonsville, Md. H4 172-3
Burtrum, Minn. K4 116-7
Burtts Corner*, N.B. H4 275
Burwell, Nebr. F9 124-5
Busby, Mont. H12 222-3
Busby, Tenn. K5 188-9
Busch, Ark. A3 150-1
Bush, La. G10 168-9
Bush, Miss. J6 176-7
Bush City, Kans. H15 108-9
Bushes, La. C6 168-9
Bushnell, Fla. E10 156-7
Bushnell, Ill. F5 96-7
Bushnell, Nebr. G1 124-5
Bushnell, S. Dak. E16 136-7
Bushong, Kans. G13 108-9
Bushton, Kans. G8 108-9
Bushyhead, Okla. C14 234-5
Bussey, Ark. J4 150-1
Bussey, Ia. I9 104-5
Butler, Ala. J2 146-7
Butler, Ga. J4 160-1
Butler, Ind. B12 100-1
Butler, Ky. E11 164-5
Butler, Md. B11 172-3
Butler, Mo. F3 120-1
Butler, N.J. C6 76-7
Butler, O. E8 132-3
Butler, Okla. E8 234-5
Butler, Pa. G2 84-5
Butler, S. Dak. C14 136-7
Butler, Wis. I4 140-1
Butler, co., Ala. K6 146-7
Butler, co., Ia. C9 104-5
Butler, co., Kans. I12 108-9
Butler, co., Ky. I7 164-5
Butler, co., Mo. J10 120-1
Butler, co., Nebr. G13 124-5
Butler, co., O. H3 132-3
Butler, co., Pa. G2 84-5
Butlerville, Ark. E8 150-1
Butlerville, Ind. K10 100-1
Butner, N.C. G7 180-1
Butte, Alaska F11 254-5
Butte.., Mont. G5 222-3
Butte, Nebr. C10 124-5
Butte, N. Dak. E7 128-9
Butte, co., Calif. G4 210-1
Butte, co., Ida. L8 218-9
Butte, co., S. Dak. D2 136-7
Butte City, Ida. L8 218-9
Butte des Morts, Wis. F3 140-1
Butte Falls, Ore. J6 238-9
Butte-Silver Bow, co., Mont. G5 222-3
Butterfield, Minn. O4 116-7
Butterfield, Mo. I4 120-1
Butternut, Wis. C10 140-1
Butters, N.C. G10 180-1
Buttonwillow, Calif. L6 210-1
Butts, co., Ga. H5 160-1
Buttzville, N.J. D3 76-7
Buxton, Kans. J14 108-9
Buxton, Me. O8 64-5
Buxton, N.C. E16 180-1
Buxton, N. Dak. E14 128-9
Buxton, Ore. B5 238-9
Buzzards Bay, Mass. H12 68-9
Buzzards Bay, Mass. G13 68-9
Byars, Okla. G12 234-5
Bybee, Tenn. H14 188-9
Byers, Colo. D13 214-5
Byers, Kans. I7 108-9
Byesville, O. F9 132-3
Byfield, Mass. A12 68-9
Byhalia, Miss. A7 176-7
Bylas, Ariz. I10 206-7
Byng, Okla. G12 234-5
Byng Inlet Area, Ont. H7 284-5
Bynum, Mont. C5 222-3
Bynum, N.C. I6 180-1
Byram, Miss. I6 176-7
Byram*, N.J. C5 76-7
Byrdstown, Tenn. A10 188-9
Byrne, Ida. L10 218-9
Byromville, Ga. K5 160-1
Byron, Ark. B8 150-1
Byron, Ga. J5 160-1
Byron, Ill. B8 96-7
Byron, Me. J2 64-5
Byron, Mich. H3 112-3
Byron, Minn. O7 116-7
Byron, Nebr. J12 124-5
Byron, Okla. C9 234-5
Byron, Wis. G4 140-1
Byron, Wyo. B9 250-1
Byron Center, Mich. I12 112-3

C

Caballo, N. Mex. J4 230-1
Cabano, Que. E15 290-1
Cabarrus, co., N.C. E7 180-1
Cabazon*, Calif. G11 210-1
Cabell, co., W. Va. G2 200-1

364 Cabin John – Cap-de-la Madeleine

Cabin John, Md. I3 172-3
Cabinet, Ida. C3 218-9
Cabins, W. Va. F9 200-1
Cable, Wis. C9 140-1
Cabool, Mo. I7 120-1
Cabot, Ark. E7 150-1
Cabot, Vt. E7 90-1
Cabri, Sask. N5 294-5
Cache, Okla. H9 234-5
Cache, co., Ut. D6 242-3
Cache Bay, Ont. H8 284-5
Cache Creek, B.C. I7 268-9
Cactus, Ariz. H6 206-7
Cactus, Tex. A5 192-3
Cactus Flat, Ariz. J10 206-7
Cactus Springs, Nev. L8 226-7
Caddo, Ala. B5 146-7
Caddo, La. A1 168-9
Caddo, Okla. I13 234-5
Caddo, co., La. B1 168-9
Caddo, co., Okla. F9 234-5
Caddo Gap, Ark. G3 150-1
Caddo Mills, Tex. B16 192-3
Caddo Valley*, Ark. H5 150-1
Caddoa, Colo. H15 214-5
Cade, La. H5 168-9
Cade, Okla. I14 234-5
Cades, S.C. E13 184-5
Cades, Tenn. B3 188-9
Cades Cove, Tenn. J15 188-9
Cadillac, Mich. G12 112-3
Cadillac, Que. H1 290-1
Cadillac, Sask. O5 294-5
Cadiz, Ind. G10 100-1
Cadiz, Ky. J4 164-5
Cadiz, O. E11 132-3
Cadmus, Kans. G16 108-9
Cadomin, Alta. J5 264-5
Cadott, Wis. F9 140-1
Cadotte Lake*, Alta. F6 264-5
Cadwell, Ga. J7 160-1
Cadys Corners, Mass. E5 68-9
Cadys Falls, Vt. D6 90-1
Caesarea*, Ont. B16 284-5
Caesars Head, S.C. E1 184-5
Cahaba, Ala. I5 146-7
Cahokia, Ill. K6 96-7
Cahone, Colo. I5 214-5
Cainesville, Mo. A4 120-1
Caineville, Ut. K7 242-3
Cainsville, Tenn. H8 188-9
Cairo, Ga. N4 160-1
Cairo, Ill. O8 96-7
Cairo, Kans. I8 108-9
Cairo, Ky. H5 164-5
Cairo, Mo. C6 120-1
Cairo, Nebr. H10 124-5
Cairo, O. D4 132-3
Cairo, Okla. H13 234-5
Cairo, Ore. F16 238-9
Cairo, W. Va. E4 200-1
Calabogie, Ont. H13 284-5
Calahoo, Alta. I7 264-5
Calais, Me. H10 64-5
Calais*, Vt. E6 90-1
Calamine, Ark. B9 150-1
Calamine, Wis. K11 140-1
Calamus, Ia. G15 104-5
Calapooya, Ore. J2 238-9
Calaveras, co., Calif. I4 210-1
Calcasieu, La. F4 168-9
Calcasieu, co., La. H2 168-9
Calcis, Ala. F7 146-7
Calder, Ida. D3 218-9
Calder, Sask. M10 294-5
Caldwell, Ark. E10 150-1
Caldwell, Ida. L2 218-9
Caldwell, Kans. K10 108-9
Caldwell, N.J. D7 76-7
Caldwell, N.C. J1 180-1
Caldwell, O. G10 132-3
Caldwell, Tex. G9 192-3
Caldwell, W. Va. I6 200-1
Caldwell, co., Ky. J4 164-5
Caldwell, co., La. C5 168-9
Caldwell, co., Mo. C4 120-1
Caldwell, co., N.C. D6 180-1
Caldwell, co., Tex. G8 192-3
Cale, Ark. I4 150-1
Caledon, Ont. C14 284-5
Caledonia*, Mich. I12 112-3
Caledonia, Minn. O9 116-7
Caledonia, Miss. E10 176-7
Caledonia, Mo. G9 120-1
Caledonia, N.Y. E4 80-1
Caledonia, N. Dak. F14 128-9
Caledonia, N.S. F5 281
Caledonia, O. D6 132-3
Caledonia, Wis. J5 140-1
Caledonia, co., Vt. E8 90-1
Calera, Ala. G6 146-7
Calera, Okla. I13 234-5
Calexico, Calif. O10 210-1
Calgary, Alta. M7 264-5
Calhan, Colo. F13 214-5
Calhoun, Ala. J7 146-7
Calhoun, Ark. J4 150-1
Calhoun, Ga. E2 160-1
Calhoun, Ky. H6 164-5
Calhoun, La. B5 168-9
Calhoun, Mo. F4 120-1
Calhoun, Okla. F16 234-5
Calhoun, Tenn. K12 188-9
Calhoun, co., Ala. D8 146-7
Calhoun, co., Ark. I6 150-1
Calhoun, co., Fla. B6 156-7
Calhoun, co., Ga. M3 160-1
Calhoun, co., Ill. I5 96-7
Calhoun, co., Ia. E5 104-5
Calhoun, co., Mich. J12 112-3
Calhoun, co., Miss. D8 176-7
Calhoun, co., S.C. F10 184-5
Calhoun, co., Tex. I9 192-3
Calhoun, co., W. Va. F4 200-1
Calhoun City, Miss. D8 176-7
Calhoun Falls, S.C. K1 184-5
Calico Rock, Ark. B7 150-1
Caliente, Nev. J10 226-7
Califon, N.J. E4 76-7
California, Ky. E12 164-5
California, Md. H11 172-3
California, Mo. E6 120-1
California, Pa. J2 84-5
California City, Calif. M7 210-1
Calio, N. Dak. C10 128-9
Calion, Ark. J6 150-1
Calipatria, Calif. O10 210-1
Calista, Kans. I9 108-9
Calistoga, Calif. A7 210-1
Callahan, Fla. B11 156-7
Callahan, co., Tex. E7 192-3
Callander, Ont. H8 284-5
Callands, Va. J8 196-7
Callao, Mo. C6 120-1
Callao, Va. G14 196-7
Callaway, Fla. C5 156-7
Callaway, Ky. J13 164-5
Callaway, Md. H11 172-3
Callaway, Minn. H2 116-7
Callaway, Nebr. G8 124-5
Callaway, Va. J8 196-7
Callaway, co., Mo. E7 120-1
Callender, Ia. E6 104-5
Callison, S.C. E7 184-5
Calloway, co., Ky. K3 164-5
Calmar, Alta. J7 264-5
Calmar, Ia. B12 104-5
Calmer, Ark. H7 150-1
Calpella, Calif. G2 210-1
Calpet, Wyo. H6 250-1
Calstock, Ont. E6 284-5
Calumet, Ia. C3 104-5
Calumet, La. I7 168-9
Calumet, Mich. B8 112-3
Calumet, Minn. H6 116-7
Calumet, Okla. E10 234-5
Calumet, Que. I10 290-1
Calumet, co., Wis. G14 140-1
Calumet City, Ill. N4 96-7
Calumet-Norvelt*, Pa. I3 84-5
Calumet Park, Ill. N4 96-7
Calva, Ariz. I9 206-7
Calvary, Ga. O4 160-1
Calvert, Ala. L3 146-7
Calvert, Kans. D6 108-9
Calvert, Md. B13 172-3
Calvert, Tex. F9 192-3
Calvert, co., Md. G11 172-3
Calvert City, Ky. J3 164-5
Calverton*, Md. D10 172-3
Calverton, Va. B2 196-7
Calverton Park*, Mo. E10 120-1
Calvin, La. C4 168-9
Calvin, N. Dak. B10 128-9
Calvin, Okla. G13 234-5
Calwa, Calif. K5 210-1
Calypso, N.C. F12 180-1
Camak, Ga. G8 160-1
Camanche, Ia. G16 104-5
Camargo*, Ky. G12 164-5
Camargo, Okla. D7 234-5
Camarillo, Calif. G7 210-1
Camarillo Heights*, Calif. G7 210-1
Camas, Ida. K9 218-9
Camas, Mont. D2 222-3
Camas, Wash. J8 246-7
Camas, co., Ida. M5 218-9
Camas Prairie, Mont. D2 222-3
Camas Valley, Ore. H4 238-9
Cambria, Calif. L4 210-1
Cambria, Ill. M8 96-7
Cambria, Ind. F7 100-1
Cambria, Va. I7 196-7
Cambria, Wis. H2 140-1
Cambria, co., Pa. I5 84-5
Cambrian Park*, Calif. J3 210-1
Cambridge, Ida. J2 218-9
Cambridge, Ill. D6 96-7
Cambridge, Ia. F8 104-5
Cambridge, Kans. J12 108-9
Cambridge*, Ky. G9 164-5
Cambridge, Me. I5 64-5
Cambridge, Md. G13 172-3
Cambridge, Mass. D11 68-9
Cambridge, Minn. K6 116-7
Cambridge, Nebr. J8 124-5
Cambridge, N.Y. E12 80-1
Cambridge*, N.S. D6 281
Cambridge, O. F9 132-3
Cambridge, Okla. G8 234-5
Cambridge, Ont. D13 284-5
Cambridge, Vt. D5 90-1
Cambridge, Wis. J2 140-1
Cambridge Bay, N.W. Terr. B2 296
Cambridge City, Ind. H11 100-1
Cambridge-Narrows, N.B. I5 275
Cambridge Springs, Pa. D2 84-5
Cambridgeport, Vt. M6 90-1
Camden, Ala. J5 146-7
Camden, Ark. I5 150-1
Camden, Del. F4 153
Camden, Ind. E7 100-1
Camden, Me. L6 64-5
Camden, Mich. K13 112-3
Camden, Miss. H7 176-7
Camden, Mo. D4 120-1
Camden, N.J. I3 76-7
Camden, N.Y. E8 80-1
Camden, N.C. C15 180-1
Camden, O. I13 132-3
Camden, S.C. D11 184-5
Camden, Tenn. B5 188-9
Camden, W. Va. E5 200-1
Camden, co., Ga. N10 160-1
Camden, co., Mo. G6 120-1
Camden, co., N.J. K4 76-7
Camden, co., N.C. B15 180-1
Camden-on-Gauley, W. Va. G5 200-1
Camden Point, Mo. H14 120-1
Camdenton, Mo. G6 120-1
Cameo, Colo. F6 214-5
Cameron, Ariz. D7 206-7
Cameron, La. I2 168-9
Cameron, Mo. F16 120-1
Cameron, Mont. H6 222-3
Cameron, N.C. J6 180-1
Cameron, Okla. F16 234-5
Cameron, S.C. F11 184-5
Cameron, Tex. F9 192-3
Cameron, W. Va. C5 200-1
Cameron, Wis. D8 140-1
Cameron, co., La. I3 168-9
Cameron, co., Pa. E7 84-5
Cameron, co., Tex. K8 192-3
Cameron Falls, Ont. F4 284-5
Camilla, Ga. M4 160-1
Camillus, N.Y. E7 80-1
Cammack, Ind. G10 100-1
Cammack Village, Ark. I15 150-1
Camp, Ark. A8 150-1
Camp, La. A3 168-9
Camp, co., Tex. D10 192-3
Camp Barrett*, Va. F12 196-7
Camp Bird, Colo. H7 214-5
Camp Creek, W. Va. J4 200-1
Camp Crook, S. Dak. B1 136-7
Camp Douglas, Wis. H11 140-1
Camp Forsyth*, Kans. E12 108-9
Camp Funston*, Kans. E12 108-9
Camp Hill, Ala. H9 146-7
Camp Hill, Pa. I10 84-5
Camp Houston, Okla. C8 234-5
Camp Lake, Wis. K15 140-1
Camp Lejeune Central*, N.C. G13 180-1
Camp Morton*, Man. J4 272-3
Camp Point, Ill. G4 96-7
Camp Romaca, Mass. C2 68-9
Camp Sherman, Ore. E8 238-9
Camp Springs, Md. J5 172-3
Camp Verde, Ariz. G7 206-7
Camp Wood, Ariz. F5 206-7
Camp Wood, Tex. G6 192-3
Campaign, Tenn. I10 188-9
Campbell, Ala. J3 146-7
Campbell*, Alaska F11 254-5
Campbell, Calif. D8 210-1
Campbell, Minn. J2 116-7
Campbell, Mo. J11 120-1
Campbell, Nebr. J10 124-5
Campbell, O. C11 132-3
Campbell, co., Ky. E12 164-5
Campbell, co., S. Dak. B9 136-7
Campbell, co., Tenn. A12 188-9
Campbell, co., Va. I9 196-7
Campbell, co., Wyo. D14 250-1
Campbell River, B.C. J5 268-9
Campbell Station, Ark. C9 150-1
Campbellford, Ont. J12 284-5
Campbell's Bay, Que. J1 290-1
Campbellsburg, Ind. L8 100-1
Campbellsburg*, Ky. F10 164-5
Campbellsport, Wis. H4 140-1
Campbellsville, Ky. I10 164-5
Campbellsville, Tenn. J6 188-9
Campbellton, Fla. A6 156-7
Campbellton, N.B. D4 275
Campbellton, Nfld. M10 278-9
Campbelltown, Pa. I11 84-5
Campbelltown Heights*, Alta. I8 264-5
Camper, Man. G13 272-3
Camperville, Man. F11 272-3
Campion, Colo. E3 214-5
Campo, Colo. J16 214-5
Campobello, S.C. E3 184-5
Campti, La. D3 168-9
Campton, Ga. F5 160-1
Campton, Ky. H13 164-5
Campton, N.H. I6 72-3
Campville, Conn. D6 60-1
Camrose, Alta. J8 264-5
Camsell Portage*, Sask. A5 294-5
Cana, Va. K6 196-7
Canaan*, Conn. A5 60-1
Canaan, Conn. A5 60-1
Canaan, Ind. L11 100-1
Canaan, Me. J5 64-5
Canaan, Miss. A8 176-7
Canaan, N.H. J4 72-3
Canaan, Vt. B11 90-1
Canaan Road, N.B. H6 275
Canaan Valley, Conn. A5 60-1
Canadian, Okla. F14 234-5
Canadian, Tex. A6 192-3
Canadian, co., Okla. E10 234-5
Canadian R., Okla. F10 234-5
Canadys, S.C. H11 184-5
Canajoharie, N.Y. E10 80-1
Canal Flats, B.C. J10 268-9
Canal Fulton, O. E15 132-3
Canal Point, Fla. D14 156-7
Canal Winchester, O. G7 132-3
Canalou, Mo. I11 120-1
Canandaigua, N.Y. F5 80-1
Canaseraga, N.Y. G4 80-1
Canastota, N.Y. E8 80-1
Canby, Minn. M2 116-7
Canby, Ore. G2 238-9
Candia, N.H. N7 72-3
Candiac*, Que. J13 290-1
Candiac, Sask. N9 294-5
Candle, Alaska D9 254-5
Candler, co., Ga. J9 160-1
Candlewood*, N.J. H7 76-7
Candlewood Knolls, Conn. F4 60-1
Cando, N. Dak. C10 128-9
Cando, Sask. K5 294-5
Candor, N.Y. G7 80-1
Candor, N.C. J4 180-1
Cane Beds, Ariz. B5 206-7
Cane Savannah, S.C. E12 184-5
Cane Springs, Ariz. F3 206-7
Cane Valley, Ky. I10 164-5
Canehill, Ark. B2 150-1
Canelo, Ariz. M9 206-7
Caney, Ark. G5 150-1
Caney, Kans. K14 108-9
Caney, Ky. H14 164-5
Caney, La. F2 168-9
Caney, Okla. H13 234-5
Caney Branch, Tenn. H15 188-9
Caney Spring, Tenn. J7 188-9
Caneyville, Ky. I7 164-5
Canfield, Ark. J3 150-1
Canfield, Colo. F3 214-5
Canfield, O. C11 132-3
Canim Lake, B.C. H8 268-9
Canisteo, N.Y. G4 80-1
Canistota, S. Dak. G15 136-7
Canjilon, N. Mex. C6 230-1
Cankton, La. H5 168-9
Canmer, Ky. I9 164-5
Canmore, Alta. M6 264-5
Cannel City, Ky. H14 164-5
Cannelburg, Ind. L5 100-1
Cannelton, Ind. O6 100-1
Cannelton-Carbondale, W. Va. I15 200-1
Cannifton*, Ont. J12 284-5
Cannington*, Ont. B15 284-5
Cannon, Del. I3 153
Cannon, N. Mex. G11 230-1
Cannon, co., Tenn. C8 188-9
Cannon Ball, N. Dak. I7 128-9
Cannon Beach, Ore. B4 238-9
Cannon Beach Junction, Ore. A4 238-9
Cannon Falls, Minn. N7 116-7
Cannondale, Conn. I4 60-1
Cannonsburg, Ky. F15 164-5
Cannonsburg, Mich. I12 112-3
Cannonville, Ut. M6 242-3
Canobie, N.B. E6 275
Canobie Lake, N.H. O8 72-3
Canoe, Ala. M4 146-7
Canoe Lake, Sask. G5 294-5
Canon, Ga. E7 160-1
Canon City, Colo. G11 214-5
Cañon Plaza, N. Mex. C6 230-1
Canonchet, R.I. G2 87
Canonsburg, Pa. I1 84-5
Canoochee, Ga. I9 160-1
Canora, Sask. L10 294-5
Canova, S. Dak. G14 136-7
Canso, N.S. D10 281
Canterbury, Conn. D14 60-1
Canterbury, Del. G4 153
Canterbury, N.B. I3 275
Canterbury, N.H. L6 72-3
Canton, Conn. C8 60-1
Canton, Ga. E3 160-1
Canton, Ill. F6 96-7
Canton, Kans. G10 108-9
Canton, Ky. J4 164-5
Canton, Me. K3 64-5
Canton, Mass. K4 68-9
Canton, Minn. O8 116-7
Canton, Miss. H6 176-7
Canton, Mo. B8 120-1
Canton, N.Y. B8 80-1
Canton, N.C. E3 180-1
Canton, N. Dak. C13 128-9
Canton, O. D10 132-3
Canton, Okla. D9 234-5
Canton, Pa. D11 84-5
Canton, S. Dak. H16 136-7
Canton, Tex. E10 192-3
Canton, Wis. D9 140-1
Canton Begin*, Que. B11 290-1
Canton Center, Conn. C7 60-1
Cantonment*, Fla. B3 156-7
Cantril, Ia. J11 104-5
Cantwell, Alaska E11 254-5
Canute, Okla. F7 234-5
Canutillo, Tex. E1 192-3
Canvas, W. Va. H5 200-1
Canwood, Sask. J6 294-5
Canyon*, B.C. K10 268-9
Canyon, Tex. B5 192-3
Canyon, co., Ida. L2 218-9
Canyon City, Ore. E12 238-9
Canyon Creek, Alta. G6 264-5
Canyon Creek, Mont. E6 222-3
Canyon Diablo, Ariz. E8 206-7
Canyon Ferry Lake, Mont. F6 222-3
Canyon Junction, Wyo. F2 250-1
Canyonville, Ore. I5 238-9
Cap-à-l'Aigle, Que. E13 290-1
Cap-aux-Meules, Que. I7 290-1
Cap-Bateau*, N.B. E7 275
Cap-Chat, Que. H5 290-1
Cap-de-Cocagne, N.B. H7 275
Cap-de-la Madeleine, Que. H14 290-1

Cap-de-la-Madeleine-Nord-Est*, Que. H14 290-1
Cap-Lumière, N.B. G7 275
Cap-Pelé, N.B. H8 275
Cap-Santé, Que. G10 290-1
Cap-St.-Ignace, Que. F12 290-1
Capac, Mich. G6 112-3
Capaldo, Kans. J16 108-9
Cape Breton, co., N.S. C11 281
Cape Breton Isl., N.S. B11 281
Cape Broyle, Nfld. O11 278-9
Cape Canaveral, Fla. E13 156-7
Cape Carteret, N.C. F14 180-1
Cape Charles, Va. I15 196-7
Cape Cod, Mass. F16 68-9
Cape Coral*, Fla. H11 156-7
Cape Dorset, N.W. Terr. C3 296
Cape Egmont, P.E.I. E4 287
Cape Elizabeth, Me. N3 64-5
Cape Fear, N.C. H12 180-1
Cape Girardeau, Mo. H12 120-1
Cape Girardeau, co., Mo. H11 120-1
Cape Hatteras, N.C. E16 180-1
Cape Horn, Ida. K5 218-9
Cape Lisburne*, Alaska B8 254-5
Cape May, N.J. O3 76-7
Cape May, N.J. O4 76-7
Cape May, co., N.J. O4 76-7
Cape May Court House, N.J. O4 76-7
Cape May Point, N.J. O3 76-7
Cape Neddick, Me. O2 64-5
Cape Pole, Alaska H15 254-5
Cape Porpoise, Me. O3 64-5
Cape Rosier, Me. L7 64-5
Cape Sable Isl., N.S. G4 281
Cape St. Claire*, Md. E12 172-3
Cape St. George-Petit Jardin-Grand Jardin*, Nfld. N7 278-9
Cape Tormentine, N.B. H8 275
Cape Traverse*, P.E.I. F5 287
Cape Vincent, N.Y. C7 80-1
Cape Wolfe, P.E.I. C3 287
Capehart*, S.C. J11 184-5
Capeville, Va. F5 196-7
Capistrano Beach*, Calif. I9 210-1
Capitan, N. Mex. I7 230-1
Capitol, Mont. H16 222-3
Capitol Heights, Ia. G8 104-5
Capitol Heights, Md. J5 172-3
Capitola*, Calif. J3 210-1
Caplan*, Que. I6 290-1
Capleville, Tenn. K1 188-9
Capon Bridge, W. Va. E10 200-1
Capon Springs, W. Va. E10 200-1
Capreol, Ont. G7 284-5
Caprock, N. Mex. I11 230-1
Capron, Ill. A9 96-7
Capron, Okla. C9 234-5
Capron, Va. H2 196-7
Capshaw, Ala. B6 146-7
Captain Cook, Hawaii J12 258-9
Capulin, Colo. J10 214-5
Capulin, N. Mex. C10 230-1
Caputa, S. Dak. F3 136-7
Caramat*, Ont. F4 284-5
Caraquet, N.B. E6 275
Caratunk, Me. H4 64-5
Caraway, Ark. C11 150-1
Carberry, Man. J11 272-3
Carbon, Alta. L8 264-5
Carbon, Ind. I5 100-1
Carbon, Ia. I5 104-5
Carbon, co., Mont. H10 222-3
Carbon, co., Pa. G14 84-5
Carbon, co., Ut. H9 242-3
Carbon, co., Wyo. I11 250-1
Carbon Cliff, Ill. C5 96-7
Carbon Hill, Ala. D4 146-7
Carbonado, Wash. K3 246-7
Carbondale*, Alta. O7 264-5
Carbondale*, Alta. I8 264-5
Carbondale, Colo. E8 214-5
Carbondale, Ill. N8 96-7
Carbondale, Kans. F14 108-9
Carbondale, Pa. D14 84-5
Carbonear, Nfld. N11 278-9
Carbonton, N.C. I5 180-1
Carbonville, Ut. H8 242-3
Carcross, Y.T. C2 297
Cardale, Man. I10 272-3
Cardiff, Ala. E6 146-7
Cardiff, Colo. E8 214-5
Cardiff, N.J. M5 76-7
Cardiff*, Ont. I11 284-5
Cardiff-by-the-Sea, Calif. J10 210-1
Cardigan, P.E.I. F9 287
Cardin, Okla. B15 234-5
Cardinal, Man. J12 272-3
Cardinal, Ont. I15 284-5
Cardinal, Va. E4 196-7
Cardington, O. E7 132-3
Cardonia, Ind. I5 100-1
Cardston, Alta. O8 264-5
Cardville, Me. I7 64-5
Cardwell, Mo. K10 120-1
Cardwell, Mont. G6 222-3
Cardwell, Va. H12 196-7
Carencro, La. H5 168-9
Caretta, W. Va. J3 200-1
Carey, Ida. M7 218-9
Carey, O. D6 132-3
Careywood, Ida. C3 218-9
Caribou, Me. C9 64-5
Caribou, co., Ida. N10 218-9
Carievale, Sask. O11 294-5
Carignan*, Que. J12 290-1
Carl, Ga. F5 160-1
Carl Junction, Mo. H3 120-1
Carlanna, Alaska H16 254-5
Carle Place*, N.Y. K11 80-1
Carleton, Mich. J14 112-3
Carleton, Nebr. I12 124-5
Carleton, Okla. E9 234-5
Carleton, P.E.I. F5 287
Carleton*, Que. I5 290-1
Carleton, co., N.B. G3 275
Carleton Place, Ont. I14 284-5
Carlile, Wyo. C15 250-1
Carlin, Nev. D8 226-7
Carlinville, Ill. I6 96-7
Carlisle, Ark. F8 150-1
Carlisle, Ind. K4 100-1
Carlisle, Ia. H8 104-5
Carlisle, Ky. F12 164-5
Carlisle, La. E15 168-9
Carlisle, Mass. F2 68-9
Carlisle, Miss. J4 176-7
Carlisle, O. I14 132-3
Carlisle*, Ont. D14 284-5
Carlisle, Pa. I10 84-5
Carlisle, S.C. H7 184-5
Carlisle, Tenn. A5 188-9
Carlisle, co., Ky. J2 164-5
Carlisle Barracks, Pa. I10 84-5
Carlock, Tenn. K13 188-9
Carlos, Ind. G11 100-1
Carlos, Minn. K3 116-7
Carlowrie*, Man. K4 272-3
Carlowville, Ala. J5 146-7
Carlsbad, Calif. I10 210-1
Carlsbad, N. Mex. K10 230-1
Carlsbad Caverns, N. Mex. L9 230-1
Carlsbad Springs, Ont. H15 284-5
Carlsborg, Wash. D7 246-7
Carlshend, Mich. D10 112-3
Carlstadt, N.J. B11 76-7
Carlton, Ga. F7 160-1
Carlton, Kans. G11 108-9
Carlton, Minn. I8 116-7
Carlton, Ore. G1 238-9
Carlton, Sask. K6 294-5
Carlton, Wash. D11 246-7
Carlton, co., Minn. I7 116-7
Carlyle, Ill. K8 96-7
Carlyle, Kans. H15 108-9
Carlyle, Mont. E16 222-3
Carlyle, Sask. O10 294-5
Carmacks, Y.T. C2 297
Carman, Man. J13 272-3
Carmangay, Alta. N8 264-5
Carmanville, Nfld. M10 278-9
Carmel, Ind. D2 100-1
Carmel, La. C2 168-9
Carmel, Me. J6 64-5
Carmel, N.J. M3 76-7
Carmel, N.Y. I11 80-1
Carmel, Sask. K7 294-5
Carmel-by-the-Sea, Calif. K3 210-1
Carmel Valley, Calif. K3 210-1
Carmen, Ariz. M8 206-7
Carmen, Ida. I7 218-9
Carmen, Okla. C9 234-5
Carmi, Ill. M10 96-7
Carmichael, Calif. A9 210-1
Carmody Hills-Pepper Mill Village*, Md. E10 172-3
Carnation, Wash. E8 246-7
Carnduff, Sask. O11 294-5
Carnegie, Ga. L3 160-1
Carnegie, Okla. G9 234-5
Carnegie, Pa. B6 84-5
Carneiro, Kans. G9 108-9
Carnes, Miss. M8 176-7
Carnesville, Ga. E6 160-1
Carney, Mich. E10 112-3
Carney, Okla. E12 234-5
Carneys Point, N.J. K1 76-7
Carnigan, Ga. M11 160-1
Carnot-Moon*, Pa. H2 84-5
Carnue, N. Mex. F6 230-1
Caro, Mich. E5 112-3
Carol City, Fla. H16 156-7
Carol Stream, Ill. M2 96-7
Caroleen, N.C. E5 180-1
Carolina*, Ala. M7 146-7
Carolina, R.I. H3 87
Carolina Beach, N.C. H12 180-1
Caroline, Alta. K7 264-5
Caroline, Wis. D2 140-1
Caroline, co., Md. F13 172-3
Caroline, co., Va. G13 196-7
Caron, Sask. N7 294-5
Carp, Nev. K10 226-7
Carp, Ont. H14 284-5
Carp Lake, Mich. E13 112-3
Carpenter, Ia. B9 104-5
Carpenter, Miss. J5 176-7
Carpenter, Okla. F7 234-5
Carpenter, S. Dak. D13 136-7
Carpenter, Wyo. J16 250-1
Carpentersville, Ill. L1 96-7
Carpenterville, Ore. J3 238-9
Carpinteria, Calif. N6 210-1
Carpio, N. Dak. C5 128-9
Carrabassett, Me. I3 64-5
Carrabelle, Fla. C7 156-7
Carragana, Sask. K9 294-5
Carrboro, N.C. H6 180-1
Carrick*, Man. K4 272-3
Carrier, Okla. C10 234-5
Carrier Mills, Ill. N9 96-7
Carriere, Miss. N7 176-7
Carrington, N. Dak. F10 128-9
Carrizo, Ariz. F10 206-7
Carrizo Springs, Tex. I6 192-3
Carrizozo, N. Mex. I7 230-1
Carroll, Ia. F5 104-5
Carroll, Me. H9 64-5
Carroll, Man. J11 272-3
Carroll, Nebr. E13 124-5
Carroll, N.H. F6 72-3
Carroll, O. G7 132-3
Carroll, co., Ark. A4 150-1
Carroll, co., Ga. G2 160-1
Carroll, co., Ill. B6 96-7
Carroll, co., Ind. E6 100-1
Carroll, co., Ia. F4 104-5
Carroll, co., Ky. E10 164-5
Carroll, co., Md. B9 172-3
Carroll, co., Miss. F6 176-7
Carroll, co., Mo. D5 120-1
Carroll, co., N.H. I7 72-3
Carroll, co., O. D10 132-3
Carroll, co., Tenn. B4 188-9
Carroll, co., Va. J6 196-7
Carrolls, Wash. I7 246-7
Carrolls Crossing, N.B. G5 275
Carrollton, Ala. F3 146-7
Carrollton, Ark. A4 150-1
Carrollton, Ga. G2 160-1
Carrollton, Ill. I5 96-7
Carrollton, Ky. E10 164-5
Carrollton, Mich. E3 112-3
Carrollton, Miss. E6 176-7
Carrollton, Mo. D5 120-1
Carrollton, O. E10 132-3
Carrollton, Tex. C14 192-3
Carrollton, Va. G3 196-7
Carrolltown, Pa. H6 84-5
Carrot River, Sask. J9 294-5
Carrsville, Ky. I3 164-5
Carrsville, Va. H3 196-7
Carrville, Ala. H8 146-7
Carryville, Ark. A12 150-1
Carseland, Alta. M8 264-5
Carson, Calif. H8 210-1
Carson, Ia. I3 104-5
Carson, Miss. K7 176-7
Carson, N. Dak. I6 128-9
Carson, Okla. F13 234-5
Carson, Ore. D15 238-9
Carson, Va. F1 196-7
Carson, Wash. J8 246-7
Carson, co., Tex. B5 192-3
Carson City, Mich. I13 112-3
Carson City, Nev. G2 226-7
Carson R., Nev. G2 226-7
Carsonville, Mich. E7 112-3
Carstairs, Alta. L7 264-5
Carter, Ky. F14 164-5
Carter, Miss. G5 176-7
Carter, Mont. C7 222-3
Carter, Okla. F7 234-5
Carter, S. Dak. H9 136-7
Carter, Tenn. A16 188-9
Carter, Wyo. J5 250-1
Carter, co., Ky. F14 164-5
Carter, co., Mo. I9 120-1
Carter, co., Mont. G16 222-3
Carter, co., Okla. I11 234-5
Carter, co., Tenn. B16 188-9
Carter Lake, Ia. H2 104-5
Carter Nine, Okla. C12 234-5
Carteret, N.J. F7 76-7
Carteret, co., N.C. F14 180-1
Cartersburg, Ind. H7 100-1
Cartersville, Ga. E3 160-1
Cartersville, Mont. F13 222-3
Cartersville, Okla. F16 234-5
Cartersville, S.C. D13 184-5
Cartersville, Va. H11 196-7
Carterville, Ill. N8 96-7
Carterville, Mo. I3 120-1
Carthage, Ark. H6 150-1
Carthage, Ill. F4 96-7
Carthage, Ind. H10 100-1
Carthage, Me. J3 64-5
Carthage, Miss. H7 176-7
Carthage, Mo. H3 120-1
Carthage, N.Y. C8 80-1
Carthage, N.C. E9 180-1
Carthage, S. Dak. F14 136-7
Carthage, Tenn. B9 188-9
Carthage, Tex. E11 192-3
Cartier*, Ont. G7 284-5
Cartwright*, Man. K11 272-3
Cartwright, Nfld. H8 278-9
Cartwright, N. Dak. E1 128-9
Caruthers, Calif. K5 210-1
Caruthersville, Mo. K11 120-1
Carver, Mass. G13 68-9
Carver, Minn. C9 116-7
Carver, co., Minn. M6 116-7
Carver Ranch Estates*, Fla. I13 156-7
Carville, La. B10 168-9
Cary, Ga. J6 160-1
Cary, Ill. K2 96-7
Cary, Ky. J13 164-5
Cary, Me. F9 64-5
Cary, Miss. G4 176-7
Cary, N.C. I7 180-1
Carytown*, Mo. H3 120-1
Caryville, Fla. B5 156-7
Caryville, Mass. K2 68-9
Caryville, Tenn. G11 188-9
Casa, Ark. H12 150-1
Casa Blanca, N. Mex. F4 230-1
Casa Grande, Ariz. J7 206-7
Casanova, Va. B2 196-7
Casar, N.C. E5 180-1
Cascabel, Ariz. K9 206-7
Cascade, Colo. K3 214-5
Cascade, Ida. J3 218-9
Cascade, Ia. E14 104-5
Cascade, Mont. D6 222-3
Cascade, N.H. F8 72-3
Cascade, Va. K8 196-7
Cascade, W. Va. B16 200-1
Cascade, Wis. G5 140-1
Cascade, co., Mont. E6 222-3
Cascade Gorge, Ore. I6 238-9
Cascade Locks, Ore. B7 238-9
Cascade Range 14-15
Cascade Summit, Ore. G7 238-9
Cascadia, Ore. J2 238-9
Cascilla, Miss. D6 176-7
Casco, Me. M8 64-5
Casco, Wis. D6 140-1
Casco Bay, Me. O10 64-5
Cascumpec, P.E.I. C4 287
Caselton, Nev. I10 226-7
Caseville, Mich. G14 112-3
Casey, Ill. I11 96-7
Casey, Ia. H5 104-5
Casey, co., Ky. I10 164-5
Caseyville, Ill. K6 96-7
Caseyville, Ky. H4 164-5
Cash, Ark. C10 150-1
Cash, Va. E4 196-7
Cash Point, Tenn. E7 188-9
Cashiers, N.C. F3 180-1
Cashion*, Ariz. I6 206-7
Cashion, Okla. E10 234-5
Cashmere, Wash. F11 246-7
Cashton, Wis. H10 140-1
Casitas Springs*, Calif. N6 210-1
Casnovia*, Mich. I11 112-3
Casper, Wyo. F13 250-1
Caspian, Mich. D8 112-3
Caspiana, La. C2 168-9
Cass, W. Va. G7 200-1
Cass, co., Ill. G6 96-7
Cass, co., Ind. D7 100-1
Cass, co., Ia. H4 104-5
Cass, co., Mich. K11 112-3
Cass, co., Minn. H5 116-7
Cass, co., Mo. E3 120-1
Cass, co., Nebr. H15 124-5
Cass, co., N. Dak. G13 128-9
Cass, co., Tex. D11 192-3
Cass City, Mich. H15 112-3
Cass Lake, Minn. H4 116-7
Cassa, Wyo. G15 250-1
Cassadaga, N.Y. G1 80-1
Cassatt, S.C. D12 184-5
Casselberry, Fla. E12 156-7
Casselman, Ont. H15 284-5
Casselton, N. Dak. G14 128-9
Cassia, co., Ida. O7 218-9
Cassiar, B.C. B4 268-9
Cassity, W. Va. F15 200-1
Cassoday, Kans. H12 108-9
Cassopolis, Mich. K11 112-3
Casstown, O. F4 132-3
Cassville, Ga. E3 160-1
Cassville, Ind. E8 100-1
Cassville, Mo. J4 120-1
Cassville, W. Va. A14 200-1
Cassville, Wis. K10 140-1
Castalia, Ia. C12 104-5
Castalia, N.B. K4 275
Castalia, N.C. C12 180-1
Castalia, O. B7 132-3
Castalian Springs, Tenn. G8 188-9
Castana, Ia. F2 104-5
Castile, N.Y. F4 80-1
Castine, Me. K7 64-5
Castle*, Calif. D11 210-1
Castle, Okla. F13 234-5
Castle, Ore. B11 238-9
Castle Butte, Ariz. E9 206-7
Castle Dale, Ut. I7 242-3
Castle Hayne, N.C. G12 180-1
Castle Hill, Me. C8 64-5
Castle Hills, Tex. J2 192-3
Castle Hot Springs, Ariz. H6 206-7
Castle Rock, Colo. I3 214-5
Castle Rock, Minn. D11 116-7
Castle Rock, S. Dak. D2 136-7
Castle Rock, Ut. E7 242-3
Castle Rock, Wash. I7 246-7
Castle Shannon*, Pa. I2 84-5
Castleberry, Ala. L6 146-7
Castleford, Ida. O5 218-9
Castlegar, B.C. J9 268-9
Castleton, Ont. K11 284-5
Castleton, Vt. J4 90-1
Castleton-on-Hudson, N.Y. F11 80-1
Castlewood, S. Dak. D15 136-7
Castlewood, Va. J3 196-7
Castor, Alta. K9 264-5
Castor, La. C3 168-9
Castro, co., Tex. C4 192-3
Castro Valley, Calif. C8 210-1
Castroville, Calif. J3 210-1
Castroville, Tex. J1 192-3
Caswell, Me. B9 64-5
Caswell, co., N.C. C9 180-1
Caswellem*, Alta. I8 264-5
Cat Creek, Mont. E11 222-3
Catahoula, La. H6 168-9
Catahoula, co., La. D6 168-9
Cataldo, Ida. D3 218-9
Catalina, Nfld. M11 278-9
Cataract, Wis. H10 140-1
Catasauqua, Pa. H14 84-5
Cataula, Ga. J3 160-1
Cataumet, Mass. H14 68-9
Catawba, N.C. I1 180-1
Catawba, O. F5 132-3
Catawba, S.C. B10 184-5
Catawba, Va. I7 196-7
Catawba, W. Va. B15 200-1
Catawba, Wis. D10 140-1
Catawba, co., N.C. E6 180-1

Catawissa, Pa. G12 84-5
Cateechee, S.C. B5 184-5
Cates, Ind. G4 100-1
Catesby, Okla. C6 234-5
Catharine, Kans. F7 108-9
Catharpin, Va. A2 196-7
Cathay, N. Dak. F10 128-9
Cathcart, Ont. E13 284-5
Cathedral City, Calif. H12 210-1
Catherine, Ala. I4 146-7
Cathlamet, Wash. I6 246-7
Catlettsburg, Ky. F15 164-5
Catlin, Ill. G11 96-7
Cato, N.Y. E6 80-1
Cato, Wis. F5 140-1
Catonsville, Md. F6 172-3
Catoosa, Okla. D14 234-5
Catoosa, co., Ga. D2 160-1
Catron, Mo. J11 120-1
Catron, co., N. Mex. H3 230-1
Catskill, N.Y. G11 80-1
Cattaraugus, N.Y. G2 80-1
Cattaraugus, co., N.Y. G2 80-1
Caulksville, Ark. D3 150-1
Causapscal, Que. I5 290-1
Causey, N. Mex. H11 230-1
Cauthornville, Va. H13 196-7
Cauthron, Ark. E2 150-1
Cavalier, N. Dak. B13 128-9
Cavalier, co., N. Dak. B11 128-9
Cave, S.C. H9 184-5
Cave City, Ark. B8 150-1
Cave City, Ky. I8 164-5
Cave Creek, Ariz. H6 206-7
Cave Junction, Ore. J4 238-9
Cave Springs, Ark. A2 150-1
Cave Springs, Ga. F2 160-1
Ca-Vel, N.C. C10 180-1
Cavendish, Ida. F3 218-9
Cavendish, Vt. K6 90-1
Cavetown, Md. B8 172-3
Cavour, S. Dak. E13 136-7
Cavour, Wis. D14 140-1
Cawker City, Kans. D8 108-9
Cawood, Ky. J14 164-5
Cawston, B.C. J8 268-9
Cayce, Ky. K2 164-5
Cayce, S.C. E10 184-5
Caycuse, B.C. K6 268-9
Cayley, Alta. N8 264-5
Cayucos, Calif. L4 210-1
Cayuga, Ind. G4 100-1
Cayuga, N.Y. F6 80-1
Cayuga, N. Dak. J13 128-9
Cayuga, co., N.Y. F6 80-1
Cayuga Heights, N.Y. G6 80-1
Cayuse, Ore. B13 238-9
Cazenovia, N.Y. E7 80-1
Cazenovia, Wis. I11 140-1
Cebolla, N. Mex. C6 230-1
Cecelia, La. H5 168-9
Cecil, Ala. I8 146-7
Cecil, Ark. D3 150-1
Cecil, Ga. N6 160-1
Cecil, O. C3 132-3
Cecil, Ore. B11 238-9
Cecil, Wis. C3 140-1
Cecil, co., Md. B13 172-3
Cecile, La. B2 168-9
Cecilia, Ky. D1 164-5
Cecilton, Md. C13 172-3
Cedar, Kans. D7 108-9
Cedar, Mich. F12 112-3
Cedar, Ut. H8 242-3
Cedar, co., Ia. G13 104-5
Cedar, co., Mo. G4 120-1
Cedar, co., Nebr. D13 124-5
Cedar Bluff, Ala. C9 146-7
Cedar Bluff, Va. I4 196-7
Cedar Bluffs, Kans. C4 108-9
Cedar Bluffs, Nebr. I1 124-5
Cedar Brook, N.J. K4 76-7
Cedar City, Mo. E7 120-1
Cedar City, Ut. L4 242-3
Cedar Creek, Ariz. H9 206-7
Cedar Creek, Ark. F3 150-1
Cedar Creek, Nebr. J2 124-5
Cedar Crest, N. Mex. F6 230-1
Cedar Falls, Ia. D10 104-5
Cedar Falls, N.C. I4 180-1
Cedar Falls, Wash. F9 246-7
Cedar Fort, Ut. F6 242-3
Cedar Grove, Fla. C5 156-7
Cedar Grove, Ind. J12 100-1
Cedar Grove, Me. M11 64-5
Cedar Grove, Md. G2 172-3
Cedar Grove, N.J. B9 76-7
Cedar Grove, N.C. G6 180-1
Cedar Grove, Tenn. C4 188-9
Cedar Grove, W. Va. I14 200-1
Cedar Grove, Wis. H5 140-1
Cedar Hammock
[-Bradenton South],
Fla. J2 156-7
Cedar Heights*, Pa. J15 84-5
Cedar Hill, Tenn. F6 188-9
Cedar Hill, Tex. D14 192-3
Cedar Hill Lakes*, Mo. F10 120-1
Cedar Island, N.C. F15 180-1
Cedar Key, Fla. D9 156-7
Cedar Knolls, N.J. D6 76-7
Cedar Lake, Ala. B6 146-7
Cedar Lake, Ind. B4 100-1
Cedar Mills, Minn. B7 116-7
Cedar Mountain, N.C. E4 180-1
Cedar Park*, Tex. G8 192-3
Cedar Point, Kans. H12 108-9
Cedar Rapids, Ia. F12 104-5
Cedar Rapids, Nebr. F11 124-5
Cedar Ridge, Ariz. C7 206-7
Cedar Run, N.J. K7 76-7
Cedar Spring, Ariz. E9 206-7
Cedar Springs, Ga. M2 160-1
Cedar Springs, Mich. I12 112-3
Cedar Springs, Ont. F11 284-5
Cedar Vale, Kans. K12 108-9
Cedarbluff, Miss. E9 176-7
Cedarbrook-Melrose
Park*, Pa. J15 84-5
Cedarburg, Wis. I15 140-1
Cedaredge, Colo. F7 214-5
Cedarhurst*, N.Y. K11 80-1
Cedartown, Ga. F2 160-1
Cedarvale, B.C. E4 268-9
Cedarvale, N. Mex. G7 230-1
Cedarville, Ark. C2 150-1
Cedarville, Calif. D5 210-1
Cedarville, Ill. A7 96-7
Cedarville*, Ky. I16 164-5
Cedarville, Mass. G14 68-9
Cedarville, Mich. D13 112-3
Cedarville, N.J. M2 76-7
Cedarville, O. H16 132-3
Cedarville, W. Va. F5 200-1
Cedarwood, Colo. H12 214-5
Cedarwood Park, N.J. I7 76-7
Cedonia, Wash. D14 246-7
Cedoux, Sask. N9 294-5
Celeste, Tex. A16 192-3
Celestine, Ind. N6 100-1
Celilo, Ore. B9 238-9
Celina, O. E3 132-3
Celina, Tenn. A10 188-9
Celina, Tex. A15 192-3
Celista, B.C. I8 268-9
Celo, N.C. D4 180-1
Celoron, N.Y. G1 80-1
Cement, Okla. G10 234-5
Cement City, Mich. J13 112-3
Cementville, Ind. N9 100-1
Centenary, S.C. E14 184-5
Centennial, Wyo. J13 250-1
Center, Colo. I10 214-5
Center, Ga. F6 160-1
Center, Ind. F8 100-1
Center, Ky. I9 164-5
Center, Mo. C8 120-1
Center, Nebr. D12 124-5
Center, N. Dak. G6 128-9
Center, Okla. G12 234-5
Center, Tenn. J5 188-9
Center, Tex. E11 192-3
Center City, Minn. L7 116-7
Center Cross, Va. H14 196-7
Center Groton, Conn. G13 60-1
Center Harbor, N.H. J7 72-3
Center Hill, Ala. D6 146-7
Center Hill, Ark. D8 150-1
Center Hill, Fla. E4 156-7
Center Junction, Ia. F14 104-5
Center Line, Mich. I6 112-3
Center Lovell, Me. L2 64-5
Center Montville, Me. K6 64-5
Center Moriches, N.Y. J13 80-1
Center Ossipee, N.H. J8 72-3
Center Point, Ala. E6 146-7
Center Point, Ark. H3 150-1
Center Point, Ind. J5 100-1
Center Point, Ia. E12 104-5
Center Point, La. E5 168-9
Center Point, Tenn. K5 188-9
Center Point, W. Va. D5 200-1
Center Ridge, Ark. D6 150-1
Center Ridge, Miss. J8 176-7
Center Sandwich, N.H. I7 72-3
Centerbrook, Conn. G11 60-1
Centerburg, O. E7 132-3
Centereach, N.Y. J12 80-1
Centerfield, Ut. I6 242-3
Centerton, Ark. A2 150-1
Centerton, Ind. I7 100-1
Centertown, Ky. I6 164-5
Centertown, Mo. E6 120-1
Centertown, Tenn. I9 188-9
Centerview, Mo. E4 120-1
Centerville, Ark. E5 150-1
Centerville, Del. A3 153
Centerville, Ga. J5 160-1
Centerville, Ida. L4 218-9
Centerville, Ind. H11 100-1
Centerville, Ia. J9 104-5
Centerville, Kans. H15 108-9
Centerville*, Ky. I16 164-5
Centerville, La. I6 168-9
Centerville, Me. J10 64-5
Centerville, Mass. H15 68-9
Centerville, Minn. A11 116-7
Centerville, Mo. H9 120-1
Centerville, Nev. G2 226-7
Centerville, N.C. C12 180-1
Centerville, O. I15 132-3
Centerville, Pa. J2 84-5
Centerville, R.I. G2 87
Centerville, S. Dak. I15 136-7
Centerville, Tenn. I5 188-9
Centerville, Tex. F10 192-3
Centerville, Ut. E6 242-3
Centerville, Vt. D6 90-1
Centerville, Wash. J10 246-7
Centerville, Wis. H9 140-1
Centerville-Dublin
Gulch*, Mont. G5 222-3
Centrahoma, Okla. H13 234-5
Central, Alaska D12 254-5
Central, Ariz. J10 206-7
Central, Ark. H2 150-1
Central, Ark. G5 150-1
Central, Ida. N10 218-9
Central, La. C11 168-9
Central, N. Mex. K3 230-1
Central, S.C. B5 184-5
Central, Tenn. B3 188-9
Central, Ut. J6 242-3
Central, Ut. M3 242-3
Central Barren, Ind. N8 100-1
Central Bedeque*, P.E.I. E5 287
Central Blissville, N.B. I4 275
Central Butte, Sask. M6 294-5
Central City*, Ark. D2 150-1
Central City, Colo. G1 214-5
Central City, Ill. K8 96-7
Central City, Ia. E13 104-5
Central City, Ky. I6 164-5
Central City, Nebr. H12 124-5
Central City, Pa. J5 84-5
Central City, S. Dak. E2 136-7
Central Falls, N.C. I4 180-1
Central Falls, R.I. B6 87
Central Heights, Ariz. I8 206-7
Central Heights, Ia. B8 104-5
Central Islip, N.Y. J12 80-1
Central Lake, Mich. F12 112-3
Central Pacolet, S.C. F5 184-5
Central Park*, Alta. K7 264-5
Central Park, Wash. G6 246-7
Central Patricia, Ont. D3 284-5
Central Point, Ore. J6 238-9
Central Point West*, Ore. J6 238-9
Central Square, N.Y. E7 80-1
Central Station, W. Va. E5 200-1
Central Valley, Calif. E3 210-1
Central Village, Conn. D14 60-1
Centralhatchee, Ga. H2 160-1
Centralia, Ill. K8 96-7
Centralia, Ia. D14 104-5
Centralia, Kans. D13 108-9
Centralia, Mo. D7 120-1
Centralia, Okla. C14 234-5
Centralia, Pa. G12 84-5
Centralia, Wash. H7 246-7
Centralia, W. Va. G5 200-1
Centre, Ala. D9 146-7
Centre, co., Pa. G8 84-5
Centre Calling Lake*,
Alta. G8 264-5
Centre Hall, Pa. G8 84-5
Centre St. Simon, N.B. E7 275
Centreville, Ala. G5 146-7
Centreville, Ill. K6 96-7
Centreville, Md. E13 172-3
Centreville, Mich. K12 112-3
Centreville, Miss. L4 176-7
Centreville, N.B. G3 275
Centreville, N.S. E4 281
Centreville, Va. A3 196-7
Centropolis, Kans. F15 108-9
Centuria, Wis. D7 140-1
Century, Fla. A3 156-7
Century, W. Va. D14 200-1
Cereal, Alta. L10 264-5
Ceredo, W. Va. H9 200-1
Ceres, Calif. D10 210-1
Ceres, Okla. C11 234-5
Ceres, Va. J5 196-7
Ceresco, Nebr. J1 124-5
Cerrillos, N. Mex. E6 230-1
Cerritos*, Calif. N7 210-1
Cerro, N. Mex. C7 230-1
Cerro Gordo, Ill. H9 96-7
Cerro Gordo, N.C. G10 180-1
Cerro Gordo, co., Ia. C8 104-5
Cerulean Springs, Ky. J5 164-5
Cestos, Okla. D8 234-5
Ceylon, Minn. O4 116-7
Ceylon, Sask. O8 294-5
Chackbay, La. D11 168-9
Chacon, N. Mex. D8 230-1
Chadbourn, N.C. G10 180-1
Chadron, Nebr. C3 124-5
Chadwick, Ill. B6 96-7
Chadwick Acres*, N.C. G13 180-1
Chaffee, Mo. H11 120-1
Chaffee, N. Dak. H13 128-9
Chaffee, co., Colo. G10 214-5
Chagrin Falls, O. B15 132-3
Chaleur Bay, N.B. D5 275
Chalfant*, Pa. I2 84-5
Chalfont, Pa. I15 84-5
Chalk Level, Tenn. G14 188-9
Chalk River, Ont. H9 284-5
Chalkville, Ala. E6 146-7
Chalkyitsik, Alaska C12 254-5
Challis, Ida. J6 218-9
Chalmers, Ind. E6 100-1
Chalmette, La. D15 168-9
Chalybeate, Miss. A9 176-7
Chalybeate, N.C. J7 180-1
Chalybeate Springs, Ga. I3 160-1
Chama, Colo. J11 214-5
Chama, N. Mex. B6 230-1
Chamberino, N. Mex. L5 230-1
Chamberlain, Sask. M7 294-5
Chamberlain, S. Dak. G10 136-7
Chamberlain Settlement*,
N.B. E6 275
Chambers, Ariz. E11 206-7
Chambers, La. F4 168-9
Chambers, Nebr. E10 124-5
Chambers, co., Ala. G10 146-7
Chambers, co., Tex. G11 192-3
Chambersburg, Pa. J8 84-5
Chamblee, Ga. B11 160-1
Chambly*, Que. J12 290-1
Chambly, co., Que. J3 290-1
Chambord, Que. C10 290-1
Chamisal, N. Mex. D7 230-1
Chamois, Mo. E8 120-1
Champ, Md. H14 172-3
Champaign, Ill. G10 96-7
Champaign, co., Ill. G10 96-7
Champaign, co., O. F5 132-3
Champion, Alta. N8 264-5
Champion, Mich. D9 112-3
Champion, Nebr. I5 124-5
Champlain, N.Y. A11 80-1
Champlain, Que. G9 290-1
Champlain, Va. G13 196-7
Champlain, co., Que. I3 290-1
Champlain Park*, N.Y. A11 80-1
Champlin, Minn. A10 116-7
Chance, Ala. K4 146-7
Chance, Md. H13 172-3
Chance, Okla. D16 234-5
Chance, S. Dak. B5 136-7
Chance Cove, Nfld. N10 278-9
Chance Harbour, N.B. J5 275
Chancellor, Ala. L8 146-7
Chancellor, S. Dak. H15 136-7
Chancellor, Va. C2 196-7
Chandalar, Alaska C11 254-5
Chandler, Ariz. I6 206-7
Chandler, Ind. O4 100-1
Chandler, Minn. O2 116-7
Chandler, Okla. E12 234-5
Chandler, Que. I6 290-1
Chandler*, Tex. E10 192-3
Chandler Heights, Ariz. I7 206-7
Chandler Springs, Ala. F8 146-7
Chandlerville, Ill. G6 96-7
Chaneliak, Alaska E8 254-5
Change Islands, Nfld. L10 278-9
Changewater, N.J. E4 76-7
Chanhassen, Minn. B9 116-7
Channahon*, Ill. D10 96-7
Channel-Port aux
Basques, Nfld. O7 278-9
Channing, Mich. D9 112-3
Channing, Tex. A4 192-3
Chantilly, Va. A3 196-7
Chanute, Kans. I15 108-9
Chanute, Tenn. A10 188-9
Chapais, Que. H2 290-1
Chapeau, Que. J1 290-1
Chapel Hill, N.C. H6 180-1
Chapel Hill, Tenn. I7 188-9
Chapel Oaks-Cedar
Heights*, Md. E10 172-3
Chapeltown, Del. F3 153
Chapin, Ia. C8 104-5
Chapin, S.C. K7 184-5
Chapleau, Ont. G6 284-5
Chaplin, Conn. C13 60-1
Chaplin, Ky. C4 164-5
Chaplin, Sask. N6 294-5
Chapman, Ala. K6 146-7
Chapman, Kans. F11 108-9
Chapman, Me. C8 64-5
Chapman, Nebr. H11 124-5
Chapmansboro, Tenn. G6 188-9
Chapmanville, W. Va. J12 200-1
Chappell, Nebr. H3 124-5
Chappells, S.C. K5 184-5
Chaptico, Md. H10 172-3
Chardon, O. A16 132-3
Charenton, La. I6 168-9
Charette, Que. J3 290-1
Charing, Ga. J4 160-1
Charing Cross, Ont. F11 284-5
Chariton, Ia. I8 104-5
Chariton, co., Mo. C5 120-1
Charlack*, Mo. E10 120-1
Charlemagne*, Que. I12 290-1
Charlemont, Mass. B4 68-9
Charleroi, Pa. J2 84-5
Charles, Ga. K8 160-1
Charles, co., Md. G9 172-3
Charles City, Ia. C10 104-5
Charles City, Va. I13 196-7
Charles City, co., Va. I13 196-7
Charles Mix, co., S. Dak. H11 136-7
Charles Town, W. Va. E12 200-1
Charlesbourg, Que. F11 290-1
Charleston, Ariz. M10 206-7
Charleston, Ark. D3 150-1
Charleston, Ill. I10 96-7
Charleston, Kans. I4 108-9
Charleston, Me. I6 64-5
Charleston, Miss. D6 176-7
Charleston, Mo. I12 120-1
Charleston, Nev. B9 226-7
Charleston, Ore. H3 238-9
Charleston, S.C. I13 184-5
Charleston, Tenn. J2 188-9
Charleston, Tenn. K12 188-9
Charleston, Ut. F7 242-3
Charleston*, Vt. B9 90-1
Charleston, W. Va. G3 200-1
Charleston, co., S.C. I12 184-5
Charleston Base*, S.C. H13 184-5
Charleston Park, Nev. M8 226-7
Charleston Yard*, S.C. H13 184-5
Charlestown, Ind. M9 100-1
Charlestown*, Md. B13 172-3
Charlestown, Mass. H5 68-9
Charlestown, N.H. M3 72-3
Charlestown, R.I. H3 87
Charlevoix, Mich. E12 112-3
Charlevoix, co., Mich. E12 112-3
Charlevoix-Est, co., Que. D13 290-1
Charlevoix-Ouest, co.,
Que. D12 290-1
Charleys Branch, Tenn. G11 188-9
Charlie Lake, B.C. E8 268-9
Charlo, Mont. D3 222-3
Charlo*, N.B. D5 275
Charlotte, Ark. C9 150-1
Charlotte, Ia. F15 104-5
Charlotte, Me. I11 64-5
Charlotte, Mich. J13 112-3
Charlotte, N.C. E7 180-1

Charlotte, Tenn. B6 188-9
Charlotte, Tex. H7 192-3
Charlotte, Vt. F4 90-1
Charlotte, co., Fla. H11 156-7
Charlotte, co., N.B. J4 275
Charlotte, co., Va. J10 196-7
Charlotte Courthouse, Va. J10 196-7
Charlotte Hall, Md. G10 172-3
Charlottesville, Ind. H10 100-1
Charlottesville, Va. G10 196-7
Charlottetown, P.E.I. F7 287
Charlotteville, Ga. K8 160-1
Charlton, Mass. E7 68-9
Charlton, Ont. G8 284-5
Charlton, co., Ga. N9 160-1
Charmco, W. Va. H5 200-1
Charny, Que. G11 290-1
Charter Oak, Ia. F5 104-5
Chartley, Mass. F11 68-9
Chase, Ala. B7 146-7
Chase, B.C. I8 268-9
Chase, Kans. H8 108-9
Chase, La. C6 168-9
Chase, Md. E8 172-3
Chase, Mich. H12 112-3
Chase*, Tex. I8 192-3
Chase, co., Kans. H12 108-9
Chase, co., Nebr. I5 124-5
Chase City, Va. J10 196-7
Chaseburg, Wis. I9 140-1
Chaseley, N. Dak. F9 128-9
Chaska, Minn. B9 116-7
Chaska, Tenn. F11 188-9
Chassell, Mich. C8 112-3
Chastang, Ala. M3 146-7
Chataignier, La. G4 168-9
Chatawa, Miss. M5 176-7
Chatcolet, Ida. D2 218-9
Château-Richer, Que. F11 290-1
Chateaugay, N.Y. A10 80-1
Châteauguay*, Que. J3 290-1
Châteauguay, co., Que. J12 290-1
Chater*, Man. J2 272-3
Chatfield, Ark. E11 150-1
Chatfield, Man. H14 272-3
Chatfield, Minn. O8 116-7
Chatfield, O. D7 132-3
Chatham, Ill. H7 96-7
Chatham, La. C4 168-9
Chatham, Mass. H16 68-9
Chatham, Mich. D10 112-3
Chatham, Miss. G4 176-7
Chatham, N.B. F6 275
Chatham, N.H. G9 72-3
Chatham*, N.J. E6 76-7
Chatham, N.J. E6 76-7
Chatham, N.Y. G11 80-1
Chatham, Ont. F10 284-5
Chatham, Va. J9 196-7
Chatham, co., Ga. K11 160-1
Chatham, co., N.C. D9 180-1
Chatham Head, N.B. F6 275
Chatom, Ala. L2 146-7
Chatsworth, Ga. D3 160-1
Chatsworth, Ill. E10 96-7
Chatsworth, Ia. C1 104-5
Chatsworth, N.J. J6 76-7
Chatsworth, Ont. B13 284-5
Chattahoochee, Fla. B6 156-7
Chattahoochee, co., Ga. J2 160-1
Chattahoochee R., Ga. K2 160-1
Chattanooga, Okla. H9 234-5
Chattanooga, Tenn. D10 188-9
Chattaroy, Wash. E16 246-7
Chattaroy, W. Va. K10 200-1
Chattooga, co., Ga. E2 160-1
Chatwood, Pa. B9 84-5
Chaumont, N.Y. C7 80-1
Chauncey, Ga. K7 160-1
Chauncey, O. H8 132-3
Chautauqua, Kans. K13 108-9
Chautauqua, co., Kans. K13 108-9
Chautauqua, co., N.Y. G1 80-1
Chautauqua Lake, N.Y. G1 80-1
Chauvin, Alta. J10 264-5
Chauvin, La. J8 168-9
Chaves, co., N. Mex. I10 230-1
Cheatham, co., Tenn. A7 188-9
Chebanse, Ill. E11 96-7
Chebeaque Island, Me. O9 64-5
Cheboygan, Mich. E13 112-3
Cheboygan, co., Mich. E13 112-3
Check, Va. J7 196-7
Checotah, Okla. F14 234-5
Cheddar, S.C. H1 184-5
Chef Menteur, La. C15 168-9
Chefornak, Alaska F8 254-5
Chehalis, Wash. H7 246-7
Chelan, Sask. K9 294-5
Chelan, Wash. E11 246-7
Chelan, co., Wash. E10 246-7
Chelan Falls, Wash. E12 246-7
Chelmsford, Mass. B10 68-9
Chelsea, Ala. F6 146-7
Chelsea, Ia. F11 104-5
Chelsea, Me. L5 64-5
Chelsea, Mass. H5 68-9
Chelsea, Mich. J3 112-3
Chelsea, Okla. C14 234-5
Chelsea, S. Dak. C12 136-7
Chelsea, Vt. H7 90-1
Chelsea, Wis. E11 140-1
Cheltenham, Md. K5 172-3
Chemainus, B.C. D12 268-9
Chemeketa Park-Redwood Estates*, Calif. J3 210-1
Chemult, Ore. H8 238-9
Chemung, co., N.Y. G6 80-1
Chenango, co., N.Y. F8 80-1
Chenequa*, Wis. J14 140-1
Chenequa North*, Wis. J14 140-1
Chénéville, Que. H10 290-1
Cheney, Kans. I10 108-9
Cheney, Wash. F15 246-7
Cheney Res., Kans. I9 108-9
Cheneyville, La. F5 168-9
Cheniere, La. B5 168-9
Chenoa, Ill. E9 96-7
Chenoweth*, Ore. B9 238-9
Chepachet, R.I. B3 87
Cheraw, Colo. H14 214-5
Cheraw, Miss. L7 176-7
Cheraw, S.C. B13 184-5
Cheriton, Va. F5 196-7
Cherokee, Ala. B3 146-7
Cherokee, Ia. D3 104-5
Cherokee, Kans. J16 108-9
Cherokee, N.C. E2 180-1
Cherokee, Okla. C9 234-5
Cherokee, S.C. E4 184-5
Cherokee, co., Ala. D9 146-7
Cherokee, co., Ga. F3 160-1
Cherokee, co., Ia. D3 104-5
Cherokee, co., Kans. K16 108-9
Cherokee, co., N.C. E1 180-1
Cherokee, co., Okla. D15 234-5
Cherokee, co., S.C. A8 184-5
Cherokee, co., Tex. E10 192-3
Cherokee Falls, S.C. A9 184-5
Cherokee Village [-Hidden Valley], Ark. A9 150-1
Cherry, Ariz. F6 206-7
Cherry, N.C. D15 180-1
Cherry, Tenn. J2 188-9
Cherry, co., Nebr. D6 124-5
Cherry Creek, B.C. I8 268-9
Cherry Creek, Ida. O9 218-9
Cherry Creek, Nev. E10 226-7
Cherry Creek, N.Y. G2 80-1
Cherry Creek, S. Dak. E6 136-7
Cherry Grove, Ore. F1 238-9
Cherry Grove, W. Va. G8 200-1
Cherry Hill, Ark. F3 150-1
Cherry Hill, Md. B13 172-3
Cherry Hill, N.J. N11 76-7
Cherry Hills Village, Colo. H3 214-5
Cherry Point*, N.C. F14 180-1
Cherry Run, W. Va. D11 200-1
Cherry Valley, Ark. D10 150-1
Cherry Valley*, Calif. N8 210-1
Cherry Valley, Ill. A8 96-7
Cherry Valley, N.Y. F9 80-1
Cherry Valley, Ont. K13 284-5
Cherry Valley, Tenn. B8 188-9
Cherryfield, Me. J9 64-5
Cherryland*, Calif. I3 210-1
Cherryvale, Kans. J14 108-9
Cherryville, Mo. G8 120-1
Cherryville, N.C. E6 180-1
Cherrywood Village*, Ky. G9 164-5
Chesaning, Mich. F2 112-3
Chesapeake, O. K8 132-3
Chesapeake, Va. J15 196-7
Chesapeake, W. Va. I14 200-1
Chesapeake and Delaware Canal, Del. C3 153
Chesapeake Bay, Md. E11 172-3
Chesapeake Beach, Md. F11 172-3
Chesapeake City, Md. B14 172-3
Chesaw, Wash. B13 246-7
Chesham, N.H. N4 72-3
Cheshire, Conn. F8 60-1
Cheshire, Mass. C2 68-9
Cheshire, O. I8 132-3
Cheshire, Ore. K1 238-9
Cheshire, co., N.H. O3 72-3
Cheshire Harbor, Mass. B2 68-9
Chesilhurst, N.J. K4 76-7
Chesley, Ont. B12 284-5
Chesnee, S.C. A8 184-5
Chester, Ark. C2 150-1
Chester, Calif. F4 210-1
Chester, Conn. G11 60-1
Chester, Ga. J7 160-1
Chester, Ida. K10 218-9
Chester, Ill. M7 96-7
Chester, Ia. A11 104-5
Chester, Me. H7 64-5
Chester, Md. E12 172-3
Chester, Mass. D3 68-9
Chester, Miss. F8 176-7
Chester, Mont. B7 222-3
Chester, Nebr. J12 124-5
Chester, N.H. N8 72-3
Chester*, N.J. D5 76-7
Chester, N.J. D5 76-7
Chester, N.Y. I10 80-1
Chester*, N.S. E6 281
Chester, Okla. D8 234-5
Chester, Pa. K15 84-5
Chester, S.C. B9 184-5
Chester, S. Dak. F15 136-7
Chester, Ut. H6 242-3
Chester, Vt. L6 90-1
Chester, Va. E1 196-7
Chester, W. Va. A6 200-1
Chester, co., Pa. K13 84-5
Chester, co., S.C. C9 184-5
Chester, co., Tenn. C4 188-9
Chester Center, Mass. D3 68-9
Chesterfield, Conn. G12 60-1
Chesterfield, Ida. N10 218-9
Chesterfield, Ind. G10 100-1
Chesterfield, Mass. D4 68-9
Chesterfield, N.H. O2 72-3
Chesterfield, N.J. H5 76-7
Chesterfield, S.C. B12 184-5
Chesterfield, Tenn. C4 188-9
Chesterfield, Va. I12 196-7
Chesterfield, co., S.C. B12 184-5
Chesterfield, co., Va. I12 196-7
Chesterfield Inlet, N.W. Terr. C3 296
Chesterhill, O. H9 132-3
Chestermere Lake*, Alta. M7 264-5
Chesterton, Ind. A5 100-1
Chestertown, Md. D13 172-3
Chesterville, Me. K4 64-5
Chesterville, Miss. C9 176-7
Chesterville, Ont. H15 284-5
Chestnut, La. C3 168-9
Chestnut Hill, Conn. D12 60-1
Chestnut Hill, Mass. I4 68-9
Chestnut Hill, Tenn. H14 188-9
Chestnut Mound, Tenn. A9 188-9
Chestnut Mountain, Ga. E5 160-1
Chesuncook, Me. E5 64-5
Cheswick, Pa. A7 84-5
Cheswold, Del. E3 153
Chetek, Wis. E9 140-1
Chéticamp, N.S. A10 281
Chetopa, Kans. K15 108-9
Chetwynd, B.C. E7 268-9
Chevak, Alaska E8 254-5
Cheverly, Md. I5 172-3
Cheviot, O. K13 132-3
Chevy Chase, Md. I3 172-3
Chevy Chase*, Md. E9 172-3
Chevy Chase Heights*, Pa. H4 84-5
Chevy Chase Section Four*, Md. E9 172-3
Chevy Chase View, Md. I3 172-3
Chewalla, Tenn. D4 188-9
Chewelah, Wash. D15 246-7
Chewey, Okla. D16 234-5
Chewsville, Md. B7 172-3
Cheyenne, Okla. E7 234-5
Cheyenne, Wyo. J15 250-1
Cheyenne, co., Colo. F15 214-5
Cheyenne, co., Kans. C2 108-9
Cheyenne, co., Nebr. G2 124-5
Cheyenne Wells, Colo. F16 214-5
Chi Chil Tah, N. Mex. F2 230-1
Chiapuk, Ariz. K6 206-7
Chiawuli Tak, Ariz. L7 206-7
Chibougamau, Que. H3 290-1
Chicago, Ill. B11 96-7
Chicago Heights, Ill. O4 96-7
Chicago Ridge, Ill. N3 96-7
Chicago Sanitary & Ship Canal, Ill. N2 96-7
Chichester, N.H. M7 72-3
Chickaloon, Alaska F11 254-5
Chickamauga, Ga. D2 160-1
Chickamaw Beach, Minn. I5 116-7
Chickasaw, Ala. N3 146-7
Chickasaw, La. A7 168-9
Chickasaw, O. E3 132-3
Chickasaw, co., Ia. B11 104-5
Chickasaw, co., Miss. D9 176-7
Chickasha, Okla. G10 234-5
Chicken, Alaska D13 254-5
Chico, Calif. G3 210-1
Chico, Tex. D8 192-3
Chico Hot Springs, Mont. H7 222-3
Chico North*, Calif. G3 210-1
Chico West*, Calif. G3 210-1
Chicopee, Mass. E5 68-9
Chicora, Miss. K10 176-7
Chicora, Pa. G3 84-5
Chicot, Ark. J9 150-1
Chicot, co., Ark. K9 150-1
Chicoutimi, Que. I4 290-1
Chicoutimi, co., Que. G4 290-1
Chidester, Ark. I5 150-1
Chiefland, Fla. D9 156-7
Chignik, Alaska H9 254-5
Chignik Lagoon, Alaska H9 254-5
Chignik Lake, Alaska H9 254-5
Childers, Okla. C14 234-5
Childersburg, Ala. F7 146-7
Childress, Tex. C6 192-3
Childress, co., Tex. B6 192-3
Childs, Ariz. G7 206-7
Childs, Ariz. K5 206-7
Childs, Md. B13 172-3
Chilesburg, Va. G12 196-7
Chilhowee, Mo. E4 120-1
Chilhowie, Va. J5 196-7
Chili, Ind. D8 100-1
Chili, Wis. F11 140-1
Chilili, N. Mex. F6 230-1
Chillicothe, Ill. E7 96-7
Chillicothe, Ia. I10 104-5
Chillicothe, Mo. C4 120-1
Chillicothe, O. H6 132-3
Chillicothe, Tex. C7 192-3
Chillicothe West*, O. H6 132-3
Chilliwack, B.C. J7 268-9
Chillum, Md. I4 172-3
Chilly, Ida. K7 218-9
Chilmark, Mass. J13 68-9
Chilocco, Okla. B11 234-5
Chiloquin, Ore. I7 238-9
Chilton, Wis. H14 140-1
Chilton, co., Ala. H6 146-7
Chimacum, Wash. G1 246-7
Chimayo, N. Mex. D7 230-1
Chimney Rock, Colo. J8 214-5
China, Me. K5 64-5
China*, Tex. G11 192-3
China Grove, Ala. J8 146-7
China Grove*, N.C. E7 180-1
China Lake, Calif. L8 210-1
Chinchalo, Ore. I8 238-9
Chincoteague, Va. G16 196-7
Chincoteague Bay, Md. H15 172-3
Chinle, Ariz. C10 206-7
Chino, Calif. G9 210-1
Chino Valley, Ariz. F5 206-7
Chinook, Mont. B9 222-3
Chinook, Wash. H5 246-7
Chinquapin, N.C. F12 180-1
Chipewyan Lake*, Alta. E8 264-5
Chipita Park, Colo. K3 214-5
Chipley, Fla. B5 156-7
Chipman*, Alta. I8 264-5
Chipman, N.B. H5 275
Chipola, La. F8 168-9
Chippenhook, Vt. J4 90-1
Chippewa, co., Mich. D12 112-3
Chippewa, co., Minn. L3 116-7
Chippewa, co., Wis. E9 140-1
Chippewa Falls, Wis. F9 140-1
Chippewa Lake, Mich. H12 112-3
Chippewa-on-the-Lake, O. D13 132-3
Chisago, co., Minn. K7 116-7
Chisago City, Minn. L7 116-7
Chisholm, Me. K3 64-5
Chisholm, Minn. G7 116-7
Chismville, Ark. D3 150-1
Chistochina, Alaska E12 254-5
Chitek Lake, Sask. I5 294-5
Chitina, Alaska F12 254-5
Chittenango*, N.Y. E8 80-1
Chittenden, Vt. I5 90-1
Chittenden, co., Vt. E5 90-1
Chitwood, Ore. D4 238-9
Chivington, Colo. G15 214-5
Chloe, W. Va. F4 200-1
Chloride, Ariz. E3 206-7
Chloride, N. Mex. J4 230-1
Choccolocco, Ala. E9 146-7
Chocorua, N.H. I8 72-3
Chocowinity, N.C. E14 180-1
Choctaw, Ala. I3 146-7
Choctaw, Ark. D6 150-1
Choctaw, Miss. E4 176-7
Choctaw, Okla. J3 234-5
Choctaw, co., Ala. J2 146-7
Choctaw, co., Miss. F8 176-7
Choctaw, co., Okla. I14 234-5
Choctaw Bluff, Ala. L4 146-7
Choiceland, Sask. J8 294-5
Chokio, Minn. K2 116-7
Cholona, Nev. C3 226-7
Chopin, La. E3 168-9
Chortitz, Man. K13 272-3
Chortitz, Sask. N5 294-5
Chosen, Fla. D14 156-7
Choska, Okla. E14 234-5
Choteau, Mont. C6 222-3
Choudrant, La. B4 168-9
Choulic, Ariz. M7 206-7
Chouteau, Okla. D15 234-5
Chouteau, co., Mont. C7 222-3
Chowan, co., N.C. C14 180-1
Chowchilla, Calif. J5 210-1
Chrisman, Ill. H11 96-7
Chrisney, Ind. O5 100-1
Christian, Alaska C12 254-5
Christian, W. Va. K12 200-1
Christian, co., Ill. I8 96-7
Christian, co., Ky. J5 164-5
Christian, co., Mo. I5 120-1
Christian Hollow, N.H. N3 72-3
Christiana, Del. B3 153
Christiana, Pa. J13 84-5
Christiana, Tenn. I8 188-9
Christiansburg, O. F4 132-3
Christiansburg, Va. I7 196-7
Christie, Okla. D16 234-5
Christina, Mont. D9 222-3
Christina Lake, B.C. K9 268-9
Christine, N. Dak. H14 128-9
Christmas, Ariz. J9 206-7
Christmasville, Tenn. B4 188-9
Christopher, Ill. M8 96-7
Christopher Lake, Sask. J7 294-5
Chromo, Colo. J9 214-5
Chrysler, Ala. L4 146-7
Chuathbaluk*, Alaska F9 254-5
Chubbuck, Ida. N9 218-9
Chuckanut, Wash. C8 246-7
Chuckey, Tenn. G15 188-9
Chugiak*, Alaska F11 254-5
Chugwater, Wyo. I15 250-1
Chuichu, Ariz. J7 206-7
Chula, Ga. M6 160-1
Chula, Mo. B5 120-1
Chula Vista, Calif. K11 210-1
Chulahoma, Miss. B7 176-7
Chunchula, Ala. M2 146-7
Chunky, Miss. I9 176-7
Church Butte, Wyo. J6 250-1
Church Creek, Md. G13 172-3
Church Hill, Md. D13 172-3
Church Hill, Miss. K3 176-7
Church Hill, Tenn. F15 188-9
Church Point, La. G5 168-9
Church Road, Va. F1 196-7
Church Rock, N. Mex. E2 230-1
Churchbridge, Sask. M10 294-5
Churchill, Man. B5 272-3
Churchill*, O. C11 132-3
Churchill*, Pa. I2 84-5
Churchill, co., Nev. F4 226-7
Churchill Falls, Nfld. H3 278-9
Churchill R., Man. C4 272-3
Churchill R., Sask. G8 294-5
Churchs Ferry, N. Dak. D10 128-9
Churchton, Tenn. B3 188-9
Churchville, Md. B12 172-3
Churchville, N.Y. E4 80-1
Churchville, Va. G9 196-7

Churdan, Ia.	F5	104-5
Churubusco, Ind.	C10	100-1
Chute-aux-Outardes, Que.	A15	290-1
Cibecue, Ariz.	H9	206-7
Cibola, Ariz.	I2	206-7
Cicero, Ill.	M4	96-7
Cicero, Ind.	G8	100-1
Cimarron, Colo.	G7	214-5
Cimarron, Kans.	I4	108-9
Cimarron, N. Mex.	C8	230-1
Cimarron, co., Okla.	C1	234-5
Cincinnati, Ia.	K9	104-5
Cincinnati, O.	I3	132-3
Cinco, W. Va.	H14	200-1
Cinco Bayou, Fla.	B4	156-7
Cinda, Ky.	I14	164-5
Cinderella, W. Va.	I2	200-1
Cinebar, Wash.	H7	246-7
Cinnaminson, N.J.	M11	76-7
Circle, Alaska	D12	254-5
Circle, Mont.	D14	222-3
Circle Pines*, Minn.	L6	116-7
Circle Springs, Alaska	D12	254-5
Circleville, Kans.	D14	108-9
Circleville, O.	G6	132-3
Circleville, Ut.	K5	242-3
Circleville, W. Va.	G8	200-1
Cisco, Ga.	C3	160-1
Cisco, Tex.	E7	192-3
Cisco, Ut.	I10	242-3
Cisne, Ill.	K10	96-7
Cissna Park, Ill.	F11	96-7
Citra, Okla.	G13	234-5
Citronelle, Ala.	M2	146-7
Citrus, co., Fla.	E10	156-7
Citrus Heights, Calif.	A9	210-1
City View, S.C.	F2	184-5
Civit, Okla.	G11	234-5
Clackamas, co., Ore.	D7	238-9
Claflin, Kans.	G8	108-9
Claggettsville, Md.	F3	172-3
Claiborne, Ala.	K4	146-7
Claiborne, La.	B5	168-9
Claiborne, Md.	E12	172-3
Claiborne, co., La.	A3	168-9
Claiborne, co., Miss.	J4	176-7
Claiborne, co., Tenn.	A13	188-9
Clair, N.B.	F1	275
Clair, Sask.	L8	294-5
Clair Haven, Mich.	I7	112-3
Clair Haven West*, Mich.	I15	112-3
Claire City, S. Dak.	A15	136-7
Clairfield, Tenn.	F12	188-9
Clairmont, Alta.	G4	264-5
Clairton, Pa.	B7	84-5
Clallam, co., Wash.	D6	246-7
Clallam Bay, Wash.	D5	246-7
Clam Gulch*, Alaska	F11	254-5
Clancy, Mont.	F6	222-3
Clandeboye, Man.	I14	272-3
Clandonald, Alta.	I10	264-5
Clanton, Ala.	G6	146-7
Clanwilliam, Man.	I11	272-3
Clara, Miss.	K9	176-7
Clara City, Minn.	M3	116-7
Clare, Ia.	D6	104-5
Clare, La.	E2	168-9
Clare, Mich.	H13	112-3
Clare, co., Mich.	G13	112-3
Claremont*, Calif.	G9	210-1
Claremont, Minn.	O7	116-7
Claremont, N.H.	L3	72-3
Claremont, N.C.	I1	180-1
Claremont, S.C.	E11	184-5
Claremont, S. Dak.	B13	136-7
Claremont, Va.	F2	196-7
Claremore, Okla.	D14	234-5
Clarence, Ala.	D7	146-7
Clarence, Ia.	F14	104-5
Clarence, La.	D3	168-9
Clarence, Mo.	C7	120-1
Clarence, N.Y.	E3	80-1
Clarence Cannon Res., Mo.	D7	120-1
Clarence Center*, N.Y.	E3	80-1
Clarence Creek*, Ont.	H15	284-5
Clarendon, Ark.	F9	150-1
Clarendon, N.C.	H10	180-1
Clarendon, Tex.	B5	192-3
Clarendon, Vt.	J5	90-1
Clarendon, co., S.C.	F12	184-5
Clarendon Hills*, Ill.	B10	96-7
Clarendon Springs, Vt.	J4	90-1
Clarenville, Nfld.	N10	278-9
Claresholm, Alta.	N8	264-5
Claresholm Airport*, Alta.	N8	264-5
Clareton, Wyo.	D15	250-1
Clarinda, Ia.	J4	104-5
Clarington, O.	G11	132-3
Clarion, Ia.	D7	104-5
Clarion, Pa.	F4	84-5
Clarion, co., Pa.	F4	84-5
Clarissa, Minn.	J4	116-7
Clarita, Okla.	H13	234-5
Clark, Colo.	B8	214-5
Clark, Mo.	D7	120-1
Clark, Nev.	F2	226-7
Clark, N.J.	E7	76-7
Clark, N.C.	E13	180-1
Clark, S. Dak.	D14	136-7
Clark, Wyo.	B8	250-1
Clark, co., Ark.	H4	150-1
Clark, co., Ida.	K9	218-9
Clark, co., Ill.	I11	96-7
Clark, co., Ind.	M9	100-1
Clark, co., Kans.	J5	108-9
Clark, co., Ky.	G12	164-5
Clark, co., Mo.	A7	120-1
Clark, co., Nev.	M10	226-7
Clark, co., O.	G5	132-3
Clark, co., S. Dak.	D13	136-7
Clark, co., Wash.	J8	246-7
Clark, co., Wis.	F10	140-1
Clark Fork, Ida.	C3	218-9
Clark Mills*, N.Y.	E8	80-1
Clark Point*, Ont.	B11	284-5
Clarkdale, Ariz.	F6	206-7
Clarkdale, Ga.	B9	160-1
Clarke, Ore.	B11	238-9
Clarke, co., Ala.	K3	146-7
Clarke, co., Ga.	F6	160-1
Clarke, co., Ia.	I7	104-5
Clarke, co., Miss.	J9	176-7
Clarke, co., Va.	E11	196-7
Clarkedale, Ark.	D12	150-1
Clarke's Beach*, Nfld.	N11	278-9
Clarkesville, Ga.	D6	160-1
Clarkfield, Minn.	M3	116-7
Clarkia, Ida.	E3	218-9
Clarkrange, Tenn.	H9	188-9
Clarks, La.	C5	168-9
Clarks, Nebr.	G12	124-5
Clarks Corner, Conn.	D13	60-1
Clarks Falls, Conn.	F15	60-1
Clarks Green, Pa.	E14	84-5
Clarks Grove, Minn.	O6	116-7
Clark's Harbour, N.S.	G4	281
Clarks Hill, Ind.	F6	100-1
Clarks Hill, S.C.	F7	184-5
Clarks Mills, Wis.	F5	140-1
Clarks Point, Alaska	G9	254-5
Clarks Summit, Pa.	E14	84-5
Clarksboro, N.J.	J2	76-7
Clarksburg, Ind.	I10	100-1
Clarksburg, Md.	G2	172-3
Clarksburg, Mass.	B3	68-9
Clarksburg, Mo.	E6	120-1
Clarksburg, N.J.	H6	76-7
Clarksburg, O.	H6	132-3
Clarksburg*, Ont.	B13	284-5
Clarksburg, Tenn.	C4	188-9
Clarksburg, W. Va.	E6	200-1
Clarksdale, Miss.	C5	176-7
Clarksdale, Mo.	F15	120-1
Clarkson, Ky.	I8	164-5
Clarkson, Miss.	E8	176-7
Clarkson, Nebr.	F13	124-5
Clarkson Valley*, Mo.	E10	120-1
Clarkston, Ga.	B11	160-1
Clarkston, Mich.	H5	112-3
Clarkston, Ut.	C6	242-3
Clarkston, Wash.	H16	246-7
Clarksville, Ark.	D4	150-1
Clarksville, Del.	J6	153
Clarksville, Ind.	N9	100-1
Clarksville, Ia.	D10	104-5
Clarksville, Md.	G4	172-3
Clarksville*, Mich.	I12	112-3
Clarksville, Mo.	D9	120-1
Clarksville, N.H.	B7	72-3
Clarksville, O.	J16	132-3
Clarksville, Okla.	E14	234-5
Clarksville, Tenn.	F6	188-9
Clarksville, Tex.	D10	192-3
Clarksville, Va.	K10	196-7
Clarkton, Mo.	J11	120-1
Clarkton, N.C.	G11	180-1
Clarkville, Ida.	C3	218-9
Clarno, Ore.	D10	238-9
Clarno, Wis.	K12	140-1
Clarysville, Md.	B3	172-3
Clatonia, Nebr.	I14	124-5
Clatskanie, Ore.	A5	238-9
Clatsop, co., Ore.	A5	238-9
Claud, Okla.	H11	234-5
Claude, Tex.	B5	192-3
Claudelle, Kans.	D7	108-9
Claudville, Va.	K7	196-7
Claunch, N. Mex.	H7	230-1
Clavet, Sask.	L6	294-5
Clawson, Ida.	L11	218-9
Clawson, Mich.	I6	112-3
Clawson, Ut.	I7	242-3
Claxton, Ga.	K9	160-1
Clay, Ark.	D8	150-1
Clay, Ky.	I4	164-5
Clay, La.	B4	168-9
Clay, W. Va.	H16	200-1
Clay, co., Ala.	F9	146-7
Clay, co., Ark.	A11	150-1
Clay, co., Fla.	C11	156-7
Clay, co., Ga.	L2	160-1
Clay, co., Ill.	K10	96-7
Clay, co., Ind.	J5	100-1
Clay, co., Ia.	B4	104-5
Clay, co., Kans.	E11	108-9
Clay, co., Ky.	I13	164-5
Clay, co., Minn.	H2	116-7
Clay, co., Miss.	E9	176-7
Clay, co., Mo.	D3	120-1
Clay, co., Nebr.	I12	124-5
Clay, co., N.C.	E2	180-1
Clay, co., S. Dak.	I15	136-7
Clay, co., Tenn.	A9	188-9
Clay, co., Tex.	D8	192-3
Clay, co., W. Va.	G4	200-1
Clay Camp, Nev.	M7	226-7
Clay Center, Kans.	E11	108-9
Clay Center, Nebr.	I12	124-5
Clay Center, O.	B6	132-3
Clay City, Ill.	K10	96-7
Clay City, Ind.	J5	100-1
Clay City, Ky.	H12	164-5
Clay Springs, Ariz.	G9	206-7
Clay Spur, Wyo.	D16	250-1
Claycomo, Mo.	I15	120-1
Clayhatchee, Ala.	L9	146-7
Claymont, Del.	A4	153
Claypool, Ariz.	I8	206-7
Claypool, Ind.	C9	100-1
Claysburg, Pa.	I6	84-5
Claysville, Pa.	J1	84-5
Clayton, Ala.	J9	146-7
Clayton*, Calif.	I3	210-1
Clayton, Del.	E3	153
Clayton, Ga.	D6	160-1
Clayton, Ida.	K6	218-9
Clayton, Ill.	G4	96-7
Clayton, Ind.	H7	100-1
Clayton, Ia.	C13	104-5
Clayton, Kans.	D5	108-9
Clayton, La.	D6	168-9
Clayton, Mass.	F2	68-9
Clayton, Mich.	K13	112-3
Clayton, Mo.	B16	120-1
Clayton, N.J.	K3	76-7
Clayton, N. Mex.	C11	230-1
Clayton, N.Y.	B7	80-1
Clayton, N.C.	I8	180-1
Clayton, O.	H14	132-3
Clayton, Okla.	H15	234-5
Clayton, Ont.	H14	284-5
Clayton, S.C.	I7	184-5
Clayton, S. Dak.	H14	136-7
Clayton, Tenn.	A3	188-9
Clayton, Wash.	E15	246-7
Clayton, Wis.	E8	140-1
Clayton, co., Ga.	G4	160-1
Clayton, co., Ia.	D13	104-5
Clayton Lake, Me.	C5	64-5
Clayville, N.Y.	E8	80-1
Clayville, R.I.	D3	87
Clayville, Va.	I12	196-7
Cle Elum, Wash.	F10	246-7
Clear Brook, Va.	D11	196-7
Clear Creek, Ind.	K7	100-1
Clear Creek, W. Va.	K15	200-1
Clear Creek, co., Colo.	E10	214-5
Clear Fork, W. Va.	J3	200-1
Clear Lake, Ind.	A12	100-1
Clear Lake, Ia.	B8	104-5
Clear Lake, Minn.	L5	116-7
Clear Lake, Okla.	C6	234-5
Clear Lake, S. Dak.	D16	136-7
Clear Lake, Ut.	I4	242-3
Clear Lake, Wis.	E8	140-1
Clear Lake Shores*, Tex.	H10	192-3
Clear Spring, Md.	B6	172-3
Clear Springs, Ind.	K8	100-1
Clearbrook, B.C.	C15	268-9
Clearbrook, Minn.	G3	116-7
Clearco, W. Va.	H5	200-1
Clearcreek, Ut.	H7	242-3
Clearfield, Ia.	J5	104-5
Clearfield, Ky.	G13	164-5
Clearfield, Pa.	F6	84-5
Clearfield, S. Dak.	I9	136-7
Clearfield, Ut.	E6	242-3
Clearfield, co., Pa.	F6	84-5
Clearlake, Wash.	C8	246-7
Clearlake Highlands, Calif.	H3	210-1
Clearlake Oaks, Calif.	G3	210-1
Clearmont, Mo.	A2	120-1
Clearmont, Wyo.	B12	250-1
Clearview, Okla.	F13	234-5
Clearview, W. Va.	B5	200-1
Clearwater, B.C.	H8	268-9
Clearwater, Fla.	F9	156-7
Clearwater, Ida.	G4	218-9
Clearwater, Kans.	J11	108-9
Clearwater, Man.	K12	272-3
Clearwater, Minn.	L5	116-7
Clearwater, Nebr.	E11	124-5
Clearwater, Ore.	H7	238-9
Clearwater, S.C.	F8	184-5
Clearwater, Wash.	E5	246-7
Clearwater, co., Ida.	F4	218-9
Clearwater, co., Minn.	G3	116-7
Clearwater Lake*, Man.	C4	272-3
Clearwater Lake, Wis.	C13	140-1
Cleary, Miss.	I6	176-7
Cleaton, Ky.	I6	164-5
Cleator, Ariz.	G6	206-7
Clebit, Okla.	H15	234-5
Cleburne, Tex.	E13	192-3
Cleburne, co., Ala.	D9	146-7
Cleburne, co., Ark.	C7	150-1
Cleghorn, Ia.	C3	104-5
Clem, Ga.	G2	160-1
Clem, Ore.	C10	238-9
Clem, W. Va.	G5	200-1
Clementon, N.J.	O11	76-7
Clements, Kans.	H12	108-9
Clements, Md.	H11	172-3
Clements, Minn.	N4	116-7
Clementsport, N.S.	E4	281
Clementsville, Ida.	L11	218-9
Clementsville, Ky.	I10	164-5
Clemmons, N.C.	H3	180-1
Clemons, Ia.	F9	104-5
Clemscott, Okla.	H11	234-5
Clemson, S.C.	B5	184-5
Clendenin, W. Va.	G4	200-1
Cleo Springs, Okla.	D9	234-5
Cleona, Pa.	I12	84-5
Cleora, Okla.	C15	234-5
Clermont, Fla.	F5	156-7
Clermont, Ga.	E5	160-1
Clermont, Ia.	C12	104-5
Clermont, Ky.	C2	164-5
Clermont, N.J.	N4	76-7
Clermont, Que.	E13	290-1
Clermont, co., O.	I4	132-3
Clermont Harbor, Miss.	O8	176-7
Cleveland, Ala.	D7	146-7
Cleveland, Ark.	D6	150-1
Cleveland, Ga.	D5	160-1
Cleveland, Ida.	O10	218-9
Cleveland, Kans.	J9	108-9
Cleveland, Me.	A8	64-5
Cleveland, Minn.	N5	116-7
Cleveland, Miss.	E5	176-7
Cleveland, Mo.	K15	120-1
Cleveland, Mont.	C10	222-3
Cleveland, N. Mex.	D8	230-1
Cleveland, N.Y.	E7	80-1
Cleveland, N.C.	I2	180-1
Cleveland, N. Dak.	G10	128-9
Cleveland, O.	B9	132-3
Cleveland, Okla.	D13	234-5
Cleveland, Ore.	H5	238-9
Cleveland, S.C.	E1	184-5
Cleveland, Tenn.	D11	188-9
Cleveland, Tex.	F15	192-3
Cleveland, Ut.	I8	242-3
Cleveland, Va.	J4	196-7
Cleveland, W. Va.	G13	200-1
Cleveland, Wis.	G5	140-1
Cleveland, co., Ark.	H7	150-1
Cleveland, co., N.C.	E5	180-1
Cleveland, co., Okla.	F11	234-5
Cleveland Heights, O.	B15	132-3
Clevenger, Tenn.	H14	188-9
Clever, Mo.	I5	120-1
Cleves, O.	K12	132-3
Clewiston, Fla.	H12	156-7
Cliff, N. Mex.	J2	230-1
Cliffield, Va.	I5	196-7
Clifford, Ind.	J9	100-1
Clifford, Ky.	G15	164-5
Clifford, Mich.	F6	112-3
Clifford, N. Dak.	F13	128-9
Clifford, Ont.	C12	284-5
Clifford, Va.	H9	196-7
Cliffordvale, N.B.	F3	275
Cliffside, N.C.	E5	180-1
Cliffside Park, N.J.	C12	76-7
Clifftop, W. Va.	J16	200-1
Cliffwood [-Cliffwood Beach], N.J.	G10	76-7
Clifton, Ariz.	J11	206-7
Clifton, Colo.	F6	214-5
Clifton, Ida.	O10	218-9
Clifton, Ill.	E11	96-7
Clifton, Kans.	D11	108-9
Clifton, La.	F9	168-9
Clifton, Me.	J7	64-5
Clifton, N.J.	B10	76-7
Clifton, Ore.	A5	238-9
Clifton, S.C.	F5	184-5
Clifton, Tex.	E8	192-3
Clifton, Va.	B3	196-7
Clifton, Wis.	H11	140-1
Clifton City, Tenn.	D5	188-9
Clifton Corners, Me.	J7	64-5
Clifton Forge, Va.	H8	196-7
Clifton Heights*, Pa.	J15	84-5
Clifton Hill, Mo.	C6	120-1
Clifton Knolls*, N.Y.	F11	80-1
Clifton Springs, N.Y.	E5	80-1
Cliftonville, Miss.	F10	176-7
Clifty, Ark.	A3	150-1
Clifty, Ky.	J6	164-5
Climax, Colo.	E10	214-5
Climax, Ga.	N4	160-1
Climax, Kans.	I13	108-9
Climax*, Mich.	J12	112-3
Climax, Minn.	G1	116-7
Climax, N.C.	H4	180-1
Climax, Sask.	O5	294-5
Climax Springs, Mo.	F5	120-1
Clinch, co., Ga.	N7	160-1
Clinchburg, Va.	J4	196-7
Clinchco, Va.	I3	196-7
Clinchport, Va.	J2	196-7
Clines Corners, N. Mex.	F7	230-1
Clinton, Ala.	G3	146-7
Clinton, Ark.	C6	150-1
Clinton, B.C.	I7	268-9
Clinton, Conn.	H10	60-1
Clinton, Ga.	I6	160-1
Clinton, Ill.	G8	96-7
Clinton, Ind.	I4	100-1
Clinton, Ia.	F16	104-5
Clinton, Kans.	F15	108-9
Clinton, Ky.	K2	164-5
Clinton, La.	F7	168-9
Clinton, Me.	J5	64-5
Clinton, Md.	K5	172-3
Clinton, Mass.	C9	68-9
Clinton, Mich.	J14	112-3
Clinton, Minn.	L2	116-7
Clinton, Miss.	I5	176-7
Clinton, Mo.	F4	120-1
Clinton, Mont.	E4	222-3
Clinton, Nebr.	D4	124-5
Clinton*, N.J.	E4	76-7
Clinton, N.J.	E4	76-7
Clinton*, N.Y.	E8	80-1
Clinton, N.C.	F11	180-1
Clinton, O.	E14	132-3
Clinton, Okla.	F8	234-5
Clinton, Ont.	C12	284-5
Clinton, P.E.I.	E6	287
Clinton, S.C.	I4	184-5
Clinton, Tenn.	H11	188-9
Clinton, Ut.	E6	242-3
Clinton, Wash.	G2	246-7
Clinton, Wis.	K2	140-1
Clinton, co., Ill.	K7	96-7
Clinton, co., Ind.	F7	100-1
Clinton, co., Ia.	F15	104-5
Clinton, co., Ky.	K10	164-5
Clinton, co., Mich.	I13	112-3
Clinton, co., Mo.	C3	120-1
Clinton, co., N.Y.	A11	80-1
Clinton, co., O.	H5	132-3

Clinton, co., Pa. F8 84-5
Clinton Creek, Y.T. B1 297
Clintonville, Ky. B8 164-5
Clintonville, W. Va. I5 200-1
Clintonville, Wis. F13 140-1
Clints Well, Ariz. G7 206-7
Clintwood, Va. I3 196-7
Clio, Ala. K9 146-7
Clio, Ia. K8 104-5
Clio, Mich. F4 112-3
Clio, S.C. C14 184-5
Clio, W. Va. G4 200-1
Clipper, Wash. C8 246-7
Clitherall, Minn. J3 116-7
Clive, Alta. K8 264-5
Clive, Ia. G7 104-5
Clive, Ut. F4 242-3
Clontarf, Minn. L3 116-7
Clopton, Ala. K10 146-7
Cloquet, Minn. I8 116-7
Cloridorme*, Que. H6 290-1
Closter, N.J. C8 76-7
Cloud, co., Kans. E10 108-9
Cloud Chief, Okla. F8 234-5
Cloud Lake*, Fla. D16 156-7
Cloudcroft, N. Mex. J7 230-1
Cloudy, Okla. H15 234-5
Cloutierville, La. E3 168-9
Clover, Ida. O6 218-9
Clover, S.C. A9 184-5
Clover, Va. J10 196-7
Clover, W. Va. F4 200-1
Clover Bend, Ark. B10 150-1
Clover Lick, W. Va. H7 200-1
Clover Pass*, Alaska H16 254-5
Clovercroft, Tenn. H7 188-9
Cloverdale, Ala. A4 146-7
Cloverdale, Calif. H2 210-1
Cloverdale, Ida. L3 218-9
Cloverdale, Ind. I6 100-1
Cloverdale, Mich. J12 112-3
Cloverdale, Ore. C4 238-9
Cloverdale, Va. I8 196-7
Cloverland, Ind. I5 100-1
Cloverleaf, Man. I15 272-3
Cloverport, Ky. H7 164-5
Cloverport, Tenn. K4 188-9
Clovis, Calif. J5 210-1
Clovis, N. Mex. G11 230-1
Clow, Ark. H3 150-1
Cluny, Alta. M8 264-5
Cluster Springs, Va. K10 196-7
Clute, Tex. K13 192-3
Clutier, Ia. F10 104-5
Clyattville, Ga. O6 160-1
Clyburn, S.C. C11 184-5
Clyde, Alta. I8 264-5
Clyde, Ida. K8 218-9
Clyde, Kans. D10 108-9
Clyde, Mich. I4 112-3
Clyde, Mo. B3 120-1
Clyde, N.Y. E6 80-1
Clyde, N.C. E3 180-1
Clyde, N. Dak. B10 128-9
Clyde, O. C6 132-3
Clyde, Okla. C10 234-5
Clyde, Tex. E7 192-3
Clyde Hill, Wash. H3 246-7
Clyde Park, Mont. G8 222-3
Clyde River, P.E.I. F7 287
Clyman, Wis. I3 140-1
Clymer, Pa. H5 84-5
Clyo, Ga. J11 160-1
Co-Operative, Ky. K11 164-5
Coachella, Calif. N9 210-1
Coahoma, Miss. C5 176-7
Coahoma, Tex. E5 192-3
Coahoma, co., Miss. C5 176-7
Coal, co., Okla. G13 234-5
Coal City, Ill. D10 96-7
Coal City, Ind. J5 100-1
Coal City, W. Va. I4 200-1
Coal Creek, Colo. G11 214-5
Coal Fire, Ala. F3 146-7
Coal Fork, W. Va. H14 200-1
Coal Grove, O. J7 132-3
Coal Harbour, B.C. I4 268-9
Coal Hill, Ark. D3 150-1
Coal Mountain, Ga. E4 160-1
Coal Mountain, W. Va. I3 200-1
Coal Run*, Ky. H15 164-5
Coal Valley, Ala. E5 146-7
Coal Valley, Ill. D5 96-7
Coaldale, Alta. N9 264-5
Coaldale, Colo. G10 214-5
Coaldale, Pa. G13 84-5
Coaledo, Ore. H3 238-9
Coalfield, Tenn. H10 188-9
Coalgate, Okla. H13 234-5
Coalhurst, Alta. N8 264-5
Coaling, Ala. G5 146-7
Coalinga, Calif. K5 210-1
Coalmont, Ala. F6 146-7
Coalmont, B.C. J8 268-9
Coalmont, Colo. C9 214-5
Coalmont, Ind. J5 100-1
Coalmont, Tenn. K10 188-9
Coalridge, Mont. A16 222-3
Coalton, O. I7 132-3
Coalton, Okla. F14 234-5
Coalville, Ia. E6 104-5
Coalville, Ut. E7 242-3
Coalwood, Mont. G14 222-3
Coalwood, W. Va. J3 200-1
Coast Ranges 14-15
Coates, Minn. C11 116-7
Coatesville, Ind. H6 100-1
Coatesville, Pa. J14 84-5
Coaticook, Que. J15 290-1
Coats, Kans. J7 108-9
Coats, N.C. J7 180-1
Cobalt, Conn. E10 60-1
Cobalt, Ida. I6 218-9
Cobalt, Ont. G8 284-5
Cobalt City, Mo. H10 120-1
Cobb, Ga. K5 160-1
Cobb, Ky. J4 164-5
Cobb, Wis. J11 140-1
Cobb, co., Ga. F3 160-1
Cobb Island, Md. H10 172-3
Cobble Hill, B.C. D12 268-9
Cobbs Creek, Va. E4 196-7
Cobbtown, Ga. K9 160-1
Cobden, Ill. N8 96-7
Cobden, Minn. N4 116-7
Cobden, Ont. H13 284-5
Coble, Tenn. C6 188-9
Cobleskill, N.Y. F10 80-1
Coboconk*, Ont. A16 284-5
Cobourg, Ont. K11 284-5
Cobre, Nev. C10 226-7
Coburg, Ia. J3 104-5
Coburg, Ore. K1 238-9
Coburn, W. Va. B13 200-1
Coburn Gore, Me. H2 64-5
Cocagne Nord*, N.B. H7 275
Cochenour*, Ont. D2 284-5
Cochesett, Mass. F12 68-9
Cochin, Sask. J5 294-5
Cochise, Ariz. K10 206-7
Cochise, co., Ariz. L11 206-7
Cochiti Pueblo, N. Mex. E6 230-1
Cochituate, Mass. I2 68-9
Cochran, Ga. J6 160-1
Cochran, Ore. B5 238-9
Cochran, co., Tex. D4 192-3
Cochrane, Alta. M7 264-5
Cochrane, Ont. F7 284-5
Cochrane, Wis. G8 140-1
Cochranton, Pa. E2 84-5
Cocke, co., Tenn. B14 188-9
Cockeysville, Md. C11 172-3
Cockrell Hill, Tex. D14 192-3
Cockrum, Miss. B7 176-7
Cocoa, Fla. F12 156-7
Cocoa Beach, Fla. F13 156-7
Cocoa West*, Fla. F12 156-7
Cocodrie, La. J8 168-9
Cocolalla, Ida. C3 218-9
Coconino, co., Ariz. E7 206-7
Coconut Creek*, Fla. I13 156-7
Codell, Kans. E7 108-9
Coderre, Sask. N7 294-5
Codes Corner*, Ont. J14 284-5
Codette, Sask. J8 294-5
Codington, co., S. Dak. C14 136-7
Cody, Nebr. C6 124-5
Cody, Wyo. C8 250-1
Codyville, Me. H10 64-5
Coeburn, Va. J3 196-7
Coesse, Ind. C10 100-1
Coeur d'Alene, Ida. D2 218-9
Coeur d'Alene Lake, Ida. D2 218-9
Coffee, co., Ala. L8 146-7
Coffee, co., Ga. L7 160-1
Coffee, co., Tenn. C8 188-9
Coffee Creek, Mont. D8 222-3
Coffee Springs, Ala. L8 146-7
Coffeen, Ill. J8 96-7
Coffeeville, Ala. K3 146-7
Coffeeville, Miss. D7 176-7
Coffey, Mo. B4 120-1
Coffey, co., Kans. H14 108-9
Coffeyville, Kans. K14 108-9
Cofield, N.C. C14 180-1
Cogar, Okla. F10 234-5
Cogdell, Ga. N8 160-1
Coggon, Ia. E13 104-5
Coghill, Tenn. K13 188-9
Cogswell, N. Dak. J13 128-9
Cohagen, Mont. E13 222-3
Cohasset, Ala. L6 146-7
Cohasset, Mass. J7 68-9
Cohasset, Minn. H6 116-7
Cohasset, Va. H11 196-7
Cohoctah, Mich. H3 112-3
Cohocton, N.Y. F5 80-1
Cohoe, Alaska F11 254-5
Cohoes, N.Y. F11 80-1
Cohutta, Ga. C3 160-1
Coila, Miss. F6 176-7
Coin, Ia. J4 104-5
Cokato, Minn. A8 116-7
Coke, co., Tex. E6 192-3
Cokedale, Colo. J12 214-5
Coker, Ala. F4 146-7
Coker Creek, Tenn. K14 188-9
Cokesbury, Md. I15 172-3
Cokesbury, S.C. J3 184-5
Cokesbury Church, Del. I4 153
Coketon, W. Va. E8 200-1
Cokeville, Wyo. H5 250-1
Colbert, Ga. F6 160-1
Colbert, Okla. I13 234-5
Colbert, Wash. E16 246-7
Colbert, co., Ala. B3 146-7
Colbert Heights, Ala. B4 146-7
Colborne, Ont. K12 284-5
Colburn, Ida. B3 218-9
Colburn, Ind. E6 100-1
Colby, Kans. E3 108-9
Colby, Wis. F11 140-1
Colbyville, Vt. E6 90-1
Colchester, Conn. E12 60-1
Colchester, Ill. F5 96-7
Colchester, Ont. G9 284-5
Colchester, Vt. D4 90-1
Colchester, co., N.S. C7 281
Colcord, Okla. D16 234-5
Cold Bay, Alaska I8 254-5
Cold Lake, Alta. H10 264-5
Cold Spring, Ky. E11 164-5
Cold Spring, Mass. E3 68-9
Cold Spring, Mass. D6 68-9
Cold Spring, Minn. L5 116-7
Cold Spring, N.J. O4 76-7
Cold Spring, N.Y. A14 80-1
Cold Spring Harbor, N.Y. D16 80-1
Cold Springs, Ala. D5 146-7
Cold Springs, Okla. G8 234-5
Cold Stream, W. Va. E10 200-1
Colden Hill*, N.Y. I10 80-1
Coldspring, Tex. G10 192-3
Coldwater, Kans. J6 108-9
Coldwater, Ky. K3 164-5
Coldwater, Mich. K13 112-3
Coldwater, Miss. B6 176-7
Coldwater, O. E3 132-3
Coldwater, Ont. A14 284-5
Coldwater, Tenn. K7 188-9
Coldwell Corner, Del. D2 153
Cole, Okla. G11 234-5
Cole, co., Mo. F7 120-1
Cole Camp, Mo. F5 120-1
Colebrook, Conn. B6 60-1
Colebrook, N.H. C6 72-3
Coleharbor, N. Dak. F6 128-9
Coleman, Alta. O7 264-5
Coleman, Fla. E10 156-7
Coleman, Ga. L3 160-1
Coleman, Md. C13 172-3
Coleman, Mich. H13 112-3
Coleman, Okla. H13 234-5
Coleman, P.E.I. C3 287
Coleman, Tex. E7 192-3
Coleman, Wis. E15 140-1
Coleman, co., Tex. E7 192-3
Coleman Falls, Va. I9 196-7
Colemans Lake, Ga. I8 160-1
Colerain, N.C. C14 180-1
Coleraine, Minn. H6 116-7
Coleraine*, Que. I15 290-1
Coleridge, Nebr. D13 124-5
Coleridge, N.C. I5 180-1
Coles, Miss. L4 176-7
Coles, co., Ill. I10 96-7
Coles Point, Va. G14 196-7
Colesburg, Ia. D13 104-5
Colesburg, Ky. D2 164-5
Colesburg, Tenn. H5 188-9
Colesville*, Md. D10 172-3
Coleville, Sask. L4 294-5
Colfax, Calif. G4 210-1
Colfax, Ill. F9 96-7
Colfax, Ind. G6 100-1
Colfax, Ia. G8 104-5
Colfax, La. E4 168-9
Colfax, N. Dak. I14 128-9
Colfax, Wash. G16 246-7
Colfax, W. Va. B14 200-1
Colfax, Wis. E8 140-1
Colfax, co., Nebr. F13 124-5
Colfax, co., N. Mex. C9 230-1
Colgate, N. Dak. F13 128-9
Colgate, Sask. O9 294-5
Colinton, Alta. H8 264-5
Collacott Subdivision*, Sask. M10 294-5
Collbran, Ala. C9 146-7
Collbran, Colo. E7 214-5
College, Alaska D11 254-5
College Bridge*, N.B. H7 275
College City, Ark. B10 150-1
College Corner, O. G2 132-3
College Grove, Tenn. I7 188-9
College Heights, Alta. K8 264-5
College Heights, Ark. I8 150-1
College Heights, S.C. C13 184-5
College Hill, Ky. H12 164-5
College Park, Ga. C10 160-1
College Park, Md. I4 172-3
College Place, Wash. I14 246-7
College Springs, Ia. J4 104-5
College Station, Tex. G9 192-3
Collegedale, Tenn. K11 188-9
Collegeville, Ind. D5 100-1
Collegeville*, Minn. K5 116-7
Collegeville, Pa. A10 84-5
Colleton, co., S.C. H11 184-5
Collette, N.B. G6 275
Collettsville, N.C. D5 180-1
Collettville*, B.C. J8 268-9
Colleyville, Tex. C13 192-3
Collier, co., Fla. I11 156-7
Collier Manor-Cresthaven*, Fla. I13 156-7
Colliers*, Nfld. N11 278-9
Colliers, W. Va. B6 200-1
Collierville, Tenn. K2 188-9
Collin, co., Tex. D9 192-3
Collingdale, Pa. B10 84-5
Collingswood, N.J. N10 76-7
Collingsworth, co., Tex. B6 192-3
Collingwood, Ont. B13 284-5
Collins, Ark. I8 150-1
Collins, Ga. K9 160-1
Collins, Ia. F8 104-5
Collins, Miss. K7 176-7
Collins, Mo. G4 120-1
Collins, Mont. C6 222-3
Collins, Wis. F5 140-1
Collins Bay, Ont. J13 284-5
Collins Park, Del. B3 153
Collinston, La. B6 168-9
Collinsville, Ala. C8 146-7
Collinsville, Conn. C7 60-1
Collinsville, Ill. K6 96-7
Collinsville, Miss. H9 176-7
Collinsville, Okla. D14 234-5
Collinsville*, Tex. D9 192-3
Collinsville, Va. J8 196-7
Collinwood, Tenn. D5 188-9
Collirene, Ala. I6 146-7
Collyer, Kans. F5 108-9
Colma, Calif. C7 210-1
Colman, S. Dak. F15 136-7
Colmar Manor, Md. I4 172-3
Colo, Ia. F8 104-5
Cologne, Minn. C9 116-7
Cologne, N.J. L5 76-7
Cologne, Va. E3 196-7
Coloma, Mich. J11 112-3
Coloma, Wis. F1 140-1
Colome, S. Dak. H10 136-7
Colon*, Mich. K12 112-3
Colon, Nebr. I1 124-5
Colon, N.C. I6 180-1
Colona, Colo. G7 214-5
Colona, Ill. C6 96-7
Colonia, N.J. E7 76-7
Colonial Acres, Mass. H15 68-9
Colonial Beach, Va. C4 196-7
Colonial Heights*, Tenn. F16 188-9
Colonial Heights, Va. F1 196-7
Colonial Hills*, Fla. F9 156-7
Colonias, N. Mex. F9 230-1
Colonie, N.Y. F11 80-1
Colonsay, Sask. L7 294-5
Colony, Kans. H15 108-9
Colony, Okla. F8 234-5
Colony, Wyo. B16 250-1
Colony Town, Miss. F5 176-7
Colora, Md. B13 172-3
Colorado, co., Tex. G9 192-3
Colorado City, Ariz. A5 206-7
Colorado City, Tex. E5 192-3
Colorado R., Ariz. E2 206-7
Colorado R., Colo. E6 214-5
Colorado R., Ut. J10 242-3
Colorado Springs, Colo. F12 214-5
Colored Hill*, W. Va. J4 200-1
Colquitt, Ga. N3 160-1
Colquitt, La. A3 168-9
Colquitt, co., Ga. M5 160-1
Colrain, Mass. B4 68-9
Colstrip, Mont. G13 222-3
Colt, Ark. E10 150-1
Colter, Wyo. D10 250-1
Colter Bay, Wyo. I2 250-1
Colton, Calif. G10 210-1
Colton, Ore. C7 238-9
Colton, S. Dak. G15 136-7
Colton, Ut. G7 242-3
Colton, Wash. H16 246-7
Colton Hollow, Mass. E6 68-9
Colts Neck, N.J. G7 76-7
Columbia, Ala. L10 146-7
Columbia, Conn. D12 60-1
Columbia, Del. K3 153
Columbia, Ill. L6 96-7
Columbia, Ky. J10 164-5
Columbia, La. C5 168-9
Columbia, Me. J9 64-5
Columbia, Md. G5 172-3
Columbia, Miss. L7 176-7
Columbia, Mo. D7 120-1
Columbia, N.H. C6 72-3
Columbia, N.J. C3 76-7
Columbia, N.C. D15 180-1
Columbia, Pa. J12 84-5
Columbia, S.C. E10 184-5
Columbia, S. Dak. B12 136-7
Columbia, Tenn. C7 188-9
Columbia, Ut. H9 242-3
Columbia, Va. H11 196-7
Columbia, co., Ark. J4 150-1
Columbia, co., Fla. C10 156-7
Columbia, co., Ga. G8 160-1
Columbia, co., N.Y. G11 80-1
Columbia, co., Ore. A6 238-9
Columbia, co., Pa. F12 84-5
Columbia, co., Wash. H15 246-7
Columbia, co., Wis. I12 140-1
Columbia City, Ind. C10 100-1
Columbia City, Ore. B6 238-9
Columbia Falls, Me. J9 64-5
Columbia Falls, Mont. B3 222-3
Columbia Furnace, Va. E10 196-7
Columbia Gardens, Mont. G5 222-3
Columbia Heights*, Minn. M6 116-7
Columbia Heights, Wash. I7 246-7
Columbia Icefield, Alta. K5 264-5
Columbia R., B.C. H9 268-9
Columbia R., Wash. I5 246-7
Columbiana, Ala. F7 146-7
Columbiana, O. D11 132-3
Columbiana, co., O. D11 132-3
Columbiaville, Mich. F5 112-3
Columbine, Colo. B8 214-5
Columbine Valley, Colo. H3 214-5
Columbus, Ark. I3 150-1
Columbus, Ga. J2 160-1
Columbus, Ind. J9 100-1
Columbus, Kans. K16 108-9
Columbus, Ky. J2 164-5
Columbus, La. E2 168-9
Columbus, Miss. E10 176-7
Columbus, Mont. G9 222-3
Columbus, Nebr. G13 124-5
Columbus, N.J. I5 76-7
Columbus, N. Mex. M4 230-1
Columbus, N.C. E4 180-1
Columbus, N. Dak. B4 128-9
Columbus, O. F6 132-3
Columbus, Tex. G9 192-3
Columbus, Wis. I2 140-1
Columbus, co., N.C. H11 180-1
Columbus Base, Miss. E10 176-7

Columbus City, Ala. C7 146-7
Columbus City, Ia. H13 104-5
Columbus Grove, O. D4 132-3
Columbus Junction, Ia. H13 104-5
Colusa, Calif. G3 210-1
Colusa, co., Calif. G3 210-1
Colver, Pa. H5 84-5
Colville, Wash. C15 246-7
Colwell, Ia. B10 104-5
Colwell, Ont. B14 284-5
Colwich, Kans. I10 108-9
Colwyn*, Pa. J15 84-5
Comal, co., Tex. G8 192-3
Comanche, Mont. G10 222-3
Comanche, Okla. H10 234-5
Comanche, Tex. E7 192-3
Comanche, co., Kans. K6 108-9
Comanche, co., Okla. H8 234-5
Comanche, co., Tex. E7 192-3
Comber*, Ont. F10 284-5
Combes*, Tex. K8 192-3
Combined Locks*, Wis. G14 140-1
Combs, Ark. C3 150-1
Combs, Ky. I14 164-5
Comeau*, Man. J3 272-3
Comer, Ala. J10 146-7
Comer, Ga. F7 160-1
Comertown, Mont. A16 222-3
Comfort, N.C. F13 180-1
Comfort, W. Va. J14 200-1
Comfrey, Minn. N4 116-7
Comins, Mich. F13 112-3
Commack, N.Y. J12 80-1
Commerce*, Calif. G8 210-1
Commerce, Ga. E6 160-1
Commerce, Miss. B5 176-7
Commerce, Mo. H12 120-1
Commerce, Okla. B15 234-5
Commerce, Tex. D10 192-3
Commerce City, Colo. G3 214-5
Commercial*, N.J. N3 76-7
Commercial Point, O. G6 132-3
Commiskey, Ind. L9 100-1
Commonwealth, Wis. C14 140-1
Como, Colo. E10 214-5
Como, La. C6 168-9
Como, Miss. B6 176-7
Como, N.C. C14 180-1
Como, Tenn. B4 188-9
Como*, Wis. K14 140-1
Comobabi, Ariz. L7 206-7
Comox, B.C. J5 268-9
Compton, Ark. B4 150-1
Compton, Calif. G8 210-1
Compton, Md. H11 172-3
Compton*, Que. J15 290-1
Compton, co., Que. J15 290-1
Comstock*, Mich. J12 112-3
Comstock, Minn. I1 116-7
Comstock, Nebr. F9 124-5
Comstock, Wis. D8 140-1
Comstock Park*, Mich. I12 112-3
Conasauga, Tenn. K12 188-9
Conception Bay South*, Nfld. N11 278-9
Conception Harbour*, Nfld. N11 278-9
Conception Junction, Mo. B3 120-1
Conchas Dam, N. Mex. E10 230-1
Conchas Res., N. Mex. E9 230-1
Concho, Ariz. G10 206-7
Concho, Okla. E10 234-5
Concho, co., Tex. F6 192-3
Conconully, Wash. C12 246-7
Concord, Ark. C8 150-1
Concord, Calif. B8 210-1
Concord, Del. J4 153
Concord, Ga. H4 160-1
Concord, Ky. E13 164-5
Concord, La. A6 168-9
Concord, Md. F14 172-3
Concord, Mass. G2 68-9
Concord, Mich. K1 112-3
Concord*, Mo. E10 120-1
Concord, Nebr. D13 124-5
Concord, N.H. M6 72-3
Concord, N.C. E7 180-1
Concord, Tenn. I7 188-9
Concord, Vt. E9 90-1
Concord, Va. I9 196-7
Concord, Wis. J3 140-1
Concord North, N.C. J2 180-1
Concordia, Kans. D10 108-9
Concordia, Mo. D4 120-1
Concordia, co., La. E6 168-9
Concrete, Wash. C9 246-7
Conda, Ida. N11 218-9
Conde, S. Dak. C13 136-7
Condon, Mont. D4 222-3
Condon, Ore. C10 238-9
Condon, Tenn. G12 188-9
Conecuh, co., Ala. L6 146-7
Conehatta, Miss. H8 176-7
Conejos, Colo. J10 214-5
Conejos, co., Colo. J10 214-5
Conestee, S.C. G2 184-5
Conestogo*, Ont. D13 284-5
Conesville, Ia. H13 104-5
Conesville, O. F9 132-3
Conetoe, N.C. D13 180-1
Confluence, Pa. K4 84-5
Congamond, Mass. F4 68-9
Congaree, S.C. E11 184-5
Conger, Minn. O6 116-7
Congers, N.Y. B14 80-1
Congress, Ariz. G5 206-7
Congress, Sask. O7 294-5
Conicville, Va. E10 196-7
Conklin, Alta. G9 264-5
Conley, Ga. C11 160-1
Connaught Heights*, Sask. J5 294-5
Conneaut, O. A11 132-3
Conneautville, Pa. D1 84-5
Connecticut R., Conn. E9 60-1
Connecticut R., N.H. K3 72-3
Connecticut R., Vt. L7 90-1
Connell, Wash. H13 246-7
Connellsville, Pa. J3 84-5
Conner, Ida. O7 218-9
Conner, Mont. G3 222-3
Connersville, Ind. I11 100-1
Conning Towers-Nautilus Park*, Conn. G13 60-1
Connor, Me. B9 64-5
Connors, N.B. F1 275
Connorsville, Wis. E8 140-1
Conover, N.C. I1 180-1
Conover, Wis. C12 140-1
Conovertown, N.J. M6 76-7
Conowingo, Md. B12 172-3
Conquest, Sask. L6 294-5
Conrad, Ia. E9 104-5
Conrad, Mont. C6 222-3
Conrath, Wis. E10 140-1
Conroe, Tex. F13 192-3
Conroy, Ia. G11 104-5
Consecon, Ont. K12 284-5
Conshohocken, Pa. A10 84-5
Consort, Alta. K10 264-5
Constance Bay & Buckhams Bay*, Ont. H15 284-5
Constantine, Mich. K12 112-3
Consul, Sask. O4 294-5
Contact, Nev. A10 226-7
Contee, Md. H5 172-3
Continental, Ariz. L8 206-7
Continental, O. C4 132-3
Continental Divide 14-15, 16-17
Continental Divide, N. Mex. E3 230-1
Contoocook, N.H. M6 72-3
Contra Costa, co., Calif. I3 210-1
Contreras, N. Mex. G5 230-1
Convene, Me. N7 64-5
Convent, La. C11 168-9
Convent Station, N.J. D6 76-7
Converse, Ind. E9 100-1
Converse, La. D2 168-9
Converse, S.C. E5 184-5
Converse, Tex. J3 192-3
Converse, co., Wyo. F14 250-1
Convoy, O. D3 132-3
Conway, Ark. E6 150-1
Conway*, Fla. E12 156-7
Conway, Ia. J5 104-5
Conway, Kans. G10 108-9
Conway, Ky. I12 164-5
Conway, La. A4 168-9
Conway, Mass. C4 68-9
Conway, Mich. E12 112-3
Conway, Miss. G7 176-7
Conway, Mo. H6 120-1
Conway, N.H. H8 72-3
Conway, N.C. C13 180-1
Conway, N. Dak. D13 128-9
Conway, Pa. H1 84-5
Conway*, P.E.I. C4 287
Conway, S.C. E15 184-5
Conway, Wash. E2 246-7
Conway, co., Ark. D6 150-1
Conway Springs, Kans. J10 108-9
Conyers, Ga. G5 160-1
Conyngham, Pa. G13 84-5
Coochs Bridge, Del. B2 153
Coodys Bluff, Okla. C14 234-5
Cook, Minn. F7 116-7
Cook, Nebr. I15 124-5
Cook, Wash. J9 246-7
Cook, co., Ga. N6 160-1
Cook, co., Ill. B11 96-7
Cook, co., Minn. F10 116-7
Cooke, co., Tex. D8 192-3
Cooke City, Mont. I9 222-3
Cookeville, Tenn. B10 188-9
Cookietown, Okla. H9 234-5
Cooking Lake*, Alta. J8 264-5
Cooks, Mich. D11 112-3
Cooks Corner, Mass. D5 68-9
Cooks Mills, Me. M8 64-5
Cooks Springs, Ala. E7 146-7
Cookshire, Que. J15 290-1
Cookson, Okla. E15 234-5
Cookstown, N.J. I5 76-7
Cookstown, Ont. B14 284-5
Cooksville, Md. F4 172-3
Cooksville, Wis. J1 140-1
Cookville, Vt. G8 90-1
Cool Ridge, W. Va. J4 200-1
Cool Spring, Del. I5 153
Cool Valley*, Mo. E10 120-1
Cooleemee, N.C. H2 180-1
Coolidge, Ariz. J7 206-7
Coolidge, Ga. N5 160-1
Coolidge, Kans. H1 108-9
Coolidge*, Tex. E9 192-3
Coolidge Dam, Ariz. I9 206-7
Coolin, Ida. B2 218-9
Coolville, O. H9 132-3
Coon Rapids, Ia. F5 104-5
Coon Rapids, Minn. A10 116-7
Coon Valley, Wis. H10 140-1
Cooper, Ala. H7 146-7
Cooper, Ky. J11 164-5
Cooper, Me. I10 64-5
Cooper, Tex. D10 192-3
Cooper, co., Mo. E6 120-1
Cooper City, Fla. G16 156-7
Cooper Landing, Alaska F11 254-5
Cooper Road*, La. B1 168-9
Coopers, S.C. E14 184-5
Coopers Mills, Me. L5 64-5
Cooperstown, N.Y. F9 80-1
Cooperstown, N. Dak. F12 128-9
Cooperstown, Wis. E5 140-1
Coopersville, Ky. J11 164-5
Coopersville, Mich. I12 112-3
Cooperton, Okla. G8 234-5
Coos, co., N.H. D7 72-3
Coos, co., Ore. H4 238-9
Coos Bay, Ore. E3 238-9
Coos Junction, N.H. E6 72-3
Coosa, co., Ala. G7 146-7
Coosa R., Ala. G7 146-7
Coosada, Ala. I7 146-7
Coosawhatchie, S.C. I10 184-5
Cooter, Mo. K11 120-1
Cooter Point, La. D6 168-9
Copalis Beach, Wash. F5 246-7
Copalis Crossing, Wash. G5 246-7
Copan, Okla. B13 234-5
Cope, Colo. E15 214-5
Cope, S.C. G10 184-5
Copeland, Ida. A3 218-9
Copeland, Kans. J4 108-9
Copemish, Mich. G11 112-3
Copen, W. Va. F5 200-1
Copenhagen, N.Y. C8 80-1
Copiague, N.Y. K12 80-1
Copiah, co., Miss. J5 176-7
Copicut Hill, Mass. H12 68-9
Coplay*, Pa. H14 84-5
Coplin, Me. I3 64-5
Coppell, Ont. F6 284-5
Coppell, Tex. C14 192-3
Copper Basin, Nev. D6 226-7
Copper Canyon, Nev. D6 226-7
Copper Center, Alaska F12 254-5
Copper City, Mich. B9 112-3
Copper Hill, Va. J7 196-7
Copper Valley, Va. J7 196-7
Copperas Cove, Tex. F8 192-3
Copperdale, Colo. G2 214-5
Copperfield, Nev. F1 226-7
Copperfield, Ore. D16 238-9
Copperhill, Tenn. K13 188-9
Coppermine, N.W. Terr. B2 296
Coppersburg, Pa. H15 84-5
Coppock, Ia. I12 104-5
Coquille, Ore. H3 238-9
Cora, Wyo. F6 250-1
Coral Cove*, Fla. G10 156-7
Coral Gables, Fla. H16 156-7
Coral Hills*, Md. F10 172-3
Coral Springs*, Fla. I13 156-7
Coralville, Ia. G12 104-5
Coram, Mont. B3 222-3
Coraopolis, Pa. A5 84-5
Corapeake, N.C. B14 180-1
Corbeil, Ont. H8 284-5
Corbett, Okla. G11 234-5
Corbin, Kans. K10 108-9
Corbin, Ky. J12 164-5
Corbin, Va. G12 196-7
Corbin City, N.J. N4 76-7
Corcoran, Calif. K6 210-1
Corcoran*, Minn. A9 116-7
Cord, Ark. C9 150-1
Cordaville*, Mass. D10 68-9
Cordele, Ga. K5 160-1
Cordell, Okla. F8 234-5
Corder, Mo. D4 120-1
Cordero, Nev. A5 226-7
Cordes, Ariz. G6 206-7
Cordesville, S.C. G13 184-5
Cordova, Ala. E5 146-7
Cordova, Alaska F12 254-5
Cordova, Ill. C6 96-7
Cordova, Md. E13 172-3
Cordova, Nebr. H13 124-5
Cordova, N.C. F9 180-1
Cordova, S.C. G10 184-5
Cordova, Tenn. K2 188-9
Cordova Mines, Ont. J12 284-5
Core, W. Va. A14 200-1
Corea, Me. K9 64-5
Corey, La. C5 168-9
Corfu, N.Y. E3 80-1
Corinna, Me. I6 64-5
Corinne, Okla. H15 234-5
Corinne, Ut. D6 242-3
Corinth*, Ark. E4 150-1
Corinth, Ga. H2 160-1
Corinth, Ky. F11 164-5
Corinth, Ky. J7 164-5
Corinth, Me. I6 64-5
Corinth, Miss. A10 176-7
Corinth, N.Y. E11 80-1
Corinth*, Vt. G8 90-1
Corinth, W. Va. D8 200-1
Corinth Center, Vt. G8 90-1
Corley, W. Va. F5 200-1
Cormack, Nfld. M8 278-9
Cormierville, N.B. G7 275
Cormorant, Man. A10 272-3
Corn, Okla. F8 234-5
Cornatzer, N.C. H2 180-1
Cornelia, Ga. D6 160-1
Cornelius, N.C. J1 180-1
Cornelius*, Ore. C6 238-9
Cornell, Mich. D10 112-3
Cornell, Wis. E9 140-1
Corner Brook, Nfld. M7 278-9
Cornerstone, Ark. G8 150-1
Cornersville, Md. G12 172-3
Cornersville, Tenn. J7 188-9
Cornerville, Ark. I8 150-1
Corning, Ark. A11 150-1
Corning, Calif. F3 210-1
Corning, Ia. I5 104-5
Corning, Kans. D13 108-9
Corning, Mo. B1 120-1
Corning, N.Y. G5 80-1
Corning, O. G8 132-3
Corning, Sask. N9 294-5
Cornish, Me. N7 64-5
Cornish*, N.H. K3 72-3
Cornish, Okla. I11 234-5
Cornish, Ut. C6 242-3
Cornishville, Ky. D5 164-5
Cornlea, Nebr. F12 124-5
Cornstalk, W. Va. I6 200-1
Cornucopia, Ore. D15 238-9
Cornucopia, Wis. A9 140-1
Cornville, Ariz. F6 206-7
Cornville, Me. J5 64-5
Cornwall, Conn. C5 60-1
Cornwall, N.Y. A13 80-1
Cornwall, Ont. I16 284-5
Cornwall, Pa. I12 84-5
Cornwall, P.E.I. F7 287
Cornwall, Vt. H4 90-1
Cornwall Bridge, Conn. C4 60-1
Cornwall Center, Conn. C5 60-1
Cornwall Hollow, Conn. C5 60-1
Cornwallis, W. Va. E4 200-1
Cornwell, S.C. C10 184-5
Cornwells Heights, Pa. A12 84-5
Corolla, N.C. C16 180-1
Corona, Ala. E4 146-7
Corona, Calif. H10 210-1
Corona, N. Mex. H7 230-1
Corona, S. Dak. B15 136-7
Coronaca, S.C. J3 184-5
Coronach, Sask. O7 294-5
Coronado, Calif. J10 210-1
Coronation, Alta. K9 264-5
Corpus Christi, Tex. I8 192-3
Corral, Ida. M5 218-9
Corrales, N. Mex. F6 230-1
Correctionville, Ia. E2 104-5
Correll, Minn. L2 116-7
Corrigan, Tex. F11 192-3
Corriganville, Md. B3 172-3
Corrinne, W. Va. J4 200-1
Corry, Pa. C3 84-5
Corryton, Tenn. H12 188-9
Corsica, S. Dak. H12 136-7
Corsicana, Tex. E9 192-3
Corson, S. Dak. G16 136-7
Corson, co., S. Dak. B6 136-7
Cortaro, Ariz. K8 206-7
Corte Madera, Calif. C7 210-1
Cortelyou, Ala. L3 146-7
Cortez, Colo. I6 214-5
Cortland, Ind. K9 100-1
Cortland, Nebr. I14 124-5
Cortland, N.Y. F7 80-1
Cortland, O. B11 132-3
Cortland, co., N.Y. F7 80-1
Corton, W. Va. G4 200-1
Corum, Okla. H10 234-5
Corunna, Ind. B11 100-1
Corunna, Mich. G2 112-3
Corunna*, Ont. E10 284-5
Corvallis, Mont. F3 222-3
Corvallis, Ore. E5 238-9
Corwin, Kans. K9 108-9
Corwin, O. J15 132-3
Corwin Springs, Mont. H7 222-3
Corwith, Ia. C7 104-5
Cory, Ind. J5 100-1
Corydon, Ind. N8 100-1
Corydon, Ia. J8 104-5
Corydon, Ky. H5 164-5
Coryell, co., Tex. F8 192-3
Cosby, Mo. B3 120-1
Cosby, S.C. I9 184-5
Cosby, Tenn. H14 188-9
Cosgrave, Nev. C5 226-7
Coshocton, O. E9 132-3
Coshocton, co., O. E9 132-3
Cosmopolis, Wash. G5 246-7
Cosmos, Minn. M4 116-7
Costa Mesa, Calif. H9 210-1
Costigan, Me. I7 64-5
Costilla, N. Mex. B7 230-1
Costilla, co., Colo. I11 214-5
Cotati, Calif. B7 210-1
Côte-St.-Luc*, Que. I12 290-1
Coteau, N. Dak. B4 128-9
Coteau-du-Lac*, Que. J11 290-1
Coteau-Landing, Que. J11 290-1
Coteau Road*, N.B. E7 275
Cotesfield, Nebr. G10 124-5
Cotopaxi, Colo. G10 214-5
Cottage City*, Md. E10 172-3
Cottage Grove, Ala. G8 146-7
Cottage Grove, Ind. I12 100-1
Cottage Grove*, Minn. M7 116-7
Cottage Grove, Ore. G5 238-9
Cottage Grove, Tenn. A4 188-9
Cottage Grove, Wis. J2 140-1
Cottage Hills, Ill. K6 96-7
Cottageville, S.C. H12 184-5
Cottageville, W. Va. F3 200-1
Cottam*, Ont. G10 284-5
Cotter, Ark. A6 150-1
Cotter, Ia. H13 104-5
Cottle, co., Tex. C6 192-3
Cotton, Ga. N4 160-1
Cotton, co., Okla. H9 234-5
Cotton Center, Ariz. J5 206-7
Cotton Plant, Ark. E9 150-1
Cotton Valley, La. A2 168-9
Cottondale, Ala. F4 146-7
Cottondale, Fla. B6 156-7
Cottonport, La. F5 168-9
Cottonton, Ala. J10 146-7
Cottontown, Tenn. G7 188-9

Cottonwood – Crystal Springs 371

Cottonwood, Ala. M10 146-7
Cottonwood, Ariz. F6 206-7
Cottonwood, Calif. F3 210-1
Cottonwood, Ida. G3 218-9
Cottonwood, Minn. M3 116-7
Cottonwood, Okla. H13 234-5
Cottonwood, S. Dak. F5 136-7
Cottonwood*, Ut. F6 242-3
Cottonwood, co., Minn. O3 116-7
Cottonwood Falls, Kans. G12 108-9
Cottonwood Grove, Tenn. B2 188-9
Cottonwood Landing, Nev. O10 226-7
Cottonwood Point, Mo. K11 120-1
Cottrell, Ore. C7 238-9
Cotuit, Mass. H14 68-9
Cotulla, Tex. I7 192-3
Couchtown, S.C. F8 184-5
Couchwood, La. A2 168-9
Couderay, Wis. D9 140-1
Coudersport, Pa. D7 84-5
Coulee, N. Dak. C5 128-9
Coulee City, Wash. F13 246-7
Coulee Dam, Wash. E13 246-7
Coulter, Ia. D8 104-5
Coulterville, Ill. L7 96-7
Counce, Tenn. D4 188-9
Council, Ida. J3 218-9
Council, N.C. G11 180-1
Council Bluffs, Ia. H2 104-5
Council Grove, Kans. G12 108-9
Council Hill, Okla. E14 234-5
Country Club, Mo. C2 120-1
Country Club Heights*, Ind. G9 100-1
Country Club Hills, Ill. O4 96-7
Country Club Hills*, Mo. E10 120-1
Country Estates*, Fla. F9 156-7
Country Harbour Mines, N.S. D9 281
Country Homes, Wash. E16 246-7
Country Knolls*, N.Y. F11 80-1
Country Life Acres*, Mo. E10 120-1
Countryside*, Ill. C11 96-7
Countryside*, Kans. F16 108-9
County Line, Ala. D6 146-7
Countyline, Okla. H11 234-5
Coupeville, Wash. F1 246-7
Courcelles*, Que. I16 290-1
Courtdale*, Pa. E13 84-5
Courtenay, B.C. J5 268-9
Courtenay, N. Dak. G11 128-9
Courtenay, S.C. B5 184-5
Courtland, Ala. B5 146-7
Courtland, Ariz. L10 206-7
Courtland, Kans. D9 108-9
Courtland, Minn. N5 116-7
Courtland, Miss. C6 176-7
Courtland, Ont. E13 284-5
Courtland, Va. J13 196-7
Courtney, N.C. H2 180-1
Courtney, Okla. I11 234-5
Courtrock, Ore. E12 238-9
Coushatta, La. C2 168-9
Coutts, Alta. O9 264-5
Cove, Ark. G2 150-1
Cove, Ore. C14 238-9
Cove, Ut. C6 242-3
Cove City, N.C. E13 180-1
Cove City*, Tex. G12 192-3
Cove Creek Cascades, Tenn. I15 188-9
Cove Fort, Ut. J5 242-3
Cove Gap, W. Va. J11 200-1
Cove Orchard, Ore. F1 238-9
Cove Point, Md. G12 172-3
Covedale, O. I3 132-3
Covehead Road, P.E.I. E7 287
Covel, W. Va. J4 200-1
Covelo, Calif. F2 210-1
Covena, Ga. J8 160-1
Coventry, Conn. C11 60-1
Coventry*, R.I. E5 87
Coventry, Vt. C8 90-1
Coventry Center, R.I. E3 87
Coverdale, Ont. K11 284-5
Coverdales Crossroad, Del. I4 153
Covert, Mich. J11 112-3
Covesville, Va. H10 196-7
Covin, Ala. E3 146-7
Covina*, Calif. G9 210-1
Covington, Ga. G5 160-1
Covington, Ind. G4 100-1
Covington, Ky. D11 164-5
Covington, La. A14 168-9
Covington, Mich. C8 112-3
Covington, O. F3 132-3
Covington, Okla. D10 234-5
Covington, Tenn. C2 188-9
Covington, Va. H8 196-7
Covington, co., Ala. L7 146-7
Covington, co., Miss. K7 176-7
Cow Creek, Wyo. E15 250-1
Cow Head, Nfld. L8 278-9
Cowan, Ind. G10 100-1
Cowan, Ky. F12 164-5
Cowan, Man. F10 272-3
Cowan, Tenn. D9 188-9
Cowansville, Que. J13 290-1
Coward, S.C. E13 184-5
Cowarts, Ala. L10 146-7
Cowden, Okla. F8 234-5
Cowdrey, Colo. B9 214-5
Cowen, W. Va. G5 200-1
Coweta, Okla. E14 234-5
Coweta, co., Ga. G3 160-1
Cowgill, Mo. C4 120-1
Cowgill Corner, Del. F4 153
Cowichan Bay, B.C. D12 268-9
Cowiche, Wash. H10 246-7
Cowles, Nebr. J11 124-5
Cowles, N. Mex. E7 230-1
Cowley, Alta. O7 264-5
Cowley, Wyo. B9 250-1
Cowley, co., Kans. J11 108-9
Cowlic, Ariz. L6 206-7
Cowlington, Okla. F16 234-5
Cowlitz, co., Wash. I7 246-7
Cowpens, S.C. A8 184-5
Cox City, Okla. G10 234-5
Coxheath*, N.S. B11 281
Cox's Cove, Nfld. M7 278-9
Coxs Creek, Ky. C3 164-5
Coxs Mills, W. Va. E5 200-1
Coxsackie, N.Y. G11 80-1
Coy, Ala. J4 146-7
Coy, Ark. G8 150-1
Coyle, Okla. E11 234-5
Coyote, N. Mex. D6 230-1
Coyote Springs, Wyo. I12 250-1
Coyville, Kans. I14 108-9
Cozad, Nebr. H8 124-5
Cozahome, Ark. B6 150-1
Crab Orchard, Ky. I11 164-5
Crab Orchard, Nebr. I15 124-5
Crab Orchard, Tenn. H9 188-9
Crab Orchard, W. Va. K15 200-1
Crabapple, Ga. A11 160-1
Crabtree, Ore. I1 238-9
Crabtree, Pa. B8 84-5
Crabtree, Que. H12 290-1
Craddockville, Va. H15 196-7
Crafton, Pa. A6 84-5
Craftsbury, Vt. D7 90-1
Cragford, Ala. F9 146-7
Craig, Ala. I6 146-7
Craig, Alaska H16 254-5
Craig, Colo. C7 214-5
Craig, Ia. C1 104-5
Craig, Mo. B1 120-1
Craig, Mont. E5 222-3
Craig, Nebr. F14 124-5
Craig, co., Okla. C15 234-5
Craig, co., Va. I7 196-7
Craig Beach, O. C11 132-3
Craig Springs, Va. I7 196-7
Craigellachie, B.C. I9 268-9
Craighead, co., Ark. C10 150-1
Craigleith, Ont. B13 284-5
Craigmont, Ida. G3 218-9
Craigsville, Va. G9 196-7
Craigsville, W. Va. H5 200-1
Craigville, Ind. D11 100-1
Craigville, Mass. H15 68-9
Craik, Sask. M7 294-5
Crainville, Ill. M8 96-7
Cramerton*, N.C. E6 180-1
Cranberry, N.C. C5 180-1
Cranberry Isles, Me. L8 64-5
Cranberry Portage, Man. A9 272-3
Cranbrook, B.C. J10 268-9
Cranbury, N.J. G6 76-7
Crandall, Ga. D3 160-1
Crandall, Ind. N8 100-1
Crandall, Man. I10 272-3
Crandall, Miss. J10 176-7
Crandall, Tex. D16 192-3
Crandon, Wis. D13 140-1
Crane, Ind. L6 100-1
Crane, Mo. I4 120-1
Crane, Mont. D16 222-3
Crane, Ore. G13 238-9
Crane, Tex. F4 192-3
Crane, co., Tex. F4 192-3
Crane Hill, Ala. D5 146-7
Crane Lake, Minn. F7 116-7
Crane River, Man. G12 272-3
Crane Valley, Sask. O7 294-5
Cranfield, Miss. K3 176-7
Cranford, N.J. E7 76-7
Cranston, R.I. D5 87
Crapaud, P.E.I. F6 287
Crapo, Md. H13 172-3
Crary, N. Dak. D11 128-9
Crater Lake, Ore. H7 238-9
Crates, Ore. B9 238-9
Craven, Sask. M8 294-5
Craven, co., N.C. E13 180-1
Cravens, La. F3 168-9
Crawford, Ala. I10 146-7
Crawford, Colo. G7 214-5
Crawford, Ga. F6 160-1
Crawford, Me. I10 64-5
Crawford, Miss. F10 176-7
Crawford, Nebr. D2 124-5
Crawford, Okla. E7 234-5
Crawford, Tenn. B10 188-9
Crawford, W. Va. F13 200-1
Crawford, co., Ark. C2 150-1
Crawford, co., Ga. I4 160-1
Crawford, co., Ill. J11 96-7
Crawford, co., Ind. N7 100-1
Crawford, co., Ia. F3 104-5
Crawford, co., Kans. J16 108-9
Crawford, co., Mich. F13 112-3
Crawford, co., Mo. F8 120-1
Crawford, co., O. D7 132-3
Crawford, co., Pa. D2 84-5
Crawford, co., Wis. J9 140-1
Crawford Bay, B.C. J10 268-9
Crawford House, N.H. G7 72-3
Crawfordsville, Ark. D11 150-1
Crawfordsville, Ind. G6 100-1
Crawfordsville, Ia. I13 104-5
Crawfordsville, Ore. J1 238-9
Crawfordville, Fla. C7 156-7
Crawfordville, Ga. G7 160-1
Crayne, Ky. I4 164-5
Creagerstown, Md. B8 172-3
Creal Springs, Ill. N9 96-7
Crediton*, Ont. D12 284-5
Creede, Colo. H8 214-5
Creedmoor, N.C. H7 180-1
Creek, co., Okla. E12 234-5
Creelman, Sask. O9 294-5
Creemore, Ont. B14 284-5
Creighton, Mo. F4 120-1
Creighton, Nebr. D12 124-5
Creighton, Sask. H10 294-5
Cremo, W. Va. F4 200-1
Cremona, Alta. L7 264-5
Crenshaw, Miss. B6 176-7
Crenshaw, co., Ala. K7 146-7
Creola, Ala. M3 146-7
Creole, La. I3 168-9
Cresaptown, Md. B3 172-3
Cresbard, S. Dak. C11 136-7
Crescent, Ga. M11 160-1
Crescent, Ia. H2 104-5
Crescent, Okla. E10 234-5
Crescent, Ore. G8 238-9
Crescent City, Calif. D1 210-1
Crescent City, Fla. D11 156-7
Crescent City, Ill. E11 96-7
Crescent Junction, Ut. J10 242-3
Crescent Lake, Me. M8 64-5
Crescent Lake, Ore. G7 238-9
Crescent Mills, Mass. E4 68-9
Crescent North*, Calif. D1 210-1
Crescent Park*, Ky. E11 164-5
Crescent Springs*, Ky. D11 164-5
Cresco, Ia. B11 104-5
Cresskill, N.J. C8 76-7
Cresson, Pa. H6 84-5
Cressona, Pa. H12 84-5
Crest Forest*, Calif. N8 210-1
Crest Hill, Ill. O2 96-7
Crested Butte, Colo. F8 214-5
Crestline, Calif. G10 210-1
Crestline, Kans. J16 108-9
Crestline, Nev. J11 226-7
Crestline, O. D7 132-3
Creston, B.C. K10 268-9
Creston, Ill. B8 96-7
Creston, Ind. B4 100-1
Creston, Ia. I6 104-5
Creston, La. C3 168-9
Creston, Nebr. F13 124-5
Creston, O. E13 132-3
Creston, S.C. F11 184-5
Creston, Wash. E14 246-7
Creston, W. Va. F4 200-1
Creston, Wyo. I10 250-1
Creston Junction, Wyo. I10 250-1
Crestone, Colo. H10 214-5
Crestview, Fla. B4 156-7
Crestview*, Ky. D11 164-5
Crestview, S.C. D13 184-5
Crestview Acres*, Sask. J7 294-5
Crestview Hills*, Ky. E11 164-5
Crestwood*, Ill. C11 96-7
Crestwood, Ky. A3 164-5
Crestwood, Mo. C15 120-1
Creswell, N.C. D15 180-1
Creswell, Ore. F6 238-9
Crete, Ill. O4 96-7
Crete, Nebr. I14 124-5
Creve Coeur, Ill. F7 96-7
Creve Coeur*, Mo. E10 120-1
Crew Lake, La. B6 168-9
Crewe, Va. I11 196-7
Crewport, Wash. H11 246-7
Crews, Ala. D3 146-7
Cricket, N.C. G1 180-1
Cridersville, O. D4 132-3
Criehaven, Me. M7 64-5
Criglersville, Va. C1 196-7
Crimora, Va. G10 196-7
Criner, Okla. G11 234-5
Cripple Creek, Colo. F11 214-5
Cripple Creek, Va. J6 196-7
Crisfield, Md. I14 172-3
Crisp, N.C. D13 180-1
Crisp, co., Ga. L5 160-1
Crittenden, Ky. E11 164-5
Crittenden, Va. G4 196-7
Crittenden, co., Ark. D11 150-1
Crittenden, co., Ky. I4 164-5
Critz, Va. K7 196-7
Crivitz, Wis. E15 140-1
Crocheron, Md. H13 172-3
Crocker, Mo. G7 120-1
Crocker, S. Dak. C13 136-7
Crockett, Tex. F10 192-3
Crockett, Va. J5 196-7
Crockett, co., Tenn. C3 188-9
Crockett, co., Tex. F5 192-3
Crockett Mills, Tenn. B3 188-9
Crocketts Bluff, Ark. G9 150-1
Crocketville, S.C. H10 184-5
Croft, N.C. J1 180-1
Crofton, B.C. D12 268-9
Crofton, Ky. J5 164-5
Crofton*, Md. E11 172-3
Crofton, Nebr. D12 124-5
Croghan, N.Y. C8 80-1
Cromer, Man. J9 272-3
Cromwell, Ala. I2 146-7
Cromwell, Conn. E9 60-1
Cromwell, Ind. B10 100-1
Cromwell, Ia. I5 104-5
Cromwell, Ky. I7 164-5
Cromwell, Minn. I7 116-7
Cromwell, Okla. F13 234-5
Crook, Colo. B15 214-5
Crook, co., Ore. F10 238-9
Crook, co., Wyo. B15 250-1
Crooked Creek, Alaska F9 254-5
Crooked River, Sask. J9 294-5
Crooks, S. Dak. G15 136-7
Crooks Gap, Wyo. G10 250-1
Crookston, Minn. G1 116-7
Crookston, Nebr. C7 124-5
Crooksville, O. G8 132-3
Crookton, Ariz. E5 206-7
Croom, Md. K6 172-3
Cropper, Ky. A4 164-5
Cropwell, Ala. E7 146-7
Crosby, Minn. I5 116-7
Crosby, Miss. L4 176-7
Crosby, N. Dak. B3 128-9
Crosby, Tex. G15 192-3
Crosby, co., Tex. D5 192-3
Crosbyton, Tex. C5 192-3
Crosland, Ga. M5 160-1
Cross, S.C. G12 184-5
Cross, co., Ark. D10 150-1
Cross Anchor, S.C. H5 184-5
Cross Canyon, Ariz. D11 206-7
Cross City, Fla. D9 156-7
Cross Hill, S.C. J4 184-5
Cross Junction, Va. D11 196-7
Cross Keys, N.J. K3 76-7
Cross Keys, S.C. H5 184-5
Cross Lake, Man. A13 272-3
Cross Lake, Minn. I5 116-7
Cross Plains, Ind. K11 100-1
Cross Plains, Tenn. F7 188-9
Cross Plains, Tex. E7 192-3
Cross Plains, Wis. I1 140-1
Cross Point, Que. I5 290-1
Cross Roads, Ark. G6 150-1
Cross Roads, Ark. G10 150-1
Cross Roads, Ark. H2 150-1
Cross Roads, Miss. A10 176-7
Cross Timbers, Mo. G5 120-1
Cross Village, Mich. E12 112-3
Crossett, Ark. K7 150-1
Crossfield, Alta. L7 264-5
Crossgate*, Ky. G9 164-5
Crossnore, N.C. D5 180-1
Crossroads, La. C2 168-9
Crossroads, Miss. M7 176-7
Crossroads, N. Mex. I11 230-1
Crossroads, P.E.I. F7 287
Crosstown, Mo. G11 120-1
Crosstown, Tenn. J2 188-9
Crossville, Ala. C8 146-7
Crossville, Ala. E3 146-7
Crossville, Ill. L10 96-7
Crossville, Tenn. H9 188-9
Crosswicks, N.J. H5 76-7
Croswell, Mich. F7 112-3
Crothersville, Ind. L9 100-1
Croton-on-Hudson, N.Y. B14 80-1
Crouch, Ida. K4 218-9
Crouch, Va. H13 196-7
Crouse, N.C. E6 180-1
Crouseville, Me. C8 64-5
Crow Agency, Mont. G12 222-3
Crow Wing, co., Minn. J5 116-7
Crowder, Miss. C6 176-7
Crowder, Mo. I11 120-1
Crowder, Okla. F14 234-5
Crowell, Tex. C6 192-3
Crowheart, Wyo. E8 250-1
Crowley, Colo. H13 214-5
Crowley, La. H4 168-9
Crowley, Ore. H14 238-9
Crowley, Tex. D13 192-3
Crowley, co., Colo. G13 214-5
Crown City, O. J8 132-3
Crown King, Ariz. G6 206-7
Crown Point, Ind. B4 100-1
Crownpoint, N. Mex. E3 230-1
Crownsville, Md. H7 172-3
Crowsnest*, Sask. M9 294-5
Crowville, La. C6 168-9
Croydon, N.H. K4 72-3
Croydon, Ut. E7 242-3
Crozet, Va. G10 196-7
Crozier, La. J8 168-9
Crozier, Va. H12 196-7
Cruger, Miss. F6 176-7
Crum, W. Va. K10 200-1
Crumlin, Ont. E12 284-5
Crump, Tenn. D4 188-9
Crumpton, Md. D13 172-3
Crumrod, Ark. H10 150-1
Crumstown, Ind. A7 100-1
Crutchfield, Ky. K2 164-5
Crutwell, Sask. J7 294-5
Cruzville, N. Mex. I2 230-1
Crysler*, Ont. H16 284-5
Crystal, Ida. K2 218-9
Crystal, Ida. N9 218-9
Crystal, Me. F8 64-5
Crystal, Mich. I13 112-3
Crystal, Minn. A10 116-7
Crystal, Nev. L10 226-7
Crystal, N. Mex. D2 230-1
Crystal, N. Dak. C13 128-9
Crystal, Okla. H14 234-5
Crystal Bay, Nev. G1 226-7
Crystal Beach, Fla. H1 156-7
Crystal City, Man. K12 272-3
Crystal City, Mo. D15 120-1
Crystal City, Tex. H6 192-3
Crystal Falls, Mich. D9 112-3
Crystal Hill, Va. J10 196-7
Crystal Lake, Conn. B11 60-1
Crystal Lake, Ill. K1 96-7
Crystal Lake, Ia. B7 104-5
Crystal Lake Park*, Mo. E10 120-1
Crystal Lakes, O. H15 132-3
Crystal River, Fla. E10 156-7
Crystal Springs, Ark. F4 150-1
Crystal Springs, Fla. G4 156-7

Crystal Springs, Kans. J9 108-9
Crystal Springs, Miss. J5 176-7
Crystal Springs, Sask. K7 294-5
Crystal Valley, Ga. J3 160-1
Cub Run, Ky. I8 164-5
Cuba, Ala. I2 146-7
Cuba, Ill. F6 96-7
Cuba, Kans. D10 108-9
Cuba, Ky. K3 164-5
Cuba, Mo. F8 120-1
Cuba, N. Mex. D5 230-1
Cuba, N.Y. G3 80-1
Cuba, Tenn. K1 188-9
Cuba City, Wis. K11 140-1
Cubero, N. Mex. F4 230-1
Cucamonga*, Calif. N8 210-1
Cuchara, Colo. I11 214-5
Cuchillo, N. Mex. J4 230-1
Cudahy*, Calif. N7 210-1
Cudahy, Wis. J5 140-1
Cudworth, Sask. K7 294-5
Cuero, Tex. H8 192-3
Cuervo, N. Mex. F9 230-1
Cuevas, Miss. O8 176-7
Culberson, N.C. F1 180-1
Culberson, co., Tex. F2 192-3
Culbertson, Mont. B15 222-3
Culbertson, Nebr. J6 124-5
Culdesac, Ida. F3 218-9
Cullen, La. A2 168-9
Cullen, Va. I10 196-7
Culleoka, Tenn. J6 188-9
Culler, Ark. F8 150-1
Cullison, Kans. I7 108-9
Cullman, Ala. C6 146-7
Cullman, co., Ala. D6 146-7
Culloden, Ga. I4 160-1
Culloden, W. Va. H11 200-1
Cullomburg, Ala. K2 146-7
Cullowhee, N.C. E3 180-1
Culp Creek, Ore. G6 238-9
Culpeper, Va. C1 196-7
Culpeper, co., Va. F11 196-7
Cultus Lake, B.C. C16 268-9
Culver, Ind. C7 100-1
Culver, Kans. F10 108-9
Culver, Ore. E9 238-9
Culver City*, Calif. G8 210-1
Culvers Lake, N.J. B4 76-7
Cumbee, Fla. H5 156-7
Cumberland, B.C. J5 268-9
Cumberland*, Ind. H8 100-1
Cumberland, Ia. H5 104-5
Cumberland, Ky. J14 164-5
Cumberland*, Me. N9 64-5
Cumberland, Md. B4 172-3
Cumberland, N.J. M4 76-7
Cumberland, O. G9 132-3
Cumberland, Okla. I12 234-5
Cumberland*, Ont. H15 284-5
Cumberland*, R.I. A5 87
Cumberland, Va. I11 196-7
Cumberland, Wash. F8 246-7
Cumberland, Wis. D8 140-1
Cumberland, co., Ill. I10 96-7
Cumberland, co., Ky. J10 164-5
Cumberland, co., Me. M2 64-5
Cumberland, co., N.J. M3 76-7
Cumberland, co., N.C. F10 180-1
Cumberland, co., N.S. C6 281
Cumberland, co., Pa. J9 84-5
Cumberland, co., Tenn. B11 188-9
Cumberland, co., Va. H11 196-7
Cumberland Bay, N.B. H5 275
Cumberland Beach*, Ont. A14 284-5
Cumberland Center, Me. N9 64-5
Cumberland City, Tenn. A6 188-9
Cumberland Furnace, Tenn. G5 188-9
Cumberland Gap, Tenn. F13 188-9
Cumberland Heights, Tenn. J10 188-9
Cumberland Hill, R.I. A5 87
Cumberland House, Sask. I10 294-5
Cumberland Springs, Tenn. J11 188-9
Cumby, Tex. D10 192-3
Cuming, co., Nebr. E14 124-5
Cumming, Ga. A12 160-1
Cumming, Ia. H7 104-5
Cummings, Kans. D15 108-9
Cummings, N. Dak. F14 128-9
Cummings, S.C. I10 184-5
Cummington, Mass. C3 68-9
Cumnock, N.C. I6 180-1
Cundiff, Ky. J10 164-5
Cundiyo, N. Mex. D7 230-1
Cundys Harbor, Me. N10 64-5
Cunningham, Kans. I8 108-9
Cunningham, Ky. J2 164-5
Cunningham, Tenn. G5 188-9
Cunningham, Wash. G13 246-7
Cupar, Sask. M8 294-5
Cupertino, Calif. D8 210-1
Cuprum, Ida. I2 218-9
Curdsville, Ky. H5 164-5
Curlew, Ia. C5 104-5
Curlew, Wash. B14 246-7
Currant, Nev. H9 226-7
Currie, Minn. O3 116-7
Currie, Nev. E10 226-7
Currie, N.C. G12 180-1
Currituck, N.C. C15 180-1
Currituck, co., N.C. B15 180-1
Curry, Ala. F8 146-7
Curry, Alaska E11 254-5
Curry, co., N. Mex. G11 230-1
Curry, co., Ore. J3 238-9
Curryville, Mo. D8 120-1
Curtin, Ore. G5 238-9
Curtin, W. Va. G6 200-1
Curtis, Ark. H5 150-1
Curtis, Nebr. I7 124-5
Curtis, Okla. D8 234-5
Curtis, Wash. H6 246-7
Curtis, Wyo. H15 250-1
Curtiss, Ariz. L9 206-7
Curtiss, Wis. F11 140-1
Curtiss Station, Miss. C6 176-7
Curtisville*, Pa. H2 84-5
Curve, Tenn. I3 188-9
Curwensville, Pa. G6 84-5
Cushing, Ia. E3 104-5
Cushing, Me. L6 64-5
Cushing, Nebr. G11 124-5
Cushing, Okla. E12 234-5
Cushing, Wis. D7 140-1
Cushman, Ark. C8 150-1
Cushman, Mass. C5 68-9
Cushman, Mont. F10 222-3
Cushman, Ore. F4 238-9
Cusick, Wash. D16 246-7
Cusseta, Ala. H10 146-7
Cusseta, Ga. J3 160-1
Custar, O. C5 132-3
Custer, Ky. H8 164-5
Custer, Mich. H11 112-3
Custer, Mont. G12 222-3
Custer, S. Dak. G2 136-7
Custer, Wash. B7 246-7
Custer, Wis. D1 140-1
Custer, co., Colo. H11 214-5
Custer, co., Ida. K6 218-9
Custer, co., Mont. F14 222-3
Custer, co., Nebr. G8 124-5
Custer, co., Okla. E8 234-5
Custer, co., S. Dak. G2 136-7
Custer City, Okla. E8 234-5
Cut Bank, Mont. B5 222-3
Cut Knife, Sask. K4 294-5
Cut Off, La. J9 168-9
Cutbank, Sask. M6 294-5
Cuthbert, Ga. L3 160-1
Cutler, Calif. K6 210-1
Cutler, Ind. E7 100-1
Cutler, Me. J11 64-5
Cutler Ridge, Fla. I16 156-7
Cutlerville*, Mich. I12 112-3
Cutten, Calif. E1 210-1
Cutter, Ariz. I9 206-7
Cuttingsville, Vt. K5 90-1
Cuttyhunk, Mass. I12 68-9
Cuyahoga, co., O. B9 132-3
Cuyahoga Falls, O. D15 132-3
Cuyahoga Heights*, O. B9 132-3
Cuyamungue, N. Mex. D7 230-1
Cuyuna, Minn. I5 116-7
Cuzco, Ind. M6 100-1
Cuzzart, W. Va. D8 200-1
Cyclone, W. Va. K13 200-1
Cygnet, O. C5 132-3
Cylinder, Ia. C5 104-5
Cylon, Wis. E7 140-1
Cynthiana, Ind. N3 100-1
Cynthiana, Ky. A8 164-5
Cypert, Ark. G10 150-1
Cypress, Ala. G4 146-7
Cypress*, Calif. H9 210-1
Cypress, Fla. B6 156-7
Cypress, La. D3 168-9
Cypress Gardens*, Fla. F11 156-7
Cypress Inn, Tenn. D5 188-9
Cypress Quarters*, Fla. G12 156-7
Cypress River*, Man. J12 272-3
Cyr, Me. B9 64-5
Cyr, Mont. E3 222-3
Cyril, Okla. G9 234-5
Cyrus, Minn. K3 116-7
Czar, Alta. K10 264-5
Czar, W. Va. G14 200-1

D

Dabneys, Va. H12 196-7
Dacoma, Okla. C9 234-5
Dacono, Colo. F3 214-5
Dacula, Ga. F5 160-1
Dacusville, S.C. F1 184-5
Dade, co., Fla. J13 156-7
Dade, co., Ga. D1 160-1
Dade, co., Mo. H4 120-1
Dade City, Fla. F4 156-7
Dade City East*, Fla. E10 156-7
Dade City North*, Fla. E10 156-7
Dadeville, Ala. G9 146-7
Dadeville, Mo. H4 120-1
Dafter, Mich. D13 112-3
Daggett, Calif. M8 210-1
Daggett, Mich. E9 112-3
Daggett, co., Ut. E9 242-3
Dagmar, Mont. B16 222-3
Dagsboro, Del. J5 153
Dahlen, N. Dak. D12 128-9
Dahlgren, Va. C4 196-7
Dahlonega, Ga. D5 160-1
Daigle, Me. A8 64-5
Dailey, Colo. B15 214-5
Dailey, W. Va. F15 200-1
Daingerfield, Tex. D11 192-3
Dairy, Ore. J8 238-9
Daisetta, Tex. G16 192-3
Daisy, Ark. G3 150-1
Daisy, Ga. K10 160-1
Daisy, Okla. H14 234-5
Daisy, Wash. D14 246-7
Dakota, Minn. O9 116-7
Dakota, co., Minn. M7 116-7
Dakota, co., Nebr. D14 124-5
Dakota City, Ia. D6 104-5
Dakota City, Nebr. D14 124-5
Dalark, Ark. H5 150-1
Dalcour, La. D15 168-9
Dale, Ind. N6 100-1
Dale, Okla. J4 234-5
Dale*, Pa. I5 84-5
Dale, S.C. I11 184-5
Dale, Wis. E3 140-1
Dale, co., Ala. K9 146-7
Dale City*, Va. F12 196-7
Dale Creek, Wyo. J14 250-1
Daleview, Mont. A15 222-3
Daleville, Ala. L9 146-7
Daleville, Ind. G10 100-1
Daleville, Miss. H9 176-7
Daleville, Va. I8 196-7
Daleyville, Wis. J12 140-1
Dalhart, Tex. A4 192-3
Dalhousie, N.B. D5 275
Dalkena, Wash. D16 246-7
Dallam, co., Tex. A4 192-3
Dallas, Ark. F2 150-1
Dallas, Ga. F3 160-1
Dallas, Ia. I8 104-5
Dallas, Me. I2 64-5
Dallas, N.C. J1 180-1
Dallas, Ore. D5 238-9
Dallas, Pa. E13 84-5
Dallas, S. Dak. H10 136-7
Dallas, Tex. D9 192-3
Dallas, W. Va. C6 200-1
Dallas, Wis. E8 140-1
Dallas, co., Ala. I5 146-7
Dallas, co., Ark. H6 150-1
Dallas, co., Ia. G6 104-5
Dallas, co., Mo. G5 120-1
Dallas, co., Tex. E9 192-3
Dallas Center, Ia. G7 104-5
Dallas City, Ill. F4 96-7
Dallastown, Pa. J11 84-5
Dalles, The, Ore. B9 238-9
Dallesport, Wash. J10 246-7
Dalmeny, Sask. K6 294-5
Dalton, Ark. A9 150-1
Dalton, Ga. D2 160-1
Dalton, Kans. J11 108-9
Dalton, Mass. C2 68-9
Dalton, Minn. J2 116-7
Dalton, Mo. D5 120-1
Dalton, Nebr. G2 124-5
Dalton, N.H. F6 72-3
Dalton, O. F14 132-3
Dalton, Pa. E14 84-5
Dalton, Wis. G2 140-1
Dalton Gardens, Ida. C2 218-9
Dalworthington Gardens, Tex. D13 192-3
Daly City, Calif. C7 210-1
Dalzell, S.C. E12 184-5
Damar, Kans. E6 108-9
Damariscotta*, Me. M12 64-5
Damariscotta [-Newcastle], Me. M12 64-5
Damascus, Ala. L6 146-7
Damascus, Ark. D6 150-1
Damascus, Ga. M3 160-1
Damascus, Md. F3 172-3
Damascus, Va. J4 196-7
Dameron, Md. H12 172-3
Dames Quarter, Md. H13 172-3
Damon, Okla. G15 234-5
Dana, Ind. H4 100-1
Dana, Ia. F6 104-5
Dana, N.C. E4 180-1
Dana, Sask. K7 294-5
Dana Point, Calif. H9 210-1
Danburg, Ga. F8 160-1
Danbury, Conn. G4 60-1
Danbury, Ia. E3 104-5
Danbury, Nebr. J7 124-5
Danbury, N.H. K5 72-3
Danbury, N.C. C8 180-1
Danbury*, Tex. H10 192-3
Danbury, Wis. C7 140-1
Danby, Vt. K5 90-1
Danby Four Corners, Vt. K4 90-1
Dancyville, Tenn. K3 188-9
Dandridge, Tenn. H13 188-9
Dane, Wis. I1 140-1
Dane, co., Wis. J12 140-1
Danforth, Me. G9 64-5
Dania, Fla. G16 156-7
Daniel, Wyo. F6 250-1
Daniel Junction, Wyo. F6 250-1
Daniels, Ida. O9 218-9
Daniels, Md. F5 172-3
Daniels, co., Mont. A14 222-3
Daniel's Harbour, Nfld. L8 278-9
Daniels-Rhyne, N.C. E6 180-1
Danielson, Conn. C14 60-1
Danielsville, Ga. F6 160-1
Danieltown, Va. J11 196-7
Dannebrog, Nebr. H11 124-5
Dannemora, N.Y. A11 80-1
Danner, Ore. H15 238-9
Dansby, Ark. E11 150-1
Dansville, Mich. I2 112-3
Dansville, N.Y. F4 80-1
Dant, Ore. D9 238-9
Dante, S. Dak. I13 136-7
Dante, Va. J3 196-7
Danube, Minn. M4 116-7
Danvers, Ill. F8 96-7
Danvers, Mass. B12 68-9
Danvers, Minn. L3 116-7
Danvers, Mont. D9 222-3
Danville, Ala. C5 146-7
Danville, Ark. E4 150-1
Danville, Ga. J6 160-1
Danville, Ill. G11 96-7
Danville, Ind. H7 100-1
Danville, Ia. J13 104-5
Danville, Kans. J9 108-9
Danville, Ky. D6 164-5
Danville, La. C3 168-9
Danville, N.H. O8 72-3
Danville, O. E8 132-3
Danville, Pa. G11 84-5
Danville, Que. I14 290-1
Danville, Vt. E8 90-1
Danville, Va. K9 196-7
Danville, Wash. B14 246-7
Danville, W. Va. J13 200-1
Danwood, S.C. D13 184-5
Daphne, Ala. N3 146-7
Darbun, Miss. L6 176-7
Darby, Mont. G3 222-3
Darby, Pa. B11 84-5
Darbydale, O. G6 132-3
D'Arcy, Sask. L5 294-5
Dardanelle, Ark. D5 150-1
Darden, Tenn. C5 188-9
Dare, co., N.C. D16 180-1
Dares Beach, Md. G11 172-3
Darfur, Minn. O4 116-7
Darien, Conn. J4 60-1
Darien, Ga. M10 160-1
Darien*, Ill. B10 96-7
Darien, Wis. K3 140-1
Dark Cove, Nfld. M10 278-9
Dark Cove-Middle Brook-Gambo*, Nfld. M10 278-9
Dark Harbor, Me. L6 64-5
Darke, co., O. F3 132-3
Darling, Miss. C6 176-7
Darlingford, Man. K13 272-3
Darlington, Ala. J5 146-7
Darlington, Ida. L7 218-9
Darlington, Ind. G6 100-1
Darlington, La. F8 168-9
Darlington, Md. B12 172-3
Darlington, Mo. B3 120-1
Darlington*, N.B. D5 275
Darlington, N.J. B7 76-7
Darlington, S.C. D13 184-5
Darlington, Wis. K11 140-1
Darlington, co., S.C. C13 184-5
Darlove, Miss. F4 176-7
Darmstadt, Ind. O4 100-1
Darnell, La. B6 168-9
Darnestown, Md. H2 172-3
Darnley, P.E.I. D5 287
Darr, Nebr. H8 124-5
Darrington, Wash. D9 246-7
Darrow, La. C10 168-9
Dartmouth, Mass. H12 68-9
Dartmouth, N.S. E7 281
Darwin, Minn. A7 116-7
Darwin, Okla. H14 234-5
Dasher, Ga. O6 160-1
Dashwood*, Ont. D11 284-5
Dassel, Minn. A7 116-7
Date Creek, Ariz. G5 206-7
Dateland, Ariz. J4 206-7
Datil, N. Mex. H3 230-1
Datto, Ark. A10 150-1
Daufuskie Island, S.C. K10 184-5
Daulnay*, N.B. E6 275
Dauphin, Man. I2 272-3
Dauphin, Pa. I10 84-5
Dauphin, co., Pa. I11 84-5
Dauphin Isl., Ala. O2 146-7
Dauphin Island, Ala. O3 146-7
Daus, Tenn. K10 188-9
Davant, La. J10 168-9
Davella, Ky. H15 164-5
Daveluyville*, Que. H15 290-1
Davenport, Fla. G6 156-7
Davenport, Ia. G14 104-5
Davenport, Nebr. I12 124-5
Davenport, N. Dak. H14 128-9
Davenport, Okla. E12 234-5
Davenport, Va. I4 196-7
Davenport, Wash. E14 246-7
Davey, Nebr. J1 124-5
David City, Nebr. G13 124-5
Davidson, N.C. J1 180-1
Davidson, Okla. H8 234-5
Davidson, Sask. M7 294-5
Davidson, Tenn. B10 188-9
Davidson, co., N.C. D8 180-1
Davidson, co., Tenn. B7 188-9
Davidsonville, Md. I7 172-3
Davie, Fla. G16 156-7
Davie, co., N.C. D7 180-1
Davie Bay*, B.C. J6 268-9
Daviess, co., Ind. L5 100-1
Daviess, co., Ky. H6 164-5
Daviess, co., Mo. B4 120-1
Davin, Sask. N8 294-5
Davis, Calif. A9 210-1
Davis, N.C. F15 180-1
Davis, Okla. H11 234-5
Davis*, Sask. J7 294-5
Davis, S. Dak. H15 136-7
Davis, W. Va. E8 200-1
Davis, co., Ia. J11 104-5
Davis, co., Ut. E6 242-3
Davis City, Ia. J7 104-5
Davis Corner, Del. F3 153
Davis Dam, Ariz. E2 206-7
Davis Mill, N.B. F3 275
Davis Station, S.C. F12 184-5
Davisboro, Ga. I8 160-1
Davisburg, Mich. H4 112-3
Davison, Mich. G4 112-3
Davison, co., S. Dak. G13 136-7
Daviston, Ala. G9 146-7
Davisville, R.I. F5 87
Davisville, W. Va. E3 200-1
Davy, W. Va. J3 200-1

Dawes, co., Nebr. C2 124-5
Dawson, Ala. C8 146-7
Dawson, Ga. L4 160-1
Dawson, Ia. G6 104-5
Dawson, Md. C3 172-3
Dawson, Minn. M2 116-7
Dawson, Nebr. J16 124-5
Dawson, N. Dak. H9 128-9
Dawson, Ore. E5 238-9
Dawson, Tex. E9 192-3
Dawson, W. Va. I5 200-1
Dawson, Y.T. B1 297
Dawson, co., Ga. E4 160-1
Dawson, co., Mont. D15 222-3
Dawson, co., Nebr. H8 124-5
Dawson, co., Tex. D4 192-3
Dawson Bay*, Man. H2 272-3
Dawson Creek, B.C. E8 268-9
Dawson Settlement, N.B. H7 275
Dawson Springs, Ky. I5 164-5
Dawsonville, Ga. E4 160-1
Dawsonville, Md. H2 172-3
Dawsonville, N.B. D4 275
Day, co., S. Dak. C14 136-7
Daykin, Nebr. I13 124-5
Daylight, Ind. O4 100-1
Days Creek, Ore. H5 238-9
Days Ferry, Me. N11 64-5
Daysland, Alta. J9 264-5
Dayton, Ala. I4 146-7
Dayton, Ida. O10 218-9
Dayton, Ind. F6 100-1
Dayton, Ia. E6 104-5
Dayton, Ky. D11 164-5
Dayton, Me. N2 64-5
Dayton, Md. G4 172-3
Dayton, Minn. A10 116-7
Dayton, Mont. C3 222-3
Dayton, Nev. G2 226-7
Dayton, N.J. G6 76-7
Dayton, O. G4 132-3
Dayton, Ore. G1 238-9
Dayton, Tenn. J11 188-9
Dayton, Tex. G15 192-3
Dayton, Va. F10 196-7
Dayton, Wash. H15 246-7
Dayton, Wis. J1 140-1
Dayton, Wyo. B11 250-1
Daytona Beach, Fla. D12 156-7
Daytona Beach Shores*, Fla. D12 156-7
Dayville, Conn. C14 60-1
Dayville, Mass. D3 68-9
Dayville, Ore. E11 238-9
Dazey, N. Dak. G12 128-9
De Ann, Ark. I4 150-1
De Armanville, Ala. E9 146-7
De Baca, co., N. Mex. H9 230-1
De Bary, Fla. E11 156-7
De Beque, Colo. E6 214-5
De Borgia, Mont. D2 222-3
De Forest, Wis. I1 140-1
De Funiak Springs, Fla. B5 156-7
De Graff, Minn. L3 116-7
De Graff, O. E4 132-3
De Grasse*, Que. G6 290-1
De Grau, Nfld. N7 278-9
De Kalb, Ill. B9 96-7
De Kalb, Miss. G10 176-7
De Kalb, Mo. G14 120-1
De Kalb, S.C. D11 184-5
De Kalb, Tex. D11 192-3
De Kalb, co., Ala. B9 146-7
De Kalb, co., Ill. B9 96-7
De Kalb, co., Mo. B3 120-1
De Kalb, co., Tenn. C9 188-9
De Lamere, N. Dak. I13 128-9
De Land, Fla. D12 156-7
De Leon, Tex. E7 192-3
De Leon Springs, Fla. D11 156-7
De Lisle, Miss. O8 176-7
De Moss Springs, Ore. C9 238-9
De Mossville, Ky. E11 164-5
De Pere, Wis. E4 140-1
De Queen, Ark. H2 150-1
De Quincy, La. G2 168-9
De Ridder, La. F2 168-9
De Rossett, Tenn. B10 188-9
De Smet, S. Dak. E14 136-7
De Soto, Ga. K4 160-1
De Soto, Ill. M8 96-7
De Soto, Ia. H7 104-5
De Soto, Kans. F15 108-9
De Soto, Miss. J9 176-7
De Soto, Mo. F10 120-1
De Soto, Tex. D14 192-3
De Soto, Wis. I9 140-1
De Soto, co., Fla. H11 156-7
De Soto, co., La. C2 168-9
De Soto, co., Miss. A6 176-7
De Tour, Mich. D14 112-3
De Valls Bluff, Ark. F9 150-1
De Weese, Miss. H9 176-7
De Witt, Ark. G9 150-1
De Witt, Ia. G15 104-5
De Witt, Nebr. I14 124-5
De Witt*, N.Y. E7 80-1
De Witt, Va. F1 196-7
De Witt, co., Ill. G9 96-7
De Witt, co., Tex. H8 192-3
Deadhorse*, Alaska B11 254-5
Deadhorse Wells, Nev. G4 226-7
Deadwood, Ore. F4 238-9
Deadwood, S. Dak. E2 136-7
Deaf Smith, co., Tex. B4 192-3
Deal, N.J. H8 76-7
Deal Island, Md. H13 172-3
Deale, Md. K7 172-3
Dean, La. A5 168-9
Dean, Mont. H9 222-3
Dean, S.C. D5 184-5
Deans, N.J. G6 76-7
Deans Market, Ark. C2 150-1
Deansville, W. Va. E13 200-1
Dearborn, Mich. J6 112-3
Dearborn, Mo. G14 120-1
Dearborn, co., Ind. J11 100-1
Dearborn Heights*, Mich. J15 112-3
Dearing, Ga. G8 160-1
Dearing, Kans. K14 108-9
Deary, Ida. E3 218-9
Death Valley, Calif. K8 210-1
Deatsville, Ala. H7 146-7
Deatsville, Ky. C2 164-5
Deauville, Que. J14 290-1
Deaver, Wyo. B9 250-1
Debden, Sask. J6 294-5
Debec, N.B. H3 275
Debert, N.S. D7 281
Deblois, Me. J9 64-5
Decatur, Ala. B6 146-7
Decatur, Ark. A2 150-1
Decatur, Ga. G4 160-1
Decatur, Ill. H8 96-7
Decatur, Ind. D12 100-1
Decatur, Mich. J11 112-3
Decatur, Miss. H8 176-7
Decatur, Nebr. E15 124-5
Decatur, Tenn. J12 188-9
Decatur, Tex. B12 192-3
Decatur, Wash. C7 246-7
Decatur, co., Ga. N3 160-1
Decatur, co., Ind. J10 100-1
Decatur, co., Ia. J7 104-5
Decatur, co., Kans. D4 108-9
Decatur, co., Tenn. C5 188-9
Decatur City, Ia. J7 104-5
Decaturville, Tenn. C5 188-9
Decherd, Tenn. D9 188-9
Decker, Ind. M4 100-1
Decker, Man. I10 272-3
Decker, Mich. E6 112-3
Decker, Mont. I13 222-3
Decker Lake, B.C. F5 268-9
Deckers, Colo. I2 214-5
Deckerville, Ark. D11 150-1
Deckerville, Mich. H15 112-3
Declo, Ida. O7 218-9
Decorah, Ia. B12 104-5
Decoy, Ky. H14 164-5
Decoy, Nev. D10 226-7
Dedham, Ia. F5 104-5
Dedham, Me. J7 64-5
Dedham, Mass. D11 68-9
Dee, Ore. B8 238-9
Deedsville, Ind. D8 100-1
Deemer, Miss. H8 176-7
Deenwood, Ga. M8 160-1
Deep Brook, N.S. E4 281
Deep Creek Lake, Md. B1 172-3
Deep Gap, N.C. C6 180-1
Deep River, Conn. G11 60-1
Deep River, Ind. B5 100-1
Deep River, Ia. G11 104-5
Deep River, Ont. H9 284-5
Deep River, Wash. H5 246-7
Deep Run, N.C. F12 180-1
Deep Water, W. Va. J15 200-1
Deephaven, Minn. B10 116-7
Deepstep, Ga. H7 160-1
Deepwater, Mo. F4 120-1
Deepwater, N.J. K1 76-7
Deer, Ark. C5 150-1
Deer Creek, Ill. F8 96-7
Deer Creek, Minn. J3 116-7
Deer Creek, Okla. C11 234-5
Deer Harbor, Wash. C7 246-7
Deer Island, Ore. B6 238-9
Deer Isle, Me. L7 64-5
Deer Lake, Nfld. M8 278-9
Deer Lodge, Mont. F5 222-3
Deer Lodge, Tenn. G10 188-9
Deer Park, Ala. L2 146-7
Deer Park*, Ill. A10 96-7
Deer Park, La. E6 168-9
Deer Park, Md. C2 172-3
Deer Park, N.Y. J12 80-1
Deer Park, O. K14 132-3
Deer Park, Tex. H14 192-3
Deer Park, Wash. E15 246-7
Deer Park, Wis. E7 140-1
Deer River, Minn. H6 116-7
Deer Trail, Colo. E13 214-5
Deerfield, Ill. K3 96-7
Deerfield, Kans. H3 108-9
Deerfield, Mass. C5 68-9
Deerfield, Mich. K13 112-3
Deerfield, Mo. G3 120-1
Deerfield, N.H. M8 72-3
Deerfield*, N.J. M3 76-7
Deerfield, Tenn. K5 188-9
Deerfield, Va. G9 196-7
Deerfield*, Wis. J13 140-1
Deerfield Beach, Fla. F16 156-7
Deerhorn, Man. H13 272-3
Deering, Alaska C9 254-5
Deering, Mo. K11 120-1
Deering, N.H. N5 72-3
Deering, N. Dak. C7 128-9
Deerwood, Minn. J5 116-7
Deeson, Miss. D4 176-7
Deeth, Nev. C9 226-7
Defas Park*, Ut. G6 242-3
Defense Heights*, Md. E10 172-3
Defiance, Ia. G3 104-5
Defiance, O. C4 132-3
Defiance, co., O. B3 132-3
Defoe, Ky. A5 164-5
Deford, Mich. H15 112-3
Dégelis, Que. E15 290-1
DeKalb, co., Ga. G4 160-1
DeKalb, co., Ind. B11 100-1
Dekoven, Ky. H4 164-5
Del Aire*, Calif. N7 210-1
Del Bonita, Mont. A5 222-3
Del City, Okla. J2 234-5
Del Mar, Calif. J10 210-1
Del Norte, Colo. I9 214-5
Del Norte, co., Calif. D1 210-1
Del Rey Oaks*, Calif. K3 210-1
Del Rio, Tenn. H15 188-9
Del Rio, Tex. H5 192-3
Dela, Okla. H14 234-5
Delacroix, La. D16 168-9
Delafield, Wis. J4 140-1
Delanco, N.J. I4 76-7
Delaney, Ark. C3 150-1
Delaneys Corner, Del. E2 153
Delano, Calif. L6 210-1
Delano, Minn. A9 116-7
Delano, Tenn. K13 188-9
Delaplain, Nev. A10 226-7
Delaplaine, Ark. B10 150-1
Delaplane, Va. A2 196-7
Delavan, Ill. F7 96-7
Delavan, Kans. G12 108-9
Delavan, Minn. O5 116-7
Delavan, Wis. K3 140-1
Delavan Lake, Wis. K3 140-1
Delaware, Ark. D4 150-1
Delaware, Ind. K11 100-1
Delaware, Ia. E13 104-5
Delaware*, N.J. G4 76-7
Delaware, O. E6 132-3
Delaware, Okla. C14 234-5
Delaware, co., Ind. F10 100-1
Delaware, co., Ia. E13 104-5
Delaware, co., N.Y. G9 80-1
Delaware, co., O. E7 132-3
Delaware, co., Okla. C16 234-5
Delaware, co., Pa. J15 84-5
Delaware City, Del. C3 153
Delbarton, W. Va. K11 200-1
Delburne, Alta. K8 264-5
Delcambre, La. I5 168-9
Delco, N.C. G12 180-1
Delevan, N.Y. F3 80-1
Delhi, Calif. D11 210-1
Delhi, Colo. I13 214-5
Delhi, Ia. E13 104-5
Delhi, La. B6 168-9
Delhi, Minn. M3 116-7
Delhi, N.Y. G9 80-1
Delhi, Okla. F7 234-5
Delhi*, Ont. E13 284-5
Delia, Alta. L9 264-5
Delia, Kans. E13 108-9
Delight, Ark. H4 150-1
Delisle, Sask. L6 294-5
Dell, Ark. C12 150-1
Dell, Mont. I5 222-3
Dell Rapids, S. Dak. G16 136-7
Delle, Ut. E4 242-3
Dellrose, Tenn. K7 188-9
Dellroy, O. E10 132-3
Dellslow, W. Va. A15 200-1
Dellvale, Kans. D5 108-9
Dellview, N.C. E6 180-1
Dellwood, Minn. A11 116-7
Dellwood*, Mo. E10 120-1
Delmar, Ala. C4 146-7
Delmar, Del. K3 153
Delmar, Ia. F15 104-5
Delmar, Md. G15 172-3
Delmar, Ore. H3 238-9
Delmas, Sask. J5 294-5
Delmont, N.J. N4 76-7
Delmont*, Pa. I3 84-5
Delmont, S. Dak. H13 136-7
Deloit, Ia. F3 104-5
Delong, Ind. C7 100-1
Deloraine, Man. K10 272-3
Deloro, Ont. J12 284-5
Delphi, Ind. E6 100-1
Delphia, Mont. F11 222-3
Delphia, S.C. B9 184-5
Delphos, Ia. J6 104-5
Delphos, Kans. E10 108-9
Delphos, O. D4 132-3
Delran*, N.J. I4 76-7
Delray, W. Va. E10 200-1
Delray Beach, Fla. E16 156-7
Delson*, Que. J12 290-1
Delta, Ala. F9 146-7
Delta, Colo. F7 214-5
Delta, Ia. H11 104-5
Delta, La. C8 168-9
Delta, Man. I13 272-3
Delta, Mo. H11 120-1
Delta, O. B4 132-3
Delta, S.C. H6 184-5
Delta, Ut. I5 242-3
Delta, co., Colo. F7 214-5
Delta, co., Mich. E10 112-3
Delta, co., Tex. D10 192-3
Delta City, Miss. G4 176-7
Delta Junction*, Alaska E12 254-5
Deltaville, Va. E4 196-7
Delton, Mich. J12 112-3
Deltona*, Fla. E12 156-7
Demaine, Sask. M6 294-5
Demarest, N.J. C8 76-7
Deming, N. Mex. L4 230-1
Deming, Wash. C8 246-7
Demopolis, Ala. H3 146-7
Demorest, Ga. D6 160-1
DeMotte, Ind. C5 100-1
Dempsey, Okla. F6 234-5
Dempster, S. Dak. D15 136-7
Denair*, Calif. I4 210-1
Denare Beach, Sask. H10 294-5
Dendron, Va. F2 196-7
Denham, Ind. C6 100-1
Denham, Minn. J7 116-7
Denham, Miss. K10 176-7
Denham Springs, La. A10 168-9
Denhoff, N. Dak. F8 128-9
Denholm, Sask. K5 294-5
Denio, Nev. A4 226-7
Denison, Ia. F3 104-5
Denison, Kans. E14 108-9
Denison, Tex. C9 192-3
Denman, Okla. G15 234-5
Denmark, Ia. J13 104-5
Denmark, Me. N7 64-5
Denmark, Miss. C8 176-7
Denmark, Ore. I3 238-9
Denmark, S.C. G10 184-5
Denmark, Tenn. J4 188-9
Denmark, Wis. E5 140-1
Dennard, Ark. C6 150-1
Dennehotso, Ariz. B10 206-7
Denning, Ark. D3 150-1
Dennis, Kans. J15 108-9
Dennis*, Mass. G6 68-9
Dennis, Miss. B11 176-7
Dennis*, N.J. N4 76-7
Dennis, Okla. C15 234-5
Dennis Acres*, Mo. I3 120-1
Dennis Port, Mass. H16 68-9
Dennison*, Minn. N7 116-7
Dennison, O. E10 132-3
Dennistown, Me. G3 64-5
Dennisville, N.J. N4 76-7
Dennysville, Me. I11 64-5
Densmore, Kans. D6 108-9
Dent, Minn. I3 116-7
Dent, co., Mo. H8 120-1
Denton, Ga. L8 160-1
Denton, Kans. D15 108-9
Denton, Md. E14 172-3
Denton, Mo. K11 120-1
Denton, Mont. D8 222-3
Denton, Nebr. H14 124-5
Denton, N.C. I3 180-1
Denton, Tex. B13 192-3
Denton, co., Tex. D9 192-3
Dentsville, Md. G10 172-3
Dentsville, S.C. E10 184-5
Denver, Ark. A4 150-1
Denver, Colo. D11 214-5
Denver, Ind. D8 100-1
Denver, Ia. D11 104-5
Denver, Mo. A3 120-1
Denver, N.C. I1 180-1
Denver, Pa. I13 84-5
Denver, S.C. C5 184-5
Denver, Tenn. B5 188-9
Denver, co., Colo. D11 214-5
Denver City, Tex. D4 192-3
Denville, N.J. D6 76-7
Denzil, Sask. K4 294-5
Deora, Colo. I15 214-5
Depauw, Ind. N8 100-1
Depew, N.Y. E2 80-1
Depew, Okla. E12 234-5
Depoe Bay, Ore. D4 238-9
Deport, Tex. D10 192-3
Deposit, N.Y. H8 80-1
Depoy, Ky. I6 164-5
Deptford*, N.J. J3 76-7
Depue, Ill. D8 96-7
Deputy, Ind. L9 100-1
Derby, Colo. G3 214-5
Derby, Conn. H6 60-1
Derby, Ia. J8 104-5
Derby, Kans. J11 108-9
Derby, Me. H6 64-5
Derby, Miss. M7 176-7
Derby*, Vt. B8 90-1
Derby Center, Vt. B8 90-1
Derby Line, Vt. B8 90-1
Derita, N.C. J1 180-1
Derma, Miss. D8 176-7
Dermott, Ark. I9 150-1
Deroche, B.C. C15 268-9
Derry, La. E3 168-9
Derry, N.H. O7 72-3
Derry, N. Mex. K4 230-1
Derry, Pa. I4 84-5
DeRuyter, N.Y. F7 80-1
Derwent, Alta. I10 264-5
Des Allemands, La. D13 168-9
Des Arc, Ark. E9 150-1
Des Arc, Mo. H10 120-1
Des Lacs, N. Dak. D6 128-9
Des Moines, Ia. G8 104-5
Des Moines, N. Mex. C10 230-1
Des Moines, Wash. J2 246-7
Des Moines, co., Ia. J13 104-5
Des Moines R., Ia. F7 104-5
Des Peres, Mo. B15 120-1
Des Plaines, Ill. L3 96-7
Desbarats, Ont. H6 284-5
Desbiens, Que. C10 290-1
Deschaillons-sur-St.-Laurent*, Que. G10 290-1
Deschambault*, Que. G10 290-1
Deschambault Lake, Sask. H9 294-5
Deschutes, Ore. F9 238-9
Deschutes, co., Ore. G9 238-9
Deseret, Ut. I5 242-3
Deseronto, Ont. K13 284-5
Desert Hot Springs, Calif. G12 210-1
Desert View Highlands*, Calif. N7 210-1
Desert Wells, Nev. F4 226-7
Desha, Ark. C8 150-1

Desha, co., Ark. I9 150-1
Deshler, Nebr. J12 124-5
Deshler, O. C4 132-3
Desloge, Mo. F15 120-1
Desmarais, Alta. F7 264-5
Desmet, Ida. E2 218-9
Despard, W. Va. C14 200-1
Destin, Fla. B4 156-7
Detour, Md. B9 172-3
Detroit, Ala. D3 146-7
Detroit, Kans. F11 108-9
Detroit, Me. J6 64-5
Detroit, Mich. J15 112-3
Detroit, Ore. D7 238-9
Detroit, Tex. C10 192-3
Detroit Beach, Mich. K14 112-3
Detroit Lakes, Minn. I3 116-7
Deuel, co., Nebr. G4 124-5
Deuel, co., S. Dak. D15 136-7
Deux-Montagnes, Que. I12 290-1
Deux-Montagnes, co., Que. I11 290-1
Devenport, Ala. J7 146-7
Devereux, Ga. H7 160-1
Deville, La. E5 168-9
Devils Lake, N. Dak. D10 128-9
Devils Lake, N. Dak. D11 128-9
Devils Slide, Ut. E7 242-3
Devils Tower, Wyo. B15 250-1
Devine, Tex. K1 192-3
Devol, Okla. I9 234-5
Devola, O. H10 132-3
Devon, Alta. J8 264-5
Devon, Kans. I16 108-9
Devon, Mont. B7 222-3
Devondale*, Ky. G9 164-5
Devonia, Tenn. H11 188-9
Dewar, Ia. D11 104-5
Dewar, Okla. F14 234-5
Dewberry, Alta. I10 264-5
Deweese, Nebr. I11 124-5
Dewey, Ariz. G6 206-7
Dewey, Okla. C13 234-5
Dewey, co., Okla. D7 234-5
Dewey, co., S. Dak. C8 136-7
Dewey Beach, Del. I6 153
Deweyville*, Ut. C6 242-3
DeWitt, Mich. H1 112-3
Dewitt, Mo. D5 120-1
Dewy Rose, Ga. E7 160-1
Dexter, Ga. J7 160-1
Dexter, Ia. H6 104-5
Dexter, Kans. K12 108-9
Dexter, Ky. J3 164-5
Dexter, Me. I6 64-5
Dexter, Mich. J3 112-3
Dexter, Minn. O7 116-7
Dexter, Mo. I11 120-1
Dexter, N. Mex. J9 230-1
Dexter, N.Y. C7 80-1
Diablo, Calif. C8 210-1
Diagonal, Ia. J6 104-5
Diamond, Ill. D10 96-7
Diamond, La. J10 168-9
Diamond, Mo. I3 120-1
Diamond, Ore. H13 238-9
Diamond, Wash. G16 246-7
Diamond, Wyo. I15 250-1
Diamond Bar*, Calif. N7 210-1
Diamond Bluff, Wis. F7 140-1
Diamond City, Ark. A5 150-1
Diamond Head, Hawaii K6 258-9
Diamond Hill, R.I. A5 87
Diamond Lake*, Ill. A10 96-7
Diamond Lake, Ore. H7 238-9
Diamondville, Wyo. I5 250-1
Diana, W. Va. G6 200-1
Diaz, Ark. C9 150-1
Dibble, Okla. G10 234-5
D'Iberville, Miss. N9 176-7
Diboll, Tex. F11 192-3
Dibrell, Tenn. C9 188-9
Dickens, Ia. B4 104-5
Dickens, Nebr. H6 124-5
Dickens, Tex. D5 192-3
Dickens, co., Tex. C5 192-3
Dickenson, co., Va. I3 196-7
Dickerson, Md. G1 172-3
Dickerson, N.C. G7 180-1
Dickert, Ala. G9 146-7
Dickey, Ga. M3 160-1
Dickey, N. Dak. H11 128-9
Dickey, co., N. Dak. J11 128-9
Dickeyville, Wis. K10 140-1
Dickinson, Ala. K4 146-7
Dickinson, N. Dak. G3 128-9
Dickinson, Tex. I15 192-3
Dickinson, co., Ia. B4 104-5
Dickinson, co., Kans. F11 108-9
Dickinson, co., Mich. D9 112-3
Dickson, Okla. I12 234-5
Dickson, Tenn. H5 188-9
Dickson, W. Va. I10 200-1
Dickson, co., Tenn. B6 188-9
Dickson City, Pa. E14 84-5
Didsbury, Alta. L7 264-5
Diehlstadt, Mo. I12 120-1
Dieppe, N.B. H7 275
Dierks, Ark. H3 150-1
Dietrich, Ida. N6 218-9
Digby, N.S. E4 281
Digby, co., N.S. E4 281
Diggins, Mo. I6 120-1
Diggs, Va. E4 196-7
Dighton, Kans. G4 108-9
Dighton, Mass. G11 68-9
Dike, Ia. E10 104-5
Dildo*, Nfld. N11 278-9
Dilke, Sask. M7 294-5
Dilkon, Ariz. E9 206-7
Dill City, Okla. F8 234-5
Dillard, Ga. C6 160-1
Dillard, Ore. H5 238-9
Diller, Nebr. J14 124-5
Dilley, Tex. H7 192-3
Dillingham, Alaska G9 254-5
Dillon, Colo. E10 214-5
Dillon, Mont. H5 222-3
Dillon, S.C. C14 184-5
Dillon, co., S.C. C14 184-5
Dillonvale, O. F11 132-3
Dillsboro, Ind. K11 100-1
Dillsboro, N.C. E2 180-1
Dillsburg, Pa. J10 84-5
Dillwyn, Va. H10 196-7
Dilworth, Minn. I1 116-7
Dimmit, co., Tex. I6 192-3
Dimmitt, Tex. C4 192-3
Dimock, S. Dak. H13 136-7
Dimondale, Mich. I1 112-3
Dingess, W. Va. K11 200-1
Dingle, Ida. O11 218-9
Dingwall, N.S. A11 281
Dinosaur, Colo. C5 214-5
Dinsmore, Sask. M6 294-5
Dinuba, Calif. K6 210-1
Dinwiddie, Va. I12 196-7
Dinwiddie, co., Va. I12 196-7
Diomede*, Alaska C7 254-5
Disautel, Wash. D13 246-7
Disco, Mich. H6 112-3
Dishman, Wash. E16 246-7
Disko, Ind. C9 100-1
Disley, Sask. N8 294-5
Disney, Okla. C15 234-5
Disputanta, Ky. I12 164-5
Disputanta, Va. F2 196-7
Disraëli, Que. I16 290-1
Disston, Ore. G6 238-9
District Heights, Md. J5 172-3
Divernon, Ill. I7 96-7
Divide, Colo. K2 214-5
Divide, Mont. G5 222-3
Divide, co., N. Dak. B2 128-9
Dividend, Ut. G6 242-3
Dividing Creek, N.J. N3 76-7
Dix, Nebr. G2 124-5
Dix Hills*, N.Y. J12 80-1
Dixboro, Mich. J4 112-3
Dixfield, Me. K3 64-5
Dixiana, S.C. E10 184-5
Dixie, Ala. M6 146-7
Dixie, Ark. B11 150-1
Dixie, Ark. E9 150-1
Dixie, Ga. O5 160-1
Dixie, Ida. H4 218-9
Dixie, La. B1 168-9
Dixie, Wash. I15 246-7
Dixie, W. Va. I15 200-1
Dixie, co., Fla. D9 156-7
Dixie Gardens, La. B2 168-9
Dixie Inn, La. B2 168-9
Dixie Union, Ga. M8 160-1
Dixie Valley, Nev. F4 226-7
Dixmont, Me. J6 64-5
Dixmont Center, Me. J6 64-5
Dixmoor*, Ill. C11 96-7
Dixon, Calif. A8 210-1
Dixon, Ill. B7 96-7
Dixon, Ia. G14 104-5
Dixon, Ky. H5 164-5
Dixon, Mo. G7 120-1
Dixon, Mont. D3 222-3
Dixon, Nebr. D13 124-5
Dixon, N. Mex. D7 230-1
Dixon, Wyo. K10 250-1
Dixon, co., Nebr. D13 124-5
Dixon Springs, Tenn. A9 188-9
Dixons Mills, Ala. J4 146-7
Dixville, Que. K15 290-1
D'Lo, Miss. J6 176-7
Doaktown, N.B. G5 275
Doaneville, Conn. E14 60-1
Dobbs Ferry, N.Y. C14 80-1
Dobson, N.C. C7 180-1
Docena*, Ala. E6 146-7
Dock Junction, Ga. M10 160-1
Dockton, Wash. J2 246-7
Doctors Inlet, Fla. C11 156-7
Dodding Subdivision*, B.C. H6 268-9
Doddridge, Ark. K3 150-1
Doddridge, co., W. Va. E5 200-1
Doddsville, Miss. E5 176-7
Dodge, Nebr. F14 124-5
Dodge, N. Dak. F4 128-9
Dodge, Wis. G9 140-1
Dodge, co., Ga. K6 160-1
Dodge, co., Minn. O7 116-7
Dodge, co., Nebr. F14 124-5
Dodge, co., Wis. I13 140-1
Dodge Center, Minn. O7 116-7
Dodge City, Kans. I5 108-9
Dodge Corner, Mass. B4 68-9
Dodgeville, Wis. J11 140-1
Dodgingtown, Conn. G5 60-1
Dodsland, Sask. L4 294-5
Dodson, La. C4 168-9
Dodson, Mont. B11 222-3
Doe Hill, Va. F9 196-7
Doebay, Wash. C7 246-7
Doerun, Ga. M5 160-1
Dogpatch, Ark. B5 150-1
Dogue, Va. C3 196-7
Dola, W. Va. C13 200-1
Doland, S. Dak. D13 136-7
Dolbeau, Que. B10 290-1
Dolgeville, N.Y. E9 80-1
Dollar, Ore. J2 238-9
Dollar Bay, Mich. C8 112-3
Dollard, Sask. O5 294-5
Dollard-des-Ormeaux*, Que. I12 290-1
Dolliver, Ia. A5 104-5
Dolores, Colo. I6 214-5
Dolores, co., Colo. H6 214-5
Dolph, Ark. B7 150-1
Dolphin, Va. J12 196-7
Dolton, Ill. N4 96-7
Dolton, S. Dak. H14 136-7
Domain*, Man. K4 272-3
Domaine-Laurentien*, Que. I11 290-1
Domaine-Quevillon*, Que. I12 290-1
Dome, Ariz. J2 206-7
Dome Peak, N.W. Terr. C1 296
Domingo, N. Mex. E6 230-1
Dominguez*, Calif. N7 210-1
Dominion, Md. E12 172-3
Dominion, N.S. B12 281
Dominion City, Man. K14 272-3
Domremy, Sask. K7 294-5
Don Luis, Ariz. M10 206-7
Donahue, Ia. G15 104-5
Donald, B.C. I10 268-9
Donald, Ore. G2 238-9
Donalda, Alta. K8 264-5
Donalds, S.C. I2 184-5
Donaldson, Ark. G5 150-1
Donaldson, Ind. B7 100-1
Donaldson, Minn. E1 116-7
Donaldsonville, La. C10 168-9
Donalsonville, Ga. N3 160-1
Doncaster, Md. G9 172-3
Doña Ana, N. Mex. L5 230-1
Doña Ana, co., N. Mex. K5 230-1
Donelson, Tenn. H7 188-9
Doneraile, S.C. D13 184-5
Dongola, Ill. O8 96-7
Doniphan, Kans. D15 108-9
Doniphan, Mo. J9 120-1
Doniphan, Nebr. H11 124-5
Doniphan, co., Kans. D15 108-9
Donken, Mich. C8 112-3
Donkey Creek, Wyo. C15 250-1
Donkin*, N.S. B12 281
Donley, co., Tex. B5 192-3
Donna, Tex. K8 192-3
Donnacona, Que. G10 290-1
Donnan, Ia. C12 104-5
Donnellson, Ia. J13 104-5
Donnelly, Alaska E12 254-5
Donnelly, Alta. G5 264-5
Donnelly, Ida. J3 218-9
Donnelly, Minn. K2 116-7
Donnelsville, O. G16 132-3
Donner, La. E11 168-9
Donnybrook, N. Dak. C5 128-9
Donora, Pa. I2 84-5
Donovan, Ga. I8 160-1
Dooley, Mont. A16 222-3
Dooling, Ga. K5 160-1
Doolittle, Mo. G7 120-1
Dooly, co., Ga. K5 160-1
Doon, Ia. B1 104-5
Door, co., Wis. E16 140-1
Dora, Ala. E5 146-7
Dora, Ark. C2 150-1
Dora, N. Mex. H11 230-1
Dora, Ore. H4 238-9
Doran, Minn. J2 116-7
Doran, Va. I4 196-7
Doraville, Ga. B11 160-1
Dorcas, W. Va. F9 200-1
Dorchester, Mass. I5 68-9
Dorchester, Nebr. I13 124-5
Dorchester, N.B. I7 275
Dorchester, N.H. J5 72-3
Dorchester, N.J. N3 76-7
Dorchester*, Ont. E12 284-5
Dorchester, Wis. E11 140-1
Dorchester, co., Md. G13 172-3
Dorchester, co., Que. H16 290-1
Dorchester, co., S.C. G11 184-5
Dorchester Crossing, N.B. H7 275
Doré Lake, Sask. H6 294-5
Dorena, Ore. G6 238-9
Dorintosh, Sask. H5 294-5
Dorion, Que. J11 290-1
Dormont*, Pa. I2 84-5
Dorothy, N.J. M4 76-7
Dorothy, W. Va. K14 200-1
Dorr, Mich. I12 112-3
Dorrance, Kans. F8 108-9
Dorris, Calif. D3 210-1
Dorrs Corner, Md. H6 172-3
Dorset, Vt. L4 90-1
Dorsey, Miss. C10 176-7
Dorval*, Que. I12 290-1
Dos Cabezas, Ariz. K11 206-7
Dos Palos, Calif. J5 210-1
Doskie, Miss. A10 176-7
Dosquet, Que. G15 290-1
Dossville, Miss. G7 176-7
Doster, Ala. K9 146-7
Doswell, Va. H12 196-7
Dot Lake, Alaska E12 254-5
Dothan, Ala. L10 146-7
Doty, Wash. H6 246-7
Double Adobe, Ariz. M10 206-7
Double Bridges, Tenn. B2 188-9
Double Springs, Ala. D5 146-7
Douds, Ia. J11 104-5
Dougherty, Ia. C9 104-5
Dougherty, Okla. H12 234-5
Dougherty, co., Ga. M4 160-1
Douglas, Ala. D7 146-7
Douglas, Ariz. M11 206-7
Douglas, Ga. M7 160-1
Douglas, Man. J11 272-3
Douglas, Mass. F8 68-9
Douglas, Mich. J11 112-3
Douglas, Nebr. I15 124-5
Douglas, N. Dak. E6 128-9
Douglas, Okla. D10 234-5
Douglas, Ont. H13 284-5
Douglas, Wash. E11 246-7
Douglas, W. Va. E8 200-1
Douglas, Wyo. G14 250-1
Douglas, co., Colo. E12 214-5
Douglas, co., Ga. G3 160-1
Douglas, co., Ill. H10 96-7
Douglas, co., Kans. F15 108-9
Douglas, co., Minn. J3 116-7
Douglas, co., Mo. I6 120-1
Douglas, co., Nebr. G15 124-5
Douglas, co., Nev. G2 226-7
Douglas, co., Ore. G5 238-9
Douglas, co., S. Dak. H12 136-7
Douglas, co., Wash. E12 246-7
Douglas, co., Wis. B8 140-1
Douglas Hill, Me. N7 64-5
Douglas Lake, B.C. J8 268-9
Douglas Lake, Tenn. B13 188-9
Douglass, Kans. J11 108-9
Douglass Hills No. 1*, Ky. A2 164-5
Douglastown*, N.B. F6 275
Douglasville, Ga. G3 160-1
Dousman, Wis. J3 140-1
Dove Creek, Colo. H5 214-5
Dover, Ark. D5 150-1
Dover, Del. F4 153
Dover, Fla. H3 156-7
Dover, Ga. J10 160-1
Dover, Ida. B3 218-9
Dover, Ind. J12 100-1
Dover, Ky. E12 164-5
Dover, Mass. J3 68-9
Dover, Minn. O8 116-7
Dover, Mo. D4 120-1
Dover, Mont. D8 222-3
Dover, N.H. M9 72-3
Dover*, N.J. I7 76-7
Dover, N.J. D5 76-7
Dover, Nfld. M10 278-9
Dover, N.C. E13 180-1
Dover, O. E10 132-3
Dover, Okla. E10 234-5
Dover, Pa. J11 84-5
Dover, Tenn. A5 188-9
Dover, Vt. N5 90-1
Dover Base*, Del. F4 153
Dover-Foxcroft, Me. H6 64-5
Dovesville, S.C. C13 184-5
Dovray, Minn. O3 116-7
Dow, Okla. G14 234-5
Dow City, Ia. F3 104-5
Dowagiac, Mich. K11 112-3
Dowdy, Ark. C9 150-1
Dowell, Md. H12 172-3
Dowelltown*, Tenn. B9 188-9
Dowling, Mich. J12 112-3
Downe*, N.J. N3 76-7
Downers Grove, Ill. M2 96-7
Downey, Calif. G8 210-1
Downey, Ida. O10 218-9
Downieville, Calif. G4 210-1
Downing, Mo. A7 120-1
Downing, Wis. E8 140-1
Downingtown, Pa. B9 84-5
Downs, Ill. F9 96-7
Downs, Kans. D8 108-9
Downs Chapel, Del. E3 153
Downsville, La. B4 168-9
Downsville, Md. B7 172-3
Downsville, Wis. F8 140-1
Dows, Ia. D8 104-5
Doyle, Tenn. C10 188-9
Doylestown, O. E14 132-3
Doylestown, Pa. I15 84-5
Doylestown, Wis. H2 140-1
Doyleville, Colo. G9 214-5
Doyline, La. B2 168-9
Dozier, Ala. K7 146-7
Dracut, Mass. B10 68-9
Dragerton, Ut. H8 242-3
Dragon, Ut. H11 242-3
Dragonville, Va. H14 196-7
Dragoon, Ariz. L10 206-7
Drain, Ore. G5 238-9
Drake, Ariz. F6 206-7
Drake, Colo. D2 214-5
Drake, N. Dak. E8 128-9
Drake, Sask. L8 294-5
Drake, S.C. C14 184-5
Drakes Branch, Va. J10 196-7
Drakes Crossing, Ore. H2 238-9
Drakesboro, Ky. I6 164-5
Drakesville, Ia. J10 104-5
Drakeville, Conn. C6 60-1
Draper, S. Dak. F8 136-7
Draper, Va. J6 196-7
Drasco, Ark. C8 150-1
Dravosburg*, Pa. I2 84-5
Drawbridge, Md. G13 172-3
Drayden, Md. H11 172-3
Drayton, N. Dak. C14 128-9
Drayton, Ont. C13 284-5
Drayton, S.C. F4 184-5
Drayton Plains, Mich. I5 112-3
Drayton Valley, Alta. J5 264-5
Dresden, Kans. D4 108-9
Dresden, Me. M11 64-5
Dresden, O. F8 132-3
Dresden, Ont. F11 284-5
Dresden, Tenn. B4 188-9
Dresser, Wis. E7 140-1

Dresslerville – East Ellijay 375

Dresslerville, Nev...... G2 226-7
Drew, Me.......... G8 64-5
Drew, Miss.......... E5 176-7
Drew, co., Ark....... I8 150-1
Drewryville, Va....... H1 196-7
Drewsey, Ore........ F13 238-9
Drexel, Mo.......... F3 120-1
Drexel, N.C.......... D5 180-1
Dreyfus, Ky.......... E8 164-5
Driftwood, Okla....... C9 234-5
Driftwood Trailer Court*, Sask.............. J7 294-5
Driggs, Ark.......... D3 150-1
Driggs, Ida.......... L11 218-9
Drinkwater, Sask...... N8 294-5
Driscoll, N. Dak....... H8 128-9
Driscoll, Tex......... I8 192-3
Driver, Ark.......... C12 150-1
Driver, Va........... G4 196-7
Droop, W. Va........ H6 200-1
Dropmore*, Man...... I1 272-3
Druid Hills*, Ky....... G9 164-5
Drumbo*, Ont........ D13 284-5
Drumheller, Alta...... L8 264-5
Drummond, Ida....... K11 218-9
Drummond, Mont...... E4 222-3
Drummond*, N.B...... F3 275
Drummond, Okla...... D10 234-5
Drummond, Wis....... B9 140-1
Drummond, co., Que... I14 290-1
Drummond Island, Mich. D14 112-3
Drummonds, Tenn..... J1 188-9
Drummondville, Que... I14 290-1
Drummondville-Sud*, Que.............. I14 290-1
Drumright, Okla....... D12 234-5
Drury, Mass.......... B3 68-9
Dry Branch, Ga....... I6 160-1
Dry Branch, W. Va..... I14 200-1
Dry Creek, La........ G3 168-9
Dry Creek, Miss....... K7 176-7
Dry Creek, W. Va..... K14 200-1
Dry Fork, Va......... J9 196-7
Dry Lake, Nev........ M10 226-7
Dry Mills, Me......... N9 64-5
Dry Prong, La........ D4 168-9
Dry Ridge, Ky........ E11 164-5
Dry Tortugas, Fla...... K9 156-7
Dryden, Ark......... C10 150-1
Dryden, Me.......... K3 64-5
Dryden, Mich......... G6 112-3
Dryden, N.Y......... G7 80-1
Dryden, Ont......... E2 284-5
Dryden, Ore......... J5 238-9
Dryden, Va.......... J2 196-7
Dryden, Wash........ F11 246-7
Dryfork, W. Va....... F8 200-1
Du Bois, Pa......... F5 84-5
Du Page, co., Ill...... B10 96-7
Du Pont, Ga......... N7 160-1
Du Quoin, Ill......... M8 96-7
Duarte*, Calif........ G9 210-1
Dubach, La.......... B4 168-9
Dubard, Miss........ E6 176-7
Dubberly, La........ B3 168-9
Dubbs, Miss......... B5 176-7
Dublin, Ala.......... J8 146-7
Dublin*, Calif........ I3 210-1
Dublin, Ga.......... J7 160-1
Dublin, Ind.......... H11 100-1
Dublin, Ky.......... J2 164-5
Dublin, Md.......... B12 172-3
Dublin, Miss......... D5 176-7
Dublin, N.H......... O4 72-3
Dublin, N.C......... G11 180-1
Dublin, O........... F6 132-3
Dublin, Tex......... E8 192-3
Dublin, Va.......... I5 196-7
Dublin Hill, Del....... I3 153
Dubois, Ida......... K9 218-9
Dubois, Ind......... M6 100-1
Dubois, Nebr......... J15 124-5
Dubois, Wyo......... E7 250-1
Dubois, co., Ind....... N6 100-1
Duboistown, Pa....... F10 84-5
Dubose, S.C......... E12 184-5
Dubre, Ky.......... J9 164-5
Dubreuilville, Ont..... F5 284-5
Dubuc, Sask......... M10 294-5
Dubuisson, La........ G5 168-9
Dubuque, Ia......... D15 104-5
Dubuque, co., Ia...... E14 104-5
Duchesne, Ut........ G8 242-3
Duchesne, co., Ut..... G8 242-3
Duchess, Alta........ M9 264-5
Duck, W. Va......... G5 200-1
Duck Bay, Man....... E11 272-3
Duck Hill, Miss....... E7 176-7
Duck Lake, Sask....... K7 294-5
Duck River, Tenn...... I5 188-9
Ducktown, Ga........ E4 160-1
Ducktown, Tenn....... K13 188-9
Ducktown Station, Tenn. K13 188-9
Duckwater, Nev....... G8 226-7
Dudley, Ga.......... J7 160-1
Dudley, Mass......... F8 68-9
Dudley, Mo.......... I11 120-1
Dudley, N.C......... E12 180-1
Dudley, S.C......... B11 184-5
Dudleyville, Ala....... G9 146-7
Due West, S.C....... J2 184-5
Duenweg, Mo........ I3 120-1
Duff, Sask.......... M9 294-5
Duffee, Miss......... I9 176-7
Dufferin, co., Ont...... B14 284-5
Duffield, Va......... J2 196-7
Dufresne*, Man....... K4 272-3
Dufrost*, Man........ K14 272-3
Dufur, Ore.......... C9 238-9
Dugald*, Man........ J14 272-3
Dugger, Ind......... K5 100-1
Dugspur, Va......... J6 196-7
Duguayville*, N.B..... E7 275
Dugway, Ut......... G4 242-3
Duke, Ala.......... D8 146-7
Duke, Okla......... H7 234-5
Dukedom, Tenn....... A4 188-9
Dukes, co., Mass...... I13 68-9
Dulac, La........... J8 168-9
Dulce, N. Mex........ B5 230-1
Duluth, Ga.......... A12 160-1
Duluth, Minn......... I8 116-7
Dumas, Ark......... H8 150-1
Dumas, Ga.......... K3 160-1
Dumas, Miss......... B9 176-7
Dumas, Tex......... A5 192-3
Dumfries, Va......... B3 196-7
Dummer, N.H........ E8 72-3
Dummerston*, Vt...... N6 90-1
Dumont, Ia.......... D9 104-5
Dumont, Minn........ K2 116-7
Dumont, N.J......... A12 76-7
Dunbar, Ky.......... I7 164-5
Dunbar, Nebr......... H15 124-5
Dunbar, Pa.......... J3 84-5
Dunbar, S.C......... C14 184-5
Dunbar, W. Va........ H13 200-1
Dunbar, Wis......... D14 140-1
Dunbarton, La........ D6 168-9
Dunbarton Center, N.H. M6 72-3
Dunblane, Sask....... M6 294-5
Duncan, Ariz......... J11 206-7
Duncan, B.C......... D12 268-9
Duncan, Miss........ D4 176-7
Duncan, Nebr........ G12 124-5
Duncan, Okla........ H10 234-5
Duncan, Ore......... B13 238-9
Duncan, S.C......... F3 184-5
Duncan, W. Va....... F3 200-1
Duncan, Wyo........ E7 250-1
Duncannon, Pa....... I10 84-5
Duncansville, Pa...... I6 84-5
Duncanville, Ala...... G4 146-7
Duncanville, Tex...... D14 192-3
Duncombe, Ia........ E7 104-5
Dundalk, Md......... F7 172-3
Dundalk, Ont........ B13 284-5
Dundarrach, N.C...... F10 180-1
Dundas, Minn........ N6 116-7
Dundas, Ont......... D14 284-5
Dundas, Va.......... J11 196-7
Dundee, Fla......... H6 156-7
Dundee, Ia.......... D13 104-5
Dundee, Ky......... H7 164-5
Dundee, Mich........ K14 112-3
Dundee, Minn........ O3 116-7
Dundee, Miss........ B5 176-7
Dundee, N.Y......... F5 80-1
Dundee, Ore......... G1 238-9
Dundee, Wis......... H4 140-1
Dundon, W. Va....... H16 200-1
Dundurn, Sask........ L6 294-5
Dundy, co., Nebr...... J5 124-5
Dune Acres, Ind....... A5 100-1
Dunedin, Fla......... H1 156-7
Dunedin, Ont........ B14 284-5
Dunellen, N.J........ F6 76-7
Dunes*, Ore......... F4 238-9
Dungannon, Va....... J3 196-7
Dungeness, Wash...... D7 246-7
Dunham, Que........ J13 290-1
Dunkerton, Ia........ D11 104-5
Dunkirk, Ind......... F11 100-1
Dunkirk, Md......... K6 172-3
Dunkirk, Mont........ B6 222-3
Dunkirk, N.Y......... F1 80-1
Dunkirk, O.......... D5 132-3
Dunkley, B.C........ G7 268-9
Dunklin, co., Mo...... K11 120-1
Dunlap, Ill........... E7 96-7
Dunlap, Ind.......... A9 100-1
Dunlap, Ia.......... G3 104-5
Dunlap, Kans........ G13 108-9
Dunlap, Tenn........ K10 188-9
Dunlap Lake-Dewey Park*, Ill........ K6 96-7
Dunlow, W. Va....... J10 200-1
Dunmore, Alta........ N10 264-5
Dunmore, Pa......... E14 84-5
Dunmore, W. Va...... G7 200-1
Dunn, La............ B6 168-9
Dunn, N.C.......... J7 180-1
Dunn, co., N. Dak...... F4 128-9
Dunn, co., Wis........ F8 140-1
Dunn Center, N. Dak... F4 128-9
Dunn Corner, R.I...... I2 87
Dunn Loring, Va....... A3 196-7
Dunnell, Minn........ O4 116-7
Dunnellon, Fla........ D10 156-7
Dunning, Nebr........ F8 124-5
Dunnottar, Man....... I14 272-3
Dunns, W. Va........ J4 200-1
Dunnsville, Va........ H13 196-7
Dunnville, Ky........ I10 164-5
Dunnville, Ont........ E14 284-5
Dunphy, Nev......... D7 226-7
Dunrea, Man......... J11 272-3
Dunreith, Ind........ H10 100-1
Dunseith, N. Dak...... B8 128-9
Dunsford, Ont........ B16 284-5
Dunsmuir, Calif....... E3 210-1
Dunstable, Mass...... B10 68-9
Dunville, Nfld........ O10 278-9
Dunwoody, Ga........ B11 160-1
Duparquet, Que....... H1 290-1
Duplex, Tenn......... I7 188-9
Duplin, co., N.C...... F12 180-1
Dupo, Ill............ L6 96-7
Dupont, Ind......... L10 100-1
Dupont, La.......... F5 168-9
Dupont, O........... C4 132-3
Dupont*, Pa......... E14 84-5
Dupont, Wash........ K1 246-7
Dupont Manor*, Del.... F4 153
Dupree, S. Dak....... C6 136-7
Dupuyer, Mont....... C5 222-3
Duquesne, Ariz....... M9 206-7
Duquesne, Mo........ I3 120-1
Duquesne, Pa........ B7 84-5
Duran, N. Mex........ G8 230-1
Durand, Ga.......... I3 160-1
Durand, Ill........... A8 96-7
Durand, Mich........ G3 112-3
Durand, Wis......... F8 140-1
Durango, Colo........ J7 214-5
Durango, Ia......... D14 104-5
Durant, Ia.......... G14 104-5
Durant, Miss......... G7 176-7
Durant, Okla......... I13 234-5
Durants Neck, N.C..... C15 180-1
Durban, Man......... F9 272-3
Durbin, W. Va........ G7 200-1
Durham, Ark......... B3 150-1
Durham, Calif........ G3 210-1
Durham, Conn........ F9 60-1
Durham, Kans........ G11 108-9
Durham, Me......... M9 64-5
Durham, N.H......... M9 72-3
Durham, N.C......... D10 180-1
Durham, Okla........ E6 234-5
Durham, Ont........ B13 284-5
Durham*, Ore........ C6 238-9
Durham, co., N.C...... D10 180-1
Durham Bridge, N.B.... H4 275
Durham Center, Conn... F9 60-1
Durkee, Ore......... E15 238-9
Durkee, Wyo........ C10 250-1
Duroc, Wyo......... I16 250-1
Durrell*, Nfld........ L10 278-9
Duryea, Pa.......... E14 84-5
Duson, La........... H5 168-9
Dustin, Okla......... F13 234-5
Dusty, N. Mex........ I4 230-1
Dusty, Wash......... G15 246-7
Dutch Harbor, Alaska.. I6 254-5
Dutch John, Ut....... E10 242-3
Dutch Mills, Ark...... B2 150-1
Dutch Neck, N.J...... G5 76-7
Dutch Neck Crossroad, Del.............. E4 153
Dutchess, co., N.Y..... H11 80-1
Duthie, Ida.......... D4 218-9
Dutton, Ala.......... B8 146-7
Dutton, Mont........ C6 222-3
Dutton, Ont......... E12 284-5
Dutton, Va.......... E4 196-7
Duty, La............ D5 168-9
Duval, Sask......... M8 294-5
Duval, co., Fla....... D11 156-7
Duval, co., Tex....... I7 192-3
Duvall, Wash........ E8 246-7
Duxbury, Mass....... F13 68-9
Duxbury, Vt......... F6 90-1
Dwarf, Ky.......... I14 164-5
Dwight, Ill.......... E10 96-7
Dwight, Kans........ F12 108-9
Dwight, Mass........ D5 68-9
Dwight, Nebr........ H13 124-5
Dwight, N. Dak....... I15 128-9
Dwyer, N. Mex....... K3 230-1
Dwyer, Wyo......... H15 250-1
Dyckesville, Wis....... D5 140-1
Dycusburg, Ky........ I4 164-5
Dyer, Ark........... D2 150-1
Dyer, Ind........... B4 100-1
Dyer, Nev........... J4 226-7
Dyer, Tenn.......... B3 188-9
Dyer, co., Tenn....... B2 188-9
Dyer Brook, Me....... E8 64-5
Dyersburg, Tenn....... B2 188-9
Dyersville, Ia........ D14 104-5
Dyess, Ark.......... C12 150-1
Dyke, Va........... G10 196-7
Dysart, Ia.......... F11 104-5
Dysart, Sask......... M8 294-5

E

E, Me.............. D9 64-5
Eads, Colo.......... G15 214-5
Eads, Tenn.......... K2 188-9
Eagan*, Minn........ M7 116-7
Eagan, Tenn......... F12 188-9
Eagar, Ariz......... G11 206-7
Eagle, Alaska........ D13 254-5
Eagle, Colo.......... E9 214-5
Eagle, Ida........... D4 218-9
Eagle, Ida........... L3 218-9
Eagle, Mich.......... I13 112-3
Eagle, Nebr.......... K1 124-5
Eagle, Wis........... J3 140-1
Eagle, co., Colo...... D9 214-5
Eagle Bend, Minn...... J4 116-7
Eagle Butte, S. Dak.... C7 136-7
Eagle City, Okla...... E9 234-5
Eagle Creek, Ore...... C7 238-9
Eagle Grove, Ia....... D7 104-5
Eagle Harbor, Md...... G11 172-3
Eagle Heights*, B.C.... J5 268-9
Eagle Lake, Fla....... H5 156-7
Eagle Lake, Me....... B7 64-5
Eagle Lake, Minn...... N5 116-7
Eagle Lake, Ont....... H8 284-5
Eagle Lake, Tex....... H9 192-3
Eagle Mills, Ark...... I6 150-1
Eagle Mountain, Calif.. N10 210-1
Eagle Nest, N. Mex.... C8 230-1
Eagle Pass, Tex....... H6 192-3
Eagle Point, Ore...... J6 238-9
Eagle River*, Alaska.... F11 254-5
Eagle River, Mich...... B9 112-3
Eagle River, Ont...... E2 284-5
Eagle River, Wis....... C13 140-1
Eagle Rock, N.C...... I8 180-1
Eagle Rock, Va....... H8 196-7
Eagle Springs, N.C..... J5 180-1
Eaglesham, Alta....... F4 264-5
Eaglewood*, N.J...... K7 76-7
Eagleton Village*, Tenn.. I12 188-9
Eagletown, Ind....... G8 100-1
Eagletown, Okla...... I16 234-5
Eagleville, Conn...... C12 60-1
Eagleville, Mo........ A4 120-1
Eagleville, Tenn....... I7 188-9
Eakly, Okla......... F9 234-5
Ear Falls, Ont........ E2 284-5
Earl, N.C........... E6 180-1
Earl, Okla.......... H12 234-5
Earl, Wis........... C8 140-1
Earl Grey, Sask....... M8 294-5
Earl Park, Ind........ E4 100-1
Earle, Ark.......... D11 150-1
Earle, S.C.......... F14 184-5
Earleville, Md........ C13 172-3
Earlham, Ia.......... H6 104-5
Earlimart, Calif....... L6 210-1
Earling, Ia.......... G3 104-5
Earling, W. Va........ K12 200-1
Earlington, Ky........ I5 164-5
Earlsboro, Okla....... F12 234-5
Earlton, Kans........ I15 108-9
Earlton, Ont......... G8 284-5
Earlville, Ill......... C8 96-7
Earlville, Ia......... D13 104-5
Earlville, N.Y........ F8 80-1
Early, Ia........... E4 104-5
Early, Tex.......... E7 192-3
Early, co., Ga....... M2 160-1
Early Branch, S.C..... I10 184-5
Earlysville, Va....... G10 196-7
Earth, Tex.......... C4 192-3
Easley, S.C......... F1 184-5
Easleyville, La........ F8 168-9
East Alliance, O...... D10 132-3
East Alton, Ill........ K6 96-7
East Amana, Ia....... G12 104-5
East Amwell*, N.J..... G4 76-7
East Andover, Me...... J2 64-5
East Andover, N.H..... K5 72-3
East Angus, Que....... J15 290-1
East Auburndale*, Fla... F11 156-7
East Aurora, N.Y..... F3 80-1
East Baldwin, Me...... N7 64-5
East Bank, W. Va..... I14 200-1
East Barnard, Vt...... I6 90-1
East Barre, Vt....... G7 90-1
East Baton Rouge, co., La.............. G7 168-9
East Bay, N.S........ B11 281
East Bend, N.C...... G2 180-1
East Berlin, Conn..... E9 60-1
East Berlin, Pa....... J10 84-5
East Bernard*, Tex..... G9 192-3
East Bernstadt, Ky..... I12 164-5
East Berwick*, Pa..... F12 84-5
East Bethel, Minn...... L6 116-7
East Bloomfield*, N.Y.. F5 80-1
East Blue Hill, Me..... K7 64-5
East Blythe, Calif...... N11 210-1
East Boothbay, Me..... N11 64-5
East Boston, Mass..... H5 68-9
East Boxford, Mass..... B12 68-9
East Brady, Pa....... G3 84-5
East Braintree, Man.... J16 272-3
East Braintree, Mass.... J6 68-9
East Brewton, Ala..... M5 146-7
East Bridgewater, Mass.. F12 68-9
East Brimfield, Mass.... E7 68-9
East Brookfield, Mass... E7 68-9
East Brooklyn, Conn.... C14 60-1
East Broughton*, Que... H15 290-1
East Broughton Station*, Que.............. H15 290-1
East Brownfield, Me.... N7 64-5
East Brunswick, N.J.... F6 76-7
East Burke, Vt....... D9 90-1
East Calais, Vt....... E7 90-1
East Camden, Ark...... I6 150-1
East Canaan, Conn..... A5 60-1
East Canton, O....... F16 132-3
East Carroll, co., La.... B7 168-9
East Cayuga Heights*, N.Y.............. F6 80-1
East Charleston, Vt.... C9 90-1
East Charlotte, Vt..... F4 90-1
East Chicago, Ind...... A4 100-1
East Chicago Heights, Ill. O4 96-7
East Cleveland, O...... B15 132-3
East Cleveland*, Tenn... D11 188-9
East Coleman*, Alta.... O7 264-5
East Compton*, Calif... N7 210-1
East Concord, Vt...... E10 90-1
East Conemaugh, Pa.... I5 84-5
East Corinth, Me...... I6 64-5
East Corinth, Vt...... G8 90-1
East Coulee, Alta...... L9 264-5
East Deerfield, Mass.... C5 68-9
East Dennis, Mass...... G15 68-9
East Derry, N.H...... O7 72-3
East Detroit, Mich..... J6 112-3
East Dixfield, Me...... K3 64-5
East Dorset, Vt....... L4 90-1
East Douglas, Mass..... E9 68-9
East Dover, Vt....... N6 90-1
East Dublin, Ga....... J7 160-1
East Dubuque, Ill...... A5 96-7
East Dummerston, Vt... N6 90-1
East Dundee, Ill....... L1 96-7
East Eddington, Me..... J7 64-5
East Ellijay, Ga....... D4 160-1

East Ely, Nev. G10 226-7
East Enterprise, Ind. L11 100-1
East Fairview, N. Dak. E1 128-9
East Falmouth, Mass. H14 68-9
East Faxon, Pa. F10 84-5
East Feliciana, co., La. F7 168-9
East Flat Rock*, N.C. E4 180-1
East Fork, Miss. L5 176-7
East Franklin, Me. K8 64-5
East Franklin, Vt. B5 90-1
East Freetown, Mass. G12 68-9
East Gaffney, S.C. A8 184-5
East Galesburg, Ill. E6 96-7
East Gardiner, Ore. G4 238-9
East Gastonia*, N.C. F6 180-1
East Germantown, Ind. H11 100-1
East Glacier Park, Mont. B4 222-3
East Glastonbury, Conn. D10 60-1
East Glenville*, N.Y. E10 80-1
East Granby, Conn. B9 60-1
East Grand Forks, Minn. F1 116-7
East Grand Rapids, Mich. I12 112-3
East Granville, Vt. G6 90-1
East Greenville, Pa. I14 84-5
East Greenwich*, N.J. K2 76-7
East Greenwich, R.I. E5 87
East Griffin, Ga. H4 160-1
East Gull Lake, Minn. J5 116-7
East Haddam, Conn. F11 60-1
East Half Hollow Hills*, N.Y. J12 80-1
East Hampstead, N.H. O8 72-3
East Hampton, Conn. E10 60-1
East Hampton, N.Y. J14 80-1
East Hanover*, N.J. D6 76-7
East Hardwick, Vt. D7 90-1
East Hartford, Conn. D9 60-1
East Hartland, Conn. B8 60-1
East Harwich, Mass. H16 68-9
East Haven, Conn. H8 60-1
East Haven, Vt. D9 90-1
East Haverhill, N.H. H5 72-3
East Hazelcrest*, Ill. C11 96-7
East Helena, Mont. F6 222-3
East Herkimer*, N.Y. E9 80-1
East Hills*, N.Y. J11 80-1
East Hiram, Me. N7 64-5
East Hodge*, La. C4 168-9
East Holden, Me. J7 64-5
East Hope, Ida. B3 218-9
East Islip*, N.Y. K12 80-1
East Johnson, Vt. D6 90-1
East Jordan, Mich. F12 112-3
East Juliette, Ga. H5 160-1
East Keansburg, N.J. H11 76-7
East Killingly, Conn. C15 60-1
East Kingsford*, Mich. E9 112-3
East Kingston, N.H. N9 72-3
East La Mirada*, Calif. N7 210-1
East Lake, Mich. G11 112-3
East Lake, N.C. D16 180-1
East Lake-Orient Park*, Fla. D11 156-7
East Lansdowne*, Pa. J15 84-5
East Lansing, Mich. H1 112-3
East Las Vegas, Nev. M10 226-7
East Laurinburg, N.C. F9 180-1
East Layton*, Ut. E6 242-3
East Lebanon, Me. O2 64-5
East Lee, Mass. D2 68-9
East Lempster, N.H. M4 72-3
East Leverett, Mass. C5 68-9
East Limington, Me. O7 64-5
East Litchfield, Conn. D6 60-1
East Livermore, Me. K3 64-5
East Liverpool, O. D12 132-3
East Liverpool North*, O. D11 132-3
East Longmeadow, Mass. F5 68-9
East Los Angeles, Calif. G8 210-1
East Lyme, Conn. G12 60-1
East Lyndon, Vt. D9 90-1
East Lynn, W. Va. I10 200-1
East Lynne, Mo. K16 120-1
East Machias, Me. J10 64-5
East Madison, Me. J4 64-5
East Mansfield, Mass. F11 68-9
East Marion [-Clinchfield], N.C. D5 180-1
East Massapequa*, N.Y. K11 80-1
East McKeesport*, Pa. I2 84-5
East Meadow, N.Y. E16 80-1
East Middlebury, Vt. H4 90-1
East Middletown*, N.Y. I10 80-1
East Mill Creek, Ut. F6 242-3
East Millinocket, Me. G7 64-5
East Millstone, N.J. F5 76-7
East Moline, Ill. C5 96-7
East Monmouth, Me. L4 64-5
East Montpelier, Vt. F7 90-1
East Moriches, N.Y. J13 80-1
East Morris, Conn. D6 60-1
East Naples*, Fla. I11 156-7
East Neck*, N.Y. J12 80-1
East New Market, Md. G13 172-3
East New Portland, Me. I4 64-5
East Newark, N.J. D10 76-7
East Newnan*, Ga. H3 160-1
East Newport, Me. J6 64-5
East Northport, N.Y. J12 80-1
East Olympia, Wash. G7 246-7
East Orange, N.J. C10 76-7
East Orange, Vt. G7 90-1
East Orland, Me. K7 64-5
East Otis, Mass. E3 68-9
East Palatka, Fla. C11 156-7
East Palestine, O. D12 132-3
East Palo Alto*, Calif. J3 210-1
East Parsonfield, Me. O7 64-5
East Patchogue*, N.Y. J12 80-1
East Peacham, Vt. F8 90-1
East Peoria, Ill. F7 96-7
East Peru, Ia. I7 104-5
East Peru, Me. K3 64-5
East Petersburg, Pa. J12 84-5
East Pittsburgh*, Pa. I2 84-5
East Pittston, Me. L5 64-5
East Plymouth, Conn. D7 60-1
East Point, Ga. C10 160-1
East Point, Ky. H15 164-5
East Point, La. C2 168-9
East Point, P.E.I. D11 287
East Poland, Me. M9 64-5
East Portal, Colo. G1 214-5
East Portal, Mont. D1 222-3
East Porterville*, Calif. K6 210-1
East Poultney, Vt. J4 90-1
East Prairie, Mo. I12 120-1
East Princeton, Mass. C8 68-9
East Providence, R.I. C6 87
East Putnam, Conn. B15 60-1
East Putney, Vt. M7 90-1
East Quogue*, N.Y. J12 80-1
East Rainelle, W. Va. I5 200-1
East Randolph, N.Y. G2 80-1
East Randolph, Vt. H6 90-1
East Richford, Vt. B6 90-1
East Ridge, Tenn. K11 188-9
East R., N.Y. E14 80-1
East River, Conn. H9 60-1
East Riverside-Kinghurst*, N.B. J5 275
East Rochester, N.Y. E5 80-1
East Rockaway*, N.Y. K11 80-1
East Rockingham, N.C. F9 180-1
East Rupert, Vt. L4 90-1
East Rutherford, N.J. B11 76-7
East Ryegate, Vt. F8 90-1
East Saugatuck, Mich. J11 112-3
East Sebago, Me. N8 64-5
East Selkirk, Man. I15 272-3
East Shelburne, Mass. B4 68-9
East Sioux Falls, S. Dak. G16 136-7
East Somerset*, Ky. J11 164-5
East Sparta, O. D10 132-3
East Spencer, N.C. I2 180-1
East St. Johnsbury, Vt. E9 90-1
East St. Louis, Ill. K6 96-7
East Stone Gap, Va. J3 196-7
East Stoneham, Me. L2 64-5
East Stroudsburg, Pa. F15 84-5
East Sullivan, Me. K8 64-5
East Sumner, Me. K3 64-5
East Swanzey, N.H. O3 72-3
East Syracuse, N.Y. E7 80-1
East Tawas, Mich. G14 112-3
East Thermopolis, Wyo. E9 250-1
East Thetford, Vt. I8 90-1
East Thompson, Conn. A15 60-1
East Topsham, Vt. G8 90-1
East Troy, Wis. K4 140-1
East Uniacke, N.S. D7 281
East Union, Me. L6 64-5
East Uniontown*, Pa. J3 84-5
East Vandergrift*, Pa. H3 84-5
East Vassalboro, Me. K5 64-5
East Vernonia, Ore. B5 238-9
East Vestal*, N.Y. G7 80-1
East View, W. Va. C13 200-1
East Village, Conn. G6 60-1
East Wallingford, Vt. K5 90-1
East Walpole, Mass. K4 68-9
East Washington, Pa. I1 84-5
East Waterboro, Me. N2 64-5
East Waterford, Me. L2 64-5
East Wenatchee, Wash. F11 246-7
East Wenatchee Bench*, Wash. F11 246-7
East Whately, Mass. C5 68-9
East Willington, Conn. C12 60-1
East Williston*, N.Y. J11 80-1
East Wilton, Me. J3 64-5
East Windsor*, Conn. D9 60-1
East Windsor, Mass. C3 68-9
East Windsor*, N.J. G5 76-7
East Windsor Hill, Conn. C10 60-1
East Winn, Me. H8 64-5
East Winter Haven*, Fla. F11 156-7
East Winthrop, Me. K4 64-5
East Wolfeboro, N.H. J8 72-3
East Woodstock, Conn. B14 60-1
Eastaboga, Ala. E8 146-7
Eastabuchie, Miss. K8 176-7
Eastampton*, N.J. I5 76-7
Eastanollee, Ga. D6 160-1
Eastborough, Kans. I11 108-9
Eastbrook, Me. J8 64-5
Eastchester*, N.Y. J11 80-1
Eastend, Sask. O4 294-5
Eastern Valley, Ala. F6 146-7
Easterville, Man. D11 272-3
Eastford, Conn. B13 60-1
Eastgate, Nev. G5 226-7
Eastgate, Wash. I3 246-7
Eastham, Mass. G16 68-9
Easthampton, Mass. D4 68-9
Eastlake, Colo. F3 214-5
Eastlake, O. A15 132-3
Eastland, Tex. E7 192-3
Eastland, co., Tex. E7 192-3
Eastlawn Gardens*, Pa. G15 84-5
Eastman, Ga. K6 160-1
Eastman, Que. J14 290-1
Eastman, Wis. J10 140-1
Easton, Calif. K5 210-1
Easton, Conn. H5 60-1
Easton, Kans. E15 108-9
Easton, Me. C9 64-5
Easton, Md. F13 172-3
Easton, Mass. F11 68-9
Easton, Minn. O5 116-7
Easton, Mo. G15 120-1
Easton, N.H. G5 72-3
Easton, Pa. H15 84-5
Easton, Wash. F10 246-7
Easton, Wis. H12 140-1
Easton Center, Me. C9 64-5
Easton Green, Mass. F11 68-9
Eastover, S.C. E11 184-5
Eastpoint, Fla. C6 156-7
Eastport, Ida. A3 218-9
Eastport, Me. I11 64-5
Eastport, Mich. F12 112-3
Eastport, N.Y. J13 80-1
Eastport, Nfld. M10 278-9
Eastside, Miss. O10 176-7
Eastside, Ore. H4 238-9
Eastsound, Wash. C7 246-7
Eastview, Ky. H8 164-5
Eastview*, Tenn. D4 188-9
Eastville, Ga. F6 160-1
Eastville, Va. E5 196-7
Eastwood, Ky. A3 164-5
Eastwood*, Mich. J12 112-3
Eaton, Colo. D4 214-5
Eaton, Ind. F10 100-1
Eaton, Me. G9 64-5
Eaton*, N.H. I8 72-3
Eaton, O. G3 132-3
Eaton, Tenn. B3 188-9
Eaton, co., Mich. J13 112-3
Eaton Crossroad, Tenn. I11 188-9
Eaton Estates, O. C13 132-3
Eaton Park, Fla. H5 156-7
Eaton Rapids, Mich. J13 112-3
Eatonia, Sask. M4 294-5
Eatonton, Ga. H6 160-1
Eatontown, N.J. G8 76-7
Eatonville, Fla. E7 156-7
Eatonville, Wash. G8 246-7
Eau Claire*, Mich. K11 112-3
Eau Claire, Wis. F9 140-1
Eau Claire, co., Wis. F9 140-1
Eau Claire Southeast*, Wis. F9 140-1
Eau Galle, Wis. F8 140-1
Eben Junction, Mich. D10 112-3
Ebenezer, Miss. G6 176-7
Ebenezer, P.E.I. E7 287
Ebenezer, Sask. L10 294-5
Ebensburg, Pa. H4 84-5
Ebony, Va. K11 196-7
Ebro, Fla. B5 156-7
Eccles, W. Va. K15 200-1
Echeta, Wyo. C13 250-1
Echo, Ala. K9 146-7
Echo, La. F5 168-9
Echo, Minn. M3 116-7
Echo, Ore. B12 238-9
Echo Bay, Ont. H6 284-5
Echo Lake, Colo. H1 214-5
Echo Lake*, N.S. E7 281
Echola, Ala. F4 146-7
Echols, co., Ga. O7 160-1
Echota, Okla. E16 234-5
Eckerman, Mich. D12 112-3
Eckerty, Ind. N7 100-1
Eckhart Mines, Md. B3 172-3
Eckleson, N. Dak. G12 128-9
Eckley, Colo. D15 214-5
Eckman, N. Dak. C7 128-9
Eckman, W. Va. J3 200-1
Eckville, Alta. K7 264-5
Eclectic, Ala. H8 146-7
Eclipse, Va. G4 196-7
Economy, Ind. G11 100-1
Economy, Pa. A5 84-5
Ecorse, Mich. K6 112-3
Ecru, Miss. C9 176-7
Ector, co., Tex. E4 192-3
Edam, Sask. J5 294-5
Edberg, Alta. J8 264-5
Edcouch*, Tex. K8 192-3
Eddiceton, Miss. K4 176-7
Eddington, Me. J7 64-5
Eddiville, Ida. D3 218-9
Eddy, Ala. C7 146-7
Eddy, Okla. C11 234-5
Eddy, co., N. Mex. K10 230-1
Eddy, co., N. Dak. E10 128-9
Eddystone*, Pa. K15 84-5
Eddyville, Ia. I10 104-5
Eddyville, Ky. J4 164-5
Eddyville, Nebr. H9 124-5
Eddyville, Ore. E4 238-9
Eden, Ariz. J10 206-7
Eden, Ga. K11 160-1
Eden, Ida. N6 218-9
Eden, Ind. H9 100-1
Eden, Man. I11 272-3
Eden, Md. H14 172-3
Eden, Mich. I1 112-3
Eden, Miss. G5 176-7
Eden, Mont. D7 222-3
Eden, N.Y. F2 80-1
Eden, N.C. C9 180-1
Eden, S. Dak. B14 136-7
Eden, Tex. F6 192-3
Eden, Vt. C6 90-1
Eden, Wis. G4 140-1
Eden, Wyo. H7 250-1
Eden Mills, Vt. C7 90-1
Eden Prairie*, Minn. M6 116-7
Eden Valley, Minn. L4 116-7
Edenton, N.C. C14 180-1
Edenville, Mich. H13 112-3
Edenwold, Sask. M8 294-5
Edesville, Md. D12 172-3
Edgar, Nebr. I12 124-5
Edgar, Wis. F11 140-1
Edgar, co., Ill. H11 96-7
Edgar Springs, Mo. G8 120-1
Edgard, La. C12 168-9
Edgarton, W. Va. J2 200-1
Edgartown, Mass. I14 68-9
Edge Hill, Ga. H8 160-1
Edgecliff, Tex. D12 192-3
Edgecomb, Me. N11 64-5
Edgecombe, co., N.C. D12 180-1
Edgefield*, La. C2 168-9
Edgefield, S.C. E8 184-5
Edgefield, co., S.C. F7 184-5
Edgehill, Va. C4 196-7
Edgeley, N. Dak. I11 128-9
Edgeley, Sask. M9 294-5
Edgemere, Ida. C2 218-9
Edgemere, Md. G8 172-3
Edgemont, Ark. C7 150-1
Edgemont, Calif. G10 210-1
Edgemont, S. Dak. H1 136-7
Edgemoor, S.C. B10 184-5
Edgemoor, Tenn. H11 188-9
Edger, Mont. H10 222-3
Edgerly, La. H2 168-9
Edgerton, Alta. J10 264-5
Edgerton, Ind. C12 100-1
Edgerton, Kans. F15 108-9
Edgerton, Minn. O2 116-7
Edgerton, Mo. H15 120-1
Edgerton, O. B3 132-3
Edgerton, Wis. J2 140-1
Edgerton, Wyo. E13 250-1
Edgewater, Ala. E6 146-7
Edgewater, B.C. I10 268-9
Edgewater, Colo. G3 214-5
Edgewater, Fla. D12 156-7
Edgewater, Md. I7 172-3
Edgewater, N.J. C12 76-7
Edgewater Park, Miss. N9 176-7
Edgewater Park, N.J. I4 76-7
Edgewood, B.C. J9 268-9
Edgewood, Fla. F7 156-7
Edgewood, Ind. G9 100-1
Edgewood, Ia. D13 104-5
Edgewood*, Ky. E11 164-5
Edgewood, Md. C12 172-3
Edgewood*, O. A11 132-3
Edgewood*, Pa. G11 84-5
Edgewood*, Pa. I2 84-5
Edgewood*, Tex. D10 192-3
Edgeworth, Pa. A5 84-5
Edina, Minn. B10 116-7
Edina, Mo. B7 120-1
Edinboro, Pa. C2 84-5
Edinburg, Ill. H8 96-7
Edinburg, Ind. J9 100-1
Edinburg, Me. H7 64-5
Edinburg, Miss. G8 176-7
Edinburg, N. Dak. C12 128-9
Edinburg, Tex. K8 192-3
Edinburg, Va. E10 196-7
Edison, Ga. L3 160-1
Edison, Nebr. J8 124-5
Edison*, N.J. F6 76-7
Edison, O. E7 132-3
Edison, Wash. C8 246-7
Edisto Island, S.C. I12 184-5
Edler, Colo. J15 214-5
Edmond, Kans. D5 108-9
Edmond, Okla. I2 234-5
Edmond, W. Va. J16 200-1
Edmonds, Ida. L10 218-9
Edmonds, Wash. H2 246-7
Edmondson, Ark. E11 150-1
Edmonson, co., Ky. I8 164-5
Edmonston, Md. I4 172-3
Edmonton, Alta. I8 264-5
Edmonton, Ky. J9 164-5
Edmonton Beach*, Alta. J7 264-5
Edmore, Mich. H12 112-3
Edmore, N. Dak. C11 128-9
Edmund, S.C. E9 184-5
Edmund, Wis. J11 140-1
Edmunds, co., S. Dak. B10 136-7
Edmundson*, Mo. E10 120-1
Edmundston, N.B. E2 275
Edna, Kans. K15 108-9
Edna, Okla. E13 234-5
Edna, Tex. H9 192-3
Edna Bay, Alaska H15 254-5
Edneyville, N.C. E4 180-1
Edon, O. B3 132-3
Edrans, Man. I12 272-3
Edson, Alta. I5 264-5
Edson, Kans. E2 108-9
Edson, Wyo. I12 250-1
Edwall, Wash. F15 246-7
Edward, N.C. E14 180-1
Edwards, Calif. M7 210-1
Edwards, Colo. E9 214-5
Edwards, Miss. I5 176-7
Edwards, N.Y. B8 80-1
Edwards, co., Ill. L10 96-7
Edwards, co., Kans. I16 108-9
Edwards, co., Tex. G6 192-3
Edwardsburg, Mich. K11 112-3
Edwardsport, Ind. L5 100-1
Edwardsville, Ala. E9 146-7
Edwardsville, Del. G3 153
Edwardsville, Ill. K6 96-7
Edwardsville, Ind. N9 100-1
Edwardsville, Kans. E16 108-9
Edwardsville, Pa. F13 84-5
Edwardsville, Va. G14 196-7
Edwin, Ala. K10 146-7
Eek, Alaska F8 254-5
Eel River Bridge*, N.B. F6 275
Eel River Crossing*, N.B. D4 275
Effie, La. E5 168-9
Effie, Minn. G6 116-7
Effingham, Ill. J9 96-7

Effingham, Kans. D15 108-9
Effingham, N.H. J9 72-3
Effingham, S.C. D13 184-5
Effingham, co., Ga. K11 160-1
Effingham, co., Ill. J9 96-7
Effingham Falls, N.H. I8 72-3
Efland, N.C. H6 180-1
Egan, La. H4 168-9
Egan, S. Dak. F16 136-7
Eganville, Ont. H13 284-5
Egbert, Wyo. J16 250-1
Egegik, Alaska G9 254-5
Egeland, N. Dak. C10 128-9
Egg Harbor*, N.J. L5 76-7
Egg Harbor, Wis. E16 140-1
Egg Harbor City, N.J. L5 76-7
Eggleston, Va. I6 196-7
Egin, Ida. L10 218-9
Eglin, Fla. B4 156-7
Eglon, Wash. G2 246-7
Egmondville, Ont. D12 284-5
Egmont, B.C. A11 268-9
Egmont Bay, P.E.I. D3 287
Egnar, Colo. H5 214-5
Egremont, Mass. E1 68-9
Egypt, Ark. C10 150-1
Egypt, Mass. J8 68-9
Egypt, Miss. D9 176-7
Egypt Lake*, Fla. F10 156-7
Ehrenberg, Ariz. H2 206-7
Ehrhardt, S.C. H10 184-5
Eidson, Tenn. F14 188-9
Eielson*, Alaska D12 254-5
Eightmile, Ore. C11 238-9
Eighty-Eight, Ky. J8 164-5
Eitzen, Minn. O9 116-7
Ekalaka, Mont. G16 222-3
Eklutna*, Alaska F11 254-5
Ekonk, Conn. E14 60-1
Ekron, Ky. G8 164-5
Ekuk, Alaska G9 254-5
Ekwok, Alaska G9 254-5
El Cajon, Calif. J11 210-1
El Campo, Tex. H9 192-3
El Campo South*, Tex. H9 192-3
El Centro, Calif. O10 210-1
El Cerrito, Calif. C7 210-1
El Dorado, Ark. J6 150-1
El Dorado, Kans. I12 108-9
El Dorado, co., Calif. H5 210-1
El Dorado Springs, Mo. G4 120-1
El Encanto Heights*, Calif. M5 210-1
El Granada*, Calif. J3 210-1
El Lago*, Tex. G10 192-3
El Llanito, N. Mex. F6 230-1
El Mirage, Ariz. H6 206-7
El Monte, Calif. G9 210-1
El Paso, Ark. E7 150-1
El Paso, Ill. E8 96-7
El Paso, Tex. E1 192-3
El Paso, Wis. F7 140-1
El Paso, co., Colo. F12 214-5
El Paso, co., Tex. E1 192-3
El Paso de Robles, Calif. L4 210-1
El Portal*, Fla. H16 156-7
El Prado, N. Mex. C7 230-1
El Ranchero Vill-Golf Lake Estates*, Fla. G10 156-7
El Reno, Okla. F10 234-5
El Rio, Calif. G6 210-1
El Rito, N. Mex. C6 230-1
El Segundo*, Calif. G8 210-1
El Toro*, Calif. O8 210-1
El Toro Station*, Calif. O8 210-1
El Vado, N. Mex. C5 230-1
El Verano, Calif. B7 210-1
Elaine, Ark. G10 150-1
Elamville, Ala. K9 146-7
Eland, Wis. C2 140-1
Elba, Ala. L8 146-7
Elba, Ida. O7 218-9
Elba, Minn. O8 116-7
Elba, Nebr. G11 124-5
Elba, N.Y. E3 80-1
Elbe, Wash. G8 246-7
Elberfeld, Ind. N4 100-1
Elberon, Ia. F11 104-5
Elberon, Va. F3 196-7
Elbert, Colo. F12 214-5
Elbert, co., Colo. E13 214-5
Elbert, co., Ga. F7 160-1
Elberta, Ala. O4 146-7
Elberta, Ga. J5 160-1
Elberta, Mich. F11 112-3
Elberta, Ut. G6 242-3
Elberton, Ga. F7 160-1
Elberton, Wash. G16 246-7
Elbethel, Tenn. J7 188-9
Elbing, Kans. H11 108-9
Elbow, Sask. M6 294-5
Elbow Lake, Minn. J2 116-7
Elbridge*, N.Y. E6 80-1
Elbridge, Tenn. B2 188-9
Elburn, Ill. M1 96-7
Elburz, Nev. C9 226-7
Elcho, Wis. D13 140-1
Elderon, Wis. D1 140-1
Eldersburg-Flohrville*, Md. C10 172-3
Eldoes Trailer Park*, Alta. G4 264-5
Eldon, Ia. J11 104-5
Eldon, Mo. F6 120-1
Eldon, P.E.I. F8 287
Eldora, Colo. F1 214-5
Eldora, Ia. E9 104-5
Eldorado, Ill. M10 96-7
Eldorado, Md. G14 172-3
Eldorado, Nebr. I12 124-5
Eldorado, O. H13 132-3
Eldorado, Okla. H7 234-5
Eldorado, Tex. F6 192-3
Eldorado, Wis. G3 140-1
Eldorado Springs, Colo. F2 214-5
Eldred, Pa. C6 84-5
Eldridge, Ala. D4 146-7
Eldridge, Ia. G15 104-5
Eldridge, N. Dak. G11 128-9
Eleanor, W. Va. G2 200-1
Electra, Tex. C7 192-3
Electric City, Wash. E13 246-7
Electric Mills, Miss. G10 176-7
Electron, Wash. G8 246-7
Eleele, Hawaii D4 258-9
Elephant Butte, N. Mex. J5 230-1
Elephant Butte Res., N. Mex. J5 230-1
Eleva, Wis. F9 140-1
Eleven Mile Corner, Ariz. J7 206-7
Elfin Cove*, Alaska G14 254-5
Elfrida, Ariz. L10 206-7
Elfros, Sask. L9 294-5
Elgin, Ala. A5 146-7
Elgin, Ariz. L9 206-7
Elgin, Ill. B10 96-7
Elgin, Ia. C12 104-5
Elgin, Kans. K13 108-9
Elgin, Man. J10 272-3
Elgin, Minn. N8 116-7
Elgin, Nebr. E11 124-5
Elgin, Nev. K10 226-7
Elgin, N. Dak. I5 128-9
Elgin, Okla. G9 234-5
Elgin, Ore. B14 238-9
Elgin, S.C. B11 184-5
Elgin, S.C. D11 184-5
Elgin, Tenn. G10 188-9
Elgin, Tex. G8 192-3
Elgin, Ut. I9 242-3
Elgin, co., Ont. F11 284-5
Elgood, W. Va. J5 200-1
Eli, Nebr. C5 124-5
Elida, N. Mex. H11 230-1
Elida, O. D4 132-3
Elie*, Man. J13 272-3
Elim, Alaska D8 254-5
Eliot, Me. O2 64-5
Elizabeth*, Alta. H10 264-5
Elizabeth, Colo. I4 214-5
Elizabeth, Ga. B10 160-1
Elizabeth, Ill. A6 96-7
Elizabeth, Ind. O9 100-1
Elizabeth, La. F3 168-9
Elizabeth, Minn. J2 116-7
Elizabeth, Miss. F4 176-7
Elizabeth, N.J. E7 76-7
Elizabeth, Pa. B7 84-5
Elizabeth, W. Va. E4 200-1
Elizabeth City, N.C. C15 180-1
Elizabethton, Tenn. G17 188-9
Elizabethtown, Ill. N10 96-7
Elizabethtown, Ind. K9 100-1
Elizabethtown, Ky. H8 164-5
Elizabethtown, N.Y. B11 80-1
Elizabethtown, N.C. G11 180-1
Elizabethtown, Pa. J11 84-5
Elizabethville, Pa. H11 84-5
Elizaville, Ky. F13 164-5
Elk*, N.J. K3 76-7
Elk, Wash. D16 246-7
Elk, Wyo. I2 250-1
Elk, co., Kans. J13 108-9
Elk, co., Pa. E6 84-5
Elk City, Ida. H4 218-9
Elk City, Kans. J14 108-9
Elk City, Nebr. I2 124-5
Elk City, Okla. F7 234-5
Elk City, W. Va. D15 200-1
Elk Creek, Nebr. I15 124-5
Elk Creek, Va. J5 196-7
Elk Falls, Kans. J13 108-9
Elk Garden, W. Va. D9 200-1
Elk Grove, Calif. A9 210-1
Elk Grove Village, Ill. L3 96-7
Elk Hill, Va. H11 196-7
Elk Horn, Ia. G4 104-5
Elk Horn, Ky. I10 164-5
Elk Lake, Ont. G7 284-5
Elk Mills, Md. B14 172-3
Elk Mills, Tenn. B16 188-9
Elk Mound, Wis. F8 140-1
Elk Mountain, Wyo. I12 250-1
Elk Park, Mont. G5 222-3
Elk Park, N.C. C5 180-1
Elk Point, Alta. I10 264-5
Elk Point, S. Dak. J16 136-7
Elk Rapids, Mich. F12 112-3
Elk River, Ida. E3 218-9
Elk River, Minn. L6 116-7
Elk Run Heights, Ia. E11 104-5
Elk Springs, Colo. C6 214-5
Elk Valley, Tenn. F11 188-9
Elkader, Ia. C13 104-5
Elkatawa, Ky. H13 164-5
Elkford, B.C. J11 268-9
Elkhart, Ind. A8 100-1
Elkhart, Ia. G8 104-5
Elkhart, Kans. K1 108-9
Elkhart, Tex. F10 192-3
Elkhart, co., Ind. A9 100-1
Elkhart Lake, Wis. G5 140-1
Elkhead, Ore. G5 238-9
Elkhorn, Man. I9 272-3
Elkhorn, Mont. F6 222-3
Elkhorn, Nebr. I2 124-5
Elkhorn, Ore. D7 238-9
Elkhorn, Wis. K14 140-1
Elkhorn City, Ky. I16 164-5
Elkhorn R., Nebr. E11 124-5
Elkin, N.C. G1 180-1
Elkins, Ark. B3 150-1
Elkins, N.H. L5 72-3
Elkins, N. Mex. I10 230-1
Elkins, W. Va. F7 200-1
Elkland, Pa. C9 84-5
Elkmont, Ala. A6 146-7
Elko, B.C. J11 268-9
Elko, Ga. J5 160-1
Elko, Minn. C10 116-7
Elko, Nev. C8 226-7
Elko, S.C. G9 184-5
Elko, co., Nev. C8 226-7
Elkol, Wyo. I5 250-1
Elkport, Ia. D13 104-5
Elkridge, Md. G6 172-3
Elkton, Ky. J6 164-5
Elkton, Md. B14 172-3
Elkton, Mich. H14 112-3
Elkton, Minn. O7 116-7
Elkton, Ore. G5 238-9
Elkton, S. Dak. E16 136-7
Elkton, Tenn. D7 188-9
Elkton, Va. F10 196-7
Elkview*, W. Va. G3 200-1
Elkville, Ill. M8 96-7
Elkwater, Alta. N11 264-5
Elkwood, Va. B2 196-7
Ellabell, Ga. K10 160-1
Ellamore, W. Va. E15 200-1
Ellaville, Ga. K4 160-1
Ellenboro*, N.C. E5 180-1
Ellenboro, W. Va. E4 200-1
Ellendale, Del. H4 153
Ellendale, Minn. O6 116-7
Ellendale, N. Dak. J11 128-9
Ellendale, Tenn. K1 188-9
Ellensburg, Wash. G11 246-7
Ellenton, Fla. J2 156-7
Ellenton, Ga. N6 160-1
Ellenville, N.Y. H10 80-1
Ellenwood, Ga. D11 160-1
Ellerbe, N.C. K4 180-1
Ellerslie, Ga. J3 160-1
Ellerslie, Md. B4 172-3
Ellerslie, P.E.I. D4 287
Ellerton, Md. B8 172-3
Ellettsville, Ind. J7 100-1
Ellicott, Colo. F12 214-5
Ellicott City, Md. C10 172-3
Ellicottville, N.Y. G3 80-1
Ellijay, Ga. D4 160-1
Ellington, Conn. B10 60-1
Ellington, Mo. H9 120-1
Ellinwood, Kans. H8 108-9
Elliot Lake, Ont. H6 284-5
Elliott, Ia. I4 104-5
Elliott, Md. H13 172-3
Elliott, Miss. E7 176-7
Elliott, N. Dak. I13 128-9
Elliott, S.C. D12 184-5
Elliott, co., Ky. G14 164-5
Elliottsville, Me. H5 64-5
Elliottville, Ky. G14 164-5
Ellis, Ida. J6 218-9
Ellis, Kans. F6 108-9
Ellis, Nebr. J14 124-5
Ellis, S. Dak. G15 136-7
Ellis, co., Kans. F6 108-9
Ellis, co., Okla. D6 234-5
Ellis, co., Tex. E9 192-3
Ellisforde, Wash. C12 246-7
Ellison, W. Va. J4 200-1
Ellison Bay, Wis. E16 140-1
Elliston, Ky. E11 164-5
Elliston, Mont. F5 222-3
Elliston, Va. I7 196-7
Ellistown, Miss. C9 176-7
Ellisville, Mass. G14 68-9
Ellisville, Miss. K8 176-7
Ellisville, Mo. C15 120-1
Ellisville, Wis. E5 140-1
Ellisville Junction, Miss. K8 176-7
Elloree, S.C. F11 184-5
Ellport, Pa. G1 84-5
Ellsinore, Mo. I9 120-1
Ellston, Ia. J6 104-5
Ellsworth, Conn. C4 60-1
Ellsworth, Ia. E8 104-5
Ellsworth, Kans. G9 108-9
Ellsworth, Me. K8 64-5
Ellsworth, Mich. F12 112-3
Ellsworth, Minn. O2 116-7
Ellsworth, Nebr. E4 124-5
Ellsworth, N.H. I5 72-3
Ellsworth, Pa. J2 84-5
Ellsworth, S. Dak. F3 136-7
Ellsworth, Wis. F7 140-1
Ellsworth, co., Kans. G9 108-9
Ellwood City, Pa. G1 84-5
Elm City, N.C. D12 180-1
Elm Creek, Man. J13 272-3
Elm Creek, Nebr. I9 124-5
Elm Grove, La. B2 168-9
Elm Grove, Mass. B4 68-9
Elm Grove, Wis. J4 140-1
Elm Hall, Mich. H13 112-3
Elm Springs, Ark. B2 150-1
Elm Springs Colony, S. Dak. H13 136-7
Elma, Ia. B10 104-5
Elma, Man. J16 272-3
Elma, N.Y. F2 80-1
Elma, Wash. G6 246-7
Elmdale, Kans. G12 108-9
Elmdale, Minn. K5 116-7
Elmendorf*, Alaska F11 254-5
Elmer, La. F4 168-9
Elmer, Mo. B6 120-1
Elmer, N.J. L3 76-7
Elmer, Okla. H7 234-5
Elmer City, Wash. E13 246-7
Elmhurst, Ill. M3 96-7
Elmira, Ida. B3 218-9
Elmira, Ind. A11 100-1
Elmira, Mich. F13 112-3
Elmira, Mo. G16 120-1
Elmira, N.Y. G6 80-1
Elmira, Ont. C13 284-5
Elmira, Ore. F5 238-9
Elmira, P.E.I. E11 287
Elmira, W. Va. G5 200-1
Elmira Heights, N.Y. G6 80-1
Elmira Heights North*, N.Y. G6 80-1
Elmo, Mo. A2 120-1
Elmo, Mont. C3 222-3
Elmo, Ut. H8 242-3
Elmo, Wyo. I12 250-1
Elmodel, Ga. M3 160-1
Elmont, Kans. E14 108-9
Elmont, N.Y. E15 80-1
Elmore, Ala. H7 146-7
Elmore, Minn. O5 116-7
Elmore, O. B6 132-3
Elmore*, Vt. D7 90-1
Elmore, co., Ala. H8 146-7
Elmore, co., Ida. M4 218-9
Elmore City, Okla. H11 234-5
Elmsdale*, N.S. D7 281
Elmsdale, P.E.I. C3 287
Elmsdale, P.E.I. C3 287
Elmsford, N.Y. C15 80-1
Elmvale, Ont. A14 284-5
Elmville, Conn. C14 60-1
Elmwood, Ill. E6 96-7
Elmwood, Nebr. K2 124-5
Elmwood, Okla. C5 234-5
Elmwood, Ont. B12 284-5
Elmwood, Tenn. B9 188-9
Elmwood, W. Va. F3 200-1
Elmwood, Wis. F8 140-1
Elmwood Park, Ill. M3 96-7
Elmwood Park, N.J. A10 76-7
Elmwood Park, Wis. K5 140-1
Elmwood Place, O. K13 132-3
Elnora, Alta. K8 264-5
Elnora, Ind. L5 100-1
Eloise, Fla. H5 156-7
Elon College, N.C. H5 180-1
Elora, Ont. C13 284-5
Elora, Tenn. E8 188-9
Eloy, Ariz. J7 206-7
Elphinstone, Man. H10 272-3
Elrod, Ala. F4 146-7
Elrosa, Minn. K4 116-7
Elrose, Sask. M5 294-5
Elroy, Wis. H11 140-1
Elsa*, Tex. K8 192-3
Elsa, Y.T. B2 297
Elsah, Ill. J6 96-7
Elsberry, Mo. D9 120-1
Elsie, Mich. G1 112-3
Elsie, Nebr. H5 124-5
Elsie, Ore. B5 238-9
Elsinboro*, N.J. L1 76-7
Elsinore, Ut. J5 242-3
Elsmere, Del. A3 153
Elsmere, Ky. E11 164-5
Elsmere, Nebr. E8 124-5
Elsmore, Kans. I15 108-9
Elstow, Sask. L7 294-5
Elton, La. G4 168-9
Elton, W. Va. I5 200-1
Elton, Wis. E13 140-1
Eltopia, Wash. H13 246-7
Elva, Man. K9 272-3
Elverton, Tenn. H10 188-9
Elvins, Mo. G10 120-1
Elwell, Mich. H13 112-3
Elwood, Ill. D10 96-7
Elwood, Ind. F9 100-1
Elwood, Kans. D16 108-9
Elwood, Nebr. I8 124-5
Elwood, N.J. L5 76-7
Elwood*, N.Y. J12 80-1
Elwood, Ore. C7 238-9
Elwood*, Ut. C5 242-3
Ely, Ia. F12 104-5
Ely, Minn. F8 116-7
Ely, Nev. G10 226-7
Ely, Vt. H8 90-1
Elyria, Kans. H10 108-9
Elyria, Nebr. F10 124-5
Elyria, O. B8 132-3
Elysburg, Pa. G11 84-5
Elysian, Minn. N6 116-7
Emanguk*, Alaska E8 254-5
Emanuel, co., Ga. J8 160-1
Embarrass, Wis. D3 140-1
Embden, Me. I4 64-5
Emblem, Wyo. C9 250-1
Embree, Nfld. M9 278-9
Embreeville Junction*, Tenn. A15 188-9
Embro*, Ont. D13 284-5
Embrun*, Ont. H15 284-5
Emelle, Ala. H2 146-7
Emerado, N. Dak. E13 128-9
Emerald, Nebr. H14 124-5
Emerald, Wis. E8 140-1
Emerald Grove, Wis. K2 140-1
Emerald Isle, N.C. G14 180-1
Emerald [Junction], P.E.I. E6 287
Emerson, Ark. K4 150-1
Emerson, Ga. A9 160-1
Emerson, Ia. I3 104-5
Emerson, Man. K14 272-3
Emerson, Nebr. E14 124-5

Emerson, N.J. A11 76-7
Emerson, N.C. G11 180-1
Emery, S. Dak. G14 136-7
Emery, Ut. J7 242-3
Emery, co., Ut. I8 242-3
Emery Mills, Me. N2 64-5
Emeryville, Calif. C7 210-1
Emida, Ida. E3 218-9
Emigrant, Mont. H7 222-3
Emily, Minn. I5 116-7
Eminence, Ind. I7 100-1
Eminence*, Ky. F10 164-5
Eminence, Mo. I8 120-1
Emison, Ind. L4 100-1
Emlyn, Ky. K12 164-5
Emma, Mo. D5 120-1
Emmaus, Pa. H14 84-5
Emmerton, Va. H14 196-7
Emmet, Ark. I4 150-1
Emmet, Nebr. D10 124-5
Emmet, co., Ia. B5 104-5
Emmet, co., Mich. E12 112-3
Emmetsburg, Ia. C5 104-5
Emmett, Ida. L3 218-9
Emmett, Kans. E13 108-9
Emmett, Mich. G7 112-3
Emmitsburg, Md. B9 172-3
Emmons, Minn. O6 116-7
Emmons, W. Va. I13 200-1
Emmons, co., N. Dak. I8 128-9
Emo, Ont. F1 284-5
Emory, Tex. D10 192-3
Emory, Va. J4 196-7
Emory Gap, Tenn. H10 188-9
Emory Grove, Md. G3 172-3
Empire, Ala. E6 146-7
Empire, Calif. C10 210-1
Empire, Colo. G1 214-5
Empire, Ga. J6 160-1
Empire, La. J11 168-9
Empire, Mich. F11 112-3
Empire, Nev. D2 226-7
Empire, O. E11 132-3
Empire City, Okla. H10 234-5
Emporia, Kans. G13 108-9
Emporia, Va. J12 196-7
Emporium, Pa. E7 84-5
Empress, Alta. M11 264-5
Emsworth*, Pa. H2 84-5
Emyvale, P.E.I. F6 287
Enaville, Ida. D3 218-9
Encampment, Wyo. J12 250-1
Encinal, N. Mex. F4 230-1
Encinitas, Calif. J10 210-1
Encino, N. Mex. G7 230-1
Endako, B.C. F6 268-9
Endeavor, Wis. G1 140-1
Endeavour, Sask. K10 294-5
Enderby, B.C. I9 268-9
Enderlin, N. Dak. H13 128-9
Enders, Nebr. I5 124-5
Endersby, Ore. C9 238-9
Endicott, Nebr. J13 124-5
Endicott, N.Y. G7 80-1
Endicott, Wash. G15 246-7
Endicott, W. Va. D5 200-1
Endwell, N.Y. G7 80-1
Energy, Ill. N8 96-7
Enetai, Wash. I1 246-7
Enfield, Conn. B10 60-1
Enfield, Ill. M10 96-7
Enfield, Me. H7 64-5
Enfield, N.H. J4 72-3
Enfield, N.C. C12 180-1
Enfield*, N.S. D7 281
Engadine, Mich. D12 112-3
Engelhard, N.C. E16 180-1
England, Ark. F7 150-1
England*, La. E4 168-9
Englee, Nfld. K9 278-9
Englefeld, Sask. K8 294-5
Englehart, Ont. G8 284-5
Englevale, Kans. I16 108-9
Englevale, N. Dak. I12 128-9
Englewood, Colo. H3 214-5
Englewood, Fla. H10 156-7
Englewood*, Ind. L7 100-1
Englewood, Kans. K5 108-9
Englewood, La. B7 168-9
Englewood, N.J. B12 76-7
Englewood, O. H14 132-3
Englewood, Tenn. J13 188-9
Englewood Cliffs, N.J. D8 76-7
English, Ind. N7 100-1
English, Ky. F10 164-5
English, W. Va. J3 200-1
English Bay, Alaska G11 254-5
English Creek, N.J. M5 76-7
Englishtown, N.J. G6 76-7
Enid, Miss. D6 176-7
Enid, Mont. C15 222-3
Enid, Okla. D10 234-5
Enigma, Ga. M6 160-1
Enilda, Alta. G6 264-5
Enka, N.C. E4 180-1
Ennice, N.C. B7 180-1
Ennis, Mont. H6 222-3
Ennis, Tex. E15 192-3
Enoch, Ut. L4 242-3
Enoch, W. Va. H16 200-1
Enoka, La. B7 168-9
Enola, Ark. E7 150-1
Enola, Nebr. F12 124-5
Enon, Ala. I9 146-7
Enon, Miss. L6 176-7
Enon, N.C. G2 180-1
Enon, O. H16 132-3
Enondale, Miss. H10 176-7
Enoree, S.C. H4 184-5
Enos, Okla. I12 234-5
Enosburg*, Vt. B5 90-1
Enosburg Falls, Vt. B5 90-1
Enrose, Ida. L2 218-9
Ensenada, N. Mex. C6 230-1
Ensign, Kans. I4 108-9
Ensley, Fla. B3 156-7
Ensor, Tenn. B9 188-9
Enterprise, Ala. L8 146-7
Enterprise, Calif. E3 210-1
Enterprise, Kans. F11 108-9
Enterprise, La. D5 168-9
Enterprise, Miss. I9 176-7
Enterprise, Ore. C15 238-9
Enterprise, Tenn. J6 188-9
Enterprise, Tenn. G15 188-9
Enterprise, Ut. M3 242-3
Enterprise, W. Va. C14 200-1
Enterprise, Wis. D12 140-1
Entiat, Wash. E11 246-7
Entwistle, Alta. I6 264-5
Enumclaw, Wash. F8 246-7
Enville, Okla. I12 234-5
Enville, Tenn. D4 188-9
Eola, La. F5 168-9
Eolia, Mo. D9 120-1
Eoline, Ala. G5 146-7
Epes, Ala. H3 146-7
Ephesus*, Ga. H2 160-1
Ephraim, Ut. I6 242-3
Ephraim, Wis. E16 140-1
Ephrata, Pa. I13 84-5
Ephrata, Wash. F12 246-7
Epiphany, S. Dak. G14 136-7
Epoufette, Mich. D12 112-3
Epping, N.H. N8 72-3
Epping, N. Dak. D2 128-9
Epps, La. B6 168-9
Epsie, Mont. H14 222-3
Epsom, N.H. M7 72-3
Epworth, Ga. C4 160-1
Epworth, Ia. E14 104-5
Epworth, Va. H13 196-7
Equality, Ala. H8 146-7
Equality, Ill. N10 96-7
Eram, Okla. E14 234-5
Eramosa, Ont. C14 284-5
Erath, La. I5 168-9
Erath, co., Tex. E8 192-3
Erhard, Minn. I2 116-7
Erial, N.J. O11 76-7
Erick, Okla. F6 234-5
Erickson, B.C. K10 268-9
Erickson, Man. H11 272-3
Ericsburg, Minn. E6 116-7
Ericson, Nebr. F10 124-5
Erie, Colo. F3 214-5
Erie, Ill. C6 96-7
Erie, Kans. J15 108-9
Erie, Mich. K14 112-3
Erie, N. Dak. G13 128-9
Erie, Pa. B2 84-5
Erie, co., N.Y. F3 80-1
Erie, co., O. C7 132-3
Erie, co., Pa. C2 84-5
Erie Beach, Ont. F11 284-5
Erieau, Ont. F11 284-5
Eriksdale, Man. H13 272-3
Erin, Ont. C14 284-5
Erin, Tenn. A6 188-9
Erin Springs, Okla. G11 234-5
Erlands Point*, Wash. E7 246-7
Erlanger, Ky. E11 164-5
Erma, N.J. O4 76-7
Ermine, Ky. I15 164-5
Ernestville, Tenn. H16 188-9
Ernfold, Sask. N6 294-5
Ernul, N.C. E14 180-1
Eros, La. B4 168-9
Errington*, B.C. J5 268-9
Errol, N.H. D8 72-3
Errol, Ont. E11 284-5
Erskine, Alta. K8 264-5
Erskine, Minn. G2 116-7
Erskine, Ore. C9 238-9
Ervay, Wyo. F11 250-1
Erving, Mass. B6 68-9
Erwin, N.C. J7 180-1
Erwin, S. Dak. E14 136-7
Erwin, Tenn. G16 188-9
Erwin, W. Va. C16 200-1
Erwinville, La. G6 168-9
Erwood, Sask. J10 294-5
Esbon, Kans. D8 108-9
Escalante, Ut. L6 242-3
Escalon, Calif. C10 210-1
Escambia, co., Ala. L5 146-7
Escambia, co., Fla. A3 156-7
Escanaba, Mich. E10 112-3
Escatawpa, Miss. N10 176-7
Escondida, N. Mex. H5 230-1
Escondido, Calif. I11 210-1
Escoumins, Que. C14 290-1
Escuminac, N.B. F7 275
Eska, Alaska F11 254-5
Eskdale, W. Va. J14 200-1
Eskimo Point, N.W. Terr. C2 296
Eskridge, Kans. F13 108-9
Esmeralda, co., Nev. J5 226-7
Esmond, N. Dak. D9 128-9
Esmond, R.I. B4 87
Esmond, S. Dak. F13 136-7
Esmont, Va. H10 196-7
Esom Hill, Ga. F2 160-1
Española, N. Mex. D6 230-1
Espanola, Ont. H7 284-5
Espanong, N.J. C5 76-7
Esparto*, Calif. H3 210-1
Espy, Pa. G12 84-5
Essex, Conn. G11 60-1
Essex, Ia. J3 104-5
Essex, Md. F7 172-3
Essex, Mass. B13 68-9
Essex, Mo. I11 120-1
Essex, Mont. B4 222-3
Essex, Ont. F10 284-5
Essex*, Vt. E4 90-1
Essex, co., Mass. B12 68-9
Essex, co., N.J. D7 76-7
Essex, co., N.Y. D11 80-1
Essex, co., Ont. G10 284-5
Essex, co., Vt. C10 90-1
Essex, co., Va. G13 196-7
Essex Fells, N.J. D7 76-7
Essex Junction, Vt. E4 90-1
Essexville, Mich. H14 112-3
Estabrook, Colo. I2 214-5
Estacada, Ore. C7 238-9
Estancia, N. Mex. G7 230-1
Estcourt Station, Me. A6 64-5
Estell Manor, N.J. M4 76-7
Estelline, S. Dak. E15 136-7
Ester, Alaska D11 254-5
Esterbrook, Wyo. G14 250-1
Esterhazy, Sask. M10 294-5
Estes Park, Colo. E1 214-5
Estesmill, Miss. H8 176-7
Estevan, Sask. O10 294-5
Esther, La. I5 168-9
Esther, Mo. G10 120-1
Estherville, Ia. B5 104-5
Estherwood, La. H4 168-9
Estill, Miss. F4 176-7
Estill, S.C. I9 184-5
Estill, co., Ky. H12 164-5
Estill Springs, Tenn. D8 188-9
Estillfork, Ala. A8 146-7
Esto, Fla. A5 156-7
Eston, Sask. M4 294-5
Estral Beach, Mich. J15 112-3
Estrella, Ariz. J5 206-7
Etam, W. Va. C16 200-1
Étang-du-Nord, Que. I7 290-1
Ethan, S. Dak. G13 136-7
Ethel, Ark. G9 150-1
Ethel, La. G7 168-9
Ethel, Miss. F8 176-7
Ethel, Mo. B6 120-1
Ethel, Wash. H7 246-7
Ethel, W. Va. K12 200-1
Ethelbert, Man. F10 272-3
Ethelsville, Ala. F3 146-7
Ether, N.C. J4 180-1
Ethete, Wyo. F8 250-1
Ethridge, Mont. B6 222-3
Ethridge, Tenn. J5 188-9
Etlan, Va. B1 196-7
Etna, Calif. D2 210-1
Etna, Me. J6 64-5
Etna, Nev. J10 226-7
Etna, N.H. J3 72-3
Etna, Pa. A6 84-5
Etna, Ut. C2 242-3
Etna, Wyo. F5 250-1
Etna Green, Ind. B8 100-1
Eton, Ga. D3 160-1
Etowah, Ark. C12 150-1
Etowah, Tenn. K13 188-9
Etowah, co., Ala. D8 146-7
Etta, Miss. C8 176-7
Ettrick, Va. F1 196-7
Ettrick, Wis. G9 140-1
Eubank, Ky. I11 164-5
Eucha, Okla. D15 234-5
Euclid, O. A15 132-3
Euclid Center, Mich. J11 112-3
Euclid Heights, Ark. K12 150-1
Eudora, Ark. K9 150-1
Eudora, Kans. F15 108-9
Eufaula, Ala. J10 146-7
Eufaula, Okla. F14 234-5
Eufaula Res., Okla. F14 234-5
Eugene, Mo. F7 120-1
Eugene, Ore. F5 238-9
Eugenia, Ont. B13 284-5
Euharlee, Ga. A8 160-1
Euless, Tex. C14 192-3
Eulonia, Ga. M10 160-1
Eunice, La. G4 168-9
Eunice, N. Mex. K12 230-1
Eunola, Ala. M9 146-7
Eupora, Miss. E8 176-7
Eure, N.C. C14 180-1
Eureka, Calif. E1 210-1
Eureka, Colo. H7 214-5
Eureka, Ill. E8 96-7
Eureka, Ind. O5 100-1
Eureka, Kans. I13 108-9
Eureka, Mich. G1 112-3
Eureka, Mo. C14 120-1
Eureka, Mont. A2 222-3
Eureka, Nev. F8 226-7
Eureka, N.C. E12 180-1
Eureka, N.W. Terr. A3 296
Eureka, N.S. C8 281
Eureka, S.C. B9 184-5
Eureka, S.C. F8 184-5
Eureka, S. Dak. A10 136-7
Eureka, Ut. G5 242-3
Eureka, Wash. I14 246-7
Eureka, W. Va. D4 200-1
Eureka, Wis. F3 140-1
Eureka, co., Nev. E7 226-7
Eureka Springs, Ark. A3 150-1
Eureka Springs, Miss. C7 176-7
Eustis, Fla. E11 156-7
Eustis, Me. H3 64-5
Eustis, Nebr. I8 124-5
Eutaw, Ala. G3 146-7
Eutawville, S.C. G12 184-5
Eva, Ala. C6 146-7
Eva, La. E6 168-9
Eva, Okla. C3 234-5
Eva, Tenn. B5 188-9
Évain, Que. H1 290-1
Evan, Minn. N4 116-7
Evangeline, La. H4 168-9
Evangeline*, N.B. E7 275
Evangeline, co., La. G4 168-9
Evans, Colo. E4 214-5
Evans, Ga. G9 160-1
Evans, La. F2 168-9
Evans, Wash. C15 246-7
Evans, W. Va. F3 200-1
Evans, co., Ga. K9 160-1
Evans City, Pa. G2 84-5
Evans Mills, N.Y. C7 80-1
Evansburg, Alta. I6 264-5
Evansdale, Ia. E11 104-5
Evanston, Ill. L4 96-7
Evanston, Ky. H14 164-5
Evanston, Wyo. J5 250-1
Evansville*, Alaska D11 254-5
Evansville, Ark. C2 150-1
Evansville, Ill. M6 96-7
Evansville, Ind. O4 100-1
Evansville, Minn. J3 116-7
Evansville, Miss. B5 176-7
Evansville, Vt. C8 90-1
Evansville, Wis. K1 140-1
Evansville, Wyo. F13 250-1
Evaro, Mont. E3 222-3
Evart, Mich. H12 112-3
Evarts, Ky. J14 164-5
Eveleth, Minn. G7 116-7
Evelyn, La. C2 168-9
Evendale*, O. H3 132-3
Evening Shade, Ark. B8 150-1
Evensville, Tenn. J12 188-9
Everest, Kans. D14 108-9
Everett, Ga. M10 160-1
Everett, Mass. H5 68-9
Everett*, Ont. B14 284-5
Everett, Pa. J6 84-5
Everett, Wash. E8 246-7
Everetts, N.C. D13 180-1
Everetts Corner, Del. F2 153
Everettville, W. Va. B15 200-1
Everglades, Fla. J12 156-7
Everglades, Fla. J12 156-7
Evergreen, Ala. L6 146-7
Evergreen, Colo. H2 214-5
Evergreen, La. F5 168-9
Evergreen, Miss. C10 176-7
Evergreen, N.C. G10 180-1
Evergreen, Va. I10 196-7
Evergreen Park, Ill. N4 96-7
Evergreen Place*, Man. I3 272-3
Evergreen Trailer Park*, Alta. I8 264-5
Everly, Ia. B4 104-5
Everman, Tex. D13 192-3
Everson, Pa. J3 84-5
Everson, Wash. B8 246-7
Everton, Ark. B5 150-1
Everton, Ind. I11 100-1
Everton, Mo. H4 120-1
Evesboro, N.J. N12 76-7
Evesham*, N.J. J4 76-7
Evesham, Sask. K4 294-5
Evington, Va. I9 196-7
Ewa, Hawaii J4 258-9
Ewa Beach, Hawaii J4 258-9
Ewan, N.J. K2 76-7
Ewan, Wash. G15 246-7
Ewanville, N.J. I5 76-7
Ewell, Md. I13 172-3
Ewells Mill, Vt. E8 90-1
Ewen, Mich. C8 112-3
Ewing, Ky. F12 164-5
Ewing, Mo. B8 120-1
Ewing, Nebr. E11 124-5
Ewing*, N.J. G4 76-7
Ewing, Va. J1 196-7
Excel, Ala. L5 146-7
Excelsior, Ark. D2 150-1
Excelsior, Minn. B9 116-7
Excelsior, Wis. J10 140-1
Excelsior Springs, Mo. H16 120-1
Exchange, W. Va. F5 200-1
Exeland, Wis. D9 140-1
Exeter, Calif. K6 210-1
Exeter, Me. I6 64-5
Exeter, Mo. J4 120-1
Exeter, Nebr. I13 124-5
Exeter, N.H. N9 72-3
Exeter, Ont. D12 284-5
Exeter*, Pa. E13 84-5
Exeter, R.I. F4 87
Exeter, Va. J2 196-7
Exie, Ky. I9 164-5
Exira, Ia. G5 104-5
Exline, Ia. J9 104-5
Exline, Md. B5 172-3
Exmore, Va. H15 196-7
Experiment, Ga. H4 160-1
Export, Pa. B8 84-5
Expose, Miss. L7 176-7
Exshaw, Alta. M6 264-5
Extension, B.C. C11 268-9
Extension, La. D6 168-9
Eyebrow, Sask. M7 294-5
Eyota, Minn. O8 116-7
Ezel, Ky. G13 164-5

F

Fabens, Tex. E1 192-3
Faber, Va. H10 196-7
Fabius, Ala. B9 146-7
Fabyan, Conn. A14 60-1

Fabyan, N.H. G7 72-3
Fackler, Ala. B8 146-7
Factory Village, N.H. C7 72-3
Fadette, Ala. M9 146-7
Fair Bluff, N.C. G10 180-1
Fair Grove, Mo. H5 120-1
Fair Haven, Mich. H7 112-3
Fair Haven, N.J. G8 76-7
Fair Haven, N.Y. E6 80-1
Fair Haven, Vt. J3 90-1
Fair Hill, Md. B13 172-3
Fair Lawn, N.J. A10 76-7
Fair Oaks, Ark. D10 150-1
Fair Oaks, Calif. A10 210-1
Fair Oaks, Ga. B10 160-1
Fair Oaks, Ind. C5 100-1
Fair Oaks*, Okla. D14 234-5
Fair Plain, Mich. J11 112-3
Fair Play, Mo. G4 120-1
Fair Play, S.C. C5 184-5
Fair Port, Va. H14 196-7
Fairacres, N. Mex. L5 230-1
Fairbank, Ariz. L10 206-7
Fairbank, Ia. D11 104-5
Fairbank, Md. F12 172-3
Fairbanks, Alaska D11 254-5
Fairbanks, Ind. J4 100-1
Fairbanks, La. B5 168-9
Fairbanks, Me. J3 64-5
Fairborn, O. H15 132-3
Fairburn, Ga. D10 160-1
Fairburn, S. Dak. G3 136-7
Fairbury, Ill. E9 96-7
Fairbury, Nebr. J13 124-5
Fairchance, Pa. K3 84-5
Fairchild*, Wash. E15 246-7
Fairchild, Wis. F10 140-1
Fairdale, Ky. B2 164-5
Fairdale, N. Dak. C12 128-9
Fairdale, Ore. C5 238-9
Fairdale*, Pa. J2 84-5
Fairfax, Ala. H10 146-7
Fairfax, Calif. B7 210-1
Fairfax, Del. A4 153
Fairfax, Ia. F12 104-5
Fairfax, Man. J10 272-3
Fairfax, Minn. N4 116-7
Fairfax, Mo. A1 120-1
Fairfax, O. K14 132-3
Fairfax, Okla. C12 234-5
Fairfax, S.C. H9 184-5
Fairfax, S. Dak. I11 136-7
Fairfax, Vt. D5 90-1
Fairfax, Va. A3 196-7
Fairfax, co., Va. F12 196-7
Fairfield, Ala. E6 146-7
Fairfield, Calif. B8 210-1
Fairfield, Conn. I5 60-1
Fairfield, Ida. M5 218-9
Fairfield, Ill. L10 96-7
Fairfield, Ia. I12 104-5
Fairfield, Ky. C3 164-5
Fairfield, Me. K5 64-5
Fairfield, Miss. C9 176-7
Fairfield, Mont. D6 222-3
Fairfield, Nebr. I11 124-5
Fairfield*, N.J. M2 76-7
Fairfield*, N.J. C7 76-7
Fairfield, N.C. E15 180-1
Fairfield, O. K13 132-3
Fairfield, Tenn. J8 188-9
Fairfield, Tenn. I5 188-9
Fairfield, Tex. E9 192-3
Fairfield, Ut. G6 242-3
Fairfield, Vt. C5 90-1
Fairfield, Va. H9 196-7
Fairfield, Wash. F16 246-7
Fairfield, co., Conn. H5 60-1
Fairfield, co., O. G7 132-3
Fairfield, co., S.C. C9 184-5
Fairforest, S.C. F4 184-5
Fairground, Ont. E13 284-5
Fairgrove, Mich. H14 112-3
Fairhaven, Md. K7 172-3
Fairhaven, Mass. I12 68-9
Fairhaven, Minn. L5 116-7
Fairhaven, N.B. J4 275
Fairhope, Ala. N3 146-7
Fairhope-Arnold City*, Pa. J3 84-5
Fairisle*, N.B. F6 275
Fairland, Ind. I9 100-1
Fairland, Okla. C15 234-5
Fairlawn*, O. C9 132-3
Fairlawn, Va. I7 196-7
Fairlee, Md. D12 172-3
Fairlee, Vt. H8 90-1
Fairlight, Sask. N11 294-5
Fairmeade*, Ky. G9 164-5
Fairmont*, Ill. J6 96-7
Fairmont, Minn. O5 116-7
Fairmont, Nebr. I12 124-5
Fairmont, N.C. G10 180-1
Fairmont, Okla. D10 234-5
Fairmont, S.C. F4 184-5
Fairmont, Wash. G3 246-7
Fairmont, W. Va. D6 200-1
Fairmont City, Ill. K6 96-7
Fairmount, Del. J6 153
Fairmount, Ga. E3 160-1
Fairmount, Ill. G11 96-7
Fairmount, Ind. F9 100-1
Fairmount, Md. I14 172-3
Fairmount*, N.Y. E6 80-1
Fairmount, N. Dak. J15 128-9
Fairmount, Tenn. K11 188-9
Fairmount Heights, Md. J5 172-3
Fairplains, N.C. G1 180-1
Fairplay, Colo. E10 214-5
Fairplay, Md. B7 172-3
Fairport, Kans. F7 108-9
Fairport, N.Y. E5 80-1
Fairport Harbor, O. A10 132-3
Fairton, N.J. M2 76-7
Fairvale*, N.B. I5 275
Fairview, Ala. C6 146-7
Fairview, Alta. F4 264-5
Fairview, Ark. A6 150-1
Fairview, Ida. O10 218-9
Fairview, Ill. F6 96-7
Fairview, Kans. C14 108-9
Fairview*, Ky. E11 164-5
Fairview, Md. B7 172-3
Fairview, Mich. F13 112-3
Fairview, Mo. I3 120-1
Fairview, Mont. C16 222-3
Fairview, N.J. C12 76-7
Fairview, N.Y. H11 80-1
Fairview, Okla. D9 234-5
Fairview, Ore. B7 238-9
Fairview, Ore. H4 238-9
Fairview, Pa. C1 84-5
Fairview, S. Dak. H16 136-7
Fairview, Tenn. H6 188-9
Fairview, Ut. H7 242-3
Fairview*, Wash. H11 246-7
Fairview, W. Va. A14 200-1
Fairview, Wyo. G5 250-1
Fairview-Ferndale*, Pa. G11 84-5
Fairview Heights*, Ill. K6 96-7
Fairview Park, Ind. I4 100-1
Fairview Park, O. B13 132-3
Fairview Subdivision*, Alta. N8 264-5
Fairwater, Wis. G2 140-1
Fairway, Kans. F16 108-9
Fairy Glen, Sask. J8 294-5
Faison, N.C. F12 180-1
Faith, N.C. I2 180-1
Faith, S. Dak. C5 136-7
Falcon, Ark. J4 150-1
Falcon, Colo. F12 214-5
Falcon, Miss. C6 176-7
Falcon, N.C. K7 180-1
Falcon Heights*, Minn. M6 116-7
Falcon Heights*, Ore. J8 238-9
Falcon Lake*, Man. J16 272-3
Falconer, N.Y. G2 80-1
Falfurrias, Tex. J8 192-3
Falher, Alta. G5 264-5
Falkland*, B.C. I8 268-9
Falkland, N.C. D13 180-1
Falkner, Miss. A9 176-7
Falkville, Ala. C6 146-7
Fall Branch, Tenn. G15 188-9
Fall City, Wash. F8 246-7
Fall Creek, Ore. F6 238-9
Fall Creek, Wis. F9 140-1
Fall River, Kans. I13 108-9
Fall River, Mass. H11 68-9
Fall River*, N.S. E7 281
Fall River, Wis. H2 140-1
Fall River, co., S. Dak. H2 136-7
Fall River Mills, Calif. E4 210-1
Fall Rock, Ky. I13 164-5
Fallbrook, Calif. I10 210-1
Falling Springs, W. Va. I6 200-1
Falling Waters, W. Va. D12 200-1
Fallis, Okla. E11 234-5
Fallon, Mont. E15 222-3
Fallon, Nev. F3 226-7
Fallon, co., Mont. F16 222-3
Fallon Station*, Nev. F3 226-7
Falls, co., Tex. F9 192-3
Falls Church, Va. A4 196-7
Falls City, Ida. N6 218-9
Falls City, Nebr. J16 124-5
Falls City, Ore. D5 238-9
Falls Creek, Pa. F5 84-5
Falls Mill, W. Va. F12 200-1
Falls Mills, Va. I5 196-7
Falls View-Charlton Heights, W. Va. I15 200-1
Falls Village, Conn. B5 60-1
Fallsburg, Ky. G15 164-5
Fallston, Md. B12 172-3
Fallston, N.C. E6 180-1
Falmouth, Ind. H10 100-1
Falmouth, Ky. E12 164-5
Falmouth, Me. O9 64-5
Falmouth, Mass. H13 68-9
Falmouth, Mich. G12 112-3
Falmouth*, N.S. D6 281
Falmouth, Va. C3 196-7
Falmouth Foreside, Me. O9 64-5
False Pass, Alaska I7 254-5
Falun, Kans. G10 108-9
Falun, Wis. D7 140-1
Fame, Okla. F14 234-5
Fancy Farm, Ky. J2 164-5
Fannin, Miss. I6 176-7
Fannin, co., Ga. C4 160-1
Fannin, co., Tex. C9 192-3
Fannystelle, Man. J13 272-3
Fanrock, W. Va. J3 200-1
Fanshawe, Okla. G15 234-5
Fanwood, N.J. E6 76-7
Far Hills, N.J. E5 76-7
Faraday, Ore. C7 238-9
Farber, Mo. D8 120-1
Fargo, Ark. E9 150-1
Fargo, Mich. G7 112-3
Fargo, N. Dak. G14 128-9
Fargo, Okla. D7 234-5
Faribault, Minn. N6 116-7
Faribault, co., Minn. O5 116-7
Farina, Ill. K9 96-7
Farisita, Colo. I11 214-5
Farley, Ia. E14 104-5
Farley, Mass. B5 68-9
Farley, Mo. I14 120-1
Farley, N. Mex. C10 230-1
Farlington, Kans. I16 108-9
Farmer, N.C. I4 180-1
Farmer, S. Dak. G14 136-7
Farmer, Wash. E12 246-7
Farmer City, Ill. G9 96-7
Farmers, Ky. G13 164-5
Farmers Branch, Tex. C14 192-3
Farmersburg, Ind. J4 100-1
Farmersburg, Ia. C13 104-5
Farmersville, Ala. J6 146-7
Farmersville, Calif. K6 210-1
Farmersville, Mass. H14 68-9
Farmersville, O. I14 132-3
Farmersville, Tex. B16 192-3
Farmerville, La. A4 168-9
Farmingdale, Me. L4 64-5
Farmingdale, N.J. H7 76-7
Farmingdale, N.Y. E16 80-1
Farmington, Ark. B2 150-1
Farmington, Conn. D8 60-1
Farmington, Del. H3 153
Farmington, Ga. G6 160-1
Farmington, Ill. F6 96-7
Farmington, Ia. J12 104-5
Farmington, Ky. K3 164-5
Farmington, Me. J3 64-5
Farmington*, Mich. J5 112-3
Farmington, Minn. C11 116-7
Farmington, Mo. G10 120-1
Farmington, Mont. C6 222-3
Farmington, N.H. L8 72-3
Farmington, N. Mex. C3 230-1
Farmington, N.C. H2 180-1
Farmington, Tenn. J7 188-9
Farmington, Ut. E6 242-3
Farmington, Wash. G16 246-7
Farmington, W. Va. B14 200-1
Farmington Falls, Me. J4 64-5
Farmington Hills, Mich. J5 112-3
Farmland, Ind. G11 100-1
Farmville, N.C. E13 180-1
Farmville, Va. I11 196-7
Farnam, Nebr. I8 124-5
Farner, Tenn. K13 188-9
Farnham, N.Y. F2 80-1
Farnham, Que. J13 290-1
Farnham, Ut. H8 242-3
Farnham, Va. H14 196-7
Farnhamville, Ia. E6 104-5
Farnums, Mass. C2 68-9
Farnumsville, Mass. E9 68-9
Faro, Y.T. C2 297
Farragut, Ia. J3 104-5
Farragut, Tenn. I11 188-9
Farrah, Wyo. B16 250-1
Farrar, Ga. G5 160-1
Farrell, Miss. C5 176-7
Farrell, Pa. F1 84-5
Farris, Okla. H14 234-5
Farson, Wyo. H7 250-1
Farthing, Wyo. I15 250-1
Farwell, Mich. H13 112-3
Farwell, Minn. K3 116-7
Farwell, Nebr. G10 124-5
Farwell, Tex. C4 192-3
Fassett*, Que. I10 290-1
Fatima, Que. I7 290-1
Faulk, co., S. Dak. C11 136-7
Faulkner, Md. G10 172-3
Faulkner, co., Ark. E7 150-1
Faulkton, S. Dak. C11 136-7
Faunsdale, Ala. I4 146-7
Fauquier, B.C. J9 268-9
Fauquier, Ont. F7 284-5
Fauquier, co., Va. E11 196-7
Faust, Alta. G6 264-5
Faust, Ut. G5 242-3
Fawcett, Alta. H7 264-5
Faxon, Okla. H9 234-5
Faxon, Pa. F10 84-5
Faxon, Tenn. B5 188-9
Fay, Okla. E8 234-5
Fayette, Ala. E3 146-7
Fayette, Ia. C12 104-5
Fayette, Me. K4 64-5
Fayette, Miss. K4 176-7
Fayette, Mo. D6 120-1
Fayette, O. B4 132-3
Fayette, Ut. I6 242-3
Fayette, co., Ala. E4 146-7
Fayette, co., Ga. G3 160-1
Fayette, co., Ill. J9 96-7
Fayette, co., Ind. H11 100-1
Fayette, co., Ia. C12 104-5
Fayette, co., Ky. G11 164-5
Fayette, co., O. G6 132-3
Fayette, co., Pa. K3 84-5
Fayette, co., Tenn. D2 188-9
Fayette, co., Tex. G9 192-3
Fayette, co., W. Va. I4 200-1
Fayette City, Pa. J3 84-5
Fayetteville, Ala. G7 146-7
Fayetteville, Ark. B2 150-1
Fayetteville, Ga. G4 160-1
Fayetteville, N.Y. E7 80-1
Fayetteville, N.C. F10 180-1
Fayetteville, O. K16 132-3
Fayetteville, Ore. J1 238-9
Fayetteville, Pa. J9 84-5
Fayetteville, Tenn. D8 188-9
Fayetteville, W. Va. H4 200-1
Fayston*, Vt. F5 90-1
Faywood, N. Mex. K3 230-1
Featherston, Okla. F14 234-5
Featherville, Ida. L5 218-9
Federal, Wyo. J15 250-1
Federal Dam, Minn. H5 116-7
Federal Heights*, Colo. G3 214-5
Federal Way, Wash. J2 246-7
Federalsburg, Md. F14 172-3
Fedora, S. Dak. F13 136-7
Felch, Mich. D9 112-3
Felchville, Vt. K7 90-1
Felicity, O. I4 132-3
Fellows, Calif. M6 210-1
Fellowsville, W. Va. C16 200-1
Fellsburg, Kans. I7 108-9
Fellsburg*, Pa. I3 84-5
Fellsmere, Fla. G13 156-7
Felps, La. F8 168-9
Felsenthal, Ark. K7 150-1
Felt, Ida. L11 218-9
Felt, Okla. C1 234-5
Felton, Ark. F10 150-1
Felton, Calif. J3 210-1
Felton, Del. G3 153
Felton, Minn. H2 116-7
Fence, Wis. D14 140-1
Fence Lake, N. Mex. G2 230-1
Fender, Ark. B10 150-1
Fenelon, Nev. C10 226-7
Fenelon Falls, Ont. A16 284-5
Fenn, Ida. G3 218-9
Fennimore, Wis. J11 140-1
Fennville, Mich. J11 112-3
Fenton, Ia. B6 104-5
Fenton, La. H3 168-9
Fenton, Mich. H4 112-3
Fenton, Mo. C15 120-1
Fentress, co., Tenn. A11 188-9
Fenwick, Conn. H11 60-1
Fenwick, Mich. I12 112-3
Fenwick, W. Va. H5 200-1
Fenwick Island, Del. K7 153
Fenwood, Sask. M9 294-5
Fenwood, Wis. F11 140-1
Ferdig, Mont. B6 222-3
Ferdinand, Ida. G3 218-9
Ferdinand, Ind. N6 100-1
Ferdinand*, Vt. C10 90-1
Fergus, Mont. D10 222-3
Fergus, Ont. C13 284-5
Fergus, co., Mont. D10 222-3
Fergus Falls, Minn. J2 116-7
Ferguson, Ia. F9 104-5
Ferguson, Ky. J11 164-5
Ferguson, Mo. B16 120-1
Ferguson, N.C. C6 180-1
Ferguson, W. Va. J10 200-1
Ferintosh, Alta. J8 264-5
Ferland, Ont. E4 284-5
Ferland, Sask. O6 294-5
Ferme-Neuve, Que. I2 290-1
Fermont*, Que. G6 290-1
Fern Creek, Ky. B2 164-5
Fern Crest Village, Fla. G16 156-7
Fern Park, Fla. E12 156-7
Fernan Lake, Ida. D3 218-9
Fernandina Beach, Fla. B11 156-7
Fernbank, Ala. E3 146-7
Ferncliff, Va. G11 196-7
Ferndale, Ark. I14 150-1
Ferndale, Calif. E1 210-1
Ferndale*, Md. D11 172-3
Ferndale, Mich. J6 112-3
Ferndale, Pa. I5 84-5
Ferndale, Wash. C7 246-7
Ferney, S. Dak. C13 136-7
Fernie, B.C. J11 268-9
Fernley, Nev. F3 226-7
Fernwood, Ida. E3 218-9
Fernwood, Miss. L5 176-7
Fernwood, N.Y. D7 80-1
Ferrelview, Mo. H15 120-1
Ferriday, La. D6 168-9
Ferrier Acres*, Alta. K6 264-5
Ferris, Tex. D15 192-3
Ferris, Wyo. H11 250-1
Ferrisburg, Vt. F4 90-1
Ferron, Ut. I7 242-3
Ferrum, Va. J8 196-7
Ferry, co., Wash. D14 246-7
Ferry Lake, La. A1 168-9
Ferryland, Nfld. O11 278-9
Ferrysburg, Mich. I11 112-3
Ferryville, Wis. I9 140-1
Fertile, Ia. B8 104-5
Fertile, Minn. G2 116-7
Fessenden, N. Dak. E9 128-9
Festina, Ia. B12 104-5
Festus, Mo. F10 120-1
Fidelity*, Mo. H3 120-1
Field, Ont. H8 284-5
Fieldale, Va. J8 196-7
Fielding, Ut. C6 242-3
Fields, La. G2 168-9
Fields, Ore. J13 238-9
Fieldsboro, Del. D3 153
Fieldsboro, N.J. H5 76-7
Fierro, N. Mex. K3 230-1
Fife, Va. H11 196-7
Fife, Wash. J2 246-7
Fife Lake, Mich. G12 112-3
Fife Lake, Sask. O7 294-5
Fifield, Wis. C11 140-1
Fifth Ward, La. F5 168-9
Fifty Lakes, Minn. I5 116-7
Fiftysix, Ark. B7 150-1
Figure Five, Ark. C2 150-1
Filbert, S.C. A9 184-5
Filbert, W. Va. J3 200-1
Filer, Ida. O6 218-9
Filer City, Mich. G11 112-3
Filion, Mich. H15 112-3
Filley, Nebr. I14 124-5
Fillmore, Calif. F7 210-1
Fillmore, Ind. I6 100-1
Fillmore, La. B2 168-9

Fillmore, Mo. B2 120-1
Fillmore, N.Y. F3 80-1
Fillmore, N. Dak. D9 128-9
Fillmore, Okla. H13 234-5
Fillmore, Sask. N9 294-5
Fillmore, Ut. I5 242-3
Fillmore, co., Minn. O8 116-7
Fillmore, co., Nebr. I12 124-5
Fincastle, Tenn. G12 188-9
Fincastle, Va. I8 196-7
Finch, Ont. H16 284-5
Finchville, Ky. B4 164-5
Finderne, N.J. F5 76-7
Findlater, Sask. M7 294-5
Findlay, Ill. I9 96-7
Findlay, O. C5 132-3
Finesville, N.J. E3 76-7
Fingal, N. Dak. H13 128-9
Fingal, Ont. E12 284-5
Finger, Tenn. D4 188-9
Fingerville, S.C. E4 184-5
Finksburg, Md. C10 172-3
Finland, Minn. G9 116-7
Finland, S.C. G10 184-5
Finlayson, Minn. J7 116-7
Finley, Ky. I10 164-5
Finley, N. Dak. F12 128-9
Finley, Okla. H14 234-5
Finley, Tenn. B2 188-9
Finley, Wash. I13 246-7
Finleyson, Ga. K6 160-1
Finly, Ind. H9 100-1
Finn, Mont. E5 222-3
Finn Rock, Ore. F7 238-9
Finney, co., Kans. H4 108-9
Finnville, Mass. J6 68-9
Fir Mountain, Sask. O6 294-5
Fircrest, Wash. J2 246-7
Fire Lake*, Alaska F11 254-5
Firebaugh, Calif. J5 210-1
Firebrick, Ky. E14 164-5
Firesteel, S. Dak. B6 136-7
Firestone, Colo. F3 214-5
Firth, Ida. M9 218-9
Firth, Nebr. I14 124-5
Firthcliffe*, N.Y. I10 80-1
Fish Creek, Wis. E16 140-1
Fish Haven, Ida. O11 218-9
Fisher, Ark. D10 150-1
Fisher, Ill. G10 96-7
Fisher, La. E2 168-9
Fisher, Minn. G1 116-7
Fisher, Ore. E4 238-9
Fisher, Wash. J7 246-7
Fisher, W. Va. E9 200-1
Fisher, co., Tex. D6 192-3
Fisher Bay, Man. G14 272-3
Fisher Branch, Man. G14 272-3
Fisher-Eldora*, Pa. I2 84-5
Fishers Hill, Va. E11 196-7
Fishers Station, Ind. D3 100-1
Fishersville, Va. G10 196-7
Fisherville, Ky. B3 164-5
Fisherville, Mass. E9 68-9
Fisherville, Tenn. K2 188-9
Fishing Creek, Md. H12 172-3
Fishkill, N.Y. I11 80-1
Fishtail, Mont. H9 222-3
Fishville, La. E4 168-9
Fisk, Mo. I10 120-1
Fiskdale*, Mass. E7 68-9
Fiske, Sask. L5 294-5
Fiskeville, R.I. D4 87
Fitchburg, Mass. B8 68-9
Fitchville, Conn. E13 60-1
Fitler, Miss. H4 176-7
Fittstown, Okla. H12 234-5
Fitzgerald, Ga. L6 160-1
Fitzhugh, Ark. D9 150-1
Fitzhugh, Okla. G12 234-5
Fitzpatrick, Ala. I8 146-7
Fitzroy Harbour, Ont. H14 284-5
Fitzwilliam, N.H. O4 72-3
Fitzwilliam Depot, N.H. O4 72-3
Five Forks, W. Va. F4 200-1
Five Islands, Me. N11 64-5
Five Points, Ala. G10 146-7
Five Points, Del. I6 153
Five Points*, Fla. B10 156-7
Five Points, N. Mex. F5 230-1
Five Points, Tenn. D6 188-9
Flag Pond, Tenn. H16 188-9
Flagler, Colo. E15 214-5
Flagler, co., Fla. D11 156-7
Flagler Beach, Fla. D12 156-7
Flagstaff, Ariz. E7 206-7
Flagtown, N.J. F5 76-7
Flaherty, Ky. H8 164-5
Flaming Gorge Res., Wyo. J7 250-1
Flanagan, Ill. E9 96-7
Flanders, Conn. D4 60-1
Flanders, N.J. D5 76-7
Flanders, N.Y. J13 80-1
Flandreau, S. Dak. F16 136-7
Flanigan, Nev. E2 226-7
Flasher, N. Dak. I6 128-9
Flat, Alaska E9 254-5
Flat Creek, Tenn. J8 188-9
Flat Creek [-Wegra-Praco], Ala. E5 146-7
Flat Lick, Ky. J13 164-5
Flat River, Mo. F15 120-1
Flat River, P.E.I. G8 287
Flat Rock, Ala. B9 146-7
Flat Rock, Ind. J9 100-1
Flat Rock, Mich. K5 112-3
Flat Rock, N.C. C7 180-1
Flat Rock, N.C. E4 180-1
Flat Top*, W. Va. J4 200-1
Flat Woods, Tenn. C5 188-9
Flathead, co., Mont. B3 222-3
Flathead Lake, Mont. C3 222-3
Flatlands, N.B. D4 275
Flatonia*, Tex. G8 192-3
Flats, Nebr. F5 124-5
Flatwillow, Mont. E11 222-3
Flatwood, Ala. J4 146-7
Flatwood, Ala. I7 146-7
Flatwoods, Ky. F15 164-5
Flatwoods, La. E3 168-9
Flatwoods, W. Va. F5 200-1
Flaxcombe, Sask. L4 294-5
Flaxton, N. Dak. B4 128-9
Flaxville, Mont. A15 222-3
Fleetwood, Okla. I10 234-5
Fleetwood, Pa. H14 84-5
Fleming, Colo. B15 214-5
Fleming, Ky. I15 164-5
Fleming*, Mo. D4 120-1
Fleming, Sask. N11 294-5
Fleming, co., Ky. F13 164-5
Fleming Park*, Alta. J7 264-5
Flemings Corner, Del. H3 153
Flemings Landing, Del. D4 153
Flemingsburg, Ky. F13 164-5
Flemington, Ga. L10 160-1
Flemington, Mo. G5 120-1
Flemington, N.J. F4 76-7
Flemington, Pa. F9 84-5
Flemington, W. Va. C14 200-1
Flensburg, Minn. K4 116-7
Flesherton, Ont. B13 284-5
Fletcher, Nev. I3 226-7
Fletcher, N.C. E4 180-1
Fletcher, O. F4 132-3
Fletcher, Okla. G9 234-5
Fletcher, Vt. D5 90-1
Fletcher Park, Wyo. H14 250-1
Fleur de Lys, Nfld. L9 278-9
Flin Flon, Man. F1 272-3
Flin Flon, Sask. H10 294-5
Flint, Mich. I14 112-3
Flint, Okla. D16 234-5
Flint City, Ala. B6 146-7
Flint Hill, N.C. G2 180-1
Flint Hill, Va. B1 196-7
Flintstone, Md. B4 172-3
Flintville, Tenn. D8 188-9
Flippen, Ga. D11 160-1
Flippin, Ark. A6 150-1
Flippin, Ky. K8 164-5
Flippin, Tenn. I2 188-9
Floe, W. Va. G4 200-1
Flomaton, Ala. M5 146-7
Floodwood, Minn. H7 116-7
Flora, Ill. K9 96-7
Flora, Ind. E7 100-1
Flora, La. D3 168-9
Flora, Miss. H6 176-7
Flora, Ore. B15 238-9
Flora Vista, N. Mex. C3 230-1
Florahome, Fla. C11 156-7
Floral, Ark. C8 150-1
Floral City, Fla. E10 156-7
Floral Park*, Mont. G5 222-3
Floral Park, N.Y. E15 80-1
Florala, Ala. M7 146-7
Flordell Hills*, Mo. E10 120-1
Florence, Ala. B4 146-7
Florence, Ariz. J7 206-7
Florence, Ark. I8 150-1
Florence, Colo. G11 214-5
Florence, Ind. L12 100-1
Florence, Kans. H11 108-9
Florence, Ky. E11 164-5
Florence, Md. F3 172-3
Florence, Minn. N2 116-7
Florence, Miss. I6 176-7
Florence, Mont. F3 222-3
Florence*, N.J. I4 76-7
Florence, N.J. O12 76-7
Florence*, N.S. B11 281
Florence, Ore. F4 238-9
Florence, S.C. D13 184-5
Florence, S. Dak. C14 136-7
Florence*, Tex. F8 192-3
Florence, Vt. I4 90-1
Florence, Wis. C14 140-1
Florence, co., S.C. D13 184-5
Florence, co., Wis. C14 140-1
Florence-Graham*, Calif. G8 210-1
Florence Juntion, Ariz. I7 206-7
Florence [-Roebling], N.J. H4 76-7
Florenceville*, N.B. G3 275
Floresville, Tex. K3 192-3
Florham Park, N.J. D6 76-7
Florida, Mass. B3 68-9
Florida, N. Mex. H5 230-1
Florida, N.Y. I10 80-1
Florida, O. C4 132-3
Florida City, Fla. J15 156-7
Florida Keys, Fla. K12 156-7
Florida Ridge*, Fla. G13 156-7
Florien, La. E2 168-9
Florin*, Calif. H4 210-1
Floris, Ia. J11 104-5
Floris, Okla. C5 234-5
Florissant, Colo. K2 214-5
Florissant, Mo. B15 120-1
Flossmoor, Ill. O4 96-7
Flournoy, La. B1 168-9
Flourtown*, Pa. J15 84-5
Flovilla, Ga. H5 160-1
Flowell, Ut. I5 242-3
Flower, W. Va. F5 200-1
Flower Hill*, N.Y. J11 80-1
Flower Mound*, Tex. D9 192-3
Flower Station, Del. J3 153
Floweree, Mont. D7 222-3
Flowery Branch, Ga. E5 160-1
Flowood*, Miss. I6 176-7
Floyd, Ark. E7 150-1
Floyd, Ia. B10 104-5
Floyd, La. B7 168-9
Floyd, N. Mex. H11 230-1
Floyd, Va. J7 196-7
Floyd, co., Ga. E2 160-1
Floyd, co., Ind. N9 100-1
Floyd, co., Ia. C9 104-5
Floyd, co., Ky. H15 164-5
Floyd, co., Tex. C5 192-3
Floyd, co., Va. J7 196-7
Floyd Dale, S.C. D14 184-5
Floydada, Tex. C5 192-3
Floyds Knobs, Ind. N9 100-1
Fluker, La. F8 168-9
Flushing, Mich. G3 112-3
Flushing, O. F10 132-3
Fluvanna, co., Va. H11 196-7
Flying H, N. Mex. J8 230-1
Flynns Lick, Tenn. B9 188-9
Foam Lake, Sask. L9 294-5
Foard, co., Tex. C6 192-3
Fob, Okla. I12 234-5
Fogo, Nfld. L10 278-9
Fola, W. Va. H16 200-1
Folcroft*, Pa. K15 84-5
Foley, Ala. O4 146-7
Foley, Minn. K5 116-7
Foley, Mo. A14 120-1
Foleyet, Ont. F6 284-5
Folkston, Ga. N9 160-1
Follansbee, W. Va. B5 200-1
Folly Beach, S.C. I13 184-5
Folsom, Calif. A10 210-1
Folsom, Ky. E11 164-5
Folsom, La. G9 168-9
Folsom, N.J. L4 76-7
Folsom, N. Mex. B10 230-1
Folsom, W. Va. B13 200-1
Folsomdale, Ky. J3 164-5
Folsomville, Ind. N5 100-1
Fond du Lac, Sask. B6 294-5
Fond du Lac, Wis. H14 140-1
Fond du Lac, co., Wis. H14 140-1
Fonda, Ia. D5 104-5
Fonda, N.Y. E10 80-1
Fondale, La. C5 168-9
Foneswood, Va. G13 196-7
Fontaine, Ark. B10 150-1
Fontana, Calif. G10 210-1
Fontana, Kans. G16 108-9
Fontana Dam, N.C. E1 180-1
Fontana on Geneva Lake, Wis. K3 140-1
Fontanelle, Ia. H5 104-5
Fontanet, Ind. I5 100-1
Fontenelle, Wyo. H6 250-1
Footville, Wis. K1 140-1
Forada, Minn. K3 116-7
Foraker, Ind. B9 100-1
Foraker, Okla. C12 234-5
Forbes, N. Dak. J11 128-9
Forbing, La. B2 168-9
Forbing Park, Ariz. F5 206-7
Forbus, Tenn. F9 188-9
Ford, Kans. I5 108-9
Ford, Va. I12 196-7
Ford, Wash. E15 246-7
Ford, co., Ill. F10 96-7
Ford, co., Kans. I5 108-9
Ford City, Calif. L6 210-1
Ford City, Pa. G3 84-5
Fordland, Mo. I6 120-1
Fordoche, La. G6 168-9
Fords Corner, Del. F3 153
Fords Prairie, Wash. G7 246-7
Fordsville, Ky. H7 164-5
Fordville, N. Dak. D12 128-9
Fordwich*, Ont. C12 284-5
Fordyce, Ark. I6 150-1
Fordyce, Nebr. D13 124-5
Foreman, Ark. I2 150-1
Foremost, Alta. O10 264-5
Forest, Del. D3 153
Forest, Ind. F7 100-1
Forest, La. A7 168-9
Forest, Miss. I8 176-7
Forest, O. D5 132-3
Forest, Ont. E11 284-5
Forest, Va. I9 196-7
Forest, co., Pa. E4 84-5
Forest, co., Wis. D13 140-1
Forest Acres, S.C. E10 184-5
Forest City, Ia. B8 104-5
Forest City, Me. G9 64-5
Forest City, Mo. B2 120-1
Forest City, N.C. E5 180-1
Forest City, Pa. D14 84-5
Forest Dale, Vt. H4 90-1
Forest Grove, B.C. H8 268-9
Forest Grove, Mont. E10 222-3
Forest Grove, Ore. B5 238-9
Forest Heights, Md. J4 172-3
Forest Hill, La. F4 168-9
Forest Hill, Md. B12 172-3
Forest Hill, Miss. I6 176-7
Forest Hill, Tenn. K2 188-9
Forest Hill, Tex. D13 192-3
Forest Hill, W. Va. J5 200-1
Forest Hills*, Fla. F9 156-7
Forest Hills*, Ky. G9 164-5
Forest Hills*, Pa. I2 84-5
Forest Hills, Tenn. H6 188-9
Forest Home, Ala. J6 146-7
Forest Homes, Ill. J6 96-7
Forest Junction, Wis. F4 140-1
Forest Lake, Minn. L7 116-7
Forest Lake, S.C. E10 184-5
Forest Park, Ga. D11 160-1
Forest Park*, Ill. B11 96-7
Forest Park*, O. H3 132-3
Forest Park, Okla. J2 234-5
Forest River, N. Dak. D13 128-9
Forest Station, Me. G9 64-5
Forest View*, Ill. C11 96-7
Forestburg, Alta. K9 264-5
Forestburg, S. Dak. F13 136-7
Forestdale*, Ala. E6 146-7
Forestdale, Mass. H14 68-9
Forestdale, R.I. A4 87
Foreston, Minn. K6 116-7
Foreston, S.C. F13 184-5
Forestville, Md. J5 172-3
Forestville, Mich. H15 112-3
Forestville, N.Y. F2 80-1
Forestville, Que. B14 290-1
Forestville, Wis. D6 140-1
Forgan, Okla. C5 234-5
Forge Village, Mass. B10 68-9
Forget, Sask. O10 294-5
Fork, Md. C12 172-3
Fork, N.C. H2 180-1
Fork, S.C. D15 184-5
Fork Mountain, Tenn. H10 188-9
Fork Ridge, Tenn. F12 188-9
Fork River, Man. G11 272-3
Fork Shoals, S.C. H2 184-5
Fork Union, Va. H11 196-7
Forked Island, La. I4 168-9
Forked River, N.J. J7 76-7
Forkland, Ala. H3 146-7
Forks, Wash. E5 246-7
Forks of Elkhorn, Ky. A5 164-5
Forks, The, Me. H4 64-5
Forksville, Va. J11 196-7
Forkville, Miss. H7 176-7
Forman, N. Dak. J13 128-9
Formosa, Ark. D6 150-1
Formosa, Ont. B12 284-5
Formoso, Kans. D9 108-9
Forney, Tex. D16 192-3
Forrest, Ill. E10 96-7
Forrest, Man. I11 272-3
Forrest, N. Mex. G11 230-1
Forrest, co., Miss. L8 176-7
Forrest City, Ark. E10 150-1
Forreston, Ill. B7 96-7
Forsyth, Ga. H5 160-1
Forsyth, Ill. H8 96-7
Forsyth, Mo. J5 120-1
Forsyth, Mont. F13 222-3
Forsyth, co., Ga. E4 160-1
Forsyth, co., N.C. C8 180-1
Fort Adams, Miss. L2 176-7
Fort Ann, N.Y. D11 80-1
Fort Apache, Ariz. H10 206-7
Fort Ashby, W. Va. D10 200-1
Fort Assiniboine, Alta. H7 264-5
Fort Atkinson, Ia. B12 104-5
Fort Atkinson, Wis. J3 140-1
Fort Augustus*, P.E.I. E8 287
Fort Belvoir, Va. B4 196-7
Fort Bend, co., Tex. H10 192-3
Fort Benning, Ga. J3 160-1
Fort Benton, Mont. C8 222-3
Fort Blackmore, Va. J3 196-7
Fort Bliss, Tex. E1 192-3
Fort Bragg, Calif. G1 210-1
Fort Bragg*, N.C. F10 180-1
Fort Branch, Ind. N4 100-1
Fort Bridger, Wyo. J6 250-1
Fort Calhoun, Nebr. I2 124-5
Fort Campbell North*, Ky. K5 164-5
Fort Campbell South*, Tenn. A6 188-9
Fort Carson*, Colo. G12 214-5
Fort-Chimo, Que. C5 290-1
Fort Chipewyan, Alta. C9 264-5
Fort Churchill*, Man. B5 272-3
Fort Cobb, Okla. G9 234-5
Fort Collins, Colo. C11 214-5
Fort Collins West*, Colo. D3 214-5
Fort-Coulonge, Que. J1 290-1
Fort-Coulonge-Nord-Est*, Que. J1 290-1
Fort Covington, N.Y. A10 80-1
Fort Davis, Ala. I9 146-7
Fort Davis, Tex. F3 192-3
Fort Defiance, Ariz. D11 206-7
Fort Deposit, Ala. J7 146-7
Fort Devens, Mass. C9 68-9
Fort Dix, N.J. I5 76-7
Fort Dodge, Ia. D6 104-5
Fort Douglas, Ark. C5 150-1
Fort Duchesne, Ut. G9 242-3
Fort Edward, N.Y. E11 80-1
Fort Erie, Ont. E15 284-5
Fort Fairfield, Me. C9 64-5
Fort Frances, Ont. F2 284-5
Fort Fraser, B.C. F6 268-9
Fort Fred Steele, Wyo. I11 250-1
Fort Gaines, Ga. L2 160-1
Fort Garland, Colo. I11 214-5
Fort Gay, W. Va. J9 200-1
Fort Gibson, Okla. E15 234-5
Fort Good Hope, N.W. Terr. B1 296
Fort Gordon, Ga. H9 160-1
Fort Grant, Ariz. J10 206-7
Fort Greely, Alaska E12 254-5
Fort Hall, Ida. M9 218-9
Fort Harrison, Mont. F6 222-3
Fort Hood, Tex. F8 192-3
Fort Howard, Md. G8 172-3
Fort Huachuca*, Ariz. L10 206-7
Fort Hunt*, Va. F13 196-7

Fort Irwin, Calif. L9 210-1
Fort Jennings, O. D4 132-3
Fort Jesup, La. D2 168-9
Fort Johnson*, N.Y. . . . E10 80-1
Fort Jones, Calif. D2 210-1
Fort Kent, Alta. H10 264-5
Fort Kent, Me. A7 64-5
Fort Kent Mills, Me. . . . A7 64-5
Fort Klamath, Ore. I7 238-9
Fort Knox*, Ky. G8 164-5
Fort Langley, B.C. C14 268-9
Fort Laramie, Wyo. H16 250-1
Fort Lauderdale, Fla. . . . I13 156-7
Fort Lawn, S.C. B10 184-5
Fort Lawrence, N.S. C6 281
Fort Leavenworth*, Kans. E15 108-9
Fort Lee, N.J. B12 76-7
Fort Lee, Va. F1 196-7
Fort Leonard Wood*, Mo. G7 120-1
Fort Lewis, Wash. F7 246-7
Fort Liard, N.W. Terr. . . C1 296
Fort Logan, Mont. E7 222-3
Fort Loramie, O. E3 132-3
Fort Lupton, Colo. F4 214-5
Fort Lyon, Colo. H15 214-5
Fort MacKay, Alta. E9 264-5
Fort Macleod, Alta. N8 264-5
Fort Madison, Ia. J13 104-5
Fort McClellan, Ala. E8 146-7
Fort McDowell, Ariz. . . . H7 206-7
Fort McKinley*, O. G3 132-3
Fort McMurray, Alta. . . . E9 264-5
Fort McPherson, N.W. Terr. B1 296
Fort Meade, Fla. I5 156-7
Fort Meade, Md. H5 172-3
Fort Mill, S.C. A10 184-5
Fort Mitchell, Ky. D11 164-5
Fort Mitchell, Va. J10 196-7
Fort Morgan, Ala. O3 146-7
Fort Morgan, Colo. C13 214-5
Fort Motte, S.C. F11 184-5
Fort Myers, Fla. H11 156-7
Fort Myers Beach, Fla. . . I11 156-7
Fort Myers Shores, Fla. . H11 156-7
Fort Myers Southeast*, Fla. H11 156-7
Fort Myers Southwest*, Fla. H11 156-7
Fort Myers Villas (-Pine Manor), Fla. I11 156-7
Fort Necessity, La. C6 168-9
Fort Nelson, B.C. C7 268-9
Fort Oglethorpe, Ga. . . . C2 160-1
Fort Payne, Ala. C9 146-7
Fort Peck, Mont. C13 222-3
Fort Peck Lake, Mont. . . C13 222-3
Fort Pierce, Fla. G13 156-7
Fort Pierce Northwest*, Fla. G13 156-7
Fort Pierre, S. Dak. E8 136-7
Fort Pillow, Tenn. J2 188-9
Fort Plain, N.Y. F9 80-1
Fort Qu'Appelle, Sask. . . M9 294-5
Fort Randall Dam, S. Dak. I12 136-7
Fort Ransom, N. Dak. . . H12 128-9
Fort Recovery, O. E3 132-3
Fort Reno, Okla. F10 234-5
Fort Richardson*, Alaska F11 254-5
Fort Riley-Camp Whiteside*, Kans. . . . E12 108-9
Fort Ripley, Minn. J5 116-7
Fort Ritchie, Md. A8 172-3
Fort Ritner, Ind. L8 100-1
Fort Robinson, Nebr. . . . D2 124-5
Fort Rock, Ore. H9 238-9
Fort Rucker, Ala. L9 146-7
Fort Sam Houston, Tex. . J2 192-3
Fort Saskatchewan, Alta. . I8 264-5
Fort Scott, Kans. I16 108-9
Fort Seybert, W. Va. . . . G9 200-1
Fort Shaw, Mont. D6 222-3
Fort Shawnee*, O. D4 132-3
Fort Sill, Okla. G9 234-5
Fort Simpson, N.W. Terr. C1 296
Fort Smith, Ark. D2 150-1
Fort Smith, N.W. Terr. . C2 296
Fort Spring, W. Va. I6 200-1
Fort St. James, B.C. F6 268-9
Fort St. John, B.C. E8 268-9
Fort Stanton, N. Mex. . . I7 230-1
Fort Stewart, Ga. K10 160-1
Fort Stockton, Tex. F4 192-3
Fort Sumner, N. Mex. . . G10 230-1
Fort Supply, Okla. C7 234-5
Fort Thomas, Ariz. J10 206-7
Fort Thomas, Ky. D11 164-5
Fort Thompson, S. Dak. . F10 136-7
Fort Totten, N. Dak. . . . E10 128-9
Fort Towson, Okla. I15 234-5
Fort Valley, Ga. J5 160-1
Fort Vermilion, Alta. . . . C6 264-5
Fort Wainwright, Alaska . D12 254-5
Fort Walton Beach, Fla. . B4 156-7
Fort Washakie, Wyo. . . . F8 250-1
Fort Wayne, Ind. C11 100-1
Fort White, Fla. C9 156-7
Fort Wingate, N. Mex. . . E2 230-1
Fort Worth, Tex. D8 192-3
Fort Wright-Lookout Heights*, Ky. D11 164-5
Fort Yates, N. Dak. J7 128-9
Fort Yukon, Alaska C12 254-5
Forteau, Nfld. J8 278-9
Fortescue, Mo. B1 120-1
Fortierville, Que. G10 290-1
Fortine, Mont. A2 222-3
Fortsonia, Ga. F7 160-1
Fortuna, Calif. E1 210-1
Fortuna, N. Dak. B2 128-9
Fortuna Ledge, Alaska . . E8 254-5
Fortune, Nfld. O9 278-9
Fortune Branch, Ore. . . . I5 238-9
Fortville, Ind. H9 100-1
Forty Fort, Pa. E13 84-5
Forum, Ark. B3 150-1
Foss, Okla. F8 234-5
Fossil, Ore. D10 238-9
Fosston, Minn. G3 116-7
Fosston, Sask. K9 294-5
Foster, Ky. E12 164-5
Foster, Mo. F3 120-1
Foster, Nebr. E12 124-5
Foster, Okla. H11 234-5
Foster, Ore. J2 238-9
Foster*, R.I. C2 87
Foster, W. Va. J13 200-1
Foster, Wis. F9 140-1
Foster, co., N. Dak. F10 128-9
Foster Center, R.I. C2 87
Foster City*, Calif. I3 210-1
Foster City, Mich. D9 112-3
Foster Village, Hawaii . . J5 258-9
Fosters, Ala. G4 146-7
Fosters Corner, Me. N8 64-5
Fostoria, Ala. J6 146-7
Fostoria, Ia. B4 104-5
Fostoria, Kans. E12 108-9
Fostoria, Mich. F5 112-3
Fostoria, O. C6 132-3
Fouke, Ark. J3 150-1
Foules, La. D6 168-9
Fountain, Ala. K4 146-7
Fountain, Colo. G12 214-5
Fountain, Ind. F5 100-1
Fountain, Mich. G11 112-3
Fountain, Minn. O8 116-7
Fountain, N.C. D13 180-1
Fountain, co., Ind. G5 100-1
Fountain City, Ind. G12 100-1
Fountain City, Tenn. . . . H12 188-9
Fountain City, Wis. G8 140-1
Fountain Green, Ut. H6 242-3
Fountain Head*, Md. . . . A7 172-3
Fountain Hill, Ark. J8 150-1
Fountain Hill, Pa. H15 84-5
Fountain Inn, S.C. G3 184-5
Fountain Lake, Ark. K12 150-1
Fountain Run, Ky. K8 164-5
Fountain Valley, Calif. . . H9 210-1
Fountaintown, Ind. H9 100-1
Four Buttes, Mont. A14 222-3
Four Corners, Mont. . . . B6 222-3
Four Corners, Ore. H1 238-9
Four Corners, Wyo. C16 250-1
Four Forks, La. C1 168-9
Four Holes, S.C. G12 184-5
Four Lakes, Wash. F15 246-7
Four Oaks, N.C. J8 180-1
Four Roads, N.B. E7 275
Four States, W. Va. B13 200-1
Fourche, Ark. H14 150-1
Fourmile, Ky. J13 164-5
Fowblesburg, Md. B10 172-3
Fowler, Calif. K6 210-1
Fowler, Colo. H13 214-5
Fowler, Ind. E5 100-1
Fowler, Kans. J5 108-9
Fowler, La. B5 168-9
Fowler, Mich. I13 112-3
Fowler Beach, Del. H5 153
Fowlerton, Ind. F10 100-1
Fowlerville, Mich. I2 112-3
Fowlkes, Tenn. B2 188-9
Fowltown, Ga. O3 160-1
Fox, Ark. C7 150-1
Fox, Okla. H11 234-5
Fox, Ore. E12 238-9
Fox Chapel*, Pa. H2 84-5
Fox Creek, Alta. H5 264-5
Fox Creek, Ida. L11 218-9
Fox Farm*, Wyo. J15 250-1
Fox Island, Wash. J1 246-7
Fox Lake, Ill. J2 96-7
Fox Lake, Wis. H2 140-1
Fox Lake Hills*, Ill. A10 96-7
Fox Point, Wis. I5 140-1
Fox River*, Ill. B10 96-7
Fox River Grove, Ill. . . . K2 96-7
Fox Valley, Ore. I2 238-9
Fox Valley, Sask. N4 294-5
Foxboro, Ont. J12 284-5
Foxborough, Mass. E11 68-9
Foxholm, N. Dak. C6 128-9
Foxhome, Minn. J2 116-7
Foxpark, Wyo. J13 250-1
Foxvale, Mass. F11 68-9
Foxville, Vt. G7 90-1
Foxwarren, Man. H9 272-3
Foxwells, Va. D4 196-7
Foxworth, Miss. L7 176-7
Foyil, Okla. C14 234-5
Frackville, Pa. G12 84-5
Framingham, Mass. D10 68-9
Frampton*, Que. J4 290-1
Frances, Ky. I4 164-5
Frances, Wash. H6 246-7
Francestown, N.H. N5 72-3
Francesville, Ind. D6 100-1
Francis, Okla. G12 234-5
Francis, Sask. N9 294-5
Francis, Ut. F7 242-3
Francis Creek, Wis. F5 140-1
Francis Peninsula*, B.C. . J6 268-9
Francisco, Ind. N4 100-1
Francoeur*, Que. G11 290-1
Franconia, N.H. G5 72-3
Franconia, Va. B4 196-7
Frank, Alta. O7 264-5
Frank, N.C. C5 180-1
Frankenmuth, Mich. E4 112-3
Frankewing, Tenn. K7 188-9
Frankford, Del. K5 153
Frankford, Mo. C8 120-1
Frankford*, N.J. B5 76-7
Frankford, Ont. K12 284-5
Frankfort, Ala. B3 146-7
Frankfort, Ill. O3 96-7
Frankfort, Ind. F7 100-1
Frankfort, Kans. D12 108-9
Frankfort, Ky. G11 164-5
Frankfort, Me. J7 64-5
Frankfort, Mich. F11 112-3
Frankfort, N.Y. E9 80-1
Frankfort, O. H6 132-3
Frankfort, S. Dak. D12 136-7
Franklin, Ala. K5 146-7
Franklin, Ariz. J11 206-7
Franklin, Ark. B8 150-1
Franklin, Conn. E13 60-1
Franklin, Ga. H2 160-1
Franklin, Ida. O10 218-9
Franklin, Ind. I8 100-1
Franklin, Ia. J13 104-5
Franklin, Ky. K7 164-5
Franklin, La. I6 168-9
Franklin, Me. J8 64-5
Franklin, Man. I11 272-3
Franklin, Mass. E10 68-9
Franklin, Mich. I5 112-3
Franklin, Minn. G7 116-7
Franklin, Minn. N4 116-7
Franklin, Mo. D6 120-1
Franklin, Mont. F9 222-3
Franklin, Nebr. J10 124-5
Franklin, N.H. K6 72-3
Franklin*, N.J. E3 76-7
Franklin*, N.J. F3 76-7
Franklin*, N.J. F5 76-7
Franklin*, N.J. K3 76-7
Franklin, N.J. B5 76-7
Franklin, N.Y. G8 80-1
Franklin, N.C. E2 180-1
Franklin, O. I14 132-3
Franklin, Okla. K3 234-5
Franklin, Pa. E2 84-5
Franklin, Tenn. B7 188-9
Franklin, Tex. F9 192-3
Franklin, Vt. B5 90-1
Franklin, Va. H2 196-7
Franklin, W. Va. G8 200-1
Franklin, Wis. J5 140-1
Franklin, co., Ala. B3 146-7
Franklin, co., Ark. C3 150-1
Franklin, co., Fla. C6 156-7
Franklin, co., Ga. E6 160-1
Franklin, co., Ida. O10 218-9
Franklin, co., Ill. M9 96-7
Franklin, co., Ind. I12 100-1
Franklin, co., Ia. D8 104-5
Franklin, co., Kans. G15 108-9
Franklin, co., Ky. F11 164-5
Franklin, co., La. C6 168-9
Franklin, co., Me. I3 64-5
Franklin, co., Mass. B4 68-9
Franklin, co., Miss. K4 176-7
Franklin, co., Mo. F9 120-1
Franklin, co., Nebr. J10 124-5
Franklin, co., N.Y. B10 80-1
Franklin, co., N.C. D11 180-1
Franklin, co., O. G6 132-3
Franklin, co., Pa. J8 84-5
Franklin, co., Tenn. D8 188-9
Franklin, co., Tex. D10 192-3
Franklin, co., Vt. C5 90-1
Franklin, co., Va. J8 196-7
Franklin, co., Wash. H14 246-7
Franklin Grove, Ill. B8 96-7
Franklin Lakes, N.J. C7 76-7
Franklin Mts., N.W. Terr. C1 296
Franklin Park, Ill. M3 96-7
Franklin Park, N.J. F6 76-7
Franklin Park*, Pa. H2 84-5
Franklin River, B.C. J5 268-9
Franklin Springs, Ga. . . . E6 160-1
Franklin Square, N.Y. . . E15 80-1
Franklinton, La. F9 168-9
Franklinton, N.C. H8 180-1
Franklinville, N.J. L3 76-7
Franklinville, N.Y. G3 80-1
Franklinville, N.C. I4 180-1
Frankston, Tex. E10 192-3
Franksville, Wis. K5 140-1
Frankton, Ind. F9 100-1
Franktown, Colo. I4 214-5
Frankville, Ala. K3 146-7
Frannie, Wyo. B9 250-1
Franquelin, Que. A16 290-1
Fraser, Colo. D10 214-5
Fraser, Ia. F7 104-5
Fraser, Mich. I6 112-3
Fraser, Minn. G7 116-7
Fraser Lake, B.C. F6 268-9
Fraserdale*, Ont. F6 284-5
Fraserwood, Man. H14 272-3
Fraterville, Tenn. G11 188-9
Frazee, Minn. I3 116-7
Frazer, Mont. C14 222-3
Frazeysburg, O. F8 132-3
Frazier Park, Calif. M6 210-1
Fraziers Bottom, W. Va. . G2 200-1
Fraziers Well, Ariz. D4 206-7
Freda, Mich. C8 112-3
Frederic, Mich. F13 112-3
Frederic, Wis. D7 140-1
Frederica, Del. G4 153
Frederick, Colo. F3 214-5
Frederick, Kans. G9 108-9
Frederick, Md. C8 172-3
Frederick, Okla. H8 234-5
Frederick, S. Dak. A12 136-7
Frederick, co., Md. C9 172-3
Frederick, co., Va. E11 196-7
Frederick Corner, Mass. . B10 68-9
Fredericks Hall, Va. G12 196-7
Fredericksburg, Ind. M8 100-1
Fredericksburg, Ia C11 104-5
Fredericksburg, O. D9 132-3
Fredericksburg, Pa. D2 84-5
Fredericksburg, Tex. . . . G7 192-3
Fredericksburg, Va. G12 196-7
Fredericktown, Ky. D3 164-5
Fredericktown, Mo. H10 120-1
Fredericktown, O. E7 132-3
Fredericktown, Pa. J2 84-5
Fredericton, N.B. H4 275
Fredericton Junction, N.B. I4 275
Frederika, Ia. C11 104-5
Fredon, N.J. C4 76-7
Fredonia, Ariz. B5 206-7
Fredonia, Ark. F9 150-1
Fredonia, Ia. H13 104-5
Fredonia, Kans. J14 108-9
Fredonia, Ky. I4 164-5
Fredonia, N.Y. G1 80-1
Fredonia, N. Dak. I10 128-9
Fredonia, Wis. H5 140-1
Fredrickson Trailer Court*, Alta. J7 264-5
Free Soil, Mich. G11 112-3
Free Trade, Miss. H8 176-7
Free Union, Va. G10 196-7
Freeborn, Minn. O6 116-7
Freeborn, co., Minn. . . . O6 116-7
Freeburg, Ill. L6 96-7
Freeburg, Mo. F7 120-1
Freeburn, Ky. H16 164-5
Freedom, Calif. J3 210-1
Freedom, Ind. J6 100-1
Freedom, Me. K6 64-5
Freedom, N.H. I8 72-3
Freedom, Okla. C8 234-5
Freedom*, Pa. H1 84-5
Freedom, Ut. H6 242-3
Freedom, Wis. E4 140-1
Freedom, Wyo. F5 250-1
Freehold*, N.J. H7 76-7
Freehold, N.J. H7 76-7
Freeland, Md. B11 172-3
Freeland, Mich. H13 112-3
Freeland, N.C. H11 180-1
Freeland, Pa. F13 84-5
Freeland, P.E.I. C4 287
Freeland, Wash. G2 246-7
Freeland, Wyo. G12 250-1
Freelandville, Ind. L5 100-1
Freeman, Ariz. J6 206-7
Freeman, Mo. E3 120-1
Freeman, S. Dak. H14 136-7
Freeman, Va. J12 196-7
Freeman, Wash. F16 246-7
Freemansburg*, Pa. H15 84-5
Freemanville, Ala. M4 146-7
Freemont, Ky. J3 164-5
Freemont, Mich. H11 112-3
Freeny, Miss. H8 176-7
Freeport, Fla. B4 156-7
Freeport, Ill. A7 96-7
Freeport, Kans. K9 108-9
Freeport, Me. N10 64-5
Freeport, Mich. I12 112-3
Freeport, Minn. K4 116-7
Freeport, N.Y. F16 80-1
Freeport, O. F10 132-3
Freeport, Pa. H3 84-5
Freeport, Tex. K14 192-3
Freer, Tex. I7 192-3
Freestone, co., Tex. E9 192-3
Freetown, Ind. K8 100-1
Freetown, Mass. G11 68-9
Freetown, N.Y. J14 80-1
Freetown*, P.E.I. E6 287
Freeville, N.Y. F7 80-1
Freewood Acres, N.J. . . . H7 76-7
Freistatt, Mo. I4 120-1
Frelinghuysen*, N.J. . . . C4 76-7
Fremont, Calif. D8 210-1
Fremont, Ind. A11 100-1
Fremont, Ia. I10 104-5
Fremont, Mo. I9 120-1
Fremont, Nebr. G14 124-5
Fremont, N.H. N8 72-3
Fremont, N.C. E12 180-1
Fremont, O. C6 132-3
Fremont, Ut. K6 242-3
Fremont, Wis. E2 140-1
Fremont, co., Colo. G11 214-5
Fremont, co., Ida. K10 218-9
Fremont, co., Ia. J3 104-5
Fremont, co., Wyo. F7 250-1
French Camp, Miss. F8 176-7
French Creek, W. Va. . . . F14 200-1
French Lick, Ind. M7 100-1
French Settlement, La. . . B11 168-9
Frenchboro, Me. L8 64-5
Frenchburg, Ky. G13 164-5
Frenchglen, Ore. I13 238-9
Frenchman, Nev. G4 226-7
Frenchman Bay, Me. . . . K8 64-5
Frenchman Butte, Sask. . I4 294-5
Frenchmans Bayou, Ark. D12 150-1
Frenchton, W. Va. F13 200-1
Frenchtown, Mont. E3 222-3
Frenchtown, N.J. F3 76-7
Frenchville, Me. A8 64-5
Frenier, La. C13 168-9
Freshwater, Colo. K1 214-5

Freshwater*, Nfld. O10 278-9
Fresno, Ark. H8 150-1
Fresno, Calif. J5 210-1
Fresno, Mont. B8 222-3
Fresno, co., Calif. J6 210-1
Frewen, Wyo. I10 250-1
Frewsburg, N.Y. G2 80-1
Friars Point, Miss. C5 176-7
Friday Harbor, Wash. C7 246-7
Fridley, Minn. A10 116-7
Friedensfeld*, Man. K3 272-3
Friedensruh, Man. K13 272-3
Friend, Nebr. I13 124-5
Friend, Ore. C9 238-9
Friendly, W. Va. D4 200-1
Friendship, Ark. G5 150-1
Friendship, Ind. K11 100-1
Friendship, La. C3 168-9
Friendship, Me. M5 64-5
Friendship, Md. K7 172-3
Friendship, Miss. C9 176-7
Friendship, N.Y. G3 80-1
Friendship, Okla. G8 234-5
Friendship, Tenn. B3 188-9
Friendship, Wis. H12 140-1
Friendsville, Md. B1 172-3
Friendsville, Tenn. I14 188-9
Friendswood, Ind. G1 100-1
Friendswood, Tex. I14 192-3
Frierson, La. C2 168-9
Fries, Va. J5 196-7
Fries Mill, N.J. K3 76-7
Friesland, Wis. H2 140-1
Frio, co., Tex. H7 192-3
Friona, Tex. B4 192-3
Frisco, Colo. E10 214-5
Frisco, N.C. E16 180-1
Frisco, Tex. B14 192-3
Frisco City, Ala. L5 146-7
Fritch, Tex. A5 192-3
Fritz Creek*, Alaska G11 254-5
Frobisher, Sask. O10 294-5
Frobisher Bay, N.W. Terr. C4 296
Frogmore, La. D6 168-9
Frogmore, S.C. J11 184-5
Frogville, Okla. I15 234-5
Frohna, Mo. G11 120-1
Froid, Mont. B15 222-3
Fromberg, Mont. H10 222-3
Front Royal, Va. E11 196-7
Frontenac, Kans. J16 108-9
Frontenac*, Mo. E10 120-1
Frontenac, co., Ont. J13 284-5
Frontenac, co., Que. I16 290-1
Frontier, Mich. K13 112-3
Frontier, Sask. O5 294-5
Frontier, Wyo. I5 250-1
Frontier, co., Nebr. I7 124-5
Frost, La. A11 168-9
Frost, Minn. O5 116-7
Frost, W. Va. H7 200-1
Frost Bridge, Miss. K10 176-7
Frostburg, Md. B3 172-3
Frostproof, Fla. I6 156-7
Fruit Heights*, Ut. E6 242-3
Fruita, Colo. F5 214-5
Fruitdale, Ala. L2 146-7
Fruitdale, Ore. J5 238-9
Fruitdale, S. Dak. D2 136-7
Fruithurst, Ala. E9 146-7
Fruitland, Ida. K2 218-9
Fruitland, Ia. H13 104-5
Fruitland, Md. H14 172-3
Fruitland, N. Mex. C3 230-1
Fruitland, Tenn. B3 188-9
Fruitland, Ut. G8 242-3
Fruitland, Wash. D14 246-7
Fruitland Park, Fla. E11 156-7
Fruitland Park, Miss. M8 176-7
Fruitport, Mich. I11 112-3
Fruitvale, B.C. K9 268-9
Fruitvale, Colo. F6 214-5
Fruitvale, Ida. J3 218-9
Fruitvale, Tenn. J4 188-9
Fruitvale, Wash. H11 246-7
Fruitville, Fla. K3 156-7
Frye, Me. J2 64-5
Fryeburg, La. B3 168-9
Fryeburg, Me. L1 64-5
Fulda, Ind. O6 100-1
Fulda, Minn. O3 116-7
Fulgham, Ky. K1 164-5
Fulks Run, Va. F10 196-7
Fuller Springs*, Tex. F11 192-3
Fullerton, Calif. G9 210-1
Fullerton, Ky. E14 164-5
Fullerton, Nebr. G12 124-5
Fullerton, N. Dak. I11 128-9
Fullerton, Pa. H14 84-5
Fulton, Ala. K4 146-7
Fulton, Ark. I3 150-1
Fulton, Ill. B6 96-7
Fulton, Ind. D8 100-1
Fulton, Kans. H16 108-9
Fulton, Ky. K2 164-5
Fulton, Md. G4 172-3
Fulton, Miss. C10 176-7
Fulton, Mo. E7 120-1
Fulton, N.Y. E6 80-1
Fulton, O. E7 132-3
Fulton, Ore. B13 238-9
Fulton, S. Dak. G13 136-7
Fulton, Tenn. J1 188-9
Fulton, Tex. I9 192-3
Fulton, Wis. J2 140-1
Fulton, co., Ark. A8 150-1
Fulton, co., Ga. G3 160-1
Fulton, co., Ill. F6 96-7
Fulton, co., Ind. D7 100-1
Fulton, co., Ky. K2 164-5
Fulton, co., N.Y. E10 80-1
Fulton, co., O. B4 132-3
Fulton, co., Pa. K7 84-5
Fultondale, Ala. E6 146-7
Fultonville, N.Y. E10 80-1
Fultz, Ky. F14 164-5
Funk, Nebr. I9 124-5
Funkley, Minn. G5 116-7
Funkstown, Md. B7 172-3
Funston, Ga. M5 160-1
Funston, La. C1 168-9
Fuquay-Varina, N.C. I7 180-1
Furdale*, Sask. K6 294-5
Furlow, Ark. F7 150-1
Furman, Ala. J6 146-7
Furman, S.C. I10 184-5
Furnace Village, Mass. F11 68-9
Furnas, co., Nebr. J8 124-5
Fyffe, Ala. C8 146-7

G

Gaastra, Mich. D8 112-3
Gabaldon, N. Mex. E8 230-1
Gabbs, Nev. G5 226-7
Gable, S.C. E12 184-5
Gabriola, B.C. C12 268-9
Gackle, N. Dak. H10 128-9
Gadsden, Ala. D8 146-7
Gadsden, Ariz. K1 206-7
Gadsden, S.C. E11 184-5
Gadsden, Tenn. I4 188-9
Gadsden, co., Fla. B7 156-7
Gaffney, S.C. A8 184-5
Gage, N. Mex. L3 230-1
Gage, Okla. D7 234-5
Gage, co., Nebr. I14 124-5
Gages Lake [-Wildwood], Ill. J3 96-7
Gagetown, Mich. H14 112-3
Gagetown, N.B. I5 275
Gagnon, Que. G5 290-1
Gahanna, O. F7 132-3
Gail, Tex. D5 192-3
Gaines, Mich. H3 112-3
Gaines, W. Va. F13 200-1
Gaines, co., Tex. D4 192-3
Gainesboro, Tenn. A9 188-9
Gainesboro, Va. D11 196-7
Gainesville, Ala. G3 146-7
Gainesville, Fla. C10 156-7
Gainesville, Ga. E5 160-1
Gainesville, Miss. O7 176-7
Gainesville, Mo. J6 120-1
Gainesville, Tex. D9 192-3
Gainesville, Va. A2 196-7
Gainesville Cotton Mills, Ga. E5 160-1
Gainsborough, Sask. O11 294-5
Gaither, Md. F4 172-3
Gaithersburg, Md. G3 172-3
Gaitherville, Tenn. K5 188-9
Gakona, Alaska E12 254-5
Galahad, Alta. K9 264-5
Galata, Mont. B7 222-3
Galatia, Ill. M9 96-7
Galatia, Kans. G7 108-9
Galax, Va. J6 196-7
Galbraith, La. E3 168-9
Galchutt, N. Dak. I14 128-9
Galen, Mont. F5 222-3
Galena, Alaska D10 254-5
Galena, Ida. L6 218-9
Galena, Ill. A5 96-7
Galena, Ind. N9 100-1
Galena, Kans. K16 108-9
Galena, Md. C13 172-3
Galena, Mo. I5 120-1
Galena, O. F7 132-3
Galena, Ore. D13 238-9
Galena Park, Tex. H14 192-3
Gales Ferry, Conn. G13 60-1
Galesburg, Ill. E6 96-7
Galesburg, Kans. J15 108-9
Galesburg*, Mich. J12 112-3
Galesburg, N. Dak. F13 128-9
Galestown, Md. G14 172-3
Galesville, Md. J7 172-3
Galesville, Wis. H9 140-1
Galeton, Colo. D4 214-5
Galeton, Pa. D8 84-5
Galiano Island*, B.C. K6 268-9
Galice, Ore. I4 238-9
Galien, Mich. K11 112-3
Galilee, R.I. I4 87
Galion, La. A6 168-9
Galion, O. D7 132-3
Galisteo, N. Mex. E7 230-1
Galivants Ferry, S.C. D15 184-5
Gallant, Ala. D7 146-7
Gallatin, Mo. B4 120-1
Gallatin, Tenn. A8 188-9
Gallatin, co., Ill. M10 96-7
Gallatin, co., Ky. E10 164-5
Gallatin, co., Mont. H7 222-3
Gallatin Gateway, Mont. H7 222-3
Gallaway, Tenn. K2 188-9
Gallia, co., O. J8 132-3
Galliano, La. J9 168-9
Gallina, N. Mex. D5 230-1
Gallion, Ala. H4 146-7
Gallipolis, O. J8 132-3
Gallipolis Ferry, W. Va. F2 200-1
Gallitzin, Pa. H6 84-5
Gallman, Miss. J5 176-7
Galloway, B.C. J11 268-9
Galloway*, N.J. M6 76-7
Galloway, W. Va. D14 200-1
Galloway, Wis. D1 140-1
Gallup, N. Mex. E2 230-1
Gallup City, Mont. C6 222-3
Gallup Mills, Vt. D10 90-1
Galt, Calif. B9 210-1
Galt, Ia. D8 104-5
Galt, Mo. B5 120-1
Galt, Nev. K10 226-7
Galva, Ill. D6 96-7
Galva, Ia. D3 104-5
Galva, Kans. G10 108-9
Galva, La. B13 168-9
Galveston, Ind. E8 100-1
Galveston, Tex. J16 192-3
Galveston, co., Tex. H10 192-3
Galveston Isl., Tex. J15 192-3
Galvin, Wash. G7 246-7
Gamaliel, Ark. A7 150-1
Gamaliel, Ky. K8 164-5
Gambell, Alaska D6 254-5
Gambier, O. E8 132-3
Gambo, Nfld. M10 278-9
Gambrills, Md. H6 172-3
Gamerco, N. Mex. E2 230-1
Ganado, Ariz. D10 206-7
Ganado, Tex. H9 192-3
Gananoque, Ont. J14 284-5
Gandeeville, W. Va. F4 200-1
Gander, Nfld. M10 278-9
Gandy, Nebr. G7 124-5
Gandy, Ut. H2 242-3
Ganer, Ala. M8 146-7
Gang Mills*, N.Y. G5 80-1
Ganges, B.C. D12 268-9
Gannett, Ida. M6 218-9
Gannon Road*, N.S. B11 281
Gannvalley, S. Dak. F11 136-7
Gans, Okla. F16 234-5
Gantt, Ala. L7 146-7
Gantt*, S.C. B6 184-5
Gantts Quarry, Ala. G7 146-7
Gap, Okla. H14 234-5
Gap, Pa. J13 84-5
Gap Mills, W. Va. J6 200-1
Gap, The, Ariz. C7 206-7
Gapland, Md. C7 172-3
Garber, Ia. D13 104-5
Garber, Okla. D10 234-5
Garberville, Calif. F2 210-1
Garcia, Colo. J11 214-5
Gardar, N. Dak. C12 128-9
Garden, Mich. E11 112-3
Garden, co., Nebr. F4 124-5
Garden Acres*, Calif. I4 210-1
Garden Bay, B.C. A11 268-9
Garden City, Ala. D6 146-7
Garden City, Colo. E4 214-5
Garden City, Ga. K11 160-1
Garden City, Ida. L3 218-9
Garden City, Kans. H3 108-9
Garden City, Mich. J5 112-3
Garden City, Miss. L3 176-7
Garden City, Mo. E3 120-1
Garden City, N.Y. E16 80-1
Garden City, S. Dak. D14 136-7
Garden City, Tex. E5 192-3
Garden City, Ut. C7 242-3
Garden City Park*, N.Y. J11 80-1
Garden Grove, Calif. H9 210-1
Garden Grove, Ia. J8 104-5
Garden Plain, Kans. I10 108-9
Garden River*, Alta. C7 264-5
Garden Valley, Ida. K4 218-9
Garden View, Pa. F10 84-5
Gardena*, Calif. N7 210-1
Gardena, Ida. L3 218-9
Gardena, N. Dak. C8 128-9
Gardendale, Ala. E6 146-7
Gardenton, Man. K15 272-3
Gardi, Ga. L10 160-1
Gardiner, Me. L4 64-5
Gardiner, Mont. I7 222-3
Gardiner, Ore. G4 238-9
Gardiner, Wash. F1 246-7
Gardner, Ark. G5 150-1
Gardner, Colo. H11 214-5
Gardner, Ill. D10 96-7
Gardner, Kans. F16 108-9
Gardner, La. E4 168-9
Gardner, Mass. B7 68-9
Gardner, N. Dak. G14 128-9
Gardner City, La. I6 168-9
Gardnertown*, N.Y. I10 80-1
Gardnerville [-Minden], Nev. G2 226-7
Garfield, Ark. A3 150-1
Garfield, Colo. G9 214-5
Garfield, Ga. J9 160-1
Garfield, Ida. L10 218-9
Garfield, Kans. H7 108-9
Garfield, Ky. H7 164-5
Garfield, Me. D8 64-5
Garfield, Minn. K3 116-7
Garfield, N.J. B11 76-7
Garfield, N. Mex. K4 230-1
Garfield, Wash. G16 246-7
Garfield, co., Colo. E6 214-5
Garfield, co., Mont. D12 222-3
Garfield, co., Nebr. F10 124-5
Garfield, co., Okla. D10 234-5
Garfield, co., Ut. L7 242-3
Garfield, co., Wash. H15 246-7
Garfield Heights, O. B15 132-3
Garibaldi, Ore. B4 238-9
Garibaldi Estates Subdivision*, B.C. H5 268-9
Garibaldi Highlands Subdivision*, B.C. H5 268-9
Garita, N. Mex. F9 230-1
Garland, Ala. K6 146-7
Garland, Ark. J3 150-1
Garland, Kans. I16 108-9
Garland, Me. I6 64-5
Garland*, Man. I2 272-3
Garland, Mont. G14 222-3
Garland, Nebr. H13 124-5
Garland, N.C. F11 180-1
Garland, Okla. F15 234-5
Garland, Tenn. J2 188-9
Garland, Tex. C15 192-3
Garland, Ut. C5 242-3
Garland, Wyo. B9 250-1
Garland, co., Ark. F5 150-1
Garnavillo, Ia. C13 104-5
Garneill, Mont. E9 222-3
Garner, Ark. E8 150-1
Garner, Ia. C8 104-5
Garner, Ky. I15 164-5
Garner, N.C. I7 180-1
Garnet, Mont. E4 222-3
Garnet, Nev. M10 226-7
Garnett, Kans. H15 108-9
Garnett, S.C. I9 184-5
Garnett Settlement, N.B. J5 275
Garnish, Nfld. O9 278-9
Garrard, Ky. I13 164-5
Garrard, co., Ky. H11 164-5
Garret Grove, Ark. F10 150-1
Garretson, S. Dak. G16 136-7
Garrett, Ind. B11 100-1
Garrett, Ky. G8 164-5
Garrett, Wash. I14 246-7
Garrett, Wyo. H14 250-1
Garrett, co., Md. B2 172-3
Garrett Bridge, Ark. H8 150-1
Garrett Park, Md. H3 172-3
Garretts Bend, W. Va. I12 200-1
Garrettsville, O. C16 132-3
Garrick, Sask. J8 294-5
Garrison, Ia. F11 104-5
Garrison, Ky. F14 164-5
Garrison, Md. E6 172-3
Garrison, Minn. J6 116-7
Garrison, Mont. F5 222-3
Garrison, Nebr. G13 124-5
Garrison, N. Dak. E6 128-9
Garrison, Tex. E11 192-3
Garrison, Ut. I2 242-3
Garrison, W. Va. J14 200-1
Garrison Dam, N. Dak. F6 128-9
Garrisonville, Va. C3 196-7
Garryowen, Mont. H12 222-3
Garson, Man. I15 272-3
Garvin, Minn. N3 116-7
Garvin, Okla. I16 234-5
Garvin, co., Okla. G11 234-5
Garwin, Ia. F10 104-5
Garwood, N.J. E7 76-7
Gary, Ind. A5 100-1
Gary, Minn. G2 116-7
Gary, S. Dak. D16 136-7
Gary, W. Va. J3 200-1
Garysburg*, N.C. C13 180-1
Garyville, La. C12 168-9
Garza, co., Tex. D5 192-3
Garza-Little Elm Res., Tex. B14 192-3
Gas, Kans. I15 108-9
Gas City, Ind. E10 100-1
Gas City, Okla. H10 234-5
Gasburg, Va. K12 196-7
Gasconade, Mo. E8 120-1
Gasconade, co., Mo. F8 120-1
Gascons-Ouest, Que. I6 290-1
Gascoyne, N. Dak. I3 128-9
Gaspé, Que. H6 290-1
Gaspé-Est, co., Que. H6 290-1
Gaspé-Ouest, co., Que. H6 290-1
Gaspereaux, P.E.I. F10 287
Gassaway, Tenn. B9 188-9
Gassaway, W. Va. G5 200-1
Gassetts, Vt. K6 90-1
Gassoway, La. A7 168-9
Gassville, Ark. A6 150-1
Gaston, Ind. F10 100-1
Gaston, N.C. C12 180-1
Gaston, Ore. F1 238-9
Gaston, S.C. E10 184-5
Gaston, W. Va. E13 200-1
Gaston, co., N.C. E6 180-1
Gastonburg, Ala. I4 146-7
Gastonia, N.C. J1 180-1
Gastonia North*, N.C. F6 180-1
Gate, Okla. C6 234-5
Gate, Wash. G6 246-7
Gate City, Va. J3 196-7
Gates, Nebr. F9 124-5
Gates, N.C. B14 180-1
Gates, Ore. D7 238-9
Gates, Tenn. I3 188-9
Gates, co., N.C. B14 180-1
Gates Mills*, O. B10 132-3
Gatesville, Miss. J6 176-7
Gatesville, N.C. C14 180-1
Gatesville, Tex. F8 192-3
Gateway, Ark. A3 150-1
Gateway, Colo. G5 214-5
Gateway, Ore. D9 238-9
Gatineau, Que. I9 290-1
Gatineau, co., Que. I2 290-1
Gatliff, Ky. K12 164-5
Gatlinburg, Tenn. C13 188-9
Gattman, Miss. D11 176-7
Gauley Bridge, W. Va. I16 200-1
Gauley Mills, W. Va. G5 200-1
Gault, Miss. C7 176-7
Gaultois, Nfld. N9 278-9
Gautier, Miss. N10 176-7
Gay, Ga. H3 160-1
Gay, Okla. I14 234-5
Gay, W. Va. F3 200-1

Gay Head, Mass. J13 68-9
Gaylesville, Ala. C9 146-7
Gaylord, Kans. D7 108-9
Gaylord, Mich. F13 112-3
Gaylord, Minn. N5 116-7
Gaylord, Ore. H4 238-9
Gaylordsville, Conn. E4 60-1
Gays Mills, Wis. I10 140-1
Gaysville, Vt. I6 90-1
Gayville, S. Dak. I15 136-7
Gearhart, Ore. A4 238-9
Geary, N.B. I4 275
Geary, Okla. E9 234-5
Geary, co., Kans. F12 108-9
Geauga, co., O. B10 132-3
Gebo, Wyo. D9 250-1
Geddes, S. Dak. H12 136-7
Geeville, Miss. B9 176-7
Geiger, Ala. G2 146-7
Geiger Heights*, Wash. E16 246-7
Geismar, La. B10 168-9
Geistown, Pa. I5 84-5
Gem, Ida. D4 218-9
Gem, Kans. E3 108-9
Gem, W. Va. F5 200-1
Gem, co., Ida. K3 218-9
Gem Lake*, Minn. L7 116-7
Gem Village, Colo. J7 214-5
Gene Autry, Okla. H12 234-5
Genelle, B.C. K9 268-9
General Wayne*, Pa. J15 84-5
Genesee, Ida. F2 218-9
Genesee, Mich. G4 112-3
Genesee, co., Mich. I14 112-3
Genesee, co., N.Y. E3 80-1
Geneseo, Ill. D6 96-7
Geneseo, Kans. G9 108-9
Geneseo, N.Y. F4 80-1
Geneva, Ala. M8 146-7
Geneva, Ga. J3 160-1
Geneva, Ida. O11 218-9
Geneva, Ill. B10 96-7
Geneva, Ind. E11 100-1
Geneva, Ia. D9 104-5
Geneva, Ky. H5 164-5
Geneva, Minn. O6 116-7
Geneva, Nebr. I12 124-5
Geneva, N.Y. F5 80-1
Geneva, O. A11 132-3
Geneva, Ore. E8 238-9
Geneva, co., Ala. M8 146-7
Geneva-on-the-Lake, O. A11 132-3
Genevia, Ark. J16 150-1
Genoa, Ark. J3 150-1
Genoa, Colo. E14 214-5
Genoa, Ill. B9 96-7
Genoa, Nebr. G12 124-5
Genoa, Nev. G2 226-7
Genoa, O. B6 132-3
Genoa, W. Va. I10 200-1
Genoa, Wis. I9 140-1
Genoa City, Wis. K14 140-1
Genola, Minn. K5 116-7
Genola, Ut. G6 242-3
Genou, Mont. C7 222-3
Gentian, Ga. J2 160-1
Gentry, Ark. A2 150-1
Gentry, Mo. A3 120-1
Gentry, Tenn. B9 188-9
Gentry, co., Mo. B3 120-1
Gentryville, Ind. O5 100-1
George*, Calif. N8 210-1
George, Ia. B2 104-5
George, N.C. C13 180-1
George, Wash. G12 246-7
George, co., Miss. M10 176-7
George West, Tex. I8 192-3
Georges Mills, N.H. K4 72-3
Georgetown, Ala. M2 146-7
Georgetown, Ark. B3 150-1
Georgetown, Ark. E9 150-1
Georgetown, Calif. H4 210-1
Georgetown, Colo. G1 214-5
Georgetown, Conn. H4 60-1
Georgetown, Del. I4 153
Georgetown, Ga. L2 160-1
Georgetown, Ida. O11 218-9
Georgetown, Ill. G11 96-7
Georgetown, Ind. N8 100-1
Georgetown, Ky. A7 164-5
Georgetown, La. D4 168-9
Georgetown, Me. N11 64-5
Georgetown, Md. C13 172-3
Georgetown, Mass. B12 68-9
Georgetown, Minn. H1 116-7
Georgetown, Miss. J6 176-7
Georgetown, Mont. F4 222-3
Georgetown, O. I4 132-3
Georgetown, P.E.I. F9 287
Georgetown, S.C. G15 184-5
Georgetown, Tenn. K12 188-9
Georgetown, Tex. G8 192-3
Georgetown, co., S.C. F14 184-5
Georgetown Harbour, P.E.I. F10 287
Georgia*, Vt. C4 90-1
Georgia Plains, Vt. C4 90-1
Georgian Bay, Ont. I7 284-5
Georgiana, Ala. K6 146-7
Georgiaville, R.I. B4 87
Gerald, Mo. F8 120-1
Gerald, Sask. M10 294-5
Geraldine, Ala. C8 146-7
Geraldine, Mont. D8 222-3
Geraldton, Ont. E4 284-5
Gerber, Calif. F3 210-1
Gering, Nebr. F1 124-5
Gerlach, Nev. D2 226-7
Germania, Wis. G1 140-1
Germann, Ariz. I7 206-7
Germantown, Conn. G4 60-1
Germantown, Ill. K7 96-7
Germantown, Ky. E12 164-5
Germantown, Md. G2 172-3
Germantown, O. I14 132-3
Germantown, Tenn. K1 188-9
Germantown*, Wis. J14 140-1
Germfask, Mich. D11 112-3
Geronimo, Ariz. J10 206-7
Geronimo, Okla. H9 234-5
Gerrardstown, W. Va. D11 200-1
Gerton, N.C. E4 180-1
Gerty, Okla. G13 234-5
Gervais, Ore. G1 238-9
Gethsemane, Ark. G8 150-1
Gettysburg, O. F3 132-3
Gettysburg, Pa. K10 84-5
Gettysburg, S. Dak. C9 136-7
Geuda Springs, Kans. K11 108-9
Geyser, Mont. D8 222-3
Geyserville, Calif. A6 210-1
Gheens, La. I9 168-9
Ghent, Ky. E10 164-5
Ghent, Minn. N2 116-7
Ghent, W. Va. J4 200-1
Gholson, Miss. G9 176-7
Gibbon, Minn. N4 116-7
Gibbon, Nebr. H10 124-5
Gibbon, Ore. B13 238-9
Gibbons, Alta. I8 264-5
Gibbonsville, Ida. H7 218-9
Gibbs, Mo. B6 120-1
Gibbs, Tenn. A3 188-9
Gibbs Crossing, Mass. D6 68-9
Gibbsboro, N.J. O11 76-7
Gibbstown, N.J. J2 76-7
Gibbsville, Wis. G5 140-1
Gibraltar, Mich. K6 112-3
Gibsland, La. B3 168-9
Gibson, Ga. H8 160-1
Gibson, Ia. H11 104-5
Gibson, La. I7 168-9
Gibson, Miss. D9 176-7
Gibson, Mo. J11 120-1
Gibson*, N.C. F9 180-1
Gibson, Okla. E15 234-5
Gibson, Tenn. B3 188-9
Gibson, Wyo. H15 250-1
Gibson, co., Ind. N3 100-1
Gibson, co., Tenn. B3 188-9
Gibson City, Ill. F10 96-7
Gibsonburg, O. B6 132-3
Gibsons, B.C. B12 268-9
Gibsonton, Fla. I3 156-7
Gibsonville*, N.C. D9 180-1
Giddings, Tex. G9 192-3
Gideon, Mo. J11 120-1
Gideon, Okla. D15 234-5
Gifford, Fla. G13 156-7
Gifford, Ida. F3 218-9
Gifford, Ill. G10 96-7
Gifford, Ind. C5 100-1
Gifford, S.C. H9 184-5
Gifford, Wash. D14 246-7
Gift, Tenn. J2 188-9
Gift Lake, Alta. F6 264-5
Gig Harbor, Wash. J2 246-7
Gila, N. Mex. J2 230-1
Gila, co., Ariz. H8 206-7
Gila Bend, Ariz. J5 206-7
Gila Center, Ariz. J2 206-7
Gila R., Ariz. J7 206-7
Gilark, La. B2 168-9
Gilbert*, Ariz. I7 206-7
Gilbert, Ark. B6 150-1
Gilbert, Ia. F7 104-5
Gilbert, La. C6 168-9
Gilbert, Minn. G8 116-7
Gilbert, S.C. E9 184-5
Gilbert, W. Va. J2 200-1
Gilbert Plains, Man. G10 272-3
Gilberton*, Pa. G12 84-5
Gilbertown, Ala. J2 146-7
Gilbertsville, Ky. J3 164-5
Gilbertsville, N.Y. G8 80-1
Gilbertville, Ia. E11 104-5
Gilbertville, Mass. D6 68-9
Gilboa, W. Va. H16 200-1
Gilby, N. Dak. D13 128-9
Gilchrist, Ore. G8 238-9
Gilchrist, co., Fla. C9 156-7
Gilcrest, Colo. E4 214-5
Gildford, Mont. B8 222-3
Gilead, Conn. D11 60-1
Gilead, La. G8 168-9
Gilead, Me. K1 64-5
Gilead, Nebr. J13 124-5
Giles, co., Tenn. D7 188-9
Giles, co., Va. I6 196-7
Gilford, N.H. K7 72-3
Gilford Park, N.J. I7 76-7
Gilkey, N.C. E5 180-1
Gill, Mass. B5 68-9
Gill, W. Va. J11 200-1
Gillam, Man. D5 272-3
Gillespie, Ariz. I5 206-7
Gillespie, Ill. J7 96-7
Gillespie, co., Tex. G7 192-3
Gillett, Ark. H9 150-1
Gillett, Wis. C4 140-1
Gillett Grove, Ia. C4 104-5
Gillette, N.J. E6 76-7
Gillette, Wyo. C14 250-1
Gillham, Ark. G2 150-1
Gilliam, La. A1 168-9
Gilliam, Mo. D5 120-1
Gilliam, co., Ore. C10 238-9
Gillies Bay*, B.C. H5 268-9
Gillis, La. G2 168-9
Gillisonville, S.C. I10 184-5
Gills Rock, Wis. E16 140-1
Gillsburg, Miss. M5 176-7
Gillsville, Ga. E5 160-1
Gilluly, Ut. G7 242-3
Gilman, Colo. E9 214-5
Gilman, Conn. E12 60-1
Gilman, Ill. E10 96-7
Gilman, Ia. F10 104-5
Gilman, Minn. K5 116-7
Gilman, Mont. D5 222-3
Gilman, Vt. E10 90-1
Gilman, Wis. E10 140-1
Gilman City, Mo. B4 120-1
Gilmania, S.C. I10 184-5
Gilmanton, N.H. L7 72-3
Gilmanton, Wis. G8 140-1
Gilmanton Iron Works, N.H. L7 72-3
Gilmer, Tex. D10 192-3
Gilmer, W. Va. F5 200-1
Gilmer, co., Ga. D4 160-1
Gilmer, co., W. Va. F5 200-1
Gilmore, Ark. D11 150-1
Gilmore, Ida. J8 218-9
Gilmore, Okla. F16 234-5
Gilmore City, Ia. D6 104-5
Gilpin, co., Colo. D10 214-5
Gilroy, Calif. J4 210-1
Gilsum, N.H. N3 72-3
Gilt Edge, Tenn. J1 188-9
Giltner, Nebr. H11 124-5
Gimli, Man. H14 272-3
Gin City, Ark. K3 150-1
Ginns Corner, Del. D3 153
Ginty Corner, Mass. F11 68-9
Girard, Ga. H10 160-1
Girard, Ill. I7 96-7
Girard, Kans. J16 108-9
Girard, La. B6 168-9
Girard, O. C11 132-3
Girard, Pa. C1 84-5
Girardville, Pa. G12 84-5
Girardville, Que. B9 290-1
Girdler, Ky. J13 164-5
Girdletree, Md. I15 172-3
Giroux*, Man. J15 272-3
Girouxville, Alta. G5 264-5
Girvin, Sask. M7 294-5
Gitano, Miss. J8 176-7
Given, W. Va. F3 200-1
Givhans, S.C. G12 184-5
Glace, W. Va. I6 200-1
Glace Bay, N.S. B12 281
Glacier, Wash. B8 246-7
Glacier, co., Mont. B5 222-3
Gladbrook, Ia. F10 104-5
Glade, Kans. D6 108-9
Glade, La. E5 168-9
Glade Park, Colo. F5 214-5
Glade Spring, Va. J4 196-7
Gladehill, Va. J8 196-7
Glades, co., Fla. H12 156-7
Gladesville, W. Va. B15 200-1
Gladeville, Tenn. H8 188-9
Gladewater, Tex. E10 192-3
Gladmar, Sask. O8 294-5
Gladstone, Man. I12 272-3
Gladstone, Mich. E10 112-3
Gladstone, Mo. D3 120-1
Gladstone, Nebr. J13 124-5
Gladstone, N. Mex. C10 230-1
Gladstone, N. Dak. G4 128-9
Gladstone*, Ore. C6 238-9
Gladstone, Va. H10 196-7
Gladwin, Mich. G13 112-3
Gladwin, co., Mich. G13 112-3
Glady, W. Va. F16 200-1
Gladys, Va. I9 196-7
Glancy, Miss. J5 176-7
Glandorf, O. C4 132-3
Glasco, Kans. E9 108-9
Glasco*, N.Y. G11 80-1
Glascock, co., Ga. H8 160-1
Glasford, Ill. F7 96-7
Glasgo, Conn. F14 60-1
Glasgow, Del. B2 153
Glasgow, Ky. J8 164-5
Glasgow, Mo. D6 120-1
Glasgow, Mont. C13 222-3
Glasgow, Va. H9 196-7
Glasgow, W. Va. I14 200-1
Glaslyn, Sask. J5 294-5
Glass, Man. J14 272-3
Glass Hill, S.C. E15 184-5
Glassboro, N.J. K3 76-7
Glasscock, co., Tex. E5 192-3
Glassport, Pa. B6 84-5
Glasston, N. Dak. C13 128-9
Glastenbury*, Vt. M4 90-1
Glastonbury, Conn. D10 60-1
Gleason, Tenn. B4 188-9
Gleason, Wis. E12 140-1
Gleasondale, Mass. H1 68-9
Gleeson, Ariz. L10 206-7
Gleichen, Alta. M8 264-5
Glen, Miss. A10 176-7
Glen, Mont. H5 222-3
Glen, N.H. H8 72-3
Glen, W. Va. H15 200-1
Glen Allan, Miss. G4 176-7
Glen Allen, Ala. D4 146-7
Glen Allen, Va. D1 196-7
Glen Alpine, N.C. D5 180-1
Glen Arm, Md. C11 172-3
Glen Avon, Calif. G10 210-1
Glen Burnie, Md. G6 172-3
Glen Cairn*, Ont. H10 284-5
Glen Canyon, Ut. N6 242-3
Glen Canyon Dam, Ariz. A7 206-7
Glen Carbon, Ill. K6 96-7
Glen Cove, Me. L6 64-5
Glen Cove, N.Y. D16 80-1
Glen Daniel, W. Va. K15 200-1
Glen Dean, Ky. H7 164-5
Glen Easton, W. Va. C5 200-1
Glen Echo, Md. I3 172-3
Glen Echo Park*, Mo. E10 120-1
Glen Elder, Kans. D9 108-9
Glen Ellyn, Ill. M2 96-7
Glen Ewen, Sask. O10 294-5
Glen Flora, Wis. D10 140-1
Glen Gardner, N.J. E4 76-7
Glen Haven, Colo. D2 214-5
Glen Haven, Wis. K9 140-1
Glen Jean [-Hilltop], W. Va. K16 200-1
Glen Lyn, Va. I6 196-7
Glen Lyon, Pa. F13 84-5
Glen Miller, Ont. K12 284-5
Glen Mills, Mass. A12 68-9
Glen Park, N.Y. C7 80-1
Glen Raven, N.C. H5 180-1
Glen Ridge*, Fla. D16 156-7
Glen Ridge, N.J. C10 76-7
Glen Robertson, Ont. H16 284-5
Glen Rock, N.J. A10 76-7
Glen Rock, Pa. K11 84-5
Glen Rodgers, W. Va. K14 200-1
Glen Rose, Tex. E8 192-3
Glen Ross, Ont. J12 284-5
Glen St. Mary, Fla. B10 156-7
Glen Ullin, N. Dak. H5 128-9
Glen Walter, Ont. I16 284-5
Glen Wilton, Va. H8 196-7
Glenada, Ore. F4 238-9
Glenaire, Mo. I15 120-1
Glenallen, Mo. H11 120-1
Glenalum, W. Va. J2 200-1
Glenarden, Md. I5 172-3
Glenavon, Sask. N9 294-5
Glenbain, Sask. O6 294-5
Glenbank*, B.C. J10 268-9
Glenbar, Ariz. J10 206-7
Glenbeulah, Wis. G5 140-1
Glenboro, Man. J12 272-3
Glenbrook, Nev. G1 226-7
Glenbrook, Ore. E5 238-9
Glenburn*, Me. I7 64-5
Glenburn, N. Dak. C6 128-9
Glenburn Center, Me. I7 64-5
Glencliff, N.H. H5 72-3
Glencoe, Ala. D8 146-7
Glencoe, Ark. A8 150-1
Glencoe, Ill. K4 96-7
Glencoe, Ky. E10 164-5
Glencoe, Minn. C8 116-7
Glencoe, N. Mex. I8 230-1
Glencoe, Okla. D12 234-5
Glencoe, Ont. E11 284-5
Glencross, S. Dak. B7 136-7
Glendale, Ariz. I6 206-7
Glendale, Ark. H7 150-1
Glendale*, B.C. H7 268-9
Glendale, Calif. G8 210-1
Glendale*, Colo. G3 214-5
Glendale, Ida. O10 218-9
Glendale, Ky. E1 164-5
Glendale, Mass. D1 68-9
Glendale, Mo. B15 120-1
Glendale, Nev. L10 226-7
Glendale, N.H. K7 72-3
Glendale, O. K14 132-3
Glendale, Ore. I5 238-9
Glendale, R.I. A3 87
Glendale, S.C. F5 184-5
Glendale, Tenn. J6 188-9
Glendale, Ut. M5 242-3
Glendale, W. Va. C5 200-1
Glendale, Wis. I5 140-1
Glendale Falls, Mass. D3 68-9
Glendale Heights*, Ill. B10 96-7
Glendale Springs, N.C. C6 180-1
Glendevey, Colo. B10 214-5
Glendive, Mont. E15 222-3
Glendo, Wyo. G15 250-1
Glendola, N.J. H8 76-7
Glendon, Alta. H9 264-5
Glendon, N.C. J5 180-1
Glendora*, Calif. G9 210-1
Glendora, Mich. K11 112-3
Glendora, Miss. D6 176-7
Glendora, N.J. O10 76-7
Gleneden Beach, Ore. D4 238-9
Glenelg, Md. F4 172-3
Glenella, Man. H12 272-3
Glenfield, N. Dak. F11 128-9
Glenfork, W. Va. K14 200-1
Glengary, W. Va. D11 200-1
Glenham*, N.Y. I11 80-1
Glenham, S. Dak. B8 136-7
Glenhayes, W. Va. J9 200-1
Glenisle, Colo. I1 214-5
Glenlea*, Man. K4 272-3
Glenmary, Tenn. G10 188-9
Glenmere*, Sask. N7 294-5
Glenmont, O. E8 132-3
Glenmora, La. F4 168-9
Glenmore, Va. H10 196-7
Glenn, Mich. J11 112-3
Glenn, co., Calif. G3 210-1
Glenn Springs, S.C. G5 184-5
Glennallen, Alaska F12 254-5
Glennie, Mich. F14 112-3
Glenns Ferry, Ida. N5 218-9
Glennville, Ga. K9 160-1
Glenoak, Okla. C14 234-5
Glenolden*, Pa. J15 84-5
Glenoma, Wash. H8 246-7
Glenora, B.C. C3 268-9
Glenora, Man. K12 272-3

384 Glenpool – Grande Prairie

Glenpool, Okla. E13 234-5
Glenridge, Mass. J3 68-9
Glenrio, N. Mex. F12 230-1
Glenrock, Wyo. F13 250-1
Glenrosa*, B.C. J9 268-9
Glens Falls, N.Y. E11 80-1
Glens Fork, Ky. J10 164-5
Glenside, Pa. A11 84-5
Glenside, Sask. L6 294-5
Glentana, Mont. A13 222-3
Glentworth, Sask. O6 294-5
Glenview, Ill. L3 96-7
Glenview Hills*, Ky. A2 164-5
Glenview Manor*, Ky. G9 164-5
Glenville, Ala. J10 146-7
Glenville, Conn. J3 60-1
Glenville, Minn. O6 116-7
Glenville, Nebr. I11 124-5
Glenville, N.C. E3 180-1
Glenville, W. Va. F5 200-1
Glenwillow, O. C15 132-3
Glenwood, Ala. K8 146-7
Glenwood, Alta. O8 264-5
Glenwood*, Alta. J5 264-5
Glenwood, Ark. G4 150-1
Glenwood, Ga. K8 160-1
Glenwood, Ill. O4 96-7
Glenwood, Ind. I11 100-1
Glenwood, Ia. I2 104-5
Glenwood, Me. F8 64-5
Glenwood, Md. F4 172-3
Glenwood, Minn. K3 116-7
Glenwood, Mo. A6 120-1
Glenwood, N.J. A6 76-7
Glenwood, N. Mex. J2 230-1
Glenwood*, Nfld. M10 278-9
Glenwood, N.C. E5 180-1
Glenwood, Ore. F1 238-9
Glenwood, Ut. J6 242-3
Glenwood, Va. K9 196-7
Glenwood, Wash. I9 246-7
Glenwood, W. Va. G2 200-1
Glenwood Beach*, Ont. B15 284-5
Glenwood City, Wis. E8 140-1
Glenwood Springs, Colo. E8 214-5
Glezon, Ind. M5 100-1
Glidden, Ia. F5 104-5
Glidden, Sask. M4 294-5
Glidden, Wis. C10 140-1
Glide, Ore. H5 238-9
Glimp, Tenn. J2 188-9
Globe, Ariz. I8 206-7
Glocester*, R.I. B3 87
Gloria Glens Park, O. D13 132-3
Glorieta, N. Mex. E7 230-1
Gloster, La. C1 168-9
Gloster, Miss. L4 176-7
Gloucester, Mass. B13 68-9
Gloucester*, N.J. N10 76-7
Gloucester, Va. I14 196-7
Gloucester, co., N.B. E5 275
Gloucester, co., N.J. K3 76-7
Gloucester, co., Va. I14 196-7
Gloucester City, N.J. N10 76-7
Gloucester Point, Va. F4 196-7
Glouster, O. H8 132-3
Glover, Miss. A6 176-7
Glover, Okla. I16 234-5
Glover, Vt. C8 90-1
Glovergap, W. Va. A13 200-1
Gloversville, N.Y. E10 80-1
Glovertown, Nfld. M10 278-9
Gloverville, S.C. F8 184-5
Glymphville, S.C. I7 184-5
Glynco*, Ga. M10 160-1
Glyndon, Md. C10 172-3
Glyndon, Minn. I1 116-7
Glynn, co., Ga. M10 160-1
Glynn Haven, Ga. M11 160-1
Gnadenhutten, O. E10 132-3
Gnadenthal, Man. K13 272-3
Goble, Ore. A6 238-9
Gobler, Mo. K11 120-1
Gobles*, Mich. J12 112-3
Goby, Va. C3 196-7
Godbout, Que. A16 290-1
Goddard, Kans. I10 108-9
Goderich, Ont. C11 284-5
Godfrey, Ga. G6 160-1
Godfrey, Ill. J6 96-7
Gods River*, Man. F5 272-3
Godwin, N.C. J7 180-1
Godwin, Tenn. I6 188-9
Goehner, Nebr. H13 124-5
Goessel, Kans. H11 108-9
Goff, Kans. D13 108-9
Goffs, W. Va. E4 200-1
Goffstown, N.H. N6 72-3
Gogama, Ont. G7 284-5
Gogebic, co., Mich. D7 112-3
Goin, Tenn. G12 188-9
Golansville, Va. G12 196-7
Golconda, Ill. O10 96-7
Golconda, Nev. C5 226-7
Gold Acres, Nev. E7 226-7
Gold Bar, Wash. E9 246-7
Gold Beach, Ore. J3 238-9
Gold Bridge, B.C. I7 268-9
Gold Butte, Nev. M11 226-7
Gold Creek, Ark. H15 150-1
Gold Dust, La. F5 168-9
Gold Hill, Nev. G2 226-7
Gold Hill, N.C. I3 180-1
Gold Hill, Ore. J5 238-9
Gold Hill, Ut. G3 242-3
Gold Point, Nev. K6 226-7
Gold Point, N.C. D13 180-1
Gold Reed, Nev. J7 226-7
Gold River*, B.C. H5 268-9
Goldcreek, Mont. F5 222-3
Golddust, Tenn. I1 188-9
Golden, B.C. I10 268-9
Golden, Colo. G2 214-5
Golden, Ida. H4 218-9
Golden, Miss. B11 176-7
Golden, Okla. I16 234-5
Golden Beach, Fla. G16 156-7
Golden City, Mo. H3 120-1
Golden Gate, Calif. C7 210-1
Golden Hill, Minn. O8 116-7
Golden Lake, Ont. H12 284-5
Golden Meadow, La. J9 168-9
Golden Prairie, Sask. N4 294-5
Golden Prairie, Wyo. J16 250-1
Golden Valley*, Minn. M6 116-7
Golden Valley, N. Dak. F5 128-9
Golden Valley, co., Mont. F9 222-3
Golden Valley, co., N. Dak. H1 128-9
Goldendale, Wash. J10 246-7
Goldens Bridge, N.Y. A15 80-1
Goldfield, Ia. D7 104-5
Goldfield, Nev. J6 226-7
Goldman, La. D7 168-9
Goldonna, La. C3 168-9
Goldsboro, Md. E14 172-3
Goldsboro, N.C. E12 180-1
Goldsby, Okla. F11 234-5
Goldsmith, Ind. F8 100-1
Goldston, N.C. I5 180-1
Goldthwaite, Tex. F7 192-3
Goldvein, Va. C2 196-7
Goleta, Calif. N5 210-1
Golf*, Fla. E16 156-7
Golf Manor, O. K14 132-3
Golfview*, Fla. D16 156-7
Goliad, Tex. H8 192-3
Goliad, co., Tex. H8 192-3
Golovin, Alaska D8 254-5
Goltry, Okla. C9 234-5
Golts, Md. C14 172-3
Golva, N. Dak. H1 128-9
Gondola Point, N.B. I5 275
Gonic, N.H. L9 72-3
Gonor, Man. I14 272-3
Gonvick, Minn. G3 116-7
Gonzales, Calif. K4 210-1
Gonzales, La. B11 168-9
Gonzales, Tex. H8 192-3
Gonzales, co., Tex. H8 192-3
Gonzales Ranch, N. Mex. F8 230-1
Goochland, Va. H11 196-7
Goochland, co., Va. H11 196-7
Good Hart, Mich. E12 112-3
Good Hope*, Ala. C6 146-7
Good Hope, Ga. F5 160-1
Good Hope, Miss. H7 176-7
Good Luck*, Md. E10 172-3
Good Pine, La. D5 168-9
Good Springs, Ala. A5 146-7
Good Thunder, Minn. O5 116-7
Goode, Va. I9 196-7
Goodell, Ia. C8 104-5
Goodells, Mich. G7 112-3
Gooderham, Ont. A16 284-5
Goodeve, Sask. M9 294-5
Goodhue, Minn. N7 116-7
Goodhue, co., Minn. N7 116-7
Gooding, Ida. N5 218-9
Gooding, co., Ida. N5 218-9
Goodison, Mich. H6 112-3
Goodland, Ind. D5 100-1
Goodland, Kans. E1 108-9
Goodland, Okla. I14 234-5
Goodlands, Man. K10 272-3
Goodlettsville, Tenn. G7 188-9
Goodman, Ala. L8 146-7
Goodman, Miss. G6 176-7
Goodman, Mo. I3 120-1
Goodman, Wis. D14 140-1
Goodnews Bay, Alaska G8 254-5
Goodnight, Okla. E11 234-5
Goodrich, Colo. C13 214-5
Goodrich, Mich. G4 112-3
Goodrich, N. Dak. F8 128-9
Goodrich Falls, N.H. G8 72-3
Goodridge, Minn. F3 116-7
Goodsoil, Sask. H4 294-5
Goodspring, Tenn. K6 188-9
Goodsprings, Ala. E5 146-7
Goodsprings, Nev. N9 226-7
Goodview, Minn. O9 116-7
Goodwater, Ala. G8 146-7
Goodwater, Okla. I16 234-5
Goodwater, Sask. O9 294-5
Goodway, Ala. L4 146-7
Goodwell, Okla. C3 234-5
Goodwill, Md. I15 172-3
Goodwin, Ark. E10 150-1
Goodwin, S. Dak. D15 136-7
Goodwin Mill*, N.B. E6 275
Goodwins Mills, Me. N2 64-5
Goodyear*, Ariz. I5 206-7
Goose Creek*, Ky. A2 164-5
Goose Creek, S.C. H13 184-5
Goose Egg, Wyo. G12 250-1
Goose Lake, Ia. F15 104-5
Goose Rocks Beach, Me. O3 64-5
Gooseprairie, Wash. G9 246-7
Goosport, La. H3 168-9
Gopher, Ore. C5 238-9
Gordo, Ala. F3 146-7
Gordon, Ala. L10 146-7
Gordon, Ga. I6 160-1
Gordon, Kans. J11 108-9
Gordon, La. A3 168-9
Gordon*, Man. J4 272-3
Gordon, Nebr. C4 124-5
Gordon, W. Va. J13 200-1
Gordon, Wis. C8 140-1
Gordon, co., Ga. E2 160-1
Gordonsburg, Tenn. J5 188-9
Gordonsville, Ala. I6 146-7
Gordonsville, Tenn. B9 188-9
Gordonsville, Va. G11 196-7
Gordonville, Mo. H11 120-1
Gore, Okla. E15 234-5
Gore Bay, Ont. H7 284-5
Gore Springs, Miss. E7 176-7
Goretown, S.C. D16 184-5
Goreville, Ill. N9 96-7
Gorgas, Ala. E5 146-7
Gorham, Kans. F7 108-9
Gorham, Me. O8 64-5
Gorham, N.H. F8 72-3
Gorlitz, Sask. L10 294-5
Gorman, Md. C2 172-3
Gorman, Tenn. B5 188-9
Gorman, Tex. E7 192-3
Gormania, W. Va. E8 200-1
Gorrie*, Ont. C12 284-5
Gorst, Wash. I1 246-7
Gortner, Md. C1 172-3
Gorum, La. E3 168-9
Goshen, Ala. K8 146-7
Goshen, Ark. B3 150-1
Goshen, Calif. K6 210-1
Goshen, Conn. C5 60-1
Goshen, Ida. M10 218-9
Goshen, Ind. A9 100-1
Goshen, Mass. C4 68-9
Goshen, N.H. L4 72-3
Goshen, N.J. O4 76-7
Goshen, N.Y. I10 80-1
Goshen, O. K15 132-3
Goshen, Ore. F6 238-9
Goshen, Ut. G6 242-3
Goshen, Vt. H4 90-1
Goshen, Va. G8 196-7
Goshen, co., Wyo. I16 250-1
Goshen Hill, Conn. E12 60-1
Goshen Springs, Miss. H6 176-7
Goshute, Ut. G2 242-3
Gosnell, Ark. B12 150-1
Gosnold*, Mass. I13 68-9
Gosper, co., Nebr. I8 124-5
Gosport, Ind. J6 100-1
Goss, Miss. L7 176-7
Goss Heights, Mass. D3 68-9
Gossville, N.H. M7 72-3
Gotebo, Okla. G8 234-5
Gotham, Wis. J11 140-1
Gothenburg, Nebr. H8 124-5
Goudeau, La. F5 168-9
Gough, Ga. H9 160-1
Gough, S.C. G13 184-5
Gould, Ark. H8 150-1
Gould, Colo. C10 214-5
Gould, Okla. G7 234-5
Gould City, Mich. D12 112-3
Goulds, Fla. I15 156-7
Goulds*, Nfld. O11 278-9
Gouldsboro, Me. K9 64-5
Gouldtown, N.J. M2 76-7
Gouverneur, N.Y. B8 80-1
Govan, Sask. M8 294-5
Govan, S.C. G10 184-5
Govan, Wash. E13 246-7
Gove, Kans. F4 108-9
Gove, co., Kans. F4 108-9
Government Camp, Ore. C8 238-9
Gowanda, N.Y. G2 80-1
Gowen, Okla. G14 234-5
Gower, Mo. C3 120-1
Gowganda, Ont. G7 284-5
Gowrie, Ia. E6 104-5
Grabill, Ind. C11 100-1
Grace, Ida. N10 218-9
Grace, Miss. G4 176-7
Grace City, N. Dak. F11 128-9
Gracefield, Que. J2 290-1
Graceham, Md. B8 172-3
Gracemont, Okla. F9 234-5
Graceville, Fla. A5 156-7
Graceville, Minn. K2 116-7
Gracewood, Ga. H9 160-1
Gracey, Ky. J5 164-5
Grady, Ala. J8 146-7
Grady, Ark. H8 150-1
Grady, Miss. E8 176-7
Grady, N. Mex. F11 230-1
Grady, Okla. I10 234-5
Grady, co., Ga. N4 160-1
Grady, co., Okla. G10 234-5
Gradyville, Ky. J9 164-5
Graettinger, Ia. B5 104-5
Graf, Ia. D14 104-5
Grafton*, Alta. O7 264-5
Grafton, Ill. J5 96-7
Grafton, Ia. B9 104-5
Grafton, Mass. E9 68-9
Grafton, Nebr. I12 124-5
Grafton*, N.B. H3 275
Grafton, N.H. K5 72-3
Grafton, N. Dak. C13 128-9
Grafton, O. C13 132-3
Grafton, Ont. K11 284-5
Grafton, Ut. M4 242-3
Grafton, Vt. L6 90-1
Grafton, Va. F4 196-7
Grafton, W. Va. E7 200-1
Grafton, Wis. I5 140-1
Grafton, co., N.H. J4 72-3
Graham, Ala. F10 146-7
Graham, Ga. L8 160-1
Graham, Ky. I5 164-5
Graham, Mo. B2 120-1
Graham, N.C. D9 180-1
Graham, Okla. H11 234-5
Graham, Tenn. I5 188-9
Graham, Tex. D7 192-3
Graham, Wash. K3 246-7
Graham, co., Ariz. I10 206-7
Graham, co., Kans. E5 108-9
Graham, co., N.C. E1 180-1
Graham Heights*, W. Va. D6 200-1
Graham Isl., B.C. F2 268-9
Grahamdale*, Man. I3 272-3
Grahamville, Ky. I2 164-5
Grahn, Ky. F14 164-5
Grain Valley, Mo. J16 120-1
Grainfield, Kans. E4 108-9
Grainger, co., Tenn. B13 188-9
Graingers, N.C. E13 180-1
Grainola, Okla. B12 234-5
Grainton, Nebr. H6 124-5
Grambling, La. B4 168-9
Gramercy, La. C12 168-9
Gramling, S.C. E8 184-5
Grammer, Ind. K9 100-1
Granada, Colo. H16 214-5
Granada, Minn. O5 116-7
Granbury, Tex. E8 192-3
Granby, Colo. D10 214-5
Granby, Conn. B8 60-1
Granby, Mass. D5 68-9
Granby, Mo. I3 120-1
Granby, Que. J13 290-1
Granby, Vt. D10 90-1
Granby-Nord, Que. J13 290-1
Granby-Ruisseau*, Que. I7 290-1
Granby-Sud*, Que. J13 290-1
Granby-Sud-Est*, Que. J13 290-1
Grand, co., Colo. D10 214-5
Grand, co., Ut. I10 242-3
Grand Bank, Nfld. O9 278-9
Grand Bay, Ala. N2 146-7
Grand Bay*, N.B. J5 275
Grand Bayou, La. C2 168-9
Grand Beach, Mich. K10 112-3
Grand Bend, Ont. D11 284-5
Grand Blanc, Mich. G4 112-3
Grand Cane, La. C1 168-9
Grand Canyon, Ariz. C6 206-7
Grand Canyon, Ariz. C6 206-7
Grand Centre, Alta. H10 264-5
Grand Chenier, La. I3 168-9
Grand Coteau, La. G5 168-9
Grand Coulee, Sask. N8 294-5
Grand Coulee, Wash. E13 246-7
Grand-Étang, N.S. B10 281
Grand Falls, Me. H8 64-5
Grand Falls, N.B. F3 275
Grand Falls, Nfld. M9 278-9
Grand Forks, B.C. K9 268-9
Grand Forks, N. Dak. E14 128-9
Grand Forks, co., N. Dak. E13 128-9
Grand Forks Base*, N. Dak. E13 128-9
Grand Glaise, Ark. D9 150-1
Grand Gulf, Miss. J4 176-7
Grand Harbour, N.B. K4 275
Grand Haven, B.C. E8 268-9
Grand Haven, Mich. I11 112-3
Grand Island, Nebr. H11 124-5
Grand Isle, La. K10 168-9
Grand Isle, Me. A8 64-5
Grand Isle, Vt. C3 90-1
Grand Isle, co., Vt. C3 90-1
Grand Junction, Colo. F6 214-5
Grand Junction, Ia. F6 104-5
Grand Junction, Mich. J11 112-3
Grand Junction, Tenn. K3 188-9
Grand Lake, Colo. C10 214-5
Grand Lake, La. H2 168-9
Grand Lake, N.B. I5 275
Grand Lake Road*, N.S. B11 281
Grand Lake Stream, Me. H9 64-5
Grand Lake Towne*, Okla. D15 234-5
Grand Ledge, Mich. I13 112-3
Grand Manan Isl., N.B. K4 275
Grand Marais, Man. H15 272-3
Grand Marais, Mich. C11 112-3
Grand Marais, Minn. G11 116-7
Grand Marsh, Wis. H12 140-1
Grand Meadow, Minn. O7 116-7
Grand Mound, Ia. G15 104-5
Grand Pass, Mo. D5 120-1
Grand Prairie, Tex. D14 192-3
Grand Prairie Trail*, Alta. J5 264-5
Grand Pré, N.S. D6 281
Grand Rapids, Man. C12 272-3
Grand Rapids, Mich. I12 112-3
Grand Rapids, Minn. H6 116-7
Grand Rapids, O. B5 132-3
Grand Ridge, Fla. B6 156-7
Grand Ridge, Ill. D9 96-7
Grand River, Ia. J7 104-5
Grand River, O. A16 132-3
Grand Rivers, Ky. J3 164-5
Grand Ronde, Ore. D5 238-9
Grand Saline*, Tex. D10 192-3
Grand Terrace*, Calif. N8 210-1
Grand Tower, Ill. N7 96-7
Grand Tracadie, P.E.I. E8 287
Grand Traverse, co., Mich. F12 112-3
Grand Valley, Colo. E7 214-5
Grand Valley, Ont. C13 284-5
Grand View, Ida. N3 218-9
Grand View, Wis. B9 140-1
Grande-Anse*, N.B. E6 275
Grande Cache, Alta. I3 264-5
Grande-Entrée, Que. I7 290-1
Grande Pointe, Man. J14 272-3
Grande Prairie, Alta. G4 264-5

Grande-Rivière, Que. H6 290-1
Grande-Vallée, Que. H6 290-1
Grandes-Bergeronnes, Que. C14 290-1
Grandfield, Okla. H8 234-5
Grandin, Mo. I9 120-1
Grandin, N. Dak. F14 128-9
Grand'Mère, Que. G9 290-1
Grandmuir Estates*, Alta. J7 264-5
Grandview, Ark. A4 150-1
Grandview, Ill. H7 96-7
Grandview, Ind. O5 100-1
Grandview, Ia. H13 104-5
Grandview, Man. G10 272-3
Grandview, Mo. J15 120-1
Grandview, Tenn. I12 188-9
Grandview, Tex. E13 192-3
Grandview, Wash. I12 246-7
Grandview, W. Va. K16 200-1
Grandview Heights, O. F6 132-3
Grandview Plaza*, Kans. E11 108-9
Grandville, Mich. I12 112-3
Grandy, N.C. C16 180-1
Grange, Ark. B9 150-1
Granger, Ind. A8 100-1
Granger, Ia. G7 104-5
Granger, Mo. A7 120-1
Granger, Tex. F8 192-3
Granger, Wash. H11 246-7
Granger, Wyo. I6 250-1
Granger [-Hunter], Ut. F6 242-3
Grangeville, Ida. G3 218-9
Grangeville, La. G8 168-9
Granisle, B.C. E4 268-9
Granite, Colo. F9 214-5
Granite, N.H. J8 72-3
Granite, Okla. G7 234-5
Granite, Ore. D13 238-9
Granite, co., Mont. F4 222-3
Granite Canyon, Wyo. J15 250-1
Granite City, Ill. K6 96-7
Granite Falls, Minn. M3 116-7
Granite Falls, N.C. D6 180-1
Granite Falls, Wash. D8 246-7
Granite Park*, Ut. F6 242-3
Granite Point, Nev. E4 226-7
Granite Quarry, N.C. I2 180-1
Graniteville, S.C. F8 184-5
Graniteville, Vt. G7 90-1
Grannis, Ark. G2 150-1
Grano, N. Dak. C6 128-9
Granogue, Del. A3 153
Grant, Ala. B7 146-7
Grant, Colo. H1 214-5
Grant, Ida. L10 218-9
Grant, Ia. I4 104-5
Grant, La. F3 168-9
Grant, Mich. H12 112-3
Grant, Mont. I4 222-3
Grant, Nebr. H5 124-5
Grant, Okla. I14 234-5
Grant, Tenn. B9 188-9
Grant, Va. J5 196-7
Grant, co., Ark. G6 150-1
Grant, co., Ind. E9 100-1
Grant, co., Kans. J2 108-9
Grant, co., Ky. E11 164-5
Grant, co., La. D4 168-9
Grant, co., Minn. K2 116-7
Grant, co., Nebr. F5 124-5
Grant, co., N. Mex. K2 230-1
Grant, co., N. Dak. I6 128-9
Grant, co., Okla. C10 234-5
Grant, co., Ore. E12 238-9
Grant, co., S. Dak. C16 136-7
Grant, co., Wash. F12 246-7
Grant, co., W. Va. E9 200-1
Grant, co., Wis. K10 140-1
Grant City, Mo. A3 120-1
Grant Park, Ill. D11 96-7
Grant Town, W. Va. B14 200-1
Grant Village, Wyo. G2 250-1
Grantham, N.H. K4 72-3
Granthams Landing*, B.C. J6 268-9
Granton, Wis. F11 140-1
Grants, N. Mex. F3 230-1
Grants Lick, Ky. E11 164-5
Grants Mills, R.I. A5 87
Grants Pass, Ore. J5 238-9
Grants Pass Southwest*, Ore. J5 238-9
Grantsburg, Wis. D7 140-1
Grantsdale, Mont. F3 222-3
Grantsville, Md. B2 172-3
Grantsville, Ut. F5 242-3
Grantsville, W. Va. F4 200-1
Grantville*, Alta. L8 264-5
Grantville, Ga. H3 160-1
Grantville, Kans. E14 108-9
Grantwood*, Mo. E10 120-1
Granum, Alta. N8 264-5
Granville, Ariz. I11 206-7
Granville, Ill. D8 96-7
Granville, Ia. C2 104-5
Granville, Mass. F3 68-9
Granville, N.Y. D12 80-1
Granville, N. Dak. D7 128-9
Granville, O. F7 132-3
Granville, Tenn. B9 188-9
Granville, Vt. H5 90-1
Granville, W. Va. A15 200-1
Granville, co., N.C. C11 180-1
Granville Lake*, Man. D2 272-3
Grapeland, Tex. F10 192-3
Grapeview, Wash. J1 246-7
Grapevine, Tex. C14 192-3
Grasmere, Ida. O4 218-9
Grasmere, N.H. N6 72-3
Grasonville, Md. E12 172-3
Grass Creek, Wyo. D9 250-1
Grass Lake, Mich. K2 112-3
Grass Range, Mont. E10 222-3
Grass Valley, Calif. G4 210-1
Grass Valley, Ore. C9 238-9
Grasshopper Junction, Ariz. E2 206-7
Grasston, Minn. K7 116-7
Grassy Butte, N. Dak. F3 128-9
Grassy Lake, Alta. N9 264-5
Gratiot, Wis. K11 140-1
Gratiot, co., Mich. I13 112-3
Gratis, Ga. F5 160-1
Gratis, O. I13 132-3
Graton, Calif. A6 210-1
Gratz, Ky. F10 164-5
Gravel Hill, Del. I5 153
Gravel Ridge, Ark. I16 150-1
Gravel Switch, Ky. E5 164-5
Gravelbourg, Sask. O6 294-5
Gravelford, Ore. H4 238-9
Gravelly, Ark. E3 150-1
Gravenhurst, Ont. A15 284-5
Graves, co., Ky. K3 164-5
Graves Mill, Va. F11 196-7
Graveston, Tenn. H12 188-9
Gravette, Ark. A2 150-1
Gravity, Ia. J5 104-5
Grawn, Mich. F12 112-3
Gray, Ga. I6 160-1
Gray, Ida. M11 218-9
Gray, Ia. G4 104-5
Gray, Ky. J12 164-5
Gray, La. E11 168-9
Gray, Me. N9 64-5
Gray, Okla. C5 234-5
Gray, Sask. N8 294-5
Gray, Tenn. G16 188-9
Gray, Va. G1 196-7
Gray, co., Kans. I4 108-9
Gray, co., Tex. B5 192-3
Gray Court, S.C. H3 184-5
Gray Hawk, Ky. I12 164-5
Gray Horse, Okla. C12 234-5
Gray Mountain, Ariz. D7 206-7
Grayland, Wash. G5 246-7
Grayling*, Alaska F9 254-5
Grayling, Mich. F13 112-3
Graymoor*, Ky. G9 164-5
Grays, S.C. I10 184-5
Grays Harbor, co., Wash. F5 246-7
Grays Hill, S.C. J11 184-5
Grays River, Wash. H6 246-7
Grayslake, Ill. J2 96-7
Grayson, Ala. C5 146-7
Grayson, Ga. F5 160-1
Grayson, Ky. F14 164-5
Grayson, La. C5 168-9
Grayson, Mo. G15 120-1
Grayson*, Okla. F14 234-5
Grayson, Sask. M10 294-5
Grayson, co., Ky. I8 164-5
Grayson, co., Tex. D9 192-3
Grayson, co., Va. J5 196-7
Graysonia, Ark. H4 150-1
Graysville, Ala. E6 146-7
Graysville, Ga. C2 160-1
Graysville, Ind. K4 100-1
Graysville*, Man. K3 272-3
Graysville, Tenn. J11 188-9
Grayville, Ill. L11 96-7
Greasewood, Ariz. D10 206-7
Great Barrington, Mass. E1 68-9
Great Bear Lake, N.W. Terr. C1 296
Great Bend, Kans. G8 108-9
Great Bend, N. Dak. I14 128-9
Great Cacapon, W. Va. D11 200-1
Great Divide, Colo. B7 214-5
Great Egg Harbor R., N.J. L4 76-7
Great Falls, Man. I16 272-3
Great Falls, Mont. D7 222-3
Great Falls, S.C. C10 184-5
Great Meadows, N.J. D4 76-7
Great Mills, Md. H11 172-3
Great Neck, N.Y. E15 80-1
Great Neck Estates*, N.Y. J11 80-1
Great Neck Plaza*, N.Y. J11 80-1
Great Pond, Me. I8 64-5
Great Salt Lake, Ut. D4 242-3
Great Slave Lake, N.W. Terr. C1 296
Great Smoky Mts. 14-15
Greater Hendersonville*, Tenn. A8 188-9
Greaterville, Ariz. L8 206-7
Greeley, Colo. C12 214-5
Greeley, Ia. D13 104-5
Greeley, Kans. G15 108-9
Greeley, Nebr. G11 124-5
Greeley, co., Kans. G1 108-9
Greeley, co., Nebr. F11 124-5
Greeley Landing, Me. H6 64-5
Greeleyville, S.C. F13 184-5
Greely*, Ont. H14 284-5
Green, Kans. E11 108-9
Green*, N.J. C4 76-7
Green*, Ore. H5 238-9
Green, co., Ky. I9 164-5
Green, co., Wis. K12 140-1
Green Acres*, Sask. J6 294-5
Green Acres, Wash. E16 246-7
Green Bank, N.J. L5 76-7
Green Bay, Va. I11 196-7
Green Bay, Wis. F15 140-1
Green Bay, Wis. G15 140-1
Green Brook, N.J. E6 76-7
Green Camp, O. E6 132-3
Green City, Mo. B5 120-1
Green Court, Alta. I6 264-5
Green Cove Springs, Fla. C11 156-7
Green Creek, N.J. O4 76-7
Green Farms, Conn. I5 60-1
Green Forest, Ark. A4 150-1
Green Hall, Ky. I13 164-5
Green Haven, Md. G7 172-3
Green Hill, Ala. A4 146-7
Green Hill, R.I. I4 87
Green Island, Ia. F16 104-5
Green Island, N.Y. F11 80-1
Green Isle, Minn. C8 116-7
Green Lake, Me. J7 64-5
Green Lake, Sask. H5 294-5
Green Lake, Wis. H13 140-1
Green Lake, co., Wis. H13 140-1
Green Mountain, Ia. F9 104-5
Green Mountain Falls, Colo. K3 214-5
Green Mts. 14-15
Green Oaks, Ill. K3 96-7
Green Pond, Ala. F5 146-7
Green Pond, N.J. C6 76-7
Green Pond, S.C. I11 184-5
Green Ridge, Mo. E5 120-1
Green Ridge Park, Mass. C2 68-9
Green R., Ut. J9 242-3
Green River, Ut. I9 242-3
Green River, Vt. O6 90-1
Green River, Wyo. I7 250-1
Green Rock, Ill. D6 96-7
Green Sea, S.C. D16 184-5
Green Spring, Del. E3 153
Green Spring, W. Va. D10 200-1
Green Springs, O. C6 132-3
Green Sulphur Springs, W. Va. I5 200-1
Green Tree*, Pa. I2 84-5
Green Valley, Ill. F7 96-7
Green Valley*, Ont. H16 284-5
Green Valley, Wis. C4 140-1
Green Village, N.J. D6 76-7
Greenacres, Calif. L6 210-1
Greenacres City, Fla. E16 156-7
Greenback, Tenn. I14 188-9
Greenbank, Wash. F2 246-7
Greenbelt, Md. I5 172-3
Greenbrier, Ala. B6 146-7
Greenbrier, Ark. D6 150-1
Greenbrier, Tenn. G7 188-9
Greenbrier, co., W. Va. H5 200-1
Greenbush, Me. I7 64-5
Greenbush, Mich. F14 112-3
Greenbush, Minn. E2 116-7
Greenbush, Wis. G4 140-1
Greencastle, Ind. I6 100-1
Greencastle, Mo. B6 120-1
Greencastle, Pa. K8 84-5
Greencreek, Ida. G3 218-9
Greendale, Ind. K12 100-1
Greendale*, Mo. E10 120-1
Greendale, Ut. E10 242-3
Greendale, Wis. J5 140-1
Greene, Ia. C9 104-5
Greene, Me. L3 64-5
Greene, N.Y. G7 80-1
Greene, R.I. E2 87
Greene, co., Ala. G3 146-7
Greene, co., Ark. B11 150-1
Greene, co., Ga. G6 160-1
Greene, co., Ill. I5 96-7
Greene, co., Ind. K5 100-1
Greene, co., Ia. F6 104-5
Greene, co., Miss. L9 176-7
Greene, co., Mo. H5 120-1
Greene, co., N.Y. G10 80-1
Greene, co., N.C. E12 180-1
Greene, co., O. G5 132-3
Greene, co., Pa. K1 84-5
Greene, co., Tenn. B14 188-9
Greene, co., Va. G10 196-7
Greeneville, Tenn. G15 188-9
Greenfield, Sask. K6 294-5
Greenfield, Ark. C10 150-1
Greenfield, Calif. K4 210-1
Greenfield, Calif. L6 210-1
Greenfield, Ill. I6 96-7
Greenfield, Ind. H9 100-1
Greenfield, Ia. H5 104-5
Greenfield, Me. I8 64-5
Greenfield, Mass. B5 68-9
Greenfield, Minn. A9 116-7
Greenfield, Mo. H4 120-1
Greenfield, N.H. N5 72-3
Greenfield, N. Mex. J9 230-1
Greenfield, N.S. F5 281
Greenfield, O. H6 132-3
Greenfield, Okla. E9 234-5
Greenfield, Tenn. B3 188-9
Greenfield, Wis. I5 140-1
Greenfield Park*, Que. I12 290-1
Greenhills, O. K13 132-3
Greenland, Ark. B2 150-1
Greenland, Mich. C8 112-3
Greenland, N.H. N9 72-3
Greenland, W. Va. E9 200-1
Greenlawn, N.Y. J12 80-1
Greenleaf, Ida. L2 218-9
Greenleaf, Kans. D11 108-9
Greenleaf, Ore. F4 238-9
Greenleaf, Wis. E4 140-1
Greenlee, co., Ariz. I11 206-7
Greenmount, Md. B10 172-3
Greenmountain, N.C. D4 180-1
Greenough, Mont. E4 222-3
Greenport, N.Y. J13 80-1
Greens Acres*, Ont. H14 284-5
Greensboro, Ala. H4 146-7
Greensboro, Fla. B6 156-7
Greensboro, Ga. G6 160-1
Greensboro, Ind. H10 100-1
Greensboro, Md. E14 172-3
Greensboro, N.C. D9 180-1
Greensboro, Vt. D8 90-1
Greensboro Bend, Vt. D8 90-1
Greensburg, Ind. J10 100-1
Greensburg, Kans. J6 108-9
Greensburg, Ky. I9 164-5
Greensburg, La. F8 168-9
Greensburg, Pa. I3 84-5
Greensfork, Ind. H11 100-1
Greenspond, Nfld. M11 278-9
Greensville, co., Va. J12 196-7
Greentop, Mo. A6 120-1
Greentown, Ind. E8 100-1
Greenup, Ill. I10 96-7
Greenup, Ky. F15 164-5
Greenup, co., Ky. F14 164-5
Greenvale, Tenn. H8 188-9
Greenview, Ill. G7 96-7
Greenview, W. Va. J13 200-1
Greenville, Ala. J7 146-7
Greenville, Calif. F4 210-1
Greenville, Fla. B8 156-7
Greenville, Ga. H3 160-1
Greenville, Ill. J8 96-7
Greenville, Ind. N8 100-1
Greenville, Ia. C4 104-5
Greenville, Ky. I6 164-5
Greenville, Me. G5 64-5
Greenville, Mich. I12 112-3
Greenville, Miss. F4 176-7
Greenville, Mo. I10 120-1
Greenville, N.H. O5 72-3
Greenville, N.C. D13 180-1
Greenville, O. F3 132-3
Greenville, Pa. E1 84-5
Greenville, R.I. B4 87
Greenville, S.C. B6 184-5
Greenville, Tex. B16 192-3
Greenville, Ut. K4 242-3
Greenville, Va. G9 196-7
Greenville, co., S.C. B6 184-5
Greenville Junction, Me. G4 64-5
Greenville North, Miss. F4 176-7
Greenwald, Minn. K4 116-7
Greenway, Ark. A12 150-1
Greenway, S. Dak. A10 136-7
Greenwich, Conn. J3 60-1
Greenwich*, N.J. E3 76-7
Greenwich*, N.J. J2 76-7
Greenwich, N.J. M2 76-7
Greenwich, N.Y. E11 80-1
Greenwich, O. C7 132-3
Greenwich, Ut. K6 242-3
Greenwood*, Alta. M7 264-5
Greenwood, Ark. D2 150-1
Greenwood, B.C. K9 268-9
Greenwood, Del. H3 153
Greenwood, Fla. A6 156-7
Greenwood, Ida. O7 218-9
Greenwood, Ind. G2 100-1
Greenwood, La. B1 168-9
Greenwood, Me. K2 64-5
Greenwood*, Minn. L5 116-7
Greenwood, Miss. E6 176-7
Greenwood, Mo. J16 120-1
Greenwood, Nebr. K1 124-5
Greenwood, S.C. D7 184-5
Greenwood, S. Dak. I12 136-7
Greenwood, W. Va. E5 200-1
Greenwood, Wis. F10 140-1
Greenwood, co., Kans. I13 108-9
Greenwood, co., S.C. D7 184-5
Greenwood Estates*, Alta. I8 264-5
Greenwood Lake, N.Y. I10 80-1
Greenwood Springs, Miss. D10 176-7
Greenwood Village, Colo. H3 214-5
Greer, Ariz. H11 206-7
Greer, Ida. F3 218-9
Greer, S.C. F3 184-5
Greer, W. Va. B16 200-1
Greer, co., Okla. G7 234-5
Greers Ferry, Ark. D7 150-1
Gregg, co., Tex. E11 192-3
Gregory, Ark. E9 150-1
Gregory, Mich. J2 112-3
Gregory, S. Dak. H10 136-7
Gregory*, Tex. I8 192-3
Gregory, co., S. Dak. H11 136-7
Gregson, Mont. G5 222-3
Grenada, Miss. E7 176-7
Grenada, co., Miss. E7 176-7
Grenfell, Sask. N10 294-5
Grenola, Kans. J12 108-9
Grenora, N. Dak. C1 128-9
Grenville, N. Mex. C11 230-1
Grenville, Que. I10 290-1
Grenville, S. Dak. B14 136-7
Gresham, Nebr. H13 124-5
Gresham, Ore. C7 238-9
Gresham, S.C. E14 184-5
Gresham, Wis. C3 140-1
Gretna, Fla. B7 156-7
Gretna, Kans. D7 108-9
Gretna, La. D14 168-9
Gretna, Man. K14 272-3
Gretna, Nebr. J2 124-5
Gretna, Va. J9 196-7
Grey, co., Ont. B13 284-5
Grey Eagle, Minn. K4 116-7
Grey Gables, Mass. G13 68-9
Greybull, Wyo. C10 250-1
Greycliffe, Mont. G9 222-3
Greystone, Colo. C6 214-5
Greystone, Conn. E7 60-1

Grider, Ark. C12 150-1
Gridley, Calif. G4 210-1
Gridley, Ill. E9 96-7
Gridley, Kans. H14 108-9
Griffin, Ga. H4 160-1
Griffin, Ind. N3 100-1
Griffin, La. C6 168-9
Griffin, Sask. O9 294-5
Griffing Park*, Tex. G11 192-3
Griffith, Ariz. E3 206-7
Griffith, Ind. A4 100-1
Griffith Creek, Tenn. K10 188-9
Griffithsville, W. Va. I12 200-1
Griffithville, Ark. E8 150-1
Grifton, N.C. E13 180-1
Griggs, Okla. C2 234-5
Griggs, co., N. Dak. F12 128-9
Griggstown, N.J. F5 76-7
Griggsville, Ill. H5 96-7
Grigston, Kans. G3 108-9
Grimes, Ala. L9 146-7
Grimes, Calif. G3 210-1
Grimes, Ia. G7 104-5
Grimes, Okla. F7 234-5
Grimes, co., Tex. G10 192-3
Grimesland, N.C. E13 180-1
Grimms, Wis. F5 140-1
Grimms Landing, W. Va. F2 200-1
Grimsby, Ont. D14 284-5
Grimshaw, Alta. F5 264-5
Grimsley, Tenn. G9 188-9
Grindrod, B.C. I9 268-9
Grindstone, Me. G7 64-5
Grinnell, Ia. G10 104-5
Grinnell, Kans. E4 108-9
Griquet, Nfld. J9 278-9
Grisdale, Wash. F6 246-7
Grise Fiord, N.W. Terr. A3 296
Grissom, Ind. E8 100-1
Griswold*, Conn. E14 60-1
Griswold, Ia. I4 104-5
Griswold, Man. J10 272-3
Groesbeck, Tex. F9 192-3
Gronlid, Sask. J8 294-5
Groom, Tex. B5 192-3
Groom Creek, Ariz. G6 206-7
Gros-Morne, Que. H6 290-1
Groseclose, Va. J5 196-7
Gross, Ida. K3 218-9
Gross, Nebr. C10 124-5
Grosse Ile*, Mich. K6 112-3
Grosse Isle*, Man. J4 272-3
Grosse Pointe, Mich. J7 112-3
Grosse Pointe Farms, Mich. J7 112-3
Grosse Pointe Park, Mich. J7 112-3
Grosse Pointe Shores*, Mich. J15 112-3
Grosse Pointe Woods, Mich. J7 112-3
Grosse Tete, La. H6 168-9
Grosses-Roches*, Que. H5 290-1
Grossmont-Mount Helix*, Calif. O8 210-1
Grosvenor Dale, Conn. B14 60-1
Groton, Conn. G13 60-1
Groton, Mass. B9 68-9
Groton, N.H. J5 72-3
Groton, N.Y. F6 80-1
Groton, S. Dak. B13 136-7
Groton, Vt. F8 90-1
Grotto, Wash. E9 246-7
Grottoes, Va. G10 196-7
Grouard Mission*, Alta. G6 264-5
Grouse Creek, Ut. C3 242-3
Grove, Kans. E14 108-9
Grove, Me. I10 64-5
Grove, Okla. C16 234-5
Grove Beach, Conn. H10 60-1
Grove City*, Fla. H10 156-7
Grove City, Minn. L4 116-7
Grove City, O. G6 132-3
Grove City, Pa. F2 84-5
Grove Hill, Ala. K4 146-7
Groveland, Fla. F5 156-7
Groveland, Mass. A12 68-9
Groveoak, Ala. C8 146-7
Groveport, O. G7 132-3
Grover, Colo. B13 214-5
Grover, N.C. E6 180-1
Grover, S.C. H11 184-5
Grover, S. Dak. D14 136-7
Grover, Ut. K7 242-3
Grover, Wyo. F5 250-1
Grover City, Calif. M4 210-1
Grover Hill, O. C3 132-3
Grovertown, Ind. B7 100-1
Groves, Tex. G11 192-3
Groveton, N.H. E6 72-3
Groveton, Tex. F10 192-3
Groveton*, Va. E13 196-7
Grovetown, Ga. G9 160-1
Grovont, Wyo. J2 250-1
Growler, Ariz. J3 206-7
Growler Pass, Ariz. K5 206-7
Grubbs, Ark. C10 150-1
Gruetli*, Tenn. D10 188-9
Grulla, Tex. K7 192-3
Grundy, Va. I4 196-7
Grundy, co., Ill. D10 96-7
Grundy, co., Ia. E10 104-5
Grundy, co., Mo. B4 120-1
Grundy, co., Tenn. D9 188-9
Grundy Center, Ia. E10 104-5
Grunthal, Man. K14 272-3
Grunthal, Sask. K6 294-5
Gruver, Ia. B5 104-5
Gruver, Tex. A5 192-3
Grygla, Minn. F3 116-7
Gu Achi, Ariz. K6 206-7
Gu Komelik, Ariz. K6 206-7
Gu Oidak, Ariz. L6 206-7
Gu Vo, Ariz. L5 206-7
Gu-Win, Ala. D3 146-7
Guadalupe, Ariz. I6 206-7
Guadalupe, Calif. M5 210-1
Guadalupe, co., N. Mex. G9 230-1
Guadalupe, co., Tex. H8 192-3
Guadalupita, N. Mex. D8 230-1
Guage, Ky. H14 164-5
Gualala, Calif. H2 210-1
Guardian, W. Va. G6 200-1
Guelph, N. Dak. J12 128-9
Guelph, Ont. D13 284-5
Guemes, Wash. C7 246-7
Guerette, Me. B8 64-5
Guernsey, Ia. G11 104-5
Guernsey, Sask. L8 294-5
Guernsey, Wyo. H15 250-1
Guernsey, co., O. F10 132-3
Guess, S.C. B12 184-5
Gueydan, La. H4 168-9
Guide Rock, Nebr. J11 124-5
Guigues*, Que. I1 290-1
Guild, N.H. L4 72-3
Guild, Tenn. K10 188-9
Guildhall, Vt. D11 90-1
Guilford, Conn. H9 60-1
Guilford, Ind. J12 100-1
Guilford, Me. I5 64-5
Guilford, Md. G5 172-3
Guilford, Mo. B2 120-1
Guilford, N.C. H4 180-1
Guilford, Vt. N6 90-1
Guilford, co., N.C. C9 180-1
Guilford College*, N.C. H4 180-1
Guin, Ala. D3 146-7
Guion, Ark. B8 150-1
Gulf, N.C. I6 180-1
Gulf, co., Fla. C6 156-7
Gulf Breeze, Fla. B3 156-7
Gulf Crest, Ala. M2 146-7
Gulf Gate Estates*, Fla. G10 156-7
Gulf Harbors*, Fla. F9 156-7
Gulf Shores, Ala. O4 146-7
Gulf Stream*, Fla. E16 156-7
Gulfport, Fla. I2 156-7
Gulfport, Miss. O9 176-7
Gulkana, Alaska E12 254-5
Gulkana Airport, Alaska E12 254-5
Gull Lake, Alta. K7 264-5
Gull Lake*, Man. J4 272-3
Gull Lake, Sask. N5 294-5
Gull Rock, N.C. E16 180-1
Gulliver, Mich. D11 112-3
Gully, Minn. G3 116-7
Gum Ridge, La. B6 168-9
Gum Spring, Va. H11 196-7
Gum Springs, Ark. H5 150-1
Gumboro, Del. K5 153
Gunlock, Ut. M2 242-3
Gunn, Alta. I7 264-5
Gunn City, Mo. K16 120-1
Gunnison, Colo. G8 214-5
Gunnison, Miss. D4 176-7
Gunnison, Ut. I6 242-3
Gunnison, co., Colo. F8 214-5
Gunsight, Mont. B5 222-3
Gunter, Ore. G5 238-9
Gunter, Tex. A15 192-3
Guntersville, Ala. C7 146-7
Guntersville Lake, Ala. B8 146-7
Gunton, Man. I14 272-3
Guntown, Miss. C9 176-7
Gurdon, Ark. H5 150-1
Gurley, Ala. B7 146-7
Gurley, Nebr. G2 124-5
Gurleyville, Conn. C12 60-1
Gurnee, Ill. J3 96-7
Gurney, Wis. B10 140-1
Gusher, Ut. F9 242-3
Gustavus, Alaska G15 254-5
Gustine, Calif. D10 210-1
Guston, Ky. H8 164-5
Guthrie, Ariz. J11 206-7
Guthrie, Ky. K6 164-5
Guthrie, La. B5 168-9
Guthrie, Okla. E11 234-5
Guthrie, Tex. D6 192-3
Guthrie, co., Ia. G6 104-5
Guthrie Center, Ia. G5 104-5
Guthriesville, S.C. B9 184-5
Guttenberg, Ia. D14 104-5
Guttenberg, N.J. C12 76-7
Guy, Ark. D7 150-1
Guyan, W. Va. J3 200-1
Guyencourt, Del. A3 153
Guymon, Okla. C3 234-5
Guys, Tenn. D4 188-9
Guysborough, N.S. D10 281
Guysborough, co., N.S. D9 281
Guyton, Ga. J10 160-1
Gwendolen, Ore. C10 238-9
Gwenford, Ida. O9 218-9
Gwinn, Mich. D10 112-3
Gwinner, N. Dak. I13 128-9
Gwinnett, co., Ga. F4 160-1
Gwynn, Va. E4 196-7
Gwynneville, Ind. I9 100-1
Gypsum, Colo. E8 214-5
Gypsum, Kans. G10 108-9
Gypsumville, Man. F12 272-3
Gypsy, W. Va. C13 200-1

H

Haakon, co., S. Dak. E6 136-7
Habersham, Ga. D6 160-1
Habersham, Tenn. F11 188-9
Habersham, co., Ga. D5 160-1
Hachita, N. Mex. L3 230-1
Hacienda, Fla. G16 156-7
Hacienda Heights*, Calif. N7 210-1
Hackberry, Ariz. E3 206-7
Hackberry, La. H2 168-9
Hackensack, Minn. H5 116-7
Hackensack, N.J. B11 76-7
Hacker Valley, W. Va. G6 200-1
Hackett, Ark. D2 150-1
Hackettstown, N.J. D4 76-7
Hackleburg, Ala. C4 146-7
Hackney, Kans. K11 108-9
Hackneyville, Ala. G8 146-7
Hacoda, Ala. M8 146-7
Hadar, Nebr. E13 124-5
Haddam, Conn. F10 60-1
Haddam, Kans. D11 108-9
Haddock, Ga. H6 160-1
Haddon, N.J. N11 76-7
Haddon Heights, N.J. N11 76-7
Haddonfield, N.J. N11 76-7
Hadensville, Va. H11 196-7
Hadley, Ind. H7 100-1
Hadley, Mass. D5 68-9
Hadley, Mich. G5 112-3
Hadley, Minn. O2 116-7
Hadlock, Wash. G1 246-7
Hadlyme, Conn. G11 60-1
Hafford, Sask. K6 294-5
Hagaman, N.Y. E10 80-1
Hagan, Ga. K9 160-1
Hagarville, Ark. D4 150-1
Hagen, Sask. J7 294-5
Hagensborg, B.C. H5 268-9
Hager City, Wis. F7 140-1
Hagerhill, Ky. H15 164-5
Hagerman, Ida. N5 218-9
Hagerman, N. Mex. J10 230-1
Hagerstown, Ind. H11 100-1
Hagerstown, Md. B7 172-3
Hagewood, La. D3 168-9
Hagood, S.C. E11 184-5
Hague, N. Dak. J8 128-9
Hague, Sask. K6 294-5
Hague, Va. G14 196-7
Hahira, Ga. N6 160-1
Hahnville, La. C13 168-9
Haigler, Nebr. J4 124-5
Haiku, Hawaii G11 258-9
Haile, La. A5 168-9
Hailey, Ida. L6 218-9
Haileybury, Ont. G8 284-5
Haileyville, Okla. G14 234-5
Hailstone, Ut. F7 242-3
Haina, Hawaii H13 258-9
Haines, Alaska G15 254-5
Haines, Ore. D14 238-9
Haines City, Fla. H6 156-7
Haines Junction, Y.T. C1 297
Hainesport, N.J. I4 76-7
Hairy Hill, Alta. I9 264-5
Hakalau, Hawaii I14 258-9
Halawa Heights, Hawaii J5 258-9
Halbrite, Sask. O9 294-5
Halbstadt, Man. K14 272-3
Halbur, Ia. F4 104-5
Haldeman, Ky. G13 164-5
Haldimand, Ont. E14 284-5
Hale, Mich. G14 112-3
Hale, Mo. C5 120-1
Hale, co., Ala. H4 146-7
Hale, co., Tex. C5 192-3
Hale Center, Tex. C5 192-3
Haleburg, Ala. L10 146-7
Haledon, N.J. A10 76-7
Haleiwa, Hawaii G3 258-9
Hales Corners, Wis. J5 140-1
Hales Crossing, Mass. B5 68-9
Halethorpe, Md. G6 172-3
Haleyville, Ala. C4 146-7
Haleyville, N.J. N3 76-7
Half Hollow Hills*, N.Y. J12 80-1
Half Moon Bay, Calif. D7 210-1
Half Way, Mo. G5 120-1
Halfmoon Bay, B.C. B12 268-9
Halfmoon Junction*, N.Y. F11 80-1
Halfway, Ky. J8 164-5
Halfway, Md. B7 172-3
Halfway, Ore. D15 238-9
Halfway Point-Benoit's Cove-John's Beach*, Nfld. M7 278-9
Haliburton, Ont. A16 284-5
Haliburton, co., Ont. I11 284-5
Halibut Cove, Alaska G11 254-5
Halifax, Mass. F12 68-9
Halifax, N.C. C13 180-1
Halifax, N.S. E7 281
Halifax, Vt. O6 90-1
Halifax, Va. J10 196-7
Halifax, co., N.C. C12 180-1
Halifax, co., N.S. D8 281
Halifax, co., Va. J10 196-7
Haliimaile, Hawaii G11 258-9
Halkirk, Alta. K9 264-5
Hall, Ind. I7 100-1
Hall, Md. J6 172-3
Hall, Mont. F4 222-3
Hall, W. Va. E14 200-1
Hall, co., Ga. E5 160-1
Hall, co., Nebr. H10 124-5
Hall, co., Tex. C6 192-3
Hall Park*, Okla. F11 234-5
Hall Quarry, Me. K8 64-5
Hall Summit, La. C2 168-9
Hallam, Nebr. I14 124-5
Hallam, Pa. J11 84-5
Hallandale, Fla. G16 156-7
Hallburg, W. Va. G4 200-1
Hallebourg, Ont. F6 284-5
Halleck, Nev. C9 226-7
Hallett, Okla. D12 234-5
Hallettsville, Tex. H9 192-3
Halley, Ark. I9 150-1
Halliday, Ark. B11 150-1
Halliday, N. Dak. F4 128-9
Hallie*, Wis. F9 140-1
Hallieford, Va. E4 196-7
Hallock, Minn. D1 116-7
Hallowell, Kans. K16 108-9
Hallowell, Me. L4 64-5
Halls, Tenn. B2 188-9
Halls Crossroads, Tenn. H12 188-9
Halls Summit, Kans. G14 108-9
Hallsboro, N.C. G11 180-1
Hallstead, Pa. C14 84-5
Hallsville, Mo. D7 120-1
Hallsville*, Tex. E11 192-3
Halltown, Ala. C3 146-7
Halltown, Mo. H4 120-1
Halltown, W. Va. E12 200-1
Hallville, Conn. F13 60-1
Hallwood, Va. G16 196-7
Halma, Minn. E2 116-7
Halpine*, Md. D9 172-3
Halsell, Ala. I2 146-7
Halsey, Nebr. F7 124-5
Halsey, Ore. J1 238-9
Halstad, Minn. G1 116-7
Halstead, Kans. H10 108-9
Haltom City, Tex. C13 192-3
Halton Hills, Ont. C14 284-5
Ham Lake, Minn. L6 116-7
Ham-Nord, Que. I15 290-1
Ham-Sud, Que. I15 290-1
Hamar, N. Dak. E11 128-9
Hamberg, N. Dak. E9 128-9
Hamblen, co., Tenn. B14 188-9
Hambleton, W. Va. D16 200-1
Hamburg, Ark. J8 150-1
Hamburg, Conn. G11 60-1
Hamburg, Ind. M9 100-1
Hamburg, Ia. K3 104-5
Hamburg, La. F5 168-9
Hamburg, Mich. J3 112-3
Hamburg, Minn. C8 116-7
Hamburg, Miss. K4 176-7
Hamburg, N.J. B5 76-7
Hamburg, N.Y. F2 80-1
Hamburg, Pa. H13 84-5
Hamburg, Wis. E11 140-1
Hamden, Conn. G8 60-1
Hamden, O. I7 132-3
Hamer, Ida. L9 218-9
Hamer, S.C. C15 184-5
Hamersville, O. I4 132-3
Hamill, S. Dak. G10 136-7
Hamilton, Ala. D3 146-7
Hamilton, Alaska E8 254-5
Hamilton, Colo. C7 214-5
Hamilton, Ga. I3 160-1
Hamilton, Ill. F3 96-7
Hamilton, Ind. A12 100-1
Hamilton, Ia. I9 104-5
Hamilton, Kans. H13 108-9
Hamilton, Mass. B12 68-9
Hamilton, Mich. J11 112-3
Hamilton, Miss. E10 176-7
Hamilton, Mo. C4 120-1
Hamilton, Mont. F3 222-3
Hamilton*, N.J. H5 76-7
Hamilton*, N.J. M5 76-7
Hamilton, N.Y. F8 80-1
Hamilton, N.C. D13 180-1
Hamilton, N. Dak. B13 128-9
Hamilton, O. H3 132-3
Hamilton, Ont. J8 284-5
Hamilton, Ore. D12 238-9
Hamilton, R.I. F5 87
Hamilton, Tex. E8 192-3
Hamilton, Va. E12 196-7
Hamilton, Wash. C8 246-7
Hamilton, co., Fla. B9 156-7
Hamilton, co., Ill. M9 96-7
Hamilton, co., Ind. G8 100-1
Hamilton, co., Ia. E7 104-5
Hamilton, co., Kans. H1 108-9
Hamilton, co., Nebr. H12 124-5
Hamilton, co., N.Y. D10 80-1
Hamilton, co., O. H3 132-3
Hamilton, co., Tenn. D10 188-9
Hamilton, co., Tex. F8 192-3
Hamilton City, Calif. G2 210-1
Hamilton Dome, Wyo. D9 250-1
Hamilton Fort, Ut. L4 242-3
Hamilton Inlet, Nfld. G7 278-9
Hamiota, Man. I10 272-3
Hamler, O. C4 132-3
Hamlet, Ark. H16 150-1
Hamlet, Ind. B7 100-1
Hamlet, Nebr. I6 124-5
Hamlet, N.C. F9 180-1
Hamlet, Ore. B5 238-9
Hamlin, Kans. C14 108-9
Hamlin, Me. B9 64-5
Hamlin, Tex. D6 192-3
Hamlin, W. Va. H2 200-1
Hamlin, co., S. Dak. D15 136-7
Hammer, S. Dak. A15 136-7
Hammett, Ida. N4 218-9
Hammon, Okla. E7 234-5
Hammond, Ind. A4 100-1
Hammond, La. G9 168-9
Hammond, Me. E9 64-5
Hammond, Minn. N8 116-7
Hammond, Mont. H15 222-3
Hammond, Ore. A4 238-9
Hammond, Wis. E7 140-1

Hammond East*, La. G8 168-9
Hammonds Plains, N.S. E7 281
Hammondsport, N.Y. G5 80-1
Hammondville, Ala. B9 146-7
Hammonton, N.J. K4 76-7
Hamner, Ala. H2 146-7
Hampden, Me. J7 64-5
Hampden, Mass. E5 68-9
Hampden, Nfld. L8 278-9
Hampden, N. Dak. C11 128-9
Hampden, co., Mass. E4 68-9
Hampden Highlands, Me. J7 64-5
Hampden Sydney, Va. I10 196-7
Hampshire, Ill. B9 96-7
Hampshire, Tenn. J5 188-9
Hampshire, Wyo. E15 250-1
Hampshire, co., Mass. D4 68-9
Hampshire, co., W. Va. E10 200-1
Hampstead, Md. B10 172-3
Hampstead, N.H. O8 72-3
Hampstead, N.C. G13 180-1
Hampstead*, Que. I12 290-1
Hampton, Ark. I6 150-1
Hampton, Conn. D13 60-1
Hampton, Fla. C10 156-7
Hampton, Ga. E11 160-1
Hampton, Ill. C5 96-7
Hampton, Ia. D8 104-5
Hampton, Ky. I3 164-5
Hampton, Minn. C11 116-7
Hampton, Nebr. H12 124-5
Hampton, N.B. I5 275
Hampton, N.H. N9 72-3
Hampton*, N.J. B4 76-7
Hampton, N.J. E4 76-7
Hampton, Ore. G10 238-9
Hampton, P.E.I. F6 287
Hampton, S.C. H10 184-5
Hampton, Tenn. B16 188-9
Hampton, Va. F4 196-7
Hampton, Wyo. I6 250-1
Hampton, co., S.C. I10 184-5
Hampton Bays, N.Y. J13 80-1
Hampton Beach, N.H. O9 72-3
Hampton Falls, N.H. N9 72-3
Hamptonville, N.C. H2 180-1
Hamtramck, Mich. J6 112-3
Hana, Hawaii G12 258-9
Hanahan*, S.C. H13 184-5
Hanalei, Hawaii D4 258-9
Hanamaulu, Hawaii D5 258-9
Hanapepe, Hawaii D4 258-9
Hanby Corner, Del. A4 153
Hanceville, Ala. D6 146-7
Hancock, Conn. E7 60-1
Hancock, Ia. H3 104-5
Hancock, Me. K8 64-5
Hancock, Md. B6 172-3
Hancock, Mass. C2 68-9
Hancock, Mich. C8 112-3
Hancock, Minn. L3 116-7
Hancock, N.H. N4 72-3
Hancock, N.Y. H8 80-1
Hancock, Vt. H5 90-1
Hancock, W. Va. D11 200-1
Hancock, Wis. F1 140-1
Hancock, co., Ga. H7 160-1
Hancock, co., Ill. F4 96-7
Hancock, co., Ind. H9 100-1
Hancock, co., Ia. C7 104-5
Hancock, co., Ky. H7 164-5
Hancock, co., Me. I8 64-5
Hancock, co., Miss. N7 176-7
Hancock, co., O. C5 132-3
Hancock, co., Tenn. A14 188-9
Hancock, co., W. Va. A5 200-1
Hancock Point, Me. K8 64-5
Hancocks Bridge, N.J. L1 76-7
Hand, co., S. Dak. E11 136-7
Handel, Sask. L5 294-5
Handley, W. Va. I15 200-1
Handsom, Va. H2 196-7
Haney, B.C. C14 268-9
Hanford, Calif. K6 210-1
Hanford Northwest*, Calif. K5 210-1
Hanford South*, Calif. K5 210-1
Hanging Limb, Tenn. B10 188-9
Hanging Rock, O. J7 132-3
Hankinson, N. Dak. J14 128-9
Hanks, N. Dak. C2 128-9
Hanksville, Ut. K8 242-3
Hanksville, Vt. F5 90-1
Hanley, Sask. L6 294-5
Hanley Falls, Minn. M3 116-7
Hanley Hills*, Mo. E10 120-1
Hanlontown, Ia. B8 104-5
Hanna, Alta. L9 264-5
Hanna, Ind. B6 100-1
Hanna, La. C2 168-9
Hanna, Okla. F14 234-5
Hanna, Ut. F8 242-3
Hanna, Wyo. I12 250-1
Hanna City, Ill. F7 96-7
Hannaford, N. Dak. F12 128-9
Hannagan Meadow, Ariz. H11 206-7
Hannah, N. Dak. B11 128-9
Hannibal, Mo. C8 120-1
Hannibal, N.Y. E6 80-1
Hannibal, Wis. E10 140-1
Hannon, Ala. I9 146-7
Hanover, Conn. E13 60-1
Hanover, Ill. A6 96-7
Hanover, Ind. L10 100-1
Hanover, Kans. C11 108-9
Hanover, Me. K2 64-5
Hanover, Mass. K7 68-9
Hanover, Mich. K1 112-3
Hanover, Minn. A9 116-7
Hanover, Mont. E9 222-3
Hanover, N.H. J3 72-3
Hanover, N.J. D6 76-7
Hanover, N. Mex. K3 230-1
Hanover, O. F8 132-3
Hanover, Ont. B12 284-5
Hanover, Pa. K10 84-5
Hanover, Va. H12 196-7
Hanover, Wis. K2 140-1
Hanover, co., Va. H12 196-7
Hanover Park, Ill. L2 96-7
Hanoverton, O. D11 132-3
Hansboro, N. Dak. B10 128-9
Hansell, Ia. D9 104-5
Hansen, Ida. O6 218-9
Hansen, Nebr. I11 124-5
Hansford, co., Tex. A5 192-3
Hanska, Minn. N5 116-7
Hanson, Ky. I5 164-5
Hanson, Mass. E12 68-9
Hanson, co., S. Dak. G13 136-7
Hanston, Kans. H6 108-9
Hansville, Wash. G2 246-7
Hants, co., N.S. D7 281
Hantsport, N.S. D6 281
Hapeville, Ga. C10 160-1
Happy, Tex. B5 192-3
Happy Camp, Calif. D2 210-1
Happy Jack, Ariz. F7 206-7
Happy Valley*, Ore. C7 238-9
Happy Valley-Goose Bay, Nfld. H6 278-9
Happys Inn, Mont. C2 222-3
Harahan, La. D14 168-9
Haralson, Ga. H3 160-1
Haralson, co., Ga. F2 160-1
Harbeson, Del. I5 153
Harbine, Nebr. J14 124-5
Harbor, Ore. K3 238-9
Harbor Beach, Mich. H15 112-3
Harbor Springs, Mich. E12 112-3
Harborside, Me. K7 64-5
Harborton, Va. H15 196-7
Harbour Breton, Nfld. O9 278-9
Harbour Grace, Nfld. N11 278-9
Harbour Main*, Nfld. O11 278-9
Harbour Main*, Nfld. O11 278-9
Harbuck, Tenn. K13 188-9
Harcourt, Ia. E6 104-5
Harcourt, N.B. G6 275
Harcuvar, Ariz. H3 206-7
Hardaway, Ala. I8 146-7
Hardee, co., Fla. G11 156-7
Hardeeville, S.C. J10 184-5
Hardeman, co., Tenn. D3 188-9
Hardeman, co., Tex. C6 192-3
Harden City, Okla. H12 234-5
Hardesty, Okla. C4 234-5
Hardieville, Alta. N8 264-5
Hardin, Ill. J5 96-7
Hardin, Ky. J3 164-5
Hardin, Mo. D4 120-1
Hardin, Mont. G12 222-3
Hardin, co., Ill. N10 96-7
Hardin, co., Ia. E8 104-5
Hardin, co., Ky. H8 164-5
Hardin, co., O. E5 132-3
Hardin, co., Tenn. D5 188-9
Hardin, co., Tex. G11 192-3
Harding, Kans. H16 108-9
Harding*, Man. J1 272-3
Harding, Minn. J5 116-7
Harding*, N.J. E6 76-7
Harding, co., N. Mex. D10 230-1
Harding, co., S. Dak. B2 136-7
Hardinsburg, Ind. M8 100-1
Hardinsburg, Ky. H7 164-5
Hardisty, Alta. K9 264-5
Hardman, Ore. C11 238-9
Hardscrabble, Del. J4 153
Hardtner, Kans. K8 108-9
Hardwick, Ga. H6 160-1
Hardwick, Mass. D6 68-9
Hardwick, Minn. O2 116-7
Hardwick, N.J. C4 76-7
Hardwick, Vt. E7 90-1
Hardwood, Mich. D9 112-3
Hardwood Ridge, N.B. H5 275
Hardy, Ark. A9 150-1
Hardy, Ia. D6 104-5
Hardy, Miss. D7 176-7
Hardy, Nebr. J12 124-5
Hardy, Okla. B12 234-5
Hardy, Va. I8 196-7
Hardy, co., W. Va. F9 200-1
Hardys Trailer Camp*, Sask. J10 294-5
Hardyston*, N.J. B5 76-7
Hardyville, Ky. I9 164-5
Hardyville, Va. E4 196-7
Hare Bay, Nfld. M10 278-9
Hares Corner, Del. B3 153
Harford, co., Md. B12 172-3
Hargrave, Man. J9 272-3
Harjo, Okla. F12 234-5
Harker Heights*, Tex. F8 192-3
Harkers Island, N.C. F15 180-1
Harlan, Ind. C12 100-1
Harlan, Ia. G3 104-5
Harlan, Kans. D8 108-9
Harlan, Ky. J14 164-5
Harlan, Ore. E4 238-9
Harlan, co., Ky. J14 164-5
Harlan, co., Nebr. J9 124-5
Harlem, Fla. H12 156-7
Harlem, Ga. G8 160-1
Harlem, Mont. B10 222-3
Harley Dome, Ut. I11 242-3
Harleysville, Pa. I15 84-5
Harleyville, S.C. G12 184-5
Harlingen, Tex. K8 192-3
Harlow, N. Dak. D9 128-9
Harlowton, Mont. F9 222-3
Harman, W. Va. F8 200-1
Harmans, Md. G6 172-3
Harmon, La. C2 168-9
Harmon, Okla. D7 234-5
Harmon, co., Okla. G6 234-5
Harmons School, Del. J6 153
Harmony, Ark. C4 150-1
Harmony, Ind. I5 100-1
Harmony, Me. I5 64-5
Harmony, Md. F13 172-3
Harmony, Minn. O8 116-7
Harmony, N.J. E3 76-7
Harmony, N.C. H2 180-1
Harmony, Pa. G2 84-5
Harmony, R.I. B4 87
Harmony, Tenn. K8 188-9
Harmony, W. Va. F3 200-1
Harmonyville, Vt. M6 90-1
Harms, Tenn. K7 188-9
Harnett, co., N.C. E10 180-1
Harney, Nev. D7 226-7
Harney, Ore. G13 238-9
Harney, co., Ore. I12 238-9
Harper, Ia. H11 104-5
Harper, Kans. J9 108-9
Harper, Ore. F15 238-9
Harper, Wash. I2 246-7
Harper, W. Va. K15 200-1
Harper, co., Kans. K9 108-9
Harper, co., Okla. C7 234-5
Harper Woods, Mich. J7 112-3
Harpers Ferry, Ia. B13 104-5
Harpers Ferry, W. Va. E12 200-1
Harpersville, Ala. F7 146-7
Harperville, Miss. H8 176-7
Harpster, O. D6 132-3
Harpswell*, Me. O10 64-5
Harpswell Center, Me. N10 64-5
Harrah, Okla. J3 234-5
Harrah, Wash. H11 246-7
Harrell, Ark. I6 150-1
Harrells, N.C. F12 180-1
Harrellsville, N.C. C14 180-1
Harriet, Ark. B6 150-1
Harrietsfield*, N.S. E7 281
Harrietta, Mich. G12 112-3
Harriman, N.Y. A13 80-1
Harriman, Tenn. H10 188-9
Harriman, Wyo. K14 250-1
Harrington, Del. H3 153
Harrington, Me. J9 64-5
Harrington*, P.E.I. E7 287
Harrington, Wash. F14 246-7
Harrington Park, N.J. A12 76-7
Harris, Ala. B6 146-7
Harris, Ariz. E3 206-7
Harris, Ia. A3 104-5
Harris, Kans. H15 108-9
Harris, Minn. K7 116-7
Harris, Mo. A5 120-1
Harris, N.C. E5 180-1
Harris, Okla. I16 234-5
Harris, R.I. D4 87
Harris, Sask. L5 294-5
Harris, S.C. J3 184-5
Harris, co., Ga. I3 160-1
Harris, co., Tex. G10 192-3
Harrisburg, Ark. D10 150-1
Harrisburg, Ill. N9 96-7
Harrisburg, Mo. D6 120-1
Harrisburg, Nebr. F1 124-5
Harrisburg, N.C. J2 180-1
Harrisburg, O. G6 132-3
Harrisburg, Ore. J1 238-9
Harrisburg, Pa. I11 84-5
Harrisburg, S. Dak. H16 136-7
Harrisburg, Tenn. I13 188-9
Harrison, Ark. B5 150-1
Harrison, Ga. I7 160-1
Harrison, Ida. D2 218-9
Harrison, Me. M7 64-5
Harrison, Mich. G13 112-3
Harrison, Mont. G6 222-3
Harrison, Nebr. D1 124-5
Harrison*, N.J. K2 76-7
Harrison, N.J. D10 76-7
Harrison, O. H2 132-3
Harrison, S. Dak. H12 136-7
Harrison, Tenn. K11 188-9
Harrison, W. Va. G5 200-1
Harrison, co., Ind. N8 100-1
Harrison, co., Ia. G2 104-5
Harrison, co., Ky. F12 164-5
Harrison, co., Miss. N8 176-7
Harrison, co., Mo. A4 120-1
Harrison, co., O. E10 132-3
Harrison, co., Tex. E11 192-3
Harrison, co., W. Va. E6 200-1
Harrison Hot Springs, B.C. B16 268-9
Harrisonburg, La. D6 168-9
Harrisonburg, Va. F10 196-7
Harrisonville, Ga. H2 160-1
Harrisonville, Ky. B5 164-5
Harrisonville, Mo. E3 120-1
Harrisonville, N.J. K2 76-7
Harriston, Miss. K4 176-7
Harriston, Ont. C13 284-5
Harristown, Ill. H8 96-7
Harrisville, Conn. B14 60-1
Harrisville, Mich. F14 112-3
Harrisville, Miss. J6 176-7
Harrisville, N.H. N4 72-3
Harrisville, N.Y. C8 80-1
Harrisville, O. F11 132-3
Harrisville, R.I. A3 87
Harrisville, Ut. D6 242-3
Harrisville, W. Va. E4 200-1
Harrisville, Wis. G1 140-1
Harrod, O. D4 132-3
Harrods Creek, Ky. A2 164-5
Harrodsburg, Ind. K7 100-1
Harrodsburg, Ky. D5 164-5
Harrogate, Tenn. F13 188-9
Harrold, S. Dak. E10 136-7
Harrop, B.C. J10 268-9
Harrow, Ont. G9 284-5
Harrowby*, Man. I1 272-3
Harrowsmith, Ont. J13 284-5
Harry S. Truman Res., Mo. F3 120-1
Harsens Island, Mich. I8 112-3
Harshaw, Ariz. M9 206-7
Hart, Mich. H11 112-3
Hart, Tex. C4 192-3
Hart, co., Ga. E7 160-1
Hart, co., Ky. I8 164-5
Hartfield, Va. E4 196-7
Hartford, Ala. M9 146-7
Hartford, Ark. E2 150-1
Hartford, Conn. D9 60-1
Hartford, Ga. K6 160-1
Hartford, Ill. K6 96-7
Hartford, Ia. H8 104-5
Hartford, Kans. H13 108-9
Hartford, Ky. I6 164-5
Hartford, Me. K3 64-5
Hartford, Mich. J11 112-3
Hartford, N.J. I4 76-7
Hartford, O. F7 132-3
Hartford, S. Dak. G15 136-7
Hartford, Tenn. I14 188-9
Hartford, Vt. J7 90-1
Hartford, W. Va. F2 200-1
Hartford, Wis. I14 140-1
Hartford, co., Conn. C9 60-1
Hartford City, Ind. F10 100-1
Hartington, Nebr. D13 124-5
Hartland, Conn. B7 60-1
Hartland, Me. J5 64-5
Hartland, Mich. I4 112-3
Hartland, Minn. O6 116-7
Hartland, N.B. H3 275
Hartland, Vt. J7 90-1
Hartland, W. Va. H16 200-1
Hartland, Wis. I4 140-1
Hartley, Ia. B3 104-5
Hartley, co., Tex. A4 192-3
Hartline, Wash. E13 246-7
Hartly, Del. F3 153
Hartman, Ark. D4 150-1
Hartman, Colo. H16 214-5
Hartney, Man. J10 272-3
Harts, W. Va. J11 200-1
Hartsburg, Mo. E7 120-1
Hartsdale, N.Y. C15 80-1
Hartsel, Colo. F10 214-5
Hartselle, Ala. C6 146-7
Hartshorne, Okla. G14 234-5
Hartsville, Ind. J9 100-1
Hartsville, Mass. E2 68-9
Hartsville, S.C. C13 184-5
Hartsville, Tenn. A8 188-9
Hartville, Mo. H6 120-1
Hartville, O. E16 132-3
Hartville, Wyo. H15 250-1
Hartwell, Ga. E7 160-1
Hartwick, Ia. G11 104-5
Hartwood, Va. C2 196-7
Harty, Ont. F6 284-5
Harvard, Ida. E2 218-9
Harvard, Ill. A9 96-7
Harvard, Mass. G1 68-9
Harvard, Nebr. I11 124-5
Harvest, Ala. A6 146-7
Harvey, Ark. F3 150-1
Harvey, Ill. N4 96-7
Harvey, Ia. H9 104-5
Harvey*, La. I9 168-9
Harvey, Mich. D10 112-3
Harvey, N.B. I4 275
Harvey, N. Dak. E9 128-9
Harvey, co., Kans. H11 108-9
Harvey Cedars, N.J. K7 76-7
Harveys Lake, Pa. E13 84-5
Harveysburg, O. J14 132-3
Harveyville, Kans. F13 108-9
Harvie Heights*, Alta. M6 264-5
Harviell, Mo. J10 120-1
Harwich, Mass. H16 68-9
Harwich Port, Mass. H16 68-9
Harwinton, Conn. D7 60-1
Harwood, Md. J7 172-3
Harwood, Mo. G3 120-1
Harwood Heights, Ill. L3 96-7
Hasbrouck Heights, N.J. B11 76-7
Haskell, Ark. K14 150-1
Haskell, Okla. E14 234-5
Haskell, Tex. D6 192-3
Haskell, co., Kans. J3 108-9
Haskell, co., Okla. F15 234-5
Haskell, co., Tex. D6 192-3
Haskett*, Man. K3 272-3
Haskins, O. B5 132-3
Haslett, Mich. H1 112-3
Hassayampa, Ariz. I5 206-7
Hassell, N.C. D13 180-1
Hastings, Fla. C11 156-7
Hastings, Ia. I3 104-5
Hastings, Mich. J12 112-3
Hastings, Minn. M7 116-7
Hastings, Nebr. I11 124-5
Hastings, N. Dak. H12 128-9
Hastings, Okla. H10 234-5
Hastings, Ont. J11 284-5
Hastings, Pa. H6 84-5
Hastings, co., Ont. J12 284-5

Hastings-on-Hudson, N.Y. D14 80-1
Hasty, Ark. B5 150-1
Hasty, Colo. H15 214-5
Haswell, Colo. G14 214-5
Hat Creek, Wyo. F16 250-1
Hatboro, Pa. A11 84-5
Hatboro West*, Pa. I15 84-5
Hatch, Ida. N10 218-9
Hatch, N. Mex. K5 230-1
Hatch, Ut. L5 242-3
Hatchechubbee, Ala. I10 146-7
Hatchville, Mass. H14 68-9
Hatfield, Ark. G2 150-1
Hatfield, Ind. O5 100-1
Hatfield, Mass. D5 68-9
Hatfield, Minn. O2 116-7
Hatfield, Pa. I15 84-5
Hatfield, Wis. G10 140-1
Hatfield Point, N.B. I5 275
Hathaway, La. H4 168-9
Hathaway, Mont. F13 222-3
Hathorne, Mass. A12 68-9
Hatley, Miss. D10 176-7
Hatley, Wis. C1 140-1
Hatteras, N.C. E16 180-1
Hattertown, Conn. G5 60-1
Hattiesburg, Miss. L8 176-7
Hattiesburg South*, Miss. L8 176-7
Hattieville, Ark. D6 150-1
Hatton, Ala. B5 146-7
Hatton, Ark. G2 150-1
Hatton, Ky. A5 164-5
Hatton, N. Dak. E13 128-9
Hatton, Ut. J5 242-3
Hatton, Wash. G13 246-7
Hatzic, B.C. C15 268-9
Hatzic Prairie*, B.C. J6 268-9
Haubstadt, Ind. N4 100-1
Haugan, Mont. D1 222-3
Haugen, Wis. D8 140-1
Haughton, La. B2 168-9
Hauppauge, N.Y. J12 80-1
Hauser, Ida. C2 218-9
Hauser, Ore. G3 238-9
Haute-Aboujagane, N.B. H7 275
Hauterive, Que. A16 290-1
Hauula, Hawaii G5 258-9
Havana, Ala. G4 146-7
Havana, Ark. E4 150-1
Havana, Fla. B7 156-7
Havana, Ill. G6 96-7
Havana, Kans. K14 108-9
Havana, N. Dak. J13 128-9
Havelock, Ia. C5 104-5
Havelock, N.B. H6 275
Havelock, N.C. F14 180-1
Havelock, Ont. J12 284-5
Haven, Kans. I10 108-9
Havensville, Kans. D13 108-9
Haverhill*, Fla. D16 156-7
Haverhill, Mass. A11 68-9
Haverhill, N.H. H4 72-3
Haverill, Ia. F9 104-5
Haversham, R.I. I2 87
Haverstraw, N.Y. B14 80-1
Haviland, Kans. J7 108-9
Haviland*, N.Y. H11 80-1
Havre, Mont. B9 222-3
Havre-Aubert, Que. I7 290-1
Havre Boucher, N.S. C10 281
Havre de Grace, Md. B13 172-3
Havre-St.-Pierre, Que. G6 290-1
Haw River*, N.C. C9 180-1
Hawaii, co., Hawaii J13 258-9
Hawaii Kai*, Hawaii J7 258-9
Hawaiian Gardens*, Calif. N7 210-1
Hawarden, Ia. C1 104-5
Hawarden, Sask. L6 294-5
Hawesville, Ky. G6 164-5
Hawi, Hawaii H12 258-9
Hawk Junction, Ont. G5 284-5
Hawk Point, Mo. D9 120-1
Hawk Springs, Wyo. I16 250-1
Hawk, The, N.S. G4 281
Hawkesbury, Ont. H16 284-5
Hawkeye, Ia. C12 104-5
Hawkins*, Tex. D10 192-3
Hawkins, Wis. D10 140-1
Hawkins, co., Tenn. A14 188-9
Hawkinsville, Ga. K6 160-1
Hawks, Mich. E14 112-3
Hawley, Mass. C3 68-9
Hawley, Minn. I2 116-7
Hawley, Okla. C10 234-5
Hawley, Pa. E15 84-5
Hawleyville, Conn. G5 60-1
Haworth, N.J. A12 76-7
Haworth, Okla. I16 234-5
Hawthorn, Fla. D10 156-7
Hawthorn Woods, Ill. K2 96-7
Hawthorne, Calif. G8 210-1
Hawthorne, Nev. H3 226-7
Hawthorne, N.J. A10 76-7
Haxtun, Colo. C15 214-5
Hay, Wash. H15 246-7
Hay Creek, Ore. E9 238-9
Hay Lakes, Alta. J8 264-5
Hay River, N.W. Terr. C1 296
Hay Springs, Nebr. D3 124-5
Hayden, Ala. D6 146-7
Hayden, Ariz. J8 206-7
Hayden, Colo. C8 214-5
Hayden, Conn. C9 60-1
Hayden, Ida. C2 218-9
Hayden, Ind. K9 100-1
Hayden, N. Mex. D11 230-1
Hayden, Okla. C14 234-5
Hayden Lake, Ida. C2 218-9
Haydenville, Mass. D4 68-9
Hayes, La. H3 168-9
Hayes, S. Dak. E7 136-7
Hayes, co., Nebr. I6 124-5
Hayes Center, Nebr. I6 124-5
Hayesville, Ia. H11 104-5
Hayesville, N.C. F1 180-1
Hayesville, O. D8 132-3
Hayesville, Ore. H1 238-9
Hayfield, Minn. O7 116-7
Hayfield, Va. D11 196-7
Hayfork, Calif. E2 210-1
Haymarket, Va. A2 196-7
Haynes, Ark. E10 150-1
Haynes, N. Dak. J4 128-9
Haynesville, La. A3 168-9
Haynesville, Me. F9 64-5
Haynesville, Va. G14 196-7
Hayneville, Ala. I7 146-7
Hays, Kans. F6 108-9
Hays, Mont. C10 222-3
Hays, N.C. G1 180-1
Hays, co., Tex. G8 192-3
Haysi, Va. I3 196-7
Haysville, Ind. M6 100-1
Haysville, Kans. J11 108-9
Haysville, Tenn. A8 188-9
Hayti, Mo. K11 120-1
Hayti*, Pa. K13 84-5
Hayti, S. Dak. D15 136-7
Hayti Heights*, Mo. K11 120-1
Hayton, Wis. F4 140-1
Hayward, Calif. C8 210-1
Hayward, Minn. O6 116-7
Hayward, Okla. D11 234-5
Hayward, Wis. C9 140-1
Haywood, Man. J13 272-3
Haywood, N.C. I6 180-1
Haywood, Okla. G14 234-5
Haywood, Va. C1 196-7
Haywood, co., N.C. E3 180-1
Haywood, co., Tenn. C2 188-9
Haywood City*, Mo. I11 120-1
Hazard, Ky. I14 164-5
Hazard, Nebr. H10 124-5
Hazardville, Conn. B10 60-1
Hazel, Ky. K3 164-5
Hazel, S. Dak. D14 136-7
Hazel Crest, Ill. N4 96-7
Hazel Dell, Sask. L9 294-5
Hazel Green, Ala. A7 146-7
Hazel Green, Ky. H13 164-5
Hazel Green, Wis. K11 140-1
Hazel Hill, N.S. D10 281
Hazel Park, Mich. J6 112-3
Hazel Patch, Ky. I12 164-5
Hazel Run, Minn. M3 116-7
Hazelbrook*, P.E.I. F8 287
Hazelgreen, W. Va. E4 200-1
Hazelhurst, Wis. D12 140-1
Hazelridge*, Man. I15 272-3
Hazelton, B.C. E5 268-9
Hazelton, Ida. N6 218-9
Hazelton, Kans. K8 108-9
Hazelton, N. Dak. I8 128-9
Hazelton, W. Va. D8 200-1
Hazelwood, Ind. I7 100-1
Hazelwood*, Mo. E10 120-1
Hazelwood, N.C. E3 180-1
Hazelwood, Ore. F2 238-9
Hazen, Ala. I5 146-7
Hazen, Ark. F8 150-1
Hazen, Nev. F3 226-7
Hazen, N. Dak. F6 128-9
Hazenmore, Sask. O6 294-5
Hazlehurst, Ga. L8 160-1
Hazlehurst, Miss. J5 176-7
Hazlet, N.J. H10 76-7
Hazlet, Sask. N5 294-5
Hazleton, Ind. M4 100-1
Hazleton, Ia. D12 104-5
Hazleton, Pa. G13 84-5
Hazlettville, Del. F3 153
Head of Island, La. B11 168-9
Head of the Harbor*, N.Y. J12 80-1
Head Waters, Va. G9 196-7
Headland, Ala. L10 146-7
Headquarters, Ida. F4 218-9
Headrick, Okla. H8 234-5
Heads, Miss. E4 176-7
Heafford Junction, Wis. D12 140-1
Healdsburg, Calif. A6 210-1
Healdton, Okla. H11 234-5
Healdville, Vt. K6 90-1
Healing Springs, Ala. K2 146-7
Healing Springs, Va. G8 196-7
Healy, Alaska E11 254-5
Healy, Kans. G4 108-9
Heard, co., Ga. H2 160-1
Heards, Va. H10 196-7
Hearne, Tex. F9 192-3
Hearst, Ont. E6 284-5
Heart Butte, Mont. B5 222-3
Heart's Content, Nfld. N11 278-9
Heart's Delight-Islington*, Nfld. N11 278-9
Heart's Desire*, Ont. H14 284-5
Heartwell, Nebr. I10 124-5
Heartwellville, Vt. N5 90-1
Heaters, W. Va. F5 200-1
Heath, Ala. L7 146-7
Heath, Ky. J2 164-5
Heath, Mass. B4 68-9
Heath, Mont. E9 222-3
Heath, O. F8 132-3
Heath Springs, S.C. C11 184-5
Heathsville, Va. G14 196-7
Heaton, N. Dak. F9 128-9
Heavener, Okla. G16 234-5
Hebbardsville, Ky. H5 164-5
Hebbronville, Tex. J7 192-3
Hebbville, Md. F6 172-3
Heber, Ariz. G9 206-7
Heber, Ut. F7 242-3
Heber Springs, Ark. D7 150-1
Hebert, La. C5 168-9
Hébertville-Station*, Que. C11 290-1
Hebo, Ore. C4 238-9
Hebron, Conn. E11 60-1
Hebron, Ill. A9 96-7
Hebron, Ind. B5 100-1
Hebron, Ky. D11 164-5
Hebron, Me. L3 64-5
Hebron, Md. G14 172-3
Hebron, Nebr. J12 124-5
Hebron, N.H. J5 72-3
Hebron, N. Dak. G5 128-9
Hebron, O. F7 132-3
Hebron, W. Va. E4 200-1
Hebron, Wis. J3 140-1
Heceta Beach, Ore. F4 238-9
Heceta Junction, Ore. F4 238-9
Hecla, S. Dak. A13 136-7
Hector, Ark. D5 150-1
Hector, Minn. M4 116-7
Hedding, N.J. H4 76-7
Hedgesville, W. Va. D11 200-1
Hedgeville, Mont. F9 222-3
Hedley, B.C. J8 268-9
Hedrick, Ia. I11 104-5
Hedville, Kans. F10 108-9
Hedwig Village*, Tex. H13 192-3
Heeney, Colo. D9 214-5
Heflin, Ala. E9 146-7
Heflin, La. B3 168-9
Hegeler [-Home Gardens], Ill. G11 96-7
Heglar, Ida. O8 218-9
Heiberger, Ala. H5 146-7
Heidelberg, Ky. H13 164-5
Heidelberg, Minn. N6 116-7
Heidelberg, Miss. J9 176-7
Heidelberg*, Ont. D13 284-5
Heidelberg*, Pa. I2 84-5
Heidrick, Ky. J13 164-5
Heil, N. Dak. I5 128-9
Heimdal, N. Dak. E9 128-9
Heise, Ida. L10 218-9
Heiskell, Tenn. H11 188-9
Heisler, Alta. K9 264-5
Heislerville, N.J. N3 76-7
Heisson, Wash. J7 246-7
Heizer, Kans. G7 108-9
Heldt, Wyo. H16 250-1
Helen, Ga. D5 160-1
Helen, Md. G11 172-3
Helen, W. Va. I4 200-1
Helena, Ala. F6 146-7
Helena, Ark. G11 150-1
Helena, Ga. K7 160-1
Helena, Mont. F6 222-3
Helena, O. C6 132-3
Helena, Okla. C9 234-5
Helena, S.C. J6 184-5
Helenville, Wis. J3 140-1
Helix, Ore. B13 238-9
Hellertown, Pa. H15 84-5
Hellier, Ky. I15 164-5
Helmer, Ida. E3 218-9
Helmer, Ind. A11 100-1
Helmetta, N.J. G6 76-7
Helmsburg, Ind. J8 100-1
Helmville, Mont. E5 222-3
Heloise, Tenn. B2 188-9
Helper, Ut. H8 242-3
Helton, Ky. J14 164-5
Heltonville, Ind. K7 100-1
Helvetia, W. Va. G14 200-1
Heman, Ida. K10 218-9
Hemet, Calif. H11 210-1
Hemet East*, Calif. N8 210-1
Hemingford, Nebr. E2 124-5
Hemingway, S.C. E14 184-5
Hemlock, Ind. F8 100-1
Hemlock, Mich. E2 112-3
Hemlock, W. Va. F14 200-1
Hemmingford, Que. J12 290-1
Hemp, Ga. D4 160-1
Hemphill, Tex. F11 192-3
Hemphill, co., Tex. A6 192-3
Hempstead, N.Y. E16 80-1
Hempstead, Tex. G10 192-3
Hempstead, co., Ark. H3 150-1
Hempwallace, Ark. G4 150-1
Henagar, Ala. B9 146-7
Henderson, Ala. K8 146-7
Henderson, Ark. A7 150-1
Henderson, Colo. G3 214-5
Henderson, Ga. J5 160-1
Henderson, Ia. I3 104-5
Henderson, Ky. H5 164-5
Henderson, La. H6 168-9
Henderson, Md. D14 172-3
Henderson, Mich. G2 112-3
Henderson, Minn. N5 116-7
Henderson, Nebr. H12 124-5
Henderson, Nev. M10 226-7
Henderson, N.C. C11 180-1
Henderson, Tenn. C4 188-9
Henderson, Tex. E11 192-3
Henderson, W. Va. F2 200-1
Henderson, co., Ill. E4 96-7
Henderson, co., Ky. H5 164-5
Henderson, co., N.C. E4 180-1
Henderson, co., Tenn. C4 188-9
Henderson, co., Tex. E10 192-3
Hendersonville, N.C. E4 180-1
Hendersonville, S.C. I11 184-5
Hendersonville, Tenn. G7 188-9
Hendersonville West*, N.C. E4 180-1
Hendley, Nebr. J8 124-5
Hendon, Sask. K9 294-5
Hendricks, Minn. N2 116-7
Hendricks, W. Va. E16 200-1
Hendricks, co., Ind. H7 100-1
Hendron, Tenn. H12 188-9
Hendrum, Minn. H1 116-7
Hendry, co., Fla. I12 156-7
Henefer, Ut. E7 242-3
Henlawson, W. Va. K12 200-1
Henley, Mo. F7 120-1
Hennepin, Ill. D8 96-7
Hennepin, Okla. H11 234-5
Hennepin, co., Minn. M6 116-7
Hennessey, Okla. D10 234-5
Henniker, N.H. M5 72-3
Henning, Minn. J3 116-7
Henning, Tenn. J2 188-9
Henribourg, Sask. J7 294-5
Henrico, co., Va. I12 196-7
Henrietta, Mo. D4 120-1
Henrietta, Tenn. G6 188-9
Henrietta, Tex. C8 192-3
Henrietta [-Avondale], N.C. E5 180-1
Henriette, Minn. K7 116-7
Henrieville, Ut. M6 242-3
Henry, Ida. N11 218-9
Henry, Ill. D8 96-7
Henry, La. I5 168-9
Henry, Nebr. E1 124-5
Henry, Nev. A10 226-7
Henry, S. Dak. D14 136-7
Henry, Tenn. B4 188-9
Henry, Va. J8 196-7
Henry, co., Ala. K10 146-7
Henry, co., Ga. G4 160-1
Henry, co., Ill. D6 96-7
Henry, co., Ind. H10 100-1
Henry, co., Ia. I13 104-5
Henry, co., Ky. F10 164-5
Henry, co., Mo. F4 120-1
Henry, co., O. C4 132-3
Henry, co., Tenn. B4 188-9
Henry, co., Va. K8 196-7
Henryetta, Okla. F13 234-5
Henryville, Ind. M9 100-1
Henryville, Que. J13 290-1
Henryville, Tenn. J5 188-9
Hensall, Ont. D12 284-5
Henshaw, Ky. H4 164-5
Hensley, Ark. K16 150-1
Hepburn, Ia. J4 104-5
Hepburn, Sask. K6 294-5
Hephzibah, Ga. H9 160-1
Hephzibah Heights, Mass. E2 68-9
Hepler, Kans. I16 108-9
Heppner, Ore. C11 238-9
Heppner Junction, Ore. B11 238-9
Hepworth, Ont. A12 284-5
Hepzibah, W. Va. C13 200-1
Herb Lake, Man. F2 272-3
Herbert, Sask. N6 294-5
Herbster, Wis. A9 140-1
Herchmer, Man. C5 272-3
Herculaneum, Mo. D15 120-1
Hercules, Calif. B7 210-1
Herd, Okla. C13 234-5
Hereford, Ariz. M10 206-7
Hereford, Colo. B13 214-5
Hereford, Md. B11 172-3
Hereford, Ore. E14 238-9
Hereford, Tex. B4 192-3
Herington, Kans. G11 108-9
Herkimer, Kans. C12 108-9
Herkimer, N.Y. E9 80-1
Herkimer, co., N.Y. D9 80-1
Herman, Mich. C9 112-3
Herman, Minn. K2 116-7
Herman, Nebr. F15 124-5
Herman Brothers Trailer Court*, Sask. N8 294-5
Hermann, Mo. E8 120-1
Hermansville, Mich. E9 112-3
Hermanville, Miss. J4 176-7
Hermiston, Ore. B12 238-9
Hermitage, Ark. J7 150-1
Hermitage, La. G7 168-9
Hermitage, Mo. G5 120-1
Hermitage Springs, Tenn. A9 188-9
Hermon, Me. J6 64-5
Hermosa, S. Dak. G3 136-7
Hermosa, Wyo. J14 250-1
Hermosa Beach*, Calif. H8 210-1
Hernando, Fla. E10 156-7
Hernando, Miss. B6 176-7
Hernando, co., Fla. E10 156-7
Herndon, Kans. C3 108-9
Herndon, Ky. K5 164-5
Herndon, Va. A3 196-7
Herndon Heights, W. Va. J4 200-1
Herod, Ga. L4 160-1
Herold, W. Va. G5 200-1
Heron, Mont. C1 222-3
Heron Lake, Minn. O3 116-7
Hérouxville*, Que. I12 290-1
Herreid, S. Dak. A9 136-7
Herrick, S. Dak. I11 136-7
Herricks*, N.Y. J11 80-1
Herriman, Ut. F6 242-3
Herrin, Ill. M8 96-7
Herring, Okla. E7 234-5
Herring Cove, Alaska H16 254-5
Herring Cove*, N.S. E7 281
Herron, Mich. F14 112-3
Herschel, Sask. L5 294-5
Herscher, Ill. E10 96-7

Hersey, Me. E8 64-5
Hersey, Mich. H12 112-3
Hersey, Wis. E8 140-1
Hershey, Nebr. G6 124-5
Hershey, Pa. I11 84-5
Hertford, N.C. C15 180-1
Hertford, co., N.C. C13 180-1
Hesper, Ia. A12 104-5
Hesperia, Calif. F10 210-1
Hesperia, Mich. H11 112-3
Hesperus, Colo. J7 214-5
Hess, Okla. H7 234-5
Hessel, Mich. D13 112-3
Hessmer, La. F5 168-9
Hesston, Kans. H10 108-9
Hester, Okla. G7 234-5
Hesterville, Miss. F7 176-7
Heth, Ark. E11 150-1
Hetland, S. Dak. E15 136-7
Hettie, W. Va. F13 200-1
Hettinger, N. Dak. J4 128-9
Hettinger, co., N. Dak. I4 128-9
Heuvelton, N.Y. B8 80-1
Heward, Sask. O9 294-5
Hewitt, Minn. J4 116-7
Hewitt, N.J. B7 76-7
Hewitt, Wis. F11 140-1
Hewlett*, N.Y. K11 80-1
Hewlett Bay Park*, N.Y. K11 80-1
Hewlett Harbor*, N.Y. K11 80-1
Hewlett Neck*, N.Y. K11 80-1
Heyburn, Ida. O7 218-9
Heyworth, Ill. G8 96-7
Hi-Nella, N.J. O11 76-7
Hialeah, Fla. H16 156-7
Hialeah Gardens*, Fla. H16 156-7
Hiattville, Kans. I16 108-9
Hiawassee, Ga. C5 160-1
Hiawatha, Colo. B6 214-5
Hiawatha, Ia. F12 104-5
Hiawatha, Kans. C14 108-9
Hiawatha, Ut. H7 242-3
Hiawatha Park*, Ont. H15 284-5
Hibbard, Ida. L10 218-9
Hibbing, Minn. G7 116-7
Hibernia, N.J. C6 76-7
Hickam Housing, Hawaii J4 258-9
Hickey, Tenn. B9 188-9
Hickiwan, Ariz. K5 206-7
Hickman, Del. H3 153
Hickman, Ky. K1 164-5
Hickman, Nebr. I14 124-5
Hickman, Tenn. B9 188-9
Hickman, co., Ky. K2 164-5
Hickman, co., Tenn. C6 188-9
Hickman's Harbour, Nfld. N11 278-9
Hickok, Kans. J2 108-9
Hickory, La. A16 168-9
Hickory, Miss. I9 176-7
Hickory, N.C. D6 180-1
Hickory, Okla. H12 234-5
Hickory, co., Mo. G5 120-1
Hickory Corners, Mich. J12 112-3
Hickory East, N.C. D6 180-1
Hickory Flat, Ala. G10 146-7
Hickory Flat, Ark. D8 150-1
Hickory Flat, Miss. B8 176-7
Hickory Grove, Ky. J3 164-5
Hickory Grove, N.C. J2 180-1
Hickory Grove, S.C. B9 184-5
Hickory Grove, S.C. E15 184-5
Hickory Hills, Ill. N3 96-7
Hickory North*, N.C. D6 180-1
Hickory Plains, Ark. E8 150-1
Hickory Ridge, Ark. D10 150-1
Hickory Tavern, S.C. H3 184-5
Hickory Valley, Tenn. K3 188-9
Hickory Withe, Tenn. K2 188-9
Hickox, Ga. N9 160-1
Hicks, La. E3 168-9
Hickson, N. Dak. H14 128-9
Hicksville, Mass. H12 68-9
Hicksville, N.Y. E16 80-1
Hicksville, O. C3 132-3
Hico, La. A4 168-9
Hico, Tex. E8 192-3
Hico, W. Va. J16 200-1
Hidalgo*, Tex. K8 192-3
Hidalgo, co., N. Mex. M2 230-1
Hidalgo, co., Tex. K8 192-3
Hidden Hills*, Calif. N6 210-1
Hiddenite, N.C. H1 180-1
Hideaway Park, Colo. D10 214-5
Higbee, Mo. D6 120-1
Higden, Ark. D7 150-1
Higdon, Ala. A9 146-7
Higdon, Ga. D4 160-1
Higganum, Conn. F10 60-1
Higgins, Okla. G15 234-5
Higgins Beach, Me. N3 64-5
Higgins Lake, Mich. G13 112-3
Higginson, Ark. E8 150-1
Higginsport, O. J4 132-3
Higginsville, Mo. D4 120-1
Higgston, Ga. K8 160-1
High Bluff, Man. I13 272-3
High Bridge, Ky. C6 164-5
High Bridge, N.J. E4 76-7
High Hill, Mo. E8 120-1
High Level, Alta. C5 264-5
High Point, Ala. C7 146-7
High Point, Miss. F8 176-7
High Point, N.C. D8 180-1
High Prairie, Alta. G5 264-5
High River, Alta. M7 264-5
High Rock, N.C. I3 180-1
High Rolls Mountain Park, N. Mex. J7 230-1
High Shoals, N.C. J1 180-1
High Springs, Fla. C10 156-7
High View, W. Va. E10 200-1
Highfalls, N.C. J5 180-1
Highfield, Md. B8 172-3
Highfield*, Pa. G2 84-5
Highfill, Ark. A2 150-1
Highgate, Ont. F11 284-5
Highgate*, Vt. B4 90-1
Highgate Falls, Vt. B4 90-1
Highgate Springs, Vt. B4 90-1
Highland, Ark. H3 150-1
Highland, Calif. G10 210-1
Highland, Ill. K7 96-7
Highland, Ind. A4 100-1
Highland, Kans. C15 108-9
Highland, La. A7 168-9
Highland, Me. I4 64-5
Highland, Md. G4 172-3
Highland, Mich. I4 112-3
Highland, N.Y. H11 80-1
Highland, Ore. C7 238-9
Highland, Tenn. D5 188-9
Highland, W. Va. E4 200-1
Highland, Wis. J11 140-1
Highland, co., O. I5 132-3
Highland, co., Va. G8 196-7
Highland Acres*, Del. F4 153
Highland Beach, Fla. F16 156-7
Highland Beach, Md. I8 172-3
Highland City, Fla. H5 156-7
Highland Falls, N.Y. A14 80-1
Highland Grove, Ont. I11 284-5
Highland Heights, Ky. E11 164-5
Highland Heights*, O. B10 132-3
Highland Home, Ala. J7 146-7
Highland Lake*, Ala. D7 146-7
Highland Park, Fla. I6 156-7
Highland Park, Ill. K3 96-7
Highland Park, Mich. J6 112-3
Highland Park, N.J. F6 76-7
Highland Park*, Pa. H9 84-5
Highland Park*, Pa. G15 84-5
Highland Park, Tex. C15 192-3
Highland Park Subdivision*, Ont. B14 284-5
Highland Springs, Va. E1 196-7
Highland View, Fla. C6 156-7
Highlands, N.J. H12 76-7
Highlands, N.C. F3 180-1
Highlands, Tex. H15 192-3
Highlands, co., Fla. G12 156-7
Highley Heights*, Mo. G10 120-1
Highlight, Wyo. D14 250-1
Highmore, S. Dak. E10 136-7
Highspire, Pa. I11 84-5
Hightown, Va. F8 196-7
Hightstown, N.J. H6 76-7
Highwood, Ill. K3 96-7
Highwood, Mont. D7 222-3
Higley, Ariz. I7 206-7
Hiko, Nev. J9 226-7
Hiland, Wyo. F11 250-1
Hiland Park, Fla. C5 156-7
Hilbert, Wis. F4 140-1
Hilbre*, Man. I3 272-3
Hilda, S.C. G9 184-5
Hildebran, N.C. D6 180-1
Hildebrand, Ore. J8 238-9
Hilden, N.S. D7 281
Hildreth, Nebr. I10 124-5
Hilea, Hawaii K13 258-9
Hiles, Wis. D13 140-1
Hilgard, Ore. C14 238-9
Hilger, Mont. D9 222-3
Hilham, Tenn. A10 188-9
Hill, Mont. B7 222-3
Hill, N.H. K6 72-3
Hill, co., Mont. A9 222-3
Hill, co., Tex. E8 192-3
Hill City, Ga. D2 160-1
Hill City, Ida. M5 218-9
Hill City, Kans. E5 108-9
Hill City, Minn. H6 116-7
Hill City, S. Dak. F2 136-7
Hill County Village*, Tex. G7 192-3
Hill Spring, Alta. O8 264-5
Hillburn, N.Y. C13 80-1
Hillcrest, Alta. O7 264-5
Hillcrest, Ill. B8 96-7
Hillcrest, Mass. H11 68-9
Hillcrest, N.Y. C13 80-1
Hillcrest*, Pa. F1 84-5
Hillcrest, Tenn. F16 188-9
Hillcrest*, Tex. H10 192-3
Hillcrest Heights, Fla. I6 156-7
Hillcrest Heights, Md. J4 172-3
Hillcrest Trailer Park, Man. J4 272-3
Hilldale*, Ut. M4 242-3
Hillemann, Ark. E10 150-1
Hiller*, Pa. J2 84-5
Hillery-Batestown*, Ill. G11 96-7
Hillhead, S. Dak. A14 136-7
Hillhouse, Miss. D4 176-7
Hillhouse Addition, Mo. G6 120-1
Hilliard, Fla. B11 156-7
Hilliard, O. F6 132-3
Hillis*, N.Y. H11 80-1
Hillisburg, Ind. F7 100-1
Hillman, Mich. F14 112-3
Hillman, Minn. J5 116-7
Hillpoint, Wis. I11 140-1
Hillridge*, Man. J3 272-3
Hillrose, Colo. C14 214-5
Hills, Ia. G13 104-5
Hills, Minn. O2 116-7
Hills and Dales, O. E15 132-3
Hills Borough Park*, P.E.I. E7 287
Hillsboro, Ala. B5 146-7
Hillsboro, Ga. H5 160-1
Hillsboro, Ill. J7 96-7
Hillsboro, Ind. G5 100-1
Hillsboro, Ind. G10 100-1
Hillsboro, Ia. J12 104-5
Hillsboro, Kans. H11 108-9
Hillsboro, Ky. F13 164-5
Hillsboro, Md. E13 172-3
Hillsboro, Miss. H7 176-7
Hillsboro, Mo. F10 120-1
Hillsboro, N.H. M5 72-3
Hillsboro, N. Mex. J4 230-1
Hillsboro, N. Dak. F14 128-9
Hillsboro, O. H5 132-3
Hillsboro, Ore. F1 238-9
Hillsboro, Tenn. D9 188-9
Hillsboro, Tex. E9 192-3
Hillsboro, Va. E12 196-7
Hillsboro, W. Va. H6 200-1
Hillsboro, Wis. I11 140-1
Hillsboro Beach, Fla. F16 156-7
Hillsborough, Calif. D7 210-1
Hillsborough, N.B. H7 275
Hillsborough*, N.H. M5 72-3
Hillsborough*, N.J. F5 76-7
Hillsborough, N.C. D10 180-1
Hillsborough, co., Fla. F10 156-7
Hillsborough, co., N.H. N5 72-3
Hillsburgh*, Ont. C13 284-5
Hillsdale, Ind. O4 100-1
Hillsdale, Ind. H4 100-1
Hillsdale, Kans. G16 108-9
Hillsdale, Mich. K13 112-3
Hillsdale*, Mo. E10 120-1
Hillsdale, N.J. C8 76-7
Hillsdale, Okla. C10 234-5
Hillsdale, Tenn. A9 188-9
Hillsdale, Wis. E8 140-1
Hillsdale, Wyo. J16 250-1
Hillsdale, co., Mich. K13 112-3
Hillside, Ariz. G5 206-7
Hillside, Colo. G10 214-5
Hillside*, Ill. B11 96-7
Hillside, N.J. D10 76-7
Hillside Gardens, Ont. H15 284-5
Hillsview, S. Dak. B10 136-7
Hillsville, Va. J6 196-7
Hilltonia, Ga. I10 160-1
Hilltop, Minn. A10 116-7
Hilo, Hawaii I14 258-9
Hilshire Village*, Tex. G10 192-3
Hilton, Ga. M2 160-1
Hilton, N.Y. E4 80-1
Hilton Beach, Ont. H6 284-5
Hilton Head Isl., S.C. J11 184-5
Hilton Head Island, S.C. J11 184-5
Hiltons, Va. J3 196-7
Hima, Ky. J13 164-5
Himes, Wyo. B9 250-1
Hinchcliff, Miss. C6 176-7
Hinckley, Ill. C9 96-7
Hinckley, Me. J5 64-5
Hinckley, Minn. J7 116-7
Hinckley, Ut. I5 242-3
Hindman, Ky. I14 164-5
Hinds, co., Miss. I5 176-7
Hindsville, Ark. B3 150-1
Hines, Ore. G12 238-9
Hines Creek, Alta. F4 264-5
Hinesburg, Vt. F4 90-1
Hineston, La. F4 168-9
Hinesville, Ga. L10 160-1
Hingham, Mass. I7 68-9
Hingham, Mont. B8 222-3
Hingham, Wis. H5 140-1
Hinkley, Calif. M8 210-1
Hinsdale, Ill. M3 96-7
Hinsdale, Mass. C2 68-9
Hinsdale, Mont. B12 222-3
Hinsdale, N.H. O2 72-3
Hinsdale, co., Colo. H8 214-5
Hinsonton, Ga. N5 160-1
Hinton, Alta. J5 264-5
Hinton, Ia. D1 104-5
Hinton, Okla. F9 234-5
Hinton, W. Va. I5 200-1
Hiram, Ga. B9 160-1
Hiram, Me. N7 64-5
Hiram, O. C16 132-3
Hiseville, Ky. J9 164-5
Hitchcock, Okla. E9 234-5
Hitchcock, Sask. O9 294-5
Hitchcock, S. Dak. E12 136-7
Hitchcock, Tex. J15 192-3
Hitchcock, co., Nebr. J6 124-5
Hitchins, Ky. F14 164-5
Hitchita*, Okla. E14 234-5
Hiteman, Ia. I9 104-5
Hitterdal, Minn. H2 116-7
Hiwannee, Miss. J10 176-7
Hiwasse, Ark. A2 150-1
Hiwassee, Va. J6 196-7
Hiwassee Dam, N.C. E1 180-1
Hix, W. Va. I5 200-1
Hixon, B.C. G7 268-9
Hixson, Tenn. K11 188-9
Hixton, Wis. G10 140-1
Hoagland, Ind. D11 100-1
Hoback Junction, Wyo. K2 250-1
Hobart, Ind. A5 100-1
Hobart, N.Y. G9 80-1
Hobart, Okla. G8 234-5
Hobart, Wash. F8 246-7
Hobbs, Ind. F9 100-1
Hobbs, Md. E14 172-3
Hobbs, N. Mex. K12 230-1
Hobbsville, N.C. C14 180-1
Hobe Sound*, Fla. H13 156-7
Hoberg, Mo. I4 120-1
Hobgood, N.C. D13 180-1
Hoboken, Ga. M9 160-1
Hoboken, N.J. D11 76-7
Hobson, Mont. E9 222-3
Hobson, Va. G4 196-7
Hobson City, Ala. E8 146-7
Hobucken, N.C. E14 180-1
Hochatown, Okla. H16 234-5
Hochfeld, Man. K13 272-3
Hockanum, Mass. D5 68-9
Hockerville, Okla. B15 234-5
Hockessin, Del. A3 153
Hocking, co., O. H7 132-3
Hockinson, Wash. J7 246-7
Hockley, co., Tex. D4 192-3
Hode, Ky. G15 164-5
Hodgdon, Me. E9 64-5
Hodge, La. C4 168-9
Hodgeman, co., Kans. H5 108-9
Hodgens, Okla. G16 234-5
Hodgenville, Ky. E2 164-5
Hodges, Ala. C3 146-7
Hodges, Mont. E16 222-3
Hodges, S.C. J3 184-5
Hodgeville, Sask. N6 294-5
Hodgkins, Ill. M3 96-7
Hodgson, Man. G14 272-3
Hoehne, Colo. J13 214-5
Hoey, Sask. J7 294-5
Hoffman, Minn. K3 116-7
Hoffman, N.C. K5 180-1
Hoffman, Okla. F14 234-5
Hoffman Estates, Ill. L2 96-7
Hog Shooter, Okla. C14 234-5
Hogan, Nev. C10 226-7
Hogansville, Ga. H2 160-1
Hogeland, Mont. A10 222-3
Hogsett, W. Va. F2 200-1
Hohenwald, Tenn. J5 188-9
Hohokus, N.J. C8 76-7
Hoisington, Kans. G8 108-9
Hokah, Minn. O9 116-7
Hoke, co., N.C. F10 180-1
Hokes Bluff, Ala. D8 146-7
Holabird, S. Dak. E10 136-7
Holbein*, Sask. J7 294-5
Holberg, B.C. I4 268-9
Holborn, Nev. C10 226-7
Holbrook, Ariz. F9 206-7
Holbrook, Ida. O9 218-9
Holbrook, Mass. K6 68-9
Holbrook, Nebr. J8 124-5
Holbrook [-Holtsville], N.Y. J12 80-1
Holbrook Junction, Nev. H2 226-7
Holcomb, Kans. H3 108-9
Holcomb, Miss. E6 176-7
Holcomb, Mo. J11 120-1
Holcomb, N.Y. F5 80-1
Holcombe, Wis. E9 140-1
Holcut, Miss. B10 176-7
Holden, Alta. J9 264-5
Holden, La. A12 168-9
Holden, Me. J7 64-5
Holden, Mass. D8 68-9
Holden, Mo. E4 120-1
Holden, Ut. I5 242-3
Holden, Vt. I5 90-1
Holden, W. Va. K11 200-1
Holden Beach*, N.C. H11 180-1
Holden Heights*, Fla. E11 156-7
Holdenville, Okla. G13 234-5
Holderness, N.H. J6 72-3
Holdfast, Sask. M7 294-5
Holdingford, Minn. K5 116-7
Holdman, Ore. B12 238-9
Holdrege, Nebr. I9 124-5
Holgate, O. C4 132-3
Holiday Gardens*, Fla. F9 156-7
Holiday Hills*, Fla. F9 156-7
Holiday Hills*, Ill. A10 96-7
Holikachuk, Alaska E9 254-5
Holladay, Tenn. C5 188-9
Holladay, Ut. F6 242-3
Holland, Ark. E7 150-1
Holland, Ind. N5 100-1
Holland, Ia. E10 104-5
Holland, Ky. K8 164-5
Holland, Man. J12 272-3
Holland, Mass. F7 68-9
Holland, Mich. I11 112-3
Holland, Minn. N2 116-7
Holland, Mo. K11 120-1
Holland, Nebr. I14 124-5
Holland, N.J. E3 76-7
Holland, O. B5 132-3
Holland, Ore. J5 238-9
Holland, Tex. F8 192-3
Holland, Vt. B9 90-1
Holland, Va. H13 196-7
Holland, Wis. E4 140-1
Holland Gin, Ala. A6 146-7
Holland Landing, Ont. B15 284-5
Holland Patent, N.Y. E8 80-1
Hollandale, Minn. O6 116-7
Hollandale, Miss. F4 176-7
Hollandale, Wis. J11 140-1
Hollandsburg, Ind. H5 100-1
Hollandsville, Del. G3 153
Hollansburg, O. G12 132-3
Hollenberg, Kans. C11 108-9
Holley, N.Y. E4 80-1
Holley, Ore. J2 238-9
Holliday, Mo. C7 120-1
Holliday, Tex. C7 192-3
Hollidaysburg, Pa. I6 84-5
Hollins, Ala. G8 146-7
Hollins, Va. I8 196-7
Hollis, Alaska H16 254-5
Hollis*, Me. N2 64-5

Hollis, N.H. O6 72-3
Hollis, Okla. G6 234-5
Hollis Center, Me. N2 64-5
Hollister, Calif. J4 210-1
Hollister, Ida. O6 218-9
Hollister, Mo. J5 120-1
Hollister, N.C. C12 180-1
Hollister, Okla. H8 234-5
Hollister, Wis. E13 140-1
Holliston, Mass. J2 68-9
Holloman, N. Mex. J6 230-1
Hollow Creek*, Ky. A2 164-5
Hollow Rock, Tenn. B4 188-9
Holloway, La. E5 168-9
Holloway, Minn. L2 116-7
Holloway, O. F10 132-3
Holly, Colo. H16 214-5
Holly, Mich. H4 112-3
Holly, Wash. F7 246-7
Holly Beach, La. I2 168-9
Holly Bluff, Miss. G5 176-7
Holly Grove, Ark. F9 150-1
Holly Hill, Fla. D12 156-7
Holly Hill, S.C. G12 184-5
Holly Oak, Del. A4 153
Holly Park, N.J. J7 76-7
Holly Pond, Ala. D6 146-7
Holly Ridge, La. B6 168-9
Holly Ridge, Miss. F4 176-7
Holly Ridge, N.C. G13 180-1
Holly Springs, Ark. I6 150-1
Holly Springs, Ga. A10 160-1
Holly Springs, Miss. B8 176-7
Holly Springs, N.C. I7 180-1
Hollyhill, Ky. K12 164-5
Hollytree, Ala. B7 146-7
Hollyvilla*, Ky. G9 164-5
Hollyville, Del. I5 153
Hollywood, Ala. B8 146-7
Hollywood, Ark. H4 150-1
Hollywood, Fla. G16 156-7
Hollywood, Ga. D6 160-1
Hollywood, La. H2 168-9
Hollywood, Md. H11 172-3
Hollywood, Miss. B5 176-7
Hollywood, Mo. K10 120-1
Hollywood, S.C. I12 184-5
Hollywood, W. Va. J6 200-1
Hollywood Park*, Tex. H8 192-3
Holman, N. Mex. D8 230-1
Holman Island, N.W. Terr. B2 296
Holmdel, N.J. G7 76-7
Holmdel Gardens*, Kans. H9 108-9
Holmen, Wis. H9 140-1
Holmes, co., Fla. A5 156-7
Holmes, co., Miss. G6 176-7
Holmes, co., O. E8 132-3
Holmes Beach, Fla. J2 156-7
Holmesville, Miss. L5 176-7
Holmesville, Nebr. J14 124-5
Holmesville, O. D9 132-3
Holmfield, Man. K11 272-3
Holmquist, S. Dak. B14 136-7
Holmwood, La. H3 168-9
Holstein, Ia. D3 104-5
Holstein, Nebr. I10 124-5
Holston, Va. J4 196-7
Holt, Ala. F4 146-7
Holt, Fla. B4 156-7
Holt, Mich. I1 112-3
Holt, Minn. E2 116-7
Holt, Mo. H16 120-1
Holt, co., Mo. B2 120-1
Holt, co., Nebr. D10 124-5
Holtland, Tenn. I7 188-9
Holton, Ind. K10 100-1
Holton, Kans. D14 108-9
Holton, La. G9 168-9
Holts Summit*, Mo. E7 120-1
Holtville, Ala. H7 146-7
Holtville, Calif. O10 210-1
Holtville, N.B. G4 275
Holtyre, Ont. F7 284-5
Holualoa, Hawaii J12 258-9
Holub, Ark. F10 150-1
Holum, La. C5 168-9
Holy Cross, Alaska E9 254-5
Holy Cross, Ia. D14 104-5
Holy Trinity, Ala. I11 146-7
Holyoke, Colo. C16 214-5
Holyoke, Mass. E5 68-9
Holyrood, Kans. G9 108-9
Holyrood*, Nfld. O11 278-9
Home, Kans. D12 108-9
Home Corner, Ind. E9 100-1
Home Gardens, Calif. H10 210-1
Homeacre-Lyndora*, Pa. G2 84-5
Homedale, Ida. L2 218-9
Homeland*, Calif. N8 210-1
Homeland, Ga. N9 160-1
Homer, Alaska G11 254-5
Homer, Ga. E6 160-1
Homer, Ill. G11 96-7
Homer, Ind. I10 100-1
Homer, La. A3 168-9
Homer, Mich. J13 112-3
Homer, Minn. O9 116-7
Homer, Nebr. E14 124-5
Homer, N.Y. F7 80-1
Homer City, Pa. H4 84-5
Homerville, Ga. N7 160-1
Homestead, Fla. J15 156-7
Homestead, Ia. G12 104-5
Homestead, Mont. B15 222-3
Homestead, Okla. D9 234-5
Homestead, Ore. C16 238-9
Homestead*, Pa. I2 84-5
Homestead, R.I. F6 87
Homestead Base, Fla. I15 156-7
Homestown*, Mo. J11 120-1
Hometown, Ill. N4 96-7
Hometown*, Pa. G13 84-5
Hometown, W. Va. G3 200-1
Homewood, Ala. F6 146-7
Homewood, Ill. O4 96-7
Homewood, Kans. G15 108-9
Homewood*, Man. K3 272-3
Homewood, Miss. I7 176-7
Homewood, S.C. E15 184-5
Hominy, Okla. D13 234-5
Hon, Ark. E2 150-1
Honaker, Va. J4 196-7
Honaunau, Hawaii J12 258-9
Hondo, N. Mex. J8 230-1
Hondo, Tex. H7 192-3
Honea Path, S.C. I2 184-5
Honeoye Falls, N.Y. E4 80-1
Honesdale, Pa. D15 84-5
Honey Brook, Pa. J13 84-5
Honey Creek, Ind. G10 100-1
Honey Creek, Wis. K4 140-1
Honey Grove, Tex. D10 192-3
Honey Harbour, Ont. A14 284-5
Honey Hill, S.C. G14 184-5
Honeymoon Bay, B.C. K6 268-9
Honeyville, Ut. C6 242-3
Honga, Md. H12 172-3
Honobia, Okla. H15 234-5
Honokaa, Hawaii H13 258-9
Honokahua, Hawaii F10 258-9
Honokowai, Hawaii G10 258-9
Honolulu, Hawaii F8 258-9
Honolulu, co., Hawaii I4 258-9
Honomu, Hawaii I14 258-9
Honor, Mich. F11 112-3
Honoraville, Ala. J7 146-7
Honouliuli, Hawaii J4 258-9
Hood, co., Tex. E8 192-3
Hood River, Ore. B8 238-9
Hood River, co., Ore. C8 238-9
Hoodsport, Wash. F6 246-7
Hooker, Okla. C4 234-5
Hooker, co., Nebr. F6 124-5
Hookerton, N.C. E13 180-1
Hooks, Tex. D11 192-3
Hooksett, N.H. M7 72-3
Hoolehua, Hawaii F9 258-9
Hoonah, Alaska G15 254-5
Hoopa, Calif. E2 210-1
Hooper, Colo. I10 214-5
Hooper, Nebr. F14 124-5
Hooper, Ut. E5 242-3
Hooper, Wash. G15 246-7
Hooper Bay, Alaska E7 254-5
Hoopersville, Md. H12 172-3
Hoopeston, Ill. F11 96-7
Hoople, N. Dak. C13 128-9
Hoosac Tunnel, Mass. B3 68-9
Hoosick Falls, N.Y. F12 80-1
Hoover*, Ala. E6 146-7
Hoover Res., O. F6 132-3
Hooversville, Pa. J5 84-5
Hopatcong, N.J. C5 76-7
Hope, Alaska F11 254-5
Hope, Ariz. H3 206-7
Hope, Ark. I3 150-1
Hope, B.C. J7 268-9
Hope, Ida. B3 218-9
Hope, Ind. J9 100-1
Hope, Kans. G11 108-9
Hope, Ky. G13 164-5
Hope, Me. L6 64-5
Hope, Mich. H13 112-3
Hope, N.J. C4 76-7
Hope, N. Mex. K9 230-1
Hope, N. Dak. F13 128-9
Hope, Ore. F15 238-9
Hope, R.I. D4 87
Hope Hull, Ala. I7 146-7
Hope Mills, N.C. K6 180-1
Hope Valley, R.I. G2 87
Hopedale, Ill. F8 96-7
Hopedale, Mass. K1 68-9
Hopedale, Nfld. F6 278-9
Hopedale, O. E11 132-3
Hopeton, Okla. C8 234-5
Hopeville, Conn. G14 60-1
Hopewell, Kans. I7 108-9
Hopewell, Miss. J6 176-7
Hopewell*, N.J. G4 76-7
Hopewell*, N.J. M3 76-7
Hopewell, N.J. G4 76-7
Hopewell, N.S. D8 281
Hopewell, Tenn. J1 188-9
Hopewell, Tenn. G7 188-9
Hopewell, Va. F1 196-7
Hopewell, W. Va. B14 200-1
Hopewell Cape, N.B. I7 275
Hopewell Junction*, N.Y. I11 80-1
Hopkins, Mich. J12 112-3
Hopkins, Minn. B10 116-7
Hopkins, Mo. A2 120-1
Hopkins, S.C. E10 184-5
Hopkins, Va. H16 196-7
Hopkins, co., Ky. I5 164-5
Hopkins, co., Tex. D10 192-3
Hopkins Hollow, R.I. E2 87
Hopkins Landing, B.C. B12 268-9
Hopkinsville, Ky. J5 164-5
Hopkinton, Ia. E13 104-5
Hopkinton, Mass. J1 68-9
Hopkinton, N.H. M6 72-3
Hopkinton, R.I. H2 87
Hopland, Calif. H2 210-1
Hopmere, Ore. H1 238-9
Hopper, Ark. G3 150-1
Hopwood, Pa. K3 84-5
Hoquiam, Wash. G5 246-7
Horace, Kans. G1 108-9
Horace, N. Dak. H14 128-9
Horatio, Ark. H2 150-1
Horatio, S.C. E11 184-5
Hordville, Nebr. H12 124-5
Horicon, Wis. H3 140-1
Horn, Ariz. J4 206-7
Horn Lake, Miss. A6 176-7
Hornbeak, Tenn. A3 188-9
Hornbeck, La. E2 168-9
Hornby Island*, B.C. J6 268-9
Horndean, Man. K13 272-3
Hornell, N.Y. G4 80-1
Hornepayne, Ont. F5 284-5
Horner, W. Va. E13 200-1
Hornerstown, N.J. H6 76-7
Hornersville, Mo. K11 120-1
Hornick, Ia. E2 104-5
Hornsby, Tenn. K4 188-9
Horntown, Va. G16 196-7
Horry, co., S.C. E15 184-5
Horse Cave, Ky. I8 164-5
Horse Creek, Wyo. J15 250-1
Horse Heaven, Ore. D10 238-9
Horse Shoe Run, W. Va. E8 200-1
Horsefly, B.C. H7 268-9
Horseheads, N.Y. G6 80-1
Horsepen, Va. I5 196-7
Horseshoe Beach*, Fla. C9 156-7
Horseshoe Bend*, Ark. B8 150-1
Horseshoe Bend, Ida. L3 218-9
Horseys Grove Church, Del. J3 153
Hortense, Ga. M9 160-1
Horton, Ala. C7 146-7
Horton, Kans. D14 108-9
Horton, Mich. K1 112-3
Horton, Ore. F5 238-9
Horton, Wyo. C16 250-1
Hortonia, Vt. I4 90-1
Hortonville, Wis. E3 140-1
Hoschton, Ga. F5 160-1
Hoskins, Conn. B8 60-1
Hoskins, Nebr. E13 124-5
Hoskins, Ore. D5 238-9
Hoskinston, Ky. J14 164-5
Hosmer, S. Dak. B10 136-7
Hosmer Corner, Mass. E4 68-9
Hospers, Ia. C2 104-5
Hosston, La. A1 168-9
Hot Coffee, Miss. K7 176-7
Hot Spring, co., Ark. G5 150-1
Hot Springs, Ark. G5 150-1
Hot Springs, Mont. D2 222-3
Hot Springs, N.C. D3 180-1
Hot Springs, S. Dak. H2 136-7
Hot Springs, Va. G8 196-7
Hot Springs, co., Wyo. E9 250-1
Hot Sulphur Springs, Colo. D10 214-5
Hotason Vo, Ariz. K5 206-7
Hotchkiss, Colo. F7 214-5
Hotchkissville, Conn. E5 60-1
Hotevilla, Ariz. D9 206-7
Hotwells, La. E4 168-9
Houck, Ariz. E11 206-7
Houghton, Ia. J12 104-5
Houghton, Mich. C8 112-3
Houghton, N.Y. G3 80-1
Houghton, S. Dak. A13 136-7
Houghton, co., Mich. C8 112-3
Houghton Lake, Mich. G13 112-3
Houghton Lake Heights, Mich. G13 112-3
Houghtonville, Mass. B2 68-9
Houlka, Miss. D9 176-7
Houlton, Me. E9 64-5
Houlton, Wis. E7 140-1
Houma, La. J8 168-9
Housatonic, Mass. D1 68-9
House, N. Mex. G10 230-1
House Rock, Ariz. B6 206-7
Houston, Ala. D5 146-7
Houston*, Alaska F11 254-5
Houston, Ark. H14 150-1
Houston, B.C. F5 268-9
Houston, Del. H4 153
Houston, Minn. O9 116-7
Houston, Miss. D9 176-7
Houston, Mo. H7 120-1
Houston, Pa. C5 84-5
Houston, Tex. G10 192-3
Houston, co., Ala. M10 146-7
Houston, co., Ga. J5 160-1
Houston, co., Minn. O9 116-7
Houston, co., Tenn. B5 188-9
Houston, co., Tex. F10 192-3
Houston Acres*, Ky. G9 164-5
Houston Lake, Mo. I15 120-1
Houstonia, Mo. E5 120-1
Houtzdale, Pa. G7 84-5
Hoven, S. Dak. C9 136-7
Hovey Mobile Park*, N. Dak. C11 128-9
Hovland, Minn. F11 116-7
Howard, Ala. D4 146-7
Howard, Colo. G10 214-5
Howard, Ga. J4 160-1
Howard, Kans. J13 108-9
Howard, Miss. G6 176-7
Howard, N.B. G5 275
Howard, S. Dak. F14 136-7
Howard, Wis. D4 140-1
Howard, co., Ark. H3 150-1
Howard, co., Ind. F8 100-1
Howard, co., Ia. B11 104-5
Howard, co., Md. D10 172-3
Howard, co., Mo. D6 120-1
Howard, co., Nebr. G11 124-5
Howard, co., Tex. E5 192-3
Howard City, Mich. H12 112-3
Howard City*, Nebr. G10 124-5
Howard Lake, Minn. A8 116-7
Howards Grove [-Millersville], Wis. G5 140-1
Howardstown, Ky. E2 164-5
Howardville, Mo. J11 120-1
Howe, Ida. L8 218-9
Howe, Ind. A10 100-1
Howe, Mass. A12 68-9
Howe, Nebr. I16 124-5
Howe, Okla. G16 234-5
Howe, Tex. A15 192-3
Howell, Ark. E9 150-1
Howell, Ga. N7 160-1
Howell, Mich. I3 112-3
Howell*, N.J. H7 76-7
Howell, Tenn. K7 188-9
Howell, Ut. C5 242-3
Howell, Wyo. J14 250-1
Howell, co., Mo. I7 120-1
Howells, Nebr. F13 124-5
Howertons, Va. H13 196-7
Howey-in-the-Hills*, Fla. E11 156-7
Howick*, Que. J12 290-1
Howlan, P.E.I. C3 287
Howland, Me. H7 64-5
Howlands, Mass. G12 68-9
Howley, Nfld. M8 278-9
Howton, Ala. F5 146-7
Hoxie, Ark. B10 150-1
Hoxie, Kans. E4 108-9
Hoya, Nev. L10 226-7
Hoyt, Colo. D13 214-5
Hoyt, Kans. E14 108-9
Hoyt, N.B. I4 275
Hoyt, Okla. F15 234-5
Hoyt Lakes, Minn. G8 116-7
Hoytsville, Ut. E7 242-3
Hoytville, O. C5 132-3
Huachuca City, Ariz. M9 206-7
Hub, Miss. L7 176-7
Hubbard, Ia. E8 104-5
Hubbard, Nebr. D14 124-5
Hubbard, O. C12 132-3
Hubbard, Ore. G2 238-9
Hubbard, Sask. M9 294-5
Hubbard, Tex. E9 192-3
Hubbard, co., Minn. H4 116-7
Hubbard Corner, Mass. F5 68-9
Hubbard Lake, Mich. F14 112-3
Hubbardston, Mass. C7 68-9
Hubbardston, Mich. I13 112-3
Hubbardstown, W. Va. I9 200-1
Hubbardton, Vt. I4 90-1
Hubbell, Mich. B9 112-3
Hubbell, Nebr. J13 124-5
Hubble Lake Subdivision*, Alta. J7 264-5
Huber, Ga. I6 160-1
Huber Heights*, O. G4 132-3
Huberdeau, Que. H10 290-1
Hubert, N.C. F13 180-1
Hubertus, Wis. I4 140-1
Huckleberry Corner, Mass. G13 68-9
Huddleston, Va. I8 196-7
Hudson, Colo. F4 214-5
Hudson, Fla. G2 156-7
Hudson, Ill. F8 96-7
Hudson, Ind. A11 100-1
Hudson, Ia. E10 104-5
Hudson, Kans. H8 108-9
Hudson, La. C4 168-9
Hudson, Me. I7 64-5
Hudson, Mass. H1 68-9
Hudson, Mich. K13 112-3
Hudson, N.H. O7 72-3
Hudson, N.Y. G11 80-1
Hudson, N.C. D6 180-1
Hudson, O. C15 132-3
Hudson*, Ont. E2 284-5
Hudson*, Que. I11 290-1
Hudson, S. Dak. I16 136-7
Hudson, Wis. E7 140-1
Hudson, Wyo. F9 250-1
Hudson, co., N.J. D8 76-7
Hudson Bay, Man. B7 272-3
Hudson Bay, Sask. J10 294-5
Hudson Center, N.H. O7 72-3
Hudson Falls, N.Y. E11 80-1
Hudson Hope, B.C. E7 268-9
Hudson Lake*, Ind. A7 100-1
Hudson R., N.Y. H10 80-1
Hudson Strait, Que. A4 290-1
Hudsons Bay*, Alta. L9 264-5
Hudsonville, Mich. I12 112-3
Hudsonville, Miss. A7 176-7
Hudspeth, co., Tex. E1 192-3
Huerfano, co., Colo. I11 214-5
Huetter, Ida. C2 218-9
Hueytown, Ala. F6 146-7
Huff, Ark. C8 150-1
Huff, N. Dak. H7 128-9
Huffman, Ark. B13 150-1
Huger, S.C. H13 184-5
Hughenden, Alta. K10 264-5
Hughes, Alaska D10 254-5
Hughes, Ark. E11 150-1
Hughes, co., Okla. F13 234-5
Hughes, co., S. Dak. E9 136-7
Hughes Crossroad, Del. G3 153
Hughes Springs*, Tex. D11 192-3
Hughesdale, R.I. C5 87
Hughestown*, Pa. E14 84-5
Hughesville, Md. G10 172-3
Hughesville, Mo. E5 120-1
Hughesville, Mont. E8 222-3
Hughesville, Pa. F11 84-5
Hughson, Calif. D10 210-1

Hugo, Colo. F14 214-5
Hugo, Minn. A11 116-7
Hugo, Okla. I14 234-5
Hugoton, Kans. K2 108-9
Hulaco, Ala. C7 146-7
Hulah, Okla. B13 234-5
Hulbert, Ark. E12 150-1
Hulbert, Mich. D12 112-3
Hulbert, Okla. E15 234-5
Hulen, Ky. J13 164-5
Hulen, Okla. H9 234-5
Hulett, Ga. D8 160-1
Hulett, Wyo. B15 250-1
Hull, Ga. F6 160-1
Hull, Ill. H4 96-7
Hull, Ia. B2 104-5
Hull, Mass. I6 68-9
Hull, Que. J2 290-1
Hull, co., Que. I9 290-1
Hulls Cove, Me. K8 64-5
Humansville, Mo. G4 120-1
Humarock, Mass. K8 68-9
Humbird, Wis. G10 140-1
Humble, Tex. G14 192-3
Humble City, N. Mex. K11 230-1
Humboldt, Ariz. G6 206-7
Humboldt, Ia. D6 104-5
Humboldt, Kans. I15 108-9
Humboldt, Minn. D1 116-7
Humboldt, Nebr. J15 124-5
Humboldt, Nev. D4 226-7
Humboldt, Sask. K8 294-5
Humboldt, S. Dak. G15 136-7
Humboldt, Tenn. I4 188-9
Humboldt, co., Calif. H1 210-1
Humboldt, co., Ia. D6 104-5
Humboldt, co., Nev. B4 226-7
Humboldt R., Nev. C4 226-7
Hume, Calif. J6 210-1
Hume, Mo. F3 120-1
Hume, Va. A1 196-7
Humeston, Ia. J8 104-5
Hummelstown, Pa. I11 84-5
Hummocks, The, R.I. E7 87
Humnoke, Ark. F8 150-1
Humphrey, Ark. G8 150-1
Humphrey, Ida. J9 218-9
Humphrey, Nebr. F12 124-5
Humphreys, Mo. B5 120-1
Humphreys, Okla. H8 234-5
Humphreys, co., Miss. F5 176-7
Humphreys, co., Tenn. B5 188-9
Humptulips, Wash. F5 246-7
Hundred, W. Va. A13 200-1
Hungry Horse, Mont. B3 222-3
Hunnewell, Kans. K10 108-9
Hunnewell, Mo. C7 120-1
Hunt, Ariz. F10 206-7
Hunt, Ark. D4 150-1
Hunt, co., Tex. D9 192-3
Hunter, Ala. I7 146-7
Hunter, Ark. E9 150-1
Hunter, Kans. E8 108-9
Hunter, Mo. I9 120-1
Hunter, N. Dak. G14 128-9
Hunter, Okla. C10 234-5
Hunter Creek, Ore. J3 238-9
Hunter River, P.E.I. E6 287
Hunter River*, P.E.I. E7 287
Hunterdon, co., N.J. F4 76-7
Hunters, Wash. D14 246-7
Hunters Creek Village*, Tex. H13 192-3
Huntersville, N.C. J1 180-1
Huntersville, W. Va. H7 200-1
Huntertown, Ind. C11 100-1
Hunting Valley*, O. B10 132-3
Huntingburg, Ind. N6 100-1
Huntingdon, B.C. C15 268-9
Huntingdon, Pa. H7 84-5
Huntingdon, Que. J11 290-1
Huntingdon, Tenn. B4 188-9
Huntingdon, co., Pa. H8 84-5
Huntingdon, co., Que. J11 290-1
Huntington, Ark. E2 150-1
Huntington, Ind. D10 100-1
Huntington, Mass. D3 68-9
Huntington, N.J. E3 76-7
Huntington, N.Y. J12 80-1
Huntington, Ore. E15 238-9
Huntington, Tex. F11 192-3
Huntington, Ut. I7 242-3
Huntington, Vt. F5 90-1
Huntington*, Va. E13 196-7
Huntington, W. Va. G1 200-1
Huntington, co., Ind. D10 100-1
Huntington Bay, N.Y. J12 80-1
Huntington Beach, Calif. H9 210-1
Huntington Park*, Calif. G8 210-1
Huntington Station, N.Y. J12 80-1
Huntington Woods*, Mich. I6 112-3
Huntingtown, Conn. G5 60-1
Huntland, Tenn. D8 188-9
Huntleigh*, Mo. E10 120-1
Huntley, Ill. K1 96-7
Huntley, Mont. G11 222-3
Huntley, Nebr. J9 124-5
Huntley, Wyo. H16 250-1
Huntly, Va. A1 196-7
Hunts Point, Wash. H3 246-7
Huntsville, Ala. B7 146-7
Huntsville, Ark. B3 150-1
Huntsville, Conn. B5 60-1
Huntsville, Ky. I6 164-5
Huntsville, Mo. C6 120-1
Huntsville, O. E5 132-3
Huntsville, Ont. H8 284-5
Huntsville, Tenn. G10 188-9
Huntsville, Tex. F10 192-3
Huntsville*, Ut. D6 242-3
Hurdland, Mo. B7 120-1
Hurdle Mills, N.C. G6 180-1
Hurdsfield, N. Dak. F9 128-9
Hurdtown, N.J. C5 76-7
Hurffville, N.J. O10 76-7
Hurlburt*, Fla. B4 156-7
Hurley, Miss. N10 176-7
Hurley, Mo. I5 120-1
Hurley, N. Mex. K3 230-1
Hurley*, N.Y. G11 80-1
Hurley, S. Dak. H15 136-7
Hurley, Tenn. D4 188-9
Hurley, Va. I4 196-7
Hurley, Wis. B11 140-1
Hurlock, Md. F14 172-3
Huron, Calif. K5 210-1
Huron, Ind. L6 100-1
Huron, Kans. D15 108-9
Huron, O. B7 132-3
Huron, S. Dak. E13 136-7
Huron, Tenn. C4 188-9
Huron, co., Mich. H15 112-3
Huron, co., O. C7 132-3
Huron, co., Ont. C12 284-5
Huron Park, Ont. D12 284-5
Hurricane, Ala. M3 146-7
Hurricane, La. B3 168-9
Hurricane, Miss. C8 176-7
Hurricane, Ut. M3 242-3
Hurricane, W. Va. H12 200-1
Hurricane Deck, Mo. F6 120-1
Hurst, Ill. M8 96-7
Hurst, Tex. C13 192-3
Hurst, W. Va. E5 200-1
Hurstbourne Acres*, Ky. G9 164-5
Hurstville, Ia. F15 104-5
Hurt, Va. I9 196-7
Hurtsboro, Ala. I10 146-7
Hushpuckena, Miss. D4 176-7
Husk, N.C. B6 180-1
Huslia, Alaska D10 254-5
Huson, Mont. E3 222-3
Hussar, Alta. M8 264-5
Husser, La. G9 168-9
Hustisford, Wis. I3 140-1
Hustle, Va. G13 196-7
Hustler, Wis. H11 140-1
Huston, Ida. L2 218-9
Hustonville, Ky. I11 164-5
Husum, Wash. J9 246-7
Hutchins, Tex. D15 192-3
Hutchins*, Wis. F13 140-1
Hutchinson, Kans. H9 108-9
Hutchinson, Minn. M5 116-7
Hutchinson, co., S. Dak. H13 136-7
Hutchinson, co., Tex. A5 192-3
Huttig, Ark. K7 150-1
Hutton, La. E3 168-9
Huttonsville, W. Va. G15 200-1
Huxford, Ala. L4 146-7
Huxley, Ia. F8 104-5
Huyett, Md. B7 172-3
Hyak, Wash. F9 246-7
Hyannis, Mass. H15 68-9
Hyannis, Nebr. E5 124-5
Hyannis Port, Mass. H15 68-9
Hyas, Sask. L10 294-5
Hyattstown, Md. F2 172-3
Hyattsville, Md. I4 172-3
Hyattville, Wyo. C10 250-1
Hybart, Ala. K5 146-7
Hybla Valley, Va. B4 196-7
Hybord*, Man. G2 272-3
Hydaburg, Alaska H16 254-5
Hyde, Pa. G6 84-5
Hyde, co., N.C. D15 180-1
Hyde, co., S. Dak. E10 136-7
Hyde Park, Mass. I5 68-9
Hyde Park, N.Y. H11 80-1
Hyde Park, Ont. E12 284-5
Hyde Park, Ut. C6 242-3
Hyde Park, Vt. D6 90-1
Hyden, Ky. I14 164-5
Hyder, Alaska H16 254-5
Hyder, Ariz. J4 206-7
Hydeville, Conn. B12 60-1
Hydeville, Vt. J4 90-1
Hydro, Okla. F9 234-5
Hygiene, Colo. E2 214-5
Hyman, S.C. E14 184-5
Hymer, Kans. G12 108-9
Hymera, Ind. J5 100-1
Hymers, Ont. F3 284-5
Hyndman, Pa. K5 84-5
Hypoluxo*, Fla. E16 156-7
Hyrum, Ut. D6 242-3
Hysham, Mont. F12 222-3
Hythe, Alta. G3 264-5
Hytop, Ala. A8 146-7

I

Iaeger, W. Va. J3 200-1
Ibapah, Ut. G2 242-3
Iberia, Mo. F7 120-1
Iberia, co., La. I6 168-9
Iberville, La. B10 168-9
Iberville, Que. J13 290-1
Iberville, co., La. H6 168-9
Iberville, co., Que. J13 290-1
Iberville-Jonction*, Que. J13 290-1
Icard, N.C. D6 180-1
Île des Chênes*, Man. J14 272-3
Ida, Ark. D8 150-1
Ida, La. A1 168-9
Ida, Mich. K14 112-3
Ida, co., Ia. E3 104-5
Ida Grove, Ia. E3 104-5
Idabel, Okla. I16 234-5
Idaho, co., Ida. H4 218-9
Idaho City, Ida. L4 218-9
Idaho Falls, Ida. M10 218-9
Idaho Springs, Colo. G1 214-5
Idahome, Ida. O8 218-9
Idalia, Colo. D16 214-5
Idalou, Tex. C5 192-3
Idana, Kans. E11 108-9
Idanha, Ore. D7 238-9
Idavada, Ida. O6 218-9
Idaville, Ind. D7 100-1
Idaville, Ore. B4 238-9
Ideal, Ga. J4 160-1
Ider, Ala. B9 146-7
Idlewild, Mich. H12 112-3
Idlewild, Tenn. B3 188-9
Idleyld Park, Ore. H5 238-9
Idmon, Ida. K10 218-9
Igiugig*, Alaska G10 254-5
Igloolik, N.W. Terr. B3 296
Ignace, Ont. E2 284-5
Ignacio, Colo. J7 214-5
Ihlen, Minn. O2 116-7
Ijamsville, Md. F2 172-3
Ikes Fork, W. Va. J3 200-1
Ila, Ga. E6 160-1
Île-à-la-Crosse, Sask. G5 294-5
Île-de-Montréal et Île-Jésus, co., Que. J3 290-1
Île-Perrot*, Que. J11 290-1
Îles-de-la Madeleine, co., Que. I7 290-1
Ilford, Man. D4 272-3
Iliamna, Alaska G10 254-5
Iliff, Colo. B15 214-5
Ilion, N.Y. E9 80-1
Illahe, Ore. I4 238-9
Illinois Camp, N. Mex. K10 230-1
Illinois R., Ill. G6 96-7
Illiopolis, Ill. H8 96-7
Illmo, Mo. H12 120-1
Ilwaco, Wash. H5 246-7
Imbler, Ore. C14 238-9
Imboden, Ark. B9 150-1
Imlay, Nev. D4 226-7
Imlay City, Mich. G6 112-3
Imlaystown, N.J. H6 76-7
Immokalee, Fla. I11 156-7
Imnaha, Ore. B16 238-9
Imogene, Ia. J3 104-5
Imperial, Calif. O10 210-1
Imperial, Nebr. I5 124-5
Imperial, Sask. M7 294-5
Imperial, W. Va. F14 200-1
Imperial, co., Calif. O10 210-1
Imperial Beach, Calif. K11 210-1
Imperial-Enlow*, Pa. I2 84-5
Imperial Mills, Alta. H9 264-5
Inavale, Nebr. J10 124-5
Inchelium, Wash. D14 246-7
Incline Village, Nev. G1 226-7
Independence, Calif. J7 210-1
Independence, Ind. F5 100-1
Independence, Ia. E12 104-5
Independence, Kans. J14 108-9
Independence, Ky. E11 164-5
Independence, La. G8 168-9
Independence, Minn. B9 116-7
Independence, Miss. B7 176-7
Independence, Mo. D3 120-1
Independence*, N.J. D4 76-7
Independence, O. B14 132-3
Independence, Ore. H1 238-9
Independence, Va. K5 196-7
Independence, W. Va. C15 200-1
Independence, Wis. G9 140-1
Independence, co., Ark. C8 150-1
Independence Hill, Ind. B5 100-1
Index, Ky. G14 164-5
Index, Va. G13 196-7
Index, Wash. E9 246-7
India, Miss. M8 176-7
India, Tenn. A4 188-9
Indiahoma, Okla. H8 234-5
Indialantic, Fla. F13 156-7
Indian*, Alaska F11 254-5
Indian Agency, Colo. J7 214-5
Indian Bay, Ark. G10 150-1
Indian Bayou, La. H5 168-9
Indian Beach*, N.C. F14 180-1
Indian Creek*, Fla. H16 156-7
Indian Fields, Ky. G12 164-5
Indian Harbor Beach, Fla. F13 156-7
Indian Head, Md. F9 172-3
Indian Head, Sask. N9 294-5
Indian Head Park*, Ill. M3 96-7
Indian Head Plant*, Md. F9 172-3
Indian Hill, O. K14 132-3
Indian Hills*, Ky. G9 164-5
Indian Hills Cherokee Section*, Ky. G9 164-5
Indian Mills, W. Va. J5 200-1
Indian Mission, Del. I5 153
Indian Mound, La. G7 168-9
Indian Mound, Tenn. A6 188-9
Indian Neck, Conn. H8 60-1
Indian Neck, Va. H13 196-7
Indian Point, Me. K8 64-5
Indian R., Del. J5 153
Indian River, Me. K10 64-5
Indian River, Mich. E13 112-3
Indian River, co., Fla. G13 156-7
Indian River Shores, Fla. G13 156-7
Indian Rocks Beach, Fla. I1 156-7
Indian Shores*, Fla. I1 156-7
Indian Springs, Ga. H5 160-1
Indian Springs, Md. B6 172-3
Indian Springs, Nev. L8 226-7
Indian Trail, N.C. K2 180-1
Indian Valley, Ida. J3 218-9
Indian Valley, Va. J7 196-7
Indian Village*, Ind. A8 100-1
Indian Wells, Ariz. E10 206-7
Indian Wells, Calif. N9 210-1
Indiana, Pa. H4 84-5
Indiana, co., Pa. H5 84-5
Indianapolis, Ind. H8 100-1
Indianford, Wis. K2 140-1
Indianola, Ia. H8 104-5
Indianola, Miss. F5 176-7
Indianola, Nebr. J7 124-5
Indianola, Okla. F14 234-5
Indianola, Ut. I17 242-3
Indianola, Wash. H2 246-7
Indianola Beach*, Ont. C15 284-5
Indiantown, Fla. C15 156-7
Indio, Calif. N9 210-1
Indore, W. Va. H16 200-1
Indrio, Fla. A15 156-7
Industrial, S.C. B10 184-5
Industry*, Calif. G9 210-1
Industry, Kans. E11 108-9
Industry, Me. J4 64-5
Industry, Pa. H1 84-5
Inez, Ky. G15 164-5
Ingalls, Ark. J7 150-1
Ingalls, Ind. G9 100-1
Ingalls, Kans. I4 108-9
Ingalls, Mich. E9 112-3
Ingalls, N.C. D5 180-1
Ingersoll*, Okla. C9 234-5
Ingersoll, Ont. E12 284-5
Ingham, co., Mich. J13 112-3
Inglefield, Ind. O4 100-1
Ingleside*, Ill. A10 96-7
Ingleside, Md. D13 172-3
Ingleside, Ont. I16 284-5
Ingleside*, Tex. I9 192-3
Ingleside, W. Va. J4 200-1
Inglewood, Calif. G8 210-1
Inglewood, Nebr. I1 124-5
Inglewood, Tenn. G7 188-9
Inglis, Fla. E9 156-7
Inglis, Man. H9 272-3
Ingold, N.C. F11 180-1
Ingomar, Miss. C9 176-7
Ingomar, Mont. F12 222-3
Ingonish, N.S. A11 281
Ingonish Beach, N.S. A11 281
Ingram*, Pa. H2 84-5
Ingram, Va. J9 196-7
Ingram, Wis. D10 140-1
Ingrams Mill, Miss. B7 176-7
Inkerman, N.B. E7 275
Inkerman, Ont. I15 284-5
Inkom, Ida. N9 218-9
Inkster, Mich. J5 112-3
Inkster, N. Dak. D13 128-9
Inland, Nebr. I11 124-5
Inman, Kans. H10 108-9
Inman, Nebr. D11 124-5
Inman, S.C. E3 184-5
Inman, Va. J2 196-7
Inman Mills, S.C. E3 184-5
Innerkip*, Ont. D13 284-5
Innis, La. F6 168-9
Innisfail, Alta. K7 264-5
Innisfree, Alta. J9 264-5
Inola, Okla. D14 234-5
Insinger, Sask. L9 294-5
Inspiration, Ariz. I8 206-7
Intake, Mont. D16 222-3
Interior, S. Dak. G5 136-7
Interlachen, Fla. C11 156-7
Interlaken, Mass. D1 68-9
Interlaken, N.J. H8 76-7
Interlaken, N.Y. F6 80-1
Intermont, W. Va. E10 200-1
International Falls, Minn. E6 116-7
Interprovincial Pipe Line*, Man. J2 272-3
Intervale, N.H. H8 72-3
Intracoastal City, La. I5 168-9
Intracoastal Waterway, La. I3 168-9
Intracoastal Waterway, S.C. F15 184-5
Intracoastal Waterway, Tex. J14 192-3
Inuvik, N.W. Terr. B1 296
Inver Grove Heights, Minn. B11 116-7
Invermay, Sask. L9 294-5
Invermere, B.C. J10 268-9
Inverness, Ala. J9 146-7
Inverness, Fla. E10 156-7
Inverness*, Ill. B10 96-7
Inverness, Miss. F5 176-7
Inverness, Mont. B8 222-3
Inverness, N.S. B10 281
Inverness, Que. H15 290-1
Inverness, co., N.S. B10 281
Inwood, Ind. B8 100-1
Inwood, Ia. B1 104-5
Inwood, Man. H14 272-3
Inwood, N.Y. F15 80-1
Inwood, W. Va. D11 200-1
Inyo, co., Calif. K8 210-1
Inyokern, Calif. L7 210-1
Ioka, Ut. G9 242-3
Iola, Kans. I15 108-9
Iola, Wis. E2 140-1
Iona, Ida. L10 218-9
Iona, Minn. O3 116-7
Iona, N.J. L3 76-7
Iona, Okla. H12 234-5
Iona, P.E.I. F8 287
Ione, Calif. B10 210-1
Ione, Ore. C11 238-9
Ione, Wash. C16 246-7

Ionia, Ia. C10 104-5
Ionia, Kans. D8 108-9
Ionia, Mich. I12 112-3
Ionia, Mo. F5 120-1
Ionia, co., Mich. I12 112-3
Iosco, co., Mich. G14 112-3
Iosepa, Ut. F4 242-3
Iota, La. H4 168-9
Iowa, La. H3 168-9
Iowa, co., Ia. G11 104-5
Iowa, co., Wis. J11 140-1
Iowa City, Ia. G13 104-5
Iowa Falls, Ia. D8 104-5
Iowa Park, Tex. C7 192-3
Iowa Point, Kans. C15 108-9
Iowa R., Ia. F9 104-5
Ipava, Ill. F6 96-7
Ipswich, Mass. B12 68-9
Ipswich, S. Dak. B11 136-7
Ira, Vt. J4 90-1
Iraan, Tex. F4 192-3
Irasburg, Vt. C8 90-1
Irasville, Vt. G5 90-1
Iredell, co., N.C. D7 180-1
Ireland, Ind. M6 100-1
Ireland, W. Va. F13 200-1
Irene, S. Dak. I15 136-7
Ireton, Ia. C1 104-5
Irion, co., Tex. F5 192-3
Irma, Alta. J10 264-5
Irma, Wis. E12 140-1
Irmo, S.C. K8 184-5
Iron, co., Mich. D8 112-3
Iron, co., Mo. H10 120-1
Iron, co., Ut. L3 242-3
Iron, co., Wis. B11 140-1
Iron Belt, Wis. B11 140-1
Iron Bridge, Ont. H6 284-5
Iron City, Ala. E9 146-7
Iron City, Ga. N3 160-1
Iron City, Tenn. E6 188-9
Iron Gate, Va. H8 196-7
Iron Gates, Mo. I3 120-1
Iron Junction, Minn. G7 116-7
Iron Mountain, Mich. E9 112-3
Iron Post, Okla. E13 234-5
Iron Ridge, Wis. H3 140-1
Iron River, Mich. D8 112-3
Iron River, Wis. B9 140-1
Iron Springs, Ariz. F5 206-7
Iron Springs, Ut. L3 242-3
Iron Station, N.C. J1 180-1
Ironaton, Ala. F8 146-7
Irondale*, Ala. F6 146-7
Irondale, Mo. G10 120-1
Irondale, O. E11 132-3
Ironia, N.J. D5 76-7
Ironshire, Md. H16 172-3
Ironside, Ore. E14 238-9
Ironsides, Md. G9 172-3
Ironton, Colo. H7 214-5
Ironton, Minn. J5 116-7
Ironton, Mo. H10 120-1
Ironton, O. J7 132-3
Ironton, Wis. I11 140-1
Ironwood, Mich. D7 112-3
Iroquois, Ont. I15 284-5
Iroquois, S. Dak. E13 136-7
Iroquois, co., Ill. F11 96-7
Iroquois Falls, Ont. F7 284-5
Iroquois Point, Hawaii J4 258-9
Irricana, Alta. L8 264-5
Irrigon, Ore. B11 238-9
Irvine, Alta. N11 264-5
Irvine, Ky. H12 164-5
Irving, Ill. J7 96-7
Irving, S.C. J3 184-5
Irving, Tex. C14 192-3
Irvington, Ala. N2 146-7
Irvington, Ky. H8 164-5
Irvington, Nebr. I2 124-5
Irvington, N.J. D10 76-7
Irvington, N.Y. C14 80-1
Irvington, Va. D4 196-7
Irvington, Wis. F8 140-1
Irwin, Ida. M11 218-9
Irwin, Ia. G4 104-5
Irwin, Pa. B7 84-5
Irwin, S.C. B11 184-5
Irwin, co., Ga. M6 160-1
Irwindale*, Calif. G9 210-1
Irwinton, Ga. I6 160-1
Irwinville, Ga. L6 160-1
Isabel, Kans. J8 108-9
Isabel, S. Dak. B6 136-7
Isabella, Okla. D9 234-5
Isabella, co., Mich. H13 112-3
Isanti, Minn. L6 116-7
Isanti, co., Minn. K6 116-7
Isbell, Ala. C4 146-7
Isham, Tenn. F10 188-9
Ishpeming, Mich. D9 112-3
Isla Vista*, Calif. M5 210-1
Islamorada, Fla. K13 156-7
Island, Ky. I6 164-5
Island, co., Wash. D7 246-7
Island Beach, N.J. J7 76-7
Island City, Ore. C14 238-9
Island Creek, Md. G11 172-3
Island Falls, Me. F8 64-5
Island Falls, Ont. E7 284-5
Island Heights, N.J. J7 76-7
Island Lake, Ill. K2 96-7
Island Lake, Ont. H6 284-5
Island of Rhode Island, R.I. F7 87
Island Park, Ida. J11 218-9
Island Park*, N.Y. K11 80-1
Island Park, R.I. F7 87
Island Pond, Vt. C9 90-1
Island View, Minn. E6 116-7
Islandia*, Fla. J13 156-7
Islandton, S.C. H10 184-5
Islay, Alta. J10 264-5
Isle, Minn. J6 116-7
Isle au Haut, Me. L7 64-5
Isle aux Morts, Nfld. O7 278-9
Isle La Motte, Vt. B3 90-1
Isle of Hope, Ga. K11 160-1
Isle of Palms, S.C. I13 184-5
Isle of Wight, Va. G3 196-7
Isle of Wight, co., Va. J14 196-7
Islen, Nev. J11 226-7
Isles of Shoals, N.H. N10 72-3
Islesboro, Me. K7 64-5
Islesford, Me. L8 64-5
Isleta, N. Mex. F5 230-1
Isleton, Calif. B9 210-1
Islington, Mass. J4 68-9
Islip*, N.Y. K12 80-1
Ismay, Mont. F15 222-3
Isola, Miss. F5 176-7
Issaquah, Wash. I3 246-7
Issaquena, co., Miss. G4 176-7
Issue, Md. H10 172-3
Italy*, Tex. E9 192-3
Itasca*, Ill. B10 96-7
Itasca, Tex. E9 192-3
Itasca, co., Minn. G6 116-7
Itawamba, co., Miss. C10 176-7
Ithaca, Mich. I13 112-3
Ithaca, Nebr. J1 124-5
Ithaca, N.Y. G6 80-1
Ithaca, Wis. I11 140-1
Itmann, W. Va. J4 200-1
Itta Bena, Miss. E5 176-7
Ituna, Sask. M9 294-5
Iuka, Kans. I8 108-9
Iuka, Miss. B11 176-7
Iva, S.C. D6 184-5
Ivan, Ark. H6 150-1
Ivanhoe, Calif. K6 210-1
Ivanhoe, Minn. N2 116-7
Ivanhoe, N.C. G12 180-1
Ivanhoe, Va. J6 196-7
Ivanhoe, W. Va. E14 200-1
Ivanof Bay*, Alaska H8 254-5
Ivey, Ga. I6 160-1
Ivins, Ut. M3 242-3
Ivor, Va. G3 196-7
Ivoryton, Conn. G11 60-1
Ivydale, W. Va. G4 200-1
Ivydell, Tenn. G11 188-9
Ivywild, Colo. K4 214-5
Ixonia, Wis. I3 140-1
Izard, co., Ark. B7 150-1

J

Jachin, Ala. I3 146-7
Jacinto, Miss. B10 176-7
Jacinto City, Tex. H14 192-3
Jack, Ala. K8 146-7
Jack, co., Tex. D8 192-3
Jackman, Me. G3 64-5
Jackman Station, Me. G3 64-5
Jackpot, Nev. A10 226-7
Jacks Creek, Tenn. C4 188-9
Jacksboro, Tenn. G11 188-9
Jacksboro, Tex. D8 192-3
Jackson, Ala. K3 146-7
Jackson, Calif. B11 210-1
Jackson, Ga. H5 160-1
Jackson, Ky. H13 164-5
Jackson, La. F7 168-9
Jackson, Me. J6 64-5
Jackson, Mich. J13 112-3
Jackson, Minn. O4 116-7
Jackson, Miss. I6 176-7
Jackson, Mo. H11 120-1
Jackson, Mont. H4 222-3
Jackson, Nebr. D14 124-5
Jackson, N.H. G8 72-3
Jackson*, N.J. I6 76-7
Jackson, N.C. C13 180-1
Jackson, O. I7 132-3
Jackson, R.I. D4 87
Jackson, S.C. G8 184-5
Jackson, Tenn. C3 188-9
Jackson, Wis. I4 140-1
Jackson, Wyo. E5 250-1
Jackson, co., Ala. B8 146-7
Jackson, co., Ark. C9 150-1
Jackson, co., Colo. C9 214-5
Jackson, co., Fla. A6 156-7
Jackson, co., Ga. E6 160-1
Jackson, co., Ill. M7 96-7
Jackson, co., Ind. K8 100-1
Jackson, co., Ia. E15 104-5
Jackson, co., Kans. E14 108-9
Jackson, co., Ky. I12 164-5
Jackson, co., La. B4 168-9
Jackson, co., Mich. J13 112-3
Jackson, co., Minn. O4 116-7
Jackson, co., Miss. N10 176-7
Jackson, co., Mo. E3 120-1
Jackson, co., N.C. E3 180-1
Jackson, co., O. I7 132-3
Jackson, co., Okla. H7 234-5
Jackson, co., Ore. J6 238-9
Jackson, co., S. Dak. G6 136-7
Jackson, co., Tenn. A9 188-9
Jackson, co., Tex. H9 192-3
Jackson, co., W. Va. F3 200-1
Jackson, co., Wis. G10 140-1
Jackson Center, O. E4 132-3
Jackson Hill, N.C. I3 180-1
Jackson Junction, Ia. B11 104-5
Jackson Lake, Wyo. D5 250-1
Jacksonboro, S.C. I12 184-5
Jacksonburg, W. Va. D5 200-1
Jacksonport, Ark. C9 150-1
Jacksonport, Wis. E16 140-1
Jackson's Arm, Nfld. L8 278-9
Jacksons Gap, Ala. G9 146-7
Jacksontown, N.B. H3 275
Jacksonville, Ala. E9 146-7
Jacksonville, Ark. I16 150-1
Jacksonville, Fla. B11 156-7
Jacksonville, Ga. L7 160-1
Jacksonville, Ill. H6 96-7
Jacksonville, Me. J10 64-5
Jacksonville, Mo. C6 120-1
Jacksonville, N.B. H3 275
Jacksonville, N.C. F13 180-1
Jacksonville, O. H8 132-3
Jacksonville, Ore. J6 238-9
Jacksonville, Tex. E10 192-3
Jacksonville, Vt. O5 90-1
Jacksonville Beach, Fla. B11 156-7
Jacob Lake, Ariz. B6 206-7
Jacobstown, N.J. I5 76-7
Jacobus, Pa. K11 84-5
Jacola*, Que. I1 290-1
Jacques-Cartier*, Que. I12 290-1
Jacques Cartier Passage, Que. H6 290-1
Jacquet River, N.B. D5 275
Jaffray, B.C. J11 268-9
Jaffrey, N.H. O4 72-3
Jakes Corner, Ariz. H7 206-7
Jakin, Ga. N2 160-1
Jal, N. Mex. L12 230-1
Jalapa, S.C. J6 184-5
Jamacia, Ia. G6 104-5
Jamacia, Va. H14 196-7
Jamaica, N.Y. E15 80-1
Jamaica, Vt. M5 90-1
Jamaica Bay, N.Y. F14 80-1
James, Ga. I6 160-1
James Bay, Ont. C7 284-5
James City, N.C. F14 180-1
James City, co., Va. I13 196-7
James R., Va. I13 196-7
James Town, Wyo. I7 250-1
Jamesburg, N.J. G6 76-7
Jameson, Mo. B4 120-1
Jamesport, Mo. B4 120-1
Jamestown, Ala. C9 146-7
Jamestown, Ark. C8 150-1
Jamestown, Colo. F2 214-5
Jamestown, Ind. H7 100-1
Jamestown, Kans. D9 108-9
Jamestown, Ky. J10 164-5
Jamestown, La. B3 168-9
Jamestown, Mo. E6 120-1
Jamestown, N.Y. G2 80-1
Jamestown, N.C. H4 180-1
Jamestown, N. Dak. G11 128-9
Jamestown, O. I16 132-3
Jamestown, R.I. G6 87
Jamestown, S.C. G14 184-5
Jamestown, Tenn. A11 188-9
Jamestown, Va. F3 196-7
Jamestown Res., N. Dak. G11 128-9
Jamestown West*, N.Y. G1 80-1
Jamesville, N.C. D14 180-1
Jamesville, Va. E5 196-7
Jamieson, Ore. F15 238-9
Jamison, Nebr. C9 124-5
Jamison, S.C. F11 184-5
Jan Bay*, Sask. H9 294-5
Jan Phyl Village*, Fla. F11 156-7
Jane Lew, W. Va. D13 200-1
Janesville, Calif. F5 210-1
Janesville, Ia. D10 104-5
Janesville, Minn. O6 116-7
Janesville, Wis. K13 140-1
Janie, La. E3 168-9
Jansen, Colo. J12 214-5
Jansen, Nebr. J13 124-5
Jansen, Sask. L8 294-5
Japton, Ark. B3 150-1
Jarales, N. Mex. G5 230-1
Jarbalo, Kans. E15 108-9
Jarbridge, Nev. A9 226-7
Jardine, Mont. I8 222-3
Jaroso, Colo. J10 214-5
Jarratt, Va. G1 196-7
Jarrettsville, Md. B11 172-3
Jarvisburg, N.C. C16 180-1
Jasmine Estates*, Fla. F9 156-7
Jasonville, Ind. K5 100-1
Jasper, Ala. D5 146-7
Jasper, Alta. J4 264-5
Jasper, Ark. B5 150-1
Jasper, Fla. B9 156-7
Jasper, Ga. E4 160-1
Jasper, Ind. M6 100-1
Jasper, Mich. K14 112-3
Jasper, Minn. O2 116-7
Jasper, Mo. H3 120-1
Jasper*, Ont. I14 284-5
Jasper, Tenn. K10 188-9
Jasper, Tex. F11 192-3
Jasper, co., Ga. H5 160-1
Jasper, co., Ill. J10 96-7
Jasper, co., Ind. C5 100-1
Jasper, co., Ia. G9 104-5
Jasper, co., Miss. J8 176-7
Jasper, co., Mo. H3 120-1
Jasper, co., S.C. J10 184-5
Jasper, co., Tex. F11 192-3
Java, S. Dak. B9 136-7
Java, Va. J9 196-7
Jay, Fla. A3 156-7
Jay, Me. K3 64-5
Jay, Okla. C16 234-5
Jay, Vt. B7 90-1
Jay, co., Ind. E11 100-1
Jay Em, Wyo. G16 250-1
Jayess, Miss. L6 176-7
Jayton, Tex. D6 192-3
Jean, Nev. N9 226-7
Jeanerette, La. I6 168-9
Jeannette, Pa. B8 84-5
Jedburg, S.C. H12 184-5
Jedburgh, Sask. M9 294-5
Jeddo, Mich. F8 112-3
Jeff, Ky. I14 164-5
Jeff Davis, co., Ga. L7 160-1
Jeff Davis, co., Tex. F3 192-3
Jeffers, Minn. O3 116-7
Jeffers, Mont. H6 222-3
Jefferson, Ala. I3 146-7
Jefferson, Ark. G7 150-1
Jefferson, Colo. E10 214-5
Jefferson, Ga. F6 160-1
Jefferson, Ia. F6 104-5
Jefferson, Kans. K14 108-9
Jefferson, Me. L5 64-5
Jefferson, Md. C8 172-3
Jefferson, N.H. F7 72-3
Jefferson*, N.J. C5 76-7
Jefferson, N.C. C6 180-1
Jefferson, O. A11 132-3
Jefferson, Okla. C10 234-5
Jefferson, Ore. I1 238-9
Jefferson, Pa. B6 84-5
Jefferson, S.C. C12 184-5
Jefferson, S. Dak. J16 136-7
Jefferson, Tex. D11 192-3
Jefferson, Va. H11 196-7
Jefferson, Wis. J13 140-1
Jefferson, co., Ala. E6 146-7
Jefferson, co., Ark. G7 150-1
Jefferson, co., Colo. E11 214-5
Jefferson, co., Fla. B8 156-7
Jefferson, co., Ga. H8 160-1
Jefferson, co., Ida. L9 218-9
Jefferson, co., Ill. L9 96-7
Jefferson, co., Ind. L10 100-1
Jefferson, co., Ia. J11 104-5
Jefferson, co., Kans. E15 108-9
Jefferson, co., Ky. G9 164-5
Jefferson, co., La. I9 168-9
Jefferson, co., Miss. J3 176-7
Jefferson, co., Mo. F10 120-1
Jefferson, co., Mont. G6 222-3
Jefferson, co., Nebr. J13 124-5
Jefferson, co., N.Y. C7 80-1
Jefferson, co., O. E11 132-3
Jefferson, co., Okla. I10 234-5
Jefferson, co., Ore. E9 238-9
Jefferson, co., Pa. F5 84-5
Jefferson, co., Tenn. B13 188-9
Jefferson, co., Tex. G11 192-3
Jefferson, co., Wash. E6 246-7
Jefferson, co., W. Va. E11 200-1
Jefferson, co., Wis. J13 140-1
Jefferson City, Mo. E7 120-1
Jefferson City, Mont. F6 222-3
Jefferson City, Tenn. H13 188-9
Jefferson Davis, co., La. H3 168-9
Jefferson Davis, co., Miss. K7 176-7
Jefferson Heights, La. C14 168-9
Jefferson Island, La. I5 168-9
Jefferson-Trooper*, Pa. J14 84-5
Jeffersonton, Va. B2 196-7
Jeffersontown, Ky. B3 164-5
Jeffersonville, Ga. I6 160-1
Jeffersonville, Ind. N9 100-1
Jeffersonville, Ky. G12 164-5
Jeffersonville, O. G5 132-3
Jeffersonville, Vt. D5 90-1
Jeffrey City, Wyo. G10 250-1
Jellico, Tenn. F11 188-9
Jellicoe, Ont. E4 284-5
Jelm, Wyo. J13 250-1
Jemez Pueblo, N. Mex. E5 230-1
Jemez Springs, N. Mex. E5 230-1
Jemison, Ala. G6 146-7
Jemtland, Me. B8 64-5
Jena, Ala. G4 146-7
Jena, La. D5 168-9
Jena, Tenn. J14 188-9
Jenera, O. D5 132-3
Jenison*, Mich. I11 112-3
Jenkinjones, W. Va. K3 200-1
Jenkins, Ky. I15 164-5
Jenkins, Minn. I5 116-7
Jenkins, co., Ga. I9 160-1
Jenkinsburg, Ga. H5 160-1
Jenkinsville, S.C. J8 184-5
Jenkintown, Pa. A11 84-5
Jenks, Okla. D13 234-5
Jennie, Ark. J9 150-1
Jennings, Fla. B9 156-7
Jennings, Kans. D4 108-9
Jennings, La. H4 168-9
Jennings, Mo. B16 120-1
Jennings, Okla. D12 234-5
Jennings, co., Ind. K10 100-1
Jenny Lind, Ark. D2 150-1
Jenpeg Camp*, Man. F3 272-3
Jenpeg Townsite*, Man. A13 272-3
Jensen, Ut. F10 242-3
Jensen Beach, Fla. B16 156-7
Jerauld, co., S. Dak. F12 136-7
Jere, W. Va. A15 200-1
Jericho, Ark. D12 150-1
Jericho, N.Y. E16 80-1
Jericho, S.C. I12 184-5
Jericho, Ut. H5 242-3
Jericho, Vt. E5 90-1
Jericho*, Va. J14 196-7
Jericho, Wis. F4 140-1
Jerico Springs, Mo. G4 120-1
Jermyn, Pa. E14 84-5
Jerome, Ariz. F6 206-7

Jerome, Ark. J9 150-1
Jerome, Ida. N6 218-9
Jerome, Ill. H7 96-7
Jerome, Pa. I5 84-5
Jerome, Wyo. D15 250-1
Jerome, co., Ida. N6 218-9
Jeromesville, O. F12 132-3
Jerry City, O. C5 132-3
Jersey, Ark. J7 150-1
Jersey, Ga. G5 160-1
Jersey*, Ont. C15 284-5
Jersey, co., Ill. J6 96-7
Jersey City, N.J. E8 76-7
Jersey Shore, Pa. F10 84-5
Jersey Village, Tex. H13 192-3
Jerseyside, Nfld. O10 278-9
Jerseyville, Ill. J6 96-7
Jerusalem, Ark. D5 150-1
Jerusalem, Ga. N10 160-1
Jerusalem, R.I. I4 87
Jessamine, co., Ky. H11 164-5
Jesse, Okla. H13 234-5
Jesse, W. Va. I3 200-1
Jessie, N. Dak. F12 128-9
Jessieville, Ark. F5 150-1
Jessup, Md. G6 172-3
Jessup*, Pa. E14 84-5
Jester, Okla. G7 234-5
Jesuit Bend, La. E15 168-9
Jesup, Ga. L9 160-1
Jesup, Ia. E11 104-5
Jet, Okla. C9 234-5
Jetersville, Va. I11 196-7
Jetmore, Kans. H5 108-9
Jetson, Ky. I7 164-5
Jett, Ky. B6 164-5
Jewell, Ia. E7 104-5
Jewell, Kans. D9 108-9
Jewell, Ore. A5 238-9
Jewell, co., Kans. C9 108-9
Jewell Ridge, Va. I4 196-7
Jewell Valley, Va. I4 196-7
Jewett, O. E11 132-3
Jewett City, Conn. E14 60-1
Jigger, La. C6 168-9
Jiggs, Nev. D8 226-7
Jim Falls, Wis. E9 140-1
Jim Hogg, co., Tex. J7 192-3
Jim Thorpe, Pa. G14 84-5
Jim Wells, co., Tex. J7 192-3
Jimtown, Okla. I11 234-5
Jo Daviess, co., Ill. A6 96-7
Joanna, S.C. I5 184-5
Joaquin, Tex. E11 192-3
Job, W. Va. F8 200-1
Joe Batt's Arm, Nfld. L10 278-9
Joe Batt's Arm-Barr'd Islands*, Nfld. L10 278-9
Joelton, Tenn. G7 188-9
Joes, Colo. E15 214-5
Joggins, N.S. C6 281
Jogues, Ont. F6 284-5
Johannesburg, Mich. F13 112-3
John Day, Ore. E12 238-9
John Sevier, Tenn. H12 188-9
Johns, Miss. I7 176-7
Johns Island, S.C. I13 184-5
Johnson, Ariz. L10 206-7
Johnson, Ark. B2 150-1
Johnson, Del. K6 153
Johnson, Minn. K2 116-7
Johnson, Nebr. I15 124-5
Johnson, Vt. D6 90-1
Johnson, Wash. H16 246-7
Johnson, co., Ark. C4 150-1
Johnson, co., Ga. I8 160-1
Johnson, co., Ill. N9 96-7
Johnson, co., Ind. J8 100-1
Johnson, co., Ia. G12 104-5
Johnson, co., Kans. F16 108-9
Johnson, co., Ky. G14 164-5
Johnson, co., Mo. E4 120-1
Johnson, co., Nebr. I15 124-5
Johnson, co., Tenn. A16 188-9
Johnson, co., Tex. E8 192-3
Johnson, co., Wyo. D12 250-1
Johnson Addition*, Alta. N9 264-5
Johnson City, Kans. J1 108-9
Johnson City, N.Y. G7 80-1
Johnson City*, Ore. C6 238-9
Johnson City, Tenn. A15 188-9
Johnson City, Tex. G8 192-3
Johnson City Southeast*, Tenn. A15 188-9
Johnson Corner, Mass. E4 68-9
Johnson Creek, Wis. J3 140-1
Johnsonburg, N.J. C4 76-7
Johnsonburg, Pa. E6 84-5
Johnsondale, Calif. K7 210-1
Johnsons Bayou, La. I1 168-9
Johnsonville, Ky. C4 164-5
Johnsonville, S.C. E14 184-5
Johnston, Ia. G7 104-5
Johnston*, R.I. C5 87
Johnston, S.C. E8 184-5
Johnston, co., N.C. E11 180-1
Johnston, co., Okla. H12 234-5
Johnston City, Ill. M9 96-7
Johnstons Station, Miss. L5 176-7
Johnstown, Colo. E3 214-5
Johnstown, Nebr. D8 124-5
Johnstown, N.Y. E10 80-1
Johnstown, N. Dak. D13 128-9
Johnstown, O. F7 132-3
Johnstown*, Ont. I15 284-5
Johnstown, Pa. I5 84-5
Johnstown Center, Wis. K2 140-1
Johnsville, Md. B9 172-3
Johnville, N.B. G3 275
Joice, Ia. B8 104-5
Joiner, Ark. D12 150-1
Joliet, Ill. C10 96-7
Joliet, Mont. H10 222-3
Joliette, Que. H12 290-1
Joliette, co., Que. I2 290-1
Jolietville, Ind. G8 100-1
Jolley, Ia. E5 104-5
Jonas Ridge, N.C. D5 180-1
Jones, Ala. H6 146-7
Jones, La. A6 168-9
Jones, Mich. K12 112-3
Jones, Okla. J3 234-5
Jones, co., Ga. I6 160-1
Jones, co., Ia. F14 104-5
Jones, co., Miss. K8 176-7
Jones, co., N.C. F13 180-1
Jones, co., S. Dak. F8 136-7
Jones, co., Tex. D6 192-3
Jones Chapel, Ala. C5 146-7
Jones Creek, Tex. K13 192-3
Jones Crossroad, Del. J4 153
Jones Mill, Ark. G5 150-1
Jones Mill, Tenn. A4 188-9
Jones Springs, W. Va. D11 200-1
Jonesboro, Ark. C11 150-1
Jonesboro, Ga. G4 160-1
Jonesboro, Ill. N8 96-7
Jonesboro, Ind. F10 100-1
Jonesboro, La. C4 168-9
Jonesboro, Me. J10 64-5
Jonesboro, Ore. F14 238-9
Jonesboro, Tenn. G16 188-9
Jonesburg, La. B6 168-9
Jonesburg, Mo. E8 120-1
Jonesport*, Me. K10 64-5
Jonestown, Md. G5 172-3
Jonestown, Miss. C5 176-7
Jonestown, Miss. G5 176-7
Jonestown, Pa. I12 84-5
Jonesville, Ind. K9 100-1
Jonesville, Ky. F11 164-5
Jonesville, La. D6 168-9
Jonesville, Mich. K13 112-3
Jonesville, N.C. G1 180-1
Jonesville, S.C. F6 184-5
Jonesville, Vt. E5 90-1
Jonesville, Va. J2 196-7
Jonquière, Que. C11 290-1
Joplin, Mo. I3 120-1
Joplin, Mont. B7 222-3
Joppa, Ala. C7 146-7
Joppa, Md. C12 172-3
Joppa, Tenn. G13 188-9
Joppatowne*, Md. C12 172-3
Jordan, Ala. K2 146-7
Jordan, Ala. H8 146-7
Jordan, Ark. B7 150-1
Jordan, Minn. C9 116-7
Jordan, Mont. D12 222-3
Jordan, N.Y. E6 80-1
Jordan Falls, N.S. G5 281
Jordan Mines, Va. H7 196-7
Jordan Valley, Ore. H16 238-9
Joseph, Ore. C15 238-9
Joseph, Ut. J5 242-3
Joseph City, Ariz. F9 206-7
Josephburg*, Alta. I8 264-5
Josephine, co., Ore. J5 238-9
Josephs Mills, W. Va. D5 200-1
Joshua, Tex. E13 192-3
Joshua Tree, Calif. N9 210-1
Jourdanton, Tex. H7 192-3
Joussard, Alta. G6 264-5
Joy, Ky. I3 164-5
Joy, Okla. H11 234-5
Joyce, La. D4 168-9
Joyce, Wash. D6 246-7
Juab, co., Ut. H4 242-3
Juan de Fuca Strait, B.C. K5 268-9
Juanita, Colo. J8 214-5
Jud, N. Dak. H11 128-9
Juda, Wis. K1 140-1
Judds Bridge, Conn. E5 60-1
Judique*, N.S. C10 281
Judith Basin, co., Mont. E8 222-3
Judith Gap, Mont. F9 222-3
Judkins, Ida. L11 218-9
Judson, Ind. H5 100-1
Judson, N. Dak. H6 128-9
Judsonia, Ark. D8 150-1
Julesburg, Colo. B16 214-5
Juliaetta, Ida. F2 218-9
Julian, Nebr. I16 124-5
Julian, N.C. H5 180-1
Julian, W. Va. I12 200-1
Juliette, Ga. H5 160-1
Juliustown, N.J. I5 76-7
Jumbo, Okla. H14 234-5
Jump River, Wis. E10 140-1
Junction, Tex. G6 192-3
Junction, Ut. K5 242-3
Junction City, Ark. K6 150-1
Junction City, Ga. J4 160-1
Junction City, Kans. F12 108-9
Junction City, Ky. E6 164-5
Junction City, La. A4 168-9
Junction City, Mo. H10 120-1
Junction City, O. G8 132-3
Junction City, Ore. K1 238-9
Junction City, Wis. F12 140-1
June Park, Fla. F13 156-7
Juneau, Alaska G15 254-5
Juneau, Wis. I14 140-1
Juneau, co., Wis. H11 140-1
Jungo, Nev. C4 226-7
Juniata, Nebr. I11 124-5
Juniata, co., Pa. H9 84-5
Junior, W. Va. E15 200-1
Juniper, Ga. J3 160-1
Juniper, Ida. O8 218-9
Juniper, N.B. G3 275
Junius, S. Dak. F15 136-7
Juno Beach, Fla. D16 156-7
Juntura, Ore. G14 238-9
Jupiter, Fla. C16 156-7
Jupiter, N.C. D4 180-1
Jupiter Inlet Beach Colony, Fla. C16 156-7
Jupiter Island, Fla. C16 156-7
Juskatla, B.C. F2 268-9
Justice, Ill. N3 96-7
Justice, Man. I11 272-3
Justice, W. Va. J3 200-1
Justin, Tex. B13 192-3

K

K I Sawyer*, Mich. D10 112-3
Kaawa, Hawaii H6 258-9
Kachemak*, Alaska G11 254-5
Kackley, Kans. D9 108-9
Kadoka, S. Dak. G6 136-7
Kaguyak, Alaska H10 254-5
Kahakuloa, Hawaii F10 258-9
Kahaluu, Hawaii I6 258-9
Kahana, Hawaii H5 258-9
Kahana, Hawaii F10 258-9
Kahlotus, Wash. H14 246-7
Kahoka, Mo. A8 120-1
Kahua, Hawaii H12 258-9
Kahuku, Hawaii E7 258-9
Kahului, Hawaii G11 258-9
Kaibab, Ariz. B5 206-7
Kaibito, Ariz. B8 206-7
Kailua, Hawaii I12 258-9
Kailua, Hawaii F8 258-9
Kailua, Hawaii G11 258-9
Kainaliu, Hawaii J12 258-9
Kaka, Ariz. K6 206-7
Kakabeka Falls, Ont. F3 284-5
Kake, Alaska H15 254-5
Kakhonak, Alaska G10 254-5
Kaktovik, Alaska B12 254-5
Kaladar, Ont. J13 284-5
Kalae, Hawaii F10 258-9
Kalaheo, Hawaii D4 258-9
Kalaloch, Wash. E5 246-7
Kalama, Wash. I7 246-7
Kalamazoo, Mich. J12 112-3
Kalamazoo, co., Mich. J12 112-3
Kalaupapa, Hawaii F10 258-9
Kaleden, B.C. J8 268-9
Kaleida, Man. K13 272-3
Kalem, Miss. I7 176-7
Kaleva, Mich. G11 112-3
Kalida, O. D4 132-3
Kalihiwai, Hawaii D4 258-9
Kalispell, Mont. C3 222-3
Kalkaska, Mich. F12 112-3
Kalkaska, co., Mich. F12 112-3
Kalo, Ia. E6 104-5
Kalona, Ia. H12 104-5
Kaltag, Alaska D9 254-5
Kaluaaha, Hawaii F10 258-9
Kalvesta, Kans. H4 108-9
Kamas, Ut. F7 242-3
Kamela, Ore. C13 238-9
Kamiah, Ida. G3 218-9
Kamloops, B.C. I8 268-9
Kamouraska, Que. E13 290-1
Kamouraska, co., Que. E14 290-1
Kampos, Nev. D7 226-7
Kamrar, Ia. E7 104-5
Kamsack, Sask. L10 294-5
Kanab, Ut. N5 242-3
Kanabec, co., Minn. K6 116-7
Kanarraville, Ut. M4 242-3
Kanata*, Ont. H10 284-5
Kanawha, Ia. C7 104-5
Kanawha, co., W. Va. H3 200-1
Kanawha R., W. Va. G2 200-1
Kandahar, Sask. L8 294-5
Kandiyohi, Minn. L4 116-7
Kandiyohi, co., Minn. L4 116-7
Kane*, Man. K3 272-3
Kane, Pa. D5 84-5
Kane, Wyo. B9 250-1
Kane, co., Ill. B10 96-7
Kane, co., Ut. M6 242-3
Kaneohe, Hawaii E8 258-9
Kankakee, Ill. D11 96-7
Kankakee, co., Ill. D11 96-7
Kannapolis, N.C. J2 180-1
Kannata Valley*, Sask. M8 294-5
Kanopolis, Kans. G9 108-9
Kanorado, Kans. E1 108-9
Kanosh, Ut. J5 242-3
Kansas, Ala. D4 146-7
Kansas, Ill. I11 96-7
Kansas, Okla. D16 234-5
Kansas City, Kans. E16 108-9
Kansas City, Mo. D3 120-1
Kansas Settlement, Ariz. L10 206-7
Kapaa, Hawaii D5 258-9
Kapaau, Hawaii H12 258-9
Kaplan, La. I5 168-9
Kapowsin, Wash. G8 246-7
Kapuskasing, Ont. F6 284-5
Karlin, Mich. G12 112-3
Karlsruhe, N. Dak. D7 128-9
Karlstad, Minn. E2 116-7
Karluk, Alaska H10 254-5
Karnak, Ill. O8 96-7
Karnes, co., Tex. H8 192-3
Karnes City, Tex. H8 192-3
Karns*, Tenn. B13 188-9
Kars*, Ont. I14 284-5
Karval, Colo. F14 214-5
Kasaan, Alaska H16 254-5
Kasabonika*, Ont. C4 284-5
Kashabowie, Ont. F3 284-5
Kasilof, Alaska F11 254-5
Kaskaskia, Ill. M6 96-7
Kaslo, B.C. J10 268-9
Kasota, Minn. N5 116-7
Kasper Creek*, Sask. O7 294-5
Kasson, Ind. O4 100-1
Kasson, Minn. O7 116-7
Kasson, W. Va. D15 200-1
Kathleen, Ga. J5 160-1
Kathryn, N. Dak. H12 128-9
Katie, Okla. H11 234-5
Katy, Tex. I12 192-3
Kauai, co., Hawaii D4 258-9
Kaufman, Tex. D16 192-3
Kaufman, co., Tex. E9 192-3
Kaukauna, Wis. E4 140-1
Kaumakani, Hawaii D4 258-9
Kaunakakai, Hawaii F9 258-9
Kaw City, Okla. C12 234-5
Kawaihae, Hawaii I12 258-9
Kawailoa, Hawaii G3 258-9
Kawailoa Beach, Hawaii G3 258-9
Kawainui, Hawaii I14 258-9
Kawkawa Lake*, B.C. J7 268-9
Kawkawlin, Mich. H14 112-3
Kay, co., Okla. B11 234-5
Kaycee, Wyo. D12 250-1
Kayenta, Ariz. B9 206-7
Kayford, W. Va. J14 200-1
Kaylor, S. Dak. H13 136-7
Kaysville, Ut. E6 242-3
Kayville, Sask. O8 294-5
Keaau*, Hawaii I14 258-9
Kealakekua, Hawaii J12 258-9
Kealia, Hawaii D5 258-9
Kealia, Hawaii J12 258-9
Keams Canyon, Ariz. D9 206-7
Keansburg, N.J. H10 76-7
Kearney, Mo. H16 120-1
Kearney, Nebr. I10 124-5
Kearney, Ont. H8 284-5
Kearney, co., Nebr. I10 124-5
Kearneysville, W. Va. D12 200-1
Kearns, Ont. F8 284-5
Kearns, Ut. F6 242-3
Kearny, Ariz. J8 206-7
Kearny, N.J. C10 76-7
Kearny, Wyo. C12 250-1
Kearny, co., Kans. H2 108-9
Kearsarge, N.H. H8 72-3
Keasey, Ore. B5 238-9
Keatchie, La. C1 168-9
Keating, Ore. D15 238-9
Keaton, Ky. G14 164-5
Keats, Kans. E12 108-9
Keaukaha, Hawaii I14 258-9
Keavy, Ky. J12 164-5
Kechi, Kans. I11 108-9
Kedgwick, N.B. E3 275
Keedysville, Md. C7 172-3
Keefton, Okla. E15 234-5
Keegan, Me. A9 64-5
Keego Harbor, Mich. I5 112-3
Keei, Hawaii J12 258-9
Keeler, Mich. J11 112-3
Keeler, Sask. M7 294-5
Keeler Bay, Vt. D3 90-1
Keeline, Wyo. G15 250-1
Keeling, Tenn. J2 188-9
Keeling, Va. J9 196-7
Keen Mountain, Va. I4 196-7
Keene, Ky. C6 164-5
Keene, Nebr. I10 124-5
Keene, N.H. N3 72-3
Keene, N. Dak. E3 128-9
Keene, Ont. K11 284-5
Keene, Tex. E13 192-3
Keene, Va. H10 196-7
Keeneland*, Ky. G9 164-5
Keenesburg, Colo. D12 214-5
Keeseville, N.Y. B11 80-1
Keetley, Ut. F7 242-3
Keewatin, Minn. G7 116-7
Keewatin*, Ont. F1 284-5
Kegley, W. Va. J4 200-1
Keiser, Ark. C12 150-1
Keith, co., Nebr. H5 124-5
Keithsburg, Ill. E4 96-7
Keithville, La. B1 168-9
Keizer, Ore. H1 238-9
Kekaha, Hawaii D4 258-9
Kekoskee, Wis. H3 140-1
Kelat, Ky. F12 164-5
Kelawea, Hawaii G10 258-9
Keldron, S. Dak. A6 136-7
Kelford, N.C. C13 180-1
Keller, Tex. C13 192-3
Keller, Va. H15 196-7
Keller, Wash. D14 246-7
Kellerman, Ala. F5 146-7
Kellerton, Ia. J6 104-5
Kelley, Ia. F7 104-5
Kelleys Isl., O. B7 132-3
Kelliher, Minn. F5 116-7
Kelliher, Sask. M9 294-5
Kellner, Wis. G12 140-1
Kellnersville, Wis. E5 140-1
Kellogg, Ida. D3 218-9
Kellogg, Ia. G9 104-5
Kellogg, Minn. N8 116-7
Kellogg, Ore. G5 238-9
Kellond, Okla. H14 234-5
Kelly*, Ala. L9 146-7
Kelly, Kans. D13 108-9
Kelly, La. C5 168-9
Kelly, N.C. G11 180-1
Kelly, Wyo. J2 250-1
Kelly Lake, B.C. I7 268-9
Kelly Lake, Minn. G7 116-7

Kellys, La. B4 168-9
Kellys Corner, N.H. L7 72-3
Kellys Cross, P.E.I. E6 287
Kellysville, W. Va. J5 200-1
Kellyton, Ala. G8 146-7
Kellytown, Ga. D12 160-1
Kellytown, S.C. D12 184-5
Kellyville, N.H. L3 72-3
Kellyville, Okla. E13 234-5
Kelowna, B.C. J8 268-9
Kelseyville, Calif. H2 210-1
Kelso, Ark. I9 150-1
Kelso, Mo. H12 120-1
Kelso, Ore. C7 238-9
Kelso, Tenn. K8 188-9
Kelso, Wash. I7 246-7
Kelton, S.C. B8 184-5
Kelton, Ut. C4 242-3
Kelvin, Ariz. I8 206-7
Kelvington, Sask. K9 294-5
Kelwood, Man. H11 272-3
Kemah*, Tex. H11 192-3
Kemano, B.C. G4 268-9
Kemmerer, Wyo. I5 250-1
Kemnay, Man. J10 272-3
Kemp, Okla. I13 234-5
Kemp*, Tex. E16 192-3
Kemp City, Okla. I13 234-5
Kemp Mill*, Md. D9 172-3
Kemper, S.C. D15 184-5
Kemper, co., Miss. H9 176-7
Kempton, Ind. F8 100-1
Kempton, N. Dak. E13 128-9
Kemptville, Ont. H15 284-5
Kempville, Tenn. A9 188-9
Ken Rock*, Ill. A8 96-7
Kenai, Alaska F11 254-5
Kenai Peninsula, Alaska G11 254-5
Kenansville, N.C. F12 180-1
Kenaston, Sask. L7 294-5
Kenbridge, Va. J11 196-7
Kendal, Sask. N9 294-5
Kendall, Fla. I16 156-7
Kendall, Kans. I2 108-9
Kendall, Wis. H11 140-1
Kendall, co., Ill. C10 96-7
Kendall, co., Tex. G7 192-3
Kendall Green, Mass. H3 68-9
Kendall Park*, N.J. G5 76-7
Kendallville, Ind. B11 100-1
Kendrick, Ida. F3 218-9
Kendrick, Okla. E12 234-5
Kenduskeag, Me. I6 64-5
Kenedy, Tex. H8 192-3
Kenedy, co., Tex. J8 192-3
Kenefick*, Okla. I13 234-5
Kenel, S. Dak. A8 136-7
Kenesaw, Nebr. I10 124-5
Kenhorst*, Pa. I13 84-5
Kenilworth, Ill. L4 96-7
Kenilworth*, N.J. E7 76-7
Kenilworth, Ont. C13 284-5
Kenilworth*, Pa. I14 84-5
Kenilworth, Ut. H8 242-3
Kenly, N.C. E12 180-1
Kenmare, N. Dak. C5 128-9
Kenmore, N.Y. E2 80-1
Kenmore, Wash. H3 246-7
Kenna, N. Mex. H10 230-1
Kenna, W. Va. G3 200-1
Kennan, Wis. D10 140-1
Kennard, Ind. H10 100-1
Kennard, Nebr. I2 124-5
Kennebec, S. Dak. G9 136-7
Kennebec, co., Me. K4 64-5
Kennebecasis R., N.B. I5 275
Kennebunk, Me. O2 64-5
Kennebunk Beach, Me. O2 64-5
Kennebunkport, Me. O3 64-5
Kennedale, Tex. D13 192-3
Kennedy, Ala. E3 146-7
Kennedy, Minn. E2 116-7
Kennedy, Nebr. D7 124-5
Kennedy, Sask. N10 294-5
Kennedyville, Md. C13 172-3
Kenner, La. C14 168-9
Kennesaw, Ga. A10 160-1
Kenneth, Minn. O2 116-7
Kenneth City, Fla. I2 156-7
Kennett, Mo. K11 120-1
Kennett Square, Pa. K14 84-5
Kennewick, Wash. I13 246-7
Kennydale, Wash. I3 246-7
Keno, Ore. K7 238-9
Keno Hill, Y.T. B2 297
Kenora, Ont. E1 284-5
Kenosee Park, Sask. N10 294-5
Kenosha, Wis. K15 140-1
Kenosha, co., Wis. K15 140-1
Kenova, W. Va. H9 200-1
Kensal, N. Dak. F11 128-9
Kensett, Ark. D8 150-1
Kensett, Ia. B8 104-5
Kensington*, Calif. I3 210-1
Kensington, Conn. E8 60-1
Kensington, Kans. D7 108-9
Kensington, Md. H3 172-3
Kensington, Minn. K3 116-7
Kensington, N.H. N9 72-3
Kensington*, N.Y. J11 80-1
Kensington, P.E.I. E5 287
Kensington, S.C. G15 184-5
Kensington Park*, Fla. K2 156-7
Kent, Ala. H8 146-7
Kent, Conn. D4 60-1
Kent, Ind. L10 100-1
Kent, Ia. I5 104-5
Kent, Minn. J1 116-7
Kent, O. D16 132-3
Kent, Ore. C10 238-9
Kent, Wash. J3 246-7
Kent, co., Del. F3 153
Kent, co., Md. D13 172-3
Kent, co., Mich. I12 112-3
Kent, co., N.B. G6 275
Kent, co., Ont. F11 284-5
Kent, co., R.I. E4 87
Kent, co., Tex. D5 192-3
Kent Acres-South Dover Manor*, Del. F4 153
Kent City, Mich. I12 112-3
Kent Corner, Mass. B12 68-9
Kent Furnace, Conn. D4 60-1
Kent Junction, N.B. G6 275
Kentland, Ind. D4 100-1
Kentland*, Md. E10 172-3
Kenton, Del. E3 153
Kenton, Ky. E11 164-5
Kenton, Man. I10 272-3
Kenton, Mich. D8 112-3
Kenton, O. D5 132-3
Kenton, Okla. B1 234-5
Kenton, Tenn. B3 188-9
Kenton, co., Ky. E11 164-5
Kenton Vale*, Ky. D11 164-5
Kents Hill, Me. K4 64-5
Kents Store, Va. H11 196-7
Kentuck, W. Va. G3 200-1
Kentucky Lake, Ky. J3 164-5
Kentucky Lake, Tenn. B5 188-9
Kentucky R., Ky. F10 164-5
Kentville, N.S. D6 281
Kentwood, La. F8 168-9
Kentwood*, Mich. I12 112-3
Kenvil, N.J. D5 76-7
Kenville, Man. F9 272-3
Kenvir, Ky. J14 164-5
Kenwood, Mass. B11 68-9
Kenwood*, O. I3 132-3
Kenwood, Okla. D15 234-5
Kenyon, Minn. N7 116-7
Kenyon, R.I. H3 87
Keo, Ark. F7 150-1
Keokea, Hawaii J12 258-9
Keokea, Hawaii G11 258-9
Keokee, Va. J2 196-7
Keokuk, Ia. K13 104-5
Keokuk, co., Ia. H11 104-5
Keolu Hills, Hawaii J7 258-9
Keomah*, Ia. H10 104-5
Keosauqua, Ia. J12 104-5
Keota, Colo. B13 214-5
Keota, Ia. H12 104-5
Keota, Okla. F15 234-5
Keowee, S.C. B5 184-5
Kerby, Ore. J4 238-9
Keremeos, B.C. J8 268-9
Kerens, Tex. E9 192-3
Kerens, W. Va. E16 200-1
Kerhonkson*, N.Y. G11 80-1
Kerkhoven, Minn. L3 116-7
Kerman, Calif. J5 210-1
Kermit, Tex. E3 192-3
Kermit, W. Va. K10 200-1
Kern, co., Calif. L7 210-1
Kernersville, N.C. G3 180-1
Kernville, Calif. L7 210-1
Kerr, co., Tex. G6 192-3
Kerrick, Minn. J7 116-7
Kerrobert, Sask. L4 294-5
Kerrville, Tex. G7 192-3
Kersey, Colo. C12 214-5
Kershaw, S.C. C11 184-5
Kershaw, co., S.C. C11 184-5
Keshena, Wis. F14 140-1
Kessinger, Ky. I8 164-5
Kessler, W. Va. I5 200-1
Keswick, Ia. H11 104-5
Keswick, N.B. H4 275
Keswick, Ont. B15 284-5
Keswick, Va. G11 196-7
Ketchan*, Sask. L9 294-5
Ketchikan, Alaska H16 254-5
Ketchum, Ida. L6 218-9
Ketchum, Okla. C15 234-5
Kettering, O. I15 132-3
Kettle Falls, Wash. C15 246-7
Kettle Island, Ky. J13 164-5
Kettle River, Minn. I7 116-7
Kettle Valley, B.C. K9 268-9
Keuterville, Ida. G3 218-9
Kevil, Ky. J2 164-5
Kevin, Mont. B6 222-3
Kewa, Wash. D14 246-7
Kewadin, Mich. F12 112-3
Kewanee, Ill. D6 96-7
Kewanee, Miss. I10 176-7
Kewanna, Ind. C7 100-1
Kewaskum, Wis. H4 140-1
Kewaunee, Wis. G15 140-1
Kewaunee, co., Wis. F15 140-1
Keweenaw, co., Mich. B9 112-3
Keweenaw Point, Mich. B9 112-3
Key Colony Beach, Fla. K12 156-7
Key Largo, Fla. J13 156-7
Key Largo, Fla. K13 156-7
Key West, Fla. K11 156-7
Keya Paha, co., Nebr. C8 124-5
Keyes, Calif. D10 210-1
Keyes, Okla. C2 234-5
Keymar, Md. B9 172-3
Keyport, N.J. H10 76-7
Keyport, Wash. H1 246-7
Keysburg, Ky. K7 164-5
Keyser, W. Va. D9 200-1
Keystone, Ala. F6 146-7
Keystone, Ind. E11 100-1
Keystone, Ia. F11 104-5
Keystone, Nebr. G5 124-5
Keystone, S. Dak. F2 136-7
Keystone, W. Va. J3 200-1
Keystone Heights, Fla. C10 156-7
Keysville, Ga. H9 160-1
Keysville, Va. J10 196-7
Keytesville, Mo. C6 120-1
Kezar Falls, Me. N7 64-5
Khedive, Sask. O8 294-5
Kiahsville, W. Va. J10 200-1
Kiamichi, Okla. G15 234-5
Kiana, Alaska C9 254-5
Kibler, Ark. D2 150-1
Kickapoo, La. C1 168-9
Kidder, Mo. F16 120-1
Kidder, S. Dak. A13 136-7
Kidder, co., N. Dak. G9 128-9
Kidderville, N.H. C7 72-3
Kief, N. Dak. E8 128-9
Kiefer, Okla. E13 234-5
Kiel, Wis. G5 140-1
Kieler, Wis. K10 140-1
Kiester, Minn. O6 116-7
Kihei, Hawaii G11 258-9
Kikino, Alta. H9 264-5
Kila, Mont. C3 222-3
Kilauea, Hawaii D4 258-9
Kilauea Crater, Hawaii J13 258-9
Kilbourne, La. A7 168-9
Kildare, Okla. C11 234-5
Kildeer, Ill. K2 96-7
Kilgore, Ida. K10 218-9
Kilgore, Nebr. C6 124-5
Kilgore*, Tex. E11 192-3
Kilkenny, Minn. N6 116-7
Kill Devil Hills, N.C. C16 180-1
Killaloe Station, Ont. H12 284-5
Killaly, Sask. M10 294-5
Killam, Alta. J9 264-5
Killarney, Man. K11 272-3
Killarney, Ont. H7 284-5
Killbuck, O. E9 132-3
Killdeer, N. Dak. F3 128-9
Killduff, Ia. G9 104-5
Killeen, Tex. F8 192-3
Killen, Ala. A4 146-7
Killian, La. A12 168-9
Killian, S.C. D10 184-5
Killingly*, Conn. C14 60-1
Killingly Center, Conn. C14 60-1
Killingworth, Conn. G10 60-1
Kilmarnock, Va. H14 196-7
Kilmichael, Miss. F7 176-7
Kiln, Miss. N8 176-7
Kilpatrick, Ala. C8 146-7
Kilts, Ore. D10 238-9
Kim, Colo. J14 214-5
Kimama, Ida. N7 218-9
Kimball, Ida. M9 218-9
Kimball, Kans. I15 108-9
Kimball, Nebr. G1 124-5
Kimball, S. Dak. G11 136-7
Kimball, Tenn. K10 188-9
Kimball, W. Va. J3 200-1
Kimball, co., Nebr. G1 124-5
Kimball Prairie, Minn. L5 116-7
Kimballton, Ia. G4 104-5
Kimballton, Va. I6 196-7
Kimberley, B.C. J10 268-9
Kimberlin Heights, Tenn. H12 188-9
Kimberling City*, Mo. I5 120-1
Kimberly, Ala. E6 146-7
Kimberly, Ida. O6 218-9
Kimberly, Nev. G9 226-7
Kimberly, Ore. D11 238-9
Kimberly, Wis. E4 140-1
Kimble, co., Tex. G6 192-3
Kimbrell, Ala. F5 146-7
Kimbrough, Ala. J4 146-7
Kimmell, Ind. B10 100-1
Kimmins, Tenn. I5 188-9
Kimmswick, Mo. D15 120-1
Kinards, S.C. I5 184-5
Kinbrae, Minn. O3 116-7
Kincaid, Ill. I7 96-7
Kincaid, Kans. H15 108-9
Kincaid, Sask. O6 294-5
Kincaid, W. Va. J15 200-1
Kincardine, Ont. B11 284-5
Kincheloe*, Mich. D13 112-3
Kincheloe, W. Va. D13 200-1
Kinde, Mich. G15 112-3
Kinder, La. G3 168-9
Kinderhook, N.Y. G11 80-1
Kindersley, Sask. L4 294-5
Kindred, N. Dak. H14 128-9
Kineo, Me. F5 64-5
King, Ark. H2 150-1
King*, N.C. C8 180-1
King, Wis. E2 140-1
King, co., Tex. D6 192-3
King, co., Wash. E9 246-7
King and Queen, co., Va. H14 196-7
King and Queen Court House, Va. D3 196-7
King City, Calif. K4 210-1
King City, Mo. B3 120-1
King City, Ont. C15 284-5
King City*, Ore. C6 238-9
King Cove, Alaska I8 254-5
King George, Va. C4 196-7
King George, co., Va. G13 196-7
King Hill, Ida. N5 218-9
King Island*, Alaska D7 254-5
King Kirkland, Ont. F8 284-5
King Salmon, Alaska G9 254-5
King William, Va. H13 196-7
King William, co., Va. H13 196-7
Kingcross Estates*, Ont. C15 284-5
Kingdom City*, Mo. E7 120-1
Kingfield, Me. I3 64-5
Kingfisher, Okla. E10 234-5
Kingfisher, co., Okla. D10 234-5
Kingman, Ariz. E3 206-7
Kingman, Ind. G5 100-1
Kingman, Kans. I9 108-9
Kingman, Me. G8 64-5
Kingman, co., Kans. J9 108-9
Kings, Miss. I4 176-7
Kings, co., Calif. K5 210-1
Kings, co., N.B. I6 275
Kings, co., N.Y. F14 80-1
Kings, co., N.S. E6 281
Kings, co., P.E.I. E9 287
Kings Canyon, Colo. B9 214-5
Kings Corner, Mass. C3 68-9
Kings Creek, S.C. A9 184-5
Kings Grant, N.J. O12 76-7
Kings Mountain, Ky. I11 164-5
Kings Mountain, N.C. E6 180-1
Kings Park, N.Y. J12 80-1
Kings Point, N.Y. E15 80-1
King's Point, Nfld. L9 278-9
Kings Valley, Ore. D5 238-9
Kingsboro, P.E.I. E11 287
Kingsburg*, Calif. K6 210-1
Kingsbury, Ind. A6 100-1
Kingsbury, Me. I5 64-5
Kingsbury, co., S. Dak. E14 136-7
Kingsclear, N.B. I4 275
Kingsdown, Kans. J5 108-9
Kingsey Falls, Que. I14 290-1
Kingsford, Mich. E9 112-3
Kingsford Heights, Ind. B6 100-1
Kingsland, Ark. H7 150-1
Kingsland, Ga. N10 160-1
Kingsley, Ia. D2 104-5
Kingsley*, Ky. G9 164-5
Kingsley, Mich. G12 112-3
Kingsley Dam, Nebr. G5 124-5
Kingsport, Tenn. A15 188-9
Kingsport North*, Tenn. A15 188-9
Kingston, Ark. B4 150-1
Kingston, Ga. E2 160-1
Kingston, Ida. D3 218-9
Kingston, Ky. D8 164-5
Kingston, La. C2 168-9
Kingston, Mass. F13 68-9
Kingston, Mich. E5 112-3
Kingston, Minn. A7 116-7
Kingston, Mo. C4 120-1
Kingston, N.H. N8 72-3
Kingston, N. Mex. J4 230-1
Kingston, N.Y. H11 80-1
Kingston*, N.S. D5 281
Kingston, O. H7 132-3
Kingston, Okla. I12 234-5
Kingston, Ont. K14 284-5
Kingston, Pa. F13 84-5
Kingston*, P.E.I. F7 287
Kingston, R.I. G4 87
Kingston, Tenn. I10 188-9
Kingston, Ut. K5 242-3
Kingston, Wash. H2 246-7
Kingston, W. Va. J15 200-1
Kingston, Wis. G2 140-1
Kingston Mills, Ont. J14 284-5
Kingston Springs, Tenn. H6 188-9
Kingston Village*, N.S. D6 281
Kingstree, S.C. F13 184-5
Kingsville, La. E4 168-9
Kingsville, Md. C12 172-3
Kingsville, Mo. K16 120-1
Kingsville, O. A11 132-3
Kingsville, Ont. G10 284-5
Kingsville, Tex. J8 192-3
Kingsville Station*, Tex. J8 192-3
Kingswood, Ky. H7 164-5
Kingville, S.C. E11 184-5
Kingwood, N.J. F3 76-7
Kingwood, W. Va. D7 200-1
Kinistino, Sask. J8 294-5
Kinkora, P.E.I. E5 287
Kinley, Sask. L6 294-5
Kinloch, Mo. B16 120-1
Kinmundy, Ill. K9 96-7
Kinnear, Wyo. F8 250-1
Kinnelon, N.J. C6 76-7
Kinney, Minn. G7 116-7
Kinney, co., Tex. H6 192-3
Kinoosao, Sask. E10 294-5
Kinross, Ia. H12 104-5
Kinross, Mich. D13 112-3
Kinsale, Va. G14 196-7
Kinsey, Ala. L10 146-7
Kinsey, Mont. F14 222-3
Kinsley, Kans. I6 108-9
Kinsman Corner, Mass. B12 68-9
Kinston, Ala. L8 146-7
Kinston, N.C. E13 180-1
Kinta, Okla. F15 234-5
Kinuso, Alta. G6 264-5
Kinzua, Ore. D11 238-9
Kiona, Wash. I12 246-7
Kiosk, Ont. H8 284-5
Kiowa, Colo. E12 214-5
Kiowa, Kans. K8 108-9
Kiowa, Mont. B4 222-3
Kiowa, Okla. G14 234-5
Kiowa, co., Colo. G15 214-5
Kiowa, co., Kans. J7 108-9
Kiowa, co., Okla. G8 234-5
Kipling, N.C. J7 180-1
Kipling, Sask. N10 294-5
Kipnuk, Alaska F8 254-5
Kipp, Kans. F10 108-9
Kippens, Nfld. N7 278-9
Kipton, O. C8 132-3
Kirby, Ark. G3 150-1
Kirby, Miss. K4 176-7
Kirby, Mont. H12 222-3
Kirby, Tex. J2 192-3

Kirby*, Vt. D9 90-1
Kirby, W. Va. E10 200-1
Kirby, Wyo. D9 250-1
Kirby Corner, Mass. H11 68-9
Kirbyton, Ky. J2 164-5
Kirbyville, Tex. F11 192-3
Kirk, Colo. E15 214-5
Kirkersville, O. F7 132-3
Kirkland, Ala. L5 146-7
Kirkland, Ariz. G5 206-7
Kirkland, Ga. M7 160-1
Kirkland, Ill. B9 96-7
Kirkland, N.B. H3 275
Kirkland*, Que. I12 290-1
Kirkland, Tenn. I7 188-9
Kirkland, Wash. H3 246-7
Kirkland Junction, Ariz. G5 206-7
Kirkland Lake, Ont. G8 284-5
Kirklin, Ind. G7 100-1
Kirkman, Ia. G4 104-5
Kirkmansville, Ky. J6 164-5
Kirksey, Ky. K3 164-5
Kirksey, S.C. E7 184-5
Kirksville, Ky. D7 164-5
Kirksville, Mo. B6 120-1
Kirkville, Ia. I10 104-5
Kirkwood, Del. C3 153
Kirkwood, Ill. E5 96-7
Kirkwood, Mo. C15 120-1
Kirkwood, S.C. D11 184-5
Kiro, Kans. E14 108-9
Kiron, Ia. E3 104-5
Kirtland, N. Mex. C3 230-1
Kirtland*, O. B10 132-3
Kirtland Hills, O. A16 132-3
Kirtley, Wyo. F16 250-1
Kirwin, Kans. D7 108-9
Kisatchie, La. E3 168-9
Kisbey, Sask. O10 294-5
Kismet, Kans. K3 108-9
Kissimmee, Fla. G7 156-7
Kistler, W. Va. K12 200-1
Kit Carson, Colo. F15 214-5
Kit Carson, co., Colo. E15 214-5
Kitchener, Ont. D13 284-5
Kitchner, B.C. K10 268-9
Kite, Ga. I8 160-1
Kitimat, B.C. F4 268-9
Kitsap, co., Wash. E7 246-7
Kitscoty, Alta. J10 264-5
Kittanning, Pa. G3 84-5
Kittanning Heights*, Pa. G3 84-5
Kittery, Me. O2 64-5
Kittery Point, Me. O2 64-5
Kittitas, Wash. G11 246-7
Kittitas, co., Wash. G11 246-7
Kittredge, Colo. H2 214-5
Kittrell, N.C. G8 180-1
Kitts Hummock, Del. F4 153
Kittson, co., Minn. E1 116-7
Kitty Hawk, N.C. C16 180-1
Kitwanga, B.C. E4 268-9
Kitzmiller, Md. C2 172-3
Kivalina, Alaska C8 254-5
Klagetoh, Ariz. D10 206-7
Klamath, co., Ore. I8 238-9
Klamath Agency, Ore. I7 238-9
Klamath Falls, Ore. J8 238-9
Klawock, Alaska H16 254-5
Kleberg, Tex. D15 192-3
Kleberg, co., Tex. J8 192-3
Kleefeld, Man. J14 272-3
Klein, Mont. F10 222-3
Klemme, Ia. C8 104-5
Klemmer Subdivision*, Sask. C9 294-5
Klickitat, Wash. J10 246-7
Klickitat, co., Wash. I10 246-7
Kline, S.C. H9 184-5
Kline, W. Va. F9 200-1
Klipsan Beach, Wash. H5 246-7
Klondike, Miss. H9 176-7
Klondike, Nev. J6 226-7
Klondike, Ore. B10 238-9
Klondike R., Y.T. B2 297
Klondyke, Ariz. J9 206-7
Kloten, N. Dak. E12 128-9
Klukwan, Alaska G15 254-5
Knapp, Wis. F8 140-1
Knappa, Ore. A5 238-9
Knellsville, Wis. H5 140-1
Knierim, Ia. E6 104-5
Knifley, Ky. I10 164-5
Knightdale, N.C. I8 180-1
Knightstown, Ind. H10 100-1
Knightsville, Ind. I5 100-1
Kniman, Ind. C5 100-1
Knob Fork, W. Va. A13 200-1
Knob Lick, Ky. J9 164-5
Knob Noster, Mo. E4 120-1
Knobel, Ark. A11 150-1
Knolls, Ut. F4 242-3
Knollwood*, O. G4 132-3
Knott, co., Ky. I14 164-5
Knotts Island, N.C. B16 180-1
Knottsville, Ky. H6 164-5
Knowles, Okla. C6 234-5
Knowles, Wis. H3 140-1
Knowlesville, N.B. G3 275
Knowlton, Mont. F15 222-3
Knowlton*, N.J. C3 76-7
Knox, Ind. B7 100-1
Knox*, Me. K6 64-5
Knox, N. Dak. D9 128-9
Knox*, Pa. F4 84-5
Knox, co., Ill. E6 96-7
Knox, co., Ind. M4 100-1
Knox, co., Ky. J13 164-5
Knox, co., Me. L6 64-5
Knox, co., Mo. B7 120-1
Knox, co., Nebr. D12 124-5
Knox, co., O. E8 132-3
Knox, co., Tenn. B13 188-9
Knox, co., Tex. D6 192-3
Knox Center, Me. K6 64-5
Knox City, Mo. B7 120-1
Knox City, Tex. D6 192-3
Knoxo, Miss. L6 176-7
Knoxville, Ala. G4 146-7
Knoxville, Ark. D4 150-1
Knoxville, Ga. I5 160-1
Knoxville, Ill. E6 96-7
Knoxville, Ia. H9 104-5
Knoxville, Md. C7 172-3
Knoxville, Miss. L3 176-7
Knoxville, Tenn. B13 188-9
Knutsford, P.E.I. C3 287
Ko Vaya, Ariz. L6 206-7
Koa Mill, Hawaii J12 258-9
Kobuk, Alaska C10 254-5
Kodak, Tenn. H13 188-9
Kodiak, Alaska H10 254-5
Kodiak Isl., Alaska H10 254-5
Kodiak Station*, Alaska H10 254-5
Kodol, W. Va. A12 200-1
Koele, Hawaii G10 258-9
Kohler, Wis. G5 140-1
Kokadjo, Me. G5 64-5
Kokomo, Ind. E8 100-1
Kokomo, Miss. L6 176-7
Kokrines, Alaska D10 254-5
Kola*, Man. J1 272-3
Koliganek, Alaska G9 254-5
Kolin, Mont. E9 222-3
Koloa, Hawaii D4 258-9
Koloa Landing, Hawaii D4 258-9
Kolola Springs, Miss. E10 176-7
Kolter, La. C1 168-9
Kom Vo, Ariz. L6 206-7
Komalty, Okla. G8 234-5
Komarno, Man. H14 272-3
Komatke, Ariz. I6 206-7
Komoka*, Ont. E12 284-5
Kona, N.C. D4 180-1
Konawa, Okla. G12 234-5
Kongiganak*, Alaska F8 254-5
Konkapot, Mass. E2 68-9
Koochiching, co., Minn. F6 116-7
Koontz Lake, Ind. B7 100-1
Koosharem, Ut. J6 242-3
Kooskia, Ida. G4 218-9
Kootenai, Ida. B3 218-9
Kootenai, co., Ida. C2 218-9
Koppel, Pa. G1 84-5
Kopperston, W. Va. K14 200-1
Kosciusko, Miss. G7 176-7
Kosciusko, co., Ind. B9 100-1
Koshkonong, Mo. J8 120-1
Kosmosdale, Ky. B1 164-5
Kossuth, Miss. A9 176-7
Kossuth, co., Ia. B6 104-5
Kotlik, Alaska E8 254-5
Kotzebue, Alaska C9 254-5
Kountze, Tex. G11 192-3
Kouts, Ind. B5 100-1
Koyuk, Alaska D9 254-5
Koyukuk, Alaska D9 254-5
Kraemer, La. D12 168-9
Krakow, Wis. D4 140-1
Kramer, Ind. F5 100-1
Kramer, Nebr. I14 124-5
Kramer, N. Dak. C7 128-9
Kramer Subdivision*, Ont. H12 284-5
Kranzburg, S. Dak. D15 136-7
Krebs, Okla. G14 234-5
Kremlin, Mont. B8 222-3
Kremlin, Okla. C10 234-5
Kremmling, Colo. D9 214-5
Kreole, Miss. N10 176-7
Krestova*, B.C. J9 268-9
Kronau, Sask. N8 294-5
Kronborg, Nebr. H12 124-5
Kronstal*, Man. K3 272-3
Krotz Springs, La. G6 168-9
Krupp, Wash. F13 246-7
Krydor, Sask. K6 294-5
Kualapuu, Hawaii F9 258-9
Kukui, Hawaii J14 258-9
Kukuihaele, Hawaii H13 258-9
Kukuiula, Hawaii D4 258-9
Kuliouou, Hawaii K7 258-9
Kulm, N. Dak. I10 128-9
Kulpmont, Pa. G12 84-5
Kumukumu, Hawaii D5 258-9
Kuna, Ida. M3 218-9
Kunia, Hawaii I3 258-9
Kupreanof, Alaska H15 254-5
Kure Beach, N.C. H12 180-1
Kuroki, Sask. L9 294-5
Kurthwood, La. E3 168-9
Kurtistown, Hawaii J14 258-9
Kusa, Okla. F14 234-5
Kutch, Colo. F13 214-5
Kuttawa, Ky. J4 164-5
Kutztown, Pa. H14 84-5
Kwethluk, Alaska F8 254-5
Kwigillingok, Alaska F8 254-5
Kwiguk, Alaska E8 254-5
Kyle, Sask. M5 294-5
Kyle, S. Dak. H5 136-7
Kyle, Tex. G8 192-3
Kylemore*, Sask. L9 294-5
Kyles Ford, Tenn. F14 188-9

L

La Baie*, Que. G4 290-1
La Barge, Wyo. H6 250-1
La Belle, Fla. H11 156-7
La Belle, Mo. B7 120-1
La Broquerie, Man. J15 272-3
La Canada-Flintridge*, Calif. G8 210-1
La Center, Ky. J2 164-5
La Center, Wash. J7 246-7
La Cienega, N. Mex. E6 230-1
La Conner, Wash. E2 246-7
La Coste, Tex. J1 192-3
La Crête, Alta. C6 264-5
La Crescent, Minn. O9 116-7
La Crescenta-Montrose*, Calif. N7 210-1
La Crosse, Ark. B8 150-1
La Crosse, Fla. C10 156-7
La Crosse, Ind. B6 100-1
La Crosse, Kans. G6 108-9
La Crosse, Va. J11 196-7
La Crosse, Wash. G15 246-7
La Crosse, Wis. H9 140-1
La Crosse, co., Wis. H9 140-1
La Cygne, Kans. G16 108-9
La Farge, Wis. I10 140-1
La Fayette, Ga. D2 160-1
La Feria*, Tex. K8 192-3
La Follette, Tenn. A12 188-9
La Fontaine, Ind. E9 100-1
La France, S.C. C5 184-5
La Garita, Colo. H9 214-5
La Glace, Alta. G3 264-5
La Grande, Ore. C14 238-9
La Grande, Wash. G8 246-7
La Grange, Ark. F10 150-1
La Grange, Ga. H2 160-1
La Grange, Ill. M3 96-7
La Grange, Ky. A3 164-5
La Grange, Mo. B8 120-1
La Grange, N.C. E12 180-1
La Grange, Tenn. K3 188-9
La Grange, Tex. G9 192-3
La Grange, Wyo. I16 250-1
La Grange Highlands*, Ill. B11 96-7
La Grange Park, Ill. M3 96-7
La Guadeloupe, Que. I16 290-1
La Habra, Calif. G9 210-1
La Harpe, Ill. F4 96-7
La Harpe, Kans. I15 108-9
La Jara, Colo. J10 214-5
La Jara, N. Mex. D5 230-1
La Joya*, Tex. K7 192-3
La Junta, Colo. H14 214-5
La Loche, Sask. F4 294-5
La Loma, N. Mex. F8 230-1
La Luz, N. Mex. J7 230-1
La Madera, N. Mex. C7 230-1
La Malbaie, Que. E13 290-1
La Marque, Tex. J15 192-3
La Mesa, Calif. J11 210-1
La Mesa, N. Mex. L5 230-1
La Mirada*, Calif. G9 210-1
La Moille, Ill. C8 96-7
La Monte, Mo. E5 120-1
La Motte, Ia. E15 104-5
La Moure, co., N. Dak. I12 128-9
La Palma, Ariz. J7 206-7
La Palma*, Calif. H9 210-1
La Patrie, Que. J16 290-1
La Paz, Ind. B8 100-1
La Pêche*, Que. I2 290-1
La Pérade, Que. G10 290-1
La Pine, Ore. G8 238-9
La Plant, S. Dak. C8 136-7
La Plata, Md. G10 172-3
La Plata, Mo. B6 120-1
La Plata, N. Mex. B3 230-1
La Plata, co., Colo. I7 214-5
La Platte, Nebr. J3 124-5
La Pocatière, Que. E13 290-1
La Pointe, Wis. A10 140-1
La Porte, Ind. A6 100-1
La Porte, Tex. H15 192-3
La Porte, co., Ind. A6 100-1
La Porte City, Ia. E11 104-5
La Prairie, Minn. H6 116-7
La Prairie, Que. J12 290-1
La Prele, Wyo. G14 250-1
La Présentation*, Que. I13 290-1
La Puente*, Calif. G9 210-1
La Puente, N. Mex. C6 230-1
La Push, Wash. E4 246-7
La Quinta, Calif. N9 210-1
La Reine, Que. H1 290-1
La Rivière, Man. K12 272-3
La Rochelle*, Man. K4 272-3
La Ronge, Sask. G7 294-5
La Rue, O. E6 132-3
La Sal, Ut. K10 242-3
La Sal Junction, Ut. K10 242-3
La Salle, Colo. E4 214-5
La Salle, Ill. D8 96-7
La Salle, Man. J14 272-3
La Salle, Minn. O4 116-7
La Salle, co., Ill. D8 96-7
La Salle, co., La. D5 168-9
La Salle, co., Tex. I7 192-3
La Sarre, Que. H1 290-1
La Sarre-Sud, Que. H1 290-1
La Sauses, Colo. J10 214-5
La Scie, Nfld. L9 278-9
La Selva Beach*, Calif. J3 210-1
La Station-du-Coteau*, Que. J2 290-1
La Tabatière, Que. G8 290-1
La Tour, Mo. K16 120-1
La Tuque, Que. E9 290-1
La Union, N. Mex. L5 230-1
La Vale [-Narrows Park], Md. B3 172-3
La Valle, Wis. I11 140-1
La Vergne, Tenn. H7 188-9
La Verkin, Ut. M3 242-3
La Verne*, Calif. G9 210-1
La Vernière*, Que. I7 290-1
La Veta, Colo. I11 214-5
La Villa*, Tex. K8 192-3
La Vista, Nebr. J2 124-5
Laager*, Tenn. D10 188-9
Labarre, La. G6 168-9
Labelle, Que. H10 290-1
Labelle, co., Que. J2 290-1
Labette, Kans. J15 108-9
Labette, co., Kans. K15 108-9
Labolt, S. Dak. C16 136-7
Labrador City, Nfld. I1 278-9
Lac-à-la-Tortue*, Que. G9 290-1
Lac Albanel, Que. G3 290-1
Lac-Alouette*, Que. I11 290-1
Lac-au-Saumon, Que. I5 290-1
Lac-aux-Sables*, Que. F9 290-1
Lac Baker, N.B. F1 275
Lac-Bouchette, Que. C10 290-1
Lac-Brome*, Que. J3 290-1
Lac-Carré, Que. H11 290-1
Lac-des-Aigles, Que. D15 290-1
Lac-des-Écorces*, Que. I2 290-1
Lac du Bonnet, Man. I15 272-3
Lac-Etchemin, Que. J4 290-1
Lac La Belle, Wis. I3 140-1
Lac la Biche, Alta. H9 264-5
Lac la Hache, B.C. H7 268-9
Lac La Ronge, Sask. G7 294-5
Lac-Lapierre*, Que. I11 290-1
Lac-Mégantic, Que. I16 290-1
Lac Qui Parle, co., Minn. M2 116-7
Lac-Saint-Jean-Est, co., Que. C10 290-1
Lac-Saint-Jean-Ouest, co., Que. H3 290-1
Lac-St.-Charles*, Que. E10 290-1
Lac Vert, Sask. K8 294-5
Lacadena, Sask. M5 294-5
Lacamp, La. E3 168-9
Lacassine, La. H3 168-9
Lacey*, N.J. J7 76-7
Lacey, Okla. D10 234-5
Lacey, Wash. K1 246-7
Lacey Spring, Va. F10 196-7
Laceys Spring, Ala. B7 146-7
Lachenaie*, Que. I12 290-1
Lachine, Mich. F14 112-3
Lachine*, Que. I12 290-1
Lachute, Que. I11 290-1
Lackawanna, N.Y. F2 80-1
Lackawanna, co., Pa. F14 84-5
Lackey, Ky. H15 164-5
Lackland*, Tex. H7 192-3
Laclede, Ida. B3 218-9
Laclede, Mo. C5 120-1
Laclede, co., Mo. H6 120-1
Laclu, Ont. E1 284-5
Lacolle, Que. J12 290-1
Lacomb, Ore. I2 238-9
Lacombe, Alta. K8 264-5
Lacombe, La. B15 168-9
Lacon, Ala. C6 146-7
Lacon, Ill. E8 96-7
Lacona, Ia. I8 104-5
Lacona, N.Y. D7 80-1
Laconia, Ind. O8 100-1
Laconia, N.H. K7 72-3
Laconia, Tenn. K3 188-9
Lacoochee, Fla. F4 156-7
Lacy-Lakeview, Tex. E9 192-3
Ladd, Ill. D8 96-7
Ladder Lake Subdivision*, Sask. I6 294-5
Laddonia, Mo. D8 120-1
Ladds, Tenn. K10 188-9
Ladelle, Ark. J8 150-1
Ladera Heights*, Calif. N7 210-1
Ladessa, Okla. G7 234-5
Ladoga, Ind. H6 100-1
Ladonia*, Tex. D10 192-3
Ladora, Ia. G11 104-5
Ladson, S.C. H13 184-5
Ladue, Mo. B15 120-1
Lady Lake, Fla. E11 156-7
Ladysmith, B.C. C12 268-9
Ladysmith, Va. G12 196-7
Ladysmith, Wis. D9 140-1
Ladywood*, Man. J3 272-3
Lafayette, Ala. G10 146-7
Lafayette, Calif. C8 210-1
Lafayette, Colo. F3 214-5
Lafayette, Ind. F6 100-1
Lafayette, Ky. K5 164-5
Lafayette, La. H5 168-9
Lafayette, Minn. N5 116-7
Lafayette, N.J. B5 76-7
Lafayette, O. D4 132-3
Lafayette*, Ore. C6 238-9
Lafayette, R.I. F5 87
Lafayette, Tenn. A9 188-9
Lafayette, Va. I7 196-7
Lafayette, co., Ark. J3 150-1
Lafayette, co., Fla. C9 156-7
Lafayette, co., La. H5 168-9
Lafayette, co., Miss. C8 176-7
Lafayette, co., Mo. E4 120-1
Lafayette, co., Wis. K11 140-1
Lafayette Hills-Plymouth Meeting*, Pa. J15 84-5
Lafayette Southwest*, La. H5 168-9
Lafayette Springs, Miss. C8 176-7
Lafe, Ark. B11 150-1
Lafitte, La. I9 168-9
Lafleche, Sask. O6 294-5
Lafontaine, Kans. J14 108-9
Lafontaine*, Que. I11 290-1

Lafourche, co., La. I8 168-9
Lagacéville, N.B. F6 275
Lagrange, Ind. A10 100-1
Lagrange, Me. I7 64-5
Lagrange, O. C12 132-3
Lagrange, co., Ind. A10 100-1
Lagro, Ind. D9 100-1
Laguna, Ariz. J2 206-7
Laguna, N. Mex. F4 230-1
Laguna Beach, Calif. H9 210-1
Laguna Hills*, Calif. O8 210-1
Laguna Niguel, Calif. H9 210-1
Lahaina, Hawaii G10 258-9
Lahmansville, W. Va. E9 200-1
Lahoma, Okla. D10 234-5
Laidlaw, B.C. B16 268-9
Laie, Hawaii G5 258-9
Laingsburg, Mich. H2 112-3
Laird, Colo. D16 214-5
Laird, Sask. K6 294-5
Lajord, Sask. N8 294-5
Lajoya, N. Mex. H5 230-1
Lake, Ky. J12 164-5
Lake, Mich. H12 112-3
Lake, Miss. I8 176-7
Lake*, N.Y. I10 80-1
Lake, co., Calif. G2 210-1
Lake, co., Colo. F9 214-5
Lake, co., Fla. E11 156-7
Lake, co., Ill. A10 96-7
Lake, co., Ind. B4 100-1
Lake, co., Mich. G11 112-3
Lake, co., Minn. G9 116-7
Lake, co., Mont. C3 222-3
Lake, co., O. B10 132-3
Lake, co., Ore. H10 238-9
Lake, co., S. Dak. F15 136-7
Lake, co., Tenn. A2 188-9
Lake Alfred, Fla. H5 156-7
Lake Alma, Sask. O8 294-5
Lake Aluma, Okla. J2 234-5
Lake Andes, S. Dak. I12 136-7
Lake Angelus*, Mich. I14 112-3
Lake Ann, Mich. F11 112-3
Lake Anna, Va. G11 196-7
Lake Arrowhead*, Calif. N8 210-1
Lake Arthur, La. H4 168-9
Lake Arthur, N. Mex. J9 230-1
Lake Athabasca, Alta. B9 264-5
Lake Athabasca, Sask. B5 294-5
Lake Barcroft*, Va. E13 196-7
Lake Barrington, Ill. K2 96-7
Lake Benton, Minn. N2 116-7
Lake Beulah, Wis. J4 140-1
Lake Bluff, Ill. K3 96-7
Lake Bronson, Minn. D2 116-7
Lake Buena Vista*, Fla. F11 156-7
Lake Butler, Fla. C10 156-7
Lake Candlewood, Conn. F4 60-1
Lake Carmel, N.Y. I11 80-1
Lake Carroll*, Fla. F10 156-7
Lake Catherine*, Ill. A10 96-7
Lake Champlain, Vt. D3 90-1
Lake Charles, La. H2 168-9
Lake Charles Washington McConaughy, Nebr. G5 124-5
Lake Cicott, Ind. D7 100-1
Lake City, Ark. C11 150-1
Lake City, Colo. H8 214-5
Lake City, Fla. C10 156-7
Lake City, Ga. D11 160-1
Lake City, Ia. E5 104-5
Lake City, Kans. J7 108-9
Lake City, Mich. G12 112-3
Lake City, Minn. N8 116-7
Lake City, Pa. C1 84-5
Lake City, S.C. E13 184-5
Lake City, S. Dak. A14 136-7
Lake City, Tenn. G11 188-9
Lake Clarke Shores, Fla. E16 156-7
Lake Como, Miss. J8 176-7
Lake Cormorant, Miss. A6 176-7
Lake Cowichan, B.C. D11 268-9
Lake Creek, Okla. G7 234-5
Lake Crystal, Minn. O5 116-7
Lake Cumberland, Ky. J10 164-5
Lake Dallas, Tex. B14 192-3
Lake Delton, Wis. I12 140-1
Lake Dick, Ark. G8 150-1
Lake Diefenbaker, Sask. M6 294-5
Lake Dunmore, Vt. H4 90-1
Lake Elmo*, Minn. M7 116-7
Lake Elmore, Vt. D7 90-1
Lake Elsinore, Calif. H10 210-1
Lake End, La. D2 168-9
Lake Erie 14-15
Lake Erie Beach*, N.Y. F2 80-1
Lake Forest*, Fla. I13 156-7
Lake Forest, Ill. K3 96-7
Lake Forest Park*, Wash. E8 246-7
Lake Fork, Ida. J3 218-9
Lake Frances, Ark. B1 150-1
Lake Francis, Man. I13 272-3
Lake Francis Case, S. Dak. G10 136-7
Lake Geneva, Wis. K4 140-1
Lake George, Colo. J2 214-5
Lake George, Mich. G12 112-3
Lake George, Minn. H4 116-7
Lake George, N.Y. D11 80-1
Lake Granby, Colo. C10 214-5
Lake Grove*, N.Y. J12 80-1
Lake Hamilton, Ark. G5 150-1
Lake Hamilton, Fla. H6 156-7
Lake Hart*, Ind. I7 100-1
Lake Havasu, Ariz. F2 206-7
Lake Havasu City, Ariz. G2 206-7
Lake Helen, Fla. E12 156-7
Lake Henry, Minn. L4 116-7
Lake Hiawatha, N.J. D6 76-7
Lake Hills-Murray Hills*, Tenn. E10 188-9
Lake Holloway*, Fla. H4 156-7
Lake Huron 14-15
Lake in the Hills*, Ill. K1 96-7
Lake Isabella, Calif. L7 210-1
Lake Jackson, Tex. K13 192-3
Lake Junaluska, N.C. E3 180-1
Lake Junction, Wyo. G2 250-1
Lake Katrine, N.Y. H11 80-1
Lake Kissimmee, Fla. F11 156-7
Lake Leelanau, Mich. F12 112-3
Lake Lenore, Sask. K8 294-5
Lake Lillian, Minn. M4 116-7
Lake Linden, Mich. B9 112-3
Lake Lotawana, Mo. J16 120-1
Lake Louise, Alta. L6 264-5
Lake Lure*, N.C. E5 180-1
Lake Magdalene*, Fla. F10 156-7
Lake Manitoba, Man. I3 272-3
Lake Marion, S.C. G12 184-5
Lake Mary*, Fla. E12 156-7
Lake Mead, Nev. M10 226-7
Lake Melville, Nfld. H6 278-9
Lake Mendota, Wis. I1 140-1
Lake Michigan 14-15
Lake Michigan Beach, Mich. J11 112-3
Lake Mills, Ia. B8 104-5
Lake Mills, Wis. J2 140-1
Lake Minchumina, Alaska E10 254-5
Lake Mohawk, N.J. C5 76-7
Lake Montezuma, Ariz. F7 206-7
Lake Moultrie, S.C. G13 184-5
Lake Moxie, Me. H4 64-5
Lake Nebagamon, Wis. B8 140-1
Lake Norden, S. Dak. E15 136-7
Lake Norman, N.C. E7 180-1
Lake O' The Cherokees, Okla. C15 234-5
Lake Oahe, S. Dak. C8 136-7
Lake Odessa, Mich. I12 112-3
Lake of the Ozarks, Mo. F6 120-1
Lake of the Woods, Minn. D4 116-7
Lake of the Woods, Ont. E1 284-5
Lake of the Woods, co., Minn. E4 116-7
Lake Okeechobee, Fla. H12 156-7
Lake Ontario 14-15
Lake Orion, Mich. H5 112-3
Lake Orion Heights, Mich. H5 112-3
Lake Oswego*, Ore. C6 238-9
Lake Ouachita, Ark. F4 150-1
Lake Ozark, Mo. F6 120-1
Lake Park, Fla. D16 156-7
Lake Park, Ga. O6 160-1
Lake Park, Ia. A4 104-5
Lake Park, Minn. I2 116-7
Lake Placid, Fla. K7 156-7
Lake Placid, N.Y. B10 80-1
Lake Pleasant, Mass. C5 68-9
Lake Pleasant, N.Y. D10 80-1
Lake Pocotopaug*, Conn. E10 60-1
Lake Pontchartrain, La. H9 168-9
Lake Powell, Ut. M8 242-3
Lake Preston, S. Dak. E14 136-7
Lake Providence, La. A7 168-9
Lake Quivira*, Kans. F16 108-9
Lake Rossignol, N.S. F5 281
Lake St. Clair, Mich. I15 112-3
Lake St. Croix Beach, Minn. B12 116-7
Lake Sakakawea, N. Dak. F5 128-9
Lake Shafer, Ind. D6 100-1
Lake Sharpe, S. Dak. F9 136-7
Lake Ship Heights*, Fla. F11 156-7
Lake Shore, Md. H7 172-3
Lake Shore, Minn. I5 116-7
Lake Shore, Ut. G6 242-3
Lake Sidney Lanier, Ga. E5 160-1
Lake Simcoe, Ont. A15 284-5
Lake Springfield, Ill. H7 96-7
Lake Station, Ind. A5 100-1
Lake Stevens, Wash. G3 246-7
Lake Success*, N.Y. J11 80-1
Lake Superior 14-15
Lake Tahoe, Calif. G5 210-1
Lake Tapawingo*, Mo. E3 120-1
Lake Telemark*, N.J. C6 76-7
Lake Texoma, Okla. I12 234-5
Lake Tomahawk, Wis. D12 140-1
Lake Toxaway, N.C. F3 180-1
Lake Valley, Okla. F8 234-5
Lake View, Ark. G10 150-1
Lake View, Ia. E4 104-5
Lake View, La. B1 168-9
Lake View, Me. H6 64-5
Lake View, S.C. D15 184-5
Lake Villa, Ill. J2 96-7
Lake Village, Ark. J9 150-1
Lake Village, Ind. C4 100-1
Lake Waccamaw, N.C. G11 180-1
Lake Wales, Fla. H6 156-7
Lake Waukomis, Mo. I15 120-1
Lake Wazeecha*, Wis. G12 140-1
Lake Wilson, Minn. O2 116-7
Lake Winnebago*, Mo. E3 120-1
Lake Winnebago, Wis. H14 140-1
Lake Winnipeg, Man. G3 272-3
Lake Winnipegosis, Man. H2 272-3
Lake Winnipesaukee, N.H. J7 72-3
Lake Wissota*, Wis. E9 140-1
Lake Worth, Fla. E16 156-7
Lake Worth Village, Tex. C12 192-3
Lake Zurich, Ill. K2 96-7
Lakebay, Wash. J1 246-7
Lakecreek, Ore. J6 238-9
Lakefield, Minn. O3 116-7
Lakefield, Ont. J11 284-5
Lakehurst, N.J. I7 76-7
Lakeland, Fla. F11 156-7
Lakeland, Ga. N7 160-1
Lakeland, La. G7 168-9
Lakeland, Mich. J3 112-3
Lakeland, Minn. B12 116-7
Lakeland*, Mo. F7 120-1
Lakeland Shores*, Minn. M7 116-7
Lakeland Village, Calif. H10 210-1
Lakemont, Ga. D6 160-1
Lakemont, Tenn. I11 188-9
Lakemoor, Ill. J2 96-7
Lakemore, O. D15 132-3
Lakeport, Ark. J9 150-1
Lakeport, Calif. G2 210-1
Lakeport, Mich. F8 112-3
Lakeport, N.H. K7 72-3
Lakes District*, Wash. F7 246-7
Lakeshire*, Mo. E10 120-1
Lakeshore, Miss. O8 176-7
Lakeside, Ariz. G10 206-7
Lakeside*, Calif. O8 210-1
Lakeside, Colo. G3 214-5
Lakeside, Conn. D5 60-1
Lakeside, Ia. D4 104-5
Lakeside*, Mo. F6 120-1
Lakeside, Mont. C3 222-3
Lakeside, Nebr. E4 124-5
Lakeside, N.S. E7 281
Lakeside, Ore. G4 238-9
Lakeside*, Tex. D8 192-3
Lakeside, Ut. D4 242-3
Lakeside, Va. D1 196-7
Lakeside Park*, Ky. D11 164-5
Lakesite*, Tenn. D10 188-9
Lakesville, Md. H13 172-3
Laketon, Ind. D9 100-1
Laketown, Ut. C7 242-3
Lakeview*, Ala. C8 146-7
Lakeview*, Alta. J7 264-5
Lakeview, Ark. A6 150-1
Lakeview, Ida. C3 218-9
Lakeview*, Ky. E11 164-5
Lakeview, Mich. H12 112-3
Lakeview, Mich. J12 112-3
Lakeview*, N.Y. E16 80-1
Lakeview, N.C. J5 180-1
Lakeview, O. E4 132-3
Lakeview, Ore. J10 238-9
Lakeview*, Tex. G11 192-3
Lakeview, Wash. K2 246-7
Lakeview Terrace*, Que. I2 290-1
Lakeville, Conn. B4 60-1
Lakeville, Ind. A8 100-1
Lakeville, Me. H8 64-5
Lakeville, Mass. G12 68-9
Lakeville, Mich. H6 112-3
Lakeville, Minn. C10 116-7
Lakeville*, N.B. H7 275
Lakewood, Calif. H8 210-1
Lakewood, Colo. G3 214-5
Lakewood, Ill. K1 96-7
Lakewood, Me. J4 64-5
Lakewood, Mass. C2 68-9
Lakewood, N.J. H7 76-7
Lakewood, N. Mex. K4 230-1
Lakewood, N.Y. G1 80-1
Lakewood, O. B14 132-3
Lakewood, Tenn. G7 188-9
Lakewood, Wash. F3 246-7
Lakewood, Wis. E14 140-1
Lakewood Center, Wash. K2 246-7
Lakewood Club*, Mich. H11 112-3
Lakin, Kans. I2 108-9
Lakota, Ia. B6 104-5
Lakota, N. Dak. D11 128-9
Lamaline, Nfld. O9 278-9
Lamar, Ark. D4 150-1
Lamar, Colo. H15 214-5
Lamar, Ind. O6 100-1
Lamar, La. C6 168-9
Lamar, Miss. A8 176-7
Lamar, Mo. H3 120-1
Lamar, Nebr. I4 124-5
Lamar, Okla. F13 234-5
Lamar, S.C. D13 184-5
Lamar, co., Ala. D3 146-7
Lamar, co., Ga. H4 160-1
Lamar, co., Miss. L7 176-7
Lamar, co., Tex. D10 192-3
Lamar Heights, Mo. H3 120-1
Lamartine, Ark. J4 150-1
Lamartine, Wis. G3 140-1
Lamasco, Ky. J4 164-5
Lamb, Mich. G7 112-3
Lamb, co., Tex. C4 192-3
Lambert, Miss. C6 176-7
Lambert, Mont. C15 222-3
Lambert, Okla. C9 234-5
Lambert Lake, Me. G10 64-5
Lamberton, Minn. N3 116-7
Lambertville, Mich. K14 112-3
Lambertville, N.J. G4 76-7
Lambeth*, Ont. E12 284-5
Lambrook, Ark. G10 150-1
Lambs Grove, Ia. G9 104-5
Lambsburg, Va. K6 196-7
Lambton, Que. I16 290-1
Lambton, co., Ont. E11 284-5
Lame Deer, Mont. G13 222-3
Lamèque*, N.B. E7 275
Lamesa, Tex. D4 192-3
Lamison, Ala. J4 146-7
Lamoille, Nev. D9 226-7
Lamoille, co., Vt. D6 90-1
Lamoine, Me. K8 64-5
Lamoine Beach, Me. K8 64-5
Lamona, Wash. F14 246-7
Lamoni, Ia. K7 104-5
Lamont, Alta. I8 264-5
Lamont, Calif. L6 210-1
Lamont, Ida. K11 218-9
Lamont, Ia. D12 104-5
Lamont, Kans. H13 108-9
Lamont, Miss. E4 176-7
Lamont, Okla. C11 234-5
Lamont, Wash. F15 246-7
Lamont, Wyo. H11 250-1
Lamonta, Ore. E9 238-9
LaMoure, N. Dak. I12 128-9
Lamourie, La. F4 168-9
Lampasas, Tex. F8 192-3
Lampasas, co., Tex. F8 192-3
Lampman, Sask. O10 294-5
Lampton, Miss. L7 176-7
Lanagan, Mo. J3 120-1
Lanai City, Hawaii G10 258-9
Lanark, Ill. B7 96-7
Lanark, Ont. I14 284-5
Lanark, W. Va. K16 200-1
Lanark, co., Ont. I14 284-5
Lancaster, Calif. E8 210-1
Lancaster, Kans. D15 108-9
Lancaster, Ky. E7 164-5
Lancaster, Mass. C9 68-9
Lancaster, Minn. D1 116-7
Lancaster, Mo. A6 120-1
Lancaster, N.H. E6 72-3
Lancaster, N.Y. F3 80-1
Lancaster, O. G7 132-3
Lancaster, Ont. H16 284-5
Lancaster, Ore. J1 238-9
Lancaster, Pa. J12 84-5
Lancaster, S.C. B11 184-5
Lancaster, Tenn. B9 188-9
Lancaster, Tex. D15 192-3
Lancaster, Va. H14 196-7
Lancaster, Wis. J10 140-1
Lancaster, co., Nebr. H14 124-5
Lancaster, co., Pa. K13 84-5
Lancaster, co., S.C. C11 184-5
Lancaster, co., Va. H14 196-7
Lancaster Mills, S.C. B11 184-5
Lance Creek, Wyo. F15 250-1
Lancer, Sask. M4 294-5
Lancing, Tenn. H10 188-9
Land, Ala. J2 146-7
Land O' Lakes, Wis. C13 140-1
Landa, N. Dak. B7 128-9
Landaff Center, N.H. G5 72-3
Lander, Wyo. F8 250-1
Lander, co., Nev. E6 226-7
Landes, W. Va. F9 200-1
Landess, Ind. E10 100-1
Landfall, Minn. B11 116-7
Landgrove*, Vt. L5 90-1
Landing, N.J. D5 76-7
Landis, Ark. B6 150-1
Landis, N.C. I2 180-1
Landis, Sask. K5 294-5
Landis Northeast, N.C. I2 180-1
Landmark*, Man. J14 272-3
Lando, S.C. B10 184-5
Lando Mines, W. Va. K11 200-1
Landover*, Md. E10 172-3
Landover Hills, Md. I5 172-3
Landrum, S.C. D3 184-5
Landry, N.B. E6 275
Landsford, S.C. B10 184-5
Landusky, Mont. C10 222-3
Lane, Kans. G15 108-9
Lane, Nev. G10 226-7
Lane, Okla. H14 234-5
Lane, S.C. F13 184-5
Lane, S. Dak. F12 136-7
Lane, Tenn. B2 188-9
Lane, co., Kans. G4 108-9
Lane, co., Ore. F6 238-9
Laneburg, Ark. I4 150-1
Lanesboro, Ia. F5 104-5
Lanesboro, Minn. O8 116-7
Lanesborough, Mass. C2 68-9
Lanesville, Ind. N9 100-1
Lanesville, Va. D2 196-7
Lanett, Ala. G10 146-7
Laneview, Va. H14 196-7
Lanford, S.C. H4 184-5
Lang, Sask. N8 294-5
Lang Bay*, B.C. J6 268-9
Langbank, Sask. N10 294-5
Langdale, Ala. G10 146-7
Langdon, Alta. M8 264-5
Langdon, Kans. I8 108-9
Langdon, N.H. M3 72-3
Langdon, N. Dak. B11 128-9
L'Ange-Gardien, Que. F11 290-1
Langenburg, Sask. M10 294-5
Langford, Md. D13 172-3
Langford, S. Dak. B13 136-7
Langham, Sask. K6 294-5
Langhorne, Pa. A12 84-5
Langhorne Manor*, Pa. I16 84-5
Langlade, Wis. E13 140-1
Langlade, co., Wis. E13 140-1
Langley, Ark. G3 150-1
Langley, B.C. C14 268-9
Langley, Okla. C15 234-5
Langley, S.C. F8 184-5
Langley, Wash. G2 246-7
Langley Park, Md. I4 172-3
Langlois, Ore. I3 238-9
Langruth, Man. I12 272-3
Langston, Ala. B8 146-7
Langston, Okla. E11 234-5
Langton, Ont. E13 284-5
Lanham, Nebr. J14 124-5
Lanham-Seabrook*, Md. E10 172-3
Lanier, co., Ga. N7 160-1

Lanigan, Sask. L8 294-5
Lanikai, Hawaii J7 258-9
Lankin, N. Dak. D12 128-9
Lannon*, Wis. J15 140-1
L'Annonciation, Que. J2 290-1
Lanoka Harbor, N.J. J7 76-7
Lanoraie, Que. H13 290-1
Lansdale, Pa. A10 84-5
Lansdowne, Ont. J14 284-5
Lansdowne, Pa. B11 84-5
Lansdowne-Baltimore Highlands, Md. F6 172-3
L'Anse, Mich. C9 112-3
L'Anse-au-Loup, Nfld. J8 278-9
Lansford, N. Dak. C6 128-9
Lansford, Pa. G13 84-5
Lansing, Ill. O4 96-7
Lansing, Ia. B13 104-5
Lansing, Kans. E16 108-9
Lansing, Mich. I13 112-3
Lansing, Minn. O7 116-7
Lansing, N.C. C6 180-1
Lantana, Fla. E16 156-7
Lantry, S. Dak. C6 136-7
Lantz, Md. B8 172-3
Lantz*, N.S. D7 281
Lantzville, B.C. J6 268-9
Laona, Wis. D14 140-1
Laotto, Ind. B11 100-1
Lapeer, Mich. G5 112-3
Lapeer, co., Mich. I15 112-3
Lapeer Heights*, Mich. I14 112-3
Lapel, Ind. G9 100-1
Lapile, Ark. K7 150-1
Lapine, Ala. J7 146-7
Laplace, La. C13 168-9
Laplante, N.B. E5 275
Lapoint, Ut. F9 242-3
Laporte, Colo. D3 214-5
Laporte, Minn. H4 116-7
Laporte, Pa. E12 84-5
Laprairie, co., Que. J12 290-1
Lapwai, Ida. F2 218-9
Laramie, Wyo. J14 250-1
Laramie, co., Wyo. J15 250-1
Larchmont, N.Y. D15 80-1
Larchwood, Ia. A1 104-5
Larder Lake, Ont. F8 284-5
Lardo, Ida. I3 218-9
L'Ardoise West, N.S. C11 281
Laredo, Mo. B5 120-1
Laredo, Mont. B9 222-3
Laredo, Tex. J7 192-3
Largo, Fla. H1 156-7
Larimer, co., Colo. C11 214-5
Larimore, N. Dak. E13 128-9
Lark Harbour, Nfld. M7 278-9
Larkinsville, Ala. B8 146-7
Larkspur, Calif. C7 210-1
Larkspur, Colo. I3 214-5
Larksville*, Pa. F13 84-5
Larned, Kans. H7 108-9
Larose, La. J9 168-9
Larouche, Que. C11 290-1
Larrabee, Ia. C3 104-5
Larry's River, N.S. D10 281
Larrywaug, Mass. D1 68-9
Larsen, Wis. F3 140-1
Larsen Bay, Alaska H10 254-5
Larslan, Mont. B13 222-3
Larson, N. Dak. B3 128-9
Larto, La. E5 168-9
Larue, co., Ky. H9 164-5
Larussell, Mo. I4 120-1
Larwill, Ind. C9 100-1
Las Animas, Colo. H14 214-5
Las Animas, co., Colo. I13 214-5
Las Cruces, N. Mex. L5 230-1
Las Mesitas, Colo. J10 214-5
Las Tablas, N. Mex. C7 230-1
Las Tusas, N. Mex. E8 230-1
Las Vegas, Nev. M9 226-7
Las Vegas, N. Mex. E8 230-1
LaSalle*, Que. I12 290-1
Lascassas, Tenn. H8 188-9
L'Ascension, Que. B11 290-1
Lashburn, Sask. J4 294-5
Lasker, N.C. C13 180-1
Lasqueti, B.C. J6 268-9
Lassen, co., Calif. E5 210-1
L'Assomption, Que. I12 290-1
L'Assomption, co., Que. I12 290-1
L'Assomption-Nord*, Que. I12 290-1
Lastrup, Minn. J5 116-7
Latah, Wash. F16 246-7
Latah, co., Ida. F2 218-9
Latchford, Ont. G8 284-5
Laterrière, Que. C11 290-1
Latex, La. B1 168-9
Latham, Kans. J12 108-9
Latham, Mo. E6 120-1
Latham, N.Y. F11 80-1
Latham, Tenn. A4 188-9
Lathrop, Calif. C9 210-1
Lathrop, Mo. C3 120-1
Lathrop Wells, Nev. L7 226-7
Lathrup Village, Mich. J5 112-3
Latimer, Ia. D8 104-5
Latimer, Kans. F12 108-9
Latimer, Ut. K3 242-3
Latimer, co., Okla. G15 234-5
Laton, Calif. K6 210-1
Latonia Lakes*, Ky. D11 164-5
Latrobe, Pa. I4 84-5
Latta, S.C. D14 184-5
Lattimore*, N.C. E5 180-1
Lattingtown*, N.Y. J11 80-1
Laud, Ind. C10 100-1
Lauder, Man. J10 272-3
Lauderdale, Minn. B11 116-7
Lauderdale, Miss. H10 176-7
Lauderdale, co., Ala. A4 146-7
Lauderdale, co., Miss. I9 176-7
Lauderdale, co., Tenn. C2 188-9
Lauderdale-by-the-Sea, Fla. G16 156-7
Lauderdale Lakes*, Fla. I13 156-7
Lauderhill, Fla. G16 156-7
Laughlin*, Tex. H5 192-3
Laupahoehoe, Hawaii I13 258-9
Laura, Ky. H15 164-5
Laura, O. G14 132-3
Laura, Sask. L6 294-5
Laurel, Del. J3 153
Laurel, Ind. I11 100-1
Laurel, Ia. G9 104-5
Laurel, Md. H5 172-3
Laurel, Miss. K8 176-7
Laurel, Mont. G10 222-3
Laurel, Nebr. D13 124-5
Laurel, Wash. I9 246-7
Laurel, co., Ky. I12 164-5
Laurel Bloomery, Tenn. A17 188-9
Laurel Fork, Va. J7 196-7
Laurel Glen, Conn. F15 60-1
Laurel Hill, Fla. A4 156-7
Laurel Hill, N.C. F9 180-1
Laurel Hollow*, N.Y. J11 80-1
Laurel Park, N.C. E4 180-1
Laurel Springs, N.J. O11 76-7
Laureldale, Pa. I13 84-5
Laurelville, O. H7 132-3
Laurence Harbor, N.J. G9 76-7
Laurens, Ia. C5 104-5
Laurens, S.C. C7 184-5
Laurens, co., Ga. J7 160-1
Laurens, co., S.C. C7 184-5
Laurentides*, Que. I12 290-1
Laurie*, Mo. F6 120-1
Laurier, Man. H11 272-3
Laurier, Wash. B14 246-7
Laurier-Station, Que. G11 290-1
Laurierville, Que. H15 290-1
Laurin, Mont. H6 222-3
Laurinburg, N.C. F9 180-1
Laurinburg West*, N.C. F9 180-1
Laurium, Mich. B8 112-3
Lauzon, Que. G11 290-1
Lava Hot Springs, Ida. N10 218-9
Lavaca, Ala. J3 146-7
Lavaca, Ark. D2 150-1
Lavaca, co., Tex. H9 192-3
Laval*, Que. I4 290-1
Laval, Que. I12 290-1
Lavalette, W. Va. H10 200-1
Lavallette, N.J. I8 76-7
Lavaltrie, Que. I13 290-1
Lavenham*, Man. J2 272-3
Laverne, Okla. C6 234-5
Lavillette, N.B. F6 275
Lavina, Mont. F10 222-3
Lavinia, Tenn. C4 188-9
Lavonia, Ga. E7 160-1
Lavoy, Alta. I9 264-5
Lawai, Hawaii D4 258-9
Lawen, Ore. G13 238-9
Lawhon, La. B3 168-9
Lawler, Ia. C11 104-5
Lawley, Ala. G6 146-7
Lawn, Nfld. O9 278-9
Lawndale*, Calif. G8 210-1
Lawndale, N.C. E6 180-1
Lawnside, N.J. N11 76-7
Lawrence, Ind. E3 100-1
Lawrence, Kans. F15 108-9
Lawrence, Mass. B11 68-9
Lawrence*, Mich. J11 112-3
Lawrence, Miss. I8 176-7
Lawrence, Nebr. J11 124-5
Lawrence*, N.J. G5 76-7
Lawrence*, N.J. M2 76-7
Lawrence*, N.Y. K11 80-1
Lawrence, Okla. G12 234-5
Lawrence, Ut. I7 242-3
Lawrence, Wash. C8 246-7
Lawrence, co., Ala. B5 146-7
Lawrence, co., Ark. B10 150-1
Lawrence, co., Ill. K11 96-7
Lawrence, co., Ind. L7 100-1
Lawrence, co., Ky. G15 164-5
Lawrence, co., Miss. K6 176-7
Lawrence, co., Mo. I4 120-1
Lawrence, co., O. J7 132-3
Lawrence, co., Pa. F1 84-5
Lawrence, co., S. Dak. E1 136-7
Lawrence, co., Tenn. D6 188-9
Lawrence Station, N.B. I3 275
Lawrenceburg, Ind. K12 100-1
Lawrenceburg, Ky. B5 164-5
Lawrenceburg, Tenn. D6 188-9
Lawrenceport, Ind. L7 100-1
Lawrencetown, N.S. E5 281
Lawrenceville, Ga. F5 160-1
Lawrenceville, Ill. K11 96-7
Lawrenceville, N.J. G5 76-7
Lawrenceville, O. G16 132-3
Lawrenceville*, Que. J14 290-1
Lawrenceville, Va. J12 196-7
Laws Hill, Miss. B7 176-7
Lawson, Ark. J6 150-1
Lawson, Colo. G1 214-5
Lawson, Mo. H16 120-1
Lawson Heights*, Pa. I4 84-5
Lawsonville, N.C. C8 180-1
Lawtell, La. G5 168-9
Lawtey, Fla. C10 156-7
Lawton, Ia. D1 104-5
Lawton, Ky. F14 164-5
Lawton, Mich. J12 112-3
Lawton, Nev. F1 226-7
Lawton, N. Dak. D11 128-9
Lawton, Okla. H9 234-5
Lawton, W. Va. K16 200-1
Layland, W. Va. K16 200-1
Laysville, Conn. G12 60-1
Layton, Ut. E6 242-3
Laytonsville, Md. G3 172-3
Lazear, Colo. F7 214-5
Lazy Lake*, Fla. G16 156-7
Le Center, Minn. N6 116-7
Le Claire, Ia. G15 104-5
Le Flore, Miss. E6 176-7
Le Flore, co., Okla. G16 234-5
Le Gore, Md. B9 172-3
Le Goulet*, N.B. E7 275
Le Grand, Ia. F10 104-5
Le Loup, Kans. G15 108-9
Le Mars, Ia. C1 104-5
Le Roy, Ill. G9 96-7
Le Roy, Ia. J8 104-5
Le Roy, Kans. H14 108-9
Le Roy, Minn. O8 116-7
Le Roy, N.Y. E4 80-1
Le Roy, W. Va. F3 200-1
Le Sueur, Minn. N5 116-7
Le Sueur, co., Minn. N6 116-7
Le Tourneau, Miss. I4 176-7
Lea, co., N. Mex. J11 230-1
Leaburg, Ore. K2 238-9
Leach, Okla. D15 234-5
Leach, Tenn. B4 188-9
Leachville, Ark. B12 150-1
Lead, S. Dak. E2 136-7
Lead Hill, Ark. A5 150-1
Lead Mine, W. Va. D16 200-1
Lead Mine, Wis. K11 140-1
Leader, Sask. M4 294-5
Leadington, Mo. G10 120-1
Leadore, Ida. J8 218-9
Leadville, Colo. E9 214-5
Leadville North*, Colo. F9 214-5
Leadwood, Mo. F15 120-1
Leaf, Miss. M9 176-7
Leaf River, Ill. B7 96-7
League City, Tex. I15 192-3
Leake, co., Miss. G7 176-7
Leakesville, Miss. L10 176-7
Leakey, Tex. G6 192-3
Leal, N. Dak. G12 128-9
Leamington, Ont. G10 284-5
Leamington, Ut. H5 242-3
Leander, La. F3 168-9
Leapwood, Tenn. D4 188-9
Learned, Miss. I5 176-7
Leary, Ga. M3 160-1
Leasburg, Mo. F8 120-1
Leasburg, N.C. C10 180-1
Leask, Sask. J6 294-5
Leatherwood, Ky. J14 164-5
Leavenworth, Ind. N7 100-1
Leavenworth, Kans. E16 108-9
Leavenworth, Wash. F10 246-7
Leavenworth, co., Kans. E15 108-9
Leawood, Kans. F16 108-9
Leawood, Mo. I3 120-1
Lebam, Wash. H6 246-7
Lebanon, Ala. C8 146-7
Lebanon, Conn. E12 60-1
Lebanon, Ga. A10 160-1
Lebanon, Ill. K7 96-7
Lebanon, Ind. G7 100-1
Lebanon, Kans. D8 108-9
Lebanon, Ky. E4 164-5
Lebanon, Me. O2 64-5
Lebanon, Miss. I5 176-7
Lebanon, Mo. G6 120-1
Lebanon, Nebr. J7 124-5
Lebanon, N.H. J3 72-3
Lebanon*, N.J. E4 76-7
Lebanon, N.J. E4 76-7
Lebanon, O. H4 132-3
Lebanon, Ore. I1 238-9
Lebanon, Pa. I12 84-5
Lebanon, S. Dak. C9 136-7
Lebanon, Tenn. G8 188-9
Lebanon, Va. J4 196-7
Lebanon, Wis. I3 140-1
Lebanon, co., Pa. H12 84-5
Lebanon Church, Va. E11 196-7
Lebanon Junction, Ky. C2 164-5
Lebanon South*, Ore. E6 238-9
Lebanon South*, Pa. I12 84-5
Lebeau, La. G5 168-9
Lebec, Calif. M6 210-1
Lebel-sur-Quévillon, Que. H2 290-1
LeBlanc, La. G3 168-9
Lebo, Kans. G14 108-9
Lebret, Sask. M9 294-5
Leclercville, Que. G10 290-1
Lecompte, La. F4 168-9
Lecompton, Kans. F15 108-9
Ledger, Mont. C6 222-3
Ledgewood, N.J. D5 76-7
Ledoux, N. Mex. D8 230-1
Leduc, Alta. J8 264-5
Ledyard, Conn. G13 60-1
Ledyard, Ia. B6 104-5
Lee, Fla. B9 156-7
Lee, Me. H8 64-5
Lee, Mass. D2 68-9
Lee, Nev. D9 226-7
Lee, N.H. M9 72-3
Lee, co., Ala. H10 146-7
Lee, co., Ark. F10 150-1
Lee, co., Fla. I11 156-7
Lee, co., Ga. L4 160-1
Lee, co., Ill. C8 96-7
Lee, co., Ia. J13 104-5
Lee, co., Ky. H13 164-5
Lee, co., Miss. C9 176-7
Lee, co., N.C. E10 180-1
Lee, co., S.C. D12 184-5
Lee, co., Tex. G9 192-3
Lee, co., Va. J2 196-7
Lee Bayou, La. D6 168-9
Lee City, Ky. H14 164-5
Lee Heights, La. E4 168-9
Lee Landing, La. A13 168-9
Leech*, N.B. E6 275
Leechburg, Pa. H3 84-5
Leechville, N.C. E15 180-1
Leedey, Okla. E7 234-5
Leeds*, Ala. E7 146-7
Leeds, Me. L3 64-5
Leeds, N. Dak. D9 128-9
Leeds, S.C. C9 184-5
Leeds, Ut. M3 242-3
Leeds and Grenville, co., Ont. I14 284-5
Leeds Junction, Me. L4 64-5
Leeds Point, N.J. L6 76-7
Leedy, Miss. B10 176-7
Leefe, Wyo. I4 250-1
Leelanau, co., Mich. F11 112-3
Lees, S.C. G9 184-5
Lees Camp, Ore. B5 238-9
Lees Ferry, Ariz. B7 206-7
Lees Summit, Mo. J16 120-1
Leesburg, Ala. C9 146-7
Leesburg, Fla. E11 156-7
Leesburg, Ga. L4 160-1
Leesburg, Ind. B9 100-1
Leesburg, Ky. A7 164-5
Leesburg, Miss. H7 176-7
Leesburg, N.J. N3 76-7
Leesburg, O. H5 132-3
Leesburg, Va. E12 196-7
Leesdale, Miss. K3 176-7
Leesport, Pa. H13 84-5
Leesville, Conn. F10 60-1
Leesville, La. F2 168-9
Leesville, S.C. E9 184-5
Leet, W. Va. J11 200-1
Leetes Island, Conn. H9 60-1
Leeton, Mo. E4 120-1
Leeton, Ut. F9 242-3
Leetonia, O. D11 132-3
Leetsdale*, Pa. H1 84-5
Leeville, La. J9 168-9
Leffingwell, Conn. F13 60-1
Leflore, Okla. G15 234-5
Leflore, co., Miss. E5 176-7
Lefor, N. Dak. H4 128-9
Lefors, Tex. B6 192-3
Lefroy, Ont. B14 284-5
Left Hand, W. Va. G4 200-1
Legal, Alta. I8 264-5
Leggett*, N.C. D12 180-1
Lehew, W. Va. E10 200-1
Lehi, Ut. F6 242-3
Lehigh, Ia. E7 104-5
Lehigh, Kans. G11 108-9
Lehigh, Okla. H13 234-5
Lehigh, co., Pa. H14 84-5
Lehigh Acres, Fla. I11 156-7
Lehighton, Pa. G14 84-5
Lehman, Ore. C13 238-9
Lehr, N. Dak. I10 128-9
Leicester, Mass. D8 68-9
Leicester, N.C. D4 180-1
Leicester, Vt. H4 90-1
Leigh, Nebr. F13 124-5
Leighton, Ala. B4 146-7
Leighton, Ia. H10 104-5
Leighton, Tenn. J4 188-9
Leipers Fork, Tenn. H6 188-9
Leipsic, Del. E4 153
Leipsic, O. C4 132-3
Leipzig, Sask. K5 294-5
Leisure City, Fla. J15 156-7
Leitchfield, Ky. I7 164-5
Leiter, Wyo. B13 250-1
Leiters Ford, Ind. C7 100-1
Leitersburg, Md. B7 172-3
Leith, N. Dak. I5 128-9
Leith-Hatfield*, Pa. K3 84-5
Leivasy, W. Va. H5 200-1
Lela, Okla. D12 234-5
Leland, Ill. C9 96-7
Leland, Ia. B8 104-5
Leland, Mich. F12 112-3
Leland, Miss. F4 176-7
Leland, N.C. G12 180-1
Leland, Ore. I5 238-9
Leland, Wash. G1 246-7
Leland Grove, Ill. H7 96-7
Lemay*, Mo. F10 120-1
Lemberg, Sask. M9 294-5
Lemhi, Ida. J7 218-9
Lemhi, co., Ida. I6 218-9
Lemington, Vt. C11 90-1
Lemitar, N. Mex. H5 230-1
Lemmon, S. Dak. A5 136-7
Lemon Grove, Calif. J11 210-1
Lemon Springs, N.C. J6 180-1
Lemont, Ill. N3 96-7
Lemont, Pa. G8 84-5
Lemoore, Calif. K5 210-1
Lemoore Station, Calif. K5 210-1
LeMoyen, La. G5 168-9
Lemoyne, Nebr. G5 124-5
Lemoyne, Pa. I11 84-5
LeMoyne*, Que. I12 290-1
Lempster, N.H. M3 72-3
Lena, Ill. A7 96-7
Lena, La. E4 168-9
Lena, Man. K11 272-3
Lena, Miss. H7 176-7
Lena, Ore. C12 238-9

Lena, S.C. I9 184-5
Lena, Wis. F15 140-1
Lenapah, Okla. C14 234-5
Lenape Heights*, Pa. H3 84-5
Lenawee, co., Mich. K13 112-3
Lenexa, Kans. F16 108-9
Lengby, Minn. G3 116-7
Lenna, Okla. F14 234-5
Lennep, Mont. F8 222-3
Lennig, Va. J10 196-7
Lennon, Mich. G3 112-3
Lennox*, Calif. G8 210-1
Lennox, S. Dak. H15 136-7
Lennox and Addington, co., Ont. I12 284-5
Lennox Isl., P.E.I. D5 287
Lennoxville, Que. J15 290-1
Lenoir, N.C. D6 180-1
Lenoir, co., N.C. E12 180-1
Lenoir City, Tenn. I11 188-9
Lenora, Kans. D5 108-9
Lenora, Okla. D8 234-5
Lenore, Ida. F3 218-9
Lenore, Man. I10 272-3
Lenore, W. Va. K10 200-1
Lenox, Ala. L5 146-7
Lenox, Ga. M6 160-1
Lenox, Ia. J5 104-5
Lenox, Mass. D2 68-9
Lenox, Tenn. B2 188-9
Lenox Dale, Mass. D2 68-9
Lenwood, Calif. M8 210-1
Lenz, Ore. I8 238-9
Leo, Ind. C11 100-1
Leo, Wyo. H12 250-1
Leola, Ark. H6 150-1
Leola, S. Dak. A11 136-7
Leoma, Tenn. K5 188-9
Leominster, Mass. C8 68-9
Leon, Ia. J7 104-5
Leon, Kans. I12 108-9
Leon, Okla. I11 234-5
Leon, Va. C1 196-7
Leon, W. Va. F2 200-1
Leon, co., Fla. B7 156-7
Leon, co., Tex. F10 192-3
Leon Valley, Tex. J2 192-3
Leona, Kans. D15 108-9
Leonard, Ark. B12 150-1
Leonard, Mich. H6 112-3
Leonard, Minn. G3 116-7
Leonard, Mo. B7 120-1
Leonard, N. Dak. H14 128-9
Leonard, Okla. E14 234-5
Leonard, Tex. A16 192-3
Leonardo, N.J. H11 76-7
Leonardtown, Md. H11 172-3
Leonardville, Kans. E12 108-9
Leoni, Mich. K2 112-3
Leonia, N.J. B12 76-7
Leonidas, Minn. G7 116-7
Leonville, La. G5 168-9
Leopold, Ind. O7 100-1
Leopold, W. Va. E5 200-1
Leopolis, Wis. D2 140-1
Leota, Minn. O2 116-7
Leota, Ut. G10 242-3
Leoti, Kans. G2 108-9
Leoville, Kans. D4 108-9
Leoville, Sask. I6 294-5
Lepanto, Ark. C11 150-1
L'Epiphanie*, Que. I12 290-1
Lequire, Okla. F15 234-5
Lerona, W. Va. J4 200-1
Leross, Sask. M9 294-5
Leroy, Ala. K3 146-7
Leroy, Ind. B5 100-1
LeRoy, Mich. G12 112-3
Leroy, N. Dak. B12 128-9
Leroy, Sask. L8 294-5
Leroy, Wyo. J5 250-1
Léry*, Que. J12 290-1
Les Becquets*, Que. G10 290-1
Les Caps*, Que. I7 290-1
Les Éboulements, Que. E13 290-1
Les Méchins, Que. H5 290-1
Lesage*, Que. I11 290-1
Lesage, W. Va. G2 200-1
Leshara, Nebr. I1 124-5
Leslie, Ark. C6 150-1
Leslie, Ga. K4 160-1
Leslie, Ida. L7 218-9
Leslie, Mich. J1 112-3
Leslie, Mo. F9 120-1
Leslie, Sask. L9 294-5
Leslie, W. Va. H5 200-1
Leslie, co., Ky. J13 164-5
Leslieville, Alta. K7 264-5
Lesser Slave Lake, Alta. G6 264-5
Lesser Slave Lake Settlement*, Alta. G6 264-5
Lessley, Miss. L3 176-7
Lesslie, S.C. B10 184-5
Lester, Ala. A5 146-7
Lester, Ia. A1 104-5
Lester, Wash. F9 246-7
Lester, W. Va. K15 200-1
Lester Prairie, Minn. B8 116-7
Lesterville, S. Dak. I14 136-7
Lestock, Sask. M9 294-5
Letart, W. Va. F2 200-1
Letcher, Ky. I14 164-5
Letcher, S. Dak. G13 136-7
Letcher, co., Ky. J14 164-5
Letellier, Man. K14 272-3
Letha, Ida. L2 218-9
Lethbridge, Alta. N8 264-5
Lethbridge, Nfld. N10 278-9
Letherbark, W. Va. F4 200-1
Leto*, Fla. F11 156-7
Letohatchee, Ala. J7 146-7
Leton, La. A3 168-9
Letona, Ark. D8 150-1
Letter Gap, W. Va. F5 200-1
Letts, Ia. H13 104-5
Lettsworth, La. F6 168-9
Leucadia, Calif. I10 210-1
Leupp, Ariz. E8 206-7
Levan, Ut. H6 242-3
Levant, Kans. E3 108-9
Levant, Me. J6 64-5
Levasy, Mo. I16 120-1
Levee, Ky. G13 164-5
Level Land, S.C. J1 184-5
Level Park-Oak Park*, Mich. J12 112-3
Level Plains*, Ala. L9 146-7
Levelland, Tex. C4 192-3
Levelock, Alaska G9 254-5
Levels, W. Va. D10 200-1
Leverett, Mass. C5 68-9
Leverett, Miss. D6 176-7
Levering, Mich. E13 112-3
Levesque, Ark. D10 150-1
Lévis, Que. G11 290-1
Lévis, co., Que. G11 290-1
Levittown, N.Y. E16 80-1
Levy, co., Fla. D9 156-7
Lewellen, Nebr. G4 124-5
Lewes, Del. I6 153
Lewis, Colo. I5 214-5
Lewis, Ind. J5 100-1
Lewis, Ia. H4 104-5
Lewis, Kans. I7 108-9
Lewis, Ore. B15 238-9
Lewis*, Vt. C10 90-1
Lewis, Wis. D7 140-1
Lewis, co., Ida. G3 218-9
Lewis, co., Ky. F13 164-5
Lewis, co., Mo. B8 120-1
Lewis, co., N.Y. D8 80-1
Lewis, co., Tenn. C6 188-9
Lewis, co., Wash. H8 246-7
Lewis, co., W. Va. F6 200-1
Lewis and Clark, co., Mont. E5 222-3
Lewis and Clark Lake, Nebr. C12 124-5
Lewis and Clark Village*, Mo. C2 120-1
Lewis Gardens, Va. E1 196-7
Lewis Springs, Ariz. M10 206-7
Lewisburg, Ky. J6 164-5
Lewisburg, La. G5 168-9
Lewisburg, O. H13 132-3
Lewisburg, Ore. I1 238-9
Lewisburg, Pa. G11 84-5
Lewisburg, Tenn. D7 188-9
Lewisburg, W. Va. I6 200-1
Lewisetta, Va. G14 196-7
Lewisport, Ky. G6 164-5
Lewisporte, Nfld. M9 278-9
Lewiston, Ala. G3 146-7
Lewiston, Ida. F2 218-9
Lewiston, Me. L3 64-5
Lewiston, Mich. F13 112-3
Lewiston, Minn. O9 116-7
Lewiston, Nebr. J15 124-5
Lewiston, N.Y. E2 80-1
Lewiston, N.C. C13 180-1
Lewiston, Ut. C6 242-3
Lewistown, Ill. F6 96-7
Lewistown, Md. B8 172-3
Lewistown, Mo. B7 120-1
Lewistown, Mont. E9 222-3
Lewistown, Pa. H9 84-5
Lewisville, Ark. J3 150-1
Lewisville, Ida. L10 218-9
Lewisville, Ind. H10 100-1
Lewisville, Minn. O5 116-7
Lewisville, N.C. H2 180-1
Lewisville, O. G10 132-3
Lewisville, Okla. F15 234-5
Lewisville, Tex. B14 192-3
Lexa, Ark. F10 150-1
Lexie, Miss. L6 176-7
Lexie Crossroads, Tenn. K8 188-9
Lexington, Ala. A5 146-7
Lexington, Ga. F7 160-1
Lexington, Ill. F9 96-7
Lexington, Ind. L10 100-1
Lexington, Ky. G11 164-5
Lexington, Mass. G4 68-9
Lexington, Mich. F8 112-3
Lexington, Minn. A11 116-7
Lexington, Miss. G6 176-7
Lexington, Mo. D4 120-1
Lexington, Nebr. H8 124-5
Lexington, N.C. D8 180-1
Lexington, O. D7 132-3
Lexington, Okla. G11 234-5
Lexington, Ore. C11 238-9
Lexington, S.C. E9 184-5
Lexington, Tenn. C4 188-9
Lexington, Tex. G9 192-3
Lexington, Va. H9 196-7
Lexington, co., S.C. E9 184-5
Lexington Park [-Patuxent River], Md. H11 172-3
Leyba, N. Mex. F7 230-1
Leyden, Mass. B5 68-9
Libau, Man. I15 272-3
Libby, Mont. B1 222-3
Libby Dam, Mont. B2 222-3
Liberal, Kans. K3 108-9
Liberal, Mo. H3 120-1
Liberty, Ida. O11 218-9
Liberty, Ind. I12 100-1
Liberty, Kans. K14 108-9
Liberty, Ky. I10 164-5
Liberty, Me. K5 64-5
Liberty, Mich. K1 112-3
Liberty, Miss. L4 176-7
Liberty, Mo. D3 120-1
Liberty, Nebr. J14 124-5
Liberty*, N.J. D4 76-7
Liberty, N.Y. H9 80-1
Liberty, N.C. H5 180-1
Liberty*, Pa. I2 84-5
Liberty, R.I. G4 87
Liberty, Sask. M7 294-5
Liberty, S.C. B5 184-5
Liberty, Tenn. B4 188-9
Liberty, Tenn. B9 188-9
Liberty, Tex. G16 192-3
Liberty, Wash. F10 246-7
Liberty, W. Va. G3 200-1
Liberty, co., Fla. C6 156-7
Liberty, co., Ga. K10 160-1
Liberty, co., Mont. B7 222-3
Liberty, co., Tex. G10 192-3
Liberty Bell Village, Colo. H7 214-5
Liberty Center, Ind. E10 100-1
Liberty Center, O. B4 132-3
Liberty Grove, Md. B13 172-3
Liberty Hill, Conn. E12 60-1
Liberty Hill, La. C3 168-9
Liberty Hill, S.C. C11 184-5
Liberty Hill, Tenn. G13 188-9
Liberty Lake, Wash. E16 246-7
Liberty Mills, Ind. C9 100-1
Libertytown, Md. C9 172-3
Libertytown, Md. H15 172-3
Libertyville*, Ala. L7 146-7
Libertyville, Ill. K3 96-7
Libertyville, Ia. I11 104-5
Libuse, La. E4 168-9
Licking, Mo. H7 120-1
Licking, co., O. F7 132-3
Lida, Nev. J5 226-7
Lidderdale, Ia. F5 104-5
Liddieville, La. C6 168-9
Lidgerwood, N. Dak. J14 128-9
Lidy Hot Springs, Ida. K9 218-9
Liebenthal, Kans. G6 108-9
Liesorland*, Sask. K6 294-5
Lifsey, Ga. H4 160-1
Light, Ark. B10 150-1
Lightfoot, Va. E3 196-7
Lighthouse Point, Fla. F16 156-7
Lightning Flat, Wyo. A15 250-1
Lignite, Alaska E11 254-5
Lignite, N. Dak. B4 128-9
Lignum, Va. C2 196-7
Ligonier, Ind. B10 100-1
Ligonier, Pa. I4 84-5
Ligurta, Ariz. J2 206-7
Lihue, Hawaii D5 258-9
Likely, B.C. H7 268-9
Lilbourn, Mo. J11 120-1
Lilburn, Ga. B12 160-1
Lilesville, N.C. K4 180-1
Lille, Me. A8 64-5
Lillian, Ala. O4 146-7
Lillie, La. A4 168-9
Lillington, N.C. E10 180-1
Lillis, Kans. D13 108-9
Lilliwaup, Wash. F7 246-7
Lillooet, B.C. I7 268-9
Lilly, Ga. K5 160-1
Lilly, Pa. I6 84-5
Lilly Grove, W. Va. J4 200-1
Lily, Ky. J12 164-5
Lily, S. Dak. C14 136-7
Lily, Wis. E13 140-1
Lily Bay, Me. G5 64-5
Lilydale, Minn. B11 116-7
Lima, Mont. I5 222-3
Lima, N.Y. F4 80-1
Lima, O. D4 132-3
Lima*, Okla. F13 234-5
Lima, W. Va. D5 200-1
Lima Center, Wis. K3 140-1
Limaville, O. E16 132-3
Lime, Colo. H12 214-5
Lime, Ore. E15 238-9
Lime Kiln, Md. F1 172-3
Lime Ridge, Wis. I11 140-1
Lime Rock, Conn. B4 60-1
Lime Springs, Ia. A11 104-5
Lime Village*, Alaska F10 254-5
Limedale, Ind. I6 100-1
Limerick, Me. O7 64-5
Limerick, Sask. O7 294-5
Limerock, R.I. B5 87
Limestone, Me. B9 64-5
Limestone, Man. D5 272-3
Limestone, Mich. D10 112-3
Limestone, Mont. H8 222-3
Limestone, N.Y. H3 80-1
Limestone, Tenn. G15 188-9
Limestone, co., Ala. A5 146-7
Limestone, co., Tex. F9 192-3
Limington, Me. O7 64-5
Limoges, Ont. H15 284-5
Limon, Colo. E14 214-5
Linch, Wyo. E13 250-1
Lincoln, Ala. E8 146-7
Lincoln, Ark. B2 150-1
Lincoln, Calif. H4 210-1
Lincoln, Del. H4 153
Lincoln, Ida. L10 218-9
Lincoln, Ill. G8 96-7
Lincoln, Ind. E8 100-1
Lincoln, Ia. E10 104-5
Lincoln, Kans. F9 108-9
Lincoln, Ky. J13 164-5
Lincoln, Me. H7 64-5
Lincoln, Me. I1 64-5
Lincoln, Mass. G3 68-9
Lincoln, Mich. F14 112-3
Lincoln, Mo. F5 120-1
Lincoln, Mont. E5 222-3
Lincoln, Nebr. H14 124-5
Lincoln, N.H. H6 72-3
Lincoln, N. Mex. I8 230-1
Lincoln, Ont. D15 284-5
Lincoln, Ore. K7 238-9
Lincoln*, Pa. I2 84-5
Lincoln*, R.I. B5 87
Lincoln, Vt. G5 90-1
Lincoln, Wash. E14 246-7
Lincoln, co., Ark. H8 150-1
Lincoln, co., Colo. F14 214-5
Lincoln, co., Ga. G8 160-1
Lincoln, co., Ida. M7 218-9
Lincoln, co., Kans. E9 108-9
Lincoln, co., Ky. H11 164-5
Lincoln, co., La. B4 168-9
Lincoln, co., Me. L5 64-5
Lincoln, co., Minn. N2 116-7
Lincoln, co., Miss. K5 176-7
Lincoln, co., Mo. D9 120-1
Lincoln, co., Mont. A1 222-3
Lincoln, co., Nebr. H7 124-5
Lincoln, co., Nev. J10 226-7
Lincoln, co., N. Mex. I8 230-1
Lincoln, co., N.C. E6 180-1
Lincoln, co., Okla. E11 234-5
Lincoln, co., Ore. E4 238-9
Lincoln, co., S. Dak. H16 136-7
Lincoln, co., Tenn. D7 188-9
Lincoln, co., Wash. F14 246-7
Lincoln, co., W. Va. H2 200-1
Lincoln, co., Wis. E12 140-1
Lincoln, co., Wyo. H5 250-1
Lincoln Beach, Ore. D4 238-9
Lincoln Center, Me. H7 64-5
Lincoln City, Ind. O5 100-1
Lincoln City, Ore. D4 238-9
Lincoln Heights, O. K13 132-3
Lincoln Park, Colo. G11 214-5
Lincoln Park, Ga. I4 160-1
Lincoln Park, Mich. K6 112-3
Lincoln Park, N.J. C7 76-7
Lincoln Park*, N.Y. G11 80-1
Lincoln Village*, Calif. I4 210-1
Lincoln Village*, O. F6 132-3
Lincolnia*, Va. E13 196-7
Lincolnia Heights, Va. A4 196-7
Lincolnshire, Ill. K3 96-7
Lincolnshire*, Ky. G9 164-5
Lincolnton, Ga. F8 160-1
Lincolnton, N.C. E6 180-1
Lincolnville, Ind. D9 100-1
Lincolnville, Kans. G11 108-9
Lincolnville, Me. L6 64-5
Lincolnville, S.C. H12 184-5
Lincolnville Center, Me. L6 64-5
Lincolnwood, Ill. L4 96-7
Lincroft, N.J. G8 76-7
Lind, Wash. G14 246-7
Linda, Calif. G4 210-1
Lindale, Ga. E2 160-1
Lindale*, Tex. E10 192-3
Lindale Park Subdivision*, Alta. I8 264-5
Lindbergh, Wyo. J16 250-1
Linden, Ala. I4 146-7
Linden, Alta. L8 264-5
Linden, Ariz. G9 206-7
Linden, Ind. G6 100-1
Linden, Ia. G6 104-5
Linden, Mich. H3 112-3
Linden, N.J. E9 76-7
Linden, N.C. J7 180-1
Linden, Tenn. C5 188-9
Linden, Tex. D11 192-3
Linden, Va. A1 196-7
Linden, W. Va. F4 200-1
Linden, Wis. J11 140-1
Linden Beach*, Ont. G10 284-5
Lindenhurst, Ill. J2 96-7
Lindenhurst, N.Y. K12 80-1
Lindenwold, N.J. O11 76-7
Lindon, Colo. D14 214-5
Lindon, Ut. F6 242-3
Lindrith, N. Mex. D5 230-1
Lindsay, Calif. K6 210-1
Lindsay, Mont. D15 222-3
Lindsay, Nebr. F12 124-5
Lindsay, Okla. G11 234-5
Lindsay, Ont. B16 284-5
Lindsborg, Kans. G10 108-9
Lindsey, O. B6 132-3
Lindside, W. Va. J5 200-1
Lindstrom, Minn. L7 116-7
Lindy, Nebr. D12 124-5
Lineboro, Md. B10 172-3
Linebrook, Mass. B12 68-9
Linesville, Pa. D1 84-5
Lineville, Ala. F9 146-7
Lineville, Ia. K8 104-5
Lingle, Wyo. H16 250-1
Lingo, N. Mex. I12 230-1
Lingshire, Mont. E7 222-3
Linière, Que. J4 290-1
Linkwood, Md. G13 172-3
Linn, Kans. D11 108-9
Linn, Mo. F7 120-1
Linn, W. Va. F5 200-1
Linn, co., Ia. F12 104-5
Linn, co., Kans. H16 108-9
Linn, co., Mo. B5 120-1
Linn, co., Ore. E6 238-9
Linn Creek, Mo. G6 120-1
Linn Grove, Ind. E11 100-1
Linn Grove, Ia. C4 104-5
Linneus, Me. E9 64-5

Linneus, Mo. B5 120-1
Linntown [-West Lawn], Pa. G11 84-5
Lino Lakes, Minn. A11 116-7
Linslaw, Ore. F4 238-9
Linthicum*, Md. D11 172-3
Lintlaw, Sask. L9 294-5
Linton, Ind. K5 100-1
Linton, Ky. K4 164-5
Linton, N. Dak. I8 128-9
Linton, Tenn. H6 188-9
Linville, La. A5 168-9
Linville, N.C. D5 180-1
Linville, Va. F10 196-7
Linwood, Ga. D2 160-1
Linwood, Kans. F15 108-9
Linwood, Md. B9 172-3
Linwood, Mich. H14 112-3
Linwood, Nebr. G13 124-5
Linwood, N.J. M5 76-7
Linwood, N.C. I3 180-1
Linwood, N.S. C10 281
Linwood*, Ont. D13 284-5
Lion's Bay*, B.C. G8 268-9
Lion's Head, Ont. A12 284-5
Lipscomb, Ala. F6 146-7
Lipscomb, Tex. A6 192-3
Lipscomb, co., Tex. A6 192-3
Lipton, Sask. M9 294-5
Lisbon, Conn. E13 60-1
Lisbon, Ia. F13 104-5
Lisbon, La. A3 168-9
Lisbon*, Me. M8 64-5
Lisbon, Md. F3 172-3
Lisbon, N.H. G5 72-3
Lisbon, N. Dak. I13 128-9
Lisbon, O. D11 132-3
Lisbon Falls, Me. M10 64-5
Lisbon [-Lisbon Center], Me. M9 64-5
Lisco, Nebr. G3 124-5
Liscomb, Ia. F9 104-5
Lisieux, Sask. O7 294-5
Lisle*, Ill. C10 96-7
L'Isle-Verte, Que. D14 290-1
L'Islet*, Que. F13 290-1
L'Islet, co., Que. F13 290-1
L'Islet-sur-Mer, Que. F13 290-1
Lisman, Ala. I2 146-7
Lismore, Minn. O2 116-7
Lister, B.C. K10 268-9
Listowel, Ont. C12 284-5
Litchfield, Conn. D6 60-1
Litchfield, Ill. J7 96-7
Litchfield, Me. L4 64-5
Litchfield, Mich. J13 112-3
Litchfield, Minn. L5 116-7
Litchfield, Nebr. G9 124-5
Litchfield, N.H. O7 72-3
Litchfield, co., Conn. C5 60-1
Litchfield Beach, S.C. F15 184-5
Litchfield Corners, Me. L4 64-5
Litchfield Park*, Ariz. I6 206-7
Litchville, N. Dak. H12 128-9
Lithia, Va. I8 196-7
Lithia Springs, Ga. C9 160-1
Lithium, Mo. G11 120-1
Lithonia, Ga. C12 160-1
Lithopolis, O. G7 132-3
Lititz, Pa. J12 84-5
Litroe, La. A5 168-9
Littcarr, Ky. I14 164-5
Little, Okla. F12 234-5
Little America, Wyo. I7 250-1
Little Bay Islands, Nfld. L9 278-9
Little Boars Head, N.H. N10 72-3
Little Bonanza, Ut. G10 242-3
Little Buffalo Lake, Alta. F6 264-5
Little Canada*, Minn. M7 116-7
Little Catalina, Nfld. M11 278-9
Little Chute, Wis. E4 140-1
Little City, Okla. I12 234-5
Little Compton, R.I. G8 87
Little Creek, Del. F4 153
Little Creek, La. D5 168-9
Little Current, Ont. H7 284-5
Little Deer Isle, Me. L7 64-5
Little Dover, N.S. D10 281
Little Eagle, S. Dak. B7 136-7
Little Egg Harbor*, N.J. K6 76-7
Little Falls, Minn. K5 116-7
Little Falls, N.J. B9 76-7
Little Falls, N.Y. E9 80-1
Little Falls, Wash. E15 246-7
Little Farms [River Ridge]*, La. I9 168-9
Little Ferry, N.J. B11 76-7
Little Flock*, Ark. A2 150-1
Little Grand Rapids, Man. F16 272-3
Little Heart's Ease, Nfld. N11 278-9
Little Heaven, Del. G4 153
Little Italy, Ark. I14 150-1
Little Medicine, Wyo. G13 250-1
Little Mount, Ky. B4 164-5
Little Mountain, S.C. K7 184-5
Little Orleans, Md. B5 172-3
Little Plymouth, Va. D3 196-7
Little Pond, P.E.I. E10 287
Little River, Kans. G9 108-9
Little River, S.C. E16 184-5
Little River, co., Ark. I2 150-1
Little Rock, Ark. F7 150-1
Little Rock, Ia. A2 104-5
Little Rock, Miss. H9 176-7
Little Rock, S.C. C14 184-5
Little Sands, P.E.I. G9 287
Little Shawmut*, Ala. G10 146-7
Little Silver, N.J. G8 76-7
Little Sioux, Ia. G2 104-5
Little Suamico, Wis. D5 140-1
Little Sweden, Ore. D7 238-9
Little Texas, Miss. B6 176-7
Little Valley, N.Y. G2 80-1
Little York, Ind. L9 100-1
Littlefield, Ariz. B3 206-7
Littlefield, N.H. N9 72-3
Littlefield, Tex. C4 192-3
Littlefork, Minn. E6 116-7
Littlelot, Tenn. I5 188-9
Littleport, Ia. D13 104-5
Littlerock, Wash. G7 246-7
Littlestown, Pa. K10 84-5
Littleton, Colo. H3 214-5
Littleton, Me. E9 64-5
Littleton, Mass. C9 68-9
Littleton, N.H. F5 72-3
Littleton, N.C. C12 180-1
Littleton, Va. G2 196-7
Littleton, W. Va. A13 200-1
Littleton Common, Mass. C10 68-9
Littleton Southeast*, Colo. E11 214-5
Littleville, Ala. B4 146-7
Litton, Miss. E4 176-7
Live Oak, Calif. G4 210-1
Live Oak*, Calif. J3 210-1
Live Oak, Fla. B9 156-7
Live Oak*, Tex. H9 192-3
Live Oak, co., Tex. I8 192-3
Livelong, Sask. J5 294-5
Lively, Va. H14 196-7
Livengood, Alaska D11 254-5
Livermore, Calif. C8 210-1
Livermore, Colo. B11 214-5
Livermore, Ia. C6 104-5
Livermore, Ky. I6 164-5
Livermore, Me. K3 64-5
Livermore Falls, Me. K3 64-5
Livermore Falls, N.H. I6 72-3
Liverpool, N.Y. E7 80-1
Liverpool, N.S. F6 281
Livingston, Ala. H3 146-7
Livingston, Calif. D11 210-1
Livingston, Ill. J7 96-7
Livingston, Ky. I12 164-5
Livingston, La. A11 168-9
Livingston, Mont. G8 222-3
Livingston, N.J. D7 76-7
Livingston, S.C. F10 184-5
Livingston, Tenn. A10 188-9
Livingston, Tex. F10 192-3
Livingston, Wis. J11 140-1
Livingston, co., Ill. E9 96-7
Livingston, co., Ky. I3 164-5
Livingston, co., La. H8 168-9
Livingston, co., Mich. J13 112-3
Livingston, co., Mo. C4 120-1
Livingston, co., N.Y. F4 80-1
Livingston Manor, N.Y. H9 80-1
Livonia, Ind. M8 100-1
Livonia, La. G6 168-9
Livonia, Mich. J5 112-3
Livonia, Mo. A6 120-1
Livonia, N.Y. F4 80-1
Lizella, Ga. I5 160-1
Lizemores, W. Va. H16 200-1
Lizton, Ind. H7 100-1
Llano, N. Mex. D7 230-1
Llano, Tex. F7 192-3
Llano, co., Tex. G7 192-3
Llaves, N. Mex. C5 230-1
Lloyd, Mont. B9 222-3
Lloyd Harbor, N.Y. D16 80-1
Lloyd Place*, Va. J14 196-7
Lloydminster**, Alta. J10 264-5
Lloydminster, Sask. J4 294-5
Loa, Ut. K6 242-3
Loachapoka, Ala. H9 146-7
Loami, Ill. H7 96-7
Lobeco, S.C. I11 184-5
Lobelville, Tenn. C5 188-9
Lobsterville, Mass. J13 68-9
Lobstick Lake, Nfld. H3 278-9
Locate, Mont. F15 222-3
Loch Arbour, N.J. H8 76-7
Loch Lynn Heights, Md. C1 172-3
Lochiel, Ariz. M9 206-7
Lochmere, N.H. K6 72-3
Lock Haven, Pa. F9 84-5
Lock Springs, Mo. B4 120-1
Lockbourne, O. G6 132-3
Lockbourne Base*, O. G6 132-3
Locke, Tenn. K1 188-9
Locke Mills, Me. K2 64-5
Lockehaven, N.H. J4 72-3
Lockeport, N.S. G5 281
Lockerby, Ut. L11 242-3
Lockesburg, Ark. H2 150-1
Lockhart, Ala. M7 146-7
Lockhart*, Fla. E11 156-7
Lockhart, S.C. B9 184-5
Lockhart, Tex. G8 192-3
Lockland, O. K14 132-3
Lockney, Tex. C5 192-3
Lockport, Ill. N2 96-7
Lockport, Ky. F10 164-5
Lockport, La. I8 168-9
Lockport*, Man. I14 272-3
Lockport, N.Y. E3 80-1
Lockridge, Ia. I12 104-5
Locks Village, Mass. C5 68-9
Lockwood, Mo. H4 120-1
Lockwood, Sask. L8 294-5
Lockwood, W. Va. I16 200-1
Loco, Okla. H10 234-5
Loco Hills, N. Mex. K10 230-1
Locust, N.J. H11 76-7
Locust, N.C. J2 180-1
Locust Bayou, Ark. I6 150-1
Locust Fork, Ala. D7 146-7
Locust Grove, Ark. C8 150-1
Locust Grove, Ga. H4 160-1
Locust Grove*, N.Y. J11 80-1
Locust Grove, Okla. D15 234-5
Locust Grove, Va. C2 196-7
Locust Hill, Va. E4 196-7
Locust Springs, Tenn. G15 188-9
Locustville, Va. H16 196-7
Lodge, S.C. H10 184-5
Lodge Grass, Mont. H12 222-3
Lodgepole, Alta. J6 264-5
Lodgepole, Mont. C10 222-3
Lodgepole, Nebr. G3 124-5
Lodi, Calif. B9 210-1
Lodi, N.J. B11 76-7
Lodi, O. D13 132-3
Lodi, Okla. G15 234-5
Lodi, Wis. I1 140-1
Lofgreen, Ut. G5 242-3
Log Cabin, La. A6 168-9
Log Lane Village, Colo. C13 214-5
Logan, Ala. D6 146-7
Logan, Ia. G2 104-5
Logan, Kans. D6 108-9
Logan, Mont. G7 222-3
Logan*, N.J. J2 76-7
Logan, N. Mex. E11 230-1
Logan, O. H8 132-3
Logan, Okla. C6 234-5
Logan, Ut. C6 242-3
Logan, W. Va. I2 200-1
Logan, co., Ark. D4 150-1
Logan, co., Colo. B15 214-5
Logan, co., Ill. G8 96-7
Logan, co., Kans. F3 108-9
Logan, co., Ky. J6 164-5
Logan, co., Nebr. F7 124-5
Logan, co., N. Dak. I9 128-9
Logan, co., O. E4 132-3
Logan, co., Okla. E11 234-5
Logan, co., W. Va. I2 200-1
Logan Lake*, B.C. I8 268-9
Logandale, Nev. L11 226-7
Logansport, Ind. D7 100-1
Logansport, La. C1 168-9
Logansport, W. Va. B13 200-1
Loganville, Ga. F5 160-1
Loganville, Wis. I11 140-1
Logdell, Ore. F12 238-9
Loggieville, N.B. F6 275
Logsden, Ore. D4 238-9
Logtown, Miss. O7 176-7
Lohman, Mo. E7 120-1
Lohman, Mont. B9 222-3
Lohrville, Ia. E5 104-5
Lohrville, Wis. F2 140-1
Lola, Ky. I3 164-5
Loleta, Calif. E1 210-1
Lolo, Mont. E3 222-3
Lolo Hot Springs, Mont. E3 222-3
Loma, Colo. F5 214-5
Loma, Mont. C8 222-3
Loma, Nebr. G13 124-5
Loma, N. Dak. C11 128-9
Loma Linda, Calif. G10 210-1
Lomax, Ala. G6 146-7
Lomax, Ill. F4 96-7
Lomax, Tex. H15 192-3
Lombard, Ill. M2 96-7
Lombard, Mont. G7 222-3
Lometa, Tex. F7 192-3
Lomira, Wis. H3 140-1
Lomita*, Calif. H8 210-1
Lomond, Alta. N9 264-5
Lompoc, Calif. M5 210-1
Lompoc North*, Calif. M5 210-1
Lompoc Northwest*, Calif. M5 210-1
Lonaconing, Md. B3 172-3
London, Ark. D4 150-1
London, Ky. I12 164-5
London, O. G5 132-3
London, Ont. J7 284-5
London, Ore. G5 238-9
London, Wis. J2 140-1
London Mills, Ill. F6 96-7
Londonderry, N.H. O7 72-3
Londonderry, Vt. L5 90-1
Londontowne*, Md. E11 172-3
Lone, Ky. H13 164-5
Lone Butte, B.C. I7 268-9
Lone Elm, Kans. H15 108-9
Lone Grove, Okla. I11 234-5
Lone Hickory, N.C. H2 180-1
Lone Jack, Mo. J16 120-1
Lone Mountain, Tenn. G13 188-9
Lone Oak, Ga. H3 160-1
Lone Oak, Ky. J3 164-5
Lone Oak, S.C. E4 184-5
Lone Oak, Tenn. K10 188-9
Lone Pine, Calif. K7 210-1
Lone Rock, Ia. B6 104-5
Lone Rock, Sask. J4 294-5
Lone Rock, Wis. J11 140-1
Lone Star, Kans. F15 108-9
Lone Star, La. C9 168-9
Lone Star, S.C. F11 184-5
Lone Star*, Tex. D11 192-3
Lone Tree, Ia. H13 104-5
Lone Wolf, Okla. G8 234-5
Lonepine, Mont. C3 222-3
Lonerock, Ore. D11 238-9
Lonetree, Wyo. J6 250-1
Long, Okla. E16 234-5
Long, co., Ga. L10 160-1
Long Beach, Calif. N7 210-1
Long Beach, Ind. A6 100-1
Long Beach, Minn. K3 116-7
Long Beach, Miss. O8 176-7
Long Beach*, N.J. L7 76-7
Long Beach, N.Y. F16 80-1
Long Beach, N.C. H12 180-1
Long Beach, Wash. H5 246-7
Long Branch, N.J. G8 76-7
Long Branch*, Va. E13 196-7
Long Creek, Ore. D12 238-9
Long Creek*, P.E.I. F7 287
Long Grove, Ill. K2 96-7
Long Grove, Ia. G15 104-5
Long Isl., N.Y. J14 80-1
Long Island, Kans. C6 108-9
Long Island*, Me. K7 64-5
Long Island, Tenn. F16 188-9
Long Island, Va. J9 196-7
Long Key (Layton), Fla. K12 156-7
Long Lake, Mich. G14 112-3
Long Lake*, Minn. M5 116-7
Long Lake, S. Dak. A11 136-7
Long Lake, Wash. E15 246-7
Long Lake, Wis. C14 140-1
Long Park, Colo. G5 214-5
Long Pine, Nebr. D8 124-5
Long Point, Ont. F13 284-5
Long Pond, Me. G4 64-5
Long Prairie, Minn. K4 116-7
Long Ridge, Conn. I3 60-1
Long Sault, Ont. I16 284-5
Long Society, Conn. F13 60-1
Long Spruce*, Man. D5 272-3
Long Valley, N.J. D4 76-7
Long Valley Junction, Ut. M5 242-3
Longboat Key, Fla. K2 156-7
Longbranch, Wash. J1 246-7
Longcove, Me. M6 64-5
Longcreek, S.C. B4 184-5
Longdale, Okla. D9 234-5
Longford, Kans. E11 108-9
Longhurst, N.C. C10 180-1
Longlac, Ont. E5 284-5
Longleaf, La. F4 168-9
Longmeadow, Mass. E5 68-9
Longmire, Wash. G9 246-7
Longmont, Colo. F3 214-5
Longport, N.J. N6 76-7
Longs, S.C. E16 184-5
Longstreet, La. C1 168-9
Longton, Kans. J13 108-9
Longtown, Miss. B6 176-7
Longtown, Mo. G11 120-1
Longue-Pointe-de-Mingan, Que. G6 290-1
Longueuil, Que. I12 290-1
Longview, Alta. M7 264-5
Longview, Colo. I2 214-5
Longview, La. C6 168-9
Longview, Miss. F9 176-7
Longview, N.C. D6 180-1
Longview, Tex. E11 192-3
Longview, Wash. I7 246-7
Longville, La. G2 168-9
Longville, Minn. H5 116-7
Longwood*, Fla. E12 156-7
Longwood, N.C. H11 180-1
Longwood Park*, N.C. F9 180-1
Loni Beach, Man. H14 272-3
Lonoke, Ark. F8 150-1
Lonoke, co., Ark. F8 150-1
Lonsdale, Ark. K13 150-1
Lonsdale, Minn. N6 116-7
Lonsdale, R.I. B5 87
Loogootee, Ind. L6 100-1
Lookeba, Okla. F9 234-5
Lookingglass, Ore. H5 238-9
Lookout, Ky. I15 164-5
Lookout, Mont. D1 222-3
Lookout, Okla. B7 234-5
Lookout, W. Va. J16 200-1
Lookout Mountain*, Ga. C2 160-1
Lookout Mountain, Tenn. K11 188-9
Loomis*, Calif. H4 210-1
Loomis, Nebr. I9 124-5
Loomis, S. Dak. G13 136-7
Loomis, Wash. C12 246-7
Loon Lake, Alta. F6 264-5
Loon Lake, Sask. I4 294-5
Loon Lake, Wash. D15 246-7
Loon Straits, Man. G15 272-3
Looneyville, W. Va. G4 200-1
Looxahoma, Miss. B7 176-7
Lopatcong*, N.J. E2 76-7
Lopez, Wash. C7 246-7
Lorado, Ark. B10 150-1
Lorado, W. Va. K13 200-1
Lorain, O. B8 132-3
Lorain*, Pa. I5 84-5
Lorain, co., O. C8 132-3
Loraine, N. Dak. B6 128-9
Loraine, Tex. E6 192-3
Lorane, Ore. F5 238-9
Loranger, La. G9 168-9
Loray, N.C. H1 180-1
Lords Point, Conn. G14 60-1
Lordsburg, N. Mex. L2 230-1
Lore City, O. F10 132-3
Loreauville, La. H6 168-9
Loreburn, Sask. M6 294-5
Lorella, Ore. J8 238-9
Lorentz, W. Va. E14 200-1
Lorenz Park*, N.Y. G11 80-1
Lorenzo, Ida. L10 218-9
Lorenzo, Nebr. H2 124-5
Lorenzo, Tex. C5 192-3
Loretta, Kans. G7 108-9
Loretta, Wis. C10 140-1
Lorette*, Man. K4 272-3
Loretteville, Que. F11 290-1
Loretto, Ky. E3 164-5
Loretto, Minn. A9 116-7
Loretto, Nebr. F11 124-5
Loretto, Pa. H6 84-5

Loretto, Tenn. K5 188-9
Loretto, Va. G13 196-7
L'Orignal, Ont. G16 284-5
Lorimor, Ia. I7 104-5
Loring*, Me. B9 64-5
Loring, Mont. A11 222-3
Loris, S.C. D16 184-5
Lorman, Miss. J4 176-7
Lorne, N.B. E5 275
Lorraine, Kans. G9 108-9
Lorraine*, Que. I12 290-1
Lorrainville, Que. I1 290-1
Lorton, Nebr. I15 124-5
Lorton, Va. B3 196-7
Los Alamitos*, Calif. H9 210-1
Los Alamos, Calif. M5 210-1
Los Alamos, N. Mex. D6 230-1
Los Alamos, co., N. Mex. D6 230-1
Los Altos, Calif. D8 210-1
Los Altos Hills, Calif. D8 210-1
Los Angeles, Calif. N7 210-1
Los Angeles, co., Calif. N7 210-1
Los Angeles Aqueduct, Calif. L7 210-1
Los Banos, Calif. J4 210-1
Los Fresnos*, Tex. K8 192-3
Los Gatos, Calif. D8 210-1
Los Lunas, N. Mex. G5 230-1
Los Molinos, Calif. F3 210-1
Los Montoyas, N. Mex. E8 230-1
Los Ojos, N. Mex. C6 230-1
Los Olivos, Calif. M5 210-1
Los Padillas, N. Mex. F5 230-1
Los Padres, Calif. K4 210-1
Los Pinos, N. Mex. B7 230-1
Los Ranchos de Albuquerque, N. Mex. F6 230-1
Los Vigiles, N. Mex. E8 230-1
Losantville*, Ind. G11 100-1
Losier Settlement*, N.B. E7 275
Lost Cabin, Wyo. E10 250-1
Lost City, W. Va. F9 200-1
Lost Creek, Wash. C16 246-7
Lost Creek, W. Va. D13 200-1
Lost Nation, Ia. F14 104-5
Lost River, Ida. L7 218-9
Lost River, W. Va. F9 200-1
Lost Springs, Kans. G11 108-9
Lost Springs, Wyo. G15 250-1
Lostine, Ore. B15 238-9
Lotbinière*, Que. G10 290-1
Lotbinière, co., Que. H16 290-1
Lothair, Ky. I14 164-5
Lothair, Mont. B7 222-3
Lothian, Md. J7 172-3
Lotsee*, Okla. D14 234-5
Lott, Tex. F9 192-3
Lottie, La. G6 168-9
Lottsburg, Va. G14 196-7
Louann, Ark. J5 150-1
Loudon, N.H. L7 72-3
Loudon, Tenn. C12 188-9
Loudon, co., Tenn. C12 188-9
Loudonville*, N.Y. F11 80-1
Loudonville, O. D8 132-3
Loudoun, co., Va. E12 196-7
Lougheed, Alta. J9 264-5
Louin, Miss. J8 176-7
Louis, Okla. H6 234-5
Louis Creek, B.C. I8 268-9
Louisa, Ky. G15 164-5
Louisa, La. I6 168-9
Louisa, Va. G11 196-7
Louisa, co., Ia. I13 104-5
Louisa, co., Va. G11 196-7
Louisbourg, N.S. C12 281
Louisburg, Kans. G16 108-9
Louisburg, Minn. L2 116-7
Louisburg, Mo. G5 120-1
Louisburg, N.C. C11 180-1
Louisdale, N.S. C10 281
Louise, Miss. G5 176-7
Louiseville, Que. H13 290-1
Louiseville-Est, Que. H13 290-1
Louiseville-Ouest*, Que. H13 290-1
Louisiana, Mo. C9 120-1
Louisville, Ala. K9 146-7
Louisville, Colo. F3 214-5
Louisville, Ga. I8 160-1
Louisville, Ill. K9 96-7
Louisville, Kans. E13 108-9
Louisville, Ky. G9 164-5
Louisville, Miss. F9 176-7
Louisville, Nebr. H15 124-5
Louisville, O. E16 132-3
Louisville, Tenn. I12 188-9
Loup, co., Nebr. F9 124-5
Loup City, Nebr. G10 124-5
Lourdes, Nfld. M7 278-9
Lourdes-du-Blanc-Sablon, Que. F8 290-1
Louvale, Ga. K3 160-1
Louviers, Colo. H3 214-5
Love, Sask. J8 294-5
Love, co., Okla. I12 234-5
Love Valley, N.C. H1 180-1
Lovejoy, Ga. D11 160-1
Lovelaceville, Ky. J2 164-5
Loveland, Colo. E3 214-5
Loveland, O. K14 132-3
Loveland, Okla. H8 234-5
Lovell, Me. L2 64-5
Lovell, Okla. D10 234-5
Lovell, Tenn. H11 188-9
Lovell, Wyo. B9 250-1
Lovelock, Nev. E4 226-7
Lovern, W. Va. J5 200-1
Loverna, Sask. L3 294-5
Loves Park, Ill. A8 96-7
Lovett, Ga. J7 160-1
Lovett, Ind. K10 100-1
Lovettsville, Va. D12 196-7
Loveville, Md. H11 172-3
Lovewell, Kans. C9 108-9
Lovilia, Ia. I9 104-5
Loving, N. Mex. L10 230-1
Loving, co., Tex. E3 192-3
Lovingston, Va. H10 196-7
Lovington, Ill. H9 96-7
Lovington, Ia. G7 104-5
Lovington, N. Mex. J11 230-1
Low, Ut. E4 242-3
Low Moor, Ia. G15 104-5
Lowden, Ia. G14 104-5
Lowden, Wash. I14 246-7
Lowe Farm, Man. K14 272-3
Lowell, Ark. A2 150-1
Lowell, Ind. B4 100-1
Lowell, Me. H8 64-5
Lowell, Mass. B10 68-9
Lowell*, Mich. I12 112-3
Lowell, Nebr. I10 124-5
Lowell*, N.C. E6 180-1
Lowell, O. H10 132-3
Lowell, Ore. F6 238-9
Lowell, Vt. C7 90-1
Lowell, W. Va. J5 200-1
Lowell, Wis. I3 140-1
Lowellville, O. C12 132-3
Lower*, N.J. O4 76-7
Lower Alloways Creek*, N.J. L1 76-7
Lower Argyle, N.S. G4 281
Lower Bank, N.J. L6 76-7
Lower Bridge, Ore. E8 238-9
Lower Brule, S. Dak. F10 136-7
Lower Burrell*, Pa. H3 84-5
Lower Caraquet*, N.B. E6 275
Lower Coverdale, N.B. H7 275
Lower Durham, N.B. H4 275
Lower Gilmanton, N.H. L7 72-3
Lower Granville, Vt. H5 90-1
Lower Kalskag, Alaska F9 254-5
Lower L'Ardoise, N.S. C11 281
Lower Marlboro, Md. F11 172-3
Lower Miami, Ariz. I8 206-7
Lower Montague, P.E.I. F9 287
Lower Nicola*, B.C. H6 268-9
Lower Nutria, N. Mex. F2 230-1
Lower Paia, Hawaii G11 258-9
Lower Peach Tree, Ala. J4 146-7
Lower Post, B.C. A5 268-9
Lower Red Lake, Minn. F3 116-7
Lower Village, Hawaii J4 258-9
Lower Village, Vt. E6 90-1
Lower Waterford, Vt. E9 90-1
Lower West Pubnico, N.S. G4 281
Lower Wingham, Ont. C12 284-5
Lower Woods Harbour, N.S. G4 281
Lowery, Ala. L8 146-7
Lowes, Ky. J2 164-5
Lowes Crossroad, Del. K4 153
Loweth, Mont. F8 222-3
Lowgap, N.C. C7 180-1
Lowland, N.C. E14 180-1
Lowland, Tenn. H14 188-9
Lowman, Ida. K4 218-9
Lowmoor, Va. H8 196-7
Lowndes, co., Ala. J6 146-7
Lowndes, co., Ga. N6 160-1
Lowndes, co., Miss. F10 176-7
Lowndesboro, Ala. I7 146-7
Lowndesville, S.C. D6 184-5
Lowry, Minn. K3 116-7
Lowry, S. Dak. C9 136-7
Lowry, Va. I9 196-7
Lowry City, Mo. F4 120-1
Lowrys, S.C. B9 184-5
Lowville, N.Y. C8 80-1
Lox, Wyo. F11 250-1
Loxahatchee Slough, Fla. H13 156-7
Loxley, Ala. N4 146-7
Loyal, Okla. E10 234-5
Loyal, Wis. F10 140-1
Loyall, Ky. J14 164-5
Loyalton, Calif. G5 210-1
Loyalton, S. Dak. C10 136-7
Lozeau, Mont. E2 222-3
Lu Verne, Ia. C6 104-5
Luana, Ia. C13 104-5
Lubbock, Tex. D5 192-3
Lubbock, co., Tex. C5 192-3
Lubec, Me. J11 64-5
Luber, Ark. C7 150-1
Lublin, Wis. E10 140-1
Lucama, N.C. D12 180-1
Lucan, Minn. N3 116-7
Lucan, Ont. D12 284-5
Lucas, Ia. I8 104-5
Lucas, Kans. F8 108-9
Lucas, Ky. J8 164-5
Lucas, La. B2 168-9
Lucas, Mich. G12 112-3
Lucas, Miss. K6 176-7
Lucas, O. D8 132-3
Lucas, co., Ia. I8 104-5
Lucas, co., O. B5 132-3
Luce, co., Mich. C12 112-3
Lucedale, Miss. M10 176-7
Lucerne, Calif. G2 210-1
Lucerne, Colo. D4 214-5
Lucerne, Ind. D7 100-1
Lucerne, Mo. A5 120-1
Lucerne, Pa. H4 84-5
Lucerne, Wash. D11 246-7
Lucerne, Wyo. D9 250-1
Lucerne in Maine, Me. J7 64-5
Lucerne Valley, Calif. F11 210-1
Luceville, Que. C15 290-1
Lucien, Miss. K5 176-7
Lucien, Okla. D11 234-5
Lucile, Ida. H3 218-9
Lucille, Ala. G5 146-7
Lucin, Ut. D3 242-3
Luck, Wis. D7 140-1
Luckey, O. B5 132-3
Lucknow, Ont. C12 284-5
Lucknow, S.C. D12 184-5
Lucky, La. C3 168-9
Lucky Lake, Sask. M6 294-5
Ludden, N. Dak. J12 128-9
Ludington, Mich. H11 112-3
Ludlow, Colo. I12 214-5
Ludlow, Ky. D11 164-5
Ludlow, Me. E9 64-5
Ludlow, Mass. E5 68-9
Ludlow, Miss. H7 176-7
Ludlow, Mo. C4 120-1
Ludlow, N.B. G5 275
Ludlow, Vt. K6 90-1
Ludlow Center, Mass. E5 68-9
Ludlow Falls, O. G14 132-3
Ludowici, Ga. L10 160-1
Ludville, Ga. E3 160-1
Ludwig, Ark. D4 150-1
Luella, Ga. H4 160-1
Lufkin, Tex. F11 192-3
Lugert, Okla. G7 234-5
Lugoff, S.C. D11 184-5
Luis Lopez, N. Mex. H5 230-1
Lukachukai, Ariz. C11 206-7
Luke*, Ariz. I6 206-7
Luke, Md. C3 172-3
Lukeville, Ariz. L5 206-7
Lula, Ga. E5 160-1
Lula, Miss. C5 176-7
Lula, Okla. G13 234-5
Luling, La. D13 168-9
Luling, Tex. G8 192-3
Lum, Mich. G6 112-3
Lumber, Ark. J4 150-1
Lumber Bridge, N.C. F10 180-1
Lumber City, Ga. K8 160-1
Lumberport, W. Va. C13 200-1
Lumberton, Miss. M8 176-7
Lumberton, N.J. I4 76-7
Lumberton, N. Mex. B5 230-1
Lumberton, N.C. G10 180-1
Lumberton*, Tex. G11 192-3
Lumby, B.C. J9 268-9
Lummi Island, Wash. C7 246-7
Lumpkin, Ga. K3 160-1
Lumpkin, co., Ga. D4 160-1
Lumsden, Nfld. M10 278-9
Lumsden, Sask. N8 294-5
Luna, La. C5 168-9
Luna, N. Mex. H2 230-1
Luna, co., N. Mex. L4 230-1
Luna Pier, Mich. K14 112-3
Lund, B.C. J6 268-9
Lund, Ida. N10 218-9
Lund, Nev. G10 226-7
Lund, Ut. L3 242-3
Lundar, Man. H13 272-3
Lundbreck, Alta. O7 264-5
Lundell, Ark. G10 150-1
Lunenburg, Mass. B9 68-9
Lunenburg, N.S. E6 281
Lunenburg, Vt. E10 90-1
Lunenburg, Va. J11 196-7
Lunenburg, co., N.S. E6 281
Lunenburg, co., Va. J11 196-7
Luning, Nev. H4 226-7
Lunsford, Ark. C11 150-1
Lupton, Ariz. E11 206-7
Lupton, Mich. G14 112-3
Lupton City, Tenn. K11 188-9
Lupus, Mo. E6 120-1
Luray, Kans. F8 108-9
Luray, Mo. A7 120-1
Luray, S.C. I9 184-5
Luray, Tenn. C4 188-9
Luray, Va. F10 196-7
Lurton, Ark. C5 150-1
Lusby, Md. G11 172-3
Luseland, Sask. L4 294-5
Lushton, Nebr. H12 124-5
Lusk, Wyo. F16 250-1
Lust Subdivision*, B.C. G4 268-9
Lutcher, La. C12 168-9
Lutesville, Mo. H11 120-1
Luther, Ia. F7 104-5
Luther, Mich. G12 112-3
Luther, Mont. H9 222-3
Luther, Okla. I3 234-5
Luther Corner, Mass. G11 68-9
Luthersville, Ga. H3 160-1
Lutherville [-Timonium], Md. E7 172-3
Lutie, Okla. G15 234-5
Luttrell, Tenn. G12 188-9
Lutts, Tenn. D5 188-9
Lutz, Fla. G3 156-7
Luverne, Ala. K7 146-7
Luverne, Minn. O2 116-7
Luverne, N. Dak. F12 128-9
Luxemburg, Ia. D14 104-5
Luxemburg, Wis. D5 140-1
Luxomni, Ga. B12 160-1
Luxora, Ark. C12 150-1
Luzerne, Ia. F11 104-5
Luzerne, Mich. F13 112-3
Luzerne, Pa. E13 84-5
Luzerne, co., Pa. F13 84-5
Lycan, Colo. I16 214-5
Lycoming, co., Pa. E10 84-5
Lydia, S.C. D12 184-5
Lydia Mills, S.C. I4 184-5
Lydick [-Chain-O-Lakes], Ind. A7 100-1
Lyerly, Ga. E1 160-1
Lyford, Ind. I4 100-1
Lyford, Tex. K8 192-3
Lykens, Pa. H11 84-5
Lyle, Minn. O7 116-7
Lyle, Wash. J9 246-7
Lyles, Tenn. H5 188-9
Lyleton, Man. K9 272-3
Lyman, Ida. L10 218-9
Lyman, Me. N2 64-5
Lyman, Miss. N8 176-7
Lyman, Nebr. E1 124-5
Lyman, Okla. C12 234-5
Lyman, S.C. F3 184-5
Lyman, Ut. K6 242-3
Lyman, Wash. C8 246-7
Lyman, Wyo. J6 250-1
Lyman, co., S. Dak. F9 136-7
Lyman Park-Thomason Park*, Va. F12 196-7
Lyme*, Conn. G11 60-1
Lyme, N.H. I4 72-3
Lyn, Ont. J15 284-5
Lynbrook, N.Y. F16 80-1
Lynch, Ky. J15 164-5
Lynch, Md. C13 172-3
Lynch, Nebr. C11 124-5
Lynch Heights, Del. G4 153
Lynch Station, Va. I9 196-7
Lynchburg, Miss. A6 176-7
Lynchburg, O. K16 132-3
Lynchburg, S.C. D13 184-5
Lynchburg, Tenn. K8 188-9
Lynchburg, Va. I9 196-7
Lynchville, Me. L2 64-5
Lynd, Minn. N2 116-7
Lyndeborough, N.H. O5 72-3
Lynden*, Ont. D14 284-5
Lynden, Wash. B8 246-7
Lyndhurst, N.J. C11 76-7
Lyndhurst, O. B15 132-3
Lyndhurst, S.C. H9 184-5
Lyndhurst, Va. G10 196-7
Lyndon, Ill. C6 96-7
Lyndon, Kans. G14 108-9
Lyndon, Ky. A2 164-5
Lyndon, Vt. E9 90-1
Lyndon Center, Vt. D9 90-1
Lyndon Station, Wis. H11 140-1
Lyndonville, N.Y. E3 80-1
Lyndonville, Vt. D9 90-1
Lynhurst, Ont. E12 284-5
Lynn, Ala. D4 146-7
Lynn, Ark. B9 150-1
Lynn, Ind. G12 100-1
Lynn, Mass. C12 68-9
Lynn, N.C. E4 180-1
Lynn, Ut. C3 242-3
Lynn, co., Tex. D5 192-3
Lynn Acres Mobile Home Park*, B.C. J8 268-9
Lynn Gardens, Tenn. F16 188-9
Lynn Grove, Ky. K3 164-5
Lynn Haven, Fla. B5 156-7
Lynn Lake, Man. D1 272-3
Lynn Lane, Okla. D14 234-5
Lynndyl, Ut. H5 242-3
Lynnfield, Mass. C12 68-9
Lynnview*, Ky. G9 164-5
Lynnville, Ind. N5 100-1
Lynnville, Ia. G10 104-5
Lynnville, Ky. K3 164-5
Lynnville, Tenn. J6 188-9
Lynnwood, Wash. H2 246-7
Lynnwood-Pricedale*, Pa. J3 84-5
Lynwood, Calif. G8 210-1
Lynwood*, Ill. C11 96-7
Lynxville, Wis. J10 140-1
Lyon, Miss. C5 176-7
Lyon, co., Ia. B1 104-5
Lyon, co., Kans. G13 108-9
Lyon, co., Ky. I4 164-5
Lyon, co., Minn. N2 116-7
Lyon, co., Nev. G2 226-7
Lyons, Colo. E2 214-5
Lyons, Ga. K8 160-1
Lyons, Ill. M3 96-7
Lyons, Ind. K5 100-1
Lyons, Kans. H9 108-9
Lyons*, Mich. I13 112-3
Lyons, Nebr. E14 124-5
Lyons, N.J. E5 76-7
Lyons, N.Y. E5 80-1
Lyons, O. B4 132-3
Lyons, Okla. E16 234-5
Lyons, Ont. E12 284-5
Lyons, Ore. I2 238-9
Lyons, S. Dak. G15 136-7
Lyons, Wis. K4 140-1
Lyons Falls, N.Y. D8 80-1
Lyons Plain, Conn. I5 60-1
Lyonsville, Mass. B4 68-9
Lysite, Wyo. E10 250-1
Lyster*, Que. G10 290-1
Lytle, Tex. K1 192-3
Lytton, B.C. J7 268-9
Lytton, Ia. E5 104-5

M

Ma-Me-O Beach, Alta. J7 264-5
Mabank, Tex. E16 192-3
Mabel, Minn. O9 116-7
Mabelvale, Ark. J15 150-1
Maben, Miss. E8 176-7
Maben, W. Va. J4 200-1
Mabie, W. Va. F15 200-1
Mableton, Ga. B10 160-1

Mabou, N.S. B10 281
Mabscott, W. Va. K15 200-1
Mabton, Wash. I11 246-7
Macalister, B.C. H7 268-9
Macamic, Que. H1 290-1
MacArthur, W. Va. K15 200-1
Maccan, N.S. C6 281
Macclenny, Fla. B10 156-7
MacClesfield, N.C. D13 180-1
Macdiarmid*, Ont. F4 284-5
Macdonald, Man. I13 272-3
MacDougall, N.B. H7 275
MacDowall, Sask. J7 294-5
Mace, W. Va. G7 200-1
Macedon, N.Y. E5 80-1
Macedonia, Ark. J4 150-1
Macedonia, Conn. D4 60-1
Macedonia, Ia. I3 104-5
Macedonia, O. C15 132-3
Maceo, Ky. H6 164-5
Maces Bay, N.B. J4 275
Macfarlan, W. Va. E4 200-1
MacGregor, Man. I12 272-3
MacGregor's Bay Area*, Ont. H9 284-5
Machias, Me. J10 64-5
Machias, Wash. G3 246-7
Machiasport, Me. J10 64-5
Machipongo, Va. E5 196-7
Mack, Colo. E5 214-5
Mackay, Ida. L7 218-9
Mackenzie*, B.C. F5 268-9
Mackenzie*, Mo. E10 120-1
Mackenzie Bay, Y.T. A2 297
Mackenzie R., N.W. Terr. C1 296
Mackey, Ind. N4 100-1
Mackeys, N.C. D14 180-1
Mackinac, co., Mich. D12 112-3
Mackinac Island, Mich. D13 112-3
Mackinaw, Ill. F8 96-7
Mackinaw City, Mich. E13 112-3
Macklin, Sask. K4 294-5
Macks, Ark. C9 150-1
Macks Creek, Mo. G5 120-1
Macksburg, Ia. I6 104-5
Macksville, Kans. I7 108-9
Mackville, Ky. D5 164-5
Mackville, Wis. E4 140-1
Macland, Ga. B9 160-1
Macleay, Ore. H1 238-9
MacNutt, Sask. M11 294-5
Macomb, Ill. F5 96-7
Macomb, Okla. K4 234-5
Macomb, co., Mich. I15 112-3
Macon, Ga. I5 160-1
Macon, Ill. H8 96-7
Macon, Miss. G10 176-7
Macon, Mo. C6 120-1
Macon, Nebr. J10 124-5
Macon, N.C. C12 180-1
Macon, Tenn. K2 188-9
Macon, Va. H11 196-7
Macon, co., Ala. I9 146-7
Macon, co., Ga. J4 160-1
Macon, co., Ill. H8 96-7
Macon, co., Mo. C6 120-1
Macon, co., N.C. E2 180-1
Macon, co., Tenn. A8 188-9
Macoun, Sask. O9 294-5
Macoupin, co., Ill. J6 96-7
Macrorie, Sask. M6 294-5
MacTier, Ont. I8 284-5
Macungie, Pa. H14 84-5
Macwahoc, Me. G8 64-5
Macy, Ind. D8 100-1
Macy, Nebr. E14 124-5
Madaket, Mass. J15 68-9
Madawaska, Me. A8 64-5
Madawaska, co., N.B. E2 275
Madbury, N.H. M9 72-3
Madden, Miss. H8 176-7
Maddock, N. Dak. E9 128-9
Maddox, Md. H10 172-3
Maddox, Tenn. D5 188-9
Madeira, O. K14 132-3
Madeira Beach, Fla. I1 156-7
Madelia, Minn. O5 116-7
Madera, Calif. J5 210-1
Madera, co., Calif. J5 210-1
Maderia Park, B.C. A11 268-9
Madill, Okla. I12 234-5
Madison, Ala. B6 146-7
Madison, Ark. E10 150-1
Madison, Conn. H10 60-1
Madison, Fla. B8 156-7
Madison, Ga. G6 160-1
Madison, Ill. K6 96-7
Madison, Ind. L10 100-1
Madison, Kans. H13 108-9
Madison, Me. J4 64-5
Madison, Md. G12 172-3
Madison, Minn. M2 116-7
Madison, Miss. H6 176-7
Madison, Mo. C7 120-1
Madison, Nebr. F13 124-5
Madison, N.H. I8 72-3
Madison*, N.J. G6 76-7
Madison, N.J. D6 76-7
Madison, N.C. C8 180-1
Madison, O. A10 132-3
Madison, Sask. M4 294-5
Madison, S.C. C4 184-5
Madison, S.C. F8 184-5
Madison, S. Dak. F15 136-7
Madison, Tenn. G7 188-9
Madison, Va. C1 196-7
Madison, W. Va. H3 200-1
Madison, Wis. J12 140-1
Madison, co., Ala. B7 146-7
Madison, co., Ark. B3 150-1
Madison, co., Fla. B8 156-7
Madison, co., Ga. E6 160-1
Madison, co., Ida. L10 218-9
Madison, co., Ill. J7 96-7
Madison, co., Ind. G9 100-1
Madison, co., Ia. H6 104-5
Madison, co., Ky. H11 164-5
Madison, co., La. C7 168-9
Madison, co., Miss. H6 176-7
Madison, co., Mo. H10 120-1
Madison, co., Mont. G6 222-3
Madison, co., Nebr. F12 124-5
Madison, co., N.Y. F7 80-1
Madison, co., N.C. D3 180-1
Madison, co., O. G5 132-3
Madison, co., Tenn. C3 188-9
Madison, co., Tex. F10 192-3
Madison, co., Va. F11 196-7
Madison Heights, Mich. I6 112-3
Madison Heights, Va. I9 196-7
Madison Junction, Wyo. F1 250-1
Madison Lake*, Minn. N5 116-7
Madison Mills, Va. C1 196-7
Madison North*, O. A10 132-3
Madisonville, Ky. I5 164-5
Madisonville, La. A14 168-9
Madisonville, Tenn. C12 188-9
Madisonville, Tex. F10 192-3
Madoc, Mont. A14 222-3
Madoc, Ont. J12 284-5
Madonna, Md. B11 172-3
Madran, N.B. E5 275
Madras, Ore. E9 238-9
Madrid, Ala. M10 146-7
Madrid, Ia. F7 104-5
Madrid, Me. J3 64-5
Madrid, Nebr. H5 124-5
Madrid, N. Mex. E6 230-1
Madsen*, Ont. E1 284-5
Maeser, Ut. F10 242-3
Mafeking, Man. D10 272-3
Magaguadavic, N.B. I3 275
Magalloway, Me. I1 64-5
Magazine, Ark. E3 150-1
Magdalena, N. Mex. H4 230-1
Magee, Miss. J7 176-7
Maggie Valley, N.C. E3 180-1
Magic City, Ida. M6 218-9
Magma, Ariz. I7 206-7
Magna, Ut. F6 242-3
Magness, Ark. C9 150-1
Magnet, Ark. K13 150-1
Magnet, Nebr. D12 124-5
Magnetawan*, Ont. H8 284-5
Magnetic Springs, O. A10 132-3
Magnolia, Ala. J4 146-7
Magnolia, Ark. J4 150-1
Magnolia, Del. F4 153
Magnolia, Ia. G2 104-5
Magnolia, Ky. I9 164-5
Magnolia, Md. C12 172-3
Magnolia, Mass. B13 68-9
Magnolia, Minn. O2 116-7
Magnolia, Miss. L5 176-7
Magnolia, N.J. O11 76-7
Magnolia, N.C. F12 180-1
Magnolia, O. D10 132-3
Magnolia Springs, Ala. O4 146-7
Magnolia Terminal, Ala. J4 146-7
Magoffin, co., Ky. H14 164-5
Magog, Que. J14 290-1
Magrath, Alta. O8 264-5
Mahanoy City, Pa. G13 84-5
Mahaska, Kans. C10 108-9
Mahaska, co., Ia. H10 104-5
Mahatta River, B.C. I4 268-9
Maher, Colo. G7 214-5
Mahkeenac Heights, Mass. D2 68-9
Mahned, Miss. L9 176-7
Mahnomen, Minn. H2 116-7
Mahnomen, co., Minn. G3 116-7
Mahomet, Ill. G10 96-7
Mahone, W. Va. E4 200-1
Mahone Bay, N.S. E6 281
Mahoning, co., O. D11 132-3
Mahopac, N.Y. A15 80-1
Mahtomedi*, Minn. M7 116-7
Mahwah, N.J. B7 76-7
Maiden, N.C. I1 180-1
Maiden Rock, Wis. F7 140-1
Maidstone, Sask. J4 294-5
Maidstone, Vt. D11 90-1
Maidsville, W. Va. A15 200-1
Maili, Hawaii I2 258-9
Main-à-Dieu, N.S. B12 281
Main Brook, Nfld. K9 278-9
Maineville, O. K15 132-3
Mainland, Nfld. N7 278-9
Maisonnette*, N.B. E6 275
Maitland, Fla. E7 156-7
Maitland, Mo. B2 120-1
Maitland, Ont. J15 284-5
Maize, Kans. I10 108-9
Majenica, Ind. D10 100-1
Major, Sask. L4 294-5
Major, co., Okla. D9 234-5
Makaha, Hawaii I2 258-9
Makakilo City, Hawaii J3 258-9
Makapala, Hawaii H12 258-9
Makaroff, Man. G9 272-3
Makawao, Hawaii G11 258-9
Makinak, Man. G11 272-3
Makoti, N. Dak. E5 128-9
Makuu, Hawaii J14 258-9
Makwa, Sask. I4 294-5
Malabar, Fla. F13 156-7
Malad City, Ida. O9 218-9
Malaga, Calif. K5 210-1
Malaga, N.J. L3 76-7
Malaga, N. Mex. L10 230-1
Malaga, Wash. F11 246-7
Malakoff, Tex. E10 192-3
Malakwa, B.C. I9 268-9
Malartic, Que. H1 290-1
Malcolm, Ala. L3 146-7
Malcolm, Nebr. H14 124-5
Malcom, Ia. G10 104-5
Malden, Mass. G5 68-9
Malden, Mo. J11 120-1
Malden, Wash. F16 246-7
Malden, W. Va. I14 200-1
Malesus, Tenn. J4 188-9
Malheur, co., Ore. G15 238-9
Malin, Ore. K8 238-9
Malinta, O. C4 132-3
Maljamar, N. Mex. K10 230-1
Mallaig, Alta. H9 264-5
Mallard, Ia. C5 104-5
Mallory, W. Va. K12 200-1
Malmo, Nebr. I1 124-5
Malo, Wash. C14 246-7
Malone, Ala. F9 146-7
Malone, Fla. A6 156-7
Malone, N.Y. A10 80-1
Malone, Wash. G6 246-7
Malott, Wash. D12 246-7
Maloy, Ia. J6 104-5
Malpeque*, P.E.I. D5 287
Malpeque Bay, P.E.I. D5 287
Malstrom*, Mont. D7 222-3
Malta, Ida. O8 218-9
Malta, Ill. B9 96-7
Malta, Mont. B11 222-3
Malta, O. G9 132-3
Malta Bend, Mo. D5 120-1
Maltais*, N.B. D4 275
Malvern, Ala. M9 146-7
Malvern, Ark. G5 150-1
Malvern, Ia. I3 104-5
Malvern, O. D10 132-3
Malvern, Pa. B9 84-5
Malverne*, N.Y. K11 80-1
Malvina, Miss. D4 176-7
Mamaroneck, N.Y. D15 80-1
Mamers, N.C. J6 180-1
Mamie, N.C. C16 180-1
Mammoth, Ariz. J9 206-7
Mammoth, Ut. G5 242-3
Mammoth, W. Va. I15 200-1
Mammoth, Wyo. A5 250-1
Mammoth Lakes, Calif. I6 210-1
Mammoth Spring, Ark. A8 150-1
Mamou, La. G4 168-9
Man, W. Va. K12 200-1
Manahawkin, N.J. K7 76-7
Manakin, Va. H12 196-7
Manalapan*, Fla. E16 156-7
Manalapan, N.J. H6 76-7
Manasquan, N.J. H8 76-7
Manassa, Colo. J10 214-5
Manassas, Ga. K9 160-1
Manassas, Va. B3 196-7
Manassas Park, Va. B3 196-7
Manatee, co., Fla. G10 156-7
Manawa, Ia. I2 104-5
Manawa, Wis. E2 140-1
Mancelona, Mich. F12 112-3
Manchac, La. B13 168-9
Manchester, Ala. D5 146-7
Manchester, Conn. D10 60-1
Manchester, Ga. I3 160-1
Manchester, Ind. K11 100-1
Manchester, Ia. D13 104-5
Manchester, Kans. F11 108-9
Manchester, Ky. I13 164-5
Manchester, Me. K4 64-5
Manchester, Md. B10 172-3
Manchester, Mass. B13 68-9
Manchester, Mich. K3 112-3
Manchester, Minn. O6 116-7
Manchester, Mo. C15 120-1
Manchester, N.H. N7 72-3
Manchester*, N.J. I7 76-7
Manchester, N.Y. E5 80-1
Manchester, O. J5 132-3
Manchester, Okla. B10 234-5
Manchester, Pa. J11 84-5
Manchester, Tenn. C8 188-9
Manchester, Vt. L4 90-1
Manchester, Wash. I2 246-7
Manchester, Wis. H13 140-1
Manchester Center, Vt. L4 90-1
Manchester Depot, Vt. L4 90-1
Mancos, Colo. I6 214-5
Mandan, N. Dak. H7 128-9
Mandaree, N. Dak. E4 128-9
Manderfield, Ut. K5 242-3
Manderson, S. Dak. H4 136-7
Manderson, Wyo. C10 250-1
Mandeville, Ark. I3 150-1
Mandeville, La. A14 168-9
Manfred, N. Dak. E9 128-9
Mangham, La. C6 168-9
Mango, Fla. H3 156-7
Mangohick, Va. H13 196-7
Mangonia Park, Fla. D16 156-7
Mangum, Okla. G7 234-5
Manhasset, N.Y. E15 80-1
Manhattan, Ill. O3 96-7
Manhattan, Kans. E12 108-9
Manhattan, Mont. G7 222-3
Manhattan, Nev. H6 226-7
Manhattan, N.Y. E14 80-1
Manhattan Beach*, Calif. G8 210-1
Manhattan Beach, Minn. I5 116-7
Manhattan Beach, Ore. B4 238-9
Manheim, Pa. J12 84-5
Manheim, W. Va. C16 200-1
Manibridge*, Man. C4 272-3
Manifest, La. D5 168-9
Manigotagan, Man. G15 272-3
Manila, Ark. C12 150-1
Manila, Ut. E10 242-3
Manila, W. Va. J12 200-1
Manilla, Ind. I10 100-1
Manilla, Ia. F4 104-5
Manistee, Mich. G11 112-3
Manistee, co., Mich. G11 112-3
Manistique, Mich. D11 112-3
Manito, Ill. F7 96-7
Manitou, Ky. I5 164-5
Manitou, Man. K12 272-3
Manitou, Okla. H8 234-5
Manitou Beach, Sask. L7 294-5
Manitou Beach-Devils Lake, Mich. K13 112-3
Manitou Springs, Colo. K3 214-5
Manitouwadge, Ont. F5 284-5
Manitowaning, Ont. H7 284-5
Manitowish Waters, Wis. C11 140-1
Manitowoc, Wis. G15 140-1
Manitowoc, co., Wis. G15 140-1
Maniwaki, Que. I2 290-1
Mankato, Kans. D9 108-9
Mankato, Minn. N5 116-7
Mankota, Sask. O6 294-5
Manley, Nebr. K2 124-5
Manley Hot Springs, Alaska D11 254-5
Manlius, N.Y. E7 80-1
Manly, Ia. B8 104-5
Manly, N.C. K5 180-1
Mannboro, Va. I12 196-7
Mannford*, Okla. D13 234-5
Manning, Alta. E5 264-5
Manning, Ark. H5 150-1
Manning, Ia. F4 104-5
Manning, N. Dak. G3 128-9
Manning, S.C. F12 184-5
Mannington, Ky. J5 164-5
Mannington*, N.J. K1 76-7
Mannington, W. Va. B13 200-1
Manns Harbor, N.C. D16 180-1
Mannsville, Ky. I10 164-5
Mannsville, Okla. I12 234-5
Mannville, Alta. J10 264-5
Manokin, Md. I14 172-3
Manokotak, Alaska G9 254-5
Manomet, Mass. F14 68-9
Manor, Ga. N8 160-1
Manor*, Pa. I3 84-5
Manor, Sask. O10 294-5
Manor, Tex. G8 192-3
Manor Creek*, Ky. A2 164-5
Manorhaven, N.Y. E15 80-1
Manotick*, Ont. H15 284-5
Manquin, Va. H13 196-7
Manring, Tenn. F12 188-9
Manse, Nev. M8 226-7
Manseau, Que. H15 290-1
Manset, Me. L8 64-5
Mansfield, Ark. E2 150-1
Mansfield, Conn. C12 60-1
Mansfield, Ga. G5 160-1
Mansfield, Ill. G9 96-7
Mansfield, La. C2 168-9
Mansfield, Mass. F11 68-9
Mansfield, Mo. I6 120-1
Mansfield*, N.J. D4 76-7
Mansfield, N.J. H5 76-7
Mansfield, O. D7 132-3
Mansfield, Pa. D10 84-5
Mansfield, S. Dak. C12 136-7
Mansfield, Tenn. B4 188-9
Mansfield, Tex. D13 192-3
Mansfield, Wash. E12 246-7
Mansfield and Dochart Area*, Ont. H10 284-5
Mansfield Center, Conn. D12 60-1
Mansfield Depot, Conn. C11 60-1
Manson, Ia. D5 104-5
Manson*, Man. I1 272-3
Manson, Wash. E11 246-7
Mansons Landing, B.C. J5 268-9
Mansonville*, Que. J14 290-1
Mansura, La. F5 168-9
Mantachie, Miss. C10 176-7
Mantador, N. Dak. I14 128-9
Manteca, Calif. C10 210-1
Mantee, Miss. E9 176-7
Manteno, Ill. D11 96-7
Manteo, N.C. D16 180-1
Manter, Kans. J1 108-9
Manti, Ut. I6 242-3
Mantoloking, N.J. I8 76-7
Manton, Mich. G12 112-3
Mantorville, Minn. O7 116-7
Mantua, N.J. O9 76-7
Mantua, O. C16 132-3
Mantua, Ut. D6 242-3
Mantua*, Va. E12 196-7
Manuelito, N. Mex. E2 230-1
Manuels*, N.B. F6 275
Manvel, N. Dak. D14 128-9
Manville, N.J. F5 76-7
Manville, R.I. A5 87
Manville, Wyo. F15 250-1
Many, La. D2 168-9
Many Farms, Ariz. C10 206-7
Manzanita, Ore. B4 238-9
Manzano, N. Mex. G6 230-1
Manzanola, Colo. H13 214-5
Mapes, N. Dak. D12 128-9
Maple, N.C. C15 180-1
Maple Bay, B.C. D12 268-9
Maple Bluff, Wis. I1 140-1
Maple City, Kans. K12 108-9
Maple City, Mich. F11 112-3

Maple Creek, Sask. N4 294-5
Maple Falls, Wash. B8 246-7
Maple Grove, Me. C9 64-5
Maple Grove, Minn. A9 116-7
Maple Grove*, Que. J12 290-1
Maple Grove, Tenn. A9 188-9
Maple Heights, O. B15 132-3
Maple Hill, Kans. F13 108-9
Maple Hill, N.C. G13 180-1
Maple Lake, Minn. A8 116-7
Maple Park, Ill. B9 96-7
Maple Park, Mass. A11 68-9
Maple Plain*, Minn. M5 116-7
Maple Rapids, Mich. I13 112-3
Maple Shade, N.J. M11 76-7
Maple Valley, Wash. J3 246-7
Maples, Ind. C11 100-1
Maplesville, Ala. H6 146-7
Mapleton, Ia. F2 104-5
Mapleton, Kans. H16 108-9
Mapleton, Me. C8 64-5
Mapleton, Minn. O5 116-7
Mapleton, N. Dak. G14 128-9
Mapleton, Ore. F4 238-9
Mapleton, Ut. G6 242-3
Mapleview, Minn. O7 116-7
Mapleville, R.I. A3 87
Maplewood, Ind. I17 100-1
Maplewood, La. H2 168-9
Maplewood, Me. O6 64-5
Maplewood, Minn. A11 116-7
Maplewood, Mo. B16 120-1
Maplewood, N.H. G6 72-3
Maplewood, N.J. E7 76-7
Maplewood, W. Va. K16 200-1
Maplewood, Wis. D6 140-1
Mappsville, Va. H16 196-7
Maquoketa, Ia. F15 104-5
Mara, B.C. I9 268-9
Maramec, Okla. D12 234-5
Marana, Ariz. K8 206-7
Marathon, Fla. K12 156-7
Marathon, Ia. C4 104-5
Marathon, N.Y. G7 80-1
Marathon, Ont. F5 284-5
Marathon, co., Wis. F11 140-1
Marathon City, Wis. F12 140-1
Marble, Ark. B4 150-1
Marble, Colo. F8 214-5
Marble, Minn. H6 116-7
Marble, N.C. E1 180-1
Marble, Wash. C15 246-7
Marble Canyon, Ariz. B7 206-7
Marble City, Okla. E16 234-5
Marble Cliff, O. F6 132-3
Marble Dale, Conn. E4 60-1
Marble Falls, Tex. G8 192-3
Marble Hill, Mo. H11 120-1
Marble Rock, Ia. C9 104-5
Marblehead, Mass. F7 68-9
Marblehead, O. B7 132-3
Marblehill, Ga. E4 160-1
Marblemount, Wash. C9 246-7
Marbleton, Que. I15 290-1
Marbleton, Wyo. G6 250-1
Marbury, Ala. H7 146-7
Marbury, Md. G9 172-3
Marcelin, Sask. J6 294-5
Marceline, Mo. C5 120-1
Marcella, Ark. C8 150-1
Marcella, N.J. C6 76-7
Marcellus, Mich. K12 112-3
Marcellus*, N.Y. E7 80-1
Marcellus, Wash. F14 246-7
March*, Calif. N8 210-1
Marchand, Man. J15 272-3
Marchwell, Sask. M11 294-5
Marco, Ind. K5 100-1
Marco, La. E4 168-9
Marcola, Ore. K1 238-9
Marcus, Ia. C2 104-5
Marcus, Wash. C15 246-7
Marcus Hook, Pa. K15 84-5
Mardela Springs, Md. G14 172-3
Marengo, Ill. A9 96-7
Marengo, Ind. N7 100-1
Marengo, Ia. G11 104-5
Marengo, O. E7 132-3
Marengo, Sask. L4 294-5
Marengo, Wash. G14 246-7
Marengo, Wis. B10 140-1
Marengo, co., Ala. I4 146-7
Marenisco, Mich. D7 112-3
Marfa, Tex. G3 192-3
Marfrance, W. Va. H5 200-1
Margaree Centre, N.S. B10 281
Margaree Forks, N.S. B10 281
Margaret, Ala. E7 146-7
Margaret, Man. J11 272-3
Margaretsville, N.C. B13 180-1
Margaretville, N.Y. G9 80-1
Margate, Fla. F16 156-7
Margate, P.E.I. D6 287
Margate City, N.J. M6 76-7
Margerum, Ala. B3 146-7
Margo, Sask. L9 294-5
Maria, Que. I5 290-1
Mariah Hill, Ind. N6 100-1
Marial, Ore. I4 238-9
Marianna, Ark. F10 150-1
Marianna, Fla. B6 156-7
Mariapolis, Man. K12 272-3
Mariaville, Me. J8 64-5
Maribel, Wis. E5 140-1
Maricopa, Ariz. J6 206-7
Maricopa, Calif. M6 210-1
Maricopa, co., Ariz. H4 206-7
Marie, Ark. C12 150-1
Marie, W. Va. J5 200-1
Mariemont, O. K14 132-3
Marienthal, Kans. G2 108-9
Maries, co., Mo. F7 120-1
Marietta, Ga. F3 160-1
Marietta, Minn. M2 116-7
Marietta, Miss. B10 176-7
Marietta, N.C. G10 180-1
Marietta, O. H10 132-3
Marietta, Okla. I11 234-5
Marietta, Pa. J12 84-5
Marietta, Wash. C7 246-7
Marieville, Que. J13 290-1
Marin, co., Calif. I2 210-1
Marina, Calif. K3 210-1
Marine, Ill. K7 96-7
Marine City, Mich. H8 112-3
Marine Corps Center*,
Ga. M4 160-1
Marine-on-St. Croix,
Minn. A12 116-7
Marineland, Fla. C12 156-7
Marinette, Wis. E15 140-1
Marinette, co., Wis. D14 140-1
Maringouin, La. G6 168-9
Marion, Ala. H5 146-7
Marion, Ark. E12 150-1
Marion, Conn. E7 60-1
Marion, Ida. O7 218-9
Marion, Ill. N9 96-7
Marion, Ind. E9 100-1
Marion, Ia. F12 104-5
Marion, Kans. H11 108-9
Marion, Ky. I4 164-5
Marion, La. A5 168-9
Marion, Me. I10 64-5
Marion, Mass. H13 68-9
Marion, Mich. G12 112-3
Marion, Miss. I10 176-7
Marion, Nebr. J7 124-5
Marion, N.C. D5 180-1
Marion, N. Dak. H12 128-9
Marion, O. E6 132-3
Marion, Ore. I1 238-9
Marion, S.C. D14 184-5
Marion, S. Dak. H15 136-7
Marion, Tex. I3 192-3
Marion, Va. J5 196-7
Marion, Wis. D2 140-1
Marion, co., Ala. C3 146-7
Marion, co., Ark. A6 150-1
Marion, co., Fla. D10 156-7
Marion, co., Ga. J3 160-1
Marion, co., Ill. K9 96-7
Marion, co., Ind. H8 100-1
Marion, co., Ia. H9 104-5
Marion, co., Kans. G11 108-9
Marion, co., Ky. H10 164-5
Marion, co., Miss. L7 176-7
Marion, co., Mo. C8 120-1
Marion, co., O. E6 132-3
Marion, co., Ore. D6 238-9
Marion, co., S.C. D14 184-5
Marion, co., Tenn. D9 188-9
Marion, co., Tex. D11 192-3
Marion, co., W. Va. D6 200-1
Marion East*, O. E6 132-3
Marion Forks, Ore. E7 238-9
Marion Heights, Pa. G12 84-5
Marion Junction, Ala. I5 146-7
Marionville, Mo. I4 120-1
Mariposa, Calif. J5 210-1
Mariposa, co., Calif. I5 210-1
Marissa, Ill. L7 96-7
Markdale, Ont. B13 284-5
Marked Tree, Ark. D11 150-1
Markesan, Wis. G2 140-1
Markham, Ill. N4 96-7
Markham, Ont. C15 284-5
Markham, Va. A1 196-7
Markinch, Sask. M8 294-5
Markle, Ind. D10 100-1
Markleeville, Calif. H5 210-1
Markleville, Ind. G10 100-1
Marks, Miss. C6 176-7
Marksboro, N.J. C4 76-7
Markstay*, Ont. G7 284-5
Marksville, La. F5 168-9
Marland, Okla. C11 234-5
Marlboro, Alta. I5 264-5
Marlboro, Me. K8 64-5
Marlboro, N.J. G7 76-7
Marlboro, N.Y. I11 80-1
Marlboro, S.C. C13 184-5
Marlboro, Vt. N6 90-1
Marlboro, co., S.C. C13 184-5
Marlborough, Conn. E11 60-1
Marlborough, Mass. D9 68-9
Marlborough*, Mo. E10 120-1
Marlborough, N.H. O3 72-3
Marlette, Mich. E6 112-3
Marlin, Tex. F9 192-3
Marlinton, W. Va. H7 200-1
Marlow, Ala. O3 146-7
Marlow, Ga. K11 160-1
Marlow, N.H. M3 72-3
Marlow, Okla. H10 234-5
Marlton, N.J. N12 76-7
Marmaduke, Ark. B11 150-1
Marmarth, N. Dak. I1 128-9
Marmet, W. Va. I14 200-1
Marmora, N.J. N5 76-7
Marmora, Ont. J12 284-5
Marne, Ia. H4 104-5
Marne, Mich. I12 112-3
Maroa, Ill. G8 96-7
Marquam, Ore. H2 238-9
Marquand, Mo. H10 120-1
Marquette, Ia. C13 104-5
Marquette, Kans. G10 108-9
Marquette, Man. I13 272-3
Marquette, Mich. C10 112-3
Marquette, Nebr. H12 124-5
Marquette, Wis. G2 140-1
Marquette, co., Mich. D9 112-3
Marquette, co., Wis. H12 140-1
Marquette Heights*, Ill. F7 96-7
Marquis, Sask. N7 294-5
Marrero, La. D14 168-9
Marrowbone, Ky. J9 164-5
Mars, Pa. H2 84-5
Mars Hill*, Me. D9 64-5
Mars Hill, Miss. L5 176-7
Mars Hill, N.C. D4 180-1
Mars Hill [-Blaine], Me. D9 64-5
Marsalis, La. B3 168-9
Marsden, Sask. J4 294-5
Marse, Wyo. H5 250-1
Marseilles, Ill. D9 96-7
Marsh, Mont. E15 222-3
Marsh Corner, Mass. B11 68-9
Marshall, Ark. C6 150-1
Marshall, Ill. I11 96-7
Marshall, Ind. H5 100-1
Marshall, Mich. J13 112-3
Marshall, Minn. N3 116-7
Marshall, Mo. D5 120-1
Marshall, N.C. D4 180-1
Marshall, Okla. D10 234-5
Marshall, Sask. J4 294-5
Marshall, Tex. E11 192-3
Marshall, Ut. F5 242-3
Marshall, Va. A2 196-7
Marshall, Wis. I2 140-1
Marshall, co., Ala. C7 146-7
Marshall, co., Ill. E7 96-7
Marshall, co., Ind. B7 100-1
Marshall, co., Ia. F9 104-5
Marshall, co., Kans. D12 108-9
Marshall, co., Ky. J3 164-5
Marshall, co., Minn. E2 116-7
Marshall, co., Miss. B7 176-7
Marshall, co., Okla. I12 234-5
Marshall, co., S. Dak. A14 136-7
Marshall, co., Tenn. D7 188-9
Marshall, co., W. Va. C5 200-1
Marshallton, Del. B3 153
Marshallton*, Pa. G11 84-5
Marshalltown, Ia. F9 104-5
Marshallville, Ga. J5 160-1
Marshallville, O. E14 132-3
Marshfield, Ind. F4 100-1
Marshfield, Me. J10 64-5
Marshfield, Mass. K8 68-9
Marshfield, Mo. H6 120-1
Marshfield, P.E.I. E7 287
Marshfield, Vt. E7 90-1
Marshfield, Wis. F11 140-1
Marshfield Hills, Mass. K8 68-9
Marshville, N.C. K3 180-1
Marsing, Ida. L2 218-9
Marsland, Nebr. D2 124-5
Marsoui, Que. H6 290-1
Marston, Md. C9 172-3
Marston, Mo. J11 120-1
Marston, N.C. K5 180-1
Marston Corners, Mass. B11 68-9
Mart, Tex. F9 192-3
Martell, Nebr. I14 124-5
Martell, Wis. F7 140-1
Martelle, Ia. F13 104-5
Martensdale, Ia. H7 104-5
Martensville, Sask. K6 294-5
Martha, Okla. G7 234-5
Martha, Tenn. G8 188-9
Martha's Vineyard Isl.,
Mass. I13 68-9
Marthasville, Mo. B13 120-1
Marthaville, La. D2 168-9
Martin, Ga. E6 160-1
Martin, Ky. H15 164-5
Martin, La. C3 168-9
Martin, Mich. J12 112-3
Martin, Miss. H9 176-7
Martin, N. Dak. E8 128-9
Martin, S.C. H9 184-5
Martin, S. Dak. I6 136-7
Martin, Tenn. A3 188-9
Martin, co., Fla. H13 156-7
Martin, co., Ind. M6 100-1
Martin, co., Ky. H15 164-5
Martin, co., Minn. O4 116-7
Martin, co., N.C. D14 180-1
Martin, co., Tex. E4 192-3
Martin City, Mont. B3 222-3
Martinez, Calif. B8 210-1
Martinez, Ga. G9 160-1
Martins Ferry, O. F11 132-3
Martins Point, N.S. E6 281
Martinsburg, Ind. M8 100-1
Martinsburg, Ia. I11 104-5
Martinsburg, Md. G1 172-3
Martinsburg, Mo. D8 120-1
Martinsburg, Nebr. D14 124-5
Martinsburg, Pa. I7 84-5
Martinsburg, W. Va. D11 200-1
Martinsdale, Mont. F8 222-3
Martinsville, Ill. I11 96-7
Martinsville, Ind. J7 100-1
Martinsville, Me. M6 64-5
Martinsville, Miss. J5 176-7
Martinsville, N.J. E5 76-7
Martinsville, O. K16 132-3
Martinsville, Va. J8 196-7
Martintown*, Ont. H16 284-5
Martling, Ala. C8 146-7
Marty, S. Dak. I12 136-7
Marvel, Ala. G6 146-7
Marvel, Colo. J6 214-5
Marvell, Ark. F10 150-1
Marvels Crossroad, Del. H4 153
Marvin, S. Dak. C15 136-7
Marvyn, Ala. I10 146-7
Marwayne, Alta. I10 264-5
Mary Esther, Fla. B4 156-7
Mary Ridge*, Mo. E10 120-1
Marydel, Del. F2 153
Marydel, Md. D14 172-3
Marydell, Miss. G8 176-7
Maryfield, Sask. N11 294-5
Maryhill*, Ont. D13 284-5
Maryhill Estates*, Ky. G9 164-5
Maryland City*, Md. D11 172-3
Maryland Heights*, Mo. E10 120-1
Maryland Line, Md. B11 172-3
Marys Corner, Wash. H7 246-7
Marystown, Nfld. O10 278-9
Marysvale, Ut. K5 242-3
Marysville, Calif. G4 210-1
Marysville, Ida. K11 218-9
Marysville, Ind. M10 100-1
Marysville, Ia. I9 104-5
Marysville, Kans. D12 108-9
Marysville, Mich. G8 112-3
Marysville, Mont. E5 222-3
Marysville, O. F6 132-3
Marysville, Pa. I10 84-5
Marysville, Wash. F3 246-7
Marytown, Wis. G4 140-1
Maryus, Va. F4 196-7
Maryville, Ill. K6 96-7
Maryville, Mo. A2 120-1
Maryville, S.C. G15 184-5
Maryville, Tenn. C12 188-9
Masardis, Me. D8 64-5
Mascot, Nebr. J9 124-5
Mascot, Tenn. H12 188-9
Mascot, Va. D3 196-7
Mascotte, Fla. F5 156-7
Mascouche*, Que. I12 290-1
Mascoutah, Ill. L7 96-7
Mashapaug, Conn. A13 60-1
Mashpee, Mass. H14 68-9
Mashulaville, Miss. G9 176-7
Maskell, Nebr. D13 124-5
Maskinongé*, Que. H13 290-1
Maskinongé, co., Que. I2 290-1
Mason, Mich. I1 112-3
Mason, Nev. G3 226-7
Mason, N.H. O5 72-3
Mason, O. K14 132-3
Mason, Okla. E13 234-5
Mason, Tenn. K2 188-9
Mason, Tex. F7 192-3
Mason, W. Va. E2 200-1
Mason, Wis. B10 140-1
Mason, co., Ill. G7 96-7
Mason, co., Ky. F13 164-5
Mason, co., Mich. G11 112-3
Mason, co., Tex. G7 192-3
Mason, co., Wash. F6 246-7
Mason, co., W. Va. F2 200-1
Mason City, Ill. G7 96-7
Mason City, Ia. B8 104-5
Mason City, Nebr. G9 124-5
Mason Hall, Tenn. B3 188-9
Masontown, Pa. K2 84-5
Masontown, W. Va. B16 200-1
Masonville, Ark. I9 150-1
Masonville, Colo. D2 214-5
Masonville, Ia. E12 104-5
Masonville, N.J. I4 76-7
Mass, Mich. C8 112-3
Massac, co., Ill. O9 96-7
Massachusetts Bay, Mass. D13 68-9
Massapequa, N.Y. F16 80-1
Massapequa Park*, N.Y. K11 80-1
Massena, Ia. I5 104-5
Massena, N.Y. A9 80-1
Masset, B.C. F2 268-9
Massey, Md. C14 172-3
Massey, Ont. H7 284-5
Masseys Landing, Del. J6 153
Massie, Nev. F3 226-7
Massies Mill, Va. H9 196-7
Massillon, O. F15 132-3
Massueville*, Que. I13 290-1
Mastens Corner, Del. G3 153
Mastic Beach, N.Y. J13 80-1
Masury, O. C12 132-3
Matachewan, Ont. G7 284-5
Matador, Tex. C5 192-3
Matagami, Que. H1 290-1
Matagorda, co., Tex. H10 192-3
Matamoras, Pa. E16 84-5
Matane, Que. B16 290-1
Matane, co., Que. H5 290-1
Matapédia*, Que. I5 290-1
Matapédia, co., Que. I5 290-1
Matawan*, N.J. H9 76-7
Matawan, N.J. H9 76-7
Matewan, W. Va. J2 200-1
Matfield Green, Kans. H12 108-9
Mather, Calif. I5 210-1
Mather, Man. K12 272-3
Mather, Wis. G11 140-1
Matherville, Ill. D5 96-7
Matherville, Miss. J10 176-7
Matheson, Colo. F13 214-5
Matheson, Ont. F7 284-5
Matheson Island, Man. F14 272-3
Mathews, La. E12 168-9
Mathews, Va. I14 196-7
Mathews, co., Va. H14 196-7
Mathews Corner, Del. D3 153
Mathias, W. Va. F9 200-1
Mathis, Tex. I8 192-3
Mathiston, Miss. E8 176-7
Matinecock*, N.Y. J11 80-1
Matinicus, Me. M7 64-5
Matinicus Isle*, Me. M7 64-5
Matlock, Ia. B2 104-5

Matlock, Wash. F6 246-7
Matoaca*, Va. I12 196-7
Matoaka, W. Va. J4 200-1
Matoy, Okla. I13 234-5
Mattapoisett, Mass. H13 68-9
Mattaponi, Va. E3 196-7
Mattawa, Ont. H8 284-5
Mattawa, Wash. H12 246-7
Mattawamkeag, Me. G8 64-5
Mattawan*, Mich. J12 112-3
Matteson, Ill. O4 96-7
Matthews, Ga. H8 160-1
Matthews, Ind. F10 100-1
Matthews, Md. F13 172-3
Matthews, Mo. I12 120-1
Matthews, N.C. K2 180-1
Mattice, Ont. E6 284-5
Mattituck, N.Y. J13 80-1
Mattoon, Ill. I10 96-7
Mattoon, Wis. E13 140-1
Mattson, Miss. D5 176-7
Mattydale*, N.Y. E7 80-1
Matunuck, R.I. I4 87
Mauckport, Ind. O8 100-1
Maud, Ky. D4 164-5
Maud, Okla. F12 234-5
Maud, Tex. D11 192-3
Maudlow, Mont. G7 222-3
Maugansville*, Md. A7 172-3
Maui [including Kalawao], co., Hawaii F10 258-9
Maui Isl., Hawaii F10 258-9
Mauldin, S.C. G2 184-5
Maumee, O. B5 132-3
Maumee Bay, O. A5 132-3
Mauna Loa, Hawaii I12 258-9
Maunaloa, Hawaii F9 258-9
Maunalua, Hawaii K7 258-9
Maunawai, Hawaii G3 258-9
Maunawili, Hawaii J6 258-9
Maupin, Ore. C9 238-9
Maurepas, La. B12 168-9
Maurertown, Va. E10 196-7
Maurice, Ia. C1 104-5
Maurice, La. H5 168-9
Maurice River*, N.J. N3 76-7
Mauricetown, N.J. N3 76-7
Maury, N.C. E13 180-1
Maury, co., Tenn. C7 188-9
Maury City, Tenn. I3 188-9
Mauston, Wis. H11 140-1
Maverick, Ariz. H11 206-7
Maverick, co., Tex. H6 192-3
Max, Nebr. J5 124-5
Max, N. Dak. E6 128-9
Max Meadows, Va. J6 196-7
Maxbass, N. Dak. C6 128-9
Maxeys, Ga. G6 160-1
Maxfield, Me. H7 64-5
Maxie, La. H4 168-9
Maxie, Miss. M 176-7
Maxie, Va. I4 196-7
Maxton, N.C. F10 180-1
Maxville, Mont. F4 222-3
Maxville, Ore. B15 238-9
Maxwell, Calif. G3 210-1
Maxwell, Ind. H9 100-1
Maxwell, Ia. G8 104-5
Maxwell, Nebr. H7 124-5
Maxwell, N. Mex. C9 230-1
Maxwell, Okla. G12 234-5
Maxwell Colony, S. Dak. H14 136-7
Maxwell Station, Ut. H8 242-3
Maxwelton, W. Va. I6 200-1
May, Ida. J7 218-9
May, Okla. C7 234-5
May City, Ia. B3 104-5
May Park*, Ore. C14 238-9
Maybank, Miss. K 176-7
Maybee, Mich. K14 112-3
Maybell, Colo. C7 214-5
Maybeury-Switchback*, W. Va. J3 200-1
Maybrook*, N.Y. I10 80-1
Mayday, Colo. I6 214-5
Mayday, Ga. N7 160-1
Mayer, Ariz. G6 206-7
Mayer, Minn. B8 116-7
Mayersville, Miss. G4 176-7
Mayerthorpe, Alta. I6 264-5
Mayes, co., Okla. D15 234-5
Mayesville, S.C. E12 184-5
Mayetta, Kans. E14 108-9
Mayfair, Sask. J6 294-5
Mayfield, Kans. J10 108-9
Mayfield, Ky. J3 164-5
Mayfield, Mich. F12 112-3
Mayfield, N.Y. E10 80-1
Mayfield*, O. B10 132-3
Mayfield, Okla. F6 234-5
Mayfield, Pa. E14 84-5
Mayfield, P.E.I. D6 287
Mayfield, Ut. I6 242-3
Mayfield Heights, O. B15 132-3
Mayflower, Ark. H15 150-1
Mayflower Heights, Mass. E15 68-9
Mayger, Ore. A6 238-9
Mayhew, Miss. E10 176-7
Mayhill, N. Mex. K8 230-1
Mayking, Ky. I15 164-5
Mayland, Tenn. B10 188-9
Maylene, Ala. F6 146-7
Maymont, Sask. K5 294-5
Mayna, La. E6 168-9
Maynard, Ark. A10 150-1
Maynard, Ia. D12 104-5
Maynard, Ky. J8 164-5
Maynard, Mass. G2 68-9
Maynard, Minn. M3 116-7
Maynardville, Tenn. G12 188-9
Mayne, B.C. D13 268-9
Mayo, Fla. C9 156-7
Mayo, Md. J7 172-3
Mayo, S.C. A8 184-5
Mayo, Va. K10 196-7
Mayo, Y.T. B2 297
Mayodan, N.C. C8 180-1
Mayoworth, Wyo. D12 250-1
Mays, Ind. H10 100-1
Mays Landing, N.J. M5 76-7
Maysville, Ark. A1 150-1
Maysville, Colo. G10 214-5
Maysville, Ga. E6 160-1
Maysville, Ia. G15 104-5
Maysville, Ky. F13 164-5
Maysville, Mo. B3 120-1
Maysville, N.C. F13 180-1
Maysville, Okla. G11 234-5
Maysville, W. Va. E9 200-1
Maytown*, Ala. F6 146-7
Maytown, Wash. G7 246-7
Mayview*, Mo. D4 120-1
Mayville, Mich. E5 112-3
Mayville, N.J. O4 76-7
Mayville, N.Y. G1 80-1
Mayville, N. Dak. F13 128-9
Mayville, Ore. D10 238-9
Mayville, Wis. H3 140-1
Maywood*, Calif. G8 210-1
Maywood, Ill. M3 96-7
Maywood, Nebr. I7 124-5
Maywood, N.J. B11 76-7
Maywood Park*, Ore. C6 238-9
Maza, N. Dak. C10 128-9
Mazama, Wash. C11 246-7
Mazenod, Sask. O7 294-5
Mazeppa, Minn. N7 116-7
Mazie, Okla. D15 234-5
Mazomanie, Wis. J12 140-1
Mazon, Ill. D9 96-7
McAdam, N.B. I3 275
McAdams, Miss. G7 176-7
McAdenville*, N.C. E6 180-1
McAdoo, Pa. G13 84-5
McAfee, Miss. H8 176-7
McAfee, N.J. B6 76-7
McAlester, Okla. G14 234-5
McAlister, N. Mex. G10 230-1
McAllen, Tex. K8 192-3
McAllister, Mont. H6 222-3
McAlpin, W. Va. C14 200-1
McArthur, Ark. I9 150-1
McArthur, Calif. E4 210-1
McArthur, O. H7 132-3
McAuley, Man. I9 272-3
McBain, Mich. G12 112-3
McBee, S.C. C12 184-5
McBeth, S.C. G13 184-5
McBride, B.C. G8 268-9
McBride*, Okla. I12 234-5
McBrides, Mich. H12 112-3
McBurg, Tenn. K7 188-9
McCabe, Mont. B16 222-3
McCain, N.C. K5 180-1
McCains, Tenn. J6 188-9
McCall, Ida. J3 218-9
McCall Creek, Miss. K5 176-7
McCalla, Ala. F6 146-7
McCallsburg, Ia. F8 104-5
McCallum, Miss. L8 176-7
McCamey, Tex. F4 192-3
McCammon, Ida. N9 218-9
McCanna, N. Dak. D13 128-9
McCarley, Miss. E 176-7
McCarthy, Alaska F13 254-5
McCartys, N. Mex. F4 230-1
McCaskill, Ark. H3 150-1
McCausland, Ia. G15 104-5
McCaysville, Ga. C4 160-1
McChesneytown-Loyalhanna*, Pa. I4 84-5
McChord*, Wash. K2 246-7
McClain, co., Okla. G10 234-5
McClave, Colo. H15 214-5
McCleary, Wash. G6 246-7
McClelland, Ia. H3 104-5
McClellandville, Del. B2 153
McClellanville, S.C. H14 184-5
McClintock, Man. C5 272-3
McCloud, Calif. E3 210-1
McCloud, Tenn. G15 188-9
McClure, O. B4 132-3
McClure, Pa. H9 84-5
McClure, Va. I3 196-7
McClusky, N. Dak. F8 128-9
McColl, S.C. B14 184-5
McComb, Miss. L5 176-7
McComb, O. C5 132-3
McComb South, Miss. L5 176-7
McCondy, Miss. D9 176-7
McCone, co., Mont. D14 222-3
McConnells, S.C. B9 184-5
McConnellsburg, Pa. J7 84-5
McConnelsville, O. G9 132-3
McConnico, Ariz. E3 206-7
McCook, Nebr. J7 124-5
McCook, co., S. Dak. G14 136-7
McCookville, Tenn. I13 188-9
McCool, Miss. F8 176-7
McCool Junction, Nebr. H12 124-5
McCoole, Md. C3 172-3
McCord, Sask. O6 294-5
McCordsville, Ind. E3 100-1
McCorkle, W. Va. I13 200-1
McCormick, S.C. E7 184-5
McCormick, co., S.C. E6 184-5
McCormmach, Ore. B13 238-9
McCoy, Colo. D9 214-5
McCoy, Va. I7 196-7
McCracken, Kans. G6 108-9
McCracken, co., Ky. J3 164-5
McCreary, Man. H11 272-3
McCreary, co., Ky. J11 164-5
McCredie Springs, Ore. G7 238-9
McCrory, Ark. D9 150-1
McCulloch, co., Tex. F7 192-3
McCullom Lake, Ill. J1 96-7
McCullough, Ala. L4 146-7
McCune, Kans. J16 108-9
McCurtain, Okla. F15 234-5
McCurtain, co., Okla. H16 234-5
McDade, La. C2 168-9
McDaniel, Md. F12 172-3
McDaniels, Ky. H7 164-5
McDermitt, Nev. A5 226-7
McDonald, Kans. D2 108-9
McDonald, Miss. H8 176-7
McDonald, N. Mex. J11 230-1
McDonald, N.C. G10 180-1
McDonald, O. C11 132-3
McDonald, Pa. B5 84-5
McDonald, Tenn. K12 188-9
McDonald, co., Mo. J3 120-1
McDonough, Del. C3 153
McDonough, Ga. G4 160-1
McDonough, co., Ill. F5 96-7
McDougal, Ark. A11 150-1
McDowell, Va. G9 196-7
McDowell, W. Va. J4 200-1
McDowell, co., N.C. E5 180-1
McDowell, co., W. Va. J2 200-1
McDuffie, co., Ga. G8 160-1
McEwen, Tenn. B6 188-9
McFadden, Wyo. I13 250-1
McFall, Mo. B3 120-1
McFarlan, N.C. F8 180-1
McFarland, Calif. L6 210-1
McFarland, Kans. F13 108-9
McFarland, Wis. J1 140-1
McGaffey, N. Mex. E2 230-1
McGaheysville, Va. F10 196-7
McGehee, Ark. I9 150-1
McGhee, Tenn. J14 188-9
McGill, Nev. F10 226-7
McGinty, La. A6 168-9
McGivney, N.B. H4 275
McGrady, N.C. C6 180-1
McGrath, Alaska E10 254-5
McGrath, Minn. J6 116-7
McGraw, N.Y. F7 80-1
McGraws, W. Va. I3 200-1
McGregor, Ia. C13 104-5
McGregor, Minn. I6 116-7
McGregor, N. Dak. C3 128-9
McGregor*, Ont. G10 284-5
McGregor, Tex. F8 192-3
McGrew, Nebr. F2 124-5
McGuffey, O. D5 132-3
McGuire*, N.J. I5 76-7
McGuireville, Ariz. F7 206-7
McHenry, Ill. J1 96-7
McHenry, Ky. I6 164-5
McHenry, Md. B2 172-3
McHenry, Miss. N 176-7
McHenry, N. Dak. F11 128-9
McHenry, co., Ill. A10 96-7
McHenry, co., N. Dak. D7 128-9
McHenry Shores*, Ill. J1 96-7
McIllwain, Tenn. C5 188-9
McIndoe Falls, Vt. F8 90-1
McIntire, Ia. A10 104-5
McIntosh, Ala. L3 146-7
McIntosh, Fla. D10 156-7
McIntosh, Ga. L10 160-1
McIntosh, Minn. G3 116-7
McIntosh, N. Mex. F7 230-1
McIntosh, Ont. E1 284-5
McIntosh, S. Dak. A6 136-7
McIntosh, co., Ga. M10 160-1
McIntosh, co., N. Dak. I10 128-9
McIntosh, co., Okla. F14 234-5
McIntyre, Ga. I6 160-1
McKague, Sask. K9 294-5
McKamie, Ark. J4 150-1
McKean, co., Pa. D5 84-5
McKee, Ky. I12 164-5
McKee City, N.J. M5 76-7
McKees Rocks*, Pa. H2 84-5
McKeesport, Pa. B7 84-5
McKellar, Ont. H8 284-5
McKendrick, N.B. D4 275
McKenna, Wash. G7 246-7
McKenney, Va. J12 196-7
McKennon, S.C. C12 184-5
McKenzie, Ala. K6 146-7
McKenzie, N. Dak. H8 128-9
McKenzie, Tenn. B4 188-9
McKenzie, co., N. Dak. E2 128-9
McKenzie Bridge, Ore. F7 238-9
McKey, Okla. F15 234-5
McKinley, Ala. I4 146-7
McKinley, Me. L8 64-5
McKinley, Minn. G8 116-7
McKinley, Tenn. G16 188-9
McKinley, Wyo. G15 250-1
McKinley, co., N. Mex. E3 230-1
McKinley Park, Alaska E11 254-5
McKinleyville, Calif. E1 210-1
McKinney, Ky. I11 164-5
McKinney, Tex. B15 192-3
McKinnon, Tenn. B5 188-9
McKinnon, Wyo. K6 250-1
McKittrick, Mo. E8 120-1
McKnight, Okla. G6 234-5
McLain, Miss. L9 176-7
McLain, Okla. E15 234-5
McLaughlin, S. Dak. A7 136-7
McLaurin, Miss. L8 176-7
McLean, Ill. G8 96-7
McLean, Nebr. D12 124-5
McLean*, Sask. N8 294-5
McLean, Tex. B6 192-3
McLean, Va. A4 196-7
McLean, co., Ill. F9 96-7
McLean, co., Ky. I6 164-5
McLean, co., N. Dak. E6 128-9
McLeansboro, Ill. M9 96-7
McLeansville, N.C. H5 180-1
McLemoresville, Tenn. B4 188-9
McLennan, Alta. G5 264-5
McLennan, co., Tex. F8 192-3
McLeod, Mont. G8 222-3
McLeod, N. Dak. I13 128-9
McLeod, co., Minn. M5 116-7
McLeod Lake, B.C. F7 268-9
McLeod Subdivision*, B.C. E7 268-9
McLeods, N.B. D4 275
McLoud, Okla. J3 234-5
McLouth, Kans. E15 108-9
McLure, B.C. I8 268-9
McMan, Okla. H11 234-5
McMasterville*, Que. I12 290-1
McMechen, W. Va. C5 200-1
McMillan, Mich. D12 112-3
McMillan, Miss. F8 176-7
McMillan, Okla. I12 234-5
McMillin, Wash. K3 246-7
McMinn, co., Tenn. D11 188-9
McMinnville, Ore. G1 238-9
McMinnville, Tenn. C9 188-9
McMullen, co., Tex. I7 192-3
McMunn*, Man. J5 272-3
McMurray, Wash. E3 246-7
McNab, Ark. I3 150-1
McNair, Miss. K4 176-7
McNair, Tex. H15 192-3
McNairy, Tenn. D4 188-9
McNairy, co., Tenn. D4 188-9
McNary, Ariz. G10 206-7
McNary, La. F4 168-9
McNary, Ore. B12 238-9
McNeal, Ariz. M10 206-7
McNeil, Ark. J4 150-1
McNeill, Miss. N7 176-7
McNulty*, Ore. B6 238-9
McNutt, La. E4 168-9
McPherson, Kans. G10 108-9
McPherson, co., Kans. G10 108-9
McPherson, co., Nebr. F6 124-5
McPherson, co., S. Dak. A10 136-7
McPhersonville, S.C. I10 184-5
McQuady, Ky. H7 164-5
McQueen, Okla. H7 234-5
McQueen-East Butte*, Mont. G5 222-3
McRae, Ark. E8 150-1
McRae, Ga. K7 160-1
McRoberts, Ky. I15 164-5
McShan, Ala. F3 146-7
McSherrystown, Pa. K10 84-5
McTaggart, Sask. O9 294-5
McTavish*, Man. K3 272-3
McVeigh, Ky. H16 164-5
McVille, Ala. C8 146-7
McVille, Miss. G7 176-7
McVille, N. Dak. E12 128-9
McWhorter, W. Va. D13 200-1
McWilliams, Ala. J5 146-7
McWillie, Okla. C9 234-5
Meacham, Ore. C13 238-9
Meacham, Sask. L7 294-5
Mead, Colo. E3 214-5
Mead, Nebr. J1 124-5
Mead, Okla. I13 234-5
Mead, Wash. E16 246-7
Mead, W. Va. J4 200-1
Meade, Kans. J4 108-9
Meade, Mich. H7 112-3
Meade, co., Kans. J4 108-9
Meade, co., Ky. G8 164-5
Meade, co., S. Dak. E3 136-7
Meade River, Alaska A10 254-5
Meador, W. Va. J2 200-1
Meadow, S. Dak. B5 136-7
Meadow, Ut. J5 242-3
Meadow Bank*, P.E.I. F7 287
Meadow Bridge, W. Va. I5 200-1
Meadow Creek, Ida. A3 218-9
Meadow Creek, W. Va. I5 200-1
Meadow Creek, Wyo. E13 250-1
Meadow Grove, Nebr. E12 124-5
Meadow Lake, Sask. I5 294-5
Meadow Vale*, Ky. G9 164-5
Meadow Vista, Calif. H4 210-1
Meadow Vista*, N. Mex. M6 230-1
Meadowbrook*, B.C. J10 268-9
Meadowbrook*, Ill. J6 96-7
Meadowbrook, W. Va. C13 200-1
Meadowdale, Wyo. G15 250-1
Meadowlands, Minn. H7 116-7
Meadowlands [-McGovern], Pa. I1 84-5
Meadows, Ida. I3 218-9
Meadows, N.H. F7 72-3
Meadows of Dan, Va. J7 196-7
Meadowview, Va. J4 196-7
Meadowview Estates*, Ky. G9 164-5
Meadowville, Ut. C7 242-3
Meadville, Miss. K4 176-7
Meadville, Mo. C5 120-1
Meadville, Pa. D2 84-5
Meaford, Ont. A13 284-5
Meagher, co., Mont. F7 222-3
Meakerville, Alaska F12 254-5
Meally, Ky. H15 164-5
Meansville, Ga. H4 160-1
Mears, Mich. H11 112-3
Meath Park, Sask. J7 294-5

Meaux, La. H5 168-9
Mebane*, N.C. C10 180-1
Mecca, Ind. H4 100-1
Mechanic Falls, Me. M8 64-5
Mechanicsburg, Ind. G7 100-1
Mechanicsburg, Ind. G10 100-1
Mechanicsburg, O. F5 132-3
Mechanicsburg, Pa. I10 84-5
Mechanicsville, Conn. B14 60-1
Mechanicsville, Del. B2 153
Mechanicsville, Ia. F13 104-5
Mechanicsville, Md. G10 172-3
Mechanicsville, Pa. G11 84-5
Mechanicsville, S.C. D13 184-5
Mechanicsville, Vt. F4 90-1
Mechanicsville*, Va. H13 196-7
Mechanicville, N.Y. F11 80-1
Mecklenburg, co., N.C. E7 180-1
Mecklenburg, co., Va. J10 196-7
Meckling, S. Dak. I15 136-7
Mecosta, Mich. H12 112-3
Mecosta, co., Mich. H12 112-3
Medaryville, Ind. C6 100-1
Meddybemps, Me. I10 64-5
Medfield, Mass. J3 68-9
Medford, Me. H7 64-5
Medford, Mass. G4 68-9
Medford, Minn. N6 116-7
Medford, N.J. J4 76-7
Medford, Okla. C10 234-5
Medford, Ore. J6 238-9
Medford, Tenn. G11 188-9
Medford, Wis. E11 140-1
Medford Lakes, N.J. J4 76-7
Medford West*, Ore. J6 238-9
Medfra, Alaska E10 254-5
Media, Pa. J15 84-5
Mediapolis, Ia. I14 104-5
Medical Lake, Wash. F15 246-7
Medical Springs, Ore. D15 238-9
Medicine Bow, Wyo. I13 250-1
Medicine Hat, Alta. N10 264-5
Medicine Lake*, Minn. M6 116-7
Medicine Lake, Mont. B15 222-3
Medicine Lake, Mont. B15 222-3
Medicine Lodge, Kans. J8 108-9
Medicine Park, Okla. G9 234-5
Medicine Springs, Mont. G3 222-3
Medimont, Ida. D3 218-9
Medina, Minn. A9 116-7
Medina, N.Y. E3 80-1
Medina, N. Dak. G10 128-9
Medina, O. C9 132-3
Medina, Tenn. C3 188-9
Medina, Wash. I3 246-7
Medina, Wis. E3 140-1
Medina, co., O. C9 132-3
Medina, co., Tex. H7 192-3
Medley*, Fla. J13 156-7
Medley, W. Va. E9 200-1
Medomak, Me. M5 64-5
Medon, Tenn. J4 188-9
Medora, Ind. L8 100-1
Medora, Kans. H10 108-9
Medora, Man. K10 272-3
Medora, N. Dak. G2 128-9
Medstead, Sask. J5 294-5
Meductic, N.B. H3 275
Medway, Me. G7 64-5
Medway, Mass. K2 68-9
Meeker, Colo. D7 214-5
Meeker, La. F4 168-9
Meeker, Okla. J4 234-5
Meeker, co., Minn. L4 116-7
Meeker Park, Colo. E1 214-5
Meers, Okla. G9 234-5
Meeteetse, Wyo. C8 250-1
Mégantic, co., Que. H15 290-1
Megargel, Ala. L4 146-7
Meggett, S.C. I12 184-5
Mehama, Ore. I2 238-9
Mehan, Okla. D12 234-5
Meherrin, Va. I11 196-7
Meigs, Ga. N4 160-1
Meigs, co., O. I8 132-3
Meigs, co., Tenn. C11 188-9
Meiners Oaks [-Mira Monte], Calif. F6 210-1
Meire Grove, Minn. K4 116-7
Mekinock, N. Dak. D13 128-9
Mekoryuk, Alaska F7 254-5
Melba, Ida. M3 218-9
Melber, Ky. J2 164-5
Melbeta, Nebr. F1 124-5
Melbourne, Ark. B8 150-1
Melbourne, Fla. F13 156-7
Melbourne, Ia. F9 104-5
Melbourne*, Ky. E11 164-5
Melbourne, Ont. E12 284-5
Melbourne, Que. I14 290-1
Melbourne, Wash. G6 246-7
Melbourne Beach*, Fla. F13 156-7
Melbourne Village, Fla. F12 156-7
Melcher, Ia. I8 104-5
Melder, La. F4 168-9
Meldrim, Ga. K11 160-1
Meldrum Bay, Ont. H6 284-5
Meleb, Man. H14 272-3
Melfa, Va. H15 196-7
Melfort, Sask. J8 294-5
Melita, Man. K9 272-3
Mellen, Wis. B10 140-1
Mellette, Okla. F14 234-5
Mellette, S. Dak. C12 136-7
Mellette, co., S. Dak. G7 136-7
Mellott, Ind. G5 100-1
Mellow Valley, Ala. F9 146-7
Mellwood, Ark. G10 150-1
Melocheville*, Que. J12 290-1
Melrose, Conn. B10 60-1
Melrose, Ia. I9 104-5
Melrose, La. D3 168-9
Melrose, Md. B10 172-3
Melrose, Mass. G5 68-9
Melrose, Minn. K4 116-7
Melrose, Mont. G5 222-3
Melrose, N.B. H8 275
Melrose, N. Mex. G11 230-1
Melrose, O. C3 132-3
Melrose, Ore. H5 238-9
Melrose, Wis. G10 140-1
Melrose Park*, Fla. I13 156-7
Melrose Park, Ill. M3 96-7
Melrose Park, N.Y. F6 80-1
Melstone, Mont. F11 222-3
Melton, Ala. H4 146-7
Melton, Miss. J4 176-7
Meltonia, Miss. E4 176-7
Melvern, Kans. G14 108-9
Melvern Square, N.S. D5 281
Melville, La. G6 168-9
Melville, Mont. G8 222-3
Melville*, N.Y. J12 80-1
Melville, Sask. M10 294-5
Melvin, Ala. J2 146-7
Melvin, Ia. B3 104-5
Melvin, Mich. F7 112-3
Melvin Mills, N.H. L5 72-3
Melvin Village, N.H. J7 72-3
Melvina, Wis. H10 140-1
Melvindale, Mich. J6 112-3
Memphis, Fla. J2 156-7
Memphis, Ind. M9 100-1
Memphis, Mich. G7 112-3
Memphis, Mo. A7 120-1
Memphis, Nebr. J1 124-5
Memphis, Tenn. D1 188-9
Memphis, Tex. B6 192-3
Memramcook East*, N.B. H7 275
Mena, Ark. F2 150-1
Menahga, Minn. I4 116-7
Menan, Ida. L10 218-9
Menands, N.Y. F11 80-1
Menard, Mont. G7 222-3
Menard, Tex. F6 192-3
Menard, co., Ill. G6 96-7
Menard, co., Tex. F6 192-3
Menasha, Wis. F3 140-1
Mendenhall, Miss. J7 176-7
Mendes, Ga. K9 160-1
Mendham*, N.J. D5 76-7
Mendham, N.J. D5 76-7
Mendham, Sask. M4 294-5
Mendocino, Calif. G1 210-1
Mendocino, co., Calif. G2 210-1
Mendon, Ill. G4 96-7
Mendon, Mass. K1 68-9
Mendon*, Mich. K12 112-3
Mendon, Mo. C5 120-1
Mendon, O. D3 132-3
Mendon*, Ut. C6 242-3
Mendon, Vt. J5 90-1
Mendota, Calif. J5 210-1
Mendota, Ill. C8 96-7
Mendota, Minn. B11 116-7
Mendota, Va. J3 196-7
Mendota Heights, Minn. B11 116-7
Menemsha, Mass. J13 68-9
Menifee, Ark. E6 150-1
Menifee, co., Ky. G13 164-5
Menlo, Ga. E1 160-1
Menlo, Ia. H6 104-5
Menlo, Kans. E4 108-9
Menlo, Wash. H6 246-7
Menlo Park, Calif. D8 210-1
Menno, S. Dak. H14 136-7
Meno, Okla. D9 234-5
Menoken, N. Dak. H7 128-9
Menominee, Mich. F9 112-3
Menominee, Nebr. C13 124-5
Menominee, co., Mich. E9 112-3
Menominee, co., Wis. E13 140-1
Menomonee Falls, Wis. I4 140-1
Menomonie, Wis. F8 140-1
Mentasta, Alaska E12 254-5
Mentmore, N. Mex. E2 230-1
Mentone, Ala. B9 146-7
Mentone, Ind. C8 100-1
Mentone, Tex. E3 192-3
Mentor, Kans. F10 108-9
Mentor, Ky. E12 164-5
Mentor, Minn. G2 116-7
Mentor, O. A16 132-3
Mentor-on-the-Lake, O. A16 132-3
Meota, Sask. J5 294-5
Mequon, Wis. I5 140-1
Mer Rouge, La. A6 168-9
Meramec R., Mo. G8 120-1
Merced, Calif. D11 210-1
Merced, co., Calif. J4 210-1
Mercedes, Tex. K8 192-3
Mercer, Me. J4 64-5
Mercer, Mo. A5 120-1
Mercer, N. Dak. F7 128-9
Mercer, Pa. F1 84-5
Mercer, Tenn. J4 188-9
Mercer, Wis. C11 140-1
Mercer, co., Ill. D5 96-7
Mercer, co., Ky. H10 164-5
Mercer, co., Mo. A4 120-1
Mercer, co., N.J. H5 76-7
Mercer, co., N. Dak. F5 128-9
Mercer, co., O. E3 132-3
Mercer, co., Pa. E1 84-5
Mercer, co., W. Va. J4 200-1
Mercer Island, Wash. I3 246-7
Mercersburg, Pa. K8 84-5
Mercerville [-Hamilton Square], N.J. H5 76-7
Merchant, S.C. E8 184-5
Merchantville, N.J. M11 76-7
Mercier, Kans. D14 108-9
Mercier*, Que. J12 290-1
Mercury, Nev. L8 226-7
Meredith, Colo. E9 214-5
Meredith, N.H. J7 72-3
Meredith Center, N.H. J6 72-3
Meredithville, Va. I11 196-7
Meredosia, Ill. H5 96-7
Meriden, Conn. F8 60-1
Meriden, Ia. C3 104-5
Meriden, Kans. E14 108-9
Meriden, N.H. K3 72-3
Meriden, Wyo. I16 250-1
Meridian, Ga. M11 160-1
Meridian, Ida. L3 218-9
Meridian, Miss. I10 176-7
Meridian, Okla. E11 234-5
Meridian, Pa. G2 84-5
Meridian, Tex. E8 192-3
Meridian Station*, Miss. I10 176-7
Meridianville, Ala. A7 146-7
Merigold, Miss. D5 176-7
Merino, Colo. C14 214-5
Merino, Mont. D8 222-3
Merino Village*, Mass. F8 68-9
Merion*, Pa. J15 84-5
Meriwether, S.C. F7 184-5
Meriwether, co., Ga. H3 160-1
Merkel, Tex. E6 192-3
Merlin*, Ont. F11 284-5
Merlin, Ore. J5 238-9
Mermaid*, P.E.I. E8 287
Mermentau, La. H4 168-9
Merna, Nebr. G8 124-5
Merna, Wyo. F6 250-1
Merom, Ind. K4 100-1
Merriam, Kans. F16 108-9
Merrick, N.Y. F16 80-1
Merrick, co., Nebr. G12 124-5
Merrickville, Ont. I14 284-5
Merricourt, N. Dak. I11 128-9
Merriewold Lake*, N.Y. I10 80-1
Merrifield, Minn. J5 116-7
Merrill, Ia. D1 104-5
Merrill, Me. E8 64-5
Merrill, Mich. E2 112-3
Merrill, Miss. M9 176-7
Merrill, Ore. K8 238-9
Merrill, Wis. E12 140-1
Merrillan, Wis. G10 140-1
Merrillville, Ga. N5 160-1
Merrillville, Ind. B5 100-1
Merrimac, Mass. A12 68-9
Merrimac, Wis. H1 140-1
Merrimack, N.H. O7 72-3
Merrimack, co., N.H. L6 72-3
Merrimack R., N.H. L6 72-3
Merrimacport, Mass. A12 68-9
Merriman, Nebr. C5 124-5
Merrionette Park*, Ill. C11 96-7
Merritt, B.C. J8 268-9
Merritt, Mich. G12 112-3
Merritt, N.C. F14 180-1
Merritt Island, Fla. F12 156-7
Merriweather, Mich. C7 112-3
Merrow, Conn. C11 60-1
Merry Hill, N.C. D14 180-1
Merry Oaks, N.C. I6 180-1
Merry Point, Va. H14 196-7
Merryville, La. F2 168-9
Mershon, Ga. M9 160-1
Merton*, Wis. J14 140-1
Mertzon, Tex. F5 192-3
Merville*, B.C. J5 268-9
Mervin, Sask. J4 294-5
Merwin, Mo. F3 120-1
Mesa, Ariz. I7 206-7
Mesa, Colo. F6 214-5
Mesa, Ida. J3 218-9
Mesa, Wash. H13 246-7
Mesa, co., Colo. F6 214-5
Mesachie Lake, B.C. K6 268-9
Mescal, Ariz. L9 206-7
Mescalero, N. Mex. J7 230-1
Mesena, Ga. G8 160-1
Meservey, Ia. C8 104-5
Mesic*, N.C. E14 180-1
Mesick, Mich. G12 112-3
Mesilla, N. Mex. L5 230-1
Mesilla Park, N. Mex. L5 230-1
Mesita, Colo. J11 214-5
Mesita, N. Mex. F4 230-1
Meskanaw, Sask. K8 294-5
Mesquite, Nev. L11 226-7
Mesquite, N. Mex. L5 230-1
Mesquite, Tex. C15 192-3
Messer, Okla. I15 234-5
Meta, Mo. F7 120-1
Métabetchouan*, Que. C10 290-1
Metairie, La. C14 168-9
Metaline, Wash. C16 246-7
Metaline Falls, Wash. B16 246-7
Metamora, Ill. E8 96-7
Metamora, Ind. I11 100-1
Metamora, Mich. G5 112-3
Metamora, O. A4 132-3
Metasville, Ga. G8 160-1
Metcalf, Ga. O5 160-1
Metcalfe, Miss. F4 176-7
Metcalfe*, Ont. H14 284-5
Metcalfe, co., Ky. J9 164-5
Metchosin, B.C. E12 268-9
Meteghan, N.S. F4 281
Meteghan River, N.S. F4 281
Methow, Wash. D11 246-7
Methuen, Mass. B11 68-9
Methvin, La. C3 168-9
Metiskow, Alta. K10 264-5
Metlakatla, Alaska H16 254-5
Metolius, Ore. E9 238-9
Metropolis, Ill. O9 96-7
Metropolis, Nev. C9 226-7
Metter, Ga. J9 160-1
Metuchen, N.J. F6 76-7
Metz, Mich. E14 112-3
Metz, Mo. G3 120-1
Metz, W. Va. B13 200-1
Mexia, Ala. K5 146-7
Mexia, Tex. E9 192-3
Mexican Hat, Ut. M10 242-3
Mexican Springs, N. Mex. E2 230-1
Mexican Water, Ariz. A10 206-7
Mexico, Ind. D8 100-1
Mexico, Ky. I4 164-5
Mexico, Me. K2 64-5
Mexico, Md. B10 172-3
Mexico, Mo. D7 120-1
Mexico, N.Y. D7 80-1
Mexico Beach*, Fla. C6 156-7
Meyers Bay*, Ill. A10 96-7
Meyersdale, Pa. K5 84-5
Meyersville, N.J. E6 76-7
Meyronne, Sask. O6 294-5
Miami, Ariz. I8 206-7
Miami, Fla. J13 156-7
Miami, Ind. E8 100-1
Miami, Man. K13 272-3
Miami, Mo. D5 120-1
Miami, N. Mex. C9 230-1
Miami, Okla. B15 234-5
Miami, Tex. A6 192-3
Miami, W. Va. I14 200-1
Miami, co., Ind. D8 100-1
Miami, co., Kans. G16 108-9
Miami, co., O. F4 132-3
Miami Beach, Fla. H16 156-7
Miami Beach, Ont. B14 284-5
Miami Shores, Fla. H16 156-7
Miami Springs, Fla. H16 156-7
Miamisburg, O. I14 132-3
Mica, Wash. F16 246-7
Mica Creek*, B.C. I9 268-9
Micanopy, Fla. D10 156-7
Micaville, N.C. D4 180-1
Micawber, Okla. E13 234-5
Michaud, Ida. N9 218-9
Michel*, Sask. F4 294-5
Michiana, Mich. K11 112-3
Michiana Shores, Ind. A6 100-1
Michie, Tenn. D4 188-9
Michigan, N. Dak. D12 128-9
Michigan Center, Mich. K2 112-3
Michigan City, Ind. A6 100-1
Michigan City, Miss. A8 176-7
Michigan Valley, Kans. G14 108-9
Michigantown, Ind. F7 100-1
Michipicoten, Ont. G5 284-5
Michipicoten River, Ont. G5 284-5
Mickleton, N.J. J2 76-7
Micoua*, Que. H5 290-1
Micro, N.C. E12 180-1
Midale, Sask. O9 294-5
Midas, Ida. B3 218-9
Middendorf, S.C. C12 184-5
Middle*, N.J. N4 76-7
Middle Amana, Ia. G12 104-5
Middle Arm, Nfld. L9 278-9
Middle Brook*, Nfld. M10 278-9
Middle Fork, Tenn. C4 188-9
Middle Grove, Mo. D7 120-1
Middle Haddam, Conn. F10 60-1
Middle Lake, Sask. K7 294-5
Middle River, Md. F8 172-3
Middle River, Minn. E2 116-7
Middleberg, Okla. G10 234-5
Middleborough, Mass. F12 68-9
Middlebourne, W. Va. D5 200-1
Middlebro, Man. K16 272-3
Middlebrook, Ark. A10 150-1
Middlebrook, Va. G9 196-7
Middleburg, Ky. I11 164-5
Middleburg, Md. B9 172-3
Middleburg, N.C. C11 180-1
Middleburg, Pa. G10 84-5
Middleburg, Tenn. K4 188-9
Middleburg, Va. A2 196-7
Middleburg Heights, O. C14 132-3
Middleburgh, N.Y. F10 80-1
Middlebury, Conn. F6 60-1
Middlebury, Ind. A9 100-1
Middlebury, Vt. G4 90-1
Middlebush, N.J. F6 76-7
Middlechurch*, Man. J4 272-3
Middlefield, Conn. E9 60-1
Middlefield, Mass. D3 68-9
Middlefield, O. B10 132-3
Middleford, Del. I3 153
Middlehope*, N.Y. I10 80-1
Middlepoint, O. D3 132-3
Middleport, N.Y. E3 80-1
Middleport, O. I8 132-3
Middlesboro, Ky. K13 164-5
Middlesex, N.B. H6 275
Middlesex, N.J. F6 76-7
Middlesex, N.C. D12 180-1
Middlesex, Vt. F6 90-1
Middlesex, co., Conn. G10 60-1
Middlesex, co., Mass. C10 68-9
Middlesex, co., N.J. G6 76-7
Middlesex, co., Ont. E11 284-5
Middlesex, co., Va. H14 196-7
Middleton, Ala. E8 146-7
Middleton, Ga. F7 160-1
Middleton, Ida. L2 218-9
Middleton, Ky. K7 164-5
Middleton, Mass. B12 68-9
Middleton, Mich. I13 112-3
Middleton, N.H. K8 72-3

Middleton, N.S. D5 281
Middleton, Okla. B11 234-5
Middleton, P.E.I. E5 287
Middleton, Tenn. K4 188-9
Middleton, Wis. I1 140-1
Middletown, Conn. F9 60-1
Middletown, Del. D3 153
Middletown, Ill. G7 96-7
Middletown, Ind. G10 100-1
Middletown, Ia. J13 104-5
Middletown, Ky. A3 164-5
Middletown, Md. C8 172-3
Middletown, Mo. D8 120-1
Middletown, N.J. H10 76-7
Middletown, N.Y. I10 80-1
Middletown, O. J14 132-3
Middletown, Pa. I11 84-5
Middletown, R.I. G6 87
Middletown, Va. A1 196-7
Middletown Springs, Vt. K4 90-1
Middleville, Mich. I12 112-3
Middleville, N.Y. E9 80-1
Midfield, Ala. F6 146-7
Midhurst, Ont. B14 284-5
Midkiff, W. Va. I11 200-1
Midland, Ark. E2 150-1
Midland, Ga. J3 160-1
Midland, Ind. K5 100-1
Midland, La. H4 168-9
Midland, Md. B3 172-3
Midland, Mass. K1 68-9
Midland, Mich. H13 112-3
Midland, N.C. J2 180-1
Midland, O. K16 132-3
Midland, Ont. A14 284-5
Midland, Ore. K8 238-9
Midland, Pa. A4 84-5
Midland, S. Dak. F7 136-7
Midland, Tex. E4 192-3
Midland, Va. B2 196-7
Midland, co., Mich. H13 112-3
Midland, co., Tex. E4 192-3
Midland City, Ala. L9 146-7
Midland City, Ariz. I8 206-7
Midland Park, N.J. C7 76-7
Midlothian, Ill. N4 96-7
Midlothian, Okla. I4 234-5
Midlothian, Tex. E14 192-3
Midlothian, Va. E1 196-7
Midnight, Miss. G5 176-7
Midtown, Tenn. I10 188-9
Midvale, Del. B3 153
Midvale, Ida. J2 218-9
Midvale, O. E10 132-3
Midvale, Ut. F6 242-3
Midvale, Wyo. F9 250-1
Midville, Ga. I9 160-1
Midway, Ala. J9 146-7
Midway, Ark. A6 150-1
Midway, Ark. D4 150-1
Midway, B.C. K9 268-9
Midway, Del. I6 153
Midway, Ga. L10 160-1
Midway, Ky. B6 164-5
Midway, La. A2 168-9
Midway, La. D5 168-9
Midway, Miss. G6 176-7
Midway*, Mo. I3 120-1
Midway, O. G5 132-3
Midway, Ore. C5 238-9
Midway, Pa. B5 84-5
Midway*, Pa. K10 84-5
Midway, S.C. G10 184-5
Midway, Tenn. A10 188-9
Midway, Ut. F7 242-3
Midway, Wis. H9 140-1
Midway-Canaan*, Fla. E12 156-7
Midway Park, N.C. F13 180-1
Midwest, Wyo. E13 250-1
Midwest City, Okla. J2 234-5
Mier, Ind. E9 100-1
Miesville, Minn. C12 116-7
Mifflin, Wis. J11 140-1
Mifflin, co., Pa. H8 84-5
Mifflinburg, Pa. G10 84-5
Mifflintown, Pa. H9 84-5
Mifflinville, Pa. F12 84-5
Mignon, Ala. F7 146-7
Mikado, Mich. F14 112-3
Mikado, Sask. L10 294-5
Mikana, Wis. D9 140-1
Mikkalo, Ore. C10 238-9
Milaca, Minn. K6 116-7
Milam, W. Va. F9 200-1
Milam, co., Tex. F9 192-3
Milan, Ga. K7 160-1
Milan, Ill. D5 96-7
Milan, Ind. K11 100-1
Milan, Kans. J10 108-9
Milan, Mich. K4 112-3
Milan, Minn. L2 116-7
Milan, Mo. B5 120-1
Milan, N.H. E8 72-3
Milan, N. Mex. F3 230-1
Milan, O. C7 132-3
Milan, Tenn. B4 188-9
Milan, Wash. E16 246-7
Milan, Wis. E11 140-1
Milbank, S. Dak. C16 136-7
Milbridge, Me. K9 64-5
Milburn, Ky. J2 164-5
Milburn, Nebr. F8 124-5
Milburn, Okla. H13 234-5
Milburn, Ut. H7 242-3
Milden, Sask. L6 294-5
Mildmay, Ont. B12 284-5
Mildred, Kans. H15 108-9
Mildred, Mont. E15 222-3
Mildred, Sask. J6 294-5
Mile 108 Recreational
Ranch*, B.C. H7 268-9
Mile 295 Alaska
Highway*, B.C. C7 268-9
Miles, Ia. F16 104-5
Miles, Tex. F6 192-3
Miles, Va. E4 196-7
Miles, Wash. E14 246-7
Miles City, Mont. F14 222-3
Milesburg, Pa. G8 84-5
Milestone, Sask. N8 294-5
Miley, S.C. H10 184-5
Milfay, Okla. E12 234-5
Milford, Conn. I7 60-1
Milford, Del. H4 153
Milford, Ill. F11 96-7
Milford, Ind. B9 100-1
Milford, Ind. J10 100-1
Milford, Ia. B4 104-5
Milford, Kans. E12 108-9
Milford, Ky. F12 164-5
Milford, Me. I7 64-5
Milford, Md. F6 172-3
Milford, Mass. K1 68-9
Milford, Mich. I4 112-3
Milford, Nebr. H13 124-5
Milford, N.H. O6 72-3
Milford, N.J. F3 76-7
Milford, N.Y. F9 80-1
Milford, O. K14 132-3
Milford, Pa. E16 84-5
Milford*, Tex. E9 192-3
Milford, Ut. K4 242-3
Milford, Va. G12 196-7
Milford, Wis. I2 140-1
Milford, Wyo. F8 250-1
Milford Bay, Ont. I8 284-5
Milford Center, O. F5 132-3
Milford Lake, Kans. E11 108-9
Mililani Town, Hawaii I4 258-9
Milk River, Alta. O9 264-5
Mill, La. C3 168-9
Mill Bay, B.C. E12 268-9
Mill City, Nev. D4 226-7
Mill City, Ore. I2 238-9
Mill Creek, Ind. A7 100-1
Mill Creek, Okla. H12 234-5
Mill Creek, W. Va. F15 200-1
Mill Fork, Ut. G7 242-3
Mill Gap, Va. G8 196-7
Mill Hall, Pa. F9 84-5
Mill Iron, Mont. G16 222-3
Mill Neck*, N.Y. J11 80-1
Mill Plain, Conn. I5 60-1
Mill Point, W. Va. H6 200-1
Mill River, Mass. C4 68-9
Mill River, Mass. E2 68-9
Mill Spring, Mo. I10 120-1
Mill Spring, N.C. E4 180-1
Mill Valley, Calif. C7 210-1
Mill Valley, Mass. D5 68-9
Mill Village, Vt. D7 90-1
Milladore, Wis. F12 140-1
Millard, co., Ut. I4 242-3
Millbank*, Ont. C12 284-5
Millboro, Va. G8 196-7
Millbrae, Calif. C7 210-1
Millbrook, Ala. I7 146-7
Millbrook, Mich. H12 112-3
Millbrook, N.Y. H11 80-1
Millbrook, N.C. H7 180-1
Millbrook, Ont. B16 284-5
Millburn, N.J. E7 76-7
Millbury, Mass. E8 68-9
Millbury, O. B5 132-3
Milldale, Conn. E8 60-1
Milldale, Tenn. F7 188-9
Mille Lacs, co., Minn. J6 116-7
Mille Lacs Lake, Minn. J6 116-7
Milledgeville, Ga. H6 160-1
Milledgeville, Ill. B7 96-7
Milledgeville, Tenn. D4 188-9
Millen, Ga. I9 160-1
Miller, Ala. I4 146-7
Miller, Kans. G13 108-9
Miller, Miss. A7 176-7
Miller, Mo. H4 120-1
Miller, Nebr. H9 124-5
Miller, Okla. H14 234-5
Miller, S. Dak. E11 136-7
Miller, co., Ark. J3 150-1
Miller, co., Ga. N3 160-1
Miller, co., Mo. F7 120-1
Miller Dale Colony, S.
Dak. E11 136-7
Miller House, Alaska D12 254-5
Millers Creek, N.C. C6 180-1
Millers Falls, Mass. B5 68-9
Millers Ferry, Ala. J5 146-7
Millers Tavern, Va. H13 196-7
Millersburg, Ind. A9 100-1
Millersburg, Ia. G11 104-5
Millersburg, Ky. A8 164-5
Millersburg, Mich. E13 112-3
Millersburg, O. E9 132-3
Millersburg, Pa. H11 84-5
Millersport, O. G7 132-3
Millerstown, Ky. I8 164-5
Millersville, Md. H6 172-3
Millersville, N.C. H1 180-1
Millersville, Pa. J12 84-5
Millersville, Tenn. G7 188-9
Millerton, Ia. J8 104-5
Millerton, N.Y. H11 80-1
Millerton, Okla. I15 234-5
Millerville, Ala. F8 146-7
Millerville, Minn. J3 116-7
Millet, Alta. J8 264-5
Millettville, S.C. H9 184-5
Millhousen, Ind. J10 100-1
Millhurst, N.J. H6 76-7
Millican, Ore. F9 238-9
Milligan, Fla. B4 156-7
Milligan, Nebr. I13 124-5
Milligan College, Tenn. G16 188-9
Milligan Ridge, Ark. C12 150-1
Milliken, Colo. E3 214-5
Millikin, La. A7 168-9
Millington, Conn. F11 60-1
Millington, Md. D14 172-3
Millington, Mich. F4 112-3
Millington, N.J. E6 76-7
Millington, Tenn. D1 188-9
Millinocket, Me. G7 64-5
Millis*, Mass. J2 68-9
Millis, Wyo. J5 250-1
Millis (-Clicquot), Mass. J2 68-9
Millport, Ala. E3 146-7
Millry, Ala. K2 146-7
Mills, Nebr. C9 124-5
Mills, N. Mex. D9 230-1
Mills, Ut. H6 242-3
Mills, Wyo. F12 250-1
Mills, co., Ia. I3 104-5
Mills, co., Tex. F7 192-3
Millsboro, Del. J5 153
Millstadt, Ill. L6 96-7
Millston, Wis. G10 140-1
Millstone, Conn. H13 60-1
Millstone*, N.J. H6 76-7
Millstone, N.J. F5 76-7
Millstream, N.B. I6 275
Milltown, Del. A3 153
Milltown, Ind. N8 100-1
Milltown, Ky. J9 164-5
Milltown, Mont. E3 222-3
Milltown, N.J. F6 76-7
Milltown, Nfld. N9 278-9
Milltown, Wis. D7 140-1
Milltown-Head of Bay
d'Espoir*, Nfld. N9 278-9
Millvale, Pa. A6 84-5
Millview, P.E.I. F8 287
Millville, Del. J6 153
Millville, Ia. D14 104-5
Millville, Mass. F9 68-9
Millville, Minn. N8 116-7
Millville, N.B. H3 275
Millville, N.J. M3 76-7
Millville, O. J13 132-3
Millville, Ut. C6 242-3
Millville, W. Va. E12 200-1
Millwood, Ky. I7 164-5
Millwood, Ore. E5 238-9
Millwood, Va. A1 196-7
Millwood, Wash. E16 246-7
Millwood, W. Va. F3 200-1
Milmay, N.J. M4 76-7
Milner, Colo. C8 214-5
Milner, Ga. H4 160-1
Milner, Ida. O7 218-9
Milnes Landing*, B.C. K6 268-9
Milnesand, N. Mex. I11 230-1
Milnor, N. Dak. I13 128-9
Milo, Alta. M8 264-5
Milo, Ida. L10 218-9
Milo, Ia. H8 104-5
Milo, Me. H6 64-5
Milo, Mo. G3 120-1
Milo, Okla. H11 234-5
Milo, Ore. I5 238-9
Milpitas, Calif. D8 210-1
Milroy, Ind. I10 100-1
Milroy, Minn. N3 116-7
Milroy, Pa. H9 84-5
Milstead, Ala. I8 146-7
Milstead, Ga. G5 160-1
Milton, Conn. D5 60-1
Milton, Del. I5 153
Milton, Fla. B3 156-7
Milton, Ind. H11 100-1
Milton, Ia. J11 104-5
Milton, Kans. J10 108-9
Milton, Ky. E9 164-5
Milton, La. H5 168-9
Milton, Me. K2 64-5
Milton, Mass. I5 68-9
Milton, N.H. L9 72-3
Milton*, N.Y. E11 80-1
Milton, N.C. C10 180-1
Milton, N. Dak. C12 128-9
Milton, N.S. F5 281
Milton, Okla. F16 234-5
Milton, Ont. D14 284-5
Milton, Pa. F11 84-5
Milton, Tenn. B8 188-9
Milton, Ut. E6 242-3
Milton, Vt. D4 90-1
Milton, Wash. J2 246-7
Milton, W. Va. H11 200-1
Milton, Wis. K2 140-1
Milton-Freewater, Ore. A13 238-9
Milton Mills, N.H. K9 72-3
Milton Station*, P.E.I. E7 287
Miltona, Minn. J3 116-7
Miltonvale, Kans. E10 108-9
Milverton, Ont. C12 284-5
Milwaukee, N.C. C13 180-1
Milwaukee, Wis. J15 140-1
Milwaukee, co., Wis. J15 140-1
Milwaukie, Ore. F2 238-9
Mimbres, N. Mex. K3 230-1
Miminigash, P.E.I. B3 287
Mimosa Park*, La. I9 168-9
Mims, Fla. E12 156-7
Mina, Nev. H4 226-7
Mina, S. Dak. B11 136-7
Minaki, Ont. E1 284-5
Minam, Ore. B14 238-9
Minatare, Nebr. F2 124-5
Minburn, Alta. J9 264-5
Minburn, Ia. G7 104-5
Minco, Okla. F10 234-5
Mindemoya, Ont. H7 284-5
Minden, Ia. H3 104-5
Minden, La. B3 168-9
Minden, Nebr. I10 124-5
Minden, Ont. A16 284-5
Minden, W. Va. J16 200-1
Minden City, Mich. H15 112-3
Mindenmines, Mo. H3 120-1
Mindoro, Wis. H9 140-1
Mine Centre, Ont. F2 284-5
Mine Hill, N.J. D5 76-7
Mineola, Ia. I3 104-5
Mineola, N.Y. E16 80-1
Mineola, Tex. D10 192-3
Miner, Mo. I12 120-1
Miner, Mont. H7 222-3
Miner, co., S. Dak. F14 136-7
Mineral, Ore. E15 238-9
Mineral, Va. G11 196-7
Mineral, Wash. H8 246-7
Mineral, co., Colo. I8 214-5
Mineral, co., Mont. E2 222-3
Mineral, co., Nev. H4 226-7
Mineral, co., W. Va. D9 200-1
Mineral Bluff, Ga. C4 160-1
Mineral City, O. E10 132-3
Mineral Hills, Mich. D8 112-3
Mineral Point, Mo. E14 120-1
Mineral Point, Wis. J11 140-1
Mineral Springs, Ark. H3 150-1
Mineral Springs, N.C. F7 180-1
Mineral Wells, Miss. A7 176-7
Mineral Wells, Tex. D8 192-3
Mineralwells, W. Va. E3 200-1
Minersville, Pa. H12 84-5
Minersville, Ut. K4 242-3
Minerva, Nev. H11 226-7
Minerva, O. D10 132-3
Minerva, Ore. F4 238-9
Minerva Park, O. F7 132-3
Mineville [-Witherbee],
N.Y. C11 80-1
Mingo, Ia. G8 104-5
Mingo, Kans. E3 108-9
Mingo, W. Va. G7 200-1
Mingo, co., W. Va. I2 200-1
Mingo Junction, O. E11 132-3
Minidoka, Ida. N7 218-9
Minidoka, co., Ida. N7 218-9
Minier, Ill. F8 96-7
Miniota, Man. I9 272-3
Minitonas, Man. E10 272-3
Mink Creek, Ida. O10 218-9
Minneapolis, Kans. E10 108-9
Minneapolis, Minn. M6 116-7
Minnedosa, Man. I11 272-3
Minnehaha, Wash. J7 246-7
Minnehaha, co., S. Dak. G16 136-7
Minnehaha Springs, W.
Va. H7 200-1
Minneiska, Minn. N9 116-7
Minneola, Fla. F5 156-7
Minneola, Kans. J5 108-9
Minneota, Minn. N2 116-7
Minnesota City, Minn. O9 116-7
Minnesota Lake, Minn. O5 116-7
Minnesota R., Minn. L2 116-7
Minnesott Beach*, N.C. E14 180-1
Minnetonka, Minn. B10 116-7
Minnetonka Beach*,
Minn. M7 116-7
Minnetrista*, Minn. L6 116-7
Minnewaukan, N. Dak. D10 128-9
Minnora, W. Va. F4 200-1
Minoa, N.Y. E7 80-1
Minocqua, Wis. C12 140-1
Minong, Wis. C8 140-1
Minonk, Ill. E8 96-7
Minooka, Ill. O2 96-7
Minor Hill, Tenn. D6 188-9
Minor Lane Heights*, Ky. G9 164-5
Minortown, Conn. E6 60-1
Minot, Me. M9 64-5
Minot, N. Dak. D6 128-9
Minot Base*, N. Dak. C6 128-9
Minster, O. E3 132-3
Mint Hill*, N.C. E7 180-1
Mint Spring, Va. G9 196-7
Minter, Ala. J6 146-7
Minter, Ga. J7 160-1
Minter, S.C. F2 184-5
Minter City, Miss. E6 176-7
Minto, Alaska D11 254-5
Minto, Man. J11 272-3
Minto, N.B. H5 275
Minto, N. Dak. D13 128-9
Minto Park*, Sask. E5 294-5
Minton, Sask. O8 294-5
Minturn, Ark. B10 150-1
Minturn, Colo. E9 214-5
Minturn, Me. L8 64-5
Mio, Mich. F13 112-3
Mira, La. A1 168-9
Mira Loma, Calif. G10 210-1
Mira Road*, N.S. B11 281
Mirabel, Que. I11 290-1
Miracle Valley, Ariz. M10 206-7
Miramar, Fla. G16 156-7
Miramar, Mass. F13 68-9
Miramichi Bay, N.B. F6 275
Miranda, S. Dak. D11 136-7
Mirror, Alta. K8 264-5
Mirror Lake, B.C. J10 268-9
Mirror Lake, N.H. J7 72-3
Miscou Centre, N.B. D7 275
Miscouche, P.E.I. E5 287
Misenheimer, N.C. J3 180-1
Mishawaka, Ind. A8 100-1

Mishicot, Wis. E6 140-1
Misquamicut, R.I. I2 87
Missanabie, Ont. F6 284-5
Missaukee, co., Mich. G12 112-3
Missi Falls*, Man. C3 272-3
Mission, B.C. C15 268-9
Mission, Del. J5 153
Mission, Kans. F16 108-9
Mission, S. Dak. H8 136-7
Mission, Tex. K8 192-3
Mission Hill, S. Dak. I15 136-7
Mission Hills, Kans. F16 108-9
Mission Viejo*, Calif. O8 210-1
Mission Woods*, Kans. E16 108-9
Missisquoi, co., Que. J13 290-1
Mississauga, Ont. D15 284-5
Mississippi, co., Ark. C12 150-1
Mississippi, co., Mo. I12 120-1
Mississippi Delta, La. J11 168-9
Mississippi R. 14-15
Mississippi Sound, Miss. O10 176-7
Mississippi State, Miss. F9 176-7
Missoula, Mont. E3 222-3
Missoula, co., Mont. E4 222-3
Missoula South*, Mont. E3 222-3
Missoula West*, Mont. E3 222-3
Missouri City, Mo. I16 120-1
Missouri City, Tex. I13 192-3
Missouri R., Mo. F9 120-1
Missouri Valley, Ia. G2 104-5
Mist, Ark. J8 150-1
Mist, Ore. A5 238-9
Mistassini, Que. B10 290-1
Mistatim, Sask. J9 294-5
Mistletoe, Ky. I13 164-5
Miston, Tenn. B2 188-9
Mitchell, Ga. H8 160-1
Mitchell, Ind. L7 100-1
Mitchell, Ia. B9 104-5
Mitchell, Kans. G9 108-9
Mitchell, La. D2 168-9
Mitchell*, Man. J15 272-3
Mitchell, Nebr. E1 124-5
Mitchell, Ont. D12 284-5
Mitchell, Ore. E10 238-9
Mitchell, Ore. J2 238-9
Mitchell, S. Dak. G13 136-7
Mitchell, Tenn. F7 188-9
Mitchell, co., Ga. M4 160-1
Mitchell, co., Ia. B10 104-5
Mitchell, co., Kans. E9 108-9
Mitchell, co., N.C. C4 180-1
Mitchell, co., Tex. E5 192-3
Mitchell Heights, W. Va. K12 200-1
Mitchells, Va. C1 196-7
Mitchellsburg, Ky. E5 164-5
Mitchellville, Ark. H8 150-1
Mitchellville, Ia. G8 104-5
Mitchellville, Md. I6 172-3
Mitchellville, Tenn. F7 188-9
Mittie, La. G3 168-9
Mixville, Conn. F7 60-1
Mize, Miss. J7 176-7
Mizpah, Minn. F5 116-7
Mizpah, Mont. F15 222-3
Mizpah, N.J. L4 76-7
Moab, Ut. J10 242-3
Moapa, Nev. L10 226-7
Moark, Ark. A11 150-1
Moatsville, W. Va. D15 200-1
Moberly, Mo. C6 120-1
Mobile, Ala. N3 146-7
Mobile, Ariz. J6 206-7
Mobile, co., Ala. M2 146-7
Mobile Bay, Ala. N3 146-7
Mobjack, Va. E4 196-7
Mobridge, S. Dak. B8 136-7
Mocane, Okla. B6 234-5
Moccasin, Ariz. B5 206-7
Moccasin, Mont. E9 222-3
Mockingbird Valley*, Ky. G9 164-5
Mocksville, N.C. D7 180-1
Moclips, Wash. F5 246-7
Modale, Ia. G2 104-5
Model, Colo. I13 214-5
Model, Tenn. A5 188-9
Modena, Mo. A4 120-1
Modena, Ut. L2 242-3
Modena, Wis. G8 140-1
Modest Town, Va. H16 196-7
Modesto, Calif. C10 210-1
Modoc, Ga. J8 160-1
Modoc, Ind. G11 100-1
Modoc, Kans. G3 108-9
Modoc, S.C. F7 184-5
Modoc, co., Calif. D4 210-1
Modoc Point, Ore. J7 238-9
Moenkopi, Ariz. C8 206-7
Moffat, Colo. H10 214-5
Moffat, co., Colo. C6 214-5
Moffett, Okla. F16 234-5
Moffit, N. Dak. H8 128-9
Mogadore, O. D15 132-3
Mogollon, N. Mex. I2 230-1
Mogote, Colo. J10 214-5
Mogul, Nev. F1 226-7
Mohall, N. Dak. B6 128-9
Mohave, co., Ariz. F3 206-7
Mohawk, Ariz. J3 206-7
Mohawk, Ind. H9 100-1
Mohawk, Mich. B9 112-3
Mohawk, N.Y. E9 80-1
Mohawk, Ore. K1 238-9
Mohawk, W. Va. J2 200-1
Mohawk Crossroad, Tenn. G14 188-9
Mohegan, Conn. F13 60-1
Mohegan, R.I. A3 87
Mohler, Ida. G3 218-9
Mohler, Ore. B4 238-9
Mohler, Wash. F14 246-7
Mohnton, Pa. I13 84-5
Moho, Nev. I4 226-7
Moiese, Mont. D3 222-3
Moisie*, Que. H5 290-1
Mojave, Calif. M7 210-1
Mokane, Mo. E7 120-1
Mokapu, Hawaii I7 258-9
Mokena, Ill. O3 96-7
Moko, Ark. A8 150-1
Mokuleia, Hawaii G2 258-9
Molalla, Ore. G2 238-9
Molanosa, Sask. H7 294-5
Mole Lake, Wis. D13 140-1
Moleen, Nev. D8 226-7
Molen, Ut. I7 242-3
Molena, Ga. I3 160-1
Molesworth, Ont. C12 284-5
Molina, Colo. F7 214-5
Moline, Ill. C5 96-7
Moline, Kans. J13 108-9
Moline, Mich. I12 112-3
Moline Acres*, Mo. E10 120-1
Molino, Fla. B3 156-7
Mollusk, Va. H14 196-7
Molokai Isl., Hawaii F10 258-9
Molson, Wash. B13 246-7
Molt, Mont. G10 222-3
Molunkus, Me. G8 64-5
Momence, Ill. D11 96-7
Mona, Ut. H6 242-3
Monaca, Pa. H1 84-5
Monahans, Tex. E4 192-3
Monango, N. Dak. I11 128-9
Monarch, Alta. N8 264-5
Monarch, Mont. E7 222-3
Monarch, Ut. F9 242-3
Monarch Mills, S.C. G6 184-5
Monarda, Me. F8 64-5
Moncks Corner, S.C. G13 184-5
Moncton, N.B. H7 275
Moncure, N.C. I6 180-1
Mondamin, Ia. G2 104-5
Mondovi, Wash. E15 246-7
Mondovi, Wis. F8 140-1
Monee, Ill. O4 96-7
Monero, N. Mex. B5 230-1
Monessen, Pa. J2 84-5
Moneta, Ia. B3 104-5
Moneta, Va. I8 196-7
Moneta, Wyo. F10 250-1
Monett, Mo. I4 120-1
Monetta, S.C. E8 184-5
Monette, Ark. C11 150-1
Money, Miss. E6 176-7
Mongo, Ind. A10 100-1
Monhegan, Me. M6 64-5
Monico, Wis. D13 140-1
Monie, Md. H14 172-3
Moniteau, co., Mo. F6 120-1
Monitor, Ore. G2 238-9
Monitor, Wash. F11 246-7
Monkton*, Ont. J7 284-5
Monkton, Vt. F4 90-1
Monkton Ridge, Vt. F4 90-1
Monmouth, Ill. E5 96-7
Monmouth, Ia. F14 104-5
Monmouth, Me. L4 64-5
Monmouth, Ore. H1 238-9
Monmouth, co., N.J. H7 76-7
Monmouth Beach, N.J. G8 76-7
Monmouth Junction, N.J. G5 76-7
Mono, co., Calif. I6 210-1
Mono Lake, Calif. I6 210-1
Monon, Ind. D6 100-1
Monona, Ia. C13 104-5
Monona, Wis. J1 140-1
Monona, co., Ia. F2 104-5
Monongah, W. Va. B14 200-1
Monongahela, Pa. I2 84-5
Monongahela R., W. Va. B14 200-1
Monongalia, co., W. Va. D6 200-1
Monoville, Tenn. B9 188-9
Monowi, Nebr. C11 124-5
Monponsett, Mass. F12 68-9
Monroe, Ark. F10 150-1
Monroe, Conn. H6 60-1
Monroe, Ga. F5 160-1
Monroe, Ind. D11 100-1
Monroe, Ia. H9 104-5
Monroe, La. B5 168-9
Monroe, Me. J6 64-5
Monroe*, Mass. B3 68-9
Monroe, Mich. K14 112-3
Monroe, Miss. K4 176-7
Monroe, Nebr. G12 124-5
Monroe, N.H. G4 72-3
Monroe*, N.J. G6 76-7
Monroe*, N.J. K3 76-7
Monroe, N.J. B5 76-7
Monroe, N.Y. A13 80-1
Monroe, N.C. F7 180-1
Monroe, O. J14 132-3
Monroe, Okla. G16 234-5
Monroe, Ore. E5 238-9
Monroe, S. Dak. H15 136-7
Monroe, Tenn. A10 188-9
Monroe, Ut. J6 242-3
Monroe, Va. H9 196-7
Monroe, Wash. E8 246-7
Monroe, Wis. K12 140-1
Monroe, co., Ala. K5 146-7
Monroe, co., Ark. F9 150-1
Monroe, co., Fla. J12 156-7
Monroe, co., Ga. I5 160-1
Monroe, co., Ill. L6 96-7
Monroe, co., Ind. J7 100-1
Monroe, co., Ia. I9 104-5
Monroe, co., Ky. K8 164-5
Monroe, co., Mich. K14 112-3
Monroe, co., Miss. D10 176-7
Monroe, co., Mo. C7 120-1
Monroe, co., N.Y. E4 80-1
Monroe, co., O. G11 132-3
Monroe, co., Pa. F15 84-5
Monroe, co., Tenn. D12 188-9
Monroe, co., W. Va. J5 200-1
Monroe, co., Wis. H10 140-1
Monroe Center, Wis. H11 140-1
Monroe City, Ind. M4 100-1
Monroe City, Mo. C8 120-1
Monroe Lake, Ind. K7 100-1
Monroeville, Ala. K5 146-7
Monroeville, Ind. D12 100-1
Monroeville, N.J. K3 76-7
Monroeville, O. C7 132-3
Monroeville, Pa. A7 84-5
Monrovia*, Calif. G9 210-1
Monrovia, Ind. I7 100-1
Monrovia, Kans. D15 108-9
Monrovia, Md. F2 172-3
Monse, Wash. D12 246-7
Monsey, N.Y. C13 80-1
Monson, Me. H5 64-5
Monson, Mass. E6 68-9
Mont Alto, Pa. K9 84-5
Mont Belvieu, Tex. H15 192-3
Mont-Carmel, Que. E13 290-1
Mont Clare, Pa. A10 84-5
Mont Ida, Kans. H15 108-9
Mont-Joli, Que. C16 290-1
Mont-Laurier, Que. I2 290-1
Mont-Louis, Que. H6 290-1
Mont Nebo, Sask. J6 294-5
Mont-Rolland*, Que. I11 290-1
Mont-Royal*, Que. I12 290-1
Mont-St.-Hilaire*, Que. I12 290-1
Mont-St.-Michel, Que. I2 290-1
Mont-St.-Pierre, Que. H6 290-1
Mont Vernon, N.H. O6 72-3
Montague, Calif. D3 210-1
Montague, Mass. C5 68-9
Montague, Mich. H11 112-3
Montague, N.J. A4 76-7
Montague, P.E.I. F9 287
Montague, Tex. C8 192-3
Montague, co., Tex. D8 192-3
Montague City, Mass. B5 68-9
Montalvo, Calif. G6 210-1
Montana, Alaska F11 254-5
Montana, Kans. J15 108-9
Montana City, Mont. F6 222-3
Montaqua, Mont. H10 222-3
Montara*, Calif. J3 210-1
Montcalm, co., Mich. I12 112-3
Montcalm, co., Que. I2 290-1
Montchanin, Del. A3 153
Montclair, Calif. G9 210-1
Montclair, N.J. C10 76-7
Monte Lake, B.C. I8 268-9
Monte Sereno, Calif. D8 210-1
Monte Vista, Colo. I10 214-5
Monte Vista, Miss. E8 176-7
Monteagle, Tenn. K9 188-9
Montebello, Calif. G9 210-1
Montebello, Que. I10 290-1
Montecito, Calif. M6 210-1
Montello, Nev. B11 226-7
Montello, Wis. H12 140-1
Monterey, Calif. K3 210-1
Monterey, Ind. C7 100-1
Monterey, Ky. F10 164-5
Monterey, La. E6 168-9
Monterey, Mass. E2 68-9
Monterey, Tenn. B10 188-9
Monterey, Va. F8 196-7
Monterey, co., Calif. K4 210-1
Monterey Park, Calif. G8 210-1
Monterville, W. Va. G7 200-1
Montesano, Wash. G6 246-7
Montevallo, Ala. G6 146-7
Montevallo, Mo. G3 120-1
Montevideo, Minn. M3 116-7
Monteview, Ida. L9 218-9
Montezuma, Colo. E10 214-5
Montezuma, Ga. J5 160-1
Montezuma, Ind. H4 100-1
Montezuma, Ia. G10 104-5
Montezuma, Kans. J4 108-9
Montezuma, N. Mex. E8 230-1
Montezuma, Tenn. D4 188-9
Montezuma, co., Colo. I6 214-5
Montfort, Wis. J10 140-1
Montgomery, Ala. I7 146-7
Montgomery, Ga. K11 160-1
Montgomery, Ill. N1 96-7
Montgomery, Ind. L5 100-1
Montgomery, La. D3 168-9
Montgomery, Mass. E4 68-9
Montgomery, Mich. K13 112-3
Montgomery, Minn. N6 116-7
Montgomery*, N.Y. I10 80-1
Montgomery*, O. H3 132-3
Montgomery, Pa. F11 84-5
Montgomery, Vt. B6 90-1
Montgomery, W. Va. I15 200-1
Montgomery, co., Ala. I7 146-7
Montgomery, co., Ark. F3 150-1
Montgomery, co., Ga. K8 160-1
Montgomery, co., Ill. I7 96-7
Montgomery, co., Ind. G6 100-1
Montgomery, co., Ia. I4 104-5
Montgomery, co., Kans. K14 108-9
Montgomery, co., Ky. G12 164-5
Montgomery, co., Md. D9 172-3
Montgomery, co., Miss. E7 176-7
Montgomery, co., Mo. D8 120-1
Montgomery, co., N.Y. F10 80-1
Montgomery, co., N.C. E9 180-1
Montgomery, co., O. G3 132-3
Montgomery, co., Pa. J15 84-5
Montgomery, co., Tenn. A6 188-9
Montgomery, co., Tex. G10 192-3
Montgomery, co., Va. J7 196-7
Montgomery City, Mo. D8 120-1
Monticello, Ark. I8 150-1
Monticello, Fla. B8 156-7
Monticello, Ga. H5 160-1
Monticello, Ill. G9 96-7
Monticello, Ind. D6 100-1
Monticello, Ia. E13 104-5
Monticello, Ky. J11 164-5
Monticello, Me. E9 64-5
Monticello, Minn. L6 116-7
Monticello, Miss. K6 176-7
Monticello, Mo. B8 120-1
Monticello, N. Mex. I4 230-1
Monticello, N.Y. H9 80-1
Monticello, S.C. J8 184-5
Monticello, Ut. L10 242-3
Monticello, Wis. K1 140-1
Montmagny, Que. F12 290-1
Montmagny, co., Que. G13 290-1
Montmartre, Sask. N9 294-5
Montmorenci, Ind. F5 100-1
Montmorenci, S.C. F8 184-5
Montmorency, co., Mich. F13 112-3
Montmorency I, co., Que. D11 290-1
Montmorency II (Île-de'Orléans), co., Que. F12 290-1
Montogomery, N.J. F5 76-7
Montour, Ida. L3 218-9
Montour, Ia. F10 104-5
Montour, co., Pa. F11 84-5
Montour Falls, N.Y. G6 80-1
Montoursville, Pa. F10 84-5
Montoya, N. Mex. F10 230-1
Montpelier, Ida. O11 218-9
Montpelier, Ind. E10 100-1
Montpelier, Ia. H14 104-5
Montpelier, La. G8 168-9
Montpelier, Miss. E9 176-7
Montpelier, N. Dak. H11 128-9
Montpelier, O. B3 132-3
Montpelier, Vt. F6 90-1
Montpelier, Va. H12 196-7
Montreal, Que. J3 290-1
Montreal, Wis. B11 140-1
Montréal-Est*, Que. I12 290-1
Montréal-Nord*, Que. I12 290-1
Montréal-Ouest*, Que. J12 290-1
Montreat, N.C. D4 180-1
Montrose, Ala. N3 146-7
Montrose, Ark. J8 150-1
Montrose, B.C. K9 268-9
Montrose, Colo. G7 214-5
Montrose, Ga. J7 160-1
Montrose, Ia. K13 104-5
Montrose, Kans. D9 108-9
Montrose, La. D3 168-9
Montrose*, Md. D9 172-3
Montrose, Mich. F3 112-3
Montrose, Minn. A8 116-7
Montrose, Miss. I8 176-7
Montrose, Mo. F4 120-1
Montrose, Pa. C13 84-5
Montrose, P.E.I. B4 287
Montrose, S.C. C13 184-5
Montrose, S. Dak. G15 136-7
Montrose, W. Va. E16 200-1
Montrose, co., Colo. G6 214-5
Montross, Va. G13 196-7
Montvale, N.J. C8 76-7
Montvale, Va. I8 196-7
Montverde, Fla. E5 156-7
Montville, Conn. F13 60-1
Montville, Me. K5 64-5
Montville, Mass. E2 68-9
Montville, N.J. C6 76-7
Monument, Colo. J3 214-5
Monument, Kans. E3 108-9
Monument, N. Mex. K11 230-1
Monument, Ore. D12 238-9
Monument Beach, Mass. H13 68-9
Moodus, Conn. F11 60-1
Moody*, Ala. E7 146-7
Moody*, Ga. N6 160-1
Moody*, Tex. F8 192-3
Moody, co., S. Dak. F16 136-7
Moody Corner, Mass. D5 68-9
Moodys, Okla. D15 234-5
Mooers, N.Y. A11 80-1
Moon Lake, Miss. C5 176-7
Moonachie*, N.J. B11 76-7
Moonbeam, Ont. F7 284-5
Mooncrest*, Alta. J7 264-5
Moorcroft, Wyo. C15 250-1
Moore, Ida. L8 218-9
Moore, Mont. E9 222-3
Moore, Okla. K2 234-5
Moore, S.C. F4 184-5
Moore, Ut. I7 242-3
Moore, co., N.C. E9 180-1
Moore, co., Tenn. D8 188-9
Moore, co., Tex. A5 192-3
Moore Haven, Fla. H12 156-7
Moore Res., Vt. E9 90-1
Moorefield, Ark. C8 150-1
Moorefield, Ky. F12 164-5
Moorefield, Nebr. I7 124-5
Moorefield, W. Va. E9 200-1
Mooreland, Ind. G11 100-1
Mooreland, Okla. D8 234-5
Moorepark*, Man. J2 272-3
Moores Corner, Mass. C5 68-9
Moores Hill, Ind. K11 100-1
Mooresburg, Tenn. G14 188-9
Mooresfield, R.I. G5 87
Moorestown, Mich. G12 112-3

Moorestown – Mount Willing 407

Moorestown, N.J. M12 76-7
Moorestown [-Lenola], N.J. M12 76-7
Mooresville, Ala. B6 146-7
Mooresville, Ind. G1 100-1
Mooresville, Mo. C4 120-1
Mooresville, N.C. I1 180-1
Mooresville, Tenn. J6 188-9
Mooreton, N. Dak. I14 128-9
Mooreville, Miss. C10 176-7
Moorewood, Okla. E7 234-5
Moorhead, Ia. F2 104-5
Moorhead, Minn. I1 116-7
Moorhead, Miss. F5 176-7
Moorhead, Mont. H14 222-3
Mooringsport, La. B1 168-9
Moorland, Ia. E6 104-5
Moorland*, Ky. G9 164-5
Moorman, Ky. I6 164-5
Moorpark, Calif. F7 210-1
Moose, Wyo. J2 250-1
Moose Creek*, Ont. I16 284-5
Moose Factory, Ont. D7 284-5
Moose Heights, B.C. G7 268-9
Moose Jaw, Sask. N7 294-5
Moose Lake, Man. B11 272-3
Moose Lake, Minn. J7 116-7
Moose Pass, Alaska F11 254-5
Moose River, Me. G3 64-5
Moosehead, Me. G5 64-5
Moosehead Lake, Me. G5 64-5
Moosehorn, Man. G13 272-3
Moosic, Pa. E14 84-5
Moosomin, Sask. N11 294-5
Moosonee, Ont. D7 284-5
Moosup, Conn. D14 60-1
Moosup Valley, R.I. D2 87
Mora, Ida. M3 218-9
Mora, La. E3 168-9
Mora, Minn. K6 116-7
Mora, N. Mex. D8 230-1
Mora, co., N. Mex. D8 230-1
Morada*, Calif. I4 210-1
Moraga*, Calif. I3 210-1
Moraine, O. I15 132-3
Moran, Ind. F7 100-1
Moran, Kans. I15 108-9
Moran, Mich. D13 112-3
Moran Junction, Wyo. I2 250-1
Morattico, Va. H14 196-7
Moravia, Ida. A3 218-9
Moravia, Ia. J10 104-5
Moravia, N.Y. F6 80-1
Moravia, Okla. F7 234-5
Moravian Falls, N.C. H1 180-1
Morden, Man. K13 272-3
Moreauville, La. F5 168-9
Morehead, Kans. J15 108-9
Morehead, Ky. G13 164-5
Morehead City, N.C. F14 180-1
Morehouse, Mo. I11 120-1
Morehouse, co., La. A5 168-9
Moreland, Ark. D5 150-1
Moreland, Ga. H3 160-1
Moreland, Ida. M9 218-9
Moreland, Ky. E6 164-5
Moreland, La. E4 168-9
Moreland Hills*, O. B10 132-3
Morell, P.E.I. E9 287
Morenci, Ariz. I11 206-7
Morenci, Mich. K13 112-3
Moretown, Vt. F6 90-1
Morgan, Ark. I15 150-1
Morgan, Ga. M3 160-1
Morgan, Minn. N4 116-7
Morgan, Mont. A11 222-3
Morgan, Ore. B11 238-9
Morgan, Vt. B9 90-1
Morgan, co., Ala. C6 146-7
Morgan, co., Colo. D13 214-5
Morgan, co., Ga. G6 160-1
Morgan, co., Ill. H6 96-7
Morgan, co., Ind. I7 100-1
Morgan, co., Ky. G14 164-5
Morgan, co., Mo. F6 120 1
Morgan, co., O. G9 132-3
Morgan, co., Tenn. B10 188-9
Morgan, co., Ut. D7 242-3
Morgan, co., W. Va. D10 200-1
Morgan City, La. I7 168-9
Morgan City, Miss. F5 176-7
Morgan City, Ut. E6 242-3
Morgan Hill, Calif. J3 210-1
Morgan Springs, Tenn. J11 188-9
Morgana, S.C. F7 184-5
Morganfield, Ky. H4 164-5
Morgansville, W. Va. E5 200-1
Morganton, Ark. D7 150-1
Morganton, Ga. D4 160-1
Morganton, N.C. D5 180-1
Morgantown, Ind. J8 100-1
Morgantown, Ky. I7 164-5
Morgantown, Miss. L6 176-7
Morgantown*, N.C. C9 180-1
Morgantown, Tenn. J11 188-9
Morgantown, W. Va. D7 200-1
Morganville, Kans. E11 108-9
Morganville, N.J. G7 76-7
Morganza, La. G6 168-9
Morganza, Md. H11 172-3
Moriarty*, N. Mex. F7 230-1
Morin Heights*, Que. I11 290-1
Morinville, Alta. I8 264-5
Morland, Kans. E5 108-9
Morley, Ia. F13 104-5
Morley, Mich. H12 112-3
Morley, Mo. I11 120-1
Morley, Tenn. F11 188-9
Mormon Lake, Ariz. F7 206-7
Morning Star, Ark. B6 150-1
Morning Star, Ark. K12 150-1
Morning Sun, Ia. I13 104-5
Morning View, Ky. E11 164-5
Morningdale, Mass. D8 68-9
Morningside, Md. J5 172-3
Morningside Park, Conn. G13 60-1
Moro, Ark. F10 150-1
Moro, Me. E8 64-5
Moro, Ore. C9 238-9
Moro Bay, Ark. J6 150-1
Morocco, Ind. D4 100-1
Moroni, Ut. H6 242-3
Morral, O. D6 132-3
Morrice, Mich. H2 112-3
Morrill, Kans. C14 108-9
Morrill, Ky. E8 164-5
Morrill, Me. K6 64-5
Morrill, Nebr. E1 124-5
Morrill, co., Nebr. F2 124-5
Morrilton, Ark. E6 150-1
Morrin, Alta. L8 264-5
Morris, Ala. E6 146-7
Morris, Conn. D6 60-1
Morris, Ga. L2 160-1
Morris, Ill. D9 96-7
Morris, Ind. J11 100-1
Morris, Man. K14 272-3
Morris, Minn. K2 116-7
Morris*, N.J. D6 76-7
Morris, N.Y. F8 80-1
Morris, Okla. E14 234-5
Morris, W. Va. G5 200-1
Morris, co., Kans. G12 108-9
Morris, co., N.J. D5 76-7
Morris, co., Tex. D11 192-3
Morris Chapel, Tenn. D4 188-9
Morris Plains, N.J. D6 76-7
Morrisburg, Ont. I15 284-5
Morrisey, Wyo. E16 250-1
Morrison*, Colo. H2 214-5
Morrison, Ill. C6 96-7
Morrison, Ia. E10 104-5
Morrison, Mo. E8 120-1
Morrison, Okla. D12 234-5
Morrison, Tenn. J9 188-9
Morrison, Wis. E5 140-1
Morrison, co., Minn. J5 116-7
Morrison City, Tenn. F16 188-9
Morrisonville, Ill. I7 96-7
Morrisonville, N.Y. A11 80-1
Morrisonville, Wis. I1 140-1
Morriston, Ark. B8 150-1
Morristown, Ariz. H5 206-7
Morristown, Ill. A8 96-7
Morristown, Ind. I9 100-1
Morristown, Minn. N6 116-7
Morristown, N.J. D6 76-7
Morristown, N.Y. B8 80-1
Morristown, O. F10 132-3
Morristown, S. Dak. A6 136-7
Morristown, Tenn. B14 188-9
Morristown*, Vt. D6 90-1
Morrisvale, W. Va. I12 200-1
Morrisville, Mo. H5 120-1
Morrisville, N.Y. F8 80-1
Morrisville, N.C. H7 180-1
Morrisville, Pa. I16 84-5
Morrisville*, Pa. J1 84-5
Morrisville, S.C. F14 184-5
Morrisville, Vt. D6 90-1
Morro Bay, Calif. L4 210-1
Morrow, Ga. D11 160-1
Morrow, Ida. G3 218-9
Morrow, La. F5 168-9
Morrow, O. K15 132-3
Morrow, co., O. E7 132-3
Morrow, co., Ore. C11 238-9
Morrowville, Kans. D11 108-9
Morse, La. H4 168-9
Morse, Okla. E13 234-5
Morse, Sask. N6 294-5
Morse Bluff, Nebr. I1 124-5
Morse Res., Ind. G8 100-1
Morses Line, Vt. B5 90-1
Mortlach*, Sask. N7 294-5
Mortimer, N.C. D5 180-1
Morton, Ark. D10 150-1
Morton, Ill. F7 96-7
Morton, Minn. N4 116-7
Morton, Miss. I7 176-7
Morton, Ont. J14 284-5
Morton*, Pa. K15 84-5
Morton, Tex. C4 192-3
Morton, Wash. H8 246-7
Morton, Wyo. F8 250-1
Morton, Wyo. F14 250-1
Morton, co., Kans. J1 108-9
Morton, co., N. Dak. H6 128-9
Morton Grove, Ill. L3 96-7
Mortons Gap, Ky. I5 164-5
Morven, Ga. N6 160-1
Morven, N.C. F8 180-1
Morvin, Ala. J3 146-7
Mosby, Mo. H16 120-1
Mosby, Mont. E11 222-3
Mosca, Colo. I10 214-5
Moscow, Ark. H8 150-1
Moscow, Ida. F2 218-9
Moscow, Ia. G14 104-5
Moscow, Kans. J2 108-9
Moscow, Me. I4 64-5
Moscow, Md. B3 172-3
Moscow, O. I4 132-3
Moscow, Pa. E14 84-5
Moscow, R.I. G2 87
Moscow, Tenn. K3 188-9
Moscow, Vt. E6 90-1
Moscow Mills, Mo. A13 120-1
Mosel, Nev. D7 226-7
Moseley, Va. I12 196-7
Moselle, Miss. K8 176-7
Moser River, N.S. D9 281
Moses Lake, Wash. G13 246-7
Moses Lake North*, Wash. G13 246-7
Moses Point, Alaska D8 254-5
Mosheim, Tenn. G15 188-9
Mosier, Ore. B8 238-9
Mosinee, Wis. F12 140-1
Moskee, Wyo. C16 250-1
Mosquero, N. Mex. E10 230-1
Moss, Miss. J8 176-7
Moss, Tenn. A9 188-9
Moss Point, Miss. N10 176-7
Mossbank, Sask. N7 294-5
Mossyrock, Wash. H7 246-7
Motbridge, S.C. D13 184-5
Motley, Minn. J4 116-7
Motley, co., Tex. C5 192-3
Mott, N. Dak. I4 128-9
Motters, Md. B8 172-3
Moulin-Morneault*, N.B. E2 275
Moulin-Vallière*, Que. F11 290-1
Moulton, Ala. C5 146-7
Moulton, Ida. O7 218-9
Moulton, Ia. J10 104-5
Moulton*, Tex. H9 192-3
Moultonborough*, N.H. J8 72-3
Moultonborough Falls, N.H. J7 72-3
Moultonville, N.H. J8 72-3
Moultrie, Ga. N5 160-1
Moultrie, co., Ill. I9 96-7
Mound, La. C7 168-9
Mound, Minn. B9 116-7
Mound Bayou, Miss. D4 176-7
Mound City, Ill. O8 96-7
Mound City, Kans. H16 108-9
Mound City, Mo. B2 120-1
Mound City, S. Dak. A9 136-7
Mound Valley, Kans. J15 108-9
Moundridge, Kans. H10 108-9
Mounds, Ill. O8 96-7
Mounds, Okla. E13 234-5
Mounds, Ut. H8 242-3
Mounds View, Minn. A11 116-7
Moundsville, W. Va. C5 200-1
Moundville, Ala. G4 146-7
Moundville, Mo. G3 120-1
Mount Airy, Ga. D6 160-1
Mount Airy, Md. E3 172-3
Mount Airy, N.C. C7 180-1
Mount Albert*, Ont. I8 284-5
Mount Andrew, Ala. J9 146-7
Mount Angel, Ore. H2 238-9
Mount Arlington, N.J. C5 76-7
Mount Auburn, Ind. H11 100-1
Mount Auburn, Ia. E11 104-5
Mount Ayr, Ind. D5 100-1
Mount Ayr, Ia. J6 104-5
Mount Berry, Ga. E2 160-1
Mount Bethel, N.J. E6 76-7
Mount Blanchard, O. D5 132-3
Mount Brydges*, Ont. E12 284-5
Mount Buchanan, P.E.I. G8 287
Mount Calvary, Wis. G4 140-1
Mount Carmel, Ala. J7 146-7
Mount Carmel, Ill. L11 96-7
Mount Carmel, Ind. J12 100-1
Mount Carmel, Ky. F13 164-5
Mount Carmel, La. E2 168-9
Mount Carmel, Miss. K7 176-7
Mount Carmel, Nfld. O11 278-9
Mount Carmel, Pa. G12 84-5
Mount Carmel, P.E.I. E4 287
Mount Carmel, S.C. E6 184-5
Mount Carmel, Tenn. F15 188-9
Mount Carmel, Tenn. G16 188-9
Mount Carmel, Ut. M4 242-3
Mount Carmel Junction, Ut. M4 242-3
Mount Carroll, Ill. B6 96-7
Mount Chase, Me. E8 64-5
Mount Clare, W. Va. D13 200-1
Mount Clemens, Mich. I7 112-3
Mount Comfort, Ind. E3 100-1
Mount Cory, O. D5 132-3
Mount Crawford, Va. G10 196-7
Mount Crest, Tenn. I11 188-9
Mount Croghan, S.C. B12 184-5
Mount Desert, Me. K8 64-5
Mount Desert Isl., Me. L8 64-5
Mount Dora, Fla. E11 156-7
Mount Dora, N. Mex. C11 230-1
Mount Eden, Ky. B4 164-5
Mount Edgecumbe, Alaska H15 254-5
Mount Emmons, Ut. F9 242-3
Mount Ephraim, N.J. N10 76-7
Mount Etna, Ind. D10 100-1
Mount Fern, N.J. D5 76-7
Mount Forest, Ont. C13 284-5
Mount Freedom, N.J. D5 76-7
Mount Gay, W. Va. K12 200-1
Mount Gilead, N.C. J4 180-1
Mount Gilead, O. E7 132-3
Mount Harmony, Md. F11 172-3
Mount Healthy, O. K13 132-3
Mount Herbert, P.E.I. F8 287
Mount Hermon, La. F9 168-9
Mount Heron, Va. I4 196-7
Mount Holly, Ark. J5 150-1
Mount Holly, N.J. I4 76-7
Mount Holly, N.C. J1 180-1
Mount Holly, S.C. H13 184-5
Mount Holly, Vt. K5 90-1
Mount Holly Springs, Pa. J10 84-5
Mount Hood, Ore. B8 238-9
Mt. Hood, Ore. C8 238-9
Mount Hope, Ala. C4 146-7
Mount Hope, Conn. C12 60-1
Mount Hope, Kans. I10 108-9
Mount Hope, N.J. C6 76-7
Mount Hope*, Ont. D14 284-5
Mount Hope, W. Va. K16 200-1
Mount Hope, Wis. J10 140-1
Mount Horeb, Wis. J12 140-1
Mount Ida, Ark. F3 150-1
Mount Ida, Wis. J10 140-1
Mount Idaho, Ida. G3 218-9
Mount Jackson, Va. F10 196-7
Mount Jewett, Pa. D6 84-5
Mount Joy, Pa. J12 84-5
Mount Judea, Ark. B5 150-1
Mount Juliet, Tenn. H8 188-9
Mt. Katahdin, Me. F6 64-5
Mount Kisco, N.Y. B15 80-1
Mount Landing, Va. G13 196-7
Mount Laurel, N.J. J4 76-7
Mount Lebanon, La. B3 168-9
Mount Leonard, Mo. D5 120-1
Mt. Logan, Y.T. C1 297
Mount Lookout, W. Va. H5 200-1
Mt. McKinley, Alaska E11 254-5
Mount Meigs, Ala. I8 146-7
Mount Montgomery, Nev. I4 226-7
Mount Moriah, Mo. A4 120-1
Mount Moriah, Nfld. M7 278-9
Mount Morris, Ill. B7 96-7
Mount Morris, Mich. F4 112-3
Mount Morris, N.Y. F4 80-1
Mount Morris, Wis. F2 140-1
Mount Mourne, N.C. I1 180-1
Mount Nebo, W. Va. H5 200-1
Mount Olive, Ala. G8 146-7
Mount Olive, Ark. B8 150-1
Mount Olive, Ill. J7 96-7
Mount Olive, La. C4 168-9
Mount Olive, Miss. J7 176-7
Mount Olive, N.J. D5 76-7
Mount Olive, N.C. E12 180-1
Mount Olive, Tenn. H12 188-9
Mount Oliver*, Pa. I2 84-5
Mount Olivet, Ky. F12 164-5
Mount Olympus*, Ut. F6 242-3
Mount Orab, O. I4 132-3
Mount Pearl, Nfld. N11 278-9
Mount Penn*, Pa. I13 84-5
Mount Pinson, Ala. E6 146-7
Mount Pleasant, Ark. B8 150-1
Mount Pleasant, Del. C3 153
Mount Pleasant, Ind. G10 100-1
Mount Pleasant, Ia. I13 104-5
Mount Pleasant, Md. B10 172-3
Mount Pleasant, Mich. H13 112-3
Mount Pleasant, Miss. A7 176-7
Mount Pleasant, N.C. J2 180-1
Mount Pleasant, N.S. E4 281
Mount Pleasant, O. F11 132-3
Mount Pleasant, Ont. E13 284-5
Mount Pleasant, Pa. J3 84-5
Mount Pleasant*, P.E.I. D4 287
Mount Pleasant, S.C. I13 184-5
Mount Pleasant, Tenn. J6 188-9
Mount Pleasant, Tex. D10 192-3
Mount Pleasant, Ut. H7 242-3
Mount Pleasant Church, Del. K3 153
Mount Pocono, Pa. F15 84-5
Mount Prospect, Ill. L3 96-7
Mount Pulaski, Ill. G8 96-7
Mount Rainier, Md. I4 172-3
Mt. Rainier, Wash. G9 246-7
Mount Royal, N.J. J2 76-7
Mount Rozell, Ala. A5 146-7
Mount Savage, Md. B3 172-3
Mount Shasta, Calif. E3 210-1
Mount Sherman, Ky. I9 164-5
Mount Sidney, Va. G10 196-7
Mount Signal, Calif. O10 210-1
Mount Solon, Va. G9 196-7
Mount Sterling, Ala. J3 146-7
Mount Sterling, Ill. H5 96-7
Mount Sterling, Ia. K12 104-5
Mount Sterling, Ky. G12 164-5
Mount Sterling, O. G6 132-3
Mount Sterling, Wis. I10 140-1
Mount Stewart, P.E.I. E8 287
Mount Storm, W. Va. E8 200-1
Mount Summit, Ind. G10 100-1
Mount Sunapee, N.H. L4 72-3
Mount Tabor, Vt. K5 90-1
Mount Union, Ia. I13 104-5
Mount Union, La. A4 168-9
Mount Union, Pa. I8 84-5
Mount Vernon, Ala. M3 146-7
Mount Vernon, Ark. E7 150-1
Mount Vernon, Ga. K8 160-1
Mount Vernon, Ga. D2 160-1
Mount Vernon, Ill. L9 96-7
Mount Vernon, Ind. O3 100-1
Mount Vernon, Ia. F13 104-5
Mount Vernon, Ky. I12 164-5
Mount Vernon, Me. K4 64-5
Mount Vernon, Md. H14 172-3
Mount Vernon, Mo. I4 120-1
Mount Vernon, N.Y. D15 80-1
Mount Vernon, O. E7 132-3
Mount Vernon, Ore. E12 238-9
Mount Vernon, S. Dak. G13 136-7
Mount Vernon, Tenn. J13 188-9
Mount Vernon, Tex. D10 192-3
Mount Vernon, Va. B4 196-7
Mount Vernon, Wash. D8 246-7
Mount Victory, O. E5 132-3
Mount View, Tenn. K9 188-9
Mount Washington, Ky. B3 164-5
Mount Washington, Mass. E1 68-9
Mount Willing, S.C. E8 184-5

Mount Wolf, Pa. J11 84-5
Mount Zion, Ga. G2 160-1
Mount Zion, Ill. H9 96-7
Mount Zion, W. Va. F4 200-1
Mountain, N. Dak. C12 128-9
Mountain, W. Va. E5 200-1
Mountain, Wis. E14 140-1
Mountain Brook, Ala. E6 146-7
Mountain City, Ga. C6 160-1
Mountain City, Nev. A8 226-7
Mountain City, Tenn. A16 188-9
Mountain Creek, Ala. H7 146-7
Mountain Falls, Va. E11 196-7
Mountain Green, Ut. E6 242-3
Mountain Grove, Mo. I7 120-1
Mountain Grove, Va. G8 196-7
Mountain Home, Ark. A7 150-1
Mountain Home, Ida. M4 218-9
Mountain Home, Wyo. K13 250-1
Mountain Home Base*, Ida. M4 218-9
Mountain Iron, Minn. G7 116-7
Mountain Lake, Minn. O4 116-7
Mountain Lake Park, Md. C1 172-3
Mountain Lakes, N.J. D6 76-7
Mountain Park, Ga. A10 160-1
Mountain Park, Okla. G8 234-5
Mountain Pass, Calif. L10 210-1
Mountain Pine, Ark. F5 150-1
Mountain Point, Alaska H16 254-5
Mountain Rest, S.C. B4 184-5
Mountain Springs, Nev. N9 226-7
Mountain Top, Ark. C3 150-1
Mountain Valley, Ark. F5 150-1
Mountain View, Ark. C7 150-1
Mountain View, Calif. D8 210-1
Mountain View, Colo. G3 214-5
Mountain View*, Ga. G4 160-1
Mountain View, Hawaii J14 258-9
Mountain View, Mo. I8 120-1
Mountain View, N. Mex. F6 230-1
Mountain View, Okla. G8 234-5
Mountain View, Wyo. J6 250-1
Mountain View, Wyo. F12 250-1
Mountain View Trailer Court*, Alta. L7 264-5
Mountain Village, Alaska E8 254-5
Mountainair, N. Mex. G6 230-1
Mountainboro, Ala. D8 146-7
Mountainburg, Ark. C2 150-1
Mountainside, N.J. E6 76-7
Mountlake Terrace, Wash. H2 246-7
Mountrail, co., N. Dak. D4 128-9
Mountville, Ga. H3 160-1
Mountville, Pa. J12 84-5
Mountville, S.C. J4 184-5
Mousie, Ky. I15 164-5
Mouth of Seneca, W. Va. F8 200-1
Mouth of Wilson, Va. K5 196-7
Mouzon, S.C. F13 184-5
Moville, Ia. D2 104-5
Moweaqua, Ill. H8 96-7
Mower, co., Minn. O7 116-7
Mowich, Ore. H8 238-9
Mowrystown, O. I5 132-3
Moxee City, Wash. H11 246-7
Moyer, Wyo. I5 250-1
Moyers, Okla. H14 234-5
Moyers, W. Va. G8 200-1
Moyie, B.C. J10 268-9
Moyie Springs, Ida. A3 218-9
Moyock, N.C. B15 180-1
Mozart, Sask. L9 294-5
Mozelle, Ky. J14 164-5
Mozer, W. Va. F9 200-1
Mud, W. Va. J12 200-1
Mud Bay*, Alaska H16 254-5
Mud Lake, Ida. L9 218-9
Muddy Gap, Wyo. H11 250-1
Muenster, Sask. K8 294-5
Muenster*, Tex. D8 192-3
Muhlenberg, co., Ky. J6 164-5
Muir, Mich. I13 112-3
Mukilteo, Wash. G2 246-7
Mukwonago, Wis. J4 140-1
Mulberry, Ark. D3 150-1
Mulberry*, Calif. G3 210-1
Mulberry, Fla. H4 156-7
Mulberry, Ind. F6 100-1
Mulberry, Kans. I16 108-9
Mulberry, Tenn. K8 188-9
Mulberry Grove, Ill. J8 96-7
Muldoon, Ida. L7 218-9
Muldraugh, Ky. C1 164-5
Muldrow, Okla. F16 234-5
Mule Creek, N. Mex. J2 230-1
Muleshoe, Tex. C4 192-3
Mulga, Ala. E6 146-7
Mulgrave, N.S. C10 281
Mulhall, Okla. D11 234-5
Mulhurst, Alta. J7 264-5
Mulino, Ore. G2 238-9
Mullan, Ida. D4 218-9
Mullen, Nebr. E6 124-5
Mullens, W. Va. J4 200-1
Mullett Lake, Mich. E13 112-3
Mullica*, N.J. L5 76-7
Mullica Hill, N.J. K2 76-7
Mulliken, Mich. I13 112-3
Mullins, S.C. D15 184-5
Mullinville, Kans. J6 108-9
Multnomah, co., Ore. B6 238-9
Mulvane, Kans. J11 108-9
Mulvihill*, Man. I3 272-3
Muncie, Ind. G10 100-1
Muncy, Pa. F11 84-5
Mundare*, Alta. I9 264-5
Munday, Tex. D7 192-3
Munday, W. Va. F4 200-1
Mundelein, Ill. K3 96-7
Munden, Kans. C10 108-9
Mundy Point, Va. G14 196-7
Munford, Ala. E8 146-7
Munford, Tenn. J2 188-9
Munfordville, Ky. I8 164-5
Munger, Mich. H14 112-3
Munhall, Pa. B6 84-5
Munich, N. Dak. C11 128-9
Munising, Mich. D10 112-3
Munith, Mich. J2 112-3
Munroe Falls, O. D15 132-3
Munsey Park*, N.Y. J11 80-1
Munson, Alta. L8 264-5
Munson, Mich. K13 112-3
Munsons Corners*, N.Y. F7 80-1
Munsonville, N.H. N4 72-3
Munster, Ind. A4 100-1
Munster*, Ont. H14 284-5
Murdo, S. Dak. G8 136-7
Murdochville, Que. H6 290-1
Murdock, Kans. J9 108-9
Murdock, Minn. L3 116-7
Murdock, Nebr. K2 124-5
Murfreesboro, Ark. H3 150-1
Murfreesboro, N.C. C13 180-1
Murfreesboro, Tenn. C8 188-9
Murillo, Ont. F3 284-5
Murphy, Ida. M3 218-9
Murphy, Miss. G5 176-7
Murphy, N.C. F1 180-1
Murphy, Okla. D15 234-5
Murphy, Ore. J5 238-9
Murphysboro, Ill. N8 96-7
Murray, Ida. D4 218-9
Murray, Ind. D11 100-1
Murray, Ia. I7 104-5
Murray, Ky. K3 164-5
Murray, Nebr. K3 124-5
Murray, Ut. F6 242-3
Murray, co., Ga. D3 160-1
Murray, co., Minn. O3 116-7
Murray, co., Okla. H12 234-5
Murray City, O. H8 132-3
Murray Harbour, P.E.I. G10 287
Murray Harbour North, P.E.I. G10 287
Murray River, P.E.I. G9 287
Murraysville, W. Va. E3 200-1
Murrayville, Ga. E5 160-1
Murrayville, Ill. I6 96-7
Murrells Inlet, S.C. F15 184-5
Murtaugh, Ida. O6 218-9
Muscatine, Ia. H14 104-5
Muscatine, co., Ia. H13 104-5
Muscle Shoals, Ala. B4 146-7
Muscoda, Wis. J11 140-1
Muscogee, co., Ga. J2 160-1
Muscotah, Kans. D14 108-9
Muscoy*, Calif. N8 210-1
Muse, Okla. G16 234-5
Muse, Pa. B5 84-5
Muses Mills, Ky. F13 164-5
Musgrave Harbour, Nfld. L10 278-9
Musgravetown, Nfld. N10 278-9
Muskego, Wis. J4 140-1
Muskegon, Mich. I11 112-3
Muskegon, co., Mich. H11 112-3
Muskegon Heights, Mich. I11 112-3
Muskingum, co., O. F9 132-3
Muskogee, Okla. E15 234-5
Muskogee, co., Okla. E15 234-5
Musquodoboit Harbour, N.S. E8 281
Musselshell, Mont. F11 222-3
Musselshell, co., Mont. F10 222-3
Mustang, Okla. J1 234-5
Mustoe, Va. G8 196-7
Muttontown*, N.Y. J11 80-1
Mutual, Okla. D8 234-5
Mutual, Ut. H7 242-3
Myers, Ky. F12 164-5
Myers, Mont. F12 222-3
Myers Chuck, Alaska H16 254-5
Myers Corner*, N.Y. I11 80-1
Myerstown, Pa. I12 84-5
Myersville, Md. C8 172-3
Mylo, N. Dak. C9 128-9
Mynard, Nebr. K3 124-5
Myra, W. Va. I11 200-1
Myrick, Miss. K9 176-7
Myricks, Mass. G12 68-9
Myrnam, Alta. I9 264-5
Myrtle*, Man. K3 272-3
Myrtle, Minn. O7 116-7
Myrtle, Miss. B8 176-7
Myrtle, W. Va. K11 200-1
Myrtle Beach, S.C. F16 184-5
Myrtle Beach Base*, S.C. F16 184-5
Myrtle Creek, Ore. H5 238-9
Myrtle Creek South*, Ore. H5 238-9
Myrtle Grove*, Fla. B3 156-7
Myrtle Grove, La. J10 168-9
Myrtle Point, Ore. H4 238-9
Myrtlewood, Ala. I3 146-7
Mystic, Conn. G14 60-1
Mystic, Ga. L6 160-1
Mystic, Ia. J9 104-5
Mystic Islands, N.J. L6 76-7
Myton, Ut. G9 242-3

N

Na Ah Tee, Ariz. E9 206-7
Naalehu, Hawaii K13 258-9
Naamans Corner, Del. A4 153
Nabb, Ind. M10 100-1
Nabesna, Alaska E13 254-5
Nabnasset, Mass. B10 68-9
Naborton, La. C2 168-9
Nabs Corner, Mass. J13 68-9
Naches, Wash. H10 246-7
Nackawic*, N.B. H3 275
Nacmine, Alta. L8 264-5
Naco, Ariz. M10 206-7
Nacogdoches, Tex. E11 192-3
Nacogdoches, co., Tex. E11 192-3
Nadeau, Mich. E10 112-3
Naf, Ida. O8 218-9
Nags Head, N.C. D16 180-1
Nahant, Mass. G6 68-9
Nahcotta, Wash. H5 246-7
Nahma, Mich. E10 112-3
Nahunta, Ga. M9 160-1
Naicam, Sask. K8 294-5
Nail, Ark. C4 150-1
Nail Pond, P.E.I. B4 287
Nain, Nfld. E5 278-9
Nairn, La. J10 168-9
Nairn, Ont. H7 284-5
Nakina, Ont. E14 284-5
Naknek, Alaska G9 254-5
Nakusp, B.C. J9 268-9
Nallen, W. Va. H5 200-1
Nambe, N. Mex. D7 230-1
Nampa, Alta. F5 264-5
Nampa, Ida. L3 218-9
Namskaket, Mass. G16 68-9
Namu, B.C. H4 268-9
Nanafalia, Ala. J3 146-7
Nanaimo, B.C. C11 268-9
Nanakuli, Hawaii J2 258-9
Nance, Ark. K13 150-1
Nance, co., Nebr. G12 124-5
Nancy, Ky. J11 164-5
Nanjemoy, Md. G9 172-3
Nankipoo, Tenn. B2 188-9
Nankipooh, Ga. J2 160-1
Nantasket Beach, Mass. I7 68-9
Nanticoke, Md. H13 172-3
Nanticoke, Ont. E13 284-5
Nanticoke, Pa. F13 84-5
Nanton, Alta. N8 264-5
Nantucket, Mass. J16 68-9
Nantucket, co., Mass. J16 68-9
Nantucket Isl., Mass. J16 68-9
Nanty-Glo, Pa. H5 84-5
Nanuet, N.Y. C14 80-1
Naola, Va. H9 196-7
Naoma, W. Va. K14 200-1
Naomi, La. E15 168-9
Napa, Calif. H3 210-1
Napa, co., Calif. H3 210-1
Napadogan, N.B. G4 275
Napaimiut, Alaska F9 254-5
Napakiak, Alaska F8 254-5
Napanee, Ont. J13 284-5
Napaskiak, Alaska F8 254-5
Napavine, Wash. H7 246-7
Naper, Nebr. C10 124-5
Naperville, Ill. M2 96-7
Napier, W. Va. F5 200-1
Napier Field*, Ala. L9 146-7
Napierville, Que. J12 290-1
Napierville, co., Que. J12 290-1
Napinka, Man. K10 272-3
Naplate, Ill. D9 96-7
Naples, Fla. I11 156-7
Naples, Ida. B3 218-9
Naples, Me. N8 64-5
Naples, N.Y. F4 80-1
Naples, N.C. E4 180-1
Naples, S. Dak. D14 136-7
Naples*, Tex. D11 192-3
Naples Park*, Fla. I11 156-7
Napoleon, Ind. J10 100-1
Napoleon, Mich. K2 112-3
Napoleon, Miss. O7 176-7
Napoleon, Mo. I16 120-1
Napoleon, N. Dak. I9 128-9
Napoleon, O. B4 132-3
Napoleonville, La. D10 168-9
Naponee, Nebr. J10 124-5
Napoopoo, Hawaii J12 258-9
Nappanee, Ind. B8 100-1
Nara Visa, N. Mex. E11 230-1
Naramata*, B.C. J8 268-9
Naranja, Fla. I15 156-7
Narberth*, Pa. J15 84-5
Nardin, Okla. C11 234-5
Narka, Kans. C10 108-9
Narol, Man. I14 272-3
Narragansett*, R.I. H5 87
Narragansett Bay, R.I. F6 87
Narragansett Pier, R.I. H5 87
Narrows, Va. I6 196-7
Narrows, The, P.E.I. C4 287
Naruna, Va. I9 196-7
Naschitti, N. Mex. D2 230-1
Naselle, Wash. H5 246-7
Nash, N. Dak. G13 128-9
Nash, Okla. C10 234-5
Nash*, Tex. D11 192-3
Nash, co., N.C. D12 180-1
Nashaquitsa, Mass. J13 68-9
Nashoba, Okla. H15 234-5
Nashotah*, Wis. J14 140-1
Nashua, Ia. C10 104-5
Nashua, Minn. J2 116-7
Nashua, Mont. C13 222-3
Nashua, N.H. O7 72-3
Nashville, Ark. H3 150-1
Nashville, Ga. M6 160-1
Nashville, Ill. L8 96-7
Nashville, Ind. J8 100-1
Nashville, Kans. J8 108-9
Nashville, Me. C8 64-5
Nashville, Mich. J12 112-3
Nashville, N.C. D12 180-1
Nashville, Tenn. B7 188-9
Nashwauk, Minn. G6 116-7
Nasonville, R.I. A3 87
Nasonworth, N.B. I4 275
Nassau, Del. I6 153
Nassau, Minn. L2 116-7
Nassau, N.Y. F11 80-1
Nassau, co., Fla. B11 156-7
Nassau, co., N.Y. K11 80-1
Nassau Bay*, Tex. G10 192-3
Nassawadox, Va. H15 196-7
Natalia, Tex. K1 192-3
Natchez, La. D3 168-9
Natchez, Miss. K3 176-7
Natchitoches, La. D3 168-9
Natchitoches, co., La. D3 168-9
Nathalie, Va. J10 196-7
Nathan, Ark. H3 150-1
Nathrop, Colo. G10 214-5
Natick, Mass. I3 68-9
National City, Calif. J11 210-1
National City, Mich. G14 112-3
National Mills, Man. D9 272-3
National Mine, Mich. D9 112-3
National Park, N.J. N9 76-7
Natoma, Kans. E7 108-9
Natrona, Wyo. F12 250-1
Natrona, co., Wyo. F11 250-1
Natura, Okla. E14 234-5
Natural Bridge, Ala. D4 146-7
Natural Bridge, Va. H8 196-7
Natural Steps, Ark. I15 150-1
Naturita, Colo. H6 214-5
Naubinway, Mich. D12 112-3
Naugatuck, Conn. F7 60-1
Naugatuck, W. Va. K10 200-1
Naugatuck R., Conn. D6 60-1
Nauvoo, Ala. D4 146-7
Nauvoo, Ill. F3 96-7
Navajo, Ariz. E10 206-7
Navajo, Mont. A15 222-3
Navajo, co., Ariz. E9 206-7
Navan*, Ont. H15 284-5
Navarino, Wis. D3 140-1
Navarre, Kans. F11 108-9
Navarre, O. D10 132-3
Navarro, co., Tex. E9 192-3
Navasota, Tex. G9 192-3
Navesink, N.J. H11 76-7
Navin*, Man. J4 272-3
Navina, Okla. E11 234-5
Navy Yard City, Wash. I1 246-7
Nawiliwili, Hawaii D5 258-9
Naxera, Va. E4 196-7
Naylor, Ark. E7 150-1
Naylor, Ga. N7 160-1
Naylor, Md. K6 172-3
Naylor, Mo. J10 120-1
Nazareth, Ky. C3 164-5
Nazareth, Pa. G15 84-5
Nazlini, Ariz. D11 206-7
Neah Bay, Wash. D4 246-7
Neahkahnie, Ore. B4 238-9
Neal, Kans. I13 108-9
Neavitt, Md. F12 172-3
Nebo, Ky. I5 164-5
Nebo, La. D5 168-9
Nebo, N.C. D5 180-1
Nebo, Okla. H12 234-5
Nebo Center*, Calif. M8 210-1
Nebraska, Ind. K10 100-1
Nebraska City, Nebr. H16 124-5
Necanicum Junction, Ore. B4 238-9
Necedah, Wis. H11 140-1
Neche, N. Dak. B13 128-9
Neck City, Mo. H3 120-1
Nectar, Ala. D6 146-7
Ned, Ky. F14 164-5
Nederland, Colo. F1 214-5
Nederland, Tex. G11 192-3
Needham, Ala. J2 146-7
Needham, Ind. I8 100-1
Needham, Mass. I4 68-9
Needham Heights, Mass. I4 68-9
Needles, Calif. M11 210-1
Needville, Tex. I12 192-3
Neel, Ala. C5 146-7
Neelin*, Man. K2 272-3
Neely, Miss. L9 176-7
Neelyville, Mo. J10 120-1
Neenach, Calif. M7 210-1
Neenah, Wis. F3 140-1
Neepawa, Man. I11 272-3
Neeses, S.C. F10 184-5
Negaunee, Mich. D9 112-3
Negreet, La. E2 168-9
Neguac*, N.B. F6 275
Nehalem, Ore. B4 238-9
Nehawka, Nebr. K3 124-5
Neiber, Wyo. D10 250-1
Neihart, Mont. E7 222-3
Neil Harbour, N.S. A11 281
Neilburg, Sask. K4 294-5
Neillsville, Wis. G10 140-1
Neilton, Wash. F5 246-7
Nekoma, Kans. G6 108-9
Nekoma, N. Dak. C11 128-9
Nekoosa, Wis. G11 140-1
Nelagoney, Okla. C13 234-5
Neligh, Nebr. E11 124-5
Nellieburg, Miss. I9 176-7
Nellis*, Nev. K7 226-7
Nelliston*, N.Y. F9 80-1
Nellysford, Va. H10 196-7
Nelson, B.C. J10 268-9
Nelson, Ga. E4 160-1
Nelson, Minn. K3 116-7
Nelson, Mo. D5 120-1
Nelson, Nebr. J11 124-5

Nelson, Nev. N10 226-7
Nelson, N.H. N4 72-3
Nelson, Okla. I14 234-5
Nelson, Va. K10 196-7
Nelson, Wis. G8 140-1
Nelson, co., Ky. H9 164-5
Nelson, co., N. Dak. . . . D12 128-9
Nelson, co., Va. H9 196-7
Nelson House, Man. . . . E3 272-3
Nelson Lagoon*, Alaska . I8 254-5
Nelson-Miramichi, N.B. . F6 275
Nelsonville, Ark. B9 150-1
Nelsonville, N.Y. A14 80-1
Nelsonville, O. H8 132-3
Nelsonville, Wis. E1 140-1
Nemacolin, Pa. K2 84-5
Nemaha, Ia. D4 104-5
Nemaha, Nebr. I16 124-5
Nemaha, co., Kans. D13 108-9
Nemaha, co., Nebr. I16 124-5
Nemo, S. Dak. F2 136-7
Nenana, Alaska D11 254-5
Nenana Native Village, Alaska. D11 254-5
Nenzel, Nebr. C6 124-5
Neodesha, Kans. J14 108-9
Neoga, Ill. I10 96-7
Neola, Ia. H3 104-5
Neola, Ut. F9 242-3
Neola, W. Va. I6 200-1
Neon, Ky. I14 164-5
Neopit, Wis. E13 140-1
Neosho, Mo. I3 120-1
Neosho, Wis. I3 140-1
Neosho, co., Kans. I15 108-9
Neosho Falls, Kans. . . . H14 108-9
Neosho Rapids, Kans. . . G13 108-9
Neosho R., Kans. K15 108-9
Nepaug, Conn. C7 60-1
Nephi, Ut. H6 242-3
Nephton, Ont. J11 284-5
Neponset, Mass. I5 68-9
Neptune*, N.J. H8 76-7
Neptune Beach, Fla. . . B11 156-7
Neptune City, N.J. H8 76-7
Nerinx, Ky. D3 164-5
Nerstrand, Minn. N7 116-7
Nesbit Heights*, Sask. . . K10 294-5
Nesbitt, Man. J11 272-3
Nesbitt, Miss. A6 176-7
Nesco, N.J. K5 76-7
Nesconset*, N.Y. J12 80-1
Nescopeck, Pa. F12 84-5
Neshanic Station, N.J. . . F5 76-7
Neshkoro, Wis. F2 140-1
Neshoba, Miss. H8 176-7
Neshoba, co., Miss. H8 176-7
Neskowin, Ore. C4 238-9
Nesmith, S.C. F14 184-5
Nespelem, Wash. D13 246-7
Nesquehoning, Pa. G13 84-5
Ness, co., Kans. G5 108-9
Ness City, Kans. G5 108-9
Nestor Falls, Ont. E1 284-5
Nestorville, W. Va. D15 200-1
Netarts, Ore. C4 238-9
Netawaka, Kans. D14 108-9
Netcong, N.J. D5 76-7
Netherhill, Sask. L4 294-5
Netherland, Tenn. B10 188-9
Nett Lake, Minn. F7 116-7
Nettie, W. Va. H5 200-1
Nettleton, Miss. D10 176-7
Neuanlage, Sask. K6 294-5
Neubergthal*, Man. K3 272-3
Neubert, Tenn. I12 188-9
Neudorf, Sask. M9 294-5
Neuenburg*, Man. K4 272-3
Neuhorst*, Man. K13 272-3
Neuhorst, Sask. K6 294-5
Neuse, N.C. H7 180-1
Neustadt, Ont. B12 284-5
Neuville*, Que. G1 290-1
Neva, Tenn. A16 188-9
Nevada, Ia. F8 104-5
Nevada, Mo. G3 120-1
Nevada, O. D6 132-3
Nevada, co., Ark. I4 150-1
Nevada, co., Calif. G4 210-1
Nevada City, Calif. G4 210-1
Nevada City, Mont. H6 222-3
Neville, Sask. N5 294-5
Nevils, Ga. K10 160-1
Nevis, Minn. H4 116-7
Nevisdale, Ky. K12 164-5
New Albany, Ind. N9 100-1
New Albany, Kans. J14 108-9
New Albany, Miss. B9 176-7
New Albany, O. F7 132-3
New Albin, Ia. A13 104-5
New Alexandria, O. E11 132-3
New Almelo, Kans. D5 108-9
New Alsace, Ind. J11 100-1
New Amsterdam, Ind. . . O8 100-1
New Amsterdam, Wis. . . H9 140-1
New Annan*, P.E.I. E5 287
New Ashford, Mass. B2 68-9
New Athens, Ill. L7 96-7
New Athens, O. F11 132-3
New Auburn, Minn. C7 116-7
New Auburn, Wis. E9 140-1
New Augusta, Miss. L9 176-7
New Baden, Ill. K7 96-7
New Baltimore, Mich. . . I7 112-3
New Beaver*, Pa. G1 84-5
New Bedford, Mass. . . . H12 68-9
New Bedford, N.J. H8 76-7
New Bercthal, Man. K14 272-3
New Berlin, Ill. H6 96-7
New Berlin, N.Y. F8 80-1
New Berlin, Wis. J4 140-1
New Berlinville*, Pa. . . . I14 84-5
New Bern, N.C. F14 180-1
New Bethlehem, Pa. F3 84-5
New Blaine, Ark. D4 150-1
New Bloomfield, Mo. . . . E7 120-1
New Bloomington, O. . . . E6 132-3
New Boston, Ill. D4 96-7
New Boston, Mass. E3 68-9
New Boston, Mich. K5 112-3
New Boston, N.H. N6 72-3
New Boston, O. J7 132-3
New Boston, Tex. D11 192-3
New Bothwell*, Man. . . . J14 272-3
New Braintree, Mass. . . . D7 68-9
New Braunfels, Tex. I3 192-3
New Bremen, O. E3 132-3
New Bridge, Ore. D15 238-9
New Brighton*, Minn. . . M7 116-7
New Brighton, Pa. G1 84-5
New Britain, Conn. D8 60-1
New Britain*, Pa. I15 84-5
New Brockton, Ala. L8 146-7
New Brunswick, N.J. . . . F6 76-7
New Buffalo, Mich. K11 112-3
New Cambria, Kans. F10 108-9
New Cambria, Mo. C6 120-1
New Canaan, Conn. I4 60-1
New Canada, Me. B7 64-5
New Canton, Tenn. F15 188-9
New Canton, Va. H11 196-7
New Carlisle, Ind. A7 100-1
New Carlisle, O. G15 132-3
New Carlisle, Que. I6 290-1
New Carrollton, Md. . . . I5 172-3
New Cassel*, N.Y. J11 80-1
New Castle, Colo. E7 214-5
New Castle, Del. B3 153
New Castle, Ind. H10 100-1
New Castle, Ky. F10 164-5
New Castle, N.H. N10 72-3
New Castle, Pa. F1 84-5
New Castle, Va. I7 196-7
New Castle, co., Del. . . . C3 153
New Castle Northwest*, Pa. G1 84-5
New Centerville, Ida. . . . L4 218-9
New Chicago, Ind. A5 100-1
New Church, Va. G16 196-7
New City, N.Y. B14 80-1
New Columbus, Ky. F10 164-5
New Concord, Ky. K4 164-5
New Concord, O. F9 132-3
New Corydon, Ind. E12 100-1
New Creek, W. Va. D9 200-1
New Cumberland, Pa. . . . I11 84-5
New Cumberland, W. Va. A5 200-1
New Cuyama, Calif. M5 210-1
New Denver, B.C. J9 268-9
New Diggings, Wis. K11 140-1
New Dundee, Ont. D13 284-5
New Durham, N.H. K8 72-3
New Eagle*, Pa. I2 84-5
New Edinburg, Ark. I7 150-1
New Effington, S. Dak. . A15 136-7
New Egypt, N.J. I6 76-7
New Ellenton, S.C. G8 184-5
New Empire, Nev. G2 226-7
New England, Ga. C1 160-1
New England, N. Dak. . . H3 128-9
New England, W. Va. . . . E3 200-1
New Era, La. E6 168-9
New Era, Mich. H11 112-3
New Era, Ore. G2 238-9
New Fairfield, Conn. . . . F4 60-1
New Fane, Wis. H4 140-1
New Florence, Mo. E8 120-1
New Fork, Wyo. G7 250-1
New Franklin, Mo. D6 120-1
New Freedom, Pa. K11 84-5
New Germany, Minn. . . . B8 116-7
New Germany*, N.S. . . . E6 281
New Glarus, Wis. J1 140-1
New Glasgow, N.S. C8 281
New Glasgow, P.E.I. . . . E6 287
New Gloucester, Me. . . . N9 64-5
New Goshen, Ind. I4 100-1
New Gretna, N.J. L6 76-7
New Hackensack*, N.Y. I11 80-1
New Hamburg, Mo. I11 120-1
New Hamburg*, N.Y. . . H11 80-1
New Hamburg, Ont. . . . D13 284-5
New Hampton, Ia. C11 104-5
New Hampton, Mo. B3 120-1
New Hampton, N.H. . . . J6 72-3
New Hanover*, N.J. I5 76-7
New Hanover, co., N.C. G12 180-1
New Harbor, Me. N12 64-5
New Harbour, Nfld. . . . N11 278-9
New Harmony, Ind. N3 100-1
New Harmony, Ut. M3 242-3
New Hartford, Conn. . . . C7 60-1
New Hartford, Ia. D10 104-5
New Hartford*, N.Y. . . . E8 80-1
New Haven, Conn. H7 60-1
New Haven, Ill. M10 96-7
New Haven, Ind. C11 100-1
New Haven, Ky. D2 164-5
New Haven, Mich. H7 112-3
New Haven, Mo. E9 120-1
New Haven, P.E.I. F6 287
New Haven, Vt. G4 90-1
New Haven, W. Va. F2 200-1
New Haven, Wyo. B15 250-1
New Haven, co., Conn. . G7 60-1
New Hazelton*, B.C. . . . J6 268-9
New Holland, N.C. E15 180-1
New Holland, O. G6 132-3
New Holland, Pa. J13 84-5
New Holland, S.C. F9 184-5
New Holstein, Wis. H15 140-1
New Hope, Ala. B7 146-7
New Hope, Ga. B9 160-1
New Hope, Ky. E3 164-5
New Hope, Minn. B10 116-7
New Hope, Pa. I16 84-5
New Hope, Va. G10 196-7
New Hradec, N. Dak. . . . G3 128-9
New Hudson, Mich. I4 112-3
New Hyde Park*, N.Y. . K11 80-1
New Iberia, La. H6 168-9
New Idanha, Ore. D7 238-9
New Ipswich, N.H. O5 72-3
New Johnsonville, Tenn. B5 188-9
New Kensington, Pa. . . . A7 84-5
New Kent, Va. E2 196-7
New Kent, co., Va. H13 196-7
New Knoxville, O. E4 132-3
New Laguna, N. Mex. . . . F4 230-1
New Lancaster, Kans. . . . G16 108-9
New Lebanon, Ind. K4 100-1
New Lebanon, O. H14 132-3
New Leipzig, N. Dak. . . . I5 128-9
New Lenox, Ill. O3 96-7
New Lenox, Mass. C2 68-9
New Lexington, O. G8 132-3
New Liberty, Ia. G14 104-5
New Liberty, Ky. F10 164-5
New Liberty, Okla. F7 234-5
New Lima, Okla. F12 234-5
New Limerick, Me. E9 64-5
New Line, Tenn. G14 188-9
New Lisbon, Ind. H11 100-1
New Lisbon, N.J. I5 76-7
New Lisbon, Wis. H11 140-1
New Liskeard, Ont. G8 284-5
New London, Ark. J7 150-1
New London, Conn. G13 60-1
New London, Ind. F8 100-1
New London, Ia. J13 104-5
New London, Minn. L4 116-7
New London, Mo. C8 120-1
New London, N.H. L4 72-3
New London, N.C. J3 180-1
New London, O. C8 132-3
New London, Tex. E10 192-3
New London, Wis. E3 140-1
New London, co., Conn. F13 60-1
New Lothrop, Mich. F3 112-3
New Madison, O. G12 132-3
New Madrid, Mo. J12 120-1
New Madrid, co., Mo. . . J12 120-1
New Manchester, W. Va. A5 200-1
New Marion, Ind. K10 100-1
New Market, Ala. A7 146-7
New Market, Ind. G6 100-1
New Market, Ia. J4 104-5
New Market, Ky. I10 164-5
New Market, Md. E2 172-3
New Market, Minn. C10 116-7
New Market, Tenn. H13 188-9
New Market, Va. F10 196-7
New Marlborough, Mass. E2 68-9
New Martinsville, W. Va. D5 200-1
New Maryland*, N.B. . . I4 275
New Matamoras, O. H11 132-3
New Meadows, Ida. I3 218-9
New Miami, O. J13 132-3
New Middleton, Tenn. . . B9 188-9
New Middletown, Ind. . . N8 100-1
New Middletown, O. . . . C12 132-3
New Midway, Md. B9 172-3
New Milford, Conn. E4 60-1
New Milford, N.J. A12 76-7
New Milford, Pa. C14 84-5
New Milton, W. Va. E5 200-1
New Minas*, N.S. D6 281
New Monmouth, N.J. . . H11 76-7
New Munich, Minn. K4 116-7
New Munster, Wis. K4 140-1
New Norway, Alta. J8 264-5
New Orleans, La. I9 168-9
New Oxford, Pa. K10 84-5
New Palestine, Ind. H9 100-1
New Paltz, N.Y. H10 80-1
New Paris, Ind. B9 100-1
New Paris, O. H12 132-3
New Pekin, Ind. M8 100-1
New Philadelphia, O. . . . E10 132-3
New Philadelphia, Pa. . . H13 84-5
New Pine Creek, Calif. . D5 210-1
New Pine Creek, Ore. . . K10 238-9
New Plymouth, Ida. K2 218-9
New Point, Va. E4 196-7
New Port Richey, Fla. . . G2 156-7
New Port Richey East-Richey Lakes*, Fla. . . . G2 156-7
New Portland, Me. J4 64-5
New Prague, Minn. D9 116-7
New Preston, Conn. D5 60-1
New Providence, Ia. . . . E9 104-5
New Providence, N.J. . . E6 76-7
New Providence, Tenn. . F5 188-9
New Prue*, Okla. D13 234-5
New Quebec Crater (Chubb Crater), Que. . B3 290-1
New Richland, Minn. . . . O6 116-7
New Richmond, Ind. . . . G6 100-1
New Richmond, Mich. . . J11 112-3
New Richmond, O. I4 132-3
New Richmond*, Que. . . I6 290-1
New Richmond, Wis. . . . E7 140-1
New Riegel, O. C6 132-3
New River, Ariz. H6 206-7
New River, Tenn. G10 188-9
New River, Va. I7 196-7
New River-Gieger*, N.C. G13 180-1
New Road, N.S. E7 281
New Roads, La. G6 168-9
New Rochelle, N.Y. . . . D15 80-1
New Rockford, N. Dak. . E10 128-9
New Ross, Ind. G6 100-1
New Rye, N.H. M7 72-3
New Salem, Ind. I10 100-1
New Salem, Kans. J11 108-9
New Salem, Mass. C6 68-9
New Salem, N. Dak. H6 128-9
New Salem-Buffington, Pa. J2 84-5
New Salisbury, Ind. N8 100-1
New Sarepta, Alta. J8 264-5
New Sarpy, La. C13 168-9
New Sharon, Ia. H10 104-5
New Sharon, Me. J4 64-5
New Shoreham*, R.I. . . . K4 87
New Shrewsbury, N.J. . . G8 76-7
New Site, Ala. G9 146-7
New Smyrna Beach, Fla. D12 156-7
New Square*, N.Y. J10 80-1
New Stanton*, Pa. I3 84-5
New Straitsville, O. . . . G8 132-3
New Strawn, Kans. H14 108-9
New Stuyahok, Alaska . . G9 254-5
New Sweden, Me. B8 64-5
New Tazewell, Tenn. . . . G13 188-9
New Topsail Beach, N.C. G13 180-1
New Town, N. Dak. E4 128-9
New Trenton, Ind. J12 100-1
New Trier, Minn. C11 116-7
New Tulsa*, Okla. D14 234-5
New Ulm, Minn. N5 116-7
New Underwood, S. Dak. F3 136-7
New Verda, La. D4 168-9
New Vernon, N.J. E6 76-7
New Victoria*, N.S. B11 281
New Vienna, Ia. D14 104-5
New Vienna, O. H5 132-3
New Village, N.J. E3 76-7
New Vineyard, Me. J3 64-5
New Virginia, Ia. I7 104-5
New Washington, Ind. . . M10 100-1
New Washington, O. . . . D7 132-3
New Waterford, N.S. . . . B11 281
New Waterford, O. D11 132-3
New Waverly, Ind. D8 100-1
New Westminster, B.C. . C12 268-9
New Whiteland, Ind. . . . H2 100-1
New Wilmington, Pa. . . . F1 84-5
New Windsor, Md. B9 172-3
New Windsor, N.Y. I11 80-1
New Woodville, Okla. . . I12 234-5
New York, co., N.Y. . . . E14 80-1
New York City, N.Y. . . K11 80-1
New York Mills, Minn. . I3 116-7
New York Mills*, N.Y. . E8 80-1
New York State Barge Canal, N.Y. E3 80-1
New Zealand, P.E.I. E10 287
New Zion, Ky. I12 164-5
New Zion, S.C. E13 184-5
Newagen, Me. N11 64-5
Newald, Wis. D13 140-1
Newalla, Okla. J3 234-5
Newark, Ark. C9 150-1
Newark, Calif. D8 210-1
Newark, Del. B2 153
Newark, Ill. C9 96-7
Newark, Md. H16 172-3
Newark, Mo. B7 120-1
Newark, N.J. E7 76-7
Newark, N.Y. E5 80-1
Newark, O. F8 132-3
Newark, S. Dak. A13 136-7
Newark, Vt. D9 90-1
Newark Bay, N.J. E10 76-7
Newark Valley, N.Y. . . . G7 80-1
Newaygo, Mich. H12 112-3
Newaygo, co., Mich. . . . H12 112-3
Newberg, Ore. G1 238-9
Newbern, Ala. H4 146-7
Newbern, Ind. J9 100-1
Newbern, Tenn. B3 188-9
Newbern, Va. J6 196-7
Newberne, W. Va. E5 200-1
Newberry, Calif. M9 210-1
Newberry, Fla. D10 156-7
Newberry, Ind. K5 100-1
Newberry, Mich. D12 112-3
Newberry, S.C. D8 184-5
Newberry, co., S.C. D8 184-5
Newborn, Ga. G5 160-1
Newboro, Ont. J14 284-5
Newburg, Ala. C4 146-7
Newburg, Ark. B8 150-1
Newburg, Md. H10 172-3
Newburg, Mo. G7 120-1
Newburg, N. Dak. C7 128-9
Newburg, W. Va. C16 200-1
Newburg, Wis. H5 140-1
Newburgh, Ind. O4 100-1
Newburgh, Me. J6 64-5
Newburgh, N.Y. I11 80-1
Newburgh, Ont. J13 284-5
Newburgh Center, Me. . . J6 64-5
Newburgh Heights, O. . . B14 132-3
Newbury, Mass. A12 68-9
Newbury, N.H. L4 72-3
Newbury, Ont. E11 284-5
Newbury, Vt. G9 90-1
Newburyport, Mass. A12 68-9
Newby, Okla. E13 234-5
Newcastle*, Me. M12 64-5
Newcastle, Nebr. D14 124-5
Newcastle, N.B. F6 275
Newcastle, Okla. K2 234-5
Newcastle, Ont. C16 284-5
Newcastle, Tex. D7 192-3
Newcastle, Ut. L3 242-3

Newcastle, Wyo. D16 250-1
Newcastle Creek, N.B. H5 275
Newcomb, Md. F12 172-3
Newcomb, N. Mex. D2 230-1
Newcomb, Tenn. F11 188-9
Newcomerstown, O. E9 132-3
Newdale, Ida. L10 218-9
Newdale, Man. I10 272-3
Newell, Ala. F9 146-7
Newell, Ark. J6 150-1
Newell, Calif. D4 210-1
Newell, Ia. D4 104-5
Newell, N.C. J2 180-1
Newell, S. Dak. D2 136-7
Newell, W. Va. A5 200-1
Newellton, La. C7 168-9
Newellton, N.S. G4 281
Newfane, N.Y. E2 80-1
Newfane, Vt. M6 90-1
Newfield, Conn. C6 60-1
Newfield, Conn. F9 60-1
Newfield, Me. O7 64-5
Newfield, N.J. L3 76-7
Newfields, N.H. N9 72-3
Newfolden, Minn. E2 116-7
Newfoundland, Ky. G14 164-5
Newfoundland, N.J. C6 76-7
Newhalem, Wash. C10 246-7
Newhalen, Alaska G10 254-5
Newhall*, Calif. F8 210-1
Newhall, Ia. F12 104-5
Newhebron, Miss. K6 176-7
Newhill, N.C. I6 180-1
Newhope, Ark. G3 150-1
Newington, Conn. D9 60-1
Newington, Ga. J10 160-1
Newington, N.H. M9 72-3
Newington, Ont. H16 284-5
Newington, Va. B4 196-7
Newkirk, N. Mex. F9 230-1
Newkirk, Okla. C11 234-5
Newland, N.C. C5 180-1
Newlight, La. C6 168-9
Newllano, La. F2 168-9
Newman, Calif. D10 210-1
Newman, Ill. H10 96-7
Newman, Ky. H5 164-5
Newman Grove, Nebr. F12 124-5
Newman Lake, Wash. E16 246-7
Newmanstown, Pa. I12 84-5
Newmarket, N.H. N9 72-3
Newmarket, Ont. B15 284-5
Newnan, Ga. H3 160-1
Newpoint, Ind. J10 100-1
Newport, Ark. C9 150-1
Newport, Del. B3 153
Newport, Ind. H4 100-1
Newport, Ky. D11 164-5
Newport, Me. J6 64-5
Newport, Mich. J15 112-3
Newport, Minn. B11 116-7
Newport, Nebr. D9 124-5
Newport, N.H. L4 72-3
Newport, N.Y. E9 80-1
Newport, N.C. F14 180-1
Newport, Okla. H11 234-5
Newport, Ore. E4 238-9
Newport, Pa. H10 84-5
Newport*, Que. H6 290-1
Newport, R.I. G6 87
Newport, S.C. B10 184-5
Newport, Tenn. H14 188-9
Newport*, Vt. B8 90-1
Newport, Vt. B8 90-1
Newport, Va. I7 196-7
Newport, Wash. D16 246-7
Newport, co., R.I. F6 87
Newport Beach, Calif. H9 210-1
Newport East, R.I. G6 87
Newport News, Va. J14 196-7
Newport Point, Que. H6 290-1
Newport West*, Que. H6 290-1
Newry, Me. K2 64-5
Newry, S.C. B5 184-5
Newsome*, Ala. C8 146-7
Newsoms, Va. J13 196-7
Newtok, Alaska F8 254-5
Newton, Ala. L9 146-7
Newton, Ga. M4 160-1
Newton, Ill. J10 96-7
Newton, Ia. G9 104-5
Newton, Kans. H11 108-9
Newton, Mass. D11 68-9
Newton, Miss. I8 176-7
Newton, N.H. O9 72-3
Newton, N.J. C5 76-7
Newton, N.C. D6 180-1
Newton, Tex. F11 192-3
Newton, Ut. C6 242-3
Newton, W. Va. G4 200-1
Newton, co., Ark. C4 150-1
Newton, co., Ga. G5 160-1
Newton, co., Ind. C4 100-1
Newton, co., Miss. I8 176-7
Newton, co., Mo. I3 120-1
Newton, co., Tex. F11 192-3
Newton Falls, O. C11 132-3
Newton Grove, N.C. J8 180-1
Newton Junction, N.H. O8 72-3
Newton Siding*, Man. J3 272-3
Newtonia, Mo. I3 120-1
Newtonsville, O. K15 132-3
Newtonville, Ala. E4 146-7
Newtonville, Ind. O6 100-1
Newtonville, N.J. L4 76-7
Newtown, Conn. G5 60-1
Newtown, Ind. F5 100-1
Newtown, Ky. A7 164-5
Newtown, Mo. A5 120-1
Newtown, O. K14 132-3
Newtown, Pa. A12 84-5
Newtown, Va. G13 196-7
Newville, Ala. L10 146-7
Newville, Ind. B12 100-1
Newville, Pa. J9 84-5
Newville, W. Va. G5 200-1
Newville, Wis. J2 140-1
Ney, O. B3 132-3
Nez Perce, co., Ida. F2 218-9
Nezperce, Ida. G3 218-9
Niagara, Ky. H5 164-5
Niagara, N.C. J5 180-1
Niagara, N. Dak. D12 128-9
Niagara, Ore. D7 238-9
Niagara, Wis. D15 140-1
Niagara, co., N.Y. E2 80-1
Niagara Falls, N.Y. E2 80-1
Niagara Falls, Ont. D15 284-5
Niagara-on-the-Lake, Ont. D15 284-5
Niangua, Mo. H6 120-1
Niantic, Conn. H12 60-1
Niantic, Ill. H8 96-7
Niarada, Mont. C3 222-3
Nibbe, Mont. G11 222-3
Nibley, Ut. C6 242-3
Niceville, Fla. B4 156-7
Nicholas, co., Ky. F12 164-5
Nicholas, co., W. Va. H5 200-1
Nicholas Denys, N.B. E5 275
Nicholasville, Ky. C7 164-5
Nicholls, Ga. M8 160-1
Nichols, Ia. H13 104-5
Nichols, N.Y. H6 80-1
Nichols, S.C. D15 184-5
Nichols, Wis. D3 140-1
Nichols Hills, Okla. J2 234-5
Nicholson*, B.C. I10 268-9
Nicholson, Ga. F6 160-1
Nicholson, Miss. N7 176-7
Nicholsville, Ala. J3 146-7
Nickel Centre, Ont. H7 284-5
Nickelsville, Va. J3 196-7
Nickerson, Kans. H9 108-9
Nickerson, Nebr. H1 124-5
Nicodemus, Kans. E6 108-9
Nicolaus, Calif. H4 210-1
Nicolet, Que. H14 290-1
Nicolet, co., Que. H14 290-1
Nicollet, Minn. N5 116-7
Nicollet, co., Minn. N5 116-7
Nicoma Park, Okla. J3 234-5
Nicomen Island*, B.C. J7 268-9
Nicut, Okla. E16 234-5
Nicut, W. Va. F4 200-1
Nida, Okla. I13 234-5
Nielsville, Minn. G1 116-7
Nigadoo*, N.B. E5 275
Nighthawk, Wash. B12 246-7
Nightingale, Calif. O9 210-1
Nightmute, Alaska F8 254-5
Nikep, Md. B3 172-3
Nikolai, Alaska E10 254-5
Nikolski, Alaska I6 254-5
Niland, Calif. O10 210-1
Niles, Ill. L3 96-7
Niles, Kans. F10 108-9
Niles, Mich. K11 112-3
Niles, Miss. D4 176-7
Niles, O. C11 132-3
Nimitz, W. Va. J5 200-1
Nimmons, Ark. A12 150-1
Nimmons, S.C. A5 184-5
Nimmonsburg [-Chenango Bridge], N.Y. G7 80-1
Nimrod, Minn. I4 116-7
Nimrod, Mont. E4 222-3
Nimrod, Ore. K2 238-9
Nimrod Hall, Va. G8 196-7
Nine Mile Creek, P.E.I. F7 287
Nine Mile Falls, Wash. E15 246-7
Ninette, Man. K11 272-3
Ninety Six, S.C. K4 184-5
Nineveh, Ind. J8 100-1
Ninga, Man. K11 272-3
Ninilchik, Alaska G11 254-5
Ninnekah, Okla. G10 234-5
Ninock, La. C2 168-9
Niobe, N. Dak. C5 128-9
Niobrara, Nebr. D11 124-5
Niobrara, co., Wyo. F15 250-1
Niota, Tenn. J13 188-9
Niotaze, Kans. K13 108-9
Nipawin, Sask. J8 294-5
Nipigon, Ont. F4 284-5
Nipomo, Calif. M5 210-1
Niskayuna*, N.Y. F11 80-1
Nisland, S. Dak. D2 136-7
Nissequogue*, N.Y. J12 80 1
Nisswa, Minn. I5 116-7
Nisula, Mich. C8 112-3
Niter, Ida. O10 218-9
Nitinat, B.C. K6 268-9
Nitro*, Que. J2 290-1
Nitro, W. Va. H12 200-1
Nitta Yuma, Miss. G4 176-7
Niulii, Hawaii H12 258-9
Niumalu, Hawaii D5 258-9
Niverville, Man. J14 272-3
Niwot, Colo. F2 214-5
Nixa, Mo. I5 120-1
Nixon, Nev. E2 226-7
Nixon, Ont. E13 284-5
Nixon, Tenn. D4 188-9
Nixon, Tex. J5 192-3
Noank, Conn. H14 60-1
Noatak, Alaska C9 254-5
Nobe, W. Va. F4 200-1
Nobel, Ont. H8 284-5
Noble, Ill. K10 96-7
Noble, La. D2 168-9
Noble, Okla. F11 234-5
Noble, co., Ind. B10 100-1
Noble, co., O. G10 132-3
Noble, co., Okla. D11 234-5
Noble Lake, Ark. H8 150-1
Nobleboro, Me. M12 64-5
Nobleford, Alta. N8 264-5
Nobles, Tenn. A5 188-9
Nobles, co., Minn. O2 116-7
Noblesville, Ind. G8 100-1
Nobleton, Ont. C14 284-5
Nobscot, Okla. E8 234-5
Nocona, Tex. C8 192-3
Nodaway, Ia. J4 104-5
Nodaway, co., Mo. A2 120-1
Node, Wyo. G16 250-1
Noel, Mo. J3 120-1
Noelville*, Ont. H8 284-5
Nogal, N. Mex. I7 230-1
Nogales, Ariz. M8 206-7
Nohly, Mont. C16 222-3
Nokesville, Va. B2 196-7
Nokomis, Ill. I8 96-7
Nokomis, Sask. L8 294-5
Nokomis Laurel*, Fla. H10 156-7
Nola, Ark. E3 150-1
Nola, Miss. K6 176-7
Nolan, Nev. H3 226-7
Nolan, W. Va. K10 200-1
Nolan, co., Tex. E6 192-3
Noland, Ky. H12 164-5
Nolanville*, Tex. F8 192-3
Nolensville, Tenn. H7 188-9
Nolia, Ariz. L6 206-7
Nome, Alaska D8 254-5
Nome, N. Dak. H12 128-9
Nomini Grove, Va. G14 196-7
Nominingue, Que. I2 290-1
Non, Okla. G13 234-5
Nondalton, Alaska G10 254-5
Nooksack, Wash. B8 246-7
Noonan, N. Dak. B3 128-9
Noone, N.H. O4 72-3
Noorvik, Alaska C9 254-5
Nooseneck, R.I. E3 87
Nora, Nebr. J12 124-5
Nora Springs, Ia. B9 104-5
Noranda, Que. H1 290-1
Norborne, Mo. D4 120-1
Norbourne Estates*, Ky. G9 164-5
Norcatur, Kans. D5 108-9
Norco, Calif. G10 210-1
Norco, La. C13 168-9
Norcross, Ga. B11 160-1
Norcross, Me. G7 64-5
Norcross, Minn. K2 116-7
Nordegg, Alta. K6 264-5
Nordin*, N.B. F6 275
Nordland, Wash. F1 246-7
Nordman, Ida. A2 218-9
Norembega, Ont. F7 284-5
Norene, Tenn. H8 188-9
Norfield, Miss. K5 176-7
Norfolk, Colo. B11 214-5
Norfolk, Conn. B6 60-1
Norfolk, Mass. K3 68-9
Norfolk, Nebr. E13 124-5
Norfolk, N.Y. A9 80-1
Norfolk, Va. J15 196-7
Norfolk, co., Mass. E10 68-9
Norfork, Ark. B7 150-1
Norge, Okla. G10 234-5
Norge, Va. E3 196-7
Norland, Ont. A16 284-5
Norlina, N.C. C12 180-1
Norma, La. F5 168-9
Norma, N.J. L3 76-7
Norma, N. Dak. C5 128-9
Norma, Tenn. G11 188-9
Normal, Ala. B7 146-7
Normal, Ill. F8 96-7
Norman, Ark. G3 150-1
Norman, Ind. K8 100-1
Norman, Nebr. I10 124-5
Norman, N.C. K4 180-1
Norman, Okla. F11 234-5
Norman*, Ont. H7 284-5
Norman, co., Minn. H2 116-7
Norman Park, Ga. M5 160-1
Norman Wells, N.W. Terr. B1 296
Normandale, Ont. E13 284-5
Normandin, Que. B9 290-1
Normandy*, Mo. E10 120-1
Normandy, Tenn. J8 188-9
Normandy Park, Wash. I2 246-7
Normangee, Tex. F9 192-3
Norman's Cove-Long Cove*, Nfld. N11 278-9
Normantown, Ga. J8 160-1
Normantown, W. Va. F5 200-1
Normétal, Que. H1 290-1
Noroton, Conn. J4 60-1
Noroton Heights, Conn. J4 60-1
Norphlet, Ark. J6 150-1
Norquay, Sask. L10 294-5
Norridge, Ill. L3 96-7
Norridgewock, Me. J4 64-5
Norrie, Wis. C1 140-1
Norris, Mont. H6 222-3
Norris, Okla. G15 234-5
Norris, S.C. B5 184-5
Norris, S. Dak. H7 136-7
Norris, Tenn. G11 188-9
Norris Arm, Nfld. M9 278-9
Norris City, Ill. M10 96-7
Norris Junction, Wyo. F2 250-1
Norris Point, Nfld. L7 278-9
Norristown, Ark. D5 150-1
Norristown, Ga. J8 160-1
Norristown, Pa. J15 84-5
Norrisville, Md. B11 172-3
North, S.C. F10 184-5
North, Va. E4 196-7
North Acton, Mass. F2 68-9
North Adams, Mass. B2 68-9
North Adams, Mich. K13 112-3
North Amherst, Mass. C5 68-9
North Amity, Me. F9 64-5
North Amityville*, N.Y. K12 80-1
North Andover, Mass. B11 68-9
North Andrews Terrace, Fla. I13 156-7
North Anson, Me. J4 64-5
North Apollo, Pa. A8 84-5
North Ardmore*, Pa. J15 84-5
North Arlington, N.J. C10 76-7
North Attleborough, Mass. F10 68-9
North Augusta, S.C. F7 184-5
North Aurora, Ill. M1 96-7
North Avondale, Colo. G13 214-5
North Babylon, N.Y. K12 80-1
North Bailey*, Alta. I8 264-5
North Ballston Spa*, N.Y. E11 80-1
North Baltimore, O. C5 132-3
North Barrington, Ill. K2 96-7
North Battle Mountain, Nev. D6 226-7
North Battleford, Sask. K5 294-5
North Bay, Ont. H8 284-5
North Bay, Wis. K5 140-1
North Bay Village, Fla. H16 156-7
North Beach, Md. K7 172-3
North Bedeque, P.E.I. E5 287
North Belgrade, Me. K4 64-5
North Belle Vernon*, Pa. J2 84-5
North Bellmore*, N.Y. K11 80-1
North Bellport*, N.Y. J13 80-1
North Belmont, N.C. J1 180-1
North Bend*, B.C. J6 268-9
North Bend, Nebr. I1 124-5
North Bend, O. K12 132-3
North Bend, Ore. G3 238-9
North Bend, Wash. F9 246-7
North Bend, Wis. H9 140-1
North Bennington, Vt. N3 90-1
North Bergen, N.J. C12 76-7
North Berwick, Me. O2 64-5
North Blandford, Mass. E3 68-9
North Bloomfield, Conn. C9 60-1
North Bonneville, Wash. J8 246-7
North Boston*, N.Y. F2 80-1
North Braddock, Pa. B7 84-5
North Bradley, Mich. H13 112-3
North Branch, Kans. C8 108-9
North Branch, Mich. F6 112-3
North Branch, Minn. L7 116-7
North Branch, N.H. N4 72-3
North Branch, N.J. E5 76-7
North Branford, Conn. H8 60-1
North Brentwood*, Md. I4 172-3
North Bridgton, Me. M7 64-5
North Brook, Ont. I13 284-5
North Brookfield, Mass. D7 68-9
North Brooksville, Me. K7 64-5
North Brunswick*, N.J. F6 76-7
North Buena Vista, Ia. D14 104-5
North Caldwell, N.J. B9 76-7
North Calling Lake*, Alta. G8 264-5
North Canaan*, Conn. A5 60-1
North Canton, Ga. E3 160-1
North Canton, O. E15 132-3
North Cape, P.E.I. A4 287
North Cape, Wis. K4 140-1
North Cape May, N.J. O4 76-7
North Carrollton, Miss. F6 176-7
North Catasauqua*, Pa. H15 84-5
North Cedar, Ia. D10 104-5
North Charleroi*, Pa. J2 84-5
North Charleston, S.C. H13 184-5
North Chatham, Mass. H16 68-9
North Chatham, N.H. G8 72-3
North Chester, Mass. D3 68-9
North Chesterville, Me. J4 64-5
North Chicago, Ill. J3 96-7
North Chichester, N.H. M7 72-3
North Chili, N.Y. E4 80-1
North Cohasset, Mass. I7 68-9
North College Hill, O. K13 132-3
North Collins, N.Y. F2 80-1
North Concord, Vt. E9 90-1
North Connellsville*, Pa. J3 84-5
North Conway, N.H. H8 72-3
North Cove, Wash. G5 246-7
North Crossett, Ark. J7 150-1
North Danville, Vt. E8 90-1
North Dighton, Mass. G11 68-9
North Dorset, Vt. L4 90-1
North Eagle Butte*, S. Dak. C7 136-7
North East, Md. B13 172-3
North East, Pa. B3 84-5
North East Carry, Me. F5 64-5
North Eastham, Mass. G16 68-9
North Easton, Mass. E11 68-9
North Edgecomb, Me. M11 64-5
North Egremont, Mass. E1 68-9
North English, Ia. H11 104-5
North Enid, Okla. D10 234-5
North Etowah, Tenn. K13 188-9
North Fair Oaks*, Calif. J3 210-1
North Fairfax, Vt. C4 90-1
North Fairfield, O. C7 132-3
North Fayston, Vt. F5 90-1
North Ferrisburg, Vt. F4 90-1

North Fond du Lac, Wis. G3 140-1
North Fork, Calif. J6 210-1
North Fork, Ida. H7 218-9
North Fork, Ore. G4 238-9
North Fort Myers, Fla. H11 156-7
North Fort Polk*, La. F2 168-9
North Fort Riley*, Kans. E12 108-9
North Foster, R.I. C2 87
North Franklin, Conn. E12 60-1
North Freedom, Wis. I12 140-1
North Gower*, Ont. I15 284-5
North Granby, Conn. B8 60-1
North Great River*, N.Y. K12 80-1
North Greenwich, Conn. J2 60-1
North Grosvenor Dale, Conn. B14 60-1
North Grove, Ind. E9 100-1
North Guilford, Me. H5 64-5
North Haledon, N.J. A10 76-7
North Hampton, N.H. N9 72-3
North Hampton, O. G16 132-3
North Hanover*, N.J. I5 76-7
North Hartsville, S.C. C13 184-5
North Hatley, Que. J14 290-1
North Haven, Conn. G8 60-1
North Haven, Me. L7 64-5
North Haven, N.Y. J14 80-1
North Haverhill, N.H. H4 72-3
North Havre, Mont. B9 222-3
North Head, N.B. K4 275
North Heath, Mass. B4 68-9
North Henderson, N.C. C11 180-1
North Hero, Vt. C3 90-1
North High Shoals*, Ga. F6 160-1
North Highlands, Calif. A9 210-1
North Hills-Ardsley*, Pa. J15 84-5
North Hodge, La. C4 168-9
North Hornell, N.Y. G4 80-1
North Hudson, Wis. E7 140-1
North Irwin*, Pa. I3 84-5
North Island*, Calif. O8 210-1
North Jay, Me. K3 64-5
North Johns, Ala. F5 146-7
North Judson, Ind. C6 100-1
North Kansas City, Mo. I15 120-1
North Kingstown*, R.I. F5 87
North Kingsville, O. A11 132-3
North Knife Lake, Man. C4 272-3
North La Junta, Colo. H14 214-5
North Lake, Wis. I4 140-1
North Lakeside*, B.C. G4 268-9
North Landgrove, Vt. L5 90-1
North Las Vegas, Nev. M9 226-7
North Lauderdale*, Fla. I13 156-7
North Leeds, Me. K3 64-5
North Lemmon, N. Dak. J4 128-9
North Leverett, Mass. C5 68-9
North Lewisburg, O. F5 132-3
North Liberty, Ind. A7 100-1
North Liberty, Ia. G12 104-5
North Lilbourn*, Mo. J11 120-1
North Lindenhurst*, N.Y. K12 80-1
North Little Rock, Ark. I16 150-1
North Livermore, Me. K3 64-5
North Logan*, Ut. C6 242-3
North Loup, Nebr. G10 124-5
North Lovell, Me. L2 64-5
North Lubec, Me. I11 64-5
North Lyndon, Me. B8 64-5
North Madison, Conn. G9 60-1
North Manchester, Ind. D9 100-1
North Mankato, Minn. N5 116-7
North Massapequa*, N.Y. K11 80-1
North Merrick*, N.Y. K11 80-1
North Miami, Fla. H16 156-7
North Miami, Okla. B15 234-5
North Miami Beach, Fla. H16 156-7
North Middletown, Ky. G12 164-5
North Monmouth, Me. L4 64-5
North Montpelier, Vt. F7 90-1
North Mount Vernon [-Academia], O. E7 132-3
North Muskegon, Mich. I11 112-3
North Myrtle Beach, S.C. E16 184-5
North Naples*, Fla. I11 156-7
North New Hyde Park*, N.Y. J11 80-1
North New Portland, Me. I4 64-5
North New Salem, Mass. C6 68-9
North Newton, Kans. H11 108-9
North Oaks*, Minn. A11 116-7
North Ogden, Ut. D6 242-3
North Olmsted, O. B13 132-3
North Otis, Mass. D2 68-9
North Oxford, Mass. E8 68-9
North Palm Beach, Fla. D16 156-7
North Park*, Ill. A8 96-7
North Parsonfield, Me. O6 64-5
North Patchogue*, N.Y. J13 80-1
North Pekin, Ill. F7 96-7
North Pembroke*, Mass. E13 68-9
North Pender Island*, B.C. E4 268-9
North Penobscot, Me. K7 64-5
North Pepperell, Mass. B9 68-9
North Perry, O. A10 132-3
North Plain, Conn. G11 60-1
North Plainfield, N.J. E6 76-7
North Plains, Ore. F1 238-9
North Platte, Nebr. G7 124-5
North Plymouth, Mass. F13 68-9
North Pole, Alaska D12 254-5
North Pomfret, Vt. I7 90-1
North Port, Fla. H10 156-7
North Portal, Sask. O10 294-5
North Potomac*, Md. D9 172-3
North Powder, Ore. D14 238-9
North Pownal, Me. N9 64-5
North Pownal, Vt. O3 90-1
North Prairie, Wis. J4 140-1
North Princeton, N.J. G5 76-7
North Providence, R.I. C5 87
North Pulaski*, Va. J6 196-7
North Randall*, O. B9 132-3
North Randolph, Vt. H6 90-1
North Reading, Mass. B11 68-9
North Redington Beach*, Fla. I1 156-7
North Redwood, Minn. N4 116-7
North Richland Hills, Tex. C13 192-3
North Richmond, N.H. O3 72-3
North Ridgeville, O. B13 132-3
North Rim, Ariz. C6 206-7
North River*, P.E.I. F7 287
North Riverside*, Ill. B11 96-7
North Robinson, O. D7 132-3
North Rochester, N.H. L9 72-3
North Royalton, O. C14 132-3
North Rustico, P.E.I. E7 287
North Salem, Ind. H7 100-1
North Salem, N.H. O8 72-3
North Salt Lake, Ut. E6 242-3
North San Pedro*, Tex. I8 192-3
North Sanbornton, N.H. K6 72-3
North Sandwich, N.H. I7 72-3
North Santee, S.C. G15 184-5
North Scituate, Mass. J7 68-9
North Scituate, R.I. C4 87
North Searsmont, Me. K6 64-5
North Shapleigh, Me. N1 64-5
North Sheldon, Vt. B5 90-1
North Sioux City, S. Dak. J16 136-7
North Smithfield*, R.I. A4 87
North Somers, Conn. A11 60-1
North Spring, W. Va. J3 200-1
North Springfield, Vt. K7 90-1
North Springfield*, Va. E13 196-7
North Springs, Tenn. A9 188-9
North St. Paul*, Minn. M7 116-7
North Stamford, Conn. I3 60-1
North Star, Mich. F1 112-3
North Star, O. E3 132-3
North Stonington, Conn. G14 60-1
North Stratford, N.H. D6 72-3
North Street, Mich. G8 112-3
North Sudbury, Mass. H2 68-9
North Sullivan, Me. K8 64-5
North Sunderland, Mass. C5 68-9
North Sydney, N.S. B11 281
North Syracuse, N.Y. E7 80-1
North Takoma Park*, Md. D10 172-3
North Tarrytown, N.Y. C14 80-1
North Tazewell, Va. I5 196-7
North Terre Haute, Ind. I4 100-1
North Tiverton, R.I. E7 87
North Tonawanda, N.Y. E2 80-1
North Troy, Vt. B7 90-1
North Tryon*, P.E.I. F6 287
North Tunbridge, Vt. H7 90-1
North Turner, Me. K3 64-5
North Utica, Ill. D8 96-7
North Uxbridge, Mass. E9 68-9
North Valley*, N. Mex. F6 230-1
North Valley Stream*, N.Y. F15 80-1
North Vancouver, B.C. B13 268-9
North Vandergrift*, Pa. H3 84-5
North Vassalboro, Me. K5 64-5
North Vernon, Ind. K10 100-1
North Village, N.H. O5 72-3
North Waldoboro, Me. L5 64-5
North Wales, Pa. A10 84-5
North Walpole, N.H. M2 72-3
North Wantagh*, N.Y. K11 80-1
North Wardell*, Mo. K11 120-1
North Warren, Pa. C4 84-5
North Washington, Ia. C10 104-5
North Waterboro, Me. O7 64-5
North Waterford, Me. L2 64-5
North Wayne, Me. K4 64-5
North Webster, Ind. B9 100-1
North West River, Nfld. H6 278-9
North Westchester, Conn. E11 60-1
North Westminster, Vt. M7 90-1
North Weymouth, Mass. I6 68-9
North Whitefield, Me. L5 64-5
North Wilbraham, Mass. E5 68-9
North Wildwood, N.J. O4 76-7
North Wilkesboro, N.C. G1 180-1
North Wilton, Conn. I4 60-1
North Wiltshire*, P.E.I. F7 287
North Windham, Conn. D13 60-1
North Windham, Me. N8 64-5
North Winter Haven*, Fla. F11 156-7
North Woodstock, Conn. B14 60-1
North Woodstock, Me. K2 64-5
North Woodstock, N.H. H6 72-3
North Yarmouth, Me. N9 64-5
North York, Pa. J11 84-5
North Zanesville*, O. F8 132-3
Northampton, Mass. D5 68-9
Northampton, Pa. H14 84-5
Northampton, co., N.C. C13 180-1
Northampton, co., Pa. G15 84-5
Northampton, co., Va. I15 196-7
Northboro, Ia. K3 104-5
Northborough, Mass. D9 68-9
Northbridge, Mass. E9 68-9
Northbrook, Ill. L3 96-7
Northcrest*, Tex. F8 192-3
Northeast Cape, Alaska D7 254-5
Northeast Harbor, Me. K8 64-5
Northfield, Conn. D6 60-1
Northfield*, Ill. B11 96-7
Northfield*, Ky. G9 164-5
Northfield, Me. J10 64-5
Northfield, Mass. B5 68-9
Northfield, Minn. N7 116-7
Northfield*, N.H. K6 72-3
Northfield, N.J. M5 76-7
Northfield, O. C15 132-3
Northfield, Vt. G6 90-1
Northfield Farms, Mass. B5 68-9
Northford, Conn. G8 60-1
Northfork*, W. Va. J3 200-1
Northgate, N. Dak. B4 128-9
Northglenn, Colo. G3 214-5
Northlake, Ill. M3 96-7
Northland, Mich. D9 112-3
Northmoor, Mo. I15 120-1
Northome, Minn. F5 116-7
Northport, Ala. F4 146-7
Northport, Me. K6 64-5
Northport, Mich. F12 112-3
Northport, Nebr. F2 124-5
Northport*, N.Y. J12 80-1
Northport, Wash. B15 246-7
Northridge, O. H14 132-3
Northriver Mills, W. Va. E10 200-1
Northrop, Minn. O5 116-7
Northside, N.C. H7 180-1
Northside, Sask. J7 294-5
Northumberland, N.H. E6 72-3
Northumberland, Pa. G11 84-5
Northumberland, co., N.B. G4 275
Northumberland, co., Ont. K11 284-5
Northumberland, co., Pa. G11 84-5
Northumberland, co., Va. H14 196-7
Northumberland Strait, P.E.I. E3 287
Northvale, N.J. C8 76-7
Northville, Conn. E4 60-1
Northville, Mass. E12 68-9
Northville, Mich. J5 112-3
Northville, N.Y. E10 80-1
Northville, S. Dak. C12 136-7
Northway, Alaska E13 254-5
Northwood, Ia. A8 104-5
Northwood, N.H. M8 72-3
Northwood, N. Dak. E13 128-9
Northwood*, O. B5 132-3
Northwood Ridge, N.H. M8 72-3
NorthWoodbury, Conn. F6 60-1
Northwoods*, Mo. E10 120-1
Northwoods Beach, Wis. C9 140-1
Northwye, Mo. G8 120-1
Norton, Kans. D5 108-9
Norton, Mass. F11 68-9
Norton, N.B. I5 275
Norton*, O. D9 132-3
Norton, Vt. B10 90-1
Norton, Va. J3 196-7
Norton, W. Va. E15 200-1
Norton, co., Kans. D5 108-9
Norton Grove, Mass. F11 68-9
Norton Shores*, Mich. I11 112-3
Nortonville, Kans. E15 108-9
Nortonville, Ky. I5 164-5
Nortonville, N. Dak. H11 128-9
Norvell, Ark. D11 150-1
Norvell, Mich. K2 112-3
Norwalk, Calif. G9 210-1
Norwalk, Conn. I4 60-1
Norwalk, Ia. H7 104-5
Norwalk, O. C7 132-3
Norwalk, Wis. H10 140-1
Norwalk Isl., Conn. J4 60-1
Norway, Ind. D6 100-1
Norway, Ia. F12 104-5
Norway, Kans. D10 108-9
Norway, Me. L2 64-5
Norway, Mich. E9 112-3
Norway, Ore. H4 238-9
Norway, S.C. G10 184-5
Norway House, Man. B13 272-3
Norwell, Mass. J7 68-9
Norwich, Conn. F13 60-1
Norwich, Kans. J10 108-9
Norwich, Mass. D4 68-9
Norwich, N.Y. F8 80-1
Norwich, N. Dak. D7 128-9
Norwich*, Ont. E13 284-5
Norwich, Vt. I7 90-1
Norwood, Colo. H6 214-5
Norwood*, Fla. I13 156-7
Norwood, Ga. G7 160-1
Norwood, Ill. F7 96-7
Norwood, La. F7 168-9
Norwood, Md. H4 172-3
Norwood, Mass. E11 68-9
Norwood, Minn. C8 116-7
Norwood, Mo. I6 120-1
Norwood, N.J. C8 76-7
Norwood, N.Y. A9 80-1
Norwood, N.C. J3 180-1
Norwood, O. K13 132-3
Norwood, Ont. J11 284-5
Norwood*, Pa. J15 84-5
Norwood, Tenn. H11 188-9
Norwood, Va. H10 196-7
Norwood Court*, Mo. E10 120-1
Norwoodville, Ia. G8 104-5
Notasulga, Ala. H9 146-7
Notch Hill, B.C. I8 268-9
Noti, Ore. F5 238-9
Notre Dame, Me. A9 64-5
Notre-Dame-de-la-Doré, Que. B9 290-1
Notre Dame de Lourdes, Man. J12 272-3
Notre-Dame-de-Montauban*, Que. I3 290-1
Notre-Dame-des-Champs*, Ont. H15 284-5
Notre Dame des Érables, N.B. E6 275
Notre-Dame-des-Prairies*, Que. I2 290-1
Notre-Dame-d'Hébertville, Que. C11 290-1
Notre-Dame-du-Bon-Conseil*, Que. J3 290-1
Notre-Dame-du-Lac, Que. E15 290-1
Notre-Dame-du-Laus, Que. H9 290-1
Notre-Dame-du-Nord*, Que. I1 290-1
Nottingham, N.H. M8 72-3
Nottoway, co., Va. I11 196-7
Nottoway Court House, Va. I11 196-7
Notus, Ida. L2 218-9
Nounan, Ida. O11 218-9
Nouvelle, Que. I5 290-1
Novar, Ont. H8 284-5
Novato, Calif. B7 210-1
Novelty, Mo. B7 120-1
Novi, Mich. I5 112-3
Novinger, Mo. B6 120-1
Nowata, Okla. C14 234-5
Nowata, co., Okla. B14 234-5
Nowood, Wyo. E11 250-1
Noxapater, Miss. G9 176-7
Noxie, Okla. B14 234-5
Noxon, Mont. C1 222-3
Noxontown Lake, Del. D2 153
Noxubee, co., Miss. G10 176-7
Nuckolls, co., Nebr. J11 124-5
Nucla, Colo. G6 214-5
Nueces, co., Tex. J8 192-3
Nugget, Wyo. I5 250-1
Nulato, Alaska D9 254-5
Numa, Ia. J9 104-5
Numila, Hawaii D4 258-9
Nunaka Valley, Alaska F11 254-5
Nunapitchuk*, Alaska F8 254-5
Nunda, N.Y. F4 80-1
Nunda, S. Dak. F15 136-7
Nunez, Ga. J8 160-1
Nunica, Mich. I11 112-3
Nunley, Ark. F2 150-1
Nunn, Colo. B12 214-5
Nunnelly, Tenn. I5 188-9
Nut Mountain, Sask. K9 294-5
Nutbush, Tenn. J3 188-9
Nutimik Lake*, Man. J4 272-3
Nutley, N.J. C10 76-7
Nutrioso, Ariz. H11 206-7
Nutter Fort, W. Va. C13 200-1
Nutting Lake, Mass. C11 68-9
Nuttsville, Va. H14 196-7
Nyac, Alaska F9 254-5
Nyack, N.Y. C14 80-1
Nye, Mont. H9 222-3
Nye, Ore. C12 238-9
Nye, co., Nev. I7 226-7
Nyssa, Ore. F16 238-9

O

Oacoma, S. Dak. G10 136-7
Oahe Dam, S. Dak. E8 136-7
Oak, Nebr. J12 124-5
Oak Bay, N.B. J3 275
Oak Bluff*, Man. K4 272-3
Oak Bluffs, Mass. I14 68-9
Oak Brae, Man. G11 272-3
Oak Brook*, Ill. B10 96-7
Oak City, N.C. D13 180-1
Oak City, Ut. I5 242-3
Oak Creek, Colo. C8 214-5
Oak Creek, Ut. H7 242-3
Oak Creek, Wis. J5 140-1
Oak Forest, Ill. N4 96-7
Oak Grove, Ala. F5 146-7
Oak Grove, Ark. A4 150-1
Oak Grove, Ark. D5 150-1
Oak Grove, Ark. E8 150-1
Oak Grove, Ark. I4 150-1
Oak Grove, Del. F4 153
Oak Grove, Ill. D5 96-7
Oak Grove, Ky. K5 164-5
Oak Grove, La. D2 168-9
Oak Grove, La. B3 168-9
Oak Grove, La. A7 168-9
Oak Grove, La. I3 168-9
Oak Grove, Mich. H3 112-3
Oak Grove*, Mo. F9 120-1
Oak Grove, Mo. J16 120-1
Oak Grove, Ore. B8 238-9
Oak Grove, S.C. D14 184-5
Oak Grove, Tenn. F8 188-9
Oak Hall, Va. G16 196-7
Oak Harbor, O. B6 132-3
Oak Harbor, Wash. E1 246-7
Oak Hill, Ala. J5 146-7
Oak Hill, Fla. E12 156-7
Oak Hill, Kans. E11 108-9
Oak Hill, Me. N3 64-5
Oak Hill, Mass. I4 68-9
Oak Hill, O. I7 132-3
Oak Hill, Tenn. H7 188-9
Oak Hill, W. Va. J16 200-1
Oak Lake, Man. J10 272-3
Oak Lane*, Pa. J15 84-5
Oak Lawn, Ill. N4 96-7
Oak Orchard, Del. J6 153
Oak Park, Ga. J8 160-1

Oak Park, Ill. M3 96-7
Oak Park, Mich. J6 112-3
Oak Park, Minn. K6 116-7
Oak Park Heights, Minn. A12 116-7
Oak Point, Man. H13 272-3
Oak Point, N.B. I5 275
Oak Ridge, Ala. C6 146-7
Oak Ridge, La. B6 168-9
Oak Ridge, Mo. H11 120-1
Oak Ridge, N.J. C6 76-7
Oak Ridge, Tenn. B12 188-9
Oak River, Man. I10 272-3
Oak Valley, Kans. J13 108-9
Oak Valley, R.I. A4 87
Oak View, Calif. F6 210-1
Oakbank, Man. J14 272-3
Oakboro, N.C. J3 180-1
Oakbrook Terrace*, Ill. B10 96-7
Oakburn, Man. H10 272-3
Oakdale, Calif. C10 210-1
Oakdale, Conn. F12 60-1
Oakdale, La. F4 168-9
Oakdale, Mass. D8 68-9
Oakdale*, Minn. M7 116-7
Oakdale, Nebr. E12 124-5
Oakdale*, N.Y. K12 80-1
Oakdale, Pa. B5 84-5
Oakdale, Tenn. H10 188-9
Oakdale, Wis. H11 140-1
Oakes, N. Dak. I12 128-9
Oakesdale, Wash. G16 246-7
Oakfield, Ga. L5 160-1
Oakfield, Me. E8 64-5
Oakfield, N.Y. E3 80-1
Oakfield, Tenn. C4 188-9
Oakfield, Wis. G3 140-1
Oakford, Ind. F8 100-1
Oakham, Mass. D7 68-9
Oakhaven, Ark. I3 150-1
Oakhurst, Calif. J6 210-1
Oakhurst, N.J. G8 76-7
Oakhurst, Okla. D13 234-5
Oakland, Ala. A4 146-7
Oakland, Calif. I3 210-1
Oakland, Fla. F6 156-7
Oakland, Ill. H10 96-7
Oakland, Ia. H3 104-5
Oakland, Ky. J8 164-5
Oakland, La. B2 168-9
Oakland, La. A5 168-9
Oakland, Me. K5 64-5
Oakland, Md. C1 172-3
Oakland*, Md. C10 172-3
Oakland, Minn. O7 116-7
Oakland, Miss. D6 176-7
Oakland*, Mo. E10 120-1
Oakland, Nebr. F14 124-5
Oakland, N.J. C7 76-7
Oakland, Okla. I12 234-5
Oakland, Ore. G5 238-9
Oakland*, Pa. F1 84-5
Oakland, R.I. A3 87
Oakland, Tenn. K2 188-9
Oakland, co., Mich. I14 112-3
Oakland City, Ind. N4 100-1
Oakland Park, Fla. G16 156-7
Oakland Park*, Mo. I3 120-1
Oakley*, Calif. I3 210-1
Oakley, Del. H4 153
Oakley, Ida. O7 218-9
Oakley, Kans. E3 108-9
Oakley, Mich. F2 112-3
Oakley, S.C. H13 184-5
Oakley*, Ut. E7 242-3
Oaklyn, N.J. N10 76-7
Oakman, Ala. E5 146-7
Oakman, Ga. D3 160-1
Oakmont, Pa. A7 84-5
Oakpark, Va. C1 196-7
Oakridge, Ore. G7 238-9
Oaks, Mo. I15 120-1
Oaks, Okla. D15 234-5
Oakton, Ky. K1 164-5
Oakton, Va. A3 196-7
Oaktown, Ind. L4 100-1
Oakvale, Miss. K6 176-7
Oakvale, W. Va. J5 200-1
Oakview, Mo. I15 120-1
Oakville, Conn. E6 60-1
Oakville, Ind. G10 100-1
Oakville, Ia. I14 104-5
Oakville, Ky. K7 164-5
Oakville, Man. J13 272-3
Oakville, Ont. D14 284-5
Oakville, Wash. G6 246-7
Oakway, S.C. C5 184-5
Oakwood, Ga. E5 160-1
Oakwood, Ill. G11 96-7
Oakwood, Md. B12 172-3
Oakwood, Mich. H5 112-3
Oakwood*, Mo. D3 120-1
Oakwood, N. Dak. C13 128-9
Oakwood*, O. B10 132-3
Oakwood, O. C3 132-3
Oakwood, O. H15 132-3
Oakwood, Okla. E8 234-5
Oakwood*, Ont. B16 284-5
Oakwood*, Pa. F1 84-5
Oakwood, Tenn. F5 188-9
Oakwood, Va. I4 196-7
Oakwood Beach, N.J. L1 76-7
Oakwood Heights*, Ill. J6 96-7
Oakwood Hills, Ill. K2 96-7
Oakwood Manor*, Mo. D3 120-1
Oakwood Park*, Mo. D3 120-1
Oark, Ark. C4 150-1
Oasis, Nev. C10 226-7
Oasis, Ut. I5 242-3
Oatland, S.C. F14 184-5
Oatman, Ariz. E2 206-7
Oats, S.C. D13 184-5
Oba, Ont. F6 284-5
Ober, Ind. B7 100-1
Oberlin, Kans. D4 108-9
Oberlin, La. G3 168-9
Oberlin, O. C8 132-3
Oberlin, Okla. I14 234-5
Oberon, N. Dak. E10 128-9
Obert, Nebr. D13 124-5
Obetz, O. G6 132-3
Obion, Tenn. B3 188-9
Obion, co., Tenn. A3 188-9
Oblong, Ill. J11 96-7
O'Brien, Ore. K4 238-9
O'Brien, co., Ia. C3 104-5
Obsidian, Ida. K5 218-9
Ocala, Fla. D10 156-7
Ocala, Nev. E3 226-7
Ocate, N. Mex. D8 230-1
Occoquan, Va. B3 196-7
Occum, Conn. E13 60-1
Ocean*, N.J. G8 76-7
Ocean*, N.J. J7 76-7
Ocean, co., N.J. J7 76-7
Ocean Breeze Park, Fla. B16 156-7
Ocean City*, Fla. B4 156-7
Ocean City, Md. H16 172-3
Ocean City, N.J. N5 76-7
Ocean City, Wash. G5 246-7
Ocean Falls, B.C. H4 268-9
Ocean Gate, N.J. J7 76-7
Ocean Grove, Mass. G11 68-9
Ocean Heights, Mass. I14 68-9
Ocean Isle Beach, N.C. H11 180-1
Ocean Park, Wash. H5 246-7
Ocean Ridge, Fla. E16 156-7
Ocean Shores, Wash. F5 246-7
Ocean Springs, Miss. N9 176-7
Ocean View, Del. J6 153
Ocean View, N.J. N5 76-7
Oceana, W. Va. K14 200-1
Oceana, co., Mich. H11 112-3
Oceano, Calif. M5 210-1
Oceanport, N.J. G8 76-7
Oceanside, Calif. I10 210-1
Oceanside, N.Y. F16 80-1
Oceanside, Ore. C4 238-9
Oceanville, N.J. L6 76-7
Ochelata, Okla. C13 234-5
Ocheyedan, Ia. A3 104-5
Ochiltree, co., Tex. A5 192-3
Ochlocknee, Ga. N4 160-1
Ochre River, Man. G11 272-3
Ocilla, Ga. L6 160-1
Ockley, Ind. E7 100-1
Ocmulgee R., Ga. K6 160-1
Ocoee, Fla. F6 156-7
Ocoee, Tenn. K12 188-9
Oconee, Ga. I7 160-1
Oconee, co., Ga. F6 160-1
Oconee, co., S.C. B4 184-5
Oconomowoc, Wis. I3 140-1
Oconomowoc Lake*, Wis. J14 140-1
Oconomowoc Lake
South*, Wis. J14 140-1
Oconto, Nebr. G8 124-5
Oconto, Wis. F15 140-1
Oconto, co., Wis. F14 140-1
Oconto Falls, Wis. C4 140-1
Ocracoke, N.C. E16 180-1
Octavia, Nebr. G13 124-5
Octavia, Okla. H16 234-5
Odanah, Wis. B10 140-1
Odd, W. Va. J4 200-1
Odebolt, Ia. E4 104-5
Odell, Ill. E9 96-7
Odell, Nebr. J14 124-5
Odell, Ore. B8 238-9
Odem*, Tex. I8 192-3
Oden, Ark. F3 150-1
Oden, Mich. E13 112-3
Odenton, Md. H6 172-3
Odenville, Ala. E7 146-7
Odessa, Del. D3 153
Odessa, Minn. L2 116-7
Odessa, Mo. D4 120-1
Odessa, Nebr. I9 124-5
Odessa, N.Y. G6 80-1
Odessa, Ont. J13 284-5
Odessa, Sask. N9 294-5
Odessa, Tex. E4 192-3
Odessa, Wash. F14 246-7
Odessadale, Ga. I3 160-1
Odin, Ill. K8 96-7
Odin, Kans. G8 108-9
Odin, Minn. O4 116-7
Odon, Ind. L5 100-1
O'Donnell, Tex. D5 192-3
O'Donnell, Wyo. B8 250-1
Odum, Ga. L9 160-1
Oelrichs, S. Dak. H3 136-7
Oelwein, Ia. D12 104-5
Ofahoma, Miss. H7 176-7
O'Fallon, Ill. K6 96-7
O'Fallon, Mo. B14 120-1
Offerle, Kans. I6 108-9
Offerman, Ga. M9 160-1
Offutt, Nebr. J3 124-5
Ogallah, Kans. F6 108-9
Ogallala, Nebr. H5 124-5
Ogden, Ark. I2 150-1
Ogden, Ill. G11 96-7
Ogden, Ind. H10 100-1
Ogden, Ia. F7 104-5
Ogden, Kans. E12 108-9
Ogden, Ut. D6 242-3
Ogden Dunes, Ind. A5 100-1
Ogdensburg, N.J. B5 76-7
Ogdensburg, N.Y. A8 80-1
Ogdensburg, Wis. E2 140-1
Ogema, Minn. H2 116-7
Ogema, Sask. O8 294-5
Ogema, Wis. D11 140-1
Ogemaw, Ark. J5 150-1
Ogemaw, co., Mich. G13 112-3
Ogilvie, Minn. K6 116-7
Ogilville, Ind. K8 100-1
Oglala, S. Dak. H4 136-7
Ogle, co., Ill. B7 96-7
Oglesby, Ill. D8 96-7
Oglesby, Okla. C14 234-5
Oglesby, Tenn. H7 188-9
Oglethorpe, Ga. K4 160-1
Oglethorpe, co., Ga. F7 160-1
Ogletown, Del. B3 153
Ogontz*, Pa. J15 84-5
Ogunquit, Me. O2 64-5
Ohatchee, Ala. E8 146-7
Ohaton, Alta. J8 264-5
Ohia Mill, Hawaii J12 258-9
Ohio, Colo. G9 214-5
Ohio, co., Ind. K12 100-1
Ohio, co., Ky. I6 164-5
Ohio, co., W. Va. B5 200-1
Ohio City, O. D3 132-3
Ohio R., O. H10 132-3
Ohioville, Pa. H1 84-5
Ohiowa, Nebr. I13 124-5
Ohley, W. Va. J14 200-1
Ohoopee, Ga. K9 160-1
Oil Center, N. Mex. K11 230-1
Oil City, La. A1 168-9
Oil City, Miss. H5 176-7
Oil City, Okla. H11 234-5
Oil City, Pa. E3 84-5
Oil Springs, Ky. H14 164-5
Oil Springs, Ont. E11 284-5
Oil Trough, Ark. C9 150-1
Oildale, Calif. L6 210-1
Oilmont, Mont. B6 222-3
Oilton, Okla. D12 234-5
Oilville, Va. H12 196-7
Ojai, Calif. F6 210-1
Ojibwa, Wis. D9 140-1
Ojo Caliente, N. Mex. D7 230-1
Ojo Feliz, N. Mex. D8 230-1
Okabena, Minn. O3 116-7
Okaloosa, co., Fla. B4 156-7
Okanagan Centre, B.C. J8 268-9
Okanagan Falls*, B.C. K11 268-9
Okanagan Landing, B.C. J8 268-9
Okanogan, Wash. D12 246-7
Okanogan, co., Wash. C12 246-7
Okarche, Okla. E10 234-5
Okaton, S. Dak. G7 136-7
Okauchee*, Wis. J14 140-1
Okawville, Ill. L7 96-7
Okay, Ark. I3 150-1
Okay, Okla. E15 234-5
O'Kean, Ark. B10 150-1
Okee, Wis. I1 140-1
Okeechobee, Fla. G12 156-7
Okeechobee, co., Fla. G12 156-7
Okeene, Okla. D9 234-5
Okeewemee, N.C. J4 180-1
Okemah, Okla. F13 234-5
Okemos, Mich. H1 112-3
Okesa, Okla. C13 234-5
Oketo, Kans. C12 108-9
Okfuskee, Okla. E13 234-5
Okfuskee, co., Okla. F13 234-5
Oklahoma, Pa. A8 84-5
Oklahoma, co., Okla. F11 234-5
Oklahoma City, Okla. F11 234-5
Oklee, Minn. F3 116-7
Okmulgee, Okla. E13 234-5
Okmulgee, co., Okla. E13 234-5
Okoboji, Ia. B4 104-5
Okolona, Ark. H4 150-1
Okolona, Ky. B2 164-5
Okolona, Miss. D9 176-7
Okotoks, Alta. M7 264-5
Okreek, S. Dak. H8 136-7
Oktaha, Okla. E14 234-5
Oktibbeha, co., Miss. F9 176-7
Ola, Ark. E5 150-1
Ola, Ida. K3 218-9
Ola, Nev. D11 226-7
Olalla, B.C. J8 268-9
Olalla, Wash. I2 246-7
Olamon, Me. I7 64-5
Olanta, S.C. E13 184-5
Olar, S.C. G10 184-5
Olathe, Colo. G7 214-5
Olathe, Kans. F16 108-9
Olberg, Ariz. J7 206-7
Olcott, N.Y. D2 80-1
Old Altona*, Man. K13 272-3
Old Bennington, Vt. N4 90-1
Old Bethpage*, N.Y. K11 80-1
Old Bridge, N.J. G6 76-7
Old Brookville*, N.Y. J11 80-1
Old Columbine, Ariz. J10 206-7
Old Crow, Y.T. A1 297
Old Faithful, Wyo. G1 250-1
Old Field*, N.Y. J12 80-1
Old Fields, W. Va. E9 200-1
Old Forge, Pa. E14 84-5
Old Fort, N.C. D4 180-1
Old Fort Nelson*, B.C. C7 268-9
Old Harbor, Alaska H10 254-5
Old Hickory, Tenn. G7 188-9
Old Hickory Lake, Tenn. B7 188-9
Old Horse Springs, N.
Mex. H3 230-1
Old Houlka, Miss. D9 176-7
Old House, S.C. J10 184-5
Old Lyme, Conn. H11 60-1
Old Mission, Mich. F12 112-3
Old Monroe, Mo. A14 120-1
Old Mystic, Conn. G14 60-1
Old Orchard Beach, Me. N3 64-5
Old Retrop, Okla. F7 234-5
Old Saybrook, Conn. H11 60-1
Old Shongaloo, La. A3 168-9
Old Spring Hill, Ala. I4 146-7
Old Tappan, N.J. C8 76-7
Old Town, Ia. B4 104-5
Old Town, Me. I7 64-5
Old Trap, N.C. C15 180-1
Old Westbury*, N.Y. J11 80-1
Oldenburg, Ind. J11 100-1
Oldfort, Tenn. K12 188-9
Oldham, S. Dak. F14 136-7
Oldham, co., Ky. F9 164-5
Oldham, co., Tex. B4 192-3
Oldhams, Va. G14 196-7
Oldmans*, N.J. K1 76-7
Olds, Alta. L7 264-5
Olds, Ia. I13 104-5
Oldsmar, Fla. H2 156-7
Oldtown, Ida. B2 218-9
Oldtown, Md. B4 172-3
Oldtown, Va. J5 196-7
Oldwick, N.J. E5 76-7
Olean, Mo. F6 120-1
Olean, N.Y. G3 80-1
O'Leary, P.E.I. C3 287
Olene, Ore. J8 238-9
Oleta, Okla. H15 234-5
Olex, Ore. C10 238-9
Olga, N. Dak. B12 128-9
Olga, Wash. C7 246-7
Olin, Ia. F14 104-5
Olin, N.C. H1 180-1
Olinghouse, Nev. F2 226-7
Olive, Mont. H14 222-3
Olive, Okla. D13 234-5
Olive Branch, Miss. A7 176-7
Olive Hill, Ky. F14 164-5
Olivehill, Tenn. D5 188-9
Olivehurst, Calif. G4 210-1
Oliver, B.C. J8 268-9
Oliver, Colo. F8 214-5
Oliver, Ga. J10 160-1
Oliver, Pa. J3 84-5
Oliver, Wis. B8 140-1
Oliver, co., N. Dak. G6 128-9
Oliver Springs, Tenn. H11 188-9
Olivet, Kans. G14 108-9
Olivet, Mich. J13 112-3
Olivet, S. Dak. H14 136-7
Olivette, Mo. B15 120-1
Olivia, Minn. M4 116-7
Olivia, N.C. J6 180-1
Olivier, La. I6 168-9
Olla, La. D5 168-9
Ollie, Ia. I11 104-5
Ollie, Mont. E16 222-3
Olmitz, Kans. G7 108-9
Olmos Park, Tex. J2 192-3
Olmstead, Ky. J6 164-5
Olmsted, co., Minn. O8 116-7
Olmsted Falls, O. B13 132-3
Olney, Ill. K10 96-7
Olney, Md. G3 172-3
Olney, Mont. B3 222-3
Olney, Okla. H13 234-5
Olney, Ore. A4 238-9
Olney, Tex. D7 192-3
Olney Springs, Colo. H13 214-5
Oloh, Miss. L7 176-7
Olowalu, Hawaii G10 258-9
Olpe, Kans. H13 108-9
Olsburg, Kans. E12 108-9
Olton, Tex. C4 192-3
Olustee, Fla. C10 156-7
Olustee, Okla. H7 234-5
Olvey, Ark. B5 150-1
Olympia, Ky. G13 164-5
Olympia, Wash. G7 246-7
Olympia Fields, Ill. O4 96-7
Olympian Village*, Mo. F10 120-1
Olyphant, Pa. E14 84-5
Oma, Miss. K6 176-7
Omaha, Ark. A5 150-1
Omaha, Ga. K2 160-1
Omaha, Nebr. G15 124-5
Omaha*, Tex. D11 192-3
Omak, Wash. D12 246-7
Omar, Del. K6 153
Omar, W. Va. K12 200-1
Omega, Ga. M6 160-1
Omega, Okla. E9 234-5
Omemee, N. Dak. C8 128-9
Omemee, Ont. B16 284-5
Omena, Mich. F12 112-3
Omer, Mich. G14 112-3
Omerville*, Que. J14 290-1
Omps, W. Va. D11 200-1
Omro, Wis. F3 140-1
Ona, Fla. J5 156-7
Ona, W. Va. H11 200-1
Onaga, Kans. D13 108-9
Onaka, S. Dak. C10 136-7
Onalaska, Wash. H7 246-7
Onalaska, Wis. H9 140-1
Onamia, Minn. J6 116-7
Onancock, Va. H15 196-7
Onanole, Man. H11 272-3
Onapa, Okla. F14 234-5
Onaping Falls, Ont. H7 284-5
Onaqui, Ut. G5 242-3
Onarga, Ill. E10 96-7
Onawa, Ia. F2 104-5
Onawa, Me. H5 64-5
Onaway, Ida. E2 218-9
Onaway, Mich. E13 112-3
Oneco, Conn. D15 60-1
Oneco, Fla. J2 156-7

Onego, W. Va. F8 200-1
Oneida, Ark. G10 150-1
Oneida, Ida. O10 218-9
Oneida, Ill. E6 96-7
Oneida, Ia. D13 104-5
Oneida, Kans. C13 108-9
Oneida, Ky. I13 164-5
Oneida, N.Y. E8 80-1
Oneida, Tenn. F10 188-9
Oneida, Wis. E4 140-1
Oneida, co., Ida. O9 218-9
Oneida, co., N.Y. E8 80-1
Oneida, co., Wis. D12 140-1
Oneida Castle*, N.Y. E8 80-1
O'Neil, Ore. E9 238-9
O'Neill, Mont. F15 222-3
O'Neill, Nebr. D10 124-5
Onekama, Mich. G11 112-3
Onemo, Va. E4 196-7
Oneonta, Ala. D7 146-7
Oneonta, N.Y. G9 80-1
Oneta, Okla. D14 234-5
100 Mile House, B.C. H7 268-9
Ong, Nebr. I12 124-5
Onia, Ark. C7 150-1
Oniad Lake*, N.Y. I11 80-1
Onida, S. Dak. D9 136-7
Onion Lake, Sask. I4 294-5
Onley, Va. H16 196-7
Only, Tenn. C6 188-9
Onondaga, Mich. J1 112-3
Onondaga, co., N.Y. E7 80-1
Onoway, Alta. I7 264-5
Onset, Mass. G13 68-9
Onslow, Ia. F14 104-5
Onslow, co., N.C. F13 180-1
Onsted*, Mich. K13 112-3
Ontario, Calif. G9 210-1
Ontario, Ind. A10 100-1
Ontario, Ia. F7 104-5
Ontario, O. D7 132-3
Ontario, Ore. F16 238-9
Ontario, Va. J10 196-7
Ontario, Wis. H10 140-1
Ontario, co., N.Y. F5 80-1
Onton, Ky. H5 164-5
Ontonagon, Mich. C8 112-3
Ontonagon, co., Mich. C7 112-3
Onward, Ind. E8 100-1
Onward, Miss. H4 176-7
Onyx, Ark. F4 150-1
Ookala, Hawaii I13 258-9
Oolitic, Ind. L7 100-1
Oologah, Okla. C14 234-5
Ooltewah, Tenn. K11 188-9
Oostburg, Wis. H5 140-1
Ootischenia*, B.C. J10 268-9
Oozewekwun*, Man. J2 272-3
Opa-locka, Fla. H16 156-7
Opal, Wyo. I6 250-1
Opal City, Ore. E9 238-9
Opal Cliffs*, Calif. J3 210-1
Opasatika, Ont. F6 284-5
Opelika, Ala. H10 146-7
Opelousas, La. G5 168-9
Opheim, Mont. A13 222-3
Ophir*, Colo. H7 214-5
Ophir, Ore. I3 238-9
Ophir, Ut. F5 242-3
Opihikao, Hawaii J14 258-9
Opp, Ala. L7 146-7
Oppelo, Ark. H13 150-1
Opportunity, Mont. G5 222-3
Opportunity, Wash. E16 246-7
Optima, Okla. C4 234-5
Oquawka, Ill. E4 96-7
Oquossoc, Me. I2 64-5
Ora, Ind. C7 100-1
Ora, Miss. K7 176-7
Ora, S.C. H4 184-5
Oracle, Ariz. K8 206-7
Oracle Junction, Ariz. K8 206-7
Oradell, N.J. A11 76-7
Oraibi, Ariz. D9 206-7
Oral, S. Dak. H2 136-7
Oran, Ia. D11 104-5
Oran, Mo. I11 120-1
Orange, Calif. H9 210-1
Orange, Conn. H7 60-1
Orange, Ind. I11 100-1
Orange, Mass. B6 68-9
Orange, N.H. J5 72-3
Orange, N.J. C9 76-7
Orange*, O. B10 132-3
Orange, Tex. G12 192-3
Orange, Vt. G7 90-1
Orange, Va. G11 196-7
Orange, co., Calif. N8 210-1
Orange, co., Fla. E12 156-7
Orange, co., Ind. M7 100-1
Orange, co., N.Y. I10 80-1
Orange, co., N.C. C10 180-1
Orange, co., Tex. G11 192-3
Orange, co., Vt. H7 90-1
Orange, co., Va. G11 196-7
Orange Beach, Ala. O4 146-7
Orange City, Fla. E12 156-7
Orange City, Ia. C2 104-5
Orange Cove*, Calif. K6 210-1
Orange Grove, Miss. N10 176-7
Orange Grove, Tex. I8 192-3
Orange Lake, Fla. D10 156-7
Orange Lake*, N.Y. I10 80-1
Orange Park, Fla. C11 156-7
Orangeburg, S.C. F10 184-5
Orangeburg, co., S.C. F10 184-5
Orangevale*, Calif. H4 210-1
Orangeville, Ont. C14 284-5
Orangeville, Ut. I7 242-3
Orcas, Wash. C7 246-7
Orchard, Colo. C13 214-5
Orchard, Ida. M3 218-9
Orchard, Ia. B10 104-5
Orchard, Nebr. E11 124-5
Orchard Beach, Md. G7 172-3
Orchard City, Colo. F7 214-5
Orchard Hill, Ga. H4 160-1
Orchard Hills*, Pa. H3 84-5
Orchard Lake, Mich. I5 112-3
Orchard Mesa*, Colo. F6 214-5
Orchard Park, N.Y. F2 80-1
Orchard Valley, Wyo. J15 250-1
Orchards, Wash. J7 246-7
Orchid*, Fla. F13 156-7
Orcutt, Calif. M5 210-1
Orcutts, Conn. B11 60-1
Ord, Nebr. F10 124-5
Orderville, Ut. M5 242-3
Ordnance, Ore. B12 238-9
Ordway, Colo. H14 214-5
Ore*, Tex. D11 192-3
Oreana, Ida. M3 218-9
Oreana, Ill. H9 96-7
Oreana, Nev. D4 226-7
Orebank*, Tenn. A15 188-9
Oregon, Ill. B8 96-7
Oregon, Mo. B2 120-1
Oregon, O. B6 132-3
Oregon, Wis. J1 140-1
Oregon, co., Mo. J8 120-1
Oregon City, Ore. G2 238-9
Oreland, Pa. A11 84-5
Orem, Ut. F6 242-3
Orestes, Ind. F9 100-1
Oretta, La. G2 168-9
Orford, N.H. I4 72-3
Orford Centre*, Que. J14 290-1
Orfordville, N.H. I4 72-3
Orfordville, Wis. K1 140-1
Organ, N. Mex. K6 230-1
Orgas, W. Va. J14 200-1
Orient, Ia. I6 104-5
Orient, Me. F9 64-5
Orient, O. G6 132-3
Orient, S. Dak. D11 136-7
Orient, Wash. C14 246-7
Orienta, Okla. D9 234-5
Oriental, N.C. F14 180-1
Orillia, Ont. A15 284-5
Orin, Wyo. G14 250-1
Orinda*, Calif. C8 210-1
Orion, Ala. J8 146-7
Orion, Ill. D5 96-7
Orion, Okla. D8 234-5
Oriska, N. Dak. G13 128-9
Oriskany*, N.Y. E8 80-1
Oriskany, Va. H8 196-7
Oriskany Falls*, N.Y. E8 80-1
Oriva, Wyo. C14 250-1
Orkney Springs, Va. F10 196-7
Orland, Calif. G3 210-1
Orland, Ind. A11 100-1
Orland, Me. K7 64-5
Orland Park, Ill. N3 96-7
Orlando, Fla. E11 156-7
Orlando, Okla. D11 234-5
Orlando, W. Va. F5 200-1
Orlean, Va. B1 196-7
Orleans, Ind. L7 100-1
Orleans, Ia. A4 104-5
Orleans, Mass. G16 68-9
Orleans, Nebr. J9 124-5
Orleans, Ont. H15 284-5
Orleans, Vt. C8 90-1
Orleans, co., La. H9 168-9
Orleans, co., N.Y. E3 80-1
Orleans, co., Vt. C8 90-1
Orlinda, Tenn. F7 188-9
Orlovista, Fla. F6 156-7
Orma, W. Va. F4 200-1
Orme, Tenn. K9 188-9
Ormiston, Sask. O7 294-5
Ormond Beach, Fla. D12 156-7
Ormond-by-the-Sea, Fla. D13 156-7
Ormsby, Minn. O4 116-7
Ormstown, Que. J11 290-1
Oro Blanco, Ariz. M8 206-7
Oro Valley, Ariz. K8 206-7
Orofino, Ida. F3 218-9
Orogrande, Ida. H4 218-9
Orogrande, N. Mex. L6 230-1
Oromocto, N.B. I4 275
Orondo, Wash. E11 246-7
Orono, Me. J7 64-5
Orono, Minn. B9 116-7
Oronoco, Minn. N7 116-7
Oronogo, Mo. H3 120-1
Orosi, Calif. K6 210-1
Orovada, Nev. B5 226-7
Oroville, Calif. G4 210-1
Oroville, Wash. B12 246-7
Orpha, Wyo. F14 250-1
Orr, Minn. F7 116-7
Orr, N. Dak. D13 128-9
Orr, Okla. I11 234-5
Orrick, Mo. I16 120-1
Orrin, N. Dak. D8 128-9
Orrington, Me. J7 64-5
Orrs Island, Me. O10 64-5
Orrum, N.C. G10 180-1
Orrville, Ala. I5 146-7
Orrville, O. E14 132-3
Orting, Wash. K3 246-7
Ortiz, Colo. J10 214-5
Ortley, S. Dak. B15 136-7
Orton, Ut. L5 242-3
Ortonville, Mich. H5 112-3
Ortonville, Minn. L2 116-7
Orwell, O. B11 132-3
Orwell, Vt. I3 90-1
Orwigsburg, Pa. H13 84-5
Orysa, Tenn. J2 188-9
Osage, Ark. B4 150-1
Osage, Ia. B9 104-5
Osage, Okla. D13 234-5
Osage, Sask. N9 294-5
Osage, W. Va. A15 200-1
Osage, Wyo. D16 250-1
Osage, co., Kans. F14 108-9
Osage, co., Mo. F7 120-1
Osage, co., Okla. C12 234-5
Osage Beach, Mo. F6 120-1
Osage City, Kans. G14 108-9
Osakis, Minn. K4 116-7
Osawatomie, Kans. G16 108-9
Osborn, Me. J8 64-5
Osborn, Mo. F16 120-1
Osborn, S.C. I12 184-5
Osborne, Kans. E8 108-9
Osborne, co., Kans. E8 108-9
Osborne Acres*, Alta. J7 264-5
Osburn, Ida. D4 218-9
Oscar, La. G6 168-9
Oscar, Okla. I10 234-5
Oscarville*, Alaska F8 254-5
Osceola, Ark. C12 150-1
Osceola, Ind. A8 100-1
Osceola, Ia. I7 104-5
Osceola, Mo. G4 120-1
Osceola, Nebr. G12 124-5
Osceola, Pa. G7 84-5
Osceola, S.C. B11 184-5
Osceola, Wis. E7 140-1
Osceola, co., Fla. F12 156-7
Osceola, co., Ia. B3 104-5
Osceola, co., Mich. G12 112-3
Oscoda, co., Mich. F13 112-3
Oscoda [-Au Sable], Mich. G14 112-3
Osgood, Ida. L10 218-9
Osgood, Ind. K11 100-1
Osgood, Mo. B5 120-1
Osgood, O. E3 132-3
Osgoode*, Ont. I15 284-5
Oshawa, Ont. C16 284-5
Oshkosh, Nebr. G4 124-5
Oshkosh, Wis. H14 140-1
Oshoto, Wyo. B15 250-1
Osierfield, Ga. L7 160-1
Osino, Nev. C8 226-7
Oskaloosa, Ia. H10 104-5
Oskaloosa, Kans. E15 108-9
Osler, Sask. K6 294-5
Oslo, Minn. F1 116-7
Osmond, Nebr. E12 124-5
Osnabrock, N. Dak. C12 128-9
Oso, Wash. D8 246-7
Osoyoos, B.C. K8 268-9
Osprey, Fla. H10 156-7
Osseo*, Minn. A10 116-7
Osseo, Wis. F9 140-1
Ossian, Ind. D11 100-1
Ossian, Ia. B12 104-5
Ossineke, Mich. F14 112-3
Ossining, N.Y. B14 80-1
Ossipee, N.H. J8 72-3
Ostella, Tenn. J7 188-9
Osterdock, Ia. D13 104-5
Osterville, Mass. H15 68-9
Osterwick, Man. K13 272-3
Ostrander, Minn. O8 116-7
Ostrander, O. F6 132-3
Ostrander, Wash. I7 246-7
Oswalt, Okla. I11 234-5
Oswego, Ill. N1 96-7
Oswego, Ind. C9 100-1
Oswego, Kans. K15 108-9
Oswego, Mont. C14 222-3
Oswego, N.Y. D6 80-1
Oswego, S.C. E12 184-5
Oswego, co., N.Y. D6 80-1
Osyka, Miss. M5 176-7
Otay-Castle Park*, Calif. O8 210-1
Otego, Kans. D8 108-9
Otego, N.Y. G8 80-1
Otero, co., Colo. H13 214-5
Otero, co., N. Mex. K7 230-1
Othello, Wash. G13 246-7
Otho, Ia. E6 104-5
Otis, Colo. D15 214-5
Otis, Ind. A6 100-1
Otis, Kans. G7 108-9
Otis, La. E4 168-9
Otis, Me. J8 64-5
Otis, Mass. E3 68-9
Otis*, Mass. G13 68-9
Otis, N. Mex. L10 230-1
Otis, Ore. D4 238-9
Otis Orchards, Wash. E16 246-7
Otisco, Ind. M9 100-1
Otisfield, Me. M8 64-5
Otisville, Mich. F4 112-3
Otisville, N.Y. I10 80-1
Oto, Ia. E2 104-5
Otoe, Nebr. H15 124-5
Otoe, co., Nebr. H15 124-5
Otsego, Mich. J12 112-3
Otsego, co., Mich. F13 112-3
Otsego, co., N.Y. F9 80-1
Ottawa, Ill. D9 96-7
Ottawa, Kans. G15 108-9
Ottawa, O. C4 132-3
Ottawa, Okla. B15 234-5
Ottawa, Ont. H10 284-5
Ottawa, W. Va. K13 200-1
Ottawa, co., Kans. E10 108-9
Ottawa, co., Mich. I11 112-3
Ottawa, co., O. B6 132-3
Ottawa, co., Okla. B16 234-5
Ottawa Hills, O. B5 132-3
Ottawa Lake, Mich. K14 112-3
Otter, Mont. H14 222-3
Otter Creek, Fla. D9 156-7
Otter Creek, Me. K8 64-5
Otter Lake, Mich. F5 112-3
Otter Lake*, Que. J2 290-1
Otter Rock, Ore. D4 238-9
Otter Tail, Minn. J3 116-7
Otter Tail, co., Minn. J2 116-7
Otterbein, Ind. E5 100-1
Otterburn Park*, Que. I12 290-1
Otterburne, Man. J14 272-3
Otterville, Mo. E5 120-1
Otterville*, Ont. E13 284-5
Otthon*, Sask. M10 294-5
Otto, N.C. F2 180-1
Otto, Wyo. C9 250-1
Ottoman, Va. H14 196-7
Ottosen, Ia. C6 104-5
Ottoville, O. D4 132-3
Ottumwa, Ia. I11 104-5
Ottumwa, Kans. H14 108-9
Otwell, Ark. C10 150-1
Otwell, Ind. M5 100-1
Ouachita, Ark. H5 150-1
Ouachita, co., Ark. I5 150-1
Ouachita, co., La. B5 168-9
Ouachita R., Ark. H5 150-1
Ouiatchouan*, Que. I3 290-1
Oungre, Sask. O9 294-5
Ouray, Colo. H7 214-5
Ouray, co., Colo. H7 214-5
Outagamie, co., Wis. G14 140-1
Outlook, Mont. A15 222-3
Outlook, Sask. L6 294-5
Outlook, Wash. H11 246-7
Outremont*, Que. I11 290-1
Ouzinkie, Alaska H10 254-5
Ovando, Mont. E4 222-3
Ovapa, W. Va. G4 200-1
Overall, Tenn. I8 188-9
Overall, Va. E11 196-7
Overbrook, Del. I6 153
Overbrook, Kans. F14 108-9
Overbrook, Okla. I11 234-5
Overflowing River, Man. C10 272-3
Overland, Mo. B15 120-1
Overland Park, Kans. F16 108-9
Overlea, Md. F7 172-3
Overlook-Page Manor*, O. G4 132-3
Overly, N. Dak. C8 128-9
Overton, Nebr. H9 124-5
Overton, Nev. L11 226-7
Overton, Tex. E10 192-3
Overton, co., Tenn. A10 188-9
Overton Beach, Nev. M11 226-7
Ovett, Miss. K9 176-7
Ovid, Colo. B16 214-5
Ovid, Ida. O11 218-9
Ovid, Mich. G1 112-3
Ovid, N.Y. F6 80-1
Oviedo, Fla. E12 156-7
Owanka, S. Dak. F4 136-7
Owasa, Ia. E8 104-5
Owassa, Ala. K6 146-7
Owasso, Okla. D14 234-5
Owatonna, Minn. O6 116-7
Owdoms, S.C. E8 184-5
Owego, N.Y. G7 80-1
Owen, Wis. F10 140-1
Owen, co., Ind. J6 100-1
Owen, co., Ky. F11 164-5
Owen Sound, Ont. A12 284-5
Owendale, Mich. H14 112-3
Owens, Del. H4 153
Owens, N.C. K6 180-1
Owens, Va. C14 196-7
Owens Cross Roads, Ala. B7 146-7
Owensboro, Ky. H6 164-5
Owensboro East*, Ky. H6 164-5
Owensboro West*, Ky. H6 164-5
Owensburg, Ind. K6 100-1
Owensville, Ark. J13 150-1
Owensville, Ind. N3 100-1
Owensville, Mo. F8 120-1
Owensville, O. K15 132-3
Owenton, Ky. F10 164-5
Owenton, Va. H13 196-7
Owings, Md. K7 172-3
Owings, S.C. H3 184-5
Owings-Mills, Md. E5 172-3
Owingsville, Ky. G13 164-5
Owinza, Ida. N7 218-9
Owls Head, Me. L6 64-5
Owosso, Mich. G2 112-3
Owsley, co., Ky. I13 164-5
Owyhee, Nev. A8 226-7
Owyhee, co., Ida. N3 218-9
Oxbow, Me. D7 64-5
Oxbow, Sask. O10 294-5
Oxford, Ala. E8 146-7
Oxford, Ark. B8 150-1
Oxford, Conn. G6 60-1
Oxford, Fla. E10 156-7
Oxford, Ga. G5 160-1
Oxford, Ida. O10 218-9
Oxford, Ind. E5 100-1
Oxford, Ia. G12 104-5
Oxford, Kans. J11 108-9
Oxford, La. D2 168-9
Oxford, Me. L3 64-5
Oxford, Md. F12 172-3
Oxford, Mass. E8 68-9
Oxford, Mich. H5 112-3
Oxford, Miss. C7 176-7
Oxford, Mont. F9 222-3
Oxford, Nebr. J9 124-5
Oxford, N.J. D3 76-7
Oxford, N.Y. G8 80-1

Oxford, N.C. C11 180-1
Oxford, N.S. C7 281
Oxford, O. J12 132-3
Oxford, Pa. K13 84-5
Oxford, Wis. G1 140-1
Oxford, co., Me. K2 64-5
Oxford, co., Ont. E13 284-5
Oxford Junction, Ia. F14 104-5
Oxford Mills, Ia. F14 104-5
Oxnard, Calif. G6 210-1
Oxon Hill, Md. K4 172-3
Oyama*, B.C. J10 268-9
Oyen, Alta. L10 264-5
Oyens, Ia. C2 104-5
Oyster, Va. F5 196-7
Oyster Bay, N.Y. D16 80-1
Oyster Bay Cove*, N.Y. J11 80-1
Oyster Bed Bridge, P.E.I. E7 287
Oysterville, Wash. H5 246-7
Ozan, Ark. H3 150-1
Ozark, Ala. L8 146-7
Ozark, Ark. D3 150-1
Ozark, Mo. I5 120-1
Ozark, co., Mo. J6 120-1
Ozaukee, co., Wis. I15 140-1
Ozawkie, Kans. E14 108-9
Ozona, Fla. H1 156-7
Ozona, Miss. N7 176-7
Ozona, Tex. F5 192-3
Ozone, Ark. C4 150-1
Ozone, Tenn. I9 188-9

P

Paauhau, Hawaii H13 258-9
Paauilo, Hawaii I13 258-9
Pablo, Mont. D3 222-3
Pabos-Mills*, Que. H6 290-1
Pace, Fla. A3 156-7
Pace, Miss. E4 176-7
Paces, Va. J9 196-7
Pachaug, Conn. E14 60-1
Pachuta, Miss. J9 176-7
Pacific, Mo. C14 120-1
Pacific, Wash. J3 246-7
Pacific, co., Wash. H6 246-7
Pacific Beach, Wash. F5 246-7
Pacific City, Ore. C4 238-9
Pacific Grove, Calif. K3 210-1
Pacific Junction, Ia. I2 104-5
Pacific Palisades, Hawaii I4 258-9
Pacifica, Calif. C7 210-1
Packerton, Ind. C9 100-1
Packerville, Conn. E14 60-1
Packton, La. D4 168-9
Packwaukee, Wis. G1 140-1
Packwood, Ia. I11 104-5
Packwood, Wash. H9 246-7
Pacolet, S.C. F5 184-5
Pacolet Mills, S.C. F5 184-5
Pacolet Park, S.C. F5 184-5
Pacquet, Nfld. L9 278-9
Paddock Lake, Wis. K4 140-1
Paddockwood, Sask. J7 294-5
Paden, Miss. B10 176-7
Paden, Okla. F12 234-5
Paden City, W. Va. D5 200-1
Padonia, Kans. C14 108-9
Padroni, Colo. B14 214-5
Paducah, Ky. J3 164-5
Paducah, Tex. C6 192-3
Page, Ariz. B7 206-7
Page, Ida. D3 218-9
Page, Nebr. D11 124-5
Page, N. Dak. G13 128-9
Page, Okla. G16 234-5
Page, co., Ia. J4 104-5
Page, co., Va. F10 196-7
Page City, Kans. E3 108-9
Page Springs, Ariz. F6 206-7
Pagedale, Mo. B16 120-1
Pageland, S.C. B12 184-5
Pages Corner, N.H. M6 72-3
Pagosa Junction, Colo. J8 214-5
Pagosa Springs, Colo. J8 214-5
Paguate, N. Mex. F4 230-1
Pahala, Hawaii J13 258-9
Pahaquarry*, N.J. C3 76-7
Pahaska, Wyo. C6 250-1
Pahoa, Hawaii J14 258-9
Pahokee, Fla. D14 156-7
Pahrump, Nev. M8 226-7
Paia, Hawaii G11 258-9
Paihaaloa, Hawaii I14 258-9
Pailo, Tenn. J11 188-9
Paincourt, Ont. F10 284-5
Paincourtville, La. C10 168-9
Painesdale, Mich. C8 112-3
Painesville, O. A10 132-3
Painesville Southwest*, O. A10 132-3
Painswick*, Ont. I8 284-5
Paint, Pa. I5 84-5
Paint Bank, Va. H7 196-7
Paint Lake Service Camp*, Man. E3 272-3
Paint Lick, Ky. E7 164-5
Paint Rock, Ala. B7 146-7
Paint Rock, N.C. D3 180-1
Paint Rock, Tex. F6 192-3
Painted Desert, Ariz. D8 206-7
Painted Post, N.Y. G5 80-1
Painter, Va. H15 196-7
Painters Hill*, Fla. D12 156-7
Paintsville, Ky. H15 164-5
Paisley, Ont. B12 284-5
Paisley, Ore. I10 238-9
Pajarito, N. Mex. F5 230-1
Pajaro*, Calif. J3 210-1
Pakenham, Ont. H14 284-5
Palacios, Tex. H9 192-3
Palatine, Ill. L2 96-7
Palatine Bridge*, N.Y. F10 80-1
Palatka, Fla. C11 156-7
Palco, Kans. E6 108-9
Paldi, B.C. D12 268-9
Palermo, Calif. G4 210-1
Palermo, Me. K5 64-5
Palermo, N. Dak. D4 128-9
Palermo, W. Va. I11 200-1
Palestine, Ala. D9 146-7
Palestine, Ark. E10 150-1
Palestine, Ill. J11 96-7
Palestine, Tex. E10 192-3
Palestine, W. Va. E4 200-1
Palisade, Colo. F6 214-5
Palisade, Minn. I6 116-7
Palisade, Nebr. I6 124-5
Palisade, Nev. D8 226-7
Palisades, Ida. M11 218-9
Palisades, Wash. F12 246-7
Palisades Park, N.J. B12 76-7
Pall Mall, Tenn. F9 188-9
Palling, B.C. F5 268-9
Palm Bay, Fla. F13 156-7
Palm Beach, Fla. D16 156-7
Palm Beach, co., Fla. H13 156-7
Palm Beach Gardens*, Fla. D16 156-7
Palm Beach Shores, Fla. D16 156-7
Palm City, Fla. B16 156-7
Palm Desert, Calif. N9 210-1
Palm Harbor, Fla. H1 156-7
Palm River-Clair Mel*, Fla. F10 156-7
Palm Shores*, Fla. F13 156-7
Palm Springs, Calif. H12 210-1
Palm Springs, Fla. E16 156-7
Palma, Ky. J3 164-5
Palma Sola*, Fla. J2 156-7
Palmarolle*, Que. H1 290-1
Palmdale, Calif. F8 210-1
Palmdale*, Pa. I11 84-5
Palmdale East*, Calif. M7 210-1
Palmer, Alaska F11 254-5
Palmer, Ia. D5 104-5
Palmer, Kans. D11 108-9
Palmer, Mass. E6 68-9
Palmer, Mich. D9 112-3
Palmer, Nebr. G11 124-5
Palmer, Sask. O7 294-5
Palmer, Tenn. D9 188-9
Palmer, Va. D4 196-7
Palmer, Wash. F8 246-7
Palmer Center, Mass. E6 68-9
Palmer Junction, Ore. B14 238-9
Palmer Lake, Colo. J3 214-5
Palmer Park*, Md. E10 172-3
Palmer Road*, P.E.I. B3 287
Palmer Springs, Va. K11 196-7
Palmerdale, Ala. E6 146-7
Palmers Crossing, Miss. L8 176-7
Palmers Hill, Conn. J3 60-1
Palmerston, Ont. C13 284-5
Palmersville, Tenn. A4 188-9
Palmerton, Pa. G13 84-5
Palmetto, Fla. J2 156-7
Palmetto, Ga. D9 160-1
Palmetto, La. G5 168-9
Palms, Mich. H15 112-3
Palmyra, Ark. H8 150-1
Palmyra, Ga. L4 160-1
Palmyra, Ill. I6 96-7
Palmyra, Ind. M8 100-1
Palmyra, Me. J5 64-5
Palmyra, Mo. C8 120-1
Palmyra, Nebr. H15 124-5
Palmyra, N.J. I3 76-7
Palmyra, N.Y. E5 80-1
Palmyra, N.C. C13 180-1
Palmyra, Pa. I11 84-5
Palmyra, Tenn. G5 188-9
Palmyra, Va. H11 196-7
Palmyra, Wis. J3 140-1
Palo, Ia. F12 104-5
Palo Alto, Calif. D8 210-1
Palo Alto*, Pa. H12 84-5
Palo Alto, co., Ia. C5 104-5
Palo Cedro, Calif. F3 210-1
Palo Pinto, Tex. D8 192-3
Palo Pinto, co., Tex. D7 192-3
Palo Verde, Ariz. I5 206-7
Palominas, Ariz. M10 206-7
Palos Heights, Ill. N3 96-7
Palos Hills, Ill. N3 96-7
Palos Park, Ill. N3 96-7
Palos Verdes Estates*, Calif. H8 210-1
Palos Verdes Peninsula*, Calif. N7 210-1
Palouse, Wash. G16 246-7
Pambrun, Sask. N6 294-5
Pamlico, co., N.C. E14 180-1
Pamlico Sound, N.C. E15 180-1
Pampa, Tex. B5 192-3
Pamplico, S.C. E14 184-5
Pamplin, Va. I10 196-7
Pana, Ill. I8 96-7
Panaca, Nev. J11 226-7
Panama, Ia. G3 104-5
Panama, Nebr. I14 124-5
Panama, Okla. F16 234-5
Panama City, Fla. C5 156-7
Panama City Beach, Fla. C5 156-7
Pando, Colo. E9 214-5
Pandora, Colo. H7 214-5
Pandora, O. D4 132-3
Pandora, Tenn. A16 188-9
Pangburn, Ark. D8 150-1
Pangman, Sask. O8 294-5
Pangnirtung, N.W. Terr. B4 296
Panguitch, Ut. L5 242-3
Panhandle, Tex. B5 192-3
Panola, Ala. G2 146-7
Panola, Okla. G15 234-5
Panola, S.C. F12 184-5
Panola, co., Miss. C6 176-7
Panola, co., Tex. E11 192-3
Panora, Ia. G6 104-5
Panorama Park, Ia. G15 104-5
Pansey, Ala. L10 146-7
Pantano, Ariz. L9 206-7
Pantego, N.C. D14 180-1
Pantego*, Tex. D8 192-3
Panther Burn, Miss. G4 176-7
Panton, Vt. G3 90-1
Paola, Kans. G16 108-9
Paoli, Colo. C15 214-5
Paoli, Ind. M7 100-1
Paoli, Okla. G11 234-5
Paoli, Pa. B10 84-5
Paoli, Wis. J1 140-1
Paonia, Colo. F7 214-5
Papaaloa, Hawaii I13 258-9
Papaikou, Hawaii I14 258-9
Papillion, Nebr. G15 124-5
Papineau, co., Que. H10 290-1
Papineauville, Que. I10 290-1
Paquetville, N.B. E6 275
Paradis, La. D13 168-9
Paradise, Ariz. L11 206-7
Paradise, Calif. G4 210-1
Paradise, Kans. E7 108-9
Paradise, Mich. C12 112-3
Paradise, Mont. D2 222-3
Paradise*, Nev. M9 226-7
Paradise*, Nfld. N11 278-9
Paradise, Ore. A15 238-9
Paradise, Ut. D6 242-3
Paradise Hill*, Okla. E16 234-5
Paradise Hill, Sask. J4 294-5
Paradise Valley, Alta. J10 264-5
Paradise Valley*, Ariz. I6 206-7
Paradise Valley, Nev. B5 226-7
Paradise Valley*, Wyo. F13 250-1
Paradox, Colo. G5 214-5
Paragon, Ind. J7 100-1
Paragonah, Ut. L4 242-3
Paragould, Ark. B11 150-1
Paraloma, Ark. I2 150-1
Paramount*, Calif. G8 210-1
Paramus, N.J. A11 76-7
Parchment, Mich. J12 112-3
Pardeeville, Wis. H1 140-1
Parent, Que. I2 290-1
Parhams, La. E6 168-9
Paris, Ark. D3 150-1
Paris, Ida. O11 218-9
Paris, Ill. H11 96-7
Paris, Ky. A8 164-5
Paris, Me. L3 64-5
Paris, Mich. H12 112-3
Paris, Miss. C8 176-7
Paris, Mo. C7 120-1
Paris, Ont. D13 284-5
Paris, S.C. F2 184-5
Paris, Tenn. B4 188-9
Paris, Tex. C10 192-3
Paris, Va. A1 196-7
Paris Crossing, Ind. L9 100-1
Parish, N.Y. D7 80-1
Park, Kans. E4 108-9
Park, co., Colo. F10 214-5
Park, co., Mont. H7 222-3
Park, co., Wyo. C7 250-1
Park City, Ill. J3 96-7
Park City, Kans. I11 108-9
Park City, Ky. J8 164-5
Park City, Mont. H10 222-3
Park City, Tenn. K7 188-9
Park City, Ut. F7 242-3
Park Falls, Wis. C11 140-1
Park Forest, Ill. O4 96-7
Park Hall, Md. H12 172-3
Park Headquarters, Calif. K8 210-1
Park Hill, N.H. N2 72-3
Park Hill, Okla. E15 234-5
Park Hills, Ky. D11 164-5
Park Lane, Conn. E4 60-1
Park Rapids, Minn. H4 116-7
Park Ridge, Ill. L3 96-7
Park Ridge, N.J. C8 76-7
Park Ridge, Wis. D1 140-1
Park River, N. Dak. C13 128-9
Park Valley, Ut. C3 242-3
Parkbeg, Sask. N7 294-5
Parkdale, Ark. K8 150-1
Parkdale, Colo. G11 214-5
Parkdale*, Mo. F10 120-1
Parkdale, Ore. C8 238-9
Parkdale, P.E.I. F7 287
Parke, co., Ind. H5 100-1
Parker, Ariz. G2 206-7
Parker, Colo. H4 214-5
Parker, Fla. C5 156-7
Parker, Ida. K10 218-9
Parker, Kans. G16 108-9
Parker, Okla. G13 234-5
Parker, S. Dak. H15 136-7
Parker, Wash. H11 246-7
Parker, co., Tex. D8 192-3
Parker City, Ind. G11 100-1
Parker Head, Me. N11 64-5
Parker Hill, N.H. G5 72-3
Parkers, Ark. J16 150-1
Parkers Ferry, S.C. I12 184-5
Parkers Lake, Ky. J11 164-5
Parkers Prairie, Minn. J3 116-7
Parkersburg, Ia. D10 104-5
Parkersburg, N.C. F11 180-1
Parkersburg, W. Va. E3 200-1
Parkerton, Wyo. F13 250-1
Parkertown, N.J. L7 76-7
Parkerville, Kans. F12 108-9
Parkesburg, Pa. J13 84-5
Parkhill, Ont. D11 284-5
Parkin, Ark. D11 150-1
Parkland*, Fla. I13 156-7
Parkland, Okla. E12 234-5
Parkland, Wash. K2 246-7
Parkman, Me. I5 64-5
Parkman, Wyo. B11 250-1
Parkrose, Ore. E2 238-9
Parks, Ariz. E6 206-7
Parks, Ark. F3 150-1
Parks, La. H6 168-9
Parks, Nebr. J5 124-5
Parkside*, Ky. G9 164-5
Parkside*, Pa. J15 84-5
Parkside, Sask. J6 294-5
Parksley, Va. H16 196-7
Parkston, S. Dak. H13 136-7
Parksville, B.C. J6 268-9
Parksville, Ky. E5 164-5
Parksville, S.C. E7 184-5
Parksville, Tenn. K13 188-9
Parkton, Md. C11 172-3
Parkton, N.C. F10 180-1
Parkville, Md. E7 172-3
Parkville, Mo. I14 120-1
Parkville, Pa. K10 84-5
Parkway, Mo. D13 120-1
Parkway-Sacramento South*, Calif. H4 210-1
Parkway Village, Ky. G9 164-5
Parkwood, N.C. J5 180-1
Parkwood Estates*, P.E.I. E7 287
Parlier, Calif. J5 210-1
Parlin, Colo. G9 214-5
Parma, Ida. L2 218-9
Parma, Mich. K1 112-3
Parma, Mo. J11 120-1
Parma, O. B14 132-3
Parma Heights, O. B14 132-3
Parmele, N.C. D13 180-1
Parmelee, S. Dak. H7 136-7
Parmer, co., Tex. B4 192-3
Parnell, Ark. E7 150-1
Parnell, Ia. G11 104-5
Parnell, Mo. A3 120-1
Paron, Ark. I14 150-1
Parowan, Ut. L4 242-3
Parr, S.C. J8 184-5
Parral, O. E10 132-3
Parran, Nev. F3 226-7
Parris Island*, S.C. J11 184-5
Parrish, Ala. E5 146-7
Parrish, Fla. J3 156-7
Parrott, Ga. L3 160-1
Parrott, Va. I6 196-7
Parrottsville, Tenn. H14 188-9
Parrsboro, N.S. D6 281
Parry, Sask. O8 294-5
Parry Sound, Ont. H8 284-5
Parshall, Colo. D10 214-5
Parshall, N. Dak. E5 128-9
Parshallville, Mich. I4 112-3
Parsippany, N.J. D6 76-7
Parsippany-Troy Hills*, N.J. D6 76-7
Parsley, W. Va. K11 200-1
Parsonburg, Md. G15 172-3
Parsonfield, Me. O6 64-5
Parsons, Kans. J15 108-9
Parsons, Tenn. C5 188-9
Parsons, W. Va. E7 200-1
Parson's Pond, Nfld. L8 278-9
Parthenon, Ark. B5 150-1
Partlow, Va. G12 196-7
Partoun, Ut. H2 242-3
Partridge, Kans. I9 108-9
Pas Airport, The*, Man. G1 272-3
Pas, The, Man. G1 272-3
Pasadena, Calif. G8 210-1
Pasadena, Md. H7 172-3
Pasadena, Nfld. M8 278-9
Pasadena, Tex. H14 192-3
Pasadena Hills*, Mo. E10 120-1
Pasadena Park*, Mo. E10 120-1
Pasatiempo*, Calif. J3 210-1
Pascagoula, Miss. O10 176-7
Pascagoula R., Miss. M9 176-7
Pasco, Wash. I13 246-7
Pasco, co., Fla. F10 156-7
Pasco West*, Wash. I13 246-7
Pascoag, R.I. A3 87
Pascola, Mo. J11 120-1
Paspébiac, Que. I6 290-1
Pasquotank, co., N.C. C15 180-1
Pass Christian, Miss. O8 176-7
Passadumkeag, Me. H7 64-5
Passaic, Mo. F3 120-1
Passaic*, N.J. E6 76-7
Passaic, N.J. D7 76-7
Passaic, co., N.J. B6 76-7
Passumpsic, Vt. E9 90-1
Pastura, N. Mex. G8 230-1
Patagonia, Ariz. M9 206-7
Pataskala, O. F7 132-3
Patch Grove, Wis. J10 140-1
Patchogue, N.Y. J12 80-1
Pateros, Wash. D12 246-7
Paterson, N.J. A10 76-7
Paterson, Wash. I12 246-7
Pathlow, Sask. K8 294-5
Patmos, Ark. I4 150-1
Patoka, Ind. M4 100-1
Paton, Ia. F6 104-5
Patrick, Nev. F2 226-7
Patrick, S.C. C13 184-5

Patrick, co., Va. K7 196-7
Patrick Draw, Wyo. I9 250-1
Patrick North*, Fla. E13 156-7
Patrick South*, Fla. E13 156-7
Patrick Springs, Va. K7 196-7
Patricksburg, Ind. J6 100-1
Patriot, Ind. L12 100-1
Patsville, Nev. A8 226-7
Patten, Me. F8 64-5
Pattenburg, N.J. E3 76-7
Patterson, Ark. D9 150-1
Patterson, Calif. D10 210-1
Patterson, Ga. M9 160-1
Patterson, Ida. J7 218-9
Patterson, Ia. H7 104-5
Patterson, Kans. I10 108-9
Patterson, La. E9 168-9
Patterson, N.C. D6 180-1
Patterson, Okla. G15 234-5
Patterson, Va. I4 196-7
Patterson Creek, W. Va. D10 200-1
Patterson Gardens, Mich. K14 112-3
Patterson Springs*, N.C. E5 180-1
Pattison, Miss. J4 176-7
Patton, Pa. H6 84-5
Patton*, Tex. G10 192-3
Pattonsburg, Mo. B3 120-1
Patuanak*, Sask. F5 294-5
Patuxent, Md. G11 172-3
Patuxent R., Md. D10 172-3
Patzau, Wis. B8 140-1
Paukaa, Hawaii I14 258-9
Paul, Ala. L6 146-7
Paul, Ida. N7 218-9
Paul, Nebr. I15 124-5
Paul Spur, Ariz. M10 206-7
Paulden, Ariz. F5 206-7
Paulding, Mich. D8 112-3
Paulding, Miss. J9 176-7
Paulding, O. C3 132-3
Paulding, co., Ga. F2 160-1
Paulding, co., O. C3 132-3
Paulette, Miss. G10 176-7
Paulette, Tenn. G12 188-9
Paulina, Ore. F11 238-9
Pauline, Ida. O9 218-9
Pauline, Kans. F14 108-9
Pauline, Nebr. I11 124-5
Pauline, S.C. G5 184-5
Paullina, Ia. C3 104-5
Pauloff Harbor, Alaska I7 254-5
Pauls Valley, Okla. G11 234-5
Paulsboro, N.J. J2 76-7
Paungassi*, Man. H4 272-3
Paunina, Ore. H8 238-9
Pauwela*, Hawaii G11 258-9
Pavillion, Wyo. E8 250-1
Pavo, Ga. N5 160-1
Paw Creek, N.C. J1 180-1
Paw Paw, Ill. C8 96-7
Paw Paw, Mich. J12 112-3
Paw Paw, W. Va. D10 200-1
Paw Paw Lake, Mich. J11 112-3
Pawcatuck, Conn. G15 60-1
Pawhuska, Okla. C13 234-5
Pawlet, Vt. K4 90-1
Pawleys Island, S.C. G15 184-5
Pawling, N.Y. I11 80-1
Pawnee, Ill. I7 96-7
Pawnee, Okla. D12 234-5
Pawnee, co., Kans. H7 108-9
Pawnee, co., Nebr. J15 124-5
Pawnee, co., Okla. D12 234-5
Pawnee City, Nebr. J15 124-5
Pawnee Rock, Kans. H7 108-9
Pawtucket, R.I. B6 87
Pax, W. Va. K15 200-1
Paxico, Kans. F13 108-9
Paxson, Alaska E12 254-5
Paxtang, Pa. I11 84-5
Paxton, Fla. A4 156-7
Paxton, Ill. F10 96-7
Paxton, Ind. K4 100-1
Paxton, Mass. D8 68-9
Paxton, Nebr. G5 124-5
Paxton, Ore. D9 238-9
Paxville, S.C. F12 184-5
Payette, Ida. K2 218-9
Payette, co., Ida. L2 218-9
Payne, Ga. I5 160-1
Payne, O. C3 132-3
Payne, co., Okla. D11 234-5
Paynes, Miss. D6 176-7
Paynesville, Mich. C8 112-3
Paynesville, Minn. L5 116-7
Paynesville, W. Va. J2 200-1
Payneville, Ky. G7 164-5
Payneway, Ark. D11 150-1
Paynton, Sask. J4 294-5
Payson, Ariz. G7 206-7
Payson, Ill. H4 96-7
Payson, Okla. E12 234-5
Payson, Ut. G6 242-3
Pe Ell, Wash. H6 246-7
Pea Ridge, Ala. G6 146-7
Pea Ridge, Ark. A3 150-1
Peabody, Kans. H11 108-9
Peabody, Mass. F6 68-9
Peabody, Tenn. G11 188-9
Peace R., Alta. C7 264-5
Peace River, Alta. F5 264-5
Peach, co., Ga. J5 160-1
Peach Orchard, Ark. A11 150-1
Peach Orchard, Mo. J11 120-1
Peach Springs, Ariz. D4 206-7
Peacham, Vt. F8 90-1
Peachburg, Ala. I9 146-7
Peachland, N.C. K3 180-1
Peachtree City*, Ga. G3 160-1
Peak, S.C. J7 184-5
Peakland, Tenn. J12 188-9
Peapack [-Gladstone], N.J. E5 76-7
Pear Ridge*, Tex. G11 192-3
Pearce, Ariz. L10 206-7
Pearcy, Ark. G4 150-1
Pearisburg, Va. I6 196-7
Pearl, Ida. L3 218-9
Pearl, Miss. I6 176-7
Pearl Beach, Mich. I8 112-3
Pearl City, Hawaii I4 258-9
Pearl R., Miss. J6 176-7
Pearl River, La. A16 168-9
Pearl River, N.Y. C14 80-1
Pearl River, co., Miss. M7 176-7
Pearland, Tex. I14 192-3
Pearlington, Miss. O7 176-7
Pearls Corner, N.H. L7 72-3
Pearsall, Tex. H7 192-3
Pearson, Ala. G5 146-7
Pearson, Ark. D7 150-1
Pearson, Ga. M7 160-1
Pearson, Miss. I6 176-7
Pearson, Okla. G12 234-5
Pearsonia, Okla. C13 234-5
Pearsons Corner, Del. F3 153
Pease, Minn. K6 116-7
Peason, La. E2 168-9
Pecan Island, La. I4 168-9
Pecatonica, Ill. A8 96-7
Peck, Ida. F3 218-9
Peck, La. D6 168-9
Peck, Mich. F7 112-3
Peck, Nev. J10 226-7
Peckham, Okla. C11 234-5
Pecks Mill, W. Va. K12 200-1
Pecos, N. Mex. E7 230-1
Pecos, Tex. F3 192-3
Pecos, co., Tex. F4 192-3
Pecos R., N. Mex. I9 230-1
Peculiar, Mo. K15 120-1
Pedee, Ore. D5 238-9
Pedricktown, N.J. K1 76-7
Pedro, Wyo. D16 250-1
Pedro Bay, Alaska G10 254-5
Pee Dee, N.C. J4 180-1
Peebles, O. I6 132-3
Peebles, Wis. G4 140-1
Peedee, S.C. D14 184-5
Peek, Okla. E7 234-5
Peekskill, N.Y. A14 80-1
Peel, Ark. A6 150-1
Peel R., Y.T. B2 297
Peeltree, W. Va. D14 200-1
Peeples Valley, Ariz. G5 206-7
Peerless, Mont. A14 222-3
Peerless, Ut. H8 242-3
Peerless Lake, Alta. E7 264-5
Peerless Park*, Mo. E10 120-1
Peers, Alta. I6 264-5
Peetz, Colo. D14 214-5
Peever, S. Dak. B15 136-7
Pefferlaw, Ont. B15 284-5
Peggs, Okla. D15 234-5
Pegram, Ida. O11 218-9
Pegram, Tenn. H6 188-9
Pejepscot, Me. N10 64-5
Pekin, Ill. F7 96-7
Pekin, N.C. K4 180-1
Pekin, N. Dak. E12 128-9
Pelahatchie, Miss. I7 176-7
Pelham, Ala. F6 146-7
Pelham, Ga. N4 160-1
Pelham, Mass. D6 68-9
Pelham, N.H. O7 72-3
Pelham, N.Y. J11 80-1
Pelham, N.C. C9 180-1
Pelham, Ont. E15 284-5
Pelham, S.C. F3 184-5
Pelham, Tenn. K9 188-9
Pelham Manor, N.Y. D15 80-1
Pelican, Alaska G15 254-5
Pelican, La. D2 168-9
Pelican Bay*, Man. J4 272-3
Pelican Lake, Wis. D13 140-1
Pelican Lakes, Minn. I5 116-7
Pelican Narrows, Sask. G9 294-5
Pelican Rapids, Man. D10 272-3
Pelican Rapids, Minn. I2 116-7
Pelion, S.C. F9 184-5
Pelkie, Mich. C8 112-3
Pell City, Ala. E7 146-7
Pell Lake, Wis. K14 140-1
Pella, Ia. H9 104-5
Pella, Wis. D3 140-1
Pellston, Mich. E13 112-3
Pellville, Ky. H6 164-5
Pelly, Sask. L10 294-5
Pelly Crossing, Y.T. B2 297
Pelsor, Ark. C5 150-1
Pelzer, S.C. H1 184-5
Pelzer North, S.C. H1 184-5
Pemaquid, Me. N12 64-5
Pemberton, B.C. I7 268-9
Pemberton, Minn. O6 116-7
Pemberton*, N.J. I5 76-7
Pemberton, N.J. I5 76-7
Pemberville, O. B5 132-3
Pembina, N. Dak. B13 128-9
Pembina, co., N. Dak. B13 128-9
Pembine, Wis. D15 140-1
Pembroke, Ga. K10 160-1
Pembroke, Ky. J5 164-5
Pembroke, Me. I11 64-5
Pembroke, Mass. E13 68-9
Pembroke, N.H. M7 72-3
Pembroke, N.C. G10 180-1
Pembroke, Ont. H9 284-5
Pembroke, Va. I6 196-7
Pembroke Park*, Fla. G16 156-7
Pembroke Pines, Fla. G16 156-7
Pemiscot, co., Mo. K11 120-1
Pen Argyl, Pa. G15 84-5
Penablanca, N. Mex. E6 230-1
Penacook, N.H. L6 72-3
Penalosa, Kans. I9 108-9
Peñasco, N. Mex. D7 230-1
Penawawa, Wash. H15 246-7
Penbrook, Pa. I11 84-5
Pence, Ind. F4 100-1
Pence, Wis. B11 140-1
Pence Springs, W. Va. I5 200-1
Pencil Bluff, Ark. F3 150-1
Pencoyd*, Pa. J15 84-5
Pend Oreille, co., Wash. C16 246-7
Pend Oreille Lake, Ida. C3 218-9
Pendennis, Kans. G4 108-9
Pender, Nebr. E14 124-5
Pender, co., N.C. G12 180-1
Pendergrass, Ga. E5 160-1
Pendleton, Ore. B13 238-9
Pendleton, S.C. C5 184-5
Pendleton, co., Ky. E11 164-5
Pendleton, co., W. Va. F8 200-1
Pendleton North*, Calif. O8 210-1
Pendleton South*, Calif. O8 210-1
Pendroy, Mont. C5 222-3
Penermon*, Mo. I11 120-1
Penetanguishene, Ont. A14 284-5
Penfield, Ga. G6 160-1
Penhold, Alta. K7 264-5
Penhook, Va. J8 196-7
Peninsula, O. C15 132-3
Peninsula Point*, Alaska H16 254-5
Penn, N. Dak. D10 128-9
Penn Square-Plymouth Valley*, Pa. J15 84-5
Penn Wynne*, Pa. J15 84-5
Penn Yan, N.Y. F5 80-1
Pennant, Sask. N5 294-5
Penndel, Pa. A12 84-5
Penndleton, Ind. G9 100-1
Penney Farms, Fla. C11 156-7
Pennine, Tenn. J12 188-9
Pennington, Ala. I3 146-7
Pennington, N.J. G4 76-7
Pennington, co., Minn. F2 116-7
Pennington, co., S. Dak. F3 136-7
Pennington Gap, Va. J2 196-7
Pennock, Minn. L4 116-7
Pennock Island*, Alaska H16 254-5
Penns Grove, N.J. K1 76-7
Penns Neck, N.J. G5 76-7
Pennsauken, N.J. M10 76-7
Pennsboro, W. Va. E5 200-1
Pennsburg, Pa. I14 84-5
Pennsuco*, Fla. H16 156-7
Pennsville, N.J. K1 76-7
Pennville, Ind. E11 100-1
Pennville*, Pa. K10 84-5
Penobscot, Me. K7 64-5
Penobscot, co., Me. I7 64-5
Penobscot Bay, Me. L6 64-5
Penobsquis, N.B. I6 275
Penokee, Kans. E5 108-9
Penrod, Ky. J6 164-5
Penrose, Colo. G11 214-5
Pensacola, Fla. B3 156-7
Pensacola, N.C. D4 180-1
Pensacola, Okla. C15 234-5
Pensaukee, Wis. C5 140-1
Pense, Sask. N8 294-5
Penticton, B.C. J8 268-9
Penton, N.J. L1 76-7
Pentress, W. Va. A14 200-1
Pentwater, Mich. H11 112-3
Penzance, Sask. M7 294-5
Peoria, Ariz. I6 206-7
Peoria, Ill. F7 96-7
Peoria, Miss. I5 176-7
Peoria, Okla. B16 234-5
Peoria, Ore. J1 238-9
Peoria, co., Ill. E7 96-7
Peoria Heights, Ill. E7 96-7
Peosta, Ia. E14 104-5
Peotone, Ill. O3 96-7
Pep, N. Mex. H11 230-1
Pepeekeo, Hawaii I14 258-9
Pepin, Wis. G8 140-1
Pepin, co., Wis. G8 140-1
Pepper, Del. J4 153
Pepper Pike*, O. B10 132-3
Pepperbox, Del. K4 153
Pepperell, Mass. B9 68-9
Pepperton, Ga. H5 160-1
Pequabuck, Conn. D7 60-1
Pequannock, N.J. C7 76-7
Pequop, Nev. C10 226-7
Pequot Lakes, Minn. I5 116-7
Peralta, N. Mex. F5 230-1
Percé, Que. H6 290-1
Percy, Ill. M7 96-7
Percy, Miss. G4 176-7
Percy, N.H. E7 72-3
Perdido, Ala. M4 146-7
Perdido Beach, Ala. O4 146-7
Perdue, Sask. L6 294-5
Perdue Hill, Ala. K4 146-7
Perham, Me. C8 64-5
Perham, Minn. I3 116-7
Peridot, Ariz. I9 206-7
Perkasie, Pa. I15 84-5
Perkins, Ga. I9 160-1
Perkins, Mich. D10 112-3
Perkins, Mo. I11 120-1
Perkins, Okla. E12 234-5
Perkins, W. Va. F5 200-1
Perkins, co., Nebr. H5 124-5
Perkins, co., S. Dak. B4 136-7
Perkinston, Miss. M8 176-7
Perkinstown, Wis. E10 140-1
Perkinsville, Ariz. F6 206-7
Perkinsville, Vt. K7 90-1
Perla, Ark. G6 150-1
Perley, Minn. H1 116-7
Perma, Mont. D3 222-3
Pernell, Okla. H11 234-5
Perquimans, co., N.C. C15 180-1
Perrin*, Tex. C9 192-3
Perrine, Fla. I16 156-7
Perrineville, N.J. H6 76-7
Perrinton, Mich. I13 112-3
Perris, Calif. I10 210-1
Perronville, Mich. E10 112-3
Perry, Ark. H13 150-1
Perry, Fla. C8 156-7
Perry, Ga. J5 160-1
Perry, Ia. G6 104-5
Perry, Kans. E15 108-9
Perry, La. I5 168-9
Perry, Me. I11 64-5
Perry, Mich. H2 112-3
Perry, Mo. C8 120-1
Perry, N.Y. F4 80-1
Perry, O. A10 132-3
Perry, Okla. D11 234-5
Perry, Ore. C14 238-9
Perry, S.C. F9 184-5
Perry, Ut. D6 242-3
Perry, W. Va. F10 200-1
Perry, co., Ala. H4 146-7
Perry, co., Ark. E6 150-1
Perry, co., Ill. M7 96-7
Perry, co., Ind. O6 100-1
Perry, co., Ky. I14 164-5
Perry, co., Miss. L9 176-7
Perry, co., Mo. G11 120-1
Perry, co., O. G8 132-3
Perry, co., Pa. I10 84-5
Perry, co., Tenn. C5 188-9
Perry Go Place*, Wis. K13 140-1
Perry Hall, Md. E8 172-3
Perry Park, Ky. F10 164-5
Perryman, Md. C12 172-3
Perryopolis, Pa. J3 84-5
Perrysburg, O. B5 132-3
Perrysville, Ind. G4 100-1
Perrysville, O. D8 132-3
Perryton, Tex. A6 192-3
Perrytown, Ark. I4 150-1
Perryville, Alaska H8 254-5
Perryville, Ark. E6 150-1
Perryville, Ky. D5 164-5
Perryville, La. B5 168-9
Perryville, Md. B13 172-3
Perryville, Mo. G11 120-1
Perryville, R.I. H4 87
Perryville, Tenn. C5 188-9
Pershing, Ia. H9 104-5
Pershing, Okla. C13 234-5
Pershing, co., Nev. D4 226-7
Persia, Ia. G3 104-5
Persia, Tenn. G14 188-9
Person, co., N.C. C10 180-1
Perth, Kans. K10 108-9
Perth, N. Dak. B9 128-9
Perth, Ont. I14 284-5
Perth, co., Ont. D12 284-5
Perth Amboy, N.J. F7 76-7
Perth-Andover, N.B. G3 275
Perthshire, Miss. D4 176-7
Peru, Ill. D8 96-7
Peru, Ind. D8 100-1
Peru, Kans. K13 108-9
Peru, Me. K3 64-5
Peru, Mass. C3 68-9
Peru, Nebr. I16 124-5
Peru, N.Y. B11 80-1
Peru, Vt. L5 90-1
Peshastin, Wash. F11 246-7
Peshtigo, Wis. E15 140-1
Petaca, N. Mex. C7 230-1
Petal, Miss. L8 176-7
Petaluma, Calif. B7 210-1
Petawawa, Ont. H9 284-5
Peterborough, N.H. O5 72-3
Peterborough, Ont. I9 284-5
Peterborough, co., Ont. J11 284-5
Peterman, Ala. K5 146-7
Peters Creek*, Alaska G11 254-5
Peters Landing, Tenn. C5 188-9
Petersburg, Alaska H15 254-5
Petersburg, Del. G3 153
Petersburg, Ill. G7 96-7
Petersburg, Ind. M5 100-1
Petersburg, Ky. D10 164-5
Petersburg*, Mich. K14 112-3
Petersburg, Nebr. F11 124-5
Petersburg, N.J. N5 76-7
Petersburg, N. Dak. D12 128-9
Petersburg, Okla. I11 234-5
Petersburg, Ore. B9 238-9
Petersburg, Tenn. K7 188-9
Petersburg, Tex. C5 192-3
Petersburg, Va. I12 196-7
Petersburg, W. Va. F9 200-1
Petersfield, Man. I14 272-3
Petersham, Mass. C6 68-9
Peterson, Ala. F4 146-7
Peterson, Ia. C3 104-5
Peterson, Minn. O9 116-7
Peterson*, Ut. E6 242-3
Peterson Station, Nev. G5 226-7
Peterstown, W. Va. J5 200-1
Petersville, Ala. A4 146-7
Peterview*, Nfld. M9 278-9
Petit-Cap, N.B. H8 275
Petit de Grat, N.S. C10 281
Petit-Étang, N.S. A10 281
Petit-Rocher*, N.B. E5 275

Petitcodiac, N.B. H6 275
Petite-Aldouane*, N.B. G7 275
Petite Lake*, Ill. A10 96-7
Petite-Lamèque, N.B. E7 275
Petite-Matane, Que. B16 290-1
Petite-Rivière*, Que. E12 290-1
Petite-Rivière-de-l'Île, N.B. E7 275
Petoskey, Mich. E12 112-3
Petrey, Ala. J8 146-7
Petroleum, Ind. E11 100-1
Petroleum, W. Va. E4 200-1
Petroleum, co., Mont. D11 222-3
Petrolia, Kans. I15 108-9
Petrolia, Ont. E11 284-5
Petros, Tenn. H10 188-9
Pettibone, N. Dak. G9 128-9
Pettigrew, Ark. C4 150-1
Pettis, co., Mo. E5 120-1
Pettus, W. Va. K14 200-1
Petty Harbour, Nfld. O11 278-9
Petty Harbour-Maddox Cove*, Nfld. O11 278-9
Pettyview, Ark. G5 150-1
Pevely, Mo. D15 120-1
Pewamo*, Mich. I13 112-3
Pewaukee, Wis. J4 140-1
Pewaukee West*, Wis. J14 140-1
Pewee Valley, Ky. A3 164-5
Peyton, Colo. F12 214-5
Peytona, W. Va. I13 200-1
Pfeifer, Kans. G7 108-9
Pharoah, Okla. F13 234-5
Pharr, Tex. K8 192-3
Pheba, Miss. E9 176-7
Phelps, Ky. H16 164-5
Phelps, N.Y. E5 80-1
Phelps, Wis. C13 140-1
Phelps, co., Mo. G8 120-1
Phelps, co., Nebr. I9 124-5
Phelps City, Mo. A1 120-1
Phenix, Va. I10 196-7
Phenix City, Ala. H11 146-7
Phil Campbell, Ala. C4 146-7
Philadelphia, Miss. H8 176-7
Philadelphia, N.Y. C8 80-1
Philadelphia, Pa. J15 84-5
Philadelphia, Tenn. I13 188-9
Philadelphia, co., Pa. J15 84-5
Philip, S. Dak. F6 136-7
Philipp, Miss. E6 176-7
Philippi, W. Va. E7 200-1
Philipsburg, Mont. F4 222-3
Philipsburg, Pa. G7 84-5
Philipsburg, Que. K13 290-1
Phillippy, Tenn. A2 188-9
Phillips, Me. J3 64-5
Phillips, Nebr. H11 124-5
Phillips, Okla. H13 234-5
Phillips, Tex. A5 192-3
Phillips, Wis. D11 140-1
Phillips, co., Ark. G10 150-1
Phillips, co., Colo. C16 214-5
Phillips, co., Kans. D7 108-9
Phillips, co., Mont. C11 222-3
Phillipsburg, Ga. M6 160-1
Phillipsburg, Kans. D6 108-9
Phillipsburg, Mo. H6 120-1
Phillipsburg, N.J. E2 76-7
Phillipsburg, O. H14 132-3
Phillipston, Mass. C7 68-9
Phillipsville*, N.C. E3 180-1
Philmont, N.Y. G11 80-1
Philo, Calif. G2 210-1
Philo, Ill. G10 96-7
Philo, O. G9 132-3
Philomath, Ga. G7 160-1
Philomath, Ore. E5 238-9
Philomont, Va. A2 196-7
Philpot, Ky. H6 164-5
Phippsburg, Colo. C8 214-5
Phippsburg, Me. N11 64-5
Phlox, Wis. E13 140-1
Phoenix, Ariz. I6 206-7
Phoenix*, Ill. C11 96-7
Phoenix, La. I10 168-9
Phoenix, Md. B11 172-3
Phoenix, Miss. H6 176-7
Phoenix, N.Y. E7 80-1
Phoenix, Ore. J6 238-9
Phoenixville, Conn. C13 60-1
Phoenixville, Pa. A9 84-5
Phosphate, Mont. F5 222-3
Pia Oik, Ariz. L5 206-7
Piapot, Sask. N4 294-5
Piatt, co., Ill. G9 96-7
Pibroch, Alta. I7 264-5
Pica, Ariz. E4 206-7
Picabo, Ida. M7 218-9
Picacho, Ariz. J7 206-7
Picacho, N. Mex. J8 230-1
Picadilly, Nfld. N7 278-9
Picayune, Miss. N7 176-7
Picerceton, Ind. C9 100-1
Picher, Okla. B15 234-5
Pick City, N. Dak. F6 128-9
Pickardville, Alta. I7 264-5
Pickaway, W. Va. J6 200-1
Pickaway, co., O. G6 132-3
Pickelville, Ut. C7 242-3
Pickens, Ark. D8 150-1
Pickens, Ark. I9 150-1
Pickens, Miss. G6 176-7
Pickens, Okla. H15 234-5
Pickens, S.C. B5 184-5
Pickens, W. Va. G6 200-1
Pickens, co., Ala. F3 146-7
Pickens, co., Ga. E3 160-1
Pickens, co., S.C. B5 184-5
Pickensville, Ala. F2 146-7
Pickerel, Wis. E13 140-1
Pickering, La. F2 168-9
Pickering, Mo. A2 120-1
Pickering*, Ont. C15 284-5
Pickering Beach, Del. F4 153
Pickerington, O. G7 132-3
Pickett, Wis. G3 140-1
Pickett, co., Tenn. A10 188-9
Pickford, Mich. D13 112-3
Pickle Lake*, Ont. D3 284-5
Pickrell, Nebr. I14 124-5
Pickstown, S. Dak. I12 136-7
Pico Rivera, Calif. G9 210-1
Picton, Ont. K13 284-5
Pictou, N.S. C8 281
Pictou, co., N.S. D9 281
Pictou Landing, N.S. C8 281
Picture Butte, Alta. N8 264-5
Pie, W. Va. I2 200-1
Pie Town, N. Mex. H3 230-1
Piedmont, Ala. D9 146-7
Piedmont, Calif. C8 210-1
Piedmont, Kans. I13 108-9
Piedmont, Mo. I10 120-1
Piedmont, Okla. I1 234-5
Piedmont*, Que. H11 290-1
Piedmont, S.C. G1 184-5
Piedmont, S. Dak. F2 136-7
Piedmont, W. Va. D9 200-1
Piedmont, Wyo. J5 250-1
Pierce, Colo. D4 214-5
Pierce, Ida. F4 218-9
Pierce, Ky. I9 164-5
Pierce, Nebr. E12 124-5
Pierce, Okla. F14 234-5
Pierce, co., Ga. M9 160-1
Pierce, co., Nebr. E12 124-5
Pierce, co., N. Dak. D8 128-9
Pierce, co., Wash. G8 246-7
Pierce, co., Wis. F7 140-1
Pierce City, Mo. I4 120-1
Pierceland, Sask. H4 294-5
Pierceville, Ind. K11 100-1
Pierceville, Kans. I4 108-9
Piermont, N.H. H4 72-3
Piermont, N.Y. C14 80-1
Pierpont, S. Dak. B13 136-7
Pierre, S. Dak. E8 136-7
Pierre Part, La. C9 168-9
Pierrefonds, Que. I12 290-1
Pierreville, Que. H13 290-1
Pierson, Fla. D11 156-7
Pierson, Ia. D2 104-5
Pierson, Man. K9 272-3
Pierson, Mich. H12 112-3
Pierz, Minn. K5 116-7
Pigeon, La. C9 168-9
Pigeon, Mich. H14 112-3
Pigeon Cove, Mass. B13 68-9
Pigeon Falls, Wis. G9 140-1
Pigeon Forge, Tenn. I13 188-9
Pigeon Hill, N.B. E7 275
Piggott, Ark. A12 150-1
Piggtown, Miss. H7 176-7
Pike, N.H. H4 72-3
Pike, Okla. I11 234-5
Pike, co., Ala. K8 146-7
Pike, co., Ark. G3 150-1
Pike, co., Ga. H4 160-1
Pike, co., Ill. H4 96-7
Pike, co., Ind. M5 100-1
Pike, co., Ky. H15 164-5
Pike, co., Miss. L5 176-7
Pike, co., Mo. D9 120-1
Pike, co., O. I7 132-3
Pike, co., Pa. E16 84-5
Pike City, Ark. H4 150-1
Pike Road, Ala. I8 146-7
Pike Road, N.C. D14 180-1
Pikes Peak, Colo. K2 214-5
Pikesville, Md. E6 172-3
Piketon, O. I6 132-3
Pikeville, Ky. H15 164-5
Pikeville, N.C. E12 180-1
Pikeville, Tenn. C10 188-9
Pikwitonei, Man. E4 272-3
Pilar, N. Mex. D7 230-1
Pilesgrove*, N.J. K3 76-7
Pilger, Nebr. E13 124-5
Pilger, Sask. K7 294-5
Pilgrim, Ky. H16 164-5
Pilgrim Heights, Mass. E16 68-9
Pillager, Minn. J5 116-7
Pilley's Island, Nfld. L9 278-9
Pillsbury, N. Dak. G12 128-9
Pilot, Va. J7 196-7
Pilot Butte, Sask. N8 294-5
Pilot Grove, Mo. E6 120-1
Pilot Knob, Mo. G10 120-1
Pilot Mound, Ia. F7 104-5
Pilot Mound, Man. K12 272-3
Pilot Mountain, N.C. C8 180-1
Pilot Mountain, Tenn. G10 188-9
Pilot Point, Alaska H9 254-5
Pilot Point, Tex. A14 192-3
Pilot Rock, Ore. C13 238-9
Pilot Station, Alaska E8 254-5
Pilottown, La. K11 168-9
Pilsen, Kans. G11 108-9
Pima, Ariz. J10 206-7
Pima, co., Ariz. K7 206-7
Pimento, Ind. J4 100-1
Pimlico, S.C. H13 184-5
Pinal, co., Ariz. J8 206-7
Pinawa, Man. I16 272-3
Pinch, W. Va. H14 200-1
Pincher Creek, Alta. O7 264-5
Pinckard, Ala. L9 146-7
Pinckney, Mich. J3 112-3
Pinckneyville, Ill. M8 96-7
Pinckneyville, Miss. M3 176-7
Pinconning, Mich. H14 112-3
Pincourt, Que. J11 290-1
Pindall, Ark. B5 150-1
Pine, Ariz. G7 206-7
Pine, Colo. I2 214-5
Pine, Ida. M5 218-9
Pine, La. K10 168-9
Pine, Ore. D16 238-9
Pine, co., Minn. J7 116-7
Pine Apple, Ala. J6 146-7
Pine Beach, N.J. J7 76-7
Pine Bluff, Ark. G7 150-1
Pine Bluff, Wis. J1 140-1
Pine Bluffs, Wyo. J16 250-1
Pine Brook, N.J. D7 76-7
Pine Bush, N.Y. I10 80-1
Pine Castle, Fla. F7 156-7
Pine City, Ark. F10 150-1
Pine City, Minn. K7 116-7
Pine City, Ore. B12 238-9
Pine City, Wash. F15 246-7
Pine Craft*, Fla. G10 156-7
Pine Creek, W. Va. K11 200-1
Pine Creek, Wis. G9 140-1
Pine Creek Gorge, Pa. D9 84-5
Pine Creek Settlement*, Man. H2 272-3
Pine Dock, Man. F14 272-3
Pine Falls, Man. H15 272-3
Pine Grove, La. G8 168-9
Pine Grove, N.J. J4 76-7
Pine Grove, Ore. C13 238-9
Pine Grove, Ore. C8 238-9
Pine Grove, Pa. H12 84-5
Pine Grove, Tenn. I13 188-9
Pine Grove, W. Va. D5 200-1
Pine Hall, N.C. C8 180-1
Pine Harbor, Ga. L11 160-1
Pine Hill, Ala. J4 146-7
Pine Hill, Ky. I12 164-5
Pine Hill, N.J. O11 76-7
Pine Hills*, Fla. E11 156-7
Pine House, Sask. G6 294-5
Pine Island, Minn. N7 116-7
Pine Knoll Shores*, N.C. F14 180-1
Pine Knot, Ky. K11 164-5
Pine Lake, Ga. C11 160-1
Pine Lake, Ind. A6 100-1
Pine Lawn, Mo. B16 120-1
Pine Level, Ala. J8 146-7
Pine Level, N.C. J8 180-1
Pine Log, Ga. E3 160-1
Pine Meadow, Conn. C7 60-1
Pine Mountain, Ga. I3 160-1
Pine Mountain Valley, Ga. I3 160-1
Pine Neck-West Tiana*, N.Y. J13 80-1
Pine Orchard, Conn. H8 60-1
Pine Orchard, Md. F5 172-3
Pine Park, Ga. N4 160-1
Pine Point, Me. N3 64-5
Pine Point, N.W. Terr. C1 296
Pine Prairie, La. F4 168-9
Pine Ridge, Ark. F3 150-1
Pine Ridge, Ky. H13 164-5
Pine Ridge*, Man. J4 272-3
Pine Ridge, Miss. K3 176-7
Pine Ridge, S. Dak. I4 136-7
Pine Ridge Valley Trailer Camp*, Man. J4 272-3
Pine River, Man. F10 272-3
Pine River, Minn. I5 116-7
Pine River, Wis. F2 140-1
Pine Run, Mich. F4 112-3
Pine Shores*, Fla. G10 156-7
Pine Springs, Ariz. E6 206-7
Pine Springs*, Minn. M7 116-7
Pine Tree Corner, Del. D3 153
Pine Tree Corner, Mass. H14 68-9
Pine Valley, N.J. O11 76-7
Pine Valley, Ut. M3 242-3
Pine Village, Ind. F5 100-1
Pinebluff, N.C. K5 180-1
Pinebur, Miss. L7 176-7
Pinecliffe, Colo. F2 214-5
Pinedale, Ala. I7 146-7
Pinedale, Ariz. G9 206-7
Pinedale, N. Mex. E3 230-1
Pinedale, Wyo. F6 250-1
Pinehurst, Ga. K5 160-1
Pinehurst, Ida. D3 218-9
Pinehurst, Md. H8 172-3
Pinehurst, Mass. C11 68-9
Pinehurst, N.C. K5 180-1
Pinehurst, Tex. F12 192-3
Pinehurst-Sheppard Park, S.C. H12 184-5
Pineknob, W. Va. K14 200-1
Pineland, S.C. I10 184-5
Pineland, Tex. F11 192-3
Pinellas, co., Fla. F9 156-7
Pinellas Park, Fla. I2 156-7
Pineora, Ga. J11 160-1
Piner, Ky. E11 164-5
Pineridge, S.C. E10 184-5
Pinero, Va. E4 196-7
Pinetop, Ariz. G10 206-7
Pinetops, N.C. D13 180-1
Pinetown, N.C. D14 180-1
Pineview, Ga. K6 160-1
Pineville, Ark. B7 150-1
Pineville, Ky. J13 164-5
Pineville, La. E4 168-9
Pineville, Miss. I8 176-7
Pineville, Mo. J3 120-1
Pineville, N.C. K1 180-1
Pineville, S.C. G13 184-5
Pineville, W. Va. J3 200-1
Pinewald, N.J. J7 76-7
Pinewood, Ont. F1 284-5
Pinewood, S.C. F11 184-5
Pinewood, Tenn. H5 188-9
Piney, Man. K16 272-3
Piney, W. Va. D5 200-1
Piney Flats, Tenn. G16 188-9
Piney Grove, Md. B5 172-3
Piney Park, Mo. D13 120-1
Piney Point, Md. I11 172-3
Piney Point Village*, Tex. H13 192-3
Piney River, Va. H9 196-7
Piney Woods, Miss. J6 176-7
Pingree, Ida. M9 218-9
Pingree, N. Dak. G10 128-9
Pink, Okla. K3 234-5
Pink Hill, N.C. F12 180-1
Pinnacle, Ark. I15 150-1
Pinnacle, N.C. C8 180-1
Pinola, Miss. J6 176-7
Pinole, Calif. B7 210-1
Piñon, Ariz. C9 206-7
Piñon, N. Mex. K8 230-1
Pinopolis, S.C. G13 184-5
Pinos Altos, N. Mex. K3 230-1
Pinson, Tenn. C4 188-9
Pinta, Ariz. E10 206-7
Pintendre*, Que. G11 290-1
Pinto, Md. B3 172-3
Pinto, Ut. M3 242-3
Pintura, Ut. M3 242-3
Pioche, Nev. I10 226-7
Pioneer, Ia. D6 104-5
Pioneer, La. B6 168-9
Pioneer, Mont. F5 222-3
Pioneer, O. B3 132-3
Pioneer, Tenn. G11 188-9
Pioneerville, Ida. L4 218-9
Pipe, Wis. G4 140-1
Piper, Kans. E16 108-9
Piper City, Ill. E10 96-7
Pipestem, W. Va. J5 200-1
Pipestone, Man. J9 272-3
Pipestone, Minn. O2 116-7
Pipestone, Mont. G5 222-3
Pipestone, co., Minn. O2 116-7
Pippa Passes, Ky. I15 164-5
Piqua, Kans. I14 108-9
Piqua, O. F4 132-3
Pirtleville, Ariz. M11 206-7
Piscataquis, co., Me. G5 64-5
Piscataway, Md. K4 172-3
Piscataway*, N.J. F6 76-7
Pisek, N. Dak. D13 128-9
Pisgah, Ala. B8 146-7
Pisgah, Ia. G2 104-5
Pisgah, Md. G9 172-3
Pisgah, W. Va. A16 200-1
Pisgah Forest, N.C. E3 180-1
Pisinimo, Ariz. L6 206-7
Pismo Beach, Calif. M4 210-1
Pistol River, Ore. J3 238-9
Pit Siding*, Man. C4 272-3
Pitcairn*, Pa. I3 84-5
Pitkas Point, Alaska E8 254-5
Pitkin, Colo. G9 214-5
Pitkin, La. F3 168-9
Pitkin, co., Colo. F8 214-5
Pitman, N.J. O10 76-7
Pitoikam, Ariz. L7 206-7
Pitsburg, O. G13 132-3
Pitt, co., N.C. D13 180-1
Pitts, Ga. K6 160-1
Pittsboro, Ind. H7 100-1
Pittsboro, Miss. D8 176-7
Pittsboro, N.C. D10 180-1
Pittsburg, Calif. B8 210-1
Pittsburg, Ind. E5 100-1
Pittsburg, Kans. J16 108-9
Pittsburg, Ky. I12 164-5
Pittsburg, N.H. B7 72-3
Pittsburg, Okla. G14 234-5
Pittsburg, Ore. B5 238-9
Pittsburg, Tex. D10 192-3
Pittsburg, co., Okla. G14 234-5
Pittsburgh, Pa. H2 84-5
Pittsfield, Ill. I5 96-7
Pittsfield, Me. J5 64-5
Pittsfield, Mass. C2 68-9
Pittsfield, N.H. L7 72-3
Pittsfield, Vt. I5 90-1
Pittsford, N.Y. E5 80-1
Pittsford, Vt. I4 90-1
Pittsford Mills, Vt. I4 90-1
Pittsgrove*, N.J. L3 76-7
Pittston, Me. L4 64-5
Pittston, Pa. E14 84-5
Pittston Farm, Me. F4 64-5
Pittsview, Ala. I10 146-7
Pittsville, Md. G15 172-3
Pittsville, Va. J9 196-7
Pittsville, Wis. G11 140-1
Pittsylvania, co., Va. J9 196-7
Piusville, P.E.I. C3 287
Piute, co., Ut. K5 242-3
Pixley, Calif. L6 210-1
Placentia*, Calif. G9 210-1
Placentia, Nfld. O10 278-9
Placer, co., Calif. G5 210-1
Placerville, Calif. A10 210-1
Placerville, Colo. H7 214-5
Placerville, Ida. L4 218-9
Placitas, N. Mex. J4 230-1
Plain, Miss. I6 176-7
Plain, Wash. E10 246-7
Plain, Wis. J11 140-1
Plain City, O. F6 132-3
Plain City, Ut. D6 242-3
Plain Dealing, La. A2 168-9

Plain View, Ia. G14 104-5
Plain View, Va. E3 196-7
Plainedge, N.Y. E16 80-1
Plainfield, Conn. D14 60-1
Plainfield, Ga. K7 160-1
Plainfield, Ill. N2 96-7
Plainfield, Ind. H7 100-1
Plainfield, Ia. C10 104-5
Plainfield, Mass. C3 68-9
Plainfield, Mich. I2 112-3
Plainfield, N.H. K3 72-3
Plainfield, N.J. E6 76-7
Plainfield*, Tenn. I14 188-9
Plainfield, Vt. F7 90-1
Plainfield, Wis. F1 140-1
Plains, Ga. K4 160-1
Plains, Kans. J4 108-9
Plains, Mont. D2 222-3
Plains*, Pa. F13 84-5
Plains, Tex. D4 192-3
Plains, The, O. H8 132-3
Plains, The, Va. A2 196-7
Plainsboro, N.J. G5 76-7
Plainview, Ark. E4 150-1
Plainview, Minn. N8 116-7
Plainview, Nebr. E12 124-5
Plainview, N.Y. E16 80-1
Plainview, Okla. C8 234-5
Plainview, Okla. G7 234-5
Plainview, Ore. J1 238-9
Plainview, Tex. C5 192-3
Plainville, Conn. E8 60-1
Plainville, Ga. E2 160-1
Plainville, Ind. L5 100-1
Plainville, Kans. E6 108-9
Plainville, Mass. D5 68-9
Plainville, Mass. F10 68-9
Plainwell, Mich. J12 112-3
Plaisance*, Que. I10 290-1
Plaisted, Me. B7 64-5
Plaistow, N.H. O8 72-3
Plamondon, Alta. H9 264-5
Planada, Calif. D11 210-1
Plandome*, N.Y. J11 80-1
Plandome Heights*, N.Y. J11 80-1
Plandome Manor*, N.Y. J11 80-1
Plankinton, S. Dak. G12 136-7
Plano, Ida. L10 218-9
Plano, Ill. C9 96-7
Plano, Ia. J9 104-5
Plano, Tex. B15 192-3
Plant City, Fla. H4 156-7
Plantagenet, Ont. H16 284-5
Plantation, Fla. G16 156-7
Plantation*, Ky. F9 164-5
Plantation Number 14*, Me. I10 64-5
Plantation Number 21*, Me. I10 64-5
Plantation Number 33*, Me. I8 64-5
Plantersville, Ala. H6 146-7
Plantersville, Miss. C9 176-7
Plantersville, S.C. F15 184-5
Plantsite, Ariz. J11 206-7
Plantsville, Conn. E8 60-1
Plaquemine, La. H7 168-9
Plaquemine Southwest*, La. H7 168-9
Plaquemines, co., La. J11 168-9
Plaster Rock, N.B. F3 275
Plateau, N.S. A10 281
Plateau City, Colo. E7 214-5
Platinum, Alaska G8 254-5
Platner, Colo. D15 214-5
Plato, Minn. C8 116-7
Plato, Sask. M5 294-5
Platoro, Colo. I9 214-5
Platte, S. Dak. H11 136-7
Platte, co., Mo. D2 120-1
Platte, co., Nebr. F13 124-5
Platte, co., Wyo. H15 250-1
Platte Center, Nebr. F12 124-5
Platte City, Mo. D2 120-1
Platte R., Nebr. G12 124-5
Platte Woods, Mo. I15 120-1
Plattenville, La. C10 168-9
Platter, Okla. I13 234-5
Platteville, Colo. E4 214-5
Platteville, Wis. K11 140-1
Plattsburg, Mo. C3 120-1
Plattsburgh, N.Y. A11 80-1
Plattsburgh Base*, N.Y. A11 80-1
Plattsmouth, Nebr. H15 124-5
Plattsville, Conn. H5 60-1
Plattsville*, Ont. D13 284-5
Plaucheville, La. F5 168-9
Plaza, N. Dak. D5 128-9
Plaza, Wash. F16 246-7
Pleasant City, O. G10 132-3
Pleasant Dale, Nebr. H14 124-5
Pleasant Dale, W. Va. E10 200-1
Pleasant Gap, Pa. G8 84-5
Pleasant Garden, N.C. H4 180-1
Pleasant Grove, Ala. E6 146-7
Pleasant Grove, Kans. F15 108-9
Pleasant Grove, Miss. C6 176-7
Pleasant Grove*, P.E.I. E8 287
Pleasant Grove, Tenn. K10 188-9
Pleasant Grove, Tenn. J7 188-9
Pleasant Grove, Ut. F6 242-3
Pleasant Heights*, Sask. M5 294-5
Pleasant Hill, Ala. I6 146-7
Pleasant Hill, Ark. H4 150-1
Pleasant Hill, Calif. C8 210-1
Pleasant Hill, Del. A2 153
Pleasant Hill, Ill. I4 96-7
Pleasant Hill, Ia. G8 104-5
Pleasant Hill, La. D2 168-9
Pleasant Hill, Miss. A7 176-7
Pleasant Hill, Mo. K16 120-1
Pleasant Hill, O. F3 132-3
Pleasant Hill, Okla. I16 234-5
Pleasant Hill, Ore. F6 238-9
Pleasant Hill*, Pa. I12 84-5
Pleasant Hill, Tenn. J2 188-9
Pleasant Hill, Tenn. B10 188-9
Pleasant Hill*, Va. J14 196-7
Pleasant Hills*, Md. B12 172-3
Pleasant Hills*, Pa. I2 84-5
Pleasant Hope, Mo. H5 120-1
Pleasant Island, Me. I2 64-5
Pleasant Lake, Ind. A11 100-1
Pleasant Lake, Mass. G16 68-9
Pleasant Lake, Mich. J2 112-3
Pleasant Lake, Minn. L5 116-7
Pleasant Mills, Ind. D12 100-1
Pleasant Plain, Ia. I12 104-5
Pleasant Plains, Ark. D8 150-1
Pleasant Plains, Ill. H6 96-7
Pleasant Plains, N.J. I7 76-7
Pleasant Point, Me. M6 64-5
Pleasant Pond, Me. H4 64-5
Pleasant Prairie, Wis. K5 140-1
Pleasant Ridge, Ala. C4 146-7
Pleasant Ridge, Me. I4 64-5
Pleasant Ridge*, Mich. J15 112-3
Pleasant Shade, Tenn. A9 188-9
Pleasant Site, Ala. B3 146-7
Pleasant Valley, Ark. H14 150-1
Pleasant Valley, Conn. B7 60-1
Pleasant Valley, Ia. G15 104-5
Pleasant Valley*, Ky. H15 164-5
Pleasant Valley, Mo. I15 120-1
Pleasant Valley*, N.Y. H11 80-1
Pleasant Valley, Ore. D15 238-9
Pleasant View, Colo. I5 214-5
Pleasant View, Ida. O9 218-9
Pleasant View, Ind. G3 100-1
Pleasant View, Ky. K12 164-5
Pleasant View*, P.E.I. B3 287
Pleasant View, Tenn. G6 188-9
Pleasant View, Ut. D6 242-3
Pleasantdale, Sask. K8 294-5
Pleasanton, Calif. C8 210-1
Pleasanton, Ia. K7 104-5
Pleasanton, Kans. H16 108-9
Pleasanton, Nebr. H10 124-5
Pleasanton, Tex. H7 192-3
Pleasants, co., W. Va. D4 200-1
Pleasantview Acreages*, Alta. I8 264-5
Pleasantville, Ia. H8 104-5
Pleasantville, N.J. M6 76-7
Pleasantville, N.Y. B15 80-1
Pleasantville, O. G7 132-3
Pleasantville, Pa. D3 84-5
Pleasantville, Tenn. C5 188-9
Pleasure Beach, Conn. H13 60-1
Pleasure Ridge Park, Ky. B1 164-5
Pleasureville*, Ky. F10 164-5
Plenty, Sask. L5 294-5
Plentywood, Mont. A15 222-3
Plessisville, Que. H15 290-1
Pletcher, Ala. H6 146-7
Plevna, Kans. I9 108-9
Plevna, Mont. F16 222-3
Pliny, W. Va. G2 200-1
Plover, Ia. C5 104-5
Plover, Wis. E1 140-1
Pluckemin, N.J. E5 76-7
Plum, Pa. A7 84-5
Plum Branch, S.C. E7 184-5
Plum City, Wis. F8 140-1
Plum Coulee, Man. K13 272-3
Plum Point, Md. F11 172-3
Plum Springs*, Ky. J7 164-5
Plumas, Man. I12 272-3
Plumas, co., Calif. F5 210-1
Plumerville, Ark. E6 150-1
Plummer, Ida. D2 218-9
Plummer, Minn. F2 116-7
Plummers Landing, Ky. F13 164-5
Plumsted*, N.J. I6 76-7
Plumtree, N.C. D5 180-1
Plunkett, Sask. L7 294-5
Plunkettville, Okla. H16 234-5
Plush, Ore. J11 238-9
Plymouth, Calif. A10 210-1
Plymouth, Conn. E7 60-1
Plymouth, Del. G4 153
Plymouth, Ill. G4 96-7
Plymouth, Ind. B8 100-1
Plymouth, Ia. B9 104-5
Plymouth, Me. J6 64-5
Plymouth, Mass. F13 68-9
Plymouth, Mich. J5 112-3
Plymouth, Minn. B10 116-7
Plymouth, Nebr. I14 124-5
Plymouth, N.H. J6 72-3
Plymouth, N.C. D14 180-1
Plymouth, O. D7 132-3
Plymouth, Pa. F13 84-5
Plymouth*, Ut. C5 242-3
Plymouth, Vt. J6 90-1
Plymouth, Wash. I13 246-7
Plymouth, Wis. G5 140-1
Plymouth, co., Ia. D2 104-5
Plymouth, co., Mass. G13 68-9
Plymouth Bay, Mass. F13 68-9
Plymouth Village*, Ky. G9 164-5
Plympton, Mass. F13 68-9
Plymptonville, Pa. F6 84-5
Poamoho Camp, Hawaii H4 258-9
Poca, W. Va. G3 200-1
Pocahontas, Ark. B10 150-1
Pocahontas, Ill. K7 96-7
Pocahontas, Ia. D5 104-5
Pocahontas, Miss. H6 176-7
Pocahontas, Mo. H11 120-1
Pocahontas, Tenn. K4 188-9
Pocahontas, Va. I5 196-7
Pocahontas, co., Ia. D5 104-5
Pocahontas, co., W. Va. H6 200-1
Pocasset, Mass. H13 68-9
Pocasset, Okla. K1 234-5
Pocatello, Ida. N9 218-9
Pocola*, Okla. F16 234-5
Pocomoke City, Md. I15 172-3
Pocotalago, Ga. E6 160-1
Poe, W. Va. I16 200-1
Pohakapu, Hawaii J7 258-9
Pohatcong*, N.J. E3 76-7
Pohénégamook*, Que. E14 290-1
Poinsett, co., Ark. C11 150-1
Point, La. B5 168-9
Point Alexander, Alaska H15 254-5
Point Arena, Calif. H1 210-1
Point Cedar, Ark. G4 150-1
Point Clear, Ala. O3 146-7
Point Comfort, Tex. I9 192-3
Point Cross, N.S. A10 281
Point de Bute, N.B. I8 275
Point Edward, Ont. E10 284-5
Point Harbor, N.C. C16 180-1
Point Hope, Alaska B8 254-5
Point Isabel, Ind. F9 100-1
Point Judith, R.I. I5 87
Point La Nim, N.B. D4 275
Point Lay, Alaska B9 254-5
Point Leamington, Nfld. M9 278-9
Point Lookout, Md. I12 172-3
Point Marion, Pa. K2 84-5
Point Mugu*, Calif. G6 210-1
Point of Rocks, Md. C8 172-3
Point of Rocks, Wyo. I8 250-1
Point Pleasant, N.J. I8 76-7
Point Pleasant, W. Va. F2 200-1
Point Pleasant Beach, N.J. I8 76-7
Point Roberts, Wash. B7 246-7
Point Whitshed, Alaska F12 254-5
Pointe a la Hache, La. J10 168-9
Pointe Anne, Ont. K12 284-5
Pointe-au-Pic, Que. E13 290-1
Pointe-aux-Outardes, Que. B15 290-1
Pointe-aux-Trembles*, Que. I12 290-1
Pointe-Calumet*, Que. I12 290-1
Pointe-Claire*, Que. I12 290-1
Pointe Coupee, co., La. G6 168-9
Pointe-des-Cascades*, Que. J12 290-1
Pointe du Bois, Man. I16 272-3
Pointe-du-Chêne*, N.B. H7 275
Pointe-du-Lac*, Que. H14 290-1
Pointe-Lebel, Que. A16 290-1
Pointe-Sapin, N.B. F7 275
Pointe-Verte*, N.B. E5 275
Points, W. Va. D10 200-1
Poipu, Hawaii D4 258-9
Polacca, Ariz. D9 206-7
Poland, Ind. I6 100-1
Poland, Me. M8 64-5
Poland, N.Y. E9 80-1
Poland, O. C11 132-3
Poland, Wis. E5 140-1
Poland Junction, Ariz. G6 206-7
Poland Spring, Me. M9 64-5
Polar, Wis. E13 140-1
Polaris, Mont. H4 222-3
Polebridge, Mont. A3 222-3
Polk, Nebr. H12 124-5
Polk, O. D8 132-3
Polk, Pa. E2 84-5
Polk, co., Ark. G2 150-1
Polk, co., Fla. F11 156-7
Polk, co., Ga. F2 160-1
Polk, co., Ia. G8 104-5
Polk, co., Minn. G2 116-7
Polk, co., Mo. G5 120-1
Polk, co., Nebr. G12 124-5
Polk, co., N.C. E4 180-1
Polk, co., Ore. D5 238-9
Polk, co., Tenn. D11 188-9
Polk, co., Tex. F11 192-3
Polk, co., Wis. D7 140-1
Polk City, Fla. G5 156-7
Polk City, Ia. G7 104-5
Polkton, N.C. K3 180-1
Polkville, Miss. I7 176-7
Polkville*, N.C. E5 180-1
Pollard, Ala. M5 146-7
Pollard, Ark. A12 150-1
Pollock, Ida. I3 218-9
Pollock, La. E4 168-9
Pollock, S. Dak. A8 136-7
Pollocksville, N.C. F13 180-1
Polo, Ill. B7 96-7
Polo, Mo. G16 120-1
Polonia, Wis. D1 140-1
Polson, Mont. C3 222-3
Polvadera, N. Mex. H5 230-1
Pomaria, S.C. J7 184-5
Pomerene, Ariz. L9 206-7
Pomeroy, Ia. D5 104-5
Pomeroy, O. I8 132-3
Pomeroy, Wash. H15 246-7
Pomeroyton, Ky. G13 164-5
Pomfret, Conn. B14 60-1
Pomfret, Md. G10 172-3
Pomfret, Vt. I7 90-1
Pomfret Center, Conn. C14 60-1
Pomona, Calif. G9 210-1
Pomona, Ga. H4 160-1
Pomona, Kans. G15 108-9
Pomona, Md. D13 172-3
Pomona, N.J. L5 76-7
Pomona*, N.Y. J11 80-1
Pomona, Tenn. H5 188-9
Pomona, Tenn. B10 188-9
Pomona Park, Fla. D11 156-7
Pomonkey, Md. F9 172-3
Pompano Beach, Fla. F16 156-7
Pompano Beach Highlands*, Fla. I13 156-7
Pompanoosuc, Vt. I8 90-1
Pompeii, Mich. F1 112-3
Pompeys Pillar, Mont. G11 222-3
Pompton Lakes, N.J. C7 76-7
Pompton Plains, N.J. C7 76-7
Pomquet, N.S. C9 281
Ponca, Ark. B4 150-1
Ponca, Nebr. D14 124-5
Ponca City, Okla. C11 234-5
Ponce de Leon, Fla. B5 156-7
Ponce Inlet*, Fla. D12 156-7
Poncha Springs, Colo. G10 214-5
Ponchatoula, La. A13 168-9
Pond, Miss. L2 176-7
Pond Creek, Okla. C10 234-5
Pond Gap, W. Va. I15 200-1
Pond Inlet, N.W. Terr. B3 296
Pond Meadow, Conn. H10 60-1
Pondera, co., Mont. B5 222-3
Ponderay, Ida. B3 218-9
Ponderosa, N. Mex. E5 230-1
Pondosa, Ore. D15 238-9
Ponemah, N.H. O6 72-3
Poneto, Ind. E11 100-1
Ponkapoag, Mass. J5 68-9
Ponoka, Alta. K8 264-5
Ponquogue*, N.Y. J13 80-1
Ponset, Conn. F10 60-1
Pont-Lafrance*, N.B. E6 275
Pont-Rouge, Que. G10 290-1
Pontbriand*, Que. H16 290-1
Ponteix, Sask. O6 294-5
Pontiac, Ill. E9 96-7
Pontiac, Mich. I14 112-3
Pontiac*, Que. I1 290-1
Pontiac, S.C. D10 184-5
Pontiac, co., Que. I1 290-1
Pontoon Beach, Ill. K6 96-7
Pontoosuc Gardens, Mass. C2 68-9
Pontotoc, Miss. C9 176-7
Pontotoc, Okla. H12 234-5
Pontotoc, co., Miss. C8 176-7
Pontotoc, co., Okla. H12 234-5
Pontypool*, Ont. B16 284-5
Pony, Mont. G6 222-3
Pool, W. Va. H5 200-1
Poole, Ky. H5 164-5
Poole, Nebr. H10 124-5
Pooler, Ga. K11 160-1
Poolesville, Md. G1 172-3
Pope, Ala. J4 146-7
Pope, Miss. C6 176-7
Pope, co., Ark. D5 150-1
Pope, co., Ill. O9 96-7
Pope, co., Minn. K3 116-7
Popejoy, Ia. D8 104-5
Popham Beach, Me. O11 64-5
Poplar, Calif. K6 210-1
Poplar, Mont. C15 222-3
Poplar, N.C. C4 180-1
Poplar, Wis. B8 140-1
Poplar Bluff, Mo. I10 120-1
Poplar Creek, Miss. F7 176-7
Poplar Grove, Ark. F10 150-1
Poplar Grove, Ill. A9 96-7
Poplar Grove, P.E.I. C4 287
Poplar Plains, Ky. F13 164-5
Poplar Point, Man. I13 272-3
Poplar Ridge*, Alta. J7 264-5
Poplarfield, Man. H13 272-3
Poplarville, Miss. M7 176-7
Poponesset Beach, Mass. H14 68-9
Poquetanuck, Conn. F13 60-1
Poquonock, Conn. B9 60-1
Poquonock Bridge, Conn. G13 60-1
Poquoson, Va. F4 196-7
Porcupine, S. Dak. H4 136-7
Porcupine Plain, Sask. K9 294-5
Port, Okla. F7 234-5
Port Alberni, B.C. J5 268-9
Port Albion, B.C. K5 268-9
Port Alice, B.C. J5 268-9
Port Allegany, Pa. D7 84-5
Port Allen, Hawaii D4 258-9
Port Allen, La. A9 168-9
Port Alsworth, Alaska F10 254-5
Port Angeles, Wash. D6 246-7
Port Angeles East*, Wash. D6 246-7
Port Aransas, Tex. I9 192-3
Port Arthur, Tex. G11 192-3
Port au Choix, Nfld. K8 278-9
Port au Port, Nfld. N7 278-9
Port au Port West-Aguathuna-Felix Cove*, Nfld. N7 278-9
Port Austin, Mich. G15 112-3
Port Barre, La. G5 168-9
Port Blakely, Wash. I2 246-7
Port Blandford, Nfld. N10 278-9
Port Bolster*, Ont. B15 284-5
Port Burwell, Ont. E13 284-5
Port Byron, Ill. C6 96-7
Port Byron, N.Y. E6 80-1
Port Carbon*, Pa. H13 84-5
Port Carling, Ont. I8 284-5
Port-Cartier, Que. H5 290-1
Port Charlotte, Fla. H10 156-7
Port Chester, N.Y. C15 80-1
Port Clements, B.C. F2 268-9
Port Clinton, O. B6 132-3

Port Clyde, Me. M6 64-5
Port Colborne, Ont. E15 284-5
Port Colden, N.J. D4 76-7
Port Coquitlam, B.C. C14 268-9
Port Deposit, Md. B13 172-3
Port Dickinson, N.Y. G7 80-1
Port Eads, La. K11 168-9
Port Edward, B.C. F3 268-9
Port Edwards, Wis. G12 140-1
Port Elgin, N.B. H8 275
Port Elgin, Ont. B12 284-5
Port Elizabeth, N.J. M3 76-7
Port Elmsley, Ont. I14 284-5
Port Ewen, N.Y. H11 80-1
Port Gamble, Wash. G2 246-7
Port Gibson, Miss. J4 176-7
Port Graham, Alaska G11 254-5
Port Hammond, B.C. C14 268-9
Port Hardy, B.C. I4 268-9
Port Hastings*, N.S. C10 281
Port Hawkesbury, N.S. C10 281
Port Heiden, Alaska H9 254-5
Port Henry, N.Y. C11 80-1
Port Herman, Md. C13 172-3
Port Higgins*, Alaska H16 254-5
Port Hood, N.S. C10 281
Port Hope, Mich. G15 112-3
Port Hope, Ont. K11 284-5
Port Hope Simpson, Nfld. I8 278-9
Port Hueneme, Calif. G6 210-1
Port Huron, Mich. I15 112-3
Port Isabel*, Tex. K9 192-3
Port Jefferson, N.Y. J12 80-1
Port Jefferson, O. E4 132-3
Port Jefferson Station*, N.Y. J12 80-1
Port Jervis, N.Y. I9 80-1
Port Lambton*, Ont. E10 284-5
Port Lavaca, Tex. I9 192-3
Port Leyden, N.Y. D8 80-1
Port Lions, Alaska H10 254-5
Port Loring, Ont. H8 284-5
Port Ludlow, Wash. G1 246-7
Port Mahon, Del. F4 153
Port Maitland, N.S. F4 281
Port McNeill, B.C. I4 268-9
Port McNicoll, Ont. A14 284-5
Port Mellon, B.C. B12 268-9
Port Monmouth, N.J. H11 76-7
Port Moody, B.C. C14 268-9
Port-Morien*, N.S. B12 281
Port Morris, N.J. D5 76-7
Port Murray, N.J. D4 76-7
Port Neches, Tex. G11 192-3
Port Norris, N.J. N3 76-7
Port Orange, Fla. D12 156-7
Port Orchard, Wash. I1 246-7
Port Orford, Ore. I3 238-9
Port Penn, Del. C3 153
Port Perry*, Ont. C16 284-5
Port Radium, N.W. Terr. C1 296
Port Reading, N.J. F9 76-7
Port Renfrew, B.C. K6 268-9
Port Republic, N.J. L6 76-7
Port Republic, Va. G10 196-7
Port Rexton, Nfld. N11 278-9
Port Richey, Fla. G2 156-7
Port Rowan*, Ont. F13 284-5
Port Royal, Ky. F10 164-5
Port Royal, S.C. J11 184-5
Port Royal, Va. G13 196-7
Port St. Joe, Fla. C6 156-7
Port St. Lucie, Fla. B16 156-7
Port Sandfield, Ont. I8 284-5
Port Sanilac, Mich. E8 112-3
Port Saunders, Nfld. K8 278-9
Port Stanley, Ont. E12 284-5
Port Sulphur, La. J10 168-9
Port Tobacco, Md. G10 172-3
Port Townsend, Wash. F1 246-7
Port Vincent, La. B11 168-9
Port Vue*, Pa. I2 84-5
Port Washington, N.Y. E15 80-1
Port Washington, O. E10 132-3
Port Washington, Wis. I15 140-1
Port Washington North*, N.Y. J11 80-1
Port Wentworth, Ga. K11 160-1
Port William, O. J16 132-3
Port Williams*, N.S. D6 281
Port Wing, Wis. A9 140-1
Portage, Alaska F11 254-5
Portage, Ind. A5 100-1
Portage, Me. C8 64-5
Portage*, Mich. J12 112-3
Portage, Mont. D7 222-3
Portage, O. C5 132-3
Portage, Pa. I6 84-5
Portage, Ut. C5 242-3
Portage, Wash. J2 246-7
Portage, Wis. I12 140-1
Portage, co., O. C10 132-3
Portage, co., Wis. G12 140-1
Portage Des Sioux, Mo. A15 120-1
Portage-du-Cap, Que. I7 290-1
Portage-du-Fort, Que. J1 290-1
Portage Isl., N.B. F6 275
Portage la Prairie, Man. J3 272-3
Portage Lake*, Me. C8 64-5
Portageville, Mo. J11 120-1
Portal, Ariz. L11 206-7
Portal, Ga. J9 160-1
Portal, N. Dak. B4 128-9
Portales, N. Mex. H11 230-1
Porter, Del. C3 153
Porter, Ind. A5 100-1
Porter, Me. N6 64-5
Porter, Minn. M2 116-7
Porter, N.C. J3 180-1
Porter, Okla. E14 234-5
Porter, Wash. G6 246-7
Porter, co., Ind. B5 100-1
Porterdale, Ga. G5 160-1
Porters Corners, Mont. F4 222-3
Porters Falls, W. Va. D5 200-1
Porters Lake*, N.S. E7 281
Portersville, Ala. C8 146-7
Portersville, Ind. M6 100-1
Porterville, Calif. K6 210-1
Porterville, Miss. H10 176-7
Porterville, Ut. E6 242-3
Porterville Northwest*, Calif. K6 210-1
Porterville West*, Calif. K6 210-1
Porthill, Ida. A3 218-9
Portia, Ark. B10 150-1
Portis, Kans. D8 108-9
Portland, Ark. J8 150-1
Portland, Colo. G11 214-5
Portland*, Colo. H7 214-5
Portland, Conn. E9 60-1
Portland, Ind. F11 100-1
Portland, Me. N3 64-5
Portland, Mich. I13 112-3
Portland, N. Dak. F13 128-9
Portland, Ont. I14 284-5
Portland, Ore. C6 238-9
Portland, Tenn. F8 188-9
Portland, Tex. I8 192-3
Portneuf, Ida. N9 218-9
Portneuf, Que. G10 290-1
Portneuf, co., Que. I3 290-1
Portneuf-Station*, Que. I3 290-1
Portola, Calif. G5 210-1
Portola Valley*, Calif. J3 210-1
Portsmouth, Ia. G3 104-5
Portsmouth, N.H. N10 72-3
Portsmouth, O. J6 132-3
Portsmouth, R.I. F7 87
Portsmouth, Va. G4 196-7
Portsmouth Harbor, N.H. N10 72-3
Portugal Cove*, Nfld. N11 278-9
Portville, N.Y. H3 80-1
Porum, Okla. F15 234-5
Posen*, Ill. C11 96-7
Posen, Mich. E14 112-3
Posey, co., Ind. O3 100-1
Poseyville, Ind. N3 100-1
Poskin, Wis. D8 140-1
Post, Ore. F10 238-9
Post, Tex. D5 192-3
Post Falls, Ida. C2 218-9
Post Mills, Vt. H8 90-1
Postelle, Ark. F10 150-1
Postles Corner, Del. F4 153
Poston, S.C. E14 184-5
Postville, Ia. C12 104-5
Potash, Ala. F10 146-7
Potato Creek, S. Dak. H5 136-7
Poteau, Okla. F16 234-5
Poteet, Tex. H7 192-3
Poth, Tex. H8 192-3
Potholes Res., Wash. G12 246-7
Potlatch, Ida. E2 218-9
Potlatch, Wash. F6 246-7
Potomac, Ill. G11 96-7
Potomac, Md. I3 172-3
Potomac, Mont. E4 222-3
Potomac Heights*, Md. F9 172-3
Potomac Park [-Bowling Green], Md. B4 172-3
Potomac R., Md. H10 172-3
Potomac R., Va. F12 196-7
Potomac Valley*, Md. D9 172-3
Potosi, Mo. G9 120-1
Potosi, Wis. K10 140-1
Potsdam, N.Y. A9 80-1
Potsdam, O. G14 132-3
Pottawatomie, co., Kans. E13 108-9
Pottawatomie, co., Okla. F11 234-5
Pottawattamie, co., Ia. H3 104-5
Pottawattomie Park, Ind. A6 100-1
Potter, Ark. F2 150-1
Potter, Kans. E15 108-9
Potter, Nebr. G2 124-5
Potter, Wis. F4 140-1
Potter, co., Pa. D8 84-5
Potter, co., S. Dak. C9 136-7
Potter, co., Tex. B5 192-3
Potter Hill, R.I. H2 87
Potter Place, N.H. K5 72-3
Pottersville, N.J. E5 76-7
Potterville, Ga. J4 160-1
Potterville, Mich. J13 112-3
Potterville, R.I. D3 87
Potts Camp, Miss. B8 176-7
Pottsboro, Tex. C9 192-3
Pottstown, Pa. I14 84-5
Pottsville, Ark. D5 150-1
Pottsville, Pa. H12 84-5
Potwin, Kans. I11 108-9
Pouce Coupe, B.C. E8 268-9
Pouch Cove*, Nfld. N11 278-9
Poughkeepsie, Ark. B9 150-1
Poughkeepsie, N.Y. H11 80-1
Poulan, Ga. M5 160-1
Poulsbo, Wash. H1 246-7
Poultney, Vt. J4 90-1
Pound, Va. I3 196-7
Pound, Wis. E15 140-1
Pounding Mill, Va. I4 196-7
Povungnituk, Que. B2 290-1
Powassan, Ont. H8 284-5
Poway, Calif. J11 210-1
Powder R., Wyo. D13 250-1
Powder River, Wyo. F11 250-1
Powder River, co., Mont. H14 222-3
Powder Springs, Ga. B9 160-1
Powder Springs, Tenn. G13 188-9
Powder Wash, Colo. B6 214-5
Powderhorn, Colo. G8 214-5
Powderly, Ky. I6 164-5
Powdersville, S.C. G1 184-5
Powderville, Mont. G15 222-3
Powell, Nebr. J13 124-5
Powell, O. F6 132-3
Powell, Okla. I12 234-5
Powell, Tenn. H12 188-9
Powell, Wyo. B8 250-1
Powell, co., Ky. H13 164-5
Powell, co., Mont. E4 222-3
Powell Butte, Ore. F9 238-9
Powells Crossroads, Tenn. K10 188-9
Powellsville, N.C. C14 180-1
Powellton, W. Va. J15 200-1
Powellville, Md. H15 172-3
Power, Mont. D6 222-3
Power, W. Va. B5 200-1
Power, co., Ida. N8 218-9
Powers, Ala. G4 146-7
Powers, Mich. E10 112-3
Powers, Ore. I4 238-9
Powers Lake, N. Dak. C4 128-9
Powers Lake, Wis. K4 140-1
Powersville, Ga. J5 160-1
Powersville, Mo. A5 120-1
Powerview, Man. H15 272-3
Poweshiek, co., Ia. G10 104-5
Powhatan, Ark. B9 150-1
Powhatan, La. D3 168-9
Powhatan, Va. H11 196-7
Powhatan, co., Va. H11 196-7
Powhatan Point, O. G11 132-3
Powhattan, Kans. D14 108-9
Pownal, Me. N9 64-5
Pownal*, P.E.I. F8 287
Pownal, Vt. O4 90-1
Poy Sippi, Wis. F2 140-1
Poyen, Ark. G6 150-1
Poynette, Wis. H1 140-1
Prague, Nebr. G14 124-5
Prague, Okla. F12 234-5
Prairie, Ala. I4 146-7
Prairie, Ida. M4 218-9
Prairie, Miss. E9 176-7
Prairie, co., Ark. F8 150-1
Prairie, co., Mont. E14 222-3
Prairie City, Ill. F5 96-7
Prairie City, Ia. G8 104-5
Prairie City, Ore. E13 238-9
Prairie City, S. Dak. B4 136-7
Prairie Creek, Ind. J4 100-1
Prairie du Chien, Wis. J9 140-1
Prairie du Rocher, Ill. M6 96-7
Prairie du Sac, Wis. J12 140-1
Prairie Farm, Wis. E8 140-1
Prairie Grove, Ark. B2 150-1
Prairie Hill, Mo. C6 120-1
Prairie Home, Mo. E6 120-1
Prairie Home, Nebr. K1 124-5
Prairie Point, Miss. F10 176-7
Prairie River, Sask. J9 294-5
Prairie View, Ark. D4 150-1
Prairie View, Kans. D6 108-9
Prairie View, Tex. G10 192-3
Prairie Village, Kans. F16 108-9
Prairieburg, Ia. E13 104-5
Prairieton, Ind. J4 100-1
Prairieville, Ala. H4 146-7
Prairieville, La. B10 168-9
Prathersville, Mo. H16 120-1
Pratt, Kans. I8 108-9
Pratt, W. Va. I15 200-1
Pratt, co., Kans. J8 108-9
Pratts, Va. C1 196-7
Pratts Corner, Mass. C5 68-9
Prattsburg, N.Y. F5 80-1
Prattsville, Ark. G6 150-1
Prattville, Ala. I7 146-7
Prattville, Mass. F11 68-9
Prattville, Mich. K13 112-3
Prawda*, Man. H5 272-3
Pray, Mont. H8 222-3
Preble, Ind. D11 100-1
Preble, co., O. G3 132-3
Preeceville, Sask. L10 294-5
Pregnall, S.C. G12 184-5
Prelate, Sask. M4 294-5
Premont, Tex. J8 192-3
Prenter, W. Va. J13 200-1
Prentice, Wis. D11 140-1
Prentiss, Me. G9 64-5
Prentiss, Miss. K7 176-7
Prentiss, co., Miss. B10 176-7
Prescott, Ariz. G5 206-7
Prescott, Ark. I4 150-1
Prescott, Ia. I5 104-5
Prescott, Kans. H16 108-9
Prescott, Mich. G14 112-3
Prescott, Ont. I15 284-5
Prescott, Ore. A6 238-9
Prescott, Wash. I14 246-7
Prescott, Wis. F7 140-1
Prescott and Russell, co., Ont. H16 284-5
Presho, S. Dak. G9 136-7
Presidio, co., Tex. G2 192-3
Presque Isle, Me. C9 64-5
Presque Isle, Mich. E14 112-3
Presque Isle, Wis. C12 140-1
Presque Isle, co., Mich. E13 112-3
Pressmens Home, Tenn. F14 188-9
Preston*, Conn. F14 60-1
Preston, Ga. K3 160-1
Preston, Ida. O10 218-9
Preston, Ia. F15 104-5
Preston, Kans. I8 108-9
Preston, Ky. G13 164-5
Preston, Md. F13 172-3
Preston, Minn. O8 116-7
Preston, Miss. G9 176-7
Preston, Mo. G5 120-1
Preston, Nebr. J16 124-5
Preston, Nev. G9 226-7
Preston, Okla. E13 234-5
Preston, Wash. F8 246-7
Preston, co., W. Va. D7 200-1
Preston City, Conn. F14 60-1
Prestonburg, Ky. H15 164-5
Prestonville, Ky. E10 164-5
Pretty Prairie, Kans. I9 108-9
Prewitt, N. Mex. E3 230-1
Price, Md. D13 172-3
Price, Que. C16 290-1
Price, Ut. H8 242-3
Price, co., Wis. D11 140-1
Pricedale, Miss. L6 176-7
Prices, Ala. D9 146-7
Prices Corner, Del. A3 153
Prichard, Ala. N3 146-7
Prichard, Ida. D4 218-9
Prichard, Miss. B6 176-7
Prichard, W. Va. I9 200-1
Prides Crossing, Mass. C12 68-9
Priest River, Ida. B2 218-9
Prim, Ark. C7 150-1
Primate, Sask. K4 294-5
Prime, N.B. F2 275
Primera*, Tex. K8 192-3
Primghar, Ia. C3 104-5
Primrose, Ga. H3 160-1
Primrose, Ky. H13 164-5
Primrose, Nebr. F11 124-5
Primrose*, Pa. H12 84-5
Primrose, R.I. A4 87
Prince, Nev. J10 226-7
Prince, W. Va. K16 200-1
Prince, co., P.E.I. D4 287
Prince Albert, Sask. J7 294-5
Prince Edward, co., Ont. K12 284-5
Prince Edward, co., Va. I10 196-7
Prince Frederick, Md. G11 172-3
Prince George, B.C. G7 268-9
Prince George, Va. I13 196-7
Prince George, co., Va. I13 196-7
Prince Georges, co., Md. F10 172-3
Prince of Wales, N.B. J5 275
Prince Rupert, B.C. F3 268-9
Prince William, co., Va. F12 196-7
Princes Lakes, Ind. J8 100-1
Princess Anne, Md. H14 172-3
Princess Harbour, Man. F14 272-3
Princeton, Ala. B7 146-7
Princeton, Ark. H6 150-1
Princeton, B.C. J8 268-9
Princeton, Fla. I15 156-7
Princeton, Ida. E2 218-9
Princeton, Ill. D7 96-7
Princeton, Ind. N4 100-1
Princeton, Ia. G16 104-5
Princeton, Kans. G15 108-9
Princeton, Ky. J4 164-5
Princeton, La. B2 168-9
Princeton, Me. H10 64-5
Princeton, Mass. C8 68-9
Princeton, Mich. D10 112-3
Princeton, Minn. K6 116-7
Princeton, Mo. A4 120-1
Princeton, Nebr. I14 124-5
Princeton*, N.J. G5 76-7
Princeton, N.J. G5 76-7
Princeton, N.C. E12 180-1
Princeton*, Ont. D13 284-5
Princeton, Ore. H13 238-9
Princeton, S.C. I2 184-5
Princeton, Tex. B16 192-3
Princeton, W. Va. J4 200-1
Princeton, Wis. G2 140-1
Princeton Junction, N.J. G5 76-7
Princeville, Ill. E7 96-7
Princeville, N.C. D13 180-1
Princeville, Que. H15 290-1
Principio Furnace, Md. B13 172-3
Prineville, Ore. E9 238-9
Pringle*, Pa. F13 84-5
Pringle, S. Dak. G2 136-7
Prinsburg, Minn. M3 116-7
Prior Lake, Minn. C10 116-7
Pripet, Me. K7 64-5
Pritchardville, S.C. J10 184-5
Pritchett, Colo. I15 214-5
Procious, W. Va. G4 200-1
Procter, B.C. J10 268-9
Proctor, Ark. E11 150-1
Proctor, Colo. B15 214-5
Proctor, Minn. I8 116-7
Proctor, Mont. C3 222-3
Proctor, Nev. C11 226-7
Proctor, Okla. D16 234-5
Proctor, Vt. J4 90-1
Proctor, W. Va. D5 200-1
Proctorsville, Vt. K6 90-1
Proctorville, N.C. G10 180-1
Proctorville, O. K8 132-3
Proebstel, Wash. J7 246-7
Progress, Miss. M5 176-7
Progress Village*, Fla. F10 156-7
Project City*, Calif. E3 210-1
Promise, Ore. B15 238-9
Promise City, Ia. J9 104-5
Promised Land, S.C. K3 184-5
Promontory, Ut. D5 242-3
Pronto, Nev. C4 226-7
Prophetstown, Ill. C6 96-7
Prospect, Ala. D4 146-7
Prospect, Conn. F7 60-1

Prospect, Ind. M7 100-1
Prospect, Ky. A2 164-5
Prospect, Me. K7 64-5
Prospect, O. E6 132-3
Prospect, Ore. I6 238-9
Prospect, Pa. G2 84-5
Prospect, Tenn. K12 188-9
Prospect, Va. I10 196-7
Prospect Harbor, Me. K8 64-5
Prospect Heights*, Colo. G11 214-5
Prospect Heights*, Ill. B11 96-7
Prospect Hill, N.C. G6 180-1
Prospect Park, N.J. A10 76-7
Prospect Park*, Pa. J15 84-5
Prospector, Man. B9 272-3
Prosperity, S.C. K6 184-5
Prosperity, W. Va. K15 200-1
Prosser, Nebr. I11 124-5
Prosser, Wash. I12 246-7
Protection, Kans. K6 108-9
Protivin, Ia. B11 104-5
Proulxville*, Que. J3 290-1
Provencal, La. D3 168-9
Providence, Ky. I4 164-5
Providence, N.C. C9 180-1
Providence, N.C. G7 180-1
Providence, R.I. C5 87
Providence, Tenn. H7 188-9
Providence, Ut. C6 242-3
Providence, co., R.I. C3 87
Providence Bay, Ont. H7 284-5
Providence Forge, Va. E2 196-7
Providence R., R.I. D6 87
Provincetown, Mass. E15 68-9
Provo, Ark. H2 150-1
Provo, S. Dak. H1 136-7
Provo, Ut. G6 242-3
Provost, Alta. K10 264-5
Prowers, co., Colo. H16 214-5
Pruden, Tenn. F12 188-9
Prudence Park, R.I. F6 87
Prudenville, Mich. G13 112-3
Prudhoe Bay, Alaska A11 254-5
Prudhoe Bay*, Alaska B11 254-5
Prud'homme, Sask. K7 294-5
Prue, Okla. D13 234-5
Pruitt, Ark. B5 150-1
Pruitt City, Okla. H11 234-5
Pryor, Mont. H10 222-3
Pryor Creek, Okla. D15 234-5
Pryorsburg, Ky. K2 164-5
Public Landing, Md. H16 172-3
Public Landing*, N.B. J5 275
Puce-Emeryville Area*, Ont. F9 284-5
Puckett, Miss. J7 176-7
Pueblo, Colo. H12 214-5
Pueblo, co., Colo. H12 214-5
Puerto de Luna, N. Mex. G9 230-1
Puget Sound, Wash. E8 246-7
Pugwash, N.S. C7 281
Puhi, Hawaii D4 258-9
Pukalani, Hawaii G11 258-9
Pukwana, S. Dak. G11 136-7
Pulaski, Ga. J9 160-1
Pulaski, Ia. J11 104-5
Pulaski, Miss. I7 176-7
Pulaski, N.Y. D7 80-1
Pulaski, Tenn. D6 188-9
Pulaski, Va. J6 196-7
Pulaski, Wis. D4 140-1
Pulaski, co., Ark. F6 150-1
Pulaski, co., Ga. K6 160-1
Pulaski, co., Ill. O8 96-7
Pulaski, co., Ind. C6 100-1
Pulaski, co., Ky. J11 164-5
Pulaski, co., Mo. G7 120-1
Pulaski, co., Va. J6 196-7
Pulcifer, Wis. C4 140-1
Pullman, Mich. J11 112-3
Pullman, Wash. G16 246-7
Pullman, W. Va. E5 200-1
Pulpit Harbor, Me. L7 64-5
Pumphrey*, Md. D11 172-3
Pumpkin Center, Calif. L6 210-1
Pumpkin Center, Okla. E14 234-5
Pumpkintown, W. Va. F15 200-1
Punaluu, Hawaii K13 258-9
Punaluu, Hawaii G5 258-9
Puncheon Camp, Tenn. G13 188-9
Pungoteague, Va. H15 196-7
Punnichy, Sask. L8 294-5
Punta de Agua, N. Mex. G6 230-1
Punta Gorda, Fla. H10 156-7
Punxsutawney, Pa. G5 84-5
Pupukea, Hawaii G3 258-9
Purcell, Kans. D15 108-9
Purcell, Mo. H3 120-1
Purcell, Okla. G11 234-5
Purcellville, Va. E12 196-7
Purdin, Mo. B5 120-1
Purdum, Nebr. E7 124-5
Purdy, Mo. I4 120-1
Purdy, Okla. G11 234-5
Purvis, Miss. L8 176-7
Puryear, Tenn. A4 188-9
Pushmataha, Ala. I2 146-7
Pushmataha, co., Okla. H14 234-5
Put-in-Bay, O. B7 132-3
Putnam, Ala. J3 146-7
Putnam, Conn. B14 60-1
Putnam, Okla. E8 234-5
Putnam, co., Fla. C11 156-7
Putnam, co., Ga. H6 160-1
Putnam, co., Ill. D8 96-7
Putnam, co., Ind. H6 100-1
Putnam, co., Mo. A5 120-1
Putnam, co., N.Y. I11 80-1
Putnam, co., O. D4 132-3
Putnam, co., Tenn. B10 188-9
Putnam, co., W. Va. G2 200-1
Putnam Heights, Conn. C14 60-1
Putnam Lake*, N.Y. I11 80-1
Putnamville, Ind. I6 100-1
Putnamville, Vt. F6 90-1
Putney, Ga. M4 160-1
Putney, Vt. N7 90-1
Putney, W. Va. H15 200-1
Puuanahulu, Hawaii I12 258-9
Puuiki, Hawaii G3 258-9
Puuiki, Hawaii G12 258-9
Puukolii, Hawaii G10 258-9
Puunene, Hawaii G11 258-9
Puxico, Mo. I10 120-1
Puyallup, Wash. K2 246-7
Pyatt, Ark. B5 150-1
Pyland, Miss. D8 176-7
Pylesville, Md. B12 172-3
Pymatuning Res., Pa. D1 84-5
Pyramid, Nev. E2 226-7
Pyramid Corners, Okla. C15 234-5
Pyramid Lake, Nev. E2 226-7
Pyriton, Ala. F8 146-7
Pyrmont, Ind. F6 100-1

Q

Quabbin Res., Mass. C6 68-9
Quaddick, Conn. B15 60-1
Quaker City, N.H. L3 72-3
Quaker City, O. F10 132-3
Quaker Farms, Conn. G6 60-1
Quaker Hill, Conn. G13 60-1
Quakertown, N.J. F4 76-7
Quakertown, Pa. H15 84-5
Quakertown North*, Mich. J14 112-3
Qualicum Beach*, B.C. K6 268-9
Quality, Ky. J6 164-5
Qualls, Okla. E15 234-5
Quamba, Minn. K6 116-7
Quanah, Tex. C6 192-3
Quantico, Md. G14 172-3
Quantico, Va. B3 196-7
Quantico Station*, Va. F12 196-7
Quapaw, Okla. B15 234-5
Qu'Appelle*, Sask. N9 294-5
Qu'Appelle Dam, Sask. M6 294-5
Quarry, Ia. F10 104-5
Quarryville, Pa. J13 84-5
Quartz Hill, Calif. F8 210-1
Quartz Mountain, Ore. J9 238-9
Quartzsite, Ariz. H2 206-7
Quasqueton, Ia. E12 104-5
Quathiaski Cove, B.C. J5 268-9
Quay, N. Mex. F10 230-1
Quay, Okla. D12 234-5
Quay, co., N. Mex. F10 230-1
Quealy, Wyo. I8 250-1
Quebec, Que. I3 290-1
Québec, co., Que. E10 290-1
Quebeck, Tenn. C10 188-9
Quechee, Vt. J7 90-1
Queen, Ariz. I8 206-7
Queen Anne, Md. E13 172-3
Queen Annes, co., Md. D13 172-3
Queen Charlotte, B.C. G2 268-9
Queen Charlotte Isl., B.C. G2 268-9
Queen City, Mo. A6 120-1
Queen City, Tex. D11 192-3
Queen Creek, Ariz. I7 206-7
Queen Elizabeth Isl., N.W. Terr. A2 296
Queens, N.Y. F14 80-1
Queens, W. Va. F14 200-1
Queens, co., N.B. I5 275
Queens, co., N.Y. F14 80-1
Queens, co., N.S. F5 281
Queens, co., P.E.I. E6 287
Queensborough, Ont. J12 284-5
Queenstown, Md. E12 172-3
Queenstown, N.B. I4 275
Queenswood*, Ont. H15 284-5
Queenswood Heights*, Ont. H15 284-5
Queets, Wash. E5 246-7
Quemado, N. Mex. G2 230-1
Quenemo, Kans. G14 108-9
Quentin, Miss. K4 176-7
Quesnel, B.C. G7 268-9
Questa, N. Mex. C7 230-1
Quick, W. Va. H15 200-1
Quicksand, Ky. H14 164-5
Quicksburg, Va. F10 196-7
Quidnet, Mass. J16 68-9
Quidnick, R.I. E4 87
Quiet Dell, W. Va. D14 200-1
Quijotoa, Ariz. K6 206-7
Quilcene, Wash. H1 246-7
Quill Lake, Sask. L8 294-5
Quimby, Ia. D3 104-5
Quimby, La. C7 168-9
Quimby, Me. B7 64-5
Quinapoxet, Mass. D8 68-9
Quinault, Wash. F5 246-7
Quinby*, S.C. D13 184-5
Quinby, Va. H16 196-7
Quincy, Calif. F4 210-1
Quincy, Fla. B7 156-7
Quincy, Ill. H3 96-7
Quincy, Ind. I6 100-1
Quincy, Kans. I13 108-9
Quincy, Ky. F14 164-5
Quincy, Mass. D12 68-9
Quincy, Mich. K13 112-3
Quincy, Miss. D10 176-7
Quincy, N.H. I5 72-3
Quincy, O. E4 132-3
Quincy, Ore. A5 238-9
Quincy, Wash. F12 246-7
Quincy, W. Va. I14 200-1
Quincy Southeast*, Ill. H3 96-7
Quinebaug, Conn. A14 60-1
Quinhagak, Alaska F8 254-5
Quinlan, Okla. D8 234-5
Quinlan, Tex. C16 192-3
Quinn, S. Dak. F5 136-7
Quinn River Crossing, Nev. B4 226-7
Quinnesec, Mich. E9 112-3
Quinnimont, W. Va. K16 200-1
Quinnville, R.I. B5 87
Quinter, Kans. F5 108-9
Quinton, Ala. E5 146-7
Quinton, N.J. L1 76-7
Quinton, Okla. F15 234-5
Quinton, Ore. B10 238-9
Quinton, Sask. L8 294-5
Quinton, Va. E2 196-7
Quinwood, W. Va. H5 200-1
Quispamsis*, N.B. I5 275
Quitman, Ark. D7 150-1
Quitman, Ga. O6 160-1
Quitman, La. C4 168-9
Quitman, Miss. J9 176-7
Quitman, Mo. A2 120-1
Quitman, Tex. D10 192-3
Quitman, co., Ga. L2 160-1
Quitman, co., Miss. C5 176-7
Quito, Miss. F6 176-7
Quivero, Ariz. E6 206-7
Qulin, Mo. J10 120-1
Quogue, N.Y. J13 80-1
Quonochontaug, R.I. I2 87

R

Rabbit Lake, Sask. J5 294-5
Rabbithole, Nev. D3 226-7
Rabun, Ala. M4 146-7
Rabun, co., Ga. C6 160-1
Rabun Gap, Ga. C6 160-1
Raceland, Ky. F15 164-5
Raceland, La. E12 168-9
Rachel, W. Va. B14 200-1
Racine, Minn. O8 116-7
Racine, O. I9 132-3
Racine, W. Va. I13 200-1
Racine, Wis. K15 140-1
Racine, co., Wis. K15 140-1
Raco, Mich. D13 112-3
Radcliff, Ky. C1 164-5
Radcliffe, Ia. E8 104-5
Radersburg, Mont. F6 222-3
Radford, Va. I7 196-7
Radiant, Va. C1 196-7
Radisson*, Que. F2 290-1
Radisson, Sask. K6 294-5
Radisson, Wis. D9 140-1
Radium, Colo. D9 214-5
Radium, Kans. H7 108-9
Radium Hot Springs, B.C. I10 268-9
Radium Springs, Ga. M4 160-1
Radium Springs, N. Mex. K5 230-1
Radnor, Ind. E7 100-1
Radnor, W. Va. J10 200-1
Radville, Sask. O8 294-5
Radway, Alta. I8 264-5
Rae, N.W. Terr. C1 296
Raeford, N.C. F10 180-1
Raeville, Nebr. F11 124-5
Ragan, Nebr. J9 124-5
Ragan, Wyo. J5 250-1
Ragland, Ala. E8 146-7
Raglesville, Ind. L6 100-1
Ragley, La. G2 168-9
Rago, Kans. J9 108-9
Ragsdale, Ind. L4 100-1
Ragtown, Ark. G10 150-1
Rahway, N.J. E7 76-7
Raiford, Fla. C10 156-7
Raiford, Okla. F14 234-5
Rainbow, Ore. F7 238-9
Rainbow, Ut. G10 242-3
Rainbow City, Ala. D8 146-7
Rainbow Lake, Alta. C3 264-5
Rainelle, W. Va. I5 200-1
Rainier, Ore. A6 238-9
Rainier, Wash. G7 246-7
Rains, S.C. D15 184-5
Rains, co., Tex. D10 192-3
Rainsville, Ala. C8 146-7
Rainsville, N. Mex. D8 230-1
Rainswood, Va. G14 196-7
Rainy River, Ont. F1 284-5
Raith, Ont. F3 284-5
Rake, Ia. A7 104-5
Raleigh, Ga. I3 160-1
Raleigh, Miss. J7 176-7
Raleigh, N.C. D11 180-1
Raleigh, N. Dak. I6 128-9
Raleigh, co., W. Va. I4 200-1
Ralls*, Mo. C8 120-1
Ralls, Tex. C5 192-3
Ralls, co., Mo. C8 120-1
Ralph, Ala. G4 146-7
Ralph, Ark. B6 150-1
Ralph, Mich. D9 112-3
Ralston, Alta. N10 264-5
Ralston, Ia. F5 104-5
Ralston, Nebr. J2 124-5
Ralston, Okla. C12 234-5
Ralston, Tenn. A3 188-9
Ralston, Wash. G14 246-7
Ralston, Wyo. B8 250-1
Rama, Sask. L9 294-5
Ramage, W. Va. J13 200-1
Ramah, Colo. F13 214-5
Ramah, La. G6 168-9
Ramah, N. Mex. F2 230-1
Rambin, La. C2 168-9
Ramblewood*, N.J. J4 76-7
Ramea, Nfld. O8 278-9
Ramer, Ala. J8 146-7
Ramer, Tenn. D4 188-9
Ramhurst, Ga. D3 160-1
Ramona, Calif. J11 210-1
Ramona, Kans. G11 108-9
Ramona, Okla. C13 234-5
Ramona, S. Dak. F15 136-7
Ramore, Ont. F7 284-5
Rampart, Alaska D11 254-5
Ramsay, Mich. D7 112-3
Ramsay, Mont. G5 222-3
Ramsay, Ont. G6 284-5
Ramseur, N.C. I5 180-1
Ramsey, Ill. J8 96-7
Ramsey, Ind. N8 100-1
Ramsey, Minn. A9 116-7
Ramsey, N.J. C7 76-7
Ramsey, W. Va. I16 200-1
Ramsey, co., Minn. M7 116-7
Ramsey, co., N. Dak. D11 128-9
Ranburne, Ala. E10 146-7
Ranchester, Wyo. B11 250-1
Ranchito, N. Mex. C7 230-1
Rancho Cordova, Calif. A9 210-1
Rancho Mirage, Calif. N9 210-1
Rancho Rinconada*, Calif. J3 210-1
Rancho Santa Clarita*, Calif. M7 210-1
Ranchos de Taos, N. Mex. C7 230-1
Rancocas, N.J. I4 76-7
Rand, Colo. C10 214-5
Randalia, Ia. C12 104-5
Randall, Ia. E8 104-5
Randall, Kans. D9 108-9
Randall, Minn. J5 116-7
Randall, co., Tex. B5 192-3
Randallstown, Md. F5 172-3
Randle, Wash. H8 246-7
Randleman, N.C. I4 180-1
Randlett, Okla. I9 234-5
Randlett, Ut. G9 242-3
Randolph, Ala. G6 146-7
Randolph, Ariz. J7 206-7
Randolph, Ia. J3 104-5
Randolph, Kans. E12 108-9
Randolph, Me. L4 64-5
Randolph*, Md. D9 172-3
Randolph, Mass. J5 68-9
Randolph, Minn. N7 116-7
Randolph, Miss. C8 176-7
Randolph*, Mo. D3 120-1
Randolph, Nebr. D13 124-5
Randolph, N.H. F7 72-3
Randolph*, N.J. D5 76-7
Randolph, N.Y. G2 80-1
Randolph, Tex. A16 192-3
Randolph, Ut. C7 242-3
Randolph, Vt. H6 90-1
Randolph, Va. J10 196-7
Randolph, Wis. H2 140-1
Randolph, co., Ala. F9 146-7
Randolph, co., Ark. A10 150-1
Randolph, co., Ga. L3 160-1
Randolph, co., Ill. M7 96-7
Randolph, co., Ind. F11 100-1
Randolph, co., Mo. C6 120-1
Randolph, co., N.C. D9 180-1
Randolph, co., W. Va. F7 200-1
Random Lake, Wis. H5 140-1
Ranfurly, Alta. J9 264-5
Rang-St.-Georges*, N.B. E6 275
Range, Ala. L5 146-7
Range, Colo. D8 214-5
Rangeley, Me. I2 64-5
Rangeley*, Me. J2 64-5
Rangely, Colo. D5 214-5
Ranger, Ga. E3 160-1
Ranger, Tex. E7 192-3
Ranger, W. Va. J11 200-1
Rangoon, W. Va. E14 200-1
Ranier, Minn. E6 116-7
Rankin, Ill. F11 96-7
Rankin, Mich. G4 112-3
Rankin, Miss. I6 176-7
Rankin*, Pa. I2 84-5
Rankin, Tex. F4 192-3
Rankin, co., Miss. I6 176-7
Rankin Inlet, N.W. Terr. C3 296
Ranlo*, N.C. E6 180-1
Ransom, Kans. G5 108-9
Ransom, co., N. Dak. H13 128-9
Ransomville, N.Y. E2 80-1
Ransomville, N.C. E14 180-1
Ranson, W. Va. E12 200-1
Rantoul, Ill. G10 96-7
Rantoul, Kans. G15 108-9
Rapelje, Mont. G9 222-3
Raphine, Va. G9 196-7
Rapid City, Man. I11 272-3
Rapid City, Mich. F12 112-3
Rapid City, S. Dak. F3 136-7
Rapid River, Mich. D10 112-3
Rapides, co., La. F4 168-9
Rapids City, Ill. C6 96-7
Rappahannock, co., Va. F11 196-7
Rappahannock Academy, Va. G13 196-7
Rappahannock R., Va. F11 196-7
Raritan*, N.J. F4 76-7
Raritan, N.J. F5 76-7
Ratcliff, Ark. D3 150-1
Rathbun, Ia. J9 104-5
Rathbun Res., Ia. J9 104-5

Rathdrum, Ida. C2 218-9
Rathwell, Man. J12 272-3
Ratliff City, Okla. H11 234-5
Raton, N. Mex. B9 230-1
Rattan, Okla. H15 234-5
Rattlesnake*, Mont. E3 222-3
Raub, Ind. E4 100-1
Raus, Tenn. J8 188-9
Ravalli, Mont. D3 222-3
Ravalli, co., Mont. F3 222-3
Ravana, Ark. K2 150-1
Raven, Va. I4 196-7
Raven, Wyo. D15 250-1
Raven Rock, W. Va. D4 200-1
Ravena, N.Y. G11 80-1
Ravenden, Ark. B9 150-1
Ravenden Springs, Ark. A9 150-1
Ravenel, S.C. I12 184-5
Ravenna, Ky. H12 164-5
Ravenna, Mich. I11 112-3
Ravenna, Mont. E4 222-3
Ravenna, Nebr. H10 124-5
Ravenna, O. C10 132-3
Ravensdale, Wash. F8 246-7
Ravenswood, W. Va. F3 200-1
Ravenwood, Mo. A3 120-1
Ravia, Okla. H12 234-5
Ravinia, S. Dak. I12 136-7
Rawdon, Que. H12 290-1
Rawlings, Md. B3 172-3
Rawlings, Va. J12 196-7
Rawlins, Wyo. I11 250-1
Rawlins, co., Kans. D3 108-9
Rawson, N. Dak. E2 128-9
Rawson, O. D5 132-3
Rawsonville, Vt. M5 90-1
Ray, Ariz. I8 206-7
Ray, Ind. A12 100-1
Ray, N. Dak. C3 128-9
Ray, co., Mo. D4 120-1
Ray City, Ga. N6 160-1
Raybon, Ga. M9 160-1
Rayland, O. F11 132-3
Rayle, Ga. F7 160-1
Raymer, Colo. C13 214-5
Raymond, Alta. O9 264-5
Raymond, Ga. H3 160-1
Raymond, Ida. O11 218-9
Raymond, Ill. I7 96-7
Raymond, Ia. E11 104-5
Raymond, Kans. H8 108-9
Raymond, Me. N8 64-5
Raymond, Minn. M3 116-7
Raymond, Miss. I5 176-7
Raymond, Mont. A15 222-3
Raymond, Nebr. K1 124-5
Raymond, N.H. N8 72-3
Raymond, S. Dak. D13 136-7
Raymond, Wash. H5 246-7
Raymondville, Mo. H8 120-1
Raymondville, Tex. K8 192-3
Raymore, Mo. K15 120-1
Raymore, Sask. L8 294-5
Rayne, La. H5 168-9
Raynesford, Mont. D7 222-3
Raynham, Mass. F11 68-9
Rayside-Balfour, Ont. H7 284-5
Raysville, Ind. H10 100-1
Raytown, Mo. J15 120-1
Rayville, La. B6 168-9
Rayville, Mo. H16 120-1
Raywick, Ky. E3 164-5
Rea, Mo. B2 120-1
Reader, Ark. I5 150-1
Reader, W. Va. D5 200-1
Readfield, Me. K4 64-5
Readfield, Wis. E3 140-1
Readfield Depot, Me. K4 64-5
Readhimer, La. C3 168-9
Reading, Kans. G13 108-9
Reading, Mass. F5 68-9
Reading, Mich. K13 112-3
Reading, O. K14 132-3
Reading, Pa. I13 84-5
Reading*, Vt. K6 90-1
Readington, N.J. F5 76-7
Readland, Ark. K9 150-1
Readlyn, Ia. D11 104-5
Readsboro, Vt. O5 90-1
Readstown, Wis. I10 140-1
Readyville, Tenn. C8 188-9
Reagan, Okla. H12 234-5
Reagan, Tenn. C4 188-9
Reagan, co., Tex. F5 192-3
Reager, Kans. D5 108-9
Real, co., Tex. G6 192-3
Reamstown*, Pa. I13 84-5
Reardan, Wash. E15 246-7
Reasnor, Ia. G9 104-5
Reaville, N.J. F4 76-7
Rebecca, Ga. L6 160-1
Recen, Colo. E10 214-5
Reck, Okla. I11 234-5
Recluse, Wyo. B13 250-1
Rector, Ark. B11 150-1
Rectortown, Va. A2 196-7
Red Ash, Tenn. G11 188-9
Red Ash, Va. I4 196-7
Red Bank, N.J. G8 76-7
Red Bank, N.J. N9 76-7
Red Bank, S.C. E9 184-5
Red Bank, Tenn. D10 188-9
Red Banks, Miss. B7 176-7
Red Bay, Ala. C3 146-7
Red Bird, Okla. E14 234-5
Red Bluff*, B.C. G4 268-9
Red Bluff, Calif. F3 210-1
Red Boiling Springs, Tenn. A9 188-9
Red Bud, Ill. L6 96-7
Red Buttes, Wyo. J14 250-1
Red Cliff, Colo. E9 214-5
Red Cliff, Wis. A10 140-1
Red Cloud, Nebr. J11 124-5
Red Creek, N.Y. E6 80-1
Red Creek, W. Va. F8 200-1
Red Cross, N.C. J3 180-1
Red Deer, Alta. K7 264-5
Red Deer Lake*, Man. G1 272-3
Red Devil, Alaska F9 254-5
Red Feather Lakes, Colo. B11 214-5
Red Hill, Ala. H8 146-7
Red Hill*, Pa. I14 84-5
Red Hook, N.Y. H11 80-1
Red House, Va. I10 196-7
Red House, W. Va. G2 200-1
Red Lake, Ariz. E6 206-7
Red Lake, Ont. D1 284-5
Red Lake, co., Minn. F2 116-7
Red Lake Falls, Minn. F2 116-7
Red Lake Road, Ont. E2 284-5
Red Level, Ala. L7 146-7
Red Lick, Miss. J4 176-7
Red Lion, Del. B3 153
Red Lion, Pa. J11 84-5
Red Lodge, Mont. H9 222-3
Red Oak, Ga. C10 160-1
Red Oak, Ia. I4 104-5
Red Oak, N.C. D12 180-1
Red Oak, Okla. G15 234-5
Red Oak, Tex. D15 192-3
Red Oak, Va. J10 196-7
Red Oaks Mill*, N.Y. H11 80-1
Red River, La. E5 168-9
Red River, N. Mex. C8 230-1
Red River, S.C. B10 184-5
Red River, co., La. C2 168-9
Red River, co., Tex. D10 192-3
Red River of the North, N. Dak. E14 128-9
Red Rock, Ariz. K7 206-7
Red Rock, B.C. G7 268-9
Red Rock, Okla. C11 234-5
Red Rock, Ont. F4 284-5
Red Scaffold, S. Dak. D5 136-7
Red Shirt, S. Dak. G3 136-7
Red Springs, N.C. F10 180-1
Red Sucker Lake, Man. F6 272-3
Red Sulphur Springs, W. Va. J5 200-1
Red Willow, co., Nebr. J7 124-5
Red Wing, Minn. N7 116-7
Red Wing Terrace*, Sask. J4 294-5
Redan, Ga. C12 160-1
Redart, Va. E4 196-7
Redbird, Wyo. E16 250-1
Redcliff, Alta. N10 264-5
Reddell, La. G4 168-9
Redden, Okla. H14 234-5
Reddick, Fla. D10 156-7
Redding, Calif. E3 210-1
Redding, Conn. H4 60-1
Redding, Ia. K6 104-5
Redding Ridge, Conn. H5 60-1
Redfield, Ark. K16 150-1
Redfield, Ia. G6 104-5
Redfield, Kans. I16 108-9
Redfield, S. Dak. D12 136-7
Redgranite, Wis. F2 140-1
Redhouse, Md. C1 172-3
Redings Mill, Mo. I3 120-1
Redington, Ariz. K9 206-7
Redington Beach, Fla. I1 156-7
Redington Shores, Fla. I1 156-7
Redkey, Ind. F11 100-1
Redland, N.C. H2 180-1
Redland, Okla. F16 234-5
Redlands, Calif. G10 210-1
Redmesa, Colo. J6 214-5
Redmond, Ore. E9 238-9
Redmond, Ut. I6 242-3
Redmond, Wash. H3 246-7
Redondo, Wash. J2 246-7
Redondo Beach, Calif. H8 210-1
Redrock, N. Mex. K2 230-1
Redstone, Colo. E8 214-5
Redstone, Mont. A15 222-3
Redstone, N.H. H8 72-3
Redvale, Colo. H6 214-5
Redvers, Sask. O11 294-5
Redwater, Alta. I8 264-5
Redway, Calif. F1 210-1
Redwing, Kans. G8 108-9
Redwood, Miss. H4 176-7
Redwood, Va. J8 196-7
Redwood, co., Minn. N3 116-7
Redwood City, Calif. D7 210-1
Redwood Falls, Minn. N4 116-7
Ree Heights, S. Dak. E11 136-7
Reece, Kans. I12 108-9
Reece City, Ala. D8 146-7
Reed, Ark. I9 150-1
Reed, Ky. H5 164-5
Reed, Me. G8 64-5
Reed, Okla. G7 234-5
Reed, Ore. F4 238-9
Reed City, Mich. H12 112-3
Reeder, N. Dak. I3 128-9
Reedley, Calif. K6 210-1
Reedpoint, Mont. G9 222-3
Reeds, Mo. I3 120-1
Reeds Ferry, N.H. O7 72-3
Reeds Spring, Mo. I5 120-1
Reedsburg, Wis. I11 140-1
Reedsport, Ore. G4 238-9
Reedsville, W. Va. B16 200-1
Reedsville, Wis. F5 140-1
Reedtown, Tenn. H14 188-9
Reedville, Va. H14 196-7
Reedy, W. Va. F4 200-1
Reedy Isl., Del. C3 153
Reelfoot Lake, Tenn. A2 188-9
Reeltown, Ala. H9 146-7
Reeman, Mich. H11 112-3
Reese, Mich. E4 112-3
Reese Village, Tex. D4 192-3
Reeseville*, Wis. J13 140-1
Reeves, La. G3 168-9
Reeves, co., Tex. F3 192-3
Reevesville, S.C. G11 184-5
Reform, Ala. F3 146-7
Reform, Miss. F8 176-7
Refuge Cove, Alaska H16 254-5
Refugio, Tex. I8 192-3
Refugio, co., Tex. I9 192-3
Regal, Minn. L4 116-7
Regan, N. Dak. G8 128-9
Regent, N. Dak. I4 128-9
Reger, Mo. B5 120-1
Reggio, La. D16 168-9
Regina, Mont. C11 222-3
Regina, N. Mex. D5 230-1
Regina, Sask. N8 294-5
Regina Beach, Sask. M8 294-5
Register, Ga. J9 160-1
Rehobeth, Md. I14 172-3
Rehoboth, Mass. G11 68-9
Rehoboth, N. Mex. E2 230-1
Rehoboth, Va. J11 196-7
Rehoboth Bay, Del. I6 153
Rehoboth Beach, Del. I6 153
Reichert, Okla. G16 234-5
Reidsville, Ga. K9 160-1
Reidsville, N.C. C9 180-1
Reidville, S.C. F3 184-5
Reinbeck, Ia. E10 104-5
Reindeer Lake, Sask. D9 294-5
Reinfeld, Man. K13 272-3
Reinland, Man. K13 272-3
Reisor, La. B1 168-9
Reisterstown, Md. C10 172-3
Reliance, Del. J3 153
Reliance, S. Dak. G10 136-7
Reliance, Tenn. K13 188-9
Reliance, Wyo. I8 250-1
Relief, N.C. D4 180-1
Rembert, S.C. D11 184-5
Rembrandt, Ia. C4 104-5
Remer, Minn. H5 116-7
Remerton, Ga. N6 160-1
Remington, Ind. C5 100-1
Remington, Va. B2 196-7
Remlap, Ala. E7 146-7
Remote, Ore. H4 238-9
Remsen, Ia. C2 104-5
Remsen, N.Y. E8 80-1
Remus, Mich. H12 112-3
Remy, La. C11 168-9
Rena*, Ark. D2 150-1
Rena Lara, Miss. D4 176-7
Rencona, N. Mex. F7 230-1
Rendalia, Ala. F8 146-7
Renews, Nfld. O11 278-9
Renforth*, N.B. J5 275
Renfrew, Ont. H13 284-5
Renfrew, co., Ont. H12 284-5
Renfroe, Ala. F8 146-7
Renfroe, Miss. G8 176-7
Renfrow, Okla. B10 234-5
Renick, Mo. D6 120-1
Renner, S. Dak. G16 136-7
Rennie, Man. J16 272-3
Rennox, Nev. D6 226-7
Reno, Ga. O4 160-1
Reno, Kans. F15 108-9
Reno, Nev. F2 226-7
Reno, Tex. C12 192-3
Reno, co., Kans. I9 108-9
Reno Beach*, O. B6 132-3
Renous, N.B. G5 275
Renovo, Pa. E8 84-5
Rensselaer, Ind. D5 100-1
Rensselaer, Mo. C8 120-1
Rensselaer, N.Y. F11 80-1
Rensselaer, co., N.Y. F11 80-1
Rentiesville, Okla. E14 234-5
Renton, Wash. I3 246-7
Rentz, Ga. J7 160-1
Renville, Minn. M3 116-7
Renville, co., Minn. M4 116-7
Renville, co., N. Dak. C5 128-9
Renwer, Man. E10 272-3
Renwick, Ia. C7 104-5
Repentigny, Que. I12 290-1
Replete, W. Va. F6 200-1
Repton, Ala. L5 146-7
Republic, Kans. C10 108-9
Republic, Mich. D9 112-3
Republic, Mo. I5 120-1
Republic, O. C6 132-3
Republic, Wash. C13 246-7
Republic [-Merrittstown], Pa. J2 84-5
Republic, co., Kans. C10 108-9
Republican, Ark. D6 150-1
Republican City, Nebr. J9 124-5
Republican Grove, Va. J9 196-7
Republican R., Nebr. J8 124-5
Resaca, Ga. D3 160-1
Rescue, Va. G3 196-7
Reserve, Kans. C14 108-9
Reserve, La. C12 168-9
Reserve, Mont. B16 222-3
Reserve, N. Mex. I2 230-1
Reserve, Sask. K10 294-5
Reserve, Wis. C9 140-1
Reserve Mines*, N.S. B11 281
Resolute Bay, N.W. Terr. B2 296
Rest Haven, Ga. F5 160-1
Restigouche, co., N.B. E4 275
Reston, Man. J9 272-3
Reston, Va. A3 196-7
Retreat, Wis. I9 140-1
Reubens, Ida. F3 218-9
Reva, Va. C1 196-7
Revelo, Ky. K11 164-5
Revelstoke, B.C. I9 268-9
Revere, Mass. H5 68-9
Revere, Minn. N3 116-7
Revere, Mo. A8 120-1
Revere, W. Va. F5 200-1
Revillo, S. Dak. C16 136-7
Reward, Sask. K4 294-5
Rewey, Wis. K11 140-1
Rex, N.C. F10 180-1
Rex, N.C. J1 180-1
Rexburg, Ida. L10 218-9
Rexford, Kans. D3 108-9
Rexford, Mont. A2 222-3
Rexhame, Mass. E13 68-9
Rexton, Mich. D12 112-3
Rexton, N.B. G7 275
Reydell, Ark. H8 150-1
Reydon, Okla. E6 234-5
Reyno, Ark. A10 150-1
Reynolds, Ga. J4 160-1
Reynolds, Ida. M2 218-9
Reynolds, Ill. D5 96-7
Reynolds, Ind. D6 100-1
Reynolds, Nebr. J13 124-5
Reynolds, N. Dak. E14 128-9
Reynolds, co., Mo. H9 120-1
Reynolds Bridge, Conn. E6 60-1
Reynoldsburg, O. F7 132-3
Reynoldsville, Pa. F5 84-5
Rhame, N. Dak. I2 128-9
Rhea, Ark. B2 150-1
Rhea, Okla. E8 234-5
Rhea, co., Tenn. C11 188-9
Rheatown, Tenn. G15 188-9
Rhein, Sask. L10 294-5
Rheinland, Sask. K6 294-5
Rhems, S.C. F14 184-5
Rhine, Ga. K6 160-1
Rhinebeck, N.Y. H11 80-1
Rhinehart, La. D5 168-9
Rhineland, Mo. E8 120-1
Rhineland, Sask. N5 294-5
Rhinelander, Wis. D12 140-1
Rhoadesville, Va. C2 196-7
Rhodelia, Ky. G7 164-5
Rhodell, W. Va. J4 200-1
Rhodes, Ia. F9 104-5
Rhodes, Mich. H13 112-3
Rhodes Point, Md. I13 172-3
Rhodesdale, Md. G14 172-3
Rhodhiss, N.C. D6 180-1
Rhododendron, Ore. C7 238-9
Rial Side, Mass. C12 68-9
Rialto, Calif. G10 210-1
Rib Lake, Wis. E11 140-1
Ribera, N. Mex. E8 230-1
Rice, Ariz. E10 206-7
Rice, Kans. D10 108-9
Rice, Minn. K5 116-7
Rice, Va. I11 196-7
Rice, Wash. D14 246-7
Rice, co., Kans. G9 108-9
Rice, co., Minn. N6 116-7
Rice City, R.I. D2 87
Rice Hill, Ore. G5 238-9
Rice Lake, Wis. D8 140-1
Rice Station, Ky. H12 164-5
Riceboro, Ga. L10 160-1
Riceton, Sask. N8 294-5
Riceville, Ia. B10 104-5
Riceville, Tenn. K12 188-9
Rich, Ark. F9 150-1
Rich, Miss. C5 176-7
Rich, co., Ut. D7 242-3
Rich Creek, Va. I6 196-7
Rich Hill, Mo. F3 120-1
Rich Pond, Ky. J7 164-5
Rich Square, N.C. C13 180-1
Richard, W. Va. A15 200-1
Richard City, Tenn. K9 188-9
Richards, Mo. G3 120-1
Richardson, Miss. N7 176-7
Richardson, Tex. C15 192-3
Richardson, co., Nebr. J16 124-5
Richardson Mts., Y.T. A1 297
Richardsville, Ky. J7 164-5
Richardsville*, N.B. D4 275
Richardsville, Va. C2 196-7
Richardton, N. Dak. G4 128-9
Richburg, S.C. B10 184-5
Richelieu*, Que. I13 290-1
Richelieu, co., Que. I13 290-1
Richer*, Man. J15 272-3
Richey, Mont. D15 222-3
Richfield, Ida. N6 218-9
Richfield, Kans. J1 108-9
Richfield, Minn. B10 116-7
Richfield, Nebr. J2 124-5
Richfield, N.C. J3 180-1
Richfield, Ut. J6 242-3
Richfield, Wis. I4 140-1
Richfield Springs, N.Y. F9 80-1
Richford, Vt. B6 90-1
Richgrove*, Calif. L6 210-1
Richibucto, N.B. G7 275
Richibucto-Village*, N.B. G7 275
Richland, Ga. K3 160-1
Richland, Ia. I12 104-5
Richland, Kans. F14 108-9
Richland*, Mich. J12 112-3
Richland, Miss. G6 176-7
Richland, Mo. G6 120-1
Richland, Mont. A13 222-3
Richland, Nebr. G13 124-5

Richland, N.J. L4 76-7
Richland, Okla. I1 234-5
Richland, Ore. D15 238-9
Richland*, Pa. I12 84-5
Richland, S.C. C5 184-5
Richland, S. Dak. J16 136-7
Richland, Tenn. H13 188-9
Richland, Wash. I13 246-7
Richland, co., Ill. K10 96-7
Richland, co., La. B5 168-9
Richland, co., Mont. C15 222-3
Richland, co., N. Dak. I14 128-9
Richland, co., O. D7 132-3
Richland, co., S.C. D10 184-5
Richland, co., Wis. I10 140-1
Richland Center, Wis. I11 140-1
Richland City, Ind. O5 100-1
Richland Hills, Tex. C13 192-3
Richlands, N.C. F13 180-1
Richlands, Va. I4 196-7
Richlawn*, Ky. G9 164-5
Richlea, Sask. M5 294-5
Richmond, Ark. I2 150-1
Richmond, Calif. C7 210-1
Richmond, Ill. J1 96-7
Richmond, Ind. H12 100-1
Richmond, Kans. G15 108-9
Richmond, Ky. H12 164-5
Richmond*, La. C7 168-9
Richmond, Me. M11 64-5
Richmond, Mass. D1 68-9
Richmond, Mich. H7 112-3
Richmond, Minn. L5 116-7
Richmond, Mo. D4 120-1
Richmond, N.H. O3 72-3
Richmond, O. E11 132-3
Richmond*, Ont. H15 284-5
Richmond, Ore. D11 238-9
Richmond, P.E.I. D4 287
Richmond, Que. I14 290-1
Richmond*, R.I. H2 87
Richmond, Tenn. J7 188-9
Richmond, Tex. I12 192-3
Richmond, Ut. C6 242-3
Richmond, Vt. E5 90-1
Richmond, Va. H12 196-7
Richmond, co., Ga. H9 160-1
Richmond, co., N.Y. F13 80-1
Richmond, co., N.C. F9 180-1
Richmond, co., N.S. C11 281
Richmond, co., Que. I15 290-1
Richmond, co., Va. G13 196-7
Richmond Beach, Wash. H2 246-7
Richmond Corner, Me. M10 64-5
Richmond Furnace, Mass. D1 68-9
Richmond Heights, Fla. I15 156-7
Richmond Heights, Mo. B15 120-1
Richmond Heights, O. A15 132-3
Richmond Hill, Ga. K11 160-1
Richmond Hill, Mass. G11 68-9
Richmond Hill, N.C. H5 180-1
Richmond Hill, Ont. C15 284-5
Richmondville, N.Y. F10 80-1
Richmound, Sask. N4 294-5
Richtex, S.C. K8 184-5
Richton, Miss. L9 176-7
Richton Park, Ill. O4 96-7
Richvalley, Ind. D9 100-1
Richville, Mich. E4 112-3
Richville, Minn. I3 116-7
Richville, Ut. E6 242-3
Richwood, N.J. K3 76-7
Richwood, O. E6 132-3
Richwood*, Tex. H10 192-3
Richwood, W. Va. H6 200-1
Richwood, Wis. I3 140-1
Rickardsville, Ia. D14 104-5
Ricketts, Ia. F3 104-5
Rickman, Tenn. B10 188-9
Rickreall, Ore. H1 238-9
Rico, Colo. I7 214-5
Riddle, Ida. O3 218-9
Riddle, N.C. C15 180-1
Riddle, Ore. I5 238-9
Riddleton, Tenn. B9 188-9
Riddleville, Ga. I8 160-1
Riderville, Ala. H6 146-7
Riderwood, Ala. J2 146-7
Ridge, La. H5 168-9
Ridge, Mont. H15 222-3
Ridge, Va. E1 196-7
Ridge Farm, Ill. H11 96-7
Ridge Spring, S.C. E8 184-5
Ridge Wood Heights*, Fla. G10 156-7
Ridgebury, Conn. G3 60-1
Ridgecrest, Calif. L8 210-1
Ridgecrest, La. D6 168-9
Ridgedale, Sask. J8 294-5
Ridgefield, Conn. H4 60-1
Ridgefield, N.J. B12 76-7
Ridgefield, Wash. J7 246-7
Ridgefield Park, N.J. B11 76-7
Ridgeland, Miss. I6 176-7
Ridgeland, S.C. J10 184-5
Ridgeland, Wis. E8 140-1
Ridgeley, W. Va. D9 200-1
Ridgely, Md. E13 172-3
Ridgely, Tenn. B2 188-9
Ridgeside*, Tenn. K11 188-9
Ridgetop, Tenn. G7 188-9
Ridgetown, Ont. F11 284-5
Ridgeview, S. Dak. C7 136-7
Ridgeview Heights*, Ky. E11 164-5
Ridgeville, Ga. M11 160-1
Ridgeville, Ind. F11 100-1
Ridgeville, Man. K14 272-3
Ridgeville, S.C. H12 184-5
Ridgeway, Ia. B11 104-5
Ridgeway, Mich. K14 112-3
Ridgeway, Mo. A4 120-1
Ridgeway, N.J. I7 76-7
Ridgeway, O. E5 132-3
Ridgeway, S.C. D10 184-5
Ridgeway, Va. K8 196-7
Ridgeway, W. Va. E11 200-1
Ridgeway, Wis. J11 140-1
Ridgeway Trailer Court*, Man. G13 272-3
Ridgewood, N.J. A10 76-7
Ridgewood, S.C. H12 184-5
Ridgway, Colo. H7 214-5
Ridgway, Ill. M10 96-7
Ridgway, Pa. E6 84-5
Riding Mountain, Man. H11 272-3
Ridley Park, Pa. B10 84-5
Riegelsville, N.J. E2 76-7
Riegelsville, Pa. H15 84-5
Rienzi, Miss. B10 176-7
Riepetown, Nev. G9 226-7
Rieth, Ore. B12 238-9
Riffle, W. Va. F5 200-1
Rifle, Colo. E7 214-5
Rig, W. Va. E9 200-1
Rigaud, Que. I11 290-1
Rigby, Ida. L10 218-9
Rigdon, Ind. F9 100-1
Riggins, Ida. H3 218-9
Riley, Ind. J5 100-1
Riley, Kans. E12 108-9
Riley, Ore. G12 238-9
Riley, co., Kans. E12 108-9
Riley Brook, N.B. F3 275
Rileyville, Va. F11 196-7
Rillito, Ariz. K8 206-7
Rimbey, Alta. K7 264-5
Rimersburg, Pa. F3 84-5
Rimini, Mont. F6 222-3
Rimini, S.C. F11 184-5
Rimouski, Que. C15 290-1
Rimouski, co., Que. C16 290-1
Rimouski-Est, Que. C15 290-1
Rimrock, Ariz. F7 206-7
Rinard, Ia. E5 104-5
Rincon, Ga. J11 160-1
Rincon, N. Mex. K5 230-1
Rindge, N.H. O4 72-3
Riner, Va. J7 196-7
Riner, Wyo. I10 250-1
Rineyville, Ky. D1 164-5
Ringgold, Ga. C2 160-1
Ringgold, La. C3 168-9
Ringgold, Md. B8 172-3
Ringgold, Va. K9 196-7
Ringgold, co., Ia. J6 104-5
Ringle, Wis. C1 140-1
Ringling, Mont. F7 222-3
Ringling, Okla. I11 234-5
Ringo, Kans. J16 108-9
Ringoes, N.J. F4 76-7
Ringold, Okla. H15 234-5
Ringos Mills, Ky. F13 164-5
Ringsted, Ia. B5 104-5
Ringwood, N.J. B7 76-7
Ringwood, Okla. D9 234-5
Rio, W. Va. E10 200-1
Rio, Wis. H1 140-1
Rio Arriba, co., N. Mex. C5 230-1
Rio Blanco, co., Colo. D6 214-5
Rio Creek, Wis. D6 140-1
Rio Dell, Calif. F1 210-1
Rio Grande, N.J. O4 76-7
Rio Grande, O. I8 132-3
Rio Grande, co., Colo. I9 214-5
Rio Grande City, Tex. K7 192-3
Rio Grande R., N. Mex. I5 230-1
Rio Hondo*, Tex. K8 192-3
Rio Linda, Calif. A9 210-1
Rio Vista, Calif. B9 210-1
Rion, S.C. D10 184-5
Riondel, B.C. J10 268-9
Riovista, Tenn. G17 188-9
Ripley, Me. I5 64-5
Ripley, Miss. B9 176-7
Ripley, N.Y. G1 80-1
Ripley, O. J5 132-3
Ripley, Okla. D12 234-5
Ripley, Ont. B11 284-5
Ripley, Tenn. C2 188-9
Ripley, W. Va. F3 200-1
Ripley, co., Ind. K10 100-1
Ripley, co., Mo. J9 120-1
Riplinger, Wis. F11 140-1
Ripon, Calif. C10 210-1
Ripon*, Que. I10 290-1
Ripon, Wis. H13 140-1
Rippey, Ia. F6 104-5
Ripples, N.B. H5 275
Rippon, W. Va. E12 200-1
Ripton, Vt. H4 90-1
Ririe, Ida. L10 218-9
Risco, Mo. J11 120-1
Rising City, Nebr. G13 124-5
Rising Fawn, Ga. D1 160-1
Rising Star, Tex. E7 192-3
Rising Sun, Del. F4 153
Rising Sun, Ind. K12 100-1
Rising Sun, Md. B13 172-3
Risingdale, Mass. D1 68-9
Risingsun, O. C5 132-3
Rison, Ark. H7 150-1
Rison, Md. G9 172-3
Rita, W. Va. K12 200-1
Ritchey, Mo. I3 120-1
Ritchie, co., W. Va. E4 200-1
Ritner, Ky. J11 164-5
Ritter, Ore. D12 238-9
Ritter, S.C. I11 184-5
Rittman, O. E14 132-3
Ritz, Ida. A3 218-9
Ritzville, Wash. G14 246-7
Riva, Md. I7 172-3
Rivare, Ind. D12 100-1
River Drive Park*, Ont. I8 284-5
River Edge, N.J. A11 76-7
River Falls, Ala. L7 146-7
River Falls, Wis. F7 140-1
River Forest*, Ill. B11 96-7
River Forest, Ind. G9 100-1
River Grove, Ill. M3 96-7
River Grove*, Ore. C6 238-9
River Hébert, N.S. C6 281
River Heights, Ut. C6 242-3
River Hills, Man. I16 272-3
River Hills*, Wis. I15 140-1
River John, N.S. C8 281
River Jordan, B.C. E11 268-9
River Oaks, Tex. C13 192-3
River Rouge, Mich. J6 112-3
River Vale, N.J. C8 76-7
River View, Ala. H10 146-7
Riverbank, Calif. C10 210-1
Riverbank, Conn. J3 60-1
Rivercrest*, Man. J4 272-3
Riverdale, Calif. K5 210-1
Riverdale, Ga. D10 160-1
Riverdale*, Ill. C11 96-7
Riverdale, Ia. H15 104-5
Riverdale, Kans. J10 108-9
Riverdale, Md. I4 172-3
Riverdale, Mass. B13 68-9
Riverdale, Mich. H13 112-3
Riverdale, Nebr. H9 124-5
Riverdale, N.J. C7 76-7
Riverdale, N. Dak. F6 128-9
Riverdale*, Ut. D6 242-3
Riverdale Heights-East Pines*, Md. E10 172-3
Riverhead, N.Y. J13 80-1
Riverhurst, Sask. M6 294-5
Riverland Village-Lauderdale Isles*, Fla. I13 156-7
Riverlea, O. F6 132-3
Rivermines, Mo. G10 120-1
Rivers, Man. I10 272-3
Riverside, Ala. E8 146-7
Riverside, Calif. N8 210-1
Riverside, Colo. H3 214-5
Riverside, Ga. N5 160-1
Riverside*, Ga. E2 160-1
Riverside, Ida. M9 218-9
Riverside*, Ill. B11 96-7
Riverside, Ia. H12 104-5
Riverside, Ky. I7 164-5
Riverside, Me. K4 64-5
Riverside, Mass. B5 68-9
Riverside, Mo. I15 120-1
Riverside, Nev. L11 226-7
Riverside, N.J. L11 76-7
Riverside, N.Y. G5 80-1
Riverside, N. Dak. G14 128-9
Riverside, O. H15 132-3
Riverside, Ore. G14 238-9
Riverside, Pa. G11 84-5
Riverside*, Sask. N5 294-5
Riverside, S.C. B10 184-5
Riverside, Ut. C5 242-3
Riverside, Wash. C12 246-7
Riverside, Wyo. J12 250-1
Riverside, co., Calif. N10 210-1
Riverside-Albert, N.B. I7 275
Riversville, Conn. J2 60-1
Riverton, Ala. A3 146-7
Riverton, Conn. B7 60-1
Riverton, Ill. H7 96-7
Riverton, Ia. J3 104-5
Riverton, La. C5 168-9
Riverton, Man. H14 272-3
Riverton, Minn. J5 116-7
Riverton, Nebr. J10 124-5
Riverton, N.H. F6 72-3
Riverton, N.J. M11 76-7
Riverton, Ore. H3 238-9
Riverton, Ut. F6 242-3
Riverton, Vt. F6 90-1
Riverton, Va. A1 196-7
Riverton, W. Va. F8 200-1
Riverton, Wyo. F9 250-1
Riverton Heights, Wash. I3 246-7
Rivervale, Ark. C11 150-1
Riverview*, Ala. M5 146-7
Riverview, Fla. I3 156-7
Riverview, Mich. K6 112-3
Riverview*, Mo. E10 120-1
Riverview, N.B. H7 275
Riverview, Tenn. H16 188-9
Riverview, Wyo. E16 250-1
Riverville, Va. H10 196-7
Riverwood*, Ky. A2 164-5
Riverwoods*, Ill. K3 96-7
Rives, Mo. K11 120-1
Rives, Tenn. A3 188-9
Rivesville, W. Va. B14 200-1
Riviera Beach, Fla. D16 156-7
Riviera Beach, Md. G7 172-3
Riviera Beach, N.J. I7 76-7
Rivière-à-Pierre, Que. F10 290-1
Rivière-au-Tonnerre, Que. G6 290-1
Rivière-Boisclair*, Que. J3 290-1
Rivière-du-Loup, Que. D14 290-1
Rivière-du-Loup, co., Que. D14 290-1
Rivière-du-Loup-Sud-Est*, Que. D14 290-1
Rivière-du-Moulin-Developpement*, Que. H16 290-1
Rivière-Portneuf, Que. C14 290-1
Rivière-Verte, N.B. F2 275
Rivulet, Mont. E2 222-3
Rixeyville, Va. B1 196-7
Rixies, Nev. D7 226-7
Ro Ellen, Tenn. B3 188-9
Roachdale, Ind. H6 100-1
Roan Mountain, Tenn. B16 188-9
Roane, co., Tenn. C11 188-9
Roane, co., W. Va. F4 200-1
Roann, Ind. D9 100-1
Roanoke, Ala. F10 146-7
Roanoke, Ill. E8 96-7
Roanoke, Ind. D10 100-1
Roanoke, La. H3 168-9
Roanoke, Tex. C13 192-3
Roanoke, Va. I8 196-7
Roanoke, W. Va. E13 200-1
Roanoke, co., Va. I7 196-7
Roanoke Rapids, N.C. C12 180-1
Roanoke R., Va. J9 196-7
Roaring Gap, N.C. C7 180-1
Roaring River, N.C. G1 180-1
Roaring Spring, Pa. I6 84-5
Roba, Ala. I9 146-7
Robards, Ky. H5 164-5
Robb, Alta. J5 264-5
Robbins, Ill. N4 96-7
Robbins, N.C. J5 180-1
Robbins, Tenn. G10 188-9
Robbinsdale*, Minn. L6 116-7
Robbinston, Me. I11 64-5
Robbinsville, N.J. H5 76-7
Robbinsville, N.C. E1 180-1
Robe, Wash. D9 246-7
Robeline, La. D2 168-9
Roberdel, N.C. K4 180-1
Robersonville, N.C. D13 180-1
Robert, La. A13 168-9
Robert Kerr Res., Okla. F15 234-5
Robert Lee, Tex. E6 192-3
Roberta, Ga. I5 160-1
Roberta, Okla. I13 234-5
Roberts, Ida. L9 218-9
Roberts, Miss. I8 176-7
Roberts, Mont. H10 222-3
Roberts, Ore. F9 238-9
Roberts, Wis. E7 140-1
Roberts, co., S. Dak. A15 136-7
Roberts, co., Tex. A16 192-3
Robert's Arm, Nfld. L9 278-9
Roberts Creek, B.C. B12 268-9
Roberts Landing, Mich. I8 112-3
Robertsburg, W. Va. G2 200-1
Robertsdale, Ala. N4 146-7
Robertson, Wyo. J5 250-1
Robertson, co., Ky. F12 164-5
Robertson, co., Tenn. A7 188-9
Robertson, co., Tex. F9 192-3
Robertsonville*, Que. J4 290-1
Robertstown, Ga. D5 160-1
Robertsville, Conn. B7 60-1
Robertville, N.B. E5 275
Robertville, S.C. I10 184-5
Roberval, Que. C10 290-1
Robeson, co., N.C. G10 180-1
Robesonia, Pa. I13 84-5
Robichaud, N.B. H7 275
Robin, Ida. N9 218-9
Robinhood, Me. N11 64-5
Robins, Ia. F12 104-5
Robinson, Ill. J11 96-7
Robinson, Kans. D14 108-9
Robinson, Ky. F11 164-5
Robinson, N. Dak. G9 128-9
Robinson, Tex. F9 192-3
Robinson Springs, Ala. H7 146-7
Robinsons, Me. D9 64-5
Robinsonville, Miss. B5 176-7
Robinsonville, N.B. E4 275
Robinswood*, Ky. G9 164-5
Robinwood, Miss. K6 176-7
Robley, Va. H14 196-7
Roblin, Man. G9 272-3
Robsart, Sask. O4 294-5
Robson, B.C. J9 268-9
Robstown, Tex. I8 192-3
Roby, Tex. D6 192-3
Roca, Nebr. I14 124-5
Rocanville, Sask. N11 294-5
Rochdale, Mass. E8 68-9
Rochdale*, N.Y. H11 80-1
Roche Harbor, Wash. C7 246-7
Roche Percee, Sask. O10 294-5
Rochelle, Ga. K6 160-1
Rochelle, Ill. B8 96-7
Rochelle, Va. C1 196-7
Rochelle, Wyo. E15 250-1
Rochelle Park, N.J. A11 76-7
Rocheport, Mo. D6 120-1
Rochester, Alta. H8 264-5
Rochester, Ill. H7 96-7
Rochester, Ind. C8 100-1
Rochester, Ky. I6 164-5
Rochester, Mass. G13 68-9
Rochester, Mich. I6 112-3
Rochester, Minn. O8 116-7
Rochester, N.H. L9 72-3
Rochester, N.Y. E4 80-1
Rochester, Pa. H1 84-5
Rochester, Vt. H5 90-1
Rochester, Wash. G7 246-7
Rochester, Wis. K4 140-1
Rochford, S. Dak. F2 136-7
Rociada, N. Mex. E7 230-1
Rock, Kans. J11 108-9
Rock, W. Va. J4 200-1
Rock, co., Minn. O2 116-7
Rock, co., Nebr. E9 124-5
Rock, co., Wis. K13 140-1
Rock Castle, W. Va. F3 200-1
Rock Cave, W. Va. F13 200-1
Rock City, Ala. D4 146-7

Rock Creek, B.C. K9 268-9
Rock Creek, Kans. E14 108-9
Rock Creek*, Minn. J7 116-7
Rock Creek, O. B11 132-3
Rock Creek, Ore. B10 238-9
Rock Creek, Ore. D14 238-9
Rock Elm, Wis. F8 140-1
Rock Falls, Ill. C7 96-7
Rock Falls, Ia. B9 104-5
Rock Falls, Wis. F8 140-1
Rock Forest, Que. J15 290-1
Rock Forge, W. Va. A15 200-1
Rock Hall, Md. D12 172-3
Rock Hill, Mo. C16 120-1
Rock Hill, S.C. B10 184-5
Rock Hill, Tenn. F14 188-9
Rock Island, Ill. C5 96-7
Rock Island, Okla. F16 234-5
Rock Island, Que. K14 290-1
Rock Island, Tenn. C9 188-9
Rock Island, Wash. F11 246-7
Rock Island, co., Ill. D4 96-7
Rock Lake, N. Dak. B10 128-9
Rock Mills, Ala. F10 146-7
Rock Point, Ariz. B10 206-7
Rock Point, Md. H10 172-3
Rock Port, Mo. A1 120-1
Rock Rapids, Ia. A2 104-5
Rock R., Ill. C6 96-7
Rock River, Wyo. I13 250-1
Rock Spring, Ga. D2 160-1
Rock Springs, Ariz. H6 206-7
Rock Springs, Mont. E13 222-3
Rock Springs, Wis. I11 140-1
Rock Springs, Wyo. I8 250-1
Rock, The, Ga. I4 160-1
Rock Valley, Ia. B1 104-5
Rockaway*, N.J. C6 76-7
Rockaway, N.J. D6 76-7
Rockaway, Ore. B4 238-9
Rockaway Beach, Mo. J5 120-1
Rockbridge, Wis. I11 140-1
Rockbridge, co., Va. G9 196-7
Rockbridge Baths, Va. H9 196-7
Rockcastle, co., Ky. I12 164-5
Rockcliffe Park, Ont. H15 284-5
Rockdale, Ill. O2 96-7
Rockdale, Md. F6 172-3
Rockdale, Tenn. J6 188-9
Rockdale, Tex. F9 192-3
Rockdale, Wis. J2 140-1
Rockdale, co., Ga. G4 160-1
Rocker, Mont. G5 222-3
Rockfall, Conn. F9 60-1
Rockfield, Ind. E7 100-1
Rockfield, Ky. J7 164-5
Rockfield, Wis. I4 140-1
Rockfish, Va. H10 196-7
Rockford, Ala. G7 146-7
Rockford, Ida. M9 218-9
Rockford, Ill. A8 96-7
Rockford, Ind. K9 100-1
Rockford, Ia. C9 104-5
Rockford, Mich. I12 112-3
Rockford, Minn. A9 116-7
Rockford, Nebr. J14 124-5
Rockford, N.C. G2 180-1
Rockford, O. D3 132-3
Rockford, Tenn. I12 188-9
Rockford, Wash. F16 246-7
Rockford Bay, Ida. D2 218-9
Rockglen, Sask. O7 294-5
Rockham, S. Dak. D11 136-7
Rockhaven, Sask. K4 294-5
Rockhouse, Ark. A4 150-1
Rockingham, N.H. N9 72-3
Rockingham, N.C. F9 180-1
Rockingham, Vt. L7 90-1
Rockingham, co., N.H. N8 72-3
Rockingham, co., N.C. C9 180-1
Rockingham, co., Va. F9 196-7
Rockland, Conn. G9 60-1
Rockland, Del. A3 153
Rockland, Ida. O8 218-9
Rockland, Me. L6 64-5
Rockland, Mass. K6 68-9
Rockland, Mich. C8 112-3
Rockland, Ont. H15 284-5
Rockland, Wis. H10 140-1
Rockland, co., N.Y. I11 80-1
Rockledge, Ala. D8 146-7
Rockledge, Fla. F12 156-7
Rockledge, Ga. J8 160-1
Rockledge*, Pa. J15 84-5
Rockleigh, N.J. C8 76-7
Rocklin, Calif. H4 210-1
Rockmart, Ga. F2 160-1
Rockport, Ark. G5 150-1
Rockport, Ind. O5 100-1
Rockport, Ky. I6 164-5
Rockport, Me. L6 64-5
Rockport, Mass. B13 68-9
Rockport, Miss. J6 176-7
Rockport, Tex. I9 192-3
Rockport, Wash. C9 246-7
Rockport, W. Va. E3 200-1
Rocksprings, Tex. G6 192-3
Rockton, Ill. A8 96-7
Rockvale, Colo. G11 214-5
Rockvale, Mont. H10 222-3
Rockvale, Tenn. I7 188-9
Rockville, Conn. C11 60-1
Rockville, Ind. H5 100-1
Rockville, Md. D9 172-3
Rockville, Mass. K2 68-9
Rockville, Minn. L5 116-7
Rockville, Mo. F4 120-1
Rockville, Nebr. H10 124-5
Rockville, N.B. I6 275
Rockville, N.S. G4 281
Rockville, R.I. G2 87
Rockville, Ut. M4 242-3
Rockville, Va. H12 196-7
Rockville Centre, N.Y. F16 80-1
Rockwall, Tex. C16 192-3
Rockwall, co., Tex. D9 192-3
Rockwell, Ia. C8 104-5
Rockwell, N.C. I3 180-1
Rockwell City, Ia. E5 104-5
Rockwood, Ala. C4 146-7
Rockwood, Me. G4 64-5
Rockwood, Mich. K6 112-3
Rockwood*, Ont. C14 284-5
Rockwood, Ore. F2 238-9
Rockwood, Pa. J4 84-5
Rockwood, Tenn. I10 188-9
Rockwood, Wis. F5 140-1
Rocky, Okla. F8 234-5
Rocky Bar, Ida. L5 218-9
Rocky Boy, Mont. C9 222-3
Rocky Branch, La. B5 168-9
Rocky Comfort, Mo. I3 120-1
Rocky Face, Ga. D2 160-1
Rocky Ford, Colo. H14 214-5
Rocky Ford, Ga. J10 160-1
Rocky Fork, Tenn. H16 188-9
Rocky Gap, Va. I6 196-7
Rocky Harbour, Nfld. L7 278-9
Rocky Harbour*, Nfld. L7 278-9
Rocky Hill, Conn. E9 60-1
Rocky Hill, Ky. J8 164-5
Rocky Hill, N.J. G5 76-7
Rocky Mount, Ga. H3 160-1
Rocky Mount, La. A2 168-9
Rocky Mount, N.C. D12 180-1
Rocky Mount, Va. J8 196-7
Rocky Mountain House, Alta. K7 264-5
Rocky Mts. 14-15, 16-17
Rocky Point, N.C. G12 180-1
Rocky Point, Wash. H1 246-7
Rocky Rapids, Alta. J7 264-5
Rocky Ridge, Md. B9 172-3
Rocky Ridge, O. B6 132-3
Rocky River, O. B13 132-3
Rockyford, Alta. L8 264-5
Rockypoint, Wyo. B14 250-1
Rodanthe, N.C. D16 180-1
Roddey, S.C. B10 184-5
Roddickton, Nfld. K9 278-9
Roddy, Tenn. I12 188-9
Rodentown, Ala. C8 146-7
Rodeo*, Calif. I3 210-1
Rodeo, N. Mex. M1 230-1
Roderfield, W. Va. J3 200-1
Rodessa, La. A1 168-9
Rodey, N. Mex. K5 230-1
Rodgers Forge, Md. E7 172-3
Rodman, Ia. C5 104-5
Rodman, S.C. B10 184-5
Rodney, Ia. E2 104-5
Rodney, Mich. H12 112-3
Rodney, Miss. J3 176-7
Rodney, Ont. F11 284-5
Rodney Village*, Del. F4 153
Roduco, N.C. C14 180-1
Roe, Ark. F9 150-1
Roebuck, S.C. F4 184-5
Roeland Park, Kans. E16 108-9
Roessleville*, N.Y. F11 80-1
Roeton, Ala. K9 146-7
Roff, Okla. H12 234-5
Roger Mills, co., Okla. E7 234-5
Rogers, Ark. A3 150-1
Rogers, Conn. C14 60-1
Rogers, Ky. H13 164-5
Rogers, La. E5 168-9
Rogers, Minn. A9 116-7
Rogers, Nebr. G14 124-5
Rogers, N. Mex. H11 230-1
Rogers, N. Dak. G12 128-9
Rogers, O. D11 132-3
Rogers*, Tex. F8 192-3
Rogers, co., Okla. D14 234-5
Rogers City, Mich. E14 112-3
Rogers Corner, Del. B3 153
Rogers Springs, Tenn. K4 188-9
Rogerson, Ida. O6 218-9
Rogersville, Ala. B5 146-7
Rogersville, Mo. I5 120-1
Rogersville, N.B. G6 275
Rogersville, Tenn. G14 188-9
Roggen, Colo. D12 214-5
Rogue River, Ore. J5 238-9
Rohnert Park*, Calif. H2 210-1
Rohnerville, Calif. E1 210-1
Rohrersville, Md. C7 172-3
Rohwer, Ark. I9 150-1
Rokeby*, Sask. M10 294-5
Roland, Ark. I15 150-1
Roland, Ia. F8 104-5
Roland, Man. K13 272-3
Roland*, Okla. F16 234-5
Rolesville, N.C. H8 180-1
Rolette, N. Dak. C9 128-9
Rolette, co., N. Dak. C9 128-9
Rolfe, Ia. C5 104-5
Roll, Ariz. J3 206-7
Roll, Okla. E7 234-5
Rolla, Ark. G6 150-1
Rolla, B.C. E8 268-9
Rolla, Kans. K1 108-9
Rolla, Mo. G8 120-1
Rolla, N. Dak. B9 128-9
Rolling Acres*, N.Y. E4 80-1
Rolling Fields*, Ky. G9 164-5
Rolling Fork, Miss. G4 176-7
Rolling Hills, Alta. N9 264-5
Rolling Hills*, Calif. H8 210-1
Rolling Hills*, Ky. F9 164-5
Rolling Hills Estates*, Calif. H8 210-1
Rolling Meadows, Ill. L2 96-7
Rolling Prairie, Ind. A7 100-1
Rolling Prairie, Wis. H3 140-1
Rollingdam, N.B. J3 275
Rollingstone, Minn. O9 116-7
Rollingwood*, Tex. G8 192-3
Rollins, Mont. C3 222-3
Rollins Fork, Va. G13 196-7
Rollinsford, N.H. M9 72-3
Rollinsville, Colo. G1 214-5
Rollo Bay, P.E.I. E10 287
Rolphton, Ont. H9 284-5
Roma-Los Saenz, Tex. K7 192-3
Romance, Ark. D7 150-1
Romance, W. Va. G3 200-1
Rome, Ga. E2 160-1
Rome, Ill. E7 96-7
Rome, Ia. I12 104-5
Rome, Me. K4 64-5
Rome, Miss. D5 176-7
Rome, N.Y. E8 80-1
Rome, Ore. I15 238-9
Rome, S.C. F14 184-5
Rome, Tenn. B9 188-9
Rome, Wis. J3 140-1
Rome City, Ind. B10 100-1
Romeo, Colo. J10 214-5
Romeo, Mich. H6 112-3
Romeoville, Ill. N2 96-7
Romeroville, N. Mex. E8 230-1
Romney, Ind. F6 100-1
Romney, W. Va. E10 200-1
Romulus, Mich. K5 112-3
Ronald, Wash. F10 246-7
Ronan, Mont. D3 222-3
Ronceverte, W. Va. I6 200-1
Ronda, N.C. G1 180-1
Rondo, Ark. F10 150-1
Ronkonkoma, N.Y. J12 80-1
Ronneby, Minn. K5 116-7
Roodhouse, Ill. I5 96-7
Rooks, co., Kans. E6 108-9
Roopville, Ga. G2 160-1
Roosevelt*, Ala. E6 146-7
Roosevelt, Ariz. H8 206-7
Roosevelt, La. B7 168-9
Roosevelt, Minn. D4 116-7
Roosevelt, N.J. H6 76-7
Roosevelt, N.Y. F16 80-1
Roosevelt, Okla. G8 234-5
Roosevelt, Ut. F9 242-3
Roosevelt, Wash. J11 246-7
Roosevelt, co., Mont. B14 222-3
Roosevelt, co., N. Mex. H11 230-1
Roosevelt Beach, Ore. F4 238-9
Roosevelt Park, Mich. I11 112-3
Roosterville, Mass. E3 68-9
Roper, Kans. I14 108-9
Roper, N.C. D14 180-1
Roque Bluffs, Me. J10 64-5
Rorketon, Man. G11 272-3
Rosa, Ark. C13 150-1
Rosa*, Man. K4 272-3
Rosaire, Que. F13 290-1
Rosalia, Kans. I12 108-9
Rosalia, Wash. F16 246-7
Rosalie, Ala. B9 146-7
Rosalie, Nebr. E14 124-5
Rosalind, Alta. J9 264-5
Rosamond, Calif. M7 210-1
Rosario, Wash. C7 246-7
Rosburg, Wash. H6 246-7
Rosbury, Vt. G6 90-1
Roscoe, Ga. D9 160-1
Roscoe*, Ill. A8 96-7
Roscoe, Minn. L4 116-7
Roscoe, Mo. G4 120-1
Roscoe, Mont. H9 222-3
Roscoe, Nebr. G5 124-5
Roscoe, Pa. J2 84-5
Roscoe, S. Dak. B10 136-7
Roscoe*, Tex. E6 192-3
Roscommon, Mich. G13 112-3
Roscommon, co., Mich. G13 112-3
Rose, Nebr. E9 124-5
Rose, Okla. D15 234-5
Rose Blanche, Nfld. O7 278-9
Rose Blanche-Harbour Le Cou*, Nfld. O7 278-9
Rose Bud, Ark. D7 150-1
Rose City, Mich. G13 112-3
Rose City*, Tex. G11 192-3
Rose Creek, Minn. O7 116-7
Rose Hill, Ia. H10 104-5
Rose Hill, Kans. J11 108-9
Rose Hill, Miss. I9 176-7
Rose Hill, N.C. F12 180-1
Rose Hill, Va. E13 196-7
Rose Lodge, Ore. D4 238-9
Rose Valley, Nev. I11 226-7
Rose Valley, Sask. K9 294-5
Rose Well, Ariz. D5 206-7
Roseau, Minn. D3 116-7
Roseau, co., Minn. D2 116-7
Roseau River*, Man. K4 272-3
Rosebank*, Man. K3 272-3
Roseboro, N.C. K8 180-1
Rosebud, Mo. F8 120-1
Rosebud, Mont. F13 222-3
Rosebud, S. Dak. H7 136-7
Rosebud, Tex. F9 192-3
Rosebud, co., Mont. G13 222-3
Roseburg, Ore. H5 238-9
Rosebush, Mich. H13 112-3
Rosedale, Alta. L8 264-5
Rosedale*, Alta. K8 264-5
Rosedale, Colo. E4 214-5
Rosedale, Ind. I5 100-1
Rosedale, La. G6 168-9
Rosedale*, Md. C11 172-3
Rosedale, Miss. D4 176-7
Rosedale, Okla. G11 234-5
Rosedale, Ont. A16 284-5
Rosedale, Tenn. H11 188-9
Rosedale, Va. J4 196-7
Rosedale, W. Va. F5 200-1
Rosedale Terrace*, Ont. I16 284-5
Rosefield, La. D5 168-9
Roseisle, Man. J13 272-3
Roseland, Ark. C12 150-1
Roseland*, Calif. H2 210-1
Roseland, Ind. A8 100-1
Roseland, Kans. J16 108-9
Roseland, La. G8 168-9
Roseland, Nebr. I11 124-5
Roseland, N.J. D7 76-7
Roselawn, Ind. C5 100-1
Roselle, Ill. L2 96-7
Roselle, N.J. E9 76-7
Roselle Park, N.J. E9 76-7
Rosemark, Tenn. K2 188-9
Rosemary, Alta. M9 264-5
Rosemead*, Calif. G9 210-1
Rosemère*, Que. I12 290-1
Rosemont, Ill. L3 96-7
Rosemont, Md. C7 172-3
Rosemont, Nebr. J11 124-5
Rosemont, W. Va. C14 200-1
Rosemount, Minn. C11 116-7
Rosemount*, O. J7 132-3
Rosenberg, Tex. I12 192-3
Rosendale, Mo. B2 120-1
Rosendale, N.Y. H10 80-1
Rosendale, Wis. G3 140-1
Rosenfeld, Man. K14 272-3
Rosengart*, Man. K13 272-3
Rosenhayn, N.J. L3 76-7
Rosenhof, Sask. N5 294-5
Rosenhoff*, Man. K4 272-3
Rosenort, Man. J14 272-3
Rosenort*, Man. K13 272-3
Rosepine, La. F2 168-9
Roseto, Pa. G15 84-5
Rosetown, Sask. L5 294-5
Rosetta, Miss. L3 176-7
Rosette, Ut. C3 242-3
Roseville, Calif. H4 210-1
Roseville, Ill. E5 96-7
Roseville, Mich. I6 112-3
Roseville, Minn. B11 116-7
Roseville, O. G8 132-3
Roseville Park, Del. B3 153
Rosewood, Ky. J6 164-5
Rosewood Heights, Ill. J6 96-7
Roseworth, Ida. O5 218-9
Rosholt, S. Dak. A15 136-7
Rosholt, Wis. D1 140-1
Rosiclare, Ill. N10 96-7
Rosine, Ky. I7 164-5
Rosinville, S.C. G11 184-5
Roslyn*, N.Y. J11 80-1
Roslyn*, Pa. J15 84-5
Roslyn, S. Dak. B14 136-7
Roslyn, Wash. F10 246-7
Roslyn Estates*, N.Y. J11 80-1
Roslyn Harbor*, N.Y. J11 80-1
Roslyn Heights, N.Y. E16 80-1
Rosman, N.C. E3 180-1
Ross*, Calif. B7 210-1
Ross, Man. J15 272-3
Ross, N. Dak. D4 128-9
Ross*, O. H3 132-3
Ross, Wyo. E13 250-1
Ross, co., O. H6 132-3
Ross Barnett Res., Miss. H6 176-7
Ross Fork, Mont. E9 222-3
Ross River, Y.T. C2 297
Rossburg, O. E3 132-3
Rossburn, Man. H10 272-3
Rosseau, Ont. H8 284-5
Rossendale*, Man. J2 272-3
Rosser*, Man. I14 272-3
Rosser, Tenn. B4 188-9
Rossford, O. B5 132-3
Rossie, Ia. C4 104-5
Rossland, B.C. K9 268-9
Rossmoor*, Calif. N7 210-1
Rossmore*, Ont. K12 284-5
Rosston, Ark. I4 150-1
Rosston, Okla. C6 234-5
Rossville, Ga. C2 160-1
Rossville, Ill. F11 96-7
Rossville, Ind. F7 100-1
Rossville, Ia. B13 104-5
Rossville, Kans. E13 108-9
Rossville, Tenn. K2 188-9
Rosthern, Sask. K7 294-5
Roswell, Colo. K4 214-5
Roswell, Ga. A11 160-1
Roswell, Ida. L2 218-9
Roswell, N. Mex. I9 230-1
Roswell, O. E10 132-3
Roswell, S. Dak. F14 136-7
Rotan, Tex. D6 192-3
Rothbury, Mich. H11 112-3
Rothesay, N.B. J5 275
Rothiemay, Mont. F9 222-3
Rothsay, Minn. I2 116-7
Rothschild, Wis. C1 140-1
Rothsville, Pa. J12 84-5
Rothville, Mo. C5 120-1
Rotterdam, N.Y. F11 80-1
Rougemont, N.C. G6 180-1
Rougemont*, Que. I13 290-1
Rough Rock, Ariz. C10 206-7
Rough Run, W. Va. F9 200-1
Rouleau, Sask. N8 294-5
Round Bay, Md. H7 172-3

Round Hill, Alta. J8 264-5
Round Hill, Conn. J2 60-1
Round Hill, N.S. E5 281
Round Hill, Va. E12 196-7
Round Lake, Ill. J2 96-7
Round Lake, Minn. O3 116-7
Round Lake, N.Y. E11 80-1
Round Lake Beach, Ill. J2 96-7
Round Lake Heights*, Ill. A10 96-7
Round Lake Park, Ill. J2 96-7
Round Mountain, Nev. H6 226-7
Round O, S.C. H11 184-5
Round Oak, Ga. H5 160-1
Round Pond, Ark. E11 150-1
Round Pond, Me. N12 64-5
Round Rock, Ariz. B11 206-7
Round Rock, Tex. G8 192-3
Round Valley, Ut. C7 242-3
Roundaway, Miss. D5 176-7
Roundlake, Miss. D4 176-7
Roundup, Mont. F10 222-3
Rouses Point, N.Y. A11 80-1
Rousseau, Ky. H14 164-5
Routon, Tenn. B4 188-9
Routt, co., Colo. C8 214-5
Rouville, co., Que. J13 290-1
Rouyn, Que. H1 290-1
Rouzerville, Pa. K9 84-5
Rover, Ark. E4 150-1
Rover, Tenn. I7 188-9
Row, Okla. D16 234-5
Rowan, Ia. D8 104-5
Rowan, co., Ky. G14 164-5
Rowan, co., N.C. D7 180-1
Rowan Mill*, N.C. D7 180-1
Rowayton, Conn. J4 60-1
Rowe, Mass. B3 68-9
Rowe, N. Mex. E7 230-1
Rowell, S.C. B10 184-5
Rowena, Ore. B9 238-9
Rowena, S. Dak. G16 136-7
Rowesville, S.C. G11 184-5
Rowland, Ky. E6 164-5
Rowland, Nev. A8 226-7
Rowland, N.C. G10 180-1
Rowland, Ore. J1 238-9
Rowland Heights*, Calif. N7 210-1
Rowlesburg, W. Va. C16 200-1
Rowlett, Tex. C15 192-3
Rowletts, Ky. I8 164-5
Rowley, Ia. E12 104-5
Rowley, Mass. B12 68-9
Rox, Nev. L10 226-7
Roxana, Del. K6 153
Roxana, Ill. K6 96-7
Roxboro, N.C. C10 180-1
Roxboro*, Que. I12 290-1
Roxbury, Conn. F5 60-1
Roxbury, Kans. G10 108-9
Roxbury, Me. J2 64-5
Roxbury, Mass. I5 68-9
Roxbury*, N.H. N3 72-3
Roxbury*, N.J. D5 76-7
Roxbury, Wis. J12 140-1
Roxbury Falls, Conn. F5 60-1
Roxie, Miss. K4 176-7
Roxobel, N.C. C13 180-1
Roxton Falls, Que. I14 290-1
Roy, Ida. O8 218-9
Roy, La. C3 168-9
Roy, Mont. D10 222-3
Roy, N. Mex. D10 230-1
Roy, Ut. E6 242-3
Roy, Wash. K2 246-7
Royal, Ala. D7 146-7
Royal, Ia. C4 104-5
Royal, Nebr. E11 124-5
Royal, Ut. H8 242-3
Royal Center, Ind. D7 100-1
Royal City*, Wash. G12 246-7
Royal Oak, Md. F12 172-3
Royal Oak, Mich. I6 112-3
Royal Palm Beach, Fla. D16 156-7
Royal Pines*, N.C. E4 180-1
Royalston, Mass. B6 68-9
Royalton, Ill. M8 96-7
Royalton, Ky. H14 164-5
Royalton, Minn. K5 116-7
Royalton*, Pa. I11 84-5
Royalton, Vt. I6 90-1
Royalton, Wis. E2 140-1
Royersford, Pa. A9 84-5
Royerton, Ind. F10 100-1
Royse City, Tex. C16 192-3
Royston, B.C. J5 268-9
Royston, Ga. E7 160-1
Royville*, Ky. J10 164-5
Rozel, Kans. H6 108-9
Rozet, Wyo. C14 250-1
Rubidoux*, Calif. N8 210-1
Rubottom, Okla. I11 234-5
Ruby, Alaska D10 254-5
Ruby, Ariz. M8 206-7
Ruby, La. E5 168-9
Ruby, Nebr. H13 124-5
Ruby, S.C. B12 184-5
Ruby, Va. B3 196-7
Ruby, Wash. C16 246-7
Ruby Valley, Nev. D9 226-7
Rubys Inn, Ut. L5 242-3
Ruckersville, Ga. E7 160-1
Ruckersville, Va. G11 196-7
Rudd, Ia. B9 104-5
Ruddels Mills, Ky. A8 164-5
Rudderville, Tenn. I7 188-9
Rudolph, Wis. G12 140-1
Rudy, Ark. D2 150-1
Rudyard, Mich. D13 112-3
Rudyard, Miss. C5 176-7
Rudyard, Mont. B8 222-3
Rufe, Okla. I15 234-5
Ruff, Wash. G13 246-7
Ruffin, N.C. C9 180-1
Ruffin, S.C. H11 184-5
Rufus, Ore. B9 238-9
Rugby, N. Dak. D8 128-9
Rugby, Tenn. G10 188-9
Rugby, Va. K5 196-7
Ruggs, Ore. C11 238-9
Ruidoso, N. Mex. J7 230-1
Ruidoso Downs, N. Mex. J7 230-1
Rule, Tex. D6 192-3
Ruleton, Kans. E1 108-9
Ruleville, Miss. E5 176-7
Rulo, Nebr. J16 124-5
Rumford, Me. K2 64-5
Rumford, S. Dak. I2 136-7
Rumford Center, Me. K2 64-5
Rumford Point, Me. K2 64-5
Rumney, N.H. I5 72-3
Rumsey, Alta. L8 264-5
Rumsey, Ky. H6 164-5
Rumson, N.J. G8 76-7
Runge, Tex. H8 192-3
Runnells, Ia. H8 104-5
Runnels, co., Tex. E6 192-3
Runnelstown, Miss. L8 176-7
Runnemede, N.J. O10 76-7
Runnymede, Sask. L10 294-5
Rupert, Ida. N7 218-9
Rupert, Vt. L4 90-1
Rupert, W. Va. I5 200-1
Rural, Wis. E2 140-1
Rural Hall, N.C. G3 180-1
Rural Retreat, Va. J5 196-7
Rural Valley, Pa. G4 84-5
Rush, Colo. F13 214-5
Rush, Ky. F15 164-5
Rush, co., Ind. I10 100-1
Rush, co., Kans. G7 108-9
Rush Center, Kans. G6 108-9
Rush City, Minn. K7 116-7
Rush Hill, Mo. D8 120-1
Rush Lake, Sask. N6 294-5
Rush Springs, Okla. G10 234-5
Rushford, Minn. O9 116-7
Rushford*, Minn. O9 116-7
Rushing, Ark. C7 150-1
Rushmore, Minn. O2 116-7
Rushoon, Nfld. O10 278-9
Rushsylvania, O. E5 132-3
Rushville, Ill. G5 96-7
Rushville, Ind. I10 100-1
Rushville, Mo. G13 120-1
Rushville, Nebr. D4 124-5
Rushville, N.Y. F5 80-1
Rushville, O. G8 132-3
Rusk, Tex. E10 192-3
Rusk, Wis. F8 140-1
Rusk, co., Tex. E11 192-3
Rusk, co., Wis. D9 140-1
Ruskin, Fla. I3 156-7
Ruskin, Nebr. J12 124-5
Ruso, N. Dak. E7 128-9
Russell, Ark. D8 150-1
Russell, Ga. F5 160-1
Russell, Ia. I9 104-5
Russell, Kans. F7 108-9
Russell, Ky. F15 164-5
Russell, Man. H9 272-3
Russell, Mass. E4 68-9
Russell, Minn. N2 116-7
Russell, Miss. I10 176-7
Russell, N. Dak. C7 128-9
Russell, Okla. G7 234-5
Russell*, Ont. H15 284-5
Russell, co., Ala. I10 146-7
Russell, co., Kans. F8 108-9
Russell, co., Ky. J10 164-5
Russell, co., Va. J4 196-7
Russell Gardens*, N.Y. J11 80-1
Russell Springs, Kans. F3 108-9
Russell Springs, Ky. J10 164-5
Russells Point, O. E4 132-3
Russellton*, Pa. H2 84-5
Russellville, Ala. B4 146-7
Russellville, Ark. D5 150-1
Russellville, Ind. H6 100-1
Russellville, Ky. J6 164-5
Russellville, Mass. E4 68-9
Russellville, Mo. E6 120-1
Russellville, O. I5 132-3
Russellville, S.C. G13 184-5
Russellville, Tenn. G14 188-9
Russellville, W. Va. H5 200-1
Russett, Okla. I12 234-5
Russia, O. F3 132-3
Russian Mission, Alaska E8 254-5
Russiaville, Ind. F8 100-1
Russum, Miss. J4 176-7
Rustburg, Va. I9 196-7
Ruston, La. B4 168-9
Ruston, Wash. J2 246-7
Ruth, Mich. H15 112-3
Ruth, Miss. L5 176-7
Ruth, Nev. G10 226-7
Ruth, N.C. E5 180-1
Ruther Glen, Va. G12 196-7
Rutherford, N.J. B11 76-7
Rutherford, Tenn. B3 188-9
Rutherford, co., N.C. E5 180-1
Rutherford, co., Tenn. B8 188-9
Rutherfordton, N.C. E5 180-1
Rutherton, N. Mex. C6 230-1
Ruthilda, Sask. L5 294-5
Ruthton, Minn. N2 116-7
Ruthven, Ia. B5 104-5
Ruthven, Ont. G10 284-5
Ruthville, Va. E2 196-7
Rutland, Ia. D6 104-5
Rutland, Mass. D8 68-9
Rutland, N. Dak. J13 128-9
Rutland, O. I8 132-3
Rutland, S. Dak. F15 136-7
Rutland*, Vt. J5 90-1
Rutland, Vt. J5 90-1
Rutland, co., Vt. J4 90-1
Rutledge, Ala. K7 146-7
Rutledge, Ga. G5 160-1
Rutledge, Minn. J7 116-7
Rutledge, Mo. A7 120-1
Rutledge*, Pa. J15 84-5
Rutledge, Tenn. G13 188-9
Ruttan Lake Mining Camp*, Man. D2 272-3
Ruxton, Md. E6 172-3
Ryan, Ia. E13 104-5
Ryan, Okla. I10 234-5
Ryan, W. Va. G3 200-1
Ryan Park, Wyo. J12 250-1
Ryans Slough, Calif. E1 210-1
Rycroft, Alta. G4 264-5
Rydal*, Pa. J15 84-5
Ryder, N. Dak. E5 128-9
Ryderwood, Wash. H7 246-7
Rye, Ark. I7 150-1
Rye, Colo. H12 214-5
Rye, N.H. N10 72-3
Rye, N.Y. D15 80-1
Rye Beach, N.H. N10 72-3
Rye Patch Res., Nev. D4 226-7
Rye Valley, Ore. E15 238-9
Ryegate, Mont. F9 222-3
Ryegate*, Vt. F8 90-1
Ryland, Ala. B7 146-7
Ryland Heights*, Ky. E11 164-5
Ryley, Alta. J9 264-5
Rymer, W. Va. B13 200-1
Ryndon, Nev. C8 226-7

S

Sabattus, Me. M10 64-5
Sabetha, Kans. C14 108-9
Sabillasville, Md. B8 172-3
Sabin, Minn. I1 116-7
Sabina, O. H5 132-3
Sabinal, Tex. H7 192-3
Sabine, co., La. D2 168-9
Sabine, co., Tex. F11 192-3
Sabino, Miss. C5 176-7
Sabinoso, N. Mex. E9 230-1
Sabot, Va. H12 196-7
Sabula, Ia. F16 104-5
Sac, co., Ia. E4 104-5
Sac City, Ia. E4 104-5
Sacaton, Ariz. J7 206-7
Sachem Head, Conn. H9 60-1
Sachse, Tex. C15 192-3
Sackets Harbor, N.Y. C7 80-1
Sackville, N.B. I7 275
Sackville*, N.S. E7 281
Saco, Ala. J9 146-7
Saco, Me. N3 64-5
Saco, Mont. B12 222-3
Sacramento, Calif. H4 210-1
Sacramento, Ky. I6 164-5
Sacramento, N. Mex. K7 230-1
Sacramento, co., Calif. H4 210-1
Sacre-Coeur-Saguenay*, Que. C13 290-1
Sacred Heart, Minn. M3 116-7
Sacred Heart, Okla. G12 234-5
Saddle Brook, N.J. B11 76-7
Saddle River, N.J. C8 76-7
Saddle Rock*, N.Y. J11 80-1
Saddle String, Wyo. C12 250-1
Sadie, La. A5 168-9
Sadie, Tenn. A16 188-9
Sadieville, Ky. A7 164-5
Sadlersville, Tenn. F6 188-9
Saegerstown, Pa. D2 84-5
Safety Harbor, Fla. H2 156-7
Saffell, Ark. C9 150-1
Safford, Ala. I5 146-7
Safford, Ariz. J10 206-7
Saffordville, Kans. G13 108-9
Sag Harbor, N.Y. J14 80-1
Sagadahoc, co., Me. M4 64-5
Sagamore, Mass. G14 68-9
Sage, Ark. B8 150-1
Sage, Wyo. I5 250-1
Sage Creek Junction, Ut. C7 242-3
Sageville, Ia. D15 104-5
Saginaw, Ala. F6 146-7
Saginaw, Mich. H14 112-3
Saginaw, Mo. I3 120-1
Saginaw, Ore. F5 238-9
Saginaw, Tex. C13 192-3
Saginaw, co., Mich. I13 112-3
Saginaw Bay, Mich. G13 112-3
Sagle, Ida. B3 218-9
Sago, W. Va. E14 200-1
Sagola, Mich. D9 112-3
Saguache, Colo. H10 214-5
Saguache, co., Colo. G9 214-5
Saguenay, co., Que. G6 290-1
Saguenay R., Que. C12 290-1
Sahuarita, Ariz. L8 206-7
St.-Adalbert, Que. F13 290-1
St.-Adelphe*, Que. I3 290-1
St. Adolphe, Man. J14 272-3
St.-Adolphe-d'Howard, Que. H11 290-1
St.-Adrien, Que. I15 290-1
St.-Agapitville*, Que. I3 290-1
St. Agatha, Me. A8 64-5
St. Agatha*, Ont. D13 284-5
St.-Alban*, Que. G10 290-1
St. Albans, Me. I5 64-5
St. Alban's, Nfld. N9 278-9
St. Albans*, Vt. C4 90-1
St. Albans, Vt. C4 90-1
St. Albans, W. Va. H13 200-1
St. Albans Bay, Vt. C4 90-1
St. Albert, Alta. I8 264-5
St. Albert Settlement*, Alta. I8 264-5
St.-Alexandre-de-Kamouraska, Que. E14 290-1
St.-Alexis-de-Matapédia*, Que. I5 290-1
St.-Alexis-des-Monts, Que. J3 290-1
St.-Amable*, Que. I12 290-1
St. Ambroise, Man. I13 272-3
St.-Ambroise, Que. C11 290-1
St.-Anaclet, Que. C15 290-1
St.-André-Avellin, Que. I10 290-1
St.-André-du-Lac-St.-Jean, Que. C10 290-1
St.-André-Est*, Que. I11 290-1
St. Andrews, N.B. J4 275
St. Andrews*, S.C. I13 184-5
St. Andrews West, Ont. H16 284-5
St. Ann, Mo. B15 120-1
St. Anna, Wis. G4 140-1
St. Anne, Ill. E11 96-7
St.-Anselme, Que. G12 290-1
St. Ansgar, Ia. B9 104-5
St. Anthony, Ida. K10 218-9
St. Anthony, Ind. N6 100-1
St. Anthony, Ia. F8 104-5
St. Anthony, Minn. K4 116-7
St. Anthony*, Minn. M6 116-7
St. Anthony, Nfld. J9 278-9
St. Anthony, N. Dak. H7 128-9
St.-Antoine, N.B. H7 275
St.-Antoine*, Que. I11 290-1
St.-Antoine-sur-Richelieu*, Que. I13 290-1
St.-Antonin, Que. D14 290-1
St.-Arsène, Que. D14 290-1
St. Arthur, N.B. D4 275
St.-Aubert, Que. F13 290-1
St.-Augustin, Que. G8 290-1
St.-Augustin-de-Quebec, Que. F10 290-1
St. Augustine, Fla. C11 156-7
St. Augustine Beach, Fla. C12 156-7
St.-Barthélémy, Que. H13 290-1
St.-Basile, N.B. F2 275
St.-Basile-le-Grand*, Que. I12 290-1
St.-Basile-Sud*, Que. I3 290-1
St. Benedict, Kans. C13 108-9
St. Benedict, Sask. K7 294-5
St.-Benjamin*, Que. H16 290-1
St. Bernard, La. D15 168-9
St. Bernard, Nebr. F12 124-5
St. Bernard, O. K13 132-3
St.-Bernard*, Que. G12 290-1
St. Bernard, co., La. I10 168-9
St.-Bernard-sur-Mer*, Que. D12 290-1
St. Bernard's, Nfld. O10 278-9
St. Bernice, Ind. H4 100-1
St. Bethlehem, Tenn. F5 188-9
St.-Boniface-de-Shawinigan*, Que. G9 290-1
St. Bonifacius, Minn. B9 116-7
St. Bride's, Nfld. O10 278-9
St. Brieux, Sask. K8 294-5
St.-Bruno, Que. C11 290-1
St.-Bruno-de-Montarville*, Que. I12 290-1
St.-Camille, Que. G13 290-1
St.-Casimir, Que. G10 290-1
St. Catharine, Ky. D4 164-5
St. Catharines, Ont. D15 284-5
St.-Césaire*, Que. I13 290-1
St. Charles, Ark. G9 150-1
St. Charles, Ida. O11 218-9
St. Charles, Ill. M1 96-7
St. Charles, Ia. H7 104-5
St. Charles, Ky. I5 164-5
St. Charles, Mich. F2 112-3
St. Charles, Minn. O8 116-7
St. Charles, Mo. E10 120-1
St.-Charles, Que. G12 290-1
St. Charles, S.C. D12 184-5
St. Charles, S. Dak. I11 136-7
St. Charles, Va. J2 196-7
St. Charles, co., La. I9 168-9
St. Charles, co., Mo. E9 120-1
St.-Charles-de-Drummond*, Que. I14 290-1
St.-Charles-de-Mandeville, Que. H12 290-1
St. Chrysostome, P.E.I. D4 287
St.-Chrysostome*, Que. J12 290-1
St. Clair, Ala. I7 146-7
St. Clair, Mich. H8 112-3
St. Clair, Minn. O5 116-7
St. Clair, Mo. D13 120-1
St. Clair, Pa. H12 84-5
St. Clair, Tenn. G14 188-9
St. Clair, co., Ala. E7 146-7
St. Clair, co., Ill. L6 96-7
St. Clair, co., Mich. I15 112-3
St. Clair, co., Mo. F4 120-1
St. Clair Beach, Ont. F10 284-5
St. Clair Shores, Mich. J7 112-3
St. Clair Springs, Ala. E7 146-7
St. Clairsville, O. F11 132-3
St. Claude, Man. J13 272-3
St. Clements*, Ont. J8 284-5
St. Cloud, Fla. G7 156-7
St. Cloud, Minn. K5 116-7

St. Cloud, Wis. G4 140-1
St.-Coeur-de-Marie, Que. C11 290-1
St. Columbans, Nebr. J3 124-5
St.-Côme, Que. H12 290-1
St.-Constant*, Que. J12 290-1
St. Croix, co., Wis. E7 140-1
St. Croix Falls, Wis. D7 140-1
St. Croix R., Minn. M7 116-7
St.-Cyprien, Que. J4 290-1
St.-Cyprien, Que. D15 290-1
St.-Cyrille*, Que. I14 290-1
St.-Cyrille-de-L'Islet*, Que. E13 290-1
St.-Damase*, Que. I13 290-1
St.-Damien-de-Buckland, Que. G12 290-1
St. David, Ariz. L9 206-7
St. David, Ill. F6 96-7
St. David, Me. A8 64-5
St.-David-de-Falardeau, Que. B11 290-1
St.-David-de-l'Auberivière*, Que. J4 290-1
St.-Denis, Que. I13 290-1
St.-Dominique*, Que. I13 290-1
St.-Donat-de-Montcalm*, Que. H11 290-1
St.-Donat-de-Rimouski, Que. C15 290-1
St. Donatus, Ia. E15 104-5
St.-Édouard-de-Kent, N.B. G7 275
St. Edward, Nebr. F12 124-5
St. Edward, P.E.I. B3 287
St. Eleanors, P.E.I. E5 287
St. Elias Mts., Y.T. C1 297
St.-Élie, Que. I3 290-1
St. Elizabeth, Mo. F7 120-1
St. Elmo, Ala. N2 146-7
St. Elmo, Ill. J9 96-7
St.-Elzéar*, Que. I1 290-1
St. Émile*, Que. F11 290-1
St.-Éphrem-de-Tring, Que. H16 290-1
St.-Épiphane, Que. D14 290-1
St.-Esprit, Que. I12 290-1
St.-Étienne-de-Lauzon*, Que. G11 290-1
St.-Étienne-des-Grès*, Que. G9 290-1
St. Eugene*, Ont. H16 284-5
St.-Eugène, Que. F13 290-1
St. Eustache*, Man. I13 272-3
St.-Eustache, Que. I12 290-1
St.-Fabien, Que. C15 290-1
St.-Félicien, Que. C10 290-1
St. Felix*, P.E.I. B4 287
St.-Félix-de-Valois, Que. H12 290-1
St.-Féréol-les-Neiges, Que. F12 290-1
St.-Fidèle, Que. E13 290-1
St.-Flavien, Que. G11 290-1
St. Florian, Ala. A4 146-7
St. Francis, Ark. A12 150-1
St. Francis, Kans. D1 108-9
St. Francis, Ky. E3 164-5
St. Francis, Me. B7 64-5
St. Francis*, Minn. L6 116-7
St. Francis, S. Dak. I7 136-7
St. Francis, Wis. J5 140-1
St. Francis, co., Ark. E10 150-1
St. Francisville, Ill. K11 96-7
St. Francisville, La. G7 168-9
St. Francois, co., Mo. G10 120-1
St.-François-d'Assise, Que. I5 290-1
St.-Francois-de-Madawaska*, N.B. F1 275
St.-Francois-du-Lac, Que. H13 290-1
St. Francois Xavier*, Man. J3 272-3
St. Front, Sask. K8 294-5
St.-Fulgence*, Que. C12 290-1
St. Gabriel, La. B10 168-9
St.-Gabriel, Que. H12 290-1
St.-Gédéon, Que. C10 290-1
St.-Gédéon, Que. I16 290-1
St. George, Alaska G6 254-5
St. George, Ga. O9 160-1
St. George, Kans. E12 108-9
St. George, Me. L6 64-5
St. George, Man. H15 272-3
St. George, Mo. C15 120-1
St. George, N.B. J4 275
St. George, N.Y. F13 80-1
St. George*, Ont. D13 284-5
St. George, S.C. G11 184-5
St. George, Ut. N3 242-3
St. George*, Vt. E4 90-1
St. George, W. Va. D16 200-1
St. George Island, Md. I11 172-3
St. Georges, Del. C3 153
St. George's, Nfld. N7 278-9
St.-Georges*, Que. G9 290-1
St.-Georges, Que. H16 290-1
St.-Georges-de-Cacouna, Que. D14 290-1
St. Georges Hill*, Sask. F5 294-5
St.-Georges-Ouest*, Que. H16 290-1
St.-Gérard*, Que. I13 290-1
St. Germain, Wis. C12 140-1
St.-Germain-de-Grantham*, Que. I14 290-1
St.-Gervais*, Que. F12 290-1
St.-Gilles*, Que. G10 290-1
St.-Grégoire*, Que. J12 290-1
St.-Grégoire-de-Greenlay, Que. I15 290-1
St. Gregor*, Sask. K8 294-5
St.-Guillaume, Que. I13 290-1
St. Hedwig, Tex. J3 192-3
St. Helen, Mich. G13 112-3
St. Helena, Calif. A7 210-1
St. Helena, Nebr. C13 124-5
St. Helena, co., La. G8 168-9
St. Helena Sound, S.C. J12 184-5
St. Helens, Ky. H13 164-5
St. Helens, Ore. B6 238-9
St.-Henri*, Que. J12 290-1
St. Henry, O. E3 132-3
St. Hilaire, Minn. F2 116-7
St.-Hilaire, N.B. F2 275
St.-Hilarion, Que. E12 290-1
St.-Honoré, Que. I16 290-1
St.-Honoré-de-Témiscouata, Que. E14 290-1
St.-Hubert*, Que. I12 290-1
St.-Hubert-de-Témiscouata, Que. D14 290-1
St.-Hugues, Que. I13 290-1
St.-Hyacinthe, Que. I13 290-1
Saint-Hyacinthe, co., Que. I13 290-1
St. Ignace, Mich. D13 112-3
St.-Ignace, N.B. G6 275
St. Ignace Isl., Ont. F4 284-5
St. Ignatius, Mont. D3 222-3
St.-Irénée*, N.B. E6 275
St.-Isidore, N.B. E6 275
St.-Isidore, Que. G11 290-1
St.-Isidore-de-Laprairie*, Que. J12 290-1
St. Isidore de Prescott, Ont. H16 284-5
St. Jacob, Ill. K7 96-7
St. Jacobs, Ont. D13 284-5
St.-Jacques, N.B. E2 275
St.-Jacques, Que. H12 290-1
St. Jacques-Coomb's Cove*, Nfld. O9 278-9
St. James, Ark. C8 150-1
St. James, La. C11 168-9
St. James, Md. B7 172-3
St. James, Minn. O4 116-7
St. James, Mo. G8 120-1
St. James, Nebr. D13 124-5
St. James, N.Y. J12 80-1
St. James, co., La. H8 168-9
St.-Jean, Que. J12 290-1
Saint-Jean, co., Que. J12 290-1
St. Jean Baptiste, Man. K14 272-3
St.-Jean-Baptiste-de-Restigouche, N.B. E3 275
St.-Jean-Baptiste-de-Rouville*, Que. J3 290-1
St.-Jean-Chrysostome*, Que. G10 290-1
St.-Jean-de-Boischatel, Que. F11 290-1
St.-Jean-de-Dieu, Que. D14 290-1
St.-Jean-de-Matha*, Que. H12 290-1
St.-Jean-Port-Joli, Que. F13 290-1
St.-Jean-sur-Lac*, Que. I2 290-1
St.-Jérôme, Que. I11 290-1
St. Jo*, Tex. D8 192-3
St.-Joachim, Que. F12 290-1
St. Joe, Ark. B6 150-1
St. Joe, Ida. D3 218-9
St. Joe, Ind. B12 100-1
St. John, Ind. B4 100-1
St. John, Kans. H8 108-9
St. John, Me. A7 64-5
St. John, Mo. B15 120-1
St. John, N.B. J5 275
St. John, N. Dak. B9 128-9
St. John, Ut. F5 242-3
St. John, Wash. G15 246-7
St. John, co., N.B. I6 275
St. John R., N.B. H2 275
St. John Station, Ut. F5 242-3
St. John the Baptist, co., La. H8 168-9
St. Johns, Ariz. G11 206-7
St. Johns, Mich. G1 112-3
St. John's, Nfld. N11 278-9
St. Johns, co., Fla. C11 156-7
St. John's Area*, Nfld. N11 278-9
St. Johnsbury, Vt. E8 90-1
St. Johnsville, N.Y. E9 80-1
St. Joseph, Ill. G10 96-7
St. Joseph, Ind. O3 100-1
St. Joseph, Kans. D10 108-9
St. Joseph, La. D7 168-9
St. Joseph, Man. K14 272-3
St. Joseph, Mich. J11 112-3
St. Joseph, Minn. K5 116-7
St. Joseph, Mo. C2 120-1
St.-Joseph, N.B. H7 275
St. Joseph, Tenn. D6 188-9
St. Joseph, Wis. H10 140-1
St. Joseph, co., Ind. A8 100-1
St. Joseph, co., Mich. K12 112-3
St.-Joseph-de-Beauce*, Que. H16 290-1
St.-Joseph-de-Sorel*, Que. H13 290-1
St.-Joseph-du-Moine, N.S. B10 281
St.-Jovite, Que. H11 290-1
St.-Juste-de-Bretenières, Que. G13 290-1
St.-Lambert*, Que. I13 290-1
St.-Lambert-de-Lévis*, Que. G11 290-1
St. Landry, La. F5 168-9
St. Landry, co., La. G5 168-9
St. Laurent, Man. I13 272-3
St.-Laurent*, Que. I12 290-1
St.-Laurent-d'Orléans*, Que. I4 290-1
St. Lawrence, Nfld. O9 278-9
St. Lawrence*, Pa. I13 84-5
St. Lawrence, S. Dak. E11 136-7
St. Lawrence, co., N.Y. B9 80-1
St. Lawrence R., Que. B15 290-1
St. Lazare, Man. H9 272-3
St.-Lazare, N.B. G7 275
St.-Lazare*, Que. G12 290-1
St.-Lazare-de-Vaudreuil*, Que. J11 290-1
St. Leo, Fla. G3 156-7
St. Leo, Kans. J8 108-9
St. Leo, Minn. M2 116-7
St.-Léolin, N.B. E6 275
St. Leon, Ind. J12 100-1
St. Leon, Man. K12 272-3
St.-Léon-de-Standon, Que. G12 290-1
St.-Léon-le-Grand, Que. C16 290-1
St. Leonard, Md. G11 172-3
St. Leonard, N.B. F2 275
St.-Léonard*, Que. I12 290-1
St.-Léonard-d'Aston*, Que. H14 290-1
St.-Léonard-de-Portneuf*, Que. G10 290-1
St.-Liboire, Que. I13 290-1
St. Libory, Nebr. H11 124-5
St. Louis, Mich. E1 112-3
St. Louis, Mo. E10 120-1
St. Louis, Okla. G12 234-5
St. Louis, P.E.I. B4 287
St. Louis, Sask. J7 294-5
St. Louis, co., Minn. H7 116-7
St. Louis, co., Mo. E10 120-1
St. Louis Crossing, Ind. J9 100-1
St.-Louis-de-Kent, N.B. G6 275
St.-Louis-de-Terrebonne*, Que. H11 290-1
St.-Louis-du-Ha! Ha!, Que. E14 290-1
St. Louis Park, Minn. B10 116-7
St. Louisville, O. F8 132-3
St.-Luc*, Que. J12 290-1
St.-Luc-de-Laval*, Que. G6 290-1
St.-Luc-de-Matane*, Que. B16 290-1
St. Lucas, Ia. C12 104-5
St. Lucie, Fla. A15 156-7
St. Lucie, co., Fla. G13 156-7
St.-Ludger, Que. B10 290-1
St. Lunaire-Griquet*, Nfld. J9 278-9
St.-Magloire, Que. G13 290-1
St. Malo, Man. K14 272-3
St.-Marc-des-Carrières*, Que. G10 290-1
St. Maries, Ida. D3 218-9
St. Marks, Fla. C7 156-7
St. Marks, Ga. H3 160-1
St. Martin, Man. F12 272-3
St. Martin, Md. G16 172-3
St. Martin, Minn. L4 116-7
St. Martin, co., La. H6 168-9
St.-Martin-de-Restigouche, N.B. E3 275
St. Martins*, Mo. F7 120-1
St. Martins, N.B. J6 275
St. Martinville, La. H6 168-9
St. Mary, Ky. E3 164-5
St. Mary, Mont. B5 222-3
St. Mary, Nebr. I15 124-5
St. Mary, co., La. I6 168-9
St. Mary-of-the-Woods, Ind. I4 100-1
St. Marys, Alaska E8 254-5
St. Marys, Ga. O10 160-1
St. Marys, Ia. H7 104-5
St. Marys, Kans. E13 108-9
St. Marys, Mo. G11 120-1
St. Mary's, Nfld. O11 278-9
St. Marys, O. E3 132-3
St. Mary's, Ont. D12 284-5
St. Marys, Pa. E6 84-5
St. Marys, W. Va. D4 200-1
St. Marys, co., Md. H11 172-3
St. Mary's Bay, N.S. F4 281
St. Marys City, Md. H12 172-3
St. Marys Point*, Minn. M7 116-7
St.-Mathias*, Que. J13 290-1
St. Matthews, Ky. A2 164-5
St. Matthews, S.C. F11 184-5
St. Maurice, La. D3 168-9
Saint-Maurice, co., Que. I2 290-1
St. Meinrad, Ind. N6 100-1
St.-Méthode-de-Frontenac*, Que. H16 290-1
St. Michael, Alaska E8 254-5
St. Michael, Minn. A9 116-7
St. Michael*, Pa. I5 84-5
St. Michaels, Ariz. D11 206-7
St. Michaels, Md. F12 172-3
St.-Michel-de-Bellechasse*, Que. F12 290-1
St.-Michel-des-Saints, Que. I3 290-1
St.-Moise C16 290-1
St.-Narcisse*, Que. G9 290-1
St.-Narcisse-de-Rimouski, Que. C15 290-1
St.-Nazaire*, Que. G4 290-1
St. Nazianz, Wis. F5 140-1
St.-Nicéphore*, Que. J4 290-1
St. Nicholas, P.E.I. E4 287
St.-Nicolas*, Que. J4 290-1
St.-Noël, Que. C16 290-1
St.-Odilon, Que. H16 290-1
St. Olaf, Ia. C13 104-5
St.-Omer*, Que. I5 290-1
St. Onge, S. Dak. E2 136-7
St.-Ours, Que. I13 290-1
St.-Pacôme, Que. E13 290-1
St.-Pamphile, Que. F13 290-1
St. Paris, O. F4 132-3
St.-Pascal, Que. E13 290-1
St.-Patrice-de-Beaurivage*, Que. J4 290-1
St. Paul, Alaska G6 254-5
St. Paul, Alta. I9 264-5
St. Paul, Ark. C3 150-1
St. Paul, Ind. I10 100-1
St. Paul, Ia. J13 104-5
St. Paul, Kans. J15 108-9
St. Paul, Ky. E14 164-5
St. Paul, Minn. M7 116-7
St. Paul, Nebr. G11 124-5
St.-Paul, N.B. H6 275
St. Paul*, Ore. D6 238-9
St.-Paul*, Que. I12 290-1
St. Paul, S.C. F12 184-5
St. Paul, Va. J3 196-7
St.-Paul-de-Montminy*, Que. F12 290-1
St.-Paul-l'Ermite*, Que. H12 290-1
St. Paul Park, Minn. B11 116-7
St.-Paulin*, Que. G9 290-1
St. Pauls, Mont. C10 222-3
St. Pauls, Nfld. L7 278-9
St. Pauls, N.C. F10 180-1
St. Peter, Kans. E5 108-9
St. Peter, Minn. N5 116-7
St. Peters, Mo. B14 120-1
St. Peters, P.E.I. E9 287
St. Petersburg, Fla. F10 156-7
St. Petersburg Beach, Fla. I2 156-7
St.-Philippe-de-Néri, Que. E13 290-1
St. Phillip, Mont. E16 222-3
St.-Pie, Que. J13 290-1
St. Pierre*, Man. J14 272-3
St.-Pierre*, Que. I12 290-1
St.-Pierre*, Que. H13 290-1
St.-Pierre-d'Orleans*, Que. F11 290-1
St.-Polycarpe, Que. J11 290-1
St.-Pons*, N.B. E6 275
St.-Prime, Que. C10 290-1
St.-Prosper, Que. J4 290-1
St.-Quentin, N.B. E3 275
St.-Raphaël, Que. G12 290-1
St.-Raphaël-Sur-Mer, N.B. E7 275
St.-Raymond, Que. F10 290-1
St.-Rédempteur*, Que. I12 290-1
St. Regis, Mont. D2 222-3
St. Regis Park*, Ky. G9 164-5
St.-Rémi*, Que. I12 290-1
St. Robert, Mo. G7 120-1
St.-Roch, Que. I13 290-1
St.-Roch-de-l'Achigan*, Que. I12 290-1
St.-Romuald-d'Etchemin, Que. G11 290-1
St. Rosa, Minn. K4 116-7
St. Rose, La. D13 168-9
St.-Samuel-de-Gayhurst*, Que. I16 290-1
St.-Sauveur, N.B. E6 275
St.-Sauveur-des-Monts*, Que. I12 290-1
St.-Siméon, Que. D13 290-1
St.-Siméon-de-Bonaventure, Que. I6 290-1
St. Simons Isl., Ga. M10 160-1
St. Simons Island, Ga. N11 160-1
St. Stephen, N.B. J3 275
St. Stephens, Ala. K3 146-7
St. Stephens, Minn. K5 116-7
St. Stephens, Nebr. J11 124-5
St. Stephens, S.C. G13 184-5
St. Stephens, Wyo. F9 250-1
St. Stephens Church, Va. H13 196-7
St.-Sulpice*, Que. I12 290-1
St.-Sylvestre, Que. H16 290-1
St. Tammany, La. A15 168-9
St. Tammany, co., La. H9 168-9
St. Thomas*, Mo. F7 120-1
St. Thomas, N. Dak. C13 128-9
St. Thomas, Ont. E12 284-5
St.-Thomas-d'Aquin*, Que. I13 290-1
St.-Thomas-de-Joliette*, Que. H12 290-1
St.-Thomas-Didyme, Que. B9 290-1
St.-Timothée*, Que. J11 290-1
St.-Tite, Que. G9 290-1
St.-Tite-des-Caps, Que. F12 290-1
St.-Ulric, Que. B16 290-1
St.-Urbain-de-Charlevoix, Que. E12 290-1
St.-Victor*, Que. H16 290-1
St. Victor, Sask. O7 294-5
St. Vincent*, Alta. I9 264-5
St. Vincent, Ark. D6 150-1
St. Vincent, Minn. D1 116-7
St. Vincent's, Nfld. O11 278-9
St. Vincent's-St. Stephen-Peter's River*, Nfld. N11 278-9
St. Vrain, N. Mex. G11 230-1
St. Walburg, Sask. I4 294-5
St.-Wilfred*, N.B. F6 275
St. Williams*, Ont. E13 284-5
St. Xavier, Mont. H11 222-3
St.-Zacharie, Que. J4 290-1
St.-Zénon, Que. I3 290-1
St.-Zotique*, Que. J11 290-1
Ste.-Adelaide-de-Pabos*, Que. I6 290-1
Ste.-Adèle*, Que. H11 290-1
Ste. Agathe, Man. J14 272-3

Ste.-Agathe, Que. H15 290-1
Ste.-Agathe-des-Monts, Que. H11 290-1
Ste.-Agathe-Sud*, Que. J2 290-1
Ste. Amelie, Man. H11 272-3
Ste.-Anastasie*, Que. G10 290-1
Ste.-Angèle-de-Mérici, Que. C16 290-1
Ste. Anne, Man. J15 272-3
Ste.-Anne-de-Beaupré, Que. F12 290-1
Ste.-Anne-de-Bellevue*, Que. I12 290-1
Ste.-Anne-de-Madawaska, N.B. F2 275
Ste.-Anne-de-Sorel*, Que. H13 290-1
Ste.-Anne-des-Monts, Que. H5 290-1
Ste.-Anne-des-Plaines*, Que. I12 290-1
Ste.-Anne-du-Lac, Que. I2 290-1
Ste.-Aurélie*, Que. H16 290-1
Ste.-Blandine, Que. C16 290-1
Ste.-Catherine, Que. F11 290-1
Ste.-Catherine*, Que. J12 290-1
Ste.-Claire-de-Joliette, Que. G12 290-1
Ste.-Croix, Que. G10 290-1
Ste.-Emélie-de-l'Énergie, Que. H12 290-1
Ste.-Famille, Que. F12 290-1
Ste.-Félicité, Que. H5 290-1
Ste.-Foy, Que. G11 290-1
Ste. Genevieve*, Man. K4 272-3
Ste. Genevieve, Mo. G11 120-1
Ste.-Geneviève*, Que. I12 290-1
Ste. Genevieve, co., Mo. G10 120-1
Ste.-Geneviève-de-Batiscan, Que. G9 290-1
Ste.-Hedwidge-de-Roberval, Que. C10 290-1
Ste.-Hélène-de-Kamouraska*, Que. E13 290-1
Ste.-Hénédine, Que. G12 290-1
Ste.-Jeanne-d'Arc, Que. B10 290-1
Ste.-Julie*, Que. I12 290-1
Ste.-Julienne, Que. H12 290-1
Ste.-Justine, Que. J4 290-1
Ste.-Louise, Que. F13 290-1
Ste.-Madeleine*, Que. I12 290-1
Ste.-Marguerite*, Que. H11 290-1
Ste.-Marie, Que. H16 290-1
Ste.-Marie-Sud-Ouest*, Que. H16 290-1
Ste.-Marie-sur-Mer*, N.B. E7 275
Ste.-Marthe-sur-le-Lac*, Que. I11 290-1
Ste.-Martine, Que. J12 290-1
Ste.-Monique, Que. B10 290-1
Ste.-Perpétue, Que. F13 290-1
Ste.-Pudentienne, Que. J13 290-1
Ste.-Rosalie, Que. I13 290-1
Ste. Rose du Lac, Man. G11 272-3
Ste.-Rose-Gloucester*, N.B. E6 275
Ste.-Thècle, Que. G9 290-1
Ste.-Thérèse*, Que. I12 290-1
Ste.-Therese-de-Colombier, Que. B15 290-1
Sakonnet, R.I. G7 87
Salaberry-de-Valleyfield, Que. J11 290-1
Salado, Ark. C8 150-1
Salamanca, N.Y. G2 80-1
Salamonia, Ind. F12 100-1
Salduro, Ut. E3 242-3
Sale City, Ga. M5 160-1
Sale Creek, Tenn. J11 188-9
Salem, Ala. H10 146-7
Salem, Ark. A8 150-1
Salem, Ark. G3 150-1
Salem, Conn. F12 60-1
Salem, Ida. L10 218-9
Salem, Ill. K8 96-7
Salem, Ind. M8 100-1
Salem, Ia. J12 104-5
Salem, Ky. I3 164-5
Salem, Me. I3 64-5
Salem, Md. G13 172-3
Salem, Mass. C12 68-9
Salem, Mich. J4 112-3
Salem, Mo. G8 120-1
Salem, Nebr. J16 124-5
Salem, N.H. O8 72-3
Salem, N.J. L1 76-7
Salem, N. Mex. K5 230-1
Salem, N.Y. E12 80-1
Salem, O. D11 132-3
Salem, Ont. C13 284-5
Salem, Ore. D6 238-9
Salem, S.C. B5 184-5
Salem, S.C. E14 184-5
Salem, S. Dak. G14 136-7
Salem, Ut. G6 242-3
Salem, Va. I8 196-7
Salem, W. Va. E5 200-1
Salem, Wis. K4 140-1
Salem, co., N.J. L1 76-7
Salem Depot, N.H. O8 72-3
Salem Neck, Mass. A12 68-9
Salemburg, N.C. K8 180-1
Salerno, Fla. B16 156-7
Salesville*, Ark. B7 150-1
Salida, Calif. C10 210-1
Salida, Colo. G10 214-5
Salina, Kans. F10 108-9
Salina, Okla. D15 234-5
Salina, Ut. I6 242-3
Salinas, Calif. K3 210-1
Saline, La. C3 168-9
Saline, Mich. K4 112-3
Saline, co., Ark. F6 150-1
Saline, co., Ill. N9 96-7
Saline, co., Kans. F10 108-9
Saline, co., Mo. D5 120-1
Saline, co., Nebr. I13 124-5
Saline City, Ind. J5 100-1
Salineville, O. D11 132-3
Salisbury, Conn. B4 60-1
Salisbury, Md. G14 172-3
Salisbury, Mass. A12 68-9
Salisbury, Mo. C6 120-1
Salisbury, N.B. H6 275
Salisbury, N.H. L6 72-3
Salisbury, N.C. D8 180-1
Salisbury, Ore. D14 238-9
Salisbury, Vt. H4 90-1
Salisbury Beach, Mass. A12 68-9
Salisbury Heights, N.H. L5 72-3
Salitpa, Ala. K3 146-7
Salix, Ia. E1 104-5
Salkum, Wash. H7 246-7
Salley, S.C. F9 184-5
Sallis, Miss. G7 176-7
Sallisaw, Okla. F16 234-5
Salmo, B.C. K10 268-9
Salmon, Ida. I7 218-9
Salmon Arm, B.C. I8 268-9
Salmon Beach, N.B. E6 275
Salmon Falls, N.H. M9 72-3
Salmon R., Ida. J6 218-9
Salmon River*, N.S. D7 281
Salmon River, N.S. F4 281
Salome, Ariz. H3 206-7
Salsbury Cove, Me. K8 64-5
Salt Fork, Okla. C10 234-5
Salt Lake, co., Ut. F6 242-3
Salt Lake City, Ut. E6 242-3
Salt Lick, Ky. G13 164-5
Salt Rock, W. Va. H11 200-1
Salt R., Ariz. H8 206-7
Salt Springs, Fla. D11 156-7
Salt Wells, Nev. F4 226-7
Salt Wells, Wyo. I8 250-1
Saltair*, B.C. J5 268-9
Saltcoats, Sask. M10 294-5
Salter Path, N.C. F14 180-1
Salters, S.C. F13 184-5
Saltery Bay, B.C. J6 268-9
Saltese, Mont. D1 222-3
Saltillo, Ind. L8 100-1
Saltillo, Miss. C9 176-7
Saltillo, Tenn. D5 188-9
Salton Sea, Calif. O10 210-1
Saltpetre, W. Va. J9 200-1
Saltsburg, Pa. H3 84-5
Saltville, Va. J4 196-7
Saluda, N.C. E4 180-1
Saluda, S.C. E8 184-5
Saluda, Va. H14 196-7
Saluda, co., S.C. D8 184-5
Salvador, Sask. K4 294-5
Salvisa, Ky. C5 164-5
Salvo, N.C. D16 180-1
Salyersville, Ky. H14 164-5
Samantha, Ala. F4 146-7
Samaria, Ida. O9 218-9
Samaria, S.C. E9 184-5
Samburg, Tenn. A2 188-9
Samish, Wash. C8 246-7
Samoset, Fla. J2 156-7
Sampit, S.C. G14 184-5
Sample, Ky. G7 164-5
Samples, Ark. G7 150-1
Sampson, co., N.C. E11 180-1
Sams Valley, Ore. J6 238-9
Samson, Ala. M8 146-7
Samsonville, N.S. C11 281
Samtown, La. E4 168-9
Samuels, Ida. B3 218-9
Samuels, Ky. C3 164-5
San Acacia, N. Mex. H5 230-1
San Acacio, Colo. J11 214-5
San Andreas, Calif. B11 210-1
San Angelo, Tex. F6 192-3
San Anselmo, Calif. B7 210-1
San Antonio, Fla. G3 156-7
San Antonio, N. Mex. H5 230-1
San Antonio, Tex. H7 192-3
San Augustine, Tex. F11 192-3
San Augustine, co., Tex. F11 192-3
San Benito, Tex. K8 192-3
San Benito, co., Calif. K4 210-1
San Bernardino, Calif. N8 210-1
San Bernardino, co., Calif. M9 210-1
San Bruno, Calif. C7 210-1
San Carlos, Ariz. I9 206-7
San Carlos, Calif. D7 210-1
San Carlos Res., Ariz. I9 206-7
San Clara, Man. F9 272-3
San Clemente, Calif. I9 210-1
San Cristobal, N. Mex. C7 230-1
San De Fuca, Wash. F1 246-7
San Diego, Calif. O8 210-1
San Diego, Tex. I8 192-3
San Diego, co., Calif. O9 210-1
San Dimas, Calif. N7 210-1
San Felipe Pueblo, N. Mex. E6 230-1
San Fernando, Calif. F8 210-1
San Fidel, N. Mex. F4 230-1
San Francisco, Calif. I3 210-1
San Francisco, co., Calif. I2 210-1
San Gabriel*, Calif. N7 210-1
San Geronimo, N. Mex. E8 230-1
San Ildefonso, N. Mex. D6 230-1
San Jacinto, Calif. H11 210-1
San Jacinto, Nev. A10 226-7
San Jacinto, co., Tex. G10 192-3
San Joaquin, Calif. K5 210-1
San Joaquin, co., Calif. I4 210-1
San Jon, N. Mex. F11 230-1
San Jose, Ariz. J11 206-7
San Jose, Calif. J3 210-1
San Jose, Ill. G7 96-7
San Jose, N. Mex. E7 230-1
San Juan, Colo. J12 214-5
San Juan, N. Mex. E7 230-1
San Juan, N. Mex. K3 230-1
San Juan*, Tex. K8 192-3
San Juan, co., Colo. I7 214-5
San Juan, co., N. Mex. C3 230-1
San Juan, co., Ut. K10 242-3
San Juan, co., Wash. D7 246-7
San Juan Bautista, Calif. J4 210-1
San Juan Capistrano, Calif. H9 210-1
San Juan Pueblo, N. Mex. D6 230-1
San Leandro, Calif. C8 210-1
San Lorenzo, Calif. C8 210-1
San Lorenzo, N. Mex. K3 230-1
San Luis, Ariz. K1 206-7
San Luis, Ariz. L6 206-7
San Luis, Colo. J11 214-5
San Luis, N. Mex. E5 230-1
San Luis Obispo, Calif. L5 210-1
San Luis Obispo, co., Calif. M5 210-1
San Manuel, Ariz. K9 206-7
San Marcos*, Calif. O8 210-1
San Marcos, Tex. G8 192-3
San Marino*, Calif. G8 210-1
San Martin*, Calif. J4 210-1
San Mateo, Calif. D7 210-1
San Mateo, Fla. D11 156-7
San Mateo, N. Mex. E4 230-1
San Mateo, co., Calif. J3 210-1
San Miguel, Ariz. M7 206-7
San Miguel, N. Mex. E8 230-1
San Miguel, N. Mex. L5 230-1
San Miguel, co., Colo. H6 214-5
San Miguel, co., N. Mex. E9 230-1
San Pablo, Calif. B7 210-1
San Patricio, N. Mex. I8 230-1
San Patricio, co., Tex. I8 192-3
San Pedra, Colo. J11 214-5
San Pierre, Ind. C6 100-1
San Rafael, Calif. B7 210-1
San Rafael, N. Mex. F3 230-1
San Ramon Village*, Calif. I3 210-1
San Remo*, N.Y. J12 80-1
San Saba, Tex. F7 192-3
San Saba, co., Tex. F7 192-3
San Simon, Ariz. K11 206-7
San Xavier, Ariz. L8 206-7
San Ysidro, N. Mex. E5 230-1
Sanborn, Ia. B3 104-5
Sanborn, Minn. N4 116-7
Sanborn, N. Dak. G12 128-9
Sanborn, Wis. B10 140-1
Sanborn, co., S. Dak. F13 136-7
Sanbornton, N.H. K6 72-3
Sanbornville, N.H. K9 72-3
Sand City*, Calif. K3 210-1
Sand Creek, Okla. C10 234-5
Sand Creek, Wis. E8 140-1
Sand Draw, Wyo. G9 250-1
Sand Fork, W. Va. F5 200-1
Sand Lake*, Alaska F11 254-5
Sand Lake, Mich. I12 112-3
Sand Lick, Ky. A6 164-5
Sand Pass, Nev. E2 226-7
Sand Point, Alaska I8 254-5
Sand Ridge*, N.Y. E7 80-1
Sand Ridge, W. Va. F4 200-1
Sand Rock, Ala. C9 146-7
Sand Springs, Mont. E12 222-3
Sand Springs, Okla. D13 234-5
Sandborn, Ind. L5 100-1
Sandcoulee, Mont. D7 222-3
Sanders, Ariz. E11 206-7
Sanders, Ida. E2 218-9
Sanders, Ky. E10 164-5
Sanders, Mont. F12 222-3
Sanders, Tenn. K9 188-9
Sanders, co., Mont. C1 222-3
Sanderson, Tex. G4 192-3
Sandersville, Ga. I7 160-1
Sandersville, Miss. J9 176-7
Sandfly, Ga. K11 160-1
Sandford, Ind. I4 100-1
Sandgap, Ky. I12 164-5
Sandgate, Vt. M4 90-1
Sandgates, Md. G11 172-3
Sandhill, Miss. H7 176-7
Sandia, N. Mex. F6 230-1
Sandia Park, N. Mex. F6 230-1
Sandia Pueblo, N. Mex. F6 230-1
Sandilands, Man. K15 272-3
Sandisfield, Mass. E2 68-9
Sandlake, Ore. C4 238-9
Sandoval, Ill. K8 96-7
Sandoval, co., N. Mex. E5 230-1
Sandown, N.H. N8 72-3
Sandpoint, Ida. B3 218-9
Sands Point*, N.Y. J11 80-1
Sandspit, B.C. G2 268-9
Sandston, Va. E1 196-7
Sandstone, Minn. J7 116-7
Sandstone, W. Va. I5 200-1
Sandtown, Del. G3 153
Sandusky, Ind. J10 100-1
Sandusky, Mich. E7 112-3
Sandusky, O. B7 132-3
Sandusky, co., O. C6 132-3
Sandusky Bay, O. B7 132-3
Sandusky South*, O. B7 132-3
Sandwich, Ill. C9 96-7
Sandwich, Mass. G14 68-9
Sandwich, N.H. I7 72-3
Sandy, Nev. N9 226-7
Sandy, Ore. C7 238-9
Sandy, Pa. F5 84-5
Sandy Bay, Sask. G10 294-5
Sandy Beach*, N.Y. E2 80-1
Sandy Bottom, Md. D12 172-3
Sandy City, Ut. F6 242-3
Sandy Cove*, Ont. B14 284-5
Sandy Cove Acres*, Ont. B14 284-5
Sandy Creek, Me. M7 64-5
Sandy Creek, N.Y. D7 80-1
Sandy Hook, Conn. G5 60-1
Sandy Hook, Ky. G14 164-5
Sandy Hook, Man. H14 272-3
Sandy Hook, Miss. M7 176-7
Sandy Hook, N.J. G11 76-7
Sandy Hook, Tenn. J5 188-9
Sandy Hook, Va. H11 196-7
Sandy Lake, Man. H10 272-3
Sandy Level, Va. J8 196-7
Sandy Point, Me. K7 64-5
Sandy Ridge, Ala. J7 146-7
Sandy Ridge, N.C. C8 180-1
Sandy River, Me. I2 64-5
Sandy River, S.C. C9 184-5
Sandy Spring, Md. G4 172-3
Sandy Springs, Ga. B11 160-1
Sandy Springs, S.C. C5 184-5
Sandyston*, N.J. B4 76-7
Sandyville, Ia. H8 104-5
Sandyville, W. Va. F3 200-1
Sanford, Ala. L7 146-7
Sanford, Colo. J10 214-5
Sanford, Fla. E12 156-7
Sanford, Me. N2 64-5
Sanford, Man. J14 272-3
Sanford, Mich. H13 112-3
Sanford, Miss. K8 176-7
Sanford, N.C. E10 180-1
Sanford, Va. G16 196-7
Sangamon, co., Ill. I7 96-7
Sanger, Calif. K6 210-1
Sanger, Tex. A13 192-3
Sangerville, Me. I5 64-5
Sangudo, Alta. I7 264-5
Sanibel, Fla. I11 156-7
Sanilac, co., Mich. H15 112-3
Sano, Nev. D2 226-7
Sanpete, co., Ut. I6 242-3
Sansom Park Village*, Tex. D8 192-3
Santa, Ida. E3 218-9
Santa Ana, Calif. H9 210-1
Santa Ana Air Facility*, Calif. O8 210-1
Santa Ana Pueblo, N. Mex. E6 230-1
Santa Anna, Tex. E7 192-3
Santa Barbara, Calif. M5 210-1
Santa Barbara, co., Calif. M5 210-1
Santa Barbara Channel, Calif. N5 210-1
Santa Catalina Isl., Calif. O7 210-1
Santa Clara, Calif. D8 210-1
Santa Clara, N. Mex. D6 230-1
Santa Clara, Ore. K1 238-9
Santa Clara, Ut. M3 242-3
Santa Clara, co., Calif. J3 210-1
Santa Claus, Ariz. E2 206-7
Santa Claus, Ga. K8 160-1
Santa Claus, Ind. O6 100-1
Santa Cruz, Ariz. I6 206-7
Santa Cruz, Calif. J3 210-1
Santa Cruz, N. Mex. D7 230-1
Santa Cruz, co., Ariz. M8 206-7
Santa Cruz, co., Calif. J3 210-1
Santa Fe, N. Mex. E7 230-1
Santa Fe, Tenn. I6 188-9
Santa Fe, co., N. Mex. E7 230-1
Santa Fe Springs*, Calif. G9 210-1
Santa Maria, Calif. M5 210-1
Santa Maria South*, Calif. M5 210-1
Santa Monica, Calif. G8 210-1
Santa Paula, Calif. F6 210-1
Santa Rita, Mont. B5 222-3
Santa Rita, N. Mex. K3 230-1
Santa Rosa, Calif. H2 210-1
Santa Rosa, Miss. N7 176-7
Santa Rosa, N. Mex. F9 230-1
Santa Rosa*, Tex. K8 192-3
Santa Rosa, co., Fla. B3 156-7
Santaquin, Ut. G6 242-3
Santee*, Calif. O8 210-1
Santee, Nebr. C12 124-5
Santee, S.C. F11 184-5
Santo Domingo Pueblo, N. Mex. E6 230-1
Santo Tomas, N. Mex. L5 230-1
Santuck, S.C. H6 184-5
Sapa, Miss. E8 176-7
Saponac, Me. I8 64-5
Sapphire, N.C. F3 180-1
Sappho, Wash. D5 246-7
Sappington*, Mo. E10 120-1
Sapulpa, Okla. D13 234-5
Saragossa, Ala. E5 146-7
Sarah, Miss. B6 176-7
Sarah, W. Va. H11 200-1
Sarah Ann, W. Va. K12 200-1
Saraland, Ala. M3 146-7
Saranac*, Mich. I12 112-3
Saranac Lake, N.Y. B10 80-1
Sarasota, Fla. G10 156-7
Sarasota, co., Fla. H10 156-7
Sarasota North*, Fla. G10 156-7

Sarasota South*, Fla. G10 156-7
Sarasota Southeast*, Fla. G10 156-7
Sarasota Springs*, Fla. G10 156-7
Saratoga, Ark. I3 150-1
Saratoga, Calif. D8 210-1
Saratoga, Ind. F12 100-1
Saratoga, N.C. D12 180-1
Saratoga, Wyo. J12 250-1
Saratoga, co., N.Y. E10 80-1
Saratoga Place*, Va. J14 196-7
Saratoga Springs, N.Y. E11 80-1
Sarben, Nebr. G6 124-5
Sarcoxie, Mo. I3 120-1
Sardinia, Ind. K10 100-1
Sardinia, O. I5 132-3
Sardinia, S.C. E13 184-5
Sardis, Ala. I6 146-7
Sardis, B.C. C16 268-9
Sardis, Ga. I10 160-1
Sardis, Ky. F12 164-5
Sardis, Miss. C6 176-7
Sardis, Okla. G15 234-5
Sardis, S.C. D13 184-5
Sardis, Tenn. C4 188-9
Sarepta, La. A2 168-9
Sarepta, Miss. D8 176-7
Sargeant, Minn. O7 116-7
Sargent, Ga. D8 160-1
Sargent, Nebr. F9 124-5
Sargent, co., N. Dak. J13 128-9
Sargents, Colo. G9 214-5
Sargentville, Me. L7 64-5
Sarita, Tex. J8 192-3
Sarles, N. Dak. B10 128-9
Sarnia, Ont. E10 284-5
Sarona, Wis. D8 140-1
Saronville, Nebr. I12 124-5
Sarpy, co., Nebr. G15 124-5
Sartell, Minn. K5 116-7
Sarto*, Man. K4 272-3
Sarton, W. Va. J5 200-1
Sasabe, Ariz. M7 206-7
Sasakwa, Okla. G13 234-5
Saseenos*, B.C. E4 268-9
Saskatchewan R., Sask. I10 294-5
Saskatoon, Sask. K6 294-5
Sassafras, Ky. I14 164-5
Sassafras, Md. C14 172-3
Sasser, Ga. L4 160-1
Satanta, Kans. J3 108-9
Satartia, Miss. H5 176-7
Satellite Beach, Fla. F13 156-7
Saticoy, Calif. F6 210-1
Satsop, Wash. G6 246-7
Satsuma, Ala. M3 146-7
Sauble Beach*, Ont. A12 284-5
Saucier, Miss. N8 176-7
Saugatuck, Conn. I4 60-1
Saugatuck, Mich. J11 112-3
Saugerties, N.Y. G11 80-1
Saugerties South*, N.Y. G11 80-1
Saugus, Mass. G5 68-9
Sauk, co., Wis. I12 140-1
Sauk Centre, Minn. K4 116-7
Sauk City, Wis. J12 140-1
Sauk Rapids, Minn. K5 116-7
Sauk Village, Ill. O4 96-7
Saukville, Wis. H5 140-1
Saulnierville, N.S. F4 281
Saulsbury, Tenn. K4 188-9
Sault-au-Mouton, Que. C14 290-1
Sault Ste. Marie, Mich. C13 112-3
Sault Ste. Marie, Ont. H6 284-5
Saumarez*, N.B. E6 275
Saunders, co., Nebr. G14 124-5
Saunderstown, R.I. G5 87
Saundersville, Tenn. G7 188-9
Sausalito, Calif. C7 210-1
Sautee-Nacoochee, Ga. D5 160-1
Savage, Md. G5 172-3
Savage, Minn. C10 116-7
Savage, Miss. B6 176-7
Savage, Mont. D16 222-3
Savageton, Wyo. D13 250-1
Savanna, Ill. B6 96-7
Savanna, Okla. G14 234-5
Savannah, Ga. K11 160-1
Savannah, Miss. N8 176-7
Savannah, Mo. B2 120-1
Savannah, N.Y. E6 80-1
Savannah, O. D8 132-3
Savannah, Tenn. D4 188-9
Savannah Beach, Ga. K12 160-1
Savannah R., Ga. E7 160-1
Savant Lake, Ont. E3 284-5
Savery, Wyo. K11 250-1
Savona, B.C. I8 268-9
Savona, N.Y. G5 80-1
Savonburg, Kans. I15 108-9
Savoonga, Alaska D7 254-5
Savoy, Ill. G10 96-7
Savoy, Mass. C3 68-9
Savoy, Mont. B10 222-3
Savoy*, Tex. C9 192-3
Savoy Center, Mass. B3 68-9
Sawmill, Ariz. D11 206-7
Sawmill, Ariz. H9 206-7
Sawpit, Colo. H7 214-5
Sawyer, Kans. J8 108-9
Sawyer, Mich. K11 112-3
Sawyer, N. Dak. D7 128-9
Sawyer, Okla. I15 234-5
Sawyer, co., Wis. C9 140-1
Sawyerville, Ala. H4 146-7
Sawyerville, Que. J15 290-1
Saxapahaw, N.C. H5 180-1
Saxe, Va. J10 196-7
Saxeville, Wis. F2 140-1
Saxis, Va. G15 196-7
Saxman*, Alaska H16 254-5
Saxman, Kans. H9 108-9
Saxon, S.C. F4 184-5
Saxon, Wis. B11 140-1
Saxonburg, Pa. G3 84-5
Saxonville, Mass. I2 68-9
Saxtons River, Vt. M7 90-1
Sayabec, Que. C16 290-1
Saybrook, Ill. F9 96-7
Saybrook Manor, Conn. H11 60-1
Saybrook Point, Conn. H11 60-1
Saylesville, R.I. B5 87
Sayner, Wis. C12 140-1
Sayre, Ala. E6 146-7
Sayre, Okla. F7 234-5
Sayre, Pa. C12 84-5
Sayreville, N.J. F6 76-7
Sayville, N.Y. K12 80-1
Sayward, B.C. I5 268-9
Scalp Level, Pa. I5 84-5
Scaly Mountain, N.C. F2 180-1
Scammon, Kans. J16 108-9
Scammon Bay, Alaska E7 254-5
Scandia, Kans. D10 108-9
Scandia, Minn. A12 116-7
Scandinavia, Wis. E2 140-1
Scanlon, Minn. I8 116-7
Scantic, Conn. C10 60-1
Scappoose, Ore. B6 238-9
Scarborough, Me. N3 64-5
Scarsdale, N.Y. C15 80-1
Scarville, Ia. A8 104-5
Scenic, S. Dak. G4 136-7
Sceptre, Sask. M4 294-5
Schaefferstown, Pa. I12 84-5
Schaffer, Mich. E10 112-3
Schaghticoke, N.Y. F11 80-1
Schaller, Ia. D4 104-5
Schanzenfeld*, Man. K13 272-3
Schaumburg, Ill. L2 96-7
Schefferville, Que. E5 290-1
Schell City, Mo. G3 120-1
Schellbourne, Nev. F10 226-7
Schenectady, N.Y. F11 80-1
Schenectady, co., N.Y. F10 80-1
Schenevus, N.Y. F9 80-1
Schererville, Ind. B4 100-1
Schertz, Tex. I3 192-3
Schiller Park, Ill. L3 96-7
Schlater, Miss. E5 176-7
Schlegel, Okla. D12 234-5
Schleicher, co., Tex. F6 192-3
Schleswig, Ia. F3 104-5
Schley, Va. E4 196-7
Schley, co., Ga. K4 160-1
Schneider, Ind. C4 100-1
Schnellville, Ind. N6 100-1
Schodde, Ida. N7 218-9
Schoenchen, Kans. G6 108-9
Schoenfeld, Sask. N5 294-5
Schoenwiese*, Man. K13 272-3
Schofield, Wis. C1 140-1
Schofield Barracks, Hawaii H3 258-9
Schoharie, N.Y. F10 80-1
Schoharie, co., N.Y. F10 80-1
Scholle, N. Mex. G6 230-1
Schomberg, Ont. C14 284-5
Schoolcraft, Mich. J12 112-3
Schoolcraft, co., Mich. D11 112-3
Schooleys Mountain, N.J. D4 76-7
Schoolton, Okla. F13 234-5
Schoosett, Mass. K7 68-9
Schram City, Ill. J7 96-7
Schreiber, Ont. F4 284-5
Schriever, La. E11 168-9
Schuchk, Ariz. L7 206-7
Schuchuli, Ariz. K5 206-7
Schuermann Heights*, Mo. E10 120-1
Schulenburg, Tex. G9 192-3
Schuler, Alta. M11 264-5
Schulte, Kans. J10 108-9
Schulter, Okla. F14 234-5
Schurz, Nev. G3 226-7
Schuster, Ala. J5 146-7
Schuyler, Nebr. G13 124-5
Schuyler, Va. H10 196-7
Schuyler, co., Ill. G5 96-7
Schuyler, co., Mo. A6 120-1
Schuyler, co., N.Y. G5 80-1
Schuylerville, N.Y. E11 80-1
Schuylkill, co., Pa. H12 84-5
Schuylkill Haven, Pa. H13 84-5
Schuylkill R., Pa. B10 84-5
Science Hill, Ky. I11 164-5
Scio, O. E10 132-3
Scio, Ore. I1 238-9
Scioto, co., O. I6 132-3
Scioto R., O. G6 132-3
Scipio, Ind. K9 100-1
Scipio, Okla. G14 234-5
Scipio, Ut. I6 242-3
Scircleville, Ind. F8 100-1
Scituate, Mass. J8 68-9
Scituate*, R.I. D3 87
Scituate Res., R.I. D4 87
Scobey, Miss. D7 176-7
Scobey, Mont. A14 222-3
Scofield, Ore. B5 238-9
Scofield, Ut. H7 242-3
Sconticut Neck, Mass. H12 68-9
Scooba, Miss. G10 176-7
Scossa, Nev. D4 226-7
Scotch Plains, N.J. E6 76-7
Scotchtown*, N.Y. I10 80-1
Scotchtown, N.S. B11 281
Scotia, Nebr. G10 124-5
Scotia, N.Y. F11 80-1
Scotia, S.C. I9 184-5
Scotland, Ark. D6 150-1
Scotland, Conn. D13 60-1
Scotland, Ga. K7 160-1
Scotland, Ind. K6 100-1
Scotland, Md. I12 172-3
Scotland, Mass. F12 68-9
Scotland*, Ont. E13 284-5
Scotland, S. Dak. I14 136-7
Scotland, co., Mo. A7 120-1
Scotland, co., N.C. F9 180-1
Scotland Neck, N.C. C13 180-1
Scotlandville, La. G7 168-9
Scotstown, Que. I16 290-1
Scott, Ark. F7 150-1
Scott, Ga. J8 160-1
Scott, Ill. K7 96-7
Scott, La. H5 168-9
Scott, Miss. E4 176-7
Scott, O. C3 132-3
Scott, Okla. F9 234-5
Scott, Sask. K4 294-5
Scott, co., Ark. E2 150-1
Scott, co., Ill. I8 96-7
Scott, co., Ind. L9 100-1
Scott, co., Ia. G15 104-5
Scott, co., Kans. G3 108-9
Scott, co., Ky. F11 164-5
Scott, co., Minn. M6 116-7
Scott, co., Miss. H7 176-7
Scott, co., Mo. I11 120-1
Scott, co., Tenn. A11 188-9
Scott, co., Va. J3 196-7
Scott City, Kans. G3 108-9
Scott City, Mo. H12 120-1
Scott Depot, W. Va. H12 200-1
Scott-Jonction*, Que. I4 290-1
Scott Valley, Ark. F10 150-1
Scottdale, Ga. B11 160-1
Scottdale, Pa. J3 84-5
Scotts, N.C. H1 180-1
Scotts Bluff, co., Nebr. E1 124-5
Scotts Corner, Del. I3 153
Scotts Hill, Tenn. C4 188-9
Scotts Mills, Ore. H2 238-9
Scotts Valley*, Calif. J3 210-1
Scottsbluff, Nebr. F1 124-5
Scottsboro, Ala. B8 146-7
Scottsboro, Tenn. G6 188-9
Scottsburg, Ind. L9 100-1
Scottsburg, Ore. G4 238-9
Scottsburg, Va. J10 196-7
Scottsdale, Ariz. I6 206-7
Scottsmoor, Fla. E12 156-7
Scottsville, Ark. D5 150-1
Scottsville, Kans. D9 108-9
Scottsville, Ky. J7 164-5
Scottsville, N.Y. E4 80-1
Scottsville, Va. H10 196-7
Scottville, Mich. H11 112-3
Scow Bay*, Alaska H15 254-5
Scranton, Ark. D4 150-1
Scranton, Ia. F5 104-5
Scranton, Kans. F14 108-9
Scranton, N.C. E15 180-1
Scranton, N. Dak. I3 128-9
Scranton, Pa. E14 84-5
Scranton, S.C. E13 184-5
Scraper, Okla. D15 234-5
Screven, Ga. M9 160-1
Screven, co., Ga. I10 160-1
Scribner, Nebr. F14 124-5
Scullin*, Okla. H12 234-5
Scullville, N.J. M5 76-7
Scullyville, Okla. F16 234-5
Scurry, co., Tex. D5 192-3
Sea Bright, N.J. G8 76-7
Sea Cliff, N.Y. D16 80-1
Sea Girt, N.J. H8 76-7
Sea Island, Ga. M11 160-1
Sea Isle City, N.J. N5 76-7
Sea Ranch Lakes*, Fla. F16 156-7
Sea View, Mass. K8 68-9
Sea View, P.E.I. D6 287
Seabeck, Wash. H1 246-7
Seaboard, N.C. C13 180-1
Seabrook, N.H. N9 72-3
Seabrook, N.J. L2 76-7
Seabrook, S.C. J11 184-5
Seabrook, Tex. I15 192-3
Seacow Pond, P.E.I. A4 287
Seadrift, Tex. I9 192-3
Seaford, Del. J3 153
Seaford, N.Y. F16 80-1
Seafort, Minn. N3 116-7
Seaforth, Ont. D12 284-5
Seagoville, Tex. D15 192-3
Seagraves, Tex. D4 192-3
Seagrove, N.C. I4 180-1
Seahurst, Wash. I2 246-7
Seal Beach*, Calif. H9 210-1
Seal Cove, Me. L8 64-5
Seal Cove, N.B. K4 275
Seal Cove, Nfld. L8 278-9
Seal Harbor, Me. L8 64-5
Seal Rock, Ore. E4 238-9
Seale, Ala. I10 146-7
Sealevel, N.C. F15 180-1
Sealston, Va. C3 196-7
Sealy, Tex. G9 192-3
Sealy Springs, Ala. M10 146-7
Seaman, O. I5 132-3
Searchlight, Nev. O10 226-7
Searchmont, Ont. G6 284-5
Searcy, Ark. D8 150-1
Searcy, La. D5 168-9
Searcy, co., Ark. B6 150-1
Searight, Ala. L7 146-7
Searles, Ala. F5 146-7
Searles Valley*, Calif. L8 210-1
Sears, Mich. H12 112-3
Searsboro, Ia. G10 104-5
Searsburg, Vt. N5 90-1
Searsmont, Me. K6 64-5
Searsport, Me. K6 64-5
Searsville, Mass. D4 68-9
Seaside, Calif. K3 210-1
Seaside, Ore. A4 238-9
Seaside Heights, N.J. J8 76-7
Seaside Park, N.J. J8 76-7
Seat Pleasant, Md. J5 172-3
Seattle, Wash. E8 246-7
Seattle Heights, Wash. H2 246-7
Seaview, Va. F5 196-7
Seaview, Wash. H5 246-7
Seawall, Me. L8 64-5
Seba Beach, Alta. I7 264-5
Sebago, Me. N7 64-5
Sebago Lake, Me. O8 64-5
Sebasco Estates, Me. O10 64-5
Sebastian, Fla. F13 156-7
Sebastian, co., Ark. E2 150-1
Sebastopol, Calif. A6 210-1
Sebastopol, Miss. H8 176-7
Sebec, Me. H6 64-5
Sebec Lake, Me. H5 64-5
Sebeka, Minn. I4 116-7
Sebewaing, Mich. H14 112-3
Seboeis, Me. H7 64-5
Seboomook, Me. F5 64-5
Seboyeta, N. Mex. F4 230-1
Sebree, Ky. H5 164-5
Sebrell, Va. G2 196-7
Sebring, Fla. G11 156-7
Sebring, O. D11 132-3
Sebringville, Ont. D12 284-5
Secaucus, N.J. C11 76-7
Sechelt, B.C. B12 268-9
Seco, Ky. I15 164-5
Second Falls, N.B. J4 275
Secondcreek, W. Va. I6 200-1
Secretary, Md. F13 172-3
Section, Ala. B8 146-7
Security [-Widefield], Colo. K4 214-5
Sedalia, Colo. H3 214-5
Sedalia, Ind. F7 100-1
Sedalia, Ky. K3 164-5
Sedalia, Mo. E5 120-1
Sedalia, N.C. H5 180-1
Sedan, Kans. K13 108-9
Sedan, Minn. K3 116-7
Sedan, Nebr. I12 124-5
Sedan, N. Mex. D11 230-1
Sedgewick, Alta. J9 264-5
Sedgewickville, Mo. H11 120-1
Sedgwick, Ark. B10 150-1
Sedgwick, Colo. B15 214-5
Sedgwick, Kans. I10 108-9
Sedgwick, Me. K7 64-5
Sedgwick, co., Colo. B15 214-5
Sedgwick, co., Kans. J11 108-9
Sedillo, N. Mex. F6 230-1
Sedley, Sask. N9 294-5
Sedley, Va. G2 196-7
Sedona, Ariz. F7 206-7
Sedro-Woolley, Wash. C8 246-7
Seebe, Alta. M6 264-5
Seebert, W. Va. H6 200-1
Seekonk, Mass. G10 68-9
Seeley Lake, Mont. E4 222-3
Seeleys Bay, Ont. J14 284-5
Seely, Wyo. B15 250-1
Seelyville, Ind. I5 100-1
Sego, Ut. I10 242-3
Segreganset, Mass. G11 68-9
Seguin, Kans. E4 108-9
Seguin, Tex. I4 192-3
Segundo, Colo. J12 214-5
Seibert, Colo. E15 214-5
Seigling, S.C. H9 184-5
Seiling, Okla. D8 234-5
Seivern, S.C. F9 184-5
Sekiu, Wash. D5 246-7
Selah, Wash. H11 246-7
Selawik, Alaska C9 254-5
Selby, S. Dak. B9 136-7
Selby-on-the-Bay*, Md. E11 172-3
Selbyville, Del. K6 153
Selbyville, W. Va. F14 200-1
Selden, Kans. D4 108-9
Selden, Me. F9 64-5
Selden*, N.Y. J12 80-1
Seldom, Nfld. L10 278-9
Seldovia, Alaska G11 254-5
Selfridge, N. Dak. J7 128-9
Selfridge Base*, Mich. I7 112-3
Selfridge-Capehart*, Mich. I15 112-3
Seligman, Ariz. E5 206-7
Seligman, Mo. J4 120-1
Selinsgrove, Pa. G11 84-5
Selkirk, Kans. G2 108-9
Selkirk, Man. I14 272-3
Selleck, Wash. F9 246-7
Sellers, Ala. J7 146-7
Sellers, S.C. D14 184-5
Sellersburg, Ind. M9 100-1
Sellersville, Pa. I15 84-5
Sells, Ariz. L6 206-7
Selma, Ala. I5 146-7
Selma, Ark. I8 150-1
Selma*, Calif. K6 210-1
Selma, Ind. G11 100-1
Selma, Ia. J11 104-5
Selma, Kans. H15 108-9
Selma, La. D4 168-9
Selma, N.C. I8 180-1
Selma, Ore. J4 238-9
Selma, Va. H8 196-7
Selma Park, B.C. B12 268-9
Selman, Okla. C7 234-5

Selmer, Tenn. D4 188-9
Selvin, Ind. N5 100-1
Selwyn Mts., Y.T. B2 297
Selz, N. Dak. E9 128-9
Seman, Ala. H8 146-7
Semans, Sask. L8 294-5
Seminary, Miss. K8 176-7
Seminoe Dam, Wyo. H12 250-1
Seminole, Ala. N4 146-7
Seminole, Fla. I1 156-7
Seminole, Okla. F12 234-5
Seminole, Tex. D4 192-3
Seminole, co., Fla. E12 156-7
Seminole, co., Ga. N2 160-1
Seminole, co., Okla. F12 234-5
Semmes, Ala. N2 146-7
Semora, N.C. C10 180-1
Sena, N. Mex. F8 230-1
Senath, Mo. K10 120-1
Senatobia, Miss. B6 176-7
Seneca, Ill. D9 96-7
Seneca, Kans. D13 108-9
Seneca, Mo. I3 120-1
Seneca, Nebr. E6 124-5
Seneca, N. Mex. C11 230-1
Seneca, Ore. F12 238-9
Seneca, S.C. B5 184-5
Seneca, S. Dak. C10 136-7
Seneca, Wis. J10 140-1
Seneca, co., N.Y. F6 80-1
Seneca, co., O. C6 132-3
Seneca Falls, N.Y. F6 80-1
Seneca Gardens*, Ky. G9 164-5
Senecaville, O. F10 132-3
Seney, Mich. D11 112-3
Senlac, Sask. K4 294-5
Senneterre, Que. H1 290-1
Senneville*, Que. I12 290-1
Senoia, Ga. H3 160-1
Sentinel, Ariz. J4 206-7
Sentinel, Okla. F8 234-5
Sentinel Butte, N. Dak. G1 128-9
Sept-Îles, Que. G5 290-1
Sequatchie, Tenn. K10 188-9
Sequatchie, co., Tenn. D10 188-9
Sequim, Wash. D7 246-7
Sequoyah, co., Okla. E15 234-5
Serafina, N. Mex. E8 230-1
Sergeant Bluff, Ia. E1 104-5
Sergeantsville, N.J. F4 76-7
Servia, Ind. D9 100-1
Service Creek, Ore. D11 238-9
Sesser, Ill. M8 96-7
Sessums, Miss. F9 176-7
Setauket [-South Setauket]*, N.Y. J12 80-1
Seth, W. Va. J14 200-1
Seton Portage, B.C. I7 268-9
Seven Corners*, Va. E13 196-7
Seven Fountains, Va. E11 196-7
Seven Hickories, Del. E3 153
Seven Hills, O. B14 132-3
Seven Mile, O. J13 132-3
Seven Mile Ford, Va. J5 196-7
Seven Persons*, Alta. N10 264-5
Seven Rivers, N. Mex. K9 230-1
Seven Sisters Falls, Man. I16 272-3
Seven Springs, N.C. E12 180-1
Severance, Colo. D3 214-5
Severance, Kans. D15 108-9
Severn, N.C. B13 180-1
Severn, Va. F4 196-7
Severna Park, Md. H7 172-3
Severy, Kans. I13 108-9
Sevier, Ut. J5 242-3
Sevier, co., Ark. H2 150-1
Sevier, co., Tenn. C13 188-9
Sevier, co., Ut. J6 242-3
Sevierville, Tenn. I13 188-9
Seville, Fla. D11 156-7
Seville, Ga. K6 160-1
Seville, O. E13 132-3
Sewalls Point, Fla. B16 156-7
Sewanee, Tenn. K9 188-9
Seward, Alaska F11 254-5
Seward, Kans. H8 108-9
Seward, Nebr. H13 124-5
Seward, Okla. E11 234-5
Seward, co., Kans. K3 108-9
Seward, co., Nebr. H13 124-5
Sewaren, N.J. F9 76-7
Sewell, N.J. O10 76-7
Sewickley, Pa. A5 84-5
Sexsmith, Alta. G4 264-5
Sextonville, Wis. J11 140-1
Seymour, Conn. G6 60-1
Seymour, Ind. K9 100-1
Seymour, Ia. J9 104-5
Seymour, Mo. I6 120-1
Seymour, Tenn. H12 188-9
Seymour, Tex. D7 192-3
Seymour, Wis. D4 140-1
Seymour Johnson*, N.C. E12 180-1
Seymourville*, La. H7 168-9
Seymourville*, Man. J5 272-3
Shabbona, Ill. C9 96-7
Shackelford, co., Tex. D7 192-3
Shacklefords, Va. E3 196-7
Shackleton, Sask. M5 294-5
Shacklett, Tenn. H6 188-9
Shadwell, Va. G11 196-7
Shady Bend, Kans. F9 108-9
Shady Cove, Ore. I6 238-9
Shady Dale, Ga. H6 160-1
Shady Grove, Ala. J8 146-7
Shady Grove, Ark. J15 150-1
Shady Grove, Ky. I4 164-5
Shady Pine, Ore. J8 238-9
Shady Point, Okla. F16 234-5
Shady Side, Md. J7 172-3
Shady Spring, W. Va. K16 200-1
Shady Valley, Tenn. A16 188-9
Shadyside, O. F11 132-3
Shafer, Minn. L7 116-7
Shaft Ox Corner, Del. K5 153
Shafter, Calif. L6 210-1
Shafter, Nev. C10 226-7
Shaftsburg, Mich. H2 112-3
Shaftsbury, Vt. M4 90-1
Shageluk, Alaska E9 254-5
Shailerville, Conn. F10 60-1
Shaker Heights, O. B15 132-3
Shakespeare*, Ont. D13 284-5
Shakopee, Minn. C10 116-7
Shaktoolik, Alaska D9 254-5
Shalalth, B.C. I7 268-9
Shalimar, Fla. B4 156-7
Shallotte, N.C. H11 180-1
Shallow Lake, Ont. A12 284-5
Shallow Water, Kans. G3 108-9
Shallowater, Tex. C5 192-3
Shamballah Ashrama, Colo. I3 214-5
Shambaugh, Ia. J4 104-5
Shamokin, Pa. G11 84-5
Shamokin, S.C. D11 184-5
Shamokin Dam, Pa. G11 84-5
Shamong*, N.J. J5 76-7
Shamrock, La. D2 168-9
Shamrock, Okla. E12 234-5
Shamrock, Sask. N6 294-5
Shamrock, Tex. B6 192-3
Shamrock Lake*, Ind. E10 100-1
Shaniko, Ore. D9 238-9
Shanks*, W. Va. E10 200-1
Shannock, R.I. H3 87
Shannon, Ga. E2 160-1
Shannon, Ill. B7 96-7
Shannon, Miss. D9 176-7
Shannon, N.C. F10 180-1
Shannon, co., Mo. H8 120-1
Shannon, co., S. Dak. H3 136-7
Shannon City, Ia. J6 104-5
Shannontown, S.C. E12 184-5
Shannonville, Ont. K13 284-5
Shanty Bay, Ont. B14 284-5
Shantytown, Nev. E9 226-7
Shapleigh, Me. N2 64-5
Sharbot Lake, Ont. I13 284-5
Sharkey, Ky. G13 164-5
Sharkey, co., Miss. G4 176-7
Sharon, Conn. C4 60-1
Sharon, Ga. G7 160-1
Sharon, Ida. O11 218-9
Sharon, Kans. K8 108-9
Sharon, La. A4 168-9
Sharon, Mass. K4 68-9
Sharon, Miss. H6 176-7
Sharon, N.H. O5 72-3
Sharon, N. Dak. F12 128-9
Sharon, Okla. D7 234-5
Sharon*, Ont. I8 284-5
Sharon, Pa. F1 84-5
Sharon, S.C. B9 184-5
Sharon, Tenn. B3 188-9
Sharon, Vt. I7 90-1
Sharon, Wis. K13 140-1
Sharon Grove, Ky. J6 164-5
Sharon Hill*, Pa. J15 84-5
Sharon North*, Pa. F1 84-5
Sharon Springs, Kans. F1 108-9
Sharon Valley, Conn. C4 60-1
Sharon West*, O. B11 132-3
Sharonville, O. K14 132-3
Sharp, co., Ark. B9 150-1
Sharpe, Kans. H14 108-9
Sharpe, Ky. J3 164-5
Sharpes, Fla. E12 156-7
Sharples, W. Va. K13 200-1
Sharps, Va. H14 196-7
Sharps Chapel, Tenn. G12 188-9
Sharpsburg, Ga. H3 160-1
Sharpsburg, Ia. J5 104-5
Sharpsburg, Ky. G12 164-5
Sharpsburg, Md. C7 172-3
Sharpsburg, N.C. D12 180-1
Sharpsburg, Pa. A6 84-5
Sharpsville, Ind. F8 100-1
Sharpsville, Pa. E1 84-5
Sharptown, Md. G14 172-3
Shasta, co., Calif. E3 210-1
Shattuck, Okla. D6 234-5
Shattuckville, Mass. B4 68-9
Shaughnessy, Alta. N8 264-5
Shaunavon, Sask. O5 294-5
Shavano Park, Tex. I2 192-3
Shaw*, Ill. A10 96-7
Shaw, Kans. I15 108-9
Shaw, La. E6 168-9
Shaw, Miss. E4 176-7
Shaw*, S.C. E11 184-5
Shaw, W. Va. D9 200-1
Shaw Island, Wash. C7 246-7
Shawanee, Tenn. F13 188-9
Shawano, Wis. F14 140-1
Shawano, co., Wis. F13 140-1
Shawbridge*, Que. I11 290-1
Shawinigan, Que. G9 290-1
Shawinigan-Sud*, Que. G5 290-1
Shawmut, Ala. G10 146-7
Shawmut, Me. J5 64-5
Shawmut, Mont. F9 222-3
Shawnee, Colo. I1 214-5
Shawnee, Ga. J10 160-1
Shawnee, Kans. F16 108-9
Shawnee, O. G8 132-3
Shawnee, Okla. F12 234-5
Shawnee, Wyo. G15 250-1
Shawnee, co., Kans. F14 108-9
Shawnee Hills, O. F6 132-3
Shawneetown, Ill. N10 96-7
Shawnigan Lake, B.C. E12 268-9
Shawsheen Village, Mass. B11 68-9
Shawsville, Va. I7 196-7
Shawville, Que. J2 290-1
Shay, Okla. I12 234-5
Shearerville, Ark. E11 150-1
Sheaville, Ore. H16 238-9
Sheboygan, Wis. H15 140-1
Sheboygan, co., Wis. H15 140-1
Sheboygan Falls, Wis. G5 140-1
Sheboygan South*, Wis. H15 140-1
Sheboygan West*, Wis. H15 140-1
Shedd, Ore. J1 238-9
Shediac, N.B. H7 275
Shediac Bridge, N.B. H7 275
Sheepscot, Me. M11 64-5
Sheet Harbour, N.S. E8 281
Sheffield, Ala. B4 146-7
Sheffield, Ill. D7 96-7
Sheffield, Ia. C8 104-5
Sheffield, Mass. E1 68-9
Sheffield, Mont. F14 222-3
Sheffield, N.B. I5 275
Sheffield, O. B12 132-3
Sheffield, Pa. D5 84-5
Sheffield, Vt. D8 90-1
Sheffield Lake, O. B12 132-3
Shefford, co., Que. J14 290-1
Sheguiandah, Ont. H7 284-5
Sheho, Sask. L9 294-5
Sheila*, N.B. E7 275
Shelbina, Mo. C7 120-1
Shelburn, Ind. J4 100-1
Shelburn, La. A7 168-9
Shelburn, Ore. I1 238-9
Shelburne, Mass. B4 68-9
Shelburne, N.H. F8 72-3
Shelburne, N.S. G5 281
Shelburne, Ont. B13 284-5
Shelburne, Vt. E4 90-1
Shelburne, co., N.S. F5 281
Shelburne Falls, Mass. B4 68-9
Shelburne Road Section*, Vt. E4 90-1
Shelby, Ala. G7 146-7
Shelby, Ind. C4 100-1
Shelby, Ia. H3 104-5
Shelby, Mich. H11 112-3
Shelby, Miss. D4 176-7
Shelby, Mont. B6 222-3
Shelby, Nebr. G13 124-5
Shelby, N.C. E6 180-1
Shelby, O. D7 132-3
Shelby, co., Ala. F7 146-7
Shelby, co., Ill. I8 96-7
Shelby, co., Ind. I9 100-1
Shelby, co., Ia. G3 104-5
Shelby, co., Ky. G10 164-5
Shelby, co., Mo. C7 120-1
Shelby, co., O. E4 132-3
Shelby, co., Tenn. D1 188-9
Shelby, co., Tex. E11 192-3
Shelby City, Ky. E6 164-5
Shelbyville, Ill. I9 96-7
Shelbyville, Ind. I9 100-1
Shelbyville, Ky. B4 164-5
Shelbyville, Mo. C7 120-1
Shelbyville, Tenn. C8 188-9
Shelbyville Res., Ill. I9 96-7
Sheldahl, Ia. G7 104-5
Sheldon, Ariz. J11 206-7
Sheldon, Ill. E11 96-7
Sheldon, Ia. B2 104-5
Sheldon, Mo. G3 120-1
Sheldon, N. Dak. H13 128-9
Sheldon, S.C. I11 184-5
Sheldon*, Tex. G10 192-3
Sheldon, Vt. B5 90-1
Sheldon, Wis. E10 140-1
Sheldon Point, Alaska E8 254-5
Sheldonville, Mass. F10 68-9
Shell, Wyo. C10 250-1
Shell Lake, Sask. J6 294-5
Shell Lake, Wis. D8 140-1
Shell Rock, Ia. D10 104-5
Shellbrook, Sask. J6 294-5
Shelley, B.C. F7 268-9
Shelley, Ida. M10 218-9
Shellhorn, Ala. J8 146-7
Shellman, Ga. L3 160-1
Shellman Bluff, Ga. L11 160-1
Shellmound, Miss. E6 176-7
Shellmouth, Man. H9 272-3
Shellsburg, Ia. F12 104-5
Shelly, Minn. G1 116-7
Shelmerdine, N.C. E13 180-1
Shelton, Conn. H6 60-1
Shelton, Nebr. H10 124-5
Shelton, S.C. I7 184-5
Shelton, Wash. F7 246-7
Sheltons, La. A5 168-9
Shemya Station*, Alaska I4 254-5
Shenandoah, Ia. J3 104-5
Shenandoah, Pa. G12 84-5
Shenandoah, Va. F10 196-7
Shenandoah, co., Va. E10 196-7
Shenandoah Heights*, Pa. G12 84-5
Shenandoah Junction, W. Va. D12 200-1
Shenandoah R., Va. E11 196-7
Shepardsville, Ind. I4 100-1
Shepardsville, Mich. G1 112-3
Shepherd, Mich. H13 112-3
Shepherd, Mont. G11 222-3
Shepherd, Tex. G10 192-3
Shepherdstown, W. Va. D12 200-1
Shepherdsville, Ky. C2 164-5
Sherard, Miss. C5 176-7
Sherborn, Mass. J2 68-9
Sherbrooke, N.S. D9 281
Sherbrooke, P.E.I. E5 287
Sherbrooke, Que. J15 290-1
Sherbrooke, co., Que. J15 290-1
Sherburn, Minn. O4 116-7
Sherburne, Ky. F13 164-5
Sherburne, N.Y. F8 80-1
Sherburne*, Vt. J5 90-1
Sherburne, co., Minn. L6 116-7
Sheridan, Ark. G6 150-1
Sheridan, Colo. H3 214-5
Sheridan, Ill. C9 96-7
Sheridan, Ind. G8 100-1
Sheridan, Ky. I4 164-5
Sheridan, La. F10 168-9
Sheridan, Me. C8 64-5
Sheridan, Mich. I12 112-3
Sheridan, Mo. A3 120-1
Sheridan, Mont. H5 222-3
Sheridan, Ore. C5 238-9
Sheridan, Wyo. B11 250-1
Sheridan, co., Kans. E4 108-9
Sheridan, co., Mont. A15 222-3
Sheridan, co., Nebr. D4 124-5
Sheridan, co., N. Dak. F8 128-9
Sheridan, co., Wyo. B11 250-1
Sheridan Lake, Colo. G16 214-5
Sherman, Conn. E4 60-1
Sherman, Ill. H7 96-7
Sherman, Kans. J15 108-9
Sherman, Ky. E11 164-5
Sherman, Me. F8 64-5
Sherman, Miss. C9 176-7
Sherman, N.Y. G1 80-1
Sherman, S. Dak. G16 136-7
Sherman, Tex. C9 192-3
Sherman, W. Va. F3 200-1
Sherman, co., Kans. E2 108-9
Sherman, co., Nebr. G10 124-5
Sherman, co., Ore. C9 238-9
Sherman, co., Tex. A5 192-3
Sherman Mills, Me. F8 64-5
Sherman Station, Me. F8 64-5
Sherrard, Ill. D5 96-7
Sherrard, W. Va. C5 200-1
Sherrelwood*, Colo. D12 214-5
Sherridon, Man. E1 272-3
Sherrill, Ark. G7 150-1
Sherrill, Ia. D14 104-5
Sherrill, N.Y. E8 80-1
Sherrills Ford, N.C. I1 180-1
Sherritt Gordon Mines*, Man. F2 272-3
Sherrodsville, O. E10 132-3
Sherry, Wis. F11 140-1
Sherwood, Ark. I16 150-1
Sherwood, Md. F12 172-3
Sherwood, Mich. K12 112-3
Sherwood, Miss. E8 176-7
Sherwood, N.C. C5 180-1
Sherwood, N. Dak. B6 128-9
Sherwood, O. C3 132-3
Sherwood, Okla. H16 234-5
Sherwood, Ore. G1 238-9
Sherwood, P.E.I. E7 287
Sherwood, Tenn. K9 188-9
Sherwood, Wis. F4 140-1
Sherwood Forest, Md. H7 172-3
Sherwood Park, Alta. I8 264-5
Shevlin, Minn. G3 116-7
Sheyenne, N. Dak. E10 128-9
Shiawassee, co., Mich. I13 112-3
Shickley, Nebr. I12 124-5
Shickshinny, Pa. F13 84-5
Shideler, Ind. F10 100-1
Shidler, Okla. C12 234-5
Shields, Kans. G4 108-9
Shields, N. Dak. I6 128-9
Shillington, Pa. I13 84-5
Shiloh, Ga. I3 160-1
Shiloh, Ill. K6 96-7
Shiloh, N.J. M2 76-7
Shiloh, N.C. C15 180-1
Shiloh, O. D7 132-3
Shiloh*, O. G4 132-3
Shiloh, S.C. E13 184-5
Shiloh, Tenn. G5 188-9
Shiloh, Va. C4 196-7
Shin Pond, Me. E7 64-5
Shine, Wash. G1 246-7
Shiner, Tex. H9 192-3
Shinglehouse, Pa. C7 84-5
Shingleton, Mich. D11 112-3
Shinnston, W. Va. C14 200-1
Shiocton, Wis. E3 140-1
Ship Bottom, N.J. K7 76-7
Shipman, Sask. J8 294-5
Shipman, Va. H10 196-7
Shippegan, N.B. E7 275
Shippensburg, Pa. J9 84-5
Shipps Bend, Tenn. I5 188-9
Shiprock, N. Mex. B2 230-1
Shipshewana, Ind. A10 100-1
Shiremanstown*, Pa. I10 84-5
Shirkshire, Mass. C4 68-9
Shirley, Ark. C7 150-1
Shirley, Ind. H10 100-1
Shirley*, Me. H5 64-5
Shirley, Mass. C9 68-9
Shirley, Mont. F14 222-3
Shirley, N.Y. J13 80-1
Shirley, S.C. I9 184-5
Shirley, W. Va. D5 200-1
Shirley Hill, N.H. N6 72-3
Shirley Mills, Me. H5 64-5
Shishmaref, Alaska C8 254-5
Shively, Ky. B1 164-5
Shively, W. Va. J11 200-1
Shivers, Miss. J6 176-7
Shives, Ark. J9 150-1

Shivwits, Ut. M3 242-3
Shoal, Ky. I13 164-5
Shoal Creek Drive, Mo. I3 120-1
Shoal Harbour*, Nfld. N10 278-9
Shoal Lake, Man. I10 272-3
Shoals, Ind. L6 100-1
Shoals, W. Va. H10 200-1
Shoals Junction, S.C. J2 184-5
Shock, W. Va. F5 200-1
Shoemakersville, Pa. H13 84-5
Shoffner, Ark. D9 150-1
Sholes, Nebr. E13 124-5
Shongaloo, La. A3 168-9
Shongopovi, Ariz. D9 206-7
Shonkin, Mont. D8 222-3
Shonto, Ariz. B9 206-7
Shooks Gap, Tenn. I12 188-9
Shooting Creek, N.C. F2 180-1
Shop Springs, Tenn. H8 188-9
Shopiere, Wis. K2 140-1
Shopton, Ala. J8 146-7
Shore Acres, N.J. I8 76-7
Shore Acres (-Sand Hills), Mass. J8 68-9
Shore Hills*, N.J. D5 76-7
Shoreacres*, B.C. J10 268-9
Shoreacres, Tex. I15 192-3
Shoreham, Mich. K11 112-3
Shoreham*, N.Y. J13 80-1
Shoreham, Vt. H3 90-1
Shoreline Drive*, Alaska H16 254-5
Shoreview, Minn. A11 116-7
Shorewood, Ill. O2 96-7
Shorewood, Minn. B9 116-7
Shorewood, Wis. J5 140-1
Shorewood Hills, Wis. J1 140-1
Shorewood Hills-Flower Hills*, Mich. K10 112-3
Short, Okla. E16 234-5
Short Beach, Conn. H8 60-1
Short Creek, W. Va. B5 200-1
Short Falls, N.H. M7 72-3
Shortdale*, Man. I1 272-3
Shorter, Ala. I8 146-7
Shorterville, Ala. K10 146-7
Shorts Beach, Del. H5 153
Shortsville, N.Y. E5 80-1
Shoshone, Ida. N6 218-9
Shoshone, co., Ida. E4 218-9
Shoshoni, Wyo. F9 250-1
Shoultes*, Wash. D8 246-7
Shouns, Tenn. A16 188-9
Shoup, Ida. I6 218-9
Show Low, Ariz. G10 206-7
Showell, Md. G16 172-3
Shreve, O. D8 132-3
Shreveport, La. B1 168-9
Shrewder, Okla. G7 234-5
Shrewsbury, Mass. D9 68-9
Shrewsbury*, Mo. E10 120-1
Shrewsbury*, N.J. G8 76-7
Shrewsbury, N.J. G8 76-7
Shrewsbury, Pa. K11 84-5
Shrewsbury, Vt. J5 90-1
Shubert, Nebr. J16 124-5
Shubuta, Miss. J9 176-7
Shueyville, Ia. G12 104-5
Shuford, Miss. C7 176-7
Shulerville, S.C. G14 184-5
Shullsburg, Wis. K11 140-1
Shumansville, Va. G13 196-7
Shungnak, Alaska. C10 254-5
Shuqualak, Miss. G10 176-7
Shutesbury, Mass. C5 68-9
Shutler, Ore. B10 238-9
Sias, W. Va. I11 200-1
Siasconset, Mass. J16 68-9
Sibert, Ky. I13 164-5
Sibley, Ia. B3 104-5
Sibley, La. B2 168-9
Sibley, Miss. L3 176-7
Sibley, Mo. I16 120-1
Sibley, N. Dak. G12 128-9
Sibley, co., Minn. M5 116-7
Sibylee, Wyo. H15 250-1
Sicamous*, B.C. I10 268-9
Sicard, La. B5 168-9
Sicily Island, La. D6 168-9
Sicklerville, N.J. K3 76-7
Sickles, Okla. F9 234-5
Sidell, Ill. H11 96-7
Sidnaw, Mich. C8 112-3
Sidney, Ark. B8 150-1
Sidney, B.C. E13 268-9
Sidney, Ill. G10 96-7
Sidney, Ind. C9 100-1
Sidney, Ia. J3 104-5
Sidney, Me. K4 64-5
Sidney, Man. J12 272-3
Sidney, Mich. I12 112-3
Sidney, Mont. C16 222-3
Sidney, Nebr. G2 124-5
Sidney, N.Y. G8 80-1
Sidney, O. E4 132-3
Sidon, Ark. D8 150-1
Sidon, Miss. F6 176-7
Sidonia, Tenn. B3 188-9
Sieben, Mont. E6 222-3
Siegas, N.B. F2 275
Sieper, La. E3 168-9
Sierra, co., Calif. G5 210-1
Sierra, co., N. Mex. J4 230-1
Sierra Blanca, Tex. F2 192-3
Sierra Madre*, Calif. G9 210-1
Sierra Vista, Ariz. M9 206-7
Sierraville, Calif. G5 210-1
Siesta Key*, Fla. G10 156-7
Sifton, Man. G11 272-3
Sifton, Wash. J7 246-7
Signal, Ariz. G3 206-7
Signal Hill*, Calif. H8 210-1
Signal Mountain, Tenn. K10 188-9
Sigourney, Ia. H11 104-5
Sigurd, Ut. J6 242-3
Sikes, La. C4 168-9
Sikeston, Mo. I11 120-1
Sil Nakya, Ariz. K7 206-7
Silas, Ala. K2 146-7
Sile, N. Mex. E6 230-1
Siler City, N.C. I5 180-1
Silerton, Tenn. K4 188-9
Silesia, Mont. H10 222-3
Siletz, Ore. D4 238-9
Silex, Mo. D9 120-1
Sillery, Que. G11 290-1
Sillikers, N.B. F5 275
Silo, Okla. I13 234-5
Siloam, Ga. G7 160-1
Siloam, Tenn. F8 188-9
Siloam Springs, Ark. B1 150-1
Silsbee, Tex. G11 192-3
Silt, Colo. E7 214-5
Siltcoos, Ore. F4 238-9
Silton, Sask. M8 294-5
Siluria, Ala. F6 146-7
Silvana, Wash. F3 246-7
Silver, Man. H14 272-3
Silver Bay, Minn. H9 116-7
Silver Beach, Mass. H13 68-9
Silver Bell, Ariz. K7 206-7
Silver Bow Park, Mont. G5 222-3
Silver City, Ida. M3 218-9
Silver City, Ia. I3 104-5
Silver City, Miss. G5 176-7
Silver City, Mont. E6 222-3
Silver City, Nev. G2 226-7
Silver City, N. Mex. K3 230-1
Silver City, S. Dak. F2 136-7
Silver City, Ut. G5 242-3
Silver Cliff, Colo. H11 214-5
Silver Creek, Ga. E2 160-1
Silver Creek, Miss. K6 176-7
Silver Creek, Mo. I3 120-1
Silver Creek, Nebr. G12 124-5
Silver Creek, N.Y. F2 80-1
Silver Creek, Wash. H7 246-7
Silver Creek Subdivision*, B.C. J6 268-9
Silver Gate, Mont. I8 222-3
Silver Grove*, Ky. E12 164-5
Silver Hill, Tenn. H8 188-9
Silver Hill, W. Va. D5 200-1
Silver Lake, Ind. C9 100-1
Silver Lake, Kans. E14 108-9
Silver Lake, Mass. B11 68-9
Silver Lake, Minn. B7 116-7
Silver Lake, N.H. I8 72-3
Silver Lake, O. D15 132-3
Silver Lake, Ore. H9 238-9
Silver Lake, Wis. K4 140-1
Silver Peak, Nev. J5 226-7
Silver Plume, Colo. G1 214-5
Silver Run, Ala. E8 146-7
Silver Run, Md. B9 172-3
Silver Spring, Md. I4 172-3
Silver Springs, Colo. H2 214-5
Silver Springs, Nev. F3 226-7
Silver Springs, N.Y. F4 80-1
Silver Star, Mont. G5 222-3
Silver Star, Nev. I4 226-7
Silver Zone, Nev. C10 226-7
Silverbow, Nev. J7 226-7
Silverdale, Kans. K12 108-9
Silverdale, Wash. H1 246-7
Silverhill, Ala. N4 146-7
Silverlake, Wash. H7 246-7
Silverstreet, S.C. K5 184-5
Silverthorne, Colo. D10 214-5
Silverton, B.C. J9 268-9
Silverton, Colo. H7 214-5
Silverton, Ida. D4 218-9
Silverton, N.J. I7 76-7
Silverton, O. K14 132-3
Silverton, Ore. H2 238-9
Silverton, Tex. C5 192-3
Silverton, Wash. D9 246-7
Silverton Station*, Man. J1 272-3
Silverwood, Mich. E5 112-3
Silvies, Ore. F12 238-9
Silvis, Ill. C5 96-7
Simcoe, Ont. E13 284-5
Simcoe, co., Ont. A14 284-5
Simi Valley, Calif. G7 210-1
Simla, Colo. F13 214-5
Simmesport, La. F6 168-9
Simmie, Sask. N5 294-5
Simmons, Ariz. F5 206-7
Simmonsville, R.I. C4 87
Simnasho, Ore. D8 238-9
Simon, Okla. I11 234-5
Simon, W. Va. J3 200-1
Simonsville, Vt. L6 90-1
Simpson, Kans. E9 108-9
Simpson, La. E3 168-9
Simpson, Mont. A8 222-3
Simpson, Nev. G2 226-7
Simpson, Sask. L7 294-5
Simpson, S.C. D10 184-5
Simpson, W. Va. C14 200-1
Simpson, co., Ky. J7 164-5
Simpson, co., Miss. J6 176-7
Simpsons, Va. J7 196-7
Simpsonville, Ky. A3 164-5
Simpsonville, Md. G5 172-3
Simpsonville, S.C. G2 184-5
Sims, Ark. F3 150-1
Sims, Ind. E9 100-1
Sims, N.C. D12 180-1
Simsboro, La. B4 168-9
Simsbury, Conn. C8 60-1
Sinai, S. Dak. E15 136-7
Sinamox, Ore. C9 238-9
Sinclair, Ida. A3 218-9
Sinclair, Me. B8 64-5
Sinclair, Man. J9 272-3
Sinclair, Wyo. I11 250-1
Sinclairville, N.Y. G1 80-1
Singer, La. G2 168-9
Singers Glen, Va. F10 196-7
Singleton, Miss. G7 176-7
Singleton, S.C. F11 184-5
Sinking Spring, Pa. I13 84-5
Sinsinawa, Wis. K10 140-1
Sintaluta, Sask. N9 294-5
Sinton, Tex. I8 192-3
Sioux, co., Ia. C1 104-5
Sioux, co., Nebr. D1 124-5
Sioux, co., N. Dak. I7 128-9
Sioux Center, Ia. C1 104-5
Sioux City, Ia. D1 104-5
Sioux Falls, S. Dak. G16 136-7
Sioux Lookout, Ont. E2 284-5
Sioux Pass, Mont. C16 222-3
Sioux Rapids, Ia. C4 104-5
Sipsey, Ala. E5 146-7
Siren, Wis. D7 140-1
Siskiyou, Ore. K6 238-9
Siskiyou, co., Calif. D3 210-1
Sisseton, S. Dak. B15 136-7
Sissonville, W. Va. G3 200-1
Sister Bay, Wis. E16 140-1
Sisters, Ore. E8 238-9
Sistersville, W. Va. D5 200-1
Sitka, Alaska H15 254-5
Sitka, Kans. K6 108-9
Sitkum, Ore. H4 238-9
Six Lakes, Mich. H12 112-3
Six Mile, Ga. E2 160-1
Six Mile, S.C. B5 184-5
Six Points, Ind. F1 100-1
Sixes, Ore. I3 238-9
Sixteen, Mont. F7 222-3
Skaggston, Tenn. H12 188-9
Skagit, co., Wash. D9 246-7
Skagway, Alaska F15 254-5
Skamania, Wash. J8 246-7
Skamania, co., Wash. I8 246-7
Skamokawa, Wash. H6 246-7
Skandia, Mich. D10 112-3
Skaneateles, N.Y. E6 80-1
Skanee, Mich. C9 112-3
Skedee, Okla. D12 234-5
Skellytown, Tex. B5 192-3
Skene, Miss. E4 176-7
Skiatook, Okla. D13 234-5
Skiddy, Kans. F12 108-9
Skidmore, Md. H8 172-3
Skidmore, Mo. A2 120-1
Skinner Pond, P.E.I. B4 287
Skippers, Va. K12 196-7
Skipperville, Ala. K9 146-7
Skipwith, Va. J10 196-7
Skockton, Ut. F5 242-3
Skokie, Ill. L3 96-7
Skowhegan, Me. J5 64-5
Skull Creek, Wyo. C16 250-1
Skull Valley, Ariz. G5 206-7
Skullbone, Tenn. B4 188-9
Skykomish, Wash. E9 246-7
Skyland, N.C. E4 180-1
Skylight, Ky. F9 164-5
Skyline, Ala. B8 146-7
Skyline, Minn. N5 116-7
Skyline View*, Pa. H11 84-5
Slab Fork, W. Va. K15 200-1
Slabtown*, N.Y. G5 80-1
Slade, Ky. H13 164-5
Sladesville, N.C. E15 180-1
Slagle, La. E3 168-9
Slanesville, W. Va. D10 200-1
Slapout, Okla. C6 234-5
Slate Springs, Miss. E8 176-7
Slater, Ia. G7 104-5
Slater, Mo. D5 120-1
Slater, Wyo. I15 250-1
Slater [-Marietta], S.C. E1 184-5
Slatersville, R.I. A4 87
Slaterville*, B.C. J11 268-9
Slatington, Pa. G14 84-5
Slaton, Tex. D5 192-3
Slatyfork, W. Va. G6 200-1
Slaughter, La. G7 168-9
Slaughter Beach, Del. H5 153
Slaughtersville, Ky. I5 164-5
Slave Lake, Alta. G7 264-5
Slayden, Miss. A8 176-7
Slayden, Tenn. G5 188-9
Slayton, Minn. O3 116-7
Slayton, Mont. F10 222-3
Sledge, Miss. C6 176-7
Sleepy Creek, W. Va. D11 200-1
Sleepy Eye, Minn. N4 116-7
Sleepy Hollow, Ill. L1 96-7
Sleetmute, Alaska F9 254-5
Slick, Okla. E13 234-5
Slick Rock, Colo. H5 214-5
Slickville, Pa. A8 84-5
Slidell, La. H10 168-9
Sligo, Ky. F10 164-5
Sligo, La. B2 168-9
Slinger, Wis. I4 140-1
Slippery Rock, Pa. F2 84-5
Sloan, Ia. E1 104-5
Sloan, Nev. N9 226-7
Sloan, N.Y. F2 80-1
Sloatsburg, N.Y. B13 80-1
Slocan, B.C. J9 268-9
Slocan Park*, B.C. J10 268-9
Slocomb, Ala. M9 146-7
Slocum, R.I. G4 87
Slocum Corner, Mass. I12 68-9
Slope, co., N. Dak. I2 128-9
Slovak, Ark. F8 150-1
Smackover, Ark. J6 150-1
Smale, Ark. F10 150-1
Small, Ida. K9 218-9
Small Point Beach, Me. O11 64-5
Smalltown, Mass. H14 68-9
Smallwood, S.C. D10 184-5
Smallwood Res., Nfld. G3 278-9
Smartt, Tenn. J9 188-9
Smeaton, Sask. J8 294-5
Smelterville, Ida. D3 218-9
Smethport, Pa. D6 84-5
Smilax, Ky. I14 164-5
Smiley, Sask. L4 294-5
Smith, Alta. G7 264-5
Smith, Miss. K7 176-7
Smith, Nev. H2 226-7
Smith, co., Kans. C7 108-9
Smith, co., Miss. J7 176-7
Smith, co., Tenn. B9 188-9
Smith, co., Tex. E10 192-3
Smith Center, Kans. D8 108-9
Smith Mills, Ky. H4 164-5
Smith River, Calif. D1 210-1
Smith Valley, Ind. G2 100-1
Smith Village, Okla. J2 234-5
Smithburg, W. Va. E5 200-1
Smithdale, Miss. L5 176-7
Smithers, B.C. F5 268-9
Smithers, W. Va. I15 200-1
Smithfield, Ind. G11 100-1
Smithfield, Ky. A4 164-5
Smithfield, Me. J4 64-5
Smithfield, Nebr. I8 124-5
Smithfield, N.C. E11 180-1
Smithfield, O. E11 132-3
Smithfield, Ont. K12 284-5
Smithfield, Pa. K2 84-5
Smithfield*, R.I. B4 87
Smithfield, Ut. C6 242-3
Smithfield, Va. G3 196-7
Smithfield, W. Va. B12 200-1
Smithfield Center*, Pa. H7 84-5
Smithland, Ia. E2 104-5
Smithland, Ky. I3 164-5
Smithonia, Ga. F6 160-1
Smiths, Ala. H10 146-7
Smiths, Miss. I5 176-7
Smiths Chapel, Tenn. A9 188-9
Smiths Cove, N.S. E4 281
Smiths Creek, Mich. G8 112-3
Smiths Creek, N.B. I6 275
Smiths Falls, Ont. I14 284-5
Smiths Ferry, Ida. K3 218-9
Smiths Grove, Ky. J8 164-5
Smithsburg, Md. B8 172-3
Smithton, Ark. H5 150-1
Smithton, Ill. L6 96-7
Smithton, Mo. E5 120-1
Smithtown, N.H. O9 72-3
Smithtown, N.C. G2 180-1
Smithtown, W. Va. B15 200-1
Smithville, Ark. B9 150-1
Smithville, Ark. K3 150-1
Smithville, Ga. L4 160-1
Smithville, Ind. K7 100-1
Smithville, Me. K9 64-5
Smithville, Md. F14 172-3
Smithville, Miss. D10 176-7
Smithville, Mo. D3 120-1
Smithville, N.H. O5 72-3
Smithville, O. E13 132-3
Smithville, Okla. H16 234-5
Smithville, Ont. D15 284-5
Smithville, Tenn. B9 188-9
Smithville, Tex. G9 192-3
Smithville, W. Va. E4 200-1
Smithwick, S. Dak. H3 136-7
Smoaks, S.C. H11 184-5
Smoke Creek, Nev. D2 226-7
Smoky Junction, Tenn. G11 188-9
Smoky Lake, Alta. I8 264-5
Smolan, Kans. F10 108-9
Smoot, W. Va. I5 200-1
Smoot, Wyo. G5 250-1
Smooth Rock Falls, Ont. F7 284-5
Smyre, N.C. J1 180-1
Smyrna, Del. E3 153
Smyrna, Ga. B10 160-1
Smyrna*, Me. E8 64-5
Smyrna, N.C. F15 180-1
Smyrna, S.C. A9 184-5
Smyrna, Tenn. H7 188-9
Smyrna Mills, Me. E8 64-5
Smyth, co., Va. J5 196-7
Snake R., Ida. M3 218-9
Snake R., Wash. H14 246-7
Snead, Ala. O7 146-7
Sneads, Fla. B6 156-7
Sneads Ferry, N.C. G13 180-1
Sneedville, Tenn. F14 188-9
Snelling, S.C. G9 184-5
Snellville, Ga. B12 160-1
Snider, Mont. D2 222-3
Snohomish, Wash. G3 246-7
Snohomish, co., Wash. D9 246-7
Snoqualmie, Wash. F9 246-7
Snoqualmie Falls, Wash. F9 246-7
Snover, Mich. E6 112-3
Snow, Okla. H15 234-5
Snow Hill, Ala. J6 146-7
Snow Hill, Ark. J6 150-1
Snow Hill, Md. H15 172-3
Snow Hill, N.C. E13 180-1
Snow Lake, Ark. H10 150-1
Snow Lake, Man. F2 272-3
Snowball, Ark. C6 150-1
Snowden, Sask. J8 294-5

Snowden, Va. H9 196-7
Snowdoun, Ala. I7 146-7
Snowflake, Ariz. G10 206-7
Snowflake, Man. K12 272-3
Snowmass, Colo. E8 214-5
Snowville, N.H. I8 72-3
Snowville, Ut. C5 242-3
Snowville, Va. J7 196-7
Snyder, Ark. J8 150-1
Snyder, Colo. C14 214-5
Snyder, Nebr. F14 124-5
Snyder, Okla. H8 234-5
Snyder, Tex. D5 192-3
Snyder, co., Pa. H10 84-5
Soap Lake, Wash. F12 246-7
Sobieski, Minn. K5 116-7
Sobieski, Wis. D4 140-1
Sobol, Okla. H15 234-5
Social Circle, Ga. G5 160-1
Social Hill, Ark. G5 150-1
Society Hill, Ala. I9 146-7
Society Hill, S.C. C13 184-5
Socorro, N. Mex. H5 230-1
Socorro, co., N. Mex. H5 230-1
Sod, W. Va. I12 200-1
Soda Creek, B.C. H7 268-9
Soda Springs, Ida. N10 218-9
Sodaville, Nev. I4 226-7
Sodaville, Ore. J1 238-9
Soddy-Daisy, Tenn. K11 188-9
Sodus, N.Y. E5 80-1
Sodus Point, N.Y. E5 80-1
Sointula, B.C. I4 268-9
Solana, Fla. H11 156-7
Solana Beach*, Calif. O8 210-1
Solano, N. Mex. D10 230-1
Solano, co., Calif. H3 210-1
Soldier, Ida. M5 218-9
Soldier, Ia. F2 104-5
Soldier, Kans. D13 108-9
Soldier, Ky. F14 164-5
Soldier Pond, Me. B7 64-5
Soldier Summit, Ut. G7 242-3
Soldiers Grove, Wis. I10 140-1
Soldotna, Alaska F11 254-5
Soledad, Calif. K4 210-1
Solen, N. Dak. I7 128-9
Solgohachia, Ark. D6 150-1
Solomon, Ariz. J10 206-7
Solomon, Kans. F10 108-9
Solomon, Que. I7 290-1
Solomon R., Kans. E9 108-9
Solomons, Md. H12 172-3
Solon, Ia. G13 104-5
Solon, Me. I4 64-5
Solon, O. B15 132-3
Solon Springs, Wis. B8 140-1
Solsberry, Ind. K6 100-1
Solsgirth, Man. H10 272-3
Solvang, Calif. M5 210-1
Solvay, N.Y. E7 80-1
Solway, Minn. G4 116-7
Solway, Tenn. H11 188-9
Sombra*, Ont. E10 284-5
Somerdale, N.J. O11 76-7
Somers, Conn. B11 60-1
Somers, Ia. E6 104-5
Somers, Mont. C3 222-3
Somers, Wis. K5 140-1
Somers Point, N.J. M5 76-7
Somerset, Colo. F7 214-5
Somerset, Ind. E9 100-1
Somerset, Kans. G16 108-9
Somerset, Ky. J11 164-5
Somerset, Man. K12 272-3
Somerset, Md. I3 172-3
Somerset, Mass. G11 68-9
Somerset, N.J. G4 76-7
Somerset, O. G8 132-3
Somerset, Pa. J4 84-5
Somerset, Tex. K1 192-3
Somerset*, Vt. M5 90-1
Somerset, Va. C1 196-7
Somerset, Wis. E7 140-1
Somerset, co., Me. F4 64-5
Somerset, co., Md. H14 172-3
Somerset, co., N.J. F5 76-7
Somerset, co., Pa. K5 84-5
Somerset Center, Mich. J13 112-3
Somerset Res., Vt. M5 90-1
Somersville, Conn. B10 60-1
Somersworth, N.H. M9 72-3
Somerton, Ariz. J2 206-7
Somervell, co., Tex. E8 192-3
Somerville, Ala. C6 146-7
Somerville, Ind. N4 100-1
Somerville, Me. K5 64-5
Somerville, Mass. D11 68-9
Somerville, N.J. F5 76-7
Somerville, O. I13 132-3
Somerville, Tenn. K3 188-9
Somerville, Tex. G9 192-3
Somerville, Va. B2 196-7
Somme, Sask. K9 294-5
Sommerfeld, Man. K14 272-3
Somonauk, Ill. C9 96-7
Sondheimer, La. B7 168-9
Sonnette, Mont. H14 222-3
Sonningdale, Sask. K5 294-5
Sonoita, Ariz. L9 206-7
Sonoma, Calif. B7 210-1
Sonoma, co., Calif. J2 210-1
Sonora, Ariz. I8 206-7
Sonora, Calif. C11 210-1
Sonora, Ky. E1 164-5
Sonora, Tex. G6 192-3
Sontag, Miss. K6 176-7
Sooke, B.C. E12 268-9
Sopchoppy, Fla. C7 156-7
Soper, Okla. I14 234-5
Soperton, Ga. J8 160-1
Sophia, N.C. H4 180-1
Sophia, W. Va. K15 200-1
Soquel*, Calif. J3 210-1
Sorel, Que. H13 290-1
Sorento, Ill. J7 96-7
Sorrento, B.C. I8 268-9
Sorrento, La. B11 168-9
Sorrento, Me. K8 64-5
Soso, Miss. J8 176-7
Souderton, Pa. I15 84-5
Soulanges, co., Que. J10 290-1
Sound View, Conn. H12 60-1
Sour Lake*, Tex. G11 192-3
Souris, Man. J10 272-3
Souris, N. Dak. B7 128-9
Souris, P.E.I. E10 287
Souris Line Road*, P.E.I. E11 287
Souris West, P.E.I. E10 287
South, Ala. L7 146-7
South Acton, Mass. G2 68-9
South Addison, Me. K9 64-5
South Alburg, Vt. B3 90-1
South Amana, Ia. G12 104-5
South Amboy, N.J. F7 76-7
South Amherst, O. B8 132-3
South Apopka, Fla. E11 156-7
South Ashburnham, Mass. B8 68-9
South Bailey*, Alta. I8 264-5
South Bar of Sydney River*, N.S. B11 281
South Barre, Mass. D7 68-9
South Bay, Fla. H13 156-7
South Bay*, Man. D3 272-3
South Baymouth, Ont. H7 284-5
South Beach*, Man. G13 272-3
South Belmar, N.J. H8 76-7
South Beloit, Ill. A8 96-7
South Bend, Ind. A8 100-1
South Bend, Nebr. J2 124-5
South Bend, Wash. H5 246-7
South Bennettsville, S.C. C14 184-5
South Berwick, Me. O2 64-5
South Berwick*, N.S. D6 281
South Bethany, Ind. K8 100-1
South Bloomfield, O. G6 132-3
South Boardman, Mich. F12 112-3
South Boston, Mass. H5 68-9
South Boston, Va. J10 196-7
South Bound Brook, N.J. F6 76-7
South Branch, N.J. F5 76-7
South Branch, Nfld. N7 278-9
South Brewster, Mass. G16 68-9
South Bristol, Me. N12 64-5
South Britain, Conn. F5 60-1
South Broadway*, Wash. H11 246-7
South Brook, Nfld. M8 278-9
South Brunswick*, N.J. G6 76-7
South Burlington, Vt. E4 90-1
South Byron, Wis. H3 140-1
South Calera, Ala. G6 146-7
South Cambridge, Vt. D5 90-1
South Canaan, Conn. B5 60-1
South Carmen, N. Mex. D8 230-1
South Carrollton, Ky. I6 164-5
South Carthage*, Tenn. B9 188-9
South Casco, Me. N8 64-5
South Chaplin, Conn. D13 60-1
South Charleston, O. G5 132-3
South Charleston, W. Va. H13 200-1
South Chicago Heights, Ill. O4 96-7
South China, Me. K5 64-5
South City Trailer Court*, B.C. I9 268-9
South Cle Elum, Wash. G10 246-7
South Cleveland*, Tenn. D11 188-9
South Clinton*, Tenn. H11 188-9
South Coatesville*, Pa. J14 84-5
South Coffeyville, Okla. B14 234-5
South Colby, Wash. I2 246-7
South Cole Creek, Wyo. F13 250-1
South Congaree, S.C. E10 184-5
South Connellsville, Pa. J3 84-5
South Corning, N.Y. G5 80-1
South Coventry, Conn. D11 60-1
South Creek, N.C. E14 180-1
South Danbury, N.H. K5 72-3
South Danville, N.H. O8 72-3
South Dayton, N.Y. G2 80-1
South Daytona, Fla. D12 156-7
South Deerfield, Mass. C5 68-9
South Dennis, N.J. N4 76-7
South Dover, Me. I6 64-5
South Duxbury*, Mass. F13 68-9
South Duxbury, Vt. F5 90-1
South Egremont, Mass. E1 68-9
South El Monte*, Calif. G9 210-1
South Elgin, Ill. L1 96-7
South Eliot, Me. O2 64-5
South English, Ia. H11 104-5
South Euclid, O. B15 132-3
South Fallsburg, N.Y. H9 80-1
South Farmingdale*, N.Y. J11 80-1
South Fayetteville, N.C. K7 180-1
South Flomaton*, Fla. A3 156-7
South Floral Park*, N.Y. J11 80-1
South Fork, Colo. I9 214-5
South Fork, Pa. I5 84-5
South Fort Polk*, La. F2 168-9
South Foster, R.I. C3 87
South Freeport, Me. N10 64-5
South Fulton, Tenn. A3 188-9
South Gastonia, N.C. F6 180-1
South Gate*, Calif. G8 210-1
South Gate*, Md. D11 172-3
South Gate Ridge*, Fla. G10 156-7
South Georgetown, Mass. B12 68-9
South Gifford, Mo. B6 120-1
South Glastonbury, Conn. E10 60-1
South Glens Falls, N.Y. E11 80-1
South Goldsboro*, N.C. E12 180-1
South Gorin, Mo. A7 120-1
South Gouldsboro, Me. K8 64-5
South Greenfield, Mo. H4 120-1
South Greensburg, Pa. B8 84-5
South Groveland, Mass. A11 68-9
South Hackensack*, N.J. D8 76-7
South Hadley, Mass. D5 68-9
South Hadley Falls, Mass. E5 68-9
South Hampton, N.H. N9 72-3
South Hanover, Mass. K7 68-9
South Harpswell, Me. O10 64-5
South Harriman, Tenn. H10 188-9
South Harrison*, N.J. K2 76-7
South Harwich, Mass. H16 68-9
South Haven, Kans. K10 108-9
South Haven, Mich. J11 112-3
South Haven, Minn. L5 116-7
South Hazelton*, B.C. J6 268-9
South Heart, N. Dak. G3 128-9
South Henderson, N.C. C11 180-1
South Hero, Vt. D3 90-1
South Hero Isl., Vt. D3 90-1
South Hill, Va. J11 196-7
South Hinesburg, Vt. F4 90-1
South Hiram, Me. N7 64-5
South Holbrook*, N.Y. K12 80-1
South Holland, Ill. N4 96-7
South Hooksett, N.H. N7 72-3
South Hope, Me. L6 64-5
South Houston, Tex. H14 192-3
South Hudson Falls*, N.Y. E11 80-1
South Huntington*, N.Y. J12 80-1
South Hutchinson, Kans. H9 108-9
South Indian Lake, Man. D3 272-3
South International Falls, Minn. E6 116-7
South Irvine, Ky. H12 164-5
South Jacksonville, Ill. H6 96-7
South Jordan, Ut. F6 242-3
South Junction, Man. K16 272-3
South Junction, Ore. D9 238-9
South Kensington*, Md. E9 172-3
South Kent, Conn. D4 60-1
South Killingly, Conn. C15 60-1
South Kingstown*, R.I. H4 87
South Lagrange, Me. I7 64-5
South Laguna*, Calif. H9 210-1
South Lake Tahoe, Calif. H5 210-1
South Lakeside*, B.C. G4 268-9
South Lancaster, Mass. C9 68-9
South Laurel*, Md. D10 172-3
South Lead Hill*, Ark. A5 150-1
South Lebanon, Me. O1 64-5
South Lebanon, O. K15 132-3
South Lee, Mass. D2 68-9
South Lincoln, Me. H7 64-5
South Lincoln, Vt. G5 90-1
South Lineville, Mo. A5 120-1
South Lockport*, N.Y. E3 80-1
South Londonderry, Vt. L5 90-1
South Lunenburg, Vt. E10 90-1
South Lyme, Conn. H12 60-1
South Lynchburg, S.C. E13 184-5
South Lyndeboro, N.H. O5 72-3
South Lynnfield, Mass. F6 68-9
South Lyon, Mich. J4 112-3
South Mansfield, La. C2 168-9
South Mashpee, Mass. H14 68-9
South Medford*, Ore. J6 238-9
South Merrimack, N.H. O6 72-3
South Miami, Fla. I16 156-7
South Miami Heights*, Fla. J13 156-7
South Milford, Ind. A10 100-1
South Mills, N.C. C15 180-1
South Milwaukee, Wis. J5 140-1
South Modesto*, Calif. I4 210-1
South Monroe, Mich. K14 112-3
South Mound, Kans. J15 108-9
South Mount Vernon, O. E7 132-3
South Naknek, Alaska G9 254-5
South Natick, Mass. I3 68-9
South Newbury, N.H. L4 72-3
South Newfane, Vt. N6 90-1
South Norfolk, Conn. B6 60-1
South Nyack, N.Y. C14 80-1
South of the Border, S.C. C15 184-5
South Ogden, Ut. D6 242-3
South Orange, N.J. D9 76-7
South Orleans, Mass. G16 68-9
South Oroville*, Calif. G4 210-1
South Orrington, Me. J7 64-5
South Palm Beach, Fla. E16 156-7
South Paris, Me. L3 64-5
South Park View*, Ky. G9 164-5
South Pasadena*, Calif. G8 210-1
South Pasadena, Fla. I2 156-7
South Pass City, Wyo. G8 250-1
South Patrick Shores*, Fla. F13 156-7
South Peacham, Vt. F8 90-1
South Pekin, Ill. F7 96-7
South Peninsula*, Fla. D12 156-7
South Penobscot, Me. K7 64-5
South Pittsburg, Tenn. K10 188-9
South Plainfield, N.J. F6 76-7
South Point, O. K7 132-3
South Pomfret, Vt. J7 90-1
South Portage, N.B. H4 275
South Portland, Me. O9 64-5
South Portsmouth, Ky. E14 164-5
South Portsmouth, R.I. F7 87
South Pottstown*, Pa. I14 84-5
South Prairie, Wash. K3 246-7
South Quarter, Mass. E3 68-9
South Randolph, Vt. H6 90-1
South Range, Mich. C8 112-3
South Range, Wis. B8 140-1
South River, N.J. F6 76-7
South River, Ont. H8 284-5
South Rockwood, Mich. J15 112-3
South Roxana, Ill. K6 96-7
South Royalton, Vt. I7 90-1
South Russell, O. B16 132-3
South Rustico*, P.E.I. D7 287
South Ryegate, Vt. F8 90-1
South St. Paul, Minn. B11 116-7
South Salisbury, N.C. I2 180-1
South Salt Lake, Ut. F6 242-3
South San Francisco, Calif. C7 210-1
South San Gabriel*, Calif. N7 210-1
South San Jose Hills*, Calif. N7 210-1
South San Pedro*, Tex. I8 192-3
South Scappoose, Ore. B6 238-9
South Seaside, Ore. A4 238-9
South Seaville, N.J. N4 76-7
South Sebec, Me. H6 64-5
South Seekonk, Mass. G10 68-9
South Shore, Ky. E14 164-5
South Shore, S. Dak. C15 136-7
South Sioux City, Nebr. D14 124-5
South Solon, O. G5 132-3
South Stony Brook*, N.Y. J12 80-1
South Streator*, Ill. D9 96-7
South Superior, Wyo. I8 250-1
South Taft*, Calif. L6 210-1
South Thomaston, Me. L6 64-5
South Toms River, N.J. J7 76-7
South Torrington, Wyo. H16 250-1
South Trescott, Me. J11 64-5
South Tucson, Ariz. K8 206-7
South Turlock*, Calif. J4 210-1
South Union, Ky. J7 164-5
South Uniontown*, Pa. K3 84-5
South Valley*, N. Mex. F6 230-1
South Valley Stream*, N.Y. K11 80-1
South Venice, Fla. H10 156-7
South Wadesboro*, N.C. F8 180-1
South Wallingford, Vt. K5 90-1
South Wardsboro, Vt. M5 90-1
South Warren, Me. L6 64-5
South Washington, Ind. M5 100-1
South Waterford, Me. L2 64-5
South Waverly, Pa. C11 84-5
South Wayne, Wis. K12 140-1
South Weare, N.H. N6 72-3
South Weber*, Ut. E6 242-3
South Webster, O. J7 132-3
South Weldon*, N.C. C13 180-1
South Wellfleet, Mass. F16 68-9
South Wellington, B.C. C12 268-9
South West City, Mo. J3 120-1
South West Lot 16, P.E.I. D4 287
South West Margaree, N.S. B10 281
South West Port Mouton, N.S. F5 281
South Westbury*, N.Y. J11 80-1
South Whitley, Ind. C10 100-1
South Whittier*, Calif. N7 210-1
South Williamson, Ky. H16 164-5
South Williamsport, Pa. F10 84-5
South Williamstown, Mass. B2 68-9
South Willington, Conn. C12 60-1
South Wilmington, Ill. D10 96-7
South Wilmington, N.C. H12 180-1
South Wilton, Conn. I4 60-1
South Windham, Conn. D12 60-1
South Windham, Vt. M6 90-1
South Windham [-Little Falls], Me. O8 64-5
South Windsor, Conn. C9 60-1
South Windsor, Me. L5 64-5
South Wolfeboro, N.H. K8 72-3
South Woodbury, Vt. E7 90-1
South Woodstock, Conn. B14 60-1
South Woodstock, Me. K2 64-5
South Worthington, Mass. D3 68-9
South Yarmouth, Mass. H15 68-9
South Yuba City*, Calif. G3 210-1
South Zanesville, O. G8 132-3
Southampton, Mass. E4 68-9
Southampton*, N.J. J4 76-7
Southampton, N.Y. J13 80-1
Southampton, Ont. B12 284-5
Southampton, co., Va. J13 196-7
Southard, N.J. H7 76-7
Southard, Okla. D9 234-5
Southaven, Miss. A6 176-7
Southbank, B.C. F5 268-9
Southbeach, Ore. E4 238-9
Southborough, Mass. I1 68-9
Southbridge, Mass. E7 68-9
Southbury, Conn. F5 60-1
Southern Indian Lake, Man. C3 272-3
Southern Pines, N.C. K3 180-1
Southern View, Ill. H7 96-7
Southey, Sask. M8 294-5
Southfield, Mich. J5 112-3
Southford, Conn. F6 60-1
Southgate, Ky. D11 164-5
Southgate, Mich. K6 112-3
Southington, Conn. E8 60-1
Southlake, Tex. C13 192-3
Southmont*, Pa. I5 84-5
Southold*, N.Y. J13 80-1
Southport, Conn. I5 60-1

Southport, Fla. B5 156-7
Southport*, Ind. H8 100-1
Southport, Me. N11 64-5
Southport*, N.Y. G6 80-1
Southport, N.C. H12 180-1
Southport, P.E.I. F7 287
Southside, Ala. D8 146-7
Southside, Ark. D7 150-1
Southside, Tenn. G5 188-9
Southside Place*, Tex. H13 192-3
Southwest Greensburg, Pa. B8 84-5
Southwest Harbor, Me. L8 64-5
Southwest Little Rock*, Ark. F7 150-1
Southwick, Ida. F3 218-9
Southwick, Mass. F4 68-9
Southwood, Del. A2 153
Southworth, Wash. I2 246-7
Sovereign, Sask. L5 294-5
Spackenhill*, N.Y. H11 80-1
Spalding, Ida. F2 218-9
Spalding, Mich. E10 112-3
Spalding, Nebr. F11 124-5
Spalding, Sask. K8 294-5
Spalding, co., Ga. H4 160-1
Spanaway, Wash. K2 246-7
Spangle, Wash. F16 246-7
Spangler, Pa. H5 84-5
Spaniard's Bay*, Nfld. N11 278-9
Spanish, Ont. H7 284-5
Spanish Fork, Ut. G6 242-3
Spanish Fort, Ala. N3 146-7
Spanish Lake*, Mo. E10 120-1
Spanishburg, W. Va. J4 200-1
Sparkman, Ark. H5 150-1
Sparks, Ga. N6 160-1
Sparks, Kans. C15 108-9
Sparks, Md. B11 172-3
Sparks, Nebr. C7 124-5
Sparks, Nev. F2 226-7
Sparks, Okla. E12 234-5
Sparland, Ill. E7 96-7
Sparlingville, Mich. G8 112-3
Sparr, Fla. D10 156-7
Sparrows Point, Md. G7 172-3
Sparta, Ga. H7 160-1
Sparta, Ill. M7 96-7
Sparta, Ind. K11 100-1
Sparta, Ky. E10 164-5
Sparta, Mich. I12 112-3
Sparta, Mo. I5 120-1
Sparta, N.J. C5 76-7
Sparta, N.C. C6 180-1
Sparta, Tenn. B10 188-9
Sparta, Va. G13 196-7
Sparta, Wis. H10 140-1
Spartanburg, S.C. B8 184-5
Spartanburg, co., S.C. B7 184-5
Sparwood, B.C. J11 268-9
Spaulding, Okla. G13 234-5
Spavinaw, Okla. C15 234-5
Spear Springs, Tenn. G14 188-9
Spearfish, S. Dak. E1 136-7
Spearman, Tex. A5 192-3
Spearsville, La. A4 168-9
Spearville, Kans. I5 108-9
Speed, Ind. M9 100-1
Speed, Kans. D6 108-9
Speed, N.C. D13 180-1
Speedway, Ind. F1 100-1
Speedwell, Tenn. G12 188-9
Speedwell, Va. J5 196-7
Speer, Okla. I14 234-5
Speers*, Pa. J2 84-5
Speers, Sask. K6 294-5
Speigner, Ala. H7 146-7
Spelter, W. Va. C13 200-1
Spenard, Alaska F11 254-5
Spence, Md. H15 172-3
Spence Bay, N.W. Terr. B3 296
Spencer, Ida. K9 218-9
Spencer, Ind. J6 100-1
Spencer, Ia. B4 104-5
Spencer, La. B5 168-9
Spencer, Mass. D7 68-9
Spencer, Nebr. C10 124-5
Spencer, N.Y. G6 80-1
Spencer, N.C. I2 180-1
Spencer, O. D12 132-3
Spencer, Okla. J2 234-5
Spencer, S. Dak. G14 136-7
Spencer, Tenn. I10 188-9
Spencer, Va. K8 196-7
Spencer, W. Va. F4 200-1
Spencer, Wis. F11 140-1
Spencer, co., Ind. O5 100-1
Spencer, co., Ky. G9 164-5
Spencer Mountain*, N.C. E6 180-1
Spencerport, N.Y. E4 80-1
Spencerville, Ind. B11 100-1
Spencerville, O. D4 132-3
Spencerville*, Ont. I15 284-5
Spences Bridge, B.C. I7 268-9
Sperling, Man. J13 272-3
Sperry, Okla. D13 234-5
Sperryville, Va. B1 196-7
Spiceland, Ind. H10 100-1
Spicer, Minn. L4 116-7
Spickardsville, Mo. B4 120-1
Spillman, La. F7 168-9
Spillville, Ia. B12 104-5
Spindale, N.C. E5 180-1
Spink, S. Dak. I16 136-7
Spink, co., S. Dak. D12 136-7
Spion Kop, Mont. D8 222-3
Spirit Lake, Ida. C2 218-9
Spirit Lake, Ia. A4 104-5
Spirit Lake, Ia. A4 104-5
Spirit Lake, Wash. I8 246-7
Spirit River, Alta. F4 264-5
Spiritwood, Sask. J6 294-5
Spiritwood Lake, N. Dak. G11 128-9
Spiro, Okla. F16 234-5
Spivey, Kans. J9 108-9
Spivey, Tenn. A9 188-9
Split Rock, Wyo. G10 250-1
Spofford, N.H. O3 72-3
Spofford, Ore. A13 238-9
Spokane, La. D6 168-9
Spokane, Wash. E16 246-7
Spokane, co., Wash. F15 246-7
Spoon R., Ill. F5 96-7
Spooner, Wis. D8 140-1
Spotswood, N.J. G6 76-7
Spotsylvania, Va. G12 196-7
Spotsylvania, co., Va. G12 196-7
Spotted Horse, Wyo. B13 250-1
Spottsville, Ky. H5 164-5
Spragge, Ont. H6 284-5
Sprague, Ala. J7 146-7
Sprague*, Conn. E13 60-1
Sprague, Man. K16 272-3
Sprague, Nebr. I14 124-5
Sprague, Wash. F15 246-7
Sprague, W. Va. K16 200-1
Sprague River, Ore. J8 238-9
Spragueville, Ia. F15 104-5
Spragueville, R.I. B4 87
Spray, Ore. D11 238-9
Spread Eagle, Wis. C14 140-1
Spreckelsville, Hawaii G11 258-9
Spreckerville*, Alta. G4 264-5
Spring Arbor, Mich. K1 112-3
Spring Bay, Ont. H7 284-5
Spring Brook, N. Dak. D2 128-9
Spring Canyon, Ut. H8 242-3
Spring City, Pa. A9 84-5
Spring City, Tenn. C11 188-9
Spring City, Ut. H7 242-3
Spring Creek, Okla. F9 234-5
Spring Creek, Tenn. C4 188-9
Spring Dale, W. Va. I5 200-1
Spring Gap, Md. B4 172-3
Spring Garden, Ala. D9 146-7
Spring Glen, Ut. H8 242-3
Spring Green, Wis. J11 140-1
Spring Grove, Ind. H12 100-1
Spring Grove, Ky. H4 164-5
Spring Grove, Minn. O9 116-7
Spring Grove, Pa. K11 84-5
Spring Grove, Va. F2 196-7
Spring Hill, Ala. J10 146-7
Spring Hill, Ala. K8 146-7
Spring Hill, Ark. I3 150-1
Spring Hill, Conn. C12 60-1
Spring Hill, Ia. H8 104-5
Spring Hill, Kans. F16 108-9
Spring Hill, Minn. K4 116-7
Spring Hill*, Pa. I6 84-5
Spring Hill, Tenn. I6 188-9
Spring Hope, N.C. D12 180-1
Spring Lake, Ind. H9 100-1
Spring Lake, Mich. I11 112-3
Spring Lake, N.J. H8 76-7
Spring Lake, N.C. K6 180-1
Spring Lake, Ut. G6 242-3
Spring Lake, Wis. F2 140-1
Spring Lake Heights, N.J. H8 76-7
Spring Lake Park, Minn. A10 116-7
Spring Lick, Ky. I7 164-5
Spring Mills, S.C. C11 184-5
Spring Park*, Minn. M6 116-7
Spring Place, Ga. D3 160-1
Spring Ridge, La. C1 168-9
Spring Valley, Ala. B4 146-7
Spring Valley, Ark. B3 150-1
Spring Valley*, Calif. O8 210-1
Spring Valley, Ill. D8 96-7
Spring Valley, Minn. O8 116-7
Spring Valley, N.Y. C13 80-1
Spring Valley, O. I15 132-3
Spring Valley, P.E.I. D5 287
Spring Valley, Sask. N7 294-5
Spring Valley, Tex. H13 192-3
Spring Valley, Wis. F8 140-1
Springboro, O. I14 132-3
Springbrook, Ia. E15 104-5
Springbrook, Ore. G1 238-9
Springbrook, Wis. C9 140-1
Springdale, Ark. B2 150-1
Springdale, Ida. O7 218-9
Springdale, Ia. G13 104-5
Springdale, Mont. G8 222-3
Springdale, Nev. K7 226-7
Springdale, Nfld. L9 278-9
Springdale, O. K13 132-3
Springdale, Pa. A7 84-5
Springdale, S.C. B11 184-5
Springdale, S.C. E10 184-5
Springdale, Ut. M4 242-3
Springdale, Wash. D15 246-7
Springer, N. Mex. C9 230-1
Springer, Okla. H11 234-5
Springerville, Ariz. G11 206-7
Springfield, Ark. D6 150-1
Springfield, Colo. I15 214-5
Springfield, Fla. C5 156-7
Springfield, Ga. J11 160-1
Springfield, Ida. M9 218-9
Springfield, Ill. H7 96-7
Springfield, Ky. D4 164-5
Springfield, La. A12 168-9
Springfield, Me. H8 64-5
Springfield, Mass. E5 68-9
Springfield, Mich. J12 112-3
Springfield, Minn. N4 116-7
Springfield, Mo. H5 120-1
Springfield, Nebr. J2 124-5
Springfield, N.H. K4 72-3
Springfield*, N.J. I5 76-7
Springfield, N.J. E7 76-7
Springfield, O. F5 132-3
Springfield, Ont. E12 284-5
Springfield, Ore. K1 238-9
Springfield, S.C. F9 184-5
Springfield, S. Dak. I13 136-7
Springfield, Tenn. F6 188-9
Springfield, Vt. L7 90-1
Springfield, Va. B4 196-7
Springfield, W. Va. D10 200-1
Springfield Place, Mich. J12 112-3
Springhill, Ark. E6 150-1
Springhill, La. A2 168-9
Springhill, N.S. C6 281
Springlake Park*, Okla. F11 234-5
Springlee*, Ky. G9 164-5
Springport, Ind. G10 100-1
Springport, Mich. J13 112-3
Springside, Sask. L10 294-5
Springstein*, Man. J14 272-3
Springston, Ida. D3 218-9
Springtown, Ark. A2 150-1
Springtown*, Tex. D8 192-3
Springvale, Ga. L3 160-1
Springvale, Me. N2 64-5
Springview, Nebr. C8 124-5
Springville, Ala. E7 146-7
Springville, Ind. K7 100-1
Springville, Ia. F13 104-5
Springville, La. A12 168-9
Springville, Miss. C8 176-7
Springville, N.Y. F3 80-1
Springville, Tenn. B5 188-9
Springville, Ut. G6 242-3
Springwater, Sask. L5 294-5
Sproat Lake, B.C. J5 268-9
Sprott, Ala. H5 146-7
Sproutville*, N.Y. I11 80-1
Spruce, Mich. F14 112-3
Spruce Corner, Mass. C4 68-9
Spruce Grove, Alta. I7 264-5
Spruce Head, Me. M6 64-5
Spruce Lake*, Sask. J4 294-5
Spruce Pine, Ala. C4 146-7
Spruce Pine, N.C. D5 180-1
Spruce View*, Alta. K7 264-5
Sprucedale, Ont. H8 284-5
Spry, Ut. L5 242-3
Spur, Tex. D5 192-3
Spurgeon, Ind. N5 100-1
Spy Hill, Sask. M11 294-5
Squa Pan, Me. D8 64-5
Squamish, B.C. A13 268-9
Squantum, Mass. I5 68-9
Square Butte, Mont. D8 222-3
Squatec*, Que. I4 290-1
Squaw Harbor*, Alaska I8 254-5
Squaw Lake, Minn. G5 116-7
Squire, W. Va. K3 200-1
Squirrel, Ida. K11 218-9
Stacy, Minn. L7 116-7
Stacy, N.C. F15 180-1
Stacyville, Ia. A10 104-5
Stacyville, Me. F7 64-5
Stafford, Conn. B12 60-1
Stafford, Kans. I8 108-9
Stafford*, N.J. K7 76-7
Stafford, Okla. F8 234-5
Stafford, S.C. I10 184-5
Stafford, Tex. I13 192-3
Stafford, Va. C3 196-7
Stafford, co., Kans. H8 108-9
Stafford, co., Va. F12 196-7
Stafford Springs, Conn. B12 60-1
Staffordsville, Ky. H15 164-5
Staffordsville, Va. I6 196-7
Staffordville, Conn. B12 60-1
Stainville, Tenn. G11 188-9
Staley, N.C. I5 180-1
Stallo, Miss. G8 176-7
Stambaugh, Mich. D8 112-3
Stamford, Conn. J3 60-1
Stamford, Nebr. J9 124-5
Stamford, N.Y. G9 80-1
Stamford, Tex. D6 192-3
Stamford, Vt. O4 90-1
Stamping Ground, Ky. A6 164-5
Stampley, Miss. K3 176-7
Stamps, Ark. J4 150-1
Stanardsville, Va. G10 196-7
Stanberry, Mo. B3 120-1
Standard, Alta. M8 264-5
Standard, La. D5 168-9
Standing Rock, Ala. G10 146-7
Standing Rock, N. Mex. E3 230-1
Standish, Me. O8 64-5
Standish, Mich. G14 112-3
Standrod, Ida. O8 218-9
Standrod, Ut. C3 242-3
Stanfield, Ariz. J6 206-7
Stanfield*, N.C. E8 180-1
Stanfield, Ore. B12 238-9
Stanford, Ark. B11 150-1
Stanford*, Calif. J3 210-1
Stanford, Ill. F8 96-7
Stanford, Ind. K6 100-1
Stanford, Ky. E6 164-5
Stanford, Mont. E8 222-3
Stanhope, Ia. E7 104-5
Stanhope, N.J. D5 76-7
Stanhope, P.E.I. E7 287
Stanislaus, co., Calif. I4 210-1
Stanley, Ida. K5 218-9
Stanley, Ia. D12 104-5
Stanley, Kans. F16 108-9
Stanley, Ky. H6 164-5
Stanley, La. C1 168-9
Stanley, N.B. H4 275
Stanley, N. Mex. F7 230-1
Stanley, N.C. J1 180-1
Stanley, N. Dak. D4 128-9
Stanley, Okla. H14 234-5
Stanley, Va. F10 196-7
Stanley, Wis. F10 140-1
Stanley, co., S. Dak. E7 136-7
Stanley Mission*, Sask. G8 294-5
Stanleytown, Va. J8 196-7
Stanleyville, N.C. G3 180-1
Stanly, co., N.C. E8 180-1
Stannard, Vt. D8 90-1
Stanstead, Que. K14 290-1
Stanstead, co., Que. J14 290-1
Stanton, Ala. H6 146-7
Stanton*, Calif. H9 210-1
Stanton, Del. B3 153
Stanton, Ia. I4 104-5
Stanton, Ky. H13 164-5
Stanton, Mich. I12 112-3
Stanton, Miss. K3 176-7
Stanton, Nebr. E13 124-5
Stanton, N.J. F6 76-7
Stanton, N. Dak. F6 128-9
Stanton, Tenn. J3 188-9
Stanton, Tex. E5 192-3
Stanton, co., Kans. I1 108-9
Stanton, co., Nebr. F13 124-5
Stantonsburg, N.C. E12 180-1
Stantonville, Tenn. D4 188-9
Stanwich, Conn. I3 60-1
Stanwood, Ia. F14 104-5
Stanwood, Mich. H12 112-3
Stanwood, Wash. F2 246-7
Staple, Ark. H9 150-1
Staplehurst, Nebr. H13 124-5
Staples, Minn. J4 116-7
Stapleton, Ala. N4 146-7
Stapleton, Ga. H8 160-1
Stapleton, Nebr. G7 124-5
Star, Ida. L3 218-9
Star, Miss. J6 176-7
Star, N.C. J4 180-1
Star, Okla. F15 234-5
Star City, Ark. H8 150-1
Star City, Ind. D7 100-1
Star City, Sask. J8 294-5
Star City, W. Va. A15 200-1
Star Prairie, Wis. E7 140-1
Starboard, Me. J10 64-5
Starbuck, Man. J14 272-3
Starbuck, Minn. K3 116-7
Starbuck, Wash. H15 246-7
Stargo, Ariz. J11 206-7
Stark, Kans. I15 108-9
Stark, N.H. E7 72-3
Stark, co., Ill. D7 96-7
Stark, co., N. Dak. H4 128-9
Stark, co., O. D10 132-3
Stark City, Mo. I3 120-1
Starke, Fla. C10 156-7
Starke, co., Ind. B7 100-1
Starkey, Ore. C13 238-9
Starks, La. H1 168-9
Starks, Me. J4 64-5
Starksboro, Vt. F4 90-1
Starkville, Colo. J12 214-5
Starkville, Miss. E9 176-7
Starkweather, N. Dak. C10 128-9
Starr, S.C. D5 184-5
Starr, co., Tex. K7 192-3
Starr King, N.H. F7 72-3
Starrat-Olsen, Ont. D1 284-5
Start, La. B6 168-9
Startex, S.C. F3 184-5
Startup, Wash. E9 246-7
State Center, Ia. F9 104-5
State College, Pa. G8 84-5
State Line, Ida. C2 218-9
State Line, La. F10 168-9
State Line, Mass. D1 68-9
State Line, Miss. K10 176-7
State Line, N.H. O4 72-3
State Line City, Ind. G4 100-1
State Road, Del. B3 153
State Road, Me. C8 64-5
State Road, N.C. C7 180-1
Stateburg, S.C. E11 184-5
Stateline, Nev. G1 226-7
Staten, W. Va. F4 200-1
Staten Island, N.Y. F13 80-1
Statenville, Ga. O7 160-1
Statesboro, Ga. J10 160-1
Statesville, N.C. D7 180-1
Statesville, Tenn. B8 188-9
Statham, Ga. F5 160-1
Station Camp, Ky. H12 164-5
Statts Mills, W. Va. F3 200-1
Stauffer, Ore. G11 238-9
Staunton, Ill. J7 96-7
Staunton, Ind. I5 100-1
Staunton, Va. G9 196-7
Stavely, Alta. N8 264-5
Staves, Ark. H7 150-1
Stay, Ky. H13 164-5
Stayner, Ont. B14 284-5
Stayton, Ore. I2 238-9
Staytonville, Del. H4 153
Stead, Man. I15 272-3
Stead, N. Mex. D11 230-1
Steamboat, Ariz. D10 206-7
Steamboat, Nev. F2 226-7
Steamboat, Ore. H6 238-9
Steamboat Rock, Ia. E9 104-5
Steamboat Springs, Colo. C9 214-5
Stearns, Ky. K11 164-5
Stearns, co., Minn. K4 116-7
Stebbins, Alaska E8 254-5
Stecker, Okla. G9 234-5
Stecoah, N.C. E2 180-1
Stedman, N.C. K7 180-1

Steedman, Okla. G13 234-5
Steedman, S.C. E9 184-5
Steele, Ala. D8 146-7
Steele, Mo. K11 120-1
Steele, N. Dak. H9 128-9
Steele, co., Minn. N6 116-7
Steele, co., N. Dak. F13 128-9
Steele City, Nebr. J13 124-5
Steeles, W. Va. J3 200-1
Steeles Tavern, Va. H9 196-7
Steeleville, Ill. M7 96-7
Steelmanville, N.J. M5 76-7
Steelton, Pa. I11 84-5
Steelville, Mo. G8 120-1
Steen, Minn. O2 116-7
Steens, Miss. E10 176-7
Steep Falls, Me. N7 64-5
Steep Rock, Man. G12 272-3
Steger, Ill. O4 96-7
Stehekin, Wash. D10 246-7
Steilacoom, Wash. K1 246-7
Steinauer, Nebr. J15 124-5
Steinbach, Man. J15 272-3
Steinhatchee, Fla. C8 156-7
Stella, Mo. I3 120-1
Stella, Nebr. J16 124-5
Stella, Okla. K3 234-5
Stellarton, N.S. C8 281
Stem, N.C. G7 180-1
Stendal, Ind. N5 100-1
Stenen, Sask. L10 294-5
Stephen, Minn. E1 116-7
Stephens, Ark. J5 150-1
Stephens, Ga. F6 160-1
Stephens, Tenn. H10 188-9
Stephens, co., Ga. D6 160-1
Stephens, co., Okla. H10 234-5
Stephens, co., Tex. E7 192-3
Stephens City*, Va. E11 196-7
Stephensburg, Ky. E1 164-5
Stephenson, Mich. E9 112-3
Stephenson, Va. D11 196-7
Stephenson, co., Ill. A7 96-7
Stephensport, Ky. G7 164-5
Stephensville, Wis. E3 140-1
Stephenville, Nfld. N7 278-9
Stephenville, Tex. E8 192-3
Stephenville Crossing, Nfld. N7 278-9
Steptoe, Nev. F10 226-7
Steptoe, Wash. G16 246-7
Sterling, Alaska F11 254-5
Sterling, Colo. C14 214-5
Sterling, Conn. D15 60-1
Sterling, Ida. N9 218-9
Sterling, Ill. C7 96-7
Sterling, Kans. H9 108-9
Sterling, Mass. C8 68-9
Sterling, Mich. G14 112-3
Sterling, Nebr. I15 124-5
Sterling, N. Dak. H8 128-9
Sterling, Okla. G9 234-5
Sterling, Ut. I6 242-3
Sterling, Va. A3 196-7
Sterling, co., Tex. E5 192-3
Sterling City, Tex. E5 192-3
Sterling Heights*, Mich. J15 112-3
Sterling Hill, Conn. D15 60-1
Sterlington*, La. B5 168-9
Sterrett, Ala. F7 146-7
Stetson, Me. I6 64-5
Stetsonville, Wis. E11 140-1
Stettler, Alta. K8 264-5
Steuben, Me. K9 64-5
Steuben, Wis. J10 140-1
Steuben, co., Ind. A11 100-1
Steuben, co., N.Y. G5 80-1
Steubenville, O. E11 132-3
Stevens, N.J. H4 76-7
Stevens, co., Kans. J2 108-9
Stevens, co., Minn. K2 116-7
Stevens, co., Wash. D15 246-7
Stevens Corner, Mass. C1 68-9
Stevens Mill, Vt. B6 90-1
Stevens Point, Wis. G12 140-1
Stevens Pottery, Ga. I6 160-1
Stevens Village, Alaska D11 254-5
Stevensburg, Va. C2 196-7
Stevenson, Ala. A8 146-7
Stevenson, Conn. G6 60-1
Stevenson, Md. E6 172-3
Stevenson, Wash. J8 246-7
Stevensville, Md. E12 172-3
Stevensville, Mich. K11 112-3
Stevensville, Mont. F3 222-3
Stevensville, Va. H13 196-7
Stewardson, Ill. I9 96-7
Stewart, Ala. G4 146-7
Stewart, B.C. E4 268-9
Stewart, Minn. C7 116-7
Stewart, Miss. F8 176-7
Stewart, Nev. G2 226-7
Stewart*, N.Y. I10 80-1
Stewart, Tenn. A5 188-9
Stewart, co., Ga. K2 160-1
Stewart, co., Tenn. A5 188-9
Stewart Crossing, Y.T. B2 297
Stewart Manor*, N.Y. J11 80-1
Stewart Valley, Sask. N5 294-5
Stewartstown, N.H. B6 72-3
Stewartstown, Pa. K11 84-5
Stewartsville, Ind. N3 100-1
Stewartsville, Mo. C3 120-1
Stewartsville, N.J. E3 76-7
Stewartville, Ala. G7 146-7
Stewartville, Mass. B4 68-9
Stewartville, Minn. O8 116-7
Stewiacke, N.S. D7 281
Stibnite, Ida. J5 218-9
Stickney*, Ill. C11 96-7
Stickney, N.B. H3 275
Stickney, S. Dak. G12 136-7
Stickney, W. Va. K14 200-1
Stickney Corner, Me. L5 64-5
Stidham, Okla. F14 234-5
Stigler, Okla. F15 234-5
Stiles, Wis. C4 140-1
Stilesboro, Ga. A8 160-1
Stilesville, Ind. I7 100-1
Still Pond, Md. C13 172-3
Stillman Valley, Ill. B8 96-7
Stillmore, Ga. J9 160-1
Stillwater, B.C. J6 268-9
Stillwater, Minn. A12 116-7
Stillwater, Nev. F4 226-7
Stillwater, N.J. C4 76-7
Stillwater, N.Y. E11 80-1
Stillwater, Okla. D11 234-5
Stillwater, co., Mont. G9 222-3
Stilson, Ga. J10 160-1
Stiltner, W. Va. I10 200-1
Stilwell, Okla. E16 234-5
Stinesville, Ind. J7 100-1
Stinnett, Tex. A5 192-3
Stirling, Alta. O9 264-5
Stirling, N.J. E6 76-7
Stirling, Ont. J12 284-5
Stirling City, Calif. F4 210-1
Stirrat, W. Va. K12 200-1
Stirum, N. Dak. I13 128-9
Stites, Ida. G4 218-9
Stittsville*, Ont. H14 284-5
Stitzer, Wis. J10 140-1
Stockbridge, Ga. D11 160-1
Stockbridge, Mass. D2 68-9
Stockbridge, Mich. J2 112-3
Stockbridge, Vt. I6 90-1
Stockbridge, Wis. F4 140-1
Stockdale, Tex. K4 192-3
Stockett, Mont. D7 222-3
Stockham, Nebr. H12 124-5
Stockholm, Me. B8 64-5
Stockholm, N.J. B6 76-7
Stockholm, Sask. M10 294-5
Stockholm, S. Dak. C15 136-7
Stockholm, Wis. G7 140-1
Stockley, Del. J5 153
Stockman, S.C. K6 184-5
Stockport, Ia. J12 104-5
Stockport, O. G9 132-3
Stockton, Ala. M3 146-7
Stockton, Calif. I4 210-1
Stockton, Ga. N7 160-1
Stockton, Ill. A6 96-7
Stockton, Ia. G14 104-5
Stockton, Kans. E7 108-9
Stockton, Man. J11 272-3
Stockton, Md. I15 172-3
Stockton, Minn. O9 116-7
Stockton, Mo. G4 120-1
Stockton, N.J. G3 76-7
Stockton Springs, Me. K7 64-5
Stockville, Nebr. I7 124-5
Stockwell, Ind. F6 100-1
Stoddard, Ida. M3 218-9
Stoddard, N.H. N4 72-3
Stoddard, Wis. I9 140-1
Stoddard, co., Mo. I11 120-1
Stokes, N.C. D13 180-1
Stokes, S.C. H11 184-5
Stokes, co., N.C. C8 180-1
Stokesdale, N.C. G4 180-1
Stollings, W. Va. K12 200-1
Stone, Ida. O9 218-9
Stone, co., Ark. C7 150-1
Stone, co., Miss. M9 176-7
Stone, co., Mo. I5 120-1
Stone Bluff, Ind. G5 100-1
Stone City, Colo. G12 214-5
Stone Harbor, N.J. O4 76-7
Stone Lake, Wis. C9 140-1
Stone Mountain, Ga. C12 160-1
Stone Park*, Ill. B11 96-7
Stonebluff, Okla. E14 234-5
Stoneboro, Pa. E2 84-5
Stoneboro, S.C. C11 184-5
Stonega, Va. J2 196-7
Stoneham, Colo. C14 214-5
Stoneham*, Me. L2 64-5
Stoneham, Mass. G5 68-9
Stoneham*, Que. F11 290-1
Stonehenge Project*, Ont. H15 284-5
Stoneleigh, Md. E7 172-3
Stoner, B.C. G7 268-9
Stoneville, Miss. F4 176-7
Stoneville, N.C. C9 180-1
Stonewall, Ark. B11 150-1
Stonewall, Colo. J11 214-5
Stonewall, Ga. D10 160-1
Stonewall, La. C1 168-9
Stonewall, Man. I13 272-3
Stonewall, Miss. I9 176-7
Stonewall, N.C. F14 180-1
Stonewall, Okla. G13 234-5
Stonewall, co., Tex. D6 192-3
Stonewall Trailer Court*, Man. J4 272-3
Stonewood, W. Va. D13 200-1
Stoney Creek, Ont. D14 284-5
Stoney Point*, Ont. F10 284-5
Stonington, Colo. I16 214-5
Stonington, Conn. G14 60-1
Stonington, Ill. H8 96-7
Stonington, Me. L7 64-5
Stony Beach*, Sask. N8 294-5
Stony Bottom, W. Va. G7 200-1
Stony Brook, N.Y. J12 80-1
Stony Creek, Conn. H9 60-1
Stony Creek, Va. G1 196-7
Stony Island, N.S. G4 281
Stony Lake*, Sask. J5 294-5
Stony Mountain, Man. I14 272-3
Stony Plain, Alta. I7 264-5
Stony Point*, Mich. K15 112-3
Stony Point, N.Y. B14 80-1
Stony Point, N.C. H1 180-1
Stony Prairie, O. B6 132-3
Stony River, Alaska F9 254-5
Storden, Minn. O3 116-7
Storey, co., Nev. F2 226-7
Storla, S. Dak. G12 136-7
Storm Lake, Ia. D4 104-5
Storm Lake, Ia. D4 104-5
Stormont, Dundas, and Glengarry, co., Ont. I15 284-5
Storrs, Conn. C12 60-1
Storthoaks, Sask. O11 294-5
Story, Ark. F4 150-1
Story, Okla. G11 234-5
Story, Wyo. B12 250-1
Story, co., Ia. F8 104-5
Story City, Ia. F8 104-5
Stotts City, Mo. I4 120-1
Stottville, N.Y. G11 80-1
Stoughton, Mass. K5 68-9
Stoughton, Sask. O10 294-5
Stoughton, Wis. J2 140-1
Stout, Ia. D10 104-5
Stoutland, Mo. G6 120-1
Stouts Mills, W. Va. F5 200-1
Stoutsville, Mo. C7 120-1
Stoutsville, O. G7 132-3
Stovall, Ga. I3 160-1
Stovall, Miss. C5 176-7
Stovall, N.C. C11 180-1
Stover, Mo. F5 120-1
Stow, Me. L1 64-5
Stow, Mass. G1 68-9
Stow, O. D15 132-3
Stow Creek*, N.J. M1 76-7
Stowe, Pa. A9 84-5
Stowe, Vt. E6 90-1
Strabane*, Pa. I1 84-5
Strafford*, Mo. H5 120-1
Strafford, N.H. M8 72-3
Strafford, Vt. H7 90-1
Strafford, co., N.H. L8 72-3
Straffordville, Ont. E13 284-5
Strait of Belle Isle, Nfld. J8 278-9
Strait of Georgia, B.C. J6 268-9
Strandburg, S. Dak. C15 136-7
Strandquist, Minn. E2 116-7
Strang, Nebr. I12 124-5
Strang, Okla. C15 234-5
Strange Creek, W. Va. G5 200-1
Strasbourg, Sask. M8 294-5
Strasburg, Colo. D13 214-5
Strasburg, Mo. K16 120-1
Strasburg, N. Dak. J8 128-9
Strasburg, O. E9 132-3
Strasburg, Pa. J13 84-5
Strasburg, Va. E11 196-7
Stratford, Calif. K5 210-1
Stratford, Conn. I6 60-1
Stratford, Ia. E7 104-5
Stratford, N.H. D6 72-3
Stratford, N.J. O11 76-7
Stratford, Okla. G12 234-5
Stratford, Ont. D12 284-5
Stratford, S. Dak. C12 136-7
Stratford, Tex. A5 192-3
Stratford, Wash. F13 246-7
Stratford, Wis. F11 140-1
Stratham, N.H. N9 72-3
Strathclair, Man. I10 272-3
Strathcona, Minn. E2 116-7
Strathmoor Gardens*, Ky. G9 164-5
Strathmoor Manor*, Ky. G9 164-5
Strathmoor Village*, Ky. G9 164-5
Strathmore, Alta. M8 264-5
Strathmore, Calif. K6 210-1
Strathmore*, N.J. F7 76-7
Strathroy, Ont. E11 284-5
Stratton, Colo. E15 214-5
Stratton, Me. I3 64-5
Stratton, Nebr. J6 124-5
Stratton, O. E11 132-3
Stratton, Ont. F1 284-5
Stratton, Vt. M5 90-1
Stratton Meadows*, Colo. F12 214-5
Straughn, Ind. H10 100-1
Strawberry, Ariz. G7 206-7
Strawberry, Ark. B9 150-1
Strawberry Plains, Tenn. H13 188-9
Strawberry Point, Ia. D13 104-5
Strawn, Tex. E7 192-3
Strayhorn, Miss. B6 176-7
Streamwood, Ill. L2 96-7
Streator, Ill. D9 96-7
Streator East*, Ill. D9 96-7
Streator West*, Ill. D9 96-7
Street, Md. B12 172-3
Streeter, N. Dak. H10 128-9
Streetsboro*, O. C10 132-3
Strevell, Ida. O8 218-9
Stringer, Miss. J8 176-7
Stringtown, Colo. E9 214-5
Stringtown, Miss. E4 176-7
Stringtown, Okla. H13 234-5
Stroh, Ind. A11 100-1
Strome, Alta. J9 264-5
Stromsburg, Nebr. H12 124-5
Stronach, Mich. G11 112-3
Stroner, Wyo. B15 250-1
Strong, Ark. K6 150-1
Strong, Me. J3 64-5
Strong, Miss. E10 176-7
Strong City, Kans. G12 108-9
Strong City, Okla. E7 234-5
Strongfield, Sask. M6 294-5
Stronghurst, Ill. E4 96-7
Strongs, Mich. D12 112-3
Strongsville, O. C14 132-3
Strother, S.C. I7 184-5
Stroud, Ala. G10 146-7
Stroud, Okla. E12 234-5
Stroud*, Ont. A14 284-5
Stroudsburg, Pa. G15 84-5
Struble, Ia. C1 104-5
Strum, Wis. G9 140-1
Struthers, O. C11 132-3
Stryker, Mont. B2 222-3
Stryker, O. B3 132-3
Stuart, Fla. G13 156-7
Stuart, Ia. H6 104-5
Stuart, Nebr. D9 124-5
Stuart, Okla. G13 234-5
Stuart, Va. K7 196-7
Stuartburn, Man. K15 272-3
Stuarts Draft, Va. G9 196-7
Stuckey, S.C. F14 184-5
Studley, Kans. E5 108-9
Studley, Va. D1 196-7
Stukely-Sud*, Que. J14 290-1
Stull, Kans. F14 108-9
Stumps Corner, Del. D3 153
Stumptown, W. Va. F4 200-1
Stumpy Point, N.C. D16 180-1
Sturbridge, Mass. E7 68-9
Sturgeon, Mo. D7 120-1
Sturgeon, P.E.I. F9 287
Sturgeon Bay, Wis. F16 140-1
Sturgeon Falls, Ont. H8 284-5
Sturgeon Lake, Minn. J7 116-7
Sturgeon Weir*, Sask. H10 294-5
Sturgill, Ore. D16 238-9
Sturgis, Ky. H4 164-5
Sturgis, Mich. K12 112-3
Sturgis, Miss. F9 176-7
Sturgis, Sask. L10 294-5
Sturgis, S. Dak. E2 136-7
Surtevant, Wis. K5 140-1
Stutsman, co., N. Dak. G11 128-9
Stuttgart, Ark. G8 150-1
Stuttgart, Kans. D6 108-9
Suamico, Wis. D4 140-1
Subiaco, Ark. D4 150-1
Sublett, Ida. O8 218-9
Sublett, Ky. H14 164-5
Sublette, Kans. J3 108-9
Sublette, co., Wyo. G6 250-1
Subligna, Ga. D2 160-1
Sublimity, Ore. H2 238-9
Sucarnoochee, Miss. H10 176-7
Succasunna, N.J. D5 76-7
Success, Ark. A10 150-1
Success, Sask. N5 294-5
Sudan, Tex. C4 192-3
Sudbury, Mass. H2 68-9
Sudbury, Ont. H7 284-5
Sudbury, Vt. I4 90-1
Sudlersville, Md. D14 172-3
Suffern, N.Y. C13 80-1
Suffield, Alta. N10 264-5
Suffield, Conn. B9 60-1
Suffolk, Mont. D9 222-3
Suffolk, Va. J14 196-7
Suffolk, co., Mass. D11 68-9
Suffolk, co., N.Y. J13 80-1
Sugar Camp, Wis. C12 140-1
Sugar City, Colo. H14 214-5
Sugar City, Ida. L10 218-9
Sugar Creek, Mo. I15 120-1
Sugar Creek*, Pa. E3 84-5
Sugar Grove, Ark. E3 150-1
Sugar Grove, Ill. M1 96-7
Sugar Grove, O. G7 132-3
Sugar Grove, Tenn. F8 188-9
Sugar Grove, Va. J5 196-7
Sugar Grove, W. Va. G8 200-1
Sugar Hill, Ga. A12 160-1
Sugar Hill, N.H. G5 72-3
Sugar Land, Tex. I13 192-3
Sugar Loaf, Ark. A5 150-1
Sugar Notch*, Pa. F13 84-5
Sugar Tree, Tenn. C5 188-9
Sugar Valley, Ga. D2 160-1
Sugarcreek, O. E9 132-3
Sugartown, La. F3 168-9
Sugarville, Ut. H5 242-3
Sugden, Okla. I10 234-5
Suisun City, Calif. B8 210-1
Suit, N.C. F1 180-1
Suitland [-Silver Hill], Md. J4 172-3
Sula, Mont. G3 222-3
Sulligent, Ala. D3 146-7
Sullivan, Ill. I9 96-7
Sullivan, Ind. K4 100-1
Sullivan, Ky. I4 164-5
Sullivan, Me. K8 64-5
Sullivan, Mo. F9 120-1
Sullivan, N.H. N3 72-3
Sullivan*, Que. H1 290-1
Sullivan, Wis. J3 140-1
Sullivan, co., Ind. K4 100-1
Sullivan, co., Mo. B5 120-1
Sullivan, co., N.H. L3 72-3
Sullivan, co., N.Y. I9 80-1
Sullivan, co., Pa. E12 84-5
Sullivan, co., Tenn. A15 188-9
Sullivan Gardens, Tenn. F16 188-9
Sullivans Island, S.C. I13 184-5
Sully, Ia. G9 104-5
Sully, co., S. Dak. D9 136-7
Sulphur, Ky. F10 164-5
Sulphur, La. H2 168-9
Sulphur, Nev. C3 226-7

Sulphur, Okla. H12 234-5
Sulphur Rock, Ark. C9 150-1
Sulphur Springs, Ark. A2 150-1
Sulphur Springs, Ark. H7 150-1
Sulphur Springs, Ind. G10 100-1
Sulphur Springs, Ore. G4 238-9
Sulphur Springs, Tenn. K10 188-9
Sulphur Springs, Tenn. G16 188-9
Sulphur Springs, Tex. D10 192-3
Sultan, Ont. G6 284-5
Sultan, Wash. E9 246-7
Sumas, Wash. B8 246-7
Sumatra, Mont. F12 222-3
Sumava Resorts, Ind. C4 100-1
Sumerduck, Va. C2 196-7
Sumiton, Ala. E5 146-7
Summer Lake, Ore. H9 238-9
Summer Shade, Ky. J9 164-5
Summerdale, Ala. N4 146-7
Summerfield, Ala. H5 146-7
Summerfield, Kans. C13 108-9
Summerfield, La. A4 168-9
Summerfield, N.C. G4 180-1
Summerfield, O. G10 132-3
Summerfield, Okla. G15 234-5
Summerfield, Tenn. K9 188-9
Summerford*, Nfld. L10 278-9
Summerhaven, Ariz. K8 206-7
Summerland, Calif. N6 210-1
Summerland, Miss. J8 176-7
Summers, Ark. B2 150-1
Summers, co., W. Va. J4 200-1
Summerside, Nfld. M7 278-9
Summerside, P.E.I. E5 287
Summersville, Ky. I9 164-5
Summersville, Mo. H8 120-1
Summersville, W. Va. H5 200-1
Summerton, S.C. F12 184-5
Summertown, Ga. I8 160-1
Summertown, Tenn. J5 188-9
Summerville, Ga. E2 160-1
Summerville, La. D5 168-9
Summerville, Ore. B14 238-9
Summerville, S.C. H12 184-5
Summit, Ala. C7 146-7
Summit, Alaska E11 254-5
Summit, Ark. B6 150-1
Summit, Ill. M3 96-7
Summit, Miss. L5 176-7
Summit, N.J. E6 76-7
Summit, Okla. E14 234-5
Summit, R.I. E3 87
Summit, S.C. E9 184-5
Summit, S. Dak. C15 136-7
Summit, Ut. L4 242-3
Summit, co., Colo. D10 214-5
Summit, co., O. C10 132-3
Summit, co., Ut. E8 242-3
Summit Bridge, Del. C2 153
Summit Hill, Pa. G13 84-5
Summit Lake, Wis. E13 140-1
Summit Point, W. Va. E11 200-1
Summitville, Colo. I9 214-5
Summitville, Ind. F9 100-1
Summitville, Tenn. C9 188-9
Sumner, Ga. M5 160-1
Sumner, Ill. K11 96-7
Sumner, Ia. C11 104-5
Sumner, Me. K3 64-5
Sumner, Miss. D5 176-7
Sumner, Mo. C5 120-1
Sumner, Nebr. H9 124-5
Sumner, Okla. D11 234-5
Sumner, Ore. H4 238-9
Sumner, Wash. J3 246-7
Sumner, co., Kans. K10 108-9
Sumner, co., Tenn. A8 188-9
Sumpter, Ore. D14 238-9
Sumrall, Miss. K7 176-7
Sumter, Ga. K4 160-1
Sumter, S.C. E12 184-5
Sumter, co., Ala. H2 146-7
Sumter, co., Fla. E10 156-7
Sumter, co., Ga. K4 160-1
Sumter, co., S.C. E11 184-5
Sumterville, Ala. H2 146-7
Sun, La. G10 168-9
Sun City, Ariz. H6 206-7
Sun City*, Calif. N8 210-1
Sun City, Kans. J7 108-9
Sun City Center, Fla. I3 156-7
Sun Prairie, Wis. I2 140-1
Sun River, Mont. D6 222-3
Sun Valley, Ida. L6 218-9
Sun Valley*, Nev. M9 226-7
Sunapee, N.H. L4 72-3
Sunbeam, Ida. K5 218-9
Sunbright, Tenn. G10 188-9
Sunburg, Minn. L3 116-7
Sunburst, Mont. A6 222-3
Sunbury, N.C. C14 180-1
Sunbury, O. F7 132-3
Sunbury, Pa. G11 84-5
Sunbury, co., N.B. H5 275
Suncook, N.H. M7 72-3
Sundance, Wyo. C16 250-1
Sundance Power Plant*, Alta. J7 264-5
Sunderland, Md. F11 172-3
Sunderland, Mass. C5 68-9
Sunderland*, Ont. B15 284-5
Sunderland, Vt. M4 90-1
Sundown, Man. K15 272-3
Sundown, Tex. D4 192-3
Sundre, Alta. L7 264-5
Sundridge, Ont. H8 284-5
Sunfield, Mich. I13 112-3
Sunfish Lake*, Minn. M7 116-7
Sunflower, Kans. F15 108-9
Sunflower, Miss. E5 176-7
Sunflower, co., Miss. E5 176-7
Sunflower Springs, Calif. M10 210-1
Sunizona, Ariz. L10 206-7
Sunland Park, N. Mex. M6 230-1
Sunman, Ind. J11 100-1
Sunny Acres*, Ky. D11 164-5
Sunny Brae, Calif. E1 210-1
Sunny Corner*, N.B. F5 275
Sunny Side, Ga. H4 160-1
Sunny Side*, Ont. A14 284-5
Sunny South, Ala. J4 146-7
Sunny Valley, Ore. I5 238-9
Sunnybrook, Md. B11 172-3
Sunnyland, Fla. K3 156-7
Sunnymead, Calif. G10 210-1
Sunnyside, Nfld. N10 278-9
Sunnyside, Ut. H9 242-3
Sunnyside, Wash. I11 246-7
Sunnyvale, Calif. D8 210-1
Sunnyvale, Mo. I3 120-1
Sunnyvale, Tex. C15 192-3
Sunol, Nebr. G3 124-5
Sunray, Okla. H10 234-5
Sunray, Tex. A5 192-3
Sunrise, Ariz. D10 206-7
Sunrise, Fla. I13 156-7
Sunrise, Ky. F12 164-5
Sunrise, Tex. F9 192-3
Sunrise, Wyo. G15 250-1
Sunrise Beach, Mo. F6 120-1
Sunrise Heights*, Mich. J12 112-3
Sunrise Manor*, Nev. M9 226-7
Sunset, Ariz. K9 206-7
Sunset*, Ark. E12 150-1
Sunset, La. G5 168-9
Sunset, Me. L7 64-5
Sunset, S.C. B5 184-5
Sunset, Ut. E6 242-3
Sunset Beach, Hawaii F3 258-9
Sunset Beach*, N.C. H12 180-1
Sunset Beach, Ore. A4 238-9
Sunset Heights*, Alta. J7 264-5
Sunset Hills*, Mo. E10 120-1
Sunset Mobile Village*, Alta. N10 264-5
Sunshine, Me. L7 64-5
Sunshine, Md. G4 172-3
Sunspot, N. Mex. K7 230-1
Suntrana, Alaska E11 254-5
Supai, Ariz. C5 206-7
Superior, Ariz. I8 206-7
Superior, Colo. F2 214-5
Superior, Ia. A4 104-5
Superior, Mont. D2 222-3
Superior, Nebr. J11 124-5
Superior, Wis. A8 140-1
Superior*, Wis. B8 140-1
Superior, Wyo. I8 250-1
Suplee, Ore. F11 238-9
Supply, N.C. H12 180-1
Supply, Va. G13 196-7
Supreme, La. D10 168-9
Suqualena, Miss. H9 176-7
Suquamish, Wash. H2 246-7
Surf City, N.J. K7 76-7
Surf City, N.C. G13 180-1
Surfside, Fla. H16 156-7
Surfside, Mass. J16 68-9
Surfside Beach, S.C. E15 184-5
Surginer, Ala. J4 146-7
Surgoinsville, Tenn. F15 188-9
Suring, Wis. E14 140-1
Surprise, Ariz. H6 206-7
Surprise, Nebr. H13 124-5
Surrency, Ga. L9 160-1
Surrey, N. Dak. D6 128-9
Surry, Me. K7 64-5
Surry, N.H. N3 72-3
Surry, Va. I13 196-7
Surry, co., N.C. C7 180-1
Surry, co., Va. I13 196-7
Susan, Va. E4 196-7
Susank, Kans. G7 108-9
Susanville, Calif. F5 210-1
Susanville, Ore. D13 238-9
Susitna, Alaska F11 254-5
Susquehanna, co., Pa. C13 84-5
Susquehanna Depot, Pa. C14 84-5
Susquehanna R., Pa. H10 84-5
Sussex, N.B. I6 275
Sussex, N.J. B5 76-7
Sussex, Va. J13 196-7
Sussex, Wis. I4 140-1
Sussex, Wyo. D13 250-1
Sussex, co., Del. I4 153
Sussex, co., N.J. B5 76-7
Sussex, co., Va. J13 196-7
Sussex Corner*, N.B. I6 275
Sutcliffe, Nev. E2 226-7
Sutherland, Ia. C3 104-5
Sutherland, Nebr. G6 124-5
Sutherland, Va. F1 196-7
Sutherlin, Ore. E5 238-9
Sutter, Calif. G3 210-1
Sutter, co., Calif. G3 210-1
Sutter Creek, Calif. A10 210-1
Suttle, Ala. H5 146-7
Sutton, Alaska F11 254-5
Sutton, Mass. E8 68-9
Sutton, Nebr. I12 124-5
Sutton, N.H. L5 72-3
Sutton, N. Dak. F11 128-9
Sutton, Ont. B15 284-5
Sutton, Que. J13 290-1
Sutton, Vt. D9 90-1
Sutton, W. Va. G5 200-1
Sutton, co., Tex. G6 192-3
Sutton Res., W. Va. G6 200-1
Suttons Bay, Mich. F12 112-3
Suver, Ore. I1 238-9
Suwanee, Ga. A12 160-1
Suwannee, co., Fla. B9 156-7
Suwannee River*, Fla. C9 156-7
Svensen, Ore. A5 238-9
Swain, Ark. C4 150-1
Swain, co., N.C. E2 180-1
Swainsboro, Ga. J8 160-1
Swaledale, Ia. C8 104-5
Swampers, La. C6 168-9
Swampscott, Mass. G6 68-9
Swan, Ia. H8 104-5
Swan Falls, Ida. M3 218-9
Swan Hills, Alta. H6 264-5
Swan Lake, Ark. H8 150-1
Swan Lake, Ida. O10 218-9
Swan Lake, Man. J12 272-3
Swan Lake, Miss. D6 176-7
Swan Lake, Mont. C4 222-3
Swan River, Man. H1 272-3
Swan Station, N.C. J6 180-1
Swan Valley, Ida. M11 218-9
Swannanoa, N.C. E4 180-1
Swanquarter, N.C. E15 180-1
Swans Island, Me. L8 64-5
Swansboro, N.C. F14 180-1
Swansea, Ariz. G3 206-7
Swansea, Ill. K6 96-7
Swansea, Mass. G11 68-9
Swansea, S.C. F10 184-5
Swansea Factory, Mass. G11 68-9
Swanson Corners, Mass. E4 68-9
Swanton, Md. C2 172-3
Swanton, Nebr. I13 124-5
Swanton, O. B5 132-3
Swanton, Vt. B4 90-1
Swanville, Me. K6 64-5
Swanville, Minn. K4 116-7
Swanzey, N.H. O3 72-3
Swarthmore*, Pa. J15 84-5
Swartz, La. B5 168-9
Swartz Creek, Mich. G3 112-3
Swatara, Minn. H6 116-7
Swayzee, Ind. E9 100-1
Swea City, Ia. B6 104-5
Sweatman, Miss. E7 176-7
Swedeburg, Nebr. J1 124-5
Sweden, Me. L2 64-5
Sweden, Me. B8 64-5
Swedesboro, N.J. K2 76-7
Sweeden, Ky. I8 164-5
Sweeny, Tex. K12 192-3
Sweet, Ida. L3 218-9
Sweet Briar, Va. H9 196-7
Sweet Chalybeate, Va. H7 196-7
Sweet Grass, co., Mont. G8 222-3
Sweet Hall, Va. E3 196-7
Sweet Home, Ark. J16 150-1
Sweet Home, Ore. E6 238-9
Sweet Springs, Mo. D5 120-1
Sweet Springs, W. Va. J6 200-1
Sweet Water, Ala. J3 146-7
Sweetgrass, Mont. A6 222-3
Sweetland, W. Va. I12 200-1
Sweets Corner, Mass. B2 68-9
Sweetser, Ind. E9 100-1
Sweetwater*, Fla. H16 156-7
Sweetwater, Ida. F2 218-9
Sweetwater, Nev. H3 226-7
Sweetwater, Okla. F6 234-5
Sweetwater, Tenn. J13 188-9
Sweetwater, Tex. E6 192-3
Sweetwater, co., Wyo. J8 250-1
Sweetwater Creek*, Fla. F10 156-7
Sweetwater Station, Wyo. G9 250-1
Swepsonville, N.C. H5 180-1
Swift, co., Minn. L3 116-7
Swift Current, Sask. N5 294-5
Swift River, Mass. C4 68-9
Swift Run, Va. F10 196-7
Swift Trail Junction, Ariz. J10 206-7
Swifton, Ark. C9 150-1
Swiftown, Miss. F5 176-7
Swink, Colo. H14 214-5
Swink*, Okla. I15 234-5
Swisher, Ia. G12 104-5
Swisher, co., Tex. C5 192-3
Swiss, W. Va. I16 200-1
Swisshome, Ore. F4 238-9
Swissvale, Pa. B6 84-5
Switz City, Ind. K5 100-1
Switzer, Ky. A6 164-5
Switzer, W. Va. K12 200-1
Switzerland, S.C. J10 184-5
Switzerland, co., Ind. L11 100-1
Swoope, Va. G9 196-7
Swords Creek, Va. J4 196-7
Swoyersville, Pa. E13 84-5
Sycamore, Ala. F8 146-7
Sycamore, Ga. L5 160-1
Sycamore, Ill. B9 96-7
Sycamore, Kans. J14 108-9
Sycamore, O. D6 132-3
Sycamore, S.C. H9 184-5
Sycamore Hills*, Mo. E10 120-1
Sydenham, Ont. J13 284-5
Sydney, Fla. H4 156-7
Sydney, N.S. B11 281
Sydney Mines, N.S. B11 281
Sydney River, N.S. B11 281
Sykeston, N. Dak. F10 128-9
Sykesville, Md. F4 172-3
Sykesville, Pa. F5 84-5
Sylacauga, Ala. F7 146-7
Sylva, N.C. E3 180-1
Sylvan Beach, N.Y. E7 80-1
Sylvan Grove, Kans. F8 108-9
Sylvan Lake, Alta. K7 264-5
Sylvan Lake, Mich. I5 112-3
Sylvan Springs*, Ala. F6 146-7
Sylvania, Ala. B8 146-7
Sylvania, Ga. I10 160-1
Sylvania, O. A5 132-3
Sylvania, Sask. K8 294-5
Sylvarena, Miss. J8 176-7
Sylvatus, Va. J6 196-7
Sylvester, Ga. M5 160-1
Sylvester, W. Va. J14 200-1
Sylvia, Kans. I8 108-9
Sylvia, Tenn. H5 188-9
Symco, Wis. D2 140-1
Symonds, Miss. D4 176-7
Symsonia, Ky. J3 164-5
Syosset, N.Y. E16 80-1
Syracuse, Ind. B9 100-1
Syracuse, Kans. H1 108-9
Syracuse, Mo. E6 120-1
Syracuse, Nebr. I15 124-5
Syracuse, N.Y. E7 80-1
Syracuse, O. I9 132-3
Syracuse*, Ut. E6 242-3
Syria, Va. C1 196-7
Syringa, Va. E4 196-7

T

T + E Trailer Park*, Alta. G4 264-5
Ta Ta Creek, B.C. J10 268-9
Taber, Alta. N9 264-5
Taber, Ida. M9 218-9
Tabernacle, N.J. J5 76-7
Tabernash, Colo. D10 214-5
Tabiona, Ut. F8 242-3
Table Rock, Nebr. J15 124-5
Table Rock, Wyo. I9 250-1
Table Rock Lake, Mo. J4 120-1
Tabler, Okla. G10 234-5
Tabor, Ia. J3 104-5
Tabor, S. Dak. I14 136-7
Tabor City, N.C. H10 180-1
Tacna, Ariz. J3 206-7
Tacoma, Wash. F8 246-7
Taconic, Conn. A4 60-1
Taconite, Minn. H6 116-7
Tacy, W. Va. D15 200-1
Tad, W. Va. H14 200-1
Tadmore, Sask. L10 294-5
Tadoussac, Que. D13 290-1
Taft, Calif. M6 210-1
Taft, Fla. F7 156-7
Taft, La. C13 168-9
Taft*, Okla. E14 234-5
Taft, Tenn. E7 188-9
Taft, Tex. I8 192-3
Taft Heights*, Calif. L6 210-1
Taft Southwest*, Tex. I8 192-3
Taftsville, Vt. J7 90-1
Taftville, Conn. E13 60-1
Taghum, B.C. J9 268-9
Tagus, N. Dak. D5 128-9
Tahitian Gardens*, Fla. F9 156-7
Tahlequah, Okla. E15 234-5
Tahoe City, Calif. G5 210-1
Tahoka, Tex. D5 192-3
Taholah, Wash. F5 246-7
Tahona, Okla. F16 234-5
Tahsis, B.C. J5 268-9
Tahuya, Wash. F7 246-7
Taiban, N. Mex. G10 230-1
Tajique, N. Mex. G6 230-1
Takilma, Ore. K4 238-9
Takoma Park, Md. I4 172-3
Takotna, Alaska E10 254-5
Takysie Lake, B.C. F5 268-9
Talala, Okla. C14 234-5
Talbot, Ore. I1 238-9
Talbot, co., Ga. I3 160-1
Talbot, co., Md. F13 172-3
Talbott, Tenn. H13 188-9
Talbotton, Ga. I3 160-1
Talco, Tex. D10 192-3
Talcott, W. Va. J5 200-1
Talcottville, Conn. C10 60-1
Talcville, Vt. H5 90-1
Talent, Ore. J6 238-9
Taliaferro, co., Ga. G7 160-1
Talihina, Okla. G15 234-5
Talisheek, La. A15 168-9
Talkeetna, Alaska E11 254-5
Talking Rock, Ga. E3 160-1
Tall Timbers, Md. H11 172-3
Talla Bena, La. B7 168-9
Talladega, Ala. F8 146-7
Talladega, co., Ala. F7 146-7
Talladega Springs, Ala. G7 146-7
Tallahassee, Fla. B7 156-7
Tallahatchie, co., Miss. D6 176-7
Tallant, Okla. C13 234-5
Tallapoosa, Ga. G2 160-1
Tallapoosa, Mo. J11 120-1
Tallapoosa, co., Ala. H8 146-7
Tallassee, Ala. H8 146-7
Tallassee, Tenn. J14 188-9
Talleyville, Del. A3 153
Tallmadge, O. D15 132-3
Tallman, Ore. I1 238-9
Tallula, Ill. H6 96-7
Tallula, Miss. H4 176-7
Tallulah, La. B7 168-9
Tallulah Falls, Ga. D6 160-1
Talmadge, Me. H9 64-5
Talmage, Calif. G2 210-1
Talmage, Kans. F11 108-9
Talmage, Nebr. I15 124-5
Talmage, Ut. F8 242-3
Talmo, Ga. E5 160-1
Taloga, Okla. D8 234-5
Talowah, Miss. L8 176-7
Talpa, N. Mex. C7 230-1

Tama, Ia. F10 104-5
Tama, co., Ia. F10 104-5
Tamaha, Okla. F15 234-5
Tamaqua, Pa. G13 84-5
Tamarac*, Fla. I13 156-7
Tamarack, Ida. I3 218-9
Tamarack, Minn. I7 116-7
Tamaroa, Ill. M8 96-7
Tamassee, S.C. B5 184-5
Tamms, Ill. O8 96-7
Tamora, Nebr. H13 124-5
Tampa, Fla. F10 156-7
Tampa, Kans. G11 108-9
Tampa Bay, Fla. F10 156-7
Tampico, Ill. C7 96-7
Tampico, Ind. L9 100-1
Tampico, Mont. B12 222-3
Tams, W. Va. I4 200-1
Tamworth, N.H. I8 72-3
Tamworth, Ont. J13 284-5
Tamworth, Va. H11 196-7
Tanacross, Alaska E12 254-5
Tanana, Alaska D11 254-5
Taney, co., Mo. J5 120-1
Taneytown, Md. B9 172-3
Taneyville, Mo. I5 120-1
Tangent, Alta. F5 264-5
Tangent, Ore. I1 238-9
Tangier, Okla. D7 234-5
Tangier, Va. H15 196-7
Tangipahoa, La. F8 168-9
Tangipahoa, co., La. G9 168-9
Tannehill, La. C4 168-9
Tanner, Ala. B6 146-7
Tanner, W. Va. F5 200-1
Tannersville, N.Y. G10 80-1
Tannersville, Va. J5 196-7
Tanque, Ariz. J11 206-7
Tanque Verde, Ariz. K9 206-7
Tansboro, N.J. O12 76-7
Tantallon, Sask. N10 294-5
Taopi, Minn. O7 116-7
Taos*, Mo. F7 120-1
Taos, N. Mex. C7 230-1
Taos, co., N. Mex. C7 230-1
Taos Pueblo, N. Mex. C7 230-1
Tapoco, N.C. E1 180-1
Tappahannock, Va. G13 196-7
Tappan, N.Y. C14 80-1
Tappen, N. Dak. H9 128-9
Tar Heel, N.C. F11 180-1
Tara, Ont. B12 284-5
Tarboro, Ga. N10 160-1
Tarboro, N.C. D13 180-1
Tarentum, Ala. K8 146-7
Tarentum, Pa. A7 84-5
Tariff, W. Va. G4 200-1
Tariffville, Conn. B8 60-1
Tarkiln, R.I. A3 87
Tarkio, Mo. A1 120-1
Tarkio, Mont. E2 222-3
Tarlton, O. H7 132-3
Tarnov, Nebr. F12 124-5
Tarpley, Tenn. K6 188-9
Tarpon Springs, Fla. G1 156-7
Tarrant, Ala. E6 146-7
Tarrant, co., Tex. D8 192-3
Tarry, Ark. H8 150-1
Tarryall, Colo. J1 214-5
Tarrytown, Ga. J8 160-1
Tarrytown, N.Y. C14 80-1
Tarsney Lakes*, Mo. D3 120-1
Taschereau*, Que. H1 290-1
Tasco, Kans. E4 108-9
Tasu*, B.C. F2 268-9
Tatamagouche, N.S. C7 281
Tate, Ga. E4 160-1
Tate, co., Miss. B6 176-7
Tateville, Ky. J11 164-5
Tatitlek, Alaska F12 254-5
Tattnall, co., Ga. K9 160-1
Tatum, N. Mex. J11 230-1
Tatum, S.C. C14 184-5
Tatum, Tex. E11 192-3
Tatums, Okla. H11 234-5
Tatumville, Tenn. B3 188-9
Taunton, Mass. F11 68-9
Taunton, Minn. M2 116-7
Tavares, Fla. E11 156-7
Tavernier, Fla. K13 156-7
Tavistock, N.J. N11 76-7
Tavistock*, Ont. D13 284-5
Tawas City, Mich. G14 112-3
Tay Creek, N.B. H4 275
Taycheedah, Wis. G4 140-1
Taylor, Ala. L9 146-7
Taylor, Ariz. G10 206-7
Taylor, Ark. K4 150-1
Taylor, B.C. E8 268-9
Taylor, La. B3 168-9
Taylor, Mich. K5 112-3
Taylor, Miss. C7 176-7
Taylor, Nebr. F9 124-5
Taylor, N. Dak. G4 128-9
Taylor, Okla. H10 234-5
Taylor, Pa. E14 84-5
Taylor, Tex. G8 192-3
Taylor, Wis. G9 140-1
Taylor, co., Fla. C8 156-7
Taylor, co., Ga. J4 160-1
Taylor, co., Ia. J5 104-5
Taylor, co., Ky. I10 164-5
Taylor, co., Tex. E6 192-3
Taylor, co., W. Va. E6 200-1
Taylor, co., Wis. E10 140-1
Taylor Lake Village*, Tex. G10 192-3
Taylor Mill*, Ky. D11 164-5
Taylor Springs, Ill. J7 96-7
Taylors, S.C. F2 184-5
Taylors Bridge, Del. D3 153
Taylors Falls, Minn. L7 116-7
Taylors Island, Md. G12 172-3
Taylorsville, Ga. F2 160-1
Taylorsville, Ind. J9 100-1
Taylorsville, Ky. B3 164-5
Taylorsville, Md. C9 172-3
Taylorsville, Miss. J8 176-7
Taylorsville, N.C. D6 180-1
Taylortown, La. B2 168-9
Taylortown, N.J. C6 76-7
Taylorville, Ill. I8 96-7
Taylorville, Md. H16 172-3
Taymouth, N.B. H4 275
Tazewell, Ga. J4 160-1
Tazewell, Tenn. G13 188-9
Tazewell, Va. I5 196-7
Tazewell, co., Ill. F7 96-7
Tazewell, co., Va. J5 196-7
Tchula, Miss. F6 176-7
Tea, S. Dak. H15 136-7
Teachey, N.C. F12 180-1
Teague, Tex. F9 192-3
Teaneck, N.J. B12 76-7
Teasdale, Ut. K7 242-3
Teaticket, Mass. H14 68-9
Teays, W. Va. H12 200-1
Tecolotito, N. Mex. F8 230-1
Tecumseh, Kans. F14 108-9
Tecumseh, Mich. K14 112-3
Tecumseh, Nebr. I15 124-5
Tecumseh, Okla. K4 234-5
Tecumseh, Ont. F9 284-5
Teec Nos Pas, Ariz. B11 206-7
Tees To, Ariz. E9 206-7
Teeswater, Ont. C12 284-5
Tefft, Ind. C6 100-1
Tegarden, Okla. C8 234-5
Tehachapi, Calif. M7 210-1
Tehama, Calif. F3 210-1
Tehama, co., Calif. F3 210-1
Tekamah, Nebr. F15 124-5
Tekoa, Wash. F16 246-7
Tekonsha, Mich. J13 112-3
Telegraph Creek, B.C. C3 268-9
Telfair, co., Ga. K7 160-1
Telford, Pa. I15 84-5
Telkwa, B.C. F5 268-9
Tell City, Ind. O6 100-1
Teller, Alaska D8 254-5
Teller, co., Colo. F11 214-5
Teller Mission [Brevig Mission], Alaska D8 254-5
Tellico Plains, Tenn. K14 188-9
Telluride, Colo. H7 214-5
Telocaset, Ore. C14 238-9
Témiscaming, Que. I1 290-1
Témiscamingue, co., Que. I1 290-1
Témiscouata, co., Que. E15 290-1
Tempe, Ariz. I6 206-7
Temperance, Mich. K14 112-3
Temperance Vale, N.B. H3 275
Temperanceville, Va. G16 196-7
Temple, Ark. I3 150-1
Temple, Ga. G2 160-1
Temple, Me. J3 64-5
Temple, Mich. G12 112-3
Temple, N.H. O5 72-3
Temple, Okla. H9 234-5
Temple*, Pa. I13 84-5
Temple, Tex. F8 192-3
Temple Bar, Ariz. C2 206-7
Temple City*, Calif. G9 210-1
Temple Hill, Ky. J8 164-5
Temple Terrace, Fla. H3 156-7
Templeman, Va. G14 196-7
Templeton, Calif. L4 210-1
Templeton, Ind. E5 100-1
Templeton, Ia. F4 104-5
Templeton, Mass. C7 68-9
Templeville, Md. D14 172-3
Templow, Tenn. G8 188-9
Temvik, N. Dak. I8 128-9
Ten Mile, Miss. M8 176-7
Ten Sleep, Wyo. D10 250-1
Tenafly, N.J. C8 76-7
Tenaha, Tex. E11 192-3
Tenakee Springs, Alaska G15 254-5
Tenant, Ala. F9 146-7
Tenants Harbor, Me. M6 64-5
Tendal, La. B7 168-9
Tendoy, Ida. I7 218-9
Tenino, Wash. G7 246-7
Tenmile, Ore. H5 238-9
Tennant, Ia. G3 104-5
Tennemo, Tenn. B2 188-9
Tennessee City, Tenn. H5 188-9
Tennessee Ridge, Tenn. B5 188-9
Tennessee R., Ala. A8 146-7
Tennessee R., Tenn. D10 188-9
Tenney, Minn. J2 116-7
Tennga, Ga. C3 160-1
Tennille, Ala. K9 146-7
Tennille, Ga. I7 160-1
Tennyson, Ind. O5 100-1
Tennyson, Wis. K10 140-1
Tensas, co., La. C7 168-9
Tensaw, Ala. L3 146-7
Tensed, Ida. E2 218-9
Tenstrike, Minn. G4 116-7
Tequesta, Fla. C16 156-7
Terence Bay, N.S. E7 281
Tererro, N. Mex. E7 230-1
Teresita, Okla. D15 234-5
Terhune, Ind. G8 100-1
Terlton, Okla. D12 234-5
Terra Alta, W. Va. D8 200-1
Terra Bella*, Calif. L6 210-1
Terrace, B.C. F4 268-9
Terrace Bay, Ont. F4 284-5
Terrace Heights*, Wash. H11 246-7
Terrace Park, O. K14 132-3
Terral, Okla. I10 234-5
Terraville, S. Dak. E2 136-7
Terre Haute, Ind. I4 100-1
Terre Hill, Pa. J13 84-5
Terrebonne, Ore. E9 238-9
Terrebonne, Que. I12 290-1
Terrebonne, co., La. J7 168-9
Terrebonne, co., Que. H11 290-1
Terrell, N.C. I1 180-1
Terrell, Tex. D16 192-3
Terrell, co., Ga. L3 160-1
Terrell, co., Tex. G4 192-3
Terrell Hills, Tex. J2 192-3
Terreton, Ida. L9 218-9
Terril, Ia. B4 104-5
Terry, La. A7 168-9
Terry, Miss. J6 176-7
Terry, Mont. E15 222-3
Terry, co., Tex. D4 192-3
Terry Creek, Tenn. G11 188-9
Terrytown, Nebr. F1 124-5
Terryville, Conn. D7 60-1
Tescott, Kans. F9 108-9
Tesla, W. Va. G5 200-1
Teslin, Y.T. C2 297
Tessier, Sask. L6 294-5
Tesuque, N. Mex. E7 230-1
Tête Jaune Cache, B.C. G8 268-9
Teterboro*, N.J. D8 76-7
Teterville, Kans. H12 108-9
Tetlin, Alaska E13 254-5
Teton, Ida. L10 218-9
Teton, co., Ida. L11 218-9
Teton, co., Mont. C5 222-3
Teton, co., Wyo. D6 250-1
Teton Village, Wyo. J1 250-1
Tetonia, Ida. L11 218-9
Teulon, Man. I14 272-3
Teutopolis, Ill. J9 96-7
Tewksbury, Mass. B11 68-9
Tewksbury*, N.J. E4 76-7
Texanna, Okla. F14 234-5
Texarkana, Ark. J2 150-1
Texarkana, Tex. D11 192-3
Texas, Ky. D4 164-5
Texas, co., Mo. H7 120-1
Texas, co., Okla. C3 234-5
Texas City, Tex. J15 192-3
Texas Creek, Colo. G11 214-5
Texasville, Ala. K10 146-7
Texhoma, Okla. C3 234-5
Texico, N. Mex. G12 230-1
Texola, Okla. F6 234-5
Thackerville, Okla. I11 234-5
Thalberg*, Man. J4 272-3
Thames R., Conn. G13 60-1
Thamesford*, Ont. E12 284-5
Thamesville, Ont. F11 284-5
Tharpe, Tenn. A5 188-9
Tharptown, Ala. B4 146-7
Thatcher, Ariz. J10 206-7
Thatcher, Colo. I13 214-5
Thatcher, Ida. O10 218-9
Thaxton, Miss. C8 176-7
Thaxton, Va. I8 196-7
Thayer, Ill. I7 96-7
Thayer, Ind. C5 100-1
Thayer, Ia. I7 104-5
Thayer, Kans. J15 108-9
Thayer, Mo. J8 120-1
Thayer, Nebr. H12 124-5
Thayer, co., Nebr. J12 124-5
Thayne, Wyo. F5 250-1
Thealka, Ky. H15 164-5
Theba, Ariz. J5 206-7
Thebes, Ark. J8 150-1
Thedford, Nebr. E7 124-5
Thedford, Ont. D11 284-5
Theodore, Ala. N3 146-7
Theodore, Sask. L9 294-5
Theodosia, Mo. J6 120-1
Theresa, N.Y. B7 80-1
Theresa, Wis. H3 140-1
Theriot, La. J8 168-9
Thermal, Calif. N9 210-1
Thermalito, Calif. G4 210-1
Thermopolis, Wyo. E9 250-1
Thermopylae, Mass. D5 68-9
Thessalon, Ont. H6 284-5
Thetford*, Vt. I8 90-1
Thetford Mines, Que. H16 290-1
Thetford Mines Nord-Est*, Que. H16 290-1
Thetford Mines Nord-Ouest*, Que. H16 290-1
Thetis Island, B.C. C12 268-9
Thibodaux, La. I8 168-9
Thicket Portage, Man. E3 272-3
Thida, Ark. D9 150-1
Thief River Falls, Minn. F2 116-7
Thiensville, Wis. I5 140-1
Thistle, Ut. G7 242-3
Thoeny, Mont. A12 222-3
Thomas, Md. G12 172-3
Thomas, Okla. E8 234-5
Thomas, W. Va. E8 200-1
Thomas, co., Ga. N5 160-1
Thomas, co., Kans. E3 108-9
Thomas, co., Nebr. E7 124-5
Thomas Corner, Del. D3 153
Thomasboro, Ill. G10 96-7
Thomaston, Ala. I4 146-7
Thomaston, Conn. E6 60-1
Thomaston, Ga. I4 160-1
Thomaston, Me. L6 64-5
Thomaston*, N.Y. J11 80-1
Thomastown, La. C7 168-9
Thomastown, Miss. G7 176-7
Thomasville, Ala. J4 146-7
Thomasville, Ga. N5 160-1
Thomasville, N.C. H3 180-1
Thompson, Conn. B14 60-1
Thompson, Ia. B7 104-5
Thompson, Man. E3 272-3
Thompson, Mich. D11 112-3
Thompson, Miss. L5 176-7
Thompson, Nebr. J13 124-5
Thompson, N. Dak. E14 128-9
Thompson, Ut. I10 242-3
Thompson Falls, Mont. D2 222-3
Thompson Grove, Ark. E11 150-1
Thompson Place-Tanglewilde*, Wash. G7 246-7
Thompsons Station, Tenn. I6 188-9
Thompsonville, Conn. B10 60-1
Thompsonville, Del. G5 153
Thompsonville, Mich. G11 112-3
Thompsonville, Ut. K5 242-3
Thomson, Ga. G8 160-1
Thomson, Ill. B6 96-7
Thomson, Minn. I8 116-7
Thor, Ia. D7 104-5
Thorburn*, N.S. C8 281
Thoreau, N. Mex. E3 230-1
Thorhild, Alta. I8 264-5
Thorn, Miss. D8 176-7
Thorn Hill, Tenn. G13 188-9
Thornburg, Ark. H13 150-1
Thornburg, Ia. H11 104-5
Thornburg, Va. G12 196-7
Thornbury, Ont. A13 284-5
Thorndale*, Ont. E12 284-5
Thorndale, Pa. B9 84-5
Thorndale, Tex. F9 192-3
Thorndike, Me. K6 64-5
Thorne, Nev. H4 226-7
Thorne, Ont. G8 284-5
Thorne Bay*, Alaska H16 254-5
Thornhill*, B.C. F4 268-9
Thornhill, Man. K13 272-3
Thornloe, Ont. G8 284-5
Thornton, Ark. I6 150-1
Thornton, Colo. G3 214-5
Thornton, Ida. L10 218-9
Thornton*, Ill. C11 96-7
Thornton, Ia. C8 104-5
Thornton, Miss. G6 176-7
Thornton, N.H. I6 72-3
Thornton*, Ont. B14 284-5
Thornton, R.I. C5 87
Thornton, Wash. G16 246-7
Thornton, W. Va. C15 200-1
Thornton, Wyo. C15 250-1
Thorntons Ferry, N.H. O7 72-3
Thorntown, Ind. G7 100-1
Thornville, Mich. G5 112-3
Thornville, O. G8 132-3
Thornwood*, N.Y. J11 80-1
Thorofare, N.J. O9 76-7
Thorold, Ont. D15 284-5
Thorp, Wis. F10 140-1
Thorpe, W. Va. J3 200-1
Thorsby, Ala. G6 146-7
Thorsby, Alta. J7 264-5
Thortonville*, Tex. E3 192-3
Thousand Oaks, Calif. G7 210-1
Thousandsticks, Ky. I13 164-5
Thrall, Kans. H13 108-9
Thrashers, Miss. B10 176-7
Three Bridges, N.J. F4 76-7
Three Churches, W. Va. D10 200-1
Three Creek, Ida. O5 218-9
Three Forks, Ky. J8 164-5
Three Forks, Mont. G6 222-3
Three Hills, Alta. L8 264-5
Three Lakes, Wis. D13 140-1
Three Mile Plains*, N.S. D6 281
Three Notch, Ala. J9 146-7
Three Oaks, Mich. K11 112-3
Three Points, Ariz. L8 206-7
Three Points, Tenn. H12 188-9
Three Rivers, Mass. E6 68-9
Three Rivers, Mich. K12 112-3
Three Rivers, Miss. N10 176-7
Three Rivers, N. Mex. J6 230-1
Three Rivers, Tex. I8 192-3
Three Rock Cove, Nfld. N7 278-9
Threeforks, Ky. H16 164-5
Threet, Ala. A4 146-7
Throckmorton, Tex. D7 192-3
Throckmorton, co., Tex. D7 192-3
Throop, Pa. E14 84-5
Thrums, B.C. J9 268-9
Thunder Bay, Mich. F14 112-3
Thunder Bay, Ont. F3 284-5
Thunder Butte, S. Dak. C6 136-7
Thunder Hawk, S. Dak. A5 136-7
Thunderbolt, Ga. K11 160-1
Thurlow, Mont. F13 222-3
Thurman, Ia. J2 104-5
Thurmond, N.C. C7 180-1
Thurmond, W. Va. J16 200-1
Thurmont, Md. B8 172-3
Thursday, W. Va. E4 200-1
Thurso, Que. I10 290-1
Thurston, Nebr. E14 124-5
Thurston, O. G7 132-3
Thurston, co., Nebr. E14 124-5
Thurston, co., Wash. G7 246-7
Thyatira, Miss. B7 176-7
Tiawah, Okla. D14 234-5
Tibbie, Ala. L2 146-7
Tibbs, Miss. C5 176-7
Tiber, Mont. B7 222-3
Tiburon*, Calif. I3 210-1
Tice, Fla. H11 156-7

Tichnor, Ark. H9 150-1
Tickfaw, La. G9 168-9
Ticonderoga, N.Y. C11 80-1
Tide Head*, N.B. D4 275
Tidewater, Ore. E4 238-9
Tidewater, Va. H14 196-7
Tie Plant, Miss. E7 176-7
Tie Siding, Wyo. J14 250-1
Tiernan, Ore. F4 238-9
Tierra Amarilla, N. Mex. C6 230-1
Tieton, Wash. H10 246-7
Tiffany, Colo. J7 214-5
Tiffany, Wis. K2 140-1
Tiffin, Ia. G12 104-5
Tiffin, O. C6 132-3
Tift, co., Ga. M6 160-1
Tifton, Ga. M6 160-1
Tiftona, Tenn. K10 188-9
Tigard*, Ore. C6 238-9
Tiger, Ga. D6 160-1
Tiger, Wash. C16 246-7
Tigerton, Wis. D2 140-1
Tigerville, S.C. E2 184-5
Tignall, Ga. F7 160-1
Tignish, P.E.I. B4 287
Tignish Shore*, P.E.I. B4 287
Tigrett, Tenn. B3 188-9
Tilbury, Ont. F10 284-5
Tilden, Ill. L7 96-7
Tilden, Ky. H5 164-5
Tilden, Miss. C10 176-7
Tilden, Nebr. E12 124-5
Tilden, Tex. I7 192-3
Tilford, Ky. I7 164-5
Tilford, S. Dak. E2 136-7
Tilghman, Md. F12 172-3
Tilghmanton, Md. B7 172-3
Tiline, Ky. I3 164-5
Tillamook, Ore. C4 238-9
Tillamook, co., Ore. C4 238-9
Tillamook Bay, Ore. B4 238-9
Tillar, Ark. I9 150-1
Tillatoba, Miss. D7 176-7
Tilleda, Wis. C2 140-1
Tiller, Ore. I6 238-9
Tillery, N.C. C13 180-1
Tilley, Alta. M9 264-5
Tillicum, Wash. K2 246-7
Tillman, S.C. J10 184-5
Tillman, co., Okla. H8 234-5
Tillson*, N.Y. H10 80-1
Tillsonburg, Ont. E13 284-5
Tilston, Man. J9 272-3
Tilton, Ark. D10 150-1
Tilton, Ga. D3 160-1
Tilton, Ill. G11 96-7
Tilton, Ky. F13 164-5
Tilton*, N.H. K6 72-3
Tilton [-Northfield], N.H. K6 72-3
Tiltonsville, O. F11 132-3
Timagami, Ont. G8 284-5
Timber, Ore. B5 238-9
Timber Bay*, Sask. I8 294-5
Timber Lake, S. Dak. B7 136-7
Timberlake, N.C. G6 180-1
Timberlake, O. A15 132-3
Timberlake, Tenn. C4 188-9
Timberlea, N.S. E7 281
Timberville, Va. F10 196-7
Timbo, Ark. C7 150-1
Times Beach, Mo. C15 120-1
Timken, Kans. G7 108-9
Timmins, Ont. F7 284-5
Timmonsville, S.C. D13 184-5
Timnath, Colo. D3 214-5
Timothy, Tenn. A10 188-9
Timpas, Colo. H14 214-5
Timpie, Ut. E5 242-3
Timpson, Tex. E11 192-3
Tina, Mo. C5 120-1
Tincap, Ont. J15 284-5
Tindal, S.C. E12 184-5
Tindall, Mo. B4 120-1
Tingley, Ia. J6 104-5
Tinkerville, N.H. G5 72-3
Tinley Park, Ill. N3 96-7
Tinmouth, Vt. K4 90-1
Tinnie, N. Mex. J8 230-1
Tinsley, Miss. H5 176-7
Tinsman, Ark. I7 150-1
Tintagel, B.C. F5 268-9
Tintah, Minn. J2 116-7
Tioga, La. E4 168-9
Tioga, N. Dak. C3 128-9
Tioga, Ore. H4 238-9
Tioga, W. Va. G5 200-1
Tioga, co., N.Y. G6 80-1
Tioga, co., Pa. D9 84-5
Tionesta, Pa. E4 84-5
Tipler, Wis. C14 140-1
Tiplersville, Miss. A9 176-7
Tipp City, O. G15 132-3
Tippah, co., Miss. B9 176-7
Tippecanoe, Ind. C8 100-1
Tippecanoe, co., Ind. F6 100-1
Tippett, Nev. E11 226-7
Tippo, Miss. D6 176-7
Tipton, Ind. F8 100-1
Tipton, Ia. G14 104-5
Tipton, Kans. E8 108-9
Tipton, Mich. K14 112-3
Tipton, Mo. E6 120-1
Tipton, Okla. H8 234-5
Tipton, Tenn. K2 188-9
Tipton, Wyo. I9 250-1
Tipton, co., Ind. F8 100-1
Tipton, co., Tenn. C2 188-9
Tiptonville, Tenn. A2 188-9
Tiptop, Va. I5 196-7
Tiro, O. D7 132-3
Tirzah, S.C. A10 184-5
Tisbury, Mass. I13 68-9
Tisch Mills, Wis. E6 140-1
Tisdale, Sask. J8 294-5
Tisdale Subdivision*, Sask. K8 294-5
Tishomingo, Miss. B10 176-7
Tishomingo, Okla. H12 234-5
Tishomingo, co., Miss. B10 176-7
Tiskilwa, Ill. D7 96-7
Titicus, Conn. H4 60-1
Titonka, Ia. B7 104-5
Titus, Ala. H7 146-7
Titus, co., Tex. D10 192-3
Titusville, Fla. E12 156-7
Titusville, N.J. G4 76-7
Titusville, Pa. D3 84-5
Tiverton, N.S. E4 281
Tiverton, Ont. B12 284-5
Tiverton, R.I. E7 87
Tiverton Four Corners, R.I. F7 87
Tivoli, N.Y. G11 80-1
Toadlena, N. Mex. D2 230-1
Toano, Va. E3 196-7
Toast*, N.C. C7 180-1
Tobaccoville, N.C. G3 180-1
Tobar, Nev. C10 226-7
Tobermory, Ont. I8 284-5
Tobias, Nebr. I13 124-5
Toccoa, Ga. D6 160-1
Toccoa Falls, Ga. D6 160-1
Toccopola, Miss. C8 176-7
Tocito, N. Mex. C2 230-1
Tocsin, Ind. D11 100-1
Tod Park, Ut. F5 242-3
Todd, N.C. C6 180-1
Todd, co., Ky. J6 164-5
Todd, co., Minn. J4 116-7
Todd, co., S. Dak. H7 136-7
Toddville, Md. H13 172-3
Tofield, Alta. J8 264-5
Tofino, B.C. J5 268-9
Togiak, Alaska G8 254-5
Togo, Sask. L11 294-5
Tohatchi, N. Mex. D2 230-1
Toivola, Mich. C8 112-3
Tok, Alaska E13 254-5
Tokeena Crossroads, S.C. C5 184-5
Tokeland, Wash. G5 246-7
Token Creek, Wis. I1 140-1
Toketee Falls, Ore. H6 238-9
Tokio, Ark. H3 150-1
Tokio, N. Dak. E11 128-9
Toksook Bay*, Alaska F7 254-5
Toledo, Ill. I10 96-7
Toledo, Ia. F10 104-5
Toledo, O. B5 132-3
Toledo, Ore. E4 238-9
Toledo, Wash. H7 246-7
Toll Gate, W. Va. E5 200-1
Tolland, Conn. C11 60-1
Tolland, Mass. E3 68-9
Tolland, co., Conn. C11 60-1
Tollesboro, Ky. F13 164-5
Tolleson, Ariz. I6 206-7
Tollette, Ark. H3 150-1
Tolley, N. Dak. C5 128-9
Tolna, N. Dak. E11 128-9
Tolono, Ill. G10 96-7
Tolovana Park, Ore. B4 238-9
Tolstoi, Man. K15 272-3
Tolstoy, S. Dak. C10 136-7
Toltec, Ariz. J7 206-7
Tolu, Ky. I3 164-5
Toluca, Ill. E8 96-7
Tom, Okla. I16 234-5
Tom Green, co., Tex. F6 192-3
Tomah, Wis. H10 140-1
Tomahawk, Ky. G15 164-5
Tomahawk, Wis. D12 140-1
Tomato, Ark. C13 150-1
Tomball, Tex. G13 192-3
Tombstone, Ariz. L10 206-7
Tome, N. Mex. G5 230-1
Tomnolen, Miss. E8 176-7
Tompkins, Sask. N4 294-5
Tompkins, co., N.Y. F6 80-1
Tompkinsville, Ky. K9 164-5
Tompkinsville, Md. H10 172-3
Toms Brook, Va. E10 196-7
Toms River, N.J. I7 76-7
Tonalea, Ariz. C8 206-7
Tonasket, Wash. C12 246-7
Tonawanda, N.Y. E2 80-1
Toney, Ala. A6 146-7
Toney Creek, S.C. H2 184-5
Tonganoxie, Kans. E15 108-9
Tonica, Ill. D8 96-7
Tonka Bay*, Minn. M6 116-7
Tonkawa, Okla. C11 234-5
Tonopah, Ariz. I5 206-7
Tonopah, Nev. I6 226-7
Tonopah Junction, Nev. I4 226-7
Tonset, Mass. G16 68-9
Tontitown, Ark. B2 150-1
Tonto Basin, Ariz. H7 206-7
Tontogany, O. B5 132-3
Tony, Wis. D10 140-1
Tooele, Ut. F5 242-3
Tooele, co., Ut. F4 242-3
Toole, co., Mont. B6 222-3
Toombs, co., Ga. K8 160-1
Toomey, La. H1 168-9
Toomsboro, Ga. I7 160-1
Toomsuba, Miss. I10 176-7
Toone, Tenn. K4 188-9
Topawa, Ariz. L7 206-7
Topaz, Ida. N10 218-9
Topeka, Ind. A10 100-1
Topeka, Kans. F14 108-9
Topeka, Miss. K6 176-7
Topinabee, Mich. E13 112-3
Topmost, Ky. I15 164-5
Topock, Ariz. F2 206-7
Toponas, Colo. D9 214-5
Toppenish, Wash. H11 246-7
Topsfield, Me. H9 64-5
Topsfield, Mass. B12 68-9
Topsham, Me. N10 64-5
Topsham*, Vt. G8 90-1
Topton, Miss. H10 176-7
Topton, N.C. E2 180-1
Topton, Pa. H14 84-5
Toquerville, Ut. M3 242-3
Torbay, Nfld. N11 278-9
Tornado, W. Va. H12 200-1
Toro, La. E2 168-9
Toronto, Ia. F14 104-5
Toronto, Kans. I14 108-9
Toronto, O. E11 132-3
Toronto, Ont. J8 284-5
Toronto, S. Dak. E16 136-7
Torquay, Sask. O9 294-5
Torrance, Calif. H8 210-1
Torrance, Ont. A14 284-5
Torrance, co., N. Mex. G7 230-1
Torras, La. F6 168-9
Torreon, N. Mex. G6 230-1
Torrey, Ut. K7 242-3
Torrington, Alta. L8 264-5
Torrington, Conn. C6 60-1
Torrington, Wyo. H16 250-1
Tortilla Flat, Ariz. I7 206-7
Toston, Mont. F7 222-3
Totoket, Conn. H8 60-1
Totowa, N.J. B10 76-7
Tottenham, Ont. C14 284-5
Touchet, Wash. I14 246-7
Tougaloo, Miss. I6 176-7
Toughkenamon*, Pa. K14 84-5
Touhy, Nebr. G14 124-5
Toulon, Ill. E7 96-7
Toulon, Nev. E3 226-7
Tourelle*, Que. H5 290-1
Touristville, Ky. J11 164-5
Tourville, Que. F13 290-1
Toutes Aides, Man. G11 272-3
Toutle, Wash. H7 246-7
Tovey, Ill. I7 96-7
Towaco, N.J. C6 76-7
Towanda, Kans. I11 108-9
Towanda, Pa. D12 84-5
Towaoc, Colo. J5 214-5
Tower, Mich. E13 112-3
Tower, Minn. G8 116-7
Tower City, N. Dak. G13 128-9
Tower City, Pa. H11 84-5
Tower Hill, Ill. I8 96-7
Tower Junction, Wyo. E2 250-1
Tower Lakes*, Ill. B10 96-7
Town and Country*, Mo. E10 120-1
Town and Country*, Wash. E16 246-7
Town Bank, N.J. O4 76-7
Town Creek, Ala. B5 146-7
Town Crest Village, Mass. B2 68-9
Town Line*, N.Y. E3 80-1
Town of Pines, Ind. A6 100-1
Towner, Colo. G16 214-5
Towner, N. Dak. D8 128-9
Towner, co., N. Dak. B10 128-9
Townley, Ala. F4 146-7
Towns, Ga. K7 160-1
Towns, co., Ga. D5 160-1
Townsend, Del. D3 153
Townsend, Ga. L10 160-1
Townsend, Mass. B9 68-9
Townsend, Mont. F6 222-3
Townsend, Tenn. I15 188-9
Townsend, Va. F5 196-7
Townsend, Wis. E14 140-1
Townsend Harbor, Mass. B9 68-9
Townshend, Vt. M6 90-1
Townsville, N.C. C11 180-1
Townville, S.C. C5 184-5
Towson, Md. C11 172-3
Toxey, Ala. J2 146-7
Toy, Nev. E3 226-7
Tracadie, N.B. E7 275
Tracadie*, N.B. E6 275
Tracadie, N.S. C9 281
Tracy, Calif. C9 210-1
Tracy, Ia. H9 104-5
Tracy, Minn. N3 116-7
Tracy, Mo. H14 120-1
Tracy, N.B. I4 275
Tracy, Que. H13 290-1
Tracy City, Tenn. K10 188-9
Tracy Corner, Mass. F11 68-9
Tracys Landing, Md. K7 172-3
Tracyton*, Wash. E7 246-7
Trade, Tenn. A17 188-9
Tradesville, S.C. B11 184-5
Trading Post, Kans. H16 108-9
Traer, Ia. E10 104-5
Traer, Kans. C4 108-9
Trafalgar, Ind. J8 100-1
Trafford, Ala. E6 146-7
Trafford, Pa. B7 84-5
Trail, B.C. K9 268-9
Trail, Minn. G3 116-7
Trail, Ore. I6 238-9
Trail City, S. Dak. B8 136-7
Trail Creek, Ind. A6 100-1
Trailcreek, Mont. A3 222-3
Trailer Estates, Fla. J2 156-7
Traill, co., N. Dak. F13 128-9
Trainer, Pa. K15 84-5
Tralake, Miss. F4 176-7
Trammel, Va. J3 196-7
Trampas, N. Mex. D7 230-1
Tramping Lake, Sask. K4 294-5
Transylvania, La. B7 168-9
Transylvania, co., N.C. E3 180-1
Traphill, N.C. C7 180-1
Trappe, Md. F13 172-3
Trappe*, Pa. I14 84-5
Traskwood, Ark. K14 150-1
Traunik, Mich. D10 112-3
Travelers Rest, S.C. F1 184-5
Travellers Rest, P.E.I. E5 287
Traverse, co., Minn. K2 116-7
Traverse City, Mich. F12 112-3
Travis, co., Tex. G8 192-3
Treadway, Tenn. G14 188-9
Treasure, co., Mont. G12 222-3
Treasure Island, Fla. I1 156-7
Treasureton, Ida. O10 218-9
Trebloc, Miss. D9 176-7
Treece, Kans. K16 108-9
Trees, La. A1 168-9
Treesbank*, Man. J2 272-3
Trego, Mont. B2 222-3
Trego, Nev. D3 226-7
Trego, Wis. C8 140-1
Trego, co., Kans. F5 108-9
Treherne, Man. J12 272-3
Trementina, N. Mex. E9 230-1
Tremont, Ill. F7 96-7
Tremont, Ind. A5 100-1
Tremont*, Me. K8 64-5
Tremont, Mass. G13 68-9
Tremont, Miss. C10 176-7
Tremont, Pa. H12 84-5
Tremont City, O. F5 132-3
Tremonton, Ut. C5 242-3
Trempealeau, Wis. H9 140-1
Trempealeau, co., Wis. G9 140-1
Trenary, Mich. D10 112-3
Trent, Ky. H13 164-5
Trent, S. Dak. F16 136-7
Trent Woods, N.C. F14 180-1
Trenton, Ala. B7 146-7
Trenton, Ark. G10 150-1
Trenton, Fla. D9 156-7
Trenton, Ga. D1 160-1
Trenton, Ill. K7 96-7
Trenton, Ky. K6 164-5
Trenton, Me. K8 64-5
Trenton, Mich. K6 112-3
Trenton, Mo. B4 120-1
Trenton, Nebr. J6 124-5
Trenton, N.J. H5 76-7
Trenton, N.C. F13 180-1
Trenton, N. Dak. D2 128-9
Trenton, N.S. C8 281
Trenton, O. J13 132-3
Trenton, Ont. K12 284-5
Trenton, S.C. F8 184-5
Trenton, Tenn. B3 188-9
Trenton, Ut. C6 242-3
Trentville, Tenn. H12 188-9
Trentwood, Wash. E16 246-7
Trepassey, Nfld. O11 278-9
Tres Piedras, N. Mex. C7 230-1
Tresckow, Pa. G13 84-5
Trestle Creek, Ida. B3 218-9
Treutlen, co., Ga. J8 160-1
Trevett, Me. N11 64-5
Trevilians, Va. G11 196-7
Trevlac, Ind. J7 100-1
Trevor, Wis. K15 140-1
Trevorton, Pa. G11 84-5
Treynor, Ia. I3 104-5
Trezevant, Tenn. B4 188-9
Tri City, Ky. K3 164-5
Tri City, Ore. H5 238-9
Tri Lakes, Ind. C10 100-1
Tri Par Estates*, Fla. G10 156-7
Triadelphia, W. Va. C5 200-1
Triana*, Ala. B6 146-7
Triangle, Va. B3 196-7
Triangle Lake, Ore. F5 238-9
Tribbett, Miss. F4 176-7
Tribbey, Okla. F12 234-5
Tribes Hill*, N.Y. F10 80-1
Tribune, Kans. G1 108-9
Tribune, Sask. O9 294-5
Tridell, Ut. F9 242-3
Trident, Mont. G6 222-3
Trigg, co., Ky. J4 164-5
Trilby, Fla. F4 156-7
Trimble, Mo. C3 120-1
Trimble, O. H8 132-3
Trimble, Tenn. B3 188-9
Trimble, co., Ky. F9 164-5
Trimont, Minn. O4 116-7
Trinchera, Colo. J13 214-5
Tring-Jonction, Que. H16 290-1
Trinidad, Calif. E1 210-1
Trinidad, Colo. J12 214-5
Trinidad*, Tex. E9 192-3
Trinidad, Wash. F12 246-7
Trinity, Ala. B5 146-7
Trinity, Ky. E13 164-5
Trinity, La. D6 168-9
Trinity, Nfld. M10 278-9
Trinity, N.C. H4 180-1
Trinity, Tex. F10 192-3
Trinity, co., Calif. E2 210-1
Trinity, co., Tex. F10 192-3
Trinity Bay, Nfld. N11 278-9
Trinity Springs, Ind. L6 100-1
Trio, S.C. F14 184-5
Trion, Ga. D2 160-1
Triplet, Va. K12 196-7
Triplett, Mo. C5 120-1

Triplett, N.C. C6 180-1
Tripoli, Ia. C11 104-5
Tripp, S. Dak. H13 136-7
Tripp, co., S. Dak. H9 136-7
Triton-Jim's Cove-Cards Harbour*, Nfld. L10 278-9
Triumph, Ida. L6 218-9
Triune, Tenn. I7 188-9
Trochu, Alta. L8 264-5
Trois-Pistoles, Que. D14 290-1
Trois-Rivières, Que. H14 290-1
Trois-Rivières-Ouest*, Que. H14 290-1
Trois-Ruisseaux*, N.B. H8 275
Trommald, Minn. I5 116-7
Tropic, Ut. L6 242-3
Trosky, Minn. O2 116-7
Trosper, Ky. J13 164-5
Trossachs, Sask. O8 294-5
Trotter, Wyo. B8 250-1
Trotwood, O. H14 132-3
Troup, Tex. E10 192-3
Troup, co., Ga. H2 160-1
Trousdale, Kans. I7 108-9
Trousdale, Okla. G12 234-5
Trousdale, co., Tenn. A8 188-9
Trout, La. D5 168-9
Trout, W. Va. H6 200-1
Trout Creek, Mich. D8 112-3
Trout Creek, Ont. H8 284-5
Trout Creek, Ut. H3 242-3
Trout Lake*, Alta. F7 264-5
Trout Lake, Mich. D12 112-3
Trout Lake, Wash. I9 246-7
Trout River, Nfld. M7 278-9
Troutdale, Ore. B7 238-9
Troutdale, Va. J5 196-7
Troutman, N.C. I1 180-1
Troutville, Va. I8 196-7
Trowbridge, Ont. C12 284-5
Troy, Ala. K8 146-7
Troy, Ida. F2 218-9
Troy, Ill. K7 96-7
Troy, Ind. O6 100-1
Troy, Kans. D15 108-9
Troy, Me. J6 64-5
Troy, Mich. I6 112-3
Troy, Miss. D9 176-7
Troy, Mo. D9 120-1
Troy, Mont. B1 222-3
Troy, N.H. O4 72-3
Troy, N.Y. F11 80-1
Troy, N.C. E9 180-1
Troy, O. F4 132-3
Troy, Okla. H12 234-5
Troy, Ore. A15 238-9
Troy, Pa. D11 84-5
Troy, S.C. E7 184-5
Troy, Tenn. A3 188-9
Troy, Vt. B7 90-1
Troy, Va. G11 196-7
Troy, W. Va. F5 200-1
Troy Center*, Wis. K14 140-1
Troy Hills, N.J. D6 76-7
Troy Mills, Ia. E12 104-5
Truckee, Calif. G5 210-1
True, W. Va. J5 200-1
Truesdale, Ia. D4 104-5
Truesdale, Mo. E9 120-1
Trujillo, N. Mex. E9 230-1
Truman, Minn. O5 116-7
Trumann, Ark. C11 150-1
Trumansburg, N.Y. F6 80-1
Trumbull, Conn. H6 60-1
Trumbull, Nebr. I11 124-5
Trumbull, co., O. B11 132-3
Truro, Ia. I7 104-5
Truro, Mass. F16 68-9
Truro, N.S. D7 281
Trussville, Ala. E7 146-7
Truth or Consequences, N. Mex. J4 230-1
Truxno, La. A4 168-9
Truxton, Ariz. E4 206-7
Tryon, Nebr. F6 124-5
Tryon, N.C. E4 180-1
Tryon, Okla. E12 234-5
Tschetter Colony, S. Dak. H14 136-7
Tualatin*, Ore. C6 238-9
Tuba City, Ariz. C8 206-7
Tubac, Ariz. M8 206-7
Tuckahoe, N.J. N4 76-7
Tuckahoe, N.Y. D15 80-1
Tucker, Ark. G7 150-1
Tucker, Ga. B11 160-1
Tucker, Ut. G7 242-3
Tucker, co., W. Va. E8 200-1
Tuckerman, Ark. C9 150-1
Tuckers Crossing, Miss. K9 176-7
Tuckerton, N.J. L6 76-7
Tuckertown, R.I. H4 87
Tucson, Ariz. K8 206-7
Tucumcari, N. Mex. F10 230-1
Tuffnell, Sask. L9 294-5
Tuftonboro, N.H. J8 72-3
Tugaske, Sask. M7 294-5
Tuktoyaktuk, N.W. Terr. B1 296
Tukwila, Wash. I3 246-7
Tula, Miss. C8 176-7
Tulameen, B.C. J8 268-9
Tulare, Calif. K6 210-1
Tulare, S. Dak. D12 136-7
Tulare, co., Calif. K6 210-1
Tulare East*, Calif. K6 210-1
Tulare Northwest*, Calif. K6 210-1
Tularosa, N. Mex. J7 230-1
Tulelake, Calif. D4 210-1
Tulia, Tex. C5 192-3
Tull, Ark. K14 150-1
Tullahassee, Okla. E14 234-5
Tullahoma, Tenn. J8 188-9
Tullos, La. D5 168-9
Tully, Mass. B6 68-9
Tully, N.Y. F7 80-1
Tullytown, Pa. J16 84-5
Tulsa, Okla. D13 234-5
Tulsa, co., Okla. E13 234-5
Tulu, Tenn. D4 188-9
Tuluksak, Alaska F8 254-5
Tumacacori, Ariz. M8 206-7
Tumalo, Ore. F8 238-9
Tumbling Shoals, Ark. D7 150-1
Tumtum, Wash. E15 246-7
Tumwater, Wash. K1 246-7
Tunbridge, Vt. H7 90-1
Tungsten, Nev. C4 226-7
Tungsten, N.C. C11 180-1
Tunica, La. F6 168-9
Tunica, Miss. B5 176-7
Tunica, co., Miss. B5 176-7
Tunica North, Miss. B5 176-7
Tunis Mills, Md. F12 172-3
Tunkhannock, Pa. E13 84-5
Tunnel City, Wis. H10 140-1
Tunnel Hill, Ga. D2 160-1
Tunnel Springs, Ala. K5 146-7
Tunnelton, Ind. L7 100-1
Tunnelton, W. Va. C16 200-1
Tunstall, Va. E2 196-7
Tuntatuliag, Alaska F8 254-5
Tununak, Alaska F7 254-5
Tuolumne, Calif. C12 210-1
Tuolumne, co., Calif. I5 210-1
Tupelo, Ark. D9 150-1
Tupelo, Miss. C9 176-7
Tupelo, Okla. H13 234-5
Tupper Lake, N.Y. B10 80-1
Turbeville, S.C. E13 184-5
Turbeville, Va. K9 196-7
Turin, Alta. N9 264-5
Turin, Ga. H3 160-1
Turin, Ia. F2 104-5
Turkey, N.C. F12 180-1
Turkey, Tex. C5 192-3
Turkey Creek, La. F4 168-9
Turkey Point, Ont. E13 284-5
Turley, N. Mex. C4 230-1
Turley, Okla. D13 234-5
Turley, Tenn. G11 188-9
Turlock, Calif. D10 210-1
Turner, Ark. G10 150-1
Turner, Me. L3 64-5
Turner, Mich. G14 112-3
Turner*, Ore. D6 238-9
Turner, co., Ga. L5 160-1
Turner, co., S. Dak. H15 136-7
Turner Center, Me. L3 64-5
Turner Valley, Alta. M7 264-5
Turners Falls, Mass. B5 68-9
Turnersburg, N.C. H1 180-1
Turnersville, Miss. J8 176-7
Turnersville, N.J. O10 76-7
Turnerville, Ga. D6 160-1
Turnerville, N. Mex. K3 230-1
Turney, Mo. C3 120-1
Turnor Lake*, Sask. F4 294-5
Turon, Kans. I8 108-9
Turpin, Okla. C5 234-5
Turquillo, N. Mex. D8 230-1
Turrell, Ark. D12 150-1
Turtle Creek, Pa. B7 84-5
Turtle Creek, W. Va. J12 200-1
Turtle Lake, N. Dak. F7 128-9
Turtle Lake, Wis. E8 140-1
Turtle River, Minn. G4 116-7
Turtleford, Sask. J4 294-5
Turton, S. Dak. C13 136-7
Tusayan, Ariz. D6 206-7
Tuscaloosa, Ala. F4 146-7
Tuscaloosa, co., Ala. F4 146-7
Tuscarawas, O. E10 132-3
Tuscarawas, co., O. F10 132-3
Tuscarora, Nev. B7 226-7
Tuscola, Ill. H10 96-7
Tuscola, Miss. H7 176-7
Tuscola, co., Mich. H14 112-3
Tuscor, Mont. C1 222-3
Tusculum, Tenn. G15 188-9
Tuscumbia, Ala. B4 146-7
Tuscumbia, Mo. F6 120-1
Tushka, Okla. H13 234-5
Tuskahoma, Okla. G15 234-5
Tuskegee, Ala. I9 146-7
Tuskegee, Okla. E13 234-5
Tustin*, Calif. H9 210-1
Tustin, Mich. G12 112-3
Tustin, Wis. F2 140-1
Tustin-Foothills*, Calif. N7 210-1
Tutela Heights*, Ont. E14 284-5
Tuthill, S. Dak. I6 136-7
Tuttle, Ida. N5 218-9
Tuttle, N. Dak. G8 128-9
Tuttle, Okla. K1 234-5
Tuttle Creek Lake, Kans. E12 108-9
Tutwiler, Miss. D5 176-7
Tuweep, Ariz. C5 206-7
Tuxedo, N.C. E4 180-1
Tuxedo Park, N.Y. B13 80-1
Tuxford, Sask. N7 294-5
Twain-Harte*, Calif. I5 210-1
Tway, Sask. K7 294-5
Tweed, Ont. J12 284-5
Twelve Mile, Ind. D8 100-1
Twentynine Palms, Calif. N9 210-1
Twentynine Palms Base*, Calif. N9 210-1
Twiggs, co., Ga. I6 160-1
Twilight, W. Va. K14 200-1
Twillie Trailer Court*, Sask. J7 294-5
Twillingate, Nfld. L10 278-9
Twin, Ala. D3 146-7
Twin Bridges, Mont. H5 222-3
Twin Brooks, S. Dak. C15 136-7
Twin Buttes, Ariz. L8 206-7
Twin City, Ga. J9 160-1
Twin Falls, Ida. O6 218-9
Twin Falls, co., Ida. O5 218-9
Twin Hills*, Alaska G8 254-5
Twin Lake, Mich. H11 112-3
Twin Lakes*, Calif. J3 210-1
Twin Lakes, Colo. F9 214-5
Twin Lakes, Conn. A4 60-1
Twin Lakes, Conn. A4 60-1
Twin Lakes, Ga. O6 160-1
Twin Lakes, Minn. O6 116-7
Twin Lakes, Wis. K14 140-1
Twin Mountain, N.H. G6 72-3
Twin Rocks, Ore. B4 238-9
Twin Valley, Minn. H2 116-7
Twining, Mich. G14 112-3
Twinsburg, O. C15 132-3
Twinton, Tenn. B10 188-9
Twisp, Wash. D11 246-7
Twist, Ark. D11 150-1
Two Buttes, Colo. I16 214-5
Two Guns, Ariz. E8 206-7
Two Harbors, Minn. H9 116-7
Two Hills, Alta. I9 264-5
Two Rivers, Wis. F6 140-1
Twodot, Mont. F8 222-3
Ty Ty, Ga. M5 160-1
Tyaskin, Md. H14 172-3
Tybouts Corner, Del. B3 153
Tye*, Tex. E6 192-3
Tye River, Va. H10 196-7
Tygart Lake, W. Va. C15 200-1
Tygh Valley, Ore. C9 238-9
Tyhee, Ida. N9 218-9
Tyler, Ala. I6 146-7
Tyler, Minn. N2 116-7
Tyler, Tex. E10 192-3
Tyler, Wash. F15 246-7
Tyler, co., Tex. F11 192-3
Tyler, co., W. Va. D5 200-1
Tylerton, Md. I13 172-3
Tylertown, Miss. L6 176-7
Tylerville, Conn. F10 60-1
Tyndall, Fla. C5 156-7
Tyndall, Man. I15 272-3
Tyndall, S. Dak. I13 136-7
Tyne Valley, P.E.I. D4 287
Tyner, Ind. B7 100-1
Tyner, Ky. I12 164-5
Tyner, N.C. C14 180-1
Tyner, Tenn. K11 188-9
Tyngsborough, Mass. B10 68-9
Tyonek, Alaska F11 254-5
Tyringham, Mass. D2 68-9
Tyro, Kans. K14 108-9
Tyro, Miss. B7 176-7
Tyro, Va. H9 196-7
Tyrone, Colo. I13 214-5
Tyrone, Ga. D10 160-1
Tyrone, N. Mex. K3 230-1
Tyrone, Okla. B4 234-5
Tyrone, Pa. H7 84-5
Tyronza, Ark. D11 150-1
Tyrrell, co., N.C. D15 180-1
Tyson, Vt. K6 90-1
Tyvan, Sask. N9 294-5

U

Ubly, Mich. H15 112-3
Ucluelet, B.C. K5 268-9
Ucolo, Ut. L11 242-3
Ucon, Ida. L10 218-9
Ucross, Wyo. B12 250-1
Udall, Kans. J11 108-9
Udell, Ia. J10 104-5
Uehling, Nebr. F14 124-5
Ugashik, Alaska H9 254-5
Uhrichsville, O. E10 132-3
Uinta, co., Wyo. J5 250-1
Uintah*, Ut. E6 242-3
Uintah, co., Ut. F10 242-3
Ukiah, Calif. G2 210-1
Ukiah, Ore. C12 238-9
Ulen, Ind. G7 100-1
Ulen, Minn. H2 116-7
Uler, W. Va. G4 200-1
Ulm, Ark. F9 150-1
Ulm, Wyo. B12 250-1
Ulmer, S.C. H10 184-5
Ulster, co., N.Y. H10 80-1
Ulysses, Kans. J2 108-9
Ulysses, Ky. G15 164-5
Ulysses, Nebr. H13 124-5
Umapine, Ore. A13 238-9
Umatilla, Fla. E11 156-7
Umatilla, Ore. B12 238-9
Umatilla, co., Ore. C13 238-9
Umiat, Alaska B11 254-5
Umikoa, Hawaii I13 258-9
Umpherville Settlement*, Man. C4 272-3
Umpire, Ark. G2 150-1
Umpqua, Ore. H5 238-9
Una, S.C. F4 184-5
Una, Tenn. H7 188-9
Unadilla, Ga. K5 160-1
Unadilla, Mich. J3 112-3
Unadilla, Nebr. H15 124-5
Unadilla, N.Y. G8 80-1
Unaka, N.C. E1 180-1
Unalakleet, Alaska D9 254-5
Unalaska, Alaska I6 254-5
Uncas, Okla. C12 234-5
Uncasville, Conn. G13 60-1
Underhill, Vt. D5 90-1
Underhill, Wis. C4 140-1
Underwood, Ala. G6 146-7
Underwood, Ind. M9 100-1
Underwood, Ia. H3 104-5
Underwood, Minn. J2 116-7
Underwood, N. Dak. F6 128-9
Underwood, Wash. J9 246-7
Underwood Crossroads, Ala. B4 146-7
Underwoods Corner, Del. E3 153
Uneeda, W. Va. J13 200-1
Unga, Alaska I8 254-5
Ungava Bay, Que. C5 290-1
Unger, Okla. I14 234-5
Unger, W. Va. D11 200-1
Unicoi, Tenn. G16 188-9
Unicoi, co., Tenn. B15 188-9
Union, Ala. G3 146-7
Union, Ark. B8 150-1
Union, Conn. B12 60-1
Union, Ia. E9 104-5
Union, Ky. E11 164-5
Union, La. C11 168-9
Union, Me. L6 64-5
Union, Mich. K12 112-3
Union, Miss. C9 176-7
Union, Miss. H8 176-7
Union, Mo. F9 120-1
Union, Nebr. K3 124-5
Union, N.H. K9 72-3
Union, N.J. E4 76-7
Union, N.J. D9 76-7
Union*, N.J. K7 76-7
Union, O. H14 132-3
Union, Ont. E12 284-5
Union, Ore. C14 238-9
Union*, P.E.I. E7 287
Union, S.C. G6 184-5
Union, Wash. F7 246-7
Union, W. Va. J6 200-1
Union, co., Ark. J6 150-1
Union, co., Fla. C10 156-7
Union, co., Ga. D5 160-1
Union, co., Ill. N8 96-7
Union, co., Ind. I12 100-1
Union, co., Ia. I6 104-5
Union, co., Ky. H4 164-5
Union, co., La. A4 168-9
Union, co., Miss. B9 176-7
Union, co., N.J. E6 76-7
Union, co., N. Mex. C11 230-1
Union, co., N.C. F7 180-1
Union, co., O. E6 132-3
Union, co., Ore. C14 238-9
Union, co., Pa. G10 84-5
Union, co., S.C. C8 184-5
Union, co., S. Dak. I16 136-7
Union, co., Tenn. B13 188-9
Union Bay, B.C. J5 268-9
Union Beach, N.J. H10 76-7
Union Bridge, Md. B9 172-3
Union Center, S. Dak. E4 136-7
Union Center, Wis. I11 140-1
Union Church, Miss. K4 176-7
Union City, Calif. C8 210-1
Union City, Ga. D10 160-1
Union City, Ind. G12 100-1
Union City, Ky. D8 164-5
Union City, Mich. J12 112-3
Union City, N.J. C11 76-7
Union City, O. F3 132-3
Union City, Okla. J1 234-5
Union City, Pa. C2 84-5
Union City, Tenn. A3 188-9
Union Creek, Ore. I6 238-9
Union Gap, Wash. H11 246-7
Union Grove, Ala. C7 146-7
Union Grove, N.C. H1 180-1
Union Grove, Tenn. J12 188-9
Union Grove, Wis. K5 140-1
Union Hall, Va. J8 196-7
Union Hill, La. F4 168-9
Union Lake, Mich. I4 112-3
Union Level, Va. J11 196-7
Union Mills, Ind. B6 100-1
Union Mills, N.C. E5 180-1
Union Park, Fla. F7 156-7
Union Pier, Mich. K11 112-3
Union Point, Ga. G7 160-1
Union Springs, Ala. J9 146-7
Union Springs, N.Y. F6 80-1
Union Star, Ky. G7 164-5
Union Star, Mo. B3 120-1
Union Village, R.I. A4 87
Union Village, Vt. I8 90-1
Uniondale, Ind. D11 100-1
Uniondale, N.Y. E16 80-1
Uniontown, Ala. I4 146-7
Uniontown, Ark. C2 150-1
Uniontown, Kans. I16 108-9
Uniontown, Ky. H4 164-5
Uniontown, Md. B9 172-3
Uniontown, N.J. E3 76-7
Uniontown, Pa. J3 84-5
Uniontown, Wash. H16 246-7
Unionvale, P.E.I. C3 287
Unionville, Conn. D8 60-1
Unionville, Ga. M6 160-1
Unionville, Ind. J7 100-1
Unionville, Ia. J10 104-5
Unionville, La. B4 168-9
Unionville, Md. C9 172-3
Unionville, Mich. H14 112-3
Unionville, Mo. A5 120-1
Unionville, N.Y. I10 80-1
Unionville, N.C. K2 180-1
Unionville, Tenn. I7 188-9
Unionville, Va. C1 196-7

Uniopolis, O. E4 132-3
United States Range, N.W. Terr. A3 296
Unity, Me. J5 64-5
Unity*, Me. J5 64-5
Unity, Md. G4 172-3
Unity, Mo. J15 120-1
Unity, N.H. L3 72-3
Unity, Ore. E14 238-9
Unity, Sask. K4 294-5
Unity, Wis. F11 140-1
Unityville, S. Dak. G14 136-7
Universal, Ind. I4 100-1
Universal City, Tex. I2 192-3
University*, Fla. H3 156-7
University, Miss. C7 176-7
University City, Mo. B15 120-1
University Heights, Ia. G13 104-5
University Heights, O. B15 132-3
University Park, Ia. H10 104-5
University Park, Md. I4 172-3
University Park, Tex. C15 192-3
University Park [-Tortugas], N. Mex. L5 230-1
University Place*, Wash. F7 246-7
Uno, Va. C1 196-7
Upalco, Ut. G9 242-3
Upham, N.B. I6 275
Upham, N. Dak. C7 128-9
Upland, Calif. G9 210-1
Upland, Ind. E10 100-1
Upland, Kans. F11 108-9
Upland, Nebr. I10 124-5
Upland*, Pa. J15 84-5
Uplands Park*, Mo. E10 120-1
Upper*, N.J. N5 76-7
Upper Arlington, O. F6 132-3
Upper Blackville, N.B. G5 275
Upper Brookville*, N.Y. J11 80-1
Upper Deerfield*, N.J. L2 76-7
Upper Fairmount, Md. I14 172-3
Upper Falls, Md. C12 172-3
Upper Fraser, B.C. F7 268-9
Upper Freehold*, N.J. H6 76-7
Upper Frenchville, Me. A8 64-5
Upper Gagetown*, N.B. I5 275
Upper Gloucester, Me. M9 64-5
Upper Greenwood Lake*, N.J. B6 76-7
Upper Highland, Ore. C7 238-9
Upper Island Cove*, Nfld. N11 278-9
Upper Kalskag, Alaska F9 254-5
Upper Kent, N.B. G3 275
Upper Klamath Lake, Ore. J7 238-9
Upper Liard, Y.T. C3 297
Upper Marlboro, Md. E10 172-3
Upper Maugerville*, N.B. H4 275
Upper Musquodoboit, N.S. D8 281
Upper Nyack, N.Y. C14 80-1
Upper Penns Neck*, N.J. K1 76-7
Upper Pittsgrove*, N.J. L2 76-7
Upper Saddle River, N.J. C8 76-7
Upper Sandusky, O. D6 132-3
Upper Seven Sisters*, Man. J4 272-3
Upper Sheila*, N.B. E6 275
Upper Soda, Ore. E7 238-9
Upper Tract, W. Va. F8 200-1
Upperglade, W. Va. G6 200-1
Upperville, Va. A2 196-7
Upsala, Minn. K4 116-7
Upshur, co., Tex. D10 192-3
Upshur, co., W. Va. F6 200-1
Upson, Wis. B11 140-1
Upson, co., Ga. I4 160-1
Upton, Ky. I8 164-5
Upton, Me. J1 64-5
Upton*, Mass. E9 68-9
Upton*, Que. I13 290-1
Upton, Ut. E7 242-3
Upton, Wyo. C15 250-1
Upton, co., Tex. F4 192-3
Upton (-West Upton), Mass. E9 68-9
Urania, La. D5 168-9
Uranium City, Sask. A5 294-5
Uravan, Colo. G5 214-5
Urbainville, P.E.I. D4 287
Urban, Wash. C7 246-7
Urbana, Ark. K6 150-1
Urbana, Ill. G10 96-7
Urbana, Ind. D9 100-1
Urbana, Ia. E12 104-5
Urbana, Kans. J15 108-9
Urbana, Md. F2 172-3
Urbana, Mo. G5 120-1
Urbana, O. F5 132-3
Urbancrest, O. G6 132-3
Urbandale, Ia. G7 104-5
Urbanette, Ark. A4 150-1
Urbank, Minn. J3 116-7
Urbanna, Va. D3 196-7
Uriah, Ala. L4 146-7
Urich, Mo. F4 120-1
Urie, Wyo. J6 250-1
Ursine, Nev. I11 226-7
Usibelli, Alaska E11 254-5
Usibelli Mine*, Alaska D11 254-5
Usk, B.C. F4 268-9
Usk, Wash. D16 246-7
Usquepaug, R.I. G3 87
Ustick, Ida. L3 218-9
Utah, co., Ut. G6 242-3
Utah Lake, Ut. G6 242-3
Ute, Ia. F3 104-5
Ute Park, N. Mex. C8 230-1
Utica, Ind. N10 100-1
Utica, Kans. G5 108-9
Utica, Ky. H6 164-5
Utica, Mich. I6 112-3
Utica, Minn. O8 116-7
Utica, Miss. I5 176-7
Utica, Mont. E8 222-3
Utica, Nebr. H13 124-5
Utica, N.Y. E8 80-1
Utica, O. F8 132-3
Utica, Okla. I13 234-5
Utica, S.C. C5 184-5
Utica, S. Dak. I14 136-7
Utica Institute, Miss. J5 176-7
Utleyville, Colo. I15 214-5
Utsalady, Wash. F2 246-7
Utting, Ariz. H3 206-7
Uva, Wyo. H15 250-1
Uvada, Ut. L2 242-3
Uvalda, Ga. K8 160-1
Uvalde, Tex. H6 192-3
Uvalde, co., Tex. H6 192-3
Uxbridge, Mass. E9 68-9
Uxbridge*, Ont. B15 284-5

V

Vacaville, Calif. A8 210-1
Vacherie, La. C11 168-9
Vader, Wash. H7 246-7
Vadis, W. Va. E5 200-1
Vadnais Heights*, Minn. M7 116-7
Vado, N. Mex. L6 230-1
Vaiden, Miss. F7 176-7
Vail, Ariz. L9 206-7
Vail, Colo. E9 214-5
Vail, Ia. F4 104-5
Vaiva Vo, Ariz. J6 206-7
Val-Barrette*, Que. J2 290-1
Val-Bélair*, Que. E10 290-1
Val-Brillant, Que. C16 290-1
Val-Comeau*, N.B. E6 275
Val Cote, Ont. E6 284-5
Val-d'Amour*, N.B. D4 275
Val-David, Que. H11 290-1
Val-des-Monts*, Que. H10 290-1
Val-d'Or, Que. H1 290-1
Val-Doucet, N.B. E6 275
Val Gagne, Ont. F7 284-5
Val Marie, Sask. O5 294-5
Val Verde, co., Tex. G5 192-3
Valatie, N.Y. G11 80-1
Valcourt, Que. J14 290-1
Valders, Wis. F5 140-1
Valdese, N.C. D6 180-1
Valdez, Alaska F12 254-5
Valdez, N. Mex. C7 230-1
Valdosta, Ga. N6 160-1
Vale, Ore. F15 238-9
Vale, S. Dak. D2 136-7
Vale, Tenn. B4 188-9
Vale Summit, Md. B3 172-3
Valeda, Kans. K15 108-9
Valeene, Ind. M7 100-1
Valemount, B.C. G8 268-9
Valencia, Ariz. I5 206-7
Valencia*, Calif. M7 210-1
Valencia, co., N. Mex. F3 230-1
Valentine, Ariz. E3 206-7
Valentine, Nebr. C7 124-5
Valentines, Va. K12 196-7
Valeria, Ia. G8 104-5
Valhermoso Springs, Ala. C6 146-7
Valier, Ill. M8 96-7
Valier, Mont. B6 222-3
Valinda*, Calif. N7 210-1
Valle, Ariz. D6 206-7
Valle Crucis, N.C. C5 180-1
Vallecito, Colo. I7 214-5
Vallecitos, N. Mex. C6 230-1
Vallée-Jonction*, Que. H16 290-1
Vallejo, Calif. B7 210-1
Valley, Nebr. I2 124-5
Valley, Wash. D15 246-7
Valley, Wyo. C7 250-1
Valley, co., Ida. J4 218-9
Valley, co., Mont. B13 222-3
Valley, co., Nebr. F10 124-5
Valley Bend, W. Va. F15 200-1
Valley Brook, Okla. J2 234-5
Valley Center, Kans. I11 108-9
Valley Chapel, W. Va. D13 200-1
Valley City, N. Dak. G12 128-9
Valley Cottage, N.Y. C14 80-1
Valley East*, Ont. H7 284-5
Valley Falls, Kans. E14 108-9
Valley Falls, N.Y. F11 80-1
Valley Falls, Ore. J10 238-9
Valley Falls, R.I. B5 87
Valley Falls, S.C. E4 184-5
Valley Farms, Ariz. J7 206-7
Valley Grove, W. Va. B5 200-1
Valley Head, Ala. B9 146-7
Valley Head, W. Va. G7 200-1
Valley Junction, Ore. D5 238-9
Valley Junction, Wis. H11 140-1
Valley Lee, Md. H11 172-3
Valley Mills, Tex. E8 192-3
Valley Park, Miss. H4 176-7
Valley Park*, Mo. E10 120-1
Valley Point, W. Va. A16 200-1
Valley River, Man. G11 272-3
Valley Springs, Ark. B5 150-1
Valley Springs, S. Dak. G16 136-7
Valley Station, Ky. B1 164-5
Valley Stream, N.Y. F15 80-1
Valley View, Alta. K7 264-5
Valley View, Ill. L1 96-7
Valley View, Ky. C7 164-5
Valley View*, O. B9 132-3
Valley View*, O. F6 132-3
Valley View, Pa. H11 84-5
Valley View, Tenn. H11 188-9
Valleyford, Wash. F16 246-7
Valleyfork, W. Va. G4 200-1
Valleyview, Alta. G5 264-5
Valleyview Trailer Court*, Man. G1 272-3
Valliant, Okla. I15 234-5
Vallonia, Ind. L8 100-1
Valmeyer, Ill. L6 96-7
Valmont, N. Mex. K7 230-1
Valmora, N. Mex. E8 230-1
Valmy, Nev. C6 226-7
Valmy, Wis. F16 140-1
Valparaiso, Fla. B4 156-7
Valparaiso, Ind. B5 100-1
Valparaiso, Nebr. H14 124-5
Valparaiso*, Sask. J8 294-5
Valrita*, Ont. E6 284-5
Valsetz, Ore. D5 238-9
Value, Miss. I6 176-7
Vamoosa, Okla. G12 234-5
Vamori, Ariz. L6 206-7
Van, Tex. E10 192-3
Van, W. Va. J13 200-1
Van Alstyne, Tex. A15 192-3
Van Buren, Ark. D2 150-1
Van Buren, Ind. E10 100-1
Van Buren, Me. B9 64-5
Van Buren, Mo. I9 120-1
Van Buren, O. C5 132-3
Van Buren, co., Ark. C6 150-1
Van Buren, co., Ia. J11 104-5
Van Buren, co., Mich. J11 112-3
Van Buren, co., Tenn. C10 188-9
Van Duesenville, Mass. D1 68-9
Van Etten, N.Y. G6 80-1
Van Horn, Tex. F2 192-3
Van Horne, Ia. F11 104-5
Van Keurens*, N.Y. H11 80-1
Van Lear, Ky. H15 164-5
Van Meter, Ia. H7 104-5
Van Norman, Mont. D13 222-3
Van Tassell, Wyo. G16 250-1
Van Vleck*, Tex. H10 192-3
Van Vleet, Miss. D9 176-7
Van Wert, Ia. J7 104-5
Van Wert, O. D3 132-3
Van Wert, co., O. D3 132-3
Van West*, Ga. F2 160-1
Van Wyck, S.C. B10 184-5
Van Zandt, Wash. C8 246-7
Van Zandt, co., Tex. E10 192-3
Vanadium, N. Mex. K3 230-1
Vananda, B.C. J6 268-9
Vananda, Mont. F12 222-3
Vance, Ala. F5 146-7
Vance, Miss. D5 176-7
Vance, S.C. G12 184-5
Vance, co., N.C. C11 180-1
Vanceboro, Me. G10 64-5
Vanceboro, N.C. E13 180-1
Vanceburg, Ky. F14 164-5
Vancleave, Miss. N10 176-7
Vancorum, Colo. H6 214-5
Vancouver, B.C. J6 268-9
Vancouver, Wash. J7 246-7
Vancouver Isl., B.C. I4 268-9
Vandalia, Ill. J8 96-7
Vandalia, Mich. K11 112-3
Vandalia, Mo. D8 120-1
Vandalia, Mont. B12 222-3
Vandalia, N.C. H4 180-1
Vandalia, O. H15 132-3
Vandemere, N.C. E14 180-1
Vandenburg*, Calif. M5 210-1
Vanderbilt, Mich. F13 112-3
Vandergrift, Pa. A8 84-5
Vanderhoof, B.C. F6 268-9
Vanderpool, Va. G8 196-7
Vandervoort, Ark. G2 150-1
Vandiver, Ala. F7 146-7
Vandiver, Mo. D7 120-1
Vanduser, Mo. I11 120-1
Vandyke, Del. D2 153
Vandyne, Wis. G3 140-1
Vanguard, Sask. O6 294-5
Vanier, Ont. H15 284-5
Vanier*, Que. F11 290-1
Vankleek Hill, Ont. H16 284-5
Vanleer, Tenn. G5 188-9
Vanlue, O. D5 132-3
Vanna, Ga. E7 160-1
Vanndale, Ark. D10 150-1
Vanoss, Okla. G12 234-5
Vanscoy, Sask. L6 294-5
Vantage, Wash. G11 246-7
Vardaman, Miss. D8 176-7
Varennes, Que. I12 290-1
Varina, Ia. D5 104-5
Varina, Va. E1 196-7
Varnado, La. F10 168-9
Varnell, Ga. C2 160-1
Varner, Kans. I9 108-9
Varney, W. Va. I2 200-1
Varnville, S.C. H10 184-5
Vars*, Ont. H15 284-5
Vashon, Wash. I2 246-7
Vashon Heights, Wash. I2 246-7
Vasper, Tenn. G11 188-9
Vass, N.C. J6 180-1
Vassalboro, Me. K4 64-5
Vassar, Kans. G14 108-9
Vassar, Man. K16 272-3
Vassar, Mich. E4 112-3
Vaucluse, S.C. F8 184-5
Vaudreuil, Que. J11 290-1
Vaudreuil, co., Que. J11 290-1
Vaughan, Miss. G6 176-7
Vaughan, Ont. C14 284-5
Vaughan, W. Va. I16 200-1
Vaughn, Ark. A2 150-1
Vaughn, Ga. H4 160-1
Vaughn, Miss. K5 176-7
Vaughn, N. Mex. G8 230-1
Vaughn, Wash. J1 246-7
Vauxhall, Alta. N9 264-5
Vavenby, B.C. I8 268-9
Vawn, Sask. J5 294-5
Vaya Chin, Ariz. K6 206-7
Veazie, Me. J7 64-5
Veblen, S. Dak. A14 136-7
Vedder Crossing, B.C. C16 268-9
Veedersburg, Ind. G5 100-1
Vega*, Alta. H7 264-5
Vega, Tex. B4 192-3
Vegas Creek*, Nev. M9 226-7
Vegreville, Alta. I9 264-5
Veguita, N. Mex. G5 230-1
Velarde, N. Mex. D7 230-1
Velda*, Mo. E10 120-1
Velda Village Hills*, Mo. E10 120-1
Velma, Miss. D7 176-7
Velma, Okla. H10 234-5
Velpen, Ind. N5 100-1
Velva, N. Dak. D7 128-9
Venango, Nebr. H4 124-5
Venango, co., Pa. E3 84-5
Venator, Ore. H14 238-9
Venderburgh, co., Ind. N4 100-1
Veneta, Ore. F5 238-9
Venetian Village, Ill. J2 96-7
Venetie, Alaska C12 254-5
Venice, Fla. H10 156-7
Venice, Ill. K6 96-7
Venice, La. J11 168-9
Venice, Nebr. J2 124-5
Venice, Ut. J6 242-3
Ventana, Ariz. K6 206-7
Ventnor City, N.J. M6 76-7
Ventura, Calif. F6 210-1
Ventura, Ia. B8 104-5
Ventura, co., Calif. M6 210-1
Venturia, N. Dak. J9 128-9
Vera, Okla. C14 234-5
Vera Cruz, Ind. E11 100-1
Veradale, Wash. E16 246-7
Verbena, Ala. H7 146-7
Verchères, Que. I12 290-1
Verchères, co., Que. I13 290-1
Verda, La. D4 168-9
Verdel, Nebr. C11 124-5
Verden, Okla. G10 234-5
Verdery, S.C. K3 184-5
Verdi, Kans. F10 108-9
Verdi, Nev. F1 226-7
Verdigre, Nebr. D11 124-5
Verdigris, Okla. D14 234-5
Verdon, Nebr. J16 124-5
Verdon, S. Dak. C13 136-7
Verdun, Que. J12 290-1
Verdunville, W. Va. K12 200-1
Verdure, Ut. L10 242-3
Veregin, Sask. L10 294-5
Vergas, Minn. I3 116-7
Vergennes, Vt. G4 90-1
Verlot, Wash. D9 246-7
Vermilion, Alta. J10 264-5
Vermilion, O. B8 132-3
Vermilion, co., Ill. G11 96-7
Vermilion, co., La. I4 168-9
Vermilion Bay, Ont. E2 284-5
Vermillion, Kans. D13 108-9
Vermillion, Minn. C11 116-7
Vermillion, S. Dak. J15 136-7
Vermillion, co., Ind. H4 100-1
Vermont, Ill. G5 96-7
Vermontville, Mich. J13 112-3
Vernal, Ut. F10 242-3
Verndale, Minn. J4 116-7
Verne, Ky. K12 164-5
Verne, Wyo. I6 250-1
Verner, Ont. H8 284-5
Verner, W. Va. I2 200-1
Vernon, Ala. E3 146-7
Vernon, Ariz. G10 206-7
Vernon, B.C. J8 268-9
Vernon*, Calif. G8 210-1
Vernon, Colo. D16 214-5
Vernon, Conn. C10 60-1
Vernon, Del. H3 153
Vernon, Fla. B5 156-7
Vernon, Ind. K10 100-1
Vernon, Kans. H14 108-9
Vernon, Ky. K9 164-5
Vernon, La. B4 168-9
Vernon, Mich. G3 112-3
Vernon, N.J. B6 76-7
Vernon, N.Y. E8 80-1
Vernon, Okla. F14 234-5
Vernon, Ont. H15 284-5
Vernon, Tex. C7 192-3
Vernon, Vt. O7 90-1
Vernon, co., La. E2 168-9
Vernon, co., Mo. G3 120-1
Vernon, co., Wis. I10 140-1
Vernon Center, Conn. C10 60-1
Vernon Center, Minn. O5 116-7
Vernon Hills, Ill. K3 96-7
Vernon River, P.E.I. F8 287
Vernon Valley, N.Y. J12 80-1
Vernonburg, Ga. K11 160-1
Vernonia, Ore. B5 238-9
Vero Beach, Fla. G13 156-7
Vero Beach South*, Fla. G13 156-7
Verona, Ky. E11 164-5
Verona, Me. K7 64-5
Verona, Miss. C9 176-7
Verona, Mo. I4 120-1

Verona, N.J. B9 76-7
Verona, N.C. G13 180-1
Verona, N. Dak. I12 128-9
Verona, O. H13 132-3
Verona, Ont. J13 284-5
Verona*, Pa. H2 84-5
Verona, Va. G9 196-7
Verona, Wis. J1 140-1
Verona, Wyo. B12 250-1
Verona Park*, Mich. J12 112-3
Verrett*, N.B. F2 275
Versailles, Conn. E13 60-1
Versailles, Ind. K11 100-1
Versailles, Ky. B6 164-5
Versailles, Mo. F6 120-1
Versailles, O. F3 132-3
Versailles, Pa. B7 84-5
Vershire, Vt. H7 90-1
Verwood, Sask. O7 294-5
Veseleyville, N. Dak. D13 128-9
Veseli, Minn. N6 116-7
Vesper, Kans. F9 108-9
Vesper, Wis. G11 140-1
Vesta, Ark. D3 150-1
Vesta, Minn. N3 116-7
Vesta, Va. J7 196-7
Vestaburg, Mich. H13 112-3
Vestal [-Twin Orchards], N.Y. G7 80-1
Vestavia Hills, Ala. F6 146-7
Vestry, Miss. N9 176-7
Vesuvius, Va. H9 196-7
Veteran, Alta. K10 264-5
Veteran, Wyo. H16 250-1
Vevay, Ind. L11 100-1
Veyo, Ut. M3 242-3
Vian, Okla. E15 234-5
Vibank, Sask. N9 294-5
Vibbard, Mo. H16 120-1
Viborg, S. Dak. I15 136-7
Viburnum, Mo. G9 120-1
Vicars, W. Va. F3 200-1
Vicco, Ky. I14 164-5
Viceroy, Sask. O7 294-5
Vici, Okla. D7 234-5
Vick, Ark. J7 150-1
Vick, La. E5 168-9
Vicksburg, Ariz. H3 206-7
Vicksburg, Mich. J12 112-3
Vicksburg, Miss. I4 176-7
Victor, Colo. G11 214-5
Victor, Ida. L11 218-9
Victor, Ia. G11 104-5
Victor, Mont. F3 222-3
Victor, N.Y. E5 80-1
Victor, S. Dak. A15 136-7
Victor Mills, S.C. F3 184-5
Victoria, Ark. C12 150-1
Victoria, B.C. K6 268-9
Victoria, Kans. F7 108-9
Victoria, Minn. B9 116-7
Victoria, Miss. A7 176-7
Victoria*, Nfld. N11 278-9
Victoria, P.E.I. F6 287
Victoria, Tenn. K9 188-9
Victoria, Tex. H9 192-3
Victoria, Va. J11 196-7
Victoria, co., N.B. F3 275
Victoria, co., N.S. B11 281
Victoria, co., Ont. A16 284-5
Victoria, co., Tex. H9 192-3
Victoria Beach, Man. H15 272-3
Victoria Cross*, P.E.I. F9 287
Victoria Glacier, Alta. L5 264-5
Victoria Harbour, Ont. A14 284-5
Victoriaville, Que. H15 290-1
Victorville, Calif. F10 210-1
Victory, Ky. I12 164-5
Victory, N.Y. E11 80-1
Victory, Okla. H7 234-5
Victory, Vt. E9 90-1
Victory, Wis. I9 140-1
Victory Gardens, N.J. D6 76-7
Vida, Mont. C14 222-3
Vida, Ore. K2 238-9
Vidalia, Ga. K8 160-1
Vidalia, La. E6 168-9
Vidette, Ga. H9 160-1
Vidor*, Tex. G12 192-3
Vienna, Ga. K5 160-1
Vienna, Ill. N9 96-7
Vienna, La. B4 168-9
Vienna, Me. K4 64-5
Vienna, Md. G14 172-3
Vienna, Mo. F7 120-1
Vienna, N.J. D4 76-7
Vienna, N.C. G3 180-1
Vienna, O. F5 132-3
Vienna, Ont. E13 284-5
Vienna, S. Dak. D14 136-7
Vienna, Va. A3 196-7
Vienna, W. Va. E3 200-1
View, Ida. O7 218-9
View Park-Windsor Hills*, Calif. N7 210-1
Vigo, co., Ind. J4 100-1
Viking, Alta. J9 264-5
Viking, Minn. F2 116-7
Vilas, Colo. I16 214-5
Vilas, S. Dak. F14 136-7
Vilas, co., Wis. C12 140-1
Vildo, Tenn. K4 188-9
Villa Grove, Colo. G10 214-5
Villa Grove, Ill. H10 96-7
Villa Hills*, Ill. K6 96-7
Villa Hills*, Ky. D11 164-5
Villa Park*, Calif. N7 210-1
Villa Park, Ill. M3 96-7
Villa Ranchaero, S. Dak. F3 136-7
Villa Rica, Ga. C8 160-1
Village, Ark. J5 150-1
Village, Va. G14 196-7
Village of the Branch*, N.Y. J12 80-1
Village Springs, Ala. E6 146-7
Village, The, Okla. I2 234-5
Villamont, Va. I8 196-7
Villanueva, N. Mex. F8 230-1
Villard, Minn. K3 116-7
Villas, N.J. O4 76-7
Ville-Marie, Que. I1 290-1
Ville Platte, La. G5 168-9
Villegreen, Colo. I14 214-5
Villisca, Ia. J4 104-5
Vilna, Alta. I9 264-5
Vilonia, Ark. H16 150-1
Vimy*, Alta. I7 264-5
Vimy Ridge, Ark. J15 150-1
Vina, Ala. C3 146-7
Vinalhaven, Me. L7 64-5
Vincennes, Ind. L4 100-1
Vincent, Ala. F7 146-7
Vincent, Ia. D7 104-5
Vincentown, N.J. J5 76-7
Vine, Tenn. H8 188-9
Vine Grove, Ky. D1 164-5
Vinegar Bend, Ala. L2 146-7
Vineland, N.J. L3 76-7
Vinemont, Ala. C6 146-7
Vineyard Haven, Mass. I14 68-9
Vining, Ia. F11 104-5
Vining, Kans. D11 108-9
Vining, Minn. J3 116-7
Vinings, Ga. B10 160-1
Vinita, Okla. C15 234-5
Vinita Park*, Mo. E10 120-1
Vinita Terrace*, Mo. E10 120-1
Vinland, Kans. F15 108-9
Vinson, Okla. G6 234-5
Vinson, Ore. C12 238-9
Vint Hill Farms Station*, Va. F12 196-7
Vinton, Ia. F11 104-5
Vinton, La. H2 168-9
Vinton, O. I8 132-3
Vinton, Va. I8 196-7
Vinton, co., O. H7 132-3
Viola, Ark. A7 150-1
Viola, Del. G3 153
Viola, Ida. E2 218-9
Viola, Ill. D5 96-7
Viola, Kans. J10 108-9
Viola*, N.Y. I10 80-1
Viola, Ore. C7 238-9
Viola, Tenn. J9 188-9
Viola, Wis. I10 140-1
Violet, La. D15 168-9
Violet Grove, Alta. J6 264-5
Violet Hill, Ark. B8 150-1
Viopuli, Ariz L7 206-7
Viper, Ky. I14 164-5
Virden, Ill. I7 96-7
Virden, Man. J10 272-3
Virden, N. Mex. K1 230-1
Virgil, Kans. H13 108-9
Virgil, Okla. I15 234-5
Virgil, S. Dak. E12 136-7
Virgilina, Va. K10 196-7
Virgin, Ut. M4 242-3
Virgin Arm, Nfld. L10 278-9
Virginia, Ida. O10 218-9
Virginia, Ill. H6 96-7
Virginia, Minn. G7 116-7
Virginia, Nebr. J14 124-5
Virginia Beach, Va. J15 196-7
Virginia City, Mont. H6 222-3
Virginia City, Nev. F2 226-7
Virginia Dale, Colo. B11 214-5
Virginia Gardens*, Fla. J13 156-7
Virginiatown*, Ont. G8 284-5
Virginville, W. Va. B6 200-1
Viroqua, Wis. I10 140-1
Visalia, Calif. K6 210-1
Visalia*, Ky. E11 164-5
Viscount, Sask. L7 294-5
Viscount Estate Subdivision*, Alta. I8 264-5
Vista, Calif. I10 210-1
Vista, Man. H10 272-3
Vista, Nev. F2 226-7
Vita, Man. K15 272-3
Vittoria*, Ont. E13 284-5
Vivian, La. A1 168-9
Vivian, Okla. F14 234-5
Vivian, S. Dak. F8 136-7
Vixen, La. C5 168-9
Vliets, Kans. D13 108-9
Vogar*, Man. H12 272-3
Volburg, Mont. G14 222-3
Volcano, Hawaii J13 258-9
Volga, S. Dak. E15 136-7
Volga, W. Va. E14 200-1
Volga City, Ia. C13 104-5
Volin, S. Dak. I15 136-7
Volland, Kans. F12 108-9
Volney, Va. K5 196-7
Voltaire, N. Dak. D7 128-9
Voluntown, Conn. E14 60-1
Volusia, co., Fla. D12 156-7
Vona, Colo. E15 214-5
Vonda, Sask. K7 294-5
Vonore, Tenn. J14 188-9
Voorhees*, N.J. J3 76-7
Voorheesville, N.Y. F11 80-1
Vossburg, Miss. J9 176-7
Vredenburgh, Ala. K5 146-7
Vulcan, Alta. N8 264-5
Vulcan, Mich. E9 112-3
Vya, Nev. B2 226-7

W

Wabamun, Alta. I7 264-5
Waban, Mass. H3 68-9
Wabana, Nfld. N11 278-9
Wabasca, Alta. F7 264-5
Wabash, Ark. G10 150-1
Wabash, Ind. D9 100-1
Wabash, Nebr. K2 124-5
Wabash, co., Ill. L11 96-7
Wabash, co., Ind. D9 100-1
Wabash R., Ind. M3 100-1
Wabasha, Minn. N8 116-7
Wabasha, co., Minn. N8 116-7
Wabasso, Minn. N3 116-7
Wabaunsee, Kans. E13 108-9
Wabaunsee, co., Kans. F13 108-9
Wabbaseka, Ark. G8 150-1
Wabek, N. Dak. E5 128-9
Wabeno, Wis. D14 140-1
Wabigoon, Ont. E2 284-5
Wabos, Ont. G6 284-5
Wabowden, Man. F3 272-3
Wabush, Nfld. I1 278-9
Wabuska, Nev. G3 226-7
Wachapreague, Va. H16 196-7
Waco, Ga. G2 160-1
Waco, Ky. D8 164-5
Waco, Mo. H3 120-1
Waco, Nebr. H13 124-5
Waco, N.C. E6 180-1
Waco, Tenn. J6 188-9
Waco, Tex. E8 192-3
Waconda, Ore. H1 238-9
Waconia, Minn. B9 116-7
Waddington, N.Y. A8 80-1
Waddy, Ky. B4 164-5
Wade, Me. B8 64-5
Wade, Miss. N10 176-7
Wade, N.C. K7 180-1
Wade, Okla. I13 234-5
Wade-Hampton*, S.C. F2 184-5
Wadena, Ia. C12 104-5
Wadena, Minn. J4 116-7
Wadena, Sask. L9 294-5
Wadena, co., Minn. I4 116-7
Wadesboro, N.C. F8 180-1
Wadestown, W. Va. A13 200-1
Wadesville, Ind. O3 100-1
Wadeville, N.C. J4 180-1
Wadley, Ala. G9 146-7
Wadley, Ga. I8 160-1
Wadley Falls, N.H. M9 72-3
Wadmalaw Island, S.C. I12 184-5
Wadsworth*, Ill. A10 96-7
Wadsworth, Mass. E10 68-9
Wadsworth, Nev. F2 226-7
Wadsworth, O. D14 132-3
Waelder, Tex. G8 192-3
Wagarville, Ala. L3 146-7
Wagener, S.C. F9 184-5
Wagner, Mont. B11 222-3
Wagner, S. Dak. I13 136-7
Wagon Mound, N. Mex. D9 230-1
Wagoner, Ariz. G5 206-7
Wagoner, Okla. D15 234-5
Wagoner, co., Okla. D14 234-5
Wagram, N.C. F9 180-1
Wagstaff, Kans. G16 108-9
Waha, Ida. G2 218-9
Wahak Hotrontik, Ariz. K6 206-7
Wahiawa, Hawaii E7 258-9
Wahiawa Res., Hawaii H4 258-9
Wahkiacus, Wash. J10 246-7
Wahkiakum, co., Wash. H6 246-7
Wahkon, Minn. J6 116-7
Wahneta, Fla. H5 156-7
Wahoo, Nebr. G14 124-5
Wahpeton, Ia. B4 104-5
Wahpeton, N. Dak. I15 128-9
Wahsatch, Ut. D7 242-3
Waiahukini, Hawaii K12 258-9
Waiakoa, Hawaii G11 258-9
Waialua, Hawaii E7 258-9
Waianae, Hawaii I2 258-9
Waidsboro, Va. J8 196-7
Waihee, Hawaii G11 258-9
Waikane, Hawaii H5 258-9
Waikapu, Hawaii G11 258-9
Wailea, Hawaii I14 258-9
Wailua, Hawaii D5 258-9
Wailuku, Hawaii G11 258-9
Waimalu, Hawaii J4 258-9
Waimanalo, Hawaii J7 258-9
Waimanalo Beach, Hawaii J7 258-9
Waimea, Hawaii I12 258-9
Waimea, Hawaii G3 258-9
Waimea, Hawaii D4 258-9
Waimea Camp, Hawaii G3 258-9
Wainee, Hawaii G10 258-9
Wainiha, Hawaii D4 258-9
Wainwright, Alaska A9 254-5
Wainwright, Alta. J10 264-5
Wainwright*, Okla. E14 234-5
Waiohinu, Hawaii K13 258-9
Waipahu, Hawaii J4 258-9
Waipio Acres, Hawaii I4 258-9
Waite, Me. H9 64-5
Waite Hill, O. A15 132-3
Waite Park, Minn. K5 116-7
Waiteville, W. Va. J6 200-1
Waits River, Vt. G8 90-1
Waitsburg, Wash. I14 246-7
Waitsfield, Vt. F5 90-1
Wakarusa, Ind. A8 100-1
Wakarusa, Kans. F14 108-9
Wakaw, Sask. K7 294-5
Wake, co., N.C. D11 180-1
Wake Forest, N.C. H8 180-1
Wake Village, Tex. D11 192-3
Wakeby, Mass. H14 68-9
WaKeeney, Kans. F5 108-9
Wakefield, Kans. E11 108-9
Wakefield, La. F7 168-9
Wakefield, Mass. F5 68-9
Wakefield, Mich. D7 112-3
Wakefield, Miss. B7 176-7
Wakefield, Nebr. E14 124-5
Wakefield, N.H. K9 72-3
Wakefield, Va. G2 196-7
Wakefield [-Peace Dale], R.I. H4 87
Wakeley, Wyo. B12 250-1
Wakeman, O. C8 132-3
Wakenda, Mo. D5 120-1
Wakita, Okla. C10 234-5
Wakonda, S. Dak. I15 136-7
Wakonda Beach, Ore. E4 238-9
Wakpala, S. Dak. B8 136-7
Wakulla, N.C. F10 180-1
Wakulla, co., Fla. C7 156-7
Walbridge, O. B5 132-3
Walcott, Ark. B11 150-1
Walcott, Ia. G14 104-5
Walcott, N. Dak. H14 128-9
Walcott, Wyo. I12 250-1
Waldeck, Sask. N5 294-5
Walden, Colo. B9 214-5
Walden, N.Y. I10 80-1
Walden, Ont. H7 284-5
Walden, Vt. E8 90-1
Waldenburg, Ark. D10 150-1
Waldersee, Man. H12 272-3
Waldheim, La. G10 168-9
Waldheim, Sask. K6 294-5
Waldo, Ark. J4 150-1
Waldo, Fla. C10 156-7
Waldo, Kans. E8 108-9
Waldo, Me. K6 64-5
Waldo, O. E6 132-3
Waldo, Wis. G5 140-1
Waldo, co., Me. K6 64-5
Waldoboro, Me. L5 64-5
Waldorf, Md. F10 172-3
Waldorf, Minn. O6 116-7
Waldport, Ore. E4 238-9
Waldron, Ark. E2 150-1
Waldron, Ind. I9 100-1
Waldron, Kans. K9 108-9
Waldron, Mich. K13 112-3
Waldron, Sask. M10 294-5
Waldron, Wash. C7 246-7
Waldwick, N.J. C8 76-7
Waldwick, Wis. K11 140-1
Wales, Alaska C7 254-5
Wales, Me. L4 64-5
Wales, Mass. E6 68-9
Wales, N. Dak. B11 128-9
Wales, Tenn. K6 188-9
Wales, Ut. H6 242-3
Wales, Wis. J4 140-1
Walesboro, Ind. K9 100-1
Waleska, Ga. E3 160-1
Walford, Ia. F12 104-5
Walhalla, Mich. H11 112-3
Walhalla, N. Dak. B12 128-9
Walhalla, S.C. B4 184-5
Walker, Ariz. G6 206-7
Walker, Ark. E8 150-1
Walker, Del. D3 153
Walker, Ia. E12 104-5
Walker, Kans. F7 108-9
Walker, Ky. J13 164-5
Walker, La. A11 168-9
Walker, La. C4 168-9
Walker*, Mich. I12 112-3
Walker, Minn. H4 116-7
Walker, Mo. G3 120-1
Walker, Ore. F5 238-9
Walker, W. Va. E4 200-1
Walker, co., Ala. E5 146-7
Walker, co., Ga. D2 160-1
Walker, co., Tex. F10 192-3
Walker Mill*, Md. E10 172-3
Walker Springs, Ala. K4 146-7
Walkersville, Md. C8 172-3
Walkersville, W. Va. F13 200-1
Walkerton, Ind. B7 100-1
Walkerton, Ont. B12 284-5
Walkerton, Va. H13 196-7
Walkertown, N.C. G3 180-1
Walkertown, Tenn. D4 188-9
Walkertown, Tenn. G15 188-9
Walkerville, Mich. H11 112-3
Walkerville, Mont. G5 222-3
Wall, N.J. H8 76-7
Wall*, Pa. I3 84-5
Wall, S. Dak. F5 136-7
Wall Lake, Ia. E4 104-5
Walla Walla, Wash. I14 246-7
Walla Walla, co., Wash. I14 246-7
Walla Walla East*, Wash. I14 246-7
Wallace, Ala. L5 146-7
Wallace, Ark. I2 150-1
Wallace, Ida. D4 218-9
Wallace, Ind. G5 100-1
Wallace, Kans. F2 108-9
Wallace, La. C12 168-9
Wallace, Mich. E9 112-3
Wallace, Nebr. H6 124-5
Wallace, N.C. F12 180-1
Wallace, N.S. C7 281
Wallace, S.C. B13 184-5
Wallace, S. Dak. C14 136-7
Wallace, W. Va. C13 200-1
Wallace, co., Kans. F1 108-9
Wallace Pond, Vt. B10 90-1
Wallace Ridge, La. D6 168-9
Wallaceburg, Ont. F10 284-5

Wallaceville, S.C. K8 184-5
Wallagrass, Me. B7 64-5
Walland, Tenn. I15 188-9
Wallback, W. Va. G4 200-1
Wallburg, N.C. H3 180-1
Walled Lake, Mich. I5 112-3
Waller, Tex. G10 192-3
Waller, co., Tex. G10 192-3
Walling, Tenn. C9 188-9
Wallingford, Conn. F8 60-1
Wallingford, Ia. B5 104-5
Wallingford, Ky. F13 164-5
Wallingford, Vt. K5 90-1
Wallington, N.J. B11 76-7
Wallins Creek, Ky. J14 164-5
Wallis*, Tex. G9 192-3
Wallis Sands, N.H. N10 72-3
Wallkill, N.Y. I10 80-1
Wallonia, Ky. J4 164-5
Walloon Lake, Mich. E12 112-3
Wallowa, Ore. B15 238-9
Wallowa, co., Ore. B15 238-9
Walls, Miss. A6 176-7
Wallsburg, Ut. F7 242-3
Wallula, Wash. I13 246-7
Wallville, Okla. G11 234-5
Walnut*, Calif. G9 210-1
Walnut, Ill. C7 96-7
Walnut, Ia. H4 104-5
Walnut, Kans. I15 108-9
Walnut, Miss. A9 176-7
Walnut, N.C. D3 180-1
Walnut Cove, N.C. G3 180-1
Walnut Creek, Calif. C8 210-1
Walnut Creek West*, Calif. I3 210-1
Walnut Grove, Ala. D7 146-7
Walnut Grove, Ga. G5 160-1
Walnut Grove, Minn. N3 116-7
Walnut Grove, Miss. H8 176-7
Walnut Grove, Mo. H4 120-1
Walnut Park*, Calif. N7 210-1
Walnut Ridge, Ark. B10 150-1
Walnutport, Pa. G14 84-5
Walpack*, N.J. B4 76-7
Walpole, Me. N12 64-5
Walpole, Mass. K3 68-9
Walpole, N.H. N3 72-3
Walsenburg, Colo. I12 214-5
Walsh, Colo. I16 214-5
Walsh, co., N. Dak. D13 128-9
Walsingham, Ont. E13 284-5
Walstonburg, N.C. E12 180-1
Walter, Ala. D6 146-7
Walterboro, S.C. H11 184-5
Walters, La. E5 168-9
Walters, Minn. O6 116-7
Walters, Miss. K8 176-7
Walters, Okla. H9 234-5
Walterville, Ore. K2 238-9
Walthall, Miss. E8 176-7
Walthall, co., Miss. L6 176-7
Waltham, Me. J8 64-5
Waltham, Mass. H3 68-9
Waltham, Minn. O7 116-7
Waltham, Mont. D7 222-3
Waltham*, Vt. G4 90-1
Walthill, Nebr. E14 124-5
Walthourville, Ga. L10 160-1
Waltman, Wyo. F11 250-1
Walton, Ind. E8 100-1
Walton, Kans. H11 108-9
Walton, Ky. E11 164-5
Walton, Nebr. K1 124-5
Walton, N.Y. G9 80-1
Walton, N.S. D6 281
Walton, Ore. F5 238-9
Walton, W. Va. G4 200-1
Walton, co., Fla. B5 156-7
Walton, co., Ga. G5 160-1
Walton Hills*, O. B9 132-3
Waltreak, Ark. E4 150-1
Waltz, Mich. K5 112-3
Walum, N. Dak. F12 128-9
Walworth, Wis. K14 140-1
Walworth, co., S. Dak. B9 136-7
Walworth, co., Wis. K14 140-1
Wamac, Ill. L8 96-7
Wamego, Kans. E13 108-9
Wamesit, Mass. B11 68-9
Wamic, Ore. C9 238-9
Wampsville, N.Y. E8 80-1
Wampum, Man. K16 272-3
Wampum, Pa. G1 84-5
Wamsutter, Wyo. I10 250-1
Wana, W. Va. A14 200-1
Wanamassa, N.J. H8 76-7
Wanamingo, Minn. N7 116-7
Wanaque, N.J. C7 76-7
Wanatah, Ind. B6 100-1
Wanblee, S. Dak. G6 136-7
Wanchese, N.C. D16 180-1
Wanda, Minn. N3 116-7
Wando, S.C. H13 184-5
Waneta, Ky. I12 164-5
Waneta, W. Va. G6 200-1
Wanette, Okla. G12 234-5
Wanham, Alta. G4 264-5
Wanilla, Miss. K6 176-7
Wanless*, Man. F1 272-3
Wann, Nebr. J2 124-5
Wann, Nev. M9 226-7
Wann, Okla. B14 234-5
Wantage*, N.J. B5 76-7
Wantagh, N.Y. F16 80-1
Wapakoneta, O. E4 132-3
Wapanucka, Okla. H13 234-5
Wapato, Ore. F1 238-9
Wapato, Wash. H11 246-7
Wapella, Sask. N10 294-5
Wapello, Ida. M9 218-9
Wapello, Ia. I13 104-5
Wapello, co., Ia. I10 104-5
Wapinitia, Ore. C9 238-9
Wapiti, Wyo. C7 250-1
Wapping, Conn. C10 60-1
Wapping, Mass. C5 68-9
Wappingers Falls, N.Y. I11 80-1
Wappingers Falls East*, N.Y. I11 80-1
Wappingers Lake*, N.Y. H11 80-1
Waquoit, Mass. H14 68-9
War, W. Va. K3 200-1
Warba, Minn. H6 116-7
Warburg, Alta. J7 264-5
Ward, Ala. I2 146-7
Ward, Ark. E8 150-1
Ward, Colo. F1 214-5
Ward, S.C. E8 184-5
Ward, S. Dak. F16 136-7
Ward, W. Va. I15 200-1
Ward, co., N. Dak. D6 128-9
Ward, co., Tex. E3 192-3
Ward Cove*, Alaska H16 254-5
Ward Ridge*, Fla. C6 156-7
Wardboro, Ida. O11 218-9
Wardell, Mo. J11 120-1
Warden, La. B6 168-9
Warden, Wash. G13 246-7
Wardensville, W. Va. E10 200-1
Wardner, Ida. D3 218-9
Wardsboro, Vt. M5 90-1
Wardsville*, Mo. F7 120-1
Wardsville, Ont. E11 284-5
Wardview, La. A2 168-9
Wardville, La. A5 168-9
Wardville, La. E4 168-9
Wardville, Okla. G13 234-5
Ware, Mass. D6 68-9
Ware, co., Ga. N8 160-1
Ware Neck, Va. E4 196-7
Ware Shoals, S.C. I3 184-5
Wareham*, Mass. G13 68-9
Wareham (-Wareham Center), Mass. G13 68-9
Warehouse Point, Conn. B9 60-1
Waresboro, Ga. M8 160-1
Waretown, N.J. K7 76-7
Warfield, B.C. K9 268-9
Warfield, Ky. G15 164-5
Warfield, Va. J12 196-7
Warfieldsburg, Md. B10 172-3
Warkworth*, Ont. K12 284-5
Warm River, Ida. K11 218-9
Warm Springs, Ark. A10 150-1
Warm Springs, Ga. I3 160-1
Warm Springs, Mont. F5 222-3
Warm Springs, Nev. I7 226-7
Warm Springs, Nev. F10 226-7
Warm Springs, Ore. D9 238-9
Warm Springs, Va. G8 196-7
Warman, Sask. K6 294-5
Warner, Alta. O9 264-5
Warner, N.H. L5 72-3
Warner, Okla. F15 234-5
Warner, Ore. H4 238-9
Warner, S. Dak. C12 136-7
Warner, Va. D3 196-7
Warner Robins, Ga. J5 160-1
Warners Grant*, Vt. B9 90-1
Warnerton, La. F9 168-9
Warr Acres, Okla. J2 234-5
Warren, Ark. I7 150-1
Warren, Conn. D5 60-1
Warren, Ida. I4 218-9
Warren, Ill. A6 96-7
Warren, Ind. E10 100-1
Warren, Me. L6 64-5
Warren*, Man. I14 272-3
Warren, Mass. E6 68-9
Warren, Mich. I6 112-3
Warren, Minn. F1 116-7
Warren, Mont. I10 222-3
Warren, N.H. I5 72-3
Warren*, N.J. E6 76-7
Warren, O. C11 132-3
Warren, Okla. G8 234-5
Warren, Ont. H8 284-5
Warren, Pa. C4 84-5
Warren, R.I. D7 87
Warren, Vt. G5 90-1
Warren*, Wyo. J15 250-1
Warren, co., Ga. H7 160-1
Warren, co., Ill. E5 96-7
Warren, co., Ind. F4 100-1
Warren, co., Ia. I8 104-5
Warren, co., Ky. J7 164-5
Warren, co., Miss. I4 176-7
Warren, co., Mo. E9 120-1
Warren, co., N.J. D3 76-7
Warren, co., N.Y. D11 80-1
Warren, co., N.C. B11 180-1
Warren, co., O. H4 132-3
Warren, co., Pa. D4 84-5
Warren, co., Tenn. C9 188-9
Warren, co., Va. E11 196-7
Warren Landing, Man. B13 272-3
Warrens, Wis. G10 140-1
Warrens Gore*, Vt. B9 90-1
Warrensburg, Ill. H8 96-7
Warrensburg, Mo. E4 120-1
Warrensburg, N.Y. D11 80-1
Warrensville, N.C. C6 180-1
Warrensville Heights, O. B15 132-3
Warrenton, Ala. C7 146-7
Warrenton, Ga. G8 160-1
Warrenton, Mo. E9 120-1
Warrenton, N.C. C12 180-1
Warrenton, Ore. A4 238-9
Warrenton, Va. F12 196-7
Warrentown, Mass. F12 68-9
Warrenville, Conn. C12 60-1
Warrenville, Ill. M2 96-7
Warrenville, S.C. F8 184-5
Warrick, co., Ind. N5 100-1
Warrington, Fla. B3 156-7
Warrington, Ind. H9 100-1
Warrior, Ala. E6 146-7
Warroad, Minn. D3 116-7
Warsaw, Ala. G2 146-7
Warsaw, Ill. F3 96-7
Warsaw, Ind. C9 100-1
Warsaw, Ky. E10 164-5
Warsaw, Minn. N6 116-7
Warsaw, Miss. B7 176-7
Warsaw, Mo. F5 120-1
Warsaw, N.Y. F3 80-1
Warsaw, N.C. F12 180-1
Warsaw, N. Dak. D13 128-9
Warsaw, O. E8 132-3
Warsaw, Ont. J11 284-5
Warsaw, Va. G14 196-7
Warson Woods*, Mo. E10 120-1
Warspite*, Alta. I8 264-5
Wartburg, Tenn. H10 188-9
Warthen, Ga. H7 160-1
Wartrace, Tenn. J8 188-9
Warwick, Del. J6 153
Warwick, Ga. L5 160-1
Warwick, Md. C14 172-3
Warwick, Mass. B6 68-9
Warwick, N.Y. I10 80-1
Warwick, N. Dak. E11 128-9
Warwick, Okla. I4 234-5
Warwick, Que. I14 290-1
Warwick, R.I. E6 87
Wasa*, B.C. J11 268-9
Wasaga Beach, Ont. B14 284-5
Wasagaming, Man. H11 272-3
Wasatch, co., Ut. F7 242-3
Wasco, Calif. L6 210-1
Wasco, Ore. B9 238-9
Wasco, co., Ore. C9 238-9
Wascott, Wis. C8 140-1
Waseca, Minn. O6 116-7
Waseca, Sask. J4 294-5
Waseca, co., Minn. O6 116-7
Washabaugh, co., S. Dak. G6 136-7
Washago, Ont. A15 284-5
Washakie, Ut. C5 242-3
Washakie, co., Wyo. D10 250-1
Washburn, Ark. E2 150-1
Washburn, Ill. E8 96-7
Washburn, Ia. E11 104-5
Washburn, Me. C8 64-5
Washburn, Mo. J4 120-1
Washburn, N. Dak. F7 128-9
Washburn, Tenn. G13 188-9
Washburn, Wis. B10 140-1
Washburn, co., Wis. C8 140-1
Washington, Ark. I3 150-1
Washington, Conn. E5 60-1
Washington, Ga. G7 160-1
Washington, Ill. F7 96-7
Washington, Ind. L5 100-1
Washington, Ia. H12 104-5
Washington, Kans. D11 108-9
Washington*, Ky. F13 164-5
Washington, La. G5 168-9
Washington, Me. L5 64-5
Washington, Mass. D2 68-9
Washington, Mich. H6 112-3
Washington, Miss. K3 176-7
Washington, Mo. C13 120-1
Washington, Nebr. I2 124-5
Washington, N.H. M4 72-3
Washington, N.J. C8 76-7
Washington, N.J. D3 76-7
Washington*, N.J. D3 76-7
Washington*, N.J. D4 76-7
Washington*, N.J. H5 76-7
Washington*, N.J. K3 76-7
Washington*, N.J. L6 76-7
Washington, N.C. E14 180-1
Washington, O. F10 132-3
Washington, Okla. G11 234-5
Washington, Pa. I1 84-5
Washington, Tenn. J12 188-9
Washington, Ut. M3 242-3
Washington, Vt. G7 90-1
Washington, Va. B1 196-7
Washington, W. Va. E3 200-1
Washington, co., Ala. L2 146-7
Washington, co., Ark. B2 150-1
Washington, co., Colo. D14 214-5
Washington, co., Fla. B5 156-7
Washington, co., Ga. I7 160-1
Washington, co., Ida. K2 218-9
Washington, co., Ill. L7 96-7
Washington, co., Ind. M8 100-1
Washington, co., Ia. H12 104-5
Washington, co., Kans. D11 108-9
Washington, co., Ky. H10 164-5
Washington, co., La. G9 168-9
Washington, co., Me. I10 64-5
Washington, co., Md. B6 172-3
Washington, co., Minn. L7 116-7
Washington, co., Miss. F4 176-7
Washington, co., Mo. G9 120-1
Washington, co., Nebr. G15 124-5
Washington, co., N.Y. E11 80-1
Washington, co., N.C. D14 180-1
Washington, co., O. H10 132-3
Washington, co., Okla. B14 234-5
Washington, co., Ore. B5 238-9
Washington, co., Pa. I1 84-5
Washington, co., R.I. G2 87
Washington, co., Tenn. B15 188-9
Washington, co., Tex. G9 192-3
Washington, co., Ut. M3 242-3
Washington, co., Vt. F6 90-1
Washington, co., Va. J4 196-7
Washington, co., Wis. I14 140-1
Washington Camp, Ariz. M9 206-7
Washington Court House, O. H5 132-3
Washington Crossing, N.J. G4 76-7
Washington Depot, Conn. E5 60-1
Washington Grove, Md. H3 172-3
Washington Heights*, N.Y. I10 80-1
Washington Isl., Wis. D16 140-1
Washington Island, Wis. E16 140-1
Washington North*, Pa. I1 84-5
Washington Park, Ill. K6 96-7
Washington Park, N.C. E14 180-1
Washington Terrace, Ut. E6 242-3
Washington Valley, N.J. D6 76-7
Washington West*, Pa. I1 84-5
Washingtonville, N.Y. A13 80-1
Washingtonville, O. D11 132-3
Washita, co., Okla. F8 234-5
Washoe, Mont. H9 222-3
Washoe, co., Nev. C2 226-7
Washougal, Wash. J8 246-7
Washta, Ia. D3 104-5
Washtenaw, co., Mich. J14 112-3
Washtucna, Wash. G14 246-7
Washunga, Okla. C12 234-5
Wasilla, Alaska F11 254-5
Waskada, Man. K10 272-3
Waskatenau, Alta. I8 264-5
Waskesiu Lake, Sask. I7 294-5
Waskom*, Tex. E11 192-3
Wasta, S. Dak. F4 136-7
Watauga, S. Dak. A6 136-7
Watauga, Tenn. G16 188-9
Watauga, Tex. C13 192-3
Watauga, co., N.C. C5 180-1
Watch Hill, R.I. I1 87
Watchorn, Okla. D12 234-5
Watchung, N.J. E6 76-7
Water Valley, Ky. K2 164-5
Water Valley, Miss. C7 176-7
Water View, Va. H14 196-7
Waterboro, Me. N2 64-5
Waterboro Center, Me. N2 64-5
Waterborough, N.B. I5 275
Waterbury, Conn. F7 60-1
Waterbury, Nebr. D14 124-5
Waterbury, Vt. F6 90-1
Waterdown*, Ont. D14 284-5
Wateree, S.C. E11 184-5
Waterflow, N. Mex. C3 230-1
Waterford, Calif. C11 210-1
Waterford, Conn. G13 60-1
Waterford, Ind. A6 100-1
Waterford, Ky. B3 164-5
Waterford, Me. L2 64-5
Waterford, Mich. H5 112-3
Waterford, Miss. B8 176-7
Waterford*, N.J. K4 76-7
Waterford, N.Y. F11 80-1
Waterford, Pa. C2 84-5
Waterford*, Vt. E9 90-1
Waterford, Va. E12 196-7
Waterford, Wis. K4 140-1
Waterford Works, N.J. K4 76-7
Waterhill, Tenn. H8 188-9
Waterlick, Va. A1 196-7
Waterloo, Ala. A3 146-7
Waterloo, Ark. I4 150-1
Waterloo, Ill. L6 96-7
Waterloo, Ind. B11 100-1
Waterloo, Ia. E11 104-5
Waterloo, Kans. I9 108-9
Waterloo, Md. G5 172-3
Waterloo, Mont. G5 222-3
Waterloo, Nebr. I2 124-5
Waterloo, N.H. L5 72-3
Waterloo, N.Y. F6 80-1
Waterloo, Ont. D13 284-5
Waterloo, Ore. J2 238-9
Waterloo, Que. J14 290-1
Waterloo, S.C. J4 184-5
Waterloo, Wis. I2 140-1
Waterman, Ill. C9 96-7
Waterman, Ore. E11 238-9
Waterproof, La. D7 168-9
Waters, Mich. F13 112-3
Watersmeet, Mich. D8 112-3
Waterton Park, Alta. O7 264-5
Watertown, Conn. E6 60-1
Watertown*, Fla. B10 156-7
Watertown, Mass. H4 68-9
Watertown, Minn. B9 116-7
Watertown, N.Y. C7 80-1
Watertown, S. Dak. D15 136-7
Watertown, Tenn. B8 188-9
Watertown, Wis. J14 140-1
Waterview, Ky. J9 164-5
Waterview, Md. H13 172-3
Waterville, Ia. B13 104-5
Waterville, Kans. D12 108-9
Waterville, Me. K5 64-5
Waterville, Minn. N6 116-7
Waterville, N.Y. E8 80-1
Waterville, N.C. D3 180-1
Waterville*, N.S. D6 281
Waterville, O. B5 132-3
Waterville*, Que. J14 290-1
Waterville, Tenn. K12 188-9
Waterville, Vt. D6 90-1
Waterville, Wash. E11 246-7
Waterville Valley, N.H. H6 72-3
Watervliet, Mich. J11 112-3
Watervliet, N.Y. F11 80-1
Watford, Ont. E11 284-5

Watford City, N. Dak. . . E3 128-9
Watha, N.C. G12 180-1
Wathena, Kans. D15 108-9
Watkins, Minn. L5 116-7
Watkins Glen, N.Y. G6 80-1
Watkinsville, Ga. F6 160-1
Watonga, Okla. E9 234-5
Watonwan, co., Minn. . . O4 116-7
Watova, Okla. C14 234-5
Watrous, N. Mex. E8 230-1
Watrous, Sask. L7 294-5
Watrousville, Mich. E4 112-3
Watseka, Ill. E11 96-7
Watson, Ark. H9 150-1
Watson, Mass. C4 68-9
Watson, Minn. M3 116-7
Watson, Mo. A1 120-1
Watson, Okla. H16 234-5
Watson, Sask. K8 294-5
Watson, Ut. G10 242-3
Watson Chapel, Ark. . . . H7 150-1
Watson Lake, Y.T. C3 297
Watsontown, Pa. F11 84-5
Watsonville, Calif. J3 210-1
Wattenberg, Colo. F3 214-5
Wattis, Ut. H7 242-3
Watton, Mich. C8 112-3
Watts, Okla. D16 234-5
Watts Bar Dam, Tenn. . . J12 188-9
Watts Mills, S.C. I4 184-5
Wattsville, Ala. E7 146-7
Wattsville, Va. G16 196-7
Waubaushene, Ont. A14 284-5
Waubay, S. Dak. B14 136-7
Waubeka, Wis. H5 140-1
Waubun, Minn. H2 116-7
Wauchula, Fla. J5 156-7
Waucoma, Ia. C11 104-5
Wauconda, Ill. K2 96-7
Wauconda, Wash. C13 246-7
Wauhillau, Okla. E16 234-5
Waukau, Wis. F3 140-1
Waukee, Ia. G7 104-5
Waukegan, Ill. A11 96-7
Waukesha, Wis. J14 140-1
Waukesha, co., Wis. . . . J14 140-1
Waukomis, Okla. D10 234-5
Waukon, Ia. B13 104-5
Waukon, Wash. F15 246-7
Waumandee, Wis. G8 140-1
Wauna, Ore. A5 238-9
Wauna, Wash. J1 246-7
Waunakee, Wis. I1 140-1
Wauneta, Kans. K13 108-9
Wauneta, Nebr. I8 124-5
Waupaca, Wis. G13 140-1
Waupaca, co., Wis. G13 140-1
Waupun, Wis. H3 140-1
Wauregan, Conn. D14 60-1
Waurika, Okla. I10 234-5
Wausa, Nebr. D12 124-5
Wausau, Fla. B5 156-7
Wausau, Wis. F12 140-1
Wausau West, Wis. F12 140-1
Wausaukee, Wis. E15 140-1
Wauseon, O. B4 132-3
Waushara, co., Wis. G13 140-1
Wautoma, Wis. H13 140-1
Wauwatosa, Wis. J5 140-1
Wauwinet, Mass. J16 68-9
Wauzeka, Wis. J10 140-1
Waveland, Ark. E4 150-1
Waveland, Ind. H5 100-1
Waveland, Miss. O8 176-7
Waverley, Ont. A14 284-5
Waverly, Ala. H9 146-7
Waverly, Fla. H6 156-7
Waverly, Ga. N10 160-1
Waverly, Ill. I6 96-7
Waverly, Ind. I8 100-1
Waverly, Ia. D10 104-5
Waverly, Kans. G14 108-9
Waverly, Ky. H4 164-5
Waverly, La. B7 168-9
Waverly, Minn. A8 116-7
Waverly, Mo. D5 120-1
Waverly, Nebr. K1 124-5
Waverly, N.Y. H6 80-1
Waverly, O. I6 132-3
Waverly, Tenn. B5 188-9
Waverly, Va. F2 196-7
Waverly, Wash. F16 246-7
Waverly, W. Va. E4 200-1
Waverly Hall, Ga. I3 160-1
Waves, N.C. D16 180-1
Wawa, Ont. G5 284-5
Wawaka, Ind. B10 100-1
Wawanesa, Man. J11 272-3
Wawota, Sask. N10 294-5
Wax, Ky. I8 164-5
Waxahachie, Tex. E14 192-3
Waxhaw, Miss. D4 176-7
Waxhaw, N.C. F7 180-1
Way, Miss. H6 176-7
Wayan, Ida. N11 218-9
Waycross, Ga. M8 160-1
Wayland, Ia. I12 104-5
Wayland, Ky. I15 164-5
Wayland, Mass. H2 68-9
Wayland, Mich. J12 112-3
Wayland, Mo. A8 120-1
Wayland, N.Y. F4 80-1
Waymansville, Ind. K8 100-1
Waymart, Pa. D15 84-5
Wayne, Ill. L2 96-7
Wayne, Kans. D10 108-9
Wayne, Me. K4 64-5
Wayne, Mich. J5 112-3
Wayne, Nebr. E13 124-5
Wayne, N.J. C7 76-7
Wayne, O. C5 132-3
Wayne, Okla. G11 234-5
Wayne, W. Va. H1 200-1
Wayne, Wis. H4 140-1
Wayne, co., Ga. M9 160-1
Wayne, co., Ill. L9 96-7
Wayne, co., Ind. H12 100-1
Wayne, co., Ia. J8 104-5
Wayne, co., Ky. J10 164-5
Wayne, co., Mich. J14 112-3
Wayne, co., Miss. K9 176-7
Wayne, co., Mo. H10 120-1
Wayne, co., Nebr. E13 124-5
Wayne, co., N.Y. E5 80-1
Wayne, co., N.C. E12 180-1
Wayne, co., O. D9 132-3
Wayne, co., Pa. D15 84-5
Wayne, co., Tenn. D5 188-9
Wayne, co., Ut. K8 242-3
Wayne, co., W. Va. H1 200-1
Wayne City, Ill. L9 96-7
Wayne Heights*, Pa. . . . K9 84-5
Waynesboro, Ga. H9 160-1
Waynesboro, Miss. K10 176-7
Waynesboro, Pa. K9 84-5
Waynesboro, Tenn. D5 188-9
Waynesboro, Va. G10 196-7
Waynesburg, Ky. I11 164-5
Waynesburg, O. D10 132-3
Waynesburg, Pa. J1 84-5
Waynesfield, O. E4 132-3
Waynesville, Ind. K9 100-1
Waynesville, Mo. G7 120-1
Waynesville, N.C. E3 180-1
Waynesville, O. J15 132-3
Waynetown, Ind. G5 100-1
Waynoka, Okla. C8 234-5
Wayside, Ga. H5 160-1
Wayside, Kans. K14 108-9
Wayside, Miss. F4 176-7
Wayside, Wis. E5 140-1
Wayzata*, Minn. M6 116-7
Weakley, co., Tenn. A3 188-9
Weare, N.H. M6 72-3
Weatherby, Mo. B3 120-1
Weatherby, Ore. E15 238-9
Weatherby Lake, Mo. . . . I14 120-1
Weatherford, Okla. F8 234-5
Weatherford, Tex. D8 192-3
Weatherly, Pa. G13 84-5
Weathers, Ark. B4 150-1
Weathers, Okla. G14 234-5
Weathersby, Miss. J7 176-7
Weathersfield*, Vt. K7 90-1
Weathersfield Bow, Vt. . K7 90-1
Weatland*, Que. I14 290-1
Weatogue, Conn. C8 60-1
Weaubleau, Mo. G4 120-1
Weaver, Ala. E9 146-7
Weaverville, Calif. E2 210-1
Weaverville, N.C. D4 180-1
Webb, Ala. L10 146-7
Webb, Ariz. L10 206-7
Webb, Ia. C4 104-5
Webb, Miss. D5 176-7
Webb, Okla. E8 234-5
Webb, Sask. N5 294-5
Webb, co., Tex. I7 192-3
Webb City, Ark. D3 150-1
Webb City, Mo. H3 120-1
Webb City, Okla. C12 234-5
Webber, Kans. C9 108-9
Webber City, Tenn. J5 188-9
Webbers Falls, Okla. . . . E15 234-5
Webberville, Mich. I2 112-3
Webbs Cross Roads, Ky. J10 164-5
Webbtown, Tenn. A9 188-9
Webbville, Ky. G15 164-5
Webbwood, Ont. H7 284-5
Weber, Ark. H9 150-1
Weber, co., Ut. D7 242-3
Weber City, N. Mex. . . . G11 230-1
Weber City, Va. J3 196-7
Webfoot, Ore. B10 238-9
Webster, Fla. E4 156-7
Webster, Ind. H12 100-1
Webster, Ia. H11 104-5
Webster, Ky. H7 164-5
Webster, Me. G8 64-5
Webster, Me. M10 64-5
Webster, Mass. F8 68-9
Webster, Minn. N6 116-7
Webster, Mont. F16 222-3
Webster, N.H. L6 72-3
Webster, N.Y. E5 80-1
Webster, N.C. E3 180-1
Webster, N. Dak. D10 128-9
Webster, S. Dak. C14 136-7
Webster*, Tex. I14 192-3
Webster, W. Va. C15 200-1
Webster, Wis. C7 140-1
Webster, co., Ga. K3 160-1
Webster, co., Ia. E6 104-5
Webster, co., Ky. H5 164-5
Webster, co., La. A2 168-9
Webster, co., Miss. E8 176-7
Webster, co., Mo. H6 120-1
Webster, co., Nebr. J11 124-5
Webster, co., W. Va. . . . G6 200-1
Webster City, Ia. E7 104-5
Webster Groves, Mo. . . . C15 120-1
Webster Springs, W. Va. G6 200-1
Websterville, Vt. G7 90-1
Wecota, S. Dak. C11 136-7
Weddell, S.C. D10 184-5
Wedderburn, Ore. J3 238-9
Wedgefield, S.C. E11 184-5
Wedgeport, N.S. G4 281
Wedgewood Park*, Nfld. N11 278-9
Wedington, Ark. B2 150-1
Wedowee, Ala. F9 146-7
Weed, Calif. D3 210-1
Weed, N. Mex. K7 230-1
Weed Heights, Nev. G3 226-7
Weedon-Centre, Que. . . . I15 290-1
Weedsport, N.Y. E6 80-1
Weehawken, N.J. C12 76-7
Weekapaug, R.I. I2 87
Weekes, Sask. K9 294-5
Weeki Wachee, Fla. F2 156-7
Weeks, La. I6 168-9
Weeks Mills, Me. K5 64-5
Weeksville, N.C. C15 180-1
Weeping Water, Nebr. . . H15 124-5
Weidman, Mich. H12 112-3
Weimar, Tex. G9 192-3
Weiner, Ark. C10 150-1
Weippe, Ida. F4 218-9
Weir, Kans. J16 108-9
Weir, Miss. F8 176-7
Weirdale, Sask. J7 294-5
Weirs Beach, N.H. J7 72-3
Weirton, W. Va. B5 200-1
Weisburg, Ind. J11 100-1
Weiser, Ida. K2 218-9
Weiss Lake, Ala. C9 146-7
Weissert, Nebr. G9 124-5
Weissport East*, Pa. . . . G14 84-5
Welaka, Fla. D11 156-7
Welby*, Colo. D12 214-5
Welch, Okla. B15 234-5
Welch, W. Va. J3 200-1
Welches, Ore. C7 238-9
Welchville, Me. L3 64-5
Welcome, Ark. K4 150-1
Welcome, Md. G9 172-3
Welcome, Minn. O4 116-7
Welcome, N.C. H3 180-1
Weld, Me. J3 64-5
Weld, co., Colo. C12 214-5
Welda, Kans. H15 108-9
Weldon, Ark. D9 150-1
Weldon, Ia. J7 104-5
Weldon, La. A4 168-9
Weldon, N.C. C13 180-1
Weldon, Sask. J8 294-5
Weldona, Colo. C13 214-5
Weleetka, Okla. F13 234-5
Welland, Ont. E15 284-5
Wellesley, Mass. I3 68-9
Wellesley*, Ont. D13 284-5
Wellesley Fells, Mass. . . I3 68-9
Wellesley Hills, Mass. . . I3 68-9
Wellfleet, Mass. F16 68-9
Wellfleet, Nebr. H7 124-5
Wellford, S.C. F3 184-5
Welling*, Alta. O8 264-5
Welling, Okla. E15 234-5
Wellington, Ala. E8 146-7
Wellington, Colo. B11 214-5
Wellington, Kans. J10 108-9
Wellington*, Ky. G9 164-5
Wellington, Me. I5 64-5
Wellington, Mo. D4 120-1
Wellington, Nev. H2 226-7
Wellington, O. C8 132-3
Wellington, Ont. K12 284-5
Wellington, P.E.I. D4 287
Wellington, Tex. B6 192-3
Wellington, Ut. H8 242-3
Wellington, Va. B4 196-7
Wellington, co., Ont. . . . C13 284-5
Wellman, Ia. H12 104-5
Wellpinit, Wash. E15 246-7
Wells, B.C. G7 268-9
Wells, Kans. E10 108-9
Wells, Me. O2 64-5
Wells, Mich. E10 112-3
Wells, Minn. O6 116-7
Wells, Nev. C9 226-7
Wells, Tex. F10 192-3
Wells, Vt. K4 90-1
Wells, co., Ind. E11 100-1
Wells, co., N. Dak. F9 128-9
Wells River, Vt. G9 90-1
Wellsboro, Pa. D9 84-5
Wellsburg, Ia. E9 104-5
Wellsburg, N.Y. H6 80-1
Wellsburg, N. Dak. E9 128-9
Wellsburg, W. Va. B5 200-1
Wellsford, Kans. J7 108-9
Wellston, Mich. G11 112-3
Wellston, Mo. B16 120-1
Wellston, O. I7 132-3
Wellston, Okla. I4 234-5
Wellsville, Kans. F15 108-9
Wellsville, Mo. D8 120-1
Wellsville, N.Y. G4 80-1
Wellsville, O. D11 132-3
Wellsville, Ut. D6 242-3
Wellton, Ariz. J3 206-7
Wellwood, Man. I11 272-3
Welsford, N.B. I5 275
Welsh, La. H3 168-9
Welton, Ia. F15 104-5
Welty, Okla. E13 234-5
Welwyn, Sask. N11 294-5
Wembley, Alta. G3 264-5
Wemme, Ore. C7 238-9
Wenasoga, Miss. A10 176-7
Wenatchee, Wash. F11 246-7
Wendel, W. Va. C14 200-1
Wendell, Ida. N6 218-9
Wendell, Mass. C6 68-9
Wendell, Minn. J2 116-7
Wendell, N.H. L4 72-3
Wendell, N.C. I8 180-1
Wendell Depot, Mass. . . B6 68-9
Wenden, Ariz. H4 206-7
Wendling, Ore. K2 238-9
Wendover, Ut. E2 242-3
Wendover, Wyo. H15 250-1
Wenham, Mass. B12 68-9
Wenona, Ill. E8 96-7
Wenona, Md. I13 172-3
Wenonah, N.J. O10 76-7
Wentworth, Mo. I3 120-1
Wentworth, N.H. I5 72-3
Wentworth, N.C. C9 180-1
Wentworth, S. Dak. F15 136-7
Wentworth, Wis. B8 140-1
Wentworths Location,
N.H. C8 72-3
Wentzville, Mo. B14 120-1
Weogufka, Ala. G7 146-7
Weona, Ark. D11 150-1
Wequetequock, Conn. . . G14 60-1
Werner, N. Dak. F4 128-9
Wernersville, Pa. I13 84-5
Wernerville*, Alta. I8 264-5
Wertz Dome, Wyo. H11 250-1
Weskan, Kans. F1 108-9
Weslaco, Tex. K8 192-3
Wesley, Ark. B3 150-1
Wesley, Ga. J8 160-1
Wesley, Ia. C7 104-5
Wesley, Me. I10 64-5
Wesleyan, S.C. B5 184-5
Wesleyville, Nfld. M11 278-9
Wesleyville, Pa. B2 84-5
Weso, Nev. C5 226-7
Wessington, S. Dak. . . . E12 136-7
Wessington Springs, S.
Dak. F12 136-7
Wesson, Ark. K5 150-1
Wesson, Miss. K5 176-7
West, Miss. F7 176-7
West, Tex. E9 192-3
West Alexandria, O. . . . H13 132-3
West Allis, Wis. J5 140-1
West Amityville*, N.Y. . K11 80-1
West Amwell*, N.J. . . . G4 76-7
West Appleton, Me. . . . K6 64-5
West Arichat, N.S. C10 281
West Ashford, Conn. . . . C12 60-1
West Athens*, Calif. . . . N7 210-1
West Auburndale*, Fla. . F11 156-7
West Augusta, Va. G9 196-7
West Babylon*, N.Y. . . . K12 80-1
West Baden Springs, Ind. M7 100-1
West Baldwin, Me. N7 64-5
West Baraboo, Wis. I12 140-1
West Barnstable, Mass. . . G15 68-9
West Barrington, R.I. . . . D6 87
West Bath, Me. N10 64-5
West Baton Rouge, co.,
La. G7 168-9
West Becket, Mass. D2 68-9
West Bedford, Mass. . . . G3 68-9
West Belmar, N.J. H8 76-7
West Bench*, B.C. J8 268-9
West Bend, Ala. J3 146-7
West Bend, Ia. C6 104-5
West Bend, Wis. I14 140-1
West Berkshire, Vt. B5 90-1
West Bethel, Me. K2 64-5
West Blocton, Ala. G5 146-7
West Bountiful*, Ut. . . . E6 242-3
West Bowdoin, Me. M10 64-5
West Boxford, Mass. . . . B11 68-9
West Boylston, Mass. . . . D8 68-9
West Bradenton*, Fla. . . J2 156-7
West Braintree, Vt. H6 90-1
West Branch, Ia. G13 104-5
West Branch, Mich. G13 112-3
West Brewster, Mass. . . . G16 68-9
West Bridgewater, Mass. F12 68-9
West Brookfield, Mass. . D7 68-9
West Brownsville*, Pa. . . J2 84-5
West Buechel*, Ky. G9 164-5
West Burke, Vt. D9 90-1
West Burlington, Ia. J14 104-5
West Burlington*, N.C. . C9 180-1
West Buxton, Me. O8 64-5
West Caldwell*, N.J. . . . D7 76-7
West Cape May, N.J. . . . O4 76-7
West Carroll, co., La. . . . A6 168-9
West Carrollton, O. I14 132-3
West Carson*, Calif. . . . N7 210-1
West Carthage, N.Y. . . . C8 80-1
West Castleton, Vt. J4 90-1
West Charleston, Vt. . . . B8 90-1
West Chester, Ia. H12 104-5
West Chester, Pa. J14 84-5
West Chesterfield, N.H. . O2 72-3
West Chicago, Ill. M2 96-7
West City, Ill. M9 96-7
West Clarkston-
Highland*, Wash. H16 246-7
West College Corner,
Ind. I12 100-1
West Columbia, S.C. . . . E10 184-5
West Columbia, Tex. . . . J13 192-3
West Columbia, W. Va. . F2 200-1
West Compton*, Calif. . . N7 210-1
West Concord, Mass. . . . G2 68-9
West Concord, Minn. . . . N7 116-7
West Concord, N.C. J2 180-1
West Conshohocken*, Pa. J14 84-5
West Corinth, Vt. G7 90-1
West Cornwall, Conn. . . C5 60-1
West Covina, Calif. G9 210-1
West Creek, N.J. K7 76-7
West Crossett, Ark. K7 150-1
West Cumberland, Me. . . N9 64-5
West Cummington, Mass. C3 68-9
West Danville, Vt. E8 90-1
West Dennis, Mass. H16 68-9
West Deptford*, N.J. . . . J2 76-7
West Derry*, Pa. I4 84-5

West Des Moines, Ia. H7 104-5
West Devon, P.E.I. C4 287
West Dover, Vt. N5 90-1
West Dundee, Ill. L1 96-7
West Easton*, Pa. H15 84-5
West Eau Gallie*, Fla. F12 156-7
West Elkton, O. I13 132-3
West Elmira, N.Y. G6 80-1
West End, Ark. G7 150-1
West End*, Fla. D10 156-7
West End*, Ill. A8 96-7
West End, N.Y. G9 80-1
West End, N.C. J5 180-1
West End Anniston, Ala. E8 146-7
West End-Cobb*, Ala. E8 146-7
West Enfield, Me. H7 64-5
West Epping, N.H. N8 72-3
West Fairlee, Vt. H8 90-1
West Fairview, Pa. I10 84-5
West Falmouth, Mass. H13 68-9
West Fargo, N. Dak. G14 128-9
West Farmington, Me. J3 64-5
West Farmington, O. B11 132-3
West Feliciana, co., La. F6 168-9
West Fernie*, B.C. J11 268-9
West Fitchburg, Mass. C8 68-9
West Fork, Ark. B2 150-1
West Forks, Me. H4 64-5
West Frankfort, Ill. M9 96-7
West Franklin, Me. K8 64-5
West Friendship, Md. F4 172-3
West Gardiner, Me. L4 64-5
West Glacier, Mont. B3 222-3
West Glen Park*, Ind. A5 100-1
West Glens Falls*, N.Y. D11 80-1
West Glocester, R.I. B2 87
West Glover, Vt. C8 90-1
West Goshen, Conn. C5 60-1
West Gouldsboro, Me. K9 64-5
West Granby, Conn. B8 60-1
West Granville, Mass. E3 68-9
West Green, Ga. L8 160-1
West Greene, Ala. G3 146-7
West Greenville, R.I. B4 87
West Greenwich*, R.I. E2 87
West Greenwich Center, R.I. E2 87
West Groton, Mass. B9 68-9
West Grove, Pa. K14 84-5
West Gulfport, Miss. N9 176-7
West Hamlin, W. Va. I11 200-1
West Harrison, Ind. J12 100-1
West Hartford, Conn. D8 60-1
West Hartford, Vt. I7 90-1
West Hartland, Conn. B7 60-1
West Hartsville, S.C. D13 184-5
West Hatfield, Mass. D4 68-9
West Haven, Conn. H7 60-1
West Haven, Vt. J3 90-1
West Haverstraw, N.Y. B14 80-1
West Hawk Lake, Man. J16 272-3
West Hazleton, Pa. G13 84-5
West Helena, Ark. F11 150-1
West Hempstead, N.Y. E16 80-1
West Hillsborough, N.C. H6 180-1
West Hollywood*, Calif. G8 210-1
West Hollywood, Fla. G16 156-7
West Homestead*, Pa. I2 84-5
West Irvine, Ky. H12 164-5
West Islip, N.Y. K12 80-1
West Jefferson*, Ala. E5 146-7
West Jefferson, N.C. C6 180-1
West Jefferson, O. F6 132-3
West Jordan, Ut. F6 242-3
West Keansburg, N.J. H10 76-7
West Kennebunk, Me. O2 64-5
West Kingston, R.I. G4 87
West Kittanning*, Pa. G3 84-5
West La Crosse, Wis. H9 140-1
West Lafayette, Ind. F6 100-1
West Lafayette, O. E9 132-3
West Lake Hills*, Tex. G8 192-3
West Laurel*, Md. D10 172-3
West Lawn, Pa. I13 84-5
West Lawn, Va. A4 196-7
West Lebanon, Ind. F4 100-1
West Lebanon, Me. O1 64-5
West Lebanon, N.H. J3 72-3
West Leechburg*, Pa. H3 84-5
West Leipsic, O. C4 132-3
West Levant, Me. I6 64-5
West Leyden, Mass. B4 68-9
West Liberty, Ia. G13 104-5
West Liberty, Ky. G14 164-5
West Liberty, O. F5 132-3
West Liberty, W. Va. B5 200-1
West Lima, Wis. I10 140-1
West Lincoln, Nebr. K1 124-5
West Lincoln, Vt. G4 90-1
West Line, Mo. E3 120-1
West Linn, Ore. F2 238-9
West Logan, W. Va. K12 200-1
West Long Branch, N.J. G8 76-7
West Lorne, Ont. F11 284-5
West Louisville, Ky. H6 164-5
West Lubec, Me. J11 64-5
West Manchester, O. H13 132-3
West Mansfield, Mass. F11 68-9
West Mansfield, O. E5 132-3
West Marion, N.C. D5 180-1
West Mayfield, Pa. G1 84-5
West Medway*, Mass. K2 68-9
West Melbourne, Fla. F13 156-7
West Memphis, Ark. E12 150-1
West Miami*, Fla. H16 156-7
West Middlesex, Pa. F1 84-5
West Middleton, Ind. F8 100-1
West Mifflin, Pa. B7 84-5
West Milan, N.H. E7 72-3
West Milford, N.J. B6 76-7
West Milford, W. Va. D13 200-1
West Milton, O. G14 132-3
West Milton, Vt. D4 90-1
West Milwaukee*, Wis. J15 140-1
West Mineral, Kans. J16 108-9
West Minot, Me. L3 64-5
West Modesto*, Calif. I4 210-1
West Monroe, La. B5 168-9
West Mount Vernon, Me. K4 64-5
West Mystic, Conn. G14 60-1
West New York, N.J. C12 76-7
West Newbury, Mass. A12 68-9
West Newbury, Vt. G8 90-1
West Newfield, Me. O6 64-5
West Newton, Mass. H4 68-9
West Newton, Pa. I3 84-5
West Northfield, Mass. B5 68-9
West Norwich, Vt. I7 90-1
West Nyack*, N.Y. I11 80-1
West Okoboji, Ia. B4 104-5
West Orange, Mass. B6 68-9
West Orange, N.J. C9 76-7
West Orange*, Tex. G12 192-3
West Ossipee, N.H. I8 72-3
West Otis, Mass. E2 68-9
West Palm Beach, Fla. H13 156-7
West Paris, Me. K2 64-5
West Paterson, N.J. B10 76-7
West Pawlet, Vt. K3 90-1
West Pelham, Mass. D5 68-9
West Pelzer, S.C. H1 184-5
West Pembroke, Me. I10 64-5
West Pensacola, Fla. B3 156-7
West Peoria*, Ill. F7 96-7
West Peru, Me. K3 64-5
West Peterborough, N.H. O4 72-3
West Pittsburg, Calif. B8 210-1
West Pittston, Pa. E14 84-5
West Plains, Mo. I8 120-1
West Point, Ark. E8 150-1
West Point, Ga. I2 160-1
West Point, Ia. J13 104-5
West Point, Ky. C1 164-5
West Point, Me. O10 64-5
West Point, Miss. E10 176-7
West Point, Nebr. F14 124-5
West Point, N.Y. A14 80-1
West Point*, Ut. E6 242-3
West Point, Va. E3 196-7
West Poland, Me. M8 64-5
West Portsmouth, O. J6 132-3
West Puente Valley*, Calif. N7 210-1
West Reading*, Pa. I13 84-5
West Redding, Conn. H4 60-1
West Richfield, O. C14 132-3
West Richland, Wash. I13 246-7
West Ridge, Ark. C12 150-1
West Rockingham, N.C. F9 180-1
West Rockport, Me. L6 64-5
West Roxbury, Mass. I4 68-9
West Royalty*, P.E.I. E7 287
West Rumney, N.H. I5 72-3
West Rupert, Vt. L4 90-1
West Rutland, Vt. J4 90-1
West Sacramento*, Calif. H3 210-1
West St. Paul, Minn. B11 116-7
West Salem, Ill. K11 96-7
West Salem, O. E12 132-3
West Salem, Wis. H9 140-1
West Salisbury, Vt. H4 90-1
West Sand Lake*, N.Y. F11 80-1
West Sayville*, N.Y. K12 80-1
West Scarboro, Me. N3 64-5
West Sechelt*, B.C. J6 268-9
West Selmont [-Selmont], Ala. I6 146-7
West Shiloh, Tenn. D4 188-9
West Side, Ore. K10 238-9
West Siloam Springs*, Okla. D16 234-5
West Simsbury, Conn. C8 60-1
West Slope, Ore. F2 238-9
West Springfield, Mass. E5 68-9
West Springfield*, Va. E13 196-7
West Springs, S.C. G5 184-5
West Stafford, Conn. B11 60-1
West Statesville*, N.C. D7 180-1
West Stayton, Ore. I1 238-9
West Sterling, Ill. C7 96-7
West Stockbridge, Mass. D1 68-9
West Suffield, Conn. B9 60-1
West Sullivan, Me. K8 64-5
West Summit, Mass. B3 68-9
West Sumner, Me. K3 64-5
West Swanzey, N.H. O3 72-3
West Terre Haute, Ind. I4 100-1
West Thumb, Wyo. G2 250-1
West Tisbury, Mass. I13 68-9
West Topsham, Vt. G7 90-1
West Townshend, Vt. M6 90-1
West Tremont, Me. K8 64-5
West Trenton, Me. L8 64-5
West Union, Ia. C12 104-5
West Union, Minn. K4 116-7
West Union, O. J5 132-3
West Union, S.C. B5 184-5
West Union, W. Va. E5 200-1
West Unity, O. B3 132-3
West University Place, Tex. H13 192-3
West Van Lear, Ky. H15 164-5
West View*, O. C9 132-3
West View, Pa. A6 84-5
West View Park*, Tenn. F15 188-9
West Village, Mass. C11 68-9
West Ware, Mass. D6 68-9
West Warren, Mass. E6 68-9
West Warwick, R.I. D4 87
West Wenatchee*, Wash. F11 246-7
West Whately, Mass. C4 68-9
West Whittier-Los Nietos*, Calif. N7 210-1
West Wildwood, N.J. O4 76-7
West Willington, Conn. C12 60-1
West Windsor*, N.J. G5 76-7
West Windsor*, Vt. K7 90-1
West Winfield, N.Y. F8 80-1
West Winter Haven*, Fla. F11 156-7
West Woodstock, Conn. B13 60-1
West Wyoming*, Pa. E13 84-5
West Yarmouth, Mass. H15 68-9
West Yellowstone, Mont. I7 222-3
West York, Pa. J11 84-5
West Yuma, Ariz. J1 206-7
Westampton*, N.J. I4 76-7
Westbank, B.C. J8 268-9
Westbay, Fla. B5 156-7
Westbend, Ky. G12 164-5
Westboro, Mo. A1 120-1
Westboro, Wis. E11 140-1
Westborough, Mass. D9 68-9
Westbourne, Man. I12 272-3
Westbrook, Conn. H11 60-1
Westbrook, Me. O9 64-5
Westbrook, Mass. C5 68-9
Westbrook, Minn. O3 116-7
Westbrook*, Ont. J14 284-5
Westbrooke Crescents*, Alta. J7 264-5
Westbury*, N.Y. J11 80-1
Westby, Mont. A16 222-3
Westby, Wis. I10 140-1
Westchester, Conn. F11 60-1
Westchester*, Ill. B11 96-7
Westchester, co., N.Y. I11 80-1
Westchester Station, N.S. C7 281
Westcliffe, Colo. H11 214-5
Westdale, La. C2 168-9
Westel, Tenn. I10 188-9
Westerly, R.I. I1 87
Western, Nebr. I13 124-5
Western College, Ia. G12 104-5
Western Grove, Ark. B5 150-1
Western Shore*, N.S. E6 281
Western Springs, Ill. M3 96-7
Westernport, Md. C3 172-3
Westerville, Nebr. G9 124-5
Westerville, O. F7 132-3
Westfall, Kans. F9 108-9
Westfall, Ore. F15 238-9
Westfield, Conn. E9 60-1
Westfield, Ill. I10 96-7
Westfield, Ind. G8 100-1
Westfield, Ia. D1 104-5
Westfield, Me. D9 64-5
Westfield, Mass. E4 68-9
Westfield*, N.B. J5 275
Westfield, N.J. E6 76-7
Westfield, N.Y. G1 80-1
Westfield, N. Dak. J8 128-9
Westfield, Pa. C9 84-5
Westfield, Vt. B7 90-1
Westfield, Wis. G1 140-1
Westfield Center, O. D13 132-3
Westfir, Ore. G6 238-9
Westford, Conn. B12 60-1
Westford, Mass. B10 68-9
Westford, Vt. D5 90-1
Westgate, Ia. D11 104-5
Westgate, Man. D9 272-3
Westhampton, Mass. D4 68-9
Westhampton, N.Y. J13 80-1
Westhampton Beach, N.Y. J13 80-1
Westhaven*, Ill. N3 96-7
Westhope, N. Dak. B7 128-9
Westlake, Ida. G3 218-9
Westlake, La. H2 168-9
Westlake, O. B13 132-3
Westlake, Ore. F4 238-9
Westland*, Mich. J14 112-3
Westlock, Alta. I7 264-5
Westmanland, Me. B8 64-5
Westmeath, Ont. H9 284-5
Westmere*, N.Y. F11 80-1
Westminster, Calif. H9 210-1
Westminster, Colo. G3 214-5
Westminster, Md. B10 172-3
Westminster, Mass. C8 68-9
Westminster, S.C. C4 184-5
Westminster, Vt. M7 90-1
Westminster East*, Colo. D12 214-5
Westminster South*, Md. B10 172-3
Westminster West, Vt. M6 90-1
Westmont*, Calif. N7 210-1
Westmont, Ill. M3 96-7
Westmont, Pa. I5 84-5
Westmore, Vt. C9 90-1
Westmoreland, Kans. E12 108-9
Westmoreland, N.H. N2 72-3
Westmoreland, Tenn. F8 188-9
Westmoreland, Va. G14 196-7
Westmoreland, co., Pa. I3 84-5
Westmoreland, co., Va. G13 196-7
Westmorland, Calif. O10 210-1
Westmorland, co., N.B. H6 275
Westmount*, N.S. B11 281
Westmount*, Que. I12 290-1
Weston*, Ala. D3 146-7
Weston, Colo. J12 214-5
Weston, Conn. I4 60-1
Weston, Ga. K3 160-1
Weston, Ida. O10 218-9
Weston, La. C4 168-9
Weston, Me. G9 64-5
Weston, Mass. H3 68-9
Weston, Mich. K14 112-3
Weston, Mo. H14 120-1
Weston, Nebr. J1 124-5
Weston, O. C5 132-3
Weston, Ore. B13 238-9
Weston, Vt. L5 90-1
Weston, W. Va. E6 200-1
Weston*, Wis. E12 140-1
Weston, Wyo. B14 250-1
Weston, co., Wyo. D15 250-1
Westover, Ala. F7 146-7
Westover, Md. I14 172-3
Westover, W. Va. A15 200-1
Westover Hills, Del. A3 153
Westphalia, Ind. L5 100-1
Westphalia, Ia. G3 104-5
Westphalia, Kans. H14 108-9
Westphalia*, Mich. I13 112-3
Westphalia, Mo. F7 120-1
Westpoint, Ind. F5 100-1
Westport, Conn. I5 60-1
Westport, Ind. J10 100-1
Westport, Ky. F9 164-5
Westport, Me. N11 64-5
Westport, Mass. H12 68-9
Westport, Minn. K4 116-7
Westport, N.H. O3 72-3
Westport, N.Y. C11 80-1
Westport, N.S. F3 281
Westport*, Okla. D13 234-5
Westport, Ont. I14 284-5
Westport, Ore. A5 238-9
Westport, S. Dak. B12 136-7
Westport, Tenn. B4 188-9
Westport, Wash. G5 246-7
Westport Point, Mass. I11 68-9
Westside, Ia. F4 104-5
Westvaco, Wyo. I7 250-1
Westvale*, N.Y. E7 80-1
Westview*, Man. I2 272-3
Westview*, Sask. M10 294-5
Westview*, S.C. B8 184-5
Westville, Fla. A5 156-7
Westville, Ill. G11 96-7
Westville, Ind. A6 100-1
Westville, N.H. O8 72-3
Westville, N.J. N10 76-7
Westville, N.S. C8 281
Westville, Okla. D16 234-5
Westville, S.C. C11 184-5
Westward Ho, Alta. L7 264-5
Westwater, Ut. I11 242-3
Westwego, La. D14 168-9
Westwold, B.C. I8 268-9
Westwood, Calif. F4 210-1
Westwood*, Kans. E16 108-9
Westwood*, Ky. G9 164-5
Westwood, La. C7 168-9
Westwood, Md. F11 172-3
Westwood, Mass. J4 68-9
Westwood*, Mich. J12 112-3
Westwood*, Mo. E10 120-1
Westwood, N.J. C8 76-7
Westwood Hills*, Kans. E16 108-9
Westwood Lakes, Fla. I15 156-7
Westworth*, Tex. D8 192-3
Wetaskiwin, Alta. J8 264-5
Wethersfield, Conn. D9 60-1
Wetmore, Colo. H11 214-5
Wetmore, Kans. D14 108-9
Wetmore, Mich. D11 112-3
Wetmore, Ore. D11 238-9
Wetmore, Tenn. K13 188-9
Wetonka, S. Dak. B11 136-7
Wetumka, Okla. F13 234-5
Wetumpka, Ala. H8 146-7
Wetzel, co., W. Va. D5 200-1
Wewahitchka, Fla. C6 156-7
Wewela, S. Dak. I10 136-7
Wewoka, Okla. F13 234-5
Wexford, co., Mich. G12 112-3
Weyanoke, La. F6 168-9
Weyauwega, Wis. E2 140-1
Weybridge, Vt. G4 90-1
Weyburn, Sask. O9 294-5
Weyerhaeuser, Wis. D9 140-1
Weyers Cave, Va. G10 196-7
Weymouth, Mass. J6 68-9
Weymouth, N.J. L4 76-7
Weymouth, N.S. E4 281
Weymouth North, N.S. E4 281
Whalan, Minn. O8 116-7
Whaley, S.C. G9 184-5
Whaleys, Del. K4 153
Whaleysville, Md. G15 172-3
Whaleyville, Va. K14 196-7
Whalom, Mass. C8 68-9
Wharncliffe, W. Va. J2 200-1
Wharton, N.J. D5 76-7
Wharton, O. D5 132-3
Wharton, Tex. H9 192-3
Wharton, W. Va. K13 200-1
Wharton, co., Tex. H9 192-3
What Cheer, Ia. H11 104-5
Whatcom, co., Wash. C9 246-7
Whately, Mass. C5 68-9
Whatley, Ala. K4 146-7
Wheat Ridge, Colo. G3 214-5
Wheatcroft, Ky. I4 164-5
Wheatfield, Ind. D5 100-1
Wheatland, Calif. H4 210-1
Wheatland, Ind. L5 100-1
Wheatland, Ia. G14 104-5
Wheatland, Man. I10 272-3
Wheatland, Mo. G5 120-1
Wheatland, Pa. F1 84-5
Wheatland, Wyo. H15 250-1
Wheatland, co., Mont. F9 222-3
Wheatley, Ark. E10 150-1
Wheatley, Ky. F10 164-5
Wheatley, Ont. G10 284-5
Wheaton, Ill. B10 96-7
Wheaton, Kans. D13 108-9

Wheaton, Md. H4 172-3
Wheaton, Minn. K2 116-7
Wheaton, Mo. I4 120-1
Wheel, Tenn. J7 188-9
Wheeler, Ala. B5 146-7
Wheeler, Ark. B2 150-1
Wheeler, Ind. B5 100-1
Wheeler, Kans. D2 108-9
Wheeler, Mich. E1 112-3
Wheeler, Miss. B10 176-7
Wheeler, Ore. B4 238-9
Wheeler, Tex. B6 192-3
Wheeler, Wash. G13 246-7
Wheeler, Wis. E8 140-1
Wheeler, co., Ga. K7 160-1
Wheeler, co., Nebr. F10 124-5
Wheeler, co., Ore. D10 238-9
Wheeler, co., Tex. B6 192-3
Wheelersburg, Ky. H14 164-5
Wheelersburg, O. J7 132-3
Wheeless, Okla. C1 234-5
Wheeling, Ill. K3 96-7
Wheeling, Ind. F10 100-1
Wheeling, La. D3 168-9
Wheeling, Mo. C5 120-1
Wheeling, W. Va. B5 200-1
Wheelock, N. Dak. D3 128-9
Wheelock, Vt. D9 90-1
Wheelon, Ut. C6 242-3
Wheelwright, Ky. I15 164-5
Whelen Springs, Ark. I5 150-1
Whidbey Isl., Wash. D7 246-7
Whigham, Ga. N4 160-1
Whigville, Conn. D7 60-1
Whippany, N.J. D6 76-7
Whipps Millgate*, Ky. G9 164-5
Whispering Pines*, N.C. F10 180-1
Whispering Pines Trailer Court*, Sask. J7 294-5
Whistle, Miss. K9 176-7
Whistler, B.C. I7 268-9
Whitacre, Va. D11 196-7
Whitaker*, Pa. I2 84-5
Whitakers, N.C. C12 180-1
Whitbourne, Nfld. O11 278-9
Whitby, Ont. C15 284-5
Whitcomb Summit, Mass. B3 68-9
White, Ark. K7 150-1
White, Ga. E3 160-1
White*, N.J. D3 76-7
White, S. Dak. E16 136-7
White, co., Ark. D8 150-1
White, co., Ga. D5 160-1
White, co., Ill. L10 96-7
White, co., Ind. E6 100-1
White, co., Tenn. B10 188-9
White Apple, Miss. K4 176-7
White Bead, Okla. G11 234-5
White Bear, Sask. M5 294-5
White Bear Lake, Minn. A11 116-7
White Bird, Ida. H3 218-9
White Bluff, Tenn. H6 188-9
White Brook, N.B. E3 275
White Canyon, Ut. L8 242-3
White Castle, La. B10 168-9
White City, Kans. F12 108-9
White City, Ore. J6 238-9
White City*, Sask. N8 294-5
White City*, Ut. F6 242-3
White Cloud, Kans. C15 108-9
White Cloud, Mich. H12 112-3
White Cone, Ariz. D10 206-7
White Creek, Wis. H12 140-1
White Deer, Tex. B5 192-3
White Eagle, Okla. C11 234-5
White Earth, Minn. H3 116-7
White Earth, N. Dak. C4 128-9
White Fox, Sask. J8 294-5
White Hall, Ala. I6 146-7
White Hall, Ark. G7 150-1
White Hall, Ill. I5 96-7
White Hall, Md. B11 172-3
White Hall, S.C. I11 184-5
White Hall, Va. G10 196-7
White Haven, Pa. F14 84-5
White Head, N.B. K4 275
White House, Tenn. G7 188-9
White House Plain Trailer Court*, Man. K4 272-3
White House Station, N.J. E4 76-7
White Lake*, B.C. I8 268-9
White Lake, N.C. G11 180-1
White Lake, S. Dak. G12 136-7
White Lake, Wis. E13 140-1
White Lake-Seven Harbors, Mich. H4 112-3
White Marsh, Md. E8 172-3
White Marsh, Va. F4 196-7
White Meadow Lake*, N.J. C6 76-7
White Mountain, Alaska D8 254-5
White Mts. 14-15
White Oak, Ga. N10 160-1
White Oak, Ky. G14 164-5
White Oak, Md. H4 172-3
White Oak, Miss. J7 176-7
White Oak, Mo. J11 120-1
White Oak, N.C. F11 180-1
White Oak, Okla. C15 234-5
White Oak, Pa. B7 84-5
White Oak, S.C. C10 184-5
White Oak, Tenn. F12 188-9
White Oak*, Tex. E11 192-3
White Oaks, Conn. F5 60-1
White Pigeon, Mich. K12 112-3
White Pine, Mich. C7 112-3
White Pine, Mont. C1 222-3
White Pine, Tenn. H14 188-9
White Pine, co., Nev. F9 226-7
White Plains, Ala. G10 146-7
White Plains, Ga. G7 160-1
White Plains, Ky. I5 164-5
White Plains, Md. G10 172-3
White Plains, N.Y. C15 80-1
White Plains, N.C. C7 180-1
White Plains, Va. J11 196-7
White Pond, S.C. G9 184-5
White Post, Va. A1 196-7
White R., Ark. E9 150-1
White R., Ind. K5 100-1
White River, Ont. F5 284-5
White River, S. Dak. G8 136-7
White River Junction, Vt. J7 90-1
White Rock, B.C. C14 268-9
White Rock, Nev. A8 226-7
White Rock*, N. Mex. D6 230-1
White Rock, R.I. H1 87
White Rock, S.C. K8 184-5
White Rock, S. Dak. A16 136-7
White Salmon, Wash. J9 246-7
White Sands, N. Mex. K6 230-1
White Settlement, Tex. C12 192-3
White Springs, Fla. B9 156-7
White Stone, S.C. F5 184-5
White Stone*, Va. H14 196-7
White Sulphur Springs, Ga. I3 160-1
White Sulphur Springs, Mont. F7 222-3
White Sulphur Springs, W. Va. I6 200-1
White Swan, Wash. H10 246-7
Whitechurch-Stouffville, Ont. C15 284-5
Whiteclay, Nebr. C3 124-5
Whitecourt, Alta. I6 264-5
Whitecroft*, Alta. I8 264-5
Whiteface, N.H. I7 72-3
Whitefield, Me. L5 64-5
Whitefield, N.H. F6 72-3
Whitefield, Okla. F15 234-5
Whitefish, Mont. B3 222-3
Whitefish Bay, Wis. I5 140-1
Whitefish Point, Mich. C12 112-3
Whiteford, Md. B12 172-3
Whitehall, Ark. D10 150-1
Whitehall, Ga. F6 160-1
Whitehall, La. B11 168-9
Whitehall, La. D5 168-9
Whitehall, Mich. H11 112-3
Whitehall, Mont. G6 222-3
Whitehall, N.Y. D11 80-1
Whitehall, O. F7 132-3
Whitehall, Pa. B6 84-5
Whitehall, Wis. G9 140-1
Whitehall Terrace, S.C. H13 184-5
Whitehaven, Md. H14 172-3
Whitehaven, Tenn. K1 188-9
Whitehead, N.C. C6 180-1
Whitehorse, S. Dak. C7 136-7
Whitehorse, Y.T. C2 297
Whitehouse, O. B5 132-3
Whitehouse*, Tex. E10 192-3
Whiteland, Ind. H2 100-1
Whitelaw, Alta. F4 264-5
Whitelaw, Kans. G1 108-9
Whitelaw, Wis. F5 140-1
Whiteleysburg, Del. G3 153
Whiteman*, Mo. E4 120-1
Whitemouth, Man. I16 272-3
Whiteriver, Ariz. H10 206-7
Whiterocks, Ut. F9 242-3
Whites, Miss. E10 176-7
Whites, Wash. G6 246-7
Whites Chapel*, Ala. E7 146-7
Whites City, N. Mex. L9 230-1
Whites Creek, Tenn. G7 188-9
Whitesboro, N.J. O4 76-7
Whitesboro, N.Y. E8 80-1
Whitesboro, Okla. G16 234-5
Whitesboro*, Tex. C9 192-3
Whitesburg, Ga. D8 160-1
Whitesburg, Ky. I15 164-5
Whitesburg, Tenn. G14 188-9
Whiteside, Ala. B6 146-7
Whiteside, Mo. D9 120-1
Whiteside, co., Ill. C6 96-7
Whiteson, Ore. G1 238-9
Whitestone, Ga. D3 160-1
Whitestown, Ind. G7 100-1
Whitesville, Del. K4 153
Whitesville, Ga. I2 160-1
Whitesville, Ky. H6 164-5
Whitesville, W. Va. J14 200-1
Whitetail, Mont. A15 222-3
Whitethorne, Va. I7 196-7
Whitetop, Va. K5 196-7
Whiteville, N.C. G11 180-1
Whiteville, Tenn. K3 188-9
Whitewater, Colo. F6 214-5
Whitewater, Ind. H12 100-1
Whitewater, Kans. I11 108-9
Whitewater, Mo. H11 120-1
Whitewater, Mont. B11 222-3
Whitewater, Wis. J3 140-1
Whitewood, Sask. N10 294-5
Whitewood, S. Dak. E2 136-7
Whitewood, Va. I4 196-7
Whitewright, Tex. A16 192-3
Whitfield, Ala. I3 146-7
Whitfield, co., Ga. D2 160-1
Whitfield Estates*, Fla. J2 156-7
Whiting, Ind. A4 100-1
Whiting, Ia. F1 104-5
Whiting, Kans. D14 108-9
Whiting, Me. J11 64-5
Whiting, N.J. I6 76-7
Whiting, Vt. H4 90-1
Whiting, Wis. E1 140-1
Whiting Field*, Fla. B3 156-7
Whitingham, Vt. O5 90-1
Whitinsville, Mass. E9 68-9
Whitlash, Mont. A7 222-3
Whitley, co., Ind. C10 100-1
Whitley, co., Ky. J12 164-5
Whitley City, Ky. K11 164-5
Whitleyville, Tenn. A9 188-9
Whitlock, Tenn. A4 188-9
Whitman, Mass. E12 68-9
Whitman, Nebr. E5 124-5
Whitman, N. Dak. D12 128-9
Whitman, Wyo. F16 250-1
Whitman, co., Wash. G16 246-7
Whitmer, W. Va. F8 200-1
Whitmire, S.C. I6 184-5
Whitmore Lake, Mich. J4 112-3
Whitmore Village, Hawaii H4 258-9
Whitney, Ida. O10 218-9
Whitney, Nebr. C2 124-5
Whitney, Nev. M10 226-7
Whitney, N.B. F5 275
Whitney, Ont. H11 284-5
Whitney, Ore. D14 238-9
Whitney, S.C. F4 184-5
Whitney, Tex. E8 192-3
Whitney Point, N.Y. G7 80-1
Whitneys, Mass. J2 68-9
Whitneyville, Me. J10 64-5
Whiton, Ala. C8 146-7
Whittaker, Mich. K4 112-3
Whittemore, Ia. C6 104-5
Whittemore, Mich. G14 112-3
Whitten, Ia. E9 104-5
Whittier, Alaska F11 254-5
Whittier, Calif. G9 210-1
Whittier, Ia. F13 104-5
Whittier, N.H. I7 72-3
Whittier, N.C. E2 180-1
Whitwell, Tenn. K10 188-9
Why, Ariz. K5 206-7
Whycocomagh, N.S. C10 281
Wianno, Mass. H15 68-9
Wiarton, Ont. A12 284-5
Wibaux, Mont. E16 222-3
Wibaux, co., Mont. E16 222-3
Wichita, Kans. I11 108-9
Wichita, co., Kans. G2 108-9
Wichita, co., Tex. C7 192-3
Wichita Falls, Tex. C7 192-3
Wichman, Nev. H3 226-7
Wick, W. Va. D5 200-1
Wickatunk, N.J. G7 76-7
Wickenburg, Ariz. H5 206-7
Wickersham, Wash. C8 246-7
Wickes, Ark. G2 150-1
Wickford, R.I. F5 87
Wickford Junction, R.I. F5 87
Wickliffe, Ky. J2 164-5
Wickliffe, O. A15 132-3
Wicomico, Va. F4 196-7
Wicomico, co., Md. H14 172-3
Wicomico Church, Va. H14 196-7
Wiconisco*, Pa. H11 84-5
Wide Ruins, Ariz. E11 206-7
Wideman, Ark. B7 150-1
Widen, W. Va. G5 200-1
Widener, Ark. E11 150-1
Widewater*, Alta. G7 264-5
Wiggins, Colo. C13 214-5
Wiggins, Miss. H7 176-7
Wiggins, Miss. M8 176-7
Wiggins, S.C. I11 184-5
Wikel, W. Va. J5 200-1
Wikieup, Ariz. F4 206-7
Wikwemikong*, Ont. H7 284-5
Wilbarger, co., Tex. C7 192-3
Wilber, Nebr. I13 124-5
Wilberforce, Ont. I11 284-5
Wilbraham, Mass. E5 68-9
Wilbur, Ore. H5 238-9
Wilbur, Wash. E14 246-7
Wilbur, W. Va. E5 200-1
Wilbur Park*, Mo. E10 120-1
Wilburn, Ark. D8 150-1
Wilburton, Okla. G15 234-5
Wilcox, Nebr. I9 124-5
Wilcox, Ore. C10 238-9
Wilcox, Sask. N8 294-5
Wilcox, co., Ala. J5 146-7
Wilcox, co., Ga. K6 160-1
Wild Cherry, Ark. A7 150-1
Wild Horse, Colo. F15 214-5
Wild Horse, Nev. B8 226-7
Wild Horse, Okla. D13 234-5
Wild Rice, N. Dak. H14 128-9
Wild Rose, Wis. F1 140-1
Wildcat, Okla. F14 234-5
Wildcat, W. Va. F13 200-1
Wildcat, Wyo. B13 250-1
Wilder, Ida. L2 218-9
Wilder, Minn. O3 116-7
Wilder, S.C. G13 184-5
Wilder, Tenn. B10 188-9
Wilder, Vt. I7 90-1
Wilders*, Ky. D11 164-5
Wildersville, Tenn. C4 188-9
Wilderville, Ore. J5 238-9
Wildie, Ky. I12 164-5
Wildrose, N. Dak. C3 128-9
Wildsville, La. D6 168-9
Wildwood, Alta. I6 264-5
Wildwood, Fla. E10 156-7
Wildwood, Ga. C1 160-1
Wildwood*, Ky. G9 164-5
Wildwood, N.J. O4 76-7
Wildwood Crest, N.J. O4 76-7
Wildwood Station*, Alaska G11 254-5
Wileville*, N.S. F6 281
Wiley, Colo. H15 214-5
Wiley, Ga. D6 160-1
Wiley Ford, W. Va. D10 200-1
Wileyville, W. Va. D5 200-1
Wilfrid, Ont. B15 284-5
Wilkes, co., Ga. G7 160-1
Wilkes, co., N.C. C6 180-1
Wilkes-Barre, Pa. F13 84-5
Wilkesboro, N.C. C6 180-1
Wilkesboro, Ore. F1 238-9
Wilkeson, Wash. K3 246-7
Wilkie, Sask. K5 294-5
Wilkin, co., Minn. J2 116-7
Wilkins, Nev. B10 226-7
Wilkinsburg, Pa. A6 84-5
Wilkinson, Ind. H10 100-1
Wilkinson, Miss. L3 176-7
Wilkinson, co., Ga. I6 160-1
Wilkinson, co., Miss. L3 176-7
Will, co., Ill. C10 96-7
Willacoochee, Ga. M7 160-1
Willacy, co., Tex. K8 192-3
Willaha, Ariz. D6 206-7
Willamette City, Ore. G6 238-9
Willamette R., Ore. D5 238-9
Willamina, Ore. D5 238-9
Willapa, Wash. H6 246-7
Willard, Kans. F13 108-9
Willard, Ky. G14 164-5
Willard, Mo. H5 120-1
Willard, Mont. F16 222-3
Willard, N. Mex. G7 230-1
Willard, N.C. G12 180-1
Willard, O. C7 132-3
Willard, Tenn. G8 188-9
Willard, Ut. D6 242-3
Willard, Wis. F10 140-1
Willards, Md. G15 172-3
Willcox, Ariz. K10 206-7
Willernie, Minn. A11 116-7
Willet, Miss. F4 176-7
Willette, Tenn. A9 188-9
Willey, Ia. F5 104-5
Willey House, N.H. G7 72-3
William Andrew Cecil Bennett Dam, B.C. E7 268-9
Williams, Ariz. E6 206-7
Williams*, Ariz. I7 206-7
Williams, Calif. G3 210-1
Williams, Ind. L7 100-1
Williams, Ia. E8 104-5
Williams, Minn. D4 116-7
Williams, Mont. B6 222-3
Williams, Ore. J5 238-9
Williams, S.C. H10 184-5
Williams, co., N. Dak. C2 128-9
Williams, co., O. B3 132-3
Williams Bay, Wis. K3 140-1
Williams Lake, B.C. H7 268-9
Williamsburg, Colo. G11 214-5
Williamsburg, Ind. G11 100-1
Williamsburg, Ia. G11 104-5
Williamsburg, Kans. G14 108-9
Williamsburg, Ky. J12 164-5
Williamsburg, Md. F14 172-3
Williamsburg, Mass. D4 68-9
Williamsburg, Mich. F12 112-3
Williamsburg, Miss. K7 176-7
Williamsburg, N.B. H4 275
Williamsburg, N. Mex. J4 230-1
Williamsburg, O. I4 132-3
Williamsburg*, Ont. I15 284-5
Williamsburg, Pa. I7 84-5
Williamsburg, Va. I14 196-7
Williamsburg, W. Va. I6 200-1
Williamsburg, co., S.C. F13 184-5
Williamson, Ga. H4 160-1
Williamson, Ia. I8 104-5
Williamson, N.Y. E5 80-1
Williamson, W. Va. I2 200-1
Williamson, co., Ill. N9 96-7
Williamson, co., Tenn. C7 188-9
Williamson, co., Tex. G8 192-3
Williamsport, Ind. F5 100-1
Williamsport, Ky. H15 164-5
Williamsport, Md. B7 172-3
Williamsport, O. G6 132-3
Williamsport, Pa. F10 84-5
Williamsport, Tenn. I6 188-9
Williamston, Mich. I2 112-3
Williamston, N.C. D14 180-1
Williamston, S.C. H1 184-5
Williamstown, Kans. F15 108-9
Williamstown, Ky. F11 164-5
Williamstown, Mass. B2 68-9
Williamstown, N.J. K3 76-7
Williamstown, Pa. H11 84-5
Williamstown, Vt. G7 90-1
Williamstown, W. Va. D3 200-1
Williamsville, Del. H4 153
Williamsville, Ill. H7 96-7
Williamsville, Mass. D1 68-9
Williamsville, Miss. G7 176-7
Williamsville, Mo. I10 120-1
Williamsville, N.Y. E2 80-1
Williamsville, Vt. N6 90-1
Williamsville, Va. G8 196-7
Williana, La. D4 168-9
Williford, Ark. B9 150-1
Willimantic, Conn. D12 60-1
Willimantic, Me. H5 64-5
Willingboro, N.J. I4 76-7
Willingdon, Alta. I9 264-5
Willington*, Conn. C12 60-1
Willington, S.C. E6 184-5
Willington Hill, Conn. C12 60-1
Willis, Kans. D14 108-9
Willis, Mich. K4 112-3

Willis, Okla. I12 234-5
Willis*, Tex. F13 192-3
Willis, Va. J7 196-7
Willis Wharf, Va. H15 196-7
Willisburg, Ky. D4 164-5
Williston, Fla. D10 156-7
Williston, N. Dak. D2 128-9
Williston, S.C. G9 184-5
Williston, Tenn. K3 188-9
Williston, Vt. E4 90-1
Williston Park*, N.Y. . . . J11 80-1
Williston Road Section*, Vt. E4 90-1
Willisville, Ark. I4 150-1
Willisville, Ill. M7 96-7
Willits, Calif. G2 210-1
Willmar, Minn. L4 116-7
Willoughby, O. A15 132-3
Willoughby Hills, O. . . . A15 132-3
Willow, Alaska F11 254-5
Willow, Ark. H6 150-1
Willow, Okla. G7 234-5
Willow Beach*, Ont. . . . B15 284-5
Willow Branch, Ind. H9 100-1
Willow Bunch, Sask. . . . O7 294-5
Willow City, N. Dak. . . . C8 128-9
Willow Creek, Mont. . . . G6 222-3
Willow Drive*, Alta. . . . O7 264-5
Willow Glen, La. E4 168-9
Willow Grove, Del. F3 153
Willow Grove, N.B. J5 275
Willow Grove, Pa. A11 84-5
Willow Island, Nebr. . . . H8 124-5
Willow Island, W. Va. . . E4 200-1
Willow Island, Wyo. F7 250-1
Willow Lake, S. Dak. . . . D14 136-7
Willow Point, B.C. J10 268-9
Willow River, B.C. F7 268-9
Willow River, Minn. J7 116-7
Willow Run, Mich. K4 112-3
Willow Spring, N.C. . . . I7 180-1
Willow Springs, Ill. N3 96-7
Willow Springs, Mo. . . . I7 120-1
Willow Springs, Ut. F5 242-3
Willow View, Okla. G11 234-5
Willowbrook*, Calif. . . . N7 210-1
Willowbrook*, Ill. B10 96-7
Willowbrook, Kans. H9 108-9
Willowbrook, Sask. M10 294-5
Willowdale, Kans. J9 108-9
Willowdale, Ore. D9 238-9
Willowick, O. A15 132-3
Willows, Calif. G3 210-1
Wills Point, Tex. D10 192-3
Willshire, O. D3 132-3
Willwood, Wyo. B8 250-1
Wilmar, Ark. I8 150-1
Wilmer, Ala. M2 146-7
Wilmer, B.C. I10 268-9
Wilmer, La. F9 168-9
Wilmer, Tex. D15 192-3
Wilmerding*, Pa. I2 84-5
Wilmette, Ill. L4 96-7
Wilmington, Del. A4 153
Wilmington, Ga. K11 160-1
Wilmington, Ill. O2 96-7
Wilmington, Ind. K11 100-1
Wilmington, Mass. C11 68-9
Wilmington, N.C. H12 180-1
Wilmington, O. H5 132-3
Wilmington, Vt. N5 90-1
Wilmington Island*, Ga. . K11 160-1
Wilmington Manor [-Chelsea-Leedom], Del. B3 153
Wilmont, Minn. O2 116-7
Wilmore, Kans. J7 108-9
Wilmore, Ky. C6 164-5
Wilmot, Ark. K8 150-1
Wilmot, Kans. J12 108-9
Wilmot, Mich. E5 112-3
Wilmot, N.H. K5 72-3
Wilmot, O. D9 132-3
Wilmot, P.E.I. G9 287
Wilmot, S. Dak. B15 136-7
Wilmot, Wis. K14 140-1
Wilmot Valley, P.E.I. . . . E5 287
Wilsey, Kans. G12 108-9
Wilsie, W. Va. G5 200-1
Wilson, Ark. D12 150-1
Wilson, Conn. C9 60-1
Wilson, Kans. F8 108-9
Wilson, La. F7 168-9
Wilson, Md. B7 172-3
Wilson, Mich. E10 112-3
Wilson, N.Y. E2 80-1
Wilson, N.C. D12 180-1
Wilson, Okla. I11 234-5
Wilson, Pa. H15 84-5
Wilson, S.C. F12 184-5
Wilson, Ut. D6 242-3
Wilson, W. Va. E8 200-1
Wilson, Wis. F8 140-1
Wilson, Wyo. J1 250-1
Wilson, co., Kans. J14 108-9
Wilson, co., N.C. D12 180-1
Wilson, co., Tenn. B8 188-9
Wilson, co., Tex. H8 192-3
Wilson City, Mo. I12 120-1
Wilson Creek, B.C. B12 268-9
Wilson Creek, Wash. . . . F13 246-7
Wilson Mills, N.C. I8 180-1
Wilsondale, W. Va. K10 200-1
Wilsons, Va. I12 196-7
Wilsons Beach, N.B. . . . J4 275
Wilsons Mills, Me. I1 64-5
Wilsonville, Ala. F7 146-7
Wilsonville, Conn. A14 60-1
Wilsonville, Ill. J7 96-7
Wilsonville, Nebr. J8 124-5
Wilsonville*, Ore. C6 238-9
Wilstacy, Ky. H14 164-5
Wilton, Ala. G6 146-7
Wilton, Ark. I2 150-1
Wilton, Conn. I4 60-1
Wilton, Ia. G14 104-5
Wilton, Me. K3 64-5
Wilton, Minn. G4 116-7
Wilton, N.H. O6 72-3
Wilton, N. Dak. G7 128-9
Wilton, Wis. H10 140-1
Wilton Manors, Fla. . . . G16 156-7
Wimbledon, N. Dak. . . . G11 128-9
Wimer, Ore. J5 238-9
Winamac, Ind. C7 100-1
Winborn, Miss. B8 176-7
Winchendon, Mass. B7 68-9
Winchester, Ark. I9 150-1
Winchester, Conn. C6 60-1
Winchester, Ida. G3 218-9
Winchester, Ill. H5 96-7
Winchester, Ind. G11 100-1
Winchester, Kans. E15 108-9
Winchester, Ky. C8 164-5
Winchester, Mass. G4 68-9
Winchester, Miss. K10 176-7
Winchester*, Mo. E10 120-1
Winchester*, Nev. M9 226-7
Winchester, N.H. O3 72-3
Winchester, O. I5 132-3
Winchester, Ont. I15 284-5
Winchester, Tenn. D8 188-9
Winchester, Va. E11 196-7
Winchester, Wash. F12 246-7
Winchester, Wis. C11 140-1
Winchester, Wis. F3 140-1
Winchester, Wyo. D9 250-1
Winchester Bay, Ore. . . . G4 238-9
Wind Gap, Pa. G15 84-5
Wind Lake, Wis. J4 140-1
Wind Point, Wis. K5 140-1
Wind R., Wyo. E9 250-1
Wind River, Wyo. F8 250-1
Windber, Pa. I5 84-5
Windcrest*, Tex. G7 192-3
Winder, Ga. F5 160-1
Windermere, B.C. J10 268-9
Windermere, Conn. C10 60-1
Windermere, Fla. F6 156-7
Windermere Country Estates*, Alta. I8 264-5
Windfall City, Ind. F9 100-1
Windham, Conn. D12 60-1
Windham*, Me. N8 64-5
Windham, Mont. E8 222-3
Windham, N.H. O7 72-3
Windham, O. C10 132-3
Windham, Vt. L6 90-1
Windham, co., Conn. . . . C13 60-1
Windham, co., Vt. M5 90-1
Windhorst, Kans. I6 108-9
Windom, Kans. G9 108-9
Windom, Minn. O4 116-7
Window Rock, Ariz. D11 206-7
Windsor*, Calif. H2 210-1
Windsor, Colo. D3 214-5
Windsor, Conn. C9 60-1
Windsor, Ill. D5 96-7
Windsor, Ill. I9 96-7
Windsor, Me. K5 64-5
Windsor, Mass. C3 68-9
Windsor, Mo. E4 120-1
Windsor, N.H. M4 72-3
Windsor, N.J. H5 76-7
Windsor, N.Y. G8 80-1
Windsor, Nfld. M9 278-9
Windsor, N.C. D14 180-1
Windsor, N.S. D6 281
Windsor, Ont. K6 284-5
Windsor*, Pa. J11 84-5
Windsor, Que. I14 290-1
Windsor, S.C. F9 184-5
Windsor, Vt. K7 90-1
Windsor, Va. G3 196-7
Windsor, Wis. I1 140-1
Windsor, co., Vt. J6 90-1
Windsor Forest*, Ga. . . . K11 160-1
Windsor Forks, N.S. E6 281
Windsor Heights, Ia. . . . G7 104-5
Windsor Heights, W. Va. B5 200-1
Windsor Locks, Conn. . . B9 60-1
Windsorville, Conn. C10 60-1
Windthorst, Sask. N10 294-5
Windy Hill, S.C. D13 184-5
Windy Hills*, Ky. G9 164-5
Windyhill, Md. F13 172-3
Winfall, N.C. C15 180-1
Winfield, Ala. D4 146-7
Winfield, Alta. J7 264-5
Winfield*, Ill. B10 96-7
Winfield, Ia. I13 104-5
Winfield, Kans. J11 108-9
Winfield, Mo. A14 120-1
Winfield*, N.J. E7 76-7
Winfield, Tenn. F10 188-9
Winfield, W. Va. G2 200-1
Winfred, S. Dak. F14 136-7
Wing, Ala. M7 146-7
Wing, N. Dak. G8 128-9
Wingate, Ind. G5 100-1
Wingate, Md. H13 172-3
Wingate, N.C. K2 180-1
Winger, Minn. G2 116-7
Wingham, Ont. C12 284-5
Wingo, Ky. K2 164-5
Winhall*, Vt. L5 90-1
Winifred, Kans. D12 108-9
Winifred, Mont. D9 222-3
Wink, Tex. E3 192-3
Winkelman, Ariz. J8 206-7
Winkleman, Wyo. F8 250-1
Winkler, Man. K13 272-3
Winkler, co., Tex. E3 192-3
Winlaw, B.C. J9 268-9
Winlock, Ore. D11 238-9
Winlock, Wash. H7 246-7
Winn, Me. G8 64-5
Winn, Mich. H13 112-3
Winn, co., La. C4 168-9
Winnabow, N.C. H12 180-1
Winnebago, Ill. A8 96-7
Winnebago, Minn. O5 116-7
Winnebago, Nebr. E14 124-5
Winnebago, Wis. F3 140-1
Winnebago, co., Ill. A8 96-7
Winnebago, co., Ia. A7 104-5
Winnebago, co., Wis. . . . H14 140-1
Winneconne, Wis. F3 140-1
Winnecook, Mont. F9 222-3
Winnemucca, Nev. C5 226-7
Winner, S. Dak. H9 136-7
Winneshiek, co., Ia. B12 104-5
Winnetka, Ill. L4 96-7
Winnetoon, Nebr. D12 124-5
Winnett, Mont. E11 222-3
Winnfield, La. D4 168-9
Winnie*, Tex. H16 192-3
Winnipeg, Man. J4 272-3
Winnipeg Beach, Man. . . H14 272-3
Winnipegosis, Man. F11 272-3
Winnisquam, N.H. K6 72-3
Winnsboro, La. C6 168-9
Winnsboro, S.C. C10 184-5
Winnsboro*, Tex. D10 192-3
Winnsboro Mills, S.C. . . D10 184-5
Winokur, Ga. N9 160-1
Winona, Ariz. E7 206-7
Winona, Kans. F2 108-9
Winona, Mich. C8 112-3
Winona, Minn. O9 116-7
Winona, Miss. E7 176-7
Winona, Mo. I8 120-1
Winona, Wash. G15 246-7
Winona, W. Va. J16 200-1
Winona, co., Minn. O9 116-7
Winona Lake, Ind. C9 100-1
Winooski, Vt. E4 90-1
Winside, Nebr. E13 124-5
Winsloe, P.E.I. E7 287
Winsloe North, P.E.I. . . . E7 287
Winslow, Ariz. F9 206-7
Winslow, Ark. C2 150-1
Winslow, Ind. N5 100-1
Winslow, Me. K5 64-5
Winslow, Nebr. F14 124-5
Winslow, N.J. K4 76-7
Winslow, Wash. H2 246-7
Winslows Mills, Me. L5 64-5
Winsted, Conn. B6 60-1
Winsted, Minn. B8 116-7
Winston*, Fla. H4 156-7
Winston, Ga. C9 160-1
Winston, Ky. H12 164-5
Winston, Mo. B3 120-1
Winston, Mont. F6 222-3
Winston, N. Mex. J4 230-1
Winston, Ore. H5 238-9
Winston, co., Ala. D4 146-7
Winston, co., Miss. G9 176-7
Winston-Salem, N.C. . . . C8 180-1
Winstonville, Miss. D4 176-7
Winter, Wis. D10 140-1
Winter Beach, Fla. G13 156-7
Winter Garden, Fla. F6 156-7
Winter Harbor, Me. K9 64-5
Winter Harbour, B.C. . . . I4 268-9
Winter Haven, Fla. H5 156-7
Winter Park, Colo. G1 214-5
Winter Park, Fla. E7 156-7
Winter Springs*, Fla. . . . E12 156-7
Winterboro, Ala. F8 146-7
Winterburn*, Alta. I8 264-5
Winterpock, Va. I12 196-7
Winterport, Me. J7 64-5
Winters, Calif. A8 210-1
Winters, Tex. E6 192-3
Wintersburg, Ariz. I5 206-7
Winterset, Ia. H7 104-5
Wintersville, O. E11 132-3
Winterthur, Del. A3 153
Winterton, Nfld. N11 278-9
Winterville, Ga. F6 160-1
Winterville, Me. B7 64-5
Winterville, Miss. E4 176-7
Winterville, N.C. E13 180-1
Winthrop, Ark. H2 150-1
Winthrop, Conn. G10 60-1
Winthrop, Ia. E12 104-5
Winthrop, Me. K4 64-5
Winthrop, Mass. H6 68-9
Winthrop, Minn. D7 116-7
Winthrop, Wash. C11 246-7
Winthrop Harbor, Ill. . . . J3 96-7
Winton*, Calif. J4 210-1
Winton, Minn. F8 116-7
Winton, N.C. C14 180-1
Winton, Wash. E10 246-7
Wiota, Ia. H5 104-5
Wiota, Mont. C13 222-3
Wiota, Wis. K11 140-1
Wirral, N.B. I4 275
Wirt, Okla. H11 234-5
Wirt, co., W. Va. F3 200-1
Wirtz, Va. J8 196-7
Wisacky, S.C. D12 184-5
Wisall, Mont. G8 222-3
Wiscasset, Me. M11 64-5
Wisconsin Dells, Wis. . . . I12 140-1
Wisconsin Rapids, Wis. . . G12 140-1
Wisconsin R., Wis. I12 140-1
Wisdom, Mont. G4 222-3
Wise, N.C. C12 180-1
Wise, Va. J3 196-7
Wise, co., Tex. D8 192-3
Wise, co., Va. J3 196-7
Wise River, Mont. G4 222-3
Wiseman, Alaska C11 254-5
Wiseman, Ark. B8 150-1
Wiseton, Sask. M5 294-5
Wishart, Sask. L9 294-5
Wishek, N. Dak. I9 128-9
Wishram, Wash. J10 246-7
Wisner, La. C6 168-9
Wisner, Nebr. E13 124-5
Wister, Okla. G16 234-5
Withee, Wis. F10 140-1
Witherbee, S.C. G13 184-5
Withrow, Wash. E12 246-7
Witless Bay, Nfld. O11 278-9
Witt, Ill. J8 96-7
Witten, S. Dak. H9 136-7
Wittenberg, Wis. C2 140-1
Witter, Ark. B3 150-1
Wittman, Md. F12 172-3
Wittmann, Ariz. H5 206-7
Witts Springs, Ark. C5 150-1
Wiville, Ark. E9 150-1
Wixom, Mich. I4 112-3
Woburn, Mass. G4 68-9
Woburn, Que. J16 290-1
Woden, Ia. B7 104-5
Wofford, Ky. J12 164-5
Wolbach, Nebr. G11 124-5
Wolco, Okla. C13 234-5
Wolcott, Colo. E9 214-5
Wolcott, Conn. E7 60-1
Wolcott, Ind. D5 100-1
Wolcott, N.Y. E6 80-1
Wolcott, Vt. D7 90-1
Wolcottville, Ind. A10 100-1
Wolf, Okla. G12 234-5
Wolf, Wyo. B11 250-1
Wolf Creek, Ky. G7 164-5
Wolf Creek, Mont. E6 222-3
Wolf Creek, Ore. I5 238-9
Wolf Creek Colony, S. Dak. H14 136-7
Wolf Lake, Mich. I11 112-3
Wolf Lake, Minn. I3 116-7
Wolf Pen, W. Va. J3 200-1
Wolf Point, Mont. C14 222-3
Wolfdale*, Pa. I1 84-5
Wolfe, co., Ky. H13 164-5
Wolfe, co., Que. I15 290-1
Wolfe City*, Tex. D10 192-3
Wolfeboro, N.H. K8 72-3
Wolfeboro Center, N.H. . J8 72-3
Wolfforth*, Tex. D5 192-3
Wolflake, Ind. B10 100-1
Wolford, N. Dak. C9 128-9
Wolfton, S.C. F10 184-5
Wolftown, Va. G11 196-7
Wolfville, N.S. D6 281
Wollaston, Mass. I5 68-9
Wollaston Lake, Sask. . . C9 294-5
Wolseley, Sask. N9 294-5
Wolsey, S. Dak. E12 136-7
Wolverine, Mich. E13 112-3
Wolverine Lake, Mich. . . I4 112-3
Wolverton, Minn. I1 116-7
Womack, La. C4 168-9
Womelsdorf, Pa. I13 84-5
Womelsdorf, W. Va. E15 200-1
Wonder, Ore. J5 238-9
Wonder Lake, Ill. J1 96-7
Wondervu, Colo. F2 214-5
Wonewoc, Wis. I11 140-1
Wonowon, B.C. D7 268-9
Wood, N.C. C12 180-1
Wood, S. Dak. H8 136-7
Wood, co., O. C5 132-3
Wood, co., Tex. D10 192-3
Wood, co., W. Va. E3 200-1
Wood, co., Wis. G11 140-1
Wood Dale*, Ill. B10 96-7
Wood Islands, P.E.I. G9 287
Wood Lake, Minn. M3 116-7
Wood Lake, Nebr. D8 124-5
Wood Mountain, Sask. . . O6 294-5
Wood Point, N.B. I7 275
Wood Ridge, N.J. B11 76-7
Wood River, Ill. K6 96-7
Wood River, Nebr. H10 124-5
Wood River Junction, R.I. H3 87
Wood Spur, Alaska E11 254-5
Wood Village*, Ore. B7 238-9
Woodardville, La. C2 168-9
Woodbend Crescents*, Alta. J7 264-5
Woodberry, Ark. I6 150-1
Woodbine, Ga. N10 160-1
Woodbine, Ia. G3 104-5
Woodbine, Kans. F11 108-9
Woodbine, Ky. J12 164-5
Woodbine, Md. F4 172-3
Woodbine, N.J. N4 76-7
Woodbine, Tenn. H7 188-9
Woodbourne*, N.Y. I9 80-1
Woodbridge*, Calif. I4 210-1
Woodbridge, Conn. G7 60-1
Woodbridge, N.J. F7 76-7
Woodbridge [-Marumsco], Va. B3 196-7
Woodburn, Ind. C12 100-1
Woodburn, Ia. I8 104-5
Woodburn, Ky. J7 164-5
Woodburn, Ore. G1 238-9
Woodbury, Conn. F6 60-1
Woodbury, Ga. I3 160-1

Woodbury, Ind. H9 100-1
Woodbury, Ky. I7 164-5
Woodbury*, Minn. M7 116-7
Woodbury, N.J. J3 76-7
Woodbury, Tenn. C9 188-9
Woodbury, Vt. E7 90-1
Woodbury, co., Ia. E2 104-5
Woodbury Heights, N.J. . O10 76-7
Woodcliff, Ga. I10 160-1
Woodcliff Lake, N.J. . . . C8 76-7
Woodenhawk, Del. I3 153
Woodfin*, N.C. D4 180-1
Woodford, Okla. H11 234-5
Woodford, S.C. F10 184-5
Woodford, Vt. L4 90-1
Woodford, Va. G12 196-7
Woodford, Wis. K12 140-1
Woodford, co., Ill. E9 96-7
Woodford, co., Ky. G11 164-5
Woodhaven*, Mich. J15 112-3
Woodhull, Ill. D6 96-7
Woodinville, Wash. H3 246-7
Woodlake, Calif. K6 210-1
Woodland, Ala. F10 146-7
Woodland, Calif. A8 210-1
Woodland, Del. J3 153
Woodland, Ga. I3 160-1
Woodland, La. F8 168-9
Woodland, Me. B8 64-5
Woodland, Me. I10 64-5
Woodland, Mich. I12 112-3
Woodland*, Minn. M6 116-7
Woodland, Miss. E9 176-7
Woodland*, N.J. J6 76-7
Woodland, N.C. C13 180-1
Woodland, Ut. F7 242-3
Woodland, Wash. I7 246-7
Woodland, Wis. H3 140-1
Woodland Acres, Colo. . H12 214-5
Woodland Acres*, Ont. . J11 284-5
Woodland Beach, Del. . . E4 153
Woodland Beach, Md. . . I7 172-3
Woodland Beach, Mich. . K15 112-3
Woodland Heights*, Pa. . E3 84-5
Woodland Hills*, Ky. . . . F9 164-5
Woodland Mills, Tenn. . . A3 188-9
Woodland Park*, Alta. . . J7 264-5
Woodland Park, Colo. . . J3 214-5
Woodlands, Man. I13 272-3
Woodlands Trailer
Court*, Man. J3 272-3
Woodlawn*, Ky. D11 164-5
Woodlawn*, Ky. J3 164-5
Woodlawn [-Wood-
moor], Md. F6 172-3
Woodlawn, Md. B13 172-3
Woodlawn, O. K13 132-3
Woodlawn, Tenn. F5 188-9
Woodlawn, Tenn. B10 188-9
Woodlawn, Va. J6 196-7
Woodlawn Heights, Ind. . G9 100-1
Woodlawn Park*, Ky. . . . G9 164-5
Woodlawn Park*, Okla. . F10 234-5
Woodleaf, N.C. I2 180-1
Woodlynne, N.J. N10 76-7
Woodman, Wis. J10 140-1
Woodmere, N.H. O4 72-3
Woodmere, N.Y. F15 80-1
Woodmere*, O. B10 132-3
Woodport, N.J. C5 76-7
Woodridge, Ill. N2 96-7
Woodridge, Man. K15 272-3
Woodridge, N.Y. H10 80-1
Woodrow, Colo. D14 214-5
Woodrow, Sask. O6 294-5
Woodrow, S.C. D12 184-5
Woodruff, Ariz. F10 206-7
Woodruff, Ida. O9 218-9
Woodruff, Kans. C6 108-9
Woodruff, S.C. G4 184-5
Woodruff, Ut. D7 242-3
Woodruff, Wis. C12 140-1
Woodruff, co., Ark. E9 150-1
Woods, Okla. J3 234-5
Woods, Ore. C4 238-9
Woods, co., Okla. C8 234-5
Woods Cross, Ut. E6 242-3
Woods Heights, Mo. . . . H16 120-1
Woods Hole, Mass. I13 68-9
Woods Landing, Wyo. . . J13 250-1
Woods Tavern, N.J. F5 76-7
Woodsboro, Md. B9 172-3
Woodsboro, Tex. I8 192-3
Woodsburgh*, N.Y. K11 80-1
Woodsdale*, B.C. J10 268-9
Woodsdale, N.C. C10 180-1
Woodsfield, O. G10 132-3
Woodside, Calif. D7 210-1
Woodside, Del. G4 153
Woodside, La. F6 168-9
Woodside, Mont. F3 222-3
Woodside*, S.C. F2 184-5
Woodside, Ut. I9 242-3
Woodside-Drifton, Pa. . . F13 84-5
Woodson, Ark. G7 150-1
Woodson, co., Kans. . . . I14 108-9
Woodson Terrace*, Mo. . E10 120-1
Woodstock, Ala. F5 146-7
Woodstock, Conn. B14 60-1
Woodstock, Ga. A10 160-1
Woodstock, Ill. A9 96-7
Woodstock, Me. K2 64-5
Woodstock, Md. F5 172-3
Woodstock, Minn. O2 116-7
Woodstock, N.B. H3 275
Woodstock, N.H. H6 72-3
Woodstock*, N.Y. G10 80-1
Woodstock, O. F5 132-3
Woodstock, Ont. D13 284-5
Woodstock, Vt. J7 90-1
Woodstock, Va. E10 196-7
Woodstock Valley, Conn. B13 60-1
Woodston, Kans. E7 108-9
Woodstown, N.J. K2 76-7
Woodsville, N.H. G4 72-3
Woodtick, Conn. E7 60-1
Woodville, Ala. B7 146-7
Woodville*, Calif. K6 210-1
Woodville, Conn. D5 60-1
Woodville, Ga. G7 160-1
Woodville, Me. G8 64-5
Woodville, Mass. J1 68-9
Woodville, Miss. L3 176-7
Woodville, N.C. C13 180-1
Woodville, O. B6 132-3
Woodville, Ont. B15 284-5
Woodville, S.C. H2 184-5
Woodville, Tex. F11 192-3
Woodville, Va. . . . . B1· 196-7
Woodville, W. Va. I12 200-1
Woodville, Wis. F7 140-1
Woodward, Ia. G7 104-5
Woodward, Okla. D7 234-5
Woodward, S.C. C10 184-5
Woodward, co., Okla. . . C8 234-5
Woodwards, Miss. K10 176-7
Woodway*, Tex. E8 192-3
Woodway*, Wash. E8 246-7
Woodworth, La. F4 168-9
Woodworth, N. Dak. . . . G10 128-9
Woodworth*, O. D11 132-3
Woodworth, Wis. K5 140-1
Woody Creek, Colo. . . . E8 214-5
Woody Island, Alaska. . . H10 254-5
Woody Point, Nfld. M7 278-9
Wooldridge, Mo. E6 120-1
Woolford, Md. G12 172-3
Woolsey, Ga. H4 160-1
Woolsey, Nev. D4 226-7
Woolstock, Ia. D7 104-5
Woolwich, Me. N11 64-5
Woolwich*, N.J. K2 76-7
Woolwine, Va. J7 196-7
Woonsocket, R.I. A4 87
Woonsocket, S. Dak. . . . F13 136-7
Wooster, Ark. E6 150-1
Wooster, O. D9 132-3
Wooton, Ky. I14 164-5
Wopowog, Conn. F10 60-1
Worcester, Mass. D8 68-9
Worcester, Vt. E6 90-1
Worcester, co., Md. H15 172-3
Worcester, co., Mass. . . . C7 68-9
Worden, Ark. D9 150-1
Worden, Ill. J7 96-7
Worden, Mont. G11 222-3
Worden, Ore. K7 238-9
Worland, Wyo. D11 250-1
Worley, Ida. D2 218-9
Wormleysburg*, Pa. I10 84-5
Worms, Nebr. H11 124-5
Worsham, Va. I11 196-7
Worth, Ill. N3 96-7
Worth, Mo. A3 120-1
Worth, co., Ga. L5 160-1
Worth, co., Ia. B9 104-5
Worth, co., Mo. A3 120-1
Wortham*, Tex. E9 192-3
Worthing, S. Dak. H16 136-7
Worthington, Ind. K6 100-1
Worthington, Ia. E14 104-5
Worthington, Ky. F15 164-5
Worthington, Mass. C3 68-9
Worthington, Minn. O3 116-7
Worthington, O. F6 132-3
Worthington, W. Va. . . . B14 200-1
Worthington Springs*,
Fla. C10 156-7
Worthville, Ky. F10 164-5
Worthville, N.C. I4 180-1
Worton, Md. D13 172-3
Woss Lake*, B.C. J6 268-9
Wottonville, Que. I15 290-1
Wounded Knee, S. Dak. . I4 136-7
Wrangell, Alaska H16 254-5
Wrangle Hill, Del. C3 153
Wray, Colo. D16 214-5
Wren, Ala. C5 146-7
Wren, O. D3 132-3
Wren, Ore. E5 238-9
Wrens, Ga. H8 160-1
Wrenshall, Minn. I8 116-7
Wrentham, Mass. E10 68-9
Wright, Ark. G7 150-1
Wright, Minn. I7 116-7
Wright, Wyo. D14 250-1
Wright, co., Ia. D7 104-5
Wright, co., Minn. L5 116-7
Wright, co., Mo. H6 120-1
Wright City, Mo. B13 120-1
Wright City, Okla. I15 234-5
Wright-Patterson*, O. . . H15 132-3
Wrights Crossroad, Del. . F2 153
Wrightstown, N.J. I5 76-7
Wrightstown, Wis. E4 140-1
Wrightsville, Ark. J16 150-1
Wrightsville, Ga. I7 160-1
Wrightsville, Pa. J12 84-5
Wrightsville Beach, N.C. H12 180-1
Wrigley, Ky. G14 164-5
Wrigley, Tenn. H5 188-9
Wroxton, Sask. M10 294-5
Wurtland*, Ky. F14 164-5
Wurtsboro, N.Y. I10 80-1
Wurtsmith*, Mich. F14 112-3
Wyaconda, Mo. A7 120-1
Wyalusing, Wis. J9 140-1
Wyandanch*, N.Y. K12 80-1
Wyandot, co., O. D6 132-3
Wyandotte, Mich. K6 112-3
Wyandotte, Okla. C16 234-5
Wyandotte, co., Kans. . . E16 108-9
Wyanet, Ill. D7 96-7
Wyarno, Wyo. B12 250-1
Wyatt, Ind. A8 100-1
Wyatt, La. C4 168-9
Wyatt, Mo. I12 120-1
Wyatt, W. Va. B13 200-1
Wyatte, Miss. B7 176-7
Wyckoff, N.J. C7 76-7
Wyco, W. Va. J4 200-1
Wye, Okla. K4 234-5
Wye Mills, Md. E13 172-3
Wyeclif*, Alta. I8 264-5
Wyeville, Wis. H11 140-1
Wykoff, Minn. O8 116-7
Wylie, Tex. B15 192-3
Wylliesburg, Va. J10 196-7
Wymark, Sask. N5 294-5
Wymer, W. Va. F16 200-1
Wymore, Nebr. J14 124-5
Wyndmere, N. Dak. I14 128-9
Wynnburg, Tenn. A2 188-9
Wynndel, B.C. K10 268-9
Wynne, Ark. E11 150-1
Wynnewood, Okla. H11 234-5
Wynona, Okla. C13 234-5
Wynot, Nebr. D13 124-5
Wynyard, Sask. L8 294-5
Wyocena, Wis. H1 140-1
Wyodak, Wyo. C14 250-1
Wyola, Mont. H12 222-3
Wyoma, Mass. G6 68-9
Wyoming, Del. F4 153
Wyoming, Ill. E7 96-7
Wyoming, Ia. F14 104-5
Wyoming, Mass. G5 68-9
Wyoming, Mich. I12 112-3
Wyoming, Minn. L7 116-7
Wyoming, O. K13 132-3
Wyoming, Ont. E11 284-5
Wyoming*, Pa. E13 84-5
Wyoming, R.I. G3 87
Wyoming, Wyo. I14 250-1
Wyoming, co., N.Y. F3 80-1
Wyoming, co., Pa. E13 84-5
Wyoming, co., W. Va. . . . I3 200-1
Wyomissing, Pa. I13 84-5
Wyomissing Hills*, Pa. . . I13 84-5
Wythe, co., Va. J6 196-7
Wytheville, Va. J6 196-7
Wytonville*, Man. K2 272-3
Wytopitlock, Me. G9 64-5

X

Xenia, Kans. H16 108-9
Xenia, O. G4 132-3

Y

Y City, Ark. F2 150-1
Yaak, Mont. A1 222-3
Yachats, Ore. E4 238-9
Yacolt, Wash. J8 246-7
Yadkin, co., N.C. C7 180-1
Yadkin College, N.C. . . . H3 180-1
Yadkinville, N.C. C7 180-1
Yahk, B.C. K10 268-9
Yakataga, Alaska F13 254-5
Yakima, Wash. H11 246-7
Yakima, co., Wash. H10 246-7
Yakt, Mont. B1 222-3
Yakutat, Alaska G14 254-5
Yalaha, Fla. E11 156-7
Yale, B.C. J7 268-9
Yale, Ia. G6 104-5
Yale, Mich. F7 112-3
Yale, Okla. D12 234-5
Yale, S. Dak. E13 136-7
Yale, Va. G1 196-7
Yalobusha, co., Miss. . . . D7 176-7
Yamachiche, Que. H13 290-1
Yamaska, Que. H13 290-1
Yamaska, co., Que. H13 290-1
Yamhill, Ore. G1 238-9
Yamhill, co., Ore. C5 238-9
Yampa, Colo. D8 214-5
Yampai, Ariz. E4 206-7
Yancey, co., N.C. D4 180-1
Yanceyville, N.C. C10 180-1
Yankeetown, Fla. D9 156-7
Yankeetown, Ind. O5 100-1
Yankton, S. Dak. I14 136-7
Yankton, co., S. Dak. . . . I14 136-7
Yantley, Ala. I2 146-7
Yanush, Okla. G15 234-5
Yaphank, N.Y. J13 80-1
Yarbo, Ala. K2 146-7
Yarbo, Sask. M10 294-5
Yarbro, Ark. B12 150-1
Yardley*, Pa. I16 84-5
Yardville [-White Horse],
N.J. H5 76-7
Yarker, Ont. J13 284-5
Yarmouth, Me. N9 64-5
Yarmouth, Mass. H15 68-9
Yarmouth, N.S. F4 281
Yarmouth, co., N.S. F4 281
Yarmouth Port, Mass. . . H15 68-9
Yarnaby, Okla. I13 234-5
Yarnell, Ariz. G5 206-7
Yarrow, B.C. C16 268-9
Yarrow Point, Wash. . . . H3 246-7
Yates, co., N.Y. F5 80-1
Yates Center, Kans. I14 108-9
Yates City, Ill. E6 96-7
Yatesville, Ga. I4 160-1
Yauhannah, S.C. F15 184-5
Yaupon Beach, N.C. . . . H12 180-1
Yavapai, co., Ariz. F5 206-7
Yawkey, W. Va. I12 200-1
Yazoo, co., Miss. H5 176-7
Yazoo City, Miss. G5 176-7
Yeadon, Pa. B11 84-5
Yeager, Okla. F13 234-5
Yeagertown, Pa. H9 84-5
Yeddo, Ind. G5 100-1
Yell, co., Ark. E4 150-1
Yellow Creek, Sask. K7 294-5
Yellow Grass, Sask. O8 294-5
Yellow Jacket, Colo. . . . I5 214-5
Yellow Medicine, co.,
Minn. M2 116-7
Yellow Pine, Ala. L2 146-7
Yellow Pine, Ida. I4 218-9
Yellow Spring, W. Va. . . E10 200-1
Yellow Springs, Md. . . . C8 172-3
Yellow Springs, O. H16 132-3
Yellowhead*, Sask. M10 294-5
Yellowknife, N.W. Terr. C1 296
Yellowstone, co., Mont. . G11 222-3
Yellowstone Lake, Wyo. . C6 250-1
Yellowstone National
Park, co., Mont. I8 222-3
Yellowstone R., Mont. . . F14 222-3
Yellville, Ark. B6 150-1
Yelm, Wash. G7 246-7
Yelvington, Ky. H6 164-5
Yemassee, S.C. I11 184-5
Yenome, S.C. G9 184-5
Yeoman, Ind. E6 100-1
Yerington, Nev. G3 226-7
Yermo, Calif. M9 210-1
Yeso, N. Mex. G9 230-1
Yetter, Ia. E5 104-5
Yewed, Okla. C9 234-5
Ymir, B.C. K10 268-9
Yoakum, Tex. H9 192-3
Yoakum, co., Tex. D4 192-3
Yocemento, Kans. F6 108-9
Yocum, Ky. G14 164-5
Yoder, Colo. F13 214-5
Yoder, Ind. D11 100-1
Yoder, Kans. I9 108-9
Yoder, Ore. G2 238-9
Yoder, Wyo. H16 250-1
Yolo, co., Calif. H3 210-1
Yolyn, W. Va. K12 200-1
Yoncalla, Ore. G5 238-9
Yonges Island, S.C. I12 184-5
Yonkers, N.Y. J11 80-1
Yonkers, Okla. D15 234-5
Yorba Linda, Calif. H9 210-1
York, Ala. H2 146-7
York, Me. O2 64-5
York, Nebr. H12 124-5
York, N. Dak. D9 128-9
York, Pa. J11 84-5
York, P.E.I. E7 287
York, S.C. B9 184-5
York, co., Me. M2 64-5
York, co., Nebr. H12 124-5
York, co., N.B. H4 275
York, co., Pa. J12 84-5
York, co., S.C. A9 184-5
York, co., Va. I14 196-7
York Beach, Me. O2 64-5
York Harbor, Me. O2 64-5
York Landing*, Man. . . . D4 272-3
York Point*, P.E.I. E7 287
Yorklyn, Del. A3 153
Yorkshire*, Va. E12 196-7
Yorkton, Sask. M10 294-5
Yorktown, Ark. H8 150-1
Yorktown, Ind. G10 100-1
Yorktown, Ia. J4 104-5
Yorktown*, Ky. H15 164-5
Yorktown, Tex. H8 192-3
Yorktown, Va. I14 196-7
Yorktown Heights, N.Y. B15 80-1
Yorktown [-Jefferson
Valley], N.Y. A15 80-1
Yorkville, Ill. C9 96-7
Yorkville, Ind. J11 100-1
Yorkville, N.Y. E8 80-1
Yorkville, O. F11 132-3
Yorkville, Tenn. B3 188-9
Yosemite, Ky. I11 164-5
Yost, Okla. D12 234-5
Yost, Ut. C3 242-3
Youbou, B.C. K6 268-9
Young, Ariz. G8 206-7
Young, Sask. L7 294-5
Young, co., Tex. D7 192-3
Young America, Ind. . . . E7 100-1
Young America, Minn. . . C8 116-7
Young Harris, Ga. C5 160-1
Youngs Cove, N.B. H5 275
Youngs Harbour*, Ont. . B15 284-5
Youngs Point, Mont. . . . H10 222-3
Youngstown, Alta. L10 264-5
Youngstown, N.Y. E2 80-1
Youngstown, O. C11 132-3
Youngstown*, Ont. J11 284-5
Youngsville, La. H5 168-9
Youngsville, N.C. H8 180-1
Youngsville, Pa. C4 84-5
Youngtown, Ariz. H6 206-7
Youngwood, Pa. C8 84-5
Yountville*, Calif. H3 210-1
Ypsilanti, Mich. K4 112-3
Ypsilanti, N. Dak. H11 128-9
Yreka City, Calif. D3 210-1
Yscloskey, La. D16 168-9
Yuba, Okla. I13 234-5
Yuba, Wis. I11 140-1
Yuba, co., Calif. G4 210-1
Yuba City, Calif. G4 210-1

Yucaipa, Calif. G11 210-1
Yucca, Ariz. F3 206-7
Yucca Valley, Calif. G12 210-1
Yukon, Okla. J1 234-5
Yukon R., Alaska D11 254-5
Yukon R., Y.T. B1 297
Yuma, Ariz. J2 206-7
Yuma, Colo. D15 214-5
Yuma, Ky. I10 164-5
Yuma, Tenn. C4 188-9
Yuma, co., Ariz. J3 206-7
Yuma, co., Colo. D15 214-5
Yuma Proving Ground*, Ariz. J2 206-7
Yuma Station*, Ariz. . . . J2 206-7
Yutan, Nebr. J1 124-5

Z

Zacata, Va. G14 196-7
Zachary, La. G7 168-9
Zachow, Wis. D4 140-1
Zafra, Okla. H16 234-5
Zahl, N. Dak. C2 128-9
Zaleski, O. H8 132-3
Zalma, Mo. I11 120-1
Zama, Miss. G8 176-7
Zama City*, Alta. C4 264-5
Zane, Ut. L3 242-3
Zanesville, Ind. D10 100-1
Zanesville, O. F8 132-3
Zap, N. Dak. F5 128-9
Zapata, Tex. J7 192-3
Zapata, co., Tex. J7 192-3
Zavala, co., Tex. H6 192-3
Zealand, N.B. H4 275
Zealandia, Sask. L5 294-5
Zearing, Ia. F8 104-5
Zeballos, B.C. J4 268-9
Zebulon, Ga. H4 160-1
Zebulon, N.C. H8 180-1
Zeeland, Mich. I11 112-3
Zeeland, N. Dak. J9 128-9
Zeigler, Ill. M8 96-7
Zelienople, Pa. G2 84-5
Zell, S. Dak. D12 136-7
Zellwood, Fla. E11 156-7
Zelma, Sask. L7 294-5
Zemple, Minn. H6 116-7
Zena, Okla. C15 234-5
Zenda, Kans. J9 108-9
Zenda, Wis. K14 140-1
Zenith, Kans. I8 108-9
Zenith, W. Va. J6 200-1
Zenon Park, Sask. J9 294-5
Zenoria, La. D5 168-9
Zent, Ark. E9 150-1
Zephyr Cove, Nev. G1 226-7
Zephyrhills, Fla. G4 156-7
Zetus, Miss. K5 176-7
Ziebach, co., S. Dak. . . . D6 136-7
Zihlman, Md. B3 172-3
Zillah, Wash. H11 246-7
Zilwaukee*, Mich. H14 112-3
Zimmerman, La. E4 168-9
Zimmerman, Minn. K6 116-7
Zinc, Ark. A5 150-1
Zion, Ark. B8 150-1
Zion, Ill. J3 96-7
Zion, S.C. D15 184-5
Zionsville, Ind. D1 100-1
Zionville, N.C. C5 180-1
Zoe, Okla. G16 234-5
Zolfo Springs, Fla. J5 156-7
Zortman, Mont. C10 222-3
Zumbro Falls, Minn. . . . N8 116-7
Zumbrota, Minn. N7 116-7
Zuni, N. Mex. F2 230-1
Zuni, Va. G3 196-7
Zurich, Kans. E6 108-9
Zurich, Ont. D11 284-5
Zwingle, Ia. E15 104-5
Zwolle, La. D2 168-9
Zylks, La. A1 168-9

Metric conversion table

Use this table to change measurements into or out of metric units. First, look up the unit you know in the left-hand column, then multiply the unit by the number given. Your answer will be approximately the number of units shown in the right-hand column.

When you know:	Multiply by:	To find:
Length and distance		
inches (in.)	25.00	millimeters
feet (ft.)	30.00	centimeters
yards (yd.)	0.90	meters
miles (mi.)	1.60	kilometers
millimeters (mm)	0.04	inches
centimeters (cm)	0.40	inches
meters (m)	1.10	yards
kilometers (km)	0.60	miles
Surface or area		
square inches (sq. in.)	6.50	square centimeters
square feet (sq. ft.)	0.09	square meters
square yards (sq. yd.)	0.80	square meters
square miles (sq. mi.)	2.60	square kilometers
acres	0.40	hectares
square centimeters (cm^2)	0.16	square inches
square meters (m^2)	1.20	square yards
square kilometers (km^2)	0.40	square miles
hectares (ha)	2.50	acres

When you know:	Multiply by:	To find:
Volume and capacity (liquid)		
fluid ounces (fl. oz.)	30.000	milliliters
pints (pt.), U.S.	0.470	liters
pints (pt.), imperial	0.568	liters
quarts (qt.), U.S.	0.950	liters
quarts (qt.), imperial	1.137	liters
gallons (gal.), U.S.	3.800	liters
gallons (gal.), imperial	4.546	liters
milliliters (ml)	0.034	fluid ounces
liters (l)	2.100	pints, U.S.
liters (l)	1.760	pints, imperial
liters (l)	1.060	quarts, U.S.
liters (l)	0.880	quarts, imperial
liters (l)	0.260	gallons, U.S.
liters (l)	0.220	gallons, imperial
Weight and mass		
ounces (oz.)	28.000	grams
pounds (lb.)	0.450	kilograms
short tons	0.900	metric tons
grams (g)	0.035	ounces
kilograms (kg)	2.200	pounds
metric tons (t)	1.100	short tons
Temperature		
degrees Fahrenheit (°F.)	5/9 (after subtracting 32)	degrees Celsius
degrees Celsius (°C)	9/5 (then add 32)	degrees Fahrenheit

Acknowledgments

Cover: © Gill Kenny
3 James Teason
12 Milt & Joan Mann; Paul G. Beswick, The Phelps Agency
13 Milt & Joan Mann; © Dan Fivehouse, Image Finders; Robert Davis Productions
22 © Billy E. Barnes; Robert Davis Productions; Artstreet
23 Milt & Joan Mann
24 Robert Davis Productions; Artstreet
26 © Alan McOnie, Image Finders
30 Robert Davis Productions
31 Milt & Joan Mann
32 Artstreet
33 Artstreet; WORLD BOOK photo by Steve Hale; WORLD BOOK photo by Steve Hale
35 Photo Librarium Canada Ltd.; © Alan McOnie, Image Finders
36 Photo Librarium Canada Ltd.
38 Artstreet
39 Dave Looy, Image Finders; Syncrude Canada Ltd.
40–41 © Edward M. Gifford, Image Finders
42 Photo Librarium Canada Ltd.
56 © Eli Heller, Picture Group
57 © William Weems, The Phelps Agency; Robert Davis Productions; Robert Davis Productions
58 © Bryce Flynn, Picture Group
59 © Ken Laffal, Picture Group; © John F. Urwiller, Picture Group
62 Milt & Joan Mann
63 Jadwiga Lopez; © Dan Fivehouse, Image Finders
66 Milt & Joan Mann; © Jack Spratt, Picture Group
67 © Stephen J. Sherman, Picture Group
70 Jadwiga Lopez
71 Robert Davis Productions; Artstreet
74–75 New Jersey Division of Travel & Tourism

Note: Credits should be read from left to right, top to bottom, on their respective pages.

78 © Robert Emerson, Picture Group; Milt & Joan Mann
79 Milt & Joan Mann
82 © Bruce Roberts, The Phelps Agency
83 Artstreet
86 Rhode Island Department of Economic Development
88 © George Bellerose, Picture Group
89 © Jack Spratt, Picture Group; © Dan Neary, Picture Group
92 Milt & Joan Mann
93 Milt & Joan Mann; Artstreet; Milt & Joan Mann
94 WORLD BOOK photo by Steve Hale; Artstreet
95–99 Artstreet
102–103 Milt & Joan Mann
106 Artstreet
107 Milt & Joan Mann; Robert Davis Productions
110 Milt & Joan Mann
111–114 Artstreet
115 Artstreet; Milt & Joan Mann
118 Milt & Joan Mann
119–122 Artstreet
123 Milt & Joan Mann
126 Artstreet
127 Milt & Joan Mann; Artstreet
130 Milt & Joan Mann; Robert Davis Productions
131 © Bill Grimes, The Phelps Agency
134 Milt & Joan Mann; Robert Davis Productions
135 Artstreet
138 © Don Davenport, Picture Group
139 Milt & Joan Mann; Artstreet
142 © *Southern Living*
143 © Al Stephenson, The Phelps Agency; © *Southern Living;* © *Southern Living*
144 © Joe Hayles, The Phelps Agency
145 Artstreet; © *Southern Living*
148 © *Southern Living;* Milt & Joan Mann
149 © *Southern Living*
152 Delaware River and Bay Authority
154 © Sylvia Martin, *Southern Living*

155 Artstreet; © Geoff Gilbert, *Southern Living*
158 Artstreet; © Judy A. Nemeth, *Southern Living*
159 Fred Zimmerman, The Phelps Agency
162 Robert Davis Productions
163 © Bruce Roberts, *Southern Living;* © *Southern Living*
166 © Mike Clemmer, *Southern Living*
167 © Al Stephenson, The Phelps Agency
170 © John O'Hagan, *Southern Living*
171 Milt & Joan Mann; © *Southern Living*
174–175 © Bruce Roberts
178 © Billy E. Barnes
179 © Bruce Roberts, *Southern Living;* Milt & Joan Mann
182 Milt & Joan Mann; © Van Chaplin, *Southern Living*
183 © John O'Hagan, *Southern Living*
186–187 © *Southern Living*
190 Robert Davis Productions
191 © *Southern Living;* Milt & Joan Mann
194 Artstreet
195 © *Southern Living;* Robert Davis Productions
198 © *Southern Living*
199 © Bruce Roberts, *Southern Living;* © *Southern Living*
202 Robert Davis Productions
203 Bob Haddon, Artstreet; © William Weems, The Phelps Agency; Artstreet
204 Robert Davis Productions
205 Robert Davis Productions; Artstreet
208 Artstreet; Milt & Joan Mann
209 © Chris Christo, Picture Group
212 Robert Davis Productions
213 Milt & Joan Mann; Artstreet
216 © Jerry Berndt, Picture Group
217 Sun Valley Company
220 Artstreet
221 Artstreet; Robert Davis Productions
224 Artstreet
225 Karen Yops; © R. H. Blanchet, Image Finders
228 Milt & Joan Mann; Artstreet
229 Milt & Joan Mann
232 Robert Davis Productions
233 Milt & Joan Mann; © *Southern Living*
236 Robert Davis Productions
237 © Jerry Berndt, Picture Group; Artstreet
240 Robert Davis Productions
241 Utah Travel Council
244 Bob Fiore, The Phelps Agency; Robert Davis Productions
245–248 Robert Davis Productions
249 Milt & Joan Mann
252 Artstreet
253 Alan McOnie, Image Finders; Robert Davis Productions
256 Milt & Joan Mann
257 Artstreet; Milt & Joan Mann
260 Robert Davis Productions
261 Milt & Joan Mann; © Ted Czolowski, Image Finders; © A. Farquhar, Image Finders
262 Milt & Joan Mann
263 Glenn Tooke, Image Finders; Milt & Joan Mann
266 Photo Librarium Canada Ltd.
267 Artstreet; Milt & Joan Mann
270 © A. Farquhar, Image Finders
271 Sigi Rufenacht, Image Finders; Robert Davis Productions
274 © Jack Spratt, Picture Group
276 Fred Herzog, Image Finders
277–282 Photo Librarium Canada Ltd.
283 Milt & Joan Mann
286–289 Photo Librarium Canada Ltd.
292 © R. H. Blanchet, Image Finders; © Bryce Flynn, Picture Group
293 © Edward M. Gifford, Image Finders
296 © Bryce Flynn, Picture Group
297 Sid Roberts, Image Finders
298 © Leonard Harris, Picture Group
299 Artstreet; © Robert J. Izzo, Picture Group; Artstreet
301 Milt & Joan Mann
303 © *Southern Living*
304 © R. H. Blanchet, Image Finders
305 Milt & Joan Mann
307 Bruce Roberts, The Phelps Agency
310 Ken Straiton, Image Finders
312 Photo Librarium Canada Ltd.